ASPEN PUBLISHERS

Eighth Edition _____

WILLS, TRUSTS, AND ESTATES

Jesse Dukeminier

Late Maxwell Professor of Law
University of California, Los Angeles

Robert H. Sitkoff

John L. Gray Professor of Law
Harvard University

James Lindgren

Professor of Law
Northwestern University

Wolters Kluwer
Law & Business

AUSTIN   BOSTON   CHICAGO   NEW YORK   THE NETHERLANDS

> Aspen Publishers
> Attn: Permissions Department
> 76 Ninth Avenue, 7th Floor
> New York, NY 10011-5201

To contact Customer Care, e-mail customer.care@aspenpublishers.com,
call 1-800-234-1660, fax 1-800-901-9075, or mail correspondence to:

> Aspen Publishers
> Attn: Order Department
> PO Box 990
> Frederick, MD 21705

Printed in the United States of America.

1 2 3 4 5 6 7 8 9 0

ISBN 978-0-7355-7996-5

Library of Congress Cataloging-in-Publication Data

Dukeminier, Jesse.
    Wills, trusts, and estates / Jesse Dukeminier, Robert H. Sitkoff, James Lindgren. — 8th ed.
      p. cm.
    Rev. ed. of: Wills, trusts, and estates / Jesse Dukeminier . . . [et al.]. 7th ed. c2005.
    Includes index.
      ISBN 978-0-7355-7996-5 (hardcover : alk. paper) 1. Wills—United States—Cases. 2. Estate planning—United States—Cases. 3. Future interests—United States—Cases. 4. Trusts and trustees—United States—Cases. I. Sitkoff, Robert H. II. Lindgren, James. III. Wills, trusts, and estates. IV. Title.
KF753.D85 2009
346.7305—dc22   2009025929

About Wolters Kluwer Law & Business

Wolters Kluwer Law & Business is a leading provider of research information and workflow solutions in key specialty areas. The strengths of the individual brands of Aspen Publishers, CCH, Kluwer Law International and Loislaw are aligned within Wolters Kluwer Law & Business to provide comprehensive, in-depth solutions and expert-authored content for the legal, professional and education markets.

CCH was founded in 1913 and has served more than four generations of business professionals and their clients. The CCH products in the Wolters Kluwer Law & Business group are highly regarded electronic and print resources for legal, securities, antitrust and trade regulation, government contracting, banking, pension, payroll, employment and labor, and healthcare reimbursement and compliance professionals.

Aspen Publishers is a leading information provider for attorneys, business professionals and law students. Written by preeminent authorities, Aspen products offer analytical and practical information in a range of specialty practice areas from securities law and intellectual property to mergers and acquisitions and pension/benefits. Aspen's trusted legal education resources provide professors and students with high-quality, up-to-date and effective resources for successful instruction and study in all areas of the law.

Kluwer Law International supplies the global business community with comprehensive English-language international legal information. Legal practitioners, corporate counsel and business executives around the world rely on the Kluwer Law International journals, loose-leafs, books and electronic products for authoritative information in many areas of international legal practice.

Loislaw is a premier provider of digitized legal content to small law firm practitioners of various specializations. Loislaw provides attorneys with the ability to quickly and efficiently find the necessary legal information they need, when and where they need it, by facilitating access to primary law as well as state-specific law, records, forms and treatises.

Wolters Kluwer Law & Business, a unit of Wolters Kluwer, is headquartered in New York and Riverwoods, Illinois. Wolters Kluwer is a leading multinational publisher and information services company.

For David Sanders,
who inspired Jesse Dukeminier,
who inspired the rest of us.

Jesse Dukeminier, 1925-2003

SUMMARY OF CONTENTS

*Chapter 15 was revised for the eighth edition principally by Stephanie J. Willbanks, Professor of Law at Vermont Law School.

CONTENTS

WILLS, TRUSTS, AND ESTATES

Scott, Austin W. Photograph by Fabian Bachrach. Courtesy of Art & Visual Materials, Special Collections Department, Harvard Law School Library.

Sears, Leah. Photograph. Reproduced by permission of Justice Sears.

Smith, Anna Nicole, with her son and daughter. Photograph. © Getty Images. Reproduced by permission.

Smithers, R. Brinkley. Photograph. Reproduced by permission of The Christopher D. Smithers Foundation, Inc.

Smithers Institute Building, East 93rd Street, New York City. Photograph. Reproduced by permission of The Christopher D. Smithers Foundation, Inc.

Snuff bottles. Photograph. Reproduced by permission of David Sanders.

Speelman, Marianna. Photograph. © Daily News LP. Reproduced by permission of the New York Daily News.

Tannenberg, Marvin. Cartoon. © 1966 by Playboy. Reproduced by special permission of PLAYBOY Magazine.

Troland, Leonard. Photograph. Reproduced by permission of the Harvard University Archives.

Trust portfolio allocation graph. Courtesy of Professor Max M. Schanzenbach.

Waggoner, Lawrence W. Photograph. Reproduced by permission of Professor Waggoner.

Wells, Eleazer M.P. Photograph. Reproduced from The Church Militant, April 1944, p.4 by permission of the Episcopal Diocese of Massachusetts.

Wells Fargo. Advertisement. Used with permission from Wells Fargo Bank, N.A.

Woodward, Lauren, and children. Photograph. Reproduced by permission of the Associated Press, the Salem News, and Amy Sweeney.

Yahuda, Abraham. Photograph. From the Schwadron portrait collection, Department of Archives, the National Library of Israel. Reproduced by permission of the National Library of Israel.

Hershey, Milton, and orphans. Photograph. Reprinted by permission of the Hershey Community Archives.

Janes, Rodney. Photograph from the New York Red Book, 1940 Edition. © New York Legal Publishing Corp. Reproduced by permission.

KenKut dispenser. Photograph. Reproduced by permission of KenKut Products, Inc.

Kuralt, Charles, with Patricia Shannon. Photograph. Reproduced by permission of AP/World Wide Photos.

Kutcher, Ashton, and Demi Moore. Photograph by Mark Mainz. © Getty Images. Reproduced by permission.

Landers, Ann. Photograph. Reproduced by permission of Creators Syndicate, Inc.

Langbein, John H. Photograph. Reproduced by permission of the Yale Law School Office of Public Affairs and Professor Langbein.

Leach, W. Barton. Photograph. Courtesy of Art & Visual Materials, Special Collections Department, Harvard Law School Library.

Markowitz, Harry M. Photograph. Reproduced by permission of Professor Markowitz.

Marsman, Captain Frederik. Photograph. © Dana Hall. Courtesy of the Dana Hall Archives, Wellesley, Massachusetts.

Monroe, Marilyn. Photograph. © Sam Shaw, Inc., 1954-2009. Photo by Sam Shaw, courtesy of Shaw Family Archives, Ltd. Reprinted by permission.

New Yorker, The. The New Yorker Magazine, Inc., holds copyrights in the following cartoons: (1) cartoon by Peter Arno © 1940, 1968, 1996; (2) cartoon by Peter Arno © 1942, 1970, 1998; (3) cartoon by Leo Cullum © 1995; (4) cartoon by Wm. Hamilton © 1977; (5) cartoon by Wm. Hamilton © 2001; (6) cartoon by Frank Modell © 1972; (7) cartoon by Michael Shaw © 2005; (8) cartoon by Barbara Smaller © 2005; (9) cartoon by Mick Stevens © 1994, (10) cartoon by Dean Vietor © 1992. These cartoons are reprinted by permission of the Cartoon Bank, a division of The New Yorker Magazine (cartoonbank.com). All rights reserved.

Norfolk, Duke of. Painting by Gerard Soest, 1677. © 2004 Tate, London. Reproduced by permission of the Tate Gallery, London.

Nottingham, Lord Chancellor. Painting after Godfrey Kneller, 1680. Reproduced by permission of the National Portrait Gallery, London.

O'Connor, Sandra Day. Photograph. Photograph by Dane Penland, Smithsonian Institution, Collection of the Supreme Court of the United States. Reproduced by permission of Justice O'Connor.

Paul, Alice. Photograph. Harris and Ewing, 1920. Library of Congress, Prints and Photographs Division, Digital Reproduction Number cph 3a21383.

Peters, Ellen Ash. Photograph. Reproduced by permission of Justice Peters.

Peterson, Laci and Scott. Photograph. AP Photo/Modesto Police Department Handout. Provided by AP/Wide World Photos.

Posner, Richard A. Photograph. Reproduced by permission of Judge Posner.

Roth, Renee. Photograph. Reproduced by permission of Surrogate Roth.

Rothko, Mark. Number 22. Oil on canvas, 90900(h) × 80111/800(w). 1949. The Museum of Modern Art, New York. Gift of the artist. Photograph © 1998 Kate Rothko Prizel and Christopher Rothko/Artists Rights Society (ARS), New York. Reproduced by permission of ARS.

Russell, Thelma, property at 4422 Palm Ave., La Mesa, California. Photograph. Reproduced by permission of David Sanders.

Schiavo, Terri Schindler. Photograph. Reproduced by permission of Mary Schindler.

Schanzenbach, Max M., and Robert H. Sitkoff, Did Reform of Prudent Trust Investment Laws Change Trust Portfolio Allocation?, 50 J.L. & Econ. 681 (2007). © 2007. Reprinted by permission.

Scott, Austin W., William Franklin Fratcher, and Mark L. Ascher, Scott and Ascher on Trusts (5th ed. 2006, 2007, 2008). Reprinted by permission of Aspen Publishers, Inc.

Sitkoff, Robert H., The Lurking Rule Against Accumulations of Income, 100 Nw. U. L. Rev. 501 (2006). © 2006. Adapted by permission.

Sitkoff, Robert H., and Max M. Schanzenbach, Jurisdictional Competition for Trust Funds: An Empirical Analysis of Perpetuities and Taxes, 115 Yale L.J. 356 (2005). © 2005. Reprinted by permission.

Syal, Rajeev, Tories Lose L8.3M Bequest Battle, Times (London), Oct. 16, 2007, at 27. © 2007 BBC News. Reprinted with permission.

Vallely, Joanna, 67-Year-Old Sets Record as Oldest Mother with Birth of Twins, The Scotsman, Dec. 31, 2006. © 2006 Reprinted by permission.

With His Wife in Limbo, Husband Can't Move, The New York Times, Nov. 2, 2003, §1, at 18. Reprinted by permission of Georges Borchardt, Inc.

Photographs and Illustrations

Barnes Foundation Gallery. Photograph. © The Barnes Foundation. Reproduced by permission of The Barnes Foundation.

Bishop, Princess Bernice Pauahi. Photograph. Photo by H.L. Chase. Reproduced by permission of the Bishop Museum.

Bogert, George G. Photograph. Reprinted by permission of the University of Chicago Library, Special Collections.

Bok, Chip. Cartoon. © 2003 Chip Bok and Creators Syndicate, Inc. Reproduced by permission of Chip Bok and Creators Syndicate, Inc.

Bonds, Barry. Photograph. © 1992 AP Photo/Craig Fuji. Reproduced by permission of AP/Wide World Photos.

Coolidge, Calvin. Photograph. Jan. 31, 1923. Photograph by Herbert E. French, National Photo Company Collection, Library of Congress, Prints and Photographs Division, Digital Reproduction Number cph 3a35018.

Devine, Father. Photograph by Otto Bettmann. © Bettmann/CORBIS. Reproduced by permission.

Duke, Doris. Photograph of signature on her will. From Surrogate's Court, New York County, New York.

Duke, Doris, and her butler. Photograph by Marina Garnier. Reproduced by permission of Marina Garnier.

Dukeminier Jesse. Photograph. Reproduced by permission of David Sanders.

Fletcher, Betty B. Photograph. Reproduced by permission of Judge Fletcher.

Fournier, George. Photograph. Provided by Richard D. Solman, Esq.

Ginsburg, Ruth Bader. Photograph. Photograph by Steven Petteway, Supreme Court of the United States. Reproduced from the Collection of the Supreme Court of the United States through the Curator's Office (202) 479-3298. Reproduced by permission of Justice Ginsburg.

Hannen, James. Etching. Reproduced by permission of the National Portrait Gallery.

Helmsley, Leona, and her dog, Trouble. Photograph. © 1993 AP Images. Reproduced by permission of AP/Wide World Photos.

Klick, Jonathan, and Robert H. Sitkoff, Agency Costs, Charitable Trusts, and Corporate Control: Evidence from Hershey's Kiss-Off, 108 Colum. L. Rev 749 (2008) © 2008. Adapted by permission.

Kristol, Irving, Taxes, Poverty, and Equality, The Public Interest 26-28 (no. 37, Fall 1974). © 1974. Reprinted by permission.

Landers, Ann. Column. Reproduced by permission of Esther P. Lederer and Creators Syndicate, Inc.

Langbein, John H., Curing Execution Errors and Mistaken Terms in Wills: The Reinstatement of Wills Delivers New Tools (and Duties) to Probate Lawyers, Probate and Property, Vol. 18, No. 1, January/February, 2004. © 2004. Reprinted by permission of the author.

_____, Living Probate: The Conservatorship Model, 77 Mich. L. Rev. 63 (1978). © 1978 by the Michigan Law Review. Reprinted by permission of the author and the Michigan Law Review.

_____, Excusing Harmless Errors in the Execution of Wills: A Report on Australia's Tranquil Revolution in Probate Law, 87 Colum. L. Rev. 1 (1987). © 1987 by the Directors of the Columbia Law Review Association, Inc. All rights reserved. Reprinted by permission of the author and the Columbia Law Review.

_____, Rise of the Management Trust, Trusts & Estates, Oct. 2004, at 52. Reprinted by permission of the author and Penton Media, Inc.

_____, Substantial Compliance with the Wills Act, 88 Harv. L. Rev. 489 (1975). © 1975 by the Harvard Law Review Association. Reprinted by permission of the author and the Harvard Law Review.

_____, The Nonprobate Revolution and the Future of the Law of Succession, 97 Harv. L. Rev. 1108 (1984). Reprinted by permission of the author and the Harvard Law Review.

_____, The Uniform Prudent Investor Act and the Future of Trust Investing, 81 Iowa L. Rev. 641 (1996). Reprinted by permission of the author and the Iowa Law Review via Copyright Clearance Center.

_____, The Twentieth-Century Revolution in Family Wealth Transmission, 86 Mich. L. Rev. 722 (1988). Reprinted by permission of the author and the Michigan Law Review.

National Conference of Commissioners on Uniform State Laws (NCCUSL), excerpts from the Uniform Probate Code (1969, 1990, 1993, 1997, 1998, 2004, 2008), Uniform Prudent Investor Act (1994), Uniform Statutory Rule Against Perpetuities (1986, 1990), Uniform Transfers to Minors Act (1983, 1986), and Uniform Trust Code (2000, 2004, 2005). © 1969, 1983, 1986, 1990, 1993, 1997, 1998, 2000, 2004, 2005, 2008 by NCCUSL. Reprinted by permission of NCCUSL.

Obituary of T. Frederik Marsman, The Boston Globe, Feb. 26, 1987, at 59. © 1987 Globe Newspaper Company – MA. Reproduced with permission of the Globe Newspaper Company – MA via Copyright Clearance Center.

Plotz, David, Judicial Restraint: Sol Wachtler's Worthy Sentiments on Prison, Slate, April 16, 1997. Reprinted by permission of United Media.

Posner, Richard A., Economic Analysis of Law (7th ed. 2007). © 2007 Richard A. Posner. Reprinted by permission of Judge Posner.

Saltzman, Jonathan, Fatal Tampering Case is Renewed: FBI Searches a Condo in Cambridge, The Boston Globe, Feb. 5, 2009, at B1. © 2009 Globe Newspaper Company – MA. Reproduced with permission of the Globe Newspaper Company – MA via Copyright Clearance Center.

ACKNOWLEDGMENTS

Books and Articles

American Law Institute, Restatement (Third) of Trusts (2003), Restatement (Third) of Trusts (2007), Restatement (Third) of Trusts (T.D. 2009), Restatement (Third) of Property (1999), Restatement (Third) of Property (2003), Restatement (Third) of Property (T.D. 2004), Restatement (Third) of Property (T.D. 2006). ©1999, 2003, 2004, 2006, 2007, 2009 by the American Law Institute. Reprinted by permission of the American Law Institute.

Ascher, Mark L., Curtailing Inherited Wealth, 89 Mich. L. Rev. 69 (1990). Reprinted by permission of the author and the Michigan Law Review.

Blum, Walter, and Harry Kalven, The Uneasy Case for Progressive Taxation, 19 U. Chi. L. Rev. 417 (1952). © 1952 by the University of Chicago. Reprinted by permission of Professor Blum and the University of Chicago Law Review.

Brooke, James, After Verdict, A Trial Still Grips Denver, The New York Times, March 21, 1997, at A26. © 1997 The New York Times Company. Preprinted by permission. All rights reserved.

_____, A Web of Money, Drugs, and Death, The New York Times, March 18, 1997, at A12. © 1997 The New York Times Company. Preprinted by permission. All rights reserved.

Buck, Estate of. California Superior Court Opinion, 21 U.S.F. L. Rev. 691 (1987). Reprinted by permission of the University of San Francisco Law Review.

Dukeminier, Jesse, and James Krier, The Rise of the Perpetual Trust, 50 UCLA L. Rev. 1303 (2003). Reprinted by permission of Professor Krier and the UCLA Law Review.

Gulliver, Ashbel, and Catherine Tilson, Classification of Gratuitous Transfers, 51 Yale L.J. 1 (1941). © 1941 by the Yale Law Journal. Reprinted by permission of Professor Gulliver, The Yale Law Journal Co., and Fred B. Rothman & Co.

Halbach, Edward C., Jr., An Introduction to Chapters 1-4, in Death, Taxes and Family Property (E. Halbach ed. 1977). © 1977 by West Publishing Co. Reprinted by permission of the author and West Publishing Co.

Tate, Peter Tiersma, Lee-ford Tritt, and John Van Der Wal. In addition, we must single out two colleagues to whom we owe a great debt: Stephanie Willbanks, who assisted with tax matters throughout the book and took the lead in revising Chapter 15, and Randy Roth, who generously provided extensive comments on early drafts of every chapter.

We are grateful to Stephanie Avanessian, Mike Borgia, Kristyn Bunce, Sam Flaks, Leslie Goemaat, Regina Goldman, Michal Herzfeld, Alicia James, Chris Kulawik, Stephanie Lester, Isley Markman, Costanza Nicolosi, Cara Peterman, Ted Segal, and Megan Watts for superb research assistance; to Terri Gallego-O'Rourke and Annmarie Zell for crucial library and research support; and to Molly Overholt, who processed mounds of manuscript and proofs with efficiency and good cheer. We thank Carmen Corral-Reid, Melody Davies, Eric Holt, and Carol McGeehan at Aspen for bringing rich intelligence and sound judgment to the project. Finally, we thank our partners, David Sanders (to whom this edition is dedicated), Tamara Sitkoff, and Valerie Lindgren, for their patience and support in bringing out this new edition.

Jesse Dukeminier, 1925-2003
Robert H. Sitkoff
James Lindgren

April 2009

Editors' note: All citations to state statutes and the United States Code are to such statutes as they appeared on Lexis or Westlaw at year-end 2008 unless stated otherwise. Footnotes are numbered consecutively from the beginning of each chapter. Most footnotes in quoted materials are omitted. Citations in quoted materials are regularly omitted or edited for readability. Editors' footnotes added to quoted materials are indicated by the abbreviation: — Eds.

trust investment and administration, which evolved in simpler times. As a result, the fiduciary obligation has replaced limitations on the trustee's powers as the principal mechanism for safeguarding the beneficiary from mismanagement or abuse by the trustee. Meanwhile, the burgeoning tort liability of modern times has spawned an asset protection industry and with it radical change in the rights of creditors to trust assets.

Taxation of donative transfers has changed dramatically. The unlimited marital deduction — which permits spouses to make unlimited tax-free gifts and bequests to each other — is now a central feature of estate planning. In 1986, Congress enacted the generation-skipping transfer tax, implementing a policy of wealth transfer taxation at each generation. This tax, like an invisible boomerang, has delivered a potentially lethal blow to the Rule Against Perpetuities. In 2001, Congress enacted legislation that phases out the federal wealth transfer taxes by 2010, but then in 2011 these taxes will revert to their pre-2001 form. Further legislation, striking a new compromise, seems likely in the near future.

Throughout the book we emphasize the basic theoretical structure and the general philosophy and purposes that unify the field of donative transfers. We focus on function and purpose, not form. To this end, we have pruned away mechanical matters (such as a step-by-step discussion of how to probate a will and settle an estate, which is essentially local law, easily learned from a local practice book). At the same time, we have sought the historical roots of modern law. Understanding how the law became the way it is illuminates its continuing evolution and the sometimes exasperating peculiarities inherited from the past.

Although we organize the material in topical compartments, we have also sought a more penetrating view of the subject as a tapestry of humanity. Every illustration included, every behind-the-scenes peek, every quirk of the parties' behavior has its place as a piece of ornament fitting into the larger whole. Understanding the ambivalences of the human heart and the richness of human frailty, and realizing that even the best-constructed estate plans may, with the ever-whirling wheels of change, turn into sand castles, are essential to being a *counselor* at law, as opposed to being a mere attorney.

As Jesse and Stan said in the first edition of this book, in 1972:

> In this book we deal with people, the quick as well as the dead. There is nothing like the death of a moneyed member of the family to show persons as they really are, virtuous or conniving, generous or grasping. Many a family has been torn apart by a botched-up will. Each case is a drama in human relationships — and the lawyer, as counselor, draftsman, or advocate, is an important figure in the dramatis personae. This is one reason the estates practitioner enjoys his work, and why we enjoy ours.

This observation remains true today. In a changing reality the human drama abides. Trusts and estates is a field concerned fundamentally with people and their relationships.

For their sage advice on this revision, we thank Jane Baron, Jerry Borison, Karen Boxx, Evelyn Brody, Eric Chason, Ronald Chester, Jeff Cooper, Bridget Crawford, Judith Daar, Alyssa DiRusso, Tom Eisele, Miranda Fleischer, Bradley Fogel, Frances Foster, Susan French, Martin Fried, Gail Frommer, Susan Gary, Wayne Gazur, Randy Gingiss, Howard Helsinger, Adam Hirsch, David Horton, Richard Hyman, Bruce Johnson, Kenneth Kettering, Diane Klein, Kris Knaplund, John Langbein, William LaPiana, Michael Lewyn, Ray Madoff, Bruce Mann, Nancy McLaughlin, Fran Miller, Alan Newman, Craig Oren, Eric Rakowski, Laura Rosenbury, Ron Scalise, Max Schanzenbach, Kent Schenkel, Jeffrey Schoenblum, Frederic Schwartz, Helene Shapo, Gary Spitko, Jeffrey Stake, Joshua

PREFACE

As trusts and estates lawyers, we are in the business of succession. This simple truth was brought home to us in a deeply personal way with the unexpected passing of Jesse Dukeminier in April 2003, necessitating the succession of authorship for this book. With this eighth edition, that process of succession continues. Stanley M. Johanson, who has been serving in an emeritus capacity, now formally retires from authorship. Robert H. Sitkoff and James Lindgren, new coauthors in the seventh edition, assume full responsibility for this revision. Jesse remains the first author, however, and with good reason. Much of the wit, erudition, and playfulness of the book belongs to Jesse, whose importance to us and to the field cannot be overstated.

Wills, Trusts, and Estates is designed for use in a course on trusts and decedents' estates and as an introduction to estate planning. Our basic aim in this eighth edition remains as before: to produce not merely competent practitioners in trusts and estates, but lawyers who think critically about problems in family wealth transmission and are able to compare alternative solutions.

Since the 1960s, the law of wills has undergone a thorough renovation. Initially, the change was brought on by a swelling public demand for cheaper and simpler ways of transferring property at death, avoiding expensive probate. Imaginative scholars then began to ventilate this ancient law of the dead hand, challenging assumptions and suggesting judicial and legislative innovation to simplify and rationalize it. Medical science complicated matters by creating varieties of parentage unheard of a generation earlier. Legal malpractice in drawing wills and trusts arrived with a bang. The nonprobate revolution, with its multitude of will substitutes, provided a system of private succession that began to compete with the court-supervised probate system. Scholars, science, malpractice liability, and market competition have been a potent combination for driving law reform, of which there has been much in the last generation.

The use of trusts to transmit family wealth has become commonplace, not only for rich clients, but also for those of modest wealth. In expanding, trust law has annexed future interests and powers of appointment, reducing these two subjects largely to problems in drafting and construing trust instruments. The teachings of modern finance theory and the shifting locus of wealth from land to financial assets has put pressure on the law of

LIST OF ILLUSTRATIONS

*Chapter 15 was revised for the eighth edition principally by Stephanie J. Willbanks, Professor of Law at
Vermont Law School.

Chapter 6. Nonprobate Transfers and Planning for Incapacity   393

1

INTRODUCTION

SECTION A.   THE POWER TO TRANSMIT PROPERTY AT DEATH: JUSTIFICATIONS AND LIMITATIONS

1.   *The Right to Inherit and the Right to Convey*

THOMAS JEFFERSON, 7 JEFFERSON'S WORKS 454 (Monticello ed. 1904): "The earth belongs in usufruct to the living; the dead have neither powers nor rights over it. The portion occupied by any individual ceases to be his when he himself ceases to be, and reverts to society." (Letter to James Madison, dated Sept. 6, 1789.)

2 William Blackstone, Commentaries
*10-13

The right of inheritance, or descent to the children and relations of the deceased, seems to have been allowed much earlier than the right of devising by testament. We are apt to conceive, at first view, that it has nature on its side; yet we often mistake for nature what we find established by long and inveterate custom. It is certainly a wise and effectual, but clearly a political, establishment; since the permanent right of property, vested in the ancestor himself, was no *natural*, but merely a *civil* right. . . . It is probable that [the right of inheritance arose] . . . from a plainer and more simple principle. A man's children or nearest relations are usually about him on his death-bed, and are the earliest witnesses of his decease. They become, therefore, generally the next immediate occupants, till at length, in process of time, this frequent usage ripened into general law. And therefore, also, in the earliest ages, on failure of children, a man's servants,

1

born under his roof, were allowed to be his heirs; being immediately on the spot when he died. For we find the old patriarch Abraham expressly declaring that "since God had given him no seed, his steward Eliezer, one born in his house, was his heir."[1]

While property continued only for life, testaments were useless and unknown: and, when it became inheritable, the inheritance was long indefeasible, and the children or heirs at law were incapable of exclusion by will; till at length it was found, that so strict a rule of inheritance made heirs disobedient and headstrong, defrauded creditors of their just debts, and prevented many provident fathers from dividing or charging their estates as the exigencies of their families required. This introduced pretty generally the right of disposing of one's property, or a part of it, by *testament*; that is, by written or oral instructions properly *witnessed* and authenticated, according to the *pleasure* of the deceased, which we, therefore, emphatically style his *will*. This was established in some countries much later than in others. With us in England, till modern times, a man could only dispose of one-third of his movables from his wife and children; and in general, no will was permitted of lands till the reign of Henry VIII; and then only of a certain portion: for it was not till after the Restoration that the power of devising real property became so universal as at present.

Wills, therefore, and testaments, rights of inheritance and successions, are all of them creatures of the civil or municipal laws, and accordingly are in all respects regulated by them; every distinct country having different ceremonies and requisites to make a testament completely valid; neither does anything vary more than the right of inheritance under different national establishments.

John Locke, Two Treatises of Government
Book 1, Ch. 9, §88 (Peter Laslett ed., 1988)

It might reasonably be asked here, how come Children by this right of possessing, before any other, the properties of their Parents upon their Decease. For it being Personally the Parents, when they dye, without actually Transferring their Right to another, why does it not return again to the common stock of Mankind? 'Twill perhaps be answered, that common consent hath disposed of it, to the Children. Common Practice, we see indeed does so dispose of it but we cannot say, that it is the common consent of Mankind; for that hath never been asked, nor actually given: and if common tacit Consent hath establish'd it, it would make but a positive and not Natural Right of Children to Inherit the Goods of their Parents: But where the Practice is Universal, 'tis reasonable to think the Cause is Natural. The ground then, I think, to be this. The first and strongest desire God

---

1. Genesis 15:3. [The words put in quotation marks are Blackstone's paraphrase of two verses of the Bible, which no one has yet translated from the original Hebrew to everyone's satisfaction. Blackstone's statement that servants took as heirs in the absence of children has been disputed by many scholars. "Israel does not know a general rule like this for regulating the inheritance." Gerhard Von Rad, Genesis 178 (John H. Marks trans., 1961). Abraham's declaration was never put to the test for thereafter, when Abraham was 100 years old and his wife, Sarah, was 90, Sarah gave birth to a son, Isaac. Genesis 17:15. — Eds.]

Planted in Men, and wrought into the very Principles of their Nature being that of Self-preservation, that is the Foundation of a right to the Creatures, for the particular support and use of each individual Person himself. But next to this, God Planted in Men a strong desire also of propagating their Kind, and continuing themselves in their Posterity, and this gives Children a Title, to share in the *Property* of their Parents, and a Right to Inherit their Possessions. Men are not Proprietors of what they have meerly for themselves, their Children have a Title to part of it, and have their Kind of Right joyn'd with their Parents, in the Possession which comes to be wholly theirs, when death having put an end to their Parents use of it, hath taken them from their Possessions, and this we call Inheritance.

Until the 1980s, the views of Jefferson and Blackstone prevailed over those of Locke. It was generally accepted that the right to transmit or inherit property at death was neither a natural right nor was it constitutionally protected. Thus in Irving Trust Co. v. Day, 314 U.S. 556, 562 (1942), the Supreme Court said:

> Rights of succession to property of a deceased, whether by will or by intestacy, are of statutory creation, and the dead hand rules succession only by sufferance. Nothing in the Federal Constitution forbids the legislature of a state to limit, condition, or even abolish the power of testamentary disposition over property within its jurisdiction.

But Hodel v. Irving, decided in the 1980s when the Court revived its interest in protecting private property through the Just Compensation Clause, changed all that.

Hodel v. Irving
Supreme Court of the United States, 1987
481 U.S. 704

O'CONNOR, J. The question presented is whether the original version of the "escheat" provision of the Indian Land Consolidation Act of 1983, Pub. L. 97-459, Tit. II, 96 Stat. 2519, effected a "taking" of appellees' decedents' property without just compensation.

I

Towards the end of the 19th century, Congress enacted a series of land Acts which divided the communal reservations of Indian tribes into individual allotments for Indians and unallotted lands for non-Indian settlement. This legislation seems to have been in part animated by a desire to force Indians to abandon their nomadic ways in order to "speed the Indians' assimilation into American society," Solem v. Bartlett, 465 U.S. 463, 466 (1984), and in part a result of pressure to free new lands for further white settlement. Ibid. . . . [In 1889, by an Act of Congress] each male Sioux head of household took 320 acres of land and most other individuals 160 acres. In order to protect the allottees from the improvident disposition of their lands to white settlers, the Sioux allotment statute provided that the allotted lands were to be held in trust by the United States. Until 1910 the lands of deceased allottees passed to their heirs "according to the laws of the State or Territory" where the land was located, and after 1910, allottees were permitted to dispose of their interests by will in accordance with regulations promulgated by the Secretary of the Interior. Those regulations generally served to protect Indian ownership of the allotted lands.

Justice Sandra Day O'Connor

The policy of allotment of Indian lands quickly proved disastrous for the Indians. Cash generated by land sales to whites was quickly dissipated and the Indians, rather than farm the land themselves, evolved into petty landlords, leasing their allotted lands to white ranchers and farmers and living off the meager rentals. . . . The failure of the allotment program became even clearer as successive generations came to hold the allotted lands. Thus 40-, 80-, and 160-acre parcels became splintered into multiple undivided interests in land, with some parcels having hundreds and many parcels having dozens of owners. Because the land was held in trust and often could not be alienated or partitioned the fractionation problem grew and grew over time.

A 1928 report commissioned by the Congress found the situation administratively unworkable and economically wasteful. L. Meriam, Institute for Government Research, The Problem of Indian Administration 40-41. . . . In discussing the Indian Reorganization Act of 1934, Representative Howard said:

> It is in the case of the inherited allotments, however, that the administrative costs become incredible. . . . On allotted reservations, numerous cases exist where the shares of each individual heir from lease money may be 1 cent a month. Or one heir may own minute fractional shares in 30 or 40 different allotments. The cost of leasing, bookkeeping, and distributing the proceeds in many cases far exceeds the total income. The Indians and the Indian Service personnel are thus trapped in a meaningless system of minute partition in which all thought of the possible use of land to satisfy human needs is lost in a mathematical haze of bookkeeping. 78 Cong. Rec. 11728 (1934) (remarks of Rep. Howard).

In 1934, in response to arguments such as these, the Congress acknowledged the failure of its policy and ended further allotment of Indian lands. Indian Reorganization Act of 1934, 48 Stat. 984.

But the end of future allotment by itself could not prevent the further compounding of the existing problem caused by the passage of time. Ownership continued to fragment as succeeding generations came to hold the property, since, in the order of things, each property owner was apt to have more than one heir. . . . [N]ot until the Indian Land Consolidation Act of 1983 did the Congress take action to ameliorate the problem of fractionated ownership of Indian lands.

Section 207 of the Indian Land Consolidation Act — the escheat provision at issue in this case — provided:

> No undivided fractional interest in any tract of trust or restricted land within a tribe's reservation or otherwise subjected to a tribe's jurisdiction shall descedent [sic] by intestacy or devise but shall escheat to that tribe if such interest represents 2 per centum or less of the total acreage in such tract and has earned to its owner less than $100 in the preceding year before it is due to escheat. 96 Stat. 2519.

Congress made no provision for the payment of compensation to the owners of the interests covered by §207. The statute was signed into law on January 12, 1983, and became effective immediately.

The three appellees — Mary Irving, Patrick Pumpkin Seed, and Eileen Bissonette — are enrolled members of the Oglala Sioux Tribe. They are, or represent, heirs or devisees of members of the Tribe who died in March, April, and June 1983. Eileen Bissonette's decedent, Mary Poor Bear-Little Hoop Cross, purported to will all her property, including property subject to §207, to her five minor children in whose name Bissonette claims the property. Chester Irving, Charles Leroy Pumpkin Seed, and Edgar Pumpkin Seed all died intestate. At the time of their deaths, the four decedents owned 41 fractional interests subject to the provisions of §207. The Irving estate lost two interests whose value together was approximately $100; the Bureau of Indian Affairs placed total values of approximately $2,700 on the 26 escheatable interests in the Cross estate and $1,816 on the 13 escheatable interests in the Pumpkin Seed estates. But for §207, this property would have passed, in the ordinary course, to appellees or those they represent.

Appellees filed suit in the United States District Court for the District of South Dakota, claiming that §207 resulted in a taking of property without just compensation in violation of the Fifth Amendment. . . .

II

[The Court held that the plaintiffs had standing under Article III of the Constitution.]

III

The Congress, acting pursuant to its broad authority to regulate the descent and devise of Indian trust lands, Jefferson v. Fink, 247 U.S. 288, 294 (1918), enacted §207 as a means of ameliorating, over time, the problem of extreme fractionation of certain Indian lands. By forbidding the passing on at death of small, undivided interests in Indian lands, Congress hoped that future generations of Indians would be able to make more productive use of the Indians' ancestral lands. We agree with the Government that encouraging the consolidation of Indian lands is a public purpose of high order. The fractionation problem on Indian reservations is extraordinary and may call for dramatic action to encourage consolidation. The Sisseton-Wahpeton Sioux Tribe, appearing as amicus curiae in support of the Secretary of the Interior, is a quintessential victim of fractionation. Forty-acre tracts on the Sisseton-Wahpeton Lake Traverse Reservation, leasing for about $1,000 annually, are commonly subdivided into hundreds of undivided interests, many of which generate only pennies a year in rent. The average tract has 196 owners and the average owner undivided interests in 14 tracts. The administrative headache this represents can be fathomed by examining Tract 1305, dubbed "one of the most fractionated parcels of land in the world." Lawson, Heirship: The Indian Amoeba, reprinted in Hearing on S. 2480 and S. 2663 before the Senate Select Committee on Indian Affairs, 98th Cong., 2d Sess., 85 (1984). Tract 1305 is 40 acres and produces $1,080 in income annually. It is valued at $8,000. It has 439 owners, one-third of whom receive less than $.05 in annual rent and two-thirds of whom receive less than $1. The largest interest holder receives $82.85 annually. The common denominator used to compute fractional interests in the property is 3,394,923,840,000. The smallest heir receives $.01 every 177 years. If the tract were sold (assuming the 439 owners could agree) for its estimated $8,000 value, he would be entitled to $.000418. The administrative costs of handling this tract are estimated by the Bureau of Indian Affairs at $17,560 annually. Id. at 86, 87. . . .

  Section 207 provides for the escheat of small undivided property interests that are unproductive during the year preceding the owner's death. Even if we accept the Government's assertion that the income generated by such parcels may be properly thought of as de minimis, their value may not be. While the Irving estate lost two interests whose value together was only approximately $100, the Bureau of Indian Affairs placed total values of approximately $2,700 and $1,816 on the escheatable interests in the Cross and Pumpkin Seed estates. These are not trivial sums. . . . Of course, the whole of appellees' decedents' property interests were not taken by §207. Appellees' decedents retained full beneficial use of the property during their lifetimes as well as the right to convey it inter vivos. There is no question, however, that the right to pass on valuable property to one's heirs is itself a valuable right. Depending on the age of the owner, much or most of the value of the parcel may inhere in this "remainder" interest. . . .

  The extent to which any of appellees' decedents had "investment-backed expectations" in passing on the property is dubious. Though it is conceivable that some of these interests were purchased with the expectation that the owners might pass on the remainder to their heirs at death, the property has been held in trust for the Indians for 100 years and is overwhelmingly acquired by gift, descent, or devise. Because of the highly fractionated ownership, the property is generally held for lease rather than improved and used by the owners. None of the appellees here can point to any specific investment-backed expectations beyond the fact that their ancestors agreed to accept allotment only after ceding to the United States large parts of the original Great Sioux Reservation.

Also weighing weakly in favor of the statute is the fact that there is something of an "average reciprocity of advantage," Pennsylvania Coal Co. v. Mahon, 260 U.S. 393, 415 (1922), to the extent that owners of escheatable interests maintain a nexus to the Tribe. Consolidation of Indian lands in the Tribe benefits the members of the Tribe. All members do not own escheatable interests, nor do all owners belong to the Tribe. Nevertheless, there is substantial overlap between the two groups. The owners of escheatable interests often benefit from the escheat of others' fractional interests. Moreover, the whole benefit gained is greater than the sum of the burdens imposed since consolidated lands are more productive than fractionated lands.

If we were to stop our analysis at this point, we might well find §207 constitutional. But the character of the Government regulation here is extraordinary. In Kaiser Aetna v. United States, 444 U.S. 164, 176 (1979), we emphasized that the regulation destroyed "one of the most essential sticks in the bundle of rights that are commonly characterized as property—the right to exclude others." Similarly, the regulation here amounts to virtually the abrogation of the right to pass on a certain type of property—the small undivided interest—to one's heirs. In one form or another, the right to pass on property—to one's family in particular—has been part of the Anglo-American legal system since feudal times. See United States v. Perkins, 163 U.S. 625, 627-628 (1896). The fact that it may be possible for the owners of these interests to effectively control disposition upon death through complex inter vivos transactions such as revocable trusts, is simply not an adequate substitute for the rights taken, given the nature of the property. Even the United States concedes that total abrogation of the right to pass property is unprecedented and likely unconstitutional. Moreover, this statute effectively abolishes both descent and devise of these property interests even when the passing of the property to the heir might result in consolidation of property—as for instance when the heir already owns another undivided interest in the property. Cf. 25 U.S.C. §2206(b) (1982 ed., Supp. III). Since the escheatable interests are not, as the United States argues, necessarily de minimis, nor, as it also argues, does the availability of inter vivos transfer obviate the need for descent and devise, a *total* abrogation of these rights cannot be upheld. . . .

In holding that complete abolition of both the descent and devise of a particular class of property may be a taking, we reaffirm the continuing vitality of the long line of cases recognizing the States', and where appropriate, the United States', broad authority to adjust the rules governing the descent and devise of property without implicating the guarantees of the Just Compensation Clause. See, e.g., Irving Trust Co. v. Day, 314 U.S. 556, 562 (1942). The difference in this case is the fact that both descent and devise are completely abolished; indeed they are abolished even in circumstances when the governmental purpose sought to be advanced, consolidation of ownership of Indian lands, does not conflict with the further descent of the property.

There is little doubt that the extreme fractionation of Indian lands is a serious public problem. It may well be appropriate for the United States to ameliorate fractionation by means of regulating the descent and devise of Indian lands. Surely it is permissible for the United States to prevent the owners of such interests from further subdividing them among future heirs on pain of escheat. It may be appropriate to minimize further compounding of the problem by abolishing the descent of such interests by rules of intestacy, thereby forcing the owners to formally designate an heir to prevent escheat to the Tribe. What is certainly not appropriate is to take the extraordinary step of abolishing both descent and devise of these property interests even when the passing of the property to the heir might result in consolidation of property. Accordingly, we find that this regulation, in the words of Justice Holmes, "goes too far." Pennsylvania Coal Co. v. Mahon, 260 U.S. at 415. The judgment of the Court of Appeals is

Affirmed.

QUESTIONS AND NOTES

1.   Most of the controlling cases cited by Justice O'Connor involve governmental regulation of land use. Why should tests that were designed to determine when compensation must be given for land use regulation be used when inheritance is at issue? A fundamental issue in the former area is whether the government is "forcing some people alone to bear public burdens which, in all fairness and justice, should be borne by the public as a whole." Armstrong v. United States, 364 U.S. 40, 49 (1960). Is this relevant to regulation of inheritance?

2.   In Hodel v. Irving, the Court's opinion appears to rest on the assumption that the right to transmit property at death is a separate, identifiable stick in the bundle of rights called property, and, if this right is taken away, compensation must be paid. The Court did not look at the impact of the statute upon the value of the whole bundle of property rights, including lifetime use, but only at the impact of the statute upon the right to transmit the property at death. If the issue is the economic loss suffered by the property owner as a consequence of the statute, as it is in regulatory taking cases, should not the court have considered the impact of the statute upon the whole bundle of rights rather than on one stick?

For an interesting comment on Hodel v. Irving, see Ronald Chester, Inheritance in American Legal Thought, *in* Inheritance and Wealth in America 23 (Robert K. Miller, Jr. and Stephen J. McNamee eds., 1998).

3.   In many societies wills are not permitted. With respect to Native American tribal lands, wills were unknown until Congress forced individual allotments on the tribes. Even then, before 1910 Native American allottees were not permitted to devise their lands.

In some countries (on the continent of Europe, for example), children cannot be disinherited. They are forced heirs. In Anglo-American history, the right to devise property has always been in uneasy tension with forced succession. In early feudal times, forced succession had the upper hand. Prior to 1540, when the Statute of Wills was enacted, a will of land was not permitted at law in England. The legal title to land owned at death passed to the eldest son, subject to the surviving spouse's dower or curtesy. In the United States, married women could not devise land without the consent of their husbands until the enactment of Married Women's Property Acts in the late nineteenth century. By the twentieth century, forced succession reappeared when statutes were enacted giving the surviving spouse a forced share, typically one-third, of the decedent spouse's estate. See In re Estate of Magee, 988 So. 2d 1 (Fla. App. 2007) (upholding spousal forced share against constitutional challenge). In Louisiana, where the civil law of France was introduced, minor and disabled children may not be disinherited. (On the protection of a spouse and children, see Chapter 7.)

Although §207 of the Indian Land Consolidation Act spoke of "escheat" to the tribe, in effect, the section made the tribe the successor to, or heir of, the Native American owner of the affected fractioned land. Why is forced succession by a tribe not constitutionally permissible when forced succession by family members is? If the Native Americans wanted tribal ownership restored, is there any way to change back to tribal ownership without paying individuals for their allotted lands? Is there any way to get the genie back in the bottle?

4.   While Hodel v. Irving was being argued in the Court of Appeals, Congress amended §207 of the Indian Land Consolidation Act to provide: "Nothing in this section shall prohibit the devise of such an escheatable fractional interest to any other owner of an undivided fractional interest in such parcel or tract of trust or restricted land." 25 U.S.C. §2206(b) (1994). The amendment was not retroactive and hence did not affect the operation of §207 on the property involved in the case. The amended statute was held unconstitutional in Babbitt v. Youpee, 519 U.S. 234 (1997), on the grounds that it permitted devise only among a very limited group (other owners of the parcel), which is not likely to include a lineal descendant of the decedent, often the primary object of the decedent's bounty.

In 2004, Congress passed the American Indian Probate Reform Act, effective June 2006, which takes a new approach to resolving the problem of fractionation. See 25 U.S.C. §2206 (2008). The new Act supplants state probate law with a federal probate code for most Native American reservations, though tribes are permitted to enact their own probate codes if they wish. Under the new law, trust land may be conveyed by will to other Native Americans or to the tribe. Without a will, the decedent's spouse generally receives only a life estate in one-third, with the rest going to the decedent's descendants. If an intestate decedent owns less than a 5 percent interest in a parcel, then the interest is not divided further, but rather the oldest child or grandchild takes all of it, limited only by the right of a surviving spouse to remain on the land. The tribe or the other co-owners may buy the decedent's interest during probate with the consent of the heirs, unless the decedent owns less than a 5 percent interest, in which event consent is not required so long as the heirs do not live on the land.

For further discussion, see Douglas R. Nash and Cecelia E. Burke, The Changing Landscape of Indian Estate Planning and Probate: The American Indian Probate Reform Act, 5 Seattle J. Soc. Just. 121 (2006); David M. English, A Uniform Probate Code for Indian Country at Last, Prob. & Prop., Mar./Apr. 2006, at 20. Meanwhile, litigation continues over individual Indian money trust accounts held by the federal government. See Cobell v. Kempthorne, 569 F. Supp. 2d 223 (D.D.C. 2008).

5.   For further reading on the changing institution of inheritance in this country, from its earliest days to the present, see Carole Shammas, Marylynn Salmon, and Michel Dahlin, Inheritance in America: From Colonial Times to the Present (1997); Kristine S. Knaplund, The Evolution of Women's Rights in Inheritance, 19 Hastings Women's L.J. 3 (2008).

For a fascinating study of the legal minefield of devising property to slaves in the antebellum South, see Adrienne D. Davis, The Private Law of Race and Sex: An Antebellum Perspective, 51 Stan. L. Rev. 221 (1999). The fundamental challenge was how to uphold testamentary freedom without disrupting racial hierarchies. Slaves were regarded as property, and the idea of property owning property was baffling. Professor Davis examines the wills of white men who devised property to their children borne by slave women, or to the slave women themselves, and the tensions and contradictions in legal doctrine these devises caused.

In Hodel v. Irving, the Supreme Court held that the Fifth Amendment curtailed the power of the government to *limit* the right to convey property at death. In the next case, the court grapples with the opposite question, namely, whether after the decedent's death the government can *increase* the property rights that pass as part of the decedent's estate.

Shaw Family Archives v. CMG Worldwide
United States District Court, Southern District of New York, 2007
486 F. Supp. 2d 309

McMahon, J.   . . . Marilyn Monroe, perhaps the most famous American sex symbol of the twentieth century, died testate on August 5, 1962. Her will, which did not expressly bequeath a right of publicity, contained the following residuary clause:

SIXTH: All the rest, residue and remainder of my estate, both real and personal of whatsoever nature and whatsoever situate, of which I shall die seized or possessed or to which I shall be in any way entitled, or over which I shall possess any power of appointment by Will at the time of my death, including any lapsed legacies, I give, devise and bequeath as follows:

(a) To MAY REIS the sum of $ 40,000 or 25% of the total remainder of my estate, whichever shall be the lesser.
(b) To DR. MARIANNE KRIS 25% of the balance thereof, to be used by her [for the furtherance of the work of such psychiatric institutions or groups as she shall elect]. . . .
(c) To LEE STRASBERG the entire remaining balance.

The will also named Aaron Frosch, Ms. Monroe's New York-based attorney, as the executor. It was subject to primary probate in New York County Surrogate's Court.

In 1968, six years after probate of the Monroe Estate had commenced, Lee Strasberg[2] married Anna Strasberg. Lee Strasberg died in 1982, leaving his wife Anna Strasberg as the sole beneficiary under his will. Upon the death of Mr. Frosch in 1989, the New York Surrogate's Court appointed Anna Strasberg as Administratrix . . . of the Monroe Estate. The Monroe Estate remained open until June 19, 2001, on which date the Surrogate's Court authorized the Administratrix to close the estate and transfer the residuary assets to MMLLC [Marilyn Monroe, LLC], a Delaware company formed by Ms. Strasberg to hold and manage the intellectual property assets of the residuary beneficiaries of Marilyn Monroe's will.

SFA [Shaw Family Archives, LLC] is a limited liability company organized under New York law with its primary place of business in New York. Its principals are the three children of the late photographer Sam Shaw. Among the photographs owned by SFA and comprising the Shaw Collection is a series of photographs of Marilyn Monroe, including many "canonical" Marilyn images. The copyrights to the Marilyn photographs are purportedly owned by Sam Shaw's daughters, Edith Marcus and Meta Stevens.

This dispute arises out of (1) the alleged sale of a T-shirt at a Target retail store in Indianapolis, Indiana on September 6, 2006, which bore a picture of Marilyn Monroe and the inscription of the "Shaw Family Archives" on the inside neck label and tag, and (2) the alleged maintenance of a website by SFA and Bradford [Licensing] through which customers could purchase licenses for the use of Ms. Monroe's picture, image and likeness on various commercial products. MMLLC asserts that it is the successor-in-interest to the postmortem right of publicity that was devised through the residuary clause of Ms. Monroe's will, and that the commercial use of Ms. Monroe's picture, image, and likeness by SFA and Bradford without MMLLC's consent violates its rights under Indiana's 1994 Right of Publicity Act. This statute, passed over three decades after Ms. Monroe's death, by a state with which she had (as far as the court is aware) absolutely no contact during her life, creates a descendible and freely transferable right of publicity that survives for 100 years after a personality's death. The statute purports to apply to an act or event that occurs within Indiana, regardless of a personality's domicile, residence, or citizenship. See Ind. Code §§32-36-1-1 to -20 (2007). . . .

DISCUSSION

In their cross-motion for summary judgment, the SFA parties [SFA and Bradford] argue, *inter alia,* that even if a postmortem right of publicity in Marilyn Monroe's

---

2. For more on Lee Strasberg, see footnote 16 at page 582. — Eds.

Marilyn Monroe

name, likeness and persona exists, MMLLC and CMG [Worldwide, Inc.] cannot demonstrate that they are the owners of that right because only property actually owned by a testator at the time of her death can be devised by will. Since neither New York nor California (the only possible domiciles of Ms. Monroe at the time of her death) — nor for that matter, Indiana — recognized descendible postmortem publicity rights at the time of Ms. Monroe's death in 1962, she could not transfer any such rights through her will, and MMLLC cannot be a successor-in-interest to them. Moreover, the SFA parties contend, neither the California nor the Indiana right of publicity statutes allow for the transfer of the publicity rights they recognize through the wills of personalities who were already deceased at the time of their enactment. The court agrees.

1. *Ms. Monroe did not have the testamentary capacity to devise property rights she did not own at the time of her death.*

MMLLC argues that its ownership interest in Ms. Monroe's postmortem right of publicity — assuming *arguendo* that such a right exists — stems from Ms. Monroe's valid devise of this right to Lee Strasberg through the residuary clause in her will. The court concludes — regardless of Ms. Monroe's domicile at the time of her death, and regardless of any rights purportedly conferred after her death by the Indiana Right of Publicity Act or by Cal. Civil Code §3344.1 (2007) — Ms. Monroe could not devise by will a property right she did not own at the time of her death in 1962.

Descendible postmortem publicity rights were not recognized, in New York, California, or Indiana at the time of Ms. Monroe's death in 1962. To this day, New York law does not recognize any common law right of publicity and limits its statutory publicity rights to living persons. California recognized descendible publicity rights when it passed its postmortem right of publicity statute in 1984, 22 years after Ms. Monroe's death. Prior to that time, a common law right of publicity existed, but it was not freely transferable or descendible. Indiana first recognized a descendible, postmortem right of publicity in 1994, when it passed the Indiana Right of Publicity Act. See Ind. Code §§32-36-1-1 to -20. Prior to that time, rights of publicity were inalienable in Indiana, since they could only be vindicated through a personal tort action for invasion of privacy.

Thus, at the time of her death in 1962 Ms. Monroe did not have any postmortem right of publicity under the law of any relevant state. As a result, any publicity rights she enjoyed during her lifetime were extinguished at her death by operation of law.

Nevertheless, MMLLC argues that her will should be construed as devising postmortem publicity rights that were later conferred on Ms. Monroe by statute. Such a construction is untenable.

Indiana follows the majority rule that the law of the domicile of the testator at his or her death applies to all questions of a will's construction. There are disputed issues of fact concerning whether Ms. Monroe was domiciled in New York or California at the time of her death. (There is absolutely no doubt that she was not domiciled in Indiana.) However, it is not necessary to resolve the question of domicile because neither New York nor California — the only two states in which Ms. Monroe could conceivably have been domiciled — permitted a testator to dispose by will of property she does not own at the time of her death.

It is well-settled that, under New York law, "A disposition by the testator of all his property passes all of the property he was entitled to dispose of *at the time of his death.*" N.Y. Est. Powers & Trusts Law §3-3.1 (2007) (emphasis added). The corollary principle recognized by the courts is that property not owned by the testator at the time of his death is not subject to disposition by will. . . .

California law does not differ from New York's. Section 21105 of the California Probate Code provides that, with inapplicable exceptions, "A will passes all property *the testator owns at death,* including property acquired after execution of the will." (emphasis added). . . .

Nor does §2-602 of the Uniform Probate Code, which states that a will may pass "property acquired by the estate after the testator's death," have anything to do with the present case, because neither New York nor California is among the 18 states that have adopted the Uniform Probate Code in whole or even in part.[3] This court has not found, nor has MMLLC cited, any provision in either the New York or the California probate laws that codifies §2-602. . . .

Even if, as MMLLC implies, there has been some recent shift away from the unequivocal rule that only property owned by the testator at the time of death can be passed by will (as evidenced by §2-602 of the Uniform Probate Code), it does not help MMLLC's cause. "Testamentary disposition . . . is controlled by the law in effect *as of the date of death.*" Dep't of Health Services v. Fontes, 215 Cal. Rptr. 14, 15 (App. 1985) (emphasis added). There is no question — based on the case law recited above — that at the time of Ms. Monroe's death in 1962, neither New York nor California permitted a testator to dispose by will of property she did not own at the time of her death. Any argument that the residuary clause of Ms. Monroe's will could devise a postmortem right of publicity is thus doubly doomed because the law in effect at the time of Ms. Monroe's death did not recognize descendible postmortem publicity rights and did not allow for distribution under a will of property not owned by the testator at the time of her death.

---

3. The official comment to UPC §2-602 (1990) explains: "This section is revised to assure that . . . a residuary clause in a will . . . passes property acquired by a testator's estate after his or her death." — Eds.

   2.   *Ms. Monroe did not "intend" to devise any rights she may have acquired under the Indiana or California right of publicity statute through the residuary clause of her will.*

   MMLLC argues that Marilyn Monroe intended to bequeath a postmortem right of publicity to her testamentary legatees. The argument is unpersuasive. . . . MMLLC makes much of Ms. Monroe's purported intent to include in her residuary estate all property "to which [she] shall be in any way entitled." In the absence of any other evidence concerning Ms. Monroe's intent, this boilerplate language is much too slender a reed on which to hang a devise of postmortem publicity rights that did not come into being until 22 years after her death. . . .

   Even if the language Ms. Monroe employed clearly demonstrated her intent to devise property she had no capacity to devise, the effect would be to render the disposition invalid, because she had no legal right to dispose of property that did not exist at the time of her death. . . .

   3.   *Neither the California nor the Indiana postmortem right of publicity statutes allows for testamentary disposition of the rights it recognizes by celebrities already deceased at the time of its enactment.* . . .

   MMLLC's case is doomed because both the California and Indiana postmortem right of publicity statutes recognize that an individual cannot pass by will a statutory property right that she did not possess at the time of her death. California's Civ. Code §3344.1(b)-(d) provides that, if no transfer of a personality's postmortem right of publicity has occurred before the personality's death, either "by contract or by means of a trust or testamentary documents," then the rights vest in certain statutorily specified heirs. Since a testamentary transfer has no effect until the testator's death, such a transfer could not be effectuated "before death" for purposes of the California statute. Thus, any rights bestowed by §3344.1 on a personality already deceased at the time of its enactment could not be transferred by will (which is how the purported property right came to MMLLC from the Administratrix at the time the Monroe Estate wound up). It would vest instead in the persons provided for by statute.

   The Indiana statute likewise provides that if a personality has not transferred her right of publicity by "contract," license," "gift," "trust," or "testamentary document," the right will "vest" in those individuals entitled to her property through the "[o]peration of the laws of intestate succession applicable to the state administering the estate and property of the intestate deceased personality, regardless of whether the state recognizes the property rights set forth under this chapter." See Ind. Code §§32-36-1-16 to -18. Ms. Monroe's legatees under her will are not her statutory heirs for intestacy purposes.

   Thus, even if a postmortem right of publicity in Marilyn Monroe's persona could have been created after her death, neither of the statutes that arguably bestowed that right allows for it to be transferred through the will of a "personality" who, like Ms. Monroe, was already deceased at the time of the statute's enactment. To the extent that other courts, including Joplin Enterprises v.

Allen,795 F. Supp. 349 (W.D. Wash. 1992) and Miller v. Glenn Miller Productions, 318 F. Supp. 2d 923 (C.D. Cal. 2004), assumed without explicitly deciding that California's right of publicity statute allows for the disposition of the rights it recognizes through wills of personalities already deceased at the time of its enactment, and that such disposition is permissible under the applicable probate principles, this court respectfully disagrees.

CONCLUSION

MMLLC's motion for summary judgment . . . is denied, and SFA's cross-motion for summary judgment . . . is granted.

NOTES AND QUESTIONS

1. *Epilogue.* The decision in *Shaw* excerpted above was rendered in May 2007. Five months later, California Governor Arnold Schwarzenegger signed an amendment to Cal. Civ. Code §3344.1 that added the following language:

> (b) . . . The rights recognized under this section shall be deemed to have existed at the time of death of any deceased personality who died prior to January 1, 1985, and . . . shall vest in the persons entitled to these property rights under the testamentary instrument of the deceased personality effective as of the date of his or her death. In the absence of an express transfer in a testamentary instrument of the deceased personality's rights . . . , a provision in the testamentary instrument that provides for the disposition of the residue of the deceased personality's assets shall be effective to transfer the rights recognized under this section in accordance with the terms of that provision. The rights established by this section shall also be freely transferable or descendible by contract, trust, or any other testamentary instrument by any subsequent owner of the deceased personality's rights as recognized by this section. . . .
>
> (p) The rights recognized by this section are expressly made retroactive, including to those deceased personalities who died before January 1, 1985. [Cal. Civ. Code §3344.1 (2008).]

Thus, under California law, publicity rights are devisable at death, even by general residuary clauses in wills made before 1984, when California first recognized such rights. The session law as enacted by the legislature makes the purpose of the amendment plain: "It is the intent of the Legislature to abrogate the summary judgment order[ ] entered in . . . Shaw Family Archives Ltd. v. CMG Worldwide." 2007 Cal. Legis. Serv. Ch. 439 §2 (S.B. 771). In 2008, however, federal district courts in both New York and California held that Monroe was a domiciliary of New York at her death, rendering the California statute inapplicable. Milton H. Greene Archives, Inc. v. CMG Worldwide, Inc., 568 F. Supp. 3d 1152 (C.D. Cal. 2008); Shaw Family Archives Ltd. v. CMG Worldwide, Inc., 2008 WL 4127830 (S.D.N.Y. 2008).

2. *Literature.* For an analysis of dead-hand control over the right of publicity, see William A. Drennan, Wills, Trusts, Schadenfreude, and the Wild, Wacky Right of Publicity: Exploring the Enforceability of Dead-Hand Restrictions, 58 Ark. L. Rev. 43 (2005). See also Mark G. Tratos and Stephen Weizenecker, Dead Celebrity Wars, 25 Ent. & Sports L. 1 (2007) (surveying deceased celebrity rights across the states); Stacey L. Dogan and Mark A. Lemley, What the Right of Publicity Can Learn From Trademark Law, 58 Stan. L. Rev. 1161 (2006).

For a discussion of the inheritance of copyrights, which is governed by federal law and not variable by will (what the author calls "estate-bumping"), see Lee-Ford Tritt, Liberating Estates Law from the Constraints of Copyright, 38 Rutgers L.J. 109 (2006).

3. *Tax implications?* Suppose *T* lives in a jurisdiction that recognizes a descendible right of publicity. How should that right be reckoned in computing the estate taxes due on *T*'s death? For an insightful analysis, see Ray D. Madoff, Taxing Personhood: Estate Taxes and the Compelled Commodification of Identity, 17 Va. Tax Rev. 759 (1998). What are the tax ramifications if the jurisdiction in which *T* lived did not recognize a descendible right of publicity at *T*'s death but thereafter recognizes such a right retroactively? Compare Joshua C. Tate, Marilyn Monroe's Legacy: Taxation of Postmortem Publicity Rights, 118 Yale L.J. Pocket Part 38 (2008), with Mitchell M. Gans, Bridget J. Crawford, and Jonathan G. Blattmachr, Postmortem Rights of Publicity: The Federal Estate Tax Consequences of New State-Law Property Rights, 117 Yale L.J. Pocket Part 203 (2008), and Mitchell M. Gans, Bridget J. Crawford, and Jonathan G. Blattmachr, The Estate Tax Fundamentals of Celebrity and Control, 118 Yale L.J. Pocket Part 50 (2008).

2. The Policy of Passing Wealth at Death

JOHN A. BRITTAIN, INHERITANCE AND THE INEQUALITY OF MATE-RIAL WEALTH 13 (1978): "The less the rewards of wealth are associated with one's own contribution, the better the case for taxing them. . . . Inheritance remains one of the purest forms of 'getting something for nothing.'"

Edward C. Halbach, Jr., An Introduction to Death,
Taxes and Family Property
in Death, Taxes and Family Property 3 (Edward C. Halbach, Jr., ed., 1977)[4]

What justifications are there for the private transmission of wealth from generation to generation? And how do we rationalize allowing only some

---

4. Reprinted from Death, Taxes and Family Property (Edward C. Halbach, Jr., ed., 1977) with permission of the West Publishing Company. Copyright © 1977 by West Publishing Co.

individuals, selected by accident of birth, to enjoy significant comforts and power they have not earned?

Many arguments are offered in support of the institution of inheritance. One is simply that, in a society based on private property, it may be the least objectionable arrangement for dealing with property on the owner's death. Another is that inheritance is natural and proper as both an expression and a reinforcement of family ties, which in turn are important to a healthy society and a good life. After all, a society should be concerned with the total amount of happiness it can offer, and to many of its members it is a great comfort and satisfaction to know during life that, even after death, those whom one cares about can be provided for and may be able to enjoy better lives because of the inheritance that can be left to them. Furthermore, it is argued, giving and bequeathing not only express but beget affection, or at least responsibility. Thus, society is seen as offering a better and happier life by responding to the understandable desire of an individual to provide for his or her family after death.

Just as individuals may be rewarded through this desire, it can also be used by society, via inheritance rights, to serve as an incentive to bring forth creativity, hard work, initiative and ultimately productivity that benefits others, as well as encouraging individual responsibility — encouraging those who can to make provision that society would otherwise have to make for those who are or may be dependents. Of course, some doubt the need for such incentives, at least beyond modest levels of achievement and wealth accumulation, relying on the quest for power (or for recognition) and other motivations — not to mention habit. Long after these forces have taken over to stimulate the industry of such individuals, however, society may continue to find it important to offer property inducements to the irrepressibly productive to save rather than to consume, and to go on saving long after their own lifelong future needs are provided for. And what harm is there if individuals, through socially approved channels, pursue immortality and psychological satisfactions? The direct and indirect (e.g., through life insurance and through corporate accumulations) savings of individuals are vital to the economy's capital base and thus to its level of employment and to the productivity of other individuals.

Consequently, it is concluded, inheritance may grant wealth to *donees* without regard to their competence and performance, but the economic reasons for allowing inheritance are viewed in terms of proper rewards and socially valuable incentives to the *donor*. In fact, some philosophers would insist, these rewards are required by ideals of social justice as the fruits of one's labors.

JEREMY BENTHAM, THE THEORY OF LEGISLATION 184 (C.K. Ogden ed., 1950): "[W]hen we recollect the infirmities of old age, we must be satisfied that it is necessary not to deprive it of this counterpoise of factitious attractions [prospects of inheritance by the younger giving care to the older]. In the rapid descent of life, every support on which man can lean should be left untouched, and it is well that interest serve as a monitor to duty."

Melvin L. Oliver, Thomas M. Shapiro, and Julie E. Press, "Them That's Got Shall Get": Inheritance and Achievement in Wealth Accumulation
in 5 Research in Politics and Society: The Politics of Wealth and Inequality 69
(Richard E. Ratcliff, Melvin L. Oliver, and Thomas M. Shapiro eds., 1995)

The role and extent of inherited wealth is an important issue that occupies considerable attention among economists. However, their theoretically driven models of the importance of inherited wealth support a wide and quite contradictory range of findings. One end estimates that 80 percent of great wealth is inherited. The other end estimates that inherited wealth comprises only 20 percent of the wealthy's stockpile and 80 percent is earned the old fashioned way. In any event the amount and meaning of inherited wealth is considerable. For example, the wealthiest generation of elderly people in America's history is in the process of passing along its wealth.

Between 1987 and 2011, the baby boom generation stands to inherit an estimated 6.8 trillion dollars.[5] Much of this wealth was built by their parents between the late 1940s and the late 1960s when real wages and savings rates were higher and housing costs were considerably lower. For the elderly middle class, the escalation of real estate prices over the last 20 years has meant a significant boon to their assets. Of course not all will benefit equally, or at all. The richest one percent will divide one-third of the worth of estates, each inheritance per estate receiving an average inheritance of $6 million; the next richest nine percent will divide another third for an average inheritance of about $396,000. Much of this wealth will be property. Philosopher Robert Nozick says that this "sticks out as a special kind of unearned benefit that produces unequal opportunities."

De Tocqueville warned the first new nation about the social and political dangers of inherited wealth becoming the basis of enduring privilege. He wrote: "What is the most important for democracy is not that great fortunes should not exist, but that great fortunes should not remain in the same hands. In that way there are rich men, but they do not form a class."

—————————————

The minimum wealth necessary to qualify in 2008 for the Forbes Magazine list of the 400 Richest Americans was $1.3 billion. The top two slots went to Bill Gates and Warren Buffett, with $57 and $50 billion, respectively. In total, the combined net worth of the 400 Richest Americans was $1.56 trillion. Forbes does not include inheritance as a category for source of wealth, but manifestly inheritance played an important role in the wealth of many on the list. Four of the top 10 slots, for example, are held by kin of Sam Walton, founder of Wal-Mart, and 3 of the top 20 slots are held by kin of Forrest Mars, inventor of M&M's chocolate candy.

A sense of the magnitude of gratuitous wealth transfer may be obtained from a review of federal estate and gift tax returns. The Statistics of Income Division

---

5. A more recent study estimates that between 1998 and 2052 at least $41 trillion will pass from one generation to the next. John J. Havens and Paul G. Schervish, Why the $41 Trillion Wealth Transfer Estimate is Still Valid: A Review of Challenges and Comments, 7 J. Gift Plan. 11 (Jan. 2003). — Eds.

(SOI) of the IRS estimates that in 2007 the IRS received nearly 40,000 estate tax returns reporting combined gross estates of just over $200 billion. Nearly $60 billion, more than one-quarter, is traceable to estates with a value of $20 million or more. Over $120 billion, more than half, is traceable to estates with a value of more than $5 million. The SOI also estimates that in 2007 the IRS received nearly 250,000 gift tax returns showing aggregate gifts in the amount of almost $40 billion, of which nearly $26 billion came from gifts of over $100,000. These estimates necessarily understate the total volume of gratuitous wealth transfer because they do not include many nontaxable transfers.

Most scholars have concluded that the concentration of wealth in the United States fell sharply from 1929 through the 1940s, reaching a plateau that held from the 1950s through the 1970s. In the 1980s, however, there was a sharp increase in the share of wealth held by the richest Americans, followed by a leveling off after 1989. Professor Repetti concludes: "The result was that at the end of the twentieth century, wealth was more concentrated in the United States than in the United Kingdom. This was a reversal from the early years of the twentieth century when the U.S. tradition of 'economic democracy' had resulted in a much lower concentration than the 'royalist legacy' of Britain." James R. Repetti, Democracy, Taxes and Wealth, 76 N.Y.U. L. Rev. 825, 825-826 (2001). In 2004, the richest 1 percent of Americans owned 34.3 percent of family wealth and the top 10 percent owned a staggering 71.2 percent of family wealth. Lawrence Mishel, Jared Bernstein, and Sylvia Alegretto, The State of Working America at Table 5.1 (2006/2007).

Wealth is usually defined by economists as a discounted future income stream, but in measuring this economists often ignore some important forms of wealth. Professor Langbein explains:

> These calculations presuppose that financial instruments, business interests, and real property are the only important components of wealth. Because this way of measuring wealth excludes the capitalized value of the income streams generated by human capital, and because it excludes the capitalized value of the private-pension and Social Security income streams, it materially overstates the disparity between the top wealth holders and the rest of the populace. These calculations also overlook what economists call the life-cycle effect: University of Michigan law students who will have six-figure incomes within a decade are currently reckoned as paupers. Nevertheless, the underlying point is undeniable. The top sliver of wealth holders is indeed very affluent. [John H. Langbein, The Twentieth-Century Revolution in Family Wealth Transmission, 86 Mich. L. Rev. 722, 746 (1988).]

The most powerful argument against permitting transmission of wealth is that it perpetuates wide disparities in the distribution of wealth, concentrates inherited economic power in the hands of a few, and denies equality of opportunity to the poor. For insightful discussions of these issues, see Anne L. Alstott, Equal Opportunity and Inheritance Taxation, 121 Harv. L. Rev. 469 (2007); Ronald Chester, Inheritance, Wealth and Society (1982); Remi Clignet, Death, Deeds and Descendants: Inheritance in Modern America (1992); Inheritance and Wealth in America (Robert K. Miller, Jr. and Stephen J. McNamee eds., 1998). See also Jens Beckert, Inherited Wealth (Thomas Dunlap trans., 2008).

In the United States, this argument once found a receptive ear in Congress, which for most of the last century imposed substantial estate and gift taxes on the rich. In 2001, however, Congress passed legislation that would phase out the estate tax via gradual increases in the taxable threshold and decreases in the tax rate. Under the 2001 law, still in force as this book went to press, in 2009 the estate tax will be levied on estates in excess of $3.5 million at a rate of 45 percent. In 2010, the tax is slated to disappear entirely, but then in 2011 the estate tax will be restored at its 2001 levels. With the election of President Barack Obama in 2008, however, many commentators predicted that the estate tax will be reinstated for 2010, and that Congress would settle on an exemption amount around $3.5 to $5 million and a maximum rate around 45 percent. Federal estate, gift, and generation-skipping taxes are discussed in Chapter 15.

Why do we allow the passing of property at death? After a person dies, there are several things that could happen to the person's property. Suppose that when Diana, Princess of Wales, died she left a valuable necklace. What are the options regarding Diana's necklace? Among the possibilities are:

(1) destroying it;
(2) burying it along with the Princess, as was often done with valuable jewelry in ancient Egypt;
(3) treating it as unowned and allowing a free-for-all in which the first person to grab it is the new owner;
(4) having the government confiscate it; or
(5) honoring Diana's wishes.

Since mandatory destruction is wasteful and a free-for-all would encourage people to hover around a dying person like vultures, the alternatives worth serious consideration are the last two: some form of confiscation and the current system of private succession (limited somewhat by estate taxes and, as we shall see, perhaps a mandatory share for one's surviving family). This debate raises questions about the inequality of wealth in American society and the desirability — and feasibility — of a more confiscatory approach.

Mark L. Ascher, *Curtailing Inherited Wealth*
89 Mich. L. Rev. 69 (1990)

About $150 billion pass at death each year. Yet in 1988 the federal wealth transfer taxes raised less than $8 billion. Obviously, these taxes could raise much more. If, to take the extreme example, we allowed the government to confiscate all property at death, we could almost eliminate the deficit with one stroke of a Presidential pen. This nation, however, rarely has used taxes on the transfer of wealth to raise significant revenue. Our historical hesitancy in this regard strongly suggests that we as a nation are unwilling to abolish inheritance in order to raise revenue. Nonetheless, thinking about using the federal wealth transfer taxes to abolish inheritance may not be entirely futile. It may permit an entirely new type of analysis. Conventional attempts to reform the federal wealth transfer taxes inevitably bog down in the Anglo-American tradition of freedom of testation. As begrudged intruders upon a general rule, these taxes necessarily end up playing an inconsequential role. One willing, for purposes of analysis, to discard freedom of testation could start from the proposition that property rights should end at death. Inheritance then would be tolerated only as an exception to that general rule. This article does just that. I invite the reader to join me in speculating whether it might not make sense to use the federal wealth transfer taxes to curtail inheritance, thereby increasing equality of opportunity while raising revenue.

My proposal views inheritance as something we should tolerate only when necessary — not something we should always protect. My major premise is that all property owned at death, after payment of debts and administration expenses, should be sold and the proceeds paid to the United States government. There would be six exceptions. A marital exemption, potentially unlimited, would accrue over the life of a marriage. Thus, spouses could continue to provide for each other after death. Decedents would also be allowed to provide for dependent lineal descendants. The amount available to any given descendant would, however, depend on the descendant's age and would drop to zero at an age of presumed independence. A separate exemption would allow generous provision for disabled lineal descendants of any age. Inheritance by lineal ascendants (parents, grandparents, etc.) would be unlimited. A universal exemption would allow a moderate amount of property either to pass outside the exemptions or to augment amounts passing under them. Thus, every decedent would be able to leave something to persons of his or her choice, regardless whether another exemption was available. Up to a fixed fraction of an estate could pass to charity. In addition, to prevent circumvention by lifetime giving, the gift tax would increase substantially.

My proposal strikes directly at inheritance by healthy, adult children. And for good reason. We cannot control differences in native ability. Even worse, so long as we believe in the family, we can achieve only the most rudimentary successes in evening out many types of opportunities. And we certainly cannot control many types of luck. But we can — and ought to — curb one form of luck. Children lucky enough to have been raised, acculturated, and educated by wealthy parents need not be allowed the additional good fortune of inheriting their parents' property. In this respect, we can do much better than we ever have before at equalizing opportunity. This proposal would leave "widows and orphans" essentially untouched. The disabled, grandparents, and charity would probably fare better than ever before. But inheritance by healthy, adult children would cease immediately, except to the extent of the universal exemption.

This proposal sounds radical, perhaps even communistic. Inheritance does seem to occupy a special place in the hearts of many Americans, even those who cannot realistically expect to inherit anything of significance. . . . My proposal

. . . reaches the conclusion that substantial limitations on inheritance would contribute meaningfully to the equality of opportunity we offer our children. It also concludes that such limitations are fully consistent with our notions of private property. Neither conclusion is new. What is new is a $200 billion deficit.[6] . . . If we cannot, or will not, control the deficit, this generation's primary bequest to its children will be the obligation to pay their parents' debts. . . .

My proposal starts from the proposition that inheritance should be permitted only where public policy clearly justifies it. I find that justification in six different contexts. Spousal inheritance would always be allowed, but the amount would depend upon the length of the marriage. Inheritance by dependent lineal descendants would be permitted, subject to limitations based on the beneficiary's age [under 25 years]. Large trusts for disabled lineal descendants would be encouraged. Inheritance by lineal ascendants would be unlimited. Charity could take up to 20%. And, in any event, $250,000 would be exempt [and could be spread among anyone]. Thus, many types of inheritance would continue. In fact, my proposal leaves untouched estates of $250,000 or less.

Irving Kristol, Taxes, Poverty, and Equality
Pub. Int. 26-28 (No. 37, Fall 1974)

Large disparities of income, leading in turn to large concentrations of wealth, and these leading in turn to large *inherited* concentrations of wealth — such, it has long been recognized, can pose a very special problem for democracy. The primal nightmare of a democracy is the emergence of an oligarchy that would, through the power associated with wealth, perpetuate itself, and eventually constitute a kind of aristocracy. So the question of the distribution of wealth is a proper concern for any democratic society. Whether, in the United States today, this question is acute is a matter of opinion and controversy. Since our economic historians tell us that, over the past 150 years, the distribution of wealth has probably become less unequal, it is not obvious that the subject should exercise us unduly. But let us assume, for the moment, that we decided it *was* acute enough (or was widely perceived to be acute enough) for us to do something about it. What might we do?

The question, oddly enough, is quite easy to answer: We should discourage the inheritance of large fortunes. This is a quite traditional liberal idea — Montesquieu and Jefferson would both have approved of it — nor is it such a difficult task. All we have to do is decide — and legislate — that no large fortune should outlast the lifetime of the man who made it, but rather that such a large fortune should dissolve into much smaller fortunes upon his death. Thus, we could make it a matter of public policy and law that no individual could inherit, in a lifetime, more than one million dollars — and any possessor of a large fortune must distribute it, prior to death or by testament, to his children, his

---

6. In early 2009 the Congressional Budget Office projected that the 2009 budget deficit would reach $1.845 trillion. — Eds.

relatives, his friends, anyone, but no one receiving more than that maximum legacy, which would be tax-free. (Institutional donations, of course, could be of any size.) Should he fail to do so, the government would levy a 100 per cent tax on the undistributed portion of his estate.

There would seem to be many advantages to such a policy. It does not discourage the incentive to invest and make money — anyone can still become enormously rich in his lifetime. Moreover, the foreknowledge that he would have to distribute his riches means that the wealthy man would, in his lifetime, be the recipient of much flattering attention and of many honors. He would, in addition, have the pleasure associated with the plenary power disposing of his wealth as he saw fit — rewarding some, failing to reward others. No large fortune would outlast a generation; but there would still be enough wealthy people around to support charities, private educational institutions, unpopular political causes, and minority cultural tastes — in other words, to act as a useful counterbalance to the ever-increasing weight of government and the public sector. Even the children of the rich would benefit, since it has long been recognized that the inheritance of large sums of money tends to distort the motivations and corrupt the characters of young people.

It can be predicted that any such proposal would provoke the hostility of the wealthy, who really do — it is perfectly natural — have dreams of their families moving through oligarchy to eventual aristocracy. But it can also be predicted that any such proposal would be contemptuously dismissed by great many liberal reformers. Why? The explanation is simple: When modern liberals talk about "the redistribution of income," they rarely mean a simple redistribution among individuals — more often they mean a redistribution *to the state*, which will then take the proper egalitarian measures. No proposal for the redistribution of large fortunes will get liberal support unless that money goes into the public treasury, where liberals will have much to say as to how it should be spent. That is the "dirty little secret" — the hidden agenda — behind the current chatter about the need for redistribution. The talk is about equality, the substance is about power.

QUESTIONS

In 1990, Professor Ascher proposed limiting to $250,000 (nearly $450,000 in 2009 dollars) the amount of property that could be passed to others, with partial or complete exceptions for property passing to spouses, parents, children under the age of 25, disabled persons, and charities. In 1974, Irving Kristol explored the possibility of limiting to $1 million (nearly $4.5 million in 2009 dollars) the amount that any one individual could inherit. Kristol says that it would be easy to implement his system, and though Ascher recognizes some obvious problems with his proposal, such as corresponding restrictions on gifts, he, too, presents his system as feasible. What would be the likely effects of an attempt to implement either approach? How would family and business relations change? What sorts of legal and illegal avoidance mechanisms would arise? In the long run, what might be the general economic effects of such reforms?

NOTE: INHERITANCE IN THE ERSTWHILE SOVIET UNION

In 1918, the Soviet Bolsheviks, carrying out the teaching of Marx and Engels, abolished inheritance. The 1918 law, translated into English, read: "Inheritance, testate and intestate, is abolished. Upon the death of the owner his property (movable and immovable) becomes the property of the R.S.F.S.R." [1918] 1 Sob. Uzak., RSFSR, No. 34, item 456, Apr. 26, 1918. Within four years, however, inheritance was re-established. The abolition of inheritance proved unpopular, and the Soviet rulers, on second thought, decided it was an institution encouraging savings and an incentive to work. Inheritance was also viewed as a method of providing for dependents of the deceased, relieving the state of this burden, and of furthering family unity and stability. Before the dissolution of the Soviet Union, the Soviet law of inheritance did not substantially differ from the civil law of inheritance found in Western Europe. See Frances Foster, The Development of Inheritance Law in the Soviet Union and the People's Republic of China, 33 Am. J. Comp. L. 33 (1985); Comment, Soviet Inheritance Law: Ideological Consistency or a Retreat to the West?, 23 Gonz. L. Rev. 593 (1988).

Inequality may result not only from inherited wealth, but also from uneven investment in the human capital of children across families. The following excerpts make this point brilliantly and raise the following question: If economic inheritance were abolished, would it be even more difficult to break up an upper class?

Walter J. Blum and Harry Kalven, Jr., The Uneasy Case
for Progressive Taxation
19 U. Chi. L. Rev. 417 (1952)

There is still another road leading to the problem of equality. Almost everybody professes to be in favor of one kind of equality — equality of opportunity. What remains to be investigated is the relationship between this kind of equality and economic equality. . . . In terms of the justice of rewards, the point is that no race can be fair unless the contestants start from the same mark. . . .

It might simplify matters somewhat to go directly to the heart of the problem — the children. . . . The important inequalities of opportunity are inequalities of environment, in its broadest sense, for the children. It is the inequalities in the worlds which the children inherit which count, and this inheritance is both economic and cultural. . . .

The critical economic inheritance consists of the day to day expenditures on the children; it is these expenditures which add up to money investments in the children's health, education and welfare which in the aggregate are, at least in our society, gravely disparate. No progressive inheritance tax, or combination of gift and inheritance taxes, can touch this source of economic inequalities among children. On the other hand a progressive income tax can, as one of its effects, help to minimize this form of unequal inheritance. It is income, not wealth, which is the important operative factor here, and by bringing incomes closer together the tax tends to bring money investments in children closer together.

But the gravest source of inequality of opportunity in our society is not economic but rather what is called cultural inheritance for lack of a better term. Under modern conditions the opportunities for formal education, healthful diet and medical attention to some extent can be equalized by economic means without too greatly disrupting the family. However, it still remains true that even today much of the transmission of culture, in the narrow sense, occurs through the family, and no system of public education and training can completely neutralize this form of inheritance. Here it is the economic investment in the parents and the grandparents, irrevocably in the past, which produces differential opportunities for the children. Nor is this the end of the matter. It has long been recognized that the parents make the children in their own image, and modern psychology has served to underscore how early this process begins to operate and how decisive it may be. The more subtle and profound influences upon the child resulting from love, integrity and family morale form a kind of inheritance which cannot, at least for those above the minimum subsistence level, be significantly affected by economic measures, or possibly by any others. If these influences on the members of the next generation are to be equalized, nothing short of major changes in the institution of the family can possibly suffice. At a minimum such changes would include socializing decisions not only about how children are to be raised but who is to raise them. And this in turn would call into question the very having of children.

"Having a fine old name really has been enough for me."

Drawing by Wm. Hamilton.

John H. Langbein, The Twentieth-Century Revolution in Family Wealth Transmission
86 Mich. L. Rev. 722 (1988)

The main purpose of this article is to [call attention to] the ways in which
. . . changes in the nature of wealth have become associated with changes of perhaps comparable magnitude in the timing and in the character of family wealth
transmission. My first theme . . . concerns human capital. Whereas of old, wealth
transmission from parents to children tended to center upon major items of patrimony such as the family farm or the family firm, today for the broad middle
classes, wealth transmission centers on a radically different kind of asset: the
investment in skills. In consequence, intergenerational wealth transmission no
longer occurs primarily upon the death of the parents, but rather, when the children are growing up, hence, during the parents' lifetimes. . . .

My thesis is quite simple, and, I hope, quite intuitive. I believe that, in striking
contrast to the patterns of last century and before, in modern times the business
of educating children has become the main occasion for intergenerational wealth
transfer. Of old, parents were mainly concerned to transmit the patrimony —
prototypically the farm or the firm, but more generally, that "provision in life"
that rescued children from the harsh fate of being a mere laborer. In today's economic order, it is education more than property, the new human capital rather
than the old physical capital, that similarly advantages a child. . . .

From the proposition that the main parental wealth transfer to children now
takes place inter vivos, there follows a corollary: Children of propertied parents
are much less likely to expect an inheritance. Whereas of old, children did expect
the transfer of the farm or firm, today's children expect help with educational
expenses, but they do not depend upon parental wealth transfer at death.
Lengthened life expectancies mean that the life-spans of the parents overlap the
life-spans of their adult children for much longer than used to be. Parents now
live to see their children reaching peak earnings potential, and those earnings
often exceed what the parents were able to earn. Today, children are typically
middle-aged when the survivor of their two parents dies, and middle-aged children are far less likely to be financially needy. It is still the common practice within
middle- and upper-middle-class families for parents to leave to their children (or
grandchildren) most or all of any property that happens to remain when the parents die, but there is no longer a widespread sense of parental responsibility to
abstain from consumption in order to transmit an inheritance.

For further discussion of investment in cultural and human capital within
families, see Samuel Bowles, Herbert Gintis, and Melissa Osborne Groves, eds.,
Unequal Chances: Family Background and Economic Success (2005). For stimu-
lating further discussion of arguments for and against inheritance and the reach
of the dead hand, see Ronald Chester, From Here to Eternity? Property and
the Dead Hand (2007); Adam J. Hirsch and William K.S. Wang, A Qualitative

Theory of the Dead Hand, 68 Ind. L.J. 1, 6-14 (1992); Stephen R. Munzer, A Theory of Property 380-418 (1990).

3.   The Problem of the Dead Hand

During life, a person can use her wealth to influence the conduct of her friends and family. To what extent should a person be able to use wealth to influence behavior after death? Arthur Hobhouse, more than 100 years ago, wrote a condemnation of the "cold and numbing influence of the Dead Hand":

> A clear, obvious, natural line is drawn for us between those persons and events which the Settlor knows and sees, and those which he cannot know and see. Within the former province we may push his natural affections and his capacity of judgment to make better dispositions than any external Law is likely to make for him. Within the latter, natural affection does not extend, and the wisest judgment is constantly baffled by the course of events. . . . What I consider to be not conjectural, but proved by experience in all human affairs, is, that people are the best judges of their own concerns; or if they are not, that it is better for them, on moral grounds, that they should manage their own concerns for themselves, and that it cannot be wrong continually to claim this liberty for every Generation of mortal men. [Arthur Hobhouse, The Dead Hand 188, 183-185 (1880).]

Restatement (Third) of Property: Wills and Other Donative Transfers (2003)

§10.1   DONOR'S INTENTION DETERMINES THE MEANING OF A DONATIVE DOCUMENT AND IS GIVEN EFFECT TO THE MAXIMUM EXTENT ALLOWED BY LAW

The controlling consideration in determining the meaning of a donative document is the donor's intention. The donor's intention is given effect to the maximum extent allowed by law.

COMMENT:

a. Rationale. The organizing principle of the American law of donative transfers is freedom of disposition. Property owners have the nearly unrestricted right to dispose of their property as they please. . . .

c. Effect of a donative document. Unless disallowed by law, the donor's intention not only determines the meaning but also the effect of a donative document.

American law does not grant courts any general authority to question the wisdom, fairness, or reasonableness of the donor's decisions about how to allocate his or her property. The main function of the law in this field is to facilitate rather than regulate. The law serves this function by establishing rules under which sufficiently reliable determinations can be made regarding the content of the donor's intention.

American law curtails freedom of disposition only to the extent that the donor attempts to make a disposition or achieve a purpose that is prohibited or restricted by an overriding rule of law. . . .

Among the rules of law that prohibit or restrict freedom of disposition in certain instances are those relating to spousal rights; creditors' rights; unreasonable restraints on alienation or marriage; provisions promoting separation or divorce; impermissible racial or other categoric restrictions; provisions encouraging illegal activity; and the rules against perpetuities and accumulations.

Shapira v. Union National Bank
Ohio Court of Common Pleas, Mahoning County, 1974
315 N.E.2d 825

HENDERSON, J.   This is an action for a declaratory judgment and the construction of the will of David Shapira, M.D., who died April 13, 1973, a resident of this county. By agreement of the parties, the case has been submitted upon the pleadings and the exhibit.

The portions of the will in controversy are as follows:

Item VIII. All the rest, residue and remainder of my estate, real and personal, of every kind and description and wheresoever situated, which I may own or have the right to dispose of at the time of my decease, I give, devise and bequeath to my three (3) beloved children, to wit: Ruth Shapira Aharoni, of Tel Aviv, Israel, or wherever she may reside at the time of my death; to my son Daniel Jacob Shapira, and to my son Mark Benjamin Simon Shapira in equal shares, with the following qualifications: . . .

(b) My son Daniel Jacob Shapira should receive his share of the bequest only, if he is married at the time of my death to a Jewish girl whose both parents were Jewish. In the event that at the time of my death he is not married to a Jewish girl whose both parents were Jewish, then his share of this bequest should be kept by my executor for a period of not longer than seven (7) years and if my said son Daniel Jacob gets married within the seven year period to a Jewish girl whose both parents were Jewish, my executor is hereby instructed to turn over his share of my bequest to him. In the event, however, that my said son Daniel Jacob is unmarried within the seven (7) years after my death to a Jewish girl whose both parents were Jewish, or if he is married to a non Jewish girl, then his share of my estate, as provided in item 8 above should go to The State of Israel, absolutely.

The provision for the testator's other son Mark, is conditioned substantially similarly. Daniel Jacob Shapira, the plaintiff, alleges that the condition upon his inheritance is unconstitutional, contrary to public policy and unenforceable because of its unreasonableness, and that he should be given his bequest free of the restriction. Daniel is 21 years of age, unmarried and a student at Youngstown State University. . . .

CONSTITUTIONALITY

Plaintiff's argument that the condition in question violates constitutional safeguards is based upon the premise that the right to marry is protected by the Fourteenth Amendment to the Constitution of the United States. . . . In Loving v. Virginia, 388 U.S. 1 (1967), the court held unconstitutional as violative of the

Equal Protection and Due Process Clauses of the Fourteenth Amendment an anti-miscegenation statute under which a black person and a white person were convicted for marrying. In its opinion the United States Supreme Court made the following statements, 388 U.S. at 12:

> There can be no doubt that restricting the freedom to marry solely because of racial classifi-cations violates the central meaning of the Equal Protection Clause.
>
>   . . . The freedom to marry has long been recognized as one of the vital personal rights essential to the orderly pursuit of happiness by free men.
>
>   Marriage is one of the "basic civil rights of man," fundamental to our very existence and survival. . . . The Fourteenth Amendment requires that the freedom of choice to marry not be restricted by invidious racial discriminations. Under our Constitution, the freedom to marry, or not marry, a person of another race resides with the individual and cannot be infringed by the State.

From the foregoing, it appears clear, as plaintiff contends, that the right to marry is constitutionally protected from restrictive state legislative action. Plaintiff submits, then, that under the doctrine of Shelley v. Kraemer, 334 U.S. 1 (1948), the constitutional protection of the Fourteenth Amendment is extended from direct state legislative action to the enforcement by state judicial proceedings of private provisions restricting the right to marry. Plaintiff contends that a judgment of this court upholding the condition restricting marriage would, under Shelley v. Kraemer, constitute state action prohibited by the Fourteenth Amendment as much as a state statute.

In Shelley v. Kraemer the United States Supreme Court held that the action of the states to which the Fourteenth Amendment has reference includes action of state courts and state judicial officials. Prior to this decision the court had invalidated city ordinances which denied blacks the right to live in white neighborhoods. In Shelley v. Kraemer owners of neighboring properties sought to enjoin blacks from occupying properties which they had bought, but which were subjected to privately executed restrictions against use or occupation by any persons except those of the Caucasian race. Chief Justice Vinson noted, in the course of his opinion at page 13: "These are cases in which the purposes of the agreements were secured only by judicial enforcement by state courts of the restrictive terms of the agreements."

In the case at bar, this court is not being asked to enforce any restriction upon Daniel Jacob Shapira's constitutional right to marry. Rather, this court is being asked to enforce the testator's restriction upon his son's inheritance. If the facts and circumstances of this case were such that the aid of this court were sought to enjoin Daniel's marrying a non-Jewish girl, then the doctrine of Shelley v. Kraemer would be applicable, but not, it is believed, upon the facts as they are. . . .

[T]he right to receive property by will is a creature of the law, and is not a natural right or one guaranteed or protected by either the Ohio or the United States constitution. . . . It is a fundamental rule of law in Ohio that a testator may legally entirely disinherit his children. . . . This would seem to demonstrate that, from a constitutional standpoint, a testator may restrict a child's inheritance. The court concludes, therefore, that the upholding and enforcement of the provisions of Dr. Shapira's will conditioning the bequests to his sons upon their marrying Jewish girls does not offend the Constitution of Ohio or of the United States.

PUBLIC POLICY

The condition that Daniel's share should be "turned over to him if he should marry a Jewish girl whose both parents were Jewish" constitutes a partial restraint upon marriage. If the condition were that the beneficiary not marry anyone, the restraint would be general or total, and, at least in the case of a first marriage, would be held to be contrary to public policy and void. A partial restraint of marriage which imposes only reasonable restrictions is valid, and not contrary to public policy: . . . The great weight of authority in the United States is that gifts conditioned upon the beneficiary's marrying within a particular religious class or faith are reasonable. . . .

Plaintiff contends, however, that in Ohio a condition such as the one in this case is void as against the public policy of this state. . . . Plaintiff's position that the free choice of religious practice cannot be circumscribed or controlled by contract is substantiated by Hackett v. Hackett, 150 N.E.2d 431 (Ohio App. 1958). This case held that a covenant in a separation agreement, incorporated in a divorce decree, that the mother would rear a daughter in the Roman Catholic faith was unenforceable. However, the controversial condition in the case at bar is a partial restraint upon marriage and not a covenant to restrain the freedom of religious practice; and, of course, this court is not being asked to hold the plaintiff in contempt for failing to marry a Jewish girl of Jewish parentage. . . .

It is noted, furthermore, in this connection, that the courts of Pennsylvania distinguish between testamentary gifts conditioned upon the religious faith of the beneficiary and those conditioned upon marriage to persons of a particular religious faith. In Clayton's Estate, 13 Pa. D. & C. 413 (Pa. Orphan's Ct. 1930), the court upheld a gift of a life estate conditioned upon the beneficiary's not marrying a woman of the Catholic faith. In its opinion the court distinguishes the earlier case of Drace v. Klinedinst, 118 A. 907 (Pa. 1922), in which a life estate willed to grandchildren, provided they remained faithful to a particular religion, was held to violate the public policy of Pennsylvania.[7] In *Clayton's Estate*, the court said that the condition concerning marriage did not affect the faith of the beneficiary, and that the condition, operating only on the choice of a wife, was too remote to be regarded as coercive of religious faith. . . .

The only cases cited by plaintiff's counsel in accord with [plaintiff's contention] are some English cases and one American decision. In England the courts have

---

7. In Estate of Laning, 339 A.2d 520 (Pa. 1975), the court stated that the *Drace* case was correctly decided on the grounds that the testator sought to require his grandchildren to "remain true" to the Catholic religion, and that the enforcement of a condition that they remain faithful Catholics would require the court to determine the doctrines of the Catholic church. "Such questions are clearly improper for a civil court to determine." The court went on to uphold a provision in Laning's will that the gift be distributed to certain relatives who held "membership in good standing" in the Presbyterian church. The court construed the provision to mean only a formal affiliation with the specified church, thus avoiding improper inquiry into church doctrine. — Eds.

held that partial restrictions upon marriage to persons not of the Jewish faith, or of Jewish parentage, were not contrary to public policy or invalid. Hodgson v. Halford (1879 Eng.) L.R. 11 Ch. Div. 959. Other cases in England, however, have invalidated forfeitures of similarly conditioned provisions for children upon the basis of uncertainty or indefiniteness. . . . Since the foregoing decisions, a later English case has upheld a condition precedent that a granddaughter-beneficiary marry a person of Jewish faith and the child of Jewish parents. The court . . . found . . . no difficulty with indefiniteness where the legatee married unquestionably outside the Jewish faith. Re Wolffe, [1953] 2 All Eng. 697.[8]

The American case cited by plaintiff is that of Maddox v. Maddox, 52 Va. (11 Grattan's) 804 (1854). The testator in this case willed a remainder to his niece if she remain a member of the Society of Friends. When the niece arrived at a marriageable age there were but five or six unmarried men of the society in the neighborhood in which she lived. She married a non-member and thus lost her own membership. The court held the condition to be an unreasonable restraint upon marriage and void, and that there being no gift over upon breach of the condition, the condition was in terrorem, and did not avoid the bequest. It can be seen that while the court considered the testamentary condition to be a restraint upon marriage, it was primarily one in restraint of religious faith. The court said that with the small number of eligible bachelors in the area the condition would have operated as a virtual prohibition of the niece's marrying, and that she could not be expected to "go abroad" in search of a helpmate or to be subjected to the chance of being sought after by a stranger. . . . The other ground upon which the Virginia court rested its decision, that the condition was in terrorem because of the absence of a gift over, is clearly not applicable to the case at bar, even if it were in accord with Ohio law, because of the gift over to the State of Israel contained in the Shapira will.

In arguing for the applicability of the Maddox v. Maddox test of reasonableness to the case at bar, counsel for the plaintiff asserts that the number of eligible Jewish females in this county would be an extremely small minority of the total population especially as compared with the comparatively much greater number in New York, whence have come many of the cases comprising the weight of authority upholding the validity of such clauses. There are no census figures in evidence. While this court could probably take judicial notice of the fact that the Jewish community is a minor, though important segment of our total local population, nevertheless the court is by no means justified in judicial knowledge

---

8. In In re Tuck's Settlement Trusts, [1977] 2 W.L.R. 411, a trust was set up by the first Baron Tuck, a Jew, for the benefit of his successors in the baronetcy. Anxious to ensure that his successors be Jewish, he provided for payment of income to the baronet for the time being if and when and as long as he should be of the Jewish faith and married to a wife of Jewish blood and of the Jewish faith. The trust also provided that in case of any dispute the decision of the Chief Rabbi of London would be conclusive. The court held that the conditions were not void for uncertainty. Lord Denning was of the view that if there was any uncertainty, it was cured by the Chief Rabbi clause. The other two judges declined to reach that issue.

The question — who is a Jew — is not easy to answer, not even in Israel where it has provoked continuing controversy. See Mark J. Altschul, Israel's Law of Return and the Debate of Altering, Repealing, or Maintaining Its Present Language, 2002 U. Ill. L. Rev. 1345; Meryl Hyman, Who Is a Jew? (1998). — Eds.

that there is an insufficient number of eligible young ladies of Jewish parentage in this area from which Daniel would have a reasonable latitude of choice.[9] And of course, Daniel is not at all confined in his choice to residents of this county, which is a very different circumstance in this day of travel by plane and freeway and communication by telephone, from the horse and buggy days of the 1854 Maddox v. Maddox decision. Consequently, the decision does not appear to be an appropriate yardstick of reasonableness under modern living conditions.

Plaintiff's counsel contends that the Shapira will falls within the principle of Fineman v. Central National Bank, 175 N.E.2d 837 (1961 Ohio Com. Pleas), holding that the public policy of Ohio does not countenance a bequest or devise conditioned on the beneficiary's obtaining a separation or divorce from his wife. Counsel argues that the Shapira condition would encourage the beneficiary to marry a qualified girl just to receive the bequest, and then to divorce her afterward. This possibility seems too remote to be a pertinent application of the policy against bequests conditioned upon divorce. . . . Indeed, in measuring the reasonableness of the condition in question, both the father and the court should be able to assume that the son's motive would be proper. And surely the son should not gain the advantage of the avoidance of the condition by the possibility of his own impropriety.

Finally, counsel urges that the Shapira condition tends to pressure Daniel, by the reward of money, to marry within seven years without opportunity for mature reflection, and jeopardizes his college education. It seems to the court, on the contrary, that the seven year time limit would be a most reasonable grace period, and one which would give the son ample opportunity for exhaustive reflection and fulfillment of the condition without constraint or oppression. Daniel is no more being "blackmailed into a marriage by immediate financial gain," as suggested by counsel, than would be the beneficiary of a living gift or conveyance upon consideration of a future marriage — an arrangement which has long been sanctioned by the courts of this state. Thompson v. Thompson, 17 Ohio St. 649 (1867).

In the opinion of this court, the provision made by the testator for the benefit of the State of Israel upon breach or failure of the condition is most significant for two reasons. First, it distinguishes this case from the bare forfeitures in . . . Maddox v. Maddox (including the technical in terrorem objection), and, in a way, from the vagueness and indefiniteness doctrine of some of the English cases. Second, and of greater importance, it demonstrates the depth of the testator's conviction. His purpose was not merely a negative one designed to punish his son for not carrying out his wishes. His unmistakable testamentary plan was that his possessions be used to encourage the preservation of the Jewish

9. The American Jewish Yearbook of 1976 estimates the Jewish population of Youngstown, Ohio, to be 5,400 in 1974. Taking into consideration other U.S. census data about the male-to-female ratio and the ages of the population in Youngstown, we estimate that about 500 Jewish females were in the 15-24 age group. If this estimate is correct, do you think this gives Daniel "a reasonable latitude of choice"? — Eds.

faith and blood, hopefully through his sons, but, if not, then through the State of Israel. Whether this judgment was wise is not for this court to determine. But it is the duty of this court to honor the testator's intention within the limitations of law and of public policy. The prerogative granted to a testator by the laws of this state to dispose of his estate according to his conscience is entitled to as much judicial protection and enforcement as the prerogative of a beneficiary to receive an inheritance.

It is the conclusion of this court that public policy should not, and does not preclude the fulfillment of Dr. Shapira's purpose, and that in accordance with the weight of authority in this country, the conditions contained in his will are reasonable restrictions upon marriage, and valid.

NOTES AND QUESTIONS

1. In 1994, the editors asked the attorney who represented Daniel Shapira for information about the aftermath of the case. The attorney contacted Mr. Shapira, who declined to give any information. It was a bitter experience, he said, that he wanted to forget.

2. What social objectives are accomplished by honoring control of a beneficiary's behavior by the dead hand, a hand that does not have a live mind controlling it and making a continuously informed judgment as circumstances change, that can no longer be affected by the opinions of others, and that does not suffer the consequences? Judge Posner suggests that perhaps the courts should have the power to modify conditions on testamentary gifts:

Judge Richard A. Posner

> Suppose a man leaves money to his son in trust, the trust to fail however if the son does not marry a woman of the Jewish faith by the time he is 25 years old. The judicial approach in such cases is to refuse to enforce the condition if it is "unreasonable." In the case just put it might make a difference whether the son was 18 or 24 at the time of the bequest and how large the Jewish population was in the place where he lived.
>
> This approach may seem wholly devoid of an economic foundation, and admittedly the criterion of reasonableness is here an unilluminating one. Consider, however, the possibilities for modification that would exist if the gift were inter vivos rather than testamentary. As the deadline approached, the son might come to his father and persuade him that a diligent search had revealed no marriageable Jewish girl who would accept him. The father might be persuaded to grant an extension or otherwise relax the condition. If the father is dead, this kind of "recontracting" is impossible, and the presumption that the condition is a reasonable one fails. This argues for applying the cy pres approach in private as well as charitable trust cases unless, perhaps, the testator expressly rejects a power of judicial modification. [Richard A. Posner, Economic Analysis of Law §18.7 (7th ed. 2007).]

You are Judge Posner. Daniel Shapira appears before you six-and-a-half years after his father's death and alleges that he has found no Jewish girl whom he desires who will accept him. What do you do?

Senator Joseph Lieberman, the Democratic nominee for vice president in 2000, was charged with enforcing a religious restriction while serving as the executor of his uncle's estate. Rather than enforce the terms of the will, which would have disinherited two of his cousins for marrying persons who were not born Jewish, he brokered a deal whereby the spouses of the disinherited cousins converted to Judaism and the cousins' shares were restored. Lieberman said that his uncle "knew who he was making the executor. He knew that these were my cousins and that I love them, and that by my nature I'm not as hard as the will was. He knew what I would do." Phil Kuntz and Bob Davis, A Beloved Uncle's Will Tests Diplomatic Skills of Joseph Lieberman — Document Disinherits Children Who Failed Religious Test, Wall St. J., Aug. 25, 2000, at A1. Did Lieberman betray his uncle's trust, or did he do the right thing?

3.   Restatement (Second) of Property: Donative Transfers §6.2, cmt. a (1983) provides that a "restraint unreasonably limits the transferee's opportunity to marry if a marriage permitted by the restraint is not likely to occur. The likelihood of marriage is a factual question, to be answered from the circumstances of the particular case." Suppose that Daniel Shapira were gay. Would the get-married provision in Dr. Shapira's will be enforceable?

4.   In *Shapira*, the court distinguished the *Maddox* case of 1854 on the grounds that "in this day of travel by plane and freeway and communication by telephone," precedents on reasonableness from the "horse and buggy days" have lost their vitality. The question thus arises, is satisfying the reasonableness test even easier today thanks to the availability of popular Jewish internet dating services such as JDate.com? In Tony Dokoupil, Sex and the Synagogue, Newsweek, Jan. 21, 2008, at 16, the author reports:

> The rise of interfaith marriage is a sensitive issue among American Jews, and now two powerful forces in the religion are teaming up to do something about it: rabbis and J Date, the top matchmaking Web site for Jewish singles. For the first time in its 10-year history, the site is offering a bulk rate to rabbis who want to buy membership accounts for their congregants.

Not all courts, however, apply a reasonableness test. In Estate of Feinberg, 891 N.E.2d 549 (Ill. App. 2008), the court held 2 to 1 that a trust provision providing that a descendant "who marries outside the Jewish faith (unless the spouse of such descendant has converted or converts within one year of the marriage to the Jewish faith) and his or her descendants shall be deemed to be deceased" was invalid without consideration whether the clause was reasonable. An appeal to the Illinois Supreme Court was pending as this book went to press.

5.   A will or trust provision is ordinarily invalid if it is intended or tends to encourage disruption of a family relationship. Thus, a bequest to the surviving spouse conditioned on the survivor not remarrying is invalid unless the purpose

is to provide support.[10] For example, in Estate of Robertson, 859 N.E.2d 772 (Ind. App. 2007), the court differentiated a gift in trust to the testator's wife "so long as she remains my widow," a valid limitation, from a trust that provides income to the spouse for life but terminates if the spouse remarries, an invalid condition. Should this difference in form determine whether the condition violates public policy?

Provisions encouraging separation or divorce are likewise usually held invalid, unless the dominant motive of the testator is to provide support in the event of separation or divorce. See In re Estate of Owen, 855 N.E.2d 603 (Ind. App. 2006) (voiding condition prohibiting daughter from renting residence while married to an identified person because it tended to promote divorce).

Restatement (Third) of Trusts §29(c) (2003) invalidates trusts that are "contrary to public policy." In general, the Restatement (Third) of Trusts frowns on restraints on beneficiary behavior, including restraints on marriage or religious freedom, and those that disrupt family relationships and choice of careers, but calls for balancing of conflicting social values.[11]

For a penetrating analysis of testamentary gifts conditioned on specified conduct by the beneficiary, see Jeffrey G. Sherman, Posthumous Meddling: An Instrumentalist Theory of Testamentary Restraints on Conjugal and Religious Choices, 1999 U. Ill. L. Rev. 1273. Professor Sherman rejects the balancing test of "contrary to public policy" and makes a principled analysis of why testation should be permitted and under what limitations. He concludes that testamentary conditions calculated to restrain legatees' personal conduct should not be enforced. The article is especially readable because it is laced with Sherman's delicious wit.

NOTE: INCENTIVE TRUSTS AND THE DEAD HAND

In modern practice conditional gifts such as in *Shapira* tend to be made in trust, known in the practitioner literature as an *incentive trust*, and are as likely to be

---

10. What about the reverse? The German poet Heinrich Heine is reported to have said that he wanted to make his wife's share of his estate conditional on her remarrying. The reason: "I want at least one person to truly bereave my death." In the end, none of Heine's wills ever contained such a condition, which undoubtedly he suggested as a joke. The editors gratefully acknowledge the assistance of Mike Widener of the Tarlton Law Library at the University of Texas for sorting out these details.

11. The reporter's notes to §29 include this account of an incentive for unhealthy behavior from a 1993 Associated Press story from Romania:

A man who was nagged by his wife to stop smoking has left her everything — but only if she takes up his habit as punishment for 40 years of "hell," newspapers reported Saturday.

Marin Cemenescu, who died last week in his hometown of Timisoara at age 76, stipulated in his will that to inherit his house and $30,000 estate, his 63-year-old wife Aneta must smoke five cigarets a day for the rest of her life, the Romania Libera daily reported.

"She could not stand to see me with a cigaret in my mouth, (and) I ended up smoking in the bathroom like a schoolboy," Cemenescu reportedly wrote in his will.

"My life was hell," he wrote.

The report said that Mrs. Cemenescu plans a legal challenge to the conditions of the will. "I'd rather lose everything than touch a cigaret," she told the newspaper.

The report did not specify the cause of Cemenescu's death or say whether it was related to his smoking.

focused on ensuring that the beneficiary does not adopt a slothful or wasteful existence as on religion or marriage.[12] The underlying worry has perhaps been most aptly put by the investment guru and billionaire Warren Buffett: "[T]he perfect amount to leave to children is 'enough money so that they would feel they could do anything, but not so much that they could do nothing.'" Richard I. Kirkland, Jr., Should You Leave It All to the Children?, Fortune, Sept. 29, 1986, at 18. And indeed, there is some evidence that the receipt of a large inheritance is associated with reduced workforce participation. See Douglas Holtz-Eakin, David Joulfaian, and Harvey S. Rosen, The Carnegie Conjecture: Some Empirical Evidence, 108 Q.J. Econ. 413 (1993).

Enter the incentive trust. Professor Tate explains:

> The conditions that incentive trusts might impose can be divided into three broad categories. First are conditions that encourage the beneficiaries to pursue an education. Second are conditions that provide what might be termed moral incentives: incentives that reflect the settlor's moral or religious outlook or promote a particular way of living. Some of these conditions try to encourage the beneficiaries to contribute to charitable causes, while others discourage substance abuse or promote a traditional family lifestyle. Finally, there are conditions designed to encourage the beneficiaries to have a productive career. . . . Provided that these incentives do not violate public policy, courts generally will enforce them. [Joshua C. Tate, Conditional Love: Incentive Trusts and the Inflexibility Problem, 41 Real Prop., Prob. & Tr. J. 445, 453 (2006).]

Judging by the anecdotal evidence, the use of incentive trusts is increasing. A recent survey of wealthy Americans revealed that 57 percent of those with $10 million or more in assets included an incentive trust in their estate plan. PNC Wealth Management, Wealth and Values Survey — Inheritance (2007). Although the survey methodology may be questioned, it seems clear that popular awareness and practitioner discussion of the incentive trust concept is on the rise. See David Handler and Alison E. Lothes, The Case for Principle Trusts and Against Incentive Trusts, Tr. & Est., Oct. 2008, at 30; Marjorie J. Stephens, Incentive Trusts: Considerations, Uses and Alternatives, 29 ACTEC J. 5 (2003); Catherine M. Allchin, In Some Trusts, the Heirs Must Work for the Money, N.Y. Times, Jan. 29, 2006, §3, at 36.

If drafted poorly, however, an incentive trust can backfire, producing perverse incentives never intended by the settlor.

> [T]he living can usually concoct schemes to outsmart the dead. Mr. Train recalled the saga of Tommy Manville, playboy heir to the Johns-Manville fortune. To prod him to settle down, according to Mr. Train, Mr. Manville's trust guaranteed him $250,000 when he married. "So he married 13 times," Mr. Train says. "He'd pay the woman $50,000, pocket $200,000, get a quickie divorce and then, when he needed more money, he'd get married again." [J. Peder Zane, The Rise of Incentive Trusts: Six Feet Under and Overbearing, N.Y. Times, Mar. 12, 1995, §4, at 5.]

---

12. Paris Hilton's octogenarian grandfather, the hotel magnate Barron Hilton, has adopted a more traditional strategy. He has pledged to leave nearly all of his $2.3 billion fortune to charity. See Susannah Rosenblatt, Barron Hilton to Leave Most of Fortune to Charity, L.A. Times, Dec. 27, 2007, at B3.

Changed circumstances can also frustrate the settlor's purpose if the trust is drafted to be inflexible. According to Professor Tate, practitioners sometimes recommend "provisions that pay out a certain amount of money from the trust for every dollar that the beneficiary earns on her own. This is sometimes described as the 'earn a dollar, get a dollar' arrangement." Tate, supra, at 460. But as Tate asks (id. at 464-466), what if the beneficiary is injured in an accident or suffers a debilitating illness? What if the beneficiary opts to stay at home with young children, or to care for a seriously ill child? Should the law of trust modification be refined to address problems that might arise in the use of incentive trusts?

NOTE: DESTRUCTION OF PROPERTY AT DEATH

A fundamental justification of private property is that society's total wealth usually is maximized by permitting individuals to decide what is the best use of their property. Each person, we ordinarily assume, makes rational choices to maximize her wealth; that the person will suffer economic loss from foolish or wrong decisions tends to deter irrational decisions. Hence a person can, if she wishes, destroy her property during life (subject to historic preservation or similar laws). For if she does, she bears most of the economic consequences of her decision, plus or minus. The question thus arises: Should a testator be permitted to order the destruction of property at death? Is not the main economic loss of posthumous destruction visited upon on others rather than the testator? On the other hand, if the testator expects that her wishes for post-death destruction of her property will not be followed, will she suffer a loss (in money or pleasure) during life from knowing that her destructive wishes will not be honored after her death? Consider the following examples:

(a) The testator's will directs his executor to tear down the testator's house because the testator does not want anyone else to live in it. Can the executor tear down the house? Should a court order the house destroyed? See Eyerman v. Mercantile Trust Co., 524 S.W.2d 210 (Mo. App. 1975) ("a well-ordered society cannot tolerate" waste). If the testator had anticipated this result, might she have destroyed her house during life, earlier than would have given her the most pleasure?

(b) Justice Hugo L. Black of the U.S. Supreme Court was of the view that private notes of the justices relating to Court conferences should not be published posthumously. Justice Black feared publication might inhibit free and vigorous discussion among the justices. Black was struck ill, destroyed his conference notes, resigned from the Court, and died a few weeks later. Suppose that Justice Black had died suddenly while on the bench and that his will had directed his executor to destroy his conference notes. Could the executor do this without a court order? Should a court order destruction of the notes, which might have enormous value to a Court historian? Who would have standing to object?

(c) Franz Kafka bequeathed his diaries, manuscripts, and letters to his friend Max Brod, directing him to burn everything. Brod declined to do so on the grounds that Kafka's unpublished works were of great literary value. Should Brod have ordered a bonfire? See Max Brod, Postscript, in Franz Kafka, The Trial 326 (1925, Mod. Lib. ed. 1956), discussed in William R. Bishin and Christopher D. Stone, Law, Language, and Ethics 1-9 (1972). See also Joseph L. Sax, Playing Darts with a Rembrandt: Public and Private Rights in Cultural Treasures (1999).

(d) In a 2008 replay of Kafka and Brod, after many years of publicly wrestling with the question, the son of the Russian writer Vladimir Nabokov (author of Lolita, among other novels), announced that he will publish the manuscript of his father's final, unfinished novel in spite of his father's instruction to destroy it. Previously his mother, Vladimir's wife, had likewise refused to destroy it, though she didn't publish it either, leaving it to Vladimir when she died. Suppose that Franz Schubert and Giacomo Puccini had ordered their unfinished works destroyed at death, thus depriving the world of Schubert's unfinished Symphony in B Minor and Puccini's unfinished opera Turandot. Should a court order destruction?

(e) Professor John Orth calls to our attention to Virgil, who left instructions to destroy the Aeneid ("Of arms and the man I sing"), an unfinished work. The Emperor Augustus ordered the executors to disregard the order. See Moses Hadas, A History of Latin Literature 142 (1952). Orth asks: "The course of Western literature would be unimaginable without 'arms and the man'! Who would have guided Dante in Hell?"

Building on the insight of Professor Shavell and others that, before death, the living do internalize some of the future costs of seemingly wasteful dead-hand control (see Steven Shavell, Foundations of Economic Analysis of Law 67-72 (2004)), Professor Strahilevitz argues for a conditional right to destroy property after death. Under Strahilevitz's proposal, if during life the testator put a future interest in the property up for sale and (1) the government declined to condemn the future interest and (2) the owner turned down the highest bid for the future interest, then a testamentary direction to destroy the property would be followed. Lior Jacob Strahilevitz, The Right to Destroy, 114 Yale L.J. 781, 848-852 (2005). In Strahilevitz's view, this safe harbor mechanism would provide evidence of testamentary capacity, would ensure resolution of purpose by exposing the testator during life to reputational sanction and persuasion, and would ensure that the testator internalizes the relevant costs by requiring the testator to forego during life the price that others are willing to pay to preserve the property. But what of the possibility that society in the aggregate might want to preserve the property without any single person feeling so strongly that she would offer enough to induce the testator to sell? See id. at 850, n.264.

SECTION B.   TRANSFER OF THE DECEDENT'S ESTATE

1.   *Probate and Nonprobate Property*

All the decedent's assets at death can be divided into probate and nonprobate property. *Probate property* is property that passes through probate under the decedent's will or by intestacy. *Nonprobate property* is property that passes outside of probate under an instrument other than a will. People often have the idea that probate under a will or intestacy is the usual mode of passing property at death, but this is false. Most property transferred at death passes outside of probate through a nonprobate mode of transfer. Consider the following list, which is not exhaustive, of common modes of nonprobate transfer.

(a) *Joint tenancy property, both real and personal.* Under the theory of joint tenancy, the decedent's interest vanishes at death. The survivor has the whole property relieved of the decedent's participation. No interest passes to the survivor at the decedent's death. In order for the survivor to perfect title to real estate, all the survivor need do is file a death certificate of the decedent. Bank accounts, brokerage and mutual fund accounts, and real estate are often held in joint tenancy, particularly between married couples.

(b) *Life insurance.* Life insurance proceeds of a policy on the decedent's life are paid by the insurance company to the beneficiary named in the insurance contract. The company will pay upon receipt of a death certificate of the insured.

(c) *Contracts with payable-on-death (POD) provisions.* A decedent may have a contract with a bank, an employer, or some other person or corporation to distribute property at the decedent's death to a named beneficiary. Pension plans often provide survivor benefits. Tax-deferred investment plans (IRAs, 401(k)s, and the like) often name a death beneficiary. In nearly all states, it is possible to put a death beneficiary on a brokerage account. To collect property held under a POD contract, all the beneficiary need do is file a death certificate with the custodian holding the property.

(d) *Interests in trust.* When property is put in trust, the trustee holds the property for the benefit of one or more named beneficiaries, who may have life estates or remainders or other types of interests. The trust property is distributed to the beneficiaries by the trustee in accordance with the terms of the trust instrument. Property held in a *testamentary trust* created under the decedent's will passes through probate, but property put in an *inter vivos* trust during the decedent's life does not. In most states, the inter vivos trust has displaced the testamentary trust as the preferred type of trust in sophisticated estate planning.

Distribution of nonprobate property does not involve a court proceeding, but is made in accordance with the terms of the controlling contract or trust or deed (nonprobate transfers are dealt with in Chapter 6). By contrast, as outlined below, distribution of probate property under a will or to intestate successors may require a court proceeding involving probate of a will or a finding of intestacy followed by appointment of a personal representative to settle the probate estate.

2. Administration of Probate Estates

a. The Functions of Probate

Probate performs three core functions: (1) it provides *evidence of transfer of title* to the new owners (i.e., it clears title and makes property marketable again); (2) it *protects creditors* by providing a procedure for payment of debts; and (3) it *distributes the decedent's property* to those intended after the decedent's creditors are paid. In considering the brief sketch of probate procedures that follows, think about how well those procedures serve the three core functions of probate and whether any alternative procedures would better serve those functions with greater speed and at lower cost. The latter question is brought into sharp relief by the modern reality that more property passes outside of the probate system than through it.

b. Probate Terminology and History

We begin with a summary of terminology and history. When a person dies and probate is necessary, the first step is the appointment of a *personal representative* to oversee the winding up of the decedent's affairs. The personal representative is a *fiduciary* who inventories and collects the property of the decedent; manages and protects the property during the administration of the decedent's estate; processes the claims of creditors and tax collectors; and distributes the property to those entitled. The court that supervises the administration of the probate estate is usually referred to as a *probate court*.

If the decedent dies testate and in the will names the person who is to execute (i.e., to carry out the terms of) the will and administer the probate estate, such personal representative is usually called an *executor*.[13] When the will does not name an executor, the named executor is unable or unwilling to serve, or the decedent dies intestate, the court will name a personal representative, who is generally called an *administrator*. The administrator is usually selected from a statutory list of persons who are to be given preference, typically in the following order: surviving spouse, children, parents, siblings, creditors. A person appointed as administrator must give bond. In most states, if the will names an individual rather than a corporate fiduciary as executor, the executor also must give bond unless the will waives the bond requirement, which is common.

One court in each county has jurisdiction over administration of decedents' estates. The name of the court varies from state to state. It may be called the surrogate's court, the orphan's court, the probate division of the district court or chancery court, or something else. But all of these differently named courts are referred to collectively as probate courts. And "to go through probate" means to have an estate administered in one of these courts.

A needlessly complicating factor in this field is that we have two legal vocabularies — one applicable to real property and the other to personal property. It is often suggested that these parallel vocabularies are traceable to the historic fact that the English common law courts had jurisdiction over succession to real property, whereas, until the nineteenth century, ecclesiastical courts controlled succession to personal property in England. But in most instances this is not provable. Take the phrase *last will and testament*. A common belief is that this phrase arose because a *will* disposed of real property and a *testament* disposed of personal property; therefore, one instrument disposing of both was a will and testament. The belief that *testament* referred to personal property is based on its

---

13. In some states, a nonresident corporate fiduciary cannot be appointed as executor, and many states have at least some restrictions on the appointment of a nonresident individual, such as requiring that the nonresident be a close relative or requiring that a local co-executor or agent serve along with the nonresident. See Jeffrey A. Schoenblum, 2008 Multistate Guide to Estate Planning at Tables 3.01 and 3.03.

Latin origin (*testamentum*). It is assumed that the Latin-trained ecclesiastical courts introduced the word *testament* into the language to refer to an instrument disposing of property over which they had jurisdiction. It is then assumed that the Old English word *will* was used by the common law courts and, by a process of association, came to relate to land — the type of property over which these courts had jurisdiction.

The evidence does not support these assumptions. As far back as the records go, the words have sometimes been used interchangeably. To speak of a testament disposing of land or of a will disposing of a cow would not have sounded strange to the medieval ear. Professor Mellinkoff believes the phrase *last will and testament* is traceable to the law's habit of doubling Old English words with synonyms of Old French or Latin origin (e.g., *had and received*, *mind and memory*, *free and clear*), "helped along by a distinctive rhythm." David Mellinkoff, The Language of the Law 331 (1963). In any case, the myth that a will disposes of land and a testament disposes of chattels dies terribly, terribly slowly. Today, it is perfectly proper to use the single word *will* to refer to an instrument disposing of both real and personal property.

A person dying testate *devises* real property to *devisees* and *bequeaths* personal property to *legatees*. Using *devise* to refer to land and *bequest* to refer to personalty became a lawyerly custom little more than a hundred years ago,[14] though the distinction, like that between *will* and *testament*, is sometimes erroneously thought to have had more ancient roots in the different courts handling the decedent's property. Although these linguistic distinctions still have currency, there are signs that synonymous usage is returning in respectable circles. The Restatement of Property applies *devise* to both realty and personalty. In drafting wills, "I give" is an excellent substitute for "I devise," "I bequeath," or "I give, devise, and bequeath." "I give" effectively transfers any kind of property, and no fly-specking lawyer can ever fault you for using this verb.

When intestacy occurs we use different words to describe what happens to the intestate's real property and what happens to his personal property. We say real property *descends to heirs*; personal property is *distributed to next-of-kin*. At common law, *heirs* and *next-of-kin* were not necessarily the same. For example, when primogeniture, which applied only to land, was in effect, real property descended to the eldest son, but personal property was distributed equally among all the children. Today, in almost all states, a single *statute of descent and distribution* governs intestacy. The same persons are named as intestate successors to both real and personal property. Thus, today the word *heirs* usually means those persons designated by the applicable statute to take a decedent's intestate property, both real and personal. *Next-of-kin* usually means exactly the same thing.

At common law, a surviving spouse was not an heir; he or she had only what were called *curtesy* or *dower* rights (rights to take a share of some of the decedent spouse's property). Today, in all states the statutes of descent and distribution

---

14. Cf. William Shakespeare, King John, act I, scene 1, line 109: "Upon his death-bed he by will bequeath'd/ His lands to me."

name the spouse as an intestate successor whose share depends upon who else survives; the spouse is thus an heir.

In this book, we do not use the Latin suffix indicating feminine gender for women playing important roles in our cast: testator, executor, and administrator. Although *testatrix, executrix*, and *administratrix* are still in current fashion, other *-trix* forms either have disappeared from use (e.g., *donatrix, creditrix*) or would sound odd to the contemporary ear (e.g., *public administratrix*).[15] And, of course, it does not matter whether the person in the given role is a man or a woman.[16]

We have tried to avoid words that assign a role to one sex, but we dare not hope that we have succeeded in a field so long dominated by assumptions of male superiority in property management. We believe it was Bentham who observed, "Error is never so difficult to be destroyed as when it has its root in language."

c. A Summary of Probate Procedure

(1) Opening probate

Though the general pattern of administering probate estates is quite similar in all jurisdictions, there are widespread variations in the procedural details. In each state, the procedure is governed by a collection of statutes and court rules giving meticulous instructions for each step in the process. Happily, this precludes our being concerned with specific rules and procedures and enables us to advise that you can safely postpone any concern about the particular mechanics of probating a will and administering an estate until you can "learn by doing" when that first estate file comes across your desk. When that day comes, you will find that there are available in most jurisdictions excellent probate practice books. The purpose of the following description is to provide a generalized summary.

The will should first be probated, or letters of administration should first be sought, in the jurisdiction where the decedent was domiciled at death. This is known as the *primary* or *domiciliary* jurisdiction. If real property is located in another jurisdiction, *ancillary administration* in the jurisdiction is required. The purpose of requiring ancillary administration is to prove title to real property in the situs state's recording system and to subject those assets to probate for the protection of local creditors. Ancillary administration may be costly because the state may require that a resident be appointed personal representative, with a local attorney. Executor's commissions and attorney's fees will be paid to them for handling the ancillary assets.

Each state has a detailed statutory procedure for issuance of *letters testamentary* to an executor or *letters of administration* to an administrator authorizing the person to act on behalf of the estate. Several states, mainly east of the Mississippi, follow the procedure formerly used by the English ecclesiastical courts in

---

15. See *-trix* in Oxford English Dictionary (1989).

16. The Supreme Court has held unconstitutional a statute giving preference to a male to serve as executor or administrator. Reed v. Reed, 404 U.S. 71 (1971).

distinguishing between contentious and noncontentious probate proceedings. Under the English system, the executor had a choice of probating a will *in common form* or *in solemn form*. Common form probate was an ex parte proceeding in which no notice or process was issued to any person. Due execution of the will was proved by the oath of the executor or such other witnesses as might be required. The will was admitted to probate at once, letters testamentary were granted, and the executor began administration of the estate. If no one raised any questions or objections, this procedure sufficed. However, within a period of years thereafter an interested party could file a *caveat*, compelling probate of the will in solemn form. Under probate in solemn form, notice to interested parties was given by citation, due execution of the will was proved by the testimony of the attesting witnesses, and administration of the estate involved greater court participation. Ex parte or common form procedure is recognized in many states, sometimes preserving the common form/solemn form terminology, but more often not.

(2)   Formal versus informal probate

The Uniform Probate Code (UPC), originally promulgated in 1969 and substantially revised in 1990, is representative of statutes regulating probate procedures. It provides for both notice probate and ex parte probate. The former is called *formal probate* (rather than solemn form probate), the latter *informal probate* (rather than common form probate). The person asking for letters can choose.[17]

Formal probate. Formal probate under the UPC is a litigated judicial determination after notice to interested parties. UPC §3-401. A formal proceeding may be used to probate a will, to block an informal proceeding, or to secure a declaratory judgment of intestacy. Formal proceedings become final judgments if not appealed.

In a formal probate, the court supervises the actions of the personal representative in administering the estate. This supervision can be time consuming and costly. The court must approve the inventory and appraisal of the estate; payment of debts; family allowance; granting options on real estate; sale of real estate; borrowing of funds and mortgaging of property; leasing of property; proration of federal estate tax; personal representative's commissions; attorney's fees; preliminary and final distributions; and discharge of the personal representative. The sale of real estate may require several trips to the courthouse to get an order to sell, to file notice of all offers received, to give notice that a previous low bidder

---

17. No proceeding, formal or informal, may be initiated more than three years from the date of death. UPC §3-108 (1990). If no will is probated within three years after death, the presumption of intestacy is conclusive. The three-year statute of limitations of the UPC changes the common law, which permits a will to be probated at any time, perhaps many years after the testator's death. See Annot., 2 A.L.R.4th 1315 (1980, rev. 2008).

The time for contesting probate of a will is governed by statute. The period of limitations for filing a will contest is ordinarily jurisdictional and is not tolled by any fact not provided by statute. If the constitutional and statutory requirements for notice are satisfied, when the period of limitation passes, the probate court no longer has jurisdiction to revoke probate. Probate of a will thereby becomes final. The rules on will contests under the UPC are in §§3-401 to 3-414.

has overbid the previous high bid, and, finally, to get approval of the terms of the sale to the highest bidder.

Informal probate. In informal probate, after appointment, the personal representative administers the estate without going back into court. The representative has the broad powers of a trustee in dealing with the estate property and may collect assets, clear titles, sell property, invest in other assets, pay creditors, continue any business of the decedent, and distribute the estate — all without court approval. UPC §3-715. The estate may be closed by the personal representative by filing a sworn statement that he has published notice to creditors, administered the estate, paid all claims, and sent a statement and accounting to all known distributees. UPC §3-1003.

The key assumptions that underpin the informal probate statutes are that the typical executor or administrator is a trusted family member, and that the typical beneficiary is also a family member. In such circumstances, unless there is a dispute over the will or the administration of the estate, the intensive judicial supervision that is typical of formal probate imposes needless costs on the estate and drains the judiciary's budget without an offsetting benefit. Under the UPC, informal probate is the norm, but an interested party may file a petition for formal probate at any time during the administration of the estate. UPC §3-502. In this way, the drafters of the UPC managed to have their cake and eat it too. The safeguards of formal probate are preserved for any case in which an interested party asks for them, but otherwise the personal representative may make use of the faster and cheaper informal probate alternative.

UPC §3-301 sets forth the requirements for informal probate. Without giving notice to anyone, the representative petitions for appointment; the petition contains pertinent information about the decedent and the names and addresses of the spouse, the children or other heirs, and, if a will is involved, the devisees. If the petition is for probate of a will, the original will must accompany the petition. The executor swears that, to the best of her knowledge, the will was validly executed; proof by the witnesses is not required. A will that appears to have the required signatures and that contains an attestation clause showing that requirements of execution have been met is probated by the registrar without further proof. UPC §3-303. Within 30 days after appointment, the personal representative has the duty of mailing notice to every interested person, including heirs apparently disinherited by a will. UPC §3-705.

(3)   Barring creditors of the decedent

Every state has a statute requiring creditors to file claims within a specified time period; claims filed thereafter are barred. These are known as *nonclaim statutes*. They come in two basic forms: Either (1) they bar claims not filed within a relatively short period after probate proceedings are begun, generally two to six months (four months under the UPC); or (2), whether or not probate proceedings are commenced, they bar claims not filed within a longer period after the decedent's death, generally one to five years (one year under the UPC). UPC §3-803. Under short-term statutes, creditors are usually notified of the requirement to file claims only by publication in a newspaper after probate proceedings are opened. The Supreme Court has held, however, that the Due Process Clause requires that known or reasonably ascertainable creditors receive actual notice before they are barred by a short-term statute running from the commencement of probate proceedings. Tulsa Prof. Collection Servs. v. Pope, 485 U.S. 478 (1988) (statute barring known creditors two months after newspaper publication objectionable). A one-year statute of limitations running from the decedent's death, barring creditors filing claims thereafter, is believed to be constitutional even without notice to creditors. Most states have such a statute. See Elaine H. Gagliardi, Remembering the Creditor at Death: Aligning Probate and Nonprobate Transfers, 41 Real Prop., Prob. & Tr. J. 819, 840-848 (2007).

(4) Closing the estate

The personal representative of an estate is expected to complete the administration and distribute the assets as promptly as possible. Even if all the beneficiaries are amicable, several things that must be done may prolong administration. Creditors must be paid. Titles must be cleared. Taxes must be paid and tax returns audited and accepted by the tax authorities. Real estate or a sole proprietorship may have to be sold.

Judicial approval of the personal representative's action is required to relieve the representative from liability, unless some statute of limitations runs upon a cause of action against the representative. The representative is not discharged from fiduciary responsibility until the court grants discharge.

d. The Costs of Probate

Much is heard about the excessive cost of probate — or, as some have put it, the high cost of dying.[18] The administrative costs of probate are mainly probate court fees, the commission of the personal representative, the attorney's fee, and,

---

18. Complaints about the delay and costs of probate are hardly new. Perhaps the most searing was by Charles Dickens. Speaking of Jarndyce v. Jarndyce, a chancery proceeding involving an estate that is at the center of his novel Bleak House, he wrote:

> Jarndyce and Jarndyce drones on. This scarecrow of a suit has, in course of time, become so complicated, that no man alive knows what it means. The parties to it understand it least; but it has been observed that no two Chancery lawyers can talk about it for five minutes, without coming to a total disagreement as to all the premises. . . . Scores of persons have deliriously found themselves made parties in Jarndyce and Jarndyce, without knowing how or why; whole families have inherited legendary hatreds with the suit. The little plaintiff or defendant, who was promised a new rocking-horse when Jarndyce and Jarndyce should be settled, has grown up, possessed himself of a real horse, and trotted away into the other world. [Id. ch. I.]

In the end, after the discovery and admission to probate of Jarndyce's true last will, "the whole estate is found to have been absorbed in costs." Id. ch. LXV.

sometimes, appraiser's and guardian ad litem's fees. In some states, the personal representative's commission is set by statute at a fixed percentage of the probate estate. In most states, the commission must be reasonable under the circumstances. See Robert A. Stein and Ian G. Fierstein, The Role of the Attorney in Estate Administration, 68 Minn. L. Rev. 1107 (1984). In some circumstances a lawyer who serves as executor may be entitled to fees for serving in both offices. See Cal. Prob. Code §10804 (2008); William M. McGovern, Jr. and Sheldon F. Kurtz, Wills, Trusts and Estates §12.5, at 535-536 (3d ed. 2004). On the other hand, if the personal representative is a family member, as is typical, she will usually serve without taking a commission.

A 1988 study examined fees for estate attorneys in ten large states. For an ordinary $100,000 estate, fees ranged from $2,000 in Florida to $5,000 in New York and Pennsylvania. For an ordinary $600,000 estate, the fees ranged from $9,000 in Texas and Virginia to $22,000 in New York and Pennsylvania. Fees in California, Georgia, Illinois, Michigan, and Ohio were somewhere in between these extremes. These numbers do not include the executor's commission, if any, and they assume probate of a relatively simple estate with a house and no major valuation issues or disputes. Cal. L. Revision Commn. Rep. No. L-1036/1055, at 7, Oct. 26, 1988.

A more recent snapshot of fees is provided by the Statistics of Income Division (SOI) of the IRS. According to estimates by the SOI, in 2007 the IRS received nearly 40,000 estate tax returns reporting aggregate deductions for personal representatives' fees of nearly $1.3 billion and attorneys' fees of $915 million. These deductions were taken against the just over $200 billion in aggregate reported gross estate values, and thus represent 0.65 percent and 0.46 percent respectively.

e. Is Probate Necessary?

In view of the costs of probate and the attendant delays, the question is often asked: *Can probate be avoided?* The answer is Yes, provided the property owner during life transfers all his property into a joint tenancy or an inter vivos trust, or makes arrangement for other forms of nonprobate transfer. In such circumstances, the will serves a backup function to catch overlooked property or property acquired after inter vivos changes in ownership have been made.

Even for property transferred by will or intestacy, probate is not always necessary. As a practical matter, establishment of the transferee's title is not necessary for many items of personal property, such as furniture or personal effects. A purchaser will assume that the possessor has title. Moreover, even for items of personal property for which ownership is evidenced by a document — such as an automobile certificate — summary procedures now exist to clear title and give the transferee official recognition of his rights. See, e.g., Cal. Vehicle Code §5910 (2008) (vehicle transfer without probate).

Statutes in almost every state permit heirs to avoid probate where the amount of property involved is small, often by requiring nothing more than an affidavit of the decedent's successor. See UPC §§3-1201 to 3-1204. Indeed, the chief area of divergence across the states is not whether to offer a *summary administration for small estates* (even the probate-preferring states that do not offer informal probate do offer a summary procedure for small estates), but rather how much and what kind of property can be transferred by summary administration. The figure defining a small estate, which can be collected upon affidavit, ranges from $5,000 (as in UPC §3-1201) to $100,000 (as in 755 Ill. Comp. Stat. Ann. 5/25-1 (2008)) or more. For a survey of small estate procedures across the states, see Jeffrey A. Schoenblum, 2008 Multistate Guide to Estate Planning at Table 4.

Also common are statutory provisions permitting collection of small bank accounts or wage claims, or transfer of an automobile certificate of title to the decedent's heirs, upon affidavit by the heirs. By filling out the appropriate forms and presenting them to the bank, the employer, or the department of motor vehicles, the heir is able to collect the decedent's property or acquire a new certificate of title. Statutes in some states permit filing a will for probate solely as a title document, with no formal administration to follow.

With the rising popularity of nonprobate modes of transfer, the ready availability of summary or affidavit administration for small estates, and special provisions for transfer of automobiles and other items with formal title registration, *increasingly probate is necessary only for very large estates or to clear title to real property.* A 1985 study of five states found that the percentage of decedents' estates that underwent probate administration ranged from 20 percent in California to 34 percent in Massachusetts. Robert A. Stein and Ian G. Fierstein, The Demography of Probate Administration, 15 U. Balt. L. Rev. 54 (1985). Thus, one way or another, the large majority of decedents manage to avoid probate.

PROBLEMS

1. Aaron Green died three weeks ago. His wife has come to your law firm with Green's will in hand. The will devises Green's entire estate "to my wife, Martha, if she survives me; otherwise to my children in equal shares." The will names Martha Green as executor. An interview with Mrs. Green reveals that the Green family consists of two adult sons and several grandchildren and that Green owned the following property: car ($15,000), furniture ($20,000), mutual fund ($10,000), joint checking account ($3,000), and life insurance policy naming Martha Green as beneficiary ($50,000). Mr. Green also had a pension plan naming Martha Green for survivor's benefits. Green owned no real property; he and his wife lived in a rented apartment. Green's debts consisted of last month's utility bills ($80) plus the usual consumer charge accounts: Visa card ($600 balance) and a local department store ($250). There is also a funeral bill ($8,000) and the cost of a cemetery lot ($600). Mrs. Green wants your advice: What should she do with the will? Must it be offered for probate? Must there be an administration of her husband's estate?

2. Same facts as in Problem 1 except that Green died intestate, and the state's statute of descent and distribution provides that where a decedent is survived by

a spouse and children, one-half of his real and personal property shall descend to the spouse and the remaining one-half shall descend to the children.

3.   Same facts as in Problem 1 except that Green also owned a house and lot worth $170,000 and another lot worth $16,000. The deeds to both tracts name Aaron Green as grantee. The residential property is subject to a mortgage with a current balance of $85,000; title to the other lot is free of encumbrances. Must (should?) Green's will be probated and his estate formally administered?

4.   Let us look at Aaron Green's problem from another perspective. Suppose Green comes to you and tells you that he does not have a will. He describes his family situation and the property owned by him: the property listed in Problem 1 but not the real estate described in Problem 3. His question: In view of his family situation and his modest estate, does he really need a will?

f.   Universal Succession

The English system of court-supervised administration of estates, which we inherited, was designed to protect creditors and to protect beneficiaries from an untrustworthy executor or heir. On the continent of Europe and in Louisiana, an entirely different system exists that rarely involves a court at all. It is known as *universal succession*. The heirs or the residuary devisees step into the shoes of the decedent at the decedent's death, taking the decedent's title and assuming all the decedent's liabilities and the obligation of paying legacies according to the decedent's will. If, for example, *O* dies intestate, leaving *H* as *O*'s heir, *H* succeeds to ownership of *O*'s property and must pay all of *O*'s creditors and any taxes resulting from *O*'s death. If *O* has three heirs, they take *O*'s property as tenants in common at *O*'s death, with the ordinary rights of tenants in common. The payment of a commission to a fiduciary is not necessary, and a lawyer need not be employed unless the heirs decide they need legal advice. A system of universal succession can have enormous advantages where the heirs or the residuary devisees are all adults. See European Succession Laws (David Hayton ed., 2d ed. 2002).

The UPC authorizes universal succession as an alternative to probate administration. Under UPC §§3-312 to 3-322, the heirs or the residuary devisees may petition the court for universal succession. If the court ascertains that the necessary parties are included and that the estate is not subject to any current contest or difficulty, it issues a written statement of universal succession. The universal successors then have full power of ownership to deal with the assets of the estate. They assume the liabilities of the decedent to creditors, including tax liability. The successors are personally liable to other heirs omitted from the petition or, in the case of residuary devisees, to other devisees for the amount of property due them. No state has yet adopted these provisions of the UPC.

Universal succession is, however, already available to a limited extent in the United States. Under California law, property that passes to the surviving spouse by intestacy or by will is not subject to administration unless the surviving spouse elects to have it administered. If the surviving spouse chooses not to have the property administered, the surviving spouse takes title to the property and assumes personal liability for the decedent's debts chargeable against the property. Cal. Prob. Code §§13500-13650 (2008). If probate is not necessary for property passing to a surviving spouse, why is it necessary for property passing to adult children?

SECTION C.   AN ESTATE PLANNING PROBLEM

1.   *The Client's Letter and Its Enclosures*

January 15, 20__

Dear _____:

For some time now, Wendy and I have been considering the rewriting of our wills since we now have very simple wills giving our property to each other in case of death and then to our children when the survivor of us dies. However, in this day of air crashes where Wendy and I might die simultaneously, the problems of settling our estate might be complicated.

These, in general, are the assets with which we are concerned:

Residence	cost $125,000	($100,000 mtge.)
Lot, cabin, Lake Murray, ME	cost 40,000	worth more
Chevrolet SUV	10,000	
Honda	12,000	
Household furniture, etc.	???	
Checking account	2,000 to 4,000	
Money market account at bank	7,000	
Certificate of deposit	20,000	
My IRA	30,000	
Stocks	130,000	
Mutual funds	110,000	
My life insurance	200,000	
Wendy's life insurance	240,000	
Mother's house at death	???	
Pension	???	

Wendy and I think our main objectives should be to avoid probate and to eliminate as many inheritance taxes as possible. I am enclosing copies of our present wills. These are some of the questions we would like your help on:

1.   It may be that we do not need wills at all. Can we let our property pass by inheritance or by joint and survivor arrangements? Our bank accounts and some of our stocks are set up to pass by a joint and survivor arrangement.

2.   As a sort of corollary to that first question, we have read in various places that it would be a good idea to set up a living trust to pass our house, cars, etc. With the use of a trust plus the joint and survivor arrangements, could we avoid the need for wills and probate entirely?

3.   If you think we should have wills, are our present ones all right? If not, how should they be changed?

Please let us hear from you at your earliest convenience.

Sincerely yours,

/s/ *Howard Brown*
Howard Brown

Last Will and Testament of Howard Brown

I, Howard Brown, of the city of Springfield, County of _____, and State of _____, do hereby make, publish, and declare this to be my Last Will and Testament, hereby revoking any and all other wills and codicils thereto, which I have heretofore made.

FIRST: I hereby direct that all of my just debts, funeral expenses, and expenses of administration of my estate be paid out of my estate as soon as may be practicable after my death.

SECOND: I name and appoint my wife, Wendy Brown, to be the executor of this my Last Will and Testament, and I direct that she not be required to give bond or other security.

THIRD: I give my remainder interest in my mother's house at 423 Elm St., Concord, Delaware, to my sister, Carol Gould.

FOURTH: I give, devise, and bequeath all the rest of my property, both real and personal, of whatever kind and nature and description, and wherever located, which I now own or may own at the time of my death, to my wife, Wendy Brown, should she survive me. Should she not survive me, I then give, devise, and bequeath all of my property to my children.

FIFTH: I authorize and empower my Executor, or anyone appointed to administer this, my Last Will and Testament, to sell and convert into cash any and all of my personal property without a court order and to convey any such real estate by deed without the necessity of a court order authorizing such conveyance or approving such deed.

SIXTH: In the event that my wife, Wendy Brown, predeceases me, I name and appoint my wife's sister, Lucy Preston Lipman, of San Francisco, California, as legal guardian of my children during their respective minorities.

IN TESTIMONY WHEREOF I have hereunto set my hand and seal this 27th day of November, 2008.

/s/ *Howard Brown*
Howard Brown

The above instrument, consisting of two typewritten pages, of which this is the second, with paragraphs FIRST through SIXTH, inclusive, was on the 27th day of November, 2008, signed by Howard Brown, in our presence, and he did then declare this to be his Last Will and Testament, and we at his request and in his presence and in the presence of each other, did sign this instrument as witnesses thereunto and as witnesses to his signature thereto.

WITNESSES: */s/ Michael Wong*

                                              /s/ Patricia Muñoz Garcia

[Wendy Brown's will contains reciprocal provisions, with the exception of the remainder interest in Howard's mother's house. Wendy leaves everything of hers to Howard if he survives, and if he does not survive her, to her children.]

2.   Some Preliminary Questions Raised by Brown's Letter

From time to time, we shall refer back to the Brown estate planning situation in the context of the substantive areas being considered. But before we embark on our studies, it may be profitable to reflect on some of the questions raised in, and by, Brown's letter.

QUESTIONS AND PROBLEMS

1.   Examine Howard Brown's present will in the context of the property and family situation described in his letter. Can you detect any problems that may be raised or any contingencies that are not provided for by the will provisions? Here are a few:

(a) *Article FIRST*: Does the "just debts" clause require the executor to pay off the mortgage on the Browns' home? Would this be desirable? See In re Estate of Miller, 127 F. Supp. 23 (D.D.C. 1955); In re Estate of Keil, 145 A.2d 563 (Del. 1958). See also the discussion of exoneration of liens, page 391.

(b) Would death taxes incurred at Howard Brown's death be "just debts," making this a tax apportionment clause requiring payment of all taxes, including those on the remainder interest in his mother's house, out of Howard's residuary estate? See Estate of Kyreazis, 701 P.2d 1022 (N.M. App. 1985); Internal Revenue Code of 1986, §§2206, 2207.

(c) Does the "just debts" clause require the executor to pay off debts barred by limitations or other such defenses?

(d) *Articles SECOND and FIFTH*: Has suitable provision been made for appointment of an executor in case Wendy Brown dies before Howard? Does the executor have sufficiently broad powers to enable her to administer the estate effectively?

(e) *Article FOURTH*: Is the dispositive plan provided by Howard's will sound? Should he make an outright distribution of his entire estate to Wendy, or should he consider making some other distribution?

(f) Which of the items of property listed in Howard Brown's letter will be governed by his will, and which will pass as nonprobate property unaffected by the will?

(g) *Article SIXTH*: If both Howard and Wendy Brown die before all their children attain majority, a guardianship administration will be required. Is this desirable? See pages 136-140.

2.   In view of the Browns' property and family situation, do they need wills at all? Should the Browns consider alternatives to a will or intestacy, such as joint and survivor arrangements and inter vivos trusts, as means of transferring their property at death?

Perhaps it has occurred to you by now that we don't really know very much about the Brown family or the property they own. Without further information, we cannot answer these questions. What further information should we obtain from the clients before we can proceed further?

3.   Additional Data on the Browns' Family and Property

Following receipt of the letter from Howard Brown asking for a review of the present wills of Howard and Wendy Brown, a conference was held with the clients, and the following additional information was obtained.

a.   Family Data

Members of Immediate Family		Age	Birth Date	Health
Husband	Howard Brown	43	7/12/—	good
Wife	Wendy Brown	41	6/1/—	"
Child of Wendy	Michael Walker	20	9/25/—	"
Child of both	Sarah Brown	14	11/19/—	"
Child of both	Stephanie Brown	11	8/22/—	"

Howard Brown is an industrial design engineer and manager of a department at Tresco Machine Tool Company in Springfield. He has been with this firm for the past eight years and feels that he has a secure and responsible position with the firm. His annual salary is $90,000.

Wendy Brown has a degree in modern languages and during the early years of their marriage taught German and French at a secondary school in Springfield. She then worked for several years only in the home. Four years ago Wendy decided to go to law school. Last year she finished law school and received a J.D. degree. (She did *not* take a course in wills and trusts.) Wendy has just accepted a position as an associate of Hanlon & Yutz, a medium-size law firm. Her annual salary is $100,000.

Michael is Wendy's son by her first husband, Brian Walker, whom Wendy divorced when Michael was three years old. A year later, Wendy and Howard married, and Howard has raised Michael as a member of his family, though never formally adopting him. Brian stopped making child support payments a couple of years after the divorce and moved out of state. He has not been heard from in many years. Michael has left home and is living with (but not married to) an older woman, Candace Robinson, age 33. They have a child, Andy, age 1.

Residence

Home address: 2220 Casino Lane, Springfield. 555-477-5882

Period of residence in this state: All of life since college.

Note: No problems regarding domicile. Also, note that none of present assets acquired while residing in another state. Howard owns out-of-state property — a lot in Maine and a remainder interest in his mother's house in Delaware.

Parents; collateral relatives

Howard's parents. Howard Brown's father, Frank, died of a heart attack at age 60. His mother, Margaret Brown, a widow, is 63 years old, is in good health, and lives in Concord, Delaware. Howard stated that his mother has a modest but comfortable income from property left by her husband and from social security. Howard says his father devised his home to his wife, Margaret, for life, and on her death to Howard and his sister, Carol Gould.

Howard estimated that his mother owns property worth about $300,000, of which $150,000 is represented by her residence. Howard is familiar with the terms of his mother's will; it provides for an equal distribution between Howard and Carol Gould. Howard is named as executor under the will.

Howard's collateral relatives. Howard has a younger sister, Carol Gould, who is a police officer with the Concord police department. Carol is divorced and lives with her mother; Carol has no children.

Wendy's parents. Wendy Brown's parents (Robert Preston, age 65, and Zoë Preston, age 62) are both living. Wendy stated that her father is a well-known doctor in Boston and is quite well off. When asked how well off, Wendy said he is "worth" at least $1 million (probably a very conservative estimate). Wendy may acquire a substantial inheritance upon the death of her parents.

Wendy's collateral relatives. Wendy Brown's siblings: one sister, Lucy Preston Lipman, a writer, lives in San Francisco with her husband, Jonathan Lipman. They have two children. Her brother, Simon Preston, is married to Antonia Preston, has no children, and is a salesman. Her other sister, Ruth Preston, unmarried, is a professor of archeology at Swarthmore.

Wendy Brown also has a maternal aunt, Fanny Fox of Lexington, Kentucky. Aunt Fanny is a rich widow without children and has a large house full of antiques, paintings, silver — things she and her husband collected during their marriage. Wendy will likely inherit some of Aunt Fanny's things and possibly a substantial sum of money.

Special family problems

Michael is a stepchild of Howard. Michael has an out-of-wedlock child, Andy.

b. Assets

The Browns have lived in Springfield since they were married 16 years ago. Since neither brought into the marriage any property of substantial value, there appears to be no problem in establishing their marital rights in the property they now own. All life insurance policies were taken out after the Browns married.

Tangible personal property

Tangible personalty consists of the usual furnishings in a family residence, two automobiles, outboard motor boat, personal effects such as clothing and jewelry, computers, plasma TV, and other miscellaneous items. No items of unusual value. Estimated value: $50,000

Real estate

(1) Family residence. The Browns purchased their home at 2220 Casino Lane, Springfield, 15 years ago. Although the purchase price for the property was $125,000, Howard believes that it is now worth around $300,000, but this is a guesstimate. Present balance on mortgage loan (note held by Springfield Federal Savings & Loan Assn.) is $100,000. The deed shows that title to the property was taken by "Howard Brown and Wendy Brown, as joint tenants with right of survivorship and not as tenants in common." $300,000

(2) Lot and cabin, Lake Murray, Maine. Twelve years ago the Browns purchased a lot and cabin on Lake Murray for $40,000. Title to the land was taken in Howard Brown's name alone. Based on current values, the Browns believe they could sell the property for at least $120,000. No mortgage indebtedness.   120,000

(3) Mother's house. Howard has a remainder interest in 423 Elm St., Concord, Delaware, with his sister. House worth about $150,000. Howard's (discounted) remainder roughly valued at $40,000.   40,000

Bank accounts

(1) Checking account, Springfield National Bank. The account balance fluctuates from around $2,000 to $4,000 each month. Howard and Wendy Brown are both authorized to draw checks on the account; the balance is payable to the survivor. $ 3,000

(2) Money market account, Springfield Federal Savings & Loan Assn. The account is in the name of Wendy Brown.   7,000

(3) Certificate of deposit, Springfield Federal Savings & Loan Assn., at 6 percent for four years. CD was issued in the name of "Howard Brown and Wendy Brown, as joint tenants with right of survivorship."   20,000

(4) IRA (Individual Retirement Account), Springfield Federal Savings & Loan Assn. Established by Howard Brown 15 years ago. Income taxes on contributions are deferred until the money is withdrawn or Howard reaches $70\frac{1}{2}$ or sooner dies. Current balance is $30,000. If Howard dies before withdrawal, balance is payable to Wendy Brown.   30,000

Securities

(1) 800 shares, General Corporation common stock. Given to Howard under his aunt's will six years ago. Current value: $50 per share. Registered in the name of Howard Brown as owner. $40,000

(2) 1,000 shares, Varoom Mutual Fund. When Howard's father died five years ago, his mother gave each of her children $7,500. Howard used all of this money to purchase 400 shares of the Varoom Fund, which has appreciated in value since his purchase. Howard has reinvested the ordinary income and capital gains dividends paid by the fund and now owns an additional 600 shares. Present value is $30 per share. Registered in the name of Howard Brown as owner.   30,000

(3) 2,000 shares, American Growth Mutual Fund. Over the years the Browns have invested in the American Growth Fund under some form of monthly investment plan. Their objective was to establish an educational fund for their children. The purchase price has fluctuated over the years from $28 to $42 a share. Present price is $40 a share. Howard says that he has kept

records on the price of the shares as purchased. Registered in
the name of "Howard Brown and Wendy Brown, as joint tenants
with right of survivorship and not as tenants in common."   80,000

(4) 1,500 shares, Union National Bank common stock. Was
given to Wendy Brown by her parents. Present value is $60 per
share. Registered in the name of Wendy Brown as owner.   90,000

Life insurance

(1) Mutual of New York policy #624-05-91, ordinary life, participating, acquired 14 years ago. Annual premium $2,050.
Cash surrender value this year $20,500; CSV is increasing at
about $1,600/year. $100,000
(2) Aetna Life Group policy, group term. Premiums are paid
by Howard Brown's employer.   100,000
(3) Prudential Life policy, group term. Premiums are paid by
Wendy Brown's employers.   240,000

Policies (1) and (2) name Howard Brown as "insured" and "owner." The policies name Wendy Brown as primary beneficiary and the estate of Howard Brown
as contingent beneficiary. Policy (3) names Wendy Brown as "insured" and
"owner." The policy names Howard Brown as beneficiary. It names Wendy's children as secondary beneficiaries.

Employee benefits of Howard Brown

In addition to the group insurance mentioned above, Howard Brown's
employer provides medical insurance, disability insurance, and a qualified pension plan. The plan will provide substantial retirement benefits to Howard, under
a formula based on his years of service and his average annual salary. The present
projection is that Howard would be able to retire at age 65 with an annuity of
about $65,000 in today's dollars.

The pension plan provides survivor benefits for the surviving spouse. If
Howard survives to retirement age, the pension is payable as a joint and survivor
annuity to Howard and his surviving spouse.

Employee benefits of Wendy Brown

In addition to the group insurance mentioned above, Wendy Brown's law firm,
Hanlon & Yutz, provides group medical coverage. There are no pension benefits
for first-year associates. Wendy has been in practice for only a month, but she will
join the plan after her first year at the firm. If she stays at the firm for 10 years, it
is likely that her income — already slightly exceeding Howard's — will grow substantially.

c. Liabilities

Real estate mortgages: $100,000 mortgage loan, Springfield Federal Savings & Loan Assn.

Other notes to banks, etc.: None.
Loans on insurance policies: None.
Accounts to others: "Usual" store, etc. accounts.
Other: None.

d. Assets and Liabilities: Summary

(1) Estate of Howard and Wendy Brown

Tangible personalty	$ 50,000
Realty:	
Residence (joint tenancy)	300,000
Lake Murray property (in Howard's name)	120,000
Remainder interest in mother's home (Howard)	40,000*
Bank accounts:	
Checking (joint and survivor)	3,000
Money market (in Wendy's name)	7,000
Certificate of deposit (joint tenancy)	20,000
IRA (Howard's, payable on death to Wendy)	30,000
Securities:	
General Corp. common (in Howard's name)	40,000*
Varoom Mutual Fund (in Howard's name)	30,000*
American Growth Mutual Fund (joint tenancy)	80,000
Union Natl. Bank common (in Wendy's name)	90,000*
Life insurance on Howard	200,000
Life insurance on Wendy	240,000
TOTAL ASSETS	$ 1,050,000[19]

(2) Liabilities

Mortgage loan, Springfield Federal Savings & Loan Assn.	100,000
TOTAL LIABILITIES	$ 100,000

---

19. Items marked by asterisk, which were acquired by gift or inheritance from Howard's and Wendy's respective relatives, are excluded from this total. All other assets are attributable to Howard Brown's earnings during their marriage. In a community property state, property acquired with a spouse's earnings is community property unless the spouses have changed it into another form of ownership.

(3)   Other factors:

    Probable inheritance by Howard Brown of about $150,000 from his mother. Probability of substantial inheritance by Wendy Brown from her parents and her Aunt Fanny — but no knowledge of whether this would be outright or in some form of trust.

SECTION D.   PROFESSIONAL RESPONSIBILITY

Trusts and estates practice is mined with conflicts of interest arising from duties to clients and their intended beneficiaries. Forewarned is forearmed.

1. *Duties to Intended Beneficiaries*

Simpson v. Calivas
Supreme Court of New Hampshire, 1994
650 A.2d 318

HORTON, J.   The plaintiff, Robert H. Simpson, Jr., appeals from a directed verdict, grant of summary judgment, and dismissal of his claims against the lawyer who drafted his father's will. The plaintiff's action, sounding in both negligence and breach of contract, alleged that the defendant, Christopher Calivas, failed to draft a will which incorporated the actual intent of Robert H. Simpson, Sr. to leave all his land to the plaintiff in fee simple. Sitting with a jury, the Superior Court (Dickson, J.) directed a verdict for the defendant based on the plaintiff's failure to introduce any evidence on . . . breach of duty. The trial court also granted summary judgment on collateral estoppel grounds based on findings of the Strafford County Probate Court and dismissed the action, ruling that under New Hampshire law an attorney who drafts a will owes no duty to intended beneficiaries. We reverse and remand.

    In March 1984, Robert H. Simpson, Sr. (Robert Sr.) executed a will that had been drafted by the defendant. The will left all real estate to the plaintiff except for a life estate in "our homestead located at Piscataqua Road, Dover, New Hampshire," which was left to Robert Sr.'s second wife, Roberta C. Simpson (stepmother). After Robert Sr.'s death in September 1985, the plaintiff and his stepmother filed a joint petition in the Strafford County Probate Court seeking a determination, essentially, of whether the term "homestead" referred to all the decedent's real property on Piscataqua Road (including a house, over one hundred acres of land, and buildings used in the family business), or only to the house (and, perhaps, limited surrounding acreage). The probate court found the term "homestead" ambiguous, and in order to aid construction, admitted some extrinsic evidence of the testator's surrounding circumstances, including evidence showing a close relationship between Robert Sr. and plaintiff's stepmother. The probate court, however, did not admit notes taken by the defendant during consultations with Robert Sr. that read: "House to wife as a life estate remainder to son, Robert H. Simpson, Jr. . . . Remaining land . . . to son Robert A. [*sic*] Simpson, Jr." The probate court construed the will to provide Roberta with a life estate in all the real property. After losing the will construction action — then two years after his father's death — the plaintiff negotiated with his stepmother to buy out her life estate in all the real property for $400,000.

The plaintiff then brought this malpractice action, pleading a contract count, based on third-party beneficiary theory, and a negligence count. . . .

The plaintiff raises . . . [these] issues on appeal: (1) whether the trial court erred in ruling that under New Hampshire law a drafting attorney owes no duty to an intended beneficiary; (2) whether the trial court erred in ruling that the findings of the probate court on testator intent collaterally estopped the plaintiff from bringing a malpractice action . . . .

We reverse and remand.

I. DUTY TO INTENDED BENEFICIARIES . . .

The critical issue, for purposes of this appeal, is whether an attorney who drafts a testator's will owes a duty of reasonable care to intended beneficiaries. We hold that there is such a duty.

As a general principle, "the concept of 'duty' . . . arises out of a relation between the parties and the protection against reasonably foreseeable harm." Morvay v. Hanover Insurance Co., 506 A.2d 333, 334 (N.H. 1986). The existence of a contract between parties may constitute a relation sufficient to impose a duty to exercise reasonable care, but in general, "the scope of such a duty is limited to those in privity of contract with each other." Robinson v. Colebrook Savings Bank, 254 A.2d 837, 839 (N.H. 1969). The privity rule is not ironclad, though, and we have been willing to recognize exceptions particularly where, as here, the risk to persons not in privity is apparent. In *Morvay*, for example, we held that investigators hired by an insurance company to investigate the cause of a fire owed a duty to the insureds to perform their investigation with due care despite the absence of privity. Accordingly, the insureds stated a cause of action by alleging that the investigators negligently concluded that the fire was set, thereby prompting the insurance company to deny coverage. *Morvay*, 506 A.2d at 335.

Because this issue is one of first impression, we look for guidance to other jurisdictions. The overwhelming majority of courts that have considered this issue have found that a duty runs from an attorney to an intended beneficiary of a will. Ronald E. Mallen & Jeffrey M. Smith, Legal Malpractice 3d ed. §26.4, at 595 (1989 & Supp. 1992). A theme common to these cases, similar to a theme of cases in which we have recognized exceptions to the privity rule, is an emphasis on the foreseeability of injury to the intended beneficiary. As the California Supreme

Court explained in reaffirming the duty owed by an attorney to an intended beneficiary:

> When an attorney undertakes to fulfill the testamentary instructions of his client, he realistically and in fact assumes a relationship not only with the client but also with the client's intended beneficiaries. The attorney's actions and omissions will affect the success of the client's testamentary scheme; and thus the possibility of thwarting the testator's wishes immediately becomes foreseeable. Equally foreseeable is the possibility of injury to an intended beneficiary. In some ways, the beneficiary's interests loom greater than those of the client. After the latter's death, a failure in his testamentary scheme works no practical effect except to deprive his intended beneficiaries of the intended bequests.

Heyer v. Flaig, 449 P.2d 161, 164-65 (Cal. 1969). We agree that although there is no privity between a drafting attorney and an intended beneficiary, the obvious foreseeability of injury to the beneficiary demands an exception to the privity rule.

The defendant in his brief, however, urges that if we are to recognize an exception to the privity rule, we should limit it to those cases where the testator's intent as expressed in the will — not as shown by extrinsic evidence — was frustrated by attorney error. See *Kirgan v. Parks,* 478 A.2d 713, 719 (Md. App. 1984). Under such a limited exception to the privity rule, a beneficiary whose interest violated the rule against perpetuities would have a cause of action against the drafting attorney, but a beneficiary whose interest was omitted by a drafting error would not. Similarly, application of such a rule to the facts of this case would require dismissal even if the allegations — that the defendant botched Robert Sr.'s instructions to leave all his land to his son — were true. We refuse to adopt a rule that would produce such inconsistent results for equally foreseeable harms, and hold that an intended beneficiary states a cause of action simply by pleading sufficient facts to establish that an attorney has negligently failed to effectuate the testator's intent as expressed to the attorney.

We are not the only court to reject the distinction urged by the defendant. In *Ogle v. Fuiten,* 466 N.E.2d 224, 225 (Ill. 1984), for example, nephews of the testator sued the testator's attorney for failing to provide in the will for the possibility that the testator's wife might not die in a common disaster, but might nonetheless fail to survive him by thirty days. The testator's wife died in the period not dealt with in the will, and without a provision in the will providing for this situation, the estate devolved by intestacy. On appeal after the dismissal of the nephews' claims, the court flatly rejected the argument that intended beneficiaries do not state a cause of action where the testator's alleged intent does not appear in the will.

The plaintiff also argues that the trial court erred in failing to recognize that the writ stated a cause of action in contract. We agree.

The general rule that a nonparty to a contract has no remedy for breach of contract is subject to an exception for third-party beneficiaries. Third-party beneficiary status necessary to trigger this exception exists where "the contract is so expressed as to give the promisor reason to know that a benefit to a third party is contemplated by the promisee as one of the motivating causes of his making the contract." Tamposi Associates, Inc. v. Star Market Co., 406 A.2d 132, 134 (N.H. 1979). We hold that where, as here, a client has contracted with an attorney to draft a will and the client has identified to whom he wishes his estate to pass, that identified beneficiary may enforce the terms of the contract as a third-party beneficiary.

Because we hold that a duty runs from a drafting attorney to an intended beneficiary, and that an identified beneficiary has third-party beneficiary status, the trial court erred by dismissing the plaintiff's writ.

II. COLLATERAL ESTOPPEL

The defendant insists, however, that even if a duty runs from a testator's attorney to an intended beneficiary, the superior court properly granted summary judgment on collateral estoppel grounds. We disagree. . . .

The primary question is whether the issues before the probate and superior courts were identical. We agree with defendant that comparison of the respective evidence which each court was competent to hear is one factor, but note that an identity of evidence is not dispositive of an identity of issues. Instead, determination of "identity" necessarily requires inquiry into each court's role and the nature of the respective findings.

The principal task of the probate court is to determine the testator's intent . . . limited by the requirement that it determine the "intention of the testator as shown by the language of the whole will." Dennett v. Osgood, 229 A.2d 689, 690 (N.H. 1967). In this effort, the probate court is always permitted to consider the "surrounding circumstances" of the testator, id., and where the terms of a will are ambiguous, as here, extrinsic evidence may be admitted to the extent that it does not contradict the express terms of the will. In re Estate of Sayewich, 413 A.2d 581, 584 (N.H. 1980). Direct declarations of a testator's intent, however, are generally inadmissible in all probate proceedings. Id. The defendant argues that even though his notes of his meeting with the decedent recorded the decedent's direct declarations of intent, they could have been admissible as an exception to the general rule had there been a proper proffer. We need not reach the issue of whether the defendant's notes fall within an exception to the general rule because even assuming admissibility and therefore an identity of evidence, there remain distinct issues. Quite simply, the task of the probate court is a limited one: to determine the intent of the testator as expressed in the language of the will. Obviously, the hope is that the application of rules of construction and consideration of extrinsic evidence (where authorized) will produce a finding of expressed intent that corresponds to actual intent. Further, the likelihood of such convergence presumably increases as the probate court considers more extrinsic evidence; however, even with access to all extrinsic evidence, there is no requirement or guarantee that the testator's intent as construed will match the testator's actual intent.

The defendant, however, insists that whether or not required to do so, the probate court in this case did make an explicit finding of actual intent when it concluded: "There is nothing to suggest that [the testator] intended to grant a life estate in anything less than the whole." We need not reach the issue of whether this language constitutes a finding of actual intent because collateral estoppel will not lie anyway. Collateral estoppel is only applicable if the finding in the first proceeding was essential to the judgment of that court. Restatement (Second) of Judgments §27. Inasmuch as the mandate of the probate court is simply to determine and give effect to the intent of the testator as expressed in the language of the will, a finding of actual intent is not necessary to that judgment. Accordingly, even an explicit finding of actual intent by a probate court cannot be the basis for collateral estoppel. . . .

Reversed and remanded.

NOTES AND QUESTIONS

1. *The privity defense.* In rejecting the privity defense, Vice Chancellor Megarry of England stated the argument against it succinctly:

> In broad terms, the question is whether solicitors who prepare a will are liable to a beneficiary under it if, through their negligence, the gift to the beneficiary is void. The solicitors are liable, of course, to the testator or his estate for a breach of the duty that they owed to him, though as he has suffered no financial loss it seems that his estate could recover no more than nominal damages. Yet it is said that however careless the solicitors were, they owed no duty to the beneficiary, and so they cannot be liable to her. If this is right, the result is striking. The only person who has a valid claim has suffered no loss, and the only person who has suffered a loss has no valid claim. [Ross v. Caunters, 3 All Eng. Rep. 580, 582 (Ch. 1980).]

At most ten states still follow the old rule that the lack of privity between the drafter and an intended beneficiary prevents a malpractice action by the beneficiary: Alabama, Arkansas, Maine, Maryland, Nebraska, New York, Ohio, Texas, Virginia, and, perhaps, Massachusetts. See Ronald E. Mallen and Jeffrey M. Smith, 4 Legal Malpractice §§34:4-34:7 (2008); Kevin S. Rosen and Pamela A. Bresnahan, Avoiding Malpractice in the Course of Estate Planning, 41 Heckerling Inst. on Est. Plan. ch. 8 (2007); Bradley E.S. Fogel, Attorney v. Client: Privity, Malpractice, and the Lack of Respect for the Primacy of the Attorney-Client Relationship in Estate Planning, 68 Tenn. L. Rev. 261 (2001).

2. *Malpractice and law reform.* If extrinsic evidence of the testator's actual intent is reliable enough to hold the drafter liable for misrendering that intent, why not reform the will to correct the drafting error and avoid the malpractice litigation altogether?

Many years ago Professor Dukeminier predicted that legal malpractice liability would prove to be a strong force for reform of property law. Jesse Dukeminier, Cleansing the Stables of Property: A River Found at Last, 65 Iowa L. Rev. 151 (1979). And so it is turning out. Today there are movements to excuse errors in will execution (see pages 246-264); to correct mistakes by lawyers in drafting instruments to carry out the client's intent (see pages 342-357); to cure or avoid perpetuities violations by judicial reformation of the instrument, the adoption of the wait-and-see doctrine, or the abolition of the Rule Against Perpetuities altogether (see pages 905-917); and to reform wills and trusts after the decedent's death to obtain tax advantages lost by the lawyer's mistake (see page 651). Has the fall of the privity defense played a role in inducing lawyers to support these reforms?

3. *Probate court jurisdiction.* In Simpson v. Calivas, the validity and construction of the will were matters for the probate court to decide. The negligence of the lawyer was a matter for a court of general jurisdiction, which entertains tort and contract suits. This is true in most states.

Historically, probate courts were inferior courts, with jurisdiction limited to determining the will's validity and supervising administration of the decedent's estate. Because of the small amount of business, legislatures were often unwilling to provide suitable compensation and clerical assistance, particularly in rural areas. In some states, probate judges may be laypersons, without legal training. Anyone can run for the office. The National Law Journal, Dec. 24, 1984, at 39, reported the election of an 18-year-old man, just six months out of high school, as probate judge for Valencia County, New Mexico. Because of lack of confidence in probate judges, their powers were often curtailed.

Today, most probate courts are better staffed and they are authorized to pass on more questions regarding wills, including the construction of wills. Nonetheless, most courts, like the New Hampshire Supreme Court, reject the claim that conclusions reached by the probate court about testator's intent in a construction suit are determinative in a malpractice suit. The issues and the evidentiary rules for proving intent applied in the two proceedings are different.

State probate courts, meanwhile, continue to suffer from a poor reputation, in some cases well deserved. See John H. Langbein, Don't Die in Connecticut, Hartford Courant, Oct. 23, 2005, at C1 (detailing the low standards and culture of petty corruption of Connecticut's probate courts); In re Feinberg, 833 N.E.2d 1204 (N.Y. 2005) (upholding removal of a probate court judge for misconduct). See also Bill Braun, Judge Facing Sex Charges Is Given New Assignment, Tulsa World, Apr. 29, 2008, at A13 (reporting that an Oklahoma judge accused of exposing himself to two women in a parking lot had been reassigned to the probate division pending resolution of the charges).

4. Sometimes attorneys who make drafting errors in wills have more to fear from their incompetence than a mere suit for malpractice. Because a Tennessee lawyer (a former judge who specialized in probate) mistakenly used the phrase "all monies" when intending to refer to the residue of an estate, the testator's intended beneficiary was not awarded the testator's stock investments. The intended beneficiary, who lost out on $100,000, became unhinged and shot and killed the lawyer — as well as a life insurance agent who, at the time of the murder, was trying to sell an insurance policy to the 81-year-old lawyer. See Angela K. Brown, One Word Enraged Lawyer's Killer, Comm. App., Mar. 20, 1999, at B2.

2. *Conflicts of Interest*

A. v. B.
Supreme Court of New Jersey, 1999
726 A.2d 924

POLLOCK, J.   This appeal presents the issue whether a law firm may disclose confidential information of one co-client to another co-client. Specifically, in this paternity action, the mother's former law firm, which contemporaneously represented the father and his wife in planning their estates, seeks to disclose to the wife the existence of the father's illegitimate child. . . .

I.

In October 1997, the husband and wife retained Hill Wallack, a firm of approximately sixty lawyers, to assist them with planning their estates.[20] On the commencement of the joint representation, the husband and wife each signed a letter captioned "Waiver of Conflict of Interest." In explaining the possible conflicts of interest, the letter recited that the effect of a testamentary transfer by one spouse to the other would permit the transferee to dispose of the property as he or she desired. The firm's letter also explained that information provided by one spouse could become available to the other. Although the letter did not contain an express waiver of the confidentiality of any such information, each spouse consented to and waived any conflicts arising from the firm's joint representation.

Unfortunately, the clerk who opened the firm's estate planning file misspelled the clients' surname. The misspelled name was entered in the computer program that the firm uses to discover possible conflicts of interest. The firm then prepared reciprocal wills and related documents with the names of the husband and wife correctly spelled.

In January 1998, before the husband and wife executed the estate planning documents, the mother coincidentally retained Hill Wallack to pursue a paternity claim against the husband. This time, when making its computer search for conflicts of interest, Hill Wallack spelled the husband's name correctly. Accordingly, the computer search did not reveal the existence of the firm's joint representation of the husband and wife. As a result, the estate planning department did not know that the family law department had instituted a paternity action for the mother. Similarly, the family law department did not know that the estate planning department was preparing estate plans for the husband and wife.

A lawyer from the firm's family law department wrote to the husband about the mother's paternity claim. The husband neither objected to the firm's representation of the mother nor alerted the firm to the conflict of interest. Instead, he retained Fox Rothschild to represent him in the paternity action. After initially denying paternity, he agreed to voluntary DNA testing, which revealed that he is

---

20. In an omitted portion of the opinion, the court said: "Because the Family Part has sealed the record, we refer to the parties without identifying them by their proper names." — Eds.

the father. Negotiations over child support failed, and the mother instituted the present action.

After the mother filed the paternity action, the husband and wife executed their wills at the Hill Wallack office. The parties agree that in their wills, the husband and wife leave their respective residuary estates to each other. If the other spouse does not survive, the contingent beneficiaries are the testator's issue. The wife's will leaves her residuary estate to her husband, creating the possibility that her property ultimately may pass to his issue. Under N.J.S.A. 3B:1-2;:3-48, the term "issue" includes both legitimate and illegitimate children. When the wife executed her will, therefore, she did not know that the husband's illegitimate child ultimately may inherit her property.

The conflict of interest surfaced when Fox Rothschild, in response to Hill Wallack's request for disclosure of the husband's assets, informed the firm that it already possessed the requested information. Hill Wallack promptly informed the mother that it unknowingly was representing both the husband and the wife in an unrelated matter.

Hill Wallack immediately withdrew from representing the mother in the paternity action. It also instructed the estate planning department not to disclose any information about the husband's assets to the member of the firm who had been representing the mother. The firm then wrote to the husband stating that it believed it had an ethical obligation to disclose to the wife the existence, but not the identity, of his illegitimate child. Additionally, the firm stated that it was obligated to inform the wife "that her current estate plan may devise a portion of her assets through her spouse to that child." The firm suggested that the husband so inform his wife and stated that if he did not do so, it would. . . .

II.

This appeal concerns the conflict between two fundamental obligations of lawyers: the duty of confidentiality, Rules of Professional Conduct (RPC) 1.6(a), and the duty to inform clients of material facts, RPC 1.4(b). The conflict arises from a law firm's joint representation of two clients whose interests initially were, but no longer are, compatible.

Crucial to the attorney-client relationship is the attorney's obligation not to reveal confidential information learned in the course of representation. Thus, RPC 1.6(a) states that "[a] lawyer shall not reveal information relating to representation of a client unless the client consents after consultation, except for disclosures that are impliedly authorized in order to carry out the representation." Generally, "the principle of attorney-client confidentiality imposes a sacred trust on the attorney not to disclose the client's confidential communication." State v. Land, 372 A.2d 297, 300 (N.J. 1977).

A lawyer's obligation to communicate to one client all information needed to make an informed decision qualifies the firm's duty to maintain the confidentiality of a co-client's information. RPC 1.4(b), which reflects a lawyer's duty to keep clients informed, requires that "[a] lawyer shall explain a matter to the extent reasonably necessary to permit the client to make informed decisions regarding the representation." In limited situations, moreover, an attorney is permitted or required to disclose confidential information. Hill Wallack argues that RPC 1.6 mandates, or at least permits, the firm to disclose to the wife the existence of the husband's illegitimate child. RPC 1.6(b) requires that a lawyer disclose "information relating to representation of a client" to the proper authorities if the lawyer "reasonably believes" that such disclosure is necessary to prevent the client "from committing a criminal, illegal or fraudulent act that the lawyer reasonably believes is likely to result in death or substantial bodily harm or substantial injury to the financial interest or property of another." RPC 1.6(b)(1). Despite Hill Wallack's claim that RPC 1.6(b) applies, the facts do not justify mandatory disclosure. The possible inheritance of the wife's estate by the husband's illegitimate child is too remote to constitute "substantial injury to the financial interest or property of another" within the meaning of RPC 1.6(b).

By comparison, in limited circumstances RPC 1.6(c) permits a lawyer to disclose a confidential communication. RPC 1.6(c) permits, but does not require, a lawyer to reveal confidential information to the extent the lawyer reasonably believes necessary "to rectify the consequences of a client's criminal, illegal or fraudulent act in furtherance of which the lawyer's services had been used." RPC 1.6(c)(1). Although RPC 1.6(c) does not define a "fraudulent act," the term takes on meaning from our construction of the word "fraud," found in the analogous "crime or fraud" exception to the attorney-client privilege. When construing the "crime or fraud" exception to the attorney-client privilege, "our courts have generally given the term 'fraud' an expansive reading." Fellerman v. Bradley, 493 A.2d 1239, 1245 (N.J. 1985).

We likewise construe broadly the term "fraudulent act" within the meaning of RPC 1.6(c). So construed, the husband's deliberate omission of the existence of his illegitimate child constitutes a fraud on his wife. When discussing their respective estates with the firm, the husband and wife reasonably could expect that each would disclose information material to the distribution of their estates, including the existence of children who are contingent residuary beneficiaries. The husband breached that duty. Under the reciprocal wills, the existence of the husband's illegitimate child could affect the distribution of the wife's estate, if she predeceased him. Additionally, the husband's child support payments and other financial responsibilities owed to the illegitimate child could deplete that part of his estate that otherwise would pass to his wife. . . .

The New Jersey RPCs are based substantially on the American Bar Association Model Rules of Professional Conduct ("the Model Rules"). RPC 1.6, however, exceeds the Model Rules in authorizing the disclosure of confidential information. . . . As adopted by the American Bar Association, Model Rule 1.6(b) permits a lawyer to reveal confidential information only "to the extent the lawyer reasonably believes necessary to prevent the client from committing a criminal act that the lawyer believes is likely to result in imminent death or substantial bodily harm." Unlike RPC 1.6, Model Rule 1.6 does not except information relating to the commission of a fraudulent act or that relating to a client's act that is likely to result in substantial financial injury. In no situation, moreover, does

Model Rule 1.6 require disclosure. Thus, the Model Rules provide for narrower disclosure than that authorized by RPC 1.6.[21] . . .

Under RPC 1.6, the facts support disclosure to the wife. The law firm did not learn of the husband's illegitimate child in a confidential communication from him. Indeed, he concealed that information from both his wife and the firm. The law firm learned about the husband's child through its representation of the mother in her paternity action against the husband. Accordingly, the husband's expectation of nondisclosure of the information may be less than if he had communicated the information to the firm in confidence.

In addition, the husband and wife signed letters captioned "Waiver of Conflict of Interest." These letters acknowledge that information provided by one client could become available to the other. The letters, however, stop short of explicitly authorizing the firm to disclose one spouse's confidential information to the other. Even in the absence of any such explicit authorization, the spirit of the letters supports the firm's decision to disclose to the wife the existence of the husband's illegitimate child. . . .

[A]n attorney, on commencing joint representation of co-clients, should agree explicitly with the clients on the sharing of confidential information. In such a "disclosure agreement," the co-clients can agree that any confidential information concerning one co-client, whether obtained from a co-client himself or herself or from another source, will be shared with the other co-client. Similarly, the co-clients can agree that unilateral confidences or other confidential information will be kept confidential by the attorney. Such a prior agreement will clarify the expectations of the clients and the lawyer and diminish the need for future litigation. . . .

In the context of estate planning, the [Restatement (Third) of the Law Governing Lawyers (Proposed Final Draft No. 1, 1996) ("the Restatement")] suggests that a lawyer's disclosure of confidential information communicated by one spouse is appropriate only if the other spouse's failure to learn of the information would be materially detrimental to that other spouse or frustrate the spouse's intended testamentary arrangement. Id. §112 comment l, illustrations 2, 3. The Restatement provides two analogous illustrations in which a lawyer has been jointly retained by a husband and wife to prepare reciprocal wills. The first illustration states:

> Lawyer has been retained by Husband and Wife to prepare wills pursuant to an arrangement under which each spouse agrees to leave most of their property to the other. Shortly after the wills are executed, Husband (unknown to Wife) asks Lawyer to prepare an inter vivos trust for an illegitimate child whose existence Husband has kept secret from Wife for many years and about whom Husband had not previously informed Lawyer. Husband states that Wife would be distraught at learning of Husband's infidelity and of Husband's years of silence and that disclosure of the information could destroy their marriage. Husband directs Lawyer not to

---

21. As amended in 2002, Model Rule 1.6(b) now does provide for permissive disclosure "to prevent, mitigate or rectify substantial injury to the financial interests or property of another that is reasonably certain to result or has resulted from the client's commission of a crime or fraud in furtherance of which the client has used the lawyer's services." — Eds.

inform Wife. The inter vivos trust that Husband proposes to create would not materially affect Wife's own estate plan or her expected receipt of property under Husband's will, because Husband proposes to use property designated in Husband's will for a personally favored charity. In view of the lack of material effect on Wife, Lawyer may assist Husband to establish and fund the inter vivos trust and refrain from disclosing Husband's information to Wife. [Id. §112, cmt. l, illus. 2.]

In authorizing non-disclosure, the Restatement explains that an attorney should refrain from disclosing the existence of the illegitimate child to the wife because the trust "would not materially affect Wife's own estate plan or her expected receipt of property under Husband's will." Ibid.

The other illustration states:

Same facts as [the prior Illustration], except that Husband's proposed inter vivos trust would significantly deplete Husband's estate, to Wife's material detriment and in frustration of the Spouses' intended testamentary arrangements. If Husband will neither inform Wife nor permit Lawyer to do so, Lawyer must withdraw from representing both Husband and Wife. In the light of all relevant circumstances, Lawyer may exercise discretion whether to inform Wife either that circumstances, which Lawyer has been asked not to reveal, indicate that she should revoke her recent will or to inform Wife of some or all the details of the information that Husband has recently provided so that Wife may protect her interests. Alternatively, Lawyer may inform Wife only that Lawyer is withdrawing because Husband will not permit disclosure of information that Lawyer has learned from Husband. [Id. §112, cmt. l, illus. 3.]

Because the money placed in the trust would be deducted from the portion of the husband's estate left to his wife, the Restatement concludes that the lawyer may exercise discretion to inform the wife of the husband's plans. Ibid. . . .

Similarly, the American College of Trust and Estate Counsel (ACTEC) also favors a discretionary rule. It recommends that the "lawyer should have a reasonable degree of discretion in determining how to respond to any particular case." American College of Trust and Estate Counsel, ACTEC Commentaries on the Model Rules of Professional Conduct 68 (2d ed. 1995). The ACTEC suggests that the lawyer first attempt to convince the client to inform the co-client. Ibid. . . .

The ACTEC reasons that if unsuccessful in persuading the client to disclose the information, the lawyer should consider several factors in deciding whether to reveal the confidential information to the co-client, including: (1) duties of impartiality and loyalty to the clients; (2) any express or implied agreement among the lawyer and the joint clients that information communicated by either client to the lawyer regarding the subject of the representation would be shared with the other client; (3) the reasonable expectations of the clients; and (4) the nature of the confidence and the harm that may result if the confidence is, or is not, disclosed. Id. at 68-69. . . .

Because Hill Wallack wishes to make the disclosure, we need not reach the issue whether the lawyer's obligation to disclose is discretionary or mandatory. In conclusion, Hill Wallack may inform the wife of the existence of the husband's illegitimate child. . . .

The law firm learned of the husband's paternity of the child through the mother's disclosure before the institution of the paternity suit. It does not seek to disclose the identity of the mother or the child. Given the wife's need for the information and the law firm's right to disclose it, the disclosure of the child's existence to the wife constitutes an exceptional case with "compelling reason clearly and convincingly shown."

The judgment of the Appellate Division is reversed and the matter is remanded to the Family Part.

NOTES AND QUESTION

1.   Estate planning lawyers commonly represent multiple members of the same family — such as a husband and wife — in drafting wills, trusts, and powers of attorney, and in the administration of wills and trusts. In such cases it is important to discuss with the affected parties at the outset the possible conflicts of interests and the ground rules for sharing information. A prudent practice, unfortunately infrequently used, is to speak with each client separately early in the representation to ferret out any hidden conflicts. Most estate planning lawyers at least discuss the potential for a conflict of interests with the clients, and then follow up on the discussion with an *engagement letter* or other form of waiver agreement. In some states an engagement letter is required. See Anne-Marie Rhodes, Engagement Letters, Tr. & Est., Apr. 2008, at 25.

The model engagement letter for the joint representation of spouses suggested in ACTEC Engagement Letters: A Guide for Practitioners (2d ed. 2007), provides as follows:

> It is common for a husband and wife to employ the same lawyer to assist them in planning their estates. You have taken this approach by asking me to represent both of you in your planning. It is important that you understand that, because I will be representing both of you, you are considered my client, collectively. Ethical considerations prohibit me from agreeing with either of you to withhold information from the other. Accordingly, in agreeing to this form of representation, each of you is authorizing me to disclose to the other any matters related to the representation that one of you might discuss with me or that I might acquire from any other source. In this representation, I will not give legal advice to either of you or make any changes in any of your estate planning documents without your mutual knowledge and consent. [Id. at 11.]

What result in A. v. B. if the husband and wife had signed an engagement letter containing this clause?

2.   For an excellent discussion of estate planning under the ABA Model Rules of Professional Conduct, see ACTEC Commentaries on the Model Rules of Professional Conduct (4th ed. 2006), particularly the treatment of Rules 1.2 (scope of representation), 1.6 (confidentiality), and 1.7 (conflicts of interest). As in A. v. B., courts often treat the ACTEC Commentaries as authoritative. For an up-to-date treatment of multiple client representation in estate planning, see John R. Price, The Fundamentals of Ethically Representing Multiple Clients in Estate

Planning, 62 U. Miami L. Rev. 735 (2008). For a survey of common malpractice pitfalls in estate planning, see Gerry W. Beyer, Avoiding the Estate Planning "Blue Screen of Death" — Common Non-Tax Errors and How to Prevent Them, 1 Est. Plan. & Comm. Prop. L.J. 61 (2008).

3. Estate planning matters are a common source of ethics complaints against attorneys. For example, in Illinois probate was fifth among 19 fields in the frequency of disciplinary complaints filed in 2007. Annual Report of the Illinois Attorney Registration and Disciplinary Commission (2008).

For useful student texts covering the materials in this book, see Roger W. Andersen, Understanding Trusts and Estates (3d ed. 2003); Gerry W. Beyer, Wills, Trusts, and Estates: Examples and Explanations (4th ed. 2007); Melanie B. Leslie and Stewart E. Sterk, Trusts and Estates: Concepts and Insights (2006); Jeffrey N. Pennell and Alan Newman, Estate and Trust Planning (2005); William M. McGovern and Sheldon F. Kurtz, Principles of Wills, Trusts & Estates (2005).

2

INTESTACY: AN ESTATE PLAN BY DEFAULT

SECTION A. THE BASIC SCHEME

1. Introduction

Some people die leaving a will that provides for the disposition of their property at death. These people are said to die *testate*. Other people die without a will. These people are said to die *intestate*. The law of intestacy governs the distribution of an intestate decedent's probate property. Intestacy is therefore the background law that lawyers plan around — what in legal theory are called *default rules*.

Lawyers almost always advise their clients to avoid intestacy by executing a will (and often a trust as well). In addition to identifying who will take the decedent's probate property, wills can designate guardians for minor children, identify a trustworthy individual or trust company to administer the estate, reduce probate costs by waiving a required bond (or surety on a bond), and achieve tax savings. Surveys report that about half of all adults claim to have a will.[1] Those who say that they have a will tend to be older and wealthier, and most but not all had assistance of a lawyer in the will's preparation.

In spite of the many advantages of a will, roughly half the population dies intestate. Why? One reason is that the unpleasantness of confronting mortality invites procrastination. In a 2006 poll of older adults, 20 percent acknowledged that "[t]hinking about my own death . . . scares me."[2] Insurers call death insurance

---

1. See Gallup Poll Social Series — Values and Beliefs (reporting 51%, May 2-5, 2005, survey of 1,005 adults); ABC News Poll: Planning Ahead (reporting 50%, Jul.-Aug. 2002, survey of 1,024 adults).

2. AARP Thoughts on the Afterlife Survey, Public Opinion Online database, Roper Center for Public Opinion Research, University of Connecticut (June 2006, survey of 1,011 adults 50 and older).

"life insurance," and agents are careful to omit the word *death* from their discussions with clients ("If anything should happen to you . . ." *If*, indeed!). As Freud wrote, "Our own death is indeed unimaginable, and whenever we make the attempt to imagine it we can perceive that we really survive as spectators. Hence . . . at bottom no one believes in his own death, or to put the same thing in another way, in the unconscious every one of us is convinced of his own immortality." Sigmund Freud, Our Attitude Towards Death, *in* 4 Collected Papers 304 (1925).

Another reason people do not make wills is the time and cost involved. It seems like a "big deal" to go to a lawyer, and lawyers tend not to market the advantages of wills relative to intestacy and nonprobate modes of transfer. See Michael R. McCunney and Alyssa A. DiRusso, Marketing Wills, 16 Elder L.J. 33 (2008). Today people commonly arrange to transfer their property at death by way of joint tenancy, payable-on-death designations on life insurance, pension plans, and the like, or revocable trusts created during life, avoiding probate and wills (indeed, more property is passed outside probate than through probate).

Whatever the reasons, people who do not make wills or otherwise dispose of their property by nonprobate transfers accept the intestacy law as their estate plans by default. The probate property of a person who dies without a will is governed by the state's statute of descent and distribution. If a will disposes of only part of the probate estate, then the result is a *partial intestacy* in which the part of the probate estate not disposed of by the will passes by intestacy. Generally speaking, the law of the state where the decedent was domiciled at death governs the disposition of personal property, and the law of the state where the decedent's real property is located governs the disposition of real property.

Because the law of intestacy is not exactly the same in all details in any two states, it is essential that lawyers become familiar with the intestacy statutes of the state in which they intend to practice. We reproduce here the intestacy provisions of the Uniform Probate Code (UPC) and in later chapters we excerpt the UPC or Uniform Trust Code (UTC, see pages 545-546) provisions relevant to the particular topic under discussion. The intestate succession scheme of each state is summarized in Table 8 of Jeffrey A. Schoenblum, 2008 Multistate Guide to Estate Planning (updated annually).

The UPC was originally promulgated in 1969. Subsequently, about one-third of the states adopted laws substantially conforming to major parts of the 1969 Code, and several other states enacted particular sections of the Code. Article VI of the Code, dealing with nonprobate transfers, was substantially revised in 1989. Article II of the Code, dealing with intestacy, wills, and donative transfers, was overhauled in 1990. See John H. Langbein and Lawrence W. Waggoner, Reforming the Law of Gratuitous Transfers: The New Uniform Probate Code, 55 Alb. L. Rev. 871 (1992). Some of the Code sections have since been revised further, most systematically in 2008. You should compare the probate code provisions of your own state with the UPC and consider whether the UPC approach is better than the one adopted in your state and any other alternatives.

Uniform Probate Code (1990, as amended 2008)

§2-101. INTESTATE ESTATE

(a) Any part of a decedent's estate not effectively disposed of by will passes by intestate succession to the decedent's heirs as prescribed in this Code, except as modified by the decedent's will.

(b) A decedent by will may expressly exclude or limit the right of an individual or class to succeed to property of the decedent passing by intestate succession. If that individual or a member of that class survives the decedent, the share of the decedent's intestate estate to which that individual or class would have succeeded passes as if that individual or each member of that class had disclaimed his [or her] intestate share.

§2-102. SHARE OF SPOUSE[3]

The intestate share of a decedent's surviving spouse is:

    (1) the entire intestate estate if:

        (A) no descendant or parent of the decedent survives the decedent; or

        (B) all of the decedent's surviving descendants are also descendants of the surviving spouse and there is no other descendant of the surviving spouse who survives the decedent;

    (2) the first [$300,000],[4] plus three-fourths of any balance of the intestate estate, if no descendant of the decedent survives the decedent, but a parent of the decedent survives the decedent;

    (3) the first [$225,000], plus one-half of any balance of the intestate estate, if all of the decedent's surviving descendants are also descendants of the surviving spouse and the surviving spouse has one or more surviving descendants who are not descendants of the decedent;

    (4) the first [$150,000], plus one-half of any balance of the intestate estate, if one or more of the decedent's surviving descendants are not descendants of the surviving spouse.

§2-103. SHARE OF HEIRS OTHER THAN SURVIVING SPOUSE

(a) Any part of the intestate estate not passing to a decedent's surviving spouse under Section 2-102, or the entire intestate estate if there is no surviving spouse, passes in the following order to the individuals who survive the decedent:

    (1) to the decedent's descendants by representation;

    (2) if there is no surviving descendant, to the decedent's parents equally if both survive, or to the surviving parent if only one survives;

---

3. The UPC's alternate section for community property states (§2-102A) provides for the same distribution of separate property as is provided in §2-102 and further provides that all community property passes to the surviving spouse whether or not the decedent is survived by descendants or parents. — Eds.

4. UPC §1-109, added to the Code in 2008, provides for an annual adjustment, based on the Consumer Price Index, of the dollar amounts stated in the Code. — Eds.

(3) if there is no surviving descendant or parent, to the descendants of the decedent's parents or either of them by representation;

(4) if there is no surviving descendant, parent, or descendant of a parent, but the decedent is survived on both the paternal and maternal sides by one or more grandparents or descendants of grandparents:

(A) half to the decedent's paternal grandparents equally if both survive, to the surviving paternal grandparent if only one survives, or to the descendants of the decedent's paternal grandparents or either of them if both are deceased, the descendants taking by representation; and

(B) half to the decedent's maternal grandparents equally if both survive, to the surviving maternal grandparent if only one survives, or to the descendants of the decedent's maternal grandparents or either of them if both are deceased, the descendants taking by representation;

(5) if there is no surviving descendant, parent, or descendant of a parent, but the decedent is survived by one or more grandparents or descendants of grandparents on the paternal but not the maternal side, or on the maternal but not the paternal side, to the decedent's relatives on the side with one or more surviving members in the manner described in paragraph (4).

(b) If there is no taker under subsection (a), but the decedent has:

(1) one deceased spouse who has one or more descendants who survive the decedent, the estate or part thereof passes to that spouse's descendants by representation; or

(2) more than one deceased spouse who has one or more descendants who survive the decedent, an equal share of the estate or part thereof passes to each set of descendants by representation.

§2-105. No Taker

If there is no taker under the provisions of this Article, the intestate estate passes to the [state].

QUESTION

Under all intestate succession statutes, parents of the decedent are not heirs if the decedent leaves a child. Why should this be so (especially if the child is an adult)? Why isn't the decedent's property used to support aging parents rather than an able-bodied adult child?

NOTE: THE MEANING OF HEIRS AND THE TRANSFER
OF AN EXPECTANCY

In the eyes of the law no living person has heirs; to use the Latin phrase: *nemo est haeres viventis*. The persons who would be the heirs of *A*, a living person, if *A* died within the next hour, are not the heirs of *A* but are the *heirs apparent*. They have a mere *expectancy*. This expectancy can be destroyed by A's deed or will. It is not a legal "interest" at all. A's heirs can be identified only at A's death, and only by reference to the applicable statute of descent and distribution. Being named in a will or will substitute makes the person a devisee or legatee or beneficiary, not an heir.

A mere expectancy cannot be transferred at law. However, a purported transfer of an expectancy, for an adequate consideration, may be enforceable in equity as a contract if the court views it as fair under all the circumstances. Equity scrutinizes such transactions to protect prospective heirs from unfair bargains.[5] See Hoffman v. Gregory, 204 S.W.3d 541 (Ark. 2005).

Should a release of an expectancy to the donor be subjected to less judicial scrutiny than the transfer of an expectancy to a third party? See Katheleen R. Guzman, Releasing the Expectancy, 34 Ariz. St. L.J. 775 (2002).

2. Share of Surviving Spouse

In designing an intestacy statute, the primary policy is to carry out the probable intent of the average intestate decedent. In the last 50 years, several empirical studies have been undertaken to determine popular preferences for intestate succession. Although these studies do not always agree, they unanimously support the conclusion that the spouse's share that had traditionally been given by most intestacy statutes was too small. The studies show that, when there are no children from a prior marriage, most persons want everything to go to the surviving spouse, thus excluding parents and siblings — and children. This preference is particularly strong among persons with moderate estates, who believe the surviving spouse will need the entire estate for support. The richer the person, the greater the desire that children or collaterals share with the spouse in the estate. See Mary L. Fellows, Rita J. Simon, and William Rau, Public Attitudes About Property Distribution at Death and Intestate Succession Laws in the United States, 1978 Am. B. Found. Res. J. 319, 348-364; Allison Dunham, The Method, Process and Frequency of Wealth Transmission at Death, 30 U. Chi. L. Rev. 241, 251-253 (1963); Comment, A Comparison of Iowans' Dispositive Preferences with Selected Provisions of the Iowa and Uniform Probate Codes, 63 Iowa L. Rev. 1041 (1978).

A study by John R. Price, The Transmission of Wealth at Death in a Community Property Jurisdiction, 50 Wash. L. Rev. 277, 311-313 (1975), supports giving the surviving spouse all of the decedent's interest in community property. See also Kristine S. Knaplund, The Evolution of Women's Rights in Inheritance, 19 Hastings Women's L.J. 3 (2008); Lawrence M. Friedman, Christopher J. Walker, and Ben Hernandez-Stern, The Inheritance Process in San Bernardino County, California, 1964: A Research Note, 43 Hous. L. Rev. 1445 (2007).

---

5. Undoubtedly, the most famous sale of an expectancy was the sale of Esau's birthright to Jacob for a bowl of pottage. Genesis 25:29-34. Whether this sale was enforceable under Hebrew law has been much debated by biblical scholars. See David Daube, Studies in Biblical Law 191-200 (1947); Reuben Ahroni, Why Did Esau Spurn the Birthright?, 29 Judaism 323 (1980). Under modern American law, was Esau's promise enforceable as a fair bargain?

Under current intestacy laws in most states, the surviving spouse usually receives at least a one-half share of the decedent's estate, an increase from the one-quarter or one-third of the estate that was typical a half century ago. There are many variations in the specifics, however, such as giving the surviving spouse a lump sum plus one-half of the remainder, or giving the surviving spouse a one-half share if only one child or descendants of one child survives, and a one-third share if more than one child or one child and descendants of a deceased child survive. For a critical survey, see Laura A. Rosenbury, Two Ways to End a Marriage: Divorce or Death, 2005 Utah L. Rev. 1227, 1261-1274.

The current UPC provision for the surviving spouse is relatively generous. Under UPC §2-102(1), if all the decedent's descendants are also descendants of the surviving spouse, and the surviving spouse has no other descendants, the surviving spouse takes the entire estate to the exclusion of the decedent's descendants. Giving everything to the spouse and nothing to the children under these circumstances was a novel statutory approach, but studies of estates with minor children show it to be the usual practice of those leaving wills. It also has the virtue of avoiding a guardianship for a minor child. Thanks in large part to the influence of the UPC, intestacy statutes that give the surviving spouse the entirety of the decedent's estate are no longer uncommon. The provisions in subsections (3) and (4), giving the surviving spouse less when either spouse has a child by someone other than the other spouse, were also unusual when originally proposed. The theory of §2-102 is discussed in Lawrence W. Waggoner, The Multiple-Marriage Society and Spousal Rights Under the Revised Uniform Probate Code, 76 Iowa L. Rev. 223 (1991).

If there is no descendant, roughly half of the states provide, as does UPC §2-102(2), that the surviving spouse share the estate with the decedent's parents, if any. If no parent survives, the surviving spouse usually takes all to the exclusion of collateral kin, as the UPC provides, but in a few states the spouse shares with the decedent's brothers and sisters and their descendants. See Ronald J. Scalise, Jr., Honor Thy Father and Mother? How Intestacy Law Goes Too Far in Protecting Parents, 37 Seton Hall L. Rev. 171 (2006).

A secondary policy of the intestacy laws is family protection — that is, preserving the economic health of the family after a death. With respect to spouses, a related consideration is the idea that marriage involves an economic partnership. The law of intestate succession therefore influences the discourse over the extent to which testators should be free to disinherit their spouses and other family members. In Chapter 7, when we examine the mandatory minimum share to which the law entitles a surviving spouse in spite of a contrary will by the decedent, the question arises, should the surviving spouse's *elective share* (or *forced share*) be the same as what the spouse would have taken in intestacy? For an interesting article documenting the reach of family policy in inheritance law and criticizing this focus on the family, see Frances H. Foster, The Family Paradigm of Inheritance Law, 80 N.C. L. Rev. 199 (2001).

In recent years some commentators have argued that advancing the public policy of the state and fostering positive social norms also should be relevant considerations in designing intestate succession statutes. For a discussion and critique of these goals, see Adam J. Hirsch, Default Rules in Inheritance Law: A Problem in Search of Its Context, 73 Fordham L. Rev. 1031 (2004).

PROBLEMS AND QUESTION

1.   Refer back to the estate planning problem of Howard and Wendy Brown on pages 49-50. Howard has two children by Wendy. Wendy has an additional child from a previous marriage. If Howard dies intestate, what will be Wendy's share under UPC §2-102? If it is Wendy who dies intestate, what will be Howard's share? What is the basis for the different amounts provided under §2-102(3) and (4)?

2.   Suppose *H* and *W* have been married one year. *H* dies, survived by *W* and a brother, but no parent. What is *W*'s share? Notice that the amount would not change even if *H* and *W* had been married for many years. Compare UPC §2-203(b) (1990, rev. 2008), page 499, which takes into account the length of the marriage in determining the surviving spouse's forced share. Why is this relevant for the spouse's forced share but not the intestate share? In Arkansas, if the decedent has no descendants, a spouse of fewer than three years takes a one-half share, and a spouse of three or more years takes the entire estate. See Ark. Code Ann. §28-9-214 (2008).

3.   Suppose Henry dies intestate. Anne, with whom he has been living, would like to claim a spouse's share. Is Anne entitled to such a share if she married Henry, but the marriage is bigamous? What if she did not marry Henry, but common law marriage is recognized? See William M. McGovern, Jr. and Sheldon F. Kurtz, Wills, Trusts and Estates §2.11 (3d ed. 2004). What if Anne and Henry did not marry because they perceived, as did the Princess of Cleves long ago, that there's nothing like marriage to spoil a perfect love, but Henry promised to take care of Anne? See pages 325-327, dealing with contracts to make wills. Suppose that Henry and Anne had married, but Henry had moved out and filed for divorce. What result?

NOTE: SAME-SEX MARRIAGE, DOMESTIC PARTNERS, AND INTESTATE SUCCESSION

The chief policies that underpin the spousal intestate share — giving effect to the probable intent of the decedent and protecting those whom the decedent treated as family — seem also to apply to domestic partners. In Mary L. Fellows, Monica K. Johnson, Amy Chiericozzi, Ann Hale, Christopher Lee, Robin Preble, and Michael Voran, Committed Partners and Inheritance: An Empirical Study, 16 Law & Ineq. J. 1 (1998), the authors found that a substantial majority of committed partners want the surviving partner to take a share of the decedent partner's estate, and this preference is even greater among same-sex partners. See also Mary Louise Fellows, E. Gary Spitko, and Charles Q. Strohm, An Empirical Assessment of the Potential for Will Substitutes to Improve State Intestacy Statutes, 85 Ind. L.J. (forthcoming 2009) (finding a preference for treating a committed partner as the other's heir, based on beneficiary designations in the partners' will substitutes).

The law pertaining to the intestacy rights of domestic partners is in flux, as is the related question of same-sex marriage. The rapidly changing legal landscape in part reflects the shift in public opinion, which appears to be moving toward a consensus in favor of legal recognition for gay and lesbian couples, but with disagreement over the form that this recognition should take.

> Although six in 10 Americans think some form of legal recognition is appropriate for same-sex couples, only a third [33%] of Americans think those couples should be allowed to marry. Another 27% of Americans support civil unions for same-sex couples, while 35% thinks there should be no legal recognition of same-sex relationships at all. . . . Support for legalizing same-sex marriage has remained about the same for the past two years, though it is up from 2004, when only 22% of Americans supported the idea. [CBS News Poll: The Debate Over Same-Sex Marriage (Mar. 12-16, 2009, survey of 1,142 adults).]

As this book went to press, same-sex marriage was recognized in Connecticut, Iowa, Maine, Massachusetts, New Hampshire, and Vermont, and civil unions with spousal-like intestacy rights were recognized in California[6] and New Jersey. In addition, intestate succession rights for domestic partners were recognized in the District of Columbia, Hawaii (called reciprocal beneficiaries), Oregon, Nevada, and Washington. In Colorado, spousal-like intestacy rights may be granted by an unmarried person to another person by a "designated beneficiary agreement."

An important issue in the states that recognize intestacy rights for domestic partners is the criteria for qualifying as a domestic partner. The usual answer is to make use of a registry. Under this approach, couples wanting to be treated as domestic partners must register as such with the state, which has the virtue of being clear. But might it exclude committed partners who want domestic partner treatment but do not know to register? Would a standard, looking to the nature of the relationship, be better? See E. Gary Spitko, An Accrual/Multi-Factor Approach to Intestate Inheritance Rights for Unmarried Committed Partners, 81 Or. L. Rev. 255 (2002).

In 1995, Professor Lawrence W. Waggoner proposed an amendment to the UPC — to become UPC §2-102B — that would have provided an intestate share for "committed partners." A committed partner was defined as a person "sharing

---

6. For five months in 2008, same-sex marriage was recognized in California, following a ruling by the state supreme court that limiting marriage to opposite-sex couples violated the state constitution. But a slim majority of voters in the November 2008 election supported a ballot proposition, known as Proposition 8, to amend the state constitution to limit marriage to opposite-sex couples. The state supreme court upheld the validity of Proposition 8, but the court also held that Proposition 8 did not have retroactive effect, preserving the validity of the marriages of same-sex couples who wed during the five-month window.

a common household with the decedent in a marriage-like relationship." Although Waggoner's proposal was never adopted by the Uniform Law Commission, it was not rejected either. In 2002 the Joint Editorial Board (JEB) for Uniform Trusts and Estates Acts revisited Waggoner's proposal, appointing Professor Thomas P. Gallanis as special reporter for the project and tasking him with the preparation of a model statute and an accompanying study on the inheritance rights of domestic partners. The JEB abandoned the project in 2004, but it consented to Gallanis's publishing his study and model statute. Under the Gallanis proposal, domestic partnership, entitling the partners to spousal-like intestacy and elective share rights, could be established by registration or by proof of "sharing a common household." T.P. Gallanis, Inheritance Rights for Domestic Partners, 79 Tul. L. Rev. 55 (2004). Although the UPC was extensively updated in 2008, none of the revisions addresses the rights of domestic partners, on which the UPC remains silent.

QUESTIONS, NOTE, AND PROBLEM

1. The patchwork of state laws on same-sex marriage, civil unions, and domestic partnerships raises important questions of conflicts of law. Suppose that a same-sex couple marries in Massachusetts but then moves to another state that does not recognize same-sex marriage. On the death of the first spouse, is the survivor entitled to an intestate share under the new state's intestacy law? Under Massachusetts law? See Estate of Ranftle, N.Y.L.J. 34 (Feb. 4, 2009) (N.Y. Surrogate's Court decision); Andrew Koppelman, Same Sex, Different States: When Same-Sex Marriages Cross State Lines (2006); Joanna L. Grossman, Resurrecting Comity: Revisiting the Problem of Non-Uniform Marriage Laws, 84 Or. L. Rev. 433 (2005).

2. Should property passing in intestacy to a domestic partner be eligible for the favorable federal tax treatment afforded to transfers between spouses? For a discussion of the tax consequences of same-sex marriages, civil unions, and domestic partnerships, see Patricia A. Cain, Taxing Families Fairly, 48 Santa Clara L. Rev. 805 (2008).

In 1996, Congress enacted the Defense of Marriage Act, 1 U.S.C. §7 (2008). Section 2 of the act provides that no state shall be required under the Full Faith and Credit Clause of the Constitution to give effect to a same-sex marriage contracted in another state. Section 3 provides that for all purposes of federal law "the word 'marriage' means only a legal union between one man and one woman as husband and wife, and the word 'spouse' refers only to a person of the opposite sex who is a husband or a wife." The latter section thus deprives same-sex married couples of the Social Security, tax, and welfare benefits afforded by federal law to opposite-sex married couples.

3. Suppose *H* marries *W*, a transsexual who was born a man, but had her birth certificate legally changed after undergoing sex-change surgery. Is *W* entitled to an intestate share in *H*'s estate? See Estate of Gardiner, 42 P.3d 120 (Kan. 2002)

(no). See also A. Spencer Bergstedt, Estate Planning and the Transgender Client, 30 W. New Eng. L. Rev. 675 (2008).

Simultaneous death. A person succeeds to the property of a decedent only if the person survives the decedent for an instant of time. The advent of the automobile and the airplane brought an increase in deaths of closely related persons in common disasters, particularly husbands and wives. The question thus arose: When a person dies simultaneously with his heir or devisee, does the heir or devisee succeed to the person's property?

The original Uniform Simultaneous Death Act (USDA) (1940, rev. 1953), drafted to answer this question, provided that if "there is no sufficient evidence" of the order of deaths, the beneficiary is deemed to have predeceased the donor. Thus, neither inherits from the other. The act further provided that if two joint tenants, *A* and *B*, die simultaneously, one-half of the property is distributed as if *A* survived and one-half is distributed as if *B* survived. The same rule is applied to property held in tenancy by the entirety or community property. With respect to life insurance, when the insured and the beneficiary die simultaneously, the proceeds are distributed as if the insured survived the beneficiary. Although the USDA was at first thought to offer an elegant solution to the simultaneous death problem, the courts were soon faced with the ghastly interpretive question of what constitutes "sufficient evidence" of the order of deaths. The tragic case of Janus v. Tarasewicz, infra, is illustrative. Because of cases such as *Janus*, the act was revised in 1991, as we shall see (page 86).

Before turning to *Janus*, however, it bears emphasizing that the problem of simultaneous death arises not only in intestacy, but also under wills, trusts, and other instruments transferring property at death. We nevertheless locate our discussion of it here, in connection with spousal intestate succession rights, for two reasons. First, the simultaneous death problem arises more often in intestacy than elsewhere, because well-drafted instruments typically require a beneficiary to survive the donor by a stated period of time (often 30 or 60 days). Under such a provision, a beneficiary who dies in a common disaster with the donor does not qualify to take. Second, because husbands and wives often travel together and are commonly each other's primary beneficiary, the typical simultaneous death case involves spouses.

Janus v. Tarasewicz
Illinois Appellate Court, 1985
482 N.E.2d 418

O'CONNOR, J.   This non-jury declaratory judgment action arose out of the death of a husband and wife, Stanley and Theresa Janus, who died after ingesting Tylenol capsules which had been laced with cyanide by an unknown perpetrator prior to its sale in stores. Stanley Janus was pronounced dead shortly after he was admitted to the hospital. However, Theresa Janus was placed on life support systems for almost two days before being pronounced dead. Claiming that there was no sufficient evidence that Theresa Janus survived her husband, plaintiff Alojza Janus, Stanley's mother, brought this action for the proceeds of Stanley's $100,000 life insurance policy which named Theresa as the primary beneficiary and plaintiff as the contingent beneficiary. Defendant Metropolitan Life Insurance Company paid the proceeds to defendant Jan Tarasewicz, Theresa's father and the administrator of her estate. The trial court found sufficient evidence that Theresa survived Stanley Janus. We affirm.

The facts of this case are particularly poignant and complex. Stanley and Theresa Janus had recently returned from their honeymoon when, on the evening of September 29, 1982, they gathered with other family members to mourn the death of Stanley's brother, Adam Janus, who had died earlier that day from what was later determined to be cyanide-laced Tylenol capsules.[7] While the family was at Adam's home, Stanley and Theresa Janus unknowingly took some of the contaminated Tylenol. Soon afterwards, Stanley collapsed on the kitchen floor.

Theresa was still standing when Diane O'Sullivan, a registered nurse and a neighbor of Adam Janus, was called to the scene. Stanley's pulse was weak so she began cardiopulmonary resuscitation (CPR) on him. Within minutes, Theresa Janus began having seizures. After paramedic teams began arriving, Ms. O'Sullivan went into the living room to assist with Theresa. While she was working on Theresa, Ms. O'Sullivan could hear Stanley's "heavy and labored breathing." She believed that both Stanley and Theresa died before they were taken to the ambulance, but she could not tell who died first.

Ronald Mahon, a paramedic for the Arlington Heights Fire Department, arrived at approximately 5:45 P.M. He saw Theresa faint and go into a seizure. Her pupils did not respond to light but she was breathing on her own during the time that he worked on her. Mahon also assisted with Stanley, giving him drugs to

---

7. See Jonathan Saltzman, Fatal Tampering Case is Renewed: FBI Searches a Condo in Cambridge, Boston Globe, Feb. 5, 2009, at B1:

> FBI agents and State Police investigators searched a Cambridge condominium yesterday that is the longtime home of a leading suspect in the 1982 deaths of seven people from cyanide-laced Tylenol capsules in the Chicago area, one of the most notorious unsolved crimes in the last generation.
>
> The first-floor condominium belongs to James W. Lewis, 62, . . . who spent 12 years in federal prison for trying to extort $1 million from the painkiller's manufacturers, but was never charged in the killings. . . .
>
> The seven victims of cyanide-tainted Extra-Strength Tylenol — four women, two men, and a 12-year-old girl — died in 1982 after taking capsules that had been purchased from drugstores and groceries in the Chicago area. Someone had opened the capsules and replaced some of the acetaminophen with cyanide and returned them to the shelves.
>
> The killer was never identified, but the deaths caused widespread panic and led to use of tamper-resistant wrappings on food and medical products. . . .
>
> Lewis was sentenced to prison in June 1983 for demanding $1 million from Johnson & Johnson, parent of Tylenol manufacturer McNeil Consumer Products Co., "to stop the killing.". . .
>
> Walter Tarasewicz, . . . whose sister Theresa Janus was 19 when she, her newlywed husband, and a brother-in-law were killed in the poisonings in the only case that touched several family members, said yesterday that he hopes police have developed enough information to lead to an arrest. Especially for the sake of his father, he said, who is about to turn 80 and longs to see his daughter's killer found.

— Eds.

stimulate heart contractions. Mahon later prepared the paramedic's report on Stanley. One entry in the report shows that at 18:00 hours Stanley had "zero blood pressure, zero pulse, and zero respiration." However, Mahon stated that the times in the report were merely approximations. He was able to say that Stanley was in the ambulance en route to the hospital when his vital signs disappeared.

When paramedic Robert Lockhart arrived at 5:55 P.M., both victims were unconscious with non-reactive pupils. Theresa's seizures had ceased but she was in a decerebrate posture in which her arms and legs were rigidly extended and her arms were rotated inward toward her body, thus, indicating severe neurological dysfunction. At that time, she was breathing only four or five times a minute and, shortly thereafter, she stopped breathing on her own altogether. Lockhart intubated them both by placing tubes down their tracheae to keep their air passages open. Prior to being taken to the ambulance, they were put on "ambu-bags" which is a form of artificial respiration whereby the paramedic respirates the patient by squeezing a bag. Neither Stanley nor Theresa showed any signs of being able to breathe on their own while they were being transported to Northwest Community Hospital in Arlington Heights, Illinois. However, Lockhart stated that when Theresa was turned over to the hospital personnel, she had a palpable pulse and blood pressure.

The medical director of the intensive care unit at the hospital, Dr. Thomas Kim, examined them when they arrived in the emergency room at approximately 6:30 P.M. Stanley had no blood pressure or pulse. An electrocardiogram detected electrical activity in Stanley Janus' heart but there was no synchronization between his heart's electrical activity and its pumping activity. A temporary pacemaker was inserted in an unsuccessful attempt to resuscitate him. Because he never developed spontaneous blood pressure, pulse or signs of respiration, Stanley Janus was pronounced dead at 8:15 P.M. on September 29, 1982.

Like Stanley, Theresa Janus showed no visible vital signs when she was admitted to the emergency room. However, hospital personnel were able to get her heart beating on its own again, so they did not insert a pacemaker. They were also able to establish a measurable, though unsatisfactory, blood pressure. Theresa was taken off the "ambu-bag" and put on a mechanical respirator. In Dr. Kim's opinion, Theresa was in a deep coma with "very unstable vital signs" when she was moved to the intensive care unit at 9:30 P.M. on September 29, 1982.

While Theresa was in the intensive care unit, numerous entries in her hospital records indicated that she had fixed and dilated pupils. However, one entry made at 2:32 A.M. on September 30, 1982, indicated that a nurse apparently detected a minimal reaction to light in Theresa's right pupil but not in her left pupil.

On September 30, 1982, various tests were performed in order to assess Theresa's brain function. These tests included an electroencephalogram (EEG) to measure electrical activity in her brain and a cerebral blood flow test to determine whether there was any blood circulating in her brain. In addition, Theresa exhibited no gag or cord reflexes, no response to pain or other external stimuli. As a result of these tests, Theresa Janus was diagnosed as having sustained total brain death, her life support systems then were terminated, and she was pronounced dead at 1:15 P.M. on October 1, 1982.

Death certificates were issued for Stanley and Theresa Janus more than three weeks later by a medical examiner's physician who never examined them. The certificates listed Stanley Janus' date of death as September 29, 1982, and Theresa Janus' date of death as October 1, 1982. Concluding that Theresa survived Stanley, the Metropolitan Life Insurance Company paid the proceeds of Stanley's life insurance policy to the administrator of Theresa's estate.

On January 6, 1983, plaintiff brought the instant declaratory judgment action against the insurance company and the administrators of Stanley and Theresa's estates, claiming the proceeds of the insurance policy as the contingent beneficiary of the policy. Also, the administrator of Stanley's estate filed a counterclaim against Theresa's estate seeking a declaration as to the disposition of the assets of Stanley's estate. . . .

Dr. Kenneth Vatz, a neurologist on the hospital staff, was called as an expert witness by plaintiff. Although he never actually examined Theresa, he had originally read her EEG as part of hospital routine. Without having seen her other hospital records, his initial evaluation of her EEG was that it showed some minimal electrical activity of living brain cells in the frontal portion of Theresa's brain. After reading her records and reviewing the EEG, however, he stated that the electrical activity measured by the EEG was "very likely" the result of interference from surrounding equipment in the intensive care unit. He concluded that Theresa was brain dead at the time of her admission to the hospital but he could not give an opinion as to who died first.

The trial court also heard an evidence deposition of Dr. Joseph George Hanley, a neurosurgeon who testified as an expert witness on behalf of the defendants. Based on his examination of their records, Dr. Hanley concluded that Stanley Janus died on September 29, 1982. He further concluded that Theresa Janus did not die until her vital signs disappeared on October 1, 1982. His conclusion that she did not die prior to that time was based on: (1) the observations by hospital personnel that Theresa Janus had spontaneous pulse and blood pressure which did not have to be artificially maintained; (2) the instance when Theresa Janus' right pupil allegedly reacted to light; and (3) Theresa's EEG which showed some brain function and which, in his opinion, could not have resulted from outside interference. At the conclusion of the trial, the court held that the evidence was sufficient to show that Theresa survived Stanley, but the court was not prepared to say by how long she survived him. Plaintiff and the administrator of Stanley's estate appeal. In essence, their main contention is that there is not sufficient evidence to prove that both victims did not suffer brain death prior to their arrival at the hospital on September 29, 1982.

Dual standards for determining when legal death occurs in Illinois were set forth in the case of In re Haymer, 450 N.E.2d 940 (Ill. App. 1983). There, the court determined that a comatose child attached to a mechanical life support system was legally dead on the date he was medically determined to have sustained total brain death, rather than on the date that his heart stopped functioning. . . . In a footnote, the court stated that widely accepted characteristics of brain death include: (1) unreceptivity and unresponsivity to intensely painful stimuli; (2) no spontaneous movement or breathing for at least one hour; (3) no blinking, no swallowing, and fixed and dilated pupils; (4) flat EEGs taken twice with at least a 24-hour intervening period; and (5) absence of drug intoxication or hyperthermia.[8] . . .

Regardless of which standard of death is applied, survivorship is a fact which must be proven by a preponderance of the evidence by the party whose claim depends on survivorship. In re Estate of Moran, 395 N.E.2d 579 (Ill. 1979). The operative provisions of the Illinois version of the Uniform Simultaneous Death Act provides in pertinent part:

> If the title to property or its devolution depends upon the priority of death and there is no sufficient evidence that the persons have died otherwise than simultaneously and there is no other provision in the will, trust agreement, deed, contract of insurance or other governing instrument for distribution of the property different from the provisions of this Section:
> (a) The property of each person shall be disposed of as if he had survived. . . .
> (d) If the insured and the beneficiary of a policy of life or accident insurance have so died, the proceeds of the policy shall be distributed as if the insured had survived the beneficiary.

Ill. Rev. Stat. 1981, ch. 110 1/2, par. 3-1. . . .

Although the use of sophisticated medical technology can also make it difficult to determine when death occurs, the context of this case does not require a determination as to the exact moment at which the decedents died. Rather, the trial court's task was to determine whether or not there was sufficient evidence that Theresa Janus survived her husband. Our task on review of this factually disputed case is to determine whether the trial court's finding was against the manifest weight of the evidence. . . . We hold that it was not.

In the case at bar, both victims arrived at the hospital with artificial respirators and no obvious vital signs. There is no dispute among the treating physicians and expert witnesses that Stanley Janus died in both a cardiopulmonary sense and a brain death sense when his vital signs disappeared en route to the hospital and were never reestablished. He was pronounced dead at 8:15 P.M. on September 29, 1982, only after intensive procedures such as electro-shock, medication, and the insertion of a pacemaker failed to resuscitate him.

---

8. The court's rendition of the test from *Haymer* is incorrect; the correct term is hypothermia (see 450 N.E.2d at 945 n.9), a cooling that is so severe that it prevents the body from maintaining normal temperature and can suppress physiological responses. Dr. Michael S. Young, a neurologist who noticed the *Janus* court's error while in Professor Ronald Volkmer's Spring 2008 Trusts and Estates class at Creighton University School of Law, explains the difference between hypothermia and hyperthermia thus: "I have warmed a person up in order to declare the person dead. This person had hypothermia. I have never cooled a person down in order to declare the person dead. Those people had hyperthermia." — Eds.

In contrast, these intensive procedures were not necessary with Theresa Janus because hospital personnel were able to reestablish a spontaneous blood pressure and pulse which did not have to be artificially maintained by a pacemaker or medication. Once spontaneous circulation was restored in the emergency room, Theresa was put on a mechanical respirator and transferred to the intensive care unit. Clearly, efforts to preserve Theresa Janus' life continued after more intensive efforts on Stanley's behalf had failed.

It is argued that the significance of Theresa Janus' cardiopulmonary functions, as a sign of life, was rendered ambiguous by the use of artificial respiration. In particular, reliance is placed upon expert testimony that a person can be brain dead and still have a spontaneous pulse and blood pressure which is indirectly maintained by artificial respiration. The fact remains, however, that Dr. Kim, an intensive care specialist who treated Theresa, testified that her condition in the emergency room did not warrant a diagnosis of brain death. In his opinion, Theresa Janus did not suffer irreversible brain death until much later, when extensive treatment failed to preserve her brain function and vital signs. . . .

There was also other evidence presented at trial which indicated that Theresa Janus was not brain dead on September 29, 1982. Theresa's EEG, taken on September 30, 1982, was not flat but rather it showed some delta waves of extremely low amplitude. Dr. Hanley concluded that Theresa's EEG taken on September 30 exhibited brain activity. Dr. Vatz disagreed. Since the trier of fact determines the credibility of expert witnesses and the weight to be given to their testimony . . . , the trial court in this case could have reasonably given greater weight to Dr. Hanley's opinion than to Dr. Vatz'. . . .

In conclusion, we believe that the record clearly established that the treating physicians' diagnoses of death with respect to Stanley and Theresa Janus were made in accordance with "the usual and customary standards of medical practice." Stanley Janus was diagnosed as having sustained irreversible cessation of circulatory and respiratory functions on September 29, 1982. These same physicians concluded that Theresa Janus' condition on that date did not warrant a diagnosis of death and, therefore, they continued their efforts to preserve her life. Their conclusion that Theresa Janus did not die until October 1, 1982, was based on various factors including the restoration of certain of her vital signs as well as other neurological evidence. The trial court found that these facts and circumstances constituted sufficient evidence that Theresa Janus survived her husband. It was not necessary to determine the exact moment at which Theresa died or by how long she survived him, and the trial court properly declined to do so. Viewing the record in its entirety, we cannot say that the trial court's finding of sufficient evidence of Theresa's survivorship was against the manifest weight of the evidence. . . .

Accordingly, there being sufficient evidence that Theresa Janus survived Stanley Janus, the judgment of the circuit court of Cook County is affirmed.

Affirmed.

PROBLEMS, NOTES, AND QUESTIONS

1. Suppose that *H* and *W* both drown in a boating accident. The evidence shows that *W* was a better swimmer and in better health than *H*. In addition, the autopsy shows *W* drowned after a violent death struggle while *H* passively submitted to death. Is there sufficient evidence of *W*'s survival? See In re Estate of Campbell, 641 P.2d 610 (Or. App. 1982).

H and *W* are killed in the crash of a private airplane. An autopsy reveals *W*'s brain is intact and there is carbon monoxide in her bloodstream; *H*'s brain is crushed and there is no carbon monoxide in his bloodstream. Is there sufficient evidence of *W*'s survival? See In re Bucci, 293 N.Y.S.2d 994 (Sur. 1968).

2. *The 120-hour rule.* To remedy the "no sufficient evidence" problem, UPC §§2-104 and 2-702 (1990, rev. 2008) provide that an heir or devisee or life insurance beneficiary who fails to survive by 120 hours (5 days) is deemed to have predeceased the decedent. The USDA was amended in 1991 to require survivorship by 120 hours, conforming it with the UPC. Under the amended UPC and USDA, a claimant must establish survivorship by 120 hours by clear and convincing evidence. What result in *Janus* and the cases in Note 1 under this rule?

A further advantage of the 120-hour rule is that it addresses contemporaneous deaths even if they do not arise from a common disaster. Suppose *H* dies of a heart attack. The next day, while en route to the cemetery, *W* is killed by *H*'s coffin, which was propelled into her when the hearse carrying them was hit from behind by another vehicle. See Evening Stand. (London), Nov. 12, 2008, at 26. What result under the sufficient evidence test? What result under the 120-hour rule?

3. Is survivorship by 120 hours long enough? Suppose someone is lacking in higher brain function, but the family insists that the patient's heart and lungs be kept working on a ventilator for more than 120 hours, long enough to allow the patient to inherit from someone else who died in the same common disaster. Would the 30-, 60-, or 90-day survivorship clauses common in well-drafted instruments work better?

4. If you are interested in whether a severed head retains feeling and consciousness for a few moments after severance and therefore arguably remains alive for that period, the experiments carried out by French doctors after the invention of the guillotine are instructive. The doctors were trying to discover if death by guillotine was really instantaneous and painless, as Dr. Guillotin, the inventor, claimed. See Alister Kershaw, A History of the Guillotine 80-89 (1958) (severed heads had looks of indignation or astonishment or, as agreed in advance of decapitation, winked in response to questions); Antonia Fraser, Mary Queen of Scots 539 (1969) (reporting that Mary's lips moved for a quarter of an hour after she was beheaded). More recently, Reuters carried a report of a Venezuelan man, previously declared dead, who woke up in pain during his autopsy. See Reuters, "Dead" Man Wakes Up Under Autopsy Knife (Sept. 17, 2007).

3.   *Shares of Descendants*

In all jurisdictions in this country, after the spouse's share (if any) is set aside, children and descendants of deceased children take the remainder of the decedent's property to the exclusion of everyone else. When one of several children has died before the decedent, leaving descendants, all states provide that the child's descendants shall *represent* the dead child and divide the child's share among themselves.

The following diagram illustrates how representation works. Assume that the intestate decedent, *A*, a widow, has three children. One of her three children, *C*, dies before *A*, survived by a husband and two children. *A* is survived by two children, *B* and *D*, and by five grandchildren, *E*, *F*, *G*, *H*, and *I*. Thus:

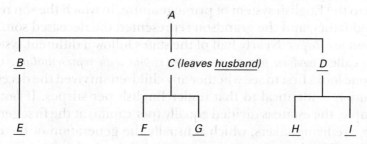

The survivors are underlined; all others are dead.

Because *C*'s children take *C*'s share by representation, *A*'s heirs are *B* (1/3), *D* (1/3), *F* (1/6), and *G* (1/6). Observe that *E*, *H*, and *I* take nothing because their parents are living. (Observe also that *C*'s spouse, the decedent's son-in-law, takes nothing. Sons-in-law and daughters-in-law are excluded as intestate successors in virtually all states.)

In more complicated contexts, there are different views about what taking by representation means. The fundamental issue is whether the division into shares should begin at the generational level immediately below the decedent or at the closest generational level with a descendant of the decedent alive. Take this case: *A* has two children, *B* and *C*. *B* predeceases *A*, leaving a child, *D*. *C* predeceases *A*, leaving two children, *E* and *F*. *A* dies intestate, leaving no surviving spouse, survived by *D*, *E*, and *F*. Thus:

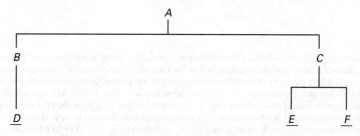

The survivors are underlined; all others are dead.

How is *A*'s estate distributed? There are three basic systems, with a twist in some states that might be considered a fourth system. See Jeffrey A. Schoenblum, 2008 Multistate Guide to Estate Planning at Table 8 (categorizing each state).

1. *English per stirpes.* About one-third of the states follow the system of English distribution *per stirpes* ("by the stocks"). Sometimes called *strict per stirpes*, the English per stirpes system of representation treats each *line* of descendants equally. The property is divided into as many shares as there are living children of the designated person and deceased children who have descendants living. The children of each deceased descendant represent their deceased parent and are moved into their parent's position beginning at the first generation below the designated person. Under this system, *A*'s property is divided into two shares at the level of *A*'s children, *D* takes *B*'s one-half by representation, and *E* and *F* split *C*'s one-half by representation. The English per stirpes system of representation owes much to the English system of primogeniture, in which the son represented the deceased father, and the grandson represented the deceased son.

2. *Modern per stirpes.* Nearly half of the states follow a different system of representation called *modern per stirpes* or *per capita with representation*. Under this approach, one looks first to see whether any children survived the decedent. If so, the distribution is identical to that under English per stirpes. If not, as in the above example, the estate is divided equally (per capita) at the first generation in which there are living takers, which is usually the generation of the decedent's grandchildren. That is, under modern per stirpes the decedent's estate is divided into shares at the generational level nearest to the decedent in which one or more descendants of the decedent are alive. Any deceased descendant on that level is represented by her descendants using an English per stirpes distribution.[9] This system treats equally each *line beginning at the closest living generation.*

In the above example, where *B* and *C* are dead, *D*, *E*, and *F* are all grandchildren of equal degree of kinship to *A*, *A*'s estate is divided equally among them in thirds. If *F* had predeceased *A*, leaving descendants, *F*'s descendants would represent *F* and take *F*'s one-third.

Two studies have indicated that an overwhelming majority of people prefer dividing the stocks at the level where someone is alive. See Mary L. Fellows, Rita J. Simon, Teal E. Snapp, and William D. Snapp, An Empirical Study of the Illinois Statutory Estate Plan, 1976 U. Ill. L.F. 717, 741 (95 percent of the persons interviewed); Comment, A Comparison of Iowans' Dispositive Preferences with Selected Provisions of the Iowa and Uniform Probate Codes, 63 Iowa L. Rev. 1041, 1111 (1978) (87 percent).

---

9. The twist that might be considered a fourth system, but that we treat as a variant on modern per stirpes, is in the representation of a deceased descendant below the closest generation with a living descendant. Modern per stirpes uses an English per stirpes distribution starting at the closest generation with a living descendant. Hence it could be called per capita with per stirpes representation. The 1969 UPC, by contrast, provided for representation as if the deceased descendant was the decedent — that is, it provided for distribution per capita with per capita representation. The distinction affects the actual distribution in only the rarest of cases. For an example and further discussion, see Restatement (Third) of Property: Wills and Other Donative Transfers §2.3, cmt. f (1999).

3.   *Per capita at each generation (1990 UPC).* The remaining states, about a dozen, follow a newer, more complicated system of distribution known as *per capita at each generation*, which has been advocated by Professor Waggoner since the early 1970s. See Lawrence W. Waggoner, A Proposed Alternative to the Uniform Probate Code's System for Intestate Distribution among Descendants, 66 Nw. U.L. Rev. 626 (1971).

Professor Lawrence W. Waggoner

Section 2-106(b) of the 1990 UPC, for which Waggoner was the reporter, adopts this approach:

> (b) [Decedent's Descendants.] If, under Section 2-103(1), a decedent's intestate estate or a part thereof passes "by representation" to the decedent's descendants, the estate or part thereof is divided into as many equal shares as there are (i) surviving descendants in the generation nearest to the decedent which contains one or more surviving descendants and (ii) deceased descendants in the same generation who left surviving descendants, if any. Each surviving descendant in the nearest generation is allocated one share. The remaining shares, if any, are combined and then divided in the same manner among the surviving descendants of the deceased descendants as if the surviving descendants who were allocated a share and their surviving descendants had predeceased the decedent.

Under UPC §2-106(b), the initial division of shares is made at the level where one or more descendants are alive (as under modern per stirpes), but the shares of deceased persons on that level are treated as one pot and are dropped down and divided equally among the representatives on the next generational level. Thus, in the situation pictured below, *D* takes a one-third share; the two-thirds that would have passed to *B* and *C* had they been living is divided equally among all the children of *B* and *C*. *E*, *F*, and *G* each take a two-ninths share.

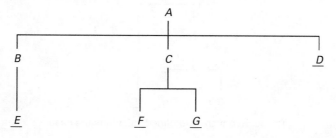

The survivors are underlined; all others are dead.

This system treats equally *each taker at each generation with the other takers at that generation*. The premise of this approach is that those equally related to the decedent should take equal shares: "Equally near, equally dear."

PROBLEM AND QUESTIONS

1.   *A* has two children, *B* and *C*. *B* predeceases *A*, leaving a child, *D*. *C* predeceases *A*, leaving two children, *E* and *F*. *E* predeceases *A*, leaving two children, *G* and *H*. Thus:

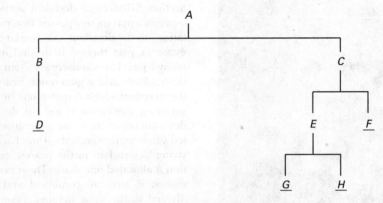

The survivors are underlined; all others are dead.

A dies intestate leaving no surviving spouse. How is *A*'s estate distributed under the English per stirpes system? Under the modern per stirpes system? Under the 1990 UPC? Under the intestacy statute of your state?

2.   Assume the same facts as in Problem 1 except that *A* has another child, *Z*, and *F* has a child, *I*. *Z* predeceases *A*, leaving no descendants. *F* survives *A*, as does *F*'s child *I*. Thus:

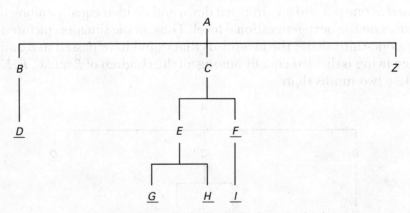

The survivors are underlined; all others are dead.

Does the presence in the family tree of the surviving *I* and the deceased *Z* change the result under any of the intestacy systems? The answer is No. *I* does not take because her parent, *F*, is alive, and because no one in *Z*'s line remains, it is ignored.

3.   Which of the three systems do you prefer? Which would your parents prefer? Are you sure? More importantly, which would most decedents prefer? A questionnaire developed by one of the advisors to the UPC drafting committee, to which 75 responses from targeted lawyers and their clients were received, revealed that 85 percent of the lawyers responding, perhaps reflecting their law school training in English property law, believed their clients wanted the English per stirpes distribution, but that 71 percent of the clients themselves wanted distribution per capita at each generation. Raymond H. Young, Meaning of "Issue" and "Descendants," 13 ACTEC Notes 225 (1988). Although this sampling is small and the methodology problematic, the study provides evidence that some lawyers simply assume what their clients want without explaining the options. See Roger W. Andersen, Informed Decisionmaking in Office Practice, 28 B.C. L. Rev. 225 (1987), arguing that a lawyer has a duty to allow a client to make informed decisions on most estate planning issues rather than assuming that the lawyer knows best.

4.   Suppose that a will devises property "to the descendants of *A* per stirpes." Which of the representation systems would a court apply in interpreting the will? The answer varies depending on the state. In some states, the courts read "per stirpes" to call for the same representational system as provided by the state's intestacy laws. In others, the courts read "per stirpes" to reference English per stirpes regardless of the form of representation provided for by the state's intestacy law. See pages 867-869.

NOTE: NEGATIVE DISINHERITANCE

An old rule of law holds that disinheritance is not possible by a declaration in a will that "my son John shall receive none of my property." To disinherit John — that is, to prevent John from taking an intestate share — John's father must devise his entire estate to other persons. If there is a partial intestacy, John will take an intestate share of the intestate property notwithstanding the provision in the will disinheriting him. See Frederic S. Schwartz, Models of the Will and Negative Disinheritance, 48 Mercer L. Rev. 1137 (1997).

UPC §2-101(b), page 73, changes this rule and authorizes a *negative will.* The barred heir is treated as if he disclaimed his intestate share, which means he is treated as having predeceased the intestate. See also Restatement (Third) of Property: Wills and Other Donative Transfers §2.7 (1999), to similar effect.

PROBLEM

T dies testate, survived by two siblings, *A* and *B*, and two nephews, *B*'s children, *X* and *Y*. *T*'s will provides that "I hereby disinherit my brother, *B*," but makes no affirmative disposition. Who takes *T*'s probate property? See Estate of Samuelson, 757 N.W.2d 44 (N.D. 2008).

4.   *Shares of Ancestors and Collaterals*

When the intestate decedent is survived by a descendant, the decedent's ancestors and collaterals do not take. In about half of the states, when there is no descendant, after deducting the spouse's share, the rest of the intestate's property is distributed to the decedent's parents, as under the UPC.

If there is no spouse or parent, the decedent's heirs will be more remote ancestors or collateral kindred. All persons who are related by blood to the decedent but who are not descendants or ancestors are called *collateral kindred*. Descendants of the decedent's parents, other than the decedent and the decedent's descendants, are called *first-line collaterals*. Descendants of the decedent's grandparents, other than the decedent's parents and their descendants, are called *second-line collaterals*. The reason for this terminology is seen by glancing at the Table of Consanguinity on the next page, which has lines descending from the decedent's ancestors.

If the decedent is not survived by a spouse, descendant, or parent, in all jurisdictions intestate property passes to brothers and sisters and their descendants. The descendants of any deceased brothers and sisters (nephews and nieces) take by representation, usually in the same manner as the decedent's descendants, as discussed at pages 88-89. See, e.g., UPC §2-106(c), which is substantially similar to §2-106(b), page 89, and calls for representation per capita at each generation. Hence:

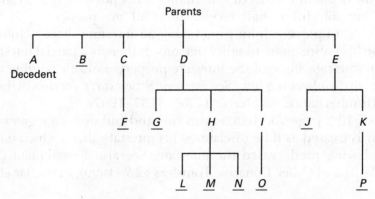

The survivors are underlined; all others are dead.

Under the English per stirpes system, division into four shares is made at the level of *A*'s brothers and sisters. So, too, under the modern per stirpes system, because one sibling, *B*, is alive. Under both of these systems, *B* takes 1/4; *F* takes 1/4; *G* takes 1/12; *L*, *M*, and *N* take 1/36; *O* takes 1/12; *J* takes 1/8; and *P* takes 1/8. Under UPC §2-106(c), *B* takes 1/4. The remaining 3/4 is divided into six shares of 1/8 each. *F*, *G*, and *J* take 1/8 each. The remaining 3/8 is divided into five sharesof 3/40. *L*, *M*, *N*, *O*, and *P* take 3/40 each.

TABLE OF CONSANGUINITY

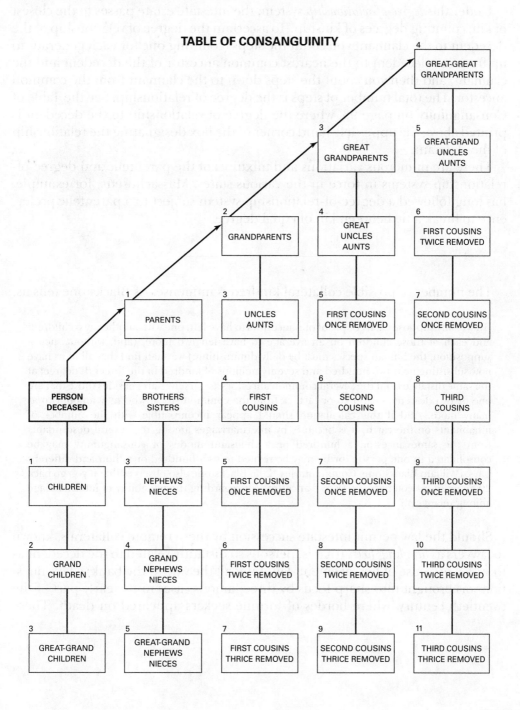

If there are no first-line collaterals, the states differ on who is next in the line of succession. Two basic schemes are used: the parentelic system and the degree-of-relationship system. Under the *parentelic* system, the intestate estate passes to grandparents and their descendants, and if none to great-grandparents and their descendants, and if none to great-great-grandparents and their descendants, and so on down each line (*parentela*) descended from an ancestor until an heir is found.

Under the *degree-of-relationship* system, the intestate estate passes to the closest of kin, counting degrees of kinship. To ascertain the degree of relationship of the decedent to the claimant you count the steps (counting one for each generation) up from the decedent to the nearest common ancestor of the decedent and the claimant, and then you count the steps down to the claimant from the common ancestor. The total number of steps is the degree of relationship. See the Table of Consanguinity on page 93, where the degree of relationship to the decedent is printed above the upper left-hand corner of the box designating the relationship of the claimant.

There are numerous variations and mixtures of the parentelic and degree-of-relationship systems in force in the various states. Massachusetts, for example, has long followed a degree-of-relationship system subject to a parentelic preference to break a tie between kin of equal degree.

The number of possible collateral kindred is immense. As Blackstone tells us:

> [I]f we only suppose each couple of our ancestors to have left, one with another, two children; and each of those children on an average to have left two more, (and, without such a supposition, the human species must be daily diminishing;) we shall find that all of us have now subsisting near two hundred and seventy millions of kindred in the fifteenth degree; at the same distance from the several common ancestors as ourselves are; besides those that are one or two descents nearer to or farther from the common stock, who may amount to as many more. And if this calculation should appear incompatible with the number of inhabitants on the earth, it is because, by intermarriages among the several descendants from the same ancestor, a hundred or a thousand modes of consanguinity may be consolidated in one person, or he may be related to us a hundred or a thousand different ways. [William Blackstone, Commentaries *205. Blackstone also observes that if you go back 20 generations you have 1,048,576 ancestors (disregarding the possibility of intermarriage among relatives)!]

Should the law permit intestate succession by these remote collaterals, known to lawyers as *laughing heirs* (that is, persons so distantly related to the decedent as to suffer no sense of bereavement, laughing all the way to the bank)? This question was brought into sharp focus by three famous cases in the early part of the twentieth century, where hordes of fortune seekers appeared on death. These were the cases of Ella Wendel, Ida Wood, and Henrietta Garrett, all of whom died during the Great Depression:

(1) Ella Wendel, a recluse, died in 1931, leaving a will devising most of her $40 million estate to charity. The only persons who may contest a will are those who would take if the will is held invalid. Some 2,303 fortune hunters strove to establish they were her next of kin, so that they might contest her will as her intestate successors. Reams of evidence were fabricated, birth and death certificates altered, and tales spun of incest and children born out of wedlock. One man was sent to jail for fabricating evidence, and Surrogate Foley referred the activities of six lawyers to the Grievance Committee of the Bar. Ultimately nine persons were established to be her cousins, and they settled out of court with the charities. In re Wendel, 257 N.Y.S. 87 (Sur. 1932); 262 N.Y.S. 41 (Sur. 1933); 287 N.Y.S. 893 (Sur. 1936). The late Justice Harlan's participation in the *Wendel* litigation is traced in Cloyd Laporte, John M. Harlan Saves the Ella Wendel Estate, 59 A.B.A. J. 868 (1973).

(2) Ida Wood, the widow of a U.S. congressman from New York, died intestate in 1932. For more than 20 years, she and her two sisters (who predeceased her) had barricaded themselves in a New York hotel room, into which no one was permitted to enter. During her life Ida had spun a web of deceit to hide who she really was. The evidence finally accepted by the court showed she had been born Ellen Walsh in Ireland, had moved with her parents to Boston, and had been her husband's mistress for ten years before they married. Once married and propelled into high society, Ida drew a curtain across her past. She made up vague stories of having been born a Mayfield and brought up in New Orleans. Her mother, and some other members of her family, took the name Mayfield, and Ida carved "Mayfield" on their tombstones. Fearful of a depression, Ida kept $500,000 in cash tied around her waist. When she died, some 1,100 persons claimed to be her next of kin — including a great many persons named Mayfield from Louisiana. Ultimately, the court established as Ida's next of kin some first cousins once removed (none of whom Ida had seen since her marriage to Wood 65 years before). In re Wood, 299 N.Y.S. 195 (Sur. 1937). The whole fascinating story is recounted in Joseph A. Cox, The Recluse of Herald Square (1964).

(3) Henrietta E. Garrett died intestate in Philadelphia in 1930, leaving an estate of over $17 million. Nearly 26,000 claims were filed by persons claiming to be her heirs. The testimony covered 390 volumes and over 115,000 pages. Finally, three persons were found to be first cousins of Henrietta. In 1953, after 23 years of litigation, the Supreme Court of Pennsylvania finally ordered the Garrett estate closed. Estate of Garrett, 94 A.2d 357 (Pa. 1953).

With these cases in mind, Professor Cavers predicted that the rules of succession would be revised to abolish laughing heirs. David F. Cavers, Change in the American Family and the "Laughing Heir," 20 Iowa L. Rev. 203 (1935). Roughly half the states have done so, typically by drawing the line at grandparents and their descendants. In these jurisdictions, there is no inheritance by relatives traced through great-grandparents and other more remote ancestors. In this, UPC §2-103(a) (1990, rev. 2008), pages 73-74, is typical.

A few states and the UPC as revised in 2008 have created a new class of heirs consisting of *stepchildren*, who take as a last resort if there are no surviving grandparents or descendants of grandparents or more closely related kin. See Ohio Rev. Code §2105.06(j) (2008); UPC §2-103(b). California goes even further. It extends intestate succession not only to stepchildren but also to mothers-in-law, fathers-in-law, brothers-in-law, and sisters-in-law — but not to sons-in-law or daughters-in-law! Cal. Prob. Code §6402(e) and (g) (2008).

If the intestate leaves no survivors entitled to take under the intestacy statute, the intestate's property *escheats* to the state. Escheats of substantial estates are rare. Relatives usually keep tabs on kinfolk of obvious wealth, and thus the larger the estate, the more likely it is that there will be heirs claiming it. Moreover, heir-hunting firms seek out unknown or uninformed heirs, offering to disclose the name of an estate to which the person may be an heir in exchange for a share of the inheritance. See Rachel Emma Silverman, Heir-Search Firms Help to Keep It in the Family — Companies Track Down Lost Beneficiaries on Behalf of Estates, Wall St. J., Feb. 21, 2007, at D2.

PROBLEMS AND NOTE

1.   The decedent is survived by his mother, his sister, and two nephews (children of a deceased brother). How is the decedent's estate distributed under UPC §2-103 (1990, rev. 2008), pages 73-74? Under the intestacy statute of your state?

2.   The decedent is survived by one first cousin on his mother's side and by two first cousins on his father's side. How is the decedent's estate distributed under UPC §2-103? Under the intestacy statute of your state? Recall that UPC §2-106, page 89, which defines representation, is based upon a goal of providing equal shares to those equally related. Is the UPC treatment of the three first cousins consistent with that goal? Why are three grandchildren or three grandnephews treated alike but not three first cousins?

3.   The decedent is survived by *A*, the first cousin of the decedent's mother, and by *B*, the granddaughter of the decedent's first cousin. (You can locate these on the Table of Consanguinity, page 93.) How is the decedent's estate distributed under UPC §2-103? Under the intestacy statute of your state?

NOTE: HALF-BLOODS

In England, which put great weight on whole-blood relations, the common law courts wholly excluded relatives of the half-blood (e.g., a half-sister) from inheriting land through intestate succession. This rule has long been abolished in all American states. In a large majority of states, and under UPC §2-107 (1990), a relative of the half-blood is treated the same as a relative of the whole-blood. In a few states, including Florida and Texas, a half-blood is given a one-half share; this was the Scottish rule and was introduced in this country in Virginia. Va. Code Ann. §64.1-2 (2008). In a few other states, a half-blood takes only when there are no whole-blood relatives of the same degree. See Miss. Code Ann. §91-1-5 (2008). In Oklahoma, half-bloods are excluded when there are whole-blood kindred in the same degree and the inheritance came to the decedent by an ancestor and the half-blood is not a descendant of the ancestor. Okla. Stat. tit. 84, §222 (2008).

PROBLEM AND NOTE

1.   *F* has one child, *A*, by his first marriage, and two children, *B* and *C*, by his second marriage. *F* is estranged from *A* and never tells his second wife or *B* and *C* of *A*'s existence. *F* and his second wife die. Then *C* dies intestate, married but without descendants. How should *C*'s property be distributed? See In re Estate of Griswold, 24 P.3d 1191 (Cal. 2001).

2.   For further discussion and a proposal for reform, see Ralph C. Brashier, Half-Bloods, Inheritance, and Family, 37 U. Mem. L. Rev. 215 (2007); Ralph C. Brashier, Consanguinity, Sibling Relationships, and the Default Rules of Inheritance Law: Reshaping Half-Blood Statutes to Reflect the Surviving Family, 58 SMU L. Rev. 137 (2005).

SECTION B.   TRANSFERS TO CHILDREN

1.   *Meaning of Children*

a.   Adopted Children

Hall v. Vallandingham
Court of Special Appeals of Maryland, 1988
540 A.2d 1162

GILBERT, C.J.   Adoption did not exist under the common law of England,[10] although it was in use "[a]mong the ancient peoples of Greece, Rome, Egypt and Babylonia." M. Leary and R. Weinberg, Law of Adoption (4th ed. 1979) 1; Lord Mackenzie, Studies in Roman Law, 130-34 (3rd ed. 1870). The primary purpose for adoption was, and still is, inheritance rights, particularly in "France, Greece, Spain and most of Latin America." Leary and Weinberg, Law of Adoption, 1. Since adoption was not a part of the common law, it owes its existence in this State, and indeed in this nation, to statutory enactments.

The first two general adoption statutes were passed in Texas and Vermont in 1850. Leary and Weinberg, Law of Adoption, 1. Maryland first enacted an Adoption Statute in Laws 1892, Ch. 244, and that law has continued in existence, in various forms, until the present time. The current statute, Maryland Code, Family Law Article Ann. §5-308 provides, in pertinent part:

---

10. According to J.W. Madden, Handbook of the Law of Persons and Domestic Relations (Wash. 1931) §106, adoption in the sense of the term as used in this country was not a part of the English law until 1926.

(b) [A]fter a decree of adoption is entered:
  (1) the individual adopted:
    (i) is the child of the petitioner for all intents and purposes;[11] and
    (ii) is entitled to all the rights and privileges of and is subject to all the obligations of
  a child born to the petitioner in wedlock;
  (2) each living natural parent of the individual adopted is:
    (i) relieved of all parental duties and obligations to the individual adopted; and
    (ii) divested of all parental rights as to the individual adopted; and
  (3) *all rights of inheritance between the individual adopted and the natural relations shall be governed by the Estates and Trusts Article.* (Emphasis supplied.)

The applicable section of the Md. Estates and Trusts Code Ann. §1-207(a), provides:

> An adopted child shall be treated as a natural child of his adopted parent or parents. On adoption, a child no longer shall be considered a child of either natural parent, except that upon adoption by the spouse of a natural parent, the child shall be considered the child of that natural parent.[12]

With that "thumbnail" history of adoption and the current statutes firmly in mind, we turn our attention to the matter sub judice.

Earl J. Vallandingham died in 1956, survived by his widow, Elizabeth, and their four children. Two years later, Elizabeth married Jim Walter Killgore, who adopted the children.

In 1983, twenty-five years after the adoption of Earl's children by Killgore, Earl's brother, William Jr., died childless, unmarried, and intestate. His sole heirs were his surviving brothers and sisters and the children of brothers and sisters who predeceased him.

Joseph W. Vallandingham, the decedent's twin brother, was appointed Personal Representative of the estate. After the Inventory and First Accounting were filed, the four natural children of Earl J. Vallandingham noted exceptions, alleging that they were entitled to the distributive share of their natural uncle's estate that their natural father would have received had he survived William. Est. & Trusts Art. §3-104(b).

The Orphan's Court transmitted the issue to the Circuit Court for St. Mary's County. That tribunal determined that the four natural children of Earl, because of their adoption by their adoptive father, Jim Walter Killgore, were not entitled to inherit from William M. Vallandingham Jr.

---

11. Notwithstanding Maryland law, a child who is eligible for social security survivor's benefits through a deceased natural parent under Federal law does not lose eligibility for the continuation of those benefits because of a subsequent adoption. 42 U.S.C. §402(d).

12. Although the statute speaks in terms of the "adopted child," the person who is adopted need not be a minor child. See Family Law Art. §5-307(a).

Patently unwilling to accept that judgment which effectively disinherited them, the children have journeyed here where they posit to us:

> Did the trial court err in construing Maryland's current law regarding natural inheritance by adopted persons so as to deny the Appellants the right to inherit through their natural paternal uncle, when said Appellants were adopted as minors by their stepfather after the death of their natural father and the remarriage of their natural mother?

When the four natural children of Earl J. Vallandingham were adopted in 1958 by Jim Killgore, then Md. Ann. Code art. 16, §78(b) clearly provided that adopted children retained the right to inherit from their natural parents and relatives.[13] That right of inheritance was removed by the Legislature in 1963 when it declared: "Upon entry of a decree of adoption, the adopted child shall lose all rights of inheritance from its parents and from their natural collateral or lineal relatives." Laws 1963, Ch. 174. Subsequently, the Legislature in 1969 enacted what is the current, above-quoted language of Est. & Trusts Art. §1-207(a). Laws 1969, Ch. 3, §4(c).

The appellants contend that since the explicit language of the 1963 Act proscribing dual inheritance by adoptees was not retained in the present law, Est. & Trusts Art. §1-207(a) implicitly permits adoptees to inherit from natural relatives, as well as the adoptive parents.

The right to receive property by devise or descent is not a natural right but a privilege granted by the State. . . . Every State possesses the power to regulate the manner or term by which property within its dominion may be transmitted by will or inheritance and to prescribe who shall or shall not be capable of receiving that property. A State may deny the privilege altogether or may impose whatever restrictions or conditions upon the grant it deems appropriate. Mager v. Grima, 49 U.S. 490 (1850).[14]

Family Law Art. §5-308(b)(1)(ii) entitles an adopted person to all the rights and privileges of a natural child insofar as the adoptive parents are concerned, but adoption does not confer upon the adopted child *more* rights and privileges than those possessed by a natural child. To construe Est. & Trusts Art. §1-207(a) so as to allow dual inheritance would bestow upon an adopted child a superior status. That status was removed in Laws 1963, Ch. 174 which, as we have said, expressly disallowed the dual inheritance capability of adopted children by providing that "the adopted child shall lose all rights of inheritance from its parents and from their natural collateral or lineal relatives." We think that the current statute, Est. & Trusts Art. §1-207(a), did not alter the substance of the 1963 act which eliminated dual inheritance. Rather, §1-207(a) merely "streamlined" the wording while retaining the meaning.

---

13. "[N]othing in this subtitle shall be construed to prevent the person adopted from inheriting from his natural parents and relatives. . . ."

14. Since the Legislature is elected by the people, it is answerable to the people, and that is the best safeguard against unreasonable laws concerning inheritance.

Family Law Art. §5-308 plainly mandates that adoption be considered a "rebirth" into a completely different relationship. Once a child is adopted, the rights of both the natural parents and relatives are terminated. L.F.M. v. Department of Social Services, 507 A.2d 1151 (Md. App. 1986). Est. & Trusts Art. §1-207(a) and Family Law Art. §5-308 emphasize the clean-cut severance from the natural bloodline. Because an adopted child has no right to inherit *from* the estate of a natural parent who dies intestate, it follows that the same child may not inherit *through* the natural parent by way of representation. What may not be done directly most assuredly may not be done indirectly. The elimination of dual inheritance in 1963 clearly established that policy, and the current language of §1-207(a) simply reflects the continuation of that policy.

We hold that because §1-207(a) eliminates the adopted child's right to inherit from the natural parent it concomitantly abrogated the right to inherit through the natural parent by way of representation.

"The Legislature giveth, and the Legislature taketh away."

Judgment affirmed.

Restatement (Third) of Property: Wills and Other Donative Transfers (1999)

§2.5   PARENT AND CHILD RELATIONSHIP

For purposes of intestate succession by, from, or through an individual:

(1) An individual is the child of his or her genetic parents, whether or not they are married to each other, except as otherwise provided in paragraph (2) or (5) or as other facts and circumstances warrant a different result.

(2) An adopted individual is a child of his or her adoptive parent or parents.

(A) If the adoption removes the child from the families of both of the genetic parents, the child is not a child of either genetic parent.

(B) If the adoption is by a relative of either genetic parent, or by the spouse or surviving spouse of such a relative, the individual remains a child of both genetic parents.

(C) If the adoption is by a stepparent, the adopted stepchild is not only a child of the adoptive stepparent but is also a child of the genetic parent who is married to the stepparent. Under several intestacy statutes, including . . . Uniform Probate Code [§2-114(b) (1990)], the adopted stepchild is also a child of the other genetic parent for purposes of inheritance from and through that parent, but not for purposes of inheritance from or through the child.

(3) A stepchild who is not adopted by his or her stepparent is not the stepparent's child.

(4) A foster child is not a child of his or her foster parent or parents.

(5) A parent who has refused to acknowledge or has abandoned his or her child, or a person whose parental rights have been terminated, is barred from inheriting from or through the child.

NOTES AND QUESTIONS

1.   Inheritance rights of an adopted child vary considerably from state to state. In some states, as in *Hall*, an adopted child inherits only from adoptive parents and their relatives; in others, an adopted child inherits from both adoptive parents and genetic parents and their relatives; in still others, as provided in UPC §2-114(b) (1990), an adopted child inherits from adoptive relatives and also from genetic relatives if the child is adopted by a stepparent. And there are many statutory variations on these three basic schemes. For a sweeping review of the development of adoption law, see Naomi Cahn, Perfect Substitutes or the Real Thing?, 52 Duke L.J. 1077 (2003).

2.   In view of the diversity and complexities of contemporary family relations created by adoptions, multiple marriages, and single parenthood, plus the increasing prevalence of unmarried domestic partners and new reproductive technologies, it is not easy to discern what the average person (the hypothetical intestate decedent) would want in many of these situations. For further discussion with reference to adoption, see E. Gary Spitko, Open Adoption, Inheritance, and the "Uncleing" Principle, 48 Santa Clara L. Rev. 765 (2008); Peter Wendel, Inheritance Rights and the Step-Partner Adoption Paradigm: Shades of the Discrimination Against Illegitimate Children, 34 Hofstra L. Rev. 351 (2005); Susan N. Gary, Adapting Intestacy Laws to Changing Families, 18 Law & Ineq. J. 1 (2000); Margaret M. Mahoney, Stepfamilies in the Law of Intestate Succession and Wills, 22 U.C. Davis L. Rev. 917 (1989); Jan E. Rein, Relatives by Blood, Adoption, and Association: Who Should Get What and Why?, 37 Vand. L. Rev. 711 (1984). For a more general treatment, see Ralph C. Brashier, Inheritance Law and the Evolving Family (2004).

3.   *The 2008 amendments to the UPC.* In 2008 the UPC provisions on inheritance between parents and children were extensively revised. Under the UPC as revised the key determination is whether there is a *parent-child relationship*. If such a relationship exists, "the parent is a parent of the child and the child is a child of the parent for the purpose of intestate succession" by, from, or through the parent or the child (§2-116). Regarding adoption, a parent-child relationship exists between an adopted child and the adoptive parent (§2-118(a)), but not between an adopted child and the child's genetic parents (§2-119(a)), the latter subject to several exceptions:

> (b) [Stepchild Adopted by Stepparent.] A parent-child relationship exists between an individual who is adopted by the spouse of either genetic parent and:
>   (1) the genetic parent whose spouse adopted the individual; and
>   (2) the other genetic parent, but only for the purpose of the right of the adoptee or
> a descendant of the adoptee to inherit from or through the other genetic parent.
> (c) [Individual Adopted by Relative of a Genetic Parent.] A parent-child relationship exists between both genetic parents and an individual who is adopted by a relative of a genetic parent, or by the spouse or surviving spouse of a relative of a genetic parent, but only for the purpose of the right of the adoptee or a descendant of the adoptee to inherit from or through either genetic parent.

(d) [Individual Adopted after Death of Both Genetic Parents.] A parent-child relationship exists between both genetic parents and an individual who is adopted after the death of both genetic parents, but only for the purpose of the right of the adoptee or a descendant of the adoptee to inherit through either genetic parent. [UPC §2-119 (2008).]

If UPC §2-119(b)(2) (2008) had been applicable in *Hall*, Earl's children, adopted by their stepfather, would have inherited from their genetic father's brother, William Jr. But William Jr. would not be able to inherit from Earl's children. In a stepparent adoption, the children can inherit from their genetic relatives, but the genetic relatives cannot inherit from the children. Is this fair?

For further discussion of the 2008 UPC provisions on parents and children, see Susan N. Gary, We Are Family: The Definition of Parent and Child for Succession Purposes, 34 ACTEC J. 171 (2008); Lee-ford Tritt, Sperms and Estates: An Unadulterated Functionally Based Approach to Parent-Child Property Succession, 62 SMU L. Rev. 367 (2009).

4.   Should a person who is related to an intestate decedent through two lines, one genetic and one adoptive, be entitled to two intestate shares? Compare UPC §2-113 (1990) (larger share only), with Jenkins v. Jenkins, 990 So. 2d 807 (Miss. App. 2008) (both shares).

We now add two wrinkles: (1) adult adoption and (2) the effect of adoption on the interpretation of wills and trusts.

(1) *Adult adoption.* Most intestacy statutes draw no distinction between the adoption of a minor and the adoption of an adult. See Tinney v. Tinney, 799 A.2d 235 (R.I. 2002) (84-year-old Newport woman adopts 38-year-old man and he shares in her intestate estate, including "Belcourt Castle, a once majestic Newport mansion"). In some states (most prominently New York), however, the adoption of one's lover is not permitted. See In re Robert Paul P., 471 N.E.2d 424 (N.Y. 1984), holding that a homosexual male, age 57, could not legally adopt his lover, age 50, although New York statutes permit the adoption of adults. The court ruled that a sexual relationship was incompatible with a parent-child relationship. For a case contrary to the New York view, see In re Adoption of Swanson, 623 A.2d 1095 (Del. 1993), holding that a 66-year-old man could adopt a 51-year-old man, his companion for 17 years, to prevent claims against their estates by collateral relatives. The Delaware court expressly rejected the New York holding. See also Terry L. Turnipseed, Scalia's Ship of Revulsion Has Sailed: Will Lawrence Protect Adults Who Adopt Lovers to Help Ensure their Inheritance from Incest Prosecution?, 32 Hamline L. Rev. (forthcoming 2009).

The adoption of an adult may be useful in preventing a will contest by denying standing to the potential contestants. The only persons who have standing to challenge the validity of a will are those who would take if the will were denied probate. To gain standing to challenge the will, the decedent's collateral relatives must first overturn the adoption. In Greene v. Fitzpatrick, 295 S.W. 896 (Ky. 1927), a wealthy bachelor adopted a married woman who had been his secretary for many years and with whom, it was alleged, the bachelor had a sexual relationship. In Collamore v. Learned, 50 N.E. 518 (Mass. 1898), a 70-year-old man adopted three persons of ages 43, 39, and 25 respectively. In both cases it was held that the adoptions could not be set aside by the persons who would have been the heirs but for the adoptions. In the second case, Justice Holmes remarked that adoption for the purpose of preventing a will contest was "perfectly proper."

(2) *Adoption and the interpretation of wills and trusts.* Is a child adopted by *A* entitled to share in a gift in a will or trust by *T* to the "children," "issue," "descendants," or "heirs" of *A*? Because adoption was unknown to the common law, "children" and "issue" necessarily connoted a blood relationship. Thus, when adoption laws were enacted in the second half of the nineteenth century, the courts struggled with the question of whether an adopted child took under the will or trust of a person who was not the adoptive parent.

The early cases, influenced by the ancient reverence for blood relationships, held that an adopted child could not take. These cases gave rise to the *stranger-to-the-adoption* rule: The adopted child is presumptively barred, whatever generic word is used, except when the donor is the adoptive parent.

As adoption became more common and more socially acceptable, courts began to carve exceptions to the stranger-to-the-adoption rule. An adopted child might be permitted to take if adopted before, but not after, the testator's death. Some courts also drew distinctions between a gift to "*A*'s children" and a gift to "*A*'s issue" or the "heirs of *A*'s body." Unlike the latter terms, which were thought to have a biological connotation, a gift to "*A*'s children" presumptively included *A*'s adopted children. Where judicial decisions were found unsatisfactory, legislatures began to intervene in favor of the adopted child. But the legislation was seldom retroactive and was sometimes ambiguous.

In most states today, a minor adopted by *A* is presumptively included in a gift by *T* to the "children," "issue," "descendants," or "heirs" of *A*. See Restatement (Third) of Property: Wills and Other Donative Transfers §14.5 (T.D. No. 4, 2004). The presumption yields to a contrary expression of intent by the donor. But the law of many states is likely to have been developed by changing judicial decisions and statutes over the twentieth century, and, since the change may not be retroactive, whether an adopted child is included may depend on what the law was at testator's death in, say, 1936. See Watson v. Baker, 829 N.E.2d 648 (Mass. 2005).

The following case adds yet another twist. Is an adult adopted by *A* included in a gift by *T* to the "children," "issue," "descendants," or "heirs" of *A*?

Minary v. Citizens Fidelity Bank & Trust Co.

Court of Appeals of Kentucky, 1967
419 S.W.2d 340

OSBORNE, J. [Amelia S. Minary died in 1932, leaving a will devising her residuary estate in trust, to pay the income to her husband and three sons, James, Thomas, and Alfred, for their respective lives. The trust was to terminate upon the death of the last surviving beneficiary, at which time the corpus was to be distributed as follows:

> After the Trust terminates, the remaining portion of the Trust Fund shall be distributed to my then surviving heirs, according to the laws of descent and distribution then in force in Kentucky, and, if no such heirs, then to the First Christian Church, Louisville, Kentucky.

The husband died, then James died without descendants, then Thomas died leaving two children: Thomas Jr. and Amelia Minary Gant. In 1934, Alfred married Myra, and in 1959 he adopted her as his child. The trust terminated upon Alfred's death without biological descendants in 1963.]

The question herein presented is, "Did Alfred's adoption of his wife Myra make her eligible to inherit under the provisions of his mother's will?" More specifically, the question is, "Is Myra included in the term 'my then surviving heirs according to the laws of descent and distribution in force in Kentucky'?"

This has revived a lively question in the jurisprudence of this state and presents two rather difficult legal problems. The first being under what conditions, if any, should an adopted child inherit from or through its adoptive parent? We have encountered little difficulty with the problem of inheriting from an adoptive parent but the question of when will an adoptive child inherit through an adoptive parent has given us considerable trouble. As late as 1945 in Copeland v. State Bank and Trust Company, 188 S.W.2d 1017 (Ky.), we held without hesitation or equivocation that the words "heirs" and "issue" as well as "children" and all other words of similar import as used in a will referred only to the natural blood relations and did not include an adopted child.

In 1950, in Isaacs v. Manning, 227 S.W.2d 418 (Ky.), we adopted the contrary position and held that an adopted child was included in the phrase "heirs at law" wherein a will devised property to designated children and then upon their death to their heirs at law. In the course of the opinion, we said, "where no language [shows] a contrary intent . . . an adopted daughter clearly falls within the class designated." In this case we distinguish the *Copeland* case, supra.

In 1953, in Major v. Kammer, 258 S.W.2d 506, we again held that an adopted child was included in the term "heirs at law," basing our decision upon the legislative changes made in the adoption laws and overruling Copeland v. State Bank and Trust Company, supra. In Edmands v. Tice, 324 S.W.2d 491, which was decided in 1959, we held that where testator used the word children, an adopted child could inherit through an adopted parent the same as if heirs at law or issue had been used. . . .

From the foregoing we conclude that when Amelia S. Minary used the phrase, "my then surviving heirs according to the laws of descent and distribution then in force in Kentucky," she included the adoptive children of her sons. This leaves us with the extremely bothersome question of: "Does the fact that Myra Minary was an adult and the wife of Alfred at the time she was adopted affect her status as an 'heir' under the will?" KRS 405.390 provides: "An adult person . . . may be adopted in the same manner as provided by law for the adoption of a child and with the same legal effect. . . ."

KRS 199.520 provides: "From and after the date of the judgment the child shall be deemed the child of petitioners and shall be considered for purposes of inheritance and succession and for all other legal considerations, the natural, legitimate child of the parents adopting it the same as if born of their bodies."

It would appear from examination of the authorities that the adoption of an adult for the purpose of making him an heir has been an accepted practice in our law for many years. However, here it should be pointed out that the practice in its ancient form made the person so adopted the legal heir of the adopting party only. This court has dealt with the problem of adopting adults for the purpose of making them heirs on several occasions. . . .

In 1957, in Bedinger v. Graybill's Executors, Ky., 302 S.W.2d 594, we had before us a case almost identical to the one here under consideration. In that case Mrs. Lulu Graybill, in 1914, set up a trust for her son Robert by will. She then provided after the death of the son that the trust "be paid over and distributed by the Trustee to the heirs at law of my said son according to the laws of descent and distribution in force in Kentucky at the time of his death." There was a devise over to others in the event that Robert died without heirs. Robert having no issue adopted his wife long after his mother's death. We held that the wife should inherit the same as an adopted child, there being no public policy against the adoption of a wife. However, it will be noted that in the course of the opinion it is carefully pointed out that the will directed the estate be paid to the "heirs at law of Robert" and did not provide that the estate should go to "my heirs," "his children" or to "his issue," indicating by this language that if the phrase had been one of the others set out the results might have been different. . . .

This case could properly be distinguished from Bedinger v. Graybill's Executors, supra, on the basis of the difference in language used in the two wills[;] however, no useful purpose could be served by so distinguishing them. The time has come to face again this problem which has persistently perplexed the court when an adult is adopted for the sole purpose of making him or her an heir and claimant to the estate of an ancestor under the terms of a testamentary instrument known and in existence at the time of the adoption. Even though the statute permits such adoption and even though it expressly provides that it shall be "with the same legal effect as the adoption of a child," we, nevertheless, are constrained to view this practice to be an act of subterfuge which in effect thwarts the intent of the ancestor whose property is being distributed and cheats the rightful heirs. We are faced with a situation wherein we must choose between carrying out the intent of deceased testators or giving a strict and rigid construction to a statute which thwarts that intent. In the *Bedinger* case there is no doubt but what the intent of the testatrix, as to the disposition of her property, was circumvented. It is our opinion that by giving a strict and literal construction to the adoption statutes, we thwarted the efforts of the deceased to dispose of her property as she saw fit.

When one rule of law does violence to another it becomes inevitable that one must then give way to the other. It is of paramount importance that a man be permitted to pass on his property at his death to those who represent the natural objects of his bounty. This is an ancient and precious right running from the dawn of civilization in an unbroken line down to the present day. Our adoption statutes are humanitarian in nature and of great importance to the welfare of the public. However, these statutes should not be given a construction that does violence to the above rule and to the extent that they violate the rule and prevent one from passing on his property in accord with his wishes, they must give way. Adoption of an adult for the purpose of bringing that person under the provisions of a pre-existing testamentary instrument when he clearly was not intended to be so covered should not be permitted and we do not view this as doing any great violence to the intent and purpose of our adoption laws.

For the foregoing reasons the action of the trial court in declaring Myra Galvin Minary an heir of Amelia S. Minary is reversed.

The judgment is reversed.

QUESTIONS, NOTES, AND PROBLEMS

1. In *Minary*, the trust was to be distributed to the testator's "surviving heirs, according to the laws of descent and distribution *then* in force in Kentucky [emphasis added]." Why leave it to future legislatures to determine who will be the beneficiaries? Why not distribute according to the laws in force on the date the trust is created? See UPC §2-711 (1990, rev. 1993), page 874.

2. The use of an adoption procedure for the purpose of creating a child to come within a class gift is in effect using adoption as a *special power of appointment* (discussed in Chapter 12). If Amelia Minary had given her sons a power to appoint at least a life estate to their spouses, Alfred's desperate shenanigans would not have been necessary and his wife would not have ended up impoverished. It is unlikely that Alfred's mother would have wanted his widow to live in penury. Likely her lawyer did not suggest a special power of appointment. Is not the testator's intent, to which the court endeavored to adhere, something of a fiction if her lawyer never brought up the subject of her sons' widows?

3. *Adult adoption and class gifts.* The cases are split on the use of adult adoption to affect a class gift. Compare Fleet National Bank v. Hunt, 944 A.2d 846 (R.I. 2008) (attempt failed), with In re Trust of Lane, 660 N.W.2d 421 (Minn. 2003) (grandson adopted his nephew to allow the nephew to take from a mutual ancestor's trust for "issue").

UPC §2-705(f) (1990, rev. 2008) excludes a person adopted after reaching the age of 18 from a class gift to the adoptive parent's children, issue, descendants, or heirs by someone other than the adoptive parent unless the adoptive parent was the adoptee's stepparent or foster parent, or the adoptive parent "functioned as a parent of the adoptee before the adoptee" turned 18. See also Restatement (Third) of Property: Wills and Other Donative Transfers §14.5 (T.D. No. 4, 2004), to similar effect.

In a state in which an adult adoptee is included in a gift to the adoptive parent's children, issue, descendants, or heirs, is there any reason for excluding a spouse who is adopted? What about an adopted lover? See Pam Belluck and Alison Leigh Cowan, Partner Adopted by an Heiress Stakes Her Claim, N.Y. Times, Mar. 19, 2007, at A1 (discussing a claim by the former lover and adopted child of the granddaughter of the founder of IBM to a share in family trusts created by him).

4.   *Children "adopted out."* So far we have considered the effect of adoption to bring the adopted person into a class gift. But what of the reverse? Does adoption remove the adoptee from a class gift to the adoptee's genetic parent's children, issue, descendants, or heirs? See In re Accounting by Fleet Bank, 884 N.E.2d 1040 (N.Y. 2008) (holding that adoptee is not included in a class gift to adoptee's genetic parent's descendants).

But suppose *T* bequeaths a fund in trust "for my wife for life, then to my descendants then living per stirpes." After *T*'s death, his son, *A*, dies, leaving a wife and a minor child, *B*. *A*'s wife remarries, and her second husband adopts the minor child *B*. *T*'s wife then dies. Is *B* entitled to share in *T*'s trust fund? Compare Newman v. Wells Fargo Bank, 926 P.2d 969 (Cal. 1996) (looking at intestacy law as it existed at time of *T*'s death to determine *T*'s intent; *B* excluded), with Lockwood v. Adamson, 566 N.E.2d 96 (Mass. 1991) (*B* shares under *T*'s will even though *B* would not inherit from *T* under intestacy law). Under UPC §2-705(b) (1990, rev. 2008), *B* would share in *T*'s trust fund because the stepparent adoption rule of §2-119(b)(2), page 101, would apply.

NOTE: DORIS DUKE AND ADOPTIVE PARENT'S REMORSE

Adoption, unlike marriage, is not revocable if the relationship turns sour. In 1988 Doris Duke, 75, one of the world's richest women, adopted Chandi Heffner, 35. Chandi had taken her name from the Hindu deity, Chandi, and was a Hare Krishna when Doris met her at a dance class. Doris Duke was the life beneficiary of two trusts created by her father, James Buchanan ("Buck") Duke, in 1917 and 1924. After Doris's death, the income from the trusts was to be payable to Doris's children. Doris had no genetic children. Subsequent to the adoption, Doris Duke had a falling out with Chandi and tried to exclude Chandi from her father's trust in her will.

Doris Duke died in 1993, a billionaire. She left her fortune to a charitable foundation, over which she put her barely-literate butler, Bernard Lafferty, in charge. After embarking on an extended spending spree, far exceeding the $500,000 a year Doris left him, the butler dropped dead some three years after Doris died. Doris's will provided:

TWENTY-ONE: As indicated in Article SEVEN, it is my intention that Chandi Heffner not be deemed to be my child for purposes of disposing of property under this my Will (or any Codicil thereto). Furthermore, it is not my intention, nor do I believe that it was ever my father's intention, that Chandi Heffner be deemed to be a child or lineal descendant of mine for purposes of disposing of the trust estate of the May 2, 1917 trust which my father established for my benefit or the Doris Duke Trust, dated December 11, 1924, which my father established for the benefit of me, certain other members of the Duke family and ultimately for charity.

I am extremely troubled by the realization that Chandi Heffner may use my 1988 adoption of her (when she was 35 years old) to attempt to benefit financially under the terms of either of the trusts created by my father. After giving the matter prolonged and serious consideration, I am convinced that I should not have adopted Chandi Heffner. I have come to the realization that her primary motive was financial gain. I firmly believe that, like me, my father would not have wanted her to have benefitted under the trusts which he created, and similarly, I do not wish her to benefit from my estate.

Her signature was shaky but bold:

Doris Duke in 1991, with her butler, Bernard Lafferty.

IN WITNESS WHEREOF, I have hereunto set my hand and affix my seal to this my Last Will and Testament on this 5th day of April, 1993.

Upon Doris Duke's death, Chandi Heffner sued the trustees of the Doris Duke Trust created by her father, Buck Duke, demanding that they pay her income as the successive life beneficiary of the Doris Duke Trust, worth $170 million at Doris's death. The trial court ruled against her, on the ground that an adult adoptee was not considered a child of the adopting parent when the trust is created by another. In re Trust of Duke, 702 A.2d 1008 (N.J. Super. 1995). Chandi Heffner also sued the trustees of the other trust created by Buck Duke and the executors of Doris Duke, claiming that Doris had promised to support her. While the litigation was proceeding, the parties settled. Chandi Heffner received $60 million from the James Buchanan Duke trusts in settlement of her claim to be a child of Doris and $5 million from the Doris Duke estate. One very expensive adoption!

For more on the Doris Duke litigation, see In re Duke, 663 N.E.2d 602 (N.Y. 1996); N.Y. Times, May 16, 1996, at B8; N.Y. Times, Nov. 5, 1996, at B8; N.Y. Times, Jan. 24, 1997, at B1 (reporting the feeding frenzy of lawyers); Susan Hansen, The Butler's Lawyers, Am. Law., Apr. 1995, at 53 (reporting sensational but unproved charges against Duke's lawyers and butler).

Thus far we have explored explicit adoptions. But the recognition of a more informal *equitable adoption* (sometimes called *virtual adoption* or *adoption by estoppel*) can also affect the distribution of property at death.

O'Neal v. Wilkes
Supreme Court of Georgia, 1994
439 S.E.2d 490

FLETCHER, J.   In this virtual adoption action, a jury found that appellant Hattie O'Neal had been virtually adopted by the decedent, Roswell Cook. On post-trial motions, the court granted a judgment notwithstanding the verdict to appellee Firmon Wilkes, as administrator of Cook's estate, on the ground that the paternal aunt who allegedly entered into the adoption contract with Cook had no legal authority to do so. We have reviewed the record and conclude that the court correctly determined that there was no valid contract to adopt.

O'Neal was born out of wedlock in 1949 and raised by her mother, Bessie Broughton, until her mother's death in 1957. At no time did O'Neal's biological father recognize O'Neal as his daughter, take any action to legitimize her, or provide support to her or her mother. O'Neal testified that she first met her biological father in 1970.

For four years after her mother's death, O'Neal lived in New York City with her maternal aunt, Ethel Campbell. In 1961, Ms. Campbell brought O'Neal to Savannah, Georgia, and surrendered physical custody of O'Neal to a woman identified only as Louise who was known to want a daughter. Shortly thereafter, Louise determined she could not care for O'Neal and took her to the Savannah home of Estelle Page, the sister of O'Neal's biological father. After a short time with Page, Roswell Cook and his wife came to Savannah from their Riceboro, Georgia home to pick up O'Neal. Page testified that she had heard that the Cooks wanted a daughter and after telling them about O'Neal, they came for her. [Mr. and Mrs. Cook were divorced in the 1970s.]

Although O'Neal was never statutorily adopted by Cook, he raised her and provided for her education and she resided with him until her marriage in 1975. While she never took the last name of Cook, he referred to her as his daughter and, later, identified her children as his grandchildren.

In November 1991, Cook died intestate. The appellee, Firmon Wilkes, was appointed as administrator of Cook's estate and refused to recognize O'Neal's asserted interest in the estate. In December 1991, O'Neal filed a petition in equity asking the court to declare a virtual adoption, thereby entitling her to the estate property she would have inherited if she were Cook's statutorily adopted child.

1. The first essential of a contract for adoption is that it be made between persons competent to contract for the disposition of the child. Winder v. Winder, 128 S.E.2d 56 (Ga. 1962); Rucker v. Moore, 199 S.E. 106 (Ga. 1938). A successful plaintiff must also prove:

Some showing of an agreement between the natural and adoptive parents, performance by the natural parents of the child in giving up custody, performance by the child by living in the home of the adoptive parents, partial performance by the foster parents in taking the child into the home and treating [it] as their child, and . . . the intestacy of the foster parent.

Williams v. Murray, 236 S.E.2d 624 (Ga. 1977), quoting *Habecker v. Young*, 474 F.2d 1229, 1230 (5th Cir. 1973). The only issue on this appeal is whether the court correctly determined that Page was without authority to contract for O'Neal's adoption.

2. O'Neal argues that Page, a paternal aunt with physical custody of her, had authority to contract for her adoption and, even if she was without such authority, any person with the legal right to contract for the adoption, be they O'Neal's biological father or maternal aunts or uncles, ratified the adoption contract by failing to object.

As a preliminary matter, we agree with O'Neal that although her biological father was living at the time the adoption contract was allegedly entered into, his consent to the contract was not necessary as he never recognized or legitimized her or provided for her support in any manner. See *Williams v. Murray*, 236 S.E.2d 624 (Ga. 1977) (mother alone may contract for adoption where the father has lost parental control or abandoned the child); OCGA §19-7-25, Code 1933, §74-203 (only mother of child born out of wedlock may exercise parental power over the child unless legitimized by the father); see also OCGA §19-8-10 (parent not entitled to notice of petition of adoption where parent has abandoned the child). What is less clear are the rights and obligations acquired by Page by virtue of her physical custody of O'Neal after her mother's death.

3. The Georgia Code defines a "legal custodian" as a person to whom legal custody has been given by court order and who has the right to physical custody of the child and to determine the nature of the care and treatment of the child and the duty to provide for the care, protection, training, and education and the physical, mental, and moral welfare of the child. OCGA §15-11-43, Code 1933, §24A-2901. A legal custodian does not have the right to consent to the adoption of a child, as this right is specifically retained by one with greater rights over the child, a child's parent or guardian. OCGA §15-11-43, Code 1933, §24A-2901 (rights of a legal custodian are subject to the remaining rights and duties of the child's parents or guardian); *Skipper v. Smith*, 238 S.E.2d 917 (Ga. 1977) (right to consent to adoption is a residual right retained by a parent notwithstanding the transfer of legal custody of the child to another person); *Jackson v. Anglin*, 19 S.E.2d 914 (Ga. 1942) (parent retains exclusive authority to consent to adoption although child is placed in temporary custody of another); *Carey v. Phillips*, 224 S.E.2d 870 (Ga. App. 1976) (parent's consent is required for adoption of child although child is in physical custody of another).

O'Neal concedes that, after her mother's death, no guardianship petition was filed by her relatives. Nor is there any evidence that any person petitioned to be appointed as her legal custodian. Accordingly, the obligation to care and provide for O'Neal, undertaken first by Campbell, and later by Page, was not a legal obligation but a familial obligation resulting in a custodial relationship properly characterized as something less than that of a legal custodian. Such a relationship carried with it no authority to contract for O'Neal's adoption. See *Skipper*, 238 S.E.2d at 919. While we sympathize with O'Neal's plight, we conclude that Page had no authority to enter into the adoption contract with Cook and the contract, therefore, was invalid.

4. Because O'Neal's relatives did not have the legal authority to enter into a contract for her adoption, their alleged ratification of the adoption contract was of no legal effect and the court did not err in granting a judgment notwithstanding the verdict in favor of the appellee. See Foster v. Cheek, 96 S.E.2d 545 (Ga. 1957) (adoption contract made between persons not competent to contract for child's adoption specifically enforceable where the parent with parental power over the child acquiesced in and ratified the adoption contract).

Judgment affirmed.

SEARS, J. dissenting. I disagree with the majority's holding that O'Neal's claim for equitable adoption is defeated by the fact that her paternal aunt was not a person designated by law as one having the authority to consent to O'Neal's adoption.

1. In Crawford v. Wilson, 78 S.E. 30 (Ga. 1913), the doctrine of equitable or virtual adoption was recognized for the first time in Georgia. Relying on the equitable principle that "equity considers that done which ought to have been done," id. at 32; see OCGA §23-1-8, we held that "an agreement to adopt a child, so as to constitute the child an heir at law on the death of the person adopting, performed on the part of the child, is enforceable upon the death of the person adopting the child as to property which is undisposed of by will," id. We held that although the death of the adopting parents precluded a literal enforcement of the contract, equity would "enforce the contract by decreeing that the child is entitled to the fruits of a legal adoption." Id. In *Crawford*, we noted that the full performance of the agreement by the child was sufficient to overcome an objection that the agreement was unenforceable because it violated the statute of frauds. Id. We further held that

Justice Leah Sears

Appointed to the Georgia Supreme Court in 1992, at age 36.

[w]here one takes an infant into his home upon a promise to adopt such as his own child, and the child performs all the duties growing out of the substituted relationship of parent and child, rendering years of service, companionship, and obedience to the foster parent, upon the faith that such foster parent stands in loco parentis, and that upon his death the child will sustain the legal relationship to his estate of a natural child, there is equitable reason that the

child may appeal to a court of equity to consummate, so far as it may be possible, the foster parent's omission of duty in the matter of formal adoption. [Id. at 33.]

Although the majority correctly states the current rule in Georgia that a contract to adopt may not be specifically enforced unless the contract was entered by a person with the legal authority to consent to the adoption of the child, *Crawford* did not expressly establish such a requirement, and I think the cases cited by the majority that have established this requirement are in error.

Instead, I would hold that where a child has fully performed the alleged contract over the course of many years or a lifetime and can sufficiently establish the existence of the contract to adopt, equity should enforce the contract over the objection of the adopting parents' heirs that the contract is unenforceable because the person who consented to the adoption did not have the legal authority to do so. Several reasons support this conclusion.

First, in such cases, the adopting parents and probably their heirs know of the defect in the contract and yet voice no objection to the contract while the child fully performs the contract and the adopting parents reap the benefits thereof. Under these circumstances, to hold that the contract is unenforceable after the child has performed is to permit a virtual fraud upon the child and should not be countenanced in equity. See 2 Corbin on Contracts, §429 (1950). Equity does not permit such action with regard to contracts that are initially unenforceable because they violate the statute of frauds, but instead recognizes that the full performance of the contract negates its initial unenforceability and renders it enforceable in equity. See 2 Corbin, supra, §§420, 421, 429, 432; Harp v. Bacon, 150 S.E.2d 655 (Ga. 1966).

Moreover, the purpose of requiring consent by a person with the legal authority to consent to an adoption, where such a person exists, is to protect that person, the child, and the adopting parents. See generally Clark, The Law of Domestic Relations, Vol. 2, Section 21.11 (2nd ed. 1987). However, as equitable adoption cases do not arise until the death of the adopting parents, the interests of the person with the [right to] consent to adopt and of the adopting parents are not in jeopardy. On the other hand, the interests of the child are unfairly and inequitably harmed by insisting upon the requirement that a person with the consent to adopt had to have been a party to the contract. That this legal requirement is held against the child is particularly inequitable because the child, the course of whose life is forever changed by such contracts, was unable to act to insure the validity of the contract when the contract was made.

Furthermore, where there is no person with the legal authority to consent to the adoption, such as in the present case, the only reason to insist that a person be appointed the child's legal guardian before agreeing to the contract to adopt would be for the protection of the child. Yet, by insisting upon this requirement after the adopting parents' deaths, this Court is harming the very person that the requirement would protect.

For all the foregoing reasons, equity ought to intervene on the child's behalf in these types of cases, and require the performance of the contract if it is sufficiently proven. See OCGA §23-1-8. In this case, I would thus not rule against O'Neal's claim for specific performance solely on the ground that her paternal aunt did not have the authority to consent to the adoption.

2. Moreover, basing the doctrine of equitable adoption in contract theory has come under heavy criticism, for numerous reasons. See Clark, supra, at 676-78; Jan Ellen Rein, Relatives by Blood, Adoption, and Association: Who Should Get What and Why (The Impact of Adoptions, Adult Adoptions, and Equitable Adoptions on Intestate Succession and Class Gifts), 37 Vand. L. Rev. 711, 770-75, 784-86 (1984). For instance, as we acknowledged in *Wilson*, supra, the contract to adopt is not being specifically enforced as the adopting parents are dead; for equitable reasons we are merely placing the child in a position that he or she would have been in if he or she had been adopted. See Rein at 774. Moreover, it is problematic whether these contracts are capable of being enforced in all respects during the child's infancy. See Rein at 773-74; Clark at 678. Furthermore, because part of the consideration for these contracts is the child's performance thereunder, the child is not merely a third-party beneficiary of a contract between the adults involved but is a party thereto. Yet, a child is usually too young to know of or understand the contract, and it is thus difficult to find a meeting of the minds between the child and the adopting parents and the child's acceptance of the contract. Rein at 772-73, 775. I agree with these criticisms and would abandon the contract basis for equitable adoption in favor of the more flexible and equitable theory advanced by the foregoing authorities. That theory focuses not on the fiction of whether there has been a contract to adopt but on the relationship between the adopting parents and the child and in particular whether the adopting parents have led the child to believe that he or she is a legally adopted member of their family. Rein at 785-87; Clark at 678, 682.

3. Because the majority fails to honor the maxim that "[e]quity considers that done which ought to be done," §23-1-8, and follows a rule that fails to protect a person with superior equities, I dissent. I am authorized to state that Justice Hunstein concurs in the result reached by this dissent.

NOTES AND QUESTION

1.   Under the *equitable adoption* doctrine, recognized in a majority of states, an oral agreement to adopt *A*, between *H* and *W* and *A*'s genetic parents, is inferred if *H* and *W* take baby *A* into their home and raise *A* as their child. As against *H* and *W*, equity treats *A* as if the contract to adopt had been performed by *H* and *W*. They are estopped to deny a formal adoption took place.

Equitable adoption permits an equitably adopted child to inherit from the foster parents. Lankford v. Wright, 489 S.E.2d 604 (N.C. 1997). On the other hand, the foster parents (and their relatives) cannot inherit from the child. Having failed to perform by in fact adopting the child, they have no claim in equity. Estate of Riggs, 440 N.Y.S.2d 450 (Sur. 1981). In Board of Educ. v. Browning, 635 A.2d 373 (Md. 1994), the court held that an equitably adopted child could not inherit through her adoptive parent to take from her adoptive parent's sister even though the sister's estate thus escheated. The court concluded that the effect of equitable adoption should be limited to inheritance from the parent who is estopped. Many courts, though not all, refuse to apply equitable adoption to testate estates. See In re Estate of Seader, 76 P.3d 1236 (Wyo. 2003).

2. Suppose in *O'Neal* that the Juvenile Court had placed Hattie in the custody of Mr. and Mrs. Cook, and that the Juvenile Court had power to consent to adoption of Hattie by the Cooks. Same result? See Welch v. Welch, 453 S.E.2d 445 (Ga. 1995) (holding no equitable adoption, by a 4 to 3 vote).

In re Estate of Ford, 82 P.3d 747 (Cal. 2004), involved a foster child who was raised from the age of two by the decedent. The court rejected the foster child's claim to an intestate share of the decedent's estate, giving the property instead to a nephew and niece who had not seen the decedent for 15 years. The court held that, under California law, equitable adoption was based on contract, and the promise or intention to adopt must be proved by clear and convincing evidence. See also Walden v. Burke, 637 S.E.2d 859 (Ga. 2006) (reaffirming the *O'Neal* requirement of contract).

Not all courts are as strict in requiring a contract. In Welch v. Wilson, 516 S.E.2d 35 (W. Va. 1999), a woman who was raised by her grandmother and step-grandfather was treated as having been equitably adopted by the step-grandfather, allowing her to inherit his entire estate. The court did not require a contract, nor did it mention estoppel, though it did note that the step-grandparent was listed as the woman's parent on school records. The court focused primarily on the ample evidence of a close, loving parent-child relationship. See also Kristine S. Knaplund, Grandparents Raising Grandchildren and the Implications for Inheritance, 48 Ariz. L. Rev. 1 (2006).

3. Hattie O'Neal was African American, and the country town of Riceboro, Georgia, where she went to live, had a population of 767, of whom 751 were African Americans. There was no lawyer in Riceboro, but there are several lawyers in the county seat, Hinesville, 17 miles away. Does this affect your view of the *O'Neal* case? See Lynda Richardson, Adoptions that Lack Papers, Not Purpose, N.Y. Times, Nov. 25, 1993, at C1, discussing the history and prevalence of informal adoptions in the African American community ("of the estimated one million black children in this country who do not live with a biological parent, nearly 800,000 have been informally adopted, usually by a grandparent"). See also Michael J. Higdon, When Informal Adoption Meets Intestate Succession: The Cultural Myopia of the Equitable Adoption Doctrine, 43 Wake Forest L. Rev. 223 (2008) (criticizing equitable adoption doctrine for insensitivity to racial and ethnic minority communities).

In *O'Neal*, the court was divided 5 to 2. Joining Justice Sears in her dissent was a white woman justice; the majority were all men, including one African American. Might women look at equitable adoption as less an application of abstract principles and more as a judgment about whether the responsibilities and care involved in a parent-child relationship had been satisfied in a particular case? See the views of Professor Rein, cited in Justice Sears's opinion, and Carol Gilligan, In a Different Voice: Psychological Theory and Women's Development (1982).

b. Posthumous Children

The typical posthumous child case involves a child who is conceived before, but born after, her father's death. Where, for purposes of inheritance or of determining property rights, it is to a child's advantage to be treated as in being from the time of conception rather than from the time of birth, the child will be so treated if born alive. The principle is an ancient one. See 1 William Blackstone, Commentaries *130. David Copperfield, the lead character in the eponymous book by Charles Dickens, reports at the outset that "I was a posthumous child. My father's eyes had closed upon the light of this world six months, when mine opened on it."

Courts have established a rebuttable presumption that the normal period of gestation is 280 days (10 lunar months). If the child claims that conception dated more than 280 days before birth, the burden of proof is usually upon the child. On supposed periods of gestation beyond 280 days, the modern record for a protracted pregnancy apparently belongs to a woman from North Carolina. In Byerly v. Tolbert, 108 S.E.2d 29 (N.C. 1959), a child was born to the decedent's widow 322 days after his death. The child (through a guardian ad litem, of course) claimed an intestate share. The trial court held as a matter of law that the infant was not a child of the decedent. On appeal, the case was reversed. Although there is a presumption that a child born more than 280 days after death is not the decedent's child, the presumption is not irrebuttable, and the child was entitled to have the issue submitted to a jury.

Uniform Parentage Act §204 (2000, rev. 2002) establishes a rebuttable presumption that a child born to a woman within 300 (rather than 280) days after the death of her husband is a child of that husband.

c. Nonmarital Children

Although innocent of any sin or crime, children of unmarried parents were given harsh, pitiless treatment by the common law.[15] A child born out of wedlock was *filius nullius*, the child of no one, and could inherit from neither father nor mother. Only the child's spouse and descendants could inherit from the child. If the child died intestate and left neither spouse nor descendants, the child's property escheated to the king or other overlord.

All states have alleviated this unsympathetic treatment of nonmarital children and now permit inheritance from the mother. But the rules respecting inheritance from the father vary. In Trimble v. Gordon, 430 U.S. 762 (1977), the Supreme Court held unconstitutional, as a denial of equal protection, an Illinois statute denying a nonmarital child inheritance rights from the father. The Court held that state discrimination against nonmarital children, though not a suspect

---

15. For a description of the legal position at common law of what was called an illegitimate child, see 1 William Blackstone, Commentaries *454 ff.; 2 id. *247 ff. In the first book of Blackstone (1 id. *457) you may find out, if you care to, how a child could be "more than ordinarily legitimate."

classification subject to the strict scrutiny test, must have a substantial justification as serving an important state interest. The valid state interest recognized by the Court was obtaining reliable proof of paternity. The Court ruled that total statutory disinheritance from the father was not rationally related to this objective. See also Lalli v. Lalli, 439 U.S. 259 (1978), upholding a New York statute permitting inheritance by a nonmarital child from the father only if the father had married the mother or had been formally adjudicated the father by a court during the father's lifetime. But see Paula A. Monopoli, Nonmarital Children and Post-Death Parentage: A Different Path for Inheritance Law?, 38 Santa Clara L. Rev. 857 (2008) (arguing that the Court's analysis has been undermined by subsequent advances in the science of paternity testing).

In the wake of these and related cases, most states amended their intestacy statutes to liberalize inheritance by nonmarital children. Most permit paternity to be established by evidence of the subsequent marriage of the parents, by acknowledgment by the father, by an adjudication during the life of the father, or by clear and convincing proof after his death. For further discussion, see Browne Lewis, Children of Men: Balancing the Inheritance Rights of Marital and Non-Marital Children, 39 U. Tol. L. Rev. 1 (2007); Linda Kelly Hill, Equal Protection Misapplied: The Politics of Gender and Legitimacy and the Denial of Inheritance, 13 Wm. & Mary J. Women & L. 129 (2006).

QUESTIONS AND NOTE

1. In the usual case, the question is whether an out-of-wedlock child can inherit from the father. But what about the reverse? Can a father of a child born out of wedlock inherit from the child? The authorities are split. See Katheleen Guzman, What Price Paternity?, 53 Okla. L. Rev. 77 (2000).

2. Should state courts develop an *equitable legitimation* doctrine (similar to equitable adoption) so that where a formal adjudication of paternity is required by statute for inheritance, a nonmarital child can inherit from the father if there is clear and convincing evidence of paternity and of the father's intent that the child be treated as an heir? See the Georgia case, Prince v. Black, 344 S.E.2d 411 (Ga. 1986) (announcing equitable legitimation doctrine) — *Georgia*, did you say? Compare O'Neal v. Wilkes, page 109. See also James R. Robinson, Untangling the "Loose Threads": Equitable Adoption, Equitable Legitimation, and Inheritance in Extralegal Family Arrangements, 48 Emory L.J. 943 (1999).

3. *DNA testing.* Should the remains of deceased persons be exhumed for DNA testing to establish paternity? In Estate of Kingsbury, 946 A.2d 389 (Me. 2008), the court ordered the deceased's body be disinterred so that a purported daughter's claim of paternity might be proven by DNA testing. In New York, on the other hand, while post-death DNA testing has been allowed on stored samples and the deceased's surviving kin, the courts have been reluctant to order exhumation. Compare In re Estate of Poldrugovaz, 851 N.Y.S.2d 254 (Sur. 2008) (allowing post-mortem DNA testing of tissue sample retained by the coroner),

and In re Estate of Gaynor, 818 N.Y.S.2d 747 (Sur. 2006) (ordering DNA testing of deceased's marital son to verify claim by purported out-of-wedlock son), with In re Estate of Janis, 600 N.Y.S.2d 416 (Sur. 1993) (refusing to order exhumation). As DNA analysis has made paternity testing both fairer and more accurate,[16] the clear trend is toward allowing it, even if exhumation of the body is required. See Ilene Sherwyn Cooper, Posthumous Paternity Testing: A Proposal to Amend EPTL 4-1.2(A)(2)(D), 69 Alb. L. Rev. 947 (2006).

Should a man who has acknowledged paternity and formed a relationship with the child later be allowed to repudiate the acknowledgement if subsequent DNA testing shows he is not the father? In Shondel J. v. Mark D. 853 N.E.2d 610 (N.Y. 2006), the court held in the negative. For further discussion, compare Melanie B. Jacobs, My Two Dads: Disaggregating Biological and Social Paternity, 38 Ariz. St. L.J. 809 (2006), with Ronald K. Henry, The Innocent Third Party: Victims of Paternity Fraud, 40 Fam. L.Q. 51 (2006).

d.   Reproductive Technology and New Forms of Parentage

At issue in Hecht v. Superior Court, 20 Cal. Rptr. 2d 275 (App. 1993), was William Kane's devise to his girlfriend, Deborah Hecht, of 15 vials of his sperm that were on deposit in a sperm bank. Kane's two adult children contested the devise and sought an order that the sperm be destroyed. The court ruled in favor of Hecht, awarding her Kane's sperm.

Would a child conceived through the use of Kane's sperm after Kane's death qualify as Kane's heir? Recall that a posthumous child (a child *en ventre sa mere*) is treated as in being from the time of conception rather than from the time of birth if it is to the child's advantage to do so and the child is born alive (see page 115). The posthumously conceived child (a child *en ventre sa frigidaire*) differs from the posthumous child in that the former is both born *and conceived after* the death of one or both of the child's genetic parents. Hence a posthumously conceived child is, by definition, a nonmarital child even though the child's parents might have been married prior to the child's conception. The California courts were able to elide the question in the subsequent litigation over Hecht's sperm,[17] but the issue has since been confronted squarely.

---

16. For a paternity case in which DNA testing was not enough, because the potential fathers were identical twin brothers, each of whom had slept with the mother, see State ex rel. Dept. Social Serv. v. Miller, 218 S.W.3d 2 (Mo. App. 2007). From the case report you may find out, if you care to, how the court resolved which of the twins was the father.

17. After the 1993 decision, the Kane children continued their litigation to deny Hecht the vials of sperm. Finally, in Hecht v. Superior Court, 59 Cal. Rptr. 2d 222 (App. 1996), the court, expressing exasperation at the children's effort to frustrate their father's will, dismissed the children's claims and ordered all the vials to be distributed to Deborah Hecht without further delay. Said the court: "We do not have before us the many legal questions raised by the possible birth of a child of Hecht through use of Kane's sperm. Thus, we do not decide, for instance, whether that child would be entitled to inherit any property as Kane's heir."

Woodward v. Commissioner of Social Security
Supreme Judicial Court of Massachusetts, 2002
760 N.E.2d 257

MARSHALL, C.J.   The United States District Court for the District of Massachusetts has certified the following question to this court.

> If a married man and woman arrange for sperm to be withdrawn from the husband for the purpose of artificially impregnating the wife, and the woman is impregnated with that sperm after the man, her husband, has died, will children resulting from such pregnancy enjoy the inheritance rights of natural children under Massachusetts' law of intestate succession?

We answer the certified question as follows: In certain limited circumstances, a child resulting from posthumous reproduction may enjoy the inheritance rights of "issue" under the Massachusetts intestacy statute. . . .

I

The undisputed facts and relevant procedural history are as follows. In January, 1993, about three and one-half years after they were married, Lauren Woodward and Warren Woodward were informed that the husband had leukemia. At the time, the couple was childless. Advised that the husband's leukemia treatment might leave him sterile, the Woodwards arranged for a quantity of the husband's semen to be medically withdrawn and preserved, in a process commonly known as "sperm banking." The husband then underwent a bone marrow transplant. The treatment was not successful. The husband died in October, 1993, and the wife was appointed administratrix of his estate.

In October, 1995, the wife gave birth to twin girls. The children were conceived through artificial insemination using the husband's preserved semen. In January, 1996, the wife applied for two forms of Social Security survivor benefits: "child's" benefits . . . and "mother's" benefits.

The Social Security Administration (SSA) rejected the wife's claims on the ground that she had not established that the twins were the husband's "children" within the meaning of the Act . . . [because] they "are not entitled to inherit from [the husband] under the Massachusetts intestacy and paternity laws." . . .

The wife appealed to the United States District Court for the District of Massachusetts, seeking a declaratory judgment to reverse the commissioner's ruling.

The United States District Court judge certified the above question to this court because "[t]he parties agree that a determination of these children's rights under the law of Massachusetts is dispositive of the case and . . . no directly applicable Massachusetts precedent exists."

II

A

We have been asked to determine the inheritance rights under Massachusetts law of children conceived from the gametes of a deceased individual and his or

***Michayla and Mackenzie Woodward, conceived with their father's sperm
after his death. Defending the court's decision, their mother, Lauren, said,
"Look at them and tell me that's not right."***

AP/Salem News/Amy Sweeney

her surviving spouse.[18] We have not previously been asked to consider whether
our intestacy statute accords inheritance rights to posthumously conceived
genetic children. Nor has any American court of last resort considered, in a published opinion, the question of posthumously conceived genetic children's inheritance rights under other States' intestacy laws. . . .

[T]he parties have articulated extreme positions. The wife's principal argument is that, by virtue of their genetic connection with the decedent, posthumously conceived children must *always* be permitted to enjoy the inheritance
rights of the deceased parent's children under our law of intestate succession.
The government's principal argument is that, because posthumously conceived
children are not "in being" as of the date of the parent's death, they are *always*
barred from enjoying such inheritance rights.

---

18. Although the certified question asks us to consider an unsettled question of law concerning the paternity
of children conceived from a deceased male's gametes, we see no principled reason that our conclusions should
not apply equally to children posthumously conceived from a deceased female's gametes.

Neither party's position is tenable. In this developing and relatively uncharted area of human relations, bright-line rules are not favored unless the applicable statute requires them. The Massachusetts intestacy statute does not. . . . On the other hand, with the act of procreation now separated from coitus, posthumous reproduction can occur under a variety of conditions that may conflict with the purposes of the intestacy law and implicate other firmly established State and individual interests. We look to our intestacy law to resolve these tensions.

B

. . . Section 1 of the intestacy statute directs that, if a decedent "leaves issue," such "issue" will inherit a fixed portion of his real and personal property, subject to debts and expenses, the rights of the surviving spouse, and other statutory payments not relevant here. See G.L. c. 190, §1. To answer the certified question, then, we must first determine whether the twins are the "issue" of the husband.

The intestacy statute does not define "issue." However, in the context of intestacy the term "issue" means all lineal (genetic) descendants, and now includes both marital and nonmarital descendants. The term "'[d]escendants' . . . has long been held to mean persons 'who by consanguinity trace their lineage to the designated ancestor.'" Lockwood v. Adamson, 566 N.E.2d 96 (Mass. 1991). . . .

We must therefore determine whether, under our intestacy law, there is any reason that children conceived after the decedent's death who are the decedent's direct genetic descendants — that is, children who "by consanguinity trace their lineage to the designated ancestor" — may not enjoy the same succession rights as children conceived before the decedent's death who are the decedent's direct genetic descendants.

To answer that question we consider whether and to what extent such children may take as intestate heirs of the deceased genetic parent consistent with the purposes of the intestacy law, and not by any assumptions of the common law. In the absence of express legislative directives, we construe the Legislature's purposes from statutory indicia and judicial decisions in a manner that advances the purposes of the intestacy law.

The question whether posthumously conceived genetic children may enjoy inheritance rights under the intestacy statute implicates three powerful State interests: [1] the best interests of children, [2] the State's interest in the orderly administration of estates, and [3] the reproductive rights of the genetic parent. Our task is to balance and harmonize these interests to effect the Legislature's over-all purposes.

1. First and foremost we consider the overriding legislative concern to promote the best interests of children. "The protection of minor children, most especially those who may be stigmatized by their 'illegitimate' status . . . has been a hallmark of legislative action and of the jurisprudence of this court." Repeatedly, forcefully, and unequivocally, the Legislature has expressed its will that all children be "entitled to the same rights and protections of the law" regardless of the accidents of their birth. Among the many rights and protections vouchsafed to all children are rights to financial support from their parents and their parents'

estates. See G.L. c. 119A, §1 ("It is the public policy of this commonwealth that dependent children shall be maintained, as completely as possible, from the resources of their parents, thereby relieving or avoiding, at least in part, the burden borne by the citizens of the commonwealth"); G.L. c. 191, §20 (establishing inheritance rights for pretermitted children); G.L. c. 196, §§1-3 (permitting allowances from estate to widows and minor children); G.L. c. 209C, §14 (permitting paternity claims to be commenced prior to birth). See also G.L. c. 190, §§1-3, 5, 7-8 (intestacy rights).

We also consider that some of the assistive reproductive technologies that make posthumous reproduction possible have been widely known and practiced for several decades. In that time, the Legislature has not acted to narrow the broad statutory class of posthumous children to restrict posthumously conceived children from taking in intestacy. Moreover, the Legislature has in great measure affirmatively supported the assistive reproductive technologies that are the only means by which these children can come into being. See G.L. c. 46, §4B (artificial insemination of married woman). See also G.L. c. 175, §47H; G.L. c. 176A, §8K; G.L. c. 176B, §4J; G.L. c. 176G, §4 (insurance coverage for infertility treatments). We do not impute to the Legislature the inherently irrational conclusion that assistive reproductive technologies are to be encouraged while a class of children who are the fruit of that technology are to have fewer rights and protections than other children.

In short, we cannot, absent express legislative directive, accept the commissioner's position that the historical context of G.L. c. 190, §8, dictates as a matter of law that all posthumously conceived children are automatically barred from taking under their deceased donor parent's intestate estate. We have consistently construed statutes to effectuate the Legislature's overriding purpose to promote the welfare of all children, notwithstanding restrictive common-law rules to the contrary. Posthumously conceived children may not come into the world the way the majority of children do. But they are children nonetheless. We may assume that the Legislature intended that such children be "entitled," in so far as possible, "to the same rights and protections of the law" as children conceived before death. See G.L. c. 209C, §1.

2. However, in the context of our intestacy laws, the best interests of the posthumously conceived child, while of great importance, are not in themselves conclusive. They must be balanced against other important State interests, not the least of which is the protection of children who are alive or conceived before the intestate parent's death. In an era in which serial marriages, serial families, and blended families are not uncommon, according succession rights under our intestacy laws to posthumously conceived children may, in a given case, have the potential to pit child against child and family against family. Any inheritance rights of posthumously conceived children will reduce the intestate share available to children born prior to the decedent's death. Such considerations, among others, lead us to examine a second important legislative purpose: to provide certainty to heirs and creditors by effecting the orderly, prompt, and accurate administration of intestate estates.

The intestacy statute furthers the Legislature's administrative goals in two principal ways: (1) by requiring certainty of filiation between the decedent and his issue, and (2) by establishing limitations periods for the commencement of claims against the intestate estate. In answering the certified question, we must consider each of these requirements of the intestacy statute in turn.

First, . . . our intestacy law mandates that, absent the father's acknowledgment of paternity or marriage to the mother, a nonmarital child must obtain a judicial determination of paternity as a prerequisite to succeeding to a portion of the father's intestate estate. . . .

Because death ends a marriage, posthumously conceived children are always nonmarital children. And because the parentage of such children can be neither acknowledged nor adjudicated prior to the decedent's death, it follows that, under the intestacy statute, posthumously conceived children must obtain a judgment of paternity as a necessary prerequisite to enjoying inheritance rights in the estate of the deceased genetic father. Although modern reproductive technologies will increase the possibility of disputed paternity claims, sophisticated modern testing techniques now make the determination of genetic paternity accurate and reliable. . . .

We now turn to the second way in which the Legislature has met its administrative goals: the establishment of a limitations period for bringing paternity claims against the intestate estate. Our discussion of this important goal, however, is necessarily circumscribed by the procedural posture of this case and by the terms of the certified question. [The parties stipulated that, in this dispute over Social Security benefits, timeliness was not at issue.] . . .

Nevertheless, the limitations question is inextricably tied to consideration of the intestacy statute's administrative goals. In the case of posthumously conceived children, the application of the one-year limitations period of G.L. c. 190, §7 is not clear; it may pose significant burdens on the surviving parent, and consequently on the child. It requires, in effect, that the survivor make a decision to bear children while in the freshness of grieving. It also requires that attempts at conception succeed quickly. Cf. Commentary, Modern Reproductive Technologies: Legal Issues Concerning Cryopreservation and Posthumous Conception, 17 J. Legal Med. 547, 549 (1996) ("It takes an average of seven insemination attempts over 4.4 menstrual cycles to establish pregnancy"). Because the resolution of the time constraints question is not required here, it must await the appropriate case, should one arise.

3. Finally, the question certified to us implicates a third important State interest: to honor the reproductive choices of individuals. We need not address the wife's argument that her reproductive rights would be infringed by denying succession rights to her children under our intestacy law. Nothing in the record even remotely suggests that she was prevented by the State from choosing to conceive children using her deceased husband's semen. The husband's reproductive rights are a more complicated matter.

In A.Z. v. B.Z., 725 N.E.2d 1051 (Mass. 2000), we . . . recognized that individuals have a protected right to control the use of their gametes. Consonant with the principles identified in A.Z. v. B.Z., a decedent's silence, or his equivocal indications of a desire to parent posthumously, "ought not to be construed as consent." See Anne Reichman Schiff, Arising from the Dead: Challenges of Posthumous Procreation, 75 N.C.L. Rev. 901, 951 (1997). The prospective donor parent must clearly and unequivocally consent not only to posthumous reproduction but also to the support of any resulting child. After the donor-parent's death, the burden rests with the surviving parent, or the posthumously conceived child's other legal representative, to prove the deceased genetic parent's affirmative consent to both requirements for posthumous parentage: posthumous reproduction and the support of any resulting child.

This two-fold consent requirement arises from the nature of alternative reproduction itself. It will not always be the case that a person elects to have his or her gametes medically preserved to create "issue" posthumously. A man, for example, may preserve his semen for myriad reasons, including, among others: to reproduce after recovery from medical treatment, to reproduce after an event that leaves him sterile, or to reproduce when his spouse has a genetic disorder or otherwise cannot have or safely bear children. That a man has medically preserved his gametes for use by his spouse thus may indicate only that he wished to reproduce after some contingency while he was alive, and not that he consented to the different circumstance of creating a child after his death. Uncertainty as to consent may be compounded by the fact that medically preserved semen can remain viable for up to ten years after it was first extracted, long after the original decision to preserve the semen has passed and when such changed circumstances as divorce, remarriage, and a second family may have intervened.

Such circumstances demonstrate the inadequacy of a rule that would make the mere genetic tie of the decedent to any posthumously conceived child, or the decedent's mere election to preserve gametes, sufficient to bind his intestate estate for the benefit of any posthumously conceived child. Without evidence that the deceased intestate parent affirmatively consented (1) to the posthumous reproduction and (2) to support any resulting child, a court cannot be assured that the intestacy statute's goal of fraud prevention is satisfied. . . .

C

The certified question does not require us to specify what proof would be sufficient to establish a successful claim under our intestacy law on behalf of a posthumously conceived child. Nor have we been asked to determine whether the wife has met her burden of proof. . . .

It is undisputed in this case that the husband is the genetic father of the wife's children. However, for the reasons stated above, that fact, in itself, cannot be sufficient to establish that the husband is the children's legal father for purposes of the devolution and distribution of his intestate property. In the United States District Court, the wife may come forward with other evidence as to her husband's consent to posthumously conceive children. She may come forward with evidence of his consent to support such children. We do not speculate as to the sufficiency of evidence she may submit at trial. . . .

III

. . . As these technologies advance, the number of children they produce will continue to multiply. So, too, will the complex moral, legal, social, and ethical questions that surround their birth. The questions present in this case cry out for lengthy, careful examination outside the adversary process, which can only address the specific circumstances of each controversy that presents itself. They demand a comprehensive response reflecting the considered will of the people.

In the absence of statutory directives, we have answered the certified question by identifying and harmonizing the important State interests implicated therein in a manner that advances the Legislature's over-all purposes. In so doing, we conclude that limited circumstances may exist, consistent with the mandates of our Legislature, in which posthumously conceived children may enjoy the inheritance rights of "issue" under our intestacy law. These limited circumstances exist where, as a threshold matter, the surviving parent or the child's other legal representative demonstrates a genetic relationship between the child and the decedent. The survivor or representative must then establish both that the decedent affirmatively consented to posthumous conception and to the support of any resulting child. Even where such circumstances exist, time limitations may preclude commencing a claim for succession rights on behalf of a posthumously conceived child. In any action brought to establish such inheritance rights, notice must be given to all interested parties.

[The clerk of the court was ordered to transmit an attested copy of this opinion to the district court.]

PROBLEMS, QUESTIONS, AND NOTES

1.   Suppose a man banks his sperm and records in writing his consent to posthumous conception with his widow, and the widow gives birth to the man's posthumously conceived daughter 21 years later. See Celia Hall, Baby Boy Born from Sperm Frozen for 21 Years, Daily Telegraph (London), May 25, 2004, at 01. Should the girl be entitled to inherit from her father? What result under *Woodward*? At what point does the need for finality in property succession trump the interests of a later-born, posthumously conceived child?

Suppose a man banks his sperm but, after he dies, there is a dispute whether he consented to posthumous conception. What proof would show that the man "affirmatively consented" under *Woodward*? What about the extraction of sperm from dead or comatose men who do not consent, and the use of such sperm by wives, girlfriends, and parents? Should a child conceived in this way be entitled to inherit from the father, who did not give his consent? In Lori B. Andrews, The Sperminator, N.Y. Times Mag., Mar. 28, 1999, at 62, the author reports that the practice of harvesting sperm from deceased men has become common (it has since been a plot device in the ABC television show Ugly Betty). See also

Katheryn D. Katz, Parenthood from the Grave: Protocols for Retrieving and Utilizing Gametes from the Dead or Dying, 2006 U. Chi. Legal F. 289.

2. *Social Security and inheritance law.* In *Woodward*, the court was asked to determine the intestacy rights of the decedent's posthumously conceived children, not for the purpose of distributing the decedent's estate, but because under federal law a child of a deceased father is eligible for Social Security survivor's benefits only if the child would inherit from the father under state law. Nearly all the litigated cases over the inheritance rights of a posthumously conceived child involve eligibility for Social Security benefits. In spite of their common issue, the cases have reached divergent results. Compare Gillett-Netting v. Barnhart, 371 F.3d 593 (9th Cir. 2004) (Arizona law, yes), and Estate of Kolacy, 753 A.2d 1257 (N.J. Super. 2000) (yes), with Finley v. Astrue, 270 S.W.3d 849 (Ark. 2008) (no), Khabbaz v. Commissioner of Social Security, 930 A.2d 1180 (N.H. 2007) (no), and Stephen v. Commissioner of Social Security, 386 F. Supp. 2d 1257 (M.D. Fla. 2005) (Florida law, no). Should Congress amend the Social Security Act to provide a uniform national rule?

3. *Legislation and law reform.* Heeding the call in *Woodward* for legislative relief, several state legislatures have responded, with California leading the way. Under Cal. Prob. Code §249.5 (2008), "a child of the decedent conceived after the death of the decedent shall be deemed to have been born in the lifetime of the decedent" if (a) the decedent consented in a signed and dated writing; (b) within four months of the decedent's death, notice of the possibility of posthumous conception is served upon "a person who has the power to control the distribution" of the decedent's property; and (c) the child "was in utero within two years of the" decedent's death and the child is not a clone of the decedent. La. Rev. Stat. 9:391.1 (2008) grants posthumously conceived children inheritance rights if born to the surviving spouse within three years of the decedent's death. Uniform Parentage Act §707 (2000, rev. 2002), adopted in a handful of states, recognizes inheritance rights for a posthumously conceived child if the parent consented to posthumous conception in writing. Fla. Stat. Ann. §742.17 (2008) provides that a posthumously conceived child inherits only if provided for expressly in the decedent's will.

UPC §2-120, added to the Code in 2008, provides that a posthumously conceived child inherits from the deceased parent if (1) during life the parent consented to posthumous conception in a signed writing or consent is otherwise proved by clear and convincing evidence, and (2) the child is in utero not later than 36 months or is born not later than 45 months after the parent's death. See Susan N. Gary, We Are Family: The Definition of Parent and Child for Succession Purposes, 34 ACTEC J. 171 (2008).

Restatement (Third) of Property: Wills and Other Donative Transfers §2.5, cmt. l (1999), takes the position that "to inherit from the decedent, a child produced from genetic material of the decedent by assisted reproductive technology must be born within a reasonable time after the decedent's death in circumstances indicating that the decedent would have approved of the child's right to inherit. A clear case would be that of a child produced by artificial insemination of the decedent's widow with his frozen sperm."

4. *Literature*. For further discussion, see Ronald Chester, Inheritance Rights of the Posthumously Conceived Child: What Exactly Does Lauren Woodward v. Commissioner of Social Security Decide?, 87 Mass. L. Rev. 49 (2002); Michael K. Elliot, Tales of Parenthood from the Crypt: The Predicament of the Posthumously Conceived Child, 39 Real Prop., Prob. & Tr. J. 47 (2004); Kristine S. Knaplund, Legal Issues of Maternity and Inheritance for the Biotech Child of the 21st Century, 43 Real Prop., Prob. & Tr. J. 393 (2008); Kristine S. Knaplund, Equal Protection, Postmortem Conception, and Intestacy, 53 U. Kan. L. Rev. 627 (2005); Browne C. Lewis, Dead Men Reproducing: Responding to the Existence of After-death Children, 16 Geo. Mason L. Rev. 403 (2009); Kathryn Venturatos Lorio, Conceiving the Inconceivable: Legal Recognition of the Posthumously Conceived Child, 34 ACTEC J. 154 (2008); Laurence C. Nolan, Critiquing Society's Response to the Needs of Posthumously Conceived Children, 82 Or. L. Rev. 1067 (2003).

For a more general treatment of new reproductive technologies and the law, see Charles P. Kindregan and Maureen McBrien, Assisted Reproductive Technology: A Lawyer's Guide to Emerging Law and Science (2006 and Supp. 2009).

Posthumously conceived children raise problems of interpretation not only for intestate succession, but also for wills and trusts.

In re Martin B.
Surrogate's Court, New York County, 2008
841 N.Y.S.2d 207

ROTH, S. This uncontested application for advice and direction in connection with seven trust agreements executed on December 31, 1969, by Martin B. (the Grantor) illustrates one of the new challenges that the law of trusts must address as a result of advances in biotechnology. Specifically, the novel question posed is whether, for these instruments, the terms "issue" and "descendants" include children conceived by means of in vitro fertilization with the cryopreserved semen of the Grantor's son who had died several years prior to such conception.

The relevant facts are briefly stated. Grantor (who was a life income beneficiary of the trusts) died on July 9, 2001, survived by his wife Abigail and their son Lindsay (who has two adult children), but predeceased by his son James, who died of Hodgkins Lymphoma on January 13, 2001. James, however, after learning of his illness, deposited a sample of his semen at a laboratory with instructions that it be cryopreserved and that, in the event of his death, it be held subject to the directions of his wife Nancy. Although at his death James had no children, three years later Nancy underwent in vitro fertilization with his cryopreserved semen and gave birth on October 15, 2004, to a boy (James Mitchell). Almost two years later, on August 14, 2006, after using the same procedure, she gave birth to another boy (Warren). It is undisputed that these infants, although conceived after the death of James, are the products of his semen.

Although the trust instruments addressed in this proceeding are not entirely identical, for present purposes the differences among them are in all but one respect immaterial. The only relevant difference is that one is expressly governed by the law of New York while the others are governed by the law of the District of Columbia. As a practical matter, however, such difference is not material since neither jurisdiction provides any statutory authority or judicial comment on the question before the court.

All seven instruments give the trustees discretion to sprinkle principal to, and among, Grantor's "issue" during Abigail's life. The instruments also provide that at Abigail's death the princi-

Surrogate Renee R. Roth

pal is to be distributed as she directs under her special testamentary power to appoint to Grantor's "issue" or "descendants" (or to certain other "eligible" appointees). In the absence of such exercise, the principal is to be distributed to or for the benefit of "issue" surviving at the time of such disposition (James's issue, in the case of certain trusts, and Grantor's issue, in the case of certain other trusts). The trustees have brought this proceeding because under such instruments they are authorized to sprinkle principal to decedent's "issue" and "descendants" and thus need to know whether James's children qualify as members of such classes.

The question thus raised is whether the two infant boys are "descendants" and "issue" for purposes of such provisions although they were conceived several years after the death of James. . . .

In this case legislative action has not kept pace with the progress of science. In the absence of binding authority, courts must turn to less immediate sources for a reflection of the public's evolving attitude toward assisted reproduction — including statutes in other jurisdictions, model codes, scholarly discussions and Restatements of the law.

We turn first to the laws of the governing jurisdictions. At present, the right of a posthumous child to inherit (EPTL 4-1.1[c] [in intestacy]) or as an after-born child under a will (EPTL 5-3.2 [under a will]) is limited to a child conceived during the decedent's lifetime. Indeed, a recent amendment to section 5-3.2 (effective July 26, 2006) was specifically intended to make it clear that a post-conceived child is excluded from sharing in the parent's estate as an "after-born" (absent some provision in the will to the contrary, EPTL 5-3.2[b]). Such limitation was intended to ensure certainty in identifying persons interested in an estate and finality in its distribution. It, however, is by its terms applicable only to wills and to "after-borns" who are children of the testators themselves and not children of third parties. Moreover, the concerns related to winding up a decedent's estate differ from those related to identifying whether a class disposition to a grantor's issue includes a child conceived after the father's death but before the disposition became effective.

With respect to future interests, both the District of Columbia and New York have statutes which ostensibly bear upon the status of a post-conceived child. In the D.C. Code, the one statutory reference to posthumous children appears in section 704 of title 42 which in relevant part provides that, "[w]here a future estate shall be limited to heirs, or issue, or children, posthumous children shall be entitled to take in the same manner as if living at the death of their parent." New York has a very similar statute, which provides in relevant part that, "[w]here a future estate is limited to children, distributees, heirs or issue, posthumous children are entitled to take in the same manner as if living at the death of their ancestors" (EPTL 6-5.7). In addition, EPTL 2-1.3(2) provides that a posthumous child may share as a member of a class if such child was conceived before the disposition became effective.

Each of the above statutes read literally would allow post-conceived children — who are indisputably "posthumous" — to claim benefits as biological offspring. But such statutes were enacted long before anyone anticipated that children could be conceived after the death of the biological parent. In other words, the respective legislatures presumably contemplated that such provisions would apply only to children *en ventre sa mere* (see e.g. Turano, Practice Commentaries, McKinney's Cons. Laws of N.Y., Book 17B, EPTL 6-5.7, at 176).

We turn now to the jurisdictions in which the inheritance rights of a post-conceived child have been directly addressed [by statute or judicial decision, on which see Notes 2 and 3 following *Woodward* at page 125]. . . .

[T]he legislatures and the courts have tried to balance competing interests. On the one hand, certainty and finality are critical to the public interests in the orderly administration of estates. On the other hand, the human desire to have children, albeit by biotechnology, deserves respect, as do the rights of the children born as a result of such scientific advances. To achieve such balance, the statutes, for example, require written consent to the use of genetic material after death and establish a cut-off date by which the child must be conceived. It is noted parenthetically that in this regard an affidavit has been submitted here stating that all of James's cryopreserved sperm has been destroyed, thereby closing the class of his children.

Finally, we turn to the instruments presently before the court. Although it cannot be said that in 1969 the Grantor contemplated that his "issue" or "descendants" would include children who were conceived after his son's death, the absence of specific intent should not necessarily preclude a determination that such children are members of the class of issue. Indeed, it is noted that the Restatement of Property suggests that "[u]nless the language or circumstances indicate that the transferor had a different intention, a child of assisted reproduction [be] treated for class-gift purposes as a child of a person who consented to function as a parent to the child and who functioned in that capacity or was prevented from doing so by an event such as death or incapacity" (Restatement [Third] of Property [Wills and Other Donative Transfers] §14.8 [Tentative Draft No. 4, 2004]).

The rationale of the Restatement . . . should be applied here, namely, if an individual considers a child to be his or her own, society through its laws should do so as well. It is noted that a similar rationale was endorsed by our State's highest court with respect to the beneficial interests of adopted children (Matter of Park, 207 N.E.2d 859 (N.Y. 1965)). Accordingly, in the instant case, these post-conceived infants should be treated as part of their father's family for all purposes. Simply put, where a governing instrument is silent, children born of this new biotechnology with the consent of their parent are entitled to the same rights "for all purposes as those of a natural child."

Although James probably assumed that any children born as a result of the use of his preserved semen would share in his family's trusts, his intention is not controlling here. For purposes of determining the beneficiaries of these trusts, the controlling factor is the Grantor's intent as gleaned from a reading of the trust agreements. Such instruments provide that, upon the death of the Grantor's wife, the trust fund would benefit his sons and their families equally. In view of such overall dispositive scheme, a sympathetic reading of these instruments warrants the conclusion that the Grantor intended all members of his bloodline to receive their share.

Based upon all of the foregoing, it is concluded that James Mitchell and Warren are "issue" and "descendants" for all purposes of these trusts.

As can be seen from all of the above, there is a need for comprehensive legislation to resolve the issues raised by advances in biotechnology. Accordingly, copies of this decision are being sent to the respective Chairs of the Judiciary Committees of the New York State Senate and Assembly.

QUESTIONS AND NOTES

1.   Suppose in *Martin B.* the remainder of James's banked sperm had not been destroyed and ten years later another child was conceived with the sperm and then born alive. Would this child qualify as a beneficiary for future distributions from James's father's trusts? Should the trustee consider the possibility of future, posthumously conceived children in the administration and portfolio management of the trust? Should the courts consider the possibility of future, posthumously conceived children — the possibility of a *fertile decedent* — in applying the Rule Against Perpetuities?

2.   *The 2008 amendments to the UPC.* As revised in 2008, the UPC states a similar rule for posthumous conception and class gifts as its rule for posthumous conception and intestate succession (see Note 3 at page 125). The key difference

is that the focus for class gifts is on the distribution date rather than the date of the parent's death. Thus, a posthumously conceived child of *A* is included in a class gift in a will or trust by *T* to the "children," "issue," "descendants," or "heirs" of *A* if (1) *A* consented to posthumous conception in a signed writing or *A*'s consent is otherwise proved by clear and convincing evidence (§§2-705(b) and 2-120(f)), and (2) the child is living on the distribution date or is in utero not later than 36 months after or is born not later than 45 months after the distribution date (§2-705(g)). If *Martin B.* arose under the UPC as revised in 2008, what result?

3. For further discussion of class closing rules and the new reproductive technologies, see Sheldon F. Kurz and Lawrence W. Waggoner, The UPC Addresses the Class-Gift and Intestacy Rights of Children of Assisted Reproductive Technologies, 35 ACTEC J. 30 (2009); Cameron Krier, Heir on the Side of Exclusion? Addressing the Problems Created by Assisted Reproductive Technologies to the Inheritance Rights of a Class Named in a Funded Trust or Probated Will, 20 Quinnipiac Prob. L.J. 47 (2006); Kristine S. Knaplund, Postmortem Conception and a Father's Last Will, 46 Ariz. L. Rev. 91 (2004).

NOTE: SURROGATE MOTHERHOOD AND MARRIED COUPLES

Who is the parent of a child born by surrogate motherhood? Surrogate motherhood can involve (1) an egg of the wife fertilized by the husband's sperm; (2) an egg of the wife fertilized by the sperm of a third party donor; (3) an egg of the surrogate mother fertilized by the husband's sperm; (4) an egg of a third party donor fertilized by the husband's sperm; or (5) an egg of a third party donor fertilized by the sperm of a third party donor. As you can see, there may be a genetic connection of both husband and wife to the child, or a genetic connection of only one of them to the child, or no genetic connection between the husband and wife and the child. The law is evolving on who is a parent, but courts are by no means in agreement, and many states have neither statutory nor case law on parentage in surrogacy matters. Article 8 of the Uniform Parentage Act (2000, rev. 2002) provides for comprehensive rules on the subject, but those rules have not been widely adopted.

In Johnson v. Calvert, 851 P.2d 776 (Cal. 1993), a husband and wife signed a contract with a woman surrogate providing that an egg of the wife fertilized by the husband's sperm would be implanted in the surrogate woman and, after the child was born, it would be taken into the home of the husband and wife as their child. The surrogate agreed to relinquish all parental rights to the child. The surrogate later changed her mind, claiming parental rights. The court held that parenthood in surrogate mother cases should not be determined by who gave birth or who contributed genetic material, but should turn on the intent of the parties as shown by the surrogacy contract. The court declared the husband and wife the sole parents. But in another jurisdiction the result might have been different. In

Michigan, for example, surrogacy for compensation is illegal, and in a custody dispute over a child born to a surrogate, the dispositive consideration is the best interests of the child. Mich. Comp. Laws §§722.859 and 722.861 (2008).

A more recent example of the difficulties in determining parentage in surrogacy cases is furnished by the so-called Erie Surrogate Triplets. The triplets, conceived from the sperm of the intended father and an unrelated egg donor, were born to a gestational surrogate in 2003. After the surrogate reneged on an agreement with the father and his fiancée to turn the triplets over to them, the surrogate, the father, and the father's fiancée — plus the egg donor, the surrogate's husband, and the company that brought them all together — became embroiled in litigation in various courts in Pennsylvania, Ohio, and Indiana. The result was that the triplets were moved, after two and half years in the surrogate's custody in Pennsylvania, to the custody of the father and his fiancée in Ohio, where the children have had no further contact with the surrogate. For a fuller rendition of the story, with policy analysis, see Robert E. Rains, What the Erie "Surrogate Triplets" Can Teach State Legislatures About the Need to Enact Article 8 of the Uniform Parentage Act (2000), 56 Clev. St. L. Rev. 1 (2008).

In some states, surrogacy agreements are prohibited or are enforceable only under certain specified conditions. This complicates matters. In Hodas v. Morin, 814 N.E.2d 320 (Mass. 2004), the court upheld the choice of Massachusetts law in a surrogacy agreement between a New York surrogate and Connecticut genetic parents, who were married, that called for the child to be born in Massachusetts. The court ruled that this provided a sufficient connection with Massachusetts to justify application of Massachusetts law, which is favorable to surrogacy and allows for a pre-birth declaratory judgment on parentage, in spite of the strong New York public policy against gestational surrogacy agreements.

Is a determination of who is a parent in custody cases and child support cases res judicata as to inheritance rights? Should the policies in the cases cited above, which are heavily influenced by the family law emphasis on the best interests of the child, also govern inheritance? See Lee-ford Tritt, Sperms and Estates: An Unadulterated Functionally Based Approach to Parent-Child Property Succession, 62 SMU L. Rev. 367 (2009).

Under the 2008 amendments to the UPC, inheritance rights turn on whether a parent-child relationship exists (see Note 3 at page 101). With respect to a child born to a surrogate (a "gestational carrier"), UPC §2-121 (2008) provides that in the absence of a court order to the contrary, the surrogate does not have a parent-child relationship with the child unless the surrogate is the child's genetic mother and no one else has a parent-child relationship with the child. An intended parent of the child, meaning a person who entered into an agreement with the surrogate stating that the person would be the parent of the child, has a parent-child relationship with the child if the person functioned as a parent of the child within two years of the child's birth.

For further discussion, see Charles P. Kindregan, Collaborative Reproduction and Rethinking Parentage, 21 J. Am. Acad. Matrimonial L. 43 (2008); Helene S. Shapo, Assisted Reproduction and the Law: Disharmony on a Divisive Social

Issue, 100 Nw. U. L. Rev. 465 (2006); Naomi R. Cahn, Parenthood, Genes, and Gametes: The Family Law and Trusts and Estates Perspectives, 32 U. Mem. L. Rev. 563 (2002); James E. Bailey, An Analytical Framework for Resolving the Issues Raised by the Interaction Between Reproductive Technology and the Law of Inheritance, 47 DePaul L. Rev. 743 (1998); Alexa E. King, Solomon Revisited: Assigning Parenthood in the Context of Collaborative Reproduction, 5 UCLA Women's L.J. 329 (1995).

NOTE: ASSISTED REPRODUCTION AND SAME-SEX COUPLES

In Adoption of Tammy, 619 N.E.2d 315 (Mass. 1993), noted in 107 Harv. L. Rev. 751 (1994), the court approved the adoption of the child, conceived by artificial insemination, of Dr. Susan Love, the eminent breast cancer surgeon, by her lesbian partner, also a surgeon. The court held that both the genetic mother and the adoptive mother had post-adoptive rights and that the adopted child would inherit from and through both mothers as the child of each. But suppose the court did not settle the inheritance rights of the parties. If the genetic mother thereafter died, survived by the child and the adoptive mother, would the child be the genetic mother's heir? See Laura M. Padilla, Flesh of My Flesh But Not My Heir: Unintended Disinheritance, 36 J. Fam. L. 219 (1997). In Elisa B. v. Superior Court, 117 P.3d 660 (Cal. 2005), the court held that a child can have only two parents, but both of those parents can be women. See also K.M. v. E.G., 117 P.3d 673 (Cal. 2005) (holding that "a woman who has supplied her ova to impregnate her lesbian partner in order to produce children who would be raised in their joint home" is a mother of the resulting children).

Under the 2008 amendments to the UPC, a child conceived by assisted reproduction other than gestational surrogacy is in a parent-child relationship (and thus entitled to inherit by, from, or through) the child's birth mother (§2-120(c)). There can also be a parent-child relationship with another person if the other person either consented in writing to assisted reproduction by the birth mother with the intent to be the other parent of the child or functioned as a parent of the child within two years of the child's birth (§2-120(f)). See Sheldon F. Kurz and Lawrence W. Waggoner, The UPC Addresses the Class-Gift and Intestacy Rights of Children of Assisted Reproductive Technologies, 35 ACTEC J. 30 (2009).

For further discussion, see Kathy T. Graham, Same-Sex Couples: Their Rights as Parents, and Their Children's Rights as Children, 48 Santa Clara L. Rev. 999 (2008); Susan Frelich Appleton, Presuming Women: Revisiting the Presumption of Legitimacy in the Same-Sex Couples Era, 86 B.U. L. Rev. 227 (2006); Richard F. Storrow, Parenthood by Pure Intention: Assisted Reproduction and the Functional Approach to Parentage, 53 Hastings L.J. 597 (2002). See also John A. Robertson, Gay and Lesbian Access to Assisted Reproductive Technology, 55 Case W. Res. L. Rev. 323 (2004).

"You just wait until your other mother gets home, young man!"

Drawing by M. Stevens.
© The New Yorker Collection 1994 Mick Stevens from cartoonbank.com.
All Rights Reserved.

2. Advancements

If a child wishes to share in the intestate distribution of a deceased parent's estate, the child must permit the administrator to include in the determination of the distributive shares the value of any property that the decedent, while living, gave the child by way of an *advancement*. At common law, any lifetime gift by the decedent to a child was presumed to be an advancement — in effect, a prepayment — of the child's intestate share. To avoid the application of the doctrine, the child had the burden of establishing that the transfer was intended as an absolute gift that was not to be counted against the child's share of the estate. The doctrine is based on the assumption that the parent would want an equal distribution of assets among the children and that true equality can be reached only if lifetime gifts by the parent are taken into account in determining the amount of the equal shares. When a parent makes an advancement to the child and the child predeceases the parent, the amount of the advancement is deducted from the shares of the child's descendants if other children of the parent survive.

If a gift is treated as an advancement, it is accounted for in distributing the decedent's estate by bringing it into *hotchpot*. Here is how hotchpot works: Assume the decedent leaves no spouse, three children, and an estate worth $50,000. One daughter, *A*, received an advancement of $10,000. To calculate the shares in the estate, the $10,000 gift is added to the $50,000, and the total of $60,000 is divided by three. *A* has already received $10,000 of her share; thus she receives only $10,000 from the estate. Her siblings each take a $20,000 share. If instead *A* had been given property worth $40,000 as an advancement, *A* would not have to give back a portion of this amount (we know that the decedent wanted *A* to have at least $40,000). *A* will stay out of hotchpot, and decedent's $50,000 will be equally divided between the other two children.

QUESTIONS AND PROBLEMS

1.   Suppose that *O* has two children, *A* and *B*. *A* owns a successful business. *B* is a single parent who struggles to make ends meet. *O* makes regular gifts to *B*, but not to *A*, because *B* is in greater need. If *O*'s lifetime transfers to *B* are deemed to be advancements, then *A* will inherit more than *B* on the death of *O*. Is this result consistent with *O*'s probable intent? Why does the law regard favorable lifetime treatment of a child as a reason to disfavor that child at the parent's death? Is not favorable lifetime treatment good evidence that the decedent would have wanted the favored child to receive at least the same share of her estate as her other children? The common law of advancements answers this question in the negative.

2.   *O* has three children. One daughter, *A*, does not leave home but lives with *O* on *O*'s farm until *O* dies. A few years before death, *O* deeds the farm to *A*. *O* dies intestate. *A* claims the gift is not an advancement but an extra gift for extraordinary services rendered to *O*. What result? See Thomas v. Thomas, 398 S.W.2d 231 (Ky. 1965).

Suppose that *O* gives his son, *B*, $20,000. *B* is ill and unable to work and support his family. Is this an advancement?

Suppose that *O*'s daughter, *C*, goes to Yale Medical School and earns a medical degree. *O* pays the tuition. Is this an advancement?

Largely because of problems of proof of the donor's intent, many states have reversed the common law presumption of advancement. In these states, a lifetime gift is presumed *not* to be an advancement unless it is shown to have been intended as such. Some states and UPC §2-109(a) (1990) go even further, requiring that the intention to make an advancement be declared in a writing signed by the grantor or grantee. See also Restatement (Third) of Property: Wills and Other Donative Transfers §2.6 (1999), to similar effect.

Uniform Probate Code (1990)

§2-109. ADVANCEMENTS

(a) If an individual dies intestate as to all or a portion of his [or her] estate, property the decedent gave during the decedent's lifetime to an individual who, at the decedent's death, is an heir[19] is treated as an advancement against the heir's intestate share only if (i) the decedent declared in a contemporaneous writing or the heir acknowledged in writing that the gift is an advancement or (ii) the decedent's contemporaneous writing or the heir's written acknowledgment otherwise indicates that the gift is to be taken into account in computing the division and distribution of the decedent's intestate estate.

(b) For purposes of subsection (a), property advanced is valued as of the time the heir came into possession or enjoyment of the property or as of the time of the decedent's death, whichever first occurs.

(c) If the recipient of the property fails to survive the decedent, the property is not taken into account in computing the division and distribution of the decedent's intestate estate, unless the decedent's contemporaneous writing provides otherwise.

_____

UPC §2-109(c) changes the common law rule if the recipient does not survive the decedent. In that case, under the UPC the advancement is not taken into account in determining the share of the recipient's descendants.

Requiring a writing to evidence an advancement in effect all but eliminates the doctrine of advancements from the law of intestate succession. The upshot is that this avoids contentious litigation between family members about little-remembered lifetime gifts. The downside is that persons who do not write wills or consult lawyers and die intestate will rarely know that a lifetime gift must be stated in writing to be an advancement to be charged against the donee's intestate share. See Mary L. Fellows, Concealing Legislative Reform in the Common-Law Tradition: The Advancements Doctrine and the Uniform Probate Code, 37 Vand. L. Rev. 671 (1984), proposing a statute requiring *all* gifts be treated as advancements absent written evidence of a contrary intent (the opposite of the UPC).

QUESTION

Which of the following rules do you think is best?

1. Gifts to children are presumptively advancements.
2. Gifts to children are presumptively not advancements.

_____

19. UPC §2-109 applies to advancements made to spouses and collaterals (such as nephews and nieces) as well as to lineal descendants. In most states, only gifts to lineal descendants are considered advancements. — Eds.

3. Gifts to children are not advancements unless stated in writing to be advancements.

4. Gifts to children are advancements unless stated in writing not to be advancements.

3.   *Guardianship and Conservatorship of Minors*

A minor has neither the legal capacity to manage property nor the legal power to make most choices about how and where to live. Clients with young children should be advised to provide for the possibility that their children might be orphaned — a possibility that must be confronted by rich and poor clients alike. It is now time to speak of guardians, conservators, and how best to avoid them if possible.

a.   Guardian of the Person

A guardian of the person has responsibility for the minor child's custody and care. As long as one parent of the child is living and competent, that parent is the natural guardian of the child's person. Hence, if only one of two parents dies, there is no need to appoint a guardian of the person (though there may be a need for a conservator or guardian of the property). If both parents die while a child is a minor and their wills do not designate a guardian, the court will appoint a guardian of the person, usually from among the nearest relatives. This person may not be whom the parents would want to have custody of the child.

Accordingly, for a parent with a minor child, one of the principal reasons for making a will is to designate a guardian of the person for the child. Most testators select a family member, often a sibling, or sometimes a friend. It is a good practice also to select an alternate. The guardian of the person for the minor decides where the minor lives, how the minor is raised and educated, and when the minor receives medical care. A guardianship of the person terminates when the minor reaches the age of majority, dies, or is adopted.

Guardianship of the person for a minor is covered by UPC §§5-201 through 5-210 (1998), which are based on the Uniform Guardianship and Protective Proceedings Act (1997).

b.   Property Management Options

Another important reason that a parent with a minor child should have a will is to deal with the management of the child's property. A guardian of the person has no authority to deal with the child's property.

Several alternatives for property management are available: guardianship of the property, conservatorship, custodianship, and trusteeship. Trusts are available only to persons who create them during life or who die testate and create one by will. If a parent dies intestate, leaving property to a minor child, a guardian of the property or a conservator must be appointed by a court, unless state law allows payment instead to a custodian under the Uniform Transfers to Minors Act or to the person who has physical custody of the child. Let us examine these alternatives for managing a minor's property.

(1) Guardianship of the property

In feudal times the guardian of a minor ward (usually the overlord) took possession of the ward's lands. The guardian had the duty of supporting the ward, but all income from rents in excess of the amount necessary for support belonged to the guardian personally. Thus guardianships (then known as wardships) were very profitable for the guardian.

After the feudal incidents, including wardship, were abolished in 1660, a new kind of guardianship was recognized, giving the ward the rents from the property and the guardian only a management fee. Nonetheless, the historical odor remained. A guardian of property was looked upon with suspicion and was required to account annually to a court of chancery. To avoid a disagreeable contest later with the ward or chancellor, guardians sought approval for their actions in advance from the chancellor. The product of this history is a system wherein the guardian is straitjacketed and the process is expensive.

The guardian of property, who does not have title to the ward's property, usually cannot change investments without a court order. The guardian has the duty of preserving the specific property left to the minor and delivering it to the ward at age 18, unless the court approves a sale, lease, or mortgage. The guardian ordinarily can use only the income from the property to support the ward; the guardian needs court approval to go into principal to support the ward. Strict court supervision over many of the guardian's acts is burdensome and time-consuming. Each trip to court incurs attorney's fees and court costs. The ward may end up with less property at the end of a guardianship than at the beginning.

In sum, guardianship for a minor's property is somewhat like going through a continuous probate until the child reaches the age of majority. It should be avoided.

(2) Conservatorship

The expense and inflexibility of a guardianship for property has led to a major reform — its replacement with a *conservator* system. Following the lead of UPC Article V (1998) and the Uniform Guardianship and Protective Proceeding Act

(1997), in many states guardianship laws have been revised to allow a more trust-like arrangement. The guardian of the property has been renamed the *conservator* and given "title as trustee" to the protected person's property, as well as investment powers similar to those of trustees. Appointment and supervision by a court is still required, but the conservator has far more flexible powers than a guardian, and only one trip to the courthouse annually for an accounting may be necessary.

The conservatorship system permits a more streamlined administration of the estate, allowing a higher net return on the assets, more flexibility in investments, and a greater chance of meeting the financial needs of the child, both while a minor and on termination of the conservatorship. The conservatorship terminates when the minor reaches the age of majority or dies before then. UPC §5-431 (1998).

In states without modern conservatorship laws, the only effective way to handle guardianship administrations is to avoid them. And, indeed, we suggest that even in states with modern conservatorship laws, the alternative arrangements of custodianship or trusteeship for a minor are preferable because the court does not become involved unless the minor contests the custodian's or trustee's actions.

(3) Custodianship

A *custodian* is a person who is given property to hold for the benefit of a minor under the Uniform Transfers to Minors Act (UTMA) (1983, rev. 1986) or its predecessor, the Uniform Gifts to Minors Act (UGMA) (1956, rev. 1966). Under these acts, some form of which has been enacted in every state, property may be transferred to a person (including the donor) as *custodian* for the benefit of the minor. A devise or gift may be made "to *X* as custodian for (name of minor) under the (name of state) Uniform Transfers to Minors Act," thereby incorporating the provisions of the state's uniform act and eliminating the necessity of drafting a trust instrument. Often the donor will choose herself as custodian for the minor, whether the donor is related to the minor or not. When setting up a custodianship, remember to use the minor's Social Security number to identify the account, so that any interest or other income will not be reported to the IRS as if it were the custodian's personal income.

The creation of a custodianship is thus quite simple. Most banks, brokers, and other financial institutions have standard forms that can be filled out by a donor making a gift to a minor or by a fiduciary making a distribution to a minor. Well-drafted wills and trusts often include a *facility of payment clause* under which assets to be distributed outright to a minor may be paid instead to a custodian or even to the parent or guardian of the minor. Even if there is no will or trust or the will or trust does not expressly authorize payment to the child's parents, many states have laws permitting a fiduciary to pay small sums to the custodial parent or to an account in the child's name alone without requiring the appointment of a guardian or conservator. See UPC §5-104 (1998) (sums not exceeding $5,000 per year).

If no such power to transfer assets to a custodian is given in a will or trust, the UTMA, but not the earlier UGMA, allows the fiduciary to make payments to a custodian nonetheless. UTMA §6. Payments to custodians over $10,000, however, require court approval.

Under UTMA §14(a), the custodian has discretionary power to expend

> for the minor's benefit so much of the custodial property as the custodian considers advisable for the use and benefit of the minor, without court order and without regard to (i) the duty or ability of the custodian personally or any other person to support the minor, or (ii) any other income or property of the minor which may be applicable or available for that purpose.

To the extent that the custodial property is not so expended, the custodian is required to transfer the property to the minor on his attaining the age of 18 or 21, depending on the circumstances, or, if the minor dies before attaining the age of 18 or 21, to the estate of the minor.

The custodian has the right to manage the property and to reinvest it. However, the custodian is a fiduciary and is subject to "the standard of care that would be observed by a prudent person dealing with property of another." UTMA §12(b). The custodian is not under the supervision of a court — as is a guardian or conservator — and no accounting to the court annually or at the end of the custodianship is necessary, but an interested party may require one if he wishes. UTMA §§12(e) and 19. A custodianship is ideal for modest gifts to a minor and is helpful in other cases when used to avoid a conservatorship or guardianship, but when a large amount of property is involved, a trust is usually preferable.

For further discussion, see Stephanie E. Heilborn and Jonathan G. Blattmachr, Planning with UTMA Accounts and Other Transfers to Minors: Part I, 34 Est. Plan. 3 (Dec. 2007), Part II, 35 Est. Plan. 11 (Jan. 2008); Jani Maurer, Uniform Transfers to Minors Act Accounts — Progress, Potential, and Pitfalls, 28 Nova L. Rev. 745 (2004).

(4) Trusts

The fourth alternative for property management on behalf of a minor is to establish a trust. A trust is the most flexible of all property arrangements, and much of the latter part of this book (see Chapters 8-14) is devoted to the law of trusts. The donor can tailor the trust specifically to family circumstances and the donor's particular desires. Under a guardianship or conservatorship, the child must receive the property at 18 and, under a custodianship, at 18 or 21, but a trust can postpone possession until the donor thinks the child is competent to manage the property. For an examination of guardianship, custodianship, and trusts, concluding that the last is preferable in most situations, see William M. McGovern, Jr., Trusts, Custodianships, and Durable Powers of Attorney, 27 Real Prop., Prob. & Tr. J. 1 (1992).

Even when a person has no children or the person's children are fully grown, most well-designed estate plans provide for a contingent trust in the event that there is a minor beneficiary, perhaps because a named adult beneficiary predeceases the testator, leaving a minor child as a substitute taker. As a result, in many law firms there is no such thing as a simple will. A well-drafted will should account for the possibility of a minor beneficiary, and in almost all cases the best way to do so is with a trust.

PROBLEM

Refer back to the estate planning problem involving Howard and Wendy Brown (pages 49-58). Assume that Howard Brown dies intestate. After payment of debts, taxes, and expenses of administration, the assets of his estate include:

	Property acquired from H's earnings during marriage[20]	*H's property acquired by gift*[20]
Tangible personalty:	$ 20,000	
Real estate:		
Residence (title is in "Howard Brown and Wendy Brown, as joint tenants with right of survivorship and not as tenants in common"); subject to mortgage of $70,000	160,000	
Lot and cabin, Lake Murray (title is in Howard alone)	75,000	
Remainder interest in mother's home		$20,000
Bank accounts:		
Checking (joint and survivor account with wife)	3,000	
Certificate of deposit ("Howard Brown and Wendy Brown, as joint tenants with right of survivorship")	20,000	
IRA (Howard's, payable on death to Wendy)	30,000	

20. The source of the property is irrelevant for intestate distribution in common law property states; how title is held at death is controlling. In community property states, property acquired from a spouse's earnings during marriage is community property and at the spouse's death passes under a different intestate scheme from separate property.

Securities:
  General Corp. stock (registered
     in Howard's name)   80,000
  Varoom Mutual Fund
     (registered in Howard's name)   30,000
    American Growth Mutual Fund
      ("Howard Brown and Wendy
      Brown, as joint tenants with
      right of survivorship and not
      as tenants in common")   40,000
Life insurance:
  (Wendy is named primary
    beneficiary; Howard's estate
    is named contingent
    beneficiary)   125,000
                                          $473,000 $130,000

Howard is survived by his wife and two minor children and a stepson. How is Howard's estate distributed under the UPC? Under the intestacy statute of your state? Should Howard have left a will?

AN EXERCISE IN LAWYERING

Wendy Brown writes you:

> Dear _____:
>
> We've had some changes in our family since we wrote our wills and our wills need changing.
> Two months ago our son, Zachary, was born. A bundle of joy — and sleepless nights! As you know, Howard and I want our property to go to the survivor, and the main reason for having wills is to provide for the children in case we die in a common disaster or before the survivor can make a will for the children.
> You drafted our wills to create a trust for our children if we die and a child is under 25. Do you think we should continue to have a single trust for all the children or should we have separate trusts for each child, permitting each child to receive the principal of the child's trust upon reaching 25? Is a "family trust" or separate trusts fairer to our newborn son? What are the pros and cons of these?
> Another problem is that my sister Lucy has separated from her husband, Jonathan, and has taken up with a man we don't like at all, Bill Hyde. She says she intends to marry him. Bill is a slick operator with a mysterious source of income. We're sick over this, because we love Lucy and hate for her to get mixed up with this guy. But if she marries Bill, we wouldn't want our children to move into their home if we die in a common disaster. My brother Simon and his wife Antonia don't have children, they both work, and wouldn't want to be in charge of a baby. Ruth is always off on digs in Turkey. Do you have any advice about who should be guardian for our children?

I enclose a copy of Howard's will that you drafted. Mine is the same, with appropriate changes in names, and except for the gift of his mother's house. Please give us your advice about these two matters.

Sincerely,

/s/ *Wendy Brown*
_____
Wendy Brown

[For more on Wendy and Howard Brown's family, see pages 49-50.]

Will of Howard Brown
(With Testamentary Trust)

ARTICLE 1

I, Howard Brown, hereby make my will, and I revoke all other wills and codicils that I have previously made.

ARTICLE 2

I give all my jewelry, clothing, household furniture and furnishings, personal automobiles, books, and other tangible articles of a household or personal nature, or my interest in any such property, not otherwise specifically disposed of by this or in any other manner, together with any insurance on the property, to my wife, Wendy Brown, if she survives me; but if my wife does not survive me, then to my children who survive me, in substantially equal shares as they may select on the basis of valuation. These gifts shall be free of all death taxes.

The executor shall represent any child under age 18 in matters relating to any distribution of tangible personal property, including selecting the assets that shall constitute that child's share. In the executor's absolute discretion, the executor may (1) sell all or part of such child's share which the executor deems unsuitable for the child's use, (2) distribute the proceeds to the Children's Trust or share of such trust for the child's benefit, or (3) deliver the unsold property without bond to the minor if sufficiently mature or to any suitable person with whom the child resides or who has control or care of the child.

ARTICLE 3

I give all my right, title, and interest in my mother's house at 423 Elm St., Concord, Delaware, to my sister Carol Gould.

ARTICLE 4

I give the residue of my estate to my wife, Wendy Brown, if she survives me. If my wife does not survive me and all my children are 25 years of age or older at my death, I give the residue of my estate to my children and to the descendants of any then-deceased child by right of representation. If my wife does not survive me and any of my children is under the age of 25 at my death, I give the residue of my estate to the trustee of the Children's Trust set forth in Article 5.

ARTICLE 5

The trustee of the Children's Trust shall hold, administer, and distribute all property allocated to the Children's Trust for the benefit of my children as follows: The trustee shall pay to or for any child as much of the income as is necessary for the child's health, education, support, or maintenance to maintain the child's accustomed manner of living. The trustee shall add to principal any net income not so distributed.

If the trustee considers the income insufficient, the trustee shall pay to or for a child as much of the principal as the trustee considers reasonably necessary for the child's health, education, support, maintenance, comfort, welfare, or happiness to maintain, at a minimum, the child's accustomed manner of living.

In making distributions, the trustee (1) may consider any other income or resources of the child, including the child's ability to obtain gainful employment and the obligation of others to support the child, known to the trustee and reasonably available for the purposes stated here; (2) may pay more to or apply more for some children than others and may make payments to or applications of benefits for one or more children to the exclusion of others; (3) may consider the value of the trust assets, the relative needs, both present and future, of each child, and the tax consequences to the trust and to any child; and (4) shall charge distributions of income and principal against the entire trust estate and not against the share of the child to whom or for whom the distribution was made.

The trustee, in the trustee's reasonable discretion, may from time to time make preliminary distributions of principal to any of my children who have attained the age of 25, if the trustee finds valid and productive reasons for making the distribution, such as the purchase of a residence or establishment of a business, and if the remaining principal and income will be adequate for the health, support, maintenance, and education of my other children. The trustee shall deduct such preliminary distributions without interest from the share ultimately distributed to such child or to such child's descendants. In the aggregate, the value of any preliminary distributions shall not exceed 50 percent of that child's putative share. The term *putative share* shall mean that portion of the entire trust estate that would be distributable to a particular child, after considering all previous loans and advances, if the entire trust were divided into separate trusts on the date that the distribution to be measured against the putative share is made.

When every child of mine has reached the age of 25 or died before reaching that age, the trustee shall divide the trust into as many equal shares as there are children of mine then living and children of mine then deceased with descendants then living.

On the division of the Children's Trust into shares, the trustee shall distribute each living child's share outright to the child and each deceased child's share to the deceased child's then-living descendants by right of representation.

ARTICLE 6

I nominate as trustee of the Children's Trust Lucy Preston Lipman. If Lucy Preston Lipman fails to qualify or ceases to act, I nominate as successor trustee [the lawyer who drew this will].

The trustee may employ custodians, attorneys, accountants, investment advisers, corporate fiduciaries, or any other agents or advisers to assist the trustee in the administration of this trust, and the trustee may rely on the advice given by these agents. The trustee shall pay reasonable compensation for all services performed by these agents from the trust estate out of either income or principal as the trustee in the trustee's reasonable discretion shall determine. These payments shall not decrease the compensation of the trustee.

No trustee shall be liable to any person interested in this trust for any act or default unless it results from the trustee's bad faith, willful misconduct, or gross negligence.

The trustee shall have the power to continue to hold any property or to abandon any property that the trustee receives or acquires.

The trustee shall have the power to retain, purchase, or otherwise acquire unproductive property.

The trustee shall have the power to manage, control, grant options on, sell (for cash or on deferred payments with or without security), convey, exchange, partition, divide, improve, and repair trust property.

The trustee shall have the power to lease trust property for terms within or beyond the terms of the trust and for any purpose, including exploration for and removal of gas, oil, and other minerals, and to enter into oil leases, pooling, and utilization agreements.

The trustee shall have the power to invest and reinvest the trust estate in every kind of property, real, personal, or mixed, and every kind of investment, specifically including, but not by way of limitation, corporate obligations of every kind, preferred or common stocks, shares in investment trusts, investment companies, mutual funds, money market funds, index funds, and mortgage participations, which persons of prudence, discretion, and intelligence acquire for their own account, and any common trust fund administered by the trustee.

The trustee shall have all the rights, powers, and privileges of an owner of the securities held in trust, including, but not by way of limitation, the power to vote, give proxies, and pay assessments; the power to participate in voting trusts and pooling agreements (whether or not extending beyond the terms of the trust); the power to enter into shareholders' agreements; the power to consent to foreclosure, reorganizations, consolidations, merger liquidations, sales, and leases, and, incident to any such action, to deposit securities with and transfer title to any protective or other committee on such terms as the trustee may deem advisable; and the power to exercise or sell stock subscription or conversion rights.

The trustee shall have the power to hold securities or other property in the trustee's name as trustee under this trust, in the trustee's own name, in the name of a nominee, or in unregistered form so that ownership will pass by delivery.

The trustee shall have the power to carry, at the expense of the trust, insurance of such kinds and in such amounts as the trustee deems advisable to protect the trust estate against any damage or loss and to protect the trustee against liability with respect to third parties.

The trustee shall have the power to loan to any person, including a trust beneficiary or the estate of a trust beneficiary, at interest rates and with or without security as the trustee deems advisable.

Upon termination of the trust, the approval of the accounts of the trustee in an instrument signed by all the adult beneficiaries and guardians of any minor beneficiaries shall be a complete discharge and release of the trustee with respect to the administration of the trust property and shall be binding on all persons.

ARTICLE 7

If my wife, Wendy Brown, does not survive me and if at my death any of my children are minors, I nominate as guardian of the persons and the property of my minor children Lucy Preston Lipman.

ARTICLE 8

The terms *child* and *children* as used in this will refer to my stepson, Michael Walker, and to my children, Sarah Brown and Stephanie Brown, and also to any child or children hereafter born to me.

ARTICLE 9

I nominate as executor of this will my wife, Wendy Brown. If for any reason she fails to qualify or ceases to act I nominate Lucy Preston Lipman to serve as executor.

My executor shall have the same powers granted the trustee under Article 6 to be exercised without court order, as well as any other powers that may be granted by law. I direct that no bond or other security shall be required of any person, including nonresidents named in this will, acting as executor, trustee, or guardian.

I have signed this will, which is typewritten on _____ sheets of paper, on this _____ day of _____, 20 _____, and, for the purposes of identification, I have also written my name on the margin of all pages before this signature page.

_____
Howard Brown

On the _____ day of _____, 20 _____, Howard Brown declared to us, the undersigned, that the foregoing instrument was his last will, and he requested us to act as witnesses to it and to his signature thereon. He then signed the will in our presence, we being present at the same time. We now, at his request, in his presence, and in the presence of each other, hereunto subscribe our names as witnesses, and each of us declares that in his or her opinion this testator is of sound and disposing mind and memory.

_____	_____
Name	Address
_____	_____
Name	Address

QUESTIONS

Note the contingent trust for children in Article 4 of Howard Brown's will. Why do you think 25 is the contingent age, rather than 18 or 21? Is the contingency, limited only to Howard's children under 25, broad enough? Suppose Howard's only surviving beneficiary is a minor grandchild. Would Howard's devise of his entire estate to that minor grandchild trigger a conservatorship? How might Article 4 be redrafted to deal with this problem?

SECTION C.   BARS TO SUCCESSION

1.   *Homicide*

In re Estate of Mahoney
Supreme Court of Vermont, 1966
220 A.2d 475

SMITH, J.   The decedent, Howard Mahoney, died intestate on May 6, 1961, of gunshot wounds. His wife, Charlotte Mahoney, the appellant here, was tried for the murder of Howard Mahoney in the Addison County Court and was convicted by jury of the crime of manslaughter in March, 1962. She is presently serving a sentence of not less than 12 nor more than 15 years at the Women's Reformatory in Rutland.

Howard Mahoney left no issue, and was survived by his wife and his father and mother. His father, Mark Mahoney, was appointed administrator of his estate which at the present time amounts to $3,885.89. After due notice and hearing, the Probate Court for the District of Franklin entered a judgment order decreeing the residue of the Estate of Howard Mahoney, in equal shares, to the father and mother of the decedent. An appeal from the judgment order and decree has been taken here by the appellant widow. The question submitted is whether a widow convicted of manslaughter in connection with the death of her husband may inherit from his estate.

The general rules of descent provide that if a decedent is married and leaves no issue, his surviving spouse shall be entitled to the whole of decedent's estate if it does not exceed $8,000. 14 Va. Stat. Ann. (V.S.A.) §551(2). Only if the decedent leaves no surviving spouse or issue does the estate descend in equal shares to the surviving father and mother. 14 V.S.A. §551(3). There is no statutory provision in Vermont regulating the descent and distribution of property from the decedent to the slayer. The question presented is one of first impression in this jurisdiction.

In a number of jurisdictions, statutes have been enacted which in certain instances, at least, prevent a person who has killed another from taking by descent or distribution from the person he has killed. . . .

Courts in those states that have no statute preventing a slayer from taking by descent or distribution from the estate of his victim, have followed three separate and different lines of decision.

(1) The legal title passed to the slayer and may be retained by him in spite of his crime. The reasoning for so deciding is that devolution of the property of a decedent is controlled entirely by the statutes of descent and distribution; further, that denial of the inheritance to the slayer because of his crime would be imposing an additional punishment for his crime not provided by statute, and would violate the constitutional provision against corruption of blood. Carpenter's Estate, 32 A. 637 (Pa. 1895); Wall v. Pfanschmidt, 106 N.E. 785 (Ill. 1914); Bird v. Plunkett et al., 95 A.2d 71 (Conn. 1953).

(2) The legal title will not pass to the slayer because of the equitable principle that no one should be permitted to profit by his own fraud, or take advantage and profit as a result of his own wrong or crime. Riggs v. Palmer, 22 N.E. 188 (N.Y. 1889); Price v. Hitaffer, 165 A. 470 (Md. 1933); Slocum v. Metropolitan Life Ins., 139 N.E. 816 (Mass. 1923). Decisions so holding have been criticized as judicially engrafting an exception on the statute of descent and distribution and being "unwarranted judicial legislation." Wall v. Pfanschmidt, supra.

(3) The legal title passes to the slayer but equity holds him to be a constructive trustee for the heirs or next of kin of the decedent. This disposition of the question presented avoids a judicial engrafting on the statutory laws of descent and distribution, for title passes to the slayer. But because of the unconscionable mode by which the property is acquired by the slayer, equity treats him as a constructive trustee and compels him to convey the property to the heirs or next of kin of the deceased.

The reasoning behind the adoption of this doctrine was well expressed by Mr. Justice Cardozo in his lecture on "The Nature of the Judicial Process." "Consistency was preserved, logic received its tribute, by holding that the legal title passed, but it was subject to a constructive trust. A constructive trust is nothing but 'the formula through which the conscience of equity finds expression.' Property is acquired in such circumstances that the holder of legal title may not in good conscience retain the beneficial interest. Equity, to express its disapproval of his conduct, converts him into a trustee."

The New Hampshire court was confronted with the same problem of the rights to the benefits of an estate by one who had slain the decedent, in the absence of a statute on the subject. Kelley v. State, 196 A.2d 68 (N.H. 1963). Speaking for an unanimous court, Chief Justice Kenison said: "But, even in the absence of statute, a court applying common law techniques can reach a sensible solution by charging the spouse, heir or legatee as a constructive trustee of the property where equity and justice demand it." Kelley v. State, supra, at 69-70. We approve of the doctrine so expressed.

However, the principle that one should not profit by his own wrong must not be extended to every case where a killer acquires property from his victim as a result of the killing. One who has killed while insane is not chargeable as a constructive trustee, or if the slayer had a vested interest in the property, it is property to which he would have been entitled if no slaying had occurred. The principle to be applied is that the slayer should not be permitted to improve his position by the killing, but should not be compelled to surrender property to which he would have been entitled if there had been no killing. The doctrine of constructive trust is involved to prevent the slayer from profiting from his crime, but not as an added criminal penalty. Kelley v. State, supra, at 70; Restatement of Restitution, §187(2), Comment a.

The appellant here was, as we have noted, convicted of manslaughter and not of murder. She calls to our attention that while the Restatement of Restitution approves the application of the constructive trust doctrine where a devisee or legatee murders the testator, that such rules are not applicable where the slayer was guilty of manslaughter. Restatement of Restitution, §187, Comment e.

The cases generally have not followed this limitation of the rule but hold that the line should not be drawn between murder and manslaughter, but between voluntary and involuntary manslaughter. Kelley v. State, supra; Chase v. Jennifer, 150 A.2d 251, 254 (Md. 1959).

We think that this is the proper rule to follow. Voluntary manslaughter is an intentional and unlawful killing, with a real design and purpose to kill, even if such killing be the result of sudden passion or great provocation. Involuntary manslaughter is caused by an unlawful act, but not accompanied with any intention to take life. State v. McDonnell, 32 Vt. 491, 545 (1860). It is the intent to kill, which when accomplished, leads to the profit of the slayer that brings into play the constructive trust to prevent the unjust enrichment of the slayer by reason of his intentional killing.

In Vermont, an indictment for murder can result in a jury conviction on either voluntary or involuntary manslaughter. State v. Averill, 81 A. 461 (Vt. 1911). The legislature has provided the sentences that may be passed upon a person convicted of manslaughter, but provides no definition of that offense, nor any statutory distinction between voluntary and involuntary manslaughter. 13 V.S.A. §2304.

The cause now before us is here on a direct appeal from the probate court. Findings of fact were made below from which it appears that the judgment of the probate court decreeing the estate of Howard Mahoney to his parents, rather than to his widow, was based upon a finding of the felonious killing of her husband by Mrs. Mahoney. However, the appellees here have asked us to affirm the decree below by imposing a constructive trust on the estate in the hands of the widow.

But the Probate Court did not decree the estate to the widow, and then make her a constructive trustee of such estate for the benefit of the parents. The judgment below decreed the estate directly to the parents, which was in direct contravention of the statutes of descent and distribution. The Probate Court was bound to follow the statutes of descent and distribution and its decree was in error and must be reversed.

The Probate Court was without jurisdiction to impose a constructive trust on the estate in the hands of the appellant, even if it had attempted to do so. Probate courts are courts of special and limited jurisdiction given by statute and do not [have powers to establish] . . . purely equitable rights and claims. . . .

However, the jurisdiction of the court of chancery may be invoked in probate matters in aid of the probate court when the powers of that court are inadequate, and it appears that the probate court cannot reasonably and adequately handle the question. The jurisdiction of the chancery court in so acting on probate matters is special and limited only to aiding the probate court. The Probate Court, in making its decree, used the record of the conviction of the appellant for manslaughter for its determination that the appellant had feloniously killed her husband. If the jurisdiction of the court of chancery is invoked by the appellees here it will be for the determination of that court, upon proof, to determine whether the appellant wilfully killed her late husband, as it will upon all other equitable considerations that may be offered in evidence, upon charging the appellant with a constructive trust. "The fact that he is convicted of murder in a criminal case does not dispense with the necessity of proof of the murder in a proceedings in equity to charge him as a constructive trustee." Restatement of Restitution, §187, Comment d.

The jurisdiction over charging the appellant with a constructive trust on the estate of Howard Mahoney lies in the court of chancery, and not in the probate court.

Decree reversed and cause remanded, with directions that the proceedings herein be stayed for sixty days to give the Administrator of the Estate of Howard Mahoney an opportunity to apply to the Franklin County Court of Chancery for relief. If application is so made, proceedings herein shall be stayed pending the final determination thereof. If application is not so made, the Probate Court for the District of Franklin shall assign to Charlotte Mahoney, surviving wife, the right and interest in and to the estate of her deceased husband which the Vermont Statutes confer.[21]

PROBLEMS, QUESTIONS, AND NOTES

1. Can a donor opt out of the slayer rules? Suppose *H*, aware of his wife *W*'s psychological instability, provides in his will that *W* should receive his entire estate even if *W* kills him. *W* then kills *H*. Does *W* take? In Wisconsin — but only in Wisconsin — the answer appears to be Yes. See Wis. Stat. Ann. §854.14(6)(b) (2008); Anne-Marie Rhodes, Consequences of Heirs' Misconduct: Moving from Rules to Discretion, 33 Ohio N.U. L. Rev. 975, 980-982 (2007). See also Marie Louise Fellows, The Slayer Rule: Not Solely a Matter of Equity, 71 Iowa L. Rev. 489 (1986).

Suppose *H* suffers from a painful and terminal illness. At *H*'s request, *W* helps *H* commit suicide. Can *W* take from *H*'s estate? See In re Estate of Schunk, 760 N.W.2d 446 (Wis. App. 2008). See also Jeffrey G. Sherman, Mercy Killing and the Right to Inherit, 61 U. Cin. L. Rev. 803 (1993).

2. Nearly every state has enacted a statute dealing with the rights of a killer in the estate of the victim, but these statutes vary in the details and usually leave gaps to be resolved by the courts. Among the many issues arising under these statutes, the following appear to give rise to the most litigation:

(a) *Does the statute apply to nonprobate transfers (joint tenancy, life insurance, pensions, and so on) as well as to wills and intestacy?* If the statute applies only to the latter, will a court nonetheless apply to nonprobate transfers a common law slayer's rule or a constructive trust to prevent the beneficiary from profiting by killing? UPC §2-803 (1990, rev. 1997), a well-drafted slayer statute, bars the killer from succeeding to nonprobate as well as probate property. It also provides that a "wrongful acquisition" of property must be treated in accordance with the equitable principle that a killer cannot profit from his wrong.

(b) *If the killer is barred from taking, who takes?* The usual view is that the killer is treated as having predeceased the victim. UPC §2-803 provides that the killer is treated as having disclaimed the property, and under the UPC disclaimer statute, §2-1106 (2002, rev. 2006), the disclaimant is treated as having "died immediately before the time of distribution." The question thus arises: If the killer is treated as having predeceased the victim, should a court give effect to a substitute gift in the killer's descendants or other heirs?

In Estate of Covert, 761 N.E.2d 571 (N.Y. 2001), Edward fatally shot his wife, Kathleen, and then turned the gun on himself, completing the tragic murder-suicide. Applying the New York slayer rule of Riggs v. Palmer, 22

---

21. In 1972, a statute was enacted in Vermont providing that an heir, devisee, or legatee who "stands convicted in any court . . . of intentionally and unlawfully killing the decedent" shall forfeit any share in the decedent's estate. Vt. Stat. Ann. tit. 14, §551(6) (2008). — Eds.

N.E. 188 (N.Y. 1889), which was famously defended by Justice Cardozo in The Nature of the Judicial Process 40-43 (1921), the court held that Edward could not take from Kathleen's estate. However, because Edward's devisees were innocent of Edward's crime, the court allowed them to take from Kathleen's estate.

Some states take a different approach. California, Rhode Island, and Virginia extend the bar by statute to the killer's descendants. Other states limit the right of the killer's descendants to take by case law. In Estate of Mueller, 655 N.E.2d 1040 (Ill. App. 1995), the decedent by will left 60 percent of his estate to his second wife and, if she predeceased him, to her children by a prior marriage. The husband was killed by a man solicited by the wife to commit the murder. The wife was barred under Illinois's slayer statute, which provided that the killer should be treated as having predeceased the victim. The court refused to apply the statute literally on the ground that this might result in the killer profiting from her wrong (inheriting from her daughters). The court held the devised property passed to the decedent's heirs. In dicta, however, the court suggested that a gift over to the killer's heirs in a will would be given effect if the killer's heirs were also the victim's heirs. But see Cook v. Grierson, 845 A.2d 1231 (Md. 2004) (intestate decedent's grandchildren cannot inherit because their father, decedent's son, was alive even though father was barred from taking as slayer).

For further discussion, see Karen J. Sneddon, Should Cain's Children Inherit Abel's Property?: Wading Into the Extended Slayer Rule Quagmire, 76 UMKC L. Rev. 101 (2007).

(c) *Is a criminal conviction required?* UPC §2-803(g) provides that a final criminal conviction of a felonious and intentional killing is conclusive. Acquittal, however, is not dispositive of the acquitted individual's status as a slayer. In the absence of a conviction, upon application of an interested person, the court must determine whether, under the preponderance of evidence standard (not the criminal law standard of beyond a reasonable doubt), the individual would be found criminally accountable for the killing. If so found, the individual is barred. The reason for using a civil standard of evidence is that probate law is concerned about a killer not profiting from her wrong, whereas criminal law is concerned with protection of the accused. Where the killer commits suicide, the killer's estate may still be barred under this section.

The UPC section appears to follow the majority view. See In re Estate of Cotton, 662 N.E.2d 63 (Ohio App. 1995), where the husband pled guilty to involuntary manslaughter in killing his wife. The court barred the husband on the ground that even though he was not convicted of an intentional and felonious killing, the civil trial court concluded that he intentionally and feloniously killed his wife and therefore the common law barred him from profiting from his wrong. A plea of guilty to a lesser crime than specified in the slayer's statute did not prevent the killer from being barred in a civil proceeding. See also In re Estate of Blodgett, 147 P.3d 702 (Alaska 2006), where the applicable slayer statute gave the trial court discretion to allow the slayer to take in the case of a felonious but unintentional killing. The court nonetheless upheld the barring of a son, who was initially charged with second degree murder for the killing of his father, but pled guilty to criminally negligent homicide.

Suppose the killer is convicted of a felonious and intentional killing but appeals the judgment. While the appeal is pending, what weight, if any, should the probate court give the fact of the conviction in applying the slayer rule? See In re Peterson, 67 Cal. Rptr. 3d 676 (App. 2007), involving the notorious Laci Peterson murder.[22] The court held that the conviction, not being final, did not conclusively bar Laci's husband and convicted killer Scott from taking, but the conviction was sufficient to make out a prima facie case of a felonious and intentional killing, putting the burden on him to overcome it, which he did not. Thus, even though his conviction was not final, Scott was barred from receiving the proceeds of a $250,000 insurance policy on Laci's life.

NOTE: THE CHINESE SYSTEM AND OTHER CONDUCT-BASED RESTRICTIONS ON INHERITANCE

In the United States, unworthy heirs — whose conduct bars inheritance — are usually limited to killers of the decedent. In nearly all other situations, inheritance is by a mechanical rule of status: kinship, marriage, or adoption. In some states, however, spouses who abandon the decedent are barred, and in a few more, parents are barred from taking from a child decedent if the parent refused to support the child. A handful of states — including California, Pennsylvania, Illinois, Oregon, and Maryland — have statutes that deny inheritance from children or elderly relatives who were abused by the heir. See Anne-Marie Rhodes, Consequences of Heirs' Misconduct: Moving from Rules to Discretion, 33 Ohio N.U. L. Rev. 975 (2007); Richard Lewis Brown, Undeserving Heirs? — The Case of the "Terminated" Parent, 40 U. Rich. L. Rev. 547 (2006); Linda Kelly Hill, No-Fault Death: Wedding Inheritance Rights to Family Values, 94 Ky. L.J. 319 (2005-2006). See also UPC §2-114 (2008), which prohibits inheritance by a parent from a child if the parental rights of the parent could have been terminated under state law for nonsupport, abandonment, abuse, or neglect.

22. When Laci Peterson disappeared on Christmas Eve, 2002, she was nearly eight months pregnant with her first child. Her husband, Scott Peterson, had started an affair with a massage therapist, Amber Frey, about a month earlier. Two weeks before Laci's disappearance, Scott told Amber that he was a widower and that the upcoming Christmas holiday would be his first without his wife. In April 2003, the badly decomposed bodies of Laci and the fetus washed up on the shore of San Francisco Bay. Convicted of Laci's murder, Scott is currently on death row at San Quentin Prison, awaiting the outcome of the appellate process.

Laci and Scott Peterson

The People's Republic of China has an entirely different scheme of inheritance, which punishes bad behavior and rewards good behavior. In an illuminating article, Frances H. Foster, Towards a Behavior-Based Model of Inheritance? The Chinese Experiment, 32 U.C. Davis L. Rev. 77 (1998), Professor Foster examines the Chinese system. The Chinese approach encompasses a broad range of misconduct, and it permits courts to reduce or eliminate a wrongdoer's share. It also rewards good behavior, even by worthy nonrelatives at the expense of the decedent's family members who do not support the decedent. It is "highly time-and-labor intensive, requiring courts to evaluate on a case-by-case basis the conduct of all potential claimants and the most appropriate division of each estate. The flexibility that is the hallmark of the behavior-based model today may prove to be its greatest drawback in the future . . . [when] increased social mobility, accumulation of private property, and a rise in the popular use of courts will bring about an increase in the number and complexity of inheritance disputes." Id. at 84-85.

Nonetheless, Foster concludes that the Chinese system has "significant advantages" over the American system, which does not penalize unworthy heirs. And it "recognizes the reality of support relationships today. It rewards contributions to the decedent's welfare by individuals outside the nuclear family, including blended and extended family members, nonmarital partners, and other unrelated parties." Id. at 125-126. Foster suggests the Chinese system may provide guidance for reforming the American inheritance system to deal with problems of parental and child neglect and rewarding exemplary conduct by, for instance, personally caring for a disabled person. See also Frances H. Foster, Linking Support and Inheritance: A New Model from China, 1999 Wis. L. Rev. 1199; Frances H. Foster, American Trust Law in a Chinese Mirror, 94 Minn. L. Rev. (forthcoming 2010).

2. *Disclaimer*

Sometimes an heir or a devisee will decline to take the property, a refusal that is called a *disclaimer*.[23] Disclaimers allow for post-mortem estate planning. The most common motivations for disclaimer are to reduce taxes or to keep property from creditors.

At common law, when a person died intestate, title to real and personal property passed to the decedent's heirs by operation of law. An intestate successor could not prevent title from passing to him. If the heir refused to accept (or, more precisely, to keep) the inheritance, the common law treated the heir's renunciation as if title had passed to the heir and then from the heir to the next intestate successor. The reason for this rule was that there must always be someone seised of the land who was liable for the feudal obligations — a reason once valid but of no importance today. On the other hand, if a person died testate, the devisee could refuse to accept the devise, thereby preventing title from passing to the devisee. A gift, whether inter vivos or by will, requires acceptance by the donee.

---

23. By traditional usage, an heir *renounces*; a beneficiary under a will *disclaims*. Today, the two words are used interchangeably as synonyms. The term *disclaimer* is the one more commonly used to describe the formal refusal to take by either an heir or a beneficiary.

These different conceptions of how title passes at death produced unexpectedly different tax results. If an heir renounced his inheritance and the common law rule applied, the situation was treated as though the heir had received the intestate share and then made a taxable gift to the persons who took by reason of the renunciation. Hardenburgh v. Commissioner, 198 F.2d 63 (8th Cir. 1952). By contrast, if a devisee disclaimed a testamentary gift, there were no gift tax consequences. Brown v. Routzahn, 63 F.2d 914 (6th Cir. 1933).

To eliminate the difference between disclaiming an intestate share and a devise, almost all states have enacted disclaimer legislation that provides that the disclaimant is treated as having died before the decedent or before the time of distribution. Thus the property does not pass to the disclaimant, and under state law the disclaimant makes no transfer of it (see UPC §§2-1105, 2-1106 (2002, rev. 2006)). This fiction allows the decedent's family to undertake post-mortem estate planning. Hence disclaimer must be kept in mind by the lawyer handling the estate. See Sims v. Hall, 592 S.E.2d 315 (S.C. App. 2003), upholding a malpractice judgment against a lawyer for failing to advise about the use of disclaimer to avoid a tax liability.

1. *Saving estate taxes.* Suppose that *O* dies intestate, survived by one sister, *A*. If *A* disclaims, *A* is treated as having predeceased *O*, and *O*'s estate will pass under the intestacy law to *A*'s child, *B*, who is *O*'s niece. Thus, to pass the property on to *A*'s child without a gift or estate tax being levied on it when it leaves *A*'s hands, *A* may decide to disclaim the inheritance. Moreover, if *B* is taxed at a lower income tax rate than *A*, then *A*'s disclaiming the inheritance will also save income taxes because any returns on the property will be taxable at *B*'s lower rate.

Most state disclaimer statutes require that a disclaimer be made within nine months of the creation of the interest being disclaimed. However, the Uniform Disclaimer of Property Interests Act (UDPIA) (1999, rev. 2006), which in 2002 was absorbed into the UPC as §§2-1101 through 2-1107 and has been adopted in about one-third of the states, does not contain a specified time limit.

The origin of the nine-month time limit was not an implementation of a considered state property law policy, but rather a reaction to the passage of Internal Revenue Code §2518 in 1976. Under §2518, only "qualified disclaimers" will avoid the gift tax liability that would have resulted if a disclaimant inherited property and then gave it away. Even if a person disclaims under applicable state law, if the disclaimer is not also "qualified" under the federal tax code, gift tax liability results. To qualify under the federal tax code, the disclaimer must be made within nine months after the interest is created or after the donee reaches 21, whichever is later. Hence, in the above example, if *A* disclaims a year after *O*'s death, *A* is treated under the tax laws as having accepted the property and having made a taxable gift to *B*. Given that disclaimers are often used for post-mortem tax planning, the decoupling of the time requirement under the UDPIA from IRC §2518 has become one of the main points of contention between the act's supporters and its critics.[24]

---

24. For debate on the UDPIA's pros and cons, compare Adam J. Hirsch, Disclaimer Law and UDPIA's Unintended Consequences, 36 Est. Plan. 34 (Apr. 2009), Adam J. Hirsch, The Uniform Acts' Loophole in

2. *Avoiding creditors.* Most disclaimer statutes provide that a disclaimer relates back *for all purposes* to the date of the decedent's death. The UDPIA "continues the effect of the relation back doctrine, not by using the specific words, but by directly stating what the relation back doctrine has been interpreted to mean." UPC §2-1106, cmt. (2002, rev. 2006). Thus, in an intestate estate, the disclaimer "takes effect . . . as of the time of the intestate's death." UPC §2-1106(b)(1).

In the example above, if *A* disclaims her interest in *O*'s estate, most cases have held that *A*'s ordinary creditors cannot reach her share of *O*'s estate. The disclaimed property is treated as passing directly to others, bypassing the disclaimant. In a subsequent bankruptcy proceeding, so long as the disclaimer was made prior to the filing of the bankruptcy petition, the federal courts respect the relation back under state disclaimer law. In re Costas, 555 F.3d 790 (9th Cir. 2009).

When, however, a bankruptcy petition is filed before the debtor disclaims, the courts almost invariably hold that the disclaimer is ineffective under federal bankruptcy law. See David B. Young, The Intersection of Bankruptcy and Probate, 49 S. Tex. L. Rev. 351, 381-394 (2007). Moreover, in a minority of states, an insolvent debtor who is not already in bankruptcy may not use a disclaimer to avoid his creditors. See UPC §2-1113, cmt. (2002, rev. 2006) (collecting authority).

For further discussion, see Adam J. Hirsch, The Problem of the Insolvent Heir, 74 Cornell L. Rev. 587 (1989) (arguing that tort creditors and child support and alimony creditors should be permitted to veto the debtor's disclaimer).

PROBLEM

O has two children, *A* and *B*. *B* dies, survived by one child, *C*. Then *O*, a widow, dies intestate. *O*'s heirs are *A* and *C*. *A* has four children. *A* disclaims. What distribution is made of *O*'s estate? UPC §2-1106(b)(3)(C) (2002, rev. 2006) provides:

> If by law or under the instrument, the descendants of the disclaimant would share in the disclaimed interest by any method of representation had the disclaimant died before the time of distribution, the *disclaimed interest* passes only to the descendants of the disclaimant who survive the time of distribution. [Emphasis added.]

While in most states individual creditors cannot reach assets disclaimed by a debtor not already in bankruptcy, the Internal Revenue Service as a creditor is treated differently.

Fraudulent Conveyance Law, 34 Est. Plan. 20 (Dec. 2007), and Adam J. Hirsch and Richard R. Gans, Disclaimer Reform and UDPIA: The Disappointing Amendments of 2006, 33 Est. Plan. 24 (Dec. 2006), with William P. LaPiana, Some Property Law Issues in the Law of Disclaimers, 38 Real Prop., Prob. & Tr. J. 207 (2003).

DRYE v. UNITED STATES, 528 U.S. 49 (1999): Irma Deliah Drye died intestate, leaving her son, Rohn F. Drye, Jr. ("Drye"), as the sole heir to her $233,000 estate. Prior to his mother's death, Drye ran up an unpaid $325,000 tax bill, prompting the IRS to file tax liens against all of Drye's "property and rights to property." To keep his mother's estate away from the IRS, Drye disclaimed his interest. This allowed the entire estate to pass to his daughter, Theresa, who was next in line under the applicable state intestacy statute.

> Theresa Drye then used the estate's proceeds to fund the Trust, of which she and, during their lifetimes, her parents are the beneficiaries. Under the Trust's terms, distributions are at the discretion of the trustee, Drye's counsel Daniel M. Traylor, and may be made only for the health, maintenance, and support of the beneficiaries. The Trust is spendthrift, and under state law, its assets are therefore shielded from creditors seeking to satisfy the debts of the Trust's beneficiaries.[25]

The question before the Court was whether Drye's disclaimer was effective to pass the property to his daughter free from the federal tax lien. Under the applicable state disclaimer law, disclaimed property bypasses the disclaimant, who is treated as having predeceased the decedent. Thus Drye argued "that state law is the proper guide to the critical determination whether his interest in his mother's estate constituted 'property' or 'rights to property.'" If so, his disclaimed interest would pass to his daughter free of the tax liens.

Speaking for a unanimous Court, Justice Ruth Bader Ginsburg rejected Drye's argument:

> The disclaiming heir . . . inevitably exercises dominion over the property. He determines who will receive the property — himself if he does not disclaim, a known other if he does. See Adam J. Hirsch, The Problem of the Insolvent Heir, 74 Cornell L. Rev. 587, 607-608 (1989). This power to channel the estate's assets warrants the conclusion that Drye held "property" or a "right to property" subject to the Government's liens. . . .
>
> Drye had the unqualified right to receive the entire value of his mother's estate (less administrative expenses), or to channel that value to his daughter. The control rein he held under state law, we hold, rendered the inheritance "property" or "rights to property belonging to him within the meaning of [the Internal Revenue Code], and hence subject to the federal tax liens that sparked this controversy.

Justice Ruth Bader Ginsburg

_____

25. Spendthrift trusts are addressed in Chapter 9 at pages 614-624. — Eds.

QUESTIONS

Suppose that Irma Deliah Drye had executed a valid will that left her entire estate to her granddaughter, Theresa, thereby disinheriting her insolvent son, Rohn. Under these facts, would the IRS have had any recourse against the assets of Irma's estate? See Robert T. Danforth, The Role of Federalism in Administering a National System of Taxation, 57 Tax Law. 625, 641-642 (2004). Suppose that Theresa promised Irma to make use of the bequest to support her father. Would the IRS be entitled to a constructive trust over the bequest to Theresa? See Cabral v. Soares, 69 Cal. Rptr. 3d 242 (App. 2007).

NOTE: DISCLAIMERS TO QUALIFY FOR MEDICAID

Under the eighteenth and nineteenth century English Poor Laws, if a person could not pay for the person's care, the person's kin could be required to do so. Today, in the United States, a person has a legal obligation to provide for the person's spouse and minor children, if able to do so, but not the person's parents or siblings.

The federal and state governments offer a range of support programs for the poor and the elderly. Perhaps the most important, which provides medical assistance to needy people, is Medicaid, a cooperative state and federal program that pays for roughly one-fifth of all hospital patients and over one-half of all nursing home residents. An applicant for Medicaid assistance must meet strict income and resource requirements, which vary from state to state. In many cases, to qualify for Medicaid, the applicant must "spend down" his assets to a few thousand dollars. See Linda S. Ershow-Levenberg, Court Approval of Medicaid Spend-Down Planning by Guardians, 6 Marq. Elder's Advisor 197 (2005); John A. Miller, Voluntary Impoverishment to Obtain Government Benefits, 13 Cornell J.L. & Pub. Poly. 81 (2003). However, giving away property may result in the disqualification of the applicant from Medicaid assistance for a certain period of time depending on the nature of the transfer. Certain transfers are exempt, such as the transfer of a home to a spouse and a transfer in trust for certain disabled persons. For a discussion of the use of trusts in Medicaid planning, see pages 638-640.

In some states, the Medicaid applicant or recipient is required to try to get transferred property returned in order to be eligible for benefits. If a Medicaid recipient dies leaving a probate estate or nonprobate transfers, the state may look to those assets to recover benefits already paid to the Medicaid recipient. See Alison Barnes, An Assessment of Medicaid Planning, 3 Hous. J. Health L. & Poly. 265 (2003); Janel C. Frank, How Far Is Too Far? Tracing Assets in Medicaid Estate Recovery, 79 N.D. L. Rev. 111 (2003).

The question thus arises, can a person who qualifies for Medicaid benefits that would be lost if the person receives an inheritance preserve his eligibility by disclaiming that inheritance? In Troy v. Hart, 697 A.2d 113 (Md. App. 1997), Paul

Lettich, a Medicaid recipient, was entitled to a $100,000 inheritance from his sister's estate. Rather than take the money, he disclaimed, making each of his other two sisters $50,000 richer. After Lettich died, the administrator of his estate sought to rescind the disclaimer and reclaim the money. The court held that Lettich was required to report his inheritance to state Medicaid authorities, whether he disclaimed it or not. Although the court held the disclaimer valid, it suggested that the amounts passing to the sisters could be subject to a claim by the state for reimbursement of Lettich's Medicaid expenses.

The law in this area is complex and has been changing rapidly. Caution is advised.

3

WILLS: CAPACITY AND CONTESTS

SECTION A.   MENTAL CAPACITY

1.   *The Test of Mental Capacity*

In the law of wills, the requirements for mental capacity are minimal. To be competent to make a will, the testator must be an adult (age 18 or older[1]) and "must be capable of knowing and understanding in a general way [1] the nature and extent of his or her property, [2] the natural objects of his or her bounty, and [3] the disposition that he or she is making of that property, and must also be capable of [4] relating these elements to one another and forming an orderly desire regarding the disposition of the property." Restatement (Third) of Property: Wills and Other Donative Transfers §8.1(b) (2003).

The test is one of *capability*, not actual knowledge. If the test were one of actual knowledge, a reasonable mistake about whether your child was alive would render you mentally incompetent because you would not know the natural objects of your bounty (your family). Nor must the testator be of average intelligence, as this would incapacitate half the population.

In re Estate of Washburn
Supreme Court of New Hampshire, 1997
690 A.2d 1024

HORTON, J.   The respondent, Barbara A. Remick, the principal beneficiary of the testatrix's April 1992 will, appeals an order of the Rockingham County

---

1. In almost all states, and under UPC §2-501 (1990), the age of majority is 18. In many states, those who are under 18 may make a will if they are married or are legally emancipated. In Georgia, one may make a will upon reaching the age of 14. Ga. Code Ann. §53-4-10 (2008).

Probate Court (O'Neill, J.) holding that the testatrix lacked the testamentary capacity necessary to execute the will. We affirm.

Katherine F. Washburn, the testatrix, executed three wills that were put in evidence before the probate court. In the first will, dated October 1986, she left $1,000 bequests to several named individuals and provided that her Portsmouth home, personal effects, and the residue of her estate should go to her sister, Margaret Fay, or in default thereof to her niece, Catherine Colonna, the petitioner in this action. In March 1992, the testatrix executed the second will, which left $1,000 bequests to certain named individuals; $5,000 to the respondent, her caretaker and companion; and the residue to petitioner. The testatrix's final will, executed approximately three weeks later in April 1992, left $5,000 bequests to the petitioner and another individual and provided that the respondent receive the residue, which included the testatrix's home and personal estate.

When the April 1992 will was offered for probate by the executor of the estate, the petitioner challenged the testamentary capacity of the testatrix to execute the will by filing a petition to re-examine the will in solemn form. The probate court held a three-day hearing on proof of the will in solemn form, during which it heard both expert and lay testimony pertaining to the testatrix's mental capacity in April 1992. The court found that the testatrix was suffering from Alzheimer's disease at the time of the execution of the April 13, 1992 will, which resulted in her inability to recollect the property she wished to dispose of and understand its general nature, and resulted in her inability to make an election upon whom and how she would bestow the property by her will. . . .

The respondent first asserts that the evidence produced by the petitioner was insufficient to rebut the presumption of due execution of the will in question. We have long held that every person is presumed to be sane, until there is some evidence shown to rebut that presumption. . . .

The petitioner offered satisfactory evidence to rebut the presumption of capacity. The medical testimony offered by Dr. Levy and Dr. Christo established that, at a minimum, the testatrix suffered from some degree of Alzheimer's in April 1992 and her behavior could have been affected. Further testimony by petitioner's lay witnesses indicated confusion, forgetfulness, and a lack of competency at the time in question. Because the petitioner met her burden of producing evidence to demonstrate a potential failure of due execution, the trial court correctly found that the presumption of competency was rebutted and the respondent had to prove capacity by a preponderance of the evidence.

Second, the respondent argues that no reasonable trier of fact could have found that the testatrix lacked the testamentary capacity to execute her will in April 1992. A thorough review of the record convinces us that the evidence supports the trial court's ruling that the testatrix lacked capacity to execute her April 1992 will. All the testifying physicians agreed that the medical evidence indicated the testatrix had Alzheimer's disease in April 1993, a year after the will's execution. The testimony revealed that Alzheimer's is a progressive disease and that the testatrix had moderate to advanced dementia in April 1993. There was also testimony that the testatrix was suffering from Alzheimer's at the time the will was executed and that the disease could have influenced her competency.

Anecdotal evidence supported the probate court's finding that the testatrix's capacity was adversely affected by the disease. The testamentary intentions of the testatrix were unclear and fluctuated. Her second and third wills were executed just over three weeks apart and contained vastly different provisions. As the probate court found, there were "discrepancies between statements the testatrix made as to how she wished to dispose of her property and the wills she signed in the spring of 1992 including the will at issue." The probate court noted the majority of witnesses testified the testatrix intended to leave the respondent her house in return for the respondent's care and that the petitioner and the respondent's daughter would be treated equally. The testimony on this point, however, conflicts with both the bequests in the March 1992 will, in which the respondent received only $5,000 and the petitioner and the respondent's daughter received different amounts, and the bequests in the April 1992 will, in which the respondent received the testatrix's $50,000 personal estate as well as her home.

There was also testimony regarding the confusion and forgetfulness of the testatrix near the time of the will's execution. The petitioner testified that at the funeral of the testatrix's sister in February 1992, the testatrix failed to recognize her niece, the petitioner's sister. Both the petitioner and the testatrix's attorney testified that the petitioner needed to supplement information the testatrix provided as to her sister's heirs. A funeral home employee stated that after her sister's funeral, the testatrix asked him to send the bill to her, although she had previously paid in person.

We conclude there was sufficient evidence for a reasonable trier of fact to determine, given all the circumstances, that the testatrix was incompetent to execute the will in question. We therefore uphold the probate court's ruling that the testatrix lacked testamentary capacity. . . .

Affirmed.

Wilson v. Lane
Supreme Court of Georgia, 2005
614 S.E.2d 88

FLETCHER, C.J. After Executrix Katherine Lane offered Jewel Jones Greer's 1997 last will and testament for probate, Floyd Wilson filed a caveat, challenging Greer's testamentary capacity. A Jasper County Superior Court jury found that Greer lacked testamentary capacity at the time she executed her will, but the trial court granted Lane's motion for judgment notwithstanding the verdict. Wilson appeals. Because we agree that there was no evidence to show that Greer lacked testamentary capacity, we affirm.

A person is mentally capable to make a will if she "has sufficient intellect to enable [her] to have a decided and rational desire as to the disposition of [her] property." In this case, the propounders introduced evidence that the will in question distributed Greer's property equally to seventeen beneficiaries, sixteen of whom are blood-relatives to Greer. The only non-relative beneficiary is Katherine Lane, who spent much of her time caring for Greer before her death in 2000. The drafting attorney testified that in his opinion, at the time the 1997 will was signed, Greer was mentally competent, and that she emphatically selected every beneficiary named in the will. Numerous other friends and acquaintances also testified that Greer had a clear mind at the time the will was signed.

Thus, the propounders established a presumption that Greer possessed testamentary capacity. The caveators, however, never presented any evidence whatsoever showing that Greer was incapable of forming a decided and rational desire as to the disposition of her property, even when the evidence is examined in the light most favorable to their case.

The caveators challenged Greer's capacity by showing that she was eccentric, aged, and peculiar in the last years of her life. They presented testimony that she had an irrational fear of flooding in her house, that she had trouble dressing and bathing herself, and that she unnecessarily called the fire department to report a non-existent fire. But "[t]he law does not withhold from the aged, the feeble, the weak-minded, the capricious, the notionate, the right to make a will, provided such person has a decided and rational desire as to the disposition of his property." Hill v. Deal, 193 S.E. 858, 861 (Ga. 1937). Although perhaps persuasive to a jury, "eccentric habits and absurd beliefs do not establish testamentary incapacity." Sarajane Love, Wills and Administration in Georgia, §45, at 82 (5th ed. 1988). All that is required to sustain the will is proof that Greer was capable of forming a certain rational desire with respect to the disposition of her assets.

In addition to Greer's eccentric habits, the caveators also introduced evidence of a guardianship petition filed for Greer a few months after the will was executed, the testimony of an expert witness, and a letter written by Greer's physician. None of that evidence, however, was sufficient to deprive Greer of her right to make a valid will, as none of it showed that she was incapable of forming a rational desire as to the disposition of her property.

The expert admitted that he had never examined Greer, and that his testimony was based solely on a cursory review of some of Greer's medical files. Further, he was equivocal in his testimony, stating only that "*it appears* that she was in some form of the early to middle stages of a dementia of the Alzheimer's type." Regardless of the stigma associated with the term "Alzheimer's," however, that testimony does not show how Greer would have been unable to form a rational desire regarding the disposition of her assets. Indeed, the expert offered no explanation of how her supposed condition would affect her competency to make a valid will.

The testimony of Greer's physician also failed to show how she lacked testamentary capacity. In 1996, the physician wrote a letter stating that Greer "was legally blind and suffered from senile dementia." But the doctor testified that he was "not sure whether she had senile dementia at the time or not, even though I wrote that." He stated further that he only wrote the letter to try and assist Greer in obtaining help with her telephone bill because she had been having trouble with her eyes. In any event, a vague reference to "senile dementia" cannot eliminate testamentary capacity. If it could, it would undermine societal confidence in the validity and sanctity of our testamentary system.

Finally, as the dissent points out, Lane filed a guardianship petition in 1998, after the will was executed, proclaiming that Greer was no longer capable of managing her own affairs alone. According to the testimony, however, the petition was filed solely in order to satisfy the Department of Family and Children Services's concerns regarding Greer's ability to continue living on her own, and thus to allow Greer to remain in her home. Even if Greer's inability to live alone existed at the time the will was executed, which was not proven by any evidence, that fact bears no relation to her ability to form a rational desire regarding the disposition of her assets. . . .

[I]n this case, no testimony, expert or otherwise, was offered to establish that at the time the will was executed, Greer suffered from a form of dementia sufficient in form or extent to render her unable to form a decided and rational desire regarding the disposition of her assets. Notwithstanding the dissent's attempt to piece together "the totality of the evidence," none of the evidence, either alone or in combination, provided any proof that Greer lacked testamentary capacity, as that term is defined in this State. At most, there was evidence that Greer was an eccentric woman whose mental health declined towards the end of her life. Accordingly, the evidence demanded a verdict upholding the validity of the will, and the trial court was correct to reverse the jury's contrary verdict. . . .

Judgment affirmed.

CARLEY, J., dissenting.   I agree that the evidence in this case would have authorized a finding that Ms. Greer possessed the requisite testamentary capacity when she executed a will in September of 1997. However, the jury found that she lacked such capacity, and we must decide whether the evidence supports that finding. I submit that, when the evidence is construed most strongly in support of the jury's verdict in favor of the Caveators, it authorized the finding that Ms. Greer did not have sufficient intellect to enable her to make a decided and rational determination concerning the disposition of her estate. Therefore, I dissent to the affirmance of the trial court's grant of the Propounder's motion for judgment notwithstanding the verdict. . . .

Here, the Caveators presented expert medical opinion testimony showing that, at the time Ms. Greer executed the will, "she was in some form of the early to middle stages of a dementia of the Alzheimer's type." A year earlier, her own physician had expressed his belief that she exhibited "senile dementia." In January of 1998, a petition was filed which alleged that Ms. Greer was an "incapacitated" adult and sought the appointment of a guardian. This petition for guardianship was supported by the affidavit of her doctor, who stated his opinion that she had "dementia-Alzheimer's type," that she suffered from "poor memory, poor judgment, [was] difficult to reason with," and that she was "incapacitated on a permanent basis." The physician's affidavit also indicated that Ms. Greer was in present need of a guardian for both her person and her property. With regard to the guardianship of her person, the doctor noted that she "lacks sufficient understanding or capacity to make significant responsible decisions concerning . . . her person or is incapable of communicating such decisions." As for the guardianship of her property, the physician indicated that she was "incapable of managing . . . her estate, and [her] property . . . will be wasted or dissipated unless proper management is provided." The Caveator's expert testified that, if, as Ms. Greer's own doctor expressed in his affidavit, she was

> having profound problems in one month where [she] would be considered incapacitated or needing a guardian then you would be able to go backwards for a number of months, probably up to a year or two, at least, and say that [she] was having some sort of problem with [her] thinking.

It was only four months between the time she signed the instrument tendered for admission into probate and the petition alleging that she was "permanently incapacitated" due to "dementia" based upon Alzheimer's disease.

In addition to the expert medical opinion evidence showing that Ms. Greer suffered from dementia attributable to Alzheimer's disease shortly before, during and shortly after the time she executed the will, the Caveators introduced evidence which was indicative of the extent to which her mental acuity had been impaired. She had an irrational fear that her home was being flooded. She even refused to get into the bathtub, and insisted on sponge baths. Visitors to her home

> couldn't flush the commode, couldn't really run the water in her kitchen sink. . . . [S]he had a phobia of water and when you went to [visit her] you dare not go in the commode, use the bathroom, you didn't cut on the water to get a drink of water or anything so you just had to sit.

There was additional evidence showing that in mid-December of 1997, only three months after executing the will, Ms. Greer was disoriented as to time and, believing that it was March, she was unaware that Christmas was imminent. She did not know her own social security number. She had a list of first names and telephone numbers, but could not provide last names for any of those on that list. As the majority notes, she called the fire department to report a non-existent fire.

"[A] court must allow the issue of testamentary capacity to go to the jury when there is a genuine conflict in the evidence regarding the testator's state of mind." Murchison v. Smith, 508 S.E.2d 641, 644 (1998). . . . While no single element of the Caveators' proof, standing alone, might otherwise be a sufficient predicate for invalidating Ms. Greer's will, when the totality of the evidence as to her mental condition during the relevant time period is considered, a jury certainly would be authorized to find that she suffered from serious dementia. If the evidence supports such a finding, then the jury was authorized to return a verdict holding that she lacked the requisite testamentary capacity. Since the evidence supports the jury's verdict in favor of the Caveators, the trial court erred in granting the Propounder's motion for judgment n.o.v.

NOTES AND QUESTION

1. *Evidentiary burdens.* Putting the burden of proof (or, more specifically, the burden of persuasion) on the proponent to show testamentary capacity, as in *Washburn*, is the minority rule. The prevailing rule, as in *Wilson* and Breeden v. Stone, infra page 171, is that once the proponent adduces prima facie evidence of due execution, the party contesting the will on the grounds of lack of capacity has the burden of persuasion. See Restatement (Third) of Property: Wills and Other Donative Transfers §8.1, cmt. f (2003); UPC §3-407 (1990).

2. *Professional responsibility.* A client whose testamentary capacity is in doubt presents a potential ethical dilemma. A lawyer may not draft a will for a person the lawyer believes to be incompetent, but the lawyer may rely on her own judgment of the client's capacity. The ACTEC commentaries explain:

> The lawyer generally should not prepare a will, trust agreement or other dispositive instrument for a client who the lawyer reasonably believes lacks the requisite capacity. On the other hand, because of the importance of testamentary freedom, the lawyer may properly assist clients whose testamentary capacity appears to be borderline. In any such case the lawyer should take steps to preserve evidence regarding the client's testamentary capacity. [ACTEC Commentaries on the Model Rules of Professional Conduct 132 (4th ed. 2006).]

For further discussion, see Jan E. Rein, Ethics and the Questionably Competent Client: What the Model Rules Say and Don't Say, 9 Stan. L. & Poly. Rev. 241 (1998).

3. *Ante-mortem probate.* Statutes in Arkansas, North Dakota, and Ohio permit probate of a will during the testator's life. These statutes authorize a person to institute during life an adversary proceeding to declare the validity of a will and the testamentary capacity and freedom from undue influence of the person executing the will. All beneficiaries named in the will and all the testator's heirs apparent must be made parties to the action. Ark. Code Ann. §28-40-202 (2008); N.D. Cent. Code §30.1-08.1-01 (2008); Ohio Rev. Code Ann. §2107.081 (2008). This procedure, which is rarely invoked, is known as "living probate" or "ante-mortem probate." When might this procedure be an attractive option? See also Pamela Champine, Expertise and Instinct in the Assessment of Testamentary Capacity, 51 Vill. L. Rev. 25 (2006) (proposing a "lifetime validation of capacity to make a will through successful performance on a standardized psychological test, known as a forensic assessment instrument, designed specifically to measure testamentary capacity").

For more on ante-mortem probate as a prophylactic against later will contests, and citations to the earlier literature, see Aloysius A. Leopold and Gerry W. Beyer, Ante-Mortem Probate: A Viable Alternative, 43 Ark. L. Rev. 131 (1990); Dara Greene, Antemortem Probate: A Mediation Model, 14 Ohio St. J. Disp. Resol. 663 (1999).

NOTE: CAPACITY THRESHOLDS

In most states capacity to make a will is governed by a different legal test and requires less mental ability than to make a contract or to complete an irrevocable lifetime gift. The capacity standards for contracts and gifts are designed to protect the incompetent contractor or donor from suffering economic loss during lifetime, which might result in impoverishment. Restatement (Third) of Property: Wills and Other Donative Transfers §8.1(c) (2003) makes this higher standard explicit: To make an irrevocable lifetime gift, not only must one have capacity to make a will, but one "must also be capable of understanding the effect that the gift may have on the future financial security of the donor and of anyone who may be dependent on the donor."

For a dead person, protection from economic loss and impoverishment is a less important consideration, one that yields to the policies of testamentary freedom and personal autonomy. Hence the standard of capacity to make a will is lower than to make a contract or an irrevocable lifetime gift. The modern view is that this lower standard of capacity applies also to the making of a revocable trust or other will substitute that is revocable until death. Maimonides School v. Coles, 881 N.E.2d 779 (Mass. App. 2008); Restatement (Third) of Property, supra, §8.1(b), cmts. d-e; Uniform Trust Code §601 (2000).

The law's disparate treatment of transfers during life versus at death is nicely illustrated by Lee v. Lee, 337 So. 2d 713 (Miss. 1976). In that case, the testator was placed under a conservatorship in 1968 because of age and physical incapacity. On May 9, 1970, testator executed a *will*; on that same date he executed and delivered a *deed* purporting to convey real property. The court held that the *deed* was void but the *will* was valid. The court reasoned that a person under a conservatorship is without the necessary contractual power to execute a deed, but such a person may nonetheless write a valid will if the trial court finds, as the trial court did here, that the will was written during a *lucid interval*. See also In re Estate of Romero, 126 P.3d 228 (Colo. App. 2005) (testamentary capacity possible in spite of conservatorship).

Interestingly, legal capacity to make a will requires a greater mental competency than is required for marriage. Estate of Park, [1953] 2 All E.R. 408, 411, is authority for the proposition that a person may have insufficient capacity to make a will on the same day as the person has sufficient capacity to marry. Marriage alone will give the surviving spouse a share of the senile spouse's estate, even though he has no capacity to devise it to her. See Hoffman v. Kohns, 385 So. 2d 1064 (Fla. App. 1980) (housekeeper marries senile man; will made one day later set aside, but marriage held valid).

For an insightful further discussion, probing the meaning of capacity across a variety of contexts, see Lawrence A. Frolik and Mary F. Radford, "Sufficient" Capacity: The Contrasting Capacity Requirements for Different Documents, 2 NAELA J. 303 (2006).

NOTE: WHY REQUIRE MENTAL CAPACITY?

At least as far back as the Romans, the law has required a person to be of sound mind to make a valid will. But why should this be so? Why isn't the power of testation extended to all persons regardless of their mental capacity?

The requirement of mental capacity assures a sane person that the disposition he desires will be carried out even if he later becomes insane and makes another will. This gives a person of sound mind the advantage of being able, while in a rational mind, to choose what will happen to his property in the future and to have confidence that this choice will be carried out. Requiring mental capacity may therefore protect a senile or incompetent testator from exploitation by cunning persons. If the incompetent could make wills, then many institutionalized people would be subject to imposition by the unscrupulous. Keep in mind, however, that what may look like exploitation to others may give the testator much pleasure.

The law also requires mental capacity to protect the decedent's family. In many ancient societies, property was viewed as tribal property or family property, rather than being owned by individuals. Although individual ownership in time

"His will reads as follows: 'Being of sound mind and disposition, I blew it all.'"

Drawing by Frank Modell.

developed, indeed triumphed, the notion persisted that the family was an economic unit with some claim on the family property. Giving effect to the expectations of inheritance tends to preserve the family as a unit for mutual support. In this way, the institution of inheritance, through the principle of reciprocity, functions as a system for providing care and support for the aged. In mental capacity cases, the principle of reciprocity is recognized when the court considers the fairness of a disposition, sometimes *sub silentio*, sometimes under the guise of considering an "unnatural" disposition.

To some extent the public acceptance of law rests upon a belief that legal institutions, including inheritance, are legitimate, and legitimacy cannot exist unless decisions are reasoned. On this view, it is important that the succession to property be perceived as a responsible, reasoned act, according the survivors their just deserts.

For further discussion of the reasons for the requirement of mental capacity and its historical and theoretical underpinnings, see Susanna L. Blumenthal, The Deviance of the Will: Policing the Bounds of Testamentary Freedom in Nineteenth-Century America, 119 Harv. L. Rev. 959 (2006) (replied to by Joel Peter Eigen, The Will of the Deviant, 119 Harv. L. Rev. F. 230 (2006)); Robert E. Mensel, Right Feeling and Knowing Right: Insanity in Testators and Criminals in Nineteenth Century American Law, 58 Okla. L. Rev. 397 (2005); Pamela R. Champine, A Sanist Will?, 46 N.Y.L. Sch. L. Rev. 547 (2002-2003); Jane B. Baron, Empathy, Subjectivity, and Testamentary Capacity, 24 San Diego L. Rev. 1043 (1987).

2. *Insane Delusion*

A person may have sufficient mental capacity generally to execute a will but be suffering from an *insane delusion* so as to cause a will to fail for lack of testamentary capacity nonetheless. If an insane delusion is shown, but the delusion did not affect the dispositions, then the will stands. Much of the litigation over insane delusion therefore focuses on causation. In the typical case, the testator's insane delusion involves a false belief about a member of the testator's family. See Dougherty v. Rubenstein, 914 A.2d 184, 196-197 (Md. App. 2007) (citing cases).

An insane delusion is a legal, not a psychiatric, concept. A delusion is a false conception of reality. An example is a belief that all Irishmen have red hair. An insane delusion — which bears on testamentary capacity — is one to which the testator adheres against all evidence and reason to the contrary. The law thus draws a distinction between an insane delusion and a mistake. An insane delusion is a belief not susceptible to correction by presenting the testator with evidence indicating the falsity of the belief. A mistake is susceptible to correction if the testator is told the truth. Under traditional law, courts do not reform or invalidate wills because of mistake (though this rule is changing, see pages 342-357), whereas they do invalidate wills or their provisions resulting from an insane delusion. See Estate of Turner, 866 N.Y.S.2d 429 (A.D. 2008) (upholding will in spite of testator's mistaken belief, rooted in a misunderstanding of the nature of a trust, that the trustee had stolen the testator's property).

Some courts have held that if there is any factual basis at all for the testator's delusion, it is not deemed insane. See Estate of Kottke, 6 P.3d 243 (Alaska 2000). The majority view, however, is that a delusion is insane even if there is some factual basis for it if a rational person in the testator's situation could not have drawn the conclusion reached by the testator. See Restatement (Third) of Property: Wills and Other Donative Transfers §8.1, cmt. s (2003).

In re Strittmater
Court of Errors and Appeals of New Jersey, 1947
53 A.2d 205

On appeal from a decree of the Prerogative Court, advised by Vice-Ordinary Bigelow, who filed the following opinion:

"This is an appeal from a decree of the Essex County Orphans Court admitting to probate the will of Louisa F. Strittmater. Appellants challenge the decree on the ground that testatrix was insane.

"The only medical witness was Dr. Sarah D. Smalley, a general practitioner who was Miss Strittmater's physician all her adult life. In her opinion, decedent suffered from paranoia of the Bleuler type of split personality.[2] The factual evidence justifies the conclusion. But I regret not having had the benefit of an analysis of the data by a specialist in diseases of the brain.

"The deceased never married. Born in 1896, she lived with her parents until their death [in] about 1928, and seems to have had a normal childhood. She was devoted to both her parents and they to her. Her admiration and love of her parents persisted after their death to 1934, at least. Yet four years later she wrote: 'My father was a corrupt, vicious, and unintelligent savage, a typical specimen of the majority of his sex. Blast his wormstinking carcass and his whole damn breed.' And in 1943, she inscribed on a photograph of her mother 'That Moronic she-devil that was my mother.'

"Numerous memoranda and comments written by decedent on the margins of books constitute the chief evidence of her mental condition. Most of them are dated in 1935, when she was 40 years old. But there are enough in later years to indicate no change in her condition. The Master who heard the case in the court below, found that the proofs demonstrated 'incontrovertably her morbid aversion to men' and 'feminism to a neurotic extreme.' This characterization seems to me not strong enough. She regarded men as a class with an insane hatred. She looked forward to the day when women would bear children without the aid of men, and all males would be put to death at birth. Decedent's inward life,

---

2. Eugen Bleuler (1857-1930), a Swiss psychiatrist, analyzed and named the condition schizophrenia, dividing it into several types, including paranoid. Bleuler believed that intense ambivalence (e.g., experiencing both love and hate toward an object) was a primary symptom of schizophrenia. He also observed that even normal persons, when preoccupied or distracted, show a number of schizophrenic symptoms, such as peculiar associations, logical blunders, and stereotypes. — Eds.

disclosed by what she wrote, found an occasional outlet such as the incident of the smashing of the clock, the killing of the pet kitten,[3] vile language, etc. On the other hand, — and I suppose this is the split personality, — Miss Strittmater, in her dealings with her lawyer, Mr. Semel, over a period of several years, and with her bank, to cite only two examples, was entirely reasonable and normal.

"Decedent, in 1925, became a member of the New Jersey branch of the National Women's Party.[4] From 1939 to 1941, and perhaps later, she worked as a volunteer one day a week in the New York office, filing papers, etc. During this period, she spoke of leaving her estate to the Party. On October 31, 1944, she executed her last will, carrying this intention into effect. A month later, December 6, she died. Her only relatives were some cousins of whom she saw very little during the last few years of her life.

"The question is whether Miss Strittmater's will is the product of her insanity. Her disease seems to have become well developed by 1936. In August of that year she wrote, 'It remains for feministic organizations like the National Women's Party, to make exposure of women's "protectors" and "lovers" for what their vicious and contemptible selves are.' She had been a member of the Women's Party for eleven years at that time, but the evidence does not show that she had taken great interest in it. I think it was her paranoic condition, especially her insane delusions about the male, that led her to leave her estate to the National Women's Party. The result is that the probate should be set aside."

PER CURIAM. The decree under review will be affirmed, for the reasons stated in the opinion of Vice-Ordinary Bigelow.

---

3. The opinion's silence leads us to wonder whether the clock was a "grandfather clock" or the kitten a "tomcat." — Eds.

4. Louisa Strittmater's intended beneficiary, the National Woman's Party (the court's reference to the National Women's Party was mistaken), was founded in 1916 by Alice Paul. It was the most radical of the leading organizations that lobbied for the Nineteenth Amendment to the U.S. Constitution, which in 1920 granted women the right to vote. After being convicted and imprisoned in 1917 for nonviolent protests in front of the White House, Paul went on a hunger strike. She was then taken to the prison hospital's psychopathic ward and treated as mentally ill — an irony given the New Jersey Supreme Court's treatment of Louisa Strittmater 30 years later. See Doris Stevens, Jailed for Freedom 215-228 (1920).

In 1921, Alice Paul drafted the Equal Rights Amendment (ERA): "Equality of Rights under the law shall not be denied or abridged by the United States or any state on account of sex." Introduced in every Congress from 1923 through the early 1970s, the ERA finally passed in 1972. The ERA was then sent to the states for ratification, but it failed because not enough states ratified it before the 1982 deadline imposed by Congress. Paul, who had a Ph.D. in economics and three law degrees (LL.B., LL.M., and D.C.L.), was a leader in lobbying Congress to add sex discrimination to the protections of Title VII in the 1964 Civil Rights Act. Until the sex amendment to Title VII passed the House of Representatives in February 1964, the National Woman's Party was the *only* national women's organization that favored adding the prohibition of sex discrimination to that statute. See Jo Freeman, How "Sex" Got into Title VII: Persistent Opportunism as a Maker of Public Policy, 9 Law & Ineq. 1 (1990).

Alice Paul died in 1977 at the age of 92. — Eds.

Alice Paul, founder of the National Woman's Party.

QUESTIONS AND NOTE

1. If *Strittmater* were to be decided today, would it come out the same way? To what extent are notions of capacity and insane delusion based on social constructions of what is "normal"?

2. In Kostic v. Chaplin, [2007] EWHC 2298 (Ch.), the court struck down one of the largest gifts ever made to a political party.

> Branislav Kostic, a pharmaceutical tycoon from Ealing, West London, left his entire fortune to the Tories after claiming that Margaret Thatcher could save the world from a satanic plot. . . .
>
> The judgment could be expensive and embarrassing for the Tories, who contested the claim from Mr Kostic's only son, Zoran. The party will now face demands for hundreds of thousands of pounds in legal costs as well as repayments of some of Mr Kostic's donations.
>
> Mr Justice Henderson [found] that Mr Kostic lacked "testamentary capacity" when he cut his son from the will. . . .
>
> Mr Kostic died aged 80 in 2005, leaving £8.3 million, which is now understood to have grown to nearer £10 million.
>
> The Belgrade-born tycoon was a loving family man until he became gripped by delusions around 1984. He read and spoke five different languages and had a wide appreciation of history, mathematics, science, philosophy, literature and the arts.
>
> His beliefs in plots to kill him soured his relationships with his wife, sister, mother, friends, advisers, bankers and colleagues. He accused his wife of stealing his passport and being a nymphomaniac with numerous male and female lovers. He believed that his mother and sister conspired to kill his father and brother-in-law. . . .
>
> In a note to Scotland Yard, he reported that a 100-strong international vice ring was attempting to poison him.
>
> In the midst of his delusions, however, he saw Mrs Thatcher's Tories as a bulwark against the "satans".
>
> Mr Kostic wrote to the Prime Minister in 1985, imploring her to save the world from "bestial monsters".
>
> "It seems to me that someone (not Gaddafi, IRA, Palestinians or Mafia, they are only the marionettes) organised many years ago a type of international university to study human weakness . . . I am sending a cheque for £5,000 to fight the evil wicked demons and SATANS and I am fully at your disposal," he wrote. . . .
>
> Lawyers for the Conservative Party Association had argued that Mr Kostic's paranoid delusions had not poisoned his affection for his son. [Rajeev Syal, Times (London), Oct. 16, 2007, at 27.]

Breeden v. Stone
Supreme Court of Colorado, 2000
992 P.2d 1167

RICE, J. . . . This case involves a contested probate of a handwritten (holographic) will executed by Spicer Breeden, the decedent.[5] Mr. Breeden died in his

---

5. Spicer Breeden was a member of one of Colorado's most prominent families, a descendant of patriarch Charles Boettcher.

home on March 19, 1996, from a self-inflicted gunshot wound two days after he was involved in a highly publicized hit-and-run accident that killed the driver of the other vehicle.[6]

Upon entering the decedent's home following his suicide, the Denver police discovered on his desk a handwritten document that read: "I want everything I have to go to Sydney Stone — 'houses,' 'jewelwry,' [sic] stocks[,] bonds, cloths [sic]. P.S. I was *Not* Driving the Vehical — [sic]." At the bottom of the handwritten document, the decedent printed, "SPICER H. BREEDEN" and signed beneath his printed name.

Sydney Stone (Respondent) offered the handwritten document for probate as the holographic will of the decedent. The decedent had previously executed a formal will in 1991 and a holographic codicil leaving his estate to persons other than Respondent.[7] Several individuals filed objections to the holographic will, including Petitioners [Spicer Breeden's sister Holly Connell, brother Vic, and father Vic, Sr.], who alleged lack of testamentary capacity. . . .

Growing up in a mountaintop mansion, Spicer Breeden could survey a shining city stamped repeatedly with the name of his mother's family fortune: Boettcher.

A Boettcher gave Denver the downtown estate where the Governor resides. Boettcher Halls grace the city's botanical gardens, theater complex and natural history museum. On the far side of the Rockies, a Boettcher, Mr. Breeden's uncle, helped transform an old mining town into a glittering ski resort: Aspen. . . .

It was 1869 when 17-year-old Charles Boettcher fled Prussia's military draft and joined his older brother selling nails in a hardware store in the Wyoming Territory. When Charles Boettcher died in 1948, he presided over a Rocky Mountain business empire: railroads, ranches, mines, meatpacking plants, cement factories, sugar mills, a life insurance company and the region's most powerful investment house.

As he neared his 96th birthday, the iron-willed entrepreneur told Time Magazine: "I like to work. I've worked hard all my life, and I suppose I'll keep working as long as I can raise a hand."

In contrast, his great-grandson, Spicer, never held a job. At age 13, Spicer Breeden inherited $2 million of the Boettcher fortune from his mother, who died of cancer. As an adult, he spent his time, court records show, using copious amounts of cocaine and racking up speeding tickets and two convictions for driving under the influence of alcohol or drugs. [James Brooke, A Web of Money, Drugs, and Death, N.Y. Times, Mar. 18, 1997, at A12.]

— Eds.

6. On March 17, 1996, while going about 110 miles an hour in his BMW, Breeden and his friend Peter Schmitz struck the car of Greg Lopez, a beloved columnist for the Rocky Mountain News, who was killed instantly. Lopez's widow gave birth to their child seven months after the accident.

The BMW stopped briefly, then sped off. After switching to an Audi sport wagon at Mr. Breeden's house, [Breeden and Schmitz] returned to bar-hopping in Denver's trendy Lower Downtown, according to testimony.

Two days later, on March 19, the police were knocking on Mr. Breeden's door, and the first television crew started broadcasting live from his front lawn. With furniture pushed against the doors and sleeping bags covering the windows, he drank rum, snorted cocaine and watched the television coverage.

Before turning his .357 Magnum revolver on his beloved chow, Gambo, wounding the dog, he scribbled a will that cut his entire family — father, brother and sister — out of his will. He left all his money, less than one-third of his mother's legacy, to [Sydney] Stone. [James Brooke, A Web of Money, Drugs, and Death, N.Y. Times, Mar. 18, 1997, at A12.]

Peter Schmitz was later acquitted of vehicular homicide. Said the jury foreman:

Very few witnesses agreed on anything; there was this jumble of information. But two witnesses for the prosecution testified that Breeden in the year before his death, had said to them that if he ever killed someone in a crash, he would shoot himself and his dog. It's chilling how predictive that was. [James Brooke, After Verdict, Trial Still Grips Denver, N.Y. Times, Mar. 21, 1997, at A26.]

— Eds.

7. In his 1991 holographic codicil, among other things Breeden wrote: "I would very much like Caroline Johnson to have Gambo, my Pet Dog." Breeden also gave Johnson $15,000 in cash. — Eds.

On September 26, 1996, the probate court formally admitted the decedent's holographic will to probate. The court made several findings based on the evidence presented. First, the court found that the decedent used cocaine and alcohol for several years prior to his death, based on the testimony of his friends Jennifer Chelwick and Michael Crow. Relying on the autopsy report and testimony from the decedent's sister, the court found that the decedent used alcohol and cocaine on the evening of March 17 and between March 17 and 19, and that substantial alcohol was consumed proximate to the time of death. Based on the testimony of a number of the decedent's friends, the court found that the decedent's moods were alternately euphoric, fearful, and depressed, and that he was excessively worried about threats against himself and his dog from government agents, friends, and others.[8]

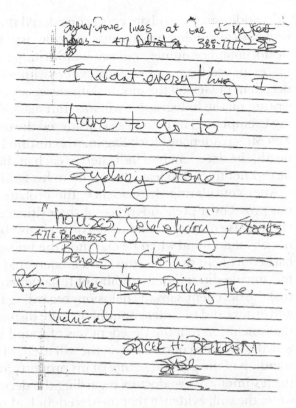

Spicer Breeden's Holographic Will

8. According to the brief filed by Spicer Breeden's brother and sister, the evidence adduced in court showed:

In August of 1995, Spicer was so delusional as a result of cocaine and alcohol abuse that he called Chelwick insisting that she come over to his house because he was covered with bugs and needed to be taken to the emergency room. In order to ease his delusional fears, Chelwick purchased Benedryl [sic] Gel and rubbed it on his arms and legs in order to calm him down and convince him he was not covered with bugs. By September of 1995, Spicer's delusions became more extreme. He thought that people were watching him, following him and that everyone was a FBI agent or DEA agent. In October of 1995, Spicer received a VCR rewinder as a gift which he promptly stomped, destroyed and threw away because he thought that Chelwick had planted a listening device in it. Other examples of Spicer's delusional behavior include being convinced that the FBI was working in conjunction with Public Service to tunnel into his house when new sewer lines were being installed in his neighborhood, that people could monitor his behavior through his television set so he climbed up on the roof and destroyed the antenna, that the cable company could monitor him through the cable wires so he cancelled his cable service, that the FBI could use information against him so he shredded bills, cards and letters, that he had individuals search his house for listening devices, and that he had friends drive by his house to ensure he was not being "watched." On other occasions, Spicer thought that Peter Schmitz ("Schmitz"), another close friend and the individual who was in the car when Greg Lopez was killed, was the Unabomber and that he had planted a bomb in his house, that Vic, Sr., his father, had planted drugs in his Porsche, and that Crow had taken all of the keys to his car and had them copied so as to be able to complete other conspiratorial schemes against him. Other examples of paranoia include . . . spreading corn flakes in the hall outside his bedroom to "crunch" if someone sought to accost him when he slept . . . and changing his locks on multiple occasions to ensure no one had access to his house. During the last six months of his life, Spicer's

In addition, the probate court considered the testimony of a number of expert witnesses, including two forensic toxicologists, two forensic psychiatrists, a forensic document examiner, and two handwriting experts. After considering conflicting evidence from the various expert witnesses, the court concluded that the decedent possessed the motor skills necessary to write his will and that his handwriting on the holographic will was unremarkable when compared to other writing exemplars. The court also considered the testimony of the decedent's friends Ken McSpadden and Rick Eagan, who testified that in the two weeks prior to his death, the decedent had indicated to each of them in separate conversations that he did not intend to leave his estate to his family.[9]

After considering the evidence, the probate court found that Petitioners did not prove by a preponderance of the evidence that, because of the decedent's chronic use of alcohol and drugs or their use between March 17 and 19, he was not of sound mind when he executed the holographic will. In addition, the probate court held that the stress and anxiety that compelled the decedent to commit suicide did not deprive him of testamentary capacity. The court also found that the decedent's insane delusions regarding his friends, government agencies, and others, did not affect or influence the disposition of his property. In reaching the conclusion that the decedent was of sound mind at the time he executed the will, the probate court relied on the will itself, which evidenced a sufficient understanding of the general nature of his property and the disposition under the will, the testimony of two doctors regarding the decedent's motor skills at the time he wrote the will, evidence that the decedent had omitted his father and sister from his will in the past, and testimony from two friends that indicated the decedent had been considering revising his will in the future. . . .

TESTAMENTARY CAPACITY . . .

Until 1973, the proponents of a will assumed the burden of proving that the testator had testamentary capacity at the time he executed a will. However, in

---

delusions caused him to believe that Vic, Sr., his father, Holly, his sister, and all his immediate friends, including Chelwick, Crow, and Schmitz were spying on him, planting drugs, bombs or listening devices in his house or cars, or otherwise threatening his life or freedom. . . .

In the middle of January 1996, Chelwick was visiting Spicer when he had a temper tantrum, threw his drink at her and held her hostage at *gun point* for four hours. . . .

On Friday, March 15, 1996, Spicer hosted a cocaine party during which large amounts of cocaine and alcohol were consumed. Spicer, along with the other participants, were so "blasted" and "wasted" that the party lasted until the last guest took a cab home at 4 a.m. on Sunday, March 17, 1996. Spicer apparently slept through the day of March 17, 1996, and later met Schmitz at the Chop House at approximately 6:30 p.m. They left the Chop House, went to Schmitz's loft, consumed cocaine and while driving to Spicer's house the fatal Lopez accident took place. Spicer then called Stone to inform her that a "bump and go" accident had taken place and if the police were to call her because his car was registered at her house that she was to inform them that he was out of town. During that same conversation, Spicer sought to purchase cocaine from Stone, which Spicer had done in the past. [Petitioners-Appellants' Opening Brief, Breeden v. Stone, Case No. 98 SC 570, at 5-9 (April 19, 1999).]

The Respondents argued that Breeden was not delusional about at least one thing: Evidently, his friend Crow was indeed an FBI informer. Respondent's Answer Brief, Breeden v. Stone, Case No. No. 98 SC 570, at 22 n.8 (May 19, 1999). — Eds.

9. In particular, McSpadden testified that at a March 14, 1996 lunch meeting, the decedent told him that he intended to leave his estate to McSpadden and Respondent.

1973, the legislature shifted this burden to the contestants of a will. Under §15-12-407, once a proponent of a will has offered prima facie proof that the will was duly executed, any contestant then assumes the burden of proving a lack of testamentary capacity, including a lack of sound mind, by a preponderance of the evidence. The issue of what constitutes sound mind has developed along two separate lines of inquiry, summarized below.

A. THE *CUNNINGHAM* TEST . . .

[This court stated] the test for sound mind in 1953 in the landmark case Cunningham v. Stender, 255 P.2d 977 (Colo. 1953), when we held that mental capacity to make a will requires that: (1) the testator understands the nature of her act; (2) she knows the extent of her property; (3) she understands the proposed testamentary disposition; (4) she knows the natural objects of her bounty; and (5) the will represents her wishes.

B. THE INSANE DELUSION TEST

This court has also held that a person who was suffering from an insane delusion at the time he executed the will may lack testamentary capacity. We first defined an insane delusion in 1924 as "a persistent belief in that which has no existence in fact, and which is adhered to against all evidence." In re Cole's Estate, 226 P. 143, 145 (Colo. 1924). We held that a party asserting that a testator was suffering from an insane delusion must meet the burden of showing that the testator suffered from such delusion.

We also have addressed the issue of the causal relationship necessary between an individual's insane delusion and his capacity to contract. See Hanks v. McNeil Coal Corp., 168 P.2d 256, 260 (Colo. 1946). In *Hanks*, [we held] that

[o]ne may have insane delusions regarding some matters and be insane on some subjects, yet [be] capable of transacting business concerning matters wherein such subjects are not concerned, and such insanity does not make one incompetent to contract unless the subject matter of the contract is so connected with an insane delusion as to render the afflicted party incapable of understanding the nature and effect of the agreement or of acting rationally in the transaction. 168 P.2d at 260.

The *Hanks* case sets out a standard for the requisite causal connection between insane delusions and contractual capacity that is equally applicable to testamentary capacity. A number of other courts have applied a similar standard in the context of testamentary capacity by phrasing the inquiry as whether the delusion *materially* affects the contested disposition in the will. See Akers v. Hodel, 871 F.2d 924, 934 (10th Cir. 1989) (holding that test under Oklahoma law is whether an insane delusion materially affected the will); Benjamin v. Woodring, 303 A.2d 779, 784 (Md. 1973) (stating that to set a will aside based on an insane delusion, will must be the consequence or product of the delusion); In re Estate of Aune, 478 N.W.2d 561, 564 (N.D. 1991) (requiring that the will is the consequence or product of an insane delusion in order to set it aside); In re Estate of Kesler, 702 P.2d 86, 88 (Utah 1985) (holding that there was substantial evidence to support that the testator suffered from insane delusions that materially affected the contested will and trust); In re Estate of Watlack, 945 P.2d 1154, 1158 (Wash. App. 1997) (finding that facts supported the conclusion that the will was the product of insane delusions); In re Estate of Evans, 265 N.W.2d 529, 534-35 (Wis. 1978) (stating that "a testamentary document will not be disallowed unless . . . the insane delusion materially affected the disposition embodied in the will").

Based on Colorado precedent and the persuasive authority from other jurisdictions discussed above, we hold that before a will can be invalidated because of a lack of testamentary capacity due to an insane delusion, the insane delusion must materially affect the disposition in the will.

C. *CUNNINGHAM* AND INSANE DELUSION TESTS ARE NOT MUTUALLY EXCLUSIVE

As the preceding case law indicates, the *Cunningham* and the insane delusion tests for sound mind have developed independently of each other.

The *Cunningham* test is most commonly applied in cases in which the objectors argue that the testator lacked general testamentary capacity due to a number of possible causes such as mental illness, physical infirmity, senile dementia, and general insanity.

The insane delusion test ordinarily involves situations in which the testator, although in possession of his general faculties, suffers from delusions that often take the form of monomania or paranoia.[10] See, e.g., Davis v. Davis, 64 Colo. 62, 170 P. 208 (1917) (father who believes his son is not his son suffers from an insane delusion).

As such, the *Cunningham* [general capacity] and insane delusion tests, although discrete, are not mutually exclusive. In order to have testamentary capacity, a testator must have a sound mind. In Colorado, a sound mind includes the presence of the *Cunningham* factors *and* the absence of insane delusions that materially affect the will. As noted above, insane delusions are often material to the making of the will, and thus will defeat testamentary capacity. However, just as in the *Hanks* case, not all insane delusions materially affect the making of a will. Nonetheless, a testator suffering from an immaterial insane delusion must still meet the *Cunningham* sound mind test.

Accordingly, we hold that an objector may challenge a testator's soundness of mind based on both or either of the *Cunningham* and insane delusion tests. . . .

E. PROBATE COURT DECISION . . .

Petitioners argue that the trial court erred by: (1) applying both the *Cunningham* and the insane delusion tests in a case which involves only insane delusions; and (2) merging the *Cunningham* and the insane delusion tests.

Upon reviewing the decision of the probate court, we hold that the court correctly applied these two exclusive tests for testamentary capacity to find that the

---

10. Monomania is defined as "insanity upon a particular subject only, and with a single delusion of the mind," while paranoia is defined as "chronic delusional insanity" that is marked by "a false premise, pursued by a logical process of reasoning to an insane conclusion." 1 William J. Bowe & Douglas H. Parker, Page on Wills §12.31 (4th ed. 1960 & Supp. 1999).

decedent was of sound mind at the time he executed his holographic will. The court found that the decedent had used alcohol and cocaine for several years prior to his death, had used alcohol and cocaine between March 17 and 19, suffered from mood swings, and worried excessively about threats against his and his dog's life. Despite these adverse findings, the court found that the decedent was of sound mind.

First, the court applied the *Cunningham* test and found that the decedent: (1) could index the major categories of the property comprising his estate; (2) knew his home and rental addresses; and (3) identified the devisee by name and provided her current address. The court noted that the will was "legible, logical in content, and reasonably set[ ] out [the decedent's] intent." In addition, the probate court considered the testimony of handwriting experts that indicated that at the time the decedent wrote the will, he was in command of his motor skills and his handwriting was unremarkable when compared to other exemplars. Based upon these factors, the trial court found that the decedent met the *Cunningham* test for sound mind.

Then, the probate court applied the insane delusion test to hold that although the decedent was suffering from insane delusions at the time he executed his will, "[his] insane delusions did not affect or influence the disposition of property made in the will." Cf. In re Haywood's Estate, 240 P.2d 1028, 1033 (Cal. App. 1952) (finding that a testator's hallucination of a headless wolf was not related to the making of the will). In so finding, the probate court considered the decedent's delusions regarding listening devices in his home and car and assassination plots against himself and his dog. In addition, the court weighed the testimony of numerous expert witnesses regarding the decedent's handwriting, his mental state near the time he executed the will, and the impact of his drug and alcohol use on his mental faculties. Further, the court considered testimony from several persons who stated that the decedent was not close to Petitioners, had infrequent contact with them, indicated to friends that he believed his father was irresponsible with money, disliked his sister's husband, and that his relationship with his brother was distant. In fact, the decedent had not made provisions for either Breeden Sr. or Connell in his earlier 1991 will. As such, the probate court concluded that the insane delusions from which the decedent suffered did not materially affect or influence the disposition made in the holographic will. . . .

In sum, the probate court order reflects that the court thoroughly considered all of the evidence presented by the parties and concluded that (1) the testator met the *Cunningham* test for sound mind and (2) the insane delusions from which the decedent was suffering did not materially affect or influence his testamentary disposition. . . .

CONCLUSION

We hold that the probate court correctly applied the two exclusive tests for testamentary capacity to find that the testator, Spicer Breeden, was of sound mind at the time he executed the holographic will. . . . Accordingly, we affirm the

decision of the court of appeals upholding the probate court's ruling that the
decedent was of sound mind . . . .

QUESTIONS AND NOTES

1. The holographic (handwritten) will in *Breeden* does not contain the word
"Will," is not dated, and makes no explicit mention of death. Should it qualify as
a will? See pages 268-285.

2. To prevail in an insane delusion contest, in most jurisdictions the contestant must show that (1) the testator labored under an insane delusion, *and* (2) the
will (or some part thereof) was a product of the insane delusion. In *Breeden*, the
court upheld the will on the grounds that Breeden's insane delusions "did not
materially affect or influence" the will's provisions. In a minority of jurisdictions,
the courts apply a lower standard for causation. In the leading case of In re
Honigman's Will, 168 N.E.2d 676 (N.Y. 1960), a sharply divided court, 4 to 3,
denied probate to a will on the grounds that its dispositive provisions "might have
been caused or affected" by the testator's insane delusion.

In *Honigman*, the testator, after coming to believe that his wife was having an
affair, left his wife only the minimum necessary to satisfy her statutory forced
share, leaving the rest to his brothers and sisters. The majority first upheld the
jury's finding that the testator was laboring under an insane delusion:

> The record is replete with testimony, supplied by a large number of disinterested persons,
> that for quite some time before his death the testator had publicly and repeatedly told friends
> and strangers alike that he believed his wife was unfaithful, often using obscene and abusive
> language. Such manifestations of suspicion were quite unaccountable, coming as they did
> after nearly 40 years of a childless yet, to all outward appearances, a congenial and harmo-
> nious marriage, which had begun in 1916. During the intervening time they had worked
> together in the successful management, operation and ownership of various restaurants, bars
> and grills and, by their joint efforts of thrift and industry, had accumulated the substantial
> fortune now at stake. . . .
>
> When, in the light of all the circumstances surrounding a long and happy marriage such
> as this, the husband publicly and repeatedly expresses suspicions of his wife's unfaithfulness;
> of misbehaving herself in a most unseemly fashion, by hiding male callers in the cellar of her
> own home, in various closets, and under the bed; of hauling men from the street up to her
> second-story bedroom by use of bed sheets; of making contacts over the household
> telephone; and of passing a clandestine note through the fence on her brother's property
> and when he claims to have heard noises which he believed to be men running about his
> home, but which he had not investigated, and which he could not verify the courts should
> have no hesitation in placing the issue of sanity in the jury's hands. To hold to the contrary
> would be to take from the jury its traditional function of passing on the facts. [Id. at
> 677-678.]

Turning to causation, the majority rejected the argument that even if the testator had an insane delusion on the question of his wife's fidelity, there were good
alternative reasons for the testator's disposition, namely, his wife's independent
fortune and his siblings' financial need. In effect, the *Honigman* court assumed

causation by putting the burden on the proponent to show that an unnatural disposition arguably within the insane delusion was not in fact a product of that delusion, a burden that the brothers and sisters could not meet.

Would the outcome in *Honigman* have been different if the court applied the *Breeden* "materially affect or influence" approach to causation? Would the outcome in *Breeden* change under the *Honigman* "might have been caused or affected" threshold for causation? Which approach is more sound?

3.   In Bradley E. S. Fogel, The Completely Insane Law of Partial Insanity: The Impact of Monomania on Testamentary Capacity, 42 Real Prop., Prob. & Tr. J. 67 (2007), Professor Fogel surveyed the case law on insane delusion and concluded that the doctrine should be abolished, leaving only the general test for capacity. Fogel writes: "Fact-finders frequently disregard some evidence in making determinations that a testator's belief is an insane delusion. This leads to arbitrary results that depend more on the fact-finder's willingness to disregard evidence (and the fact-finder's own biases) rather than on the facts of the case." Id. at 105. Do you agree? Does *Strittmater*, *Breeden*, or *Honigman* support Fogel's thesis?

In The Myth of Testamentary Freedom, 38 Ariz. L. Rev. 235 (1996), Professor Leslie argues that

> many courts do not exalt testamentary freedom above all other principles. Notwithstanding frequent declarations to the contrary, many courts are as committed to insuring that testators devise their estates in accordance with prevailing normative views as they are to effectuating testamentary intent. Those courts impose upon testators a duty to provide for those whom the court views as having a superior moral claim to the testator's assets, usually a financially dependent spouse or persons related by blood to the testator. Wills that fail to provide for those individuals typically are upheld only if the will's proponent can convince the fact-finder that the testator's deviation from normative values is morally justifiable. This unspoken rule, seeping quietly, but fervently from case law, directly conflicts with the oft-repeated axiom that testamentary freedom is the polestar of wills law.
>
> Courts impose and enforce this moral duty to family through the covert manipulation of doctrine. [Id. at 236.]

As you read the cases in this book, consider the merits of Professor Leslie's hypothesis and how you might modify it.

NOTE: DEAD MAN'S STATUTES

In an omitted portion of the *Breeden* opinion, the court upheld the trial court's exclusion of certain testimony under the state's dead man's statute. The dead man's statutes, which are still good law in a minority of states, prohibit testimony by an interested party of a decedent's oral statement in support of a claim against the decedent's estate. The purpose of these statutes is to protect the estate of a deceased person from false claims respecting business and other transactions after the deceased person's lips are sealed. The theory is that, because the decedent cannot refute the testimony of the surviving party, the surviving party's lips should be sealed too. See Shoenvogel v. Venator Group Retain, Inc., 895 So. 2d 225, 237-246 (Ala. 2004); In re Unsupervised Estate of Harris, 876 N.E.2d 1132, 1135 (Ind. App. 2007).

Dead man's statutes are highly unpopular with evidence scholars, who take the view that the statutes more often exclude evidence of a valid claim than protect the estate from a fabricated allegation. See Kenneth S. Broun, McCormick on Evidence §65 (6th ed. 2006). Today, most dead man's statutes have been abrogated and there is no such provision in the Federal Rules of Evidence. Some of the abrogating states have repealed the dead man's statute in its entirety. Others have replaced it with a more permissive rule, such as giving the court discretion to admit the testimony if the court first determines that the decedent in fact made the statement, or allowing the testimony if it is corroborated by other evidence.

For further discussion, see Ed Wallis, An Outdated Form of Evidentiary Law: A Survey of Dead Man's Statutes and a Proposal for Change, 53 Clev. St. L. Rev. 75 (2005); Wesley P. Page, Note, Dead Man Talking: A Historical Analysis of West Virginia's Dead Man's Statute and a Recommendation for Reform, 109 W. Va. L. Rev. 897 (2007).

SECTION B.   UNDUE INFLUENCE

1.   *Introduction*

Lord Justice Hannen

Undue influence is one of the most bothersome concepts in all the law. When is influence *undue?* More than a hundred years ago Lord Hannen endeavored to explain what kind of influence is undue as follows:

> To be undue influence in the eye of the law there must be — to sum it up in a word — coercion. . . . It is only when the will of the person who becomes a testator is coerced into doing that which he or she does not desire to do, that it is undue influence.
>
> The coercion may of course be of different kinds, it may be in the grossest form, such as actual confinement or violence, or a person in the last days or hours of life may have become so weak and feeble, that a very little pressure will be sufficient to bring about the desired result, and it may

even be, that the mere talking to him at that stage of illness and pressing something upon him may so fatigue the brain, that the sick person may be induced, for quietness' sake, to do anything. This would equally be coercion, though not actual violence.

These illustrations will sufficiently bring home to your minds that even very immoral considerations either on the part of the testator, or of some one else offering them, do not amount to undue influence unless the testator is in such a condition, that if he could speak his wishes to the last, he would say, "this is not my wish, but I must do it." [Wingrove v. Wingrove, 11 Prob. Div. 81 (U.K. 1885).]

Undue influence may occur where there is a confidential relationship between the parties or where there is no such relationship. Proof may be wholly inferential and circumstantial. The influence may be that of a beneficiary or that of a third person imputed to the beneficiary. If part of a will is the product of undue influence, those portions of the will that are the product of such influence may be stricken and the remainder of the will allowed to stand, if the invalid portions of the will can be separated without defeating the testator's intent or destroying the testamentary scheme. An inter vivos transfer that is a product of undue influence is likewise invalid.

Restatement (Third) of Property: Wills and Other Donative Transfers (2003)

§8.3   UNDUE INFLUENCE, DURESS, OR FRAUD

(a) A donative transfer is invalid to the extent that it was procured by undue influence, duress, or fraud.

(b) A donative transfer is procured by undue influence if the wrongdoer exerted such influence over the donor that it overcame the donor's free will and caused the donor to make a donative transfer that the donor would not otherwise have made. . . .

COMMENT:

e. Undue Influence. The doctrine of undue influence protects against overreaching by a wrongdoer seeking to take unfair advantage of a donor who is susceptible to such wrongdoing on account of the donor's age, inexperience, dependence, physical or mental weakness, or other factor. A donative transfer is procured by undue influence if the influence exerted over the donor overcame the donor's free will and caused the donor to make a donative transfer that the donor would not otherwise have made. The alleged wrongdoer need not be present when the donative document was executed in order to exert undue influence. Direct evidence of the wrongdoer's conduct and the donor's subservience is rarely available to establish the actual exertion of undue influence. The contestant's case must usually be based on circumstantial evidence, and in certain cases, is aided by a presumption of undue influence.

In the absence of direct evidence of undue influence, circumstantial evidence is sufficient to raise an inference of undue influence if the contestant proves that (1) the donor was *susceptible* to undue influence, (2) the alleged wrongdoer had an *opportunity* to exert undue influence, (3) the alleged wrongdoer had a *disposition* to exert undue influence, and (4) there was a *result* appearing to be the effect of the undue influence [emphasis added].

Shorthand formulations of undue influence, as in the Restatement provisions quoted above, inevitably beg the question because they do not tell us what influence is *undue*. While a capacity case involves an assessment of the testator's status, an undue influence case involves an assessment of conduct. Hence, in deciding when influence is "undue," judges and juries are inevitably affected by social context. Perhaps the only satisfactory way of acquiring a lawyer's feel for the contours of the undue influence doctrine is to immerse yourself in the cases.

2. *What Influence Is Undue?*

ESTATE OF LAKATOSH, 656 A.2d 1378 (Pa. Super. 1994): In March 1988, Roger Jacobs befriended the decedent, Rose Lakatosh, who was then in her 70s, living alone with only an occasional visit from her sister. "Roger lived just a few miles from Rose and visited her at least once a day and sometimes as often as two or three times a day. Roger assisted Rose around her house and drove Rose to various appointments and took her on various errands. These facts suggest that this elderly woman came to depend on Roger as the only person with whom she really had substantial contact."

A few months after they met, Roger suggested that Rose give him a power of attorney. On November 11, 1988, she executed both a power of attorney and a new will leaving all but $1,000 of her $268,000 estate to Roger, who was not present at the execution. The lawyer who drafted the will was Roger's second cousin, to whom Roger had referred Rose on an unrelated lawsuit.

Roger took advantage of his relationship with Rose:

> Concerning Rose's finances and Roger's power of attorney, Roger unlawfully converted $128,565.29 in assets from Rose's estate for his own benefit or for the benefit of others, not including Rose, from September, 1988 to June, 1990. Among other improper conversions, Roger caused approximately $72,000.00 of Rose's assets to be transferred to Patricia Fox, a woman who had been friends with Roger since February of 1984, but who was not known by Rose personally.
>
> In June, 1990, Rose was living in squalor and filth and had fallen behind in the payment of certain household bills including water/sewer bills, and County and City property taxes. On June 18, 1990 Rose executed a general revocation of the power of attorney placed in Roger Jacobs. On September 4, 1993, Rose died.

The court put the burden on Roger to rebut a presumption of undue influence:

> When the proponent of a will proves that the formalities of execution have been followed, a contestant who claims that there has been undue influence has the burden of proof. *The*

burden may be shifted so as to require the proponent to disprove undue influence. To do so, the contestant must prove by clear and convincing evidence [1] that there was a confidential relationship, [2] that the person enjoying such relationship received the bulk of the estate, and [3] that the decedent's intellect was weakened.

The three elements of this burden-shifting rule were easily met. "Roger developed a confidential relationship with Rose since he occupied a position towards Rose as an advisor, counselor and confidant, and inspired Rose's confidence that he would act in good faith for her interests." The court also held that the power of attorney "in and of itself" was sufficient for a finding that a confidential relationship existed.

Next, under the disputed will Roger received the bulk of the estate. Finally, Rose's intellect was weakened:

> Although Roger testified that Rose was in good physical and mental health on the day the will was executed and that he had no difficulty communicating with her, he also testified that, around the time of the will's execution, Rose had trouble remembering things and had no understanding of her estate or assets. Significantly, it was Roger himself who suggested that Rose execute a power of attorney so that someone could help her if it was necessary. According to Roger's testimony, he was concerned with Rose's susceptibility to being taken advantage of, and it was this concern which sparked the idea for the power of attorney. . . .
>
> Further, an audio tape, which had been made of a conversation between Rose and [her lawyer, Roger's cousin] on the day the will was executed, also evidences the notion that Rose suffered from a weakened intellect at the time. [The lawyer] testified at trial that, because Roger was to receive the bulk of Rose's estate and was not her blood relative, he thought it wise to make the tape as evidence of the will's validity, should it be challenged. Instead of reinforcing the integrity of the will, the audio tape supports the proposition that Rose suffered from a weakened intellect.
>
> The audio tape revealed that Rose was easily distracted and clearly had difficulty remaining focused on the issue of the will. Also, as pointed out by the trial court, even though [the lawyer] repeatedly attempted to re-direct Rose's attention to the issue of the will, she could not remain focused or coherent. Rose made several comments on the tape which indicate that she had a weakened intellect and that she was somewhat out of touch with reality. Specifically, Rose referred to Roger as "an angel of mercy" who "saved her life" because, before she met him, she had been "so low in hell." Rose also repeatedly claimed that her nephew, Dean Berg, threatened to rob and kill her and that he was persecuting and torturing her.
>
> Finally, proof of Rose's weakened intellect can be seen in the state in which she was living. That is, she was an elderly woman; helpless and unable to prevent the consumption of her assets by Roger during the period before and after the execution of her will, from September, 1988, to June, 1990, when she finally had Roger's power of attorney revoked. Also, Rose was living in filth in the spring of 1990, with her bills not having been paid, and, after a house fire, it was discovered that her house was in shambles with trash throughout and dead cats found in her freezer and bathtub.

The court concluded:

> As a result, the burden of disproving undue influence shifted to Roger. "Once the burden of disproving undue influence shifts to the proponent [of the will], it is incumbent upon the

proponent to demonstrate the absence of undue influence by clear and convincing evidence." Burns v. Kabboul, 595 A.2d 1153, 1163 (Pa. Super. 1991).

Consequently, we conclude that the trial court's findings rest on legally competent evidence and the trial court did not commit error or abuse its discretion in finding that Rose's will should be revoked because Roger failed to carry his burden of proving the absence of undue influence.

The court affirmed the order of the trial court, revoking the probate of Rose's will and imposing a constructive trust on Roger in the amount of $128,565.29.

NOTE: PRESUMPTIONS, BURDEN SHIFTING, AND UNDUE INFLUENCE

In most jurisdictions, undue influence cases are complicated by questions about the burden of proof (or, more specifically, the burden of persuasion). The proponent of a will has the burden of proving its validity, but this is easily done in most cases by showing due execution. The person contesting the will then has the burden of proving undue influence either directly or indirectly by proving facts that would give rise to a presumption of undue influence. To trigger this presumption, the contestant must establish the existence of a confidential relationship between the influencer and the testator plus, in most jurisdictions, one or more additional suspicious circumstances. See Restatement (Third) of Property: Wills and Other Donative Transfers §8.3, cmt. f (2003).

Confidential relationship. In a normal relationship, each party is free to be self-serving. But in certain circumstances — what the law calls a confidential relationship — the law requires one or both parties to be other-regarding because of the nature of the relationship and the potential for abuse.

> When examined more closely, the term "confidential relationship" embraces three sometimes distinct [and sometimes overlapping] relationships — fiduciary, reliant, or dominant-subservient. . . .
>
> A fiduciary relationship is one in which the confidential relationship arises from a settled category of fiduciary obligation. Some fiduciary relationships are between the donor and a hired professional. For example, an attorney is in a fiduciary relationship with his or her client. . . . [Likewise,] an agent under a power of attorney is in a fiduciary relationship with his or her principal. . . .
>
> Whether a reliant relationship exists is a question of fact. The contestant must establish that there was a relationship based on special trust and confidence, for example, that the donor was accustomed to be guided by the judgment or advice of the alleged wrongdoer or was justified in placing confidence in the belief that the alleged wrongdoer would act in the interest of the donor. Examples might include the relationship between a financial adviser and customer or between a doctor and patient.
>
> Whether a dominant-subservient relationship exists is a question of fact. The contestant must establish that the donor was subservient to the alleged wrongdoer's dominant

influence. Such a relationship might exist between a hired caregiver and an ill or feeble donor or between an adult child and an ill or feeble parent. [Restatement (Third) of Property, supra, §8.3, cmt. g.]

Suspicious circumstances. In addition to a confidential relationship, to trigger a presumption of undue influence, the contestant must usually show the existence of suspicious circumstances. In some jurisdictions, this may be satisfied by showing that the influencer procured the will. In re Estate of Moretti, 871 N.E.2d 493 (Mass. App. 2007). In other jurisdictions, as in *Lakatosh*, the extra elements are that the person in the confidential relationship received the bulk of the estate and that the decedent had a weakened intellect.

Restatement (Third) of Property, supra, §8.3, cmt. h, provides a nonexhaustive list of suspicious circumstances:

(1) the extent to which the donor was in a weakened condition, physically, mentally, or both, and therefore susceptible to undue influence;

(2) the extent to which the alleged wrongdoer participated in the preparation or procurement of the will or will substitute;

(3) whether the donor received independent advice from an attorney or from other competent and disinterested advisors in preparing the will or will substitute;

(4) whether the will or will substitute was prepared in secrecy or in haste;

(5) whether the donor's attitude toward others had changed by reason of his or her relationship with the alleged wrongdoer;

(6) whether there is a decided discrepancy between a new and previous wills or will substitutes of the donor;

(7) whether there was a continuity of purpose running through former wills or will substitutes indicating a settled intent in the disposition of his or her property; and

(8) whether the disposition of the property is such that a reasonable person would regard it as unnatural, unjust, or unfair, for example, whether the disposition abruptly and without apparent reason disinherited a faithful and deserving family member.

Burden shifting. If the presumption of undue influence is triggered, the burden shifts back to the proponent to rebut the presumption. The idea is that a person who benefits from a confidential relationship "can take precautions to ensure that proof exists that the transaction was fair and that his principal was fully informed, and he is in the best position after the transaction to explain and justify it." Cleary v. Cleary, 692 N.E.2d 955, 960 (Mass. 1998).

The question thus arises, what must the proponent show to overcome the presumption? In Jackson v. Schrader, 676 N.W.2d 599 (Iowa 2003), the court held that "the rule for rebutting the presumption of undue influence arising from a confidential relationship only requires the grantee of a transaction to prove by clear, satisfactory, and convincing evidence that the grantee acted in good faith throughout the transaction and the grantor acted freely, intelligently, and voluntarily."

NOTE

By statute, California invalidates any donative transfer to a *care custodian* of the donor. Cal. Prob. Code §21350(a)(6) (2008). The term "care custodian" is defined to include any "protective, public, sectarian, mental health, or private assistance or advocacy agency or person providing health services or social services to elders or dependent adults." Cal. Welf. & Inst. Code §15610.17(y) (2008). As we have seen, in many states, such a transfer would trigger a rebuttable presumption of undue influence. Under the California statute, however, to validate the transfer the custodian must satisfy one of the byzantine exceptions provided for by Cal. Prob. Code §21351 (2008), such as the involvement of an independent lawyer who signed a statutory "certificate of independent review." Much turns, therefore, on whether the beneficiary is a "care custodian." The California lower courts had concluded that the term only applied to professionals, but in Bernard v. Foley, 139 P.3d 1196 (Cal. 2006), the state supreme court rejected this interpretation, holding 4 to 3 that gifts to preexisting personal friends fall within the statutory proscription. For further discussion, including treatment of proposed amendments to the statute, see David Horton, The Uneasy Case for California's Care Custodian Statute, 12 Chap. L. Rev. 47 (2008).

In re Will of Moses
Supreme Court of Mississippi, 1969
227 So. 2d 829

[Fannie Traylor Moses was thrice married; each of her husbands died. During the second marriage, she struck up a friendship with Clarence Holland, an attorney 15 years her junior. After the death of her third husband, Holland became Mrs. Moses's lover as well as attorney, and this relationship continued for several years until Mrs. Moses died at age 57. During the six or seven years preceding her death, Mrs. Moses suffered from serious heart trouble, had a breast removed because of cancer, and became an alcoholic. Three years before death she made a will devising almost all of her property to Holland. This will was drafted by a lawyer, Dan Shell, who had no connection with Holland, and who did not tell Holland of the will. Mrs. Moses's closest relative was an elder sister. The sister attacked the will on the ground of undue influence. The chancellor found undue influence and denied probate. Holland appealed.]

SMITH, J. . . . A number of grounds are assigned for reversal. However, appellant's chief argument is addressed to the proposition that even if Holland, as Mrs. Moses' attorney, occupied a continuing fiduciary relationship with respect to her on May 26, 1964, the date of the execution of the document under which he claimed her estate, the presumption of undue influence was overcome because, in making the will, Mrs. Moses had the independent advice and counsel of one entirely devoted to her interests. It is argued that, for this reason, a decree should be entered here reversing the chancellor and admitting the 1964 will to probate. . . .

The evidence supports the chancellor's finding that the confidential or fiduciary relationship which existed between Mrs. Moses and Holland, her attorney, was a subsisting and continuing relationship, having . . . ended only with Mrs. Moses' death. Moreover, its effect was enhanced by the fact that throughout this period, Holland was in almost daily attendance upon Mrs. Moses on terms of the utmost intimacy. There was strong evidence that this aging woman, seriously ill, disfigured by surgery, and hopelessly addicted to alcoholic excesses, was completely bemused by the constant and amorous attentions of Holland, a man 15 years her junior. There was testimony too indicating that she entertained the pathetic hope that he might marry her. Although the evidence was not without conflict and was, in some of its aspects, circumstantial, it was sufficient to support the finding that the relationship existed on May 26, 1964, the date of the will tendered for probate by Holland.

The chancellor's factual finding of the existence of this relationship on that date is supported by evidence and is not manifestly wrong. Moreover, he was correct in his conclusion of law that such relationship gave rise to a presumption of undue influence which could be overcome only by evidence that, in making the 1964 will, Mrs. Moses had acted upon the independent advice and counsel of one entirely devoted to her interest.

Appellant takes the position that there was undisputed evidence that Mrs. Moses, in making the 1964 will did, in fact, have such advice and counsel. He relies upon the testimony of the attorney in whose office that document was prepared to support his assertion.

This attorney was and is a reputable and respected member of the bar, who had no prior connection with Holland and no knowledge of Mrs. Moses' relationship with him. He had never seen nor represented Mrs. Moses previously and never represented her afterward. He was acquainted with Holland and was aware that Holland was a lawyer.

A brief summary of his testimony, with respect to the writing of the will, follows:

Mrs. Moses had telephoned him for an appointment and had come alone to his office on March 31, 1964. She was not intoxicated and in his opinion knew what she was doing. He asked her about her property and "marital background." He did this in order, he said, to advise her as to possible renunciation by a husband. She was also asked if she had children in order to determine whether she wished to "pretermit them." As she had neither husband nor children this subject was pursued no further. He asked as to the values of various items of property in order to consider possible tax problems. He told her it would be better if she had more accurate descriptions of the several items of real and personal property comprising her estate. No further "advice or counsel" was given her.

On some later date, Mrs. Moses sent in (the attorney did not think she came personally and in any event he did not see her), some tax receipts for purposes of supplying property descriptions. He prepared the will and mailed a draft to her. Upon receiving it, she telephoned that he had made a mistake in the devise of certain realty, in that he had provided that a relatively low valued property should go to Holland rather than a substantially more valuable property which she said she wanted Holland to have. He rewrote the will, making this change, and mailed it to her, as revised, on May 21, 1964. On the one occasion when he saw Mrs. Moses, there were no questions and no discussion of any kind as to Holland being preferred to the exclusion of her blood relatives. Nor was there any inquiry or discussion as to a possible client-attorney relationship with Holland. The attorney-draftsman wrote the will according to Mrs. Moses' instructions and said that he had "no interest in" how she disposed of her property. He testified "I try to draw the will to suit their purposes and if she (Mrs. Moses) wanted to leave him (Holland) everything she had, that was her business as far as I was concerned. I was trying to represent her in putting on paper in her will her desires, and it didn't matter to me to whom she left it . . . I couldn't have cared less."

When Mrs. Moses returned to the office to execute the will, the attorney was not there and it was witnessed by two secretaries. . . .

The attorney's testimony supports the chancellor's finding that nowhere in the conversations with Mrs. Moses was there touched upon in any way the proposed testamentary disposition whereby preference was to be given a nonrelative to the exclusion of her blood relatives. There was no discussion of her relationship with Holland, nor as to who her legal heirs might be, nor as to their relationship to her, after it was discovered that she had neither a husband nor children.

It is clear from his own testimony that, in writing the will, the attorney-draftsman, did no more than write down, according to the forms of law, what Mrs. Moses told him. There was no meaningful independent advice or counsel touching upon the area in question and it is manifest that the role of the attorney in writing the will, as it relates to the present issue, was little more than that of scrivener. The chancellor was justified in holding that this did not meet the burden nor overcome the presumption.

The sexual morality of the personal relationship is not an issue. However, the intimate nature of this relationship is relevant to the present inquiry to the extent that its existence, under the circumstances, warranted an inference of undue influence, extending and augmenting that which flowed from the attorney-client relationship. Particularly is this true when viewed in the light of evidence indicating its employment for the personal aggrandizement of Holland. . . .

[T]he decree of the chancery court will be affirmed.

ROBERTSON, J., dissenting. . . . Mrs. Fannie T. Moses was the active manager of commercial property in the heart of Jackson, four apartment buildings containing ten rental units, and a 480-acre farm until the day of her death. All of the witnesses conceded that she was a good businesswoman, maintaining and repairing her properties with promptness and dispatch, and paying her bills promptly so that she would get the cash discount. She was a strong personality and pursued her own course, even though her manner of living did at times embarrass her sisters and estranged her from them.

It was not contended in this case that Holland was in any way actively concerned with the preparation or execution of the will. Appellees rely solely upon the finding of the chancellor that there were suspicious circumstances. However, the suspicious circumstances listed by the chancellor in his opinion had nothing whatsoever to do with the preparation or execution of the will. These were remote antecedent circumstances having to do with the meretricious relationship of the parties, and the fact that at times Mrs. Moses drank to excess and could be termed an alcoholic, but there is no proof in this long record that her use of alcohol affected her will power or her ability to look after her extensive real estate holdings. . . .

The majority was indeed hard put to find fault with . . . [the actions of Dan Shell, the attorney who drew the will,] on behalf of his client. . . . He ascertained that Mrs. Moses was competent to make a will; he satisfied himself that she was acting of her own free will and accord, and that she was disposing of her property exactly as she wished and intended. No more is required.

There is not one iota of testimony in the voluminous record that Clarence Holland even knew of this will, much less that he participated in the preparation or execution of it. The evidence is all to the contrary. The evidence is undisputed that she executed her last will after the fullest deliberation, with full knowledge of what she was doing, and with the independent consent and advice of an experienced and competent attorney whose sole purpose was to advise with her and prepare her will exactly as she wanted it.

In January 1967, about one month before her death and some two years and eight months after she had made her will, she called W.R. Patterson, an experienced, reliable and honorable attorney who was a friend of hers, and asked him to come by her home for a few minutes. Patterson testified:

> She said, "Well, the reason I called you out here is that I've got an envelope here with all of my important papers in it, and *that includes my last will and testament*," and says, "I would like to leave them with you if you've got a place to lock them up in your desk somewhere there in your office." . . .
>
> [A]nd she said, *"Now, Dan Shell drew my will for me two or three years ago,"* and says, *"It's exactly like I want it,"* and says, *"I had to go to his office two or three times to get it the way I wanted it, but this is the way I want it,* and if anything happens to me I want you to take all these papers and give them to Dan," and she says, "He'll know what to do with them." (Emphasis added.)

What else could she have done? She met all the tests that this Court and other courts have carefully outlined and delineated. The majority opinion says that this still was not enough, that there were "suspicious circumstances" . . . , but even these were not connected in any shape, form or fashion with the preparation or execution of her will. They had to do with her love life and her drinking habits and propensities. . . .

If full knowledge, deliberate and voluntary action, and independent consent and advice have not been proved in this case, then they just cannot be proved. . . . I think that the judgment of the lower court should be reversed and the last will and testament of Fannie T. Moses executed on May 26, 1964, admitted to probate in solemn form.

QUESTIONS AND NOTES

1.   Why is evidence of a sexual relationship outside of marriage admissible in undue influence cases? In Kelly's Estate, 46 P.2d 84, 92 (Or. 1935), the court suggested the reason was that a sexual relationship casts a suspicion of deceit and "cautions the court to examine the evidence with unusual care."

Since a person ordinarily has a sustained sexual relationship only with a partner for whom there is considerable affection, perhaps even love, why doesn't evidence of such a relationship indicate that the partner is a natural object of the decedent's bounty? In view of the increased number of committed couples living together without marriage, why should sensual pleasures without the benefit of clergy continue to be evidence of *undue* influence? See Estate of Schlagel, 89 P.3d 419 (Colo. App. 2003), upholding a husband's bequest to his wife's live-in caregiver, with whom the husband had an "intimate and romantic" relationship. The caregiver continued to live with the husband after the wife was put into a nursing home.

In Estate of Reid, 825 So. 2d 1 (Miss. 2002), the testator, an octogenarian, adopted a law student in his late twenties. The adopted son took the testator to a lawyer to effect the transfer of various property to the son and to execute a will in the son's favor. The trial court found "an intimate relationship" that "went beyond a mother/son relationship." These facts, plus the son's power of attorney, the testator's advanced age, and the son's dominance over the testator, gave rise to a presumption of undue influence that the son was not able to overcome. The court also set aside the adoption as fraudulent.

For further discussion, see Joseph W. de Furia, Jr., Testamentary Gifts Resulting from Meretricious Relationships: Undue Influence or Natural Beneficence?, 64 Notre Dame L. Rev. 200 (1989); Lawrence A. Frolik, The Biological Roots of the Undue Influence Doctrine: What's Love Got to Do with It?, 57 U. Pitt. L. Rev. 841 (1996).

2.   What role, if any, did the court's view of gender roles play in *Moses*? If Fannie Moses had been a man named Frank, and Clarence had been a woman named Clara, but otherwise the facts were essentially the same, would the result be the same? See Arlene Derenski and Sally B. Landsberg, The Age Taboo: Older Women-Younger Men Relationships (1981). Is a relationship between a young man and a woman 15 years older necessarily suspect? What about the actors Demi Moore and Ashton Kutcher? Moore is 15 years older than Kutcher.

***Ashton Kutcher
and Demi Moore***

IN RE KAUFMANN'S WILL, 247 N.Y.S.2d 664 (App. Div. 1964), aff'd, 205 N.E.2d 864 (N.Y. 1965): In 1948, at the age of 34, Robert Kaufmann, a multimillionaire by inheritance, seeking an independent life away from his family, moved from Washington to New York City. There he took up oil painting, engaged a psychoanalyst — the eminent and sought-after Dr. Janet Rioch — and met Walter Weiss, age 39, a man without material assets of consequence. Within a year after their meeting, Robert employed Walter as his financial consultant and had all his records moved to New York from the Kaufmann family office in Washington. More or less at the same time, Walter moved into Robert's apartment. In 1951 Robert bought an expensive townhouse at 42 East 74th Street. He remodeled the top floor into an office for Walter. The rest of the house was lavishly furnished as a home for Robert and Walter. Walter ran the household, overseeing the cooking, cleaning, and entertaining; answering the mail and the telephone; paying bills from Robert's bank account; and recommending doctors for Robert's various complaints. Robert was a talented artist and spent much of his time painting; he opened an art gallery where he exhibited his works and those of other artists. In their social life, Robert and Walter appeared as a couple, entertaining on a grand scale and exhibiting much love, affection, and mutual esteem. (Of course that is not to say that neither had a roving eye. Once, when Robert took a young man off to Paris, Walter followed unannounced a few days later and threw the young man out of the hotel, while Robert stood by silently.) In business matters, Robert gave Walter (who had a law degree but did not practice) his complete confidence and trust. Walter took charge of Robert's bank accounts and investments as if they belonged to the both of them. The two men lived together until 1959, when Robert died unexpectedly.

Beginning in 1951, Robert made wills in successive years, each will increasing Walter's share of his estate. In 1958, Robert executed a will, drafted by a prominent New York law firm, which left substantially all his property to Walter. Accompanying it was a letter addressed to Robert's family, signed by Robert in 1951, and passed along with each subsequent will. This letter might be described as a "coming out of the closet at death" letter. It stated that when Robert met Walter, Robert was "terribly unhappy, highly emotional and filled to the brim with a grandly variegated group of fears, guilt and assorted complexes." It stated that Walter encouraged Robert to submit to psychoanalysis and went on to say:

> Walter gave me the courage to start something which slowly but eventually permitted me to supply for myself everything my life had heretofore lacked: an outlet for my long-latent but strong creative ability in painting . . . , a balanced, healthy sex life which before had been spotty, furtive and destructive; an ability to reorientate myself to actual life and to face it calmly and realistically. All of this adds up to Peace of Mind. . . . I am eternally grateful to my dearest friend — best pal, Walter A. Weiss. What could be more wonderful than a fruitful, contented life and who more deserving of gratitude now, in the form of an inheritance, than the person who helped most in securing that life? I cannot believe my family could be anything else but glad and happy for my own comfortable self-determination and contentment and equally grateful to the friend who made it possible.
>
> Love to you all,
Bob

In 1952, Robert executed a document granting Walter exclusive power over Robert's corporeal remains and the authority to make all funeral arrangements; in addition, in the event Robert was incapacitated, Walter was granted the power to consent on Robert's behalf to the performance of any operation he deemed necessary after consultation with Robert's physicians. The instrument provided that Walter was to act as "though he were my nearest relative . . . and that his instructions and consents shall be controlling, regardless of who may object to them." The document in effect gave Walter the power that a legal spouse would have over these matters.

Robert's family in Washington deeply resented Walter's presence and his interfering business advice about the family-owned Kay Jewelry Stores, in which Robert was a major shareholder. The 1951 letter appeared to confirm the family's suspicion that a homosexual relationship existed between Robert and Walter. Upon Robert's death, his brother, Joel, sued to have the 1958 will set aside on the ground of undue influence. In his pretrial deposition, Walter denied that a homosexual relationship existed between the two men, but the appellate judges, and probably the jury as well, suspected that this was a lie. Walter did not take the stand at the trial and, therefore, was not subject to cross-examination.

After two jury trials, both finding undue influence, the majority of the appellate division agreed that the evidence was sufficient "to find that the instrument of June 19, 1958, was the end result of an unnatural, insidious influence operating on a weak-willed, trusting, inexperienced Robert whose natural warm family attachment had been attenuated by false accusations against Joel, subtle flattery suggesting an independence he had not realized and which, in fact, Weiss had stultified, and planting in Robert's mind the conviction that Joel and other members of the family were resentful of and obstructing his drive for independence." Although the earlier wills were not directly in issue, the majority thought the undue influence began before 1951 and tainted all the prior wills and gifts to Walter. The letter signed by Robert, mentioned above, was deemed to be "cogent evidence of his complete domination by Weiss," as was Walter's termination of Robert's dalliance in Paris while Robert stood mute.

The court of appeals affirmed, saying:

> Where, as here, the record indicates that testator was pliable and easily taken advantage of, as proponent admitted, that there was a long and detailed history of dominance and subservience between them, that testator relied exclusively upon proponent's knowledge and judgment in the disposition of almost all of the material circumstances affecting the conduct of his life, and proponent is willed virtually the entire estate, we consider that a question of fact was presented concerning whether the instrument offered for probate was the free, untrammeled and intelligent expression of the wishes and intentions of testator or the product of the dominance of the beneficiary.

QUESTION AND NOTES

1. If, in *Kaufmann*, Robert had been a woman named Roberta, would the result have been the same? What if the cohabitants had been married? See Jeffrey

G. Sherman, Undue Influence and the Homosexual Testator, 42 U. Pitt. L. Rev. 225, 239-248 (1981). See also Ray D. Madoff, Unmasking Undue Influence, 81 Minn. L. Rev. 571 (1997), arguing that the undue influence doctrine denies freedom of testation to those testators who deviate from prescribed testamentary norms in failing to provide for their families, and E. Gary Spitko, Gone But Not Conforming: Protecting the Abhorrent Testator from Majoritarian Cultural Norms Through Minority Culture Arbitration, 49 Case W. Res. L. Rev. 275 (1999), suggesting that a homosexual testator be permitted to direct that any will contest be adjudicated by an arbitrator appointed by the testator.

2.   For a case upholding a jury finding of no undue influence, on facts similar to those in *Kaufmann*, see Estate of Sarabia, 270 Cal. Rptr. 560 (App. 1990).

Lipper v. Weslow
Texas Court of Civil Appeals, 1963
369 S.W.2d 698

McDONALD, C.J.   This is a contest of the will of Mrs. Sophie Block, on the ground of undue influence. Plaintiffs, Julian Weslow, Jr.,[11] Julia Weslow Fortson and Alice Weslow Sale, are the 3 grandchildren of Mrs. Block by a deceased son; defendants are Mrs. Block's 2 surviving children, G. Frank Lipper and Irene Lipper Dover (half brother and half sister of plaintiffs' deceased father). (The will left the estate of testatrix to her 2 children, defendants herein; and left nothing to her grandchildren by the deceased son, plaintiffs herein.) Trial was to a jury, which found that Mrs. Block's will, signed by her on January 30, 1956, was procured by undue influence on the part of the proponent, Frank Lipper. The trial court entered judgment on the verdict, setting aside the will.

Defendants appeal, contending there is no evidence, or insufficient evidence, to support the finding that the will was procured by undue influence.

Testatrix was married 3 times. Of her first marriage she had one son, Julian Weslow (who died in 1949), who was father of plaintiffs herein. After the death of her first husband testatrix married a Mr. Lipper. Defendants are the 2 children of their marriage. After Mr. Lipper's death, testatrix married Max Block. There were no children born of this marriage. Max Block died several months after the death of testatrix.

On 30 January, 1956, Sophie Block executed the will in controversy. Such will was prepared by defendant, Frank Lipper, an attorney, one of the beneficiaries of the will, and Independent Executor of the will. The will was witnessed by 2 former business associates of Mr. Block. Pertinent provisions of the will are summarized as follows:

---

11. Julian Weslow, Jr., became a professional dog trainer, famed throughout Texas and the Southwest for "snake proofing" hunting dogs. The dog is given a zap of electricity through an electric collar when the dog sniffs a defanged rattlesnake, which strikes at the dog simultaneously. Sometimes the dog leaps two feet straight up, but in any case the dog quickly learns to give snakes a wide berth thereafter. "'This collar gives a good jolt,' explains Weslow. 'But it's certainly a lot better than a good jolt of venom.'" De-Snaking Your Dog, Life Adventures Magazine (2002). More than 10,000 dogs die each year from snake bite. See L.A. Times, Sept. 25, 1991, at C6. Weslow is said to have "de-snaked" more than 4,500 dogs. — Eds.

"That I, Mrs. Sophie Block, . . . do make, publish and declare this my last will and testament, hereby revoking all other wills by me heretofore made."

1, 2, 3 AND 4.

(Provide for payment of debts; for burial in Beth Israel Cemetery; and for minor bequests to a servant, and to an old folks' home.)

5.

(Devises the bulk of testatrix's estate to her 2 children, Mrs. Irene Lipper Dover and Frank Lipper (defendants herein), share and share alike.)

6.

(States that $7000. previously advanced to Mrs. Irene Lipper Dover, and $9300. previously advanced to Frank Lipper be taken into consideration in the final settlement of the estate; and cancels such amounts "that I gave or advanced to my deceased son, Julian.")

7.

(Appoints G. Frank Lipper Independent Executor of the estate without bond.)

8.

(Provides that if any legatee contests testatrix's will or the will of her husband, Max Block, that they forfeit all benefits under the will.)

9.

"My son, Julian A. Weslow, died on August 6, 1949, and I want to explain why I have not provided anything under this will for my daughter-in-law, Bernice Weslow, widow of my deceased son, Julian, and her children, Julian A. Weslow, Jr., Alice Weslow Sale, and Julia Weslow Fortson, and I want to go into sufficient detail in explaining my relationship in past years with my said son's widow and his children, before mentioned, and it is my desire to record such relationship so that there will be no question as to my feelings in the matter or any thought or suggestion that my children, Irene Lipper Dover and G. Frank Lipper, or my husband, Max, may have influenced me in any manner in the execution of this will. During the time that my said son, Julian, was living, the attitude of his wife, Bernice, was at times, pleasant and friendly, but the majority of the years when my said son, Julian, was living, her attitude towards me and my husband, Max, was unfriendly and frequently months would pass when she was not in my home and I did not hear from her. When my said son, Julian, was living he was treated the same as I treated my other children; and, my husband, Max, and I gave to each of our children a home and various sums of money from time to time to help in taking care of medical expenses, other unusual expenses, as well as outright gifts. Since my said son Julian's death, his widow, Bernice, and all of her children have shown a most unfriendly and distant attitude towards me, my husband, Max, and my 2 children G. Frank Lipper and Irene Lipper Dover, which attitude I cannot reconcile as I have shown them many kindnesses since they have been members of my family, and their continued unfriendly attitude towards me, my husband, Max, and my said children has hurt me deeply in my declining years, for my life would have been much happier if they had shown a disposition to want to be a part of the family and enter into a normal family relationship that usually exists with a daughter-in-law and grandchildren and great grandchildren. I have not seen my grandson, Julian A. Weslow, Jr. in several years, neither have I heard from him. My granddaughter, Alice Weslow Sale, I have not seen in several years and I have not heard from her, but I heard a report some months ago that she was now living in California and has since married William G. Sale. My granddaughter, Julia Weslow Fortson, wife of Ben Fortson, I have not seen in several years and I was told that she had a child born to her sometime in December 1952, and I have not seen the child or heard from my said granddaughter, Julia, up to this writing, and was informed by a friend that Julia has had another child recently and is now living in Louisiana, having moved from Houston; and needless to say, my said daughter-in-law, Bernice, widow of my deceased son, Julian, I have not seen in several years as she has taken little or no interest in me or my husband, Max, since the death of my son, Julian, with the exception that Christmas a year ago, if I remember correctly, she sent some flowers, which I acknowledged, and I believe she had sent some greeting cards on some occasions prior to that time. My said daughter-in-law, Bernice Weslow, has expressed to me, on several occasions, an intense hatred for my son, G. Frank Lipper, and my daughter, Irene Lipper Dover, which I cannot understand, as my said children have always shown her and her children every consideration when possible, and have expressed a desire to be friendly with her, and them. My said children, G. Frank Lipper, and Irene Lipper Dover, have at all times been attentive to me and my husband, Max, especially during the past few years when we have not been well. I will be 82 years old in June of this year and my husband, Max, will be 80 years of age in October of this year, and we have both been in failing health for the past few years and rarely leave our home, and appreciate any attention that is given us, and my husband, Max, and I cannot understand the unfriendly and distant attitude of Bernice Weslow, widow of my said son, Julian, and his children, before mentioned."

10.
(Concerns personal belongings already disposed of.)
"In Testimony Whereof, I have hereunto signed my name . . . .

"(S) *Sophie Block*"

(Here follows attestation clause and signature of the 2 witnesses.)

The record reflects that the will in question was executed 22 days before testatrix died at the age of 81 years. By its terms, it disinherits the children of testatrix's son, who died in 1949. Defendant, Frank Lipper, gets a larger share than would have been the case if the plaintiffs were not disinherited. Defendant Lipper is a lawyer, and is admittedly the scrivener of the will. There is evidence that defendant Lipper bore malice against his dead half brother. He lived next door to testatrix, and had a key to her house. The will was not read to testatrix prior to the time she signed same, and she had no discussion with anyone at the time she executed it. There is evidence that the recitations in the will that Bernice Weslow and her children were unfriendly, and never came about testatrix, were untrue. There is also evidence that the Weslows sent testatrix greeting cards and flowers from 1946 through 1954, more times than stated in the will.

Plaintiffs offered no direct evidence pertaining to the making and execution of the will on January 30, 1956, and admittedly rely wholly upon circumstantial evidence of undue influence to support the verdict.

All of the evidence is that testatrix was of sound mind at the time of the execution of the will; that she was a person of strong will; that she was in good physical health for her age; and that she was in fact physically active to the day of her death.

Mrs. Weslow's husband died in 1949; and after 1952 the Weslows came about testatrix less often than before.

The witness Lyda Friberg, who worked at the home of testatrix from 1949 to 1952, testified that in *1952* she had a conversation with Bernice Weslow in which Mrs. Weslow told her if her children didn't get their inheritance she would "sue them through every court in the Union"; that she told testatrix about this conversation, and that testatrix told her "she would have those wills fixed up so there would be no court business," and that she wasn't going to "leave them (the Weslows) a dime." The foregoing was prior to the execution of the will on January 30, 1956.

Subsequent to the execution of the will, testatrix had a conversation with her sister, Mrs. Levy. Mrs. Levy testified:

Q. Who did she say she was leaving her property to?
A. She was leaving it to her son and her daughter.
Q. What else did she say about the rest of her kin, if anything?
A. Well she said that Julian's children had been very ugly to her; that they never showed her any attention whatever; they married and she didn't know they were married; they had children and they didn't let her know. After Julian passed away, she never saw any of the family at all. They never came to see her.
Q. Did she make any statement?
A. Yes she did. When she passed away, she didn't want to leave them anything; that they did nothing for her when she was living.

Shortly before she passed away, testatrix told Mrs. Augusta Roos that she was going to leave her property to her 2 children, and further:

Q. Did she give any reason for it?
A. Yes. She said that Bernice had never been very nice to her and the children never were over.

Again, subsequent to the making of her will, testatrix talked with Effie Landry, her maid. Mrs. Landry testified:

Q. Did Mrs. Block on any occasion ever tell you anything about what was contained in her will?
A. Yes.
Q. What did she tell you about that?
A. She said she wasn't leaving the Weslow children anything.

The only question presented is whether there is any evidence of undue influence. The test of undue influence is whether such control was exercised over the mind of the testatrix as to overcome her free agency and free will and to substitute the will of another so as to cause the testatrix to do what she would not otherwise have done but for such control.

The evidence here establishes that testatrix was 81 years of age at the time of the execution of her will; that her son, defendant Lipper, who is a lawyer, wrote the will for her upon her instruction; that defendant Lipper bore malice against his deceased half brother (father of plaintiffs); that defendant Lipper lived next door to his mother and had a key to her home; that the will as written gave defendant Lipper a larger share of testatrix's estate than he would otherwise have received; that while testatrix had no discussion with anyone at the time she executed the will, she told the witness Friberg, prior to executing the will, that she was not going to leave anything to the Weslows; and subsequent to the execution of the will she told the witnesses Mrs. Levy, Mrs. Roos, and Mrs. Landry that she had not left the Weslows anything, and the reason why. The will likewise states the reasons for testatrix's action. The testatrix, although 81 years of age, was of sound mind and strong will; and in excellent physical health. There is evidence that the recitation in testatrix's will about the number of times the Weslows sent cards and flowers were incorrect, to the extent that cards and flowers were in fact sent oftener than such will recites.

The contestants established a confidential relationship, the opportunity, and perhaps a motive for undue influence by defendant Lipper. Proof of this type simply sets the stage. Contestants must go forward and prove in some fashion that the will as written resulted from the defendant Lipper substituting his mind and will for that of the testatrix. Here the will and the circumstances might raise suspicion, but it does not supply proof of the vital facts of undue influence — the substitution of a plan of testamentary disposition by another as the will of the testatrix.

All of the evidence reflected that testatrix, although 81 years of age, was of sound mind; of strong will; and in excellent physical condition. Moreover, subsequent to the execution of the will she told 3 disinterested witnesses what she had done with her property in her will, and the reason therefor. A person of sound mind has the legal right to dispose of his property as he wishes, with the burden on those attacking the disposition to prove that it was the product of undue influence.

Testatrix's will did make an unnatural disposition of her property in the sense that it preferred her 2 children over the grandchildren by a deceased son. However, the record contains an explanation from testatrix herself as to why she chose to do such. She had a right to do as she did, whether we think she was justified or not.

Plaintiffs contend that the record supports an inference that testatrix failed to receive the cards and flowers sent to her, or in the alternative that she failed to know she received same, due to conduct of defendant Lipper. Here again, defendant Lipper had the opportunity to prevent testatrix from receiving cards or flowers from the Weslows, but we think there is no evidence of probative force to support the conclusion that he in fact did such. Moreover, the will itself reflected that *some* cards and flowers were in fact received by the testatrix, the dispute in this particular area, going to the number of times that such were sent, rather than to the fact that any were sent. See also Rothermel v. Duncan, 369 S.W.2d 917 (Tex. 1963).

We conclude there is no evidence of probative force to support the verdict of the jury. The cause is reversed and rendered for defendants.

NOTES AND QUESTIONS

1. In *Lipper*, in spite of the existence of a confidential relationship and suspicious circumstances, the court put the burden on the contestants to prove undue influence. In most states, the presumption of undue influence arising from a confidential relationship and suspicious circumstances would be enough to

uphold a jury verdict of undue influence unless the proponent rebutted the presumption. If the *Lipper* court had taken this approach, would the evidence of Sophie Block's intentions adduced at trial be sufficient to rebut the presumption of undue influence?

In Delapp v. Pratt, 152 S.W.3d 530 (Tenn. App. 2004), the court upheld a jury finding of undue influence against the testator's son based on a presumption of undue influence. The son lived next door to the testator and farmed the testator's land, which was adjacent to his own; he accompanied her to the lawyer who prepared the will; he held a power of attorney from the testator; and the will favored him to the exclusion of his siblings.

2.   Mrs. Block's will included a statement (article 9) setting forth the reasons why she was not making provision for Julian's children. When the possibility of a will contest is anticipated, is this a desirable practice to follow? Or does it create litigable issues of fact? Given the stilted legalese of "said" recital, who do you think probably wrote it? Is a recital in the will any less subject to influence than the dispositive provisions?

When making a statement of reasons for disinheritance, the client should be cautioned against testamentary libel. A further problem, as Professor McMullen observes, is that "some testators use explicit testamentary statements to vent their wrath at presumptive heirs. The statements may provoke disappointed heirs to challenge the will on principle." Judith G. McMullen, Keeping Peace in the Family While You Are Resting in Peace: Making Sense of and Preventing Will Contests, 8 Marq. Elder's Advisor 61, 85 (2006). With a tip of the hat to McMullen (id. at 85-86), here are two examples related by Paul T. Whitcombe, Defamation by Will: Theories and Liabilities, 27 J. Marshall L. Rev. 749 (1994):

> (1) Before anything else is done fifty cents be paid to my son-in-law to buy for himself a good stout rope with which to hang himself, and thus rid mankind of one of the most infamous scoundrels that ever roamed this broad land or dwelt outside of a penitentiary. [Id. at 751 n.13.]
>
> (2) Unto my two daughters, Frances Marie and Denise Victoria, by reason of their unfilial attitude toward a doting father, . . . I leave the sum of $1.00 to each and a father's curse. May their lives be fraught with misery, unhappiness, and poignant sorrow. May their deaths be soon and of a lingering malignant and torturous nature. May their souls rest in hell and suffer the torments of the condemned for eternity. [Id. at 752 n.14.]

NOTE: NO-CONTEST CLAUSES

Article 8 of Mrs. Block's will in *Lipper* is an example of a *no-contest* or *in terrorem* clause. Such a clause provides that a beneficiary who contests the will shall take nothing, or a token amount, in lieu of the provisions made for the beneficiary in the will.[12] Do you see the problem with the no-contest clause in Mrs. Block's will?

---

12. In Tunstall v. Wells, 50 Cal. Rptr. 3d 468 (App. 2006), the court upheld a no-contest clause providing that if a beneficiary contested, the beneficiary's *and the beneficiary's siblings'* shares would be forfeited. Said the court,

Because Mrs. Block did not leave the plaintiffs anything in her will, they had nothing to lose by bringing the contest.

A baited no-contest clause discourages will contests by putting the prospective contestant to the choice of taking the certain but smaller provision in the will, or challenging the will for the chance at more if the will is invalidated, but at the risk of taking nothing if the will is upheld. In dealing with these clauses, courts have been pulled in opposite directions by conflicting policies. On the one hand, enforcing no-contest clauses discourages unmeritorious litigation, family quarrels, and defamation of the testator's reputation. On the other hand, enforcing no-contest clauses might inhibit a lawsuit that would prove lack of capacity or undue influence, thereby nullifying the safeguards built around the testamentary disposition of property.

Given these conflicting policies, it is no surprise that the jurisdictions diverge on how to treat no-contest clauses. Most enforce a no-contest clause unless there is probable cause for the contest. The probable cause standard, which is adopted by UPC §§2-517 and 3-905 and Restatement (Third) of Property: Wills and Other Donative Transfers §8.5 (2003), reduces the risk to the contestant of bringing a contest, but only if the contestant has a colorable basis for the claim. The courts also narrowly construe no-contest clauses to limit their reach. Harrison v. Morrow, 977 So. 2d 457 (Ala. 2007). At least two states, Indiana and Florida, do not enforce no-contest clauses at all. Others, including California, enforce no-contest clauses unless the contestant alleges forgery or subsequent revocation by a later will or codicil, or the challenge is to a provision benefitting the drafter of the will or any witness thereto. These jurisdictions take the position that a general probable cause rule encourages litigation and shifts the balance unduly in favor of contestants, though they leave undisturbed the normal litigation incentives for the excepted matters. See Donna R. Bashaw, Are In Terrorem Clauses No Longer Terrifying?, 2 NAELA J. 349 (2006).

The lawyer with a client who wishes to contest a will or trust with a no-contest clause must investigate local law carefully because there are subtle differences from state to state not only on enforceability, but also on what steps may be taken prior to a formal "contest" that triggers the clause. Many states provide for limited precontest discovery or other safe harbor proceedings to allow for a more informed decision whether to bring a full contest, triggering the clause. See Matter of Singer, 859 N.Y.S.2d 727 (A.D. 2008) (deposition of testator's attorney was not protected by the state's safe harbor precontest discovery statute).

NOTE: BEQUESTS TO ATTORNEYS

Undue influence. The will in Lipper v. Weslow was drafted by Mrs. Block's son, an attorney and a principal beneficiary under the will. Many courts, concerned

---

"the fairness of a testamentary instrument, unless it violates public policy, is not an issue for judicial review." What about a clause that forfeited the shares of the contestant and the contestant's minor children?

with the appearance of impropriety, hold that a presumption of undue influence arises when an attorney-drafter receives a legacy, except when the attorney is related to the testator. The presumption can be rebutted only by clear and convincing evidence provided by the attorney.

In New York, an attorney who is named in a will that the attorney drafted must submit an affidavit explaining the facts and circumstances of the gift, and if the surrogate is not satisfied with the explanation, a hearing is held to determine whether the attorney's bequest was the result of undue influence.

"My goodness! Your dear old uncle seems to have left everything to __me__."

Drawing by Peter Arno.

In California, after a Los Angeles Times reporter investigated the practices of a lawyer, James Gunderson, who opened up an office adjacent to Leisure World (a retirement community, not an amusement park), where he acquired 7,000 clients and prepared numerous wills and inter vivos trusts leaving him millions of dollars, the legislature enacted a statute invalidating any donative transfer to a lawyer who drafts the instrument unless the lawyer is related by blood or marriage to the testator. Cal. Prob. Code §21350 (2008). There is an exception permitting a gift to a nonrelated lawyer-drafter if the client consults an independent lawyer who attaches to the instrument a "Certificate of Independent Review," which must state that the reviewing lawyer concludes the gift is not due to undue influence, fraud, or duress. Id. §21351(b).

For a compelling account of the California scandal, see Paula A. Monopoli, American Probate: Protecting the Public, Improving the Process 39-55 (2003). See also Serge F. Kovaleski and Colin Moynihan, Many Clients of Astor Lawyer Left Him Bequests in Their Wills, N.Y. Times, Jan. 4, 2008, at B1, telling the story of New York lawyer Francis X. Morrissey, Jr., to whom quite a few of his wealthy clients made sizeable bequests in their wills, and who is now under indictment, accused of forging the signature of Brooke Astor, the doyenne of the New York social and philanthropic scene, on an amendment to her last will.

Unethical conduct. Should an attorney who draws a will containing a bequest to herself be subject to disciplinary action? John D. Randall, president of the American Bar Association from 1959 to 1960, was disbarred by the Iowa Supreme Court in 1979 for drafting a will that made him the beneficiary of a client's $4.5 million estate. Committee on Prof. Ethics v. Randall, 285 N.W.2d 161 (Iowa 1979).

Rule 1.8(c) of the Model Rules of Professional Conduct, as revised in 2002, provides as follows:

> A lawyer shall not solicit any substantial gift from a client, including a testamentary gift, or prepare on behalf of a client an instrument giving the lawyer or a person related to the lawyer any substantial gift unless the lawyer or other recipient of the gift is related to the client. For purposes of this paragraph, related persons include a spouse, child, grandchild, parent, grandparent or other relative or individual with whom the lawyer or the client maintains a close, familial relationship.

The comment to Rule 1.8 further advises:

> If effectuation of a substantial gift requires preparing a legal instrument such as a will or conveyance the client should have the detached advice that another lawyer can provide. The sole exception to this Rule is where the client is a relative of the donee.

Even when the client is a relative of the donee, "the lawyer should exercise special care if the proposed gift to the lawyer or a related person is disproportionately large in relation to the gift the client proposes to make others who are equally related." ACTEC Commentaries on the Model Rules 112 (4th ed. 2006).

In Attorney Griev. Commn. v. Brooke, 821 A.2d 414 (Md. 2003), an attorney was suspended from practice indefinitely for drafting a will for a longtime friend that gave the lawyer all of the friend's estate even though the court determined that there had been no undue influence. The friend did not have the advice of independent counsel. See also In re Filosa, 964 A.2d 1148 (R.I. 2009) (upholding public censure of lawyer who drafted a will for an unrelated person that made a substantial gift to the lawyer).

For further discussion, see Joseph W. de Furia, Jr., Testamentary Gifts from Client to the Attorney-Draftsman: From Probate Presumption to Ethical Prohibition, 66 Neb. L. Rev. 695 (1987); Chad A. Hopper, When May an Attorney Accept Gifts or Donations from Clients Without Breaching Rules Relating to Conflicts of Interest?, 24 J. Legal Prof. 445 (2000).

Fiduciary appointments. A closely related issue is whether an attorney may draw a will or trust that names the attorney as executor or trustee. Though such a designation is not a gift, the attorney may nonetheless have a personal interest in the appointment, which usually entitles the fiduciary to fees. Accordingly, the Model Rules require the client's informed consent. The comment to Rule 1.8 advises:

> In obtaining the client's informed consent to the conflict, the lawyer should advise the client concerning the nature and extent of the lawyer's financial interest in the appointment, as well as the availability of alternative candidates for the position.

See also ACTEC Commentaries on the Model Rules, supra, at 95-96, which takes the position that "a client is properly informed if the client is provided with information regarding the role and duties of the fiduciary, the ability of a lay person to serve as fiduciary with legal and other professional assistance, and the comparative costs of appointing the lawyer or another person or institution as fiduciary."

In Lawyer Disciplinary Board v. Ball, 633 S.E.2d 241 (W. Va. 2006), the court disbarred an attorney who, among other ethical lapses, accepted $1.6 million in executor's commissions from the estates of two clients whose wills he drafted, naming himself as executor, and providing that he was to be paid an unusually large percentage of the estate as his commission.

To deal with the problem of lawyers naming themselves or an affiliated lawyer as the executor under a client's will, New York enacted a statute in 1995 that limits the lawyer-executor's commissions to one-half the statutory rate unless the testator executes a separate form, which must be witnessed, indicating that the testator understood she had the option to name someone other than the lawyer as executor and to provide for a commission less than the default statutory rate. N.Y. Surr. Ct. Proc. Act §2307-a (2008).

For further discussion, see Paula A. Monopli, Drafting Attorneys as Fiduciaries: Fashioning an Optimal Ethical Rule for Conflicts of Interest, 66 U. Pitt. L. Rev. 411 (2005); Edward D. Spurgeon and Mary J. Ciccarello, The Lawyer in Other Fiduciary Roles: Policy and Ethical Considerations, 62 Fordham L. Rev. 1357 (1994); Report of the ABA Special Committee on Professional Responsibility, Preparation of Wills and Trusts That Name Drafting Lawyer as Fiduciary, 28 Real Prop., Prob. & Tr. J. 803 (1994).

3. *Planning for and Avoiding a Will Contest*

Let us now consider defensive measures that a testator or the testator's lawyer might undertake if a later contest of the testator's will is anticipated.

Contest grounds. The most common grounds for a will contest are lack of capacity and undue influence. The two are often alleged together; the testator's mental status overlaps with the susceptibility element of undue influence. Professor Langbein has pointed out several features of American probate practice that make this type of litigation more common in the United States than in England or in the European civil law countries:

(1) In civil law countries, children as well as the spouse have a forced share entitlement in the estate of a parent. The disinherited child, who is the typical plaintiff in American testamentary capacity litigation, is unknown to European law. The European parent can leave his heir disgruntled with the statutory minimum, but that share will often be large enough by comparison with the potential winnings from litigation to deaden the incentive to contest.

(2) Many American jurisdictions permit will contests on the question of capacity to be tried to a jury, which may be more disposed to work equity for the disinherited than to obey the directions of an eccentric decedent who is in any event beyond suffering. Civil jury trial has disappeared from English estate law; it was never known on the Continent.

(3) American law is unique among Western civil procedural systems in failing to charge a losing plaintiff with the attorney fees and other costs incurred by the defendant in the course of resisting the plaintiff's unjustified claim. In testamentary capacity litigation the American rule has the effect of requiring decedents' estates to subsidize the depredations of contestants. Put differently, the American rule diminishes the magnitude of a contestant's potential loss, which diminishes his disincentive to litigate an improbable claim.

(4) Civil law systems provide for the so-called authenticated will, which is executed before a quasi-judicial officer called the notary. This is not the only means of making a valid will in European countries, and because it is costly it is not widely used. But the notarial procedure does permit a testator who fears a post-mortem contest to generate during his lifetime and have preserved with the will evidence of exceptional quality regarding, *inter alia*, his capacity. The notary before whom the testator executes his will is not a judge; he does not adjudicate capacity. But he is a legally qualified and experienced officer of the state who is obliged to satisfy himself of the testator's capacity as a precondition for receiving or transcribing the testament. The authenticated will is, therefore, extremely difficult for contestants to set aside for want of capacity in post-mortem proceedings. . . .

A major reason that the impact of capacity litigation in America is so difficult to measure is that most of it is directed towards provoking pretrial settlements, typically for a fraction of what the contestants would be entitled to receive if they were to defeat the will. Especially when such tactics succeed, they do not leave traces in the law reports. Thus, the odor of the strike suit hangs heavily over this field. The beneficiaries named in the will are likely to be either charitable organizations whom the testator preferred to his relatives, or else those of his relatives and friends whom he loved most and who are most likely to want to spare his reputation from a capacity suit. They are typically put to the choice of defending a lawsuit in which a skilled plaintiff's lawyer will present evidence to a jury at a public trial touching every eccentricity that might cast doubt upon the testator's condition, or compromising the suit, thereby overriding the disposition desired by the testator and rewarding the contestants for threatening to besmirch his name. [John H. Langbein, In Living Probate: The Conservatorship Model, 77 Mich. L. Rev. 63, 64-66 (1978).]

In a 1987 study of nine years of will contests in Davidson County (Nashville), Tennessee, Professor Schoenblum found that 74 percent of contestants alleged incapacity and 73 percent alleged undue influence. Defects in execution formalities were a distant third, representing only 17 percent. Consistent with Langbein's emphasis on the significance of the jury in contest litigation, contestants won 42 percent of jury trials, but only 17 percent of bench trials. Jeffrey A. Schoenblum, Will Contests — An Empirical Study, 22 Real Prop., Prob. & Tr. J. 607 (1987).

About 35 years earlier, a study of California will contests determined that when mental capacity or undue influence was an issue, the jury found for the contestant in 77 percent of the cases, but over half of these verdicts for contestants were reversed on appeal by the California Supreme Court on grounds of insufficient evidence. Note, Will Contests on Trial, 6 Stan. L. Rev. 91, 92 (1953).

The states are split on whether undue influence or capacity claims may be tried to a jury, though "the direction of the law is away from the trial of will contests before a jury." Eunice L. Ross and Thomas J. Reed, Will Contests §14:5 (2d ed. 1999 & Supp. 2008). But see UPC §1-306 (1990) (providing for jury trial).

Warning signs. Having developed a feel for the contours of testamentary capacity and undue influence, you should now be able to recognize warning signs that a contest is more likely than usual. You should be concerned, for example, if an eccentric client's new testamentary scheme makes a radical departure from previous plans, if the testator has multiple or blended families arising from multiple marriages, if the testator imposes the sort of conditions on a bequest that are likely to cause the beneficiary to bristle, or if the testator makes a disposition to a mistress or other person or group unpopular with the testator's family.

Perhaps the biggest warning sign is an unnatural disposition, such as the omission of a close family member or an unexplainable distinction among family members of equal relation. The family often has an expectation of an inheritance, which if disappointed might invite a contest. This is particularly so if the testator disinherits or disfavors a child. In such a case, the child might read the will as a personal rejection by the parent. Professor McMullen relates an arresting example:

> In Nelson v. Daniels,[13] a disinherited son contested his mother's will alleging lack of testamentary capacity and undue influence. The will was executed sometime after the son and his mother had been embroiled in a legal dispute over some of the mother's property over which the son had had a power of appointment. The son allegedly transferred the property to himself. Despite the admitted conflict, the son apparently expected to inherit from his mother's estate, and he contested the will even though he had no material facts to support his claims. When asked if he knew of any other individual who could testify to his mother's lack of capacity, he responded: "Well, put it this way. You're not going to make me believe that my mother hated me the day she died." Thus, to the son, a portion of his mother's estate symbolized her love, and presumably her forgiveness for their past conflicts. [Judith G. McMullen, Keeping Peace in the Family While You Are Resting in Peace: Making Sense of and Preventing Will Contests, 8 Marq. Elder's Advisor 61, 81 (2006).]

---

13. No. 94CA29, 1995 WL 535200 (Ohio App. 1995).

Strategies. Where warning signs are present, a prudent lawyer will consider whether extra precautionary measures should be undertaken to prevent or, failing that, prevail in a later will contest.[14] Here are some examples:

Instead of a statement of reasons in the will, as in *Lipper*, the lawyer requests the client to write, in the client's handwriting, a *letter to the lawyer* setting forth in detail the disposition the client wishes to make. Upon receiving the letter, the lawyer replies, detailing the consequences of the disposition for the client's family, and asks for a letter setting forth the reasons for the disposition. After receiving this letter, the will is drafted as the client wants. The letters are kept in the lawyer's files to show any prospective contestant or to enter into evidence at trial, if necessary.

The lawyer arranges to record a *video discussion* between the testator and the lawyer before witnesses during which the testator explains why he wants to dispose of his property in the manner provided in his will. The discussion may include why the testator wants to disinherit an heir. But remember, any facts stated by the testator as justifying disinheritance may be contradicted by a contestant, alleging a mistake or insane delusion. Consider also that the elderly and infirm often look even worse on television and many people do not perform as well as expected once a camera is pointed in their direction. An alternative is dictation to a stenographer.

A variant on the letter and video ideas — most commonly considered when the testator wants to favor one child at the expense of another — is to hold a *family meeting* at which the testator explains to the family the testator's rationale. Particularly if the favored child has special needs or is otherwise financially disadvantaged, such a meeting can go a long way to assure that the psyches of the disfavored child are not bruised when the will is read.

The lawyer arranges for a *professional examination* of his client's level of capacity immediately before executing a will or trust. If the client has no history of mental problems, it might be better to consult his family doctor, rather than a psychiatrist, in order not to raise suspicions of mental problems. But if the client already has a psychiatric history, then an expert might be warranted.

The lawyer takes *extra precautions at the will execution*, such as using disinterested witnesses who will present well when testifying in court, perhaps friends of the testator or community leaders. The lawyer might also have more than the usual informal discussion with the client and the witnesses immediately before signing the will. The lawyer might ask the client to tell the witnesses about the

---

14. An unconventional and ultimately unsuccessful strategy to avoid a contest was employed by a Norwegian man who died in 2003.

The man . . . left a will dividing his possessions among a long list of friends because he had no direct heirs. And, to be sure that no one challenged the document, he threatened to haunt any who tampered with the document.

"I take a solemn and holy vow that, if at all possible, I will pursue you in the darkest hours of the night," he said in the will.

His half sister, who wasn't one of the beneficiaries, took her chances and challenged the will in court. Apparently, the judge doesn't believe in ghosts, because he declared the will void since the two witnesses who signed it testified they didn't know what the document was.

There have been no reports of mysterious late night occurrences from either the half sister or the judge. [You'll be Sorry!, Wis. State J., Oct. 27, 2004, at C1.]

testamentary plan and the reasoning behind it. Immediately after the will has been executed, the lawyer might ask the witnesses to sign affidavits relating their impressions of the testator and what they saw, heard, and talked about at the time of the will execution.

The lawyer suggests a *no-contest clause*, though as we have seen, the clause will have little potency unless the client is willing to make a significant bequest to the potential contestant. See pages 198-199.

Instead of transferring the property by will, the client puts the property in an *inter vivos trust* and names an institutional trustee. Although trusts, too, can be attacked on grounds of incapacity and undue influence,[15] as a practical matter it is harder to upset a trust if the settlor had a course of dealing with the trustee to evidence competence and the absence of influence. Moreover, because in most states the existence of an inter vivos trust may be kept secret from the donor's heirs (see pages 739-745), the potential contestants might not even learn of the trust's existence until it is too late to contest it. Finally, in nearly all states, trust disputes are tried before a judge, even if the equivalent will contest would be before a jury. Hence, an inter vivos trust avoids the risk that a jury will rework the donor's dispositive scheme in an attempt to do equity for a disinherited or disfavored heir.

The client makes outright *inter vivos gifts*. These, too, are subject to challenge, but unlike a transfer at death, the donor is able to testify in defense of her sanity and the absence of undue influence. Even if the donor's relations are aware that a gift has been made, they will often think twice or even three times before contesting an inter vivos gift for fear of angering the donor, who can write the family out of the donor's will.

It is sometimes suggested that the donor could *write a check* for, say, a thousand dollars or more as a gift to each potential contestant on the same day that the donor executes her will or trust. By cashing the check, the contestant invites a vigorous cross-examination in a subsequent contest on the question why he accepted the gift if he thought that the donor lacked capacity or was being unduly influenced. The drawback to this strategy is that it looks like a lawyer's gimmick, and the contestant can argue that he did not know at the time of the donor's lack of capacity or the undue influence.

NOTES AND QUESTIONS

1. For further discussion of precautionary measures, in addition to the article by Professor McMullen cited above, see Jonathan G. Blattmachr, Reducing Estate and Trust Litigation Through Disclosure, In Terrorem Clauses, Mediation, and Arbitration, 9 Cardozo J. Conf. Res. 237 (2008); Gerry W. Beyer, Estate Planning, ch. 9 (3d ed. 2004); Dennis W. Collins, Avoiding a Will Contest — The Impossible

---

15. See Lynch v. Lynch, 260 S.W.3d 834 (Mo. 2008); Uniform Trust Code §§406, 601 (2000); Restatement (Third) of Trusts §§11-12 (2003). See also Alan Newman, Revocable Trusts and the Law of Wills: An Imperfect Fit, 43 Real Prop. Tr. & Est. L.J. 523, 554-561 (2008).

Dream?, 34 Creighton L. Rev. 7 (2000); John H. Langbein, Will Contests, 103 Yale L.J. 2039 (1994).

2.   *Mediation.* The nastiness of squabbles over estates has led many practicing lawyers to suggest family mediation or arbitration of contested probate matters. These approaches have the potential to reduce litigation costs, lessen unwanted publicity, and perhaps to leave more family members speaking to each other. Should a probate court require the parties to enter into mediation (as in divorce or family disputes) before going to trial? Should you add a clause to your clients' wills requiring mediation before trial or even providing for binding arbitration of any disputes? Would the courts enforce such a clause?

Various approaches to mediating and arbitrating estate disputes are explored in Lela P. Love and Stewart E. Sterk, Leaving More Than Money: Mediation Clauses in Estate Planning Documents, 65 Wash. & Lee L. Rev. 539 (2008); Ray D. Madoff, Mediating Probate Disputes: A Study of Court Sponsored Programs, 38 Real Prop., Prob. & Tr. J. 697 (2004); Mary F. Radford, Advantages and Disadvantages of Mediation in Probate, Trust, and Guardianship Matters, 1 Pepp. Disp. Resol. L.J. 241 (2002); E. Gary Spitko, Gone But Not Conforming: Protecting the Abhorrent Testator from Majoritarian Cultural Norms Through Minority-Culture Arbitration, 49 Case W. Res. L. Rev. 275 (1999); Ronald Chester, Less Law, but More Justice? Jury Trials and Mediation as Means of Resolving Will Contests, 37 Duq. L. Rev. 173 (1999). See also the discussion of mandatory arbitration clauses in trusts at pages 608-609.

3.   On adapting parts of the civil law system to American practice, see Nicole M. Reina, Protecting Testamentary Freedom in the United States by Introducing into Law the Concept of the French Notaire, 22 N.Y.L. Sch. J. Intl. & Comp. L. 427 (2003). For a wide-ranging examination of undue influence in American, French, and German Law, see Ronald J. Scalise, Jr., Undue Influence and the Law of Wills: A Comparative Analysis, 19 Duke J. Comp. & Intl. L. 41 (2008).

SECTION C.   FRAUD

It is fairly easy to state the test for *fraud* but often difficult to apply it to particular facts. Fraud occurs where the testator is deceived by a deliberate misrepresentation and does that which he would not have done had the misrepresentation not been made. It is usually said that the misrepresentation must be made with both the *intent* to deceive the testator and the *purpose* of influencing the testamentary disposition. A provision in a will procured by fraud is invalid. The remaining portion of the will stands unless the fraud permeates the entire will or the portions invalidated by fraud are inseparable from the rest of the will.

Where the probate court cannot do justice simply by refusing probate, the will may be probated and then a court with equity powers can impose a constructive trust on one or more of the beneficiaries to remedy any unjust enrichment caused by the fraud.

If fraud occurs in the testamentary setting, it is usually either fraud in the inducement or fraud in the execution. *Fraud in the inducement* occurs when a misrepresentation causes the testator to execute or revoke a will, to refrain from executing or revoking a will, or to include particular provisions in the wrongdoer's favor. Thus:

> *Case 1.* O's heir apparent, *H*, induces *O* not to execute a will in favor of *A* by promising *O* that *H* will convey the property to *A*. At the time *H* makes the promise, *H* has no intent to convey the property to *A*. This is fraud in the inducement. If, on the other hand, at the time of his promise *H* had intended to convey the property to *A*, but *H* had changed his mind after *O*'s death and had refused to convey to *A*, no fraud is involved. However, *A* still may be able to recover from *H* on the theory of a secret trust. See page 595.

Questions of whether the legacy is the fruit of the fraud can be tricky. A fraudulently procured inheritance or bequest is invalid only if the testator would not have left the inheritance or made the bequest had the testator known the true facts. The interesting question, of course, is: What would the testator have done if the true facts had been known?

Estate of Carson, 194 P. 5 (Cal. 1920), is a dramatic illustration of the problem. In this case, J. Gamble Carson went through a marriage ceremony with Alpha O. Carson, and so she naturally assumed that they were married. After living together thereafter happily for a year, Alpha died, devising most of her estate "to my husband J. Gamble Carson." It then came to light that Alpha had been "seduced by a marital adventurer into a marriage with him which was no marriage in the eyes of the law because of the fact, which he concealed from her, that he had already had at least one, if not more, spouses, legal and illegal, who were still living and undivorced." But was the devise the fruit of the fraud? Said the court:

> Now a case can be imagined where, nothing more appearing, as in this case, than that the testatrix had been deceived into a void marriage and had never been undeceived, it might fairly be said that a conclusion that such deceit had affected a bequest to the supposed husband would not be warranted. If, for example, the parties had lived happily together for 20 years, it would be difficult to say that the wife's bequest to her supposed husband was founded on her supposed legal relation with him, and not primarily on their long and intimate association. It might well be that if undeceived at the end of that time her feeling would be, not one of resentment at the fraud upon her, but of thankfulness that she had been deceived into so many years of happiness. But, on the other hand, a case can easily be imagined where the reverse would be true. If in this case the will had been made immediately after marriage, and the testatrix had then died within a few days, the conclusion would be well-nigh irresistible, in the absence of some peculiar circumstance, that the will was founded on the supposed legal relation into which the testatrix had been deceived into believing she was entering. Between these two extreme cases come those wherein it cannot be said that either one conclusion or the other is wholly unreasonable, and in those cases the determination of the fact is for the jury. Of that sort is the present. [Id. at 8-9.]

Fraud in the execution occurs when a person intentionally misrepresents the character or contents of the instrument signed by the testator, which does not in fact carry out the testator's intent. Thus:

Case 2. *O*, with poor eyesight, asks her heir apparent, *H*, to bring her the document prepared for her as a will so that she can sign it. *H* brings *O* a document that is not *O*'s intended will, knowing it is not the document *O* wants. *O* signs it, believing it to be her will. This is fraud in the execution.

PUCKETT v. KRIDA, 1994 WL 475863, 1994 Tenn. App. LEXIS 502 (1994): Nurses Laverne Krida and Mattie Ruth Reeves were hired to provide round-the-clock care for the testator, Nancy Porch Hooper, after she returned home from being hospitalized for Alzheimer's. While under the nurses' care, Hooper's condition improved, but the nurses persuaded Hooper that her relatives were wasting her money and wanted to put her in a nursing home. Neither was true.

The trial court set aside both a deed and a will favoring the nurses as the products of fraud and undue influence. On appeal, the Court of Appeals of Tennessee affirmed, holding that the nurses had a confidential relationship with Hooper for two reasons, each sufficient on its own: (1) their status as nurses, and (2) Krida's status as Hooper's attorney-in-fact under a power of attorney. This confidential relationship, when coupled with the underlying encouragement of Hooper's false beliefs, was enough to raise a presumption of undue influence and fraud. The nurses did not successfully rebut the presumption. Said the court:

> In the instant case, the evidence shows that at the time the defendants were employed, the deceased loved her family and was very close to them. She was frugal and conservative, but entrusted the management of her financial affairs to her niece, Jean Law. The evidence is that Mrs. Law carefully managed these finances and promised to keep the deceased out of a nursing home, making every effort to do so. She never reimbursed herself for any of her expenses.
>
> Subsequent to the defendants' employment, the deceased began to believe that Jean Law wanted to put her in a nursing home and that Ms. Law had misappropriated funds. The evidence shows that neither of these beliefs were true. The evidence further shows that these false beliefs originated with the defendants who systematically separated the deceased from her family and friends and isolated her from all those individuals with whom she had previously dealt, personally and professionally. All of this was done in order to perpetuate the fraud.
>
> Defendants, either individually or collectively, made false statements to the deceased and concealed facts from her. The deceased was led to believe that her family wasted her money. When the defendants arrived in the deceased's life, her greatest fear was going to a nursing home. The evidence shows that these defendants suddenly began to exert control over the deceased by listening in on her telephone conversations and by deluding her into believing that her family intended to place her in a nursing home. Once this fear was planted, defendants fostered and nurtured it until the deceased firmly opposed those formerly most dear to her. The deceased was told by the defendants that her niece was wasting or misappropriating funds and was reimbursing herself for airline expenses and to rent fancy cars. Defendants told the deceased that her niece was wasting money and that the deceased would be left penniless. The defendants offered no proof to refute these statements, and the trial court found that Jean Law, the deceased's niece, kept meticulous records. When the defendants accepted employment to provide around-the-clock care for the deceased, they entered into a fiduciary or confidential relationship with her, and the defendant Krida assumed additional fiduciary obligations under the unrestricted power of attorney she obtained.
>
> "Since frauds are generally secret [they] have to be tracked by the footprints, marks, and signs made by the perpetrators and discovered by the light of the attending facts and circumstances." Henry R. Gibson, Gibson's Suits in Chancery §448 (William H. Inman, ed., 7th ed. 1988).

By limiting information available to the deceased and by concealing their acts from the critical examination of those whom the deceased had previously known and trusted, the defendants isolated the deceased and controlled access to her. The defendants terminated the deceased's former legal and financial relationships and arranged new ones. They made her neighbors feel unwelcome and threatened her family with legal action. They replaced her long-time tenant with a family member of one of the defendants. Furthermore, the defendants made detrimental decisions regarding the sale of the deceased's real property, to avoid contact with a realtor who had previously handled the deceased's affairs.

The dealings with the deceased's money by the defendants was irregular and unusual. Defendants offered no suitable explanation at trial to account for any of the cash funds that the deceased received while the defendant Krida managed the financial affairs.

PROBLEM

Suppose *H* asks *W* to hand him his will, intending to destroy it. *W* holds up an envelope, pretends that it contains *H*'s will, and then burns the envelope and its contents. After *H*'s death, *W* probates *H*'s will, the one she had purportedly destroyed, under which she takes *H*'s entire estate. Are *H*'s other heirs entitled to a constructive trust over so much of the assets as exceed what *W*'s intestate share would have been? See Brazil v. Silva, 185 P. 174 (Cal. 1919).

SECTION D. DURESS

When undue influence becomes overtly coercive, it is called *duress*. "A donative transfer is procured by duress if the wrongdoer threatened to perform or did perform a wrongful act that coerced the donor into making a donative transfer that the donor would not otherwise have made." Restatement (Third) of Property: Wills and Other Donative Transfers §8.3(c) (2003). The law invalidates transfers compelled by duress.

Latham v. Father Divine
Court of Appeals of New York, 1949
85 N.E.2d 168

DESMOND, J. The amended complaint herein has . . . been dismissed for insufficiency. Its principal allegations are these: plaintiffs are first cousins, but not distributees [next of kin], of Mary Sheldon Lyon, who died in October, 1946, leaving a will, executed in 1943, which gave almost her whole estate to defendant Father Divine,[16] leader of a religious cult, and to two corporate defendants in

---

16. Father Divine, a charismatic religious leader during the Depression who proclaimed his own divinity, attracted thousands of believers, mostly African American, but some, like Mary Sheldon Lyon, were white. Whatever the merits of his claim, Father Divine was a master of theater. His inspirational sermons at a Harlem

some way connected with that cult, and to an individual defendant (Patience Budd) said to be one of Father Divine's active followers; that said will has been, after a contest instituted by distributees, probated under a compromise agreement with the distributees, by the terms of which agreement, to which plaintiffs were not parties, the defendants just above referred to will receive a large sum from the estate; that after the making of said will, decedent on several occasions expressed "a desire and a determination to revoke the said will, and to execute a new will by which the plaintiffs would receive a substantial portion of the estate," "that shortly prior to the death of the deceased she had certain attorneys draft a new will in which the plaintiffs were named as legatees for a very substantial amount, totalling approximately $350,000"; that "by reason of the said false representations, the said undue influence and the said physical force" certain of the defendants "prevented the deceased from executing the said new Will"; that, shortly before decedent's death, decedent again expressed her determination to execute the proposed new will which favored plaintiffs, and that defendants "thereupon conspired to kill, and did kill, the deceased by means of a surgical operation performed by a doctor engaged by the defendants without the consent or knowledge of any of the relatives of the deceased."

Nothing is better settled than that, on such a motion as this, all the averments of the attacked pleading are taken as true. For present purposes, then, we have a case where one possessed of a large property and having already made a will leaving it to certain persons, expressed an intent to make a new testament to contain legacies to other persons, attempted to carry out that intention by having a new

---

church roused his followers to spirited expression; his exuberant and melodious services were standing room only. Father Divine went beyond the spiritual; he preached racial equality and social action against segregation. He established communes ("heavens") and religious cooperatives around the country, often in white neighborhoods, where African Americans from the ghetto could move to find work and food. Father Divine taught that there was only one race, no "Negro" and "white"; people just had darker or lighter complexions. The press of the time disparaged Father Divine as a con man of the cloth. Yet, in the last few decades, scholars searching for the roots of the African American churches' commitment to social action have come to reevaluate Father Divine. Many now view him as an influential and serious religious leader who gave his followers a feeling of goodness and worth, who crystallized the commitment of African American churches to the struggle for racial justice, and who stuck his thumb in the eye of the white establishment. He rode around in a chauffeured Rolls-Royce or, alternatively, a Duesenberg; inhabited the fanciest houses; hosted sumptuous feasts; and claimed for African Americans every perquisite of rich whites. See Jill M. Watts, God, Harlem U.S.A.: The Father Divine Story (1992); Robert Weisbrot, Father Divine and the Struggle for Racial Equality (1983).

The turn in Father Divine's fortunes, which transformed him from a minor religious figure into an adored incarnation of God, came as a result of a brush with the law in 1932. Father Divine had bought a large house in Sayville on the south shore of Long Island. On Sundays, flocks of the faithful from Harlem gathered there for some joyous prayer sessions. The white neighbors objected. Father Divine was arrested for disturbing the peace and conducting a public nuisance. This event was picked up by the national press. Father Divine was pictured as a martyr to racial prejudice. At trial, the jury found Father Divine guilty as charged. Some of Father Divine's partisans warned the judge that if he sent Father Divine to jail something terrible would happen to him. The judge, unheeding, gave Father Divine the maximum sentence of one year in jail. Three days later, the judge keeled over and died. "When the warden and the guards found out about it in the middle of the night," writes Professor Henry Louis Gates, Jr., "they raced to Father Divine's cell and woke him up. Father Divine, they said, your judge just dropped dead of a heart attack. Without missing a beat, Father Divine lifted his head and told them: 'I *hated* to do it.'" Henry L. Gates, Jr., Whose Canon Is It Anyway?, N.Y. Times, Feb. 20, 1989, §7 (Book Review), at 1. Although the story has been questioned, its repetition established Father Divine — among the believers — as an authentic voice of God.

Father Divine left New York in the 1950s and retired to a 72-acre estate outside Philadelphia. His apparent powers of retribution faded. Judge Desmond, who wrote the opinion in *Latham*, died in 1987, at the age of 91. — Eds.

Father Divine, calling the faithful to dinner.

will drawn which contained a large legacy to those others, but was, by means of misrepresentations, undue influence, force, and indeed, murder, prevented, by the beneficiaries named in the existing will, from signing the new one. Plaintiffs say that those facts, if proven, would entitle them to a judicial declaration, which their prayer for judgment demands, that defendants, taking under the already probated will, hold what they have so taken as constructive trustees for plaintiffs, whom decedent wished to, tried to, and was kept from, benefiting.

We find in New York no decision directly answering the question as to whether or not the allegations above summarized state a case for relief in equity. But reliable texts, and cases elsewhere, see 98 A.L.R. 477 et seq., answer it in the affirmative. Leading writers, 3 Scott on Trusts, pp. 2371-2376; 3 Bogert on Trusts and Trustees, part 1, §§473-474, 498, 499; 1 Perry on Trusts and Trustees [7th ed.], pp. 265, 371, in one form or another, state the law of the subject to be about as it is expressed in Comment i under §184 of the Restatement of the Law of Restitution: *"Preventing revocation of will and making new will.* Where a devisee or legatee under a will already executed prevents the testator by fraud, duress or undue influence from revoking the will and executing a new will in favor of another or from making a codicil, so that the testator dies leaving the original will in force, the devisee or legatee holds the property thus acquired upon a constructive trust for the intended devisee or legatee." . . .

While there is no New York case decreeing a constructive trust on the exact facts alleged here, there are several decisions in this court which, we think, suggest such a result and none which forbids it. Matter of O'Hara's Will, 95 N.Y. 403 (1884); Trustees of Amherst College v. Ritch, 45 N.E. 876 (N.Y. 1897); Edson v. Bartow, 48 N.E. 541 (N.Y. 1897), and Ahrens v. Jones, 62 N.E. 666 (N.Y. 1902), which need not be closely analyzed here as to their facts, all announce, in one form or another, the rule that, where a legatee has taken property under a will, after agreeing outside the will, to devote that property to a purpose intended and declared by the testator, equity will enforce a constructive trust to effectuate that purpose, lest there be a fraud on the testator. . . . In each of those four cases first above cited in this paragraph, the particular fraud consisted of the legatee's failure or refusal to carry out the testator's designs, after tacitly or expressly promising so to do. But we do not think that a breach of such an engagement is the only kind of fraud which will impel equity to action. A constructive trust will be erected whenever necessary to satisfy the demands of justice. Since a constructive trust is merely "the formula through which the conscience of equity finds expression," Beatty v. Guggenheim Exploration Co., 122 N.E. 378, 380 (N.Y. 1919), its applicability is limited only by the inventiveness of men who find new ways to enrich themselves unjustly by grasping what should not belong to them. Nothing short of true and complete justice satisfies equity, and always assuming these allegations to be true, there seems no way of achieving total justice except by the procedure used here. . . .

This is not a proceeding to probate or establish the will which plaintiffs say testatrix was prevented from signing . . . . The will Mary Sheldon Lyon did sign has been probated and plaintiffs are not contesting, but proceeding on, that probate, trying to reach property which has effectively passed thereunder. . . .

We do not agree with appellants that Riggs v. Palmer, 22 N.E. 188 (N.Y. 1889), completely controls our decision here. That was the famous case where a grandson, overeager to get the remainder interest set up for him in his grandfather's will, murdered his grandsire. After the will had been probated, two daughters of the testator who, under the will, would take if the grandson should predecease testator, sued and got judgment decreeing a constructive trust in their favor. It may be, as respondents assert, that the application of Riggs v. Palmer, supra, here would benefit not plaintiffs, but this testator's distributees. We need not pass on that now. But Riggs v. Palmer is generally helpful to appellants, since it forbade the grandson profiting by his own wrong in connection with a will; and, despite an already probated will and the Decedent Estate Law, Riggs v. Palmer used the device or formula of constructive trust to right the attempted wrong, and prevent unjust enrichment. . . .

This suit cannot be defeated by any argument that to give plaintiffs judgment would be to annul those provisions of the Statute of Wills requiring due execution by the testator. Such a contention, if valid, would have required the dismissal in a number of the suits herein cited. The answer is in Ahrens v. Jones, 62 N.E. at 668:

> The trust does not act directly upon the will by modifying the gift, for the law requires wills to be wholly in writing; but it acts upon the gift itself as it reaches the possession of the legatee,

or as soon as he is entitled to receive it. The theory is that the will has full effect by passing an absolute legacy to the legatee, and that then equity, in order to defeat fraud, raises a trust in favor of those intended to be benefited by the testator, and compels the legatee, as a trustee ex maleficio, to turn over the gift to them.

The judgment of the Appellate Division, insofar as it dismissed the complaint herein, should be reversed, and the order of Special Term affirmed, with costs in this court and in the Appellate Division.

NOTES

1. Another view of the contest of Mary Sheldon Lyon's will is presented by a biographer of Father Divine: Sara Harris, Father Divine 278-281 (1953). Harris says that Mary Sheldon Lyon was a devotee of Father Divine from 1938 to 1946 and took the spiritual name of Peace Dove. "She was sweet goodness personified. That was why, when she attended banquets, she was always granted a holy seat at God's own table. That was why the followers made a fuss over her." Harris reports that, after Father Divine lost in the court of appeals and after subsequent lower court rulings adverse to him, a settlement was reached giving Father Divine a small fraction of the amount bequeathed him. Harris suggests that the court rulings were motivated, at least in part, by racial prejudice against Father Divine and a belief that his church (called a "cult" by the court) was not quite a legitimate religious group.

2. A *constructive trust* is sometimes said to be a fraud-rectifying trust. But a constructive trust may be imposed where no fraud is involved if the court thinks that unjust enrichment would result if the person retained the property. A constructive trust is therefore not really a trust but rather is an equitable remedy. As Judge Cardozo, speaking for the Court of Appeals of New York, said: "A constructive trust is the formula through which the conscience of equity finds expression. When property has been acquired in such circumstances that the holder of the legal title may not in good conscience retain the beneficial interest, equity converts him into a trustee." Beatty v. Guggenheim Exploration Co., 122 N.E. 378, 386 (N.Y. 1919). Once converted into a constructive trustee, the holder of the property must transfer it to the constructive beneficiary. Thus, to repeat, the constructive trust is a remedy that employs the language of trusteeship. It is not itself a trust in which property is managed by a trustee for a beneficiary subject to a fiduciary obligation.

3. In Pope v. Garrett, 211 S.W.2d 559 (Tex. 1948), some, but not all, of Carrie Simmons's expectant heirs "by physical force or by creating a disturbance" prevented Carrie from executing a will in favor of her friend, Claytonia Garrett. Shortly after this incident, Carrie lapsed into a coma and died. The court imposed a constructive trust in favor of Claytonia, not only on the heirs who had participated in the disturbance but also on the innocent heirs. The court reasoned that the innocent heirs would be unjustly enriched if they were permitted to keep the property since, but for the wrongful acts, they would have inherited

nothing. See also Restatement (Third) of Restitution and Unjust Enrichment §46(1) (T.D. No. 5, 2007), which provides: "If assets that would otherwise have passed by donative transfer to the claimant are diverted to another recipient as a result of fraud, duress, undue influence, or other wrongful interference, the recipient is liable to the claimant for unjust enrichment. The misconduct that invalidates the transfer to the recipient may be the act of the recipient or of a third person."

SECTION E.   TORTIOUS INTERFERENCE WITH AN EXPECTANCY

Restatement (Second) of Torts §774B (1979) recognizes intentional interference with an expected inheritance or gift as a valid cause of action. This theory extends to expected inheritances the protection courts have accorded commercial expectancies, such as the prospect of obtaining employment or customers. Under this theory, the plaintiff must prove that the interference involved conduct tortious in itself, such as fraud, duress, or undue influence. The theory cannot be used when the challenge is based on the testator's mental incapacity.

Schilling v. Herrera
Court of Appeal of Florida, 2007
952 So. 2d 1231

Rothenberg, J. . . . Mr. [Edward] Schilling, the decedent's brother, sued Ms. [Maria] Herrera, the decedent's caretaker, for intentional interference with an expectancy of inheritance. . . . The amended complaint alleges that in December 1996, Mignonne Helen Schilling (the decedent) executed her Last Will and Testament, naming her brother and only heir-at-law, Mr. Schilling, as her personal representative and sole beneficiary, and in May 1997, she executed a Durable Power of Attorney, naming Mr. Schilling as her attorney-in-fact.

In December 1999, the decedent was diagnosed with renal disease, resulting in several hospitalizations. During this period, Mr. Schilling, who resides in New Jersey, traveled to Florida to assist the decedent. In January 2000, the decedent executed a Power of Attorney for Health Care, naming Mr. Schilling as her attorney-in-fact for health care decisions.

On January 12, 2001, when the decedent was once again hospitalized, Mr. Schilling traveled to Florida to make arrangements for the decedent's care. After being released from the hospital, the decedent was admitted to a rehabilitation hospital, then to a health care center, and then to the Clairidge House for rehabilitation. While at the Clairidge House, Ms. Herrera became involved in the decedent's care, and when the decedent was discharged from the Clairidge House on December 16, 2001, Ms. Herrera notified Mr. Schilling.

After being discharged from the Clairidge House, the decedent returned to her apartment, and Ms. Herrera began to care for her on an "occasional, as needed basis." In 2003, when the decedent's condition worsened and she was in need of additional care, Ms. Herrera converted her garage into a bedroom, and the decedent moved in. The decedent paid Ms. Herrera rent and for her services as caregiver.

When Mr. Schilling spoke to Ms. Herrera over the phone, Ms. Herrera complained that she was not getting paid enough to take care of the decedent, and on April 10, 2003, Mr. Schilling sent Ms. Herrera money. While living in the converted garage, the decedent became completely dependent on Ms. Herrera. In September 2003, without Mr. Schilling's knowledge, Ms. Herrera convinced the decedent to prepare and execute a new Power of Attorney, naming Ms. Herrera as attorney-in-fact, and to execute a new Last Will and Testament naming Ms. Herrera as personal representative and sole beneficiary of the decedent's estate.

Mr. Schilling visited the decedent in March of 2004. On August 6, 2004, the decedent died at Ms. Herrera's home.

On August 24, 2004, Ms. Herrera filed her Petition for Administration. On December 2, 2004, following the expiration of the creditor's period, Ms. Herrera petitioned for discharge of probate. On December 6, 2004, *after the expiration of the creditor's period and after Ms. Herrera had petitioned the probate court for discharge of probate, Ms. Herrera notified Mr. Schilling for the first time that the decedent, his sister, had passed away on August 6, 2004.* Shortly thereafter, in late December 2004, the Final Order of Discharge was entered by the probate court. Mr. Schilling alleges that prior to being notified of his sister's death on December 6, 2004, he attempted to contact the decedent through Ms. Herrera, but Ms. Herrera did not return his calls until the conclusion of probate proceedings and did not inform him of his sister's death, thereby depriving him of both the knowledge of the decedent's death and the opportunity of contesting the probate proceedings. Mr. Schilling further alleges that prior to the decedent's death, Ms. Herrera regularly did not immediately return his phone calls, and that Ms. Herrera's "intentional silence was part of a calculated scheme to prevent [Mr.] Schilling from contesting the Estate of Decedent, and was intended to induce [Mr.] Schilling to refrain from acting in his interests to contest the probate proceedings in a timely fashion, as [Mr.] Schilling was used to long delays in contact with [Ms.] Herrera, and did not suspect that the delay was intended to fraudulently induce [Mr.] Schilling to refrain from acting on his own behalf." Finally, Mr. Schilling alleges that he expected to inherit the decedent's estate because he was the decedent's only heir-at-law and because he was named as the sole beneficiary in the 1996 will; Ms. Herrera's fraudulent actions prevented him from receiving the decedent's estate, which he was entitled to; and but for Ms. Herrera's action of procuring the will naming her as sole beneficiary, he would have received the benefit of the estate.

After Mr. Schilling filed his amended complaint, Ms. Herrera filed a . . . motion to dismiss, arguing [that Mr. Schilling failed to state a cause of action and that he was barred from filing his claim because he failed to exhaust his probate remedies]. The trial court granted the motion to dismiss with prejudice, finding that Ms. Herrera had no duty to notify Mr. Schilling of the decedent's death as Mr. Schilling did not hire Ms. Herrera to care for the decedent, and therefore, there was "no special relationship giving rise to a proactive responsibility to provide information." The trial court also found that Mr. Schilling was barred from filing a claim for intentional interference with an expectancy of inheritance because he failed to exhaust his probate remedies. . . .

To state a cause of action for intentional interference with an expectancy of inheritance, the complaint must allege the following elements: (1) the existence of an expectancy; (2) intentional interference with the expectancy through tortious conduct; (3) causation; and (4) damages. Claveloux v. Bacotti, 778 So. 2d 399, 400 (Fla. App. 2001), citing Whalen v. Prosser, 719 So. 2d 2, 5 (Fla. App. 1998). The court in *Whalen* clearly explained that the purpose behind this tort is to protect the testator, not the beneficiary:

> Interference with an expectancy is an unusual tort because the beneficiary is authorized to sue to recover damages primarily to protect the testator's interest rather than the disappointed beneficiary's expectations. The fraud, duress, undue influence, or other independent tortious conduct required for this tort is directed at the testator. The beneficiary is not directly defrauded or unduly influenced; the testator is. Thus, the common law court has created this cause of action not primarily to protect the beneficiary's inchoate rights, but to protect the deceased testator's former right to dispose of property freely and without improper interference. In a sense, the beneficiary's action is derivative of the testator's rights. *Whalen,* 719 So. 2d at 6.

In the instant case, the trial court's ruling was based on the fact that the amended complaint fails to allege that Ms. Herrera breached a legal duty owed to Mr. Schilling. However, as the *Claveloux* court noted, there are four elements for a cause of action for intentional interference with an expectancy of inheritance, and breach of a legal duty is not one of the elements. This is consistent with the *Whalen* court's explanation that the "fraud, duress, undue influence, or other independent tortious conduct required for this tort *is directed at the testator. The beneficiary is not directly defrauded or unduly influenced; the testator is.*" Id. (emphasis added). We, therefore, review the amended complaint to determine if it sufficiently pleads a cause of action for intentional interference with an expectancy of inheritance.

In essence, the amended complaint alleges that Mr. Schilling was named as the sole beneficiary in the decedent's last will and testament; that based on this last will and testament, he expected to inherit the decedent's estate upon her death; that Ms. Herrera intentionally interfered with his expectancy of inheritance by "convincing" the decedent, while she was ill and completely dependent on Ms. Herrera, to execute a new last will and testament naming Ms. Herrera as the sole beneficiary; and that Ms. Herrera's "fraudulent actions" and "undue influence" prevented Mr. Schilling from inheriting the decedent's estate. Based on these well-pled allegations, we conclude that the amended complaint states a cause of action for intentional interference with an expectancy of inheritance. Therefore, the trial court erred, as a matter of law, in dismissing the amended complaint on that basis.

Mr. Schilling also contends that the trial court erred in finding that he was barred from filing a claim for intentional interference with an expectancy of inheritance as he failed to exhaust his probate remedies. We agree.

In finding that Mr. Schilling was barred from filing his action for intentional interference with an expectancy of inheritance, the trial court relied on DeWitt v. Duce, 408 So. 2d 216 (Fla. 1981). In *DeWitt*, the testator's will was admitted to probate after his death. Thereafter, the plaintiffs filed a petition for revocation of probate of the testator's will, but voluntarily dismissed the petition, choosing to take under the will instead of challenging the will in probate court. More than two years later, the plaintiffs filed their claim for intentional interference with an inheritance, arguing that the defendants exercised undue influence over the testator at a time when he lacked testamentary capacity, causing the testator to execute the probated will, which was less favorable to the plaintiffs and more favorable to the defendants than the testator's previous will. . . .

In answering the . . . question [whether availability of probate remedies forecloses a suit for tortious interference], the Florida Supreme Court stated that "[t]he rule is that if adequate relief is available in a probate proceeding, then that remedy must be exhausted before a tortious interference claim may be pursued." Id. at 218. The Court, however, stated that an exception to this general rule is that "[i]f the defendant's fraud is not discovered until after probate, plaintiff is allowed to bring a later action for damages since relief in probate was impossible." Id. at 219. The Court also noted that "[c]ases which allow the action for tortious interference with a testamentary expectancy are predicated on the inadequacy of probate remedies." Id. In conclusion, the Florida Supreme Court held:

> In sum, we find that [plaintiffs] had an adequate remedy in probate *with a fair opportunity to pursue it*. Because they lacked assiduity in failing to avail themselves of this remedy, we interpret Fla. Stat. Ann. §733.103(2)[17] as barring [plaintiffs] from a subsequent action in tort for wrongful interference with a testamentary expectancy, and accordingly answer the certified question in the affirmative. Id. at 221.

Therefore, the Court's holding that the plaintiffs were barred from pursuing their claim for intentional interference with an expectancy of inheritance, was based on the fact that the plaintiffs had an adequate remedy in probate; the plaintiffs had a fair opportunity to pursue their remedy; and the plaintiffs' failure to pursue their remedy was due to their lack of diligence.

---

17. In its current form, which is substantially similar, Fla. Stat. Ann. §733.103(2) (2008) provides:

> In any collateral action or proceeding relating to devised property, the probate of a will in Florida shall be conclusive of its due execution; that it was executed by a competent testator, free of fraud, duress, mistake, and undue influence; and that the will was unrevoked on the testator's death.

— Eds.

We find that *DeWitt* is factually distinguishable, and therefore inapplicable. A review of the amended complaint reflects that Mr. Schilling has alleged two separate frauds. The first alleged fraud stems from Ms. Herrera's undue influence over the deceased in procuring the will, whereas the second alleged fraud stems from Ms. Herrera's actions in preventing Mr. Schilling from contesting the will in probate court. We acknowledge that pursuant to *DeWitt,* if only the first type of fraud was involved, Mr. Schilling's collateral attack of the will would be barred. However, language contained in *DeWitt* clearly indicates that a subsequent action for intentional interference with an expectancy of inheritance may be permitted where "the circumstances surrounding the tortious conduct effectively preclude adequate relief in the probate court." Id. at 219. . . .

In the instant case, we must accept the facts alleged by Mr. Schilling as true. He alleges in the amended complaint that when the decedent began to live in Ms. Herrera's home, pursuant to powers of attorney executed by the decedent, Mr. Schilling was the decedent's attorney-in-fact; throughout the decedent's numerous illnesses, Mr. Schilling made decisions regarding the decedent's care; Mr. Schilling traveled to Miami on numerous occasions to visit the decedent, whose condition progressively worsened; Mr. Schilling stayed in contact with Ms. Herrera while the decedent was living in her home; Mr. Schilling relied on Ms. Herrera to obtain information regarding the decedent; Mr. Schilling sent money to Ms. Herrera to pay for the decedent's care; after the decedent passed away, Mr. Schilling called Ms. Herrera numerous times, but she would not return his calls; and Ms. Herrera did not inform Mr. Schilling of his sister's death until after she petitioned for discharge of probate. As the facts in the amended complaint sufficiently allege that Mr. Schilling was prevented from contesting the will in the probate court due to Ms. Herrera's fraudulent conduct, we find that the trial court erred in finding that Mr. Schilling's claim for intentional interference with an expectancy of inheritance was barred.

Accordingly, we reverse the order dismissing Mr. Schilling's amended complaint, and remand for further proceedings.

NOTES

1.   An action for tortious interference with an expectancy is not a will contest. It does not challenge the probate or validity of a will, but rather seeks to recover tort damages from a third party for tortious interference. The action is not usually subject to the typically short state statute of limitations on will contests, but rather to the tort statute of limitations, which starts running on the action at the time the plaintiff discovered or should have discovered the fraud or undue influence. In the jurisdictions that have recognized the tort, such as Florida, the courts usually require the plaintiff to pursue probate remedies first, if they are adequate, and a failure to do so usually results in barring a tortious interference suit. See Peralta v. Peralta, 131 P.3d 81 (N.M. 2005). Under this rule, if the plaintiff contests the will and loses, the plaintiff ordinarily is barred by the principle of res

judicata from suing later in tort. See Morrison v. Morrison, 663 S.E.2d 714 (Ga. 2008).

Because a suit for tortious interference with an expectancy is not a will contest, a no-contest clause (page 198) might not apply to such a suit. Punitive damages may be recovered against the wrongdoer in a suit in tort but not in a suit seeking to prevent probate of a will on the ground of undue influence or fraud.

2.   Although the trend in the cases is toward recognizing a cause of action for tortious interference with an expected inheritance or gift, in some states there is no definitive ruling and in others the courts have rejected the tort. For the position of each of the states, see the appendix to Diane J. Klein, River Deep, Mountain High, Heir Disappointed: Tortious Interference with Expectation of Inheritance—A Survey with Analysis of State Approaches in the Mountain States, 45 Idaho L. Rev. 1 (2008).

For further discussion, see Diane J. Klein, "Go West, Disappointed Heir": Tortious Interference with Expectation of Inheritance—A Survey with Analysis of State Approaches in the Pacific States, 13 Lewis & Clark L. Rev. 209 (2009); Irene D. Johnson, Tortious Interference with Expectancy of Inheritance or Gift—Suggestions for Resort to the Tort, 39 U. Tol. L. Rev. 769 (2008).

NOTE: ANNA NICOLE SMITH AND THE PROBATE EXCEPTION TO FEDERAL JURISDICTION

The most famous (and perhaps most salacious) tortious interference matter involves Vickie Lynn Marshall, better known as Anna Nicole Smith, who alleged tortious interference with a prospective lifetime gift in trust from her husband, the Texas oil magnate J. Howard Marshall. Although her claims in the Texas probate court with jurisdiction over her husband's estate were emphatically rejected, her tortious interference claim, which was litigated in federal court, was still awaiting ultimate resolution as this book went to press.

The federal litigation produced the most recent pronouncement by the Supreme Court on the probate exception to federal jurisdiction, "one of the most mysterious and esoteric branches of the law of federal jurisdiction." Dragon v. Miller, 679 F.2d 712, 713 (7th Cir. 1982) (Posner, J.). In brief, the exception prohibits the federal courts from entertaining a suit that encroaches on the traditional jurisdiction of the state probate courts. In Marshall v. Marshall, 547 U.S. 293 (2006), the Court held that Smith's claim, which did not involve the administration of an estate or the probate of a will, but rather an in personam judgment against the alleged tortfeasor, fell outside of the exception. The Court emphasized the point that any judgment in the federal suit would not disturb or interfere with the state probate court's proceedings or the administration of the decedent's estate.

The probate exception is probably based on a misunderstanding of English chancery practice. See id. at 315-318 (Stevens, J., concurring), following

John F. Winkler, The Probate Jurisdiction of the Federal Courts, 14 Prob. L.J. 77 (1997). It is also unclear how the exception will be reconciled with the proliferation of will substitutes, the result of which is that there is no longer a unified administration of all the decedent's property in the probate court anyway.

For further discussion of the probate exception, see Robert P. Dougherty, III, Note, Marshall v. Marshall: Playmates, Prenupts, and the Probate Exception, 61 Ark. L. Rev. 329 (2008); Allison Elvert Graves, Comment, Marshall v. Marshall: The Past, Present, and Future of the Probate Exception to Federal Jurisdiction, 59 Ala. L. Rev. 1643 (2008); Peter Nicolas, Fighting the Probate Mafia: A Dissection of the Probate Exception to Federal Court Jurisdiction, 74 S. Cal. L. Rev. 1479 (2001). For a treatment of problems in Smith's own estate planning, see pages 534-536.

4

WILLS: FORMALITIES AND FORMS

SECTION A.   EXECUTION OF WILLS

1.   *Attested Wills*

a.   **The Function of Formalities**

Jane B. Baron, *Gifts, Bargains, and Form*
64 Ind. L.J. 155 (1989)

Despite the benevolent motives and family settings usually associated with gifts, the accepted justification of donative formality assumes that, in giving, people are fundamentally unreliable and deceitful. Despite the self-interested aims and arm's length relationships usually associated with bargains, the accepted justification of the consideration doctrine assumes that, in business, people are trusting and trustworthy. These justifications turn the world topsy-turvy. We are to be suspected when we give, relied on when we trade.

James Lindgren, *The Fall of Formalism*
55 Alb. L. Rev. 1009 (1992)

People are not stupid. Yet for hundreds of years the law of wills has treated them as if they were. . . . The fear that they might improvidently give away their property at death has left a legacy of formalism unmatched in American law.

In the law of wills, the story told about people is that their seriously intended statements about their property can't be trusted. They are so weak, old, feeble, and subject to pressure that they need extraordinary protection from themselves.

223

Their spoken words are completely worthless. Their written statements are without meaning unless they're witnessed by two people. Even then, the witnesses must sign in the presence of the giver. And so on.

In the law of contracts, on the other hand, the story is completely different. People are intelligent and competent. They know their own mind. Other people can rely on their seriously made statements. They don't need protection from themselves. Their spoken words are enough to convey millions of dollars. And their written statements have meaning without witnesses.

Ashbel G. Gulliver and Catherine J. Tilson,
Classification of Gratuitous Transfers
51 Yale L.J. 1 (1941)

One fundamental proposition is that, under a legal system recognizing the individualistic institution of private property and granting to the owner the power to determine his successors in ownership, the general philosophy of the courts should favor giving effect to an intentional exercise of that power. . . .

If this objective is primary, the requirements of execution, which concern only the form of the transfer — what the transferor or others must do to make it legally effective — seem justifiable only as implements for its accomplishment, and should be so interpreted by the courts in these cases. They surely should not be revered as ends in themselves, enthroning formality over frustrated intent. Why do these requirements exist and what functions may they usefully perform? . . .

In the first place, the court needs to be convinced that the statements of the transferor were deliberately intended to effectuate a transfer. People are often careless in conversation and in informal writings. Even if the witnesses are entirely truthful and accurate, what is a court to conclude from testimony showing only that a father once stated that he wanted to give certain bonds to his son John? Does this remark indicate *finality of intention to transfer*, or rambling meditation about some future disposition? . . . Or suppose the evidence shows, without more, that a writing containing dispositive language was found among papers of the deceased at the time of his death? Does this demonstrate a deliberate transfer, or was it merely a tentative draft of some contemplated instrument, or perhaps random scribbling? . . . Dispositive effect should not be given to statements which were not intended to have that effect. The formalities of transfer therefore generally require the performance of some ceremonial for the purpose of impressing the transferor with the significance of his statements and thus justifying the court in reaching the conclusion, if the ceremonial is performed, that they were deliberately intended to be operative. This purpose of the requirements of transfer may conveniently be termed their *ritual function*.

Secondly, the requirements of transfer may increase the reliability of the proof presented to the court. The extent to which the quantity and effect of available evidence should be restricted by qualitative standards is, of course, a controversial matter. Perhaps any and all evidence should be freely admitted in reliance on such safeguards as cross-examination, the oath, the proficiency of handwriting experts, and the discriminating judgment of courts and juries. On the other hand, the inaccuracies of oral testimony owing to lapse of memory, mis-interpretation of the statements of others, and the more or less unconscious coloring of recollection in the light of the personal interest of the witness or of those with whom he is friendly, are very prevalent; and the possibilities of perjury and forgery cannot be disregarded. These difficulties are entitled to especially serious consideration in prescribing requirements for gratuitous transfers, because the issue of the validity of the transfer is almost always raised after the alleged transferor is dead, and therefore the main actor is usually unavailable to testify, or to clarify or contradict other evidence concerning his all-important intention. At any rate, whatever the ideal solution may be, it seems quite clear that the existing requirements of transfer emphasize the purpose of supplying satisfactory evidence to the court. This purpose may conveniently be termed their *evidentiary function*.

Thirdly, some of the requirements of the statutes of wills have the stated prophylactic purpose of safeguarding the testator, at the time of the execution of the will, against undue influence or other forms of imposition. . . . It may conveniently be termed the *protective function*. . . . This [protective function] is difficult to justify under modern conditions. . . . The protective provisions first appeared in the Statute of Frauds, from which they have been copied, perhaps sometimes blindly, by American legislatures. While there is little direct evidence, it is a reasonable assumption that, in the period prior to the Statute of Frauds, wills were usually executed on the death bed. A testator in this unfortunate situation may well need special protection against imposition. His powers of normal judgment and of resistance to improper influences may be seriously affected by a decrepit physical condition, a weakened mentality, or a morbid or unbalanced state of mind. Furthermore, in view of the propinquity of death, he would not have as much time or opportunity as would the usual inter vivos transferor to escape from the consequences of undue influence or other forms of imposition. Under modern conditions, however, wills are probably executed by most testators in the prime of life and in the presence of attorneys. [Emphasis added.]

Professor Langbein suggests that in addition to serving the cautionary function (Langbein's term for the ritual function), the evidentiary function, and the protective function, the Wills Act formalities serve a *channeling function*. Much as it is easier to determine whether a coin is a quarter if every quarter is the same size and has the same markings on it, it is easier to determine a person's wishes at death if those wishes are recorded in a standardized form.

> Compliance with the Wills Act formalities for executing witnessed wills results in considerable uniformity in the organization, language, and content of most wills. Courts are seldom left to puzzle whether the document was meant to be a will. . . .

The standardization of testation achieved under the Wills Act also benefits the testator. He does not have to devise for himself a mode of communicating his testamentary wishes to the court, and to worry whether it will be effective. Instead, he has every inducement to comply with the Wills Act formalities. The court can process his estate routinely, because his testament is conventionally and unmistakably expressed and evidenced. The lowered costs of routinized judicial administration benefit the estate and its ultimate distributees. [John H. Langbein, Substantial Compliance with the Wills Act, 88 Harv. L. Rev. 489, 494 (1975).]

Establishing that a formality serves a purpose is, however, just the beginning of determining whether it should be required.

In determining the proper level of formalities, we shouldn't ask whether this formality or that would serve the accepted purposes of formalities. Any formality would. If we required a secret handshake for willmaking that only lawyers knew, that would serve the cautionary or ritual function. In early Bavaria, to convey real property one had to box the ears of young boys.[1] Without that formality, conveyances were ineffective, even where possession occurred and the deal was never repudiated by the parties. This strange formality served all the main functions of formalities: ritual or cautionary, evidentiary, protective, and channeling. Yet it was a perverse and silly formality. Other formalities more reliably evidenced transfers.

Instead of asking whether a formality serves a function of formalities, we should ask instead whether it promotes the intent of the testator at an acceptable administrative cost. We should not box the ears of little children just because it serves the ritual function; this is misplaced formalism. [James Lindgren, The Fall of Formalism, 55 Alb. L. Rev. 1009, 1033 (1992).]

The most basic formalities for an attested will are three: (1) writing, (2) signature by the testator, and (3) attestation by witnesses. But these basic requirements for execution of wills vary considerably in detail from state to state. Some of the variations result from England having had two acts governing the execution of wills—the Statute of Frauds (1677) and the Wills Act (1837)—both of which served as models for American legislation.

Prior to enactment of the Statute of Frauds, personal property was transferable at death by either a written or an oral will, perhaps given to the priest as part of the last confession.[2] Land was made devisable "by last will and testament in writing" by the Statute of Wills in 1540, but the statute specified no signature or other formalities. The Statute of Frauds, coming 137 years later, required a written will signed by the testator in the presence of three witnesses for the testamentary disposition of land. Less stringent formalities, which need not concern us here,

---

1. Boxing the ears refers to striking someone hard on the side of the head. The idea was that, by creating a painful memory, the young boys would be good witnesses if a dispute later arose over the validity of the transfer. See Celia Wasserstein Fassberg, Form and Formalism: A Case Study, 31 Am. J. Comp. L. 627 (1983). — Eds.

2. About 20 states permit nuncupative (oral) wills — either for persons in their last illness or for military personnel or both. Typically, these statutes can be used in only very limited circumstances: they can be used only to devise personal property of small value (say, up to $1,000), and the will must be uttered before three persons, who must reduce the declaration to writing within a specified period. Oral wills admitted to probate are extremely rare. For a list of state nuncupative will statutes, see Restatement (Third) of Property: Wills and Other Donative Transfers §3.2, statutory note 3 (1999).

applied to testamentary dispositions of personalty. Having different require-ments for wills of realty and for wills of personalty proved unsatisfactory, and in 1837, England enacted a Wills Act requiring the same formalities for all wills.

The formalities required by the Wills Act of 1837 were in some ways stricter than those required by the Statute of Frauds. Under the Statute of Frauds, the three witnesses did not have to be present at the same time; each could attest separately; and the testator did not have to sign at any particular place on the document. The 1837 Wills Act reduced the number of necessary witnesses to two, but it required that the witnesses both be present when the will is signed or acknowledged; in addition, it required the will to be signed "at the foot or end," a requirement that has come to be known as *subscription*. (The exact language of the 1837 Wills Act is set out in the court's opinion in *Groffman*, page 228.) These two additional requirements of the Wills Act have given rise to much litigation.

Some states copied the Statute of Frauds; others copied the Wills Act. In a few states, the legislature added a requirement that the testator must *publish* the will by declaring before the witnesses that the instrument is his will. For each of the three main formalities—writing, signature, and attestation by witnesses—the Uniform Probate Code generally adopts whichever is the less strict requirement of the two English statutes. Moreover, in a break with prior law, as amended in 2008 the Uniform Probate Code allows for notarization as an alternative to attes-tation by witnesses.

COMPARISON OF STATUTORY FORMALITIES FOR FORMAL WILLS			
Statute of Frauds (Land) (1677)	*Wills Act (1837)*	*Uniform Probate Code (1990)*	*Uniform Probate Code (1990, rev. 2008)*
Writing	Writing	Writing	Writing
Signature	Subscription	Signature	Signature
Attestation & subscription by 3 witnesses	Attestation & subscription by 2 witnesses	Attestation & signature by 2 witnesses	Attestation & signature by 2 witnesses OR notarization

Uniform Probate Code (1990, as amended 2008)

§2-502.   EXECUTION; WITNESSED OR NOTARIZED WILLS; HOLOGRAPHIC WILLS

(a) [Witnessed or Notarized Wills.] Except as otherwise provided in subsection (b) and in Sections 2-503, 2-506, and 2-513, a will must be:

(1) in writing;

(2) signed by the testator or in the testator's name by some other individual in the testator's conscious presence and by the testator's direction; and

(3) either:

(A) signed by at least two individuals, each of whom signed within a reasonable time after the individual witnessed either the signing of the will as described in paragraph (2) or the testator's acknowledgment of that signature or acknowledgment of the will; or

(B) acknowledged by the testator before a notary public or other individual authorized by law to take acknowledgments.

(b) [Holographic Wills.] A will that does not comply with subsection (a) is valid as a holographic will, whether or not witnessed, if the signature and material portions of the document are in the testator's handwriting.

(c) [Extrinsic Evidence.] Intent that a document constitute the testator's will can be established by extrinsic evidence, including, for holographic wills, portions of the document that are not in the testator's handwriting.

Both notarized wills (authorized by UPC §2-502(a)(3)(B)) and holographic wills (authorized by UPC §2-502(b)) are treated later, beginning at pages 265 and 268, respectively. We are concerned at this point only with formal attested wills, such as under UPC §2-502(a)(1)-(3)(A).

b.   Writing, Signature, and Attestation: Strict Compliance

Under traditional law, for a will to be admitted to probate it must be in *strict compliance* with the formal requirements of the applicable Wills Act. The will must be in writing, signed by the testator, and attested by at least two witnesses,[3] plus any additional requirements that are mandated by the particular jurisdiction must be satisfied precisely.

IN RE GROFFMAN, [1969] 2 All E.R. 108 [High Court of Justice, England]: Charles Groffman died three years after executing a will at the home of his friends, the Blocks. After his death, Groffman's widow challenged the will. "My Charlie wouldn't have done that to me," she is reported to have said. If the will had been validly executed, Groffman's widow would share the estate with her daughter from her first marriage and with one of Groffman's daughters from his first marriage. But if the will were invalid, his widow would take the entire estate

----

3. Although formerly quite a few states required three witnesses, today all but Louisiana require only two. Louisiana requires two witnesses plus a notary. La. Civ. Code Ann. art. 1577 (2008). For a compendium of state witnessing requirements, see Jeffrey A. Schoenblum, 2008 Multistate Guide to Estate Planning at Table 1. For a learned and wide-ranging critique of the inconsistencies in the execution requirements across the states, see Adam J. Hirsch, Inheritance and Inconsistency, 57 Ohio St. L.J. 1057 (1997).

in intestacy. The dispute centered on the fact that Groffman and both witnesses were not present together when Groffman acknowledged his signature.

The applicable statute — the English Wills Act of 1837 — provided as follows:

> [N]o will shall be valid unless it shall be in writing and executed in manner hereinafter mentioned; . . . it shall be signed at the foot or end thereof by the testator, or by some other person in his presence and by his direction; and such signature shall be made or acknowledged by the testator in the presence of two or more witnesses present at the same time, and such witnesses shall attest and shall subscribe the will in the presence of the testator, but no form of attestation shall be necessary.

Under this statute a testator is permitted *either* to acknowledge his prior signature to both witnesses at the same time *or* to sign the will before both witnesses. Although Groffman asked his friends, Julius Leigh and David Block, together to witness his will, he did not acknowledge his signature to them both simultaneously. Instead, Groffman and the first witness, Block, left Block's lounge and went into the adjacent dining room, where Block signed the will as a witness in Groffman's presence. Then, after Block returned to the lounge, the other witness, Leigh, went into the dining room and witnessed the will with Groffman present but without Block, the first witness, also present.

Even though the court was "perfectly satisfied that the document was intended by the deceased to be executed as his will," the court nevertheless refused to admit the will to probate:

> [W]e are left with this situation — that the signature of the deceased was on the document before he asked either Mr. Block or Mr. Leigh to act as his witnesses; that Mr. Block signed his name in the presence of the deceased but not in the presence of Mr. Leigh; and that Mr. Leigh signed his name in the presence of the deceased but not in the presence of Mr. Block. The deceased did not sign in the presence of either of them; and the question is whether he acknowledged his signature in the presence of both of them. . . . As must appear from the fact that I have been satisfied that the document does represent the testamentary intentions of the deceased, I would gladly find in its favour; but I am bound to apply the statute. . . . [A]lthough I would gladly accede to the arguments for the plaintiffs if I could consistently with my judicial duty, in my view there was no acknowledgment or signature by the testator in the presence of two or more witnesses present at the same time; and I am bound to pronounce against this will.

Stevens v. Casdorph
West Virginia Supreme Court of Appeals, 1998
508 S.E.2d 610

PER CURIAM.   . . . On May 28, 1996, [Paul and Patricia Casdorph] took Mr. Homer Haskell Miller to Shawnee Bank in Dunbar, West Virginia, so that he could execute his will.[4] Once at the bank, Mr. Miller asked Debra Pauley, a bank

---

4. Mr. Miller was elderly and confined to a wheelchair.

employee and public notary, to witness the execution of his will. After Mr. Miller signed the will, Ms. Pauley took the will to two other bank employees, Judith Waldron and Reba McGinn, for the purpose of having each of them sign the will as witnesses. Both Ms. Waldron and Ms. McGinn signed the will. However, Ms. Waldron and Ms. McGinn testified during their depositions that they did not actually see Mr. Miller place his signature on the will. Further, it is undisputed that Mr. Miller did not accompany Ms. Pauley to the separate work areas of Ms. Waldron and Ms. McGinn.

Mr. Miller died on July 28, 1996. The last will and testament of Mr. Miller, which named [his nephew] Mr. Paul Casdorph as executor, left the bulk of his estate to the Casdorphs.[5] The Stevenses, [who as] nieces of Mr. Miller [would share in his intestate estate], filed the instant action to set aside the will. The Stevenses asserted in their complaint that Mr. Miller's will was not executed according to the requirements set forth in W. Va. Code §41-1-3 (1995). After some discovery, all parties moved for summary judgment. The circuit court denied the Stevenses' motion for summary judgment, but granted the Casdorphs' cross motion for summary judgment. From this ruling, the Stevenses appeal to this Court. . . .

The Stevenses' contention is simple. They argue that all evidence indicates that Mr. Miller's will was not properly executed. Therefore, the will should be voided. The procedural requirements at issue are contained in W. Va. Code §41-1-3 (1997). The statute reads:

> No will shall be valid unless it be in writing and signed by the testator, or by some other person in his presence and by his direction, in such manner as to make it manifest that the name is intended as a signature; and moreover, unless it be wholly in the handwriting of the testator, *the signature shall be made or the will acknowledged by him in the presence of at least two competent witnesses, present at the same time; and such witnesses shall subscribe the will in the presence of the testator, and of each other*, but no form of attestation shall be necessary. (Emphasis added.)

The relevant requirements of the above statute calls for a testator to sign his/her will or acknowledge such will in the presence of at least two witnesses at the same time, and such witnesses must sign the will in the presence of the testator and each other. In the instant proceeding the Stevenses assert, and the evidence supports, that Ms. McGinn and Ms. Waldron did not actually witness Mr. Miller signing his will. Mr. Miller made no acknowledgment of his signature on the will to either Ms. McGinn or Ms. Waldron. Likewise, Mr. Miller did not observe Ms. McGinn and Ms. Waldron sign his will as witnesses. Additionally, neither Ms. McGinn nor Ms. Waldron acknowledged to Mr. Miller that their signatures were on the will. It is also undisputed that Ms. McGinn and Ms. Waldron did not actually witness each other sign the will, nor did they acknowledge to each other that they had signed Mr. Miller's will. Despite the evidentiary lack of compliance

---

5. Mr. Miller's probated estate exceeded $400,000.00. The will devised $80,000.00 to Frank Paul Smith, a nephew of Mr. Miller. The remainder of the estate was left to [Paul Casdorph and his wife, Patricia].

with W. Va. Code §41-1-3, the Casdorphs argue that there was substantial compliance with the statute's requirements, insofar as everyone involved with the will knew what was occurring. The trial court found that there was substantial compliance with the statute because everyone knew why Mr. Miller was at the bank. The trial court further concluded there was no evidence of fraud, coercion or undue influence. Based upon the foregoing, the trial court concluded that the will should not be voided even though the technical aspects of W. Va. Code §41-1-3 were not followed.

Our analysis begins by noting that "the law favors testacy over intestacy." Syl. pt. 8, In re Teubert's Estate, 298 S.E.2d 456 (W. Va. 1982). However, we clearly held in syllabus point 1 of Black v. Maxwell, 46 S.E.2d 804 (W. Va. 1948), that "testamentary intent and a written instrument, executed in the manner provided by [W. Va. Code §41-1-3], existing concurrently, are essential to the creation of a valid will." *Black* establishes that mere intent by a testator to execute a written will is insufficient. The actual execution of a written will must also comply with the dictates of W. Va. Code §41-1-3. The Casdorphs seek to have this Court establish an exception to the technical requirements of the statute. In Wade v. Wade, 195 S.E. 339 (W. Va. 1938), this Court permitted a narrow exception to the stringent requirements of the W. Va. Code §41-1-3. This narrow exception is embodied in syllabus point 1 of Wade:

> Where a testator acknowledges a will and his signature thereto in the presence of two competent witnesses, one of whom then subscribes his name, the other or first witness, having already subscribed the will in the presence of the testator but out of the presence of the second witness, may acknowledge his signature in the presence of the testator and the second witness, and such acknowledgment, if there be no indicia of fraud or misunderstanding in the proceeding, will be deemed a signing by the first witness within the requirement of Code, 41-1-3, that the witnesses must subscribe their names in the presence of the testator and of each other. . . .

Wade stands for the proposition that if a witness acknowledges his/her signature on a will in the physical presence of the other subscribing witness *and the testator*, then the will is properly witnessed within the terms of W. Va. Code §41-1-3. In this case, none of the parties signed or acknowledged their signatures in the presence of each other. This case meets neither the narrow exception of *Wade* nor the specific provisions of W. Va. Code §41-1-3. . . .

In view of the foregoing, we grant the relief sought in this appeal and reverse the circuit court's order granting the Casdorphs' cross-motion for summary judgment.

Reversed.

WORKMAN, J., dissenting.   The majority once more takes a very technocratic approach to the law, slavishly worshiping form over substance. In so doing, they not only create a harsh and inequitable result wholly contrary to the indisputable intent of Mr. Homer Haskell Miller, but also a rule of law that is against the spirit and intent of our whole body of law relating to the making of wills.

There is absolutely no claim of incapacity or fraud or undue influence, nor any allegation by any party that Mr. Miller did not consciously, intentionally, and with full legal capacity convey his property as specified in his will. The challenge to the will is based solely upon the allegation that Mr. Miller did not comply with the requirement of West Virginia Code 41-1-3 that the signature shall be made or the will acknowledged by the testator in the presence of at least two competent witnesses, present at the same time. The lower court, in its very thorough findings of fact, indicated that Mr. Miller had been transported to the bank by his nephew Mr. Casdorph and the nephew's wife. Mr. Miller, disabled and confined to a wheelchair, was a shareholder in the Shawnee Bank in Dunbar, West Virginia, with whom all those present were personally familiar. When Mr. Miller executed his will in the bank lobby, the typed will was placed on Ms. Pauley's desk, and Mr. Miller instructed Ms. Pauley that he wished to have his will signed, witnessed, and acknowledged. After Mr. Miller's signature had been placed upon the will with Ms. Pauley watching, Ms. Pauley walked the will over to the tellers' area in the same small lobby of the bank. Ms. Pauley explained that Mr. Miller wanted Ms. Waldron to sign the will as a witness. The same process was used to obtain the signature of Ms. McGinn. Sitting in his wheelchair, Mr. Miller did not move from Ms. Pauley's desk during the process of obtaining the witness signatures. The lower court concluded that the will was valid and that Ms. Waldron and Ms. McGinn signed and acknowledged the will "in the presence" of Mr. Miller.

In Wade v. Wade, 195 S.E. 339 (W. Va. 1938), we addressed the validity of a will challenged for such technicalities and observed that "a narrow, rigid construction of the statute should not be allowed to stand in the way of right and justice, or be permitted to defeat a testator's disposition of his property." 195 S.E. at 340-341. We upheld the validity of the challenged will in *Wade*, noting that "each case must rest on its own facts and circumstances to which the court must look to determine whether there was a subscribing by the witnesses in the presence of the testator; that substantial compliance with the statute is all that is required." 195 S.E. at 340. A contrary result, we emphasized, "would be based on illiberal and inflexible construction of the statute, giving preeminence to letter and not to spirit, and resulting in the thwarting of the intentions of testators even under circumstances where no possibility of fraud or impropriety exists." 195 S.E. at 341.

The majority's conclusion is precisely what was envisioned and forewarned in 1938 by the drafters of the *Wade* opinion: illiberal and inflexible construction, giving preeminence to the letter of the law and ignoring the spirit of the entire body of testamentary law, resulting in the thwarting of Mr. Miller's unequivocal wishes. . . .

The majority embraces the line of least resistance. The easy, most convenient answer is to say that the formal, technical requirements have not been met and that the will is therefore invalid. End of inquiry. Yet that result is patently absurd. That manner of statutory application is inconsistent with the underlying purposes of the statute. Where a statute is enacted to protect and sanctify the execution of a will to prevent substitution or fraud, this Court's application of that statute should further such underlying policy, not impede it. When, in our efforts to strictly apply legislative language, we abandon common sense and reason in favor of technicalities, we are the ones committing the injustice.

QUESTIONS AND NOTE

1.   Why were Mr. Groffman's and Mr. Miller's wills denied probate? In each case, what formalities required by the jurisdiction's Wills Act were not satisfied?

2.   Were the ritual, evidentiary, protective, and channeling policies that underpin the Wills Act satisfied by the manners in which Groffman's and Miller's wills were executed? If so, should their wills have been denied probate? How would each case have been decided under UPC §2-502(a)?

3.   *Attestation clause.* An attestation clause recites that the will was duly executed. For an example, see paragraph 7 on page 244. Although no state requires the use of an attestation clause, such a clause gives rise to a presumption of due execution, and it is almost certainly professional malpractice not to include one. With an attestation clause, the will may be admitted to probate even though the witnesses predecease the testator or cannot recall the events of execution. Moreover, if one of the attesting witnesses testifies that the steps for due execution were not satisfied, as in *Groffman*, the attestation clause gives the lawyer for the proponent ammunition for a vigorous cross-examination, and the will can often be admitted to probate on the presumption of due execution despite such testimony. See UPC §3-406(3) (1990, rev. 2008).

NOTE: THE MEANING OF "PRESENCE" IN WILL EXECUTION

In *Casdorph*, the court found that the witnesses did not sign in the presence of the testator and the testator did not sign in the presence of the witnesses. In *Groffman*, the court found that the testator did not make or acknowledge his signature in the presence of the two witnesses at the same time. Is this necessarily true? What does *presence* mean in will execution?

In England and in some American states, the requirement that the witnesses sign in the presence of the testator is satisfied only if the testator is capable of seeing the witnesses in the act of signing. Under this *line of sight test*, the testator does not actually have to see the witnesses sign but must be able to see them were the testator to look. An exception is made for a blind testator, where the test is usually whether the testator would have been able to see the witnesses sign from where the testator was standing or sitting if the testator had the power of sight. In other American states, the line of sight rule has been rejected in favor of the *conscious presence test*. Under this test, the witness is in the presence of the testator if the testator, through sight, hearing, or general consciousness of events, comprehends that the witness is in the act of signing. UPC §2-502(a) dispenses altogether with the requirement that the witnesses sign in the testator's presence.

Consider the following problems concerning presence:

(a) Suppose the witnesses signed *T*'s will in *T*'s dining room while *T* was in her bedroom. *T* knew that the witnesses were signing and could have walked into the dining room to see them sign. Does this meet the line-of-sight test? Does this meet the conscious presence test? See McCormick v. Jeffers, 637 S.E.2d 666 (Ga. 2006); In re Estate of Fischer, 886 A.2d 996 (N.H. 2005). See also Land v. Burkhalter, 656 S.E.2d 835 (Ga. 2008).

(b) Suppose that *T*'s attorney takes *T*'s will to *T*'s home, where *T* signs the will and the attorney attests as a witness. The attorney returns to her office with the will and has her secretary call *T* on the phone. By telephone, *T* requests the secretary to witness his will; the secretary then signs as an attesting witness. Can the will be probated? See In re Jefferson, 349 So. 2d 1032 (Miss. 1977); In re McGurrin, 743 P.2d 994 (Idaho App. 1987). Suppose instead *T* requests the secretary to witness and the secretary does so with *T* watching via computer webcam. Can the will be probated? Is the line-of-sight test satisfied? What about conscious presence?

(c) Suppose that the president of a bank draws a will for a depositor. The depositor, seriously ill, drives to the bank's drive-in teller window and parks. The president takes the will to the depositor's car, where the depositor signs the will propped on his steering wheel. The bank teller, seated at a teller window overlooking the car, watches the depositor sign. The president signs as a witness in the car, then takes the will inside the teller's office where the teller, sitting in the window, signs as witness and waves to the depositor. The president then takes the will outside and shows it to the depositor, who asks the president to keep it. Has the teller signed as a witness in the presence of the testator? See In re Weber's Estate, 387 P.2d 165 (Kan. 1963), which held, 4 to 3, No, because even though the testator could see the teller, the testator could not see the pen and will on the teller's desk as the teller signed. The court thought that to apply the conscious presence test on these facts would permit it "to run wild."

To overcome the difficulties that sometimes arise in locating suitable witnesses, and to cater to the hectic schedule of his clients, one Massachusetts solo practitioner has begun holding will signing parties for groups of five or more clients who serve as witnesses for each others' wills. See Sheri Qualters, Mass. Solo Uses "Will-Signing Parties" to Expand His Practice, Natl. L.J., Feb. 26, 2007, at 10. With so much going on at one session — usually each page of a will is signed or initialed in the margin by the testator, in addition to being signed and attested by the witnesses at the end — a lawyer must be especially careful to ensure that each document is executed properly.

NOTE: THE MEANING OF "SIGNATURE" IN WILL EXECUTION

The law in all states, as well as UPC §5-502(a), requires the testator to sign the will. The purpose of the signature requirement is to provide evidence of finality, distinguishing a will from mere drafts or notes, and to provide evidence of genuineness. A signature by the testator with her full name at the end of the document will almost always satisfy the signature requirement. Problems arise when the testator's signature takes a different form.

Signature by mark, with assistance, or by another. Although it is preferable for the testator to sign her name in full, a mark, cross, abbreviation, or nickname can be sufficient. In Estate of McCabe, 274 Cal. Rptr. 43 (App. 1990), a lawyer prepared a will for James McCabe, who was very ill. Underneath the signature line was typed "James I. McCabe." The will was taken to McCabe in his hospital room. McCabe signed with an "X" because his hands were too shaky to write his name. The two attesting witnesses then signed. The court admitted the will to probate. The same result would have obtained if McCabe had written a shaky "Jim" rather than an "X." See In re Young, 397 N.E.2d 1223 (Ohio App. 1978), holding that the letter *J* subscribed by Joseph Young was sufficient when Joseph was partially paralyzed from a stroke.

If McCabe had trouble holding the pen and a witness assisted McCabe in signing his name, the signature would be valid if McCabe intended to adopt the document as his will. Restatement (Third) of Property: Wills and Other Donative Transfers §3.1, cmt. j (1999). Likewise, if someone else signed McCabe's name at McCabe's direction and in McCabe's presence, the will would be valid. Id., cmt. n.

A more interesting, and more difficult, variant is presented by Taylor v. Holt, 134 S.W.3d 830 (Tenn. App. 2003). A week before he died, Steve Godfrey composed his will on his computer. However, instead of printing the will and signing the printed copy by hand, in the presence of two witnesses he typed into the word processing file a signature in a cursive font and then printed the document. The two witnesses signed the printed document by hand, and thereafter Godfrey also had the will notarized.

The will left Godfrey's entire estate to Doris Holt, a woman he was dating. The will also expressed Godfrey's enduring love and appreciation for Doris, concluding: "Doris always remember that I do Love You and Muff."[6] Godfrey's sister, Donna Godfrey Taylor, challenged the will for want of a signature by the testator. The trial court held the will valid, and the appellate court affirmed:

> The definition of "signature" as used in the [Wills Act] is provided by Tenn. Code Ann. §1-3-105(27), which states: "As used in this code, unless the context otherwise requires: . . . 'Signature' or 'signed' includes a mark, the name being written near the mark and witnessed, or any other symbol or methodology executed or adopted by a party with intention to authenticate a writing or record, regardless of being witnessed." . . .

---

6. A letter from James C. McSween, Jr., the winning counsel in *Taylor*, to Robert H. Sitkoff, dated Oct. 9, 2008, reveals:

> I inquired of Doris Holt, concerning the identity of "Muff" mentioned in the Will. It appears that this was a pet dog that Steve Godfrey had for several years. She told me that the dog anxiously awaited his return from work late each night, and would anticipate his arrival by furiously moving from window to door at the usual hour. Muff became very despondent after the death of Steve Godfrey and died within a few weeks.

Steve Godfrey
912 Carson Springs Rd.
Newport, Tenn. 37821

**CHANCERY COURT
FILED**

January 6, 2002

JAN 2 2 2002

TIME: 11:15 Am
COCKE CO, TN
CRAIG WILD, C & M

To Whom It May Concern,

I Steve Godfrey being of sound mind and body make this my last will and
testament.

To Doris, who has stood by me through everything I leave the house and
property by the creek and all that goes with it because you loved it so much
and work so hard to make it our home and keep it paid for while I was gone,
also I want you to have my half of the lake property, the camper and other
half is yours anyway. And I really did like the steps. Doris you know how
we have talked about how I want everything done and I know you will do it
that way. So I am leaving everything I have to you, because I know you will
take care of it like you always have.

Doris, I know I don't always show you how much I love you, and how much
I appreciate you being there for me, but I do love you and I couldn't make it
without you.

I have called Hershel and Tresa to come be my witnesses so nobody can
dispute that this is my will.

Doris always remember that I do Love You and Muff.

Steve Godfrey

Hershel Williams 1-6-2002

Teresa Williams 1-6-2002

ENTERED JAN. 22, 2002

Will Book 18

Craig Wild, Clerk and Master

474

Wesley W. Webb

My Commission Expires 4/23/05

The Will in *Taylor v. Holt*

In the case at hand, Deceased did make a mark that was intended to operate as his signature. Deceased made a mark by using his computer to affix his computer generated signature, and, as indicated by the affidavits of both witnesses, this was done in the presence of the witnesses. The computer generated signature made by Deceased falls into the category of "any other symbol or methodology executed or adopted by a party with intention to authenticate a writing or record," and, if made in the presence of two attesting witnesses, as it was in this case, is sufficient to constitute proper execution of a will. Further, we note that Deceased simply used a computer rather than an ink pen as the tool to make his signature, and, therefore, complied with Tenn. Code Ann. §32-1-104 by signing the will himself. [Id. at 832-833.]

Order of signing. Another potential source of trouble is the order of signing. In general, the testator must sign or acknowledge the will before the witnesses attest, but if they all sign "as part of a single (or continuous) transaction, the exact order of signing is not critical." Restatement (Third) of Property: Wills and Other Donative Transfers §3.1, cmt. m (1999).

But what is a single or continuous transaction? In the unfortunate case of In re Colling, [1972] 1 W.L.R. 1440, a few days before his death, George Colling, in the hospital, made a will. He started to write his signature in the presence of two witnesses—Jackson, the patient in the bed next to his, and Sister Newman, a nurse. Although both witnesses were present when the testator started to sign, before the testator finished writing "Colling," Sister Newman had to attend to a patient in another part of the ward. In her absence Colling completed his signature, and Jackson witnessed the will in Colling's presence. Sister Newman then returned. Both Colling and Jackson acknowledged their signatures to her, and she then signed as the second witness. The court held, "with great regret," that the will could not be probated because the testator did not complete his signature while both witnesses were present, and the later acknowledgment did not suffice because the testator must sign or acknowledge his signature before either of the witnesses attest.

Subscription and addition after signature. Statutes in a few states have adopted the English Wills Act requirement that the testator sign the will "at the foot or end thereof," a requirement that is usually called *subscription*.

Suppose that a typewritten will is found on which is written in the testator's handwriting, below the testator's signature and above the witnesses' signatures, the following line: "I give Karen my diamond ring." Is the will entitled to probate? Initially, the answer depends upon whether the line was on the will when it was signed by the testator. If the handwritten line was added *after* the testator signed the will, the will would be admitted to probate, but the line would be ineffective as a subsequent unexecuted codicil. If added *before* the testator signed her name, would the will be admitted? Would it matter if the handwritten addition had not made a disposition of the testator's property but had said: "I appoint John executor"? See Bennett v. Ditto, 204 S.W.3d 145 (Ky. App. 2006); N.Y. Est. Powers & Trusts Law §3-2.1(a)(1) (2008).

Delayed attestation. Suppose a witness observes the testator make or acknowledge his signature, but the witness does not immediately sign the will herself.

How long may the witness delay attestation without compromising the validity of the will? In New York, a witness must attest within 30 days. N.Y. Est. Powers & Trusts Law §3-2.1(a)(4) (2008). Under UPC §2-502(a)(3)(A), the witnesses must sign "within a reasonable time."

With the erosion of the requirement that the witnesses sign in the presence of the testator, a new issue has arisen. In a surprising number of recent cases, reaching divergent results, a witness did not sign until *after the testator's death*. Can such a will be probated nonetheless? Compare In re Estate of Saueressig, 136 P.3d 201 (Cal. 2006) (holding that witnesses must sign the will before testator's death), and In re Estate of Royal, 826 P.2d 1236 (Colo. 1992) (same), with In re Estate of Miller, 149 P.3d 840 (Idaho 2006) (admitting to probate a will signed by a witness after the testator's death and more than four years after the testator signed), and In re Estate of Jung, 109 P.3d 97 (Ariz. App. 2005) (admitting to probate a will signed by a witness less than a week after the testator signed and a few days after the testator died).

Effective in 2009, Cal. Prob. Code §6110(c) requires that the witnesses sign "during the testator's lifetime," but it also authorizes the application of the harmless error rule — a curative doctrine discussed below at pages 258-264 — to defective attestation, including the failure to sign before the testator dies. The official comment to UPC §2-502(a)(3)(A) takes the position that the "reasonable" time requirement could be satisfied by a signature after the testator's death.

NOTE: THE MEANING OF "WRITING" AND VIDEO OR ELECTRONIC WILLS

In the usual case, the requirement that a will be in writing is easily satisfied because the will is written or typed on one or more sheets of paper. But a will need not be on paper. All that is required is a reasonably permanent record of the markings that make up the will. Restatement (Third) of Property: Wills and Other Donative Transfers §3.1, cmt. i (1999). The question thus arises, what about a video or electronic will?

Suppose that Robert Reed videorecords his spoken will. Then he puts the DVD in a sealed envelope, on which he signs his name and writes, "To be played in the event of my death only!" Does the DVD comply with the requirement that the will be a signed writing? Is a voice print a writing? In Estate of Reed, 672 P.2d 829 (Wyo. 1983), dealing with a videotape, the court held No. A video of an execution ceremony may be admissible, however, to prove due execution. See Ind. Code Ann. §29-1-5-3.2 (2008); La. Code of Civ. Proc. art. 2904 (2008).

The Uniform Probate Code is purposely agnostic on whether a video recording could constitute a "document or writing" sufficient to be admitted under the harmless error rule, a reform doctrine (discussed on pages 258-264) that allows a defectively executed document to be admitted to probate if there is clear and convincing evidence that it was intended to be a will.

What about a will in the form of a computer file with a unique electronic signature? In 2001, Nevada enacted a statute authorizing electronic wills, subject to some rather strict requirements, including a single original and some way of determining if the original has been altered. Nev. Rev. Stat. §133.085 (2008). An electronic will probably does not satisfy the writing or signature requirement of a traditional Wills Act, but an electronic will might nonetheless be allowed under substantial compliance or the harmless error rule. Substantial compliance, like the harmless error rule, is a reform doctrine examined at page 253.

In Rioux v. Coulombe, 19 Est. & Tr. Rep. 2d 201 (Quebec 1996), Jaqueline Rioux left a suicide note directing the police

> to an envelope which contained a computer diskette marked "this is my will/Jaqueline Rioux/february 1, 1996." The information on the diskette, when later printed out, contained unsigned directions of a testamentary nature. The testatrix had noted in her diary that she had written her will on a computer. The diskette itself contained only one file which had been saved to memory on the same day that the deceased had noted in her diary that she had made a will on computer.

The court allowed probate of the electronic will under a Quebec substantial compliance statute. That statute, however, required that the "essential" formalities be met. Were they? See Nicholas Kasirer, From Written Record to Memory in the Law of Wills, 29 Ottawa L. Rev. 39 (1997/1998).

For further discussion, see Gerry W. Beyer and Claire G. Hargrove, Digital Wills: Has the Time Come for Wills to Join the Digital Revolution?, 33 Ohio N.U. L. Rev. 865 (2007); Joseph Karl Grant, Shattering and Moving Beyond the Gutenberg Paradigm: The Dawn of the Electronic Will, 42 U. Mich. J.L. Ref. 105 (2008).

Estate of Morea
Surrogate's Court, New York, 1996
645 N.Y.S.2d 1022

HOLZMAN, S.   In this uncontested proceeding to probate a will dated December 2, 1991, the issue presented is whether the bequest to decedent's friend George Buonaroba is void under N.Y. Estates, Powers & Trust Law (EPTL) §3-3.2 in light of the fact that he was one of the three attesting witnesses and that decedent's son Kevin, whose legacy under the will is less than his intestate share as one of decedent's six surviving children, was also one of the attesting witnesses. The third attesting witness does not receive any disposition or appointment under the will. EPTL §3-3.2(a)(1) provides that an attesting witness to a will to whom a beneficial disposition is made is a competent witness who can be compelled to testify with respect to the execution of such will but that the disposition to the attesting witness is void "unless there are, at the time of execution and attestation, at least two other attesting witnesses to the will who receive no beneficial disposition or appointment thereunder."[7] The purpose of the statute is to preserve the maker's testamentary scheme to at least some extent by making all attesting witnesses competent while preserving the integrity of the process of will executions by removing the possibility that attesting witnesses who receive a disposition under the will might give false testimony in support of the will to protect their legacies.

The Legislature, in effect, has concluded that the public good is served by requiring that a few innocent attesting witnesses forfeit their legacies so that the validity of a greater number of wills might not be suspect by dint of a beneficiary under the will being one of the attesting witnesses whose testimony is required to probate the will. New York's law on this subject has been criticized as creating "a most unfortunate conclusive presumption that a beneficiary under a will who also served as an attesting witness should be dramatically and summarily punished" (Margaret Valentine Turano, 1994 Supplementary Practice Commentaries, McKinney's Cons. Laws of N.Y., Book 17B, EPTL §3-3.2 1996 Pocket Part, at 80). This "conclusive presumption" is not the law in those states that have enacted the Uniform Probate Code nor is it the law in most jurisdictions.

Here, decedent's son, Kevin, does not forfeit his legacy as a result of being both an attesting witness and a beneficiary because EPTL §3-3.2(a)(3) permits him, as a distributee, to receive the lesser of his intestate share or his legacy under the will. However, since the attesting witness, George Buonaroba, is not a distributee of the decedent, it must be determined whether the bequest to him of one-eighth of decedent's tangible personal property "that is not otherwise disposed through Paragraph Second" is void under EPTL §3-3.2.

In light of the policy that statutes are to be construed to carry out the overall legislative intent and to avoid injustice or hardship, neither the spirit nor the letter of EPTL §3-3.2 requires that George Buonaroba forfeit, through no fault of his own, the legacy that decedent wanted him to receive. The objective of EPTL §3-3.2 that there be at least two attesting witnesses who have nothing to gain by the admission of the will to probate is fulfilled in this matter by the one witness who receives no disposition or appointment and by decedent's son Kevin, who, although he received a bequest under the will, is actually adversely affected by the

---

7. EPTL §3-3.2 (2008) provides:

(a) An attesting witness to a will to whom a beneficial disposition or appointment of property is made is a competent witness and compellable to testify respecting the execution of such will as if no such disposition or appointment had been made, subject to the following:

(1) Any such disposition or appointment made to an attesting witness is void unless there are, at the time of execution and attestation, at least two other attesting witnesses to the will who receive no beneficial disposition or appointment thereunder.

(2) Subject to subparagraph (1), any such disposition or appointment to an attesting witness is effective unless the will cannot be proved without the testimony of such witness, in which case the disposition or appointment is void.

(3) Any attesting witness whose disposition is void hereunder, who would be a distributee if the will were not established, is entitled to receive so much of his intestate share as does not exceed the value of the disposition made to him in the will. . . .

— Eds.

admission of the will to probate because his intestate share would be greater than his bequest. Considering that the first definition of the word "beneficial" in Webster's Dictionary (New Twentieth Century Unabridged Second Edition) is "advantageous", it is concluded that, although Kevin received a disposition under the will, it was not beneficial to him to the extent that he would have received a larger inheritance if he testified against the validity of the will and the instrument were denied probate. Consequently, the disposition to George Buonaroba is not void under EPTL §3-3.2(a)(1) because there are at least two other witnesses to the will who receive no beneficial disposition thereunder.

NOTES

1. *Interested witnesses and purging statutes.* Because an interested witness was not permitted to testify in court in England in the early eighteenth century, a will attested by an interested witness could not be proved in probate. To alleviate this harsh outcome, in 1752 Parliament passed a statute that came to be known as the *purging statute* (25 Geo. II, ch. 6, §I). The purging statute allowed a will attested by an interested witness to be admitted to probate, but voided (purged) any bequest to the interested witness. After the purging statute, a will attested by an interested witness would be valid, but at the cost of purging the interested witness of his bequest.

The majority of states in this country have purging statutes. Most, like the New York statute excerpted in footnote 7 in *Morea*, purge only the benefit that the witness would receive under the will that is in excess of what the witness would have received in intestacy (or, under some statutes, under an earlier will). Put otherwise, the witness forfeits only the extra benefit afforded to the witness by the will. A few states, such as Massachusetts, follow the English model and purge the witness of his entire devise. Mass. Gen. Laws ch. 191, §2 (2008). For a list of state purging statutes, see Jeffrey A. Schoenblum, 2008 Multistate Guide to Estate Planning at Table 1.

The purging statutes apply only to a witness who is necessary for the will's validity. If the will is witnessed by a sufficient number of disinterested witnesses, the interested witness is said to be *supernumerary* and is entitled to take his full bequest.

2. *Interested witnesses and the UPC.* A substantial minority of states do not require that the witnesses be disinterested, following UPC §2-505(b) (1990), which provides that a will is valid even if witnessed by an interested party, and that the interested witness does not forfeit his bequest even if it is greater than that which he would have received under a prior will or by intestacy. The official comment explains the rationale:

> Interest no longer disqualifies a person as a witness, nor does it invalidate or forfeit a gift under the will. Of course, the purpose of this change is not to foster use of interested witnesses, and attorneys will continue to use disinterested witnesses in execution of wills. But the

rare and innocent use of a member of the testator's family on a home-drawn will is not penal-ized.

This approach does not increase appreciably the opportunity for fraud or undue influ-ence. A substantial devise by will to a person who is one of the witnesses to the execution of the will is itself a suspicious circumstance, and the devise might be challenged on grounds of undue influence. The requirement of disinterested witnesses has not succeeded in prevent-ing fraud and undue influence; and in most cases of undue influence, the influencer is care-ful not to sign as a witness, but to procure disinterested witnesses. [UPC §2-505, cmt.]

California has adopted a middle ground whereby a bequest to a witness trig-gers a rebuttable presumption that the bequest was procured by duress, menace, fraud, or undue influence. Cal. Prob. Code §6112 (2008).

NOTE: RECOMMENDED METHOD OF EXECUTING A WILL

In executing a will, a lawyer should not rely on the formalities required by the Wills Act in the client's home state. The client's will may be offered for probate in another state. The client may be domiciled elsewhere at death or may own real property in another state, or the will may exercise a power of appointment gov-erned by the law of another state. Under the usual conflict of laws rules, the law of the decedent's domicile at death determines the validity of the will insofar as it disposes of personal property. The law of the state where real property is located determines the validity of a disposition of real property. If a person originally domiciled in Illinois executes a will, then moves permanently to New Jersey and dies there, owning Florida real estate, some tangible personal property, and some stocks and bonds, the law of Illinois does not govern the validity of the will at all. New Jersey law determines the validity of the disposition of the tangible and intangible personalty, and Florida law governs the validity of the disposition of the real estate.[8] Almost all states have statutes recognizing as valid a will executed with the formalities required, not only by the state where the testator was domi-ciled at death, but alternatively by the state where the will was executed or the state where the testator was domiciled when the will was executed. See UPC §2-506 (1990); Restatement (Third) of Property: Wills and Other Donative Trans-fers §3.1, statutory note 1 (1999). These statutes, however, are not all uniform, and sometimes contain ambiguities and internal conflicts. A lawyer should draft a will so that there is no need to resort to such an act. Hence, the careful lawyer in our highly mobile society should draw a will and have it executed in a manner that satisfies the formal requirements in all states.[9]

---

8. The Hague Convention of 1989 discards the situs rule for real property and the domicile rule for personal property, replacing them with very different choice of law rules. The Hague Convention has not been ratified by the United States and is sharply criticized by Professor Schoenblum, this country's leading choice of law scholar in estate planning matters. See Jeffrey A. Schoenblum, Choice of Law and Succession to Wealth: A Critical Analysis of the Ramifications of the Hague Convention on Succession to Decedents' Estates, 32 Va. J. Intl. L. 83 (1991).

9. If the client owns property in a foreign country or may die domiciled there, the law of the foreign country should be examined and the will executed in compliance with such law. See Jeffrey A. Schoenblum, Multistate

If the procedure set forth below[10] is followed, the instrument will be valid in all states, no matter in which state the testator is domiciled at the date of execution or at death or where the property is located:

(1) If the will consists of more than one page, the pages are fastened together securely. The will specifies the exact number of pages of which it consists.

(2) The lawyer confirms that the testator has read the will and understands its contents.

(3) The lawyer, the testator, two (or three[11]) disinterested witnesses, and a notary public are brought together in a room from which everyone else is excluded. (If the lawyer is a notary, an additional notary is unnecessary.) The door to the room is closed. No one enters or leaves the room until the ceremony is finished.

(4) The lawyer asks the testator the following three questions:

> (a) "Is this your will?"[12]
>
> (b) "Have you read it and do you understand it?"
>
> (c) "Does it dispose of your property in accordance with your wishes?"

After each question the testator should answer "Yes" in a voice that can be heard by the three witnesses and the notary. It is neither necessary nor customary for the witnesses to know the terms of the will. If, however, the lawyer foresees a possible will contest, added precautions might be taken at this time. See page 205.

(5) The lawyer asks the testator the following question: "Do you request _____, _____, and _____ (the witnesses) to witness the signing of your will?" The testator should answer "Yes" in a voice audible to the witnesses.

(6) The witnesses should be standing or sitting so that all can see the testator sign. The testator signs on the margin of each page of the will. This is done for

---

and Multinational Estate Planning §§15.01-15.06 (25th ann. ed. 2008). See also Uniform International Wills Act, found in UPC §§2-1001 to 2-1010 (1990), and adopted in many states, which sets out the procedure to comply with the 1973 Washington Convention on Wills. The procedure recommended in the text complies with the International Wills Act, except the self-proving affidavit at the end differs slightly from the affidavit required for an international will. For further discussion of the Washington Convention, ratified by the Senate in 1991, see Recent Development, The Resurgence of the International Will: A Call for Federal Legislation, 26 Vand. J. Transnatl. L. 417 (1993).

10. This procedure is an up-to-date version of the format recommended by Professor W. Barton Leach in his Cases on Wills 44 (2d ed. 1949) and subsequently refined by Professor A. James Casner in his work, 1 Estate Planning §3.1.1, now in its sixth edition (supp. 2007-2008) and maintained by Professor Jeffrey N. Pennell.

11. Two witnesses are required; three are recommended. Every state now requires only two witnesses, except Louisiana, which requires two witnesses plus a notary (see page 228, n.3). However, a Louisiana statute provides that a will executed out of state is valid if it is valid either in the state where executed or in the state of the testator's domicile. La. Stat. Ann. §9.2401 (2008). It is common to use three witnesses, among other reasons, to reduce the harm should an interested witness be among the three. Pennsylvania is the only state that does not require witnesses at all for formal wills, so long as the testator's signature is not by a simple mark or signed by someone else at the testator's direction. Pa. Cons. Stat. tit. 20, §3132 (2008).

12. The testator's declaration that the instrument is her will is called *publication*. The purpose of publication is to assure that the testator is under no misapprehension about the instrument that the testator is signing and to impress upon the witnesses the importance of the act and their consequent duties to vouch for the validity of the instrument. Nonetheless, the requirement of publication, a formality mandated in some states, is rarely a bar to probate since the testator may indicate to the witnesses that the instrument is a will by words, signs, or conduct; even the words of another saying it is the testator's will are sufficient. It is only necessary that the evidence show that the testator and the witnesses understand that the instrument is a will. Restatement (Third) of Property: Wills and Other Donative Transfers §3.1, cmt. h (1999).

purposes of identification and to prevent subsequent substitution of pages. The testator then signs her name at the end of the will.

(7) One of the witnesses reads aloud the *attestation clause*, which attests that the foregoing things were done. Here is an example: "On the _____ day of _____, 20 _____, Wendy Brown declared to us, the undersigned, that the foregoing instrument was her last Will, and she requested us to act as witnesses to it and to her signature thereon. She then signed the Will in our presence, we being present at the same time. We now, at her request, in her presence, and in the presence of each other, hereunto subscribe our names as witnesses, and each of us declares that in his or her opinion this testator is of sound mind."

(8) Each witness then signs and writes his or her address next to the signature.

(9) A *self-proving affidavit*, typed at the end of the will, swearing before a notary public that the will was duly executed, is then signed by the testator and the witnesses before the notary public, who in turn signs and attaches the required seal. Why attach a self-proving affidavit? Due execution of a will is usually proved after the testator's death by the witnesses testifying in court or executing affidavits. If the witnesses are dead or cannot be located or have moved far away, a self-proving affidavit reciting that all the requirements of due execution have been complied with permits the will to be probated. The will is valid without such an affidavit (except in Louisiana[13]), but the affidavit makes it easier to probate the will. The affidavit must be executed in front of a notary. Almost all states recognize self-proving affidavits, an invention of the UPC that has proven very popular.

UPC §2-504 (1990, rev. 2008) authorizes two kinds of self-proving affidavits. UPC §2-504(a) authorizes a *combined* attestation clause and self-proving affidavit, so that the testator and the witnesses (and the notary) sign their names only once; this is called a *one-step* self-proving affidavit. UPC §2-504(b) authorizes a *separate* self-proving affidavit to be affixed to a will already signed and attested. The affidavit must be signed by the testator and witnesses in front of a notary *after* the testator and witnesses have signed the will. In our recommended procedure, we have followed this *two-step* process, which is permitted in more states than is the one-step process that combines the attestation clause with the self-proving affidavit.

UPC §3-406(1) (1990, rev. 2008) provides that, if a will is self-proved, questions of due execution may not be contested "unless there is evidence of fraud or forgery affecting the acknowledgment or affidavit." Section 3-406 does not limit contests on other grounds such as undue influence or lack of capacity. In states that have not adopted UPC §3-406, a self-proved will may give rise to only a rebuttable presumption of due execution. See Bruce H. Mann, Self-Proving Affidavits and Formalism in Wills Adjudication, 63 Wash. U. L.Q. 39 (1985).

(10) Although not required, the lawyer should undertake a few precautionary post-execution measures. In a quiet moment after everyone has left, the lawyer should review the will to check that all the signatures are in the correct places and that each page is initialed or signed in the margin. If an error was made, it is

---

13. See footnote 11, supra, for Louisiana law.

easier to correct by redoing the execution ceremony than by litigation after death. It is also a good practice for the lawyer to write a short memo to the file noting that the firm's usual execution procedures were followed. If the firm is retaining possession of the original (as we recommend in states where this is not expressly discouraged by local courts), the lawyer should place the original in the firm's vault or safe deposit box and put copies, noted as such, in the client files. It is a good idea to send a booklet to the client containing a photocopy of the will (marked "copy"), a cover letter stating where the original will is stored, and a copy of any earlier letters describing the estate scheme, so that after death the family might find both a copy of the will and the address of the firm having custody of the original.

NOTE: SAFEGUARDING A WILL

The many reported cases involving notations, interlineations, or other markings on wills indicate that over the years a disturbing number of testators have attempted partial revocations or, perhaps, have used their wills as memo pads on which contemplated modifications have been noted. Also, an occasional testator has taken too seriously the lawyer's advice on safeguarding the will, with the result that the will cannot be located after death.[14]

These potential difficulties have prompted some lawyers to follow the practice of retaining the client's will in the lawyer's files. The client is given a photocopy of the will, on which the location of the original will is noted. Keeping clients' wills, however, may have the appearance of soliciting business, a potentially unethical practice. In State v. Gulbankian, 196 N.W.2d 733 (Wis. 1972), the Wisconsin Supreme Court discussed the ethics of this practice and said:

---

14. Consider the case of Oscar P.'s will, a true story told in a letter to one of the editors from Mr. A.J. Robinson, an attorney in Amarillo, Texas. Mr. Robinson was counsel for one group of claimants under the will.

Two men walked into our office in late August and told us that they were Mr. P.'s nephews. They were completely covered with chigger bites from the top of their shoes to their belts. Their legs were swollen and red all over. They told us that their uncle had died in East Texas on a 40-acre farm. They said that he was found dead in his old house that did not have any doors or windows and that the floor was about to fall in, that he kept his eggs in a bucket hanging from a tree limb by wire to keep the snakes from stealing them, that he hung his milk from a tree limb, dangling in a creek, that there was no stove in the house and that he had a wheel barrow with the wheel running at about a 45 degree angle that he pushed to and from town to carry all his supplies. They had been informed that their uncle had left a will, and the entire family had descended on the place over the weekend to hunt for it. They had spent two days digging in every place that they could think of on the entire 40 acres, hunting for the will that they assumed was buried somewhere. When they were about to quit, someone decided to dig up the floor of the chicken house. Underneath the chicken house floor they found a gallon jar, and in the gallon jar was a half-gallon jar, and in the half-gallon was a quart, and in the quart was a pint, and in the pint was a half-pint, and in the half-pint was a key which appeared to fit some safe-deposit box. Upon checking all the banks in the neighboring towns, they finally found a bank that had a safe-deposit box that the key would fit. Upon opening the safe-deposit box they found P.'s holographic will. The first sentence recited that this was Oscar P.'s last will. The second sentence read: "You will find the key to my safety deposit box in a jar under the floor in the chicken house."

Oscar P. left a substantial estate.

Nor do we approve of attorneys' "safekeeping" wills. In the old days this may have been explained on the ground many people did not have a safe place to keep valuable papers, but there is little justification today because most people do have safekeeping boxes, and if not, sec. 853.09, Stats., provides for the deposit of a will with the register in probate for safekeeping during the lifetime of the testator. The correct practice is that the original will should be delivered to the testator, and should only be kept by the attorney upon specific unsolicited request of the client. [Id. at 736.]

The ACTEC Commentaries on the Model Rules take the opposite view: "A lawyer who has drawn a will or other estate planning documents for a client may offer to retain the executed originals of the documents subject to the client's instructions." ACTEC Commentaries on the Model Rules of Professional Conduct 113 (4th ed. 2006) (commentary on Rule 1.8).

Like Wisconsin, many states have statutes permitting deposit of wills with the clerk of the probate court before death. See, e.g., UPC §2-515. Depositing a will with a probate court clerk is not, however, a common practice. Few people know that such a depository is available, and, consistent with the ACTEC Commentaries, lawyers usually recommend leaving the will in the law firm's safe or safe deposit box if the client decides not to take the will home.

2. Curing Defects in the Execution of Attested Wills

a. Excusing Execution Defects by Ad Hoc Exception

Under the traditional rule of strict compliance with the Wills Act, almost any mistake in execution invalidates the will. To avoid this harsh result, some courts have occasionally excused or corrected an obvious execution defect, while others have taken the position that there can be no relief from the rule of strict compliance. To get a feel for the inconsistent treatment of defective execution — and the need for a more principled way to cure defects — consider the next two cases, which present nearly identical facts but reach opposite results.

In re Pavlinko's Estate

Supreme Court of Pennsylvania, 1959

148 A.2d 528

BELL, J.   Vasil Pavlinko died February 8, 1957; his wife, Hellen, died October 15, 1951. A testamentary writing dated March 9, 1949, which purported to be the will of Hellen Pavlinko, was signed by Vasil Pavlinko, her husband. The residuary legatee named therein, a brother of Hellen, offered the writing for probate as the will of Vasil Pavlinko, but probate was refused. The Orphans' Court, after hearing and argument, affirmed the decision of the Register of Wills.

The facts are unusual and the result very unfortunate. Vasil Pavlinko and Hellen, his wife, retained a lawyer to draw their wills and wished to leave their property to each other. By mistake Hellen signed the will which was prepared for her husband, and Vasil signed the will which was prepared for his wife, each instrument being signed at the end thereof. The lawyer who drew the will and his secretary, Dorothy Zinkham, both signed as witnesses. Miss Zinkham admitted that she was unable to speak the language of Vasil and Hellen, and that no conversation took place between them. The wills were kept by Vasil and Hellen. For some undisclosed reason, Hellen's will was never offered for probate at her death; in this case it was offered merely as an exhibit.

The instrument which was offered for probate was short. It stated: "I, *Hellen* Pavlinko, of . . . , do hereby make, publish and declare this to be *my* Last Will and Testament. . . ."

In the first paragraph she directed her executor to pay her debts and funeral expenses. In the second paragraph she gave her entire residuary estate to "my husband, Vasil Pavlinko . . . absolutely." She then provided:

> Third: If my aforesaid husband, Vasil Pavlinko, should predecease me, then and in that event, I give and bequeath:
>
> (a) To my brother-in-law, Mike Pavlinko, of McKees Rocks, Pennsylvania, the sum of Two Hundred ($200) Dollars.
>
> (b) To my sister-in-law, Maria Gerber, (nee Pavlinko), of Pittsburgh, Pennsylvania, the sum of Two Hundred ($200) Dollars.
>
> (c) The rest, residue and remainder of *my* estate, of whatsoever kind and nature and wheresoever situate, I give, devise and bequeath, absolutely, to *my brother*, Elias Martin, now residing at 520 Aidyl Avenue, Pittsburgh, Pennsylvania.
>
> I do hereby nominate, constitute and appoint my husband, Vasil Pavlinko, as Executor of this my Last Will and Testament.

It was then mistakenly signed "Vasil Pavlinko [Seal]."

While no attempt was made to probate, as Vasil's will, the writing which purported to be his will but was signed by Hellen, it could not have been probated as Vasil's will, because it was not signed by him at the end thereof.

The Wills Act of 1947 provides in clear, plain and unmistakable language in §2: "Every will, . . . shall be in writing and shall be signed *by the testator* at the end thereof," 20 P.S. §180.2, with certain exceptions not here relevant. The Court below correctly held that the paper which *recited* that it was the will of Hellen Pavlinko and intended and purported to give Hellen's estate to her husband, could not be probated as the will of Vasil and was a nullity.

In order to decide in favor of the residuary legatee, almost the entire will would have to be rewritten. The Court would have to substitute the words "Vasil Pavlinko" for "Hellen Pavlinko" and the words "my wife" wherever the words "my husband" appear in the will, and the relationship of the contingent residuary legatees would likewise have to be changed. To consider this paper — as written — as Vasil's will, it would give his entire residuary estate to "my husband, Vasil Pavlinko, absolutely" and "Third: If my husband, Vasil Pavlinko, should predecease me, then. . . I give and bequeath my residuary estate to my brother, Elias Martin." The language of this writing, which is signed at the end thereof by *Vasil* Pavlinko, is unambiguous, clear and unmistakable, and it is obvious that it is a meaningless nullity. . . .

Once a Court starts to ignore or alter or rewrite or make exceptions to clear, plain and unmistakable provisions of the Wills Act in order to accomplish equity and justice in that particular case, the Wills Act will become a meaningless, although well intentioned, scrap of paper, and the door will be opened wide to countless fraudulent claims which the Act successfully bars.

Decree affirmed. Each party shall pay their respective costs.

MUSMANNO, J., dissenting.[15] Vasil Pavlinko and his wife, Hellen Pavlinko, being unlettered in English and unlearned in the ways of the law, wisely decided

---

15. Justice Musmanno was a striking individualist, sometimes injudicious, always colorful. In dissenting from a majority holding that Henry Miller's Rabelaisian *Tropic of Cancer* was not obscene, Musmanno wrote:

"Cancer" is not a book. It is a cesspool, an open sewer, a pit of putrefaction, a slimy gathering of all that is rotten in the debris of human depravity. And in the center of all this waste and stench, besmearing himself with its foulest defilement, splashes, leaps, cavorts and wallows a bifurcated specimen that responds to the name of Henry Miller. One wonders how the human species could have produced so lecherous, blasphemous, disgusting and amoral a human being as Henry Miller. One wonders why he is received in polite society. . . . From Pittsburgh to Philadelphia, from Dan to Beersheba, and from the ramparts of the Bible to Samuel Eliot Morison's Oxford History of the American People, I dissent. [Commonwealth v. Robin, 218 A.2d 546, 561 (Pa. 1966).]

In his first five years on the Pennsylvania Supreme Court, Musmanno filed more dissenting opinions than all the other members of that court had collectively filed in the preceding 50 years. One dissent got him into a lawsuit. In another case, Chief Justice Stern ordered that Musmanno's dissent not be published in the official state reports because he had not circulated it among the court. Musmanno sought mandamus to compel the state reporter to publish his dissent. The supreme court, with Musmanno not participating, denied the writ. Musmanno v. Eldredge, 114 A.2d 511 (Pa. 1955). Justice Musmanno then moved his case to the court of last resort, the law reviews. His side of the controversy can be found in Michael A. Musmanno, Dissenting Opinions, 60 Dick. L. Rev. 139 (1956). When asked whether he read Musmanno's dissents, Chief Justice Stern replied that he was not "interested in current fiction." New Republic, Feb. 3, 1968, at 14.

Musmanno's ancestors came from Italy, and he was a leading force in establishing Columbus Day as a special day for Italian Americans. When Yale accepted the Vinland map as evidence that Norsemen and not an Italian, Christopher Columbus, were among the first Europeans to "discover" America, Musmanno immediately rose to the attack. He dropped all his duties and went to Yale to dispute the archeologists, embarked on a six-month speaking tour attacking the authenticity of the Vinland map, and wrote a book, Columbus Was First! (1966).

In 1974 the Yale Library pronounced the Vinland map a fake, based primarily on the report of a firm that found titanium in the ink, but the firm did not test authentic pre-Columbian documents for comparison, some of which have since been tested and found to contain titanium. In 1995 Yale changed its mind and announced that the Vinland map may be authentic after all. Its authenticity continues to be debated by scholars based on a range of problems besides the ink. Notwithstanding the map, scholars have reached a consensus that Musmanno's larger contention — that "Columbus Was First!" — is false. In particular, excavations at L'Anse aux Meadows in present-day Newfoundland, suggest that Vikings settled North America about five hundred years before Columbus. See Kirsten A. Seaver, Maps, Myths and Men: The Story of the Vinland Map (2004); Kenneth M. Towe, The Vinland Map Ink Is Not Medieval, 76 Analytical Chemistry 863 (2004); Jacqueline S. Olin, Evidence That the Vinland Map Is Medieval, 75 Analytical Chemistry 6745 (2003).

Justice Musmanno's last opinion was a freewheeling dissent to a reversal of a rape conviction. The majority held that it was error for the judge to tell the jurors they would have to answer to God for their actions. Commonwealth v. Holton, 247 A.2d 228 (Pa. 1968). Wrote Musmanno:

God is not dead, and judges who criticize the invocation of Divine Assistance had better begin preparing a brief to use when they stand themselves at the Eternal Bar of Justice on Judgment Day. . . . I am perfectly willing to take my chances with [the trial judge] . . . at the gates of Saint Peter and answer on our voir dire that we were always willing to invoke the name of the Lord in seeking counsel. . . . Miserere nobis Omnipotens Deus! [Id. at 242-243.]

The next day, Columbus Day 1968, Justice Musmanno dropped dead and presumably this voir dire took place. — Eds.

to have an attorney draw up their wills, since they were both approaching the age when reflecting persons must give thought to that voyage from which there is no return. They explained to the attorney, whose services they sought, that he should draw two wills which would state that when either of the partners had sailed away, the one remaining ashore would become the owner of the property of the departing voyager. Vasil Pavlinko knew but little English. However, his lawyer, fortunately, was well versed in his clients' native language, known as Little Russian or Carpathian. The attorney thus discussed the whole matter with his two visitors in their language. He then dictated appropriate wills to his stenographer in English and then, after they had been transcribed, he translated the documents, paragraph by paragraph, to Mr. and Mrs. Pavlinko, who approved of all that he had written. The wills were laid before them and each signed the document purporting to be his or her will. The attorney gave Mrs. Pavlinko the paper she had signed and handed to her husband the paper he had signed. In accordance with customs they had brought with them from the old country, Mrs. Pavlinko turned her paper over to her husband. It did not matter, however, who held the papers since they were complementary of each other. Mrs. Pavlinko left her property to Mr. Pavlinko and Mr. Pavlinko left his property to Mrs. Pavlinko. They also agreed on a common residuary legatee, Elias Martin, the brother of Mrs. Pavlinko. . . .

We have also said time[s] without number that the intent of the testator must be gathered from the four corners of his will. Whether it be from the four corners of the will signed by Vasil Pavlinko or whether from the eight corners of the wills signed by Vasil and Hellen Pavlinko, all set out before the court below, the net result is always the same, namely that the residue of the property of the last surviving member of the Pavlinko couple was to go to Elias Martin. . . .

Even if we accept the Majority's conclusion . . . that all provisions in the Pavlinko will, which refer to himself, must be regarded as nullities, . . . it does not follow that the residuary clause must perish. The fact that some of the provisions in the Pavlinko will cannot be executed does not strike down the residuary clause, which is meaningful and stands on its own two feet. We know that one of the very purposes of a residuary clause is to provide a catch-all for undisposed-of or ineffectually disposed-of property. . . . I see no insuperable obstacle to probating the will signed by Vasil Pavlinko. Even though it was originally prepared as the will of his wife, Hellen, he did adopt its testamentary provisions as his own. Some of its provisions are not effective but their ineffectuality in no way bars the legality and validity of the residuary clause which is complete in itself. I would, therefore, probate the paper signed by Vasil Pavlinko. Here, indeed, is a situation where we could, if we wished, consistent with authority and precedent, and without endangering the integrity of the Wills Act, put in to effect the time-honored proverb that 'where there's a will, there's a way.'

In re Snide
Court of Appeals of New York, 1981
418 N.E.2d 656

WACHTLER, J.[16]   This case involves the admissibility of a will to probate. The facts are simply stated and are not in dispute. Harvey Snide, the decedent, and his wife, Rose Snide, intending to execute mutual wills at a common execution ceremony, each executed by mistake the will intended for the other. There are no other issues concerning the required formalities of execution, nor is there any question of the decedent Harvey Snide's testamentary capacity, or his intention and belief that he was signing his last will and testament. Except for the obvious differences in the names of the donors and beneficiaries on the wills, they were in all other respects identical.

The proponent of the will, Rose Snide, offered the instrument Harvey actually signed for probate. The Surrogate decreed that it could be admitted, and further that it could be reformed to substitute the name "Harvey" wherever the name "Rose" appeared, and the name "Rose" wherever the name "Harvey" appeared. The Appellate Division reversed on the law, and held under a line of lower court cases dating back into the 1800's, that such an instrument may not be admitted to probate. We would reverse.

It is clear from the record, and the parties do not dispute the conclusion, that this is a case of a genuine mistake. It occurred through the presentment of the wills to Harvey and Rose in envelopes, with the envelope marked for each containing the will intended for the other. The attorney, the attesting witnesses, and Harvey and Rose, all proceed[ed] with the execution ceremony without anyone taking care to read the front pages, or even the attestation clauses of the wills, either of which would have indicated the error.

Harvey Snide is survived by his widow and three children, two of whom have reached the age of majority. These elder children have executed waivers and have consented to the admission of the instrument to probate. The minor child, however, is represented by a guardian ad litem who refuses to make such a concession. The reason for the guardian's objection is apparent. Because the will of Harvey

---

16. Judge Sol Wachtler was one of the most respected state court judges in the country until his conviction for sending threatening letters under a false name to his former mistress, apparently both to harass her and to ingratiate himself by offering his help in protecting her from the fictional harasser.

In November 1992, he was New York state's chief judge and a rising star in the Republican party, famed for his monstrous ego, his political ambition, and his jousts with Gov. Mario Cuomo. Then he was arrested for stalking his former mistress, Joy Silverman, and charged with extortion, interstate racketeering, and blackmail, among other crimes. Wachtler had written her harassing letters in the guise of a fictional alter ego, and mailed a condom to her young daughter. The judge claimed mental incapacitation: Jilted by Silverman, he'd succumbed to a manic depression that was exacerbated by an addiction to prescription amphetamines. Wachtler pled guilty to sending threats through the mail. In September 1993 — less than a year after he'd presided over New York's Court of Appeals — the 63-year-old first-time offender began serving an 11-month term in federal prison. [David Plotz, Judicial Restraint: Sol Wachtler's Worthy Sentiments on Prison, Slate, Apr. 16, 1997.]

Since serving his prison sentence, Wachtler has successfully reentered respectable society. He published a book on prison reform in 1997, see Sol Wachtler, After the Madness: A Judge's Own Prison Memoir (1997); he is an adjunct professor at Touro College Jacob D. Fuchsberg Law Center on Long Island; and his law license was reinstated in 2007. — Eds.

would pass the entire estate to Rose, the operation of the intestacy statute after a denial of probate is the only way in which the minor child will receive a present share of the estate.

The gist of the objectant's argument is that Harvey Snide lacked the required testamentary intent because he never intended to execute the document he actually signed. This argument is not novel, and in the few American cases on point it has been the basis for the denial of probate (see Nelson v. McDonald, 16 N.Y.S. 273 (Sup. 1891); Matter of Cutler, 58 N.Y.S.2d 604 (Sur. 1945); Matter of Bacon, 165 Misc. 259 (N.Y. Sur. 1937); see, also, Matter of Pavlinko, 148 A.2d 528 (Pa. 1959); Matter of Goettel, 184 Misc. 155 (N.Y. Sur. 1944)). However, cases from other common-law jurisdictions have taken a different view of the matter, and we think the view they espouse is more sound (Matter of Brander, 4 DOM L. Rep. 688 [1952]; Guardian, Trust & Executor's Co. of New Zealand v. Inwood, 65 N.Z. L. Rep. 614 [1946] [New Zealand]; see Comment, Wills, 107 U. Pa. L. Rev. 1237, 1239-1240 (1959); Kennedy, Husband and Wife Executing Wills Drawn for Each Other — Probate of Husband's Will with Substitutions, 31 Can. Bar Rev. 185).

Of course, it is essential to the validity of a will that the testator was possessed of testamentary intent, however, we decline the formalistic view that this intent attaches irrevocably to the document prepared, rather than the testamentary scheme it reflects. Certainly, had a carbon copy been substituted for the ribbon copy the testator intended to sign, it could not be seriously contended that the testator's intent should be frustrated (Matter of Epstein, 136 N.Y.S.2d 884 (Sur. 1954)). Here the situation is similar. Although Harvey mistakenly signed the will prepared for his wife, it is significant that the dispositive provisions in both wills, except for the names, were identical.

Moreover, the significance of the only variance between the two instruments is fully explained by consideration of the documents together, as well as in the undisputed surrounding circumstances. Under such facts it would indeed be ironic — if not perverse — to state that because what has occurred is so obvious, and what was intended so clear, we must act to nullify rather than sustain this testamentary scheme. The instrument in question was undoubtedly genuine, and it was executed in the manner required by the statute. Under these circumstances it was properly admitted to probate (see Matter of Pascal, 197 N.E.2d 835, 837-38 (N.Y. 1955)).

In reaching this conclusion we do not disregard settled principles, nor are we unmindful of the evils which the formalities of will execution are designed to avoid; namely, fraud and mistake. To be sure, full illumination of the nature of Harvey's testamentary scheme is dependent in part on proof outside of the will itself. However, this is a very unusual case, and the nature of the additional proof should not be ignored. Not only did the two instruments constitute reciprocal elements of a unified testamentary plan, they both were executed with statutory formality, including the same attesting witnesses, at a contemporaneous execution ceremony. There is absolutely no danger of fraud, and the refusal to read these wills together would serve merely to unnecessarily expand formalism, without any corresponding benefit. On these narrow facts we decline this unjust course.

Nor can we share the fears of the dissent that our holding will be the first step in the exercise of judicial imagination relating to the reformation of wills. Again, we are dealing here solely with identical mutual wills both simultaneously executed with statutory formality.

For the reasons we have stated, the order of the Appellate Division should be reversed, and the matter remitted to that court for a review of the facts.

JONES, J., dissenting. . . . On the basis of commendably thorough world-wide research, counsel for appellant has uncovered a total of 17 available reported cases involving mutual wills mistakenly signed by the wrong testator. Six cases arise in New York, two in Pennsylvania, three in England, one in New Zealand and five in Canada. With the exception of the two recent Surrogate's decisions (*Snide* and Matter of Iovino, N.Y.L.J., April 16, 1980, at 14, col. 5) relief was denied in the cases from New York, Pennsylvania and England. The courts that have applied the traditional doctrines have not hesitated, however, to express regret at judicial inability to remedy the evident blunder. Relief was granted in the six cases from the British Commonwealth. In these cases it appears that the court has been moved by the transparency of the obvious error and the egregious frustration of undisputed intention which would ensue from failure to correct that error. . . .

I would adhere to the precedents, and affirm the order of the Appellate Division.

NOTES AND QUESTIONS

1. Both *Pavlinko* and *Snide* raise the same issue, known in the trade as a *switched wills* case, but they reach opposite results. Why?

2. There are two different modes of correcting a switched wills error. One option is to probate the will that the decedent *intended* to sign but did not. The obvious difficulty under this approach is that the document offered for probate was not signed by the decedent. The other option is to probate the will that the decedent *actually* signed and then to reform its terms to make sense. Under this approach, in *Pavlinko* the court would substitute the name "Vasil" for "Hellen," and in *Snide* the court would substitute "Harvey" for "Rose." We return to this latter approach — reformation of wills for mistake — in Chapter 5. We take up the former approach, deeming a defective execution to be in substantial compliance with the Wills Act or excusing the execution defect as harmless error, in the next section.

3. *Guardians ad litem.* When the interests of minor children or unborn heirs are at stake, courts usually appoint a guardian ad litem, a person assigned to represent the interests of the minor or unborn heir in the litigation. In *Snide*, Harvey's two adult children waived any objections to the entire estate passing to Harvey's wife Rose under the challenged will, but the guardian ad litem for Harvey's minor child objected because the child received nothing under the will. If Harvey's will were invalid, then the estate would pass in intestacy, with the minor receiving a share. In opposing the will, the guardian ad litem opted to

maximize the child's financial position without regard for Harvey's intent or the interests of the entire family. Doubtless the guardian was concerned about his potential liability to the minor once the minor reached adulthood.

Should the guardian have considered the interests of the entire family? What is the relevance, if any, of the fact that the minor's two adult siblings, whose financial and familial interests were identical to the minor's, declined to challenge the will? Would this fact give you comfort, as guardian, to give up the minor child's claim? In Espinosa v. Sparber, Shevin, Shapo, Rosen & Heilbronner, 612 So. 2d 1378, 1379 n.1 (Fla. 1993), the court in dicta expressed the "hope" that a guardian "would not focus strictly on the financial consequences for the child, but would also consider such important factors as family harmony and stability."

For further discussion, see Martin D. Begleiter, The Guardian ad Litem in Estate Proceedings, 20 Willamette L. Rev. 643 (1984); Lawrence A. Frolik, Is the Guardian the Alter Ego of the Ward?, 27 Stetson L. Rev. 53 (2007).

b.   Curative Doctrines: Substantial Compliance and Harmless Error

As we have seen, courts have occasionally excused or corrected an obvious execution defect to avoid denying probate to a will that manifestly represents the true testamentary wishes of the decedent. In recent years, two doctrines that formalize this practice have emerged. First, under the *substantial compliance* doctrine, the court may deem a defectively executed will as being in accord with the statutory formalities if the defective execution nonetheless fulfills the purposes of those formalities. See John H. Langbein, Substantial Compliance with the Wills Act, 88 Harv. L. Rev. 489 (1975). Second, under the *harmless error rule*, also known as the *dispensing power*, the court may excuse noncompliance with statutory formalities if there is clear and convincing evidence that the decedent intended the document to be his will. See UPC §2-503 (1990, rev. 1997); Restatement (Third) of Property: Wills and Other Donative Transfers §3.3 (1999).

In re Will of Ranney
Supreme Court of New Jersey, 1991
589 A.2d 1339

[A traditional formal will ends with the testator's signature, followed by an attestation clause and the signatures of the witnesses. To make wills easier to prove in probate, most lawyers add a self-proving affidavit. A *two-step* self-proving will appends a separate affidavit to the end of the will; the witnesses (and often the testator) must sign the affidavit in addition to signing the will itself, after which the affidavit is notarized. For a *one-step* self-proving will, the testator and the attesting witnesses sign only once, with the affidavit language folded into the attestation clause, after which the will is notarized. Under either a one- or a two-step approach, the will is said to be self-proving because the affidavit provides sworn evidence of due execution. The execution of a self-proving affidavit is included in paragraph 9 of the model will execution ceremony outlined on pages 242-245.

In this case, the lawyers omitted the attestation clause and used instead an affidavit designed for a two-step self-proving will. Thus, when the witnesses signed the document, they did not attest to the execution of a will but rather signed an affidavit swearing that they had previously signed their names as witnesses during a stage in the execution ceremony that never actually occurred.

Specifically, in the presence of his wife Betty, the testator Russell G. Ranney signed on the signature line of the fourth page of his will. The fifth page of the will was an affidavit stating that

> the Testator signed and executed the instrument as his Last Will and Testament and that he signed willingly and that he executed it as his free and voluntary act for the purposes therein expressed; and that *each witness states that he or she signed the Will as witnesses* in the presence and hearing of the Testator and that to the best of his or her knowledge, the Testator was at the time 18 or more years of age, of sound mind and under no constraint or undue influence. [Emphasis added.]

Ranney, the two witnesses, and a notary each signed the affidavit, but the witnesses had not in fact signed the will itself as attesting witnesses, contrary to the assertions in the affidavit. If the lawyers had chosen the New Jersey form for a one-step self-proving will, which would have integrated the attestation clause and the affidavit together, then the witnesses would have been required to sign only once, simultaneously as witnesses to the will and as affiants swearing that they participated in the proper execution of that will.]

POLLOCK, J. . . . The acknowledgment and affidavit is almost identical to the language suggested by N.J.S.A. 3B:3-5 for a self-proving affidavit *signed subsequent to the time of execution*. The form for making a will self-proved at the time of execution, as occurred here, is set forth in the preceding section, N.J.S.A. 3B:3-4. Although the subject affidavit was executed simultaneously with the execution of the will, *the affidavit refers to the execution of the will in the past tense and incorrectly states that the witnesses had already signed the will* [emphasis added] . . . .

Russell's will gives Betty a life estate in their apartment in a building at 111 Avenue of Two Rivers in Rumson, the rental income from other apartments in that building, and the tuition and rental income from the Rumson Reading Institute, which was merged into the Ranney School after the execution of Russell's will. The will further directs that on Betty's death, the Avenue of Two Rivers property and the proceeds of the Institute are to be turned over to the trustees of the Ranney School. Additionally, Betty receives all of Russell's personal property except that necessary for the operation of the Institute.

The residue of Russell's estate is to be paid in trust to Betty, Kantor [Russell and Betty's lawyer], and Henry Bass, Russell's son-in-law, who were also appointed as executors. Betty and Harland Ranney and Suzanne Bass, Russell's two children, are to receive thirty-two percent each of the trust income, and are to share equally the net income from the operation of Ransco Corporation. Nancy Orlow, Betty's daughter and Russell's step-daughter, is to receive the remaining four percent of the trust income. Russell's will provides further that after Betty's death the income from Ransco Corporation is to be distributed equally between Harland Ranney and Suzanne Bass, and on their deaths is to be distributed to the Ranney School.

Russell died on April 4, 1987, and the Monmouth County Surrogate admitted the will to probate on April 21, 1987. . . . Subsequently, Betty . . . contested the probate of Russell's will. . . . Her sole challenge was that the will failed to comply literally with the formalities of N.J.S.A. 3B:3-2. Suzanne R. Bass, Harland Ranney, Henry Bass, and the Ranney School urged that the will be admitted to probate. . . .

Although the Appellate Division "decline[d] to hold that the placement of the witnesses' signatures is immaterial," it ruled that the self-proving affidavit was part of the will and that the witnesses' signatures on the affidavit constituted signatures on the will . . . .

We disagree with the Appellate Division that signatures on the subsequently-executed self-proving affidavit literally satisfied the requirements of N.J.S.A. 3B:3-2 as signatures on a will. We further hold, however, that the will may be admitted to probate if it substantially complies with these requirements.

II

The first question is whether Russell's will literally complies with the requirements of N.J.S.A. 3B:3-2, which provides:

> [E]very will shall be in writing, signed by the testator or in his name by some other person in his presence and at his direction, and shall be signed by at least two persons each of whom witnessed either the signing or the testator's acknowledgment of the signature or of the will.

In holding that signatures on the self-proving affidavit satisfy N.J.S.A. 3B:3-2, the Appellate Division relied on out-of-state decisions that permitted the probate of wills when the witnesses signed a self-proving affidavit, but not the will. The rationale of those cases is that a self-proving affidavit and an attestation clause are sufficiently similar to justify the conclusion that signatures on a self-proving affidavit, like signatures on the attestation clause, satisfy the requirement that the signatures be on the will. The Appellate Division found that the similarity between self-proving affidavits and attestation clauses warrants treating the affidavit attached to Russell's will as the equivalent of an attestation clause. Noting that the absence of an attestation clause does not void a will, but merely requires the proponents to prove due execution, the Appellate Division could find "no reason, either in logic or policy, to deny a similar opportunity to the proponents" of Russell's will. . . .

Self-proving affidavits and attestation clauses, although substantially similar in content, serve different functions. Bruce H. Mann, Self-Proving Affidavits and Formalism in Wills Adjudication, 63 Wash. U. L.Q. 39, 41 (1985). Attestation clauses facilitate probate by providing "prima facie evidence" that the testator voluntarily signed the will in the presence of the witnesses. An attestation clause also permits probate of a will when a witness forgets the circumstances of the will's execution or dies before the testator.

Self-proving affidavits, by comparison, are sworn statements by eyewitnesses that the will has been duly executed. Mann, supra, 63 Wash. U. L.Q. at 40. The affidavit performs virtually all the functions of an attestation clause, and has the further effect of permitting probate without requiring the appearance of either witness. Id. at 41. Wills may be made self-proving simultaneously with or after execution. N.J.S.A. 3B:3-4, -5. One difference between an attestation clause and a subsequently-signed, self-proving affidavit is that in an attestation clause, the attestant expresses the present intent to act as a witness, but in the affidavit, the affiant swears that the will has already been witnessed. This difference is more apparent than real when, as here, the affiants, with the intent to act as witnesses, sign the self-proving affidavit immediately after witnessing the testator's execution of the will.

The Legislature first authorized self-proving affidavits in the 1977 amendments to the Probate Code, specifically N.J.S.A. 3A:2A-6. Nothing in the statutory language or history intimates that the Legislature contemplated a subsequently-executed affidavit as a substitute for the attestation clause. Instead, the 1977 amendments indicate that the Legislature envisioned the will, including the attestation clause, as independent from such an affidavit. Hence, the form provided in N.J.S.A. 3B:3-5 for a subsequently-signed affidavit refers to the will as a separate instrument and states that the testator and witnesses have signed the will. Thus, the Legislature indicated its intention that subsequently-executed, self-proving affidavits be used solely in conjunction with duly-executed wills. Although the execution of Russell's will and of the self-proving affidavit apparently were contemporaneous, the affidavit follows the form provided in N.J.S.A. 3B:3-5. Consequently, the signatures of the witnesses on the subject self-proving affidavit do not literally comply with the statutory requirements.

That finding does not end the analysis. As we stated in In re Estate of Peters, 526 A.2d 1005 (N.J. 1987), in limited circumstances a will may be probated if it substantially complies with those requirements. . . .

III

Substantial compliance is a functional rule designed to cure the inequity caused by the "harsh and relentless formalism" of the law of wills. John H. Langbein, Substantial Compliance with the Wills Act, 88 Harv. L. Rev. 489, 489 (1975). . . . The underlying rationale is that the

> finding of a formal defect should lead not to automatic invalidity, but to a further inquiry: does the noncomplying document express the decedent's testamentary intent, and does its form sufficiently approximate Wills Act formality to enable the court to conclude that it serves the purposes of the Wills Act? [Langbein, supra, 88 Harv. L. Rev. at 489.]

Scholars have identified various reasons for formalities in the execution of wills. The primary purpose of those formalities is to ensure that the document reflects the uncoerced intent of the testator. Id. at 492; Mann, supra, 63 Wash. U. L.Q. at 49. Requirements that the will be in writing and signed by the testator also serve an evidentiary function by providing courts with reliable evidence of the terms of the will and of the testamentary intent. Ashbel G. Gulliver & Catherine J. Tilson, Classification of Gratuitous Transfers, 51 Yale L.J. 1, 6-7 (1941). Additionally, attestation requirements prevent fraud and undue influence. Id. at 9-10; In re Estate of Peters, supra, 526 A.2d 1005. Further, the formalities perform a "channeling function" by requiring a certain degree of uniformity in the organization, language, and content of wills. Langbein, supra, 88 Harv. L. Rev. at 494. Finally, the ceremony serves as a ritual that impresses the testator with the seriousness of the occasion. Gulliver & Tilson, supra, 51 Yale L.J. at 5.

Rigid insistence on literal compliance often frustrates these purposes. To avoid such frustration, some courts, although purporting to require literal compliance, have allowed probate of technically-defective wills. See In re Estate of Bochner, 464 N.Y.S.2d 958, 959 (Sur. 1983); In re Will of Leitstein, 260 N.Y.S.2d 406, 408 (Sur. 1965). Other courts have refused to probate wills because of technical defects despite evidence that the testator meant the document to be a will. See In re Estate of Sample, 572 P.2d 1232, 1234 (Mont. 1977) (refusing to probate will signed only on attached self-proving affidavit); Boren v. Boren, 402 S.W.2d 728, 729 (Tex. 1966) (same). Leading authorities have criticized the *Boren* rule, finding no basis in logic or policy for its blind insistence on voiding wills for "the most minute defect[s] in formal compliance . . . no matter how abundant the evidence that the defect [is] inconsequential." Langbein, supra, 88 Harv. L. Rev. at 489; accord In re Estate of Charry, 359 So. 2d 544, 545 (Fla. App. 1978) (declining to follow *Boren* rule because it elevated form over substance); Mann, supra, 63 Wash. U. L.Q. at 39-40 (characterizing *Boren* line of cases as "odd and rather perverse"); Charles I. Nelson & Jeanne M. Starck, Formalities and Formalism: A Critical Look at the Execution of Wills, 6 Pepperdine L. Rev. 331, 356-357 (1979).

We agree with those authorities. Compliance with statutory formalities is important not because of the inherent value that those formalities possess, but because of the purposes they serve. Mann, supra, 63 Wash. U. L.Q. at 60; Nelson & Starck, supra, 6 Pepperdine L. Rev. at 355. It would be ironic to insist on literal compliance with statutory formalities when that insistence would invalidate a will that is the deliberate and voluntary act of the testator. Such a result would frustrate rather than further the purpose of the formalities. Nelson & Starck, supra, 6 Pepperdine L. Rev. at 353-55. . . .

The execution of a last will and testament, however, remains a solemn event. A careful practitioner will still observe the formalities surrounding the execution of wills. When formal defects occur, proponents should prove by clear and convincing evidence that the will substantially complies with statutory requirements. See Uniform Probate Code, supra, §2-503; Restatement, supra, §33.1, cmt. g. Our adoption of the doctrine of substantial compliance should not be construed as an invitation either to carelessness or chicanery. The purpose of the doctrine is to remove procedural peccadillos as a bar to probate.

Furthermore, as previously described, a subsequently-signed self-proving affidavit serves a unique function in the probate of wills. We are reluctant to permit the signatures on such an affidavit both to validate the execution of the will and to render the will self-proving. Accordingly, if the witnesses, with the intent to attest, sign a self-proving affidavit, but do not sign the will or an attestation clause, clear and convincing evidence of their intent should be adduced to establish substantial compliance with the statute. For that reason, probate in these circumstances should proceed in solemn form. See N.J.S.A. 3B:3-23; R. 4:84-1. Probate in solemn form, which is an added precaution to assure proof of valid execution, may be initiated on an order to show cause, R. 4:84-1(b), and need not unduly delay probate of a qualified will. . . .

If, after conducting a hearing in solemn form, the trial court is satisfied that the execution of the will substantially complies with the statutory requirements, it may reinstate the judgment of the Surrogate admitting the will to probate.

The judgment of the Appellate Division is affirmed, and the matter is remanded to the Chancery Division, Probate Part.

NOTE AND QUESTION

In Estate of Fordonski, 678 N.W.2d 413 (Iowa 2004), the witnesses did not sign the will but did sign a two-step self-proving affidavit that was affixed to the will. Observing that the applicable Wills Act did not specify where the witnesses must sign, the court concluded: "Because the witnesses' signatures in the present case appear on a document attached to the dispository provisions of the will, we deem that sufficient to satisfy the formalities of execution." Though the court did not announce that it was applying a substantial compliance doctrine, did not it do so?

Uniform Probate Code (1990, as amended 1997)

§2-503. HARMLESS ERROR

Although a document or writing added upon a document was not executed in compliance with Section 2-502, the document or writing is treated as if it had been executed in compliance with that section if the proponent of the document or writing establishes by clear and convincing evidence that the decedent intended the document or writing to constitute (i) the decedent's will, (ii) a partial or complete revocation of the will, (iii) an addition to or an alteration of the will, or (iv) a partial or complete revival of his [or her] formerly revoked will or of a formerly revoked portion of the will.

In re Estate of Hall
Supreme Court of Montana, 2002
51 P.3d 1134

REGINIER, J.   . . . James Mylen Hall ("Jim") died on October 23, 1998. At the time of his death, he was 75 years old and lived in Cascade County, Montana. His wife, Betty Lou Hall ("Betty"), and two daughters from a previous marriage, Sandra Kay Ault ("Sandra") and Charlotte Rae Hall ("Charlotte"), survived him.

Jim first executed a will on April 18, 1984 (the "Original Will"). Approximately thirteen years later, Jim and Betty's attorney, Ross Cannon, transmitted to them a draft of a joint will (the "Joint Will").[17] On June 4, 1997, Jim and Betty met at Cannon's office to discuss the draft. After making several changes, Jim and Betty apparently agreed on the terms of the Joint Will. Jim and Betty were prepared to execute the Joint Will once Cannon sent them a final version.

At the conclusion of the meeting, however, Jim asked Cannon if the draft could stand as a will until Cannon sent them a final version. Cannon said that it would be valid if Jim and Betty executed the draft and he notarized it. Betty testified that no one else was in the office at the time to serve as an attesting witness. Jim and Betty, therefore, proceeded to sign the Joint Will and Cannon notarized it without anyone else present.

When they returned home from the meeting, Jim apparently told Betty to tear up the Original Will, which Betty did. After Jim's death, Betty applied to informally probate the Joint Will. Sandra objected to the informal probate and requested formal probate of the Original Will.

On August 9, 2001, Judge McKittrick heard the will contest. He issued the Order admitting the Joint Will to probate on August 27, 2001. Sandra appealed. . . .

In contested cases, the proponent of a will must establish that the testator duly executed the will. See Mont. Code Ann. (MCA) §72-3-310. For a will to be valid, two people typically must witness the testator signing the will and then sign the will themselves. See MCA §72-2-522(1)(c). If two individuals do not properly witness the document, MCA §72-2-523 provides that the document may still be treated as if it had been executed under certain circumstances. One such circumstance is if the proponent of the document establishes by clear and convincing evidence that the decedent intended the document to be the decedent's will. See MCA §72-2-523.[18]

Sandra urges this Court not to use MCA §72-2-523 "to circumvent the statute requiring two witnesses to the execution of a will." Jim and Betty's failure to use witnesses, according to Sandra, was not an innocent omission on their part. . . . She primarily argues . . . that the Joint Will should be invalid as a matter of law because no one properly witnessed it.

---

17. A joint will is one instrument executed by two persons as the will of both — one will for two people. See page 327. — Eds.

18. Section 72-2-523 is the Montana enactment of UPC §2-503. — Eds.

Sandra's numerous arguments about why the will was improperly witnessed are irrelevant to this appeal. Neither party disputes that no witnesses were present at the execution of Jim and Betty's Joint Will as required by MCA §72-2-522. In the absence of attesting witnesses, MCA §72-2-523 affords a means of validating a will for which the Montana Legislature expressly provides. The only question before this Court, therefore, is whether the District Court erred in concluding that Jim intended the Joint Will to be his will under MCA §72-2-523. We conclude that the court did not err.

The District Court made several findings of fact that supported its conclusion. In particular, it noted that the Joint Will specifically revoked all previous wills and codicils made by either Jim or Betty. Furthermore, the court found that, after they had executed the Joint Will, Jim directed Betty to destroy the Original Will.

Sandra does not dispute any of the court's factual findings. She argues only that Betty testified that she and Jim had not executed the will even after they had signed it. In making this argument, she points to the following testimony:

Question: Do you know if [Jim] gave [Sandra and Charlotte] a copy of the new will?

Answer: I don't believe he did, no.

Question: Do you know why?

Answer: Well, I guess because we didn't have the completed draft without all the scribbles on it.

Question: So he thought that will was not good yet?

Answer: No, he was sure it was good, but he didn't give it to the girls. And we didn't give it to my son. We didn't give it to anybody.

Question: Why?

Answer: Because it wasn't completely finished the way Ross was going to finish it.

This testimony may suggest that Betty believed that the Joint Will was not in a final form because of "all the scribbles on it." Nevertheless, she immediately goes on to state that she believed the will was good. When asked if it were Jim's and her intent for the Joint Will to stand as a will until they executed another one, she responded, "Yes, it was." The court could reasonably interpret this testimony to mean that Jim and Betty expected the Joint Will to stand as a will until Cannon provided one in a cleaner, more final form. Sandra points to no other evidence that suggests that Jim did not intend for the Joint Will to be his will.

For these reasons, we conclude that the District Court did not err in admitting the Joint Will into final probate. Because Jim directed Betty to destroy the Original Will, we also conclude that the District Court did not err in finding that these acts were acts of revocation of the Original Will under MCA §72-2-527.

Affirmed.

NOTE: SUBSTANTIAL COMPLIANCE VERSUS HARMLESS ERROR

The architect of both *substantial compliance* (adopted in *Ranney*) and the *harmless error rule* (also known as the *dispensing power* and applied in *Hall*) is Professor John Langbein of Yale. Langbein first proposed substantial compliance to correct execution defects but later came to believe that the harmless error rule was better. The harmless error rule (or dispensing power) is adopted by UPC §2-503 and Restatement (Third) of Property: Wills and Other Donative Transfers §3.3 (1999).

In Langbein's classic 1975 article, Substantial Compliance with the Wills Act, 88 Harv. L. Rev. 489 (1975), he proposed that courts develop a substantial compliance doctrine to cure will execution errors. Under *substantial compliance*, a will should be admitted to probate if there is clear and convincing evidence (generally the highest evidentiary standard in civil litigation) that the purposes of formalities — the evidentiary, cautionary, protective, and channeling functions — were served despite a defective execution. Langbein viewed substantial compliance as a broad palliative that would excuse most innocent execution defects, especially those involving missing or defective attestation by witnesses. In 1981, the Australian state of Queensland enacted a statute providing for probate of a will that substantially complies with the requisite formalities. Queensland Succession Act of 1981, §9(a), 1981 Queensl. Stat. No. 69.

In the same year that Langbein published his substantial compliance article, South Australia enacted a *harmless error* (or *dispensing power*) statute providing for the probate of a document that was not properly executed if the court "is satisfied . . . that the deceased intended the document to constitute his will." S. Austl. Wills Act Amendment Act (No. 2) of 1975, §9, amending Wills Act of 1936, §12(2), 8 S. Austl. Stat. 665. This act, which has been amended several times since 1975, excuses noncompliance with the Wills Act. It gives a court a dispensing power — the power to validate a document the decedent intended to be a will even though the formalities are not complied with.

After observing the South Australian experience with the dispensing power and the Queensland experience with substantial compliance, in 1987 Langbein concluded that the dispensing power was preferable to the substantial compliance doctrine. The reason was

Professor John H. Langbein

that the "courts read into their substantial compliance doctrine a near-miss standard, ignoring the central issue of whether the testator's conduct evidenced testamentary intent." John H. Langbein, Excusing Harmless Errors in the Execution of Wills: A Report on Australia's Tranquil Revolution in Probate Law, 87 Colum. L. Rev. 1, 53 (1987). For example, Langbein had intended that substantial compliance would allow most wills with defective attestation to be probated, but the Queensland courts in the 1970s and 1980s applied substantial compliance so narrowly that, because attestation generally served the purposes of formalities, they were unwilling to overlook most defects in attestation. Indeed, after public criticism of the Queensland courts' restrictive view of substantial compliance, in recent decades they have become somewhat more forgiving of execution defects. Stephanie Lester, Admitting Defective Wills to Probate, Twenty Years Later: New Evidence for the Adoption of the Harmless Error Rule, 42 Real Prop., Prob. & Tr. J. 577, 598-599 (2007).

In South Australia, by contrast, from the very beginning the dispensing power fared much better. After examining the first 41 South Australian cases after 1975, Langbein concluded:

> Implicitly, this case law has produced a ranking of the Wills Act formalities. Of the three main formalities — writing, signature, and attestation — writing turns out to be indispensable. Because section 12(2) requires a "document," nobody has tried to use the dispensing power to enforce an oral will. Failure to give permanence to the terms of your will is not harmless. Signature ranks next in importance. If you leave your will unsigned, you raise a grievous doubt about the finality and genuineness of the instrument. An unsigned will is presumptively only a draft, . . . but that presumption is rightly overcome in compelling circumstances such as in the switched-wills cases. By contrast, attestation makes a more modest contribution, primarily of a protective character, to the Wills Act policies. But the truth is that most people do not need protecting, and there is usually strong evidence that want of attestation did not result in imposition. The South Australian courts have been quick to find such evidence and to excuse attestation defects under the dispensing power.
>
> In devaluing attestation while insisting on signature and writing, the South Australian legislation and case law has brought the South Australian law of wills into a kind of alignment with the American law of will substitutes, that is, with our nonprobate system, where business practice has settled the forms for transfer. In life insurance beneficiary designations; in bank transfer arrangements such as pay-on-death accounts, joint accounts, and Totten trusts; in pension accounts; and in revocable inter vivos trusts, writing is the indispensable formality of modern practice, and signature is nearly as universal. Attestation, however, is increasingly uncommon. . . .
>
> Americans should . . . shudder that we still inflict upon our citizens the injustice of the traditional law, and we should join in this movement to rid private law of relics so embarrassing. [Langbein, supra, 87 Colum. L. Rev. at 52-54.]

In a 2007 study, Stephanie Lester reviewed 121 Australian cases decided since Langbein's study and concluded that the dispensing power has continued to fare well — with one exception. In a troubling number of cases, the court admitted a document to probate despite evidence that the document was not intended to be a will but for which there was good evidence of whom the decedent wanted to benefit. Nonetheless, Lester concluded that, "Considering the success of the harmless error rule over the past 30 years in South Australia (and more recently in New South Wales and other Australian states), jurisdictions in the United States that still use strict or substantial compliance should consider adopting" the harmless error rule. Stephanie Lester, supra at 589-598, 603. But see John V. Orth, Wills Act Formalities: How Much Compliance Is Enough?, 43 Real Prop., Trust & Est. L.J. 73 (2008) (taking issue with Lester's methods and opposing the harmless error rule).

In 1990, the harmless error rule was codified in the UPC, using the clear and convincing evidence standard. Under UPC §2-503, courts are directed to look not at whether the purposes of formalities were served (as in substantial compliance), but at whether "the decedent intended the document or writing to constitute . . . the decedent's will." A version of UPC §2-503 has been adopted in California, Colorado, Hawaii, Michigan, Montana, New Jersey, South Dakota, Utah, and Virginia.[19]

Measures similar to UPC §2-503 have been enacted in other Australian states, Manitoba, and Saskatchewan, and for a time such a provision was in force in Israel. Israeli Succession Law of 5725-1965, §25, which adopted a harmless error rule, noted in the official comment that it is a *mitzvah* to carry out the wishes of the decedent.[20] In 2004, however, §25 was amended to allow probate of a defective will only if the will has "the basic elements" and the court "has no doubt that it reflects the testator's free and true wish[es]." Id. 5764-2004 Revision (Aryeh Greenfield trans., 4th ed. 2005). The "basic elements" include a writing brought before two witnesses. Id. §25(b)(2). See Doron Menashe, Relaxed Formalism: The Validation of Flawed Wills, 40 Isr. L. Rev. 119, 125-127 (2007) (commenting on, and providing an alternative translation of, §25).

NOTES AND QUESTIONS

1. In his 1987 study, Langbein found that in every South Australian case involving attestation defects, the will was nonetheless reliable enough to be admitted to probate, a finding largely replicated by Lester in her 2007 study. If in almost every case attestation defects are going to be excused, why not use a *rule* (no attestation requirement) rather than a litigation-breeding *standard* (the dispensing power)?

19. California's harmless error rule is limited to attestation errors. In Colorado and Virginia, the harmless error rule excludes signature errors other than switched wills cases or, in Virginia, a signature on the self-proving affidavit instead of the will. See Cal. Prob. Code §6110(c)(2) (effective 2009); Colo. Rev. Stat. §15-11-503(2) (2008); Va. Code Ann. §64.1-49.1 (2008). See also In re Estate of Wiltfong, 248 P.3d 465 (Colo. App. 2006) (explaining that the Colorado version of the harmless error rule was limited to "minor flaws" in execution).

20. The term *mitzvah* resists straightforward English translation, but the basic idea is a mix of commandment and good deed.

Since the 1700s, Pennsylvania has not required attestation for formal wills, yet there is no evidence that fraud has run wild in Pennsylvania. For an argument that the minimum formalities for a will should be reduced to a writing (typed or hand-written) signed by the testator, see James Lindgren, Abolishing the Attestation Requirement for Wills, 68 N.C. L. Rev. 541 (1990); James Lindgren, The Fall of Formalism, 55 Alb. L. Rev. 1009, 1024-1033 (1992).

2. In states that have adopted the harmless error rule, the effective minimum requirement for admitting a document to probate as a will has been reduced to little more than the intent that the document be a will. Accordingly, much more pressure is put on the concept of testamentary intent, and the subject of litigation necessarily shifts. More casual documents may have to be examined to determine whether they were intended to be a will, a concern raised by Lester in her 2007 study of the more recent Australian cases.

Unfortunately, testamentary intent is not well defined or analyzed. If the requirement is understood in broad terms, such as the intent to provide for property disposition after death, then it can just as easily apply to a will substitute, such as a trust. Yet testamentary intent could be understood so narrowly that, unless the testator intended to fall within the legal category called a will, she wouldn't meet the requirement. A more coherent body of law might emerge if we had more precise terminology for the different strands of testamentary intent.

There are many possible components to testamentary intent: intent that a document be used as evidence after death, intent that a document convey no present interest, intent that it be a will, intent that it not be a will substitute, intent to execute a document, intent that it be final unless later revoked, intent that after death certain beneficiaries receive certain property, and so on. For a fumbling attempt to disentangle these threads, see Lindgren, The Fall of Formalism, supra, at 1018-1019. On finding testamentary intent, see Emily Sherwin, Clear and Convincing Evidence of Testamentary Intent: The Search for a Compromise Between Formality and Adjudicative Justice, 34 Conn. L. Rev. 453 (2002). See also C. Douglas Miller, Will Formality, Judicial Formalism, and Legislative Reform: An Examination of the New Uniform Probate Code "Harmless Error" Rule and the Movement Toward Amorphism, 43 Fla. L. Rev. 167 (1991).

3. For further discussion of the harmless error rule and the substantial compliance doctrine, see, in addition to the articles cited previously, Martin L. Fried, The Disappointed Heir: Going Beyond the Probate Process to Remedy Wrong-doing or Rectify Mistake, 39 Real Prop., Prob. & Tr. J. 357 (2004); Pamela R. Champine, My Will Be Done: Accommodating the Erring and the Atypical Testator, 80 Neb. L. Rev. 387 (2001). See also Adam J. Hirsch, Law and Proximity, 2008 U. Ill. L. Rev. 557, 589-597; Mary Louise Fellows and Gregory S. Alexander, Forty Years of Codification of Estates and Trusts Law: Lessons for the Next Generation, 40 Ga. L. Rev. 1049, 1051-1065 (2006).

3.   Notarized Wills

As amended in 2008, UPC §2-502(a)(3), page 227, provides that a will is valid if it is signed by two witnesses *or* by a notary. In the following excerpt, Professor Waggoner, the reporter for the 2008 amendments, explains the rationale for validating notarized wills.

Lawrence W. Waggoner, The UPC Authorizes Notarized Wills
34 ACTEC J. 83 (2008)

The will-execution formalities are thought to serve several functions — evidentiary, cautionary (ceremonial), channeling, and protective. A notarized will would seem to serve all of these functions. The danger that a notarized will would not reliably represent the decedent's wishes seems minimal. A notarized will would almost always be upheld under the UPC's harmless-error rule. Treating a notarized will as validly executed would allow such a will to be upheld without the need to satisfy the clear and convincing standard of proof, and would be especially beneficial in states that have not enacted a harmless-error rule.

The UPC and many non-UPC states authorize holographic wills. One of the reasons for validating a holographic will is that the larger handwriting sample yields greater assurance of the identity of the maker of the document than a mere signature. In the case of a notarized will, the notarial seal serves the same function, because one of the notary's principal duties is to verify the identity of the person signing the document.

The American notary does not serve the same function as the notary in the European civil-law countries. The civil-law notary supervises the execution of an "authenticated will," in which the notary is a quasi-judicial officer who determines whether the testator has mental capacity and is free of duress and undue influence. Compliance with the American execution formalities does no such thing: A validly executed will is still subject to contest on grounds of lack of capacity, undue influence, duress, fraud, or forgery.

Allowing notarization as an optional method of execution can benefit practice. Cases have begun to emerge in which the supervising attorney, with the client and all witnesses present, circulates one or more estate-planning documents for signature, and fails to notice that the client or, in the case of the will, one of the witnesses has unintentionally neglected to sign one of the documents. Such an omission often, but not always, arises when the attorney prepares multiple estate-planning documents — a will, a durable power of attorney, a health-care power of attorney, and perhaps a revocable trust. It is common practice, and sometimes required by state law, that the documents other than the will be notarized. It would reduce confusion and chance for error if all of the documents could be executed with the same formality.

For a variety of reasons, some individuals avoid professional advice and attempt to execute wills on their own. As long as it is clear that the decedent adopted the document as his or her will, the law has no reason to deny validity on the ground of defective execution. The harmless-error rule is one curative measure for this problem. Allowing notarization as an optional method of execution is another. The public is accustomed to thinking that a document is made "legal" by getting it notarized. To some, this conception is mistakenly but understandably carried over to executing a will. A testator who goes to the trouble of going to a bank or even a package or photocopy store to get a home-drawn will notarized shows as much of a deliberate purpose to make the will final and valid as asking a couple of individuals to sign as witnesses. In effect, the UPC as amended treats the notary as the equivalent of two attesting witnesses. The case law invalidating a notarized will after death arises from the decedent's ignorance of the statutory requirements, not in response to evidence raising doubt that the will truly represents the decedent's wishes.

NOTES, QUESTIONS, AND PROBLEM

1. In 2002, Ronald Ferree died in an apparent suicide. His 1999 "Last Will and Testament," executed on a preprinted will form, was found near his body. Portions of the will were in Ferree's handwriting and the will was notarized but not attested. One of the three named beneficiaries was a friend, Charles Creel, who would not take anything in intestacy if the will were invalid. The court held that the will did not substantially comply with the applicable Wills Act. Even if the notary were treated as a witness, there would still be only one rather than the required two. In re Will of Ferree, 848 A.2d 81 (N.J. Ch. 2003), aff'd, 848 A.2d 1 (N.J. App. 2004). Is the court's decision consistent with In re Will of Ranney, page 263? What result under UPC §2-502(a)(3)(B), page 227?

2. Suppose that only one witness, instead of the two required, signs *T*'s will, but the witness plus a notary sign the attached self-proving affidavit. Does the notary count as the second witness? Compare In re Estate of Teal, 135 S.W.3d 87 (Tex. App. 2002) (yes, notary signed as witness even though she intended to sign only as notary), with Estate of Alfaro, 703 N.E.2d 620 (Ill. App. 1998) (no, unless the notary was intending to sign as a witness rather than as a notary). What result under UPC §2-502(a)(3)(B)? Under §2-503?

3. Although generally described as a notarized will provision, by its terms UPC §2-502(a)(3)(B) is broader. It validates a will that has been "acknowledged by the testator before a notary public *or other individual authorized by law to take acknowledgments*" (emphasis added). In many states, a lawyer is permitted to take an acknowledgement by virtue of being an officer of the court. The question thus arises, in such a state, would §2-502(a)(3)(B) validate a will signed by a lawyer but not notarized and not signed by a second witness?

#8 WILL (Unmarried Individual With No Children & Two or More Beneficiaries)

Last Will and Testament
of
RONALD D. FERREE

I, RONALD FERREE _____ presently residing at
40 WATERMAN AVE, RUMSON N.J. 07760
being of full age and sound and disposing mind and memory, hereby make, publish
and declare this to be my Last Will and Testament.

FIRST: I hereby revoke any and all Wills and Codicils by me anytime
heretofore made. THERE ARE NO OTHER (RF)

SECOND: I direct that all of my just debts and funeral expenses be paid out
of my Estate as soon as practicable after my death. (RF)

THIRD: I am presently not married. (RF)

FOURTH: I hereby give, devise and bequeath all of my Estate, real, personal
and mixed, of every kind and nature whatsoever and wheresoever situated, to the
following named beneficiaries or their survivors in equal shares.

a. MICHEAL FERREE (BROTHER) 2981 HEATHER
Name and address of beneficiary
b. COURT, JENSEN BEACH, FLA 34957
Name and address of beneficiary
c. BARBRA FERREE 2981 HEATHER Ct
Name and address of beneficiary
d. COURT, JENSEN BEACH, FLA 34957
Name and address of beneficiary
e. CHARLES CREEL (MY IRA AT SMITH BARNEY)
Name and address of beneficiary 49 PARKER AVE, FAIR HAVEN N.J.

FIFTH: I nominate and appoint MICHEAL FERREE _____,
as Executor/Executrix of this Will. In the event he/she shall predecease me or fails
to serve as such Executor/Executrix, then in such event, I nominate and appoint
BARBRA FERREE _____, Executor/Executrix of this my Last
Will and Testament. I further direct that no appointee hereunder shall be required to
give any bond for the faithful performance of his/her duties.

SIXTH: I give to my Executor/Executrix, authority to exercise all the powers,
duties, rights and immunities conferred upon fiduciaries by law with full power to
sell to mortgage and to lease, and to invest and re-invest all or any part of my
Estate on such terms as he/she deems best.

IN WITNESS WHEREOF, I hereunto set my hand this 21ST day
of OCTOBER, 19 79.

Jane F. Hartman
JANE F. HARTMAN
NOTARY PUBLIC OF NEW JERSEY
My Commission Expires July 15, 2003

Ronald D. Ferree
(SIGN HERE)
RONALD D. FERREE

Signed, sealed, published and declared by the above named testator, as and for
his Last Will and Testament, in the presence of us, who at his request, in his presence,
and in the presence of one another have hereunto subscribed our names as attesting
witnesses, the day and year last written above.

_____ residing at _____
_____
_____ residing at _____
_____
_____ residing at _____
_____

Disputed Will of Ronald Ferree

4. Holographic Wills

The Jolly Testator Who Makes His Own Will[21]

Ye lawyers who live upon litigants' fees,
And who need a good many to live at your ease,
Grave or gay, wise or witty, whate'er your degree,
Plain stuff or Queen's Counsel, take counsel of me:
When a festive occasion your spirit unbends,
You should never forget the profession's best friends;
So we'll send round the wine, and a light bumper fill
To the jolly testator who makes his own will.

He premises his wish and his purpose to save
All dispute among friends when he's laid in the grave;
Then he straightway proceeds more disputes to create
Than a long summer's day would give time to relate.
He writes and erases, he blunders and blots,
He produces such puzzles and Gordian knots,
That a lawyer, intending to frame the thing ill,
Couldn't match the testator who makes his own will.

— LORD NEAVES

In slightly over half of the states, primarily in the South and West, holographic wills are permitted. A holographic will is a will written by the testator's hand and signed by the testator; attesting witnesses are not required. Holographic wills are of Roman origin and are recognized by the Code Napoleon and civil law countries. They were introduced into this country by a Virginia statute of 1751 and by the reception of the civil law into Louisiana. See generally R.H. Helmholz, The Origin of Holographic Wills in English Law, 15 Leg. Hist. 97 (1994). Holographs are authorized by UPC §2-502(b), page 227.

ASHBEL G. GULLIVER AND CATHERINE J. TILSON, CLASSIFICATION OF GRATUITOUS TRANSFERS, 51 Yale L.J. 1, 13-14 (1941): "The exemption of holographic wills from the usual statutory requirements seems almost exclusively justifiable in terms of the evidentiary function. The requirement that a holographic will be entirely written in the handwriting of the testator furnishes more complete evidence for inspection by handwriting experts than would exist if only the signature were available, and consequently tends to preclude the probate of a forged document. . . . While there is a certain ritual value in writing out the document, casual off-hand statements are frequently made in letters. The

---

21. We reproduce only the first two stanzas of Lord Neaves's poem. For the entire poem, see William L. Prosser, The Judicial Humorist 246 (1952). — Eds.

Holographic Will States (2008)

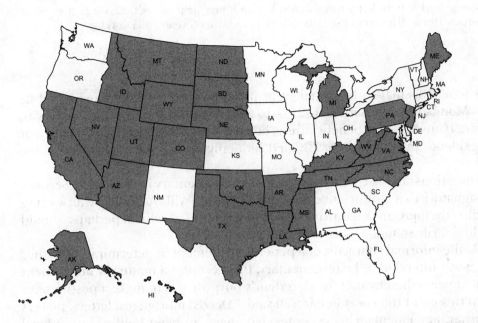

relative incompleteness of the performance of the functions of the regular statute of wills, and particularly the absence of any ritual value, may account for the fact that holographic wills are not recognized in the majority of the states, and for some decisions, in states recognizing them, requiring the most precise compliance with specified formalities."

Kimmel's Estate
Supreme Court of Pennsylvania, 1924
123 A. 405

SIMPSON, J.   One of decedent's heirs at law appeals from a decree of the orphans' court, directing the register of wills to probate the following letter:

Johnstown, Dec. 12.
The Kimmel Bro. and Famly

We are all well as you can espec fore the time of the Year. I received you kind & welcome letter from Geo & Irvin all OK glad you poot your Pork down in Pickle it is the true way to keep meet every piece gets the same, now always poot it down that way & you will not miss it & you will have good pork fore smoking you can keep it from butchern to butchern the hole year round. Boys, I wont agree with you about the open winter I think we are gone to have one of the hardest. Plenty of snow & Verry cold verry cold! I dont want to see it this way but it will come see to the old sow & take her away when the time comes well I cant say if I will come over yet. I will wright in my next letter it may be to ruff we will see in the next letter if I come I have some very valuable papers I want you to keep fore me so if enny thing hapens all the scock money in the 3 Bank liberty lones Post office stamps and my home on Horner St goes to George Darl & Irvin Kepp this letter lock it up it may help you out. Earl sent after his Christmas Tree & Trimmings I sent them he is in the Post office in Phila working.

> Will clost your Truly,
> Father.

This letter was mailed by decedent at Johnstown, Pa., on the morning of its date — Monday, December 12, 1921 — to two of his children, George and Irvin, who were named in it as beneficiaries; the envelope being addressed to them at their residence in Glencoe, Pa. He died suddenly on the afternoon of the same day.

Two questions are raised: First. Is the paper testamentary in character? Second. Is the signature to it a sufficient compliance with our Wills Act? Before answering them directly, there are a few principles, now well settled, which, perhaps, should be preliminarily stated.

While the informal character of a paper is an element in determining whether or not it was intended to be testamentary, this becomes a matter of no moment when it appears thereby that the decedent's purpose was to make a posthumous gift. On this point the court below well said: "Deeds, mortgages, letters, powers of attorney, agreements, checks, notes, etc., have all been held to be, in legal effect, wills. Hence, an assignment (Coulter v. Shelmadine, 53 A. 638 (Pa. 1902)), . . . a deed (Turner v. Scott, 51 Pa. 126 (1866), a letter of instructions (Scott's Estate, 23 A. 212 (Pa. 1892), a power of attorney (Rose v. Quick, 30 Pa. 225 (1858)), and an informal letter of requests (Knox's Estate, 18 A. 1021 (Pa. 1890)), were all held as wills."

It is equally clear that where, as here, the words "if enny thing hapens," condition the gift, they strongly support the idea of a testamentary intent; indeed they exactly state what is expressed in or must be implied from every will. True, if the particular contingency stated in a paper, as the condition upon which it shall become effective, has never in fact occurred, it will not be admitted to probate (Morrow's Appeal, 9 A. 660 (Pa. 1887); Forquer's Estate, 66 A. 92 (Pa. 1907)). In the present case, however, it is clear the contingency, "if enny thing hapens," was still existing when testator died suddenly on the same day he wrote and mailed the letter; hence, the facts not being disputed, the question of testamentary intent was one of law for the court (Davis' Estate, 118 A. 645 (Pa. 1922)).

As is often the case in holographic wills of an informal character, much of that which is written is not dispositive; and the difficulty, in ascertaining the writer's intent, arises largely from the fact that he had little, if any, knowledge of either law, punctuation, or grammar. In the present case this is apparent from the paper itself; and in this light the language now quoted must be construed:

> I think we are gone to have one of the hardest [winters]. Plenty of snow & Verry cold verry cold! I dont want to see it this way but it will come . . . well I cant say if I will come over yet. I will wright in my next letter it may be to ruff we will see in the next letter if I come I have

some very valuable papers I want you to keep fore me so if enny thing hapens all . . . [the real and personal property specified] goes to George Darl and Irvin Kepp this letter lock it up it may help you out.

When resolved into plainer English, it is clear to us that all of the quotation, preceding the words "I have some very valuable papers," relate to the predicted bad weather, a doubt as to whether decedent will be able to go to Glencoe because of it, and a possible resolution of it in his next letter; the present one stating "we will see in the next letter if I come." This being so, the clause relating to the valuable papers begins a new subject of thought, and since the clearly dispositive gifts which follow are made dependent on no other contingency than "if enny thing hapens," and death did happen suddenly on the same day, the paper, so far as respects those gifts, must be treated as testamentary.

It is difficult to understand how the decedent, probably expecting an early demise — as appears by the letter itself, and the fact of his sickness and inability to work, during the last three days of the first or second week preceding — could have possibly meant anything else than a testamentary gift, when he said "so if enny thing hapens [the property specified] goes to George Darl and Irvin"; and why, if this was not intended to be effective in and of itself, he should have sent it to two of the distributees named in it, telling them to "Kepp this letter lock it up it may help you out."

The second question to be determined . . . [is whether] the word "Father," when taken in connection with the contents of the paper, show that it was "signed by him?" . . . If the word "Father" was intended as a completed signature to this particular character of paper, it answers all the purposes of the Wills Act. That it was so intended we have no doubt. It was the method employed by decedent in signing all such letters, and was mailed by him as a finished document. . . .

True, a formal will would not be so executed; but this is not a formal will. It is a letter, signed by him in the way he executed all such letters, and, from this circumstance, his "intent to execute is apparent" beyond all question.

Decree affirmed and appeal dismissed, the costs in this court to be paid by the estate of Harry A. Kimmel, deceased.

QUESTIONS AND NOTES

1. If you had asked Mr. Kimmel before he died whether his letter was a will, what would he have answered?

2. There is a lively literature both favoring and opposing holographic wills. Opponents of holographs argue that they are inartful and breed litigation, a conclusion in part based on reviews of appellate opinions. However, in the most careful study to date of actual experiences with holographs in probate courts, Professor Stephen Clowney found that of the 145 holographic wills offered for probate in two years in Allegheny County (Pittsburgh), only 6 (4 percent) resulted in an objection or hearing of any kind. Although 43 percent did not designate an executor and 24 percent lacked a residuary clause, Clowney concluded, nonetheless, that

holographs are an indispensable tool for testators who are either unwilling or unable to commission a traditional will. Homemade testaments provide a low-cost alternative to intestacy, improve the overall quantity of will-making, function as a safety-net for testators who fall suddenly ill, and rarely result in litigation. The triumph of holographic wills also suggests, strongly, that state legislatures should consider reducing the number of requirements necessary to create a formal, attorney-authored will. . . .

The underlying truth is that scholars who base their opinion of holographs on a patchwork of humorous anecdotes and appellate level court decisions miss the rich diversity of testaments filed with the Register of Wills. The average person who chooses to execute a homemade will does not deserve to be lumped in with the occasional testator who is barely literate or takes the job less than seriously. The authors of holographic wills are not foolish or feeble or unreliable. Whether through hard work or luck, the testators in this study generally managed to scrape together sizeable assets and then chose to distribute those assets with well-written documents of their own making. This instinct to convey property to loved ones arguably should be applauded, not the subject of derision. [Stephen Clowney, In Their Own Hand: An Analysis of Holographic Wills and Homemade Willmaking, 43 Real Prop., Trust & Est. L.J. 27, 28, 46-47 (2008).]

For more skeptical views of holographic wills, see Richard Lewis Brown, The Holograph Problem — The Case Against Holographic Wills, 74 Tenn. L. Rev. 93 (2006); Gerry W. Beyer, Statuary Fill-in Will Forms: The First Decade; Theoretical Constructs and Empirical Findings, 72 Or. L. Rev. 769 (1993); Gail Boreman Bird, Sleight of Handwriting: The Holographic Will in California, 32 Hastings L.J. 605 (1981).

3. *Conditional wills.* In Kimmel's Estate, the will was upon the condition, "if enny thing hapens," meaning "if I die." Suppose a will is written to become operative if death from a particular event occurs, such as death from a surgical operation or death while on a journey. Does the testator want the will to be effective only if the event happens or to be effective at the testator's death regardless of whether his death is related to the event?

In Eaton v. Brown, 193 U.S. 411 (1904), the testator wrote a holographic will saying: "I am going on a journey and may not return. If I do not, I leave everything to my adopted son." The testator returned from her journey and died some months later. The Supreme Court, per Holmes, J., ordered the will probated. "Obviously the first sentence, 'I am going on a journey and may not ever return,' expresses the fact which was on her mind as the occasion and inducement for writing it. . . . She was thinking of the possibility of death or she would not have made a will. But that possibility at that moment took the specific shape of not returning from her journey, and so she wrote 'if I do not return,' before giving her last commands."

Most of the cases on conditional wills are in accord with Eaton v. Brown. They presume the language of condition does not mean that the will is to be probated only if the stated event happens but is, instead, merely a statement of the inducement for execution of the will, which can be probated upon death from any cause. See Estate of Martin, 635 N.W.2d 473 (S.D. 2001), holding that the statement "If anything should happen to me on this trip to Rapid City" expressed a "motive or reason for drafting the will rather than a contingency upon which the will was based." In some cases, however, the opposite result obtains. In Estate of Perez, 155 S.W.3d 599 (Tex. App. 2004), the testator wrote: "because I am sick and waiting for a heart surgery, and providing ahead of any emergency, I make the following disposition to be fulfilled in case my death occurs during the surgery." The court denied probate to the will after the testator survived the surgery but died six months later.

4.   Holographic wills are often written *in extremis,* when the testator is close to death, and sometimes under heartrending circumstances. Consider Estate of Harris, reported in W.M. Elliott, Wills — Writing Scratched on Tractor Fender — Granting of Probate, 26 Can. B. Rev. 1242 (1948):

> Recently the Surrogate Court of the Judicial District of Kerrobert in Saskatchewan granted Letters of Administration with Will Annexed of a holograph writing scratched on a tractor fender (the Estate of Cecil George Harris). . . .
>
> The facts of the Harris case were as follows. The deceased, a married man with two small children, was a wheat farmer. At noon on June 8th, 1948, he set out with a tractor and one-way disc to summer-fallow, telling his wife that he intended to work through the day and probably would not be back until almost ten in the evening. About an hour later he stopped the implements to do some oiling and make adjustments. After stepping down from the tractor seat, he put the tractor by mistake into reverse gear. As a result, it moved backwards pinning him between the two implements with his left leg caught under the left rear wheel of the tractor and the lower part of his body caught between the implements. Although he had the freedom of his arms, he was unable to reach the controls of the tractor. Eventually, the tractor engine died. He was still in this position some nine hours later when his wife, wondering at his absence, discovered him. She summoned help from the neighbors and at about 10:30 p.m. he was released and rushed to the hospital where he died, as a result of his injuries, within forty-eight hours.
>
> When the deceased was discovered he was conscious and able to give instructions for releasing him. He remained conscious until given medical attention and stated that he had been conscious during the whole of the time he was imprisoned.
>
> On June 10th . . . [a neighbor] noticed the writing scratched on the fender. It read: "In case I die in this mess, I leave all to the wife. Cecil Geo. Harris." [Id. at 1242-1243.]

The knife used to scratch the will was discovered in Harris's clothes. The fender was taken to the solicitor's office and ultimately the piece containing the will was cut off, admitted to probate, and stored with the case files. The testator's handwriting was proved by affidavit.

5.   Purported holographic wills have taken myriad forms — and shapes. In addition to tractor fenders, such wills have been written on a nurse's petticoat, a chest of drawers, a cigarette carton, a bedroom wall,[22] a napkin, a set of paper plates and the box that held them, and an eggshell. See Estate of Shelly, 950 A.2d

---

22. Herman Schmidt wrote a note on a bedroom wall to his fiancée, a belly dancer, Genevieve Decker. The 18-inch square piece of plaster containing the note was cut from the wall and offered as a will in a Philadelphia probate court. The purported will read:

> Genevieve: You take care of all my belongings. This give's you authority. Love, Herman, 8-14-1968. [Austin (Texas) American Statesman, Oct. 15, 1968.]

1021 (Pa. Super. 2008) (denying probate to a cigarette carton will); Virgil M. Harris, Ancient, Curious and Famous Wills (1911, reprint 2000); Robert S. Menchin, The Last Caprice (1963); Elmer Million, Wills: Witty, Witless, and Wicked, 7 Wayne L. Rev. 335 (1960). In the curious 1888 novel, Mr. Meeson's Will, by H. Rider Haggard, a will tattooed on the back and shoulders of a woman, Miss Smithers, was admitted to probate — as an attested will! See Catherine O. Frank, Of Testaments and Tattoos: The Wills Act of 1837 and Rider Haggard's Mr. Meeson's Will, 18 L. & Lit. 323 (2006).

If a testator writes her will by hand on a typed or preprinted will form but fails to have the form properly attested, the instrument fails as a formal will. Whether the instrument can be probated as a holograph depends on how much of the instrument is in the testator's handwriting. On this issue the courts have reached surprisingly inconsistent results.

Estate of Gonzalez
Supreme Judicial Court of Maine, 2004
855 A.2d 1146

[In August 2001, Fermin Gonzalez wanted to prepare a will before a trip to Florida. To that end, he filled in the blanks of a preprinted will form, indicating by hand his planned bequests in equal shares to three of his five children, Kerry Ann Gonzalez, Tara Maureen Gonzalez Grenon, and Kristin Julia Gonzalez. Fermin then showed his brother, Joseph, and Joseph's wife, Elizabeth, the completed form as well as a second, blank form on which he planned to copy the language from the first form more neatly. Elizabeth saw Fermin sign the first, filled-in form, but neither Elizabeth nor anyone else signed the first form as a witness. Instead, Elizabeth, Joseph, and Fermin's mother each signed their names as witnesses on the blank form, the one Fermin intended to complete more neatly based on what he had written on the first form. But before completing the second form, Fermin fell ill and died on August 21, 2001. Kerry, Tara, and Kristin petitioned to probate the first, unattested but completed form. Todd and Alison Gurney, the two children Fermin omitted, objected.]

ALEXANDER, J. . . . The document that Gonzalez signed does not qualify as a will under 18-A Me. Rev. Stat. Ann. (M.R.S.A.) §2-502 (1998), because it was not signed by any witnesses. Therefore, in order to be allowed or admitted to probate, the document must qualify as a holographic will under 18-A M.R.S.A. §2-503 (1998). A holographic will is one where "the signature and the material provisions are in the handwriting of the testator." 18-A M.R.S.A. §2-503. The comment

A235-10
R235-04

LAST WILL AND TESTAMENT

BE IT KNOWN that I, FERMIN ARENALDO GONZALEZ, _LOTS 5, 35 RUSSELL RD. W. NEWFIELD_, a resident of _____, County of YORK, _____ in the State of MAINE, being of sound mind, do make and declare this to be my Last Will and Testament expressly revoking all my prior Wills and Codicils at any time made.

I. PERSONAL REPRESENTATIVE:

I appoint JOSEPH R. GONZALEZ & WALTER GONZALEZ of 39 ROBESON ST. FRANCIA PLAN, MA., as Personal Representative of this my Last Will and provide if this Personal Representative is unable or unwilling to serve then I appoint ELIZABETH GONZALEZ of 39 ROBESON ST FRANCIA PLAN MA as alternate Personal Representative. My Personal Representative shall be authorized to carry out all provisions of this Will and pay my just debts, obligations and funeral expenses. I further provide my Personal Representative shall not be required to post surety bond in this or any other jurisdiction, and direct that no expert appraisal be made of my estate unless required by law.

II. GUARDIAN:

In the event I shall die as the sole parent of minor children, then I appoint _____ as Guardian of said minor children. If this named Guardian is unable or unwilling to serve, then I appoint _____ as alternate Guardian.

III. BEQUESTS:

I direct that after payment of all my just debts, my property be bequeathed in the manner following:

THAT THE PROPERTY ON LOT 5 W35 RUSSELL RD. W. NEWFIELD ME.

THE HOUSE CABIN AND BARN.

ALL THE CONTENTS OF MY PERSONAL PROPERTY INCLUDING MY 1953 MERCURY CAPRI CONVERTIBLE

MY 1971 FORD PUP ALONG WITH ALL JEWELRY

GOLD I.D. BRACKET, STAIN LESS STEEL ROLEX SUBMARINER WRIST WATCH, SELT PROP.

ALL POWER TOOLS INCLUDING MY WHITE QUARTER HORSE

FARM PROPERTY/TRACTOR MY HORSE A FARM QUARTER HORSE & CATTLE

[...]

BECOME THE PROPERTY OF MY THREE DAUGHTERS,

KERRY ANN GONZALEZ, TARA MAUREEN GONZALEZ BRENDON KRISTIN JULIA GONZALEZ. EACH HOLDING AN EQUAL RIGHT THAT SHOULD THEY DECIDE TO SELL ALL OF THE ABOVE THAT (10,000 (TEN THOUSAND) OF THE PROCEEDS AFTER THE SALE OF ALL OF THE ABOVE BE GIVEN TO MY FATHER & PHILIP GONZALEZ. PHILIP AND 10,000 TEN THOUSAND BE GIVEN TO MY BROTHER.

SEE PART II OF 2 GONZALEZ

Execute and attest before a notary. Caution: Louisiana residents should consult an attorney before preparing a will.

Page ___ of ___

(Rev. 1996)

[Part II continued:]

I ALSO WISH THAT SHOULD I FAEL I SHOULD LET MY BROTHERS AND PARTNERS DEVIDE TO SELL EQUALLY ANY OF THE ABOVE MENTIONED, OF MY BROTHERS JOSE, BARTOLO AND WALTER GONZALEZ TO DIVIDE THE FIRST RIGHTS TO PURCHASE ANY OF THE PROPERTY. INCLUDING HASSAN JIVAN. ALSO ORDER THAT MY DOG MARWAN & JACK RUSSELL NAMED ISARIC BE GIVEN TO MRS. ELIZABETH & VAIL OF WINFIELD COURT NH. MY PORTION BOAT & EQUIPTMENT SHOULD JOSEPH GREEN & WALTER SPLIT.

[...] THE PROPERTY JOINTLY OF MY THREE BROTHERS [...] ALONG WITH $5,000 DOLLAR FOR THE CARE OF SAID ANIMAL. I ALSO WISH THAT MR. FRANCIS LYNCH JR. OF 64 PERRY ST. E. WEYMOUTH MA. THAT MR. PROPER DRESS AND GROOMING BE IN MY WARFARE SIZE TO INSURE MY VALUE UNICORN OF SABER UPON PREPARATION FOR MY FUNERAL DRESS. IT IS MY WISH THAT THIS FORECLOSURE WHICH A [...] I ALSO WISH [...] EXCLUDED FROM ANY AND ALL 3 PERSONS SEEN AT MY FUNERAL ARRANGE NEAR THEY ARE

ALSO TO MY FUNERAL ARE MY FATHER WISH [...]
WITNESSED: JANET FRANCIS HICKEY AND JAMES F. FOLEY SR.

Witness Signature _____ Address _____

Witness Signature _____ Address _____

Witness Signature _____ Address _____

The testator has signed this will at the end and on each other separate page, and has declared and signed in our presence that it is his/her last will and testament, and in the presence of the testator and each other we have hereunto subscribed our names this _____ day of _____ (year).

ACKNOWLEDGMENT

State of _____)
County of _____)
We, _____ and _____, the testator and the witnesses, respectively, whose names are signed to the attached and foregoing instrument, were sworn and declared to the undersigned that the testator signed the instrument as his/her Last Will and that each of the witnesses, in the presence of the testator and each other, signed the will as a witness.

Testator: _____

Witness X _____

Witness _____

Witness _____

On _____ appeared _____ personally known to me (or proved to me on the basis of satisfactory evidence) to be the person(s) whose name(s) is/are subscribed to the within instrument and acknowledged to me that he/she/they executed the same in his/her/their authorized capacity(ies), and that by his/her/their signature(s) on the instrument the person(s), or the entity upon behalf of which the person(s) acted, executed the instrument.

WITNESS my hand and official seal.

Signature _____
Signature of Notary

Affiant ___ Known ___ Produced ID ___
Type of ID _____ Produced ID _____
(Seal)

Page ___ of ___

The Will in Estate of Gonzalez

from the Uniform Probate Code helps to explain the meaning of the statutory language:

> By requiring only the "material provisions" to be in the testator's handwriting (rather than requiring, as some existing statutes do, that the will be "entirely" in the testator's handwriting) a holograph may be valid even though immaterial parts such as date or introductory wording be printed or stamped. A valid holograph might even be executed on some printed will forms if the printed portion could be eliminated and the handwritten portion could evidence the testator's will.

The Gurneys argue that Gonzalez did not execute a valid holographic will because a material provision of the will — evidence of testamentary intent — appears in the preprinted portion of the document, and was not handwritten. They maintain that the handwritten words are a list of what Gonzalez wanted to do with his property, but the handwritten words do not indicate that the conveyances were testamentary in nature.

We have not yet addressed the impact that preprinted will forms have on holographic wills. Most jurisdictions have dealt with this issue in one of two ways.

Some courts have looked to the preprinted language in order to determine the context of the handwritten words. In Estate of Muder, 765 P.2d 997, 1000 (Ariz. 1988), the Supreme Court of Arizona held that a person who handwrote his wishes on a preprinted will form had effectuated a valid holographic will because the person's testamentary intent was clear.[23] The court stated:

> We hold that a testator who uses a preprinted form, and in *his own handwriting* fills in the blanks by designating his beneficiaries and apportioning his estate among them and signs it, has created a valid holographic will. Such handwritten provisions may draw testamentary context from both the printed and the handwritten language on the form. We see no need to ignore the preprinted words when the testator clearly did not, and the statute does not require us to do so. Id.

Other courts have ignored all of the preprinted words, and determined whether the handwritten words, taken alone, fulfill the requirements of a holographic will. See Estate of Black, 641 P.2d 754, 755 (Cal. 1982); Estate of Foxley, 575 N.W.2d 150, 154 (Neb. 1998).

We agree with the Supreme Court of Arizona and hold that printed portions of a will form can be incorporated into a holographic will where the trial court finds a testamentary intent, considering all of the evidence in the case. The Probate Court, after reviewing the document and hearing the evidence, explicitly found such an incorporation into the holographic will in this case: "[T]he hand-written

---

23. In Estate of Muder, at issue was a preprinted will form that was completed by hand, signed, and notarized, but attested by only one witness. The Arizona Supreme Court, 3 to 2, upheld the will as a valid holograph. The relevant handwritten dispositive language, inserted in a printed paragraph saying "I give to," read as follows: "My wife Retha F. Muder, our home and property in Shumway, Navajo County, car — pick up, travel trailer, and all other earthly possessions belonging to me, livestock, cattle, sheep, etc. Tools, savings accounts, checking accounts, retirement benefits, etc." — Eds.

material . . . implicitly adopted and incorporated the printed text on the form and converted the form into a more clear will."

The Uniform Probate Code comment states that "a holograph may be valid even though immaterial parts such as date or introductory wording be printed or stamped." The printed words in Gonzalez's will: "BE IT KNOWN that I _____, a resident of _____, County of _____, in the State of _____, being of sound mind, do make and declare this to be my Last Will and Testament expressly revoking all my prior Wills and Codicils at any time made" and "I direct that after payment of all my just debts my property be bequeathed in the manner following" are introductory phrases and may be preprinted. When filled in by the testator's handwriting, as here, they can become a valid statement of testamentary intent in a holographic will. . . .

Gonzalez's handwritten words may be read in the context of the preprinted words, and the Probate Court could properly find that the document is a valid holographic will.

The entry is: Judgment affirmed.

NOTE AND QUESTION

1.   In *Gonzalez*, the court not only considered the preprinted portions of the document to find testamentary intent, but it also held that the handwritten language incorporated the preprinted text by reference (see page 310), thereby giving effect to the preprinted text, too. In many other states, however, the court would not look to the preprinted words and the opposite result would obtain. See In re Will of Ferree, page 266 (denying probate to a partially printed, partially handwritten document); Berry v. Trible, 626 S.E.2d 440 (Va. 2006) (same).

2.   Suppose *Gonzalez* had arisen in a state that had adopted the harmless error rule. What result? See Estate of Wiltfong, 148 P.3d 465 (Colo. 2006) (holding that a partially printed, partially handwritten document was not valid as a holographic will, but was valid under the harmless error rule).

NOTE: SIGNATURE AND HANDWRITING IN HOLOGRAPHIC WILLS

To be valid, a holographic will must be written by the testator's hand and signed by the testator. Out of this simple formulation, however, arise two important interpretive problems: (a) the nature of the requirement that the testator sign the holograph, and (b) how much of the holograph must be in the testator's handwriting.

(a) *Signature.* In almost all states permitting holographs, the will may be signed at the end, at the beginning, or anywhere else on the face of the document. But if it is not signed at the end, there may be doubt about whether the decedent intended his name to be a signature. Compare Estate of Fegley, 589 P.2d 80 (Colo. App. 1978) (denying probate to a handwritten instrument reading, "I, Henrietta

Fegley, being of sound mind and disposing memory, declare this instrument to be my last will," but not otherwise signed), with Estate of MacLeod, 254 Cal. Rptr. 156 (App. 1988) (reaching a contrary result on virtually identical facts). See also Bennett v. Ditto, 204 S.W.3d 145 (Ky. App. 2006) (admitting to probate a will reading, "This was written by Donna H Wiseman on June 9, 2002," but not otherwise signed).

In Williams v. Towle, 66 Cal. Rptr. 3d 34 (App. 2007), the testator did not sign his name at the end, but he did write his name, in block letters, on the top of the first page: "Last Will Etc. or What? of Homer Eugene Williams." The court admitted the will to probate.

The Will in Williams v. Towle

(b) *The Extent of the Testator's Handwriting.* A recurring problem in determining the validity of and interpreting holographic wills is how much of the document must be written in the testator's own handwriting. The statutes fall into three categories:[24]

---

24. Though Pennsylvania has no holographic will statute, it also has no witnessing requirement for wills; thus, handwritten wills are as valid as typed wills, so long as they meet the other requirements for validity (chiefly, signature by the testator). In addition, New York and Maryland also have statutes permitting holographic wills by soldiers and sailors.

1. *First generation statutes: "entirely written, signed, and dated."* The first generation of holographic will statutes required that holographs be "entirely written, signed, and dated" in the handwriting of the testator. Under these statutes, holographs were sometimes struck down even when they included only one or two printed words. In Estate of Thorn, 192 P. 19 (Cal. 1920), the court struck down the testator's handwritten will because he had stamped the name of his home, Cragthorn, twice within its text.

In Estate of Dobson, 708 P.2d 422 (Wyo. 1985), the testator took her signed handwritten will to her local banker to discuss it with him. To make the will clearer, the banker penciled in certain numbers and parentheses and added to the devise of a tract of land, "including all mineral and oil rights," all with the consent of the testator. The court held the will could not be probated because it was not entirely in the handwriting of the decedent.

Some courts interpreted the first generation statutes as requiring that the will be "entirely dated," so that simply writing "May 1948" or "1965" was insufficient to allow probate. See Estate of Carson, 344 P.2d 612 (Cal. App. 1959) (although "May 1948" was clear, the day of the month between the month and year was illegible; will held invalid because the date was insufficient); Estate of Hazelwood, 57 Cal. Rptr. 332 (App. 1967) ("1965" was insufficient, will held invalid). Ten states still require that a holograph be entirely in the handwriting of the testator, but only two of these states require this also for the date.[25]

2. *Second generation statutes (1969 UPC): "material provisions."* The inconsistent and harsh results under statutes requiring that the entire holograph be handwritten led the drafters of the original 1969 Uniform Probate Code to require only that "the signature and the material provisions" of the holograph be in the testator's handwriting. Still, courts struggled with wills that were partially typed and partially handwritten because sometimes a material dispositive provision was wholly or partly printed and sometimes the language that indicated testamentary intent was printed rather than written out by the testator. Some courts were willing to look to the printed words to establish testamentary intent, but others were not. Seven states still have holographic will statutes based on the 1969 UPC.[26]

3. *Third generation statutes (1990 UPC): "material portions" and extrinsic evidence allowed.* Unhappy with courts continuing to strike down seemingly reliable holographs, the drafters of the 1990 UPC tried yet again to make it easier to make a valid holograph. The requirement that the "material provisions" be handwritten was changed to "material portions": "A will . . . is valid as a holographic will, whether or not witnessed, if the signature and material portions of the document are in the testator's handwriting." UPC §2-502(b), page 227. Although this would seem like a trivial change, it was apparently intended to allow the probate

---

25. Arkansas, Kentucky, Louisiana (also requires a handwritten date), Mississippi, North Carolina (but some printed language will not invalidate), Oklahoma (also requires a handwritten date), Texas, Virginia, West Virginia, and Wyoming.

26. The statutes in four states are derived from the 1969 UPC: Idaho, Maine, New Jersey, and Tennessee. California's statute is based mostly on the 1969 UPC, but it includes the extrinsic evidence rule of the 1990 UPC. Statutes in Nebraska and Nevada are loosely based on the 1969 UPC.

of a holograph even if "immaterial" parts such as the "date" or "introductory wording" are printed. UPC §2-502(b), cmt. As an example, the comment to §2-502(b) states that language such as "I give, devise and bequeath to" in a pre-printed will form should not disqualify the instrument as a valid holograph if the testator fills in the rest by hand.

The 1990 UPC also explicitly allows extrinsic evidence to be used to establish testamentary intent, thus further encouraging courts to look at the printed words in addition to the handwritten ones. "Intent that a document constitute the testator's will can be established by extrinsic evidence, including, for holographic wills, portions of the document that are not in the testator's handwriting." UPC §2-502(c), page 227. At least nine states have adopted a variant of these 1990 UPC provisions.[27]

As the next case demonstrates, the application of §2-502(c) is not limited to partially handwritten and partially typed instruments.

In re Estate of Kuralt
Supreme Court of Montana, 2000
15 P.3d 931

[Charles Kuralt was born in North Carolina in 1934. From 1970 through 1994, Kuralt was the host of the television program CBS News Sunday Morning. He became a homespun American icon and was known particularly for his "On the Road" stories based on his travels around the country in a mobile home. Kuralt specialized in "big-hearted essays on topics others thought tiny," reporting "on horse-traders and a 93-year-old brickmaker, on the wonders of nature and the nature of other wonders, like the sharecropper in Mississippi who put nine children through college or the 103-year-old entertainer who performed at nursing homes." Joe Sexton, Charles Kuralt, 62, Is Dead, N.Y. Times, July 5, 1997, at 24. Kuralt went through six motor homes while doing more than 500 On the Road stories. When in 1994 the beloved Kuralt retired from CBS News Sunday Morning, Saturday Night Live did a seemingly preposterous satire in which Norm MacDonald, as Kuralt, bid farewell, saying that he would miss all the people he had met over the years—and had sex with.[28]

Sometimes life imitates art. In 1968, six years into his marriage to Suzanne Baird (who was known as Petie), Kuralt met a woman named Pat Baker (who later went by Patricia Elizabeth Shannon) while doing an On the Road story in Reno on her efforts to build a park for African American children. Smitten, Kuralt

---

27. Alaska, Arizona (but with "material provisions"), Colorado, Hawaii, Michigan, Montana, North Dakota, South Dakota, and Utah.

28. The SNL sketch began with Norm MacDonald as Charles Kuralt talking in Kuralt's folksy manner about how much he would miss life "On the Road." After noting the beauty of the countryside, he confessed that it was the prospect of sex that had lured him to the road 37 years before and that it was what he would miss the most. He then recounted a string of sexual conquests, including the wife of Old Ned Harrigan, known for his ball of twine that was 67 feet around, and 75-year-old Thelma Ober, famous for her pumpkin pies. Saturday Night Live, Sunday Morning with Charles Kuralt, April 9, 1994, http://www.fakenews.net/archive/impressions/kuralt_94_04_09.html. — Eds.

asked her out to dinner, arriving to pick her up with a bouquet of roses in hand. A long-term romance ensued. Over the years Kuralt saw or spoke to Shannon frequently, and he provided financial support to her and her family — including buying her a vacation home in Ireland. According to Shannon, when she moved from Reno to the San Francisco Bay area in the early 1970s, she and Kuralt "went on picnics and we went sail[ing] and, you know, we acted like a family." In 1985, she moved to a log cabin that Kuralt had built for them in Montana. Larry King Live, CNN, Feb. 14, 2001.

Kuralt died on July 4, 1997, of either a heart attack or lupus (or both), after a short illness. Two weeks before he died he wrote Shannon a letter assuring her that he would see to it that she would inherit his property in Montana. This opinion was the second decision by the Montana Supreme Court on whether that letter could be probated as a holographic will.]

TRIEWEILER, J. . . . Charles Kuralt and Elizabeth Shannon maintained a long-term and intimate personal relationship. Kuralt and Shannon desired to keep their relationship secret, and were so successful in doing so that even though Kuralt's wife, Petie, knew that Kuralt owned property in Montana, she was unaware, prior to Kuralt's untimely death, of his relationship with Shannon.

Over the nearly 30-year course of their relationship, Kuralt and Shannon saw each other regularly and maintained contact by phone and mail. Kuralt was the primary source of financial support for Shannon and established close, personal relationships with Shannon's three children. Kuralt provided financial support for a joint business venture managed by Shannon and transferred a home in Ireland to Shannon as a gift.

In 1985, Kuralt purchased a 20-acre parcel of property along the Big Hole River in Madison County, near Twin Bridges, Montana. Kuralt and Shannon constructed a cabin on this 20-acre parcel. In 1987, Kuralt purchased two additional parcels along the Big Hole which adjoined the original 20-acre parcel. These two additional parcels, one upstream and one downstream of the cabin, created a parcel of approximately 90 acres and are the primary subject of this appeal.

On May 3, 1989, Kuralt executed a holographic will which stated as follows:

> May 3, 1989
>
> In the event of my death, I bequeath to Patricia Elizabeth Shannon all my interest in land, buildings, furnishings and personal belongings on Burma Road, Twin Bridges, Montana.
>
> Charles Kuralt
> 34 Bank St.
> New York, N.Y. 10014

Although Kuralt mailed a copy of this holographic will to Shannon, he subsequently executed a formal will on May 4, 1994, in New York City. This Last Will and Testament, prepared with the assistance of counsel, does not specifically mention any of the real property owned by Kuralt. The beneficiaries of Kuralt's Last Will and Testament were his wife, Petie, and the Kuralts' two children. Neither Shannon nor her children are named as beneficiaries in Kuralt's formal will.

*Elizabeth (Pat) Shannon and Charles Kuralt, bundled against the chilly
weather on Angel Island near San Francisco in the early 1970s,
sharing a picnic of wine, cheese, and fruit.*

AP/World Wide Photos

Shannon had no knowledge of the formal will until the commencement of these
proceedings.

On April 9, 1997, Kuralt deeded his interest in the original 20-acre parcel with
the cabin to Shannon. The transaction was disguised as a sale. However, Kuralt
supplied the "purchase" price for the 20-acre parcel to Shannon prior to the
transfer. After the deed to the 20-acre parcel was filed, Shannon sent Kuralt, at
his request, a blank buy-sell real estate form so that the remaining 90 acres along
the Big Hole could be conveyed to Shannon in a similar manner. Apparently, it
was again Kuralt's intention to provide the purchase price. The second transaction was to take place in September 1997 when Shannon, her son, and Kuralt
agreed to meet at the Montana cabin.

Kuralt, however, became suddenly ill and entered a New York hospital on June 18, 1997. On that same date, Kuralt wrote the letter to Shannon which is now at the center of the current dispute:

June 18, 1997

Dear Pat —

Something is terribly wrong with me and they can't figure out what. After cat-scans and a variety of cardiograms, they agree it's not lung cancer or heart trouble or blood clot. So they're putting me in the hospital today to concentrate on infectious diseases. I am getting worse, barely able to get out of bed, but still have high hopes for recovery . . . if only I can get a diagnosis! Curiouser and curiouser! I'll keep you informed. I'll have the lawyer visit the hospital to be sure you <u>inherit</u> the rest of the place in MT. if it comes to that.

I send love to you & [your youngest daughter,] Shannon. Hope things are better there!

> Love,
> C.

Enclosed with this letter were two checks made payable to Shannon, one for $8000 and the other for $9000. Kuralt did not seek the assistance of an attorney to devise the remaining 90 acres of Big Hole land to Shannon. Therefore, when Kuralt died unexpectedly, Shannon sought to probate the letter of June 18, 1997, as a valid holographic codicil to Kuralt's formal 1994 will.

The Estate opposed Shannon's Petition for Ancillary Probate based on its contention that the June 18, 1997 letter expressed only a future intent to make a will. The District Court granted partial summary judgment for the Estate on May 26, 1998. Shannon appealed from the District Court order which granted partial summary judgment to the Estate. This Court, in In re Estate of Kuralt (*Kuralt I*), 981 P.2d 771 (Mont. 1999), reversed the District Court and remanded the case for trial in order to resolve disputed issues of material fact.[29] Following an abbreviated evidentiary hearing, the District Court issued its Findings and Order. The District Court held that the June 18, 1997 letter was a valid holographic codicil to Kuralt's formal will of May 4, 1994 and accordingly entered judgment in favor of Shannon. The Estate now appeals from that order and judgment. . . .

Did the District Court err when it found that the June 18, 1997 letter expressed a present testamentary intent to transfer property in Madison County?

---

29. In dissent in *Kuralt I*, Chief Justice Turnage wrote:

The letter of June 18, 1997, and the record in this case does not meet the standard of clear and convincing evidence. . . . The June 18, 1997 letter, as set forth in the majority opinion, contains this — and only this — language relating to the question of a holographic will: "I'll have the lawyer visit the hospital to be sure you inherit the rest of the place in MT. if it comes to that." That language clearly indicates that decedent Kuralt did not intend the letter to operate as a holographic will but, rather, expressed his intent that at a future date he would have a lawyer visit him in the hospital to be sure that Patricia Shannon would, by a document thereafter to be executed, inherit "the rest of the place in MT." Such language is precatory and expresses only a desire or wish. It certainly does not constitute imperative, direct terms of bequest. [*Kuralt I*, 981 P.2d at 778.]

— Eds.

The Estate contends that the District Court made legal errors which led to a mistaken conclusion about Kuralt's intent concerning the disposition of his Montana property. The Estate argues that the District Court failed to recognize the legal effect of the 1994 will and therefore erroneously found that Kuralt, after his May 3, 1989 holographic will, had an uninterrupted intent to transfer the Montana property to Shannon. The Estate further argues that Kuralt's 1994 formal will revoked all prior wills, both expressly and by inconsistency. This manifest change of intention, according to the Estate, should have led the District Court to the conclusion that Kuralt did not intend to transfer the Montana property to Shannon upon his death.

Montana courts are guided by the bedrock principle of honoring the intent of the testator. On remand, the District Court resolved the factual question of whether Kuralt intended the letter of June 18, 1997 to effect a testamentary disposition of the Montana property. As we stated in *Kuralt I*, the "question of whether that letter contains the necessary animus testandi becomes an issue suitable for resolution by the trier of fact."[30] 981 P.2d at 778. The argument on appeal, while clothed as a legal argument, addresses factual findings made by the District Court. However, if the factual findings of the District Court are supported by substantial credible evidence and are not otherwise clearly erroneous, they will not be reversed by this Court.

The record supports the District Court's finding that the June 18, 1997 letter expressed Kuralt's intent to effect a posthumous transfer of his Montana property to Shannon. Kuralt and Shannon enjoyed a long, close personal relationship which continued up to the last letter Kuralt wrote Shannon on June 18, 1997, in which he enclosed checks to her in the amounts of $8000 and $9000. Likewise, Kuralt and Shannon's children had a long, family-like relationship which included significant financial support.

The District Court focused on the last few months of Kuralt's life to find that the letter demonstrated his testamentary intent. The conveyance of the 20-acre parcel for no real consideration and extrinsic evidence that Kuralt intended to

---

30. Montana had enacted the 1990 UPC, including the provisions on:

1. *holographic wills* ("A will that does not comply with [formalities] is valid as a holographic will, whether or not witnessed, if the signature and material portions of the document are in the testator's handwriting.");
2. *proving testamentary intent* ("Intent that the document constitute the testator's will may be established by extrinsic evidence, including, for holographic wills, portions of the document that are not in the testator's handwriting."); and
3. *the dispensing power/harmless error rule* (allowing an instrument to be admitted as a will if "the proponent of the document or writing establishes by clear and convincing evidence that the decedent intended the document or writing to constitute . . . the decedent's will").

Mont. Code Ann. §§72-2-522 to 72-2-523 (2008). — Eds.

convey the remainder of the Montana property to Shannon in a similar fashion provides substantial factual support for the District Court's determination that Kuralt intended that Shannon have the rest of the Montana property.

The June 18, 1997 letter expressed Kuralt's desire that Shannon inherit the remainder of the Montana property. That Kuralt wrote the letter *in extremis* is supported by the fact that he died two weeks later. Although Kuralt intended to transfer the remaining land to Shannon, he was reluctant to consult a lawyer to formalize his intent because he wanted to keep their relationship secret. Finally, the use of the term "inherit" underlined by Kuralt reflected his intention to make a posthumous disposition of the property. Therefore, the District Court's findings are supported by substantial evidence and are not clearly erroneous. Accordingly, we conclude that the District Court did not err when it found that the letter dated June 18, 1997 expressed a present testamentary intent to transfer property in Madison County to Patricia Shannon. . . .

[W]e agree with the District Court's conclusion that the June 18, 1997 holograph was a codicil to Kuralt's 1994 formal will. Admittedly, the June 18, 1997 letter met the threshold requirements for a valid holographic will. Moreover, the letter was a codicil as a matter of law because it made a specific bequest of the Montana property and did not purport to bequeath the entirety of the estate. See Official Comments to §72-2-527, MCA ("when the second will does not make a complete disposition of the testator's estate, the second will is more in the nature of a codicil to the first will"). The District Court was therefore correct when it concluded that the June 18, 1997 letter was a codicil. . . .

Accordingly, we affirm the judgment of the District Court.

NOTES AND QUESTIONS

1. *Epilogue.* A codicil is a testamentary instrument (i.e., a will) that amends a prior will but does not replace it. In this case Kuralt's 1994 formal will, which remained operative to the extent not amended by his 1997 letter to Shannon, provided that all estate and inheritance taxes due were to be paid out of the residuary estate. Because Kuralt's wife and children were the beneficiaries of the residue, the estate and inheritance taxes attributable to the Montana property were paid out of their share even though the property passed to Shannon. In re Estate of Kuralt, 68 P.3d 662 (Mont. 2003). Do you suppose Kuralt intended this result?

2. In *Kuralt*, there was good written evidence of whom Kuralt intended to benefit, but a serious question whether he intended the 1997 letter itself to be a will. If you had asked Kuralt whether his June 18, 1997 letter was a will, what do you think he would have said? Suppose that Kuralt had sent several letters over the years concerning his plans to redraft wills. If he then executed a new will but failed to revoke those letters, would they still be in force as wills to the extent they were not inconsistent with the later will?

SECTION B.   REVOCATION OF WILLS

1. *Revocation by Writing or Physical Act*

A will is an *ambulatory* document, which means that it is subject to modification or revocation by the testator during her lifetime. All states permit revocation of a will in one of two ways: (1) by a subsequent *writing* executed with testamentary formalities,[31] or (2) by a *physical act* such as destroying, obliterating, or burning the will. On the assumption that oral revocations would open the door for fraud, an oral declaration that a will is revoked, without more, is inoperative in all states. If a duly executed will is not revoked in a manner permitted by statute, the will is admitted to probate.[32]

The UPC's revocation section is fairly representative of statutes setting forth methods of permissible revocation.

Uniform Probate Code (1990)

§2-507.   REVOCATION BY WRITING OR BY ACT

(a) A will or any part thereof is revoked:

(1) by executing a subsequent will that revokes the previous will or part expressly or by inconsistency; or

(2) by performing a revocatory act on the will, if the testator performed the act with the intent and for the purpose of revoking the will or part or if another individual performed the act in the testator's conscious presence and by the testator's direction. For purposes of this paragraph, "revocatory act on the will" includes burning, tearing, canceling, obliterating, or destroying the will or any part of it. A burning, tearing, or canceling is a "revocatory act on the will," whether or not the burn, tear, or cancellation touched any of the words on the will. . . .

PROBLEM: REVOCATION BY INCONSISTENCY

The modern view is to treat a subsequent will that does not expressly revoke the prior will, but makes a complete disposition of the testator's estate, as presumptively replacing the prior will and revoking it by inconsistency. If the subsequent will does not make a complete disposition of the testator's estate, it is not

---

31. UPC §1-201(57) (1990) defines a *will* to include a codicil and any testamentary instrument that merely appoints an executor or revokes or revises another will. In states recognizing holographic wills, a holograph can revoke a typewritten, attested will — a principle that is implicit in Estate of Kuralt, page 280.

32. Just as UPC §2-503 excuses harmless errors in execution, it likewise excuses harmless errors in revocation.

presumed to revoke the prior will but is viewed as a *codicil*, and the property not disposed of under the codicil is disposed of in accordance with the prior will. A *codicil* is a testamentary instrument that supplements, rather than replaces, an earlier will; the codicil supersedes the will to the extent of inconsistency between them. See UPC §2-507(b)-(d) (1990); Restatement (Third) of Property: Wills and Other Donative Transfers §4.1, cmts. b-d (1999). The older view is that, in the absence of a revocation clause, a general residuary clause in a later will was not enough to revoke specific bequests in an earlier will because the earlier individual bequests and the later residuary clause were not literally inconsistent.

In 2003, *T* executes a will that gives all her property to *A*. In 2008, *T* executes a will that gives her diamond ring to *B* and her car to *C*. Even if the 2008 will makes no reference to the earlier will, the 2008 will is ordinarily treated as a *codicil*.

(a) In early 2009, *T* destroys the 2008 codicil with the intention of revoking it; *T* dies later in 2009. The 2003 will is offered for probate. Should it be admitted? See In re Estate of Hering, 166 Cal. Rptr. 298 (App. 1980).

(b) Suppose, instead, that *T* destroys the 2003 will with the intention of revoking it. After *T*'s death, the codicil is offered for probate. Should it be admitted? See Comment, Wills — Revocation by Act to the Document — Effect on Codicil, 60 Mich. L. Rev. 82 (1961).

Harrison v. Bird
Supreme Court of Alabama, 1993
621 So. 2d 972

HOUSTON, J.   The proponent of a will appeals from a judgment of the Circuit Court of Montgomery County holding that the estate of Daisy Virginia Speer, deceased, should be administered as an intestate estate and confirming the letters of administration granted by the probate court to Mae S. Bird.

The following pertinent facts are undisputed:

Daisy Virginia Speer executed a will in November 1989, in which she named Katherine Crapps Harrison as the main beneficiary of her estate. The original of the will was retained by Ms. Speer's attorney and a duplicate original was given to Ms. Harrison. On March 4, 1991, Ms. Speer telephoned her attorney and advised him that she wanted to revoke her will. Thereafter, Ms. Speer's attorney or his secretary, in the presence of each other, tore the will into four pieces. The attorney then wrote Ms. Speer a letter, informing her that he had "revoked" her will as she had instructed and that he was enclosing the pieces of the will so that she could verify that he had torn up the original. In the letter, the attorney specifically stated, "As it now stands, you are without a will."

Ms. Speer died on September 3, 1991. Upon her death, the postmarked letter from her attorney was found among her personal effects, but the four pieces of the will were not found. Thereafter, on September 17, 1991, the Probate Court of Montgomery County granted letters of administration on the estate of Ms. Speer, to Mae S. Bird, a cousin of Ms. Speer. On October 11, 1991, Ms. Harrison filed for probate a document purporting to be the last will and testament of Ms. Speer and naming Ms. Harrison as executrix. . . .

Thereafter, the circuit court ruled (1) that Ms. Speer's will was not lawfully revoked when it was destroyed by her attorney at her direction and with her consent, but not in her presence, see Ala. Code 1975, §43-8-136(b); (2) that there could be no ratification of the destruction of Ms. Speer's will, which was not accomplished pursuant to the strict requirements of §43-8-136(b); and (3) that, based on the fact that the pieces of the destroyed will were delivered to Ms. Speer's home but were not found after her death, there arose a presumption that Ms. Speer thereafter revoked the will herself. . . .

[F]inding that the presumption in favor of revocation of Ms. Speer's will had not been rebutted and therefore that the duplicate original will offered for probate by Ms. Harrison was not the last will and testament of Daisy Virginia Speer, the circuit court held that the estate should be administered as an intestate estate and confirmed the letters of administration issued by the probate court to Ms. Bird.

If the evidence establishes that Ms. Speer had possession of the will before her death, but the will is not found among her personal effects after her death, a presumption arises that she destroyed the will. See Barksdale v. Pendergrass, 319 So. 2d 267 (Ala. 1975). Furthermore, if she destroys the copy of the will in her possession, a presumption arises that she has revoked her will and all duplicates, even though a duplicate exists that is not in her possession. See Stiles v. Brown, 380 So. 2d 792 (Ala. 1980); see, also, Snider v. Burks, 4 So. 225 (Ala. 1887). However, this presumption of revocation is rebuttable and the burden of rebutting the presumption is on the proponent of the will. See *Barksdale*, supra.

Based on the foregoing, we conclude that under the facts of this case there existed a presumption that Ms. Speer destroyed her will and thus revoked it. Therefore, the burden shifted to Ms. Harrison to present sufficient evidence to rebut that presumption — to present sufficient evidence to convince the trier of fact that the absence of the will from Ms. Speer's personal effects after her death was not due to Ms. Speer's destroying and thus revoking the will. See Stiles v. Brown, supra.

From a careful review of the record, we conclude, as did the trial court, that the evidence presented by Ms. Harrison was not sufficient to rebut the presumption that Ms. Speer destroyed her will with the intent to revoke it. We, therefore, affirm the trial court's judgment. We note Ms. Harrison's argument that under the particular facts of this case, because Ms. Speer's attorney destroyed the will outside of Ms. Speer's presence, "[t]he fact that Ms. Speer may have had possession of the pieces of her will and that such pieces were not found upon her death is not sufficient to invoke the presumption [of revocation] imposed by the trial court." We find that argument to be without merit.

Affirmed.

QUESTIONS AND PROBLEMS

1.   In Harrison v. Bird, if the four torn pieces of the testator's will had been found at her death, would her attorney be liable for malpractice? Suppose the torn pieces of the will had been found among the testator's papers in a file labeled "revoked will." What result? Suppose the testator instructed the lawyer in person to destroy her will but left the lawyer's office before the lawyer did so. Would the lawyer's destruction of the will effect a valid revocation? See In re Estate of Boote, 198 S.W.3d 699 (Tenn. App. 2005).

2.   *Presumption of revocation.* Suppose that the lawyer for the testator sends her home with the only executed copy of the testator's will. The will leaves everything to her friend, *A.* After the testator's death, an heir goes into the testator's house looking for her will. The heir reports that she cannot find a will, and no will is found. What result? What sort of evidence is enough to rebut the presumption of revocation?

Restatement (Third) of Property: Wills and Other Donative Transfers §4.1, cmt. j (1999) takes the position that "the presumption is not such a strong one that clear and convincing evidence is required to rebut it." Thus, in Estate of Turner, 265 S.W.3d 709 (Tex. App. 2008), the presumption of revocation was rebutted under a preponderance of the evidence standard by the testimony of a disinterested witness who saw the will on the day of the testator's death and the fact that the testator's disinherited siblings had access to the testator's house immediately after testator's death. Some courts, however, require clear and convincing evidence. In Estate of Pallister, 611 S.E.2d 250 (S.C. 2005), the presumption of revocation was rebutted under the clear and convincing evidence standard where the relative who would have benefited by revocation had access to the testator's house and safe deposit box and had complained to the scrivener about being disinherited. The testator usually kept careful records and consulted professionals for estate planning and had expressed affection for the will beneficiaries.

NOTE: PROBATE OF LOST WILLS

In the absence of a statute to the contrary, a will that is lost, destroyed without the consent of the testator, or destroyed with the consent of the testator but not in compliance with the revocation statute can be admitted into probate if its contents are proved. A lost will can be proved by a copy in the lawyer-drafter's office or by other clear and convincing evidence.

The attacks on the World Trade Center on September 11, 2001 led to a large number of destroyed wills that were stored in these and nearby buildings. Because those wills were not destroyed by the testators with the intent to revoke, they can still be probated if their terms can be proved from copies or otherwise.

In a few states, statutes prohibit the probate of a lost or destroyed will unless the will was "in existence" at the testator's death (and destroyed thereafter) or was "fraudulently destroyed" during the testator's life. Theoretically, under such a statute a will accidentally tossed out by a housekeeper during the testator's life cannot be probated. Thus, on its face, such a statute is in conflict with the state's will revocation statute, since under the former a will not legally revoked under the latter is nevertheless barred from probate. Courts have chosen to give effect to the will revocation statutes and have gutted the proof statutes by holding *either* that a will not lawfully revoked continues in "legal existence" until the testator's death (and the word "existence" in the statute means "legal existence") *or* that a will destroyed by a method not permitted by the will revocation statute has been "fraudulently destroyed." See Estate of Irvine v. Doyle, 710 P.2d 1366 (Nev. 1985).

Thompson v. Royall
Supreme Court of Virginia, 1934
175 S.E. 748

HUDGINS, J.   The only question presented by this record is whether the will of Mrs. M. Lou Bowen Kroll had been revoked shortly before her death.

The uncontroverted facts are as follows: On the 4th day of September, 1932, Mrs. Kroll signed a will, typewritten on the five sheets of legal cap paper; the signature appeared on the last page duly attested by three subscribing witnesses. H.P. Brittain, the executor named in the will, was given possession of the instrument for safe-keeping. A codicil typed on the top third of one sheet of paper dated September 15, 1932, was signed by the testatrix in the presence of two subscribing witnesses. Possession of this instrument was given to Judge S.M.B. Coulling, the attorney who prepared both documents.

On September 19, 1932, at the request of Mrs. Kroll, Judge Coulling and Mr. Brittain took the will and the codicil to her home where she told her attorney, in the presence of Mr. Brittain and another, to destroy both. But, instead of destroying the papers, at the suggestion of Judge Coulling, she decided to retain them as memoranda, to be used as such in the event she decided to execute a new will. Upon the back of the manuscript cover, which was fastened to the five sheets by metal clasps, in the handwriting of Judge Coulling, signed by Mrs. Kroll, there is the following notation:

> This will null and void and to be only held by H.P. Brittain instead of being destroyed as a memorandum for another will if I desire to make same. This 19 Sept. 1932.
>
> *M. Lou Bowen Kroll*

The same notation was made upon the back of the sheet on which the codicil was written, except that the name S.M.B. Coulling was substituted for H.P. Brittain; this was likewise signed by Mrs. Kroll.

Mrs. Kroll died October 2, 1932, leaving numerous nephews and nieces, some of whom were not mentioned in her will, and an estate valued at approximately $200,000. On motion of some of the beneficiaries, the will and codicil were offered for probate. All the interested parties including the heirs at law were convened, and on the issue devisavit vel non [whether the purported will is valid or not] the jury found that the instruments dated September 4 and 15, 1932, were the last will and testament of Mrs. M. Lou Bowen Kroll. From an order sustaining the verdict and probating the will this writ of error was allowed.

For more than 100 years, the means by which a duly executed will may be revoked have been prescribed by statute. These requirements are found in section 5233 of the 1919 Code, the pertinent parts of which read thus:

> No will or codicil, or any part thereof, shall be revoked, unless . . . by a subsequent will or codicil, or by some writing declaring an intention to revoke the same, and executed in the manner in which a will is required to be executed, or by the testator, or some person in his presence and by his direction, cutting, tearing, burning, obliterating, canceling, or destroying the same, or the signature thereto, with the intent to revoke.

The notations, dated September 19, 1932, are not wholly in the handwriting of the testatrix, nor are her signatures thereto attached attested by subscribing witnesses; hence under the statute they are ineffectual as "some writing declaring an intention to revoke." The faces of the two instruments bear no physical evidence of any cutting, tearing, burning, obliterating, canceling, or destroying. The only contention made by appellants is that the notation written in the presence, and with the approval, of Mrs. Kroll, on the back of the manuscript cover in the one instance, and on the back of the sheet containing the codicil in the other, constitute "canceling" within the meaning of the statute.

Both parties concede that to effect revocation of a duly executed will, in any of the methods prescribed by statute, two things are necessary: (1) The doing of one of the acts specified, (2) accompanied by the intent to revoke — the animo revocandi. Proof of either, without proof of the other, is insufficient. Malone v. Hobbs, 1 Rob. (40 Va.) 346. The proof established the intention to revoke. The entire controversy is confined to the acts used in carrying out that purpose. The testatrix adopted the suggestion of her attorney to revoke her will by written memoranda, admittedly ineffectual as revocations by subsequent writings, but appellants contend the memoranda, in the handwriting of another, and testatrix' signatures, are sufficient to effect revocation by cancellation. To support this contention, appellants cite a number of authorities which hold that the modern definition of cancellation includes "any act which would destroy, revoke, recall, do away with, overrule, render null and void, the instrument."

Most of the authorities cited that approve the above or a similar meaning of the word were dealing with cancellation of simple contracts, or other instruments that require little or no formality in execution. However, there is one line of cases which apply this extended meaning of "canceling" to the revocation of wills. The leading case so holding is Warner v. Warner's Estate, 37 Vt. 356. In this case proof of the intent and the act were a notation on the same page with, and below the signature of, the testator, reading: "This will is hereby cancelled and annulled. In full this 15th day of March in the year 1859," and written lengthwise on the back of the fourth page of the foolscap paper, upon which no part of the written will appeared, were these words, "Cancelled and is null and void. (Signed) I. Warner." It was held this was sufficient to revoke the will under a statute similar to the one here under consideration.

In Evans' Appeal, 58 Pa. 238, the Pennsylvania court approved the reasoning of the Vermont court in Warner v. Warner's Estate, supra, but the force of the opinion is weakened when the facts are considered. It seems that there were lines drawn through two of the three signatures of the testator appearing in the Evans will, and the paper on which material parts of the will were written was torn in four places. It therefore appeared on the face of the instrument, when offered for probate, that there was a sufficient defacement to bring it within the meaning of both obliteration and cancellation. The construction of the statute in Warner v. Warner's Estate, supra, has been criticized by eminent text-writers on wills, and the courts in the majority of the states in construing similar statutes have refused to follow the reasoning in that case. Jarman on Wills (6th Ed.) 147, note 1; Schouler on Wills (5th Ed.) §391; Redfield on the Law of Wills (4th Ed.) 323-325; 28 R.C.L. 180; 40 Cyc. 1173; Dowling v. Gilliland, 122 N.E. 70.

The above, and other authorities that might be cited, hold that revocation of a will by cancellation within the meaning of the statute contemplates marks or lines across the written parts of the instrument or a physical defacement, or some mutilation of the writing itself, with the intent to revoke. If written words are used for the purpose, they must be so placed as to physically affect the written portion of the will, not merely on blank parts of the paper on which the will is written. If the writing intended to be the act of canceling does not mutilate, or erase, or deface, or otherwise physically come in contact with, any part of written words of the will, it cannot be given any greater weight than a similar writing on a separate sheet of paper, which identifies the will referred to, just as definitely as does the writing on the back. If a will may be revoked by writing on the back, separable from the will, it may be done by a writing not on the will. This the statute forbids. . . .

The attempted revocation is ineffectual, because testatrix intended to revoke her will by subsequent writings not executed as required by statute, and because it does not in any wise physically obliterate, mutilate, deface, or cancel any written parts of the will.

For the reasons stated, the judgment of the trial court is affirmed.

QUESTIONS AND PROBLEMS

1.   What policy is served by the court's decision in the *Thompson* case? Given the clear and uncontroverted evidence of Mrs. Kroll's intention that her will be revoked, how can the court's decision be justified? Although no one sued for legal

malpractice in the 1930s, we have been told by Judge Coulling's grandson that for the rest of his life Judge Coulling suffered greatly from shame and loss of reputation in his community because of the probate of Mrs. Kroll's will.

The UPC would change the result in *Thompson*. UPC §2-507(a)(2), page 286, allows for a cancellation regardless of whether the cancellation touches any of the words on the will. Hence the codicil, for which the words of cancellation were written on the back, would be revoked. The will presents a tougher case, because the canceling words were written on the manuscript cover attached to the will, not on the will itself.[33] Even if the will were not revoked under §2-507(a)(2), however, under the harmless error rule of §2-503, page 258, if there was clear and convincing evidence that the writing on the manuscript cover was intended to revoke the instruments — and surely there was — then the attempted revocation would be effective.

2.   Suppose that Mrs. Kroll had written, in the top margin of the will: "Cancelled. 19/9/32. M. Kroll." Would this be a valid revocation by physical act? See Maxwell v. Dawkins, 974 So. 2d 282 (Ala. 2006) (*T*'s lawyer wrote a statement of revocation in the top margin of the will, which *T* signed; court held that *T*'s signature was an act of cancellation giving effect to the language written by the lawyer). Would this be a valid revocation in states permitting holographic wills? See McCarthy v. Bank of Cal., 668 P.2d 481 (Or. App. 1983) (valid holographic revocation).

3.   Suppose that the testator writes "VOID" across the face of an unexecuted photocopy of his will. Is this a valid revocation by physical act? In Estate of Tolin, 622 So. 2d 988 (Fla. 1993), the testator showed a photocopy of his codicil (with a formal blue backing) to a friend, a retired lawyer, telling the friend he wanted to revoke the codicil. The friend, mistaking the photocopy for the original, told him he could revoke the codicil by tearing up the document. The testator did so. After the testator died, the lawyer who drafted his will and codicil produced the originals. The court held that revocation of a copy is not a valid revocation. However, because of the testator's mistake of fact, believing he was destroying the original, the court imposed a constructive trust on the codicil beneficiary for the benefit of the will beneficiary. Is this an application of the substantial compliance doctrine to the revocation of wills in the guise of a constructive trust to prevent unjust enrichment? Or is it another step toward correcting mistakes in execution and revocation of wills? In a later case, Allen v. Dalk, 826 So. 2d 245 (Fla. 2002), the Florida Supreme Court refused to extend *Tolin* to allow the probate of a will that the testator erroneously thought she had signed along with other documents.

---

33. We are indebted to Professor Robert Bartow of Temple University School of Law and Professor Melanie Jacobs of Michigan State University College of Law, and to Professor Jacobs's student Joseph Weiler, J.D. 2007, for calling this detail to our attention.

Partial revocation by physical act. Although UPC §2-507 and the statutes of many states authorize partial revocation by physical act, in several states a will cannot be revoked in part by an *act* of revocation; it can be revoked in part only by a subsequent instrument. The reasons for prohibiting partial revocation by physical act are two. First, canceling a gift to one person necessarily results in someone else taking the gift, and this "new gift" — like all bequests — can be made only by an attested writing. Second, permitting partial revocation by physical act offers opportunity for fraud. The person who takes the "new gift" may be the one who made the canceling marks. If partial revocation by act is not recognized, the will must be admitted to probate in the form in which it was originally executed if the original language can be ascertained. See Frederic S. Schwartz, Models of Will Revocation, 39 Real Prop., Prob. & Tr. J. 135 (2004).

In Estate of Malloy, 949 P.2d 804 (Wash. 1997), the court discussed the inconsistency between allowing partial revocation by physical act and requiring bequests to be attested, and held that partial revocation by physical act would not be permitted where the intent and effect of the change would result in a substantial enhancement of another bequest. A few cases have held that the testator can revoke a complete devise ("my car to *A*"), but cannot rearrange the shares in a single devise to increase the other devisee's gift. Example: "$10,000 to *A* and *B*, residue to *C*." *T* later lines out *B*'s name. *A*'s gift cannot be increased this way. The $5,000 given to *B* falls into the residuary and goes to *C*.

Restatement (Third) of Property: Wills and Other Donative Transfers §4.1, cmt. i (1999), disapproves of the *Malloy* approach and "any distinction between revocation of a complete devise and rearranging shares within a single devise or otherwise rewriting the terms of the will by deleting selected words. It is a classic example of a distinction without a difference. It is not supported by the language of the statutes specifically authorizing the revocation by act of 'a will or any part thereof.' . . . The legislature not only granted broad approval of deleting words but of the natural consequence of doing so — giving effect to the will as if the deleted words were not present."

PROBLEMS

T executes a will that devises the residue of her estate to four named relatives. After *T*'s death some years later, her will is found in a stack of papers on her desk. One of the four names in the residuary clause has been lined out with a pencil. There is no direct evidence that *T* marked out the name.

(a) What result in a state having a statute similar to UPC §2-507? See In re Byrne's Will, 271 N.W. 48 (Wis. 1937). Compare In re Estate of Funk, 654 N.E.2d 1174 (Ind. App. 1995).

(b) What result in a state that does not permit partial revocation by physical act? See Hansel v. Head, 706 So. 2d 1142 (Ala. 1997) (name obliterated with correction fluid); In re Estate of Haurin, 605 P.2d 65 (Colo. App. 1979).

(c) Suppose that *T*'s will is a holographic will in a jurisdiction permitting holographic wills. What result? See La Rue v. Lee, 60 S.E. 388 (W. Va. 1908).

2. *Dependent Relative Revocation and Revival*

Simply put, the doctrine of dependent relative revocation (DRR) is this: If the testator purports to revoke his will upon a mistaken assumption of law or fact, the revocation is ineffective if the testator would not have revoked his will had he known the truth. The underlying theory is that the testator lacks true revocatory intent if the revocation was based on a mistaken belief. A typical DRR case involves a situation where the testator destroys his will under a belief that a new will is valid but, in fact, for some reason the new will is invalid. If the court finds that the testator would not have destroyed his old will had he known the new will was ineffective, the court, applying DRR, will disregard the revocation and probate the destroyed prior will. The doctrine is one of presumptive intent, not actual intent. On DRR, see generally Restatement (Third) of Property: Wills and Other Donative Transfers §4.3 (1999) (recasting it as the doctrine of ineffective revocation).

LaCroix v. Senecal
Supreme Court of Connecticut, 1953
99 A.2d 115

BROWN J. . . . The testatrix, Celestine L. Dupre, died in Putnam on April 19, 1951, leaving as her heir at law and next of kin her niece, the plaintiff. The testatrix left a will dated March 26, 1951, and a codicil thereto dated April 10, 1951. These instruments were admitted to probate on May 22, 1951. Item five of the will reads as follows:

> All the rest, residue and remainder of my property of whatsoever the same may consist and wheresoever the same may be situated, both real and personal, I give, devise and bequeath one-half to my nephew, Nelson Lamoth of Taftville, Connecticut, to be his absolutely; the other one-half to Aurea Senecal of 200 Providence Street, Putnam, Connecticut, to be hers absolutely.

The codicil reads as follows:

> 1. I hereby revoke Item Five of said will and substitute for said Item Five the following: Item Five: All the rest, residue and remainder of property of whatsoever the same may consist and wheresoever the same may be situated, both real and personal, I give, devise and bequeath one-half to my nephew Marcisse Lamoth of Taftville, Connecticut, also known as Nelson Lamoth, to be his absolutely; the other one-half to Aurea Senecal of 200 Providence Street, Putnam, Connecticut to be hers absolutely.
> 2. I hereby republish and confirm my said will in all respects except as altered by this Codicil.

Aurea Senecal is not related to the testatrix. One of the three subscribing witnesses to the codicil was Adolphe Senecal, who at the time he witnessed the codicil was, and still is, the husband of Aurea Senecal. Section 6952 of the General Statutes, so far as material, provides as follows: "Every devise or bequest given in any will or codicil to a subscribing witness, or to the husband or wife of such subscribing witness, shall be void unless such will or codicil shall be legally attested without the signature of such witness . . . ; but the competency of such witness shall not be affected by any such devise or bequest." As the court pointed out in its memorandum of decision, any bequest to Aurea Senecal in item five of the codicil was void because her husband was a subscribing witness. The question left to be answered, therefore, was whether the devise or bequest to the defendant Aurea under item five of the original will stands. It is to be noted that the only difference between item five of the will and item five of the codicil is the substitution for the words "my nephew, Nelson Lamoth of Taftville, Connecticut," in the former, of the words "my nephew Marcisse Lamoth of Taftville, Connecticut, also known as Nelson Lamoth," in the latter. It is also to be noted that by the second paragraph of the codicil the testatrix confirmed the will "in all respects except as altered by this Codicil."

The defendants' brief suggests that the issue on this appeal is whether the doctrine of dependent relative revocation may be invoked to sustain a gift by will, when such gift has been revoked in a codicil which substantially reaffirmed the gift but was void as to it under §6952 by reason of the interest of a subscribing witness. The gist of the doctrine is that if a testator cancels or destroys a will with a present intention of making a new one immediately and as a substitute and the new will is not made or, if made, fails of effect for any reason, it will be presumed that the testator preferred the old will to intestacy, and the old one will be admitted to probate in the absence of evidence overcoming the presumption. The rule has been more simply stated in these words: "[W]here the intention to revoke is conditional and where the condition is not fulfilled, the revocation is not effective." Matter of Macomber, 87 N.Y.S.2d 308 (App. Div. 1949). As is stated in that opinion at page 312, the doctrine has had wide acceptance in both England and the United States. It is a rule of presumed intention rather than of substantive law; and is applicable in cases of partial as well as total revocation. That it can only apply when there is a clear intent of the testator that the revocation of the old is made conditional upon the validity of the new is well brought out in Sanderson v. Norcross, 136 N.E. 170 (Mass. 1922), and in Estate of Kaufman, 155 P.2d 831 (Cal. 1945), where many cases are cited.

The doctrine has long been accepted in Connecticut, notwithstanding the plaintiff's claim that we should adopt the contrary view. In 1898, Justice Simeon E. Baldwin stated in a case involving a question of this nature: "It being [the testator's] manifest intention to revoke the provision in the will only for this purpose, so far as the purpose fails of effect, the revocation must fall with it. . . . The revocation of his former provision . . . was indissolubly coupled with the creation of the substituted provision." . . .

So far as the factual situation is concerned, it would be difficult to conceive of a more deserving case for the application of the doctrine of dependent relative revocation than the one before us. There is no room for doubt that the sole purpose of the testatrix in executing the codicil was, by making the very minor change in referring to her nephew, to eliminate any uncertainty as to his identity. Obviously, it was furthest from her intention to make any change in the disposition of her residuary estate. When the will and codicil are considered together, as they must be, to determine the intent of the testatrix, it is clear that her intention to revoke the will was conditioned upon the execution of a codicil which would be effective to continue the same disposition of her residuary estate. Therefore, when it developed that the gift under the codicil to the defendant Aurea was void, the conditional intention of the testatrix to revoke the will was rendered inoperative, and the gift to Aurea under the will continued in effect. The situation is well summed up in this statement by the court in a case on all fours with the one at bar: "When a testator repeats the same dispositive plan in a new will, revocation of the old one by the new is deemed inseparably related to and dependent upon the legal effectiveness of the new." Estate of Kaufman, 155 P.2d 831 (Cal. 1945). In short, in the words of the court in Matter of Macomber, 87 N.Y.S.2d 308 (App. Div. 1949), "the facts here fit well within the classic pattern of the rule in its most reliable aspect, and it ought to be applied to the facts of this case." . . .

There is no error.

NOTES AND PROBLEMS

1.   LaCroix v. Senecal presents an easy case for applying DRR. Yet in a few states the courts have so limited the doctrine that if the same facts were presented in such a state today the court might reach the opposite result. For example, in Rosoff v. Harding, 901 So. 2d 1006 (Fla. App. 2005), the testator validly executed a new will that expressly revoked her prior will, but through a mistake in drafting the new will ineffectively exercised a power of appointment held by the testator. The power had been effectively exercised in the testator's prior will. Although the two wills had the same primary beneficiary, the confused court held that DRR could not apply because the new will was otherwise valid and it expressly revoked the prior will. Under traditional understandings of DRR, however, the later will in *Rosoff* would have been presumptively ineffective to the extent that its execution was based on the mistaken assumption that it validly exercised the power of appointment. In the words of Restatement (Third) of Property: Wills and Other Donative Transfers §4.3, cmt. e (1999), the doctrine

> may be applied when a later will that expressly revoked an earlier will contains one or more dispositive provisions that fail under applicable law. The revocation of the earlier will is presumptively ineffective to the extent necessary to give effect to the dispositive provision in the earlier will that the failed dispositive provision in the later will replaced.

See also In re Will of Sharp, 852 N.Y.S.2d 713 (Sur. 2008) (applying DRR to probate an earlier will that validy exercised a power of appointment).

For further discussion, see Frank L. Schiavo, Dependent Relative Revocation Has Gone Astray: It Should Return to Its Roots, 13 Widener L. Rev. 73 (2006); Julia E. Swenton, Note, The Missing Piece: The Forgotten Role of Testator Intent in the Application of the Doctrine of Dependent Relative Revocation in Oklahoma, 59 Okla. L. Rev. 205 (2006).

2.   Suppose clause 5 of *T*'s typewritten will provides: "I bequeath the sum of $1,000 to my nephew, Charles Blake." *T* crosses out the "$1,000" and substitutes "$1,500" — a larger bequest. *T* then writes her initials and the date in the right-hand margin opposite this entry. After *T*'s death some years later, her will is admitted to probate. Blake contends that he is entitled to $1,500 or, in the alternative, $1,000.

(a) What result in a state that recognizes holographic wills? See Estate of Phifer, 200 Cal. Rptr. 319 (App. 1984). But cf. McCarthy v. Bank of Cal., 668 P.2d 481 (Or. App. 1983). What result if, in addition, two witnesses observed the testator's modifications and then signed the will? See In re Will of Litwack, 827 N.Y.S.2d 582 (Sur. 2006).

(b) What result in a state that does not permit partial revocation by physical act?

(c) What result in a state that permits partial revocation by physical act? Should the court apply DRR? See Carpenter v. Wynn, 67 S.W.2d 688 (Ky. 1934).

(d) Suppose that *T* instead crosses out "$1,000" and substitutes "$500" — a smaller bequest. In a state that permits partial revocation by physical act, should the court apply DRR? See Ruel v. Hardy, 6 A.2d 753 (N.H. 1939).

3.   In his typewritten will, which contains a legacy of $5,000 to "John Boone," *T* crosses out "John" and writes in "Nancy." In nearly all states, Nancy cannot take because the gift to her is not attested. In a state permitting partial revocation by physical act, should the legacy to John be given effect under DRR? See In re Houghten's Estate, 17 N.W.2d 744 (Mich. 1945); Estate of Lyles, 615 So. 2d 1186 (Miss. 1993). Suppose John was Nancy's husband. How would this affect your analysis?

In a state that recognizes holographic wills, the change from John to Nancy is not a valid holograph even though *T* signs his name on the margin. Standing alone, the handwritten words are insufficient to constitute a will. Estate of Phifer, supra. On the other hand, if *T*'s will were entirely handwritten and a valid holograph, the change from John to Nancy should be permitted. See Stanley v. Henderson, 162 S.W.2d 95 (Tex. 1942); Estate of Archer, 239 Cal. Rptr. 137 (App. 1987).

4.   In *Body Heat*, a steamy 1981 *film noir* set in Florida, Matty Walker (Kathleen Turner), a blonde bent on doing away with her rich older husband, entraps a not-so-smart young lawyer, Ned Racine (William Hurt), to do the dirty work. The husband's existing will leaves half his fortune to Matty and half to his 10-year-old niece, Heather. After the husband is done in by Ned, Matty — a sometime legal secretary — produces a second will, written by Matty on stationery stolen from Ned's office, to which she has forged the signatures of her husband and — to his astonishment — Ned as a witness. (The second witness is — well, it takes too long

to explain. You'll have to rent the DVD.) This second will leaves half to Matty, but it puts Heather's half in a trust that violates the Rule Against Perpetuities. At a family conference, the husband's lawyer, oozing unction at every pore, pronounces the second will void. As a result, the lawyer says, the husband died intestate, and under Florida law Matty takes her husband's entire estate. Little Heather and her mother meekly acquiesce and disappear from the movie. Matty ends up on an island paradise with all her husband's money and a new lover; the dupe Ned is left languishing in jail.

Although critics loved the movie, which was boffo at the box office, estate lawyers might grouse about how the film handled some legal issues. Before the movie was made, Florida had adopted a wait-and-see approach for perpetuities violations (see page 900). Hence the husband's lawyer was too quick on the trigger; the trust for Heather might not turn out to be void. What's more, the screenwriter completely overlooked DRR, which might have saved Heather's share. Compare In re Estate of Jones, 352 So. 2d 1182 (Fla. App. 1977), with *Rosoff*, discussed in note 1 above.

Courts have set limits on the DRR doctrine. With rare exceptions, courts have held that DRR applies only (1) where there is an alternative plan of disposition that fails, or (2) where the mistake is recited in the terms of the revoking instrument or, possibly, is established by clear and convincing evidence. The alternative plan of disposition is usually in the form of another will, either duly or defectively executed. By so limiting the doctrine, the kind of extrinsic evidence that can be considered is narrowed.

NOTE AND PROBLEM

1. Preparing to make a new will, *T* writes "VOID" across her duly executed will. Several days later she shows the defaced will to her lawyer and instructs the lawyer to prepare a new will. The lawyer prepares a draft of the new will, but when it is shown to *T*, *T* tells the lawyer that it wrongly describes some property and is wrong in some other ways and must be changed. Before the draft can be corrected and executed, *T* dies. The lawyer testifies who the beneficiaries were to be under the new will. Does DRR apply so as to cancel the revocation of the earlier will? In Estate of Ausley, 818 P.2d 1226 (Okla. 1991), the court refused to apply DRR because the lawyer's testimony was insufficient evidence of a definite alternative plan of disposition.

2. *T*'s will bequeaths $5,000 to his old friend, Judy, and the residue of his estate to his brother, Mark. *T* later executes a codicil as follows: "I revoke the legacy to Judy, since she is dead." In fact, Judy is still living and survives *T*. Does Judy take $5,000? In Campbell v. French, 30 Eng. Rep. 1033 (Ch. 1797), on similar facts, the court held that there was no revocation, "the cause being false."

Suppose that the codicil had read: "I revoke the legacy to Judy, since I have already given her $5,000." In fact, the testator did not give Judy $5,000 during life. What result? See Witt v. Rosen, 765 S.W.2d 956 (Ark. App. 1989).

Suppose that the codicil had read: "I revoke the legacy to Judy." Evidence is offered that shows that three weeks prior to execution of the codicil, *T* was told by a friend that Judy had died, believing it to be true. In fact, Judy survives *T*. What result? Compare In re Salmonski's Estate, 238 P.2d 966 (Cal. 1951) (holding DRR was not applicable because the mistake was not recited on the face of the will), with Estate of Anderson, 65 Cal. Rptr. 2d 307 (App. 1997) (holding DRR was applicable when the mistake was inferable from the dispositive instruments and supported by the lawyer-drafter's testimony).

Estate of Alburn
Supreme Court of Wisconsin, 1963
118 N.W.2d 919

Ottilie L. Alburn, a resident of the city of Fort Atkinson, Jefferson county, died on November 13, 1960, at the age of eighty-five years. On December 5, 1960, Adele Ruedisili, a sister of deceased, filed a petition for appointment of an administrator of the estate, which petition alleged that deceased died intestate. Thereafter, Viola Henkey, a grandniece of the deceased, filed a petition for the probate of a will which deceased executed at Milwaukee, Wisconsin, in 1955 (hereinafter the "Milwaukee will"), in which Viola Henkey was named a legatee and also executrix. After the filing of these two petitions, Lulu Alburn and Doris Alburn filed a petition for the probate of a will which deceased executed at Kankakee, Illinois, in 1959 (hereinafter the "Kankakee will"). Neither of these last-named petitioners is a next-of-kin of the deceased but Lulu Alburn is a sister-in-law of deceased. Objections were filed to both the Milwaukee and Kankakee wills.

The county court held a joint hearing on all three petitions. . . . The court determined that the Kankakee will had been destroyed by deceased under the mistaken belief that by so doing she would revive the Milwaukee will which had been revoked by the revocation clause of the Kankakee will. The court applied the doctrine of dependent relative revocation and held that the Kankakee will was entitled to probate. By a judgment (denominated an "Order") entered December 28, 1961, the Kankakee will was admitted to probate. Adele Ruedisili has appealed this judgment. The proponents of the Milwaukee will have not appealed. Further facts will be stated in the opinion.

CURRIE, J.   This court is committed to the doctrine of dependent relative revocation. Estate of Eberhardt (Wis. 1957), 85 N.W.2d 483, and Estate of Callahan (Wis. 1947), 29 N.W.2d 352. The usual situation for application of this doctrine arises where a testator executes one will and thereafter attempts to revoke it by making a later testamentary disposition which for some reason proves ineffective. In both the *Eberhardt* and *Callahan* cases, however, the doctrine was applied to the unusual situation in which a testator revokes a later will under the mistaken belief that by so doing he is reinstating a prior will. In this unusual situation, the doctrine of dependent relative revocation is invoked to render the revocation ineffective. The basis of the doctrine is stated in Estate of Callahan, supra, as follows (29 N.W.2d at p. 355):

> The doctrine of dependent relative revocation is based upon the testator's inferred intention. It is held that as a matter of law the destruction of the later document is intended to be conditional where it is accompanied by the expressed intent of reinstating a former will and where there is no explanatory evidence. Of course if there is evidence that the testator intended the destruction to be absolute, there is no room for the application of the doctrine of dependent revocation.

The sole question raised by appellant on this appeal is whether the finding of the trial court that deceased revoked the Kankakee will under the mistaken belief that she was thereby reinstating the prior Milwaukee will is against the great weight and clear preponderance of the evidence. This requires that we review the pertinent evidence.

Testatrix was born in Wisconsin. For about thirty years she had resided in San Francisco, California, and later in Cleveland, Ohio. As a widow without children, she came to Milwaukee in the fall of 1954 and lived there with Viola Henkey, her grandniece. While so residing she executed the Milwaukee will on August 12, 1955. The original of this will was left with Attorney George R. Affeldt of Milwaukee, who had drafted it, where it remained until the death of testatrix. Sometime shortly prior to May 22, 1959, testatrix moved to Kankakee, Illinois, and resided there with her brother, Robert Lehmann. On May 22, 1959, she executed the Kankakee will.

On June 28, 1960, testatrix left Kankakee and came to Fort Atkinson, Wisconsin, and lived there with another brother, Edwin Lehmann, until her death in November of 1960. Testatrix was a patient at a hospital in Fort Atkinson during part of October and November of that year. Edwin testified that he had learned of the execution of the Kankakee will prior to the arrival of testatrix on June 28, 1960. On the evening of her arrival, he asked her what she had done with that will, and she replied, "What do you suppose, I got rid of it."[34] The next morning testatrix came downstairs with the torn pieces of the Kankakee will tied up in a handkerchief. Edwin provided her with a paper sack in which she deposited the pieces of the will. Edwin then took the sack with the garbage to the dump. There he opened the sack and let the pieces fly in the wind as testatrix had directed him to do.

Edwin was not questioned about any statement regarding the Milwaukee will which testatrix might have made in his presence at Fort Atkinson. He did testify that after her death he searched through her effects for a will but failed to find

---

34. The trial court in its memorandum decision found that the attempted revocation of the Kankakee will took place in Illinois but held that Wisconsin law rather than Illinois law controlled the question of whether the doctrine of dependent relative revocation should be invoked. This ruling is in accord with Restatement, Conflicts, at 389, §307, which states: "Whether an act claimed to be a revocation of a will is effective to revoke it as a will of movables is determined by the law of the state in which the deceased was domiciled at the time of his death."

one. In view of the following testimony given by Olga Lehmann, his wife, this gives rise to an inference that Edwin was searching for the Milwaukee will.

Olga Lehmann was called as a witness by counsel for proponents of the Kankakee will. . . . [She was] asked the following questions and gave the following answers thereto:

> *Q:* Did the deceased ever discuss in your presence the matter of the Milwaukee will at any other time other than the time we are just now referring to?
> *A:* Yes.
> *Q:* Who was present at that time?
> *A:* Just myself.
> *Q:* What did she tell you concerning the Milwaukee will?
> *A:* That was the one she wanted to stand.
> *Q:* Can you tell me in point of time when this might have been?
> *A:* No, we talked often.

We deem it significant that counsel for appellant did not cross-examine Olga Lehmann with respect to her testimony that testatrix said she wanted the Milwaukee will to stand. Therefore, Olga Lehmann's testimony was not qualified or limited in any way.

This statement by testatrix clearly occurred after her destruction of the Kankakee will. Appellant now attacks this statement on the ground that it was not made contemporaneously with such destruction. In Estate of Callahan, supra, however, the only evidence regarding the intent of testatrix when she destroyed her 1944 will was her husband's statement in her presence after the destruction and her silence indicating acquiescence. The husband stated that they both had destroyed their 1944 wills because they desired to put their son back in the position he occupied under their 1940 wills. Upon this evidence this court determined the doctrine of dependent relative revocation applied and affirmed the judgment of the county court which had admitted the 1944 will of testatrix to probate.

The plan of testamentary disposition under the two wills was in part as follows: The Milwaukee will contained specific bequests of jewelry and household furnishings to Viola Henkey, the grandniece of testatrix, and directed that any indebtedness owing deceased by Viola Henkey and her husband be deemed satisfied. The residuary clause bequeathed one fourth of the estate to her friend Olga Olson, one fourth to Doris Alburn, one fourth to Lulu Alburn, and one fourth to Viola Henkey. The Kankakee will included a bequest to Olga Olson of 38 shares of stock in the Bank of America National Trust & Savings Association and bequests of jewelry to Lulu and Addie Alburn. The remainder of the estate was bequeathed as follows: four tenths to Lulu Alburn, five tenths to Doris Alburn, and one tenth to Robert Lehmann, brother of testatrix. The Alburns are not related to testatrix but are relatives of her deceased husband. Viola Henkey, although a blood relative of testatrix, is not one of her next-of-kin who would inherit in the event testatrix had died intestate. The next-of-kin consist of four surviving brothers and one sister plus a large number of nieces and nephews of testatrix, the children of four deceased sisters and one deceased brother. Thus under the Milwaukee will, none of the next-of-kin were named as legatees, whereas under the Kankakee will, the only next-of-kin named a legatee was Robert, her brother. His share under the Kankakee will is somewhat less than the one-tenth share of the entire estate which he would receive if testatrix had died intestate. The bulk of the estate under both wills was bequeathed to the Alburns and Olga Olson. This plan of testamentary disposition extended as late as May, 1959.

There is no evidence of any change of circumstances occurring thereafter that would indicate any reason why testatrix should die intestate and nine tenths of her estate go to next-of-kin not named in either will. The one change in circumstance was her leaving the home of her brother Robert and moving in with her brother Edwin. This move might provide a reason for her desiring to revoke the Kankakee will, but certainly not for her wishing to die intestate. The learned trial judge, in the supplemental memorandum decision of December 26, 1961, stated, "I have a strong conviction that decedent did not want to die intestate." The evidence fully supports this conclusion despite the fact that testatrix took no steps between June 29, 1960, and her death nearly five months later to draft a new will. We deem that a reasonable inference, to be drawn from the competent evidence in this case, for her failure to make a new will is her evident belief that her Milwaukee will was still operative. Testatrix must have known that the original of the Milwaukee will was still in possession of Attorney Affeldt and believed that the only impediment to this will was the revocation clause of the Kankakee will. She also knew that the Kankakee will had been destroyed by tearing it in pieces and scattering the pieces so that they could not be found.[35]

We are constrained to conclude that the statement made to Olga Lehmann that testatrix wished her Milwaukee will to stand, the inference that she did not wish to die intestate, and the fact that she took no steps following the destruction of the Kankakee will to make a new will are sufficient evidence to support the finding that she destroyed the Kankakee will under the mistaken belief that the Milwaukee will would control the disposition of her estate. Furthermore there is no evidence which controverts this finding. Therefore, it is not against the great weight and clear preponderance of the evidence.

Counsel for respondents Alburn request a review by this court of several rulings by the trial court which excluded certain evidence pursuant to objections made by counsel for appellant Ruedisili. This excluded evidence related to further statements made by testatrix, after destruction of the Kankakee will, that she then considered her Milwaukee will to be in effect or desired this result. In view of our conclusion that the trial court's determination may be sustained upon the evidence admitted, we find it unnecessary to review these rulings.

Judgment affirmed.

---

35. The contents of the Kankakee will were proved by a carbon copy in the possession of the lawyer who had drafted it at Kankakee, Illinois.

NOTE: REVIVAL

Under Wisconsin law at the time, the will executed by Ottilie Alburn in Milwaukee in 1955 could not be revived after it had been expressly revoked by the 1959 Kankakee will. The explanation requires a brief discussion of the doctrine of revival.

The question of revival typically arises under the following facts (which were present in Estate of Alburn): Testator executes will #1. Subsequently, testator executes will #2, which revokes will #1 by an express clause or by inconsistency. Later, testator revokes will #2. Is will #1 revived?

The American states tend to fall within one of three groups. A few states take the view of the English common law courts that will #1 is not revoked unless will #2 remains in effect until the testator's death. The theory is that, since a will does not operate until the testator's death, will #2 is not legally effective during the testator's life. Therefore will #1 is not "revoked" by will #2. Technically, this theory does not involve "revival" at all because the first will has never been revoked.

The large majority of states assumes that will #2 legally revokes will #1 at the time will #2 is executed. But they divide into two groups. A majority of states holds that upon revocation of will #2, will #1 is revived if the testator so intends. The testator's intent may be shown from the circumstances surrounding revocation of will #2 or from the testator's contemporaneous or subsequent oral declarations that will #1 is to take effect. Wisconsin is now in this group of states. See Restatement (Third) of Property: Wills and Other Donative Transfers §4.2, statutory note (1999).

A minority of states takes the view that a revoked will cannot be revived unless re-executed with testamentary formalities or republished by being referred to in a later duly executed testamentary writing. At the time of the *Alburn* case, Wisconsin had this rule. See In re Eberhardt's Estate, 85 N.W.2d 483 (Wis. 1957).

Nearly half of the states have adopted a statute based on UPC §2-509, either in its 1969 or 1990 version.

Uniform Probate Code (1990)

§2-509. REVIVAL OF REVOKED WILL

(a) If a subsequent will that wholly revoked a previous will is thereafter revoked by a revocatory act under Section 2-507(a)(2), the previous will remains revoked unless it is revived. The previous will is revived if it is evident from the circumstances of the revocation of the subsequent will or from the testator's contemporary or subsequent declarations that the testator intended the previous will to take effect as executed.

(b) If a subsequent will that partly revoked a previous will is thereafter revoked by a revocatory act under Section 2-507(a)(2), a revoked part of the previous will is revived unless it is evident from the circumstances of the revocation of the subsequent will or from the testator's contemporary or subsequent declarations that the testator did not intend the revoked part to take effect as executed.

(c) If a subsequent will that revoked a previous will in whole or in part is thereafter revoked by another, later, will, the previous will remains revoked in whole or in part, unless it or its revoked part is revived. The previous will or its revoked part is revived to the extent it appears from the terms of the later will that the testator intended the previous will to take effect.

NOTE, QUESTIONS, AND PROBLEM

1.   Under UPC §2-509(a), if a subsequent will that *wholly* revoked the previous will is itself revoked by physical act, the presumption is that the previous will remains revoked. On the other hand, under UPC §2-509(b), if a subsequent will that *partly* revoked the previous will is itself revoked, the presumption is that the previous will is revived.

Suppose that Ottilie Alburn's Kankakee will, executed in 1959, had not contained an express revocation clause. Under UPC §2-509, would the presumption be that the 1955 will was revived? Does the 1959 will wholly or only partly revoke the 1955 will?

2.   In 2009, *T* dies. *T*'s heir is *H*. *T*'s safe deposit box contains the following three documents, all duly signed and witnessed according to law:

(1)   A will executed in 1999 devising all *T*'s property to *A*.
(2)   A will executed in 2006 devising all *T*'s property to *B*.
(3)   A document executed in 2007 reading: "I hereby revoke my 2006 will."

Under UPC §2-509(c), who takes *T*'s property?

3.   In a state that has enacted UPC §2-509 on revival and §2-503 to correct harmless errors in execution, is DRR still necessary? See UPC §2-507, cmt. (1990).

3.   Revocation by Operation of Law: Change in Family Circumstances

In all but a handful of states, statutes provide that a divorce revokes any provision in the decedent's will for the divorced spouse. In the remaining states, revocation occurs only if divorce is accompanied by a property settlement. These revocation statutes ordinarily apply only to wills, not to life insurance policies, pension plans, or other nonprobate transfers. See Susan N. Gary, Applying Revocation-on-Divorce Statutes to Will Substitutes, 18 Quinnipiac Prob. L.J. 83 (2004).

UPC §2-804 (1990) applies to nonprobate transfers as well as to wills. The term "governing instrument" in §2-804 is defined in UPC §1-201(18) to mean a deed, will, trust, insurance or annuity policy, account with a payable-on-death designation, pension plan, or similar nonprobate donative transfer.

Uniform Probate Code (1990, as amended 1997)

§2-804. REVOCATION OF PROBATE AND NONPROBATE TRANSFERS BY DIVORCE; NO
        REVOCATION BY OTHER CHANGES OF CIRCUMSTANCES

. . . (b) [Revocation Upon Divorce.] Except as provided by the express terms of a governing instrument, a court order, or a contract relating to the division of the marital estate made between the divorced individuals before or after the marriage, divorce, or annulment, the divorce or annulment of a marriage:

(1) revokes any revocable (i) disposition or appointment of property made by a divorced individual to his [or her] former spouse in a governing instrument and any disposition or appointment created by law or in a governing instrument to a relative of the divorced individual's former spouse, (ii) provision in a governing instrument conferring a general or nongeneral power of appointment on the divorced individual's former spouse or on a relative of the divorced individual's former spouse, and (iii) nomination in a governing instrument, nominating a divorced individual's former spouse or a relative of the divorced individual's former spouse to serve in any fiduciary or representative capacity, including a personal representative, executor, trustee, conservator, agent, or guardian; and

(2) severs the interests of the former spouses in property held by them at the time of the divorce or annulment as joint tenants with the right of survivorship [or as community property with the right of survivorship], transforming the interests of the former spouses into equal tenancies in common. . . .

(d) [Effect of Revocation.] Provisions of a governing instrument are given effect as if the former spouse and relatives of the former spouse disclaimed all provisions revoked by this section or, in the case of a revoked nomination in a fiduciary or representative capacity, as if the former spouse and relatives of the former spouse died immediately before the divorce or annulment. . . .

(f) [No Revocation for Other Change of Circumstances.] No change of circumstances other than as described in this section and in Section 2-803 effects a revocation. . . .

PROBLEM AND NOTE

1. *T* executes a will devising all his property to his wife, and if his wife does not survive him, then to his wife's son (*T*'s stepson). *T* divorces his wife and then dies. *T*'s heirs are his children by a prior marriage. A state statute revokes all provisions in a will for a divorced spouse and treats the divorced spouse as having predeceased the testator. Does the stepson take *T*'s property? Compare Estate of Nash, 220 S.W.3d 914 (Tex. 2007), with Bloom v. Selfon, 555 A.2d 75 (Pa. 1989). Who takes under UPC §2-804?

2. In Egelhoff v. Egelhoff, page 426, the U.S. Supreme Court held that federal law preempts the application of state revocation-on-divorce statutes to federally regulated pension benefits.

Marriage. If the testator executes her will and subsequently marries, statutes in a large majority of states give the spouse his intestate share, unless it appears from the will that the omission was intentional or the spouse is provided for in the will or by a will substitute with the intent that the transfer be in lieu of a testamentary provision. See UPC §2-301, page 518, which is representative. In effect, this kind of statute revokes the will to the extent of the spouse's intestate share. In a minority of states a premarital will is revoked entirely upon marriage. See page 515.

Where a surviving spouse does not take an intestate share because the spouse is mentioned in the premarital will, the spouse may be able to take an elective or forced share of the decedent spouse's estate, which is available to all surviving spouses in separate property states whether intentionally or unintentionally disinherited. We take up the elective or forced share in Chapter 7.

Birth of children. Statutes in a few states follow the old common law rule that marriage followed by birth of children revokes a will executed before marriage, but this rule has not been incorporated in the UPC and is rapidly disappearing. See Restatement (Third) of Property: Wills and Other Donative Transfers §4.1, cmt. g (1999). However, almost all states have pretermitted child statutes, giving a child born after the execution of the parent's will, and not mentioned in the will, a share in the parent's estate. See UPC §2-302, page 531. Sometimes, pretermitted child statutes include children born before the execution of the will as well as children born thereafter. A pretermitted child statute, if applicable, results in a revocation of the parent's will to the extent of the child's share.

SECTION C. COMPONENTS OF A WILL

In Section A of this chapter, we considered the formalities with which a will must be executed. We saw that if a state's Wills Act is not complied with in all its particulars, a testamentary instrument may not be entitled to probate, no matter how clearly it reflects the testator's intention that it be a will. Despite these formal requirements of transfer, however, it is possible for documents and acts lacking testamentary formalities to have the effect of determining who takes what property belonging to the testator. In this section, we are primarily concerned with two doctrines that can have this effect by permitting extrinsic evidence to resolve the identity of persons or property: (a) the doctrine of incorporation by reference, and (b) the doctrine of acts of independent significance. Before we consider these doctrines, we briefly describe two others that are sometimes confused with them: (c) the doctrine of integration of wills, and (d) the doctrine of republication by codicil.

1.   Integration of Wills

Wills are often written on more than one sheet of paper. Under the doctrine of *integration*, all papers present at the time of execution, intended to be part of the will, are integrated into the will. See Restatement (Third) of Property: Wills and Other Donative Transfers §3.5 (1999).

But which sheets of paper, present at the time of execution, were intended to be part of the will? Typically, this is obvious, for the pages of the will are physically connected with a staple or ribbon and are numbered, or, failing this, there is a sufficient connection of language carrying over from page to page to show an internal coherence of the provisions. The attorney can prevent any problem from arising under the integration doctrine by seeing to it that the will is fastened together before the testator signs and by having the testator sign or initial each numbered page of the will for identification. Litigation involving integration arises when the pages are not physically connected and there is no internal coherence, or there is evidence that a staple has been removed, or one page is in one font whereas the rest of the will is in another font.[36]

Estate of Rigsby, 843 P.2d 856 (Okla. App. 1992), is illustrative of the litigated cases. In that case, the dispute centered on whether the testator's holographic will spanned two pages. Both pages were entirely in the handwriting of the testator, and each was initialed and dated at the top. The first page began with the words, "Inasmuch as I do not have a will, I would like to make the following arrangements in the event of my death," and the second page, which listed items of personal property followed by the names of various individuals, was found folded with the first. But the two pages were not fastened together, and the testator signed only the first page, leaving two and a half inches of blank space below her signature. There was no reference on either page to the other, nor any language connecting the two pages, and the second page conflicted in part with the first. The court admitted the first page to probate, but not the second, which "could easily be interpreted as a work sheet listing Decedent's assets as a preliminary step before drafting the first page."

2.   Republication by Codicil

Publication of a will is the testator's statement to the witnesses, by words or by action, that a document is the testator's will. Under the doctrine of *republication by*

---

36. An oddball Indiana case, Keener v. Archibald, 533 N.E.2d 1268 (Ind. App. 1989), holds that the doctrine of integration is not the law in Indiana, but such a doctrine would seem to be necessary unless wills in Indiana are required to be written on one page.

codicil, a will is treated as re-executed (*re*published) as of the date of the codicil: "A will is treated as if it were executed when its most recent codicil was executed, whether or not the codicil expressly republishes the prior will, unless the effect of so treating it would be inconsistent with the testator's intent." Restatement (Third) of Property: Wills and Other Donative Transfers §3.4 (1999).

Updating the original will in this manner can have important consequences. Suppose that the testator revokes a first will by a second will and then executes a codicil to the first will. The first will is republished, and the second will is revoked by implication ("squeezed out"). See Jarvis v. Ernhart, 823 S.W.2d 154 (Mo. App. 1992). Accordingly, the doctrine of republication by codicil should not be applied automatically, but only where updating the will carries out the testator's intent, though sometimes courts have ignored this qualification. See, e.g., Azcunce v. Estate of Azcunce, 586 So. 2d 1216 (Fla. App. 1991).

Case 1 illustrates the updating of a will by republication.

> *Case 1.* The jurisdiction has a statute purging any gift to an attesting witness. In 2007 *T* executes a will devising all his property to *A*. *A* and *B* are witnesses to the will. In 2008 *T* executes a codicil devising $5,000 to *C*. *C* and *D* are witnesses to the codicil. In 2009 *T* executes a second codicil devising a diamond ring to *C*. *D* and *E* are witnesses to the second codicil. Under the doctrine of republication by codicil, the will and first codicil are deemed to be re-executed in 2009 by the second codicil, which has two disinterested witnesses. *A* and *C* are not purged of their gifts. See King v. Smith, 302 A.2d 144 (N.J. Super. 1973).

The fundamental difference between republication by codicil and the doctrine of incorporation by reference, discussed below, is that republication applies only to a prior validly executed will, whereas incorporation by reference can apply to incorporate into a will language or instruments that have never been validly executed. In the few jurisdictions that do not recognize incorporation by reference, courts have sometimes used the republication doctrine to give effect to wills that are invalid for some reason other than faulty execution. In New York, for example, which does not in general permit incorporation of unattested documents into a will, a codicil can republish and thereby give testamentary effect to a will that was invalid because of mental incapacity or undue influence, but a codicil cannot republish an instrument never duly executed with the required formalities.

In Estate of Nielson, 165 Cal. Rptr. 319 (App. 1980), the testator drew lines through the dispositive provisions of his typewritten will and wrote between the lines: "Bulk of Estate — 1. — Shrine Hospital for Crippled Children — Los Angeles, $10,000 — 2. Society for Prevention of Cruelty to Animals." Near the margin of these cancellations and interlineations were the testator's initials and date. At the top and bottom of the will were the handwritten words, "Revised by Lloyd M. Nielson November 29, 1974." The court held the handwritten words constituted a holographic codicil because they did not intend to incorporate the attested typed material. The holographic codicil republished the typewritten will, as modified.

3. Incorporation by Reference

Uniform Probate Code (1990)

§2-510. INCORPORATION BY REFERENCE

A writing in existence when a will is executed may be incorporated by reference if the language of the will manifests this intent and describes the writing sufficiently to permit its identification.

Clark v. Greenhalge

Supreme Judicial Court of Massachusetts, 1991
582 N.E.2d 949

NOLAN, J. We consider in this case whether a probate judge correctly concluded that specific, written bequests of personal property contained in a notebook maintained by a testatrix were incorporated by reference into the terms of the testatrix's will.

We set forth the relevant facts as found by the probate judge. The testatrix, Helen Nesmith, duly executed a will in 1977, which named her cousin, Frederic T. Greenhalge, II, as executor of her estate. The will further identified Greenhalge as the principal beneficiary of the estate, entitling him to receive all of Helen Nesmith's tangible personal property upon her death except those items which she "designate[d] by a memorandum left by [her] and known to [Greenhalge], or in accordance with [her] known wishes," to be given to others living at the time of her death.[37] Among Helen Nesmith's possessions was a large oil painting of a farm scene signed by T.H. Hinckley and dated 1833. The value of the painting, as assessed for estate tax purposes, was $1,800.00.

In 1972, Greenhalge assisted Helen Nesmith in drafting a document entitled "MEMORANDUM" and identified as "a list of items of personal property prepared with Miss Helen Nesmith upon September 5, 1972, for the guidance of myself in the distribution of personal tangible property." This list consisted of forty-nine specific bequests of Ms. Nesmith's tangible personal property. In 1976, Helen Nesmith modified the 1972 list by interlineations, additions and deletions. Neither edition of the list involved a bequest of the farm scene painting.

Ms. Nesmith kept a plastic-covered notebook in the drawer of a desk in her study. She periodically made entries in this notebook, which bore the title "List to be given Helen Nesmith 1979." One such entry read: "Ginny Clark farm picture hanging over fireplace. Ma's room." Imogene Conway and Joan Dragoumanos, Ms. Nesmith's private home care nurses, knew of the existence of the notebook and had observed Helen Nesmith write in it. On several occasions, Helen

---

37. The value of Ms. Nesmith's estate at the time of her death exceeded $2,000,000.00, including both tangible and nontangible assets.

**"If I could pick just one keepsake, I think
it would be the mutual funds."**

Nesmith orally expressed to these nurses her intentions regarding the disposition of particular pieces of her property upon her death, including the farm scene painting. Helen Nesmith told Conway and Dragoumanos that the farm scene painting was to be given to Virginia Clark, upon Helen Nesmith's death.

Virginia Clark and Helen Nesmith first became acquainted in or about 1940. The women lived next door to each other for approximately ten years (1945 through 1955), during which time they enjoyed a close friendship. The Nesmith-Clark friendship remained constant through the years. In more recent years, Ms. Clark frequently spent time at Ms. Nesmith's home, often visiting Helen Nesmith while she rested in the room which originally was her mother's bedroom. The farm scene painting hung in this room above the fireplace. Virginia Clark openly admired the picture.

According to Ms. Clark, sometime during either January or February of 1980, Helen Nesmith told Ms. Clark that the farm scene painting would belong to Ms. Clark after Helen Nesmith's death. Helen Nesmith then mentioned to Virginia Clark that she would record this gift in a book she kept for the purpose of memorializing her wishes with respect to the disposition of certain of her belongings.[38] After that conversation, Helen Nesmith often alluded to the fact that Ms. Clark someday would own the farm scene painting.

___

38. According to Margaret Young, another nurse employed by Ms. Nesmith, Ms. Nesmith asked Ms. Young to "print[ ] in [the] notebook, beneath [her] own handwriting, 'Ginny Clark painting over fireplace in mother's bedroom.' " Ms. Young complied with this request. Ms. Young stated that Ms. Nesmith's express purpose in having Ms. Young record this statement in the notebook was "to insure that [Greenhalge] would know that she wanted Ginny Clark to have that particular painting."

Ms. Nesmith executed two codicils to her 1977 will: one on May 30, 1980, and a second on October 23, 1980. The codicils amended certain bequests and deleted others, while ratifying the will in all other respects.

Greenhalge received Helen Nesmith's notebook on or shortly after January 28, 1986, the date of Ms. Nesmith's death. Thereafter, Greenhalge, as executor, distributed Ms. Nesmith's property in accordance with the will as amended, the 1972 memorandum as amended in 1976, and certain of the provisions contained in the notebook.[39] Greenhalge refused, however, to deliver the farm scene painting to Virginia Clark because the painting interested him and he wanted to keep it. Mr. Greenhalge claimed that he was not bound to give effect to the expressions of Helen Nesmith's wishes and intentions stated in the notebook, particularly as to the disposition of the farm scene painting. Notwithstanding this opinion, Greenhalge distributed to himself all of the property bequeathed to him in the notebook. Ms. Clark thereafter commenced an action against Mr. Greenhalge seeking to compel him to deliver the farm scene painting to her.

The probate judge found that Helen Nesmith wanted Ms. Clark to have the farm scene painting. The judge concluded that Helen Nesmith's notebook qualified as a "memorandum" of her known wishes with respect to the distribution of her tangible personal property, within the meaning of Article Fifth of Helen Nesmith's will.[40] The judge further found that the notebook was in existence at the time of the execution of the 1980 codicils, which ratified the language of Article Fifth in its entirety. Based on these findings, the judge ruled that the notebook was incorporated by reference into the terms of the will. Newton v. Seaman's Friend Soc'y, 130 Mass. 91, 93 (1881). The judge awarded the painting to Ms. Clark. . . . We . . . now hold that the probate judge correctly awarded the painting to Ms. Clark.

A properly executed will may incorporate by reference into its provisions any "document or paper not so executed and witnessed, whether the paper referred to be in the form of . . . a mere list or memorandum, . . . if it was in existence at the time of the execution of the will, and is identified by clear and satisfactory proof as the paper referred to therein." Newton v. Seaman's Friend Soc'y, supra at 93. The parties agree that the document entitled "memorandum," dated 1972 and amended in 1976, was in existence as of the date of the execution of Helen Nesmith's will. The parties further agree that this document is a memorandum regarding the distribution of certain items of Helen Nesmith's tangible personal property upon her death, as identified in Article Fifth of her will. There is no

39. Helen Nesmith's will provided that Virginia Clark and her husband, Peter Hayden Clark, receive $20,000.00 upon Helen Nesmith's death. Under the terms of the 1972 memorandum, as amended in 1976, Helen Nesmith also bequeathed to Virginia Clark a portrait of Isabel Nesmith, Helen Nesmith's sister with whom Virginia Clark had been acquainted. Greenhalge honored these bequests and delivered the money and painting to Virginia Clark.

40. Article Fifth of Helen Nesmith's will reads, in pertinent part, as follows: "that [Greenhalge] distribute such of the tangible property to and among such persons *as I may designate by a memorandum left by me and known to him, or in accordance with my known wishes*, provided that said persons are living at the time of my decease" (emphasis added).

dispute, therefore, that the 1972 memorandum was incorporated by reference into the terms of the will. *Newton*, supra.

The parties do not agree, however, as to whether the documentation contained in the notebook, dated 1979, similarly was incorporated into the will through the language of Article Fifth. Greenhalge advances several arguments to support his contention that the purported bequest of the farm scene painting written in the notebook was not incorporated into the will and thus fails as a testamentary devise. The points raised by Greenhalge in this regard are not persuasive. First, Greenhalge contends that the judge wrongly concluded that the notebook could be considered a "memorandum" within the meaning of Article Fifth, because it is not specifically identified as a "memorandum." Such a literal interpretation of the language and meaning of Article Fifth is not appropriate.

"The 'cardinal rule in the interpretation of wills, to which all other rules must bend, is that the intention of the testator shall prevail, provided it is consistent with the rules of law.'" Boston Safe Deposit & Trust Co. v. Park, 29 N.E.2d 977 (Mass. 1940), quoting McCurdy v. McCallum, 72 N.E. 75 (Mass. 1904). The intent of the testator is ascertained through consideration of "the language which [the testatrix] has used to express [her] testamentary designs," Taft v. Stearns, 125 N.E. 570 (Mass. 1920), as well as the circumstances existing at the time of the execution of the will. The circumstances existing at the time of the execution of a codicil to a will are equally relevant, because the codicil serves to ratify the language in the will which has not been altered or affected by the terms of the codicil.

Applying these principles in the present case, it appears clear that Helen Nesmith intended by the language used in Article Fifth of her will to retain the right to alter and amend the bequests of tangible personal property in her will, without having to amend formally the will. The text of Article Fifth provides a mechanism by which Helen Nesmith could accomplish the result she desired; i.e., by expressing her wishes "in a memorandum." The statements in the notebook unquestionably reflect Helen Nesmith's exercise of her retained right to restructure the distribution of her tangible personal property upon her death. That the notebook is not entitled "memorandum" is of no consequence, since its apparent purpose is consistent with that of a memorandum under Article Fifth: It is a written instrument which is intended to guide Greenhalge in "distribut[ing] such of [Helen Nesmith's] tangible personal property to and among . . . persons [who] are living at the time of her decease." In this connection, the distinction between the notebook and "a memorandum" is illusory. The appellant acknowledges that the subject documentation in the notebook establishes that Helen Nesmith wanted Virginia Clark to receive the farm scene painting upon Ms. Nesmith's death. The appellant argues, however, that the notebook cannot take effect as a testamentary instrument under Article Fifth, because the language of Article Fifth limits its application to "a" memorandum, or the 1972 memorandum. We reject this strict construction of Article Fifth. The language of Article Fifth does not preclude the existence of more than one memorandum which serves the intended purpose of that article. As previously suggested, the phrase "a memorandum" in Article Fifth appears as an expression of the manner in which Helen Nesmith could exercise her right to alter her will after its execution, but it does not denote a requirement that she do so within a particular format. To construe narrowly Article Fifth and to exclude the possibility that Helen Nesmith drafted the notebook contents as "a memorandum" under that Article, would undermine our long-standing policy of interpreting wills in a manner which best carries out the known wishes of the testatrix. See Boston Safe Deposit & Trust Co., supra. The evidence supports the conclusion that Helen Nesmith intended that the bequests in her notebook be accorded the same power and effect as those contained in the 1972 memorandum under Article Fifth. We conclude, therefore, that the judge properly accepted the notebook as a memorandum of Helen Nesmith's known wishes as referenced in Article Fifth of her will. . . .

The judge further found that the notebook was in existence on the dates Helen Nesmith executed the codicils to her will [which republished her will], . . . and that it thereby was incorporated into the will pursuant to the language and spirit of Article Fifth. . . .

Lastly, the appellant complains that the notebook fails to meet the specific requirements of a memorandum under Article Fifth of the will, because it was not "known to him" until after Helen Nesmith's death. For this reason, Greenhalge states that the judge improperly ruled that the notebook was incorporated into the will. One of Helen Nesmith's nurses testified, however, that Greenhalge was aware of the notebook and its contents, and that he at no time made an effort to determine the validity of the bequest of the farm scene painting to Virginia Clark as stated therein. There is ample support in the record, therefore, to support the judge's conclusion that the notebook met the criteria set forth in Article Fifth regarding memoranda.

We note, as did the Appeals Court, that "one who seeks equity must do equity and that a court will not permit its equitable powers to be employed to accomplish an injustice." Pitts v. Halifax Country Club, Inc., 476 N.E.2d 222 (Mass. App. 1985). To this point, we remark that Greenhalge's conduct in handling this controversy fell short of the standard imposed by common social norms, not to mention the standard of conduct attending his fiduciary responsibility as executor, particularly with respect to his selective distribution of Helen Nesmith's assets. We can discern no reason in the record as to why this matter had to proceed along the protracted and costly route that it did.[41]

Judgment affirmed.

---

41. And it had a costly aftermath for Greenhalge, the executor and residuary beneficiary of Helen Nesmith's will. A letter from Thomas D. Burns, counsel for Virginia Clark, to Jesse Dukeminier dated Sept. 27, 1993, reveals:

> While the picture was later appraised at about $35,000, its stated value by the executor Greenhalge in the inventory was only $1500. I was awarded a fee of $80,000 by the Probate Court, which I settled for $70,000 to avoid an appeal. The executor, who was a very terrible guy, refused to give up the picture and I thought the case would be on a pro bono basis, but the Probate Judge who heard the case was so incensed by Greenhalge's conduct, he awarded me my full hourly rate upon application.

— Eds.

SIMON v. GRAYSON, 102 P.2d 1081 (Cal. 1940): The testator's will, dated March 25, 1932, left $4,000 to his executors "to be paid by them as shall be directed by me in a letter that will be found in my effects and which will be addressed to my executors and dated March 25, 1932." A codicil to the will was executed November 25, 1933, which made a small change not relevant here and otherwise reaffirmed the will. After the testator's death, a letter dated July 3, 1933, addressed to the executors, was found in the testator's safe-deposit box. It stated: "In my will I have left you $4,000 to be paid to a person named in a letter. I direct you to pay the $4,000 to Esther Cohn." No letter dated March 25, 1932, was found.

The court held that the letter found in the safe-deposit box was the letter referred to in the will, despite the discrepancy in dates. It was incorporated by reference into the will, becoming an integral part of the will. Since the letter was dated prior to the date of the codicil, which republished the will, it complied with the requirement that an incorporated document be in existence on the date of the republished will. The court directed the executors to give the $4,000 to Esther Cohn's estate (she died seven days after testator).

If the testator intended to make a secret gift to Esther Cohn, he failed. A document incorporated by reference becomes part of the probate files, open to the public.

NOTES AND PROBLEMS

1.   In *Clark*, suppose that the entry in the notebook, "Ginny Clark farm picture," had been made after the 1980 codicils. Could it have been given effect? Could it have been given effect under UPC §2-503 or the substantial compliance doctrine? Under UPC §2-513, page 316?

2.   The testator executed a deed to his farm that named his niece as grantee. The deed was sealed in an envelope and placed by the testator in his safe deposit box at a local bank, where it remained until his death. Sometime later, the testator executed a will containing the following provision: "Sixth: I have already deeded my farm to my niece, Alta J. Pullman, and for that reason I do not devise my farm to her in this Will." After the testator's death, it was held that the deed was not effective to convey title to the niece because it was not delivered by the grantor during his lifetime. The niece contends that the deed was incorporated by reference by the language of clause Sixth of the will. What result? See Estate of Dimmitt, 3 N.W.2d 752 (Neb. 1942) (deed incorporated by reference!). Since the court could not openly correct the mistake by adding words to the will, the court did so in effect by a generous application of the incorporation doctrine. On correcting mistakes in wills, see Chapter 5.

3.   The doctrine of incorporation by reference is not recognized, as a general rule, in Connecticut,[42] Louisiana, or New York. To fill this lacuna, New York

---

42.   Hathaway v. Smith, 65 A. 1058 (Conn. 1907), established that the doctrine of incorporation by reference does not exist in Connecticut. An earlier, more interesting case suggested that ultimate result. In Bryan's

courts have stretched the doctrines of republication by codicil (see page 308) and integration to carry out the testator's intent. As for the latter, if, for example, the testator refers in his will to a separate memorandum disposing of his tangible personal property, and if such memorandum is attached to the other pages of his will and was present at execution, such memorandum is entitled to probate under the doctrine of integration. In re Will of Hall, 300 N.Y.S.2d 813 (Sur. 1969). Indeed, even if the memorandum is attached after the signature page, it will be deemed constructively inserted before the signature page so as to comply with a requirement that a will be signed at the end. In re Will of Powell, 395 N.Y.S.2d 334 (Sur. 1977).

Uniform Probate Code (1990)

§2-513. Separate Writing Identifying Devise of Certain Types of Tangible Personal Property

Whether or not the provisions relating to holographic wills apply, a will may refer to a written statement or list to dispose of items of tangible personal property not otherwise specifically disposed of by the will, other than money. To be admissible under this section as evidence of the intended disposition, the writing must be signed by the testator and must describe the items and the devisees with reasonable certainty. The writing may be referred to as one to be in existence at the time of the testator's death; it may be prepared before or after the execution of the will; it may be altered by the testator after its preparation; and it may be a writing that has no significance apart from its effect on the dispositions made by the will.

Appeal, 58 A. 748 (Conn. 1904), the testator, Philo S. Bennett, was a rich Connecticut friend and political ally of the Great Commoner and scourge of eastern capitalists, William Jennings Bryan, who thrice ran unsuccessfully for the presidency on the Democratic ticket. ("You shall not press down upon the brow of labor this crown of thorns. You shall not crucify mankind on a cross of gold.") While on a visit to Bryan at Lincoln, Nebraska, Bennett, with Bryan's assistance, prepared his will. The will was duly executed on May 22, 1900. It provided: "I give and bequeath unto my wife, Grace Imogene Bennett, the sum of fifty thousand dollars (50,000), in trust, however for the purposes set forth in a sealed letter which will be found with this will." Found with the will, at testator's death, was a letter dated "5/22/1900" addressed to "My Dear Wife," which referred to the $50,000 bequest in the will and stated that the $50,000 conveyed to her in trust was to be paid to William Jennings Bryan inasmuch "as his political work prevents the application of his time and talents to money making." Largely because Bennett left $20,000 to his mistress, Mrs. Bennett, angered by the will, refused to carry out Bennett's desires. Bryan sued and lost. The court held that even if incorporation by reference were recognized, the reference in the will was so vague as to be incapable of being applied to any particular instrument.

Bryan then sued Mrs. Bennett a second time, alleging that she held the $50,000 in a constructive trust for him (see page 595 on semisecret testamentary trusts). The court held that no trust arose because Mrs. Bennett had never been apprised of the terms of the will and had made no promise, an essential ingredient of a semisecret testamentary trust. Bryan v. Bigelow, 60 A. 266 (Conn. 1905).

It may be that Bryan's Appeal is an example of the old adage that hard cases make bad law. Bryan, a graduate of Northwestern University School of Law, had acted indelicately — perhaps even unethically — in participating in this secret gift to himself, and the court was probably not disposed to rule in his favor.

PROBLEM, QUESTION, AND NOTE

1.   Suppose the testator's will refers to a separate writing that instructs her executor to sell the testator's tangible personal property and to distribute the proceeds to five named persons. Is this instruction enforceable under UPC §2-513? In Last Will and Testament of Moor, 879 A.2d 648 (Del. Ch. 2005), the court held Yes, reasoning that the statutory term "dispose of" did not mandate an in-kind distribution.

2.   Should there be a limit on the value of personal property that may be passed by separate writing? In *Moor*, the court said that there is no such limit under UPC §2-513:

> One can easily imagine persons who possess items of personal property — works of art, period piece furniture, sports memorabilia — that are more valuable than their cash and securities. Because a personal property memorandum may be executed without the procedural protections of a will, there is an increased chance that such a memorandum might be induced by designing persons. Under [UPC §2-513], the public policy judgment is that this increased chance is worth taking, even if that means, for example, that grandma's expensive Ellsworth Kelly might be devised by a personal property memorandum cajoled out of her by a designing granddaughter. [879 A.2d at 654-55.]

In California, no single item passed by separate writing can have a value in excess of $5,000 and the total passed in this way cannot exceed $25,000. Cal. Prob. Code §6132 (2008).

Johnson v. Johnson
Supreme Court of Oklahoma, 1954
279 P.2d 928

PER CURIAM.   This is an appeal from a judgment of the District Court of Oklahoma County affirming the County Court of Oklahoma in denying probate to an instrument purporting to be the last will and testament of Dexter G. Johnson, who was sometimes known as D.G. Johnson.

The instrument in question was on a single sheet of paper and contained three typewritten paragraphs, started out with the words, "I, D.G. Johnson also known as Dexter G. Johnson, of Oklahoma City, Oklahoma County, State of Oklahoma do hereby make, publish and declare this to be my last Will and Testament . . . " and made numerous bequests and devises and concluded with recommending the employment of a certain attorney to probate the will. This typewritten portion was not dated nor did the testator sign his name at the conclusion thereof nor was it attested by two witnesses. At the end of the typewritten portion, at the bottom of [the] sheet of paper, appears the following, admitted to be in the handwriting of the deceased:

> To my brother James I give ten dollars only. This will shall be complete unless hereafter altered, changed or rewritten. Witness my hand this April 6, 1947. Easter Sunday, 2:30 P.M.
> D.G. Johnson
> Dexter G. Johnson

On trial de novo in the District Court the proponents of this purported will, plaintiffs in error here, introduced evidence over objections (which objections were never ruled on by the court) showing that Dexter G., or D.G. Johnson for many years was a practicing attorney in Oklahoma City; that during his practice he prepared many wills, all in proper form, for various clients; that in October, 1946, deceased told Jack G. Wiggins, his insurance counselor, that he had a will but it was out of date and needed changing; that in March, 1947, deceased told this insurance counselor that he was working on his will, making changes, and expected to complete it right away and told Mr. Wiggins in general the disposition he intended to make of his property; that in the latter part of 1946 Lowell M. Wickham, deceased's rental agent, was shown the instrument here in question at which time it had only the typewritten portions on it; that at that time deceased told him that was his will and he wanted Wickham to witness it, but he and deceased started discussing other business and neglected to do it at that time; that when Wickham left the paper was lying on deceased's desk; that some months later Wickham asked deceased about witnessing the will and deceased replied he had changed his will by codicil and did not need Wickham to sign it as witness; an offer by statement of counsel was made to show the intention of the testator in leaving his property to the persons he named as beneficiaries which was rejected by the court and is not helpful in deciding the questions raised here.

The above is a summary of all the testimony that appears in the record. None of the testimony presented to the County Court appears in the record; defendant below, contestant of the will and defendant in error here, offered no testimony.

Is this instrument one complete, integrated writing, partly typed and partly handwritten; or is it an unexecuted nonholographic will to which is appended a valid holographic codicil? If it be the former it cannot be admitted to probate because it was not signed in the presence of two subscribing witnesses as required by law.

Defendant in error urges that the instrument shows on its face that it is but one instrument and that it cannot be divided into two parts, one, the typewritten part to be called a will and the other, the handwritten part, to be called a codicil. In support of his contention he says that the typewritten portion standing alone is not a will because, though admittedly testamentary in character, it is not dated, signed, nor witnessed; that it takes the handwritten portion to complete the instrument; that by definition to have a codicil there must first be a will.

There is no question in this case that the typewritten instrument which was not signed, dated, nor attested was prepared by D.G. Johnson and that it is testamentary in character, or that he intended same as his will or that it effectively makes complete disposition of his estate. A will may be so defective, as here, that it is not entitled to probate but if testamentary in character it is a will, nonetheless. . . . Nor is there any question that the handwritten words were wholly in the handwriting of the testator.

The question next arises, do these words meet the requirements of a codicil? By definition a codicil is a supplement to, an addition to or qualification of, an existing will, made by the testator to alter, enlarge, or restrict the provisions of the

31691

129067

I, D. G. Johnson also known as Dexter G. Johnson, of Oklahoma
City, Oklahoma County, State of Oklahoma do hereby make, publish and
declare this to be my last Will and Testamnt and revoke all former wills
and codocils by me made.

FIRST: I direct my Executor to pay my just debts,last illness and burial
expense.

SECOND: I give, devise and bequeath to my sister Beulah Johnson also
known as Beulah J. Johnson and my brother V. C. Johnson also known as
Victor C. Johnson all of the rest, residue and rrmainder of my estate, real,
personal and mixed propertt, wherever situated and whatsoever kind and/or
character, subject only to the following requests of my said brother and
sister,namely and specifically that at a time when in the jydgment of my
said sister and brother they shall deem the condition of the estate in a
proper and suitable condition so to do without material injuxyxxxxx
damage to or otherwise detremental to said estate and the properties
reasonably disposed of to pay into a trust fund to be governed by my
said sister and brother the sum of Fifty thousand dollars to be used for
the erection of a new church in Montrose,Effingham County, State of
Illinois on the site where the present church now stands being the church
formerly attended by our family regularily and to build a parsonage of not
less than six rooms,nor more than eight rooms on the lots owned by me
across the street from said church site and said lots to be deeded to said
church organization for the use of the minister to preside over the church
aforesaid; also to use any sum remaining for a mauseloeum or suitable
arrangement as my said sister and brother may determine proper and fitting
for the graves of our family now buried there and any sum then remaining
to generally improve said cemetery a ll as my said sister and brother may
determine; if there be difference of opinions or desires in any matter, then
the will and desire of my sister shall prevail. and further that a fund of
Ten thousand dollars to be set up and invested in SAFE SECURITIES with
reasonable rate of interest for the use and benefit of my great neice Joanna
Johnson and a similiar sum for Joanna's sister with same conditions and
to be paid to each of them in monthly payments of Seventy-five dollars each
month beginning on their seventeenth birthday and thereafter until exhausted
ans each shall have received the full sum together with it's accruals of
ten thousand dollars or a total of twenty thousand dollars; I also request
that a fund of ten thousand dollars be set up for the purpose of paying to
my brother Joseph Evera d Johnson a monthoy stipend of fifty dollars each and
every month during his life to begin ninety days after my death and to end
with the death of my said brother or the exhaustinn of the funds if they shall.
exhaust prior to his death with any sum remaining to remine to the use and
benefit of my brother Victor C. Johnson and sister Beulah J. Johnson, and
yhe further sum of Five yhousand dollars to be paid within reasonable time
to Alma L. Kloss friend of my sister Beulah J.Johnson in appreciation for
her kindness and sincere friendship to and for my sister Beulah J. Johnson
with the request that said Alma L. Kloss invest same in some good securities,
government bonds or annuity, spkkmxxk. I further suggest that my said
sister and brother employ Claude Monnett, attorney and friend of mine be
employed for a reasonable fee, to be agreed upon by xkxxquxkixxx my sister,
brother and Mr. Monnett for complete service but should they not agree then
my said brother and sister shall employ whomsoever they may desire, being
contious that nothing to be done without their consent and knowledge

To my brother James I give ten Dollars only

This will shall be complete unless hereafter altered changed or amended

Witness My hand this April 6, 1947

Easter January 2 30 Pm

will, to explain or republish it, or to revoke it, and it must be testamentary in character. In re Whittier's Estate, 176 P.2d 281 (Wash. 1947). A codicil need not be called a codicil, In re Carr's Estate, 209 P.2d 956 (Cal. App. 1949); In re Atkinson's Estate, 294 P. 425 (Cal. App. 1930). The intention to add a codicil is controlling. Allgeier v. Brown, 251 S.W. 851 (Ky. 1952); Stewart v. Stewart, 59 N.E. 116 (Mass. 1900). The handwritten words are admittedly testamentary in character. It is clear that they made an addition to the provisions of the will theretofore existing. This codicil is on the same sheet of paper and the terms thereof, the circumstances surrounding it, as shown by the evidence indicate that the testator intended it as an addition to and republication of his will.

If it be a codicil, then, is it a valid one? It is written, dated, and signed by the testator. It meets all the requirements of a valid holographic codicil. The fact that the codicil was written on the same piece of paper as the typewritten will does not invalidate the codicil. In re Atkinson's Estate, supra.

It is admitted that a codicil republishes a previous will as modified by the codicil as of the date of the codicil. Can a valid, holographic codicil republish and validate a will which was theretofore inoperative because not dated, signed, or attested according to law?

The general principle of law is that a codicil validly executed operates as a republication of the will no matter what defects may have existed in the execution of the earlier document, that the instruments are incorporated as one, and that a proper execution of the codicil extends also to the will. That a properly executed codicil will give effect to a will which has never been signed has been specifically held in Kentucky, New Jersey, and England. See Beall v. Cunningham, 42 Ky. 390 (1843), in which it appeared that a paper wholly written by testator dated 1825 was denied probate, and thereafter there was offered for probate a typewritten will dated in 1827,[43] which was unsigned and unattested, together with a codicil dated 1832 on the same sheet of paper which was signed and attested; the opinion holds that the properly executed codicil had the effect of giving operation to the whole as one will. See also Hurley v. Blankinship, 229 S.W.2d 963 (Ky. 1950), in which a holographic will which was not signed was held validated by properly executed holographic codicils; Doe v. Evans, 149 Eng. Reprint 307 (1832), in which an unsigned typewritten will was held validated by a properly executed codicil on the same sheet of paper; see also McCurdy v. Neall, 7 A. 566 (N.J. Prerog. 1886), and Smith v. Runkle, 98 A. 1086 (N.J. App. 1916), in both of which the signatures to the wills were defective because not placed on the will in the presence of witnesses but it was held that valid codicils thereafter executed gave operation to the entire will and codicils; Rogers v. Agricola, 3 S.W.2d 26 (Ark. 1928), in which an invalid typewritten will (due to only one witness) was held validated by a subsequent holographic codicil; In re Plumel's Estate, 90 P. 192 (Cal.

---

43. Typewritten will in 1827? The first typewriters were placed on the market in 1874. Later in this paragraph the court refers to a typewritten will in Doe v. Evans, decided in 1832. In neither Beall v. Cunningham nor in Doe v. Evans was there mention of any typewriting. This anachronism was called to our attention by John Cutcher, J.D., Vanderbilt 1987, whose sharp eyes spotted it while a student in Professor Jeffrey Schoenblum's wills course at Vanderbilt. — Eds.

1907), an invalid holographic will because of printing thereon was held validated by a subsequent holographic codicil written on the back of the will.[44] . . .

The only exception is New York which modifies the general rule by holding that a properly executed codicil validates a will originally invalid for want of testamentary capacity, undue influence, or revocation but does not validate a will defectively executed because of improper attestation. It will be noted, however, that Justice Cardozo in In re Fowles Will, 118 N.E. 611 (N.Y. 1918), stated that the rule was malleable and uncertain and he anticipated that New York would abandon its limitations on the rule. . . .

We therefore hold that the valid holographic codicil incorporated the prior will by reference and republished and validated the prior will as of the date of the codicil, thus giving effect to the intention of the testator.

Reversed with directions to enter the will for probate.

CORN, J., concurring specially.[45]   I concur in the per curiam opinion. In so doing I have in mind the purpose of our law-makers in enacting statutes regulating the making of a Will. They require certain steps to be taken in the execution of a Will solely for the purpose of permitting a person to dispose of his property

44. Examine carefully the facts of the cases cited in this paragraph. Do you see why the cases cited are properly analyzed as applications of either incorporation by reference or integration and that republication by codicil is not involved? — Eds.

45. In 1964, Justices Corn and Welch were convicted of federal income tax evasion and sentenced to prison terms of 18 months and 3 years respectively. N.Y. Times, July 19, 1964, at 44; id., Nov. 14, 1964, at 14. Corn and Welch resigned their judicial positions. Subsequently Corn signed a statement in which Corn said Welch, Johnson, and he had accepted more than $150,000 in bribes for throwing cases. In 1965 Justice Johnson was convicted of corruption in office and removed from the court by the Oklahoma legislature. Id., May 14, 1965, at 40.

The newspaper accounts did not mention any evidence of bribery in the principal case of Johnson v. Johnson. Yet when a judge has been convicted of bribery in one case, the public may suspect there was bribery in others. (Indeed, when Corn was asked if he could remember any year, in the 24 he served as Justice, when he did not take money for his votes, he replied: "Well, I don't know." Id., May 11, 1965, at 18.) The votes of Corn, Welch, and Johnson were decisive in Johnson v. Johnson. Although there is no report of bribery in this case, *and none is to be inferred from this note*, does the mere appearance of possible impropriety require that the case now be reheard upon petition of the losing party?

In Johnson v. Johnson, 424 P.2d 414 (Okla. 1967), the executor of the losing party in the original case (who had since died) petitioned to have the 1954 decision vacated in view of Justice Corn's participation in that decision. Five of the supreme court justices who were on the court in 1954 disqualified themselves, and five special justices were appointed in their stead. In a unanimous decision, the court denied the petition since there was no allegation of wrongdoing in the particular case. Among the reasons given were the practical consequences of a contrary decision:

> It is apparent that if our holding were in the affirmative every decision from 1938 to January of 1959 in which Corn cast the deciding vote would have to be set aside. There are more than one thousand such cases. Rights of every kind have been settled by the decisions in such cases. Marriages have been contracted upon the basis of divorces granted, titles have been transferred and judgments paid. To now go back and reopen every such case for a possible new decision requiring new arguments and new hearings would cast intolerable and unjust burdens upon all the parties. Titles and status long thought put at rest would be thrown open to doubt. It would indeed create a "shambles" as Respondent contends. And this would be so in every case in which Corn cast the deciding vote even though no corruption occurred in such case.
>
> To us this result seems unthinkable and contrary to the most elementary principles of justice. We think it more just that those cases in which no corruption can be found should be allowed to stand, at the same time giving full right to any person who believes that any such decision has been corruptly obtained, to petition this Court for a hearing, in which, if corruption can be shown, the decision may be set aside.

Cf. Electric Auto-Lite Co. v. P. & D. Mfg. Co., 109 F.2d 566 (2d Cir. 1940), where a rehearing was granted "because of the disqualification of one member of the original court [Judge Martin T. Manton, convicted of bribery in 1939], not known at the time." — Eds.

by Will, to take effect after his death the way he desired, and to prevent someone, through fraud or by other means, from permitting this to be done. It was the purpose of our lawmakers, in passing the Act, to make it impossible for fraud or undue influence to be practiced in the execution of the Will, and in the disposition of the property disposed of by the Will. It was not the intent of our lawmakers, in enacting these statutes, if substantially complied with, to ever allow a miscarriage of justice by a wrongful disposition of the testator's property contrary to his intent. 84 O.S. 1951 §151 provides: "Intention of testator governs. — A will is to be construed according to the intention of the testator. . . . "

In the instant case, the intent expressed by the testator in the written instrument which he prepared, while of sound mind and disposing memory, is clear and beyond any question of doubt, free from fraud or undue influence of any kind. The only objection raised is that the statutes were not strictly complied with in the execution of the Will. I am of the opinion, when a person dies leaving a written instrument which he intended to be his last Will, and it is free from fraud or undue influence and in harmony with the purpose of our law-makers for enacting statutes regulating the execution of Wills, . . . it would be a miscarriage of justice to not admit the Will to probate, and thereby allow the property to be disposed of contrary to the testator's intent.[46]

To hold otherwise would, in effect, permit a contrary disposition of testator's property against the purpose for which the statutory provisions were aimed.

HALLEY, C.J., dissenting. . . . Counsel for the proponents of the purported will have come up with the ingenious idea that this instrument which is partly in typewriting and partly in handwriting is valid and should be admitted to probate for the fantastic reason that the handwriting is a codicil to the typewriting. It is my position that the typewritten part is not a will and the handwritten part is not a codicil. The handwritten part is only a continuation of the typewritten part and, combined, they constitute a will which was not attested and therefore cannot properly be admitted to probate. . . .

[T]here was nothing in the handwriting which referred to a previous will. It spoke of "this will" and not of a previous will. There is nothing about this handwriting to indicate that the testator intended it to be a codicil. He was completing his will with the handwriting.

I think he intended the typewritten portion to be a part of his will, not the completed will. A will is to be interpreted by what is found in its "four corners" and there is nothing to indicate that the testator intended it to be anything but one instrument. Parol or extrinsic evidence should not be admitted to show the contrary when the signed will is one instrument.

Under no circumstances should this be considered a codicil and I can never subscribe to the proposition that a holographic codicil will validate as a will an instrument that is typewritten, unfinished as to content, undated, unsigned and unattested. Not a case has been cited where a holographic codicil validates an

46. Is Justice Corn's view in accord with a substantial compliance doctrine or the harmless error rule of UPC §2-503? — Eds.

instrument as a will which was not dated, signed or attested and no reference made in the purported codicil to the preceding will. . . . Something is attempted to be made of the fact that the testator was a lawyer but that would prove nothing as many eminent lawyers have failed to properly prepare and execute their own wills. The will of Samuel J. Tilden is a notable example.

This will was one complete will unattested and therefore not admissible to probate and to give this will the construction that the majority has placed upon it is wholly unwarranted. Why make a mockery of the plain provision of our statutes? Property may only descend by will when the will is executed in conformity with the statutes.

I dissent.

QUESTIONS AND NOTE

1.   The majority in *Johnson* determined that there were two wills written on the same page, and that the second will (a handwritten codicil) incorporated by reference the first will (the typed will). Looking at the picture of the wills and their language, do you agree? In the purported second will, is there a reference to the first will? The language "this will" refers to — well — *this* will, not a prior will on the same page. If the only reference to the typewritten portions is the phrase "this will," does not this undermine the court's premise that there were two wills?

2.   In Berry v. Trible, 626 S.E.2d 440 (Va. 2006), after the lawyer sent the testator a typed draft will, the testator made handwritten changes on it, signing each page at the bottom. On one page the testator wrote, "I Give and bequeath all," followed by an arrow pointing to her handwritten notation of the intended beneficiary. The court held that the instrument could not be probated as a holograph, because the handwriting and the typed text were interwoven, "both physically and in sequence of thought."

4.   *Acts of Independent Significance*

Now we turn to another doctrine permitting extrinsic evidence to identify the will beneficiaries or property passing under the will. If the beneficiary or property designations are identified by acts or events that have a lifetime motive and significance apart from their effect on the will, the gift will be upheld under the doctrine of *acts of independent significance* (also called the doctrine of *nontestamentary acts*). This is true even if the phrasing of the will leaves it in the testator's power to alter the beneficiaries or the property by a nontestamentary act.

Case 2 illustrates some common applications of the acts of independent significance doctrine.

> *Case 2.* *T*'s will devises "the automobile that I own at my death" to her nephew, *N*, and gives $1,000 "to each person who shall be in my employ at my death." At the time the will is executed, *T* owns an old Toyota. Shortly before her death, *T* trades in the Toyota for a new

Lexus, with the result that *T* dies owning a $40,000 automobile rather than one worth $14,000. In the year before her death, *T* fires two long-time employees and hires three new ones. The gifts are valid. While *T*'s act in buying the Lexus had the practical effect of increasing the value of her gift to *N*, it is unlikely that this is what motivated her purchase. It is more probable that she bought the car because she wanted to drive a Lexus. Similarly, *T*'s acts in hiring and firing various employees were likely prompted by business needs rather than by a desire to make or unmake legatees under the will. Indeed, cases involving this form of devise often assume the validity of the gift without discussion of the acts of independent significance doctrine.

Uniform Probate Code (1990)

§2-512. EVENTS OF INDEPENDENT SIGNIFICANCE

A will may dispose of property by reference to acts and events that have significance apart from their effect upon the dispositions made by the will, whether they occur before or after the execution of the will or before or after the testator's death. The execution or revocation of another individual's will is such an event.

PROBLEMS

1. *T* bequeaths "the contents of my house" to *A*. In *T*'s house are a variety of belongings, including furniture, jewelry, artwork, and clothing, as well as a safe containing stock certificates and cash. Does *A* take these items? See In re Estate of Light, 895 N.E.2d 43 (Ill. App. 2008); In re Estate of Isenberg, 823 N.Y.S.2d 381 (App. Div. 2006).

T bequeaths "the contents of the right-hand drawer of my desk" to *A*. In the drawer at *T*'s death are a savings bank passbook in *T*'s name, a certificate for 100 shares of General Electric common stock, and a diamond ring. Does *A* take these items?

T bequeaths "the contents of my safe deposit box in Security Bank" to *B* and "the contents of my safe deposit box in First National Bank" to *C*. Do *B* and *C* take the items found in the respective boxes? See Annot., 5 A.L.R.3d 466 (1966, rev. 2008).

T's will provides: "I have put in my safe deposit box in Continental Bank shares of stock in several envelopes. Each envelope has on it the name of the person I desire to receive the stock contained in the envelope." At *T*'s death, several envelopes are found in *T*'s safe deposit box with the name of a person written on the envelope. Inside each is a stock certificate. For example, in one envelope is a certificate for 200 shares of Coca-Cola stock and on the envelope is written "For Ruth Moreno." Do Ruth Moreno and the other persons take the stock in the envelopes bearing their names? See Will of Le Collen, 72 N.Y.S.2d 467 (Sur. 1947); Smith v. Weitzel, 338 S.W.2d 628 (Tenn. App. 1960).

2. In 2000, Sarah executes her will devising the residue of her estate to any charitable trust established by the last will and testament of her brother, Barney.

In 2001, Barney executes his will, devising his property to the Barney Educational Trust, a charitable trust established by his will. In 2008, Barney dies. In 2009, Sarah dies. Is the Barney Educational Trust entitled to the residue of Sarah's estate? See First Natl. Bank v. Klein, 234 So. 2d 42 (Ala. 1970); In re Will of Tipler, 10 S.W.3d 244 (Tenn. App. 1998). Suppose that Barney had survived Sarah. What result? See Restatement (Third) of Property: Wills and Other Donative Transfers §3.8, statutory note (1999).

SECTION D.   CONTRACTS RELATING TO WILLS

A person may enter into a contract *to make a will* or a contract *not to revoke a will*. Contract law, not the law of wills, applies. To enforce the contract, the third-party beneficiary must sue under the law of contracts and prove a valid contract.

If, after a contract becomes binding, a party dies leaving a will not complying with the contract, the will is probated but the contract beneficiary is entitled to a remedy for the broken contract. The court might impose a constructive trust on the estate or its beneficiaries, order specific performance, award damages, or grant various forms of injunctive or declaratory relief. Whatever the vocabulary, in the usual case the remedy takes the form of either the transfer of the promised property or the payment of the value of the property that was promised by the contract. See In re Estate of Graham, 690 N.W.2d 66 (Iowa 2004); Thomas E. Atkinson, The Law of Wills §48, at 218-219 (2d ed. 1953).

1.   Contracts to Make a Will

Questions respecting contracts to make a will may arise in a variety of situations, such as a promise to make a will in exchange for an agreement to marry, to serve as nurse and housekeeper, or not to contest a will. To ameliorate problems of proof, many states now subject contracts to make a will to a Statute of Frauds provision, thus requiring such contracts to be in writing in order to be enforceable. If the contract beneficiary is not entitled to enforce the contract because of noncompliance with the Statute of Frauds, the beneficiary may nonetheless be entitled to restitution of the value to the decedent of services rendered (quantum meruit). The trick is that the beneficiary must still prove the contract, a difficulty that captured headlines in the wake of the death of Brooke Astor, the doyenne of the New York social and philanthropic scene, when several former household employees claimed to have been promised posthumous largesse. See Ianthe Jeanne Dugan, As Battle Rages Over Astor Fortune, Crumbs for the Staff, Wall St. J., Jan. 12, 2008, at A1. In the context of a promise to make a will in return for services to be rendered, the value the decedent put on the services in the oral agreement ("I promise to leave you half of my estate") is evidence of the reasonable value of those services.

"... and to my faithful valet, Sidney, whom I promised to remember
in my will — 'Hi there, Sidney' — –!"

Copyright © 1966 by Playboy.
Reproduced by special permission of PLAYBOY magazine.

QUESTION AND PROBLEMS

1.   Does Sidney have an enforceable claim against his employer's estate?

2.   *T* makes a contract with *A* to leave everything to *A* at *T*'s death if *A* will take
care of *T* for life. *T* executes a will leaving her estate to *A*. Subsequently, *A* changes
her mind and decides not to care for *T*. *T* rescinds the contract. Upon *T*'s death,
is *A* entitled to take under *T*'s will? See Trotter v. Trotter, 490 So. 2d 827 (Miss.
1986).

3.   *A* dies of AIDS. After *A*'s death, *A*'s roommate, *B*, claims half of *A*'s estate.
B alleges that *A* promised to leave *B* half his estate if *B* cared for *A* for his life. *B*
produces a document typed by *B* and signed by *A* and one witness devising

one-half of his estate to *B*. The jurisdiction has enacted UPC §2-514, page 328, requiring that the contract be evidenced by a writing signed by the decedent. Is *B* entitled to one-half of *A*'s estate? See Estate of Fritz, 406 N.W.2d 475 (Mich. App. 1987).

4.   Suppose *W* promises her husband, *H*, that she will take care of him for his life in consideration of *H* devising her Blackacre. *H* then dies, devising Blackacre to *A*. Is the contract enforceable by *W*? Is consideration given by *W*? See Borelli v. Brusseau, 16 Cal. Rptr. 2d 16 (App. 1993) (unenforceable because no consideration; *W* had legal duty to care for *H*). Compare Byrne v. Laura, 60 Cal. Rptr. 2d 908 (App. 1997) (promise by man to his live-in lover gives rise to claim for quantum meruit), with In re Estate of Braaten, 96 P.3d 1125 (Mont. 2004) (stepson did not rebut presumption that personal services rendered to a decedent by a relative are gratuitous; quantum meruit claim denied). See also Joshua C. Tate, Caregiving and the Case for Testamentary Freedom, 42 U.C. Davis L. Rev. 129, 182-189 (2008) (criticizing the blunderbuss presumption that services rendered by a caregiving family member are gratuitous).

2.   *Contracts Not to Revoke a Will*

Questions respecting contracts not to revoke a will typically arise where a husband and a wife have executed a joint will or mutual wills. A *joint will* is one instrument executed by two persons as the will of both — one will for two people. When one testator dies, the instrument is probated as the testator's will; when the other testator dies, the instrument is again probated, this time as the other testator's will. A joint will is relatively uncommon; well-counseled testators do not use them. *Mutual wills*, on the other hand, are the separate wills of two or more persons that contain similar or reciprocal (mirror-image) provisions. Mutual or reciprocal wills are quite common because spouses often want to favor each other, followed by the same set of other beneficiaries. A *joint and mutual will* refers to a joint will in which the respective testators make similar or reciprocal provisions.[47] See Atkinson, supra, §49, at 222-224.

There are no legal consequences peculiar to joint or mutual wills unless they are executed pursuant to a contract between the testators not to revoke their wills. The initial problem is proof of the contract. Most courts hold that the mere execution of a joint or mutual will does not give rise to a presumption of contract. Collins v. Estate of Collins, 619 S.E.2d 531 (N.C. App. 2005). The difficulty, however, is that in the case of a joint will, the use of a jointly executed instrument may imply an understanding or agreement and thus invites a claim of contract, the terms of which can be inferred from the will. Some courts also find an implied contract in the existence of a common dispositive scheme in mutual (reciprocal) wills, an

---

47. Unfortunately, the term *joint and mutual will* is also occasionally — and confusingly — used by courts (and sometimes even legislatures) to describe a joint will that devises the property in accordance with a contract. See, e.g., Hodges v. Callaway, 621 S.E.2d 428, 431 (Ga. 2005).

implication that is usually without basis. Considerable litigation results. See Garrett v. Read, 102 P.3d 436 (Kan. 2004) (finding contractual wills on the basis of parol testimony by scrivener of will).

A line of cases developed in which the courts searched the language of the joint or mutual will for language of agreement, sometimes finding that the use of plural first-person pronouns such as *we* and *our* implied a contract not to revoke. See Glass v. Battista, 374 N.E.2d 116 (N.Y. 1978). The danger of a lawsuit can be reduced by inserting in every joint will a provision declaring that the will was or was not executed pursuant to a contract, but the lawyer who is astute enough to be aware of this problem doubtless also knows that joint wills are notorious litigation-breeders that should not be used at all. See Timothy P. O'Sullivan, Family Harmony: An All Too Frequent Casualty of the Estate Planning Process, 8 Marq. Elder's Advisor 253, 318-320 (2007) (warning that joint wills often lead to nasty family litigation).

To extricate the courts from this unhappy interpretive exercise, many states have enacted a Statute of Frauds provision, requiring that all contracts concerning wills be recorded in writing or referenced in the will. See Estate of Lubins, 656 N.Y.S.2d 851 (Sur. 1997) (lucid recounting of the prior case law and the history of the New York statute). UPC §2-514 (1990), excerpted below, is such a statute.

Unfortunately, statutes requiring written evidence of will contracts are not always effective. A string of California cases used the doctrine of equitable estoppel to enforce oral will contracts despite a statute requiring such contracts to be in writing. In 2000, the California legislature capitulated, revising the Probate Code to allow oral will contracts if they can be proved by clear and convincing evidence. See Cal. Prob. Code §21700 (2008); Philip H. Wile, Kathleen Cordova-Lyon, and Claude D. Rohwer, Estoppel to Avoid the California Statute of Frauds, 35 McGeorge L. Rev. 319 (2004); Mark J. Phillips, Accepting the Inevitable: California Statute Finally Embraces Oral Testamentary Contracts, 4 J. Legal Advoc. & Prac. 1 (2002).

Uniform Probate Code (1990)

§2-514. CONTRACTS CONCERNING SUCCESSION

A contract to make a will or devise, or not to revoke a will or devise, or to die intestate, if executed after the effective date of this Article, may be established only by (i) provisions of a will stating material provisions of the contract, (ii) an express reference in a will to a contract and extrinsic evidence proving the terms of the contract, or (iii) a writing signed by the decedent evidencing the contract. The execution of a joint will or mutual wills does not create a presumption of a contract not to revoke the will or wills.

A contract not to revoke a will is breached if, after the contract becomes binding, a party dies leaving a will that does not comply with the contract. In the usual case, this occurs because the testator affirmatively revoked the contractual will, typically by leaving a later will with different terms. But what about the case where the testator's contractual will is revoked by operation of law arising from a change in family circumstances?

Via v. Putnam
Supreme Court of Florida, 1995
656 So. 2d 460

OVERTON, J.   . . . This case involves a dispute between a decedent's surviving spouse, who claimed a share of the decedent's estate under the pretermitted spouse statute, and the children of the decedent's first marriage, who claimed that the mutual wills executed by their parents, naming them residuary beneficiaries of their parents' estates, gave rise to a creditor's contract claim that had priority against the surviving spouse's claim against the estate. The Second District Court of Appeal held that the surviving spouse's right to receive either an elective share or pretermitted spouse's share of the decedent's estate has priority over the claims of the decedent's children. . . .

For the reasons expressed in this opinion, we approve the decision of the district court and find that Florida has a strong public policy concerning the protection of the surviving spouse of the marriage in existence at the time of the decedent's death. This policy has been continuously expressed in the law of this state and is controlling. We agree with the district court's reasoning and conclude that the children, as third-party beneficiaries under the mutual wills of their parents, should not be given creditor status . . . when their interests contravene the interests of the surviving spouse under the pretermitted spouse statute.

The record reveals the following facts. On November 15, 1985, Edgar and Joann Putnam executed mutual wills, each of which contained the following provision:

> I acknowledge that this is a mutual will made at the same time as my [spouse's] Will and each of us have executed this Will with the understanding and agreement that the survivor will not change the manner in which the residuary estate is to be distributed and that neither of us as survivors will do anything to defeat the distribution schedule set forth herein, such as disposing of assets prior to death by way of trust bank accounts, trust agreements, or in any other manner.

Each will devised that spouse's entire estate to the survivor and provided that the residuary estate would go to the children upon the survivor's death. Joann Putnam died without having done anything to defeat the terms of her mutual will. Edgar Putnam later remarried and failed to execute a subsequent will to provide for his second wife, Mary Rachel Putnam (Rachel Putnam).

Upon Edgar Putnam's death, his mutual will was admitted to probate. Rachel Putnam filed both a Petition to Determine Share of Pretermitted Spouse and an Election to Take Elective Share. In response, the children filed claims against the estate alleging that, by marrying Rachel Putnam, Edgar had breached his contract not to defeat the distribution schedule set forth in his mutual will by subjecting his assets to the statutes governing homestead property, exempt property, pretermitted share, and family allowance. . . . The trial judge, during the course of these proceedings, made the following findings. First, he found that: (a) the mutual will provision previously quoted "constituted a binding contractual agreement," of which the children are third-party beneficiaries; (b) the children properly filed a claim against the estate based upon the decedent's breach of the mutual will; and (c) the surviving spouse, Rachel Putnam, is the pretermitted spouse of Edgar Putnam. Second, the trial judge entered a summary judgment expressly finding that "Edgar J. Putnam breached his joint and mutual will that he made with Joann Putnam when he married Rachel Putnam without taking appropriate steps to protect the interests of the third-party beneficiaries under said will" and that the claims of the children "are class 7 obligations pursuant to §733.707, Florida Probate Code." The trial judge concluded that "any pretermitted spouse share or elective share that Rachel Putnam may have is subject to the class 7 obligations of this estate."

On appeal, the district court reversed and noted that, if the children's residuary beneficiary status in the mutual wills allowed them to assert creditor status against the estate, the surviving spouse in this instance would "receive nothing except family allowance and any exempt property that may pass to her free from claims of creditors." *Putnam,* 638 So. 2d at 982. The district court's decision relied on the reasoning in Shimp v. Huff, 556 A.2d 252, 263 (Md. 1989), in which Maryland's highest court, on facts essentially identical to the facts in this case, found that the public policy surrounding the marriage relationship and the elective share statute required it to rule in favor of protecting the surviving spouse's right to receive an elective share. Likewise, the Second District Court of Appeal stated that "the statutes of Florida pertaining to a surviving spouse's elective share or pretermitted share in cases discussing those rights and their predecessor, dower, suggest a strong public policy in favor of protecting a surviving spouse's right to receive an elective share or a pretermitted share." *Putnam,* 638 So. 2d at 984. The district court recognized that its holding conflicts with the Third District Court's decision in Johnson v. Girtman, 542 So. 2d 1033 (Fla. App. 1989). . . .

[The elective share statute gives the surviving spouse the right to elect against the decedent's will and take a forced share of the decedent's net estate.] The statute reads as follows:

> The elective share shall consist of an amount equal to 30 percent of the fair market value, on the date of death, of all assets referred to in §732.206, computed after deducting from the total value of the assets:
> (1) All valid claims against the estate paid or payable from the estate; and
> (2) All mortgages, liens, or security interests on the assets.

Fla. Stat. §732.207 (1993). . . .

[T]he pretermitted spouse statute[, which gives an omitted spouse a share of the decedent's estate,] reads as follows:

> When a person marries after making a will and the spouse survives the testator, the surviving spouse shall receive a share in the estate of the testator equal in value to that which the surviving spouse would have received if the testator had died intestate,[48] unless:
>
> (1) Provision has been made for, or waived by, the spouse by prenuptial or postnuptial agreement;
> (2) The spouse is provided for in the will; or
> (3) The will discloses an intention not to make provision for the spouse.
>
> The share of the estate that is assigned to the pretermitted spouse shall be obtained in accordance with Fla. Stat. §733.805.

Fla. Stat. §732.301 (1993).

The children argue that they are third-party beneficiaries of the contract between the decedent and their mother and that they deserve creditor status under §733.707. As creditors, they would have priority over the share of the pretermitted spouse and would receive the entire estate. Under this scheme, the second wife would receive only a family allowance, the exempt property, and a life estate in the homestead. . . . [I]t is our view that the legislature did not intend . . . to allow creditors' claims by third-party beneficiaries of previously executed mutual wills to take priority over the statutory rights of a pretermitted spouse and deny the pretermitted spouse any share in the decedent's estate.

We acknowledge that other jurisdictions and the Third District Court of Appeal in *Johnson* take the view that a surviving spouse's statutory share of an estate can be subordinated to claims of third-party beneficiaries of previously executed mutual wills. See *Johnson;* see also Gregory v. Estate of Gregory, 866 S.W.2d 379 (Ark. 1993); In re Estate of Stewart, 444 P.2d 337 (Cal. 1968); Keats v. Cates, 241 N.E.2d 645 (Ill. App. 1968); Baker v. Syfritt, 125 N.W. 998 (Iowa 1910); Lewis v. Lewis, 178 P. 421 (Kan. 1919); Rubenstein v. Mueller, 225 N.E.2d 540 (N.Y. 1967); Robison v. Graham, 799 P.2d 610 (Okla. 1990). These courts have advanced four different rationales for giving priority to the contract beneficiaries: (1) The surviving spouse's marital rights attach only to property legally and equitably owned by the deceased spouse, and the will contract entered into before the marriage deprives the deceased spouse of equitable title and places it in the contract beneficiary. *Lewis.* (2) When the surviving testator accepts benefits under the contractual will, an equitable trust is impressed upon the property in favor of

---

48. Under Florida law at the time, the intestate share of a surviving spouse was one-half when the decedent leaves lineal descendants from a first marriage, as in this case. Therefore, the widow could elect against her husband's will and receive 30% of his estate, or, if his will were executed before their marriage, she could claim half his estate under the pretermitted spouse statute.

If the husband executed a will after marriage, leaving his wife 10%, 50%, all, or nothing of his estate, she would have no claim as a pretermitted spouse. She would be entitled only to a 30% share under the elective share statute. — Eds.

the contract beneficiaries, and the testator is entitled to only a life estate in the property with the remainder going to the beneficiaries upon the testator's death. *Rubenstein; Gregory; Keats; Baker; Robison.* (3) When the surviving testator accepts benefits under the contractual will, the testator becomes estopped from making a different disposition of the property, despite any subsequent marriage. *Stewart.* (4) Finally, as expressed in *Johnson*, when the surviving testator breaches the will contract, the contract beneficiaries are entitled to judgment creditor status, thus giving them priority over the rights of the surviving spouse under the applicable state probate code. It is this last theory that the trial judge adopted in ruling for the children in the instant case. Under these four theories, it makes no difference whether the surviving spouse was married to the decedent for one year or twenty-five years; the surviving spouse would be entitled to no interest in the deceased spouse's probatable estate if the third-party beneficiaries' claim consumed the estate.

The Court of Appeals of Maryland, that state's highest court, recently made a detailed analysis of this issue in an opinion by Chief Judge Murphy. See Shimp v. Huff, 556 A.2d 252 (Md. 1989). That court, after reviewing the theories identified above, found that

> the question of priorities between a surviving spouse and beneficiaries under a contract to make a will should be resolved based upon the public policy which surrounds the marriage relationship and which underlies the elective share statute. . . .
>
> In addition to the public policy underlying these statutes, the public policy surrounding the marriage relationship also suggests that the surviving spouse's claim to an elective share should be afforded priority over the claims of beneficiaries of a contract to make a will. Like the majority of other courts, we have recognized the well settled principle that contracts which discourage or restrain the right to marry are void as against public policy. 556 A.2d at 263. . . .

The *Shimp* court concluded that the contract that gave rise to the claim of the third-party beneficiaries included an implied limitation. It stated: "[W]e find that the respondent's rights under the contract were limited by the possibility that the survivor might remarry and that the subsequent spouse might elect against the will." *Shimp*, 556 A.2d at 263.

The district court of appeal in the instant case found the reasoning and analysis in *Shimp* to be persuasive. We agree. . . . We emphasize that the justification for the elective share and pretermitted spouse statutes is to protect the surviving spouse of the marriage in existence at the time of death of his or her spouse. The legislature has made these shares of a deceased spouse's estate a part of the marriage contract.

Florida's pretermitted spouse statute applies only "[w]hen a person marries after making a will and the spouse survives the testator." Fla. Stat. §732.301 (1993). The statute sets forth three specific circumstances when a pretermitted spouse would not be entitled to a share of the decedent's estate: (1) when "[p]rovision has been made for, or waived by, the spouse by prenuptial or postnuptial agreement"; (2) when "[t]he spouse is provided for in the will"; or (3) when "[t]he will discloses an intention not to make provision for the spouse." Id. The trial judge found that none of these exceptions applied and that the surviving spouse in this case was a pretermitted spouse under the statute. To hold as suggested by the children would essentially amend the statutory exceptions to the pretermitted spouse statute and add a fourth exception. The legislature enacted these exceptions based on the public policy of protecting the surviving spouse of the marriage contract in existence at the time of the decedent's death. The legislature has clearly taken into account when this provision should apply and when it should not apply. We conclude that we have no authority to judicially modify the public policy protecting a surviving spouse's interest in the deceased spouse's estate by adopting this creditor-theory approach as an exception to the pretermitted spouse statute.

Accordingly, we approve the decision of the district court of appeal in this case and disapprove the decision of the Third District Court of Appeal in *Johnson* to the extent that it conflicts with this opinion. It is so ordered.

NOTES AND PROBLEMS

1.   On will contracts and their intersection with spousal rights to inheritance, see Carolyn L. Dessin, The Troubled Relationship of Will Contracts and Spousal Protection: Time for an Amicable Separation, 45 Cath. U. L. Rev. 435 (1996). See also Adam J. Hirsch, Cognitive Jurisprudence, 76 S. Cal. L. Rev. 1331, 1352-1358 (2003) (criticizing Via v. Putnam).

2.   Tricky questions of interpretation arise under contracts between spouses not to revoke their wills. Suppose that the majority rule (that the third party beneficiaries prevail over the second wife) is applicable. After Joann Putnam's death, what were Edgar's rights in the property during his lifetime? Would he have been restricted in what he could do with his own property and the property received from Joann? See In re Estate of Erickson, 841 N.E.2d 1104 (Ill. App. 2006) (beneficiaries of joint will with contract not to revoke could recover lifetime transfers of real estate that depleted the probate estate); Robison v. Graham, 799 P.2d 610 (Okla. 1990) (constructive trust imposed for beneficiaries of a contractual mutual will where the "survivor transferred most of estate into joint tenancy with new wife"); Schwartz v. Horn, 290 N.E.2d 816 (N.Y. 1972) (inter vivos gifts permitted provided that they are not inconsistent with the contract or defeat its purpose). Suppose that Edgar had thought that a round-the-world cruise would be the perfect wedding present for his new bride. Would that have been permitted? Suppose he wanted to buy Rachel an emerald bracelet from Tiffany's. Would that have been okay? Do you see the practical problem?

Does the contract in *Putnam* apply only to Edgar's property owned at Joann's death and to property inherited from her, or does it also cover property acquired by Edgar thereafter? Suppose that Edgar had inherited property from his brother after Joann died or that he won the lottery a year after Joann died. Would the contract apply to the new property? See Estate of Maloney v. Carsten, 381 N.E.2d 1263 (Ind. App. 1978).

3. *H* and *W* are doing their estate planning. They want the surviving spouse to have "everything" and "be comfortable," and they want all their property divided equally among their children (all of whom are from prior marriages) upon the death of the surviving spouse. But, knowing that the survivor will have closer ties to his or her own children, they feel uncomfortable leaving the disposition entirely in the survivor's hands. This is the basic dilemma suggested by many contractual wills. When you study trusts later in this book, you will find that *H* and *W*'s desires can be effectuated with fewer problems by creating a trust rather than by using contractual wills.

5

CONSTRUCTION OF WILLS

In speaking of the Sergeant of the Lawe, Chaucer, himself trained as a clerk in the Inns of Court, wrote:

> Therto he koude endite and make a thyng,
> Ther koude no wight pynche at his writyng.[1]

Most of the cases in this chapter — and in many of the following chapters, too — raise issues that should have been avoided by appropriate drafting. One of the objectives of this book is to help you acquire the ability of Chaucer's Sergeant of the Lawe so that no one can fault your drafting.

The goal in construing wills is to give effect to the testator's intent. In the words of Restatement (Third) of Property: Wills and Other Donative Transfers §10.1 (2003): "The controlling consideration in determining the meaning of a donative document is the donor's intention. The donor's intention is given effect to the maximum extent allowed by law." As we shall see, however, this is easier said than done.

SECTION A. MISTAKEN OR AMBIGUOUS LANGUAGE IN WILLS

1. The Traditional Approach: No Extrinsic Evidence, No Reformation

In construing wills, a majority of jurisdictions still follow (or purport to follow) two traditional rules that, operating in tandem, bar the admission of evidence to

---

1. Geoffrey Chaucer, Prologue to Canterbury Tales (line 325). Translated into modern English by Frank E. Hill, The Canterbury Tales 9 (1946):

> And he could write, and pen a deed in law
> So in his writing none could pick a flaw.

vary the terms of the will. The first is called the *plain meaning* or *no extrinsic evidence* rule. Under this rule, extrinsic evidence may be admitted to resolve some ambiguities, but the plain meaning of the words of the will cannot be disturbed by evidence that another meaning was intended.

The closely related second rule is the *no reformation* rule. Reformation is an equitable remedy that, if applied to a will, would correct a mistaken term in the will to reflect what the testator intended the will to say. The justification for refusing to reform wills is that the court is thereby compelled to interpret the words that the testator actually used, not to interpret the words that the testator is purported to have intended to use. Thus, in 1922 the Supreme Judicial Court of Massachusetts said:

> Courts have no power to reform wills. Hypothetical or imaginary mistakes of testators cannot be corrected. Omissions cannot be supplied. Language cannot be modified to meet unforeseen changes in conditions. The only means for ascertaining the intent of the testator are the words written and the acts done by him. [Sanderson v. Norcross, 136 N.E. 170, 172 (Mass. 1922).]

Mahoney v. Grainger
Supreme Judicial Court of Massachusetts, 1933
186 N.E. 86

RUGG, C.J.   This is an appeal from a decree of a probate court denying a petition for distribution of a legacy under the will of Helen A. Sullivan among her first cousins who are contended to be her heirs at law. The residuary clause was as follows: "All the rest and residue of my estate, both real and personal property, I give, devise and bequeath to my heirs at law living at the time of my decease, absolutely; to be divided among them equally, share and share alike. . . ."

The trial judge made a report of the material facts in substance as follows: The sole heir at law of the testatrix at the time of her death was her maternal aunt, Frances Hawkes Greene, who is still living and who was named in the petition for probate of her will. The will was duly proved and allowed on October 8, 1931, and letters testamentary issued accordingly. The testatrix was a single woman about sixty-four years of age, and had been a school teacher. She always maintained her own home but her relations with her aunt who was her sole heir and with several first cousins were cordial and friendly. In her will she gave general legacies in considerable sums to two of her first cousins. About ten days before her death the testatrix sent for an attorney who found her sick but intelligent about the subjects of their conversation. She told the attorney she wanted to make a will. She gave him instructions as to general pecuniary legacies. In response to the questions "Whom do you want to leave the rest of your property to? Who are your nearest relations?" she replied "I've got about twenty-five first cousins . . . let them share it equally." The attorney then drafted the will and read it to the testatrix and it was executed by her.

The trial judge ruled that statements of the testatrix "were admissible only in so far as they tended to give evidence of the material circumstances surrounding the testatrix at the time of the execution of the will; that the words heirs at law were words in common use, susceptible of application to one or many; that when applied to the special circumstances of this case that the testatrix had but one heir, notwithstanding the added words 'to be divided among them equally, share and share alike,' there was no latent ambiguity or equivocation in the will itself which would permit the introduction of the statements of the testatrix to prove her testamentary intention." Certain first cousins have appealed from the decree dismissing the petition for distribution to them.

There is no doubt as to the meaning of the words "heirs at law living at the time of my decease" as used in the will. Confessedly they refer alone to the aunt of the testatrix and do not include her cousins.

A will duly executed and allowed by the court must under the statute of wills (G.L. [Ter. Ed.] c. 191, §1 et seq.) be accepted as the final expression of the intent of the person executing it. The fact that it was not in conformity to the instructions given to the draftsman who prepared it or that he made a mistake does not authorize a court to reform or alter it or remould it by amendments. The will must be construed as it came from the hands of the testatrix. Polsey v. Newton, 85 N.E. 574 (Mass. 1908). Mistakes in the drafting of the will may be of significance in some circumstances in a trial as to the due execution and allowance of the alleged testamentary instrument. Richardson v. Richards, 115 N.E. 307 (Mass. 1917). Proof that the legatee actually designated was not the particular person intended by the one executing the will cannot be received to aid in the interpretation of a will. Tucker v. Seaman's Aid Society, 7 Metc. 188, 210 (Mass. 1843). When the instrument has been proved and allowed as a will oral testimony as to the meaning and purpose of a testator in using language must be rigidly excluded. Saucier v. Saucier, 152 N.E. 95 (Mass. 1926).

It is only where testamentary language is not clear in its application to facts that evidence may be introduced as to the circumstances under which the testator used that language in order to throw light upon its meaning. Where no doubt exists as to the property bequeathed or the identity of the beneficiary there is no room for extrinsic evidence; the will must stand as written. Barker v. Comins, 110 Mass. 477 (1872); Best v. Berry, 75 N.E. 743 (Mass. 1905).

In the case at bar there is no doubt as to the heirs at law of the testatrix. The aunt alone falls within that description. The cousins are excluded. The circumstance that the plural word "heirs" was used does not prevent one individual from taking the entire gift. Calder v. Bryant, 184 N.E. 440 (Mass. 1933).

Decree affirmed.[2]

2. Chief Justice Rugg was not a man plagued by doubts about the law, nor was he much interested in equal rights for women. In Commonwealth v. Welosky, 177 N.E. 656 (Mass. 1931), the question was whether, after women acquired the right to vote by the Nineteenth Amendment, women could serve on juries, a right conferred on "a person qualified to vote" by a Massachusetts statute enacted prior to the Nineteenth Amendment. In denying women this right, Rugg, C.J., reasoned, "The change in the legal status of women wrought by the Nineteenth Amendment was radical, drastic and unprecedented. While it is to be given full effect in its field, it is not to be extended by implication. It is unthinkable that those who first framed and selected the words for the

NOTES AND QUESTIONS

1. In Gustafson v. Svenson, 366 N.E.2d 761 (Mass. 1977), the testator devised property to Enoch Anderson or "his heirs per stirpes." Enoch predeceased the testator, leaving a wife but no descendants. Under Massachusetts law, Enoch's widow was his heir. The court held that testimony of the drafting attorney that the testator did not intend Enoch's devise to go to his widow was inadmissible since the court was of the opinion that the phrase "heirs per stirpes" was not ambiguous. Hence Enoch's widow took the devise. In 2000, the Massachusetts court went further and explicitly rejected reformation of wills other than to obtain tax advantages. Flannery v. McNamara, 738 N.E.2d 739 (Mass. 2000).

2. In Estate of Smith, 555 N.E.2d 1111 (Ill. App. 1990), the testator left a bequest to "PERRY MANOR, INC., Pinckneyville, Illinois." At the time the will was executed, Perry Manor, Inc., a Nevada corporation, operated a nursing home called Perry Manor in Pinckneyville. Before the testator died, Perry Manor, Inc., sold the nursing home to Lifecare Center of Pinckneyville, Inc. Lifecare continued to operate the nursing home and continued to call it Perry Manor. Which company do you think should get the bequest? The court held the bequest went to the Nevada corporation, which alone fit exactly the literal description of the legatee: "PERRY MANOR, INC." The words, "Pinckneyville, Illinois," which were not capitalized, merely described the location of the named legatee at the time of execution. Hence there was no ambiguity, and extrinsic evidence of the testator's intent was inadmissible. To consider such evidence, the court said, "would have the same effect as rewriting the will."

Suppose that the legatee had been described as "PERRY MANOR," without the "INC." What result? In Estate of Scale, 830 N.Y.S.2d 618 (App. Div. 2007), the testator left 10 percent of his residuary estate to "The Audubon Society of New York State." Both the National Audubon Society, which was founded in 1905 and operated in New York as Audubon New York, and the Audubon Society of New York State, Inc., which was founded in 1987 and operated under the name Audubon International, claimed the bequest. The trial court, finding a latent ambiguity in the will (see the Note on ambiguity below), awarded the bequest to the national organization based on extrinsic evidence in the form of "an affidavit of the will drafter stating that, although the testator had 'quickly, without reservation' stated upon inquiry that he intended to benefit the state organization, the testator was confused and actually intended to benefit the national organization."

On appeal, the court reversed and awarded the bequest to the New York organization. In the appellate court's view, "the testator's failure to include 'Inc.' in naming his beneficiary does not render the will ambiguous," hence the trial court

---

statute [stating qualifications for jury service] had any design that it should ever include women within its scope." Massachusetts did not change its statute, permitting women to serve as jurors, until 1949. Harvard Law School followed suit and admitted women as students in 1950.

Is Chief Justice Rugg's application of the plain meaning rule to wills consistent with his interpretation of statutes? — Eds.

should not have admitted extrinsic evidence. "[I]f courts should permit the substitution of the draft[er's] recollection of what the testator told him . . . for the language of the will itself, the instrument would cease to be the repository of the decedent's testamentary program." The court concluded: "In short, as the will unambiguously dictates, the legacy must be paid to the state organization expressly named therein." Was the will unambiguous? Would you credit the testimony of the lawyer?

The *Smith* and *Scale* cases are reminiscent of Natl. Socy. for the Prevention of Cruelty to Children v. Scottish Natl. Socy. for the Prevention of Cruelty to Children, [1915] A.C. 207. In this case, a Scotsman, who had always lived in Scotland and was interested in Scottish charities, leaving a number of bequests to them by will, bequeathed £500 to "The National Society for the Prevention of Cruelty to Children," which was the charter name of a society in London, of which the testator had never heard. Near his home was a branch office of the *Scottish* National Society for the Prevention of Cruelty to Children, whose activities he knew. Which charity should get the £500? The House of Lords held the remote charity in London should get the money because "he had by name designated it." For criticism of this case, in a classic article on the meaning of words, see Zechariah Chaffee, Jr., The Disorderly Conduct of Words, 41 Colum. L. Rev. 381, 385 (1941).

3. The plain meaning or no extrinsic evidence rule has been criticized as fundamentally misdirected.[3] Professor Wigmore, the great authority on evidence, vigorously attacked the rule, saying, "The fallacy consists in assuming that there is or ever can be *some one real* or absolute meaning. In truth there can be only *some person's* meaning: and that person, whose meaning the law is seeking, is the writer of the document. . . . [T]he 'plain meaning' is simply the meaning of the people who did *not* write the document." 9 John H. Wigmore, Evidence §2462, at 198 (James H. Chadbourn rev. 1981) (emphasis in original).

In a similar vein, Professor Thayer argued that the plain meaning rule reflects a dream, a hope, of

> that lawyer's Paradise, where all words have a fixed, precisely ascertained meaning, and where, if the writer has been careful, a lawyer having a document referred to him may sit in his chair, inspect the text, and answer all questions without raising his eyes. . . . But the fatal necessity of looking outside the text in order to identify persons and things, tends steadily to destroy such illusions and to reveal the essential imperfection of language, whether spoken or written. [James B. Thayer, A Preliminary Treatise on Evidence 428 (1898).]

For further discussion, see Kent Greenawalt, A Pluralist Approach to Interpretation: Wills and Contracts, 42 San Diego L. Rev. 533 (2005); Richard F. Storrow, Judicial Discretion and the Disappearing Distinction Between Will Interpretation and Construction, 56 Case W. Res. L. Rev. 65 (2005); Jane B. Baron, Intention, Interpretation, and Stories, 42 Duke L.J. 630 (1992); Mary L. Fellows, In Search of Donative Intent, 73 Iowa L. Rev. 611 (1988).

---

3. Another view of the plain meaning rule was expressed by A.P. Herbert's Lord Mildew: "If Parliament does not mean what it says it must say so." A.P. Herbert, Uncommon Law 313 (2d ed. 1936).

NOTE: PLAIN MEANING, AMBIGUITY, AND EXTRINSIC EVIDENCE

Under the plain meaning rule the words of the will cannot be disturbed by evidence that another meaning was intended, but in some cases extrinsic evidence may be admitted if the words of the will are ambiguous or lack a plain meaning.

Patent ambiguities. A patent ambiguity appears on the face of the will. In Succession of Neff, 716 So. 2d 410 (La. App. 1998), one clause in *T*'s will left the "disposable portion of my estate" to *T*'s daughter *A*, while the very next clause left "my entire estate" to *T*'s daughters *A* and *B*. Under traditional law, extrinsic evidence is not admissible to clarify a patent ambiguity, and the court is confined to the four corners of the will, even if as a result the will or devise fails and the property passes by intestacy. See In re Estate of Mousel, 715 N.W.2d 490 (Neb. 2006); McBride v. Sumrow, 181 S.W.3d 666 (Tenn. App. 2005). Increasingly, however, as in *Neff*, extrinsic evidence is allowed to aid in interpreting a patent ambiguity. See Andrea W. Cornelison, Dead Man Talking: Are Courts Ready to Listen? The Erosion of the Plain Meaning Rule, 35 Real Prop., Prob. & Tr. J. 811, 819-820 (2001).

Latent ambiguities. A latent ambiguity manifests itself only when the terms of the will are applied to the testator's property or designated beneficiaries. "Generally, there are two types of latent ambiguity. The first type occurs when a will clearly describes a person or thing, and two or more persons or things exactly fit that description. The second type of latent ambiguity exists when no person or thing exactly fits the description, but two or more persons or things partially fit." Phipps v. Barbera, 498 N.E.2d 411, 412 n.3 (Mass. App. 1986). Oral declarations of intent to the scrivener are admitted in most jurisdictions in cases of latent ambiguity.

The first type of latent ambiguity, when two or more persons or things fit the description in the will (e.g., a devise "to my niece Alicia," when in fact the testator has two nieces named Alicia), is called *equivocation*. Admission of extrinsic evidence first began in such cases. The courts reasoned that the extrinsic evidence merely made the terms of the will more specific without actually adding to the will's terms, which would be forbidden. See Succession of Bacot, 502 So. 2d 1118 (La. App. 1987) (will left "all to Danny"; court chose one of three homosexual lovers — all named Danny — who, extrinsic evidence showed, had the closest relationship to testator). Where there is an equivocation, direct expressions of the testator's intent are admissible in evidence.

An amusing line of equivocation cases gave rise to the *personal usage exception*. If the extrinsic evidence shows that the testator always referred to a person in an idiosyncratic manner, the evidence is admissible to show that the testator meant someone other than the person with the legal name of the legatee. Thus, in Moseley v. Goodman, 195 S.W. 590 (Tenn. 1917), the testator, in a list of bequests, left $20,000 to "Mrs. Moseley." Mrs. Lenore Moseley, the wife of the cigar store owner where the testator traded, but whom the testator had never met, claimed the bequest. The court, however, held that the bequest went to Mrs. Lillian Trimble, whom the testator called "Mrs. Moseley." Trimble's husband was a salesman in Moseley's cigar store and was called "Moseley" by the testator; his wife — dubbed

"Mrs. Moseley" by the testator — managed the apartment house where the testator lived and did kind things for him.

The second type of latent ambiguity, where the description in the will does not exactly fit any person or thing, is more common. In Ihl v. Oetting, 682 S.W.2d 865 (Mo. App. 1984), the testator devised his home to "Mr. and Mrs. Wendell Richard Hess, or the survivor of them, presently residing at No. 17 Barbara Circle." When the will was executed in 1979, Wendell Hess and his wife Glenda resided at No. 17 Barbara Circle. Soon thereafter Wendell divorced Glenda, they sold No. 17 Barbara Circle, and Wendell married Verna.

At the testator's death in 1983, Verna, relying on the rule that a will speaks as of the testator's death, claimed the "Mrs. Hess" share of the devise. She argued that no extrinsic evidence should be admitted since there was no ambiguity in the will — she alone met the description of "Mrs. Wendell Richard Hess." The court, however, found that a latent ambiguity arose from the description of the beneficiaries as "residing at No. 17 Barbara Circle." Verna Hess met the description of Mrs. Wendell Richard Hess at the time of the testator's death, but she never resided at No. 17 Barbara Circle. Glenda met the description of the Mrs. Hess residing at No. 17 Barbara Circle when the will was executed, but she no longer met that description at the time of the testator's death. The court admitted extrinsic evidence that showed an intent that the devise go to the earlier Mrs. Hess, Glenda, who shared a common interest in antiques with the testator.

Collapsing the patent/latent distinction. Determining whether an ambiguity is patent or latent is often a subjective undertaking. In Estate of Black, 27 Cal. Rptr. 418 (App. 1962), the testator, a resident of northern California, left her estate "to the University of Southern California known as The U.C.L.A." The trial court ruled there was no ambiguity and construed the gift to be "to the university in Southern California known as The U.C.L.A." The appellate court reversed, holding the devise to be ambiguous. However, the ambiguity was deemed latent, not patent, so extrinsic evidence could be admitted to resolve it.

> The provision in question is not, on its face, susceptible to one of two constructions. The language is clear, intelligible and suggests a single meaning. A reader unacquainted with the fact that there are two universities in Southern California, one known as the University of Southern California, and another commonly referred to by the initials U.C.L.A., would readily attribute to said provision the meaning that it refers to an institution named "University of Southern California," which is known by the initials U.C.L.A. [Id. at 424.]

Suppose the devise had been "to New York Law School known as N.Y.U." Patent or latent ambiguity?

As the courts have become increasingly amenable to the admission of extrinsic evidence in both patent and latent ambiguity cases, the relevance of the distinction has begun to fade. Some courts have expressly jettisoned the distinction, authorizing recourse to extrinsic evidence in all cases of ambiguity without regard to whether the ambiguity is patent or latent. See Univ. of So. Indiana v. Baker, 843 N.E.2d 528 (Ind. 2006); In re Lock Revocable Living Trust, 123 P.3d 1241

(Hawaii 2005). See also Restatement (Third) of Property: Wills and Other Donative Transfers §11.2, cmt. d (2003): "Once an ambiguity, patent or latent, is established, direct as well as circumstantial evidence of the donor's intention may be
considered in resolving the ambiguity in accordance with the donor's intention."

2.   Slouching Toward Reformation: Correcting Mistakes Without the Power to Reform Wills

The traditional refusal to reform wills rests on the premise that mischief will
ensue if the courts are allowed to reject the seemingly clear words of the will. But
how then do we explain the doctrines of undue influence, testamentary capacity
(including insane delusions), duress, and fraud? In a case involving any of these
doctrines, the court looks at evidence of the circumstances surrounding the will's
execution in order to ascertain whether the will reflects the true wishes of the testator. On this view, the rule against reformation — that is, the rule against correcting an innocent mistake in the terms of a will — is at odds with routine practice in
other areas of the law of wills.

If intentional wrongdoing causes a mistaken term in a will (*fraud*), that term can
be struck or its effect undone. If a lack of volition has an innocent cause (*lack of
capacity*), the will is not given effect. And if a bizarre mistaken belief about a member of the testator's family influences the testator's dispositive scheme, the courts
remedy this mistake by calling it an *insane delusion*. Yet if a mistaken term has an
innocent cause (*mistake*), then no relief is available to correct the error under the
rule against reformation.

The Causes and Effects of Will Defects

	Effect: Lack of Volition	Effect: Mistaken Terms
Cause: Intentional Wrongdoing	**Undue Influence, Duress** (relief granted)	**Fraud** (relief granted)
Cause: Innocent Acts	**Lack of Capacity, Insane Delusion** (relief granted)	**Mistake** (no relief)

The rule against reformation is an even greater outlier than this chart implies.
Under traditional law, courts remedy mistaken revocation of wills under the doctrine of dependent relative revocation (see page 295). If a testator fails to provide
for a living child solely because he mistakenly believes the child to be dead,

under Uniform Probate Code §2-302(c) (1990), page 531, the child receives an intestate share in the testator's estate. And if a testator forgets to update his will after a major life event, such as a divorce or the birth of a child, statutes in many states partially or completely revoke the testator's will automatically (see pages 305, 527).

In this light, consider again the rules on patent and latent ambiguity. In such cases, under the guise of resolving the ambiguity, do not the courts in effect correct mistakes by reference to extrinsic evidence? In Moseley v. Goodman, supra, the court read "Mrs. Moseley" to mean "Mrs. Trimble." Is this not a reformation of a mistake — a correction of the instrument to reflect what the testator *meant* to say?

A careful review of the cases reveals an unmistakable trend toward admitting extrinsic evidence not merely to resolve latent and, more recently, patent ambiguities, but also to correct mistaken terms to conform the will to the actual intent of the testator.

Arnheiter v. Arnheiter
Superior Court of New Jersey, Chancery Division, 1956
125 A.2d 914

SULLIVAN, J.   Burnette K. Guterl died on December 31, 1953, leaving a last will and testament which has been admitted to probate by the Surrogate of Essex County. By paragraph 2 of said will her executrix was directed "to sell my undivided one-half interest of premises known as No. 304 Harrison Avenue, Harrison, New Jersey," and use the proceeds of sale to establish trusts for each of decedent's two nieces.

This suit comes about because the decedent did not own or have any interest in 304 Harrison Avenue either at her death or at the time her will was executed. At the hearing it was established that the decedent, at the time her will was executed and also at the time of her death, owned an undivided one-half interest in 317 Harrison Avenue, Harrison, New Jersey, and that this was the only property on Harrison Avenue that she had any interest in.

Plaintiff-executrix has applied to this court to correct an obvious mistake and to change the street number in paragraph "2" of the will to read "No. 317 Harrison Avenue" instead of "No. 304 Harrison Avenue." Relief cannot be granted to the plaintiff in the precise manner sought. It matters not that an obvious mistake in the form of a misdescription is proved. A court has no power to correct or reform a will or change any of the language therein by substituting or adding words. The will of a decedent executed pursuant to statute is what it is and no court can add to it.

Plaintiff, however, is not without recourse. In the construction of wills and other instruments there is a principle "*falsa demonstratio non nocet*" (mere erroneous description does not vitiate), which applies directly to the difficulty at hand.

> Where a description of a thing or person consists of several particulars and all of them do not fit any one person or thing, less essential particulars may be rejected provided the remainder

of the description clearly fits. This is known as the doctrine of *falsa demonstratio non nocet*. Clapp, 5 N.J. Practice, §114, at 274. . . .

Turning to the problem at hand and to the description of the property as set forth in paragraph 2 of the will, we find the street number "304" to be erroneous because decedent did not own that property. If we disregard or reject that item of description, the will then directs the executrix "to sell my undivided one-half interest of premises known as Harrison Avenue, Harrison, New Jersey." Since it has been established that the decedent, at the time of her death and also when she executed her will, had an interest in only one piece of property on Harrison Avenue, Harrison, New Jersey; that her interest was an undivided one-half interest; that the property in question is 317 Harrison Avenue; and that decedent made no other specific provision in her will relating to 317 Harrison Avenue, we are led inevitably to the conclusion that even without a street number, the rest of the description in paragraph 2 of the will is sufficient to identify the property passing thereunder as 317 Harrison Avenue.

Judgment will be entered construing decedent's will as aforesaid.

QUESTIONS

What is the difference between reformation and the principle that "mere erroneous description does not vitiate"? Do not both doctrines give testamentary effect to extrinsic evidence of what the testator *meant* to say instead of what the testator *actually* said?

ESTATE OF GIBBS, 111 N.W.2d 413 (Wis. 1961): George and Lena Adele Gibbs both died in 1960. In their respective wills, they each made the following bequest:

> To Robert J. Krause, now of 4708 North 46th Street, Milwaukee, Wisconsin, if he survives me, one per cent (1%).

The Robert *J.* Krause who lived at 4708 North 46th Street in Milwaukee was quite happy to claim part of George and Lena's estates, but neither George nor Lena knew him. Their friend for three decades was Robert *W.* Krause, who lived at a different address. After the cases were consolidated, the trial court awarded both bequests to Robert *W.* Krause.

On appeal, the Wisconsin Supreme Court acknowledged the traditional rule against reformation. "It is traditional doctrine that wills must not be reformed even in the case of demonstrable mistake." The court also observed that, "Under rules as to construction of a will, unless there is ambiguity in the text of the will read in the light of surrounding circumstances, extrinsic evidence is inadmissible for the purpose of determining intent." In this case, "The terms of the bequest exactly fit appellant [Robert *J.* Krause] and no one else. There is no ambiguity."

Despite disavowing the power of reformation, and finding no ambiguity that would have justified recourse to extrinsic evidence, the court nonetheless corrected the mistake:

> Although the courts subscribe to an inflexible rule against reformation of a will, it seems that they have often strained a point in matters of identification of property or beneficiaries in order to reach a desired result by way of construction. . . .
>
> We conclude that details of identification, particularly such matters as middle initials, street addresses, and the like, which are highly susceptible to mistake, particularly in metropolitan areas, should not be accorded such sanctity as to frustrate an otherwise clearly demonstrable intent. Where such details of identification are involved, courts should receive evidence tending to show that a mistake has been made and should disregard the details when the proof establishes to the highest degree of certainty that a mistake was, in fact, made.
>
> We therefore consider that the county court properly disregarded the middle initial and street address, and determined that respondent was the Robert Krause whom testators had in mind.
>
> Orders affirmed.

QUESTION

Does the question of who takes the property under a will raise a mere detail of identification?

3.   Openly Reforming Wills for Mistake

Erickson v. Erickson
Supreme Court of Connecticut, 1998
716 A.2d 92

BORDEN, J.   The [first] issue in this appeal is whether, pursuant to General Statutes (Rev. to 1995) §45a-257(a), the trial court should have admitted extrinsic evidence regarding the decedent's intent that his will would not be revoked automatically by his subsequent marriage.[4] The named plaintiff, Alicia Erickson,[5] who is the daughter of the decedent, Ronald K. Erickson, appeals from the judgment of the trial court in favor of the defendant, Dorothy Erickson,[6] the executrix of the estate of the decedent, dismissing the plaintiff's appeal from the decree of the Probate Court for the district of Madison. The Probate Court had admitted the will of the decedent to probate. The trial court ruled that the decedent's will, which had been executed shortly before his marriage to the defendant, provided for the contingency of marriage. . . .

---

4. General Statutes (Rev. to 1995) §45a-257(a) provides: "If, after the making of a will, the testator marries . . . and no provision has been made in such will for such contingency, such marriage . . . shall operate as a revocation of such will." . . . [In 1996, §45a-257(a) was amended in line with the modern trend to give a surviving spouse who is omitted from a premarital will an intestate share, unless the omission was intentional, instead of revoking the will entirely. See page 515. — Eds.]

5. The decedent's other two daughters, Laura Erickson Kusy and Ellen Erickson Cates, did not appeal from the judgment of the trial court. Hereafter, we refer to Alicia Erickson as the plaintiff.

6. The defendant's name before her marriage to the decedent was Dorothy A. Mehring.

Certain facts in this appeal are undisputed. On September 1, 1988, the decedent executed a will. At that time, he had three daughters and was unmarried. Two days later, on September 3, 1988, he married the defendant. He died on February 22, 1996.

The six articles of his will provide as follows. The first article provides for the payment of funeral expenses and debts by the estate. The second article states that the residue of the estate will pass to the defendant. The third article provides that if the defendant predeceases the decedent, one half of the residuary estate will pass in equal parts to the decedent's three daughters, Laura Erickson Kusy, Ellen Erickson Cates and Alicia Erickson, and one half of the residuary estate will pass in equal parts to Thomas Mehring, Christopher Mehring, Maureen Mehring and Kathleen Mehring, the children of the defendant. The fourth article appoints the defendant as the executrix of the will, with Attorney Robert O'Brien as the contingent executor in the event that the defendant is unable to or refuses to serve as executrix. The fifth article gives the executrix or executor the power to dispose of property of the estate as necessary. The sixth article appoints the defendant as the guardian of any of the decedent's children who have not reached the age of eighteen at the time of his death.

The Probate Court admitted the decedent's will to probate. The plaintiff appealed from the Probate Court's judgment. Prior to trial, the plaintiff filed a motion in limine to exclude extrinsic evidence of the decedent's intent. The plaintiff argued that "§45a-257 makes the Court's inquiry very simple: to determine whether the will was revoked, the Court need examine only [the decedent's] will, his marriage certificate to [the defendant], and his death certificate. Extrinsic evidence regarding [the decedent's] intentions is inadmissible because the language of [the decedent's] will is unambiguous, and therefore under . . . §45a-257 the operation of the marriage to revoke the will is automatic and mandatory." The defendant, in opposition to the plaintiff's motion, made a detailed offer of proof to show the contrary intent of the decedent.[7] . . .

___

7. The defendant's offer of proof provided in part: "May it please the court, if [O'Brien and the defendant] were permitted to testify they would testify as follows. [O'Brien] would testify that he is an attorney before the Hartford [bar], that he was for many years prior to the marriage in 1988 the attorney for [the decedent].

"In addition to being his attorney on a variety of business and personal matters, he was also a close friend of [the decedent]. He was aware that [the decedent] was courting [the defendant] who became [his wife] and he was invited to their wedding which was scheduled for September 3, 1988.

"About one week prior to that time he received a call from [the decedent] saying he and [the defendant] immediately after the wedding were going to go to New York and then take a Concorde flight to Ireland and they wanted to arrange, as many of us do prior to events like that, for their wills to be drafted prior to the marriage ceremony.

"[The decedent] gave [O'Brien] instructions that the wills would be identical, that is, that all of his estate was to go to [the defendant]. If [the defendant] should predecease him it should go to, half should go to his children, half to [the defendant's] children. That [the defendant] should be the executrix of the will and that she would be appointed guardian of his children, and that [her] will be exactly the same.

"On Thursday, September 1, two days before the wedding, the two of them went to Hartford and executed the wills. I would offer [the defendant's] will as a piece of evidence. And I represent to the court that it is a mirror image of [the decedent's] will that you have admitted as an exhibit. She, like [the decedent], leaves everything to him. If he should predecease her half of her estate goes to his children, half to her children. He appoints her guardian of his children and appoints [her] executor of his estate.

"During the course of the execution of the wills there was no conversation whatsoever about the fact that the Saturday marriage would revoke the will that had been drafted on Thursday. The wedding to take place two days

[The trial court granted the plaintiff's motion, excluding all evidence other than the will, the marriage certificate, and the death certificate.]

With respect to the other issue at trial, namely, whether the decedent's will provided for the contingency of his marriage to the defendant, the trial court, in a de novo proceeding, concluded that the Probate Court properly had admitted the will to probate because the will provided for the contingency of marriage. The trial court reasoned that "[the decedent's] will bequeathed all of his estate to the woman he was licensed to marry and did marry two days later. In his will, he named her executrix and designated her the guardian of his daughters, whose mother had previously died. The nature of these provisions, coupled with the extreme closeness in time of the marriage constitutes clear and convincing evidence of provision for the contingency of marriage. It would be preposterous to assume that [the decedent] was instead executing a will to make provisions that were to be revoked two days later." Accordingly, the trial court rendered judgment affirming the Probate Court's judgment admitting the will, and denied the plaintiff's appeal. This appeal followed. . . .

We conclude that the will, in and of itself, did not provide for the contingency of the subsequent marriage of the decedent and, therefore, under existing case law, properly would have been revoked by that marriage pursuant to §45a-257(a). We also conclude, however, that under the circumstances of this case, the trial court improperly excluded evidence of a mistake by the scrivener that, if believed, would permit a finding that the will provided for the contingency of marriage. We therefore reverse the judgment of the trial court and order a new trial in which such evidence may be considered by the trial court.

On the basis of existing case law, the question of whether a will provides for the contingency of a subsequent marriage must be determined: (1) from the language of the will itself; and (2) without resort to extrinsic evidence of the testator's intent. Fulton Trust Co. v. Trowbridge, 11 A.2d 393 (Conn. 1940) . . . . Applying this standard, we conclude that the trial court should not have admitted the will because, notwithstanding the inferences that the trial court drew from the dates of the marriage license and the will, and from the identity of certain of the named beneficiaries in the will, there was no language in the will providing for the contingency of the subsequent marriage of the decedent. . . .

---

later would revoke the will that had been drafted on Thursday, although there was considerable discussion about the marriage itself and the festivities and the guests and things like that.

"[O'Brien] would testify that the reason that he did not place in the will any specific mention of the marriage or talk about it at all with [the defendant] or [the decedent] was because in his view when a man executes a will two days before his marriage in which he leaves everything to the woman that he's about to marry, makes her guardian of his children, makes her executrix of the estate, and if she should predecease him, leaves half of his estate to her kids, . . . [it] clearly makes provision in the will for not just a contingency, but the imminent [inevitability] of the marriage that's going to take place two days later. So he didn't think there was any necessity that he had to put in words when it was so clear that it was making [provision for his imminent marriage.] . . .

[The lawyer O'Brien would also testify that he visited the testator while he was suffering from terminal cancer. Twice O'Brien reviewed the will with the decedent and assured the decedent that his property was going to his wife. At the second such meeting, the decedent asked O'Brien to set up a corporation and distribute stock in it to his daughters, which O'Brien did. The widow would also testify to similar facts.]

This conclusion does not, however, end our inquiry in this case. In Connecticut Junior Republic v. Sharon Hospital, 448 A.2d 190 (Conn. 1982),[8] this court considered the issue of "whether extrinsic evidence of a mistake by a scrivener of a testamentary instrument is admissible in a proceeding to determine the validity of the testamentary instrument." In a three to two decision, this court held that such evidence is not admissible. Upon further consideration, we now conclude that the reasons given by the dissent in that case are persuasive and apply to the facts of the present case. We, therefore, overrule *Connecticut Junior Republic*, and hold that if a scrivener's error has misled the testator into executing a will on the belief that it will be valid notwithstanding the testator's subsequent marriage, extrinsic evidence of that error is admissible to establish the intent of the testator that his or her will be valid notwithstanding the subsequent marriage. Furthermore, if those two facts, namely, the scrivener's error and its effect on the testator's intent, are established by clear and convincing evidence, they will be sufficient to establish that "provision has been made in such will for such contingency," within the meaning of §45a-257(a).

In Connecticut Junior Republic v. Sharon Hospital, supra, this court reasserted the familiar rule that, although extrinsic evidence is not admissible to prove an intention not expressed in the will itself or to prove a devise or bequest not contained in the will, such evidence is admissible to identify a named devisee or legatee, to identify property described in the will, to clarify ambiguous language in the will, and to prove fraud, incapacity or undue influence. . . .

The dissent in that case by Justice Peters and joined by Justice Shea, concluded that it "would permit extrinsic evidence of a scrivener's error to be introduced in litigation concerned with the admissibility of a disputed will to probate." Id., 22. The dissent gave three principal reasons for its conclusion, each of which we consider to be persuasive and each of which applies to this case.

First, given that extrinsic evidence is admissible to prove that a will was executed by the testator "in reliance on erroneous beliefs induced by fraud, duress, or undue influence," there is no discernible policy difference between that case and a case in which "a will is executed in

Justice Ellen A. Peters

Her dissent in Connecticut Junior Republic becomes law.

8. In Connecticut Junior Republic v. Sharon Hospital, the testator, Richard Emerson, had his lawyer draft a second codicil to his will and first codicil to account for changes in the federal tax code. The lawyer mistakenly inserted the wrong list of charities, taken from his 1960 will, not his 1969 first codicil. Emerson, who had never requested or authorized this change, signed the second codicil in 1975. Upon his death in 1979, the probate court admitted the second codicil to probate, refusing to permit the introduction of extrinsic evidence to correct the scrivener's mistake. The Supreme Court of Connecticut affirmed. — Eds.

reliance on erroneous beliefs induced by the innocent error, by the innocent misrepresentation, of the scrivener of a will." Id., 23. In each instance, "the testamentary process is distorted by the interference of a third person who misleads the testator into making a testamentary disposition that would not otherwise have occurred." Id., 22-23. "In each instance, extrinsic evidence is required to demonstrate that a will, despite its formally proper execution, substantially misrepresents the true intent of the testator." Id., 23.

Similarly, in the present case, there is no discernible policy difference between extrinsic evidence offered to show fraud, duress or undue influence, and extrinsic evidence offered to show that a scrivener's error induced the decedent to execute a will that he believed would survive his subsequent marriage. In both instances, the testamentary process was distorted by the interference of a third person who misled the testator into executing a will that would not otherwise have been executed — in the present case, a will that would be revoked upon his marriage because it did not contain language providing for the contingency of marriage. Thus, as in the case of fraud, duress or undue influence, extrinsic evidence is required to demonstrate that the will that the testator executed did not substantially state his true intention.[9]

Second, the dissent recognized that, based on the policy of the statute of wills, the "risk of subversion of the intent of a testator, who cannot personally defend his testamentary bequest, is without doubt a serious concern." Id., 24. The dissent, however, persuasively underscored the counterbalancing "risk of blindly enforcing a testamentary disposition that substantially misstates the testator's true intent." Id. Again drawing on the analogy to the case of fraud, duress or undue influence, the dissent stated that "had the decedent's lawyer deliberately and fraudulently altered the second codicil, the relevant extrinsic evidence would unquestionably have been admitted." Id., 25. The dissent contended that "innocent misrepresentation is treated as generally equivalent to fraud in terms of its legal consequences." Id. Therefore, the dissent asserted, the "statute of wills does not compel enforcement of testamentary dispositions that a testator never intended to make." Id.

Similarly, in the present case, had the decedent's attorney deliberately and fraudulently, rather than innocently but mistakenly, misrepresented to the decedent that his will would be valid despite his subsequent marriage, it is at least arguable that the beneficiaries of that fraudulent conduct, namely, the heirs-at-law of the decedent who would inherit in the event of his intestacy, would not be permitted to take advantage of that fraud, and that a court of equity could impress a constructive trust on their inheritance. We conclude that, analogously, in this case, the extrinsic evidence should be admissible to establish the decedent's true intent.

---

9. We acknowledge that permitting extrinsic evidence of a scrivener's error will lead to the introduction of extrinsic evidence of intent, which, as we noted previously, is not permitted. For the reasons discussed herein, this common-law exception is no different, however, from the extrinsic evidence of intent permitted in cases alleging fraud, undue influence and duress.

Third, the dissent examined and rejected the two main objections to the admission of extrinsic evidence of a scrivener's error. One objection was "that whatever error the scrivener may have made was validated and ratified by the testator's act in signing his will." Id., 26. The dissent responded, correctly in our view, that, although "signing [a] will creates a strong presumption that the will accurately represents the intentions of the testator, that presumption is a rebuttable one." Id. Similarly, in the present case, although the fact that the decedent signed the will may create a rebuttable presumption that he did not intend it to survive his subsequent marriage, that presumption should be rebuttable by persuasive extrinsic evidence to the contrary.

The other objection was "that allowing extrinsic evidence of mistake will give rise to a proliferation of groundless will contests." Id. The dissent presented a two part response, with which we also agree. First, it noted that, "in the law of contracts, where the parol evidence rule has undergone considerable erosion, this risk has not been found to have been unmanageable. In the law of wills, the risk is limited by the narrowness of the exception that this case would warrant . . . [namely, to] permit the opponent of a will to introduce extrinsic evidence of the error of a scrivener, and [to] require proof of such an extrinsic error to be established by clear and convincing evidence." Id., 26-27.

Similarly, in the present case, the admissibility of such extrinsic evidence, in our view, will not prove to be any less manageable than in cases of parol evidence in contract disputes. Furthermore, we would impose the same elevated burden of proof on the proponent of the will in a case such as this. The proponent would have to establish the scrivener's error by clear and convincing evidence. . . .

[T]he dissent in *Connecticut Junior Republic* phrased the issue in that case as follows: "Must the true intent of the testator be thwarted when, because of the mistake of a scrivener, he has formally subscribed to a written bequest that substantially misstates his testamentary intention?" Id., 22. That is precisely the issue in the present case. The dissent in *Connecticut Junior Republic* answered that question in the negative, recognizing that evidence of a scrivener's mistake should be admissible where offered to establish that a written bequest should not be admitted to probate because its execution was the product of a mistake of the scrivener and, therefore, did not embody the disposition intended by the testator. Likewise, in the present case, evidence of a scrivener's mistake should be admissible to establish that a written bequest should be admitted to probate because the disposition provided by the bequest would have obtained, in accordance with the decedent's intent, but for the scrivener's mistake. . . .

Applying these principles to the facts of the present case, we conclude that the extrinsic evidence offered, if believed, could prove clearly and convincingly that there was a scrivener's error that induced the decedent to execute a will that he intended to be valid despite his subsequent marriage. The offer of proof indicates that the evidence would be susceptible to an inference by the fact finder that there had been an implied assertion by the scrivener that the will would be valid despite the decedent's subsequent marriage. This inference could have been bolstered, moreover, by the evidence of the conversations between the decedent and the scrivener shortly before the decedent's death.

The judgment is reversed and the case is remanded for a new trial.

Explicitly rejected by the court in *Erickson*, the no reformation rule is under attack. Most recently, the power to reform wills and trusts for mistake was endorsed by the American Law Institute in Restatement (Third) of Property: Wills and Other Donative Trasfers §12.1 (2003), and by the Uniform Law Commission in Uniform Trust Code §415 (2000) and Uniform Probate Code §2-805 (2008).

Uniform Probate Code (2008)

§2-805. Reformation to Correct Mistakes

The court may reform the terms of a governing instrument, even if unambiguous, to conform the terms to the transferor's intention if it is proved by clear and convincing evidence that the transferor's intent and the terms of the governing instrument were affected by a mistake of fact or law, whether in expression or inducement.

John H. Langbein, Curing Execution Errors and Mistaken Terms in Wills
18 Prob. & Prop. 28 (Jan./Feb. 2004)

In recent years a remarkable change has been emerging in the way American courts treat cases involving errors in the execution or mistakes in the content of wills. When some innocuous blunder occurred in complying with the Wills Act formalities, such as when one attesting witness went to the washroom before the other had finished signing, the courts used to apply a rule of strict compliance and hold the will invalid. Likewise, in cases of mistaken terms, for example, when the typist dropped a paragraph from the will or the drafter misrendered names or other attributes of a devise, the courts applied a no reformation rule; the will could not be corrected no matter how conclusively the mistake was shown.

Ironically, these intent-defeating results were reached in the name of legal requirements that were meant to be intent-serving. . . . The formalities [for executing wills] are not difficult to comply with, and cases of breach mostly arise when the testator does not use counsel. . . . Cases involving omitted or mistaken terms raise a similar issue — whether to restore to a will language that was to have been included within the will but was accidentally omitted or misrendered before the will was signed and attested.

THE TREND AWAY FROM FORMALISM

Leading modern authority in a number of American states has now reversed the strict compliance and no reformation rules. Both by judicial decision and by legislation, the courts have been empowered to excuse harmless execution errors and to reform mistaken terms. . . .

MISTAKEN TERMS

Section 12.1 of the [Restatement (Third) of Property: Wills and Other Donative Transfers (2003)] authorizes courts to reform mistaken terms in a will. The measure is based upon an extensive body of supporting case law, which the Restatement canvasses in its Reporter's Notes. Section 12.1 provides that a court may reform any donative document, including a will, to "conform the text to the donor's intention if it is established by clear and convincing evidence (1) that a mistake of fact or law, whether in expression or inducement, affected specific terms of the document; and (2) what the donor's intention was."

The Restatement also endorses the movement to allow courts to reform wills, trusts, and other donative documents quite apart from instances of mistake, in situations in which reformation would achieve a tax objective that the donor would have wished. Restatement §12.2 (extensive case law is reviewed in the Reporter's Notes).[10]

WHY THE CHANGE?

The reorientation toward a more intent-serving approach to the Wills Act formalities is the product of many influences. The scholarly literature that has accompanied the change has drawn attention to four main factors:

(1) the rise of the nonprobate system;
(2) experience in other jurisdictions;
(3) growing embarrassment that failure to cure well-proved mistakes inflicts unjust enrichment; and
(4) concern to spare lawyers from needless malpractice liability.

UNIFYING THE LAW OF PROBATE AND NONPROBATE TRANSFERS

Since World War II the use of nonprobate modes of transfer on death has burgeoned. Far more wealth now flows through the main will substitutes (inter vivos trusts, beneficiary designations in pension accounts, life insurance policies, and POD/TOD accounts with banks, mutual funds, and brokerage houses) than passes through probate. A dominant theme of law revision activity during this period has been to unify the constructional principles across the field of probate and nonprobate transfers. . . . The harmless error and reformation rules now

---

10. We take up reformation and modification to achieve a tax advantage, which is now explicitly authorized by UPC §2-806 (2008) and UTC §416 (2000) as well as the Restatement (Third) of Property, at page 651. — Eds.

being applied to mistakes in wills are part of this process of unification, because they are the rules that have long applied in the nonprobate system. Courts of equity have for centuries exercised the power to reform (to "rectify" in English law) mistakes in trusts, deeds of gift, and beneficiary designations. Likewise, there is a well-developed doctrine of excusing defective compliance with the contractually required formalities for change-of-beneficiary designations in the nonprobate system for life insurance policies and joint-and-survivor accounts. . . .

The ostensibly new rules being recognized by the courts and endorsed in the Restatement turn out, therefore, to be quite old; what is new is applying them to wills as well as to will substitutes. The principle being recognized in the Restatement is that wills and will substitutes entail a common issue, ascertaining the intention of a deceased transferor. The lesson of the nonprobate system, now being absorbed as the probate rule, is that in cases of mistake in execution or mistaken terms, the purposes of the formal requirements can be served by allowing the proponent of the instrument to prove by clear-and-convincing evidence that the testator intended the transfer. . . .

PREVENTING UNJUST ENRICHMENT

When an innocuous execution error defeats a will, or when a scrivener's mistake defeats a devise, the failure to implement the testator's intent not only frustrates the testator's wishes, but it also works unjust enrichment. The devisee or distributee who takes is unjustly enriched at the expense of the intended beneficiary. Preventing unjust enrichment is the central policy value of the law of restitution. The field of restitution emerged only in the twentieth century as a result of the fusion of law and equity, which allowed the common principle of preventing unjust enrichment to be generalized from the older law of quasicontract and constructive trust. The modern understanding of the importance of avoiding unjust enrichment has been an important stimulus to the development of the rules curing harmless execution errors and reforming mistaken terms.

MALPRACTICE LIABILITY

Although most execution blunders occur when laypersons attempt testation without the help of counsel, cases (such as *Snide*, [see page 250]) do occur in which counsel's negligence causes or contributes to the error. By contrast, cases of mistaken terms more often involve a lawyer-drafter, who has misrendered instructions or omitted intended terms. In these cases in which the lawyer might be liable to the intended beneficiaries for malpractice, it can be argued that making available a remedy to correct the mistake is unnecessary, because the curative doctrines benefit the lawyer, who would otherwise bear the malpractice liability. There are, however, many objections to this line of reasoning. Malpractice liability does nothing about the cases in which lawyers are not involved or not culpable. When there is a lawyer to sue, he or she may be wholly or partially judgment-proof — for example, when the lawyer is uninsured or underinsured. For devises of unique property, such as the family home or the family Bible, relief in damages cannot be adequate. Most importantly, what is wrong with the malpractice solution is that, by transforming the mistake claim into tort, it neglects the unjust enrichment intrinsic to mistake cases. Whereas most forms of malpractice cause deadweight loss that can only be remedied by compensation, in the testamentary mistake cases a benefit is transferred from the intended devisee to the mistaken devisee (or intestate taker). Because the mistaken devisee has no claim of entitlement, he or she is unjustly enriched. The malpractice solution leaves the unjust enrichment unremedied and instead creates a needless loss to be charged against the drafter. The mistake remedies (harmless error, reformation) respond to the simple truth that preventing loss is better than compensating loss.

NEW VISTAS FOR THE PROBATE LAWYER . . .

The older conventions of the strict compliance rule and the no reformation rule are now open to challenge everywhere. Lawyers processing probate matters need to be alert to the opportunity they now have to raise issues that used to be foreclosed. Sad cases of defeated intent that used to be beyond hope are now remediable, an innocuous formal defect can be excused, mistaken terms can be reformed, but only if counsel sees the issue and brings it forward.

NOTES AND QUESTIONS

1. *Reformation in the cases.* In some cases, the courts have indeed remedied mistakes by the scrivener. In Estate of Lord, 795 A.2d 700 (Me. 2002), the residuary clause was mistakenly drafted to refer to a "trust" and a "trustee" that never came into existence, but the court interpreted these words to mean "estate" and "personal representative" instead. In Estate of Getman, 15 Quinnipiac Prob. L.J. 257 (Conn. Prob. 2000), the court corrected language in a will that identified an inter vivos trust as "created this date" to "created May 9, 1999." In Estate of Ikuta, 639 P.2d 400 (Haw. 1981), the court substituted the word "youngest" for the word "oldst [oldest]" where extrinsic evidence showed that "oldst" did not make sense and was a scrivener's mistake.

Where there has been an accidental omission by the scrivener or typist, courts have sometimes inserted the missing words when convinced from the face of the will and extrinsic evidence what was intended. In Estate of Herceg, 747 N.Y.S.2d 901 (Sur. 2002), the last lines of the residuary clause were left off so that there was no indication who was to take the residue. In three prior wills, the testator had left the residue to his nephew or, if his nephew predeceased him, to his nephew's wife. The attorney-scrivener testified that the omission of the rest of the residuary clause was caused by a computer error and that no change in beneficiaries was intended by the testator, a contention supported by the will's naming the nephew's wife as an alternate executor. Endorsing Restatement (Third) of Property: Wills and Other Donative Transfers §12.1 (2003), the court held that the omission of the nephew's wife was unintentional and awarded her the residue of the estate.

There is also a growing trend in the cases, endorsed by UPC §2-806 (2008), UTC §416 (2000), and Restatement (Third) of Property, supra, §12.2, toward allowing reformation of mistake (as well as outright modification) of wills and trusts as necessary to obtain a tax advantage. For discussion, see page 651.

2. *Malpractice.* Professor Langbein argues that it is better to remedy lawyers' drafting mistakes by correcting them. Would it be preferable to hold the lawyer liable for malpractice?

When a lawyer has drafted an ambiguous will, should the lawyer be liable in malpractice for any costs and losses from litigation to construe the will? In Ventura County Humane Socy. v. Holloway, 115 Cal. Rptr. 464 (App. 1974), the court held that although an attorney is liable to testamentary beneficiaries if the beneficiaries clearly designated by the testator lose their legacy as a direct result of the attorney's negligence, the attorney is not liable for drafting an ambiguous document. "[T]he task of proving whether the claimed ambiguity was the result of negligence of the drafting attorney or whether it was the deliberate choice of the testator, would impose an insurmountable burden on the parties. . . . The duty thus created would amount to a requirement to draft litigation-proof legal documents." But see Angela M. Vallario, Shape Up or Ship Out: Accountability to Third Parties for Patent Ambiguities in Testamentary Documents, 26 Whittier L. Rev. 59 (2004) (arguing that drafting a will with patent ambiguity should be prima facie evidence of negligence).

3. *Nonprobate transfers.* Drafting mistakes in nonprobate transfers, such as inter vivos trusts, can be corrected after the settlor's death. See Bilafer v. Bilafer, 73 Cal. Rptr. 3d 880 (Cal. App. 2008) (holding that the court may reform an irrevocable trust to correct a drafting error). If we correct mistakes in inter vivos trusts, why not in wills (and testamentary trusts)? See Martin L. Fried, The Disappointed Heir: Going Beyond the Probate Process to Remedy Wrongdoing or Rectify Mistake, 39 Real Prop., Prob. & Tr. J. 357 (2004); John H. Langbein and Lawrence W. Waggoner, Reformation of Wills on the Ground of Mistake: Change of Direction in American Law?, 30 U. Pa. L. Rev. 521, 588-590 (1982).

4. *Clear and convincing evidence.* Although much is gained by allowing reformation of mistakes in wills and trusts, is anything lost? Does giving the courts the power to vary the words on the face of the will take from testators the safe harbor of a written will? Does the "clear and convincing" evidentiary threshold provide sufficient protection against abuse of the reformation power? Compare G. Sidney Buchanan, No Connecticut Yankee in the Texas Supreme Court, 40 Hous. L. Rev. 931 (2003) (arguing in the affirmative), with Pamela R. Champine, My Will Be Done: Accommodating the Erring and the Atypical Testator, 80 Neb. L. Rev. 387 (2001) (proposing that reformation be unavailable unless the testator affirmatively authorized its use). See also In re Trust Created by Isvik, 741 N.W.2d 638 (Neb. 2007) (denying reformation because evidence of alleged error was not clear and convincing).

5. *Gifts by implication.* A recurring oversight in drafting is a gap in the dispositive provisions — that is, a particular contingency (which occurs) is not

provided for. To fill such gaps, New Jersey courts developed a *doctrine of probable intent*, now validated by statute. N.J. Stat. Ann. §3B:3-33.1 (2008). If a contingency occurs for which no provision is made in the will, the court studies the family circumstances and the plan of testamentary disposition set forth in the will. The court then places itself in the position of the testator and decides how the testator probably would have responded to the contingency had she envisioned its occurrence. See Estate of Payne, 895 A.2d 428 (N.J. 2006); In re Bieley, 695 N.E.2d 1119 (N.Y. 1998).

Not everyone is enamored with the trend toward reforming wills and the admission of extrinsic evidence. In 2000, the Supreme Judicial Court of Massachusetts, which is a leader in allowing reformation to obtain tax advantages (see pages 651, 981), rejected reformation of wills for other purposes:

> [T]he reformation of a will, which would dispose of estate property based on unattested testamentary language, would violate the Statute of Wills. Strong policy reasons also militate against the requested reformation. To allow for reformation in this case would open the floodgates of litigation and lead to untold confusion in the probate of wills. It would essentially invite disgruntled individuals excluded from a will to demonstrate extrinsic evidence of the decedent's "intent" to include them. The number of groundless will contests could soar. We disagree that employing "full, clear and decisive proof" as the standard for reformation of wills would suffice to remedy such problems. Judicial resources are simply too scarce to squander on such consequences. Finally, we are not persuaded by the decisions of other jurisdictions. Therefore, we decline to join the minority and decline to follow the Restatement. [Flannery v. McNamara, 738 N.E.2d 739, 746 (Mass. 2000).]

If given the chance to decide Mahoney v. Grainger, page 336, once again, it seems clear that the Massachusetts court would reach the same result. On the other hand, as demonstrated by the next case, not even the Massachusetts court resists extrinsic evidence to vary the plain meaning of a will in *all* cases.

FLEMING v. MORRISON, 72 N.E. 499 (Mass. 1904): Francis Butterfield wanted to sleep with Mary Fleming. In order to induce her to do so, Butterfield had his lawyer, Sidney Goodrich, draft a will leaving Butterfield's entire estate to Fleming. After Butterfield signed the will and Goodrich signed as the first witness, but before the last two of the necessary three witnesses had signed, Butterfield told Goodrich "that this was a 'fake' will, made for a purpose." Butterfield then took the will to two more witnesses, acknowledged his signature to them, and they both signed as witnesses. Butterfield did not disclose to these other witnesses that he intended the will to be nothing more than a ploy to trick Fleming into sleeping with him.

On the basis of extrinsic evidence, the Massachusetts Supreme Judicial Court held the will invalid:

[The contestants argue that] the proponent of the will has failed to prove the necessary animus testandi. We are of the opinion that this contention must prevail. The finding that, before Butterfield and Goodrich "parted," Butterfield told Goodrich that the instrument which had been signed by Butterfield as and for his last will and testament, and declared by him to be such in the presence of Goodrich, and attested and subscribed by Goodrich as a witness, "was a 'fake' will, made for a purpose," is fatal to the proponent's case. This must be taken to mean that what had been done was a sham. . . . The whole finding, taken together, amounts to a finding that Butterfield had not intended the transaction which had just taken place to be in fact what it imported to be, that is to say, a finding that when Butterfield signed the instrument, and asked Goodrich to attest and subscribe it as his will, he did not, in fact, then intend it to be his last will and testament, but intended to have Mary Fleming think that he had made a will in her favor to induce her to let him sleep with her.

We are of opinion that it is competent to contradict by parol the solemn statements contained in an instrument that it is a will; that it has been signed as such by the person named as the testator, and attested and subscribed by persons signing as witnesses. . . .

[T]he animus testandi must exist when [the will] is signed or acknowledged before, and attested and subscribed by, each of the necessary three witnesses. If this is not done, the statutory requirements have not been complied with. Assuming that the acknowledgment animo testandi of a signature not originally made with that animus is enough, the will in the case at bar would have been duly executed had Butterfield subsequently acknowledged the instrument before three in place of two additional witnesses. But he did not do so. The instrument, having been acknowledged and attested and subscribed by two witnesses only, is not a valid will, within Rev. Laws, c. 135, §1.

QUESTIONS

1. If the testimony of the drafting attorney can be introduced into evidence to show that a will, which recites that it is the testator's will, is not intended as such — thus contradicting the words of the instrument — why cannot the attorney testify that the "plain meaning" of the words of the will was not the meaning intended by the testator? Does *Fleming* turn on the fact that the drafting attorney was also a witness to the will? Should Goodrich's testimony, which contradicts the attestation clause, have been allowed?

What do you think of the ethics of the lawyer Sidney Goodrich? Model Rule of Prof. Conduct 1.2(d) (2002) provides: "A lawyer shall not counsel a client to engage, or assist a client, in conduct that the lawyer knows is criminal or fraudulent."

2. Assume that, after executing the will litigated in Fleming v. Morrison, Francis Butterfield showed Mary Fleming the will, and, relying upon its validity, Mary slept with Francis. Does Mary have any remedy against Francis's estate? Contract to devise? Sexual intercourse (battery) by fraud in the inducement? Civil action for rape?

Does Mary have any cause of action against Goodrich, such as tortious interference with her expectancy (see page 215)? Would Goodrich have a duty to warn Mary under Tarasoff v. Regents of Univ. of Cal., 551 P.2d 334 (Cal. 1976) (psychotherapist has a common law duty "to use reasonable care to protect the intended victim" of a patient who "presents a serious danger of violence")? Model Rule of Prof. Conduct 1.6 (2002) permits disclosure of information relating to representation of a client to prevent "substantial bodily harm" or "a crime or fraud."

SECTION B.   DEATH OF BENEFICIARY BEFORE DEATH OF TESTATOR

1.   *Introduction*

If a devisee does not survive the testator, the devise *lapses* (that is, it fails). All gifts made by will are subject to a requirement that the devisee survive the testator, unless the testator specifies otherwise. In nearly all states, however, *antilapse statutes* have been enacted that, under certain specified circumstances, substitute another beneficiary for the predeceased devisee.

Before examining these statutes, it is important to get a firm hold on the common law rules regarding lapsed devises. These are the default rules that apply if the will does not indicate what happens when a devisee predeceases the testator and the antilapse statute is not applicable.

(1) *Specific or general devise.* If a specific or general devise lapses, the devise falls into the residue. Thus:

> *Case 1.* T's will devises her watch (a specific devise) to *A*, $10,000 (a general devise) to *B*, and the rest of her estate (the residuary devise) to *C*. *A* and *B* predecease *T*. Under the common law lapse rule, the watch and the $10,000 go to *C*.

(2) *Residuary devise.* If the residuary devise lapses, the heirs of the testator take by intestacy. If only a share of the residue lapses, such as when one of two residuary devisees predeceases the testator, at common law the lapsed residuary share passes by intestacy to the testator's heirs rather than to the remaining residuary devisees. This rule, called the *no-residue-of-a-residue* rule, is followed in Estate of Russell, infra.

> *Case 2.* After making several specific and general devises to various persons, *T* devises the residue of her estate one-half to *B* and one-half to *C*. *B* predeceases *T*. *B*'s one-half share goes to *T*'s heirs by intestacy, not to *C*.

The no-residue-of-a-residue rule, probably laid down by English courts to protect the interests of the primogenitary heir, has been roundly criticized by courts and commentators alike. In most states, this rule has been overturned by statute or judicial decision. See note 1 following the next case, Estate of Russell.

(3) *Class gift.* If the devise is to a *class* of persons, and one member of the class predeceases the testator, the surviving members of the class divide the gift. Thus:

> *Case 3.* T devises $10,000 to the children of *A* (a class gift). One child of *A*, named *B*, predeceases *T*. At *T*'s death, *T* is survived by another child of *A*, named *C*. Because this is a class gift, *C* takes *B*'s share, or the entire $10,000.

Much turns, therefore, on whether a gift to a group of persons is a class gift, a question we take up at page 375.

(4) *Void devise*. Where a devisee is already dead at the time the will is executed, or the devisee is a dog or cat or some other ineligible taker, the devise is void. The same default rules govern the disposition of a void devise as govern a lapsed devise.

Estate of Russell
Supreme Court of California, 1968
444 P.2d 353

SULLIVAN, J.   Georgia Nan Russell Hembree appeals from a judgment (Prob. Code, §1240[11]) entered in proceedings for the determination of heirship decreeing inter alia that under the terms of the will of Thelma L. Russell, deceased, all of the residue of her estate should be distributed to Chester H. Quinn.

Thelma L. Russell died testate on September 8, 1965, leaving a validly executed holographic will written on a small card. The front of the card reads:

> Turn
>   the card   March 18-1957
>   I leave everything
>   I own Real &
>   Personal to Chester
>   H. Quinn & Roxy Russell
>   Thelma L. Russell

The reverse side reads:

> My ($10.) Ten dollar gold
> Piece & diamonds I leave
> to Georgia Nan Russell.
> Alverata, Geogia [sic]

Chester H. Quinn was a close friend and companion of testatrix, who for over 25 years prior to her death had resided in one of the living units on her property and had stood in a relation of personal trust and confidence toward her. Roxy Russell was testatrix' pet dog which was alive on the date of the execution of testatrix' will but predeceased her.[12] Plaintiff is testatrix' niece and her only heir-at-law.

---

11. Hereafter unless otherwise indicated all section references are to the Probate Code.

12. Actually, the record indicates the existence of two Roxy Russells. The original Roxy was an Airedale dog which testatrix owned at the time she made her will, but which, according to Quinn, died after having had a fox tail removed from its nose, and which, according to the testimony of one Arthur Turner, owner of a pet cemetery, was buried on June 9, 1958. Roxy was replaced with another dog (breed not indicated in the record before us) which, although it answered to the name Roxy, was according to the record, in fact registered with the American Kennel Club as "Russel's [sic] Royal Kick Roxy."

Thelma Russell's Property at 4422 Palm Avenue (1999)

In her petition for determination of heirship plaintiff alleges, inter alia, that "Roxy Russell is an Airedale dog";[13] that section 27 enumerates those entitled to take by will; that "Dogs are not included among those listed in . . . Section 27. Not even Airedale dogs"; that the gift of one-half of the residue of testatrix' estate to Roxy Russell is invalid and void; and that plaintiff was entitled to such one-half as testatrix' sole heir-at-law.

At the hearing on the petition, plaintiff introduced without objection extrinsic evidence establishing that Roxy Russell was testatrix' Airedale dog which died on June 9, 1958. To this end plaintiff, in addition to an independent witness, called defendant pursuant to former Code of Civil Procedure section 2055 (now Evid. Code, §776). Upon redirect examination, counsel for Quinn then sought to introduce evidence of the latter's relationship with testatrix "in the event that your Honor feels that there is any necessity for further ascertainment of the intent above and beyond the document." Plaintiff's objections on the ground that it was inadmissible under the statute of wills and the parol evidence rule "because there is no ambiguity" and that it was inadmissible under section 105, were overruled. Over plaintiff's objection, counsel for Quinn also introduced certain documentary evidence consisting of testatrix' address book and a certain quitclaim deed "for the purpose of demonstrating the intention on the part of the deceased that she not die intestate." Of all this extrinsic evidence only the following infinitesimal portion of Quinn's testimony relates to care of the dog: "Q [Counsel for Quinn] Prior to the first Roxy's death did you ever discuss with Miss Russell taking care of Roxy if anything should ever happen to her? A Yes." Plaintiff carefully

---

13. In his "Petition for Probate of Holographic Will and for Letters of Administration with the Will Annexed," Quinn included under the names, ages and residences of the devisees and legatees of testatrix the following: "Roxy Russell, A 9 year old Airedale dog, [residing at] 4422 Palm Avenue, La Mesa, Calif." [Is this correct? Since the will was executed when the first Roxy was alive, isn't the second Roxy a pretermitted Airedale? — Eds.]

preserved an objection running to all of the above line of testimony and at the conclusion of the hearing moved to strike such evidence. Her motion was denied.

The trial court found, so far as is here material, that it was the intention of testatrix "that Chester H. Quinn was to receive her entire estate, excepting the gold coin and diamonds bequeathed to" plaintiff and that Quinn "was to care for the dog, Roxy Russell, in the event of Testatrix's death. The language contained in the Will, concerning the dog, Roxy Russell, was precatory in nature only, and merely indicative of the wish, desire and concern of Testatrix that Chester H. Quinn was to care for the dog, Roxy Russell, subsequent to Testatrix's death."[14] The court concluded that testatrix intended to and did make an absolute and outright gift to Mr. Quinn of all the residue of her estate, adding: "There occurred no lapse as to any portion of the residuary gift to Chester H. Quinn by reason of the language contained in the Will concerning the dog, Roxy Russell, such language not having the effect of being an attempted outright gift or gift in trust to the dog. The effect of such language is merely to indicate the intention of Testatrix that Chester H. Quinn was to take the entire residuary estate and to use whatever portion thereof as might be necessary to care for and maintain the dog, Roxy Russell."[15] Judgment was entered accordingly. This appeal followed.

Plaintiff's position before us may be summarized thusly: That the gift of one-half of the residue of the estate to testatrix' dog was clear and unambiguous; that such gift was void and the property subject thereof passed to plaintiff under the laws of intestate succession; and that the court erred in admitting the extrinsic evidence offered by Quinn but that in any event the uncontradicted evidence in the record did not cure the invalidity of the gift. . . .

[W]e think it is self-evident that in the interpretation of a will, a court cannot determine whether the terms of the will are clear and definite in the first place until it considers the circumstances under which the will was made so that the judge may be placed in the position of the testator whose language he is interpreting. . . . Failure to enter upon such an inquiry is failure to recognize that the "ordinary standard or 'plain meaning,' is simply the meaning of the people who did *not* write the document." (9 Wigmore on Evidence §2462 (3d ed. 1940).) . . .

---

14. The memorandum decision elaborates on this point, stating in part: "The obvious concern of the human who loves her pet is to see that it is properly cared for by someone who may be trusted to honor that concern and through resources the person may make available in the will to carry out this entreaty, desire, wish, recommendation or prayer. This, in other words, is a most logical example of a precatory provision. It is the only logical conclusion one can come to which would not do violence to the apparent intent of Mrs. Russell."

The trial court found further: "Testatrix intended that Georgia Nan Russell Hembree was not to have any other real or personal property belonging to Testatrix, other than the gold coin and diamonds." This finding also was elaborated on in the memorandum decision: "In making the will it is apparent she had Georgia on her mind. While there is other evidence in the case about Thelma Russell's frame of mind concerning her real property and her niece, which was admitted by the Court, over counsel's vigorous objection, because it concerned testatrix' frame of mind, a condition relevant to the material issue of intent, nevertheless this additional evidence was not necessary to this Court in reaching its conclusion." The additional evidence referred to included an address book of testatrix upon which she had written: "Chester, Don't let Augusta and Georgia have one penny of my place if it takes it all to fight it in Court. Thelma."

15. Said the trial court: "To ascribe to her the belief that her dog could acquire real property with all the rights and obligations incident to ownership is to describe a person who would probably be incompetent to make a will at all. There is no other evidence of incompetency and certainly incompetency is not presumed." — Eds.

[E]xtrinsic evidence of the circumstances under which a will is made (except evidence expressly excluded by statute) may be considered by the court in ascertaining what the testator meant by the words used in the will. If in the light of such extrinsic evidence, the provisions of the will are reasonably susceptible of two or more meanings claimed to have been intended by the testator, "an uncertainty arises upon the face of a will" (§105) and extrinsic evidence relevant to prove any of such meanings is admissible. . . . If, on the other hand, in the light of such extrinsic evidence, the provisions of the will are not reasonably susceptible of two or more meanings, there is no uncertainty arising upon the face of the will . . . and any proffered evidence attempting to show an intention *different* from that expressed by the words therein, giving them the only meaning to which they are reasonably susceptible, is inadmissible. . . .

Examining testatrix' will in the light of the foregoing rules, we arrive at the following conclusions: Extrinsic evidence offered by plaintiff was admitted without objection and indeed would have been properly admitted over objection to raise and resolve the latent ambiguity as to Roxy Russell and ultimately to establish that Roxy Russell was a dog. Extrinsic evidence of the surrounding circumstances was properly considered in order to ascertain what testatrix meant by the words of the will, including the words: "I leave everything I own Real & Personal to Chester H. Quinn & Roxy Russell" or as those words can now be read "to Chester H. Quinn and my dog Roxy Russell."

However, viewing the will in the light of the surrounding circumstances as are disclosed by the record, we conclude that the will cannot reasonably be construed as urged by Quinn and determined by the trial court as providing that testatrix intended to make an absolute and outright gift of the entire residue of her estate to Quinn who was "to use whatever portion thereof as might be necessary to care for and maintain the dog." No words of the will give the entire residuum to Quinn, much less indicate that the provision for the dog is merely precatory in nature. Such an interpretation is not consistent with a disposition which by its language leaves the residuum in equal shares to Quinn and the dog.[16] A disposition in equal shares to two beneficiaries cannot be equated with a disposition of the whole to one of them who may use "whatever portion thereof as might be necessary" on behalf of the other. . . .

Accordingly, since in the light of the extrinsic evidence introduced below, the terms of the will are not reasonably susceptible of the meaning claimed by Quinn to have been intended by testatrix, the extrinsic evidence offered to show such an intention should have been excluded by the trial court. Upon an independent examination of the will we conclude that the trial court's interpretation of the terms thereof was erroneous. Interpreting the provisions relating to testatrix' residuary estate in accordance with the only meaning to which they are reasonably susceptible, we conclude that testatrix intended to make a disposition of all

---

16. This is slippery work in paraphrasing. Thelma Russell did not write "in equal shares." — Eds.

of the residue of the estate to Quinn and the dog in equal shares; therefore, as tenants in common. As a dog cannot be the beneficiary under a will the attempted gift to Roxy Russell is void.[17]

There remains only the necessity of determining the effect of the void gift to the dog upon the disposition of the residuary estate. That portion of any residuary estate that is the subject of a lapsed gift to one of the residuary beneficiaries remains undisposed of by the will and passes to the heirs-at-law (§§92, 220). The rule is equally applicable with respect to a void gift to one of the residuary beneficiaries (§220). Therefore, notwithstanding testatrix' expressed intention to limit the extent of her gift by will to plaintiff one-half of the residuary estate passes to plaintiff as testatrix' only heir-at-law (§225). We conclude that the residue of testatrix' estate should be distributed in equal shares to Chester H. Quinn and Georgia Nan Russell Hembree, testatrix' niece.

The judgment is reversed. . . .

QUESTIONS AND NOTE

1. The no-residue-of-a-residue rule, which was not attacked by Chester's counsel or questioned by the court, necessitated the litigation to resolve whether Thelma meant a gift to Chester alone or to Chester and Roxy. But is the rule sound? If *T* devises her entire estate to *A* and *B*, and *B* predeceases *T* or is otherwise an ineligible taker, what result is more likely to be consistent with *T*'s probable intent: that *A* receive *T*'s entire estate, or that *A* receive one-half of *T*'s estate with the other half passing by intestacy to *T*'s heirs? The small minority of states that still follow the no-residue-of-the-residue rule assume the latter. See In re Estate of McFarland, 167 S.W.3d 299 (Tenn. 2005) (retaining the rule by 3 to 2 vote). In the vast majority of states that have rejected the rule, the assumption is that the testator would probably prefer for *A* to receive the entire residue. Consistent with this assumption, well-drafted wills almost invariably reject the rule, reallocating the share of a predeceasing residuary beneficiary to the other residuary takers. The no-residue-of-the-residue rule is rejected by UPC §2-604(b) (1990) and Restatement (Third) of Property: Wills and Other Donative Transfers §5.5, cmt. o (1999).

2. On trusts for the benefit of pet animals, and the phenomenon of gifts to pets more generally, see page 585.

17. As a consequence, the fact that Roxy Russell predeceased the testatrix is of no legal import. As appears, we have disposed of the issue raised by plaintiff's frontal attack on the eligibility of the dog to take a testamentary gift and therefore need not concern ourselves with the novel question as to whether the death of the dog during the lifetime of the testatrix resulted in a lapsed gift. (§92.)

2. *Antilapse Statutes*

Now let us turn to the effect of an antilapse statute upon a lapsed gift. In a sense, antilapse statutes are misnamed. They do not prevent a lapse; they merely substitute other beneficiaries (usually descendants) for the dead beneficiary if certain requirements are met. A typical antilapse statute provides that if a devisee is of a specified relationship to the testator and is survived by descendants who survive the testator, the descendants are substituted for the predeceased devisee. The statute changes the common law to give the predeceased devisee's gift to the devisee's descendants unless the testator provides otherwise.

Presumed intent. The theory behind the antilapse statutes is one of presumed intent. The idea is that, for certain predeceasing devisees, the testator would prefer a substitute gift to the devisee's descendants rather than for the gift to lapse. Thus:

> *Case 4.* T devises her entire estate "one-half to my son A and one-half to my daughter B." B predeceases T, leaving a child, C. At T's death, what happens to B's share? At common law, B's share would lapse and, being a residuary devise, would pass by intestacy, one-half to A and one-half to C. As a result, A would take three-quarters and C would take one-quarter. If the state has abrogated the no-residue-of-the-residue rule, B's share would go to A, leaving A with the entire estate and C with nothing. By contrast, if an antilapse statute applies, C would take B's share, leaving A with one-half and C with one-half. Antilapse statutes rest on the assumption that T would prefer a substitute gift to C than for B's share to lapse.

Scope. An antilapse statute applies to a lapsed devise *only* if the devisee bears the particular relationship to the testator specified in the statute. The assumption is that the testator would prefer a substitute gift to the devisee's descendants instead of lapse only for certain types of devisees. Some statutes apply only to descendants of the testator. Others are broader, applying to descendants of the testator's parents or grandparents, or to all kindred of the testator, and occasionally to kindred of the testator's spouse as well. In a few states, the statute applies to all devisees, whether a relative of the testator or not. The antilapse statute in the 1969 UPC applies only to a devise to a grandparent or a lineal descendant of a grandparent. The 1990 UPC adds a devise to a stepchild. Thus:

> *Case 5.* T devises her home to her niece, A, and the residue of her estate to B. A predeceases T, leaving a child, C, who survives T. Under the UPC antilapse statute, C takes T's home because A is a descendant of T's grandparent and hence comes within the required relationship. If the antilapse statute applies only to T's descendants, C does not take T's home. The devise lapses and falls into the residue given to B.

Experience suggests that most antilapse statutes are too narrowly drawn. There appears to be no empirical evidence to support limiting antilapse statutes to close relatives even though most legislatures do so. What do you think? Would the average testator want descendants to be substituted for a predeceasing devisee in every case? And why substitute *descendants* only? Why not substitute *heirs*, including a spouse? For penetrating examinations of the merits and demerits of antilapse statutes, see Susan F. French, Antilapse Statutes Are Blunt Instruments: A Blueprint for Reform, 37 Hastings L.J. 335 (1985); Patricia G. Roberts, Lapse Statutes: Recurring Construction Problems, 37 Emory L.J. 323 (1988).

UPC §2-605 (1969) is a typical antilapse statute.

Uniform Probate Code (1969)

§2-605.   ANTILAPSE; DECEASED DEVISEE; CLASS GIFTS

If a devisee who is a grandparent or a lineal descendant of a grandparent of the testator is dead at the time of execution of the will, fails to survive the testator, or is treated as if he predeceased the testator, the issue of the deceased devisee who survive the testator by 120 hours take in place of the deceased devisee and if they are all of the same degree of kinship to the devisee they take equally, but if of unequal degree then those of more remote degree take by representation. One who would have been a devisee under a class gift if he had survived the testator is treated as a devisee for purposes of this section whether his death occurred before or after the execution of the will.

Default rules. Because the antilapse statutes are designed to implement presumed intent, they state default rules that yield to a contrary expression of the testator's actual intent. Thus:

> *Case 6. T* devises her entire estate "one-half to my son *A* and one-half to my daughter *B*, but if *A* or *B* or both do not survive me, then I give such predeceasing child's share to my friend *F*." *B* predeceases *T*, leaving a child, *C*. At *T*'s death, *T*'s estate will pass one-half to *A* and one-half to *F*. The antilapse statute does not apply to *B*'s share, because *T* has provided expressly for the possibility of *B* predeceasing *T*.

In Case 6, the testator's contrary intent is stated expressly and is confirmed by the alternative devise to *F*. When the will is not as clear, however, the courts struggle with the question whether it indicates that the testator has a contrary intention. Thus:

> *Case 7. T* devises her estate "to my living brothers and sisters, *A, B, C, D,* and *E,* to share and share alike." *A, B,* and *C* predecease *T,* each leaving descendants. *T* dies. Do the descendants of *A, B,* and *C* take the respective shares of each? The question is whether the terms "living" and "share and share alike" express a requirement of survival that precludes application of the antilapse statute. In Allen v. Talley, 949 S.W.2d 59 (Tex. App. 1997), the court held that the will required survival and the antilapse statute did not apply. Under that approach, the surviving siblings, *D* and *E,* take the entire estate. See also Estate of Stangle, 788 N.Y.S.2d 241 (App. Div. 2005), holding that a devise "in equal shares to my surviving sisters and brother" precludes application of the antilapse statute.
>
> *Case 8.* Same facts as in Case 7, except the will does not include the term "living." What result? The question now is whether the term "share and share alike," by itself, indicates a

requirement of survival that precludes application of the antilapse statute. In Estate of Kuruzovich, 78 S.W.3d 226 (Mo. 2002), the court applied the antilapse statute, reasoning that "share and share alike" did not express a contrary intention. Under that approach, the surviving siblings, *D* and *E*, each take one-fifth of the estate, while the three one-fifth shares of the estate that would have gone to the deceased siblings, *A*, *B*, and *C*, pass to their respective descendants.

Words of survivorship. The promulgation of UPC §2-603 (1990, rev. 2008) introduced an additional complexity. Paragraph (b)(3) of that section provides that "words of survivorship, such as in a devise to an individual 'if he survives me,' or in a devise to 'my surviving children,' are not, in the absence of additional evidence, a sufficient indication of an intent contrary to the application of this section." Thus:

> *Case 9. T* devises Blackacre "to my son Sidney if he survives me" and devises the residue of his estate to his wife, Wilma. Sidney dies in his father's lifetime, leaving a daughter, Debby. *T* is survived by Wilma and Debby. Who takes Blackacre, Wilma or Debby? The issue is whether the words "if he survives me" evidence an intention that Sidney's child should not be substituted for Sidney. The majority of cases have held that an express requirement of survivorship, such as "if he survives me," states an intent that the antilapse statute not apply and that Debby not be substituted for her father. Under UPC §2-603(b)(3), however, the term "if he survives me" is not a sufficient expression of contrary intent, and the antilapse statute applies nonetheless, substituting Debby for her father.

The official comment to UPC §2-603 suggests the rationale for reversing the majority rule that words of survivorship establish a contrary intention:

> The argument [for the majority rule] is that attaching words of survivorship indicates that the testator thought about the matter and intentionally did not provide a substitute gift to the devisee's descendants. At best, this is an inference only, which may or may not accurately reflect the testator's actual intention. An equally plausible inference is that the words of survivorship are in the testator's will merely because the testator's lawyer used a will form with words of survivorship.

Restatement (Third) of Property: Wills and Other Donative Transfers §5.5, cmt. h (1999), amplifies on this reasoning as follows:

> An often litigated question is whether language requiring the devisee to survive the testator, without more, constitutes a sufficient expression of a contrary intent to defeat the antilapse statute. The majority view is that such language signifies a contrary intent. Because such a survival provision is often boiler-plate form-book language, the testator may not understand that such language could disinherit the line of descent headed by the deceased devisee. When the testator is older than the devisee and hence does not expect the devisee to die first, or if the devisee was childless when the will was executed, it seems especially unlikely that a provision requiring the devisee to survive the testator was intended to disinherit the devisee's descendants. . . .
>
> [T]he courts should be cautious in automatically concluding that survival language manifests a deliberate decision by the testator to disinherit the line of descent headed by a deceased devisee. . . . [T]he trier of fact should be especially reluctant to find that survival language manifests a contrary intent in cases in which the deceased devisee is one of the testator's children, or other direct descendant, and the effect of refusing to apply the antilapse statute would be to disinherit one or more grandchildren or great-grandchildren.

See also Edward C. Halbach, Jr. and Lawrence W. Waggoner, The UPC's New Survivorship and Antilapse Provisions, 55 Alb. L. Rev. 1091 (1992).

UPC §2-603(b)(3) has come under sharp criticism from commentators. Professor Ascher writes:

> Apparently, the revisers believe their own antilapse provisions are likely to reflect any particular testator's intent more faithfully than *the testator's own will*. This conclusion is not only pretentious, it disputes what should be obvious — that most testators expect *their wills* to dispose of their property *completely* — without interference from a statute of which they have never heard. Instead of allowing "if he survives me" to mean what almost everyone would expect it to mean, the revisers have translated it into, "if he survives me, and, if he does not survive me, to his issue who survive me." For those unfamiliar with estate planning esoterica, therefore, it has become yet more difficult to figure out what the words in a will actually mean. The uninitiated apparently have three options: hire a competent estate planner, go to law school, or curl up with *Alice in Wonderland*. [Mark L. Ascher, The 1990 Uniform Probate Code: Older and Better, or More Like the Internal Revenue Code?, 77 Minn. L. Rev. 639, 652-655 (1993).]

The rule of UPC §2-603(b)(3) has received a chilly reception in the state legislatures. Although it has been adopted in seven states (Alaska, Colorado, Hawaii, Michigan, Montana, New Mexico, and North Dakota), five states (Arizona, Florida, Minnesota, Utah, and Iowa (for trusts)) have enacted modified versions of §2-603 that expressly preserve the majority rule, and the two most populous states, California and Texas, have done likewise by nonuniform legislation. The Florida statute is illustrative: "Words of survivorship . . . , such as 'if he survives me,' or to 'my surviving children,' *are a sufficient indication* of an intent contrary to the application of" the antilapse statute. Fla. Stat. Ann. §732.603(3)(a) (2008) (emphasis added). Other states that have adopted the 1990 UPC, most recently Massachusetts in early 2009, have dropped §2-603 or have removed from it paragraph (b)(3).

On the other hand, UPC §2-603(b)(3), backed up by Restatement (Third) of Property, supra, §5.5, may nonetheless influence outcomes in states that have not adopted §2-603.

Ruotolo v. Tietjen
Appellate Court of Connecticut, 2006
890 A.2d 166

LAVERY, C.J.   . . . [On March 1, 1990, John N. Swanson executed a will leaving one-half of the residue of his estate "to Hazel Brennan of Guilford, Connecticut, if she survives me." Hazel Brennan, the testator's stepdaughter, died on January 2, 2001, 17 days before the testator. The applicable antilapse statute, Conn. Gen. Stat. §45a-441, provides as follows:

> When a devisee or legatee, being a child, stepchild, grandchild, brother or sister of the testator, dies before him, and no provision has been made in the will for such contingency, the issue of such devisee or legatee shall take the estate so devised or bequeathed.

Hazel Brennan's daughter, Kathleen Smaldone, sought to take Hazel's share under §45a-441. The lower court held that the testator's use of the term "if she survives me" provided for the contingency that Brennan might not survive the testator, precluding application of the antilapse statute.] We disagree and, accordingly, reverse the judgment of the Superior Court. . . .

The sole issue on appeal is whether the court properly concluded that the antilapse statute does not apply. Section 45a-441 has never been scrutinized by appellate eyes and, thus, presents a question of first impression. . . .

I

HISTORY

At common law, when a named beneficiary under a will predeceased the testator, the share of the deceased beneficiary passed not to his descendants, but rather "lapsed." See 4 W. Bowe & D. Parker, Page on the Law of Wills (Rev. ed. 2005) §35.15, at 645. . . .

In 1783, the Massachusetts legislature enacted the first antilapse statute. It provided: "When a devise of real or personal estate is made to any child or other relation of the testator, and the devisee shall die before the testator, leaving issue who survive the testator, such issue shall take the estate so devised, in the same manner as the devisee would have done, if he had survived the testator; unless a different disposition thereof shall be made or required by the will." 1783 Mass. Acts, ch. 24, §8, quoted in Susan French, "Antilapse Statutes Are Blunt Instruments: A Blueprint for Reform," 37 Hastings L.J. 335, 339 n.16 (1985). . . . Today, antilapse statutes have been enacted in every state except Louisiana. . . .

Although varying in scope, all antilapse statutes provide that when a particular devisee predeceases the testator, the devise does not fall into the residue or pass to the testator's heirs by intestacy, but rather descends to the issue of the predeceased devisee. "Although . . . commonly called 'antilapse' statutes, the label is somewhat misleading. Contrary to what the label implies, antilapse statutes do not reverse the common-law rule of lapse because they do not abrogate the law-imposed condition of survivorship. . . . What the statutes actually do is modify the devolution of lapsed devises by providing a statutory substitute gift in the case of specified relatives." Edward C. Halbach, Jr. and Lawrence Waggoner, "The UPC's New Survivorship and Antilapse Provisions," 55 Alb. L. Rev. 1091, 1101 (1992). . . .

II

OUR ANTILAPSE STATUTE

. . . The [Connecticut] antilapse statute today provides that "[w]hen a devisee or legatee, being a child, stepchild, grandchild, brother or sister of the testator, dies before him, and no provision has been made in the will for such contingency, the issue of such devisee or legatee shall take the estate so devised or bequeathed." §45a-441. Other than adding siblings and stepchildren to the class of applicable devisees and legatees [in 1987], no substantive change has been made to our antilapse statute since [it was first enacted in] 1821. . . .

Plainly, the purpose underlying our antilapse statute is the prevention of unintended disinheritance. Its passage reflects a legislative determination that, as a matter of public policy, when a testator fails to provide for the possibility that a particular beneficiary might predecease him, the lineal descendants of that beneficiary take the applicable share. . . .

Under Connecticut law, the antilapse statute applies unless a "provision has been made in the will for such contingency." A review of the antilapse statutes presently in effect in forty-eight other jurisdictions reveals that this language is unique to our statute. It is not disputed that the "contingency" referenced in §45a-441 is the death of a devisee or legatee prior to that of the testator. What is contested is the proper construction of the "provision has been made in the will" language.

The appellees contend that inclusion of words of survivorship in a will constitutes a provision for such contingency, thereby rendering the antilapse statute inapplicable. Because the bequest in the present case contains the condition "if she survives me," they claim §45a-441 is inoperative. That simple and seemingly persuasive argument fails, however, on closer examination. . . .

[A]lthough the precise wording of the condition in our antilapse statute is unique, its existence is not. Like other states, Connecticut enacted its statute to counteract the harsh results of the common-law rule of lapse. Like other states, Connecticut conditioned operation of the antilapse statute on the intent of the testator as expressed in the will. Accordingly, the critical inquiry is whether an intent contrary to §45a-441 is so manifested.

Our inquiry into whether words of survivorship evince a contrary intent sufficient to defeat the antilapse statute is guided by the following principles. Antilapse statutes "will apply unless testator's intention to exclude its operation is shown with reasonable certainty." 6 W. Bowe & D. Parker, supra, §50.11, at 96. Section 5.5 of the Restatement (Third) of Property, Wills and Other Donative Transfers (1999), addresses antilapse statutes. Comment (f) to that section provides in relevant part: "Antilapse statutes establish a strong rule of construction, designed to carry out presumed intention. They are based on the constructional preference against disinheriting a line of descent. . . . Consequently, these statutes should be given the widest possible sphere of operation and should be defeated only when the trier of fact determines that the testator wanted to disinherit the line of descent headed by the deceased devisee." 1 Restatement (Third), Property, Wills and Other Donative Transfers §5.5, cmt. f, at 383 (1999). Hence, the burden is on those who seek to deny the statutory protection rather than on those who assert it.

Finally, we are mindful that our statute was enacted to *prevent* operation of the rule of lapse. Our statute is remedial in nature and must be liberally construed. Accordingly, we resolve any doubt in favor of the operation of §45a-441.

The bequest at issue states, "one-half . . . of [the residue] property to Hazel Brennan of Guilford, Connecticut, *if she survives me*." (Emphasis added.) Our task is to determine the significance of those words of survivorship. While the present case is one of first impression in Connecticut, numerous other states have considered the question of whether words of survivorship, such as "if she survives me," demonstrate a contrary intent on the part of the testator sufficient to negate operation of the antilapse statute.

III

OTHER AUTHORITY

Whether words of survivorship alone constitute sufficient evidence of a contrary intent on the part of the testator so as to prevent application of the antilapse statute is a question on which sibling authority is split. Some courts have concluded that words of survivorship demonstrate sufficient contrary intent. Illustrative of that line of cases is Bankers Trust Co. v. Allen, 135 N.W.2d 607 (Iowa 1965). In that case, the Supreme Court of Iowa stated: "The bequest to Mary in Item III is conditioned on her surviving the testator. We have held many times . . . that our antilapse statute . . . does not apply to a bequest so conditioned. . . . This is on the theory that a bequest to one 'if she survives me' manifests an intent that the bequest would lapse if the named beneficiary dies before the testator." Id. at 611.

Underlying that view is the presumption that the testator knowingly and deliberately included the words of survivorship. As one New York court explained: "[T]hese words were used by the testator in a will drawn by an experienced attorney. Some meaning must be attributed to them — and the meaning is clear — that survivorship was a condition precedent to the receipt of the residuary estate. If words were held to be devoid of meaning, then this court would be rewriting the testator's will." In re Robinson's Will, 236 N.Y.S.2d 293, 295 (Surr. 1963). That presumption has pitfalls of its own, however.

Inclusion of words of survivorship provides neither objective evidence that a conversation about §45a-441 took place nor objective evidence that the testator considered seriously the possibility of nonsurvival or inquired about the meaning of expressions such as "lapsed bequest" and the protections of the antilapse statute. "Because such a survival provision is often boiler-plate form-book language, the testator may not understand that such language could disinherit the line of descent headed by the deceased devisee. When the testator is older than the devisee and hence does not expect the devisee to die first . . . it seems especially unlikely that a provision requiring the devisee to survive the testator was intended to disinherit the devisee's descendants." 1 Restatement (Third), supra, §5.5, cmt. h, at 385. . . .

If [the testator] intended the bequest to lapse, the testator could have explicitly so provided. The testator also could have made an alternative devise, which "indicates a contrary intent, and hence overrides an antilapse statute." 1 Restatement (Third), supra, §5.5, cmt. g, at 384. That the testator did neither in the present case informs our consideration of whether he intended disinheritance.

The argument is further weakened by the fact that, under the interpretation of §45a-441 provided by the Probate Court and the Superior Court, the result is not merely that Brennan's share lapses; her share passes to the intestate estate. Thus, at its crux, the contention of the appellees asks us to presume that, although not explicitly provided for, the testator *intended* intestacy as to Brennan's share. That argument confounds Connecticut law, which presumes that a testator designed by his will to dispose of his entire estate and to avoid intestacy as to any part of it. In addition, the bequest to Brennan was residuary in nature. "Residuary language expresses an intention to . . . avoid intestacy." Indulging in the presumption that the testator intended to avoid intestacy militates against a finding that he intended for Brennan's share to lapse.

Another presumption bears consideration. In Clifford v. Cronin, 117 A. 489 (Conn. 1922), our Supreme Court . . . stated that "the testator is presumed to know the law and that his will is drawn accordingly." . . . If we must presume that the testator was aware of our antilapse statute, we must also equally presume that he was aware that it is remedial in nature and provided a liberal construction in Connecticut. In that event, the testator would have known that any ambiguity arising from the probate of his will, absent an express indication to the contrary, would be resolved in favor of operation of the statute.

Alternatively, another line of cases from various jurisdictions concludes that words of survivorship alone are insufficient to defeat an antilapse statute. . . .

A similar case is Detzel v. Nieberding, 219 N.E.2d 327 (Ohio Prob. 1966). In *Detzel,* the will provided in relevant part, "To my beloved sister, Mary Detzel, provided she be living at the time of my death." Mary Detzel predeceased the testator. In considering the operation of Ohio's antilapse statute, the court noted that "[a]ntilapse statutes are remedial and should receive a liberal construction[.]" Accordingly, "[a]ll doubts are to be resolved in favor of the operation of the antilapse statute. . . . [T]o render [the] statute inoperative contrary intent of testator must be plainly indicated." The court continued: "To prevent operation of the Ohio antilapse statute when a devise is made to a relative conditioned upon the survival of the testator by the relative, and the relative predeceases the testator leaving issue who survive the testator, it is necessary that the testator, in apt language, make an alternative provision in his will providing that in the event such relative predeceases or fails to survive the testator such devise shall be given to another specifically named or identifiable devisee or devisees." Although we do not agree that the only way to negate operation of an antilapse statute is by providing an alternate devise, *Detzel* is persuasive nevertheless. *Detzel* has never been reversed, although another Ohio court characterized it as "clearly and completely erroneous." Shalkhauser v. Beach, 233 N.E.2d 527, 530 (Ohio Prob. 1968). The Uniform Probate Code, however, seems to agree with the logic of *Detzel*.

In 1990, a revised Uniform Probate Code was promulgated, which contained a substantially altered antilapse statute. Notably, §2-603(b)(3) provides that "words of survivorship, such as in a devise to an individual 'if he survives me,' or in a devise to 'my surviving children,' are not, in the absence of additional evidence, a sufficient indication of an intent contrary to the application of this section." Unif. Prob. Code §2-603(b)(3). The comment to that section explains that this expansion of antilapse protection was necessary because "an antilapse statute is remedial in nature. . . . [T]he remedial character of the statute means that it should be given the widest possible latitude to operate" in considering whether in an individual case there is an indication of a contrary intent sufficiently convincing to defeat the statute. The Restatement Third of Property, supra, agrees; and that proposition is consonant with Connecticut law. In sum, we agree with those jurisdictions that have held that mere words of survivorship do not defeat antilapse statutes.

IV
CONCLUSION

Our antilapse statute was enacted to prevent operation of the rule of lapse and unintended disinheritance. The statute is remedial and receives a liberal construction. Any doubts are resolved in favor of its operation. We therefore conclude that words of survivorship, such as "if she survives me," alone do not constitute a "provision" in the will for the contingency of the death of a beneficiary, as the statute requires, and thus are insufficient to negate operation of §45a-441. Our conclusion today effectuates the intent of the General Assembly in enacting this remedial statute. Should a testator desire to avoid application of the antilapse statute, the testator must either unequivocally express that intent or simply provide for an alternate bequest. Because the testator in the present case did neither, the protections of the antilapse statute apply. Accordingly, the bequest to Brennan does not lapse, but rather descends to her issue.

The judgment is reversed and the case is remanded for further proceedings consistent with this opinion.

NOTES AND QUESTIONS

1. *Epilogue.* The decision of the Appellate Court of Connecticut in *Ruotolo* was affirmed by the Connecticut Supreme Court. "The Appellate Court properly resolved [the] issue in its concise and well reasoned opinion. Because that opinion fully addresses all arguments raised in this appeal, we adopt it as a proper statement of the issue and the applicable law concerning that issue." Ruotolo v. Tietjen, 916 A.2d 1 (Conn. 2007) (per curiam).

2. In Jeffrey A. Cooper, A Lapse in Judgment: Ruotolo v. Tietjen and Interpretation of Connecticut's Anti-Lapse Statute, 20 Quinnipiac Prob. L.J. 204 (2007), Professor Cooper gives a scathing review of *Ruotolo*. He argues, among other things, that the court misread the relative weight of authority on the question whether words of survivorship preclude the application of the antilapse statute. The "case law from other jurisdictions," Cooper writes,

> reveals not an even split of authority but rather a clear majority rule that a requirement of survival, without more, generally is sufficient to negate application of an anti-lapse statute. Others

undertaking such comparative analyses similarly have concluded that the "overwhelming weight of authority" runs counter to the Appellate Court's approach. While Connecticut's courts obviously need not defer to precedents from other jurisdictions, the Appellate Court's comparative analysis of other states' anti-lapse statutes failed to properly frame the question before it and failed to make clear that the court was declining to follow a well-established majority rule. [Id. at 213.]

Cooper also asks (id. at 221), what about Erickson v. Erickson, page 345? If a drafter mistakenly uses the term "if she survives me," could that mistake be corrected by reformation?

3.   *The no-residue-of-the-residue rule revisited.* In concluding that the term "if he survives me" did not provide for the contingency that Hazel Brennan might predecease the testator, the court was influenced by the constructional preference for avoiding intestacy. If the antilapse statute did not apply, reasoned the court, then Hazel's share, being a residuary devise, would pass by intestacy by application of the no-residue-of-the-residue rule. But must this be so? In an omitted footnote, the court observed that the Restatement (Third) of Property rejects the no-residue-of-the-residue rule, and that abrogating the rule would be "consistent with the presumption that a testator intends to avoid intestacy." Yet the court did not question whether to continue to abide by the rule. Nor did any of the parties on appeal. Should they have?

A review of the appellate briefs reveals that the testator's heirs were cousins not mentioned in the will. However, the briefs also indicate that the other half of the residue was left in equal shares to four named persons, including Hazel's daughter, Kathleen. The court's decision therefore entitled Kathleen to her mother's one-half share plus her own one-eighth share. Is it likely that the testator would have preferred this outcome to Hazel's share being divided among Kathleen and the other residuary beneficiaries?

4.   *The importance of sound drafting.* A good lawyer does not rely upon presumptions. Instead she makes the client's intent clear by providing what happens if the intended devisee does not survive the testator. If there is a gift over to another devisee, she provides what happens if the second devisee predeceases the testator. Thus, for example, "to *A* if *A* survives me, but if *A* does not survive me, to *B* if *B* survives me, and if both *A* and *B* do not survive me, to be added to the residue of my estate." See John L. Garvey, Drafting Wills and Trusts: Anticipating the Birth and Death of Possible Beneficiaries, 71 Or. L. Rev. 47, 49-54 (1992).

A central purpose of UPC §2-603(b)(3) is to induce lawyers to discuss with their clients the possibility of a predeceasing beneficiary so that the client can make an informed choice that the lawyer records expressly in the will. The exemplary clause in the prior paragraph, for example, brings into sharp focus for the client the possible scenarios and who will take in each (the official comment to §2-603 provides similar exemplary language).

5.   *Boilerplate revisited.* Stamping out undesired boilerplate by statute turns out to be a difficult undertaking. After enactment, new boilerplate will arise, but that new boilerplate may not take the form that the statute's drafters had hoped. In some practices, UPC §2-603(b)(3) has prompted not the drafter's desired

conversation or the use of language such as is suggested in the prior note, but rather new boilerplate such as: "No lapse or antilapse statute shall apply to any disposition of property under this will." There is, moreover, a further problem. Some lawyers will continue to use traditional will forms that make use of language such as "if he survives me" because they are not aware of the new statutory rule. See Martin D. Begleiter, Article II of the Uniform Probate Code and the Malpractice Revolution, 59 Tenn. L. Rev. 101, 126-130 (1991) (warning of malpractice risks for lawyers using their old forms in states adopting UPC §2-603(b)(3)).

6.   In part because it reverses the rule that words of survivorship state an intent that the antilapse statute not apply, UPC §2-603 includes a complex system of priorities for primary and secondary substitute gifts to resolve the question when the descendants of the primary taker have priority over the secondary taker or the secondary taker's descendants. The curious student can find §2-603 and its official comment, which together run over 7,000 words, through the Uniform Law Commission's web page or in the Uniform Laws Annotated database in Westlaw.

NOTE: WORDS OF PURCHASE, WORDS OF LIMITATION, AND THE MEANING OF "AND" VERSUS "OR"

Suppose *T* devises property "to *A* and her heirs and assigns." As a general rule, the phrase "to *A*" is read as *words of purchase*, indicating to whom the property is devised (here, to *A*), and the phrase "and her heirs and assigns forever" is read as *words of limitation*, indicating what interest in the property is devised (here, a fee simple). On the other hand, a devise by *T* "to *A* or her heirs" can be read to include only words of purchase, indicating that *A* is the primary devisee and that *A*'s heirs are the substitute takers if *A* predeceases *T*. The crucial difference, which allows the instrument of transfer to be read to include a substitute gift, is the use of "or" instead of "and" between "*A*" and "her heirs."

In a few cases, the courts have read the term "and" as "or" to provide for a substitute gift to *A*'s heirs, thereby avoiding lapse. In Jackson v. Schultz, 151 A.2d 284 (Del. Ch. 1959), *A* was the testator's wife and *A*'s heirs were her children (the testator's step-children). The court read the term "and" as "or" to provide a substitute gift to the children, thereby avoiding an escheat to the state, as *T* had no living heirs. See also In re Mangel's Estate, 186 N.W.2d 276 (Wis. 1971), reading "and" as "or" in light of extrinsic evidence that *T* would have preferred a substitute gift to *A*'s heirs than for the gift to lapse and pass to *T*'s heirs.

Other courts have reached the opposite result on virtually identical facts. See Hofing v. Willis, 201 N.E.2d 852 (Ill. 1964); Estate of Straube, 990 S.W.2d 40 (Mo. App. 1999).

3.   Class Gifts

Under the common law lapse rule, a *class gift* is treated differently from a gift to individuals. If a class member predeceases the testator, the surviving members of the class divide the total gift, including the deceased member's share.[18] Thus, the crucial question is: What is a class? The test is often said to be whether the testator was "group minded." The testator is thought to have been group minded if he used a class label in describing the beneficiaries, such as "to *A*'s children" or "to my nephews and nieces." A gift to beneficiaries who form a natural class, but are described by their individual names, may be deemed a class gift if the court decides, after admitting extrinsic evidence, that the testator would want the survivors to divide the property rather than for a predeceasing beneficiary's share to lapse.

Restatement (Third) of Property: Wills and Other Donative Transfers
(T.D. No. 4, 2004)

§13.1   CLASS GIFT DEFINED — HOW CREATED

(a) A class gift is a disposition to beneficiaries who are described by a group label and are intended to take as a group. Taking as a group means that:

(1) the membership of the class is typically not static, but is subject to fluctuation by increase or decrease until the time when a class member is entitled to distribution; and

(2) upon distribution, the property is divided among the then-entitled class members on a fractional basis.

(b) If the terms of the disposition identify the beneficiaries only by a group label, the disposition creates a class gift, unless the language or circumstances indicate that the transferor intended the beneficiaries to take as individuals.

§13.2   CLASS GIFT DISTINGUISHED FROM DISPOSITION TO BENEFICIARIES TAKING AS INDIVIDUALS — HOW CREATED

. . . (b) If the terms of the disposition identify the beneficiaries only by name, without any reference to a group label, the disposition does not create a class gift, but is to the beneficiaries taking as individuals.

(c) If the terms of the disposition identify the beneficiaries (i) by a group label and (ii) either by name or by the number of beneficiaries who then fit the group label, the disposition is presumed not to create a class gift, but is to the beneficiaries taking as individuals. The presumption is rebutted if the language or circumstances indicate that the transferor intended the beneficiaries to take as a group.

---

18. This rule is subject to the antilapse statutes, which typically apply to class gifts, a nuance we take up at page 379.

Dawson v. Yucus
Illinois Appellate Court, 1968
239 N.E.2d 305

[Nelle G. Stewart, who died on May 29, 1965, devised her interest in her late husband's family farm to two nephews on her husband's side of the family. The second clause of her will provided:

> Through the Will of my late husband, Dr. Frank A. Stewart, I received an undivided one-fifth (1/5) interest in two hundred sixty-one and thirty-eight hundredths (261.38) acres of farm lands located in . . . Sangamon County, Illinois, and believing as I do that those farm lands should go back to my late husband's side of the house, I therefore give, devise and bequeath my one-fifth (1/5) interest in said farm lands as follows: One-half (1/2) of my interest therein to Stewart Wilson, a nephew, now living in Birmingham, Michigan and One-half (1/2) of my interest to Gene Burtle, a nephew, now living in Mission, Kansas.

Gene Burtle, one of the nephews, predeceased the testator. The residue was divided between Ina Mae Yucus and Hazel Degelow. At issue was whether the gift to the nephews Wilson and Burtle was a class gift, in which case the surviving nephew, Wilson, would take Burtle's share. If it was not a class gift, then Burtle's share would lapse, and so would pass to Yucus and Degelow as the residuary devisees. To strengthen the moral claim for finding a class, Wilson conveyed his interest in Burtle's share to Burtle's surviving children, who were substituted as plaintiffs. The court held that a class gift was not intended.]

JONES, J. . . . At the trial the court found that the death of Gene Burtle prior to that of the testatrix created a latent ambiguity and admitted extrinsic evidence relating to testatrix' intentions. . . . [Of the] relatives of Dr. Stewart, only Gene Burtle and Stewart Wilson had a close personal relationship with the testatrix. Gene Burtle died on May 15, 1963, and the testatrix knew of his death but made no changes in her previously executed will. There was evidence from four witnesses that in conversations had with testatrix she stated she wanted the one-fifth interest in the farm to go either to her husband's side of the house, or to Gene Burtle and Stewart Wilson because she felt especially close to them and none other of Dr. Stewart's relatives had any contact with her.

The trial court held, we think correctly, that clause two of testatrix' will did not create a class gift and that the gift in that clause to Gene Burtle lapsed and, pursuant to the Illinois Lapse Statute, Chapt. 3, Sec. 49, I.R.S. 1965, passed into the residue of her estate.

The definition of class gifts and pertinent rules of construction as followed by Illinois courts are set forth in the case of Strohm v. McMullen, 89 N.E.2d 383 (Ill. 1949):

> The definition of a class gift adopted by this court, as laid down by Mr. Jarman in his work on Wills, Vol. I, p. 534, 5th Am. Ed., is:
> "A gift to a class is defined . . . as a gift of an aggregate sum to a body of persons uncertain in number at the time of the gift, to be ascertained at a future time, and who are all to take in

equal or in some other definite proportions, the share of each being dependent for its amount upon the ultimate number of persons."

"A class, in its ordinary acceptation, is a number or body of persons with common characteristics or in like circumstances, or having some common attribute, and, as applied to a devise, it is generally understood to mean a number of persons who stand in the same relation to each other or to the testator." Blackstone v. Althouse, 116 N.E. 154 (Ill. 1917). And it has been definitely decided in this State that in determining whether a devise is to a class or to individuals depends upon the language of the will. If from such language it appears that the amounts of their shares are uncertain until the devise or bequest takes effect, the beneficiaries will generally be held to take as a class; but where at the time of making the gifts the number of beneficiaries is certain, and the share each is to receive is also certain, and in no way dependent for its amount upon the number who shall survive, it is not a gift to a class, but to the individuals.

There is an exception to the rule that naming the individual prevents the gift from becoming a class gift, stated in Strauss v. Strauss, 2 N.E.2d 699 (Ill. 1936), holding that the mere fact that the testator mentions by name the individuals who make up the class is not conclusive, and that if the intention to give a right of survivorship is collected from the remaining provisions of the will, as applied to the existing facts, such an intention must prevail.

Admittedly the gift in clause two is not made with the usual generic class description such as "children," "brothers," "nephews," "cousins," "issue," "descendants," or "family" but is in fact to two named individuals, conditions which militate against construction of the clause as a class gift. However, plaintiffs argue that because of the death of Gene Burtle prior to that of the testatrix a latent ambiguity exists and extrinsic evidence was properly received to show the true intention of the testatrix in clause two of her will, and that the phrase in clause two, "and believing as I do that these farm lands should go back to my husband's side of the house," together with the extrinsic evidence, clearly requires class gift construction. . . .

In this case the testatrix named the individuals, Stewart Wilson and Gene Burtle, and gave them each a one-half portion of her interest in the farm, thus making certain the number of beneficiaries and the share each is to receive. The shares in no way depend upon the number who shall survive the death of the testatrix. There is nothing in the language of the will that indicates the testatrix intended to create a class or survivorship gift. The only other provision of the will, also contained in clause two, that has any bearing on the question is the statement, "believing as I do that those farm lands should go back to my late husband's side of the house." While it is true that this language recites testatrix' desire that the one-fifth interest in the farm go back to her husband's side of the house, it does not indicate a survivorship gift was intended. Her intention to return the farm to her husband's side of the house was fulfilled when she named Stewart Wilson and Gene Burtle as the donees of the interest. . . .

Further emphasis for the result we have reached is supplied by other factors found in the will and extrinsic evidence. First, the testatrix created a survivorship gift of the residue of her estate in the ninth clause of her will, thus indicating she knew how to manifest an intent to create a class or survivorship gift; hence, the language of clause two, phrased differently, was intended to create a gift to individuals distributively. . . . Secondly, the common characteristic of the alleged class described by plaintiffs is that of relation to Dr. Stewart, or, in the words of clause two, the class is of "my late husband's side of the house." However, this characteristic is also shared by three other heirs of Dr. Stewart of the same degree of relationship to him as Stewart Wilson and Gene Burtle. It thus appears that Gene Burtle and Stewart Wilson do not constitute the alleged class but are individuals named from the class. . . .

The devise in clause two was not to persons who come within the designation of a class but was to individuals distributively. It was not so made or limited to prevent the operation of the Illinois Lapse Statute which must be given its intended effect. The court below correctly held that upon the death of Gene Burtle prior to that of the testatrix the devise to him lapsed and passed under the residuary clause of the will. The Decree will be affirmed.

Affirmed.

QUESTIONS AND NOTES

1. Does the outcome in *Dawson* support the extension of the antilapse statutes to gifts to kin of the testator's spouse?

2. The court's reasoning in *Dawson* is in accord with the weight of modern authority, which, in line with the influential Jarman treatise cited by the court, takes a rules-based approach to discerning whether the testator was group minded. Under this approach, a group label and dynamic shares indicate a class gift. Naming individuals and specifying their shares, as in *Dawson*, indicates that the testator was not group minded. But other courts and many commentators disagree. In Thomas M. Cooley, II, What Constitutes a Gift to a Class, 49 Harv. L. Rev. 903 (1936), the author argues that the rules-based approach

> obscure[s] the fact that what is known as a gift to a class is simply a legal device by which they can make a kind of distribution not specifically required by the words of the will. They imply that a class or a gift to a class is something which exists in a will and can be detected by a trained eye. It is submitted that this is not the case. What is found in the will is what the testator provided with respect to events and conditions he foresaw among the beneficiaries he indicated. From this, the court may, or may not, determine that what he did not foresee will best be carried out by the application of the device described as a gift to a class. [Id. at 931.]

In Sullivan v. Sullivan, 529 N.E.2d 890 (Mass. App. 1988), the testator devised her property "to my nephews Marshall John McDonough, and David Condon McDonough, and to my niece Martha McDonough Sullivan, in equal shares, that is one-third each." She omitted mention of two nieces from whom she was estranged. The named nephews and nieces were given fixed shares of one-third each. One mentioned nephew (Marshall) predeceased the testator without descendants. To avoid lapse, the court held the devise was to a class and that the property was to be divided equally between the survivors David and Martha. See also Iozapavichus v. Fournier, 308 A.2d 573 (Me. 1973) (holding that a gift "to

Bessie and Louise," who happened to be the testator's close friends, was a class gift on the basis of extrinsic evidence tending to show that the testator would not want Bessie's share to pass by intestacy).

3.   Restatement (Third) of Property, supra, §13.2(c) establishes a presumption that if the testator identifies the beneficiaries by group label and by name, the testator was not group minded, but the presumption may be rebutted if the "circumstances indicate that the transferor intended the beneficiaries to take as a group." Do not the circumstances in *Dawson* indicate that the testator intended her late husband's farm to pass to his nephews Stewart and Gene as a group?

4.   For further discussion of class gifts in modern law, see Lawrence W. Waggoner, Class Gifts Under the Restatement (Third) of Property, 33 Ohio N.U. L. Rev. 993 (2007); Frederic S. Schwartz, The New Restatement of Property and Class Gifts: Losing Sight of the Testator's Intention, 22 Quinnipiac Prob. L.J. 221 (2009).

NOTE: APPLICATION OF ANTILAPSE STATUTES TO CLASS GIFTS

Almost all states apply their antilapse statutes to class gifts to a single-generation class such as to "children" or "siblings,"[19] and most statutes so provide. See UPC §2-605 (1969), page 365; Restatement (Third) of Property: Wills and Other Donative Transfers §5.5, cmt. j (1999). In states where the statute is unclear, courts reason that the antilapse statutes are designed to carry out the average testator's intent and that the average testator would prefer for the deceased beneficiary's share to go to the beneficiary's descendants rather than to the surviving members of the class. However, in some states, antilapse statutes do not apply to dispositions to class members who die before execution of the will. See Tex. Prob. Code Ann. §68(a) (2008). In these states it is assumed that the testator did not have the dead class member in mind and did not want him to take. Thus:

> *Case 10. T*, a widow, dies leaving a will devising Blackacre "to my sisters," and devising her residuary estate to her stepson, *S*. When *T* executed the will, *T* had two sisters living, *A* and *B*. One sister, *C*, died before the will was executed, leaving children who survived *T. A* died during *T*'s lifetime leaving two children. *T* is survived by *B, A*'s children, *C*'s children, and *S*. Who takes Blackacre? Assuming the antilapse statute applies to devises to sisters, in most states *B* takes a one-third share, *A*'s children take a one-third share, and *C*'s children take a one-third share. In a minority of states, *C*'s children do not share because *C* was dead when the will was executed, and Blackacre goes one-half to *B* and one-half to *A*'s children. If the antilapse statute did not apply to class gifts, *B*, as the sole surviving member of the class, would take Blackacre.

---

19. There is no need to apply the antilapse statute to a gift to a multigenerational class such as to "issue" or "descendants" because a multigenerational class absorbs the concept of representation familiar from inheritance law. See page 856. Suppose *T*'s will devises his estate "to my descendants." *T* has a son, *B*, and a daughter, *C. B* dies, leaving a daughter, *D*. Then *T* dies. *D* takes *B*'s share by representation.

SECTION C.   CHANGES IN PROPERTY AFTER EXECUTION OF WILL

1.   *Ademption by Extinction*

What happens if a will includes a specific devise of an item of property, but the testator sells or gives the item away before death? Specific devises of real and personal property are subject to the doctrine of *ademption by extinction*. Thus:

> *Case 11. T's* will devises Blackacre to her son, John, and the residuary estate to her daughter, Mary. Some years later, the testator sells Blackacre and uses the sale proceeds to purchase Whiteacre, then dies without having changed her will. Under traditional law, the gift of Blackacre is adeemed (from the Latin *adimere*: to take away). Since Blackacre is not owned by the testator at her death, the devise fails. John has no claim to Whiteacre, for the will does not devise Whiteacre to him.

Ademption applies only to specific devises. Generally speaking, a *specific* devise is a disposition of a specific item of the testator's property. Examples are gifts of Blackacre or of "my three-carat diamond ring given to me by my Aunt Jane." Ademption does not apply to *general, demonstrative*, or *residuary* devises. A devise is *general* when the testator intends to confer a general benefit and not give a particular asset — for example, a legacy of $100,000 to *A*. If there is not $100,000 in cash in the testator's estate at death, the legacy is not adeemed; other property must be sold to satisfy *A*'s general legacy. A *demonstrative* devise is a hybrid: a general devise, yet payable from a specific source. Suppose that the testator's will gives *B* "the sum of $100,000 to be paid from the proceeds of sale of my Apple stock." Most courts would hold this to be a demonstrative devise. If the testator owns sufficient Apple stock at death, in raising the $100,000 the executor must comply with the testamentary direction to sell the stock. But if the testator does not own any Apple stock at death or does not own $100,000 worth of Apple stock, the devise is not adeemed. Other property must be sold in order to raise the full $100,000. A *residuary* devise conveys that portion of the testator's estate not otherwise effectively devised by other parts of the will, such as a devise to *A* of "all the rest, residue, and remainder of my property and estate."

Under the traditional *identity theory* of ademption, if a specifically devised item is not in the testator's estate, the gift is extinguished (subject to limited exceptions noted below). Under the newer *intent theory* of ademption, if the specifically devised item is not in the testator's estate, the beneficiary may nonetheless be entitled to the replacement for, or cash value of, the original item, depending on whether the beneficiary can show that this is what the testator would have wanted. Under the intent theory, in Case 11 John would be entitled to Whiteacre if he could show that *T* intended John to take Whiteacre as a replacement for Blackacre.

In re Estate of Anton

Supreme Court of Iowa, 2007

731 N.W.2d 19

APPEL, J.   In this case, we consider whether the sale of certain property by an attorney-in-fact prior to the death of the testator resulted in ademption of a specific property bequest. . . .

FACTUAL BACKGROUND

In 1972, the testator, Hestor Mary Lewis Anton (Mary), married Herbert Anton, the father of Gretchen Coy. It was the second marriage for both Herbert and Mary. During this marriage, Gretchen, Mary's stepdaughter, deeded a piece of real property to her stepmother and father. Herbert and Mary built a duplex on the property. After the death of Herbert in 1976, Mary became the sole owner of the duplex property.

In 1981, Mary executed a will. In the will, she bequeathed half of her interest in the duplex to Gretchen. The remaining half interest was bequeathed to her biological son, Robert Lewis. Mary bequeathed the remainder of her estate to Robert and her daughter, Nancy Ezarski.

In 1986, Mary was involved in a serious automobile accident. After the accident, she lived in a series of nursing homes. For a short period of time, she lived in a nursing home called Riverside. Thereafter, she moved to Green Hills Health Center in Ames, where she had a private suite. Among other things, Mary suffered from Huntington's Chorea, a malady that impacts the nervous system.

Shortly after the accident, Mary executed a durable power of attorney authorizing her daughter Nancy to manage her financial affairs.[20] The power of attorney took effect immediately. The document was a "durable" power of attorney: it explicitly stated that it would remain in full force and effect until Mary's death and would be unaffected by any mental or physical disability that might occur after its execution.

From 1986 until Mary's death on December 2, 2003, Nancy handled her mother's financial affairs. There is no evidence in the record indicating that Nancy did anything improper in connection with Mary's assets.

On Memorial Day 1998, Nancy and her mother discussed selling the family residence to provide her mother with necessary support. After this conversation, staff at the nursing home advised Nancy that she should not discuss financial matters with her mother as it would exacerbate her condition and cause distress. As a result of this input from nursing home staff, Nancy and her mother had no further discussions regarding her financial affairs.

Nancy, acting as attorney-in-fact, began selling her mother's assets in order to pay her ongoing living expenses. Mary was generally aware her assets were being

---

20. On powers of attorney, see pages 448-456. — Eds.

sold off to pay for her expenses. Her only concern was that she would have enough money to continue living at Green Hills. There was, however, no evidence that Mary was ever aware that the duplex was sold.

By 2003, the only asset remaining in Mary's estate was the duplex. The combined income from that asset and from her husband's trust was insufficient to meet her ongoing expenses. At this point, Nancy listed the duplex property for sale. Nancy then received a call from Gretchen's son, who informed Nancy of the terms of Mary's will and told her she could not sell the duplex.

In light of the phone call from Gretchen's son, Nancy took the duplex off the market and contacted an attorney, who issued an opinion stating that Nancy had the power and authority to sell the duplex. The attorney also advised, however, that the trustee of the Harold R. Lewis Trust had the discretion to distribute the principal of the trust to Mary for her health, well-being, and maintenance. Nancy then contacted the trust officer at First National Bank to inquire about obtaining a loan from the trust. She was informed that the bank preferred that all of Mary's assets be sold prior to invading the trust's principal. As a result, Nancy believed she had no other choice but to sell the property, which was accomplished on August 28, 2003.

The evidence in the record regarding Mary's capacity at the time of the sale is thin. Nurses' notes indicate that on April 16, 2003, Mary had "periods of confusion." A social service progress note dated October 9, 2003, six weeks after the sale, makes reference to "advanced dementia." Nancy herself appeared to have concerns regarding Mary's mental state. Nancy indicated in a phone conversation with Gretchen Coy in June 2003 that Mary "sleeps almost all the time." The letter to Nancy from the estate's attorney recalled Nancy's indication that Mary was not competent to handle her affairs at the time the sale of the duplex was being considered. At trial, however, Nancy testified that her mother was "not incompetent" at the time of the duplex's sale.

The net proceeds of the duplex's sale were $133,263. Nancy began to pay Mary's living expenses out of the proceeds. At the time of Mary's death, the remaining balance was $104,317.38. . . .

LEGAL BACKGROUND

A. . . .

In the early twentieth century, this court adopted the identity theory of ademption. Under the identity rule, if specifically bequeathed property was not found in the estate at the time of death, the bequest was adeemed. . . . Beginning in the 1960s, however, this court began to depart from the rigid application of the identity theory in all settings.

For example, in Estate of Bierstedt, 119 N.W.2d 234 (Iowa 1963), this court considered whether the sale by a guardian of specifically bequeathed real estate without the knowledge and consent of an incompetent testator caused ademption by extinction under the identity rule. In this case, the court rejected application of a "rigid identity rule" and applied what it called a "modified intention" approach. The court noted that the order establishing the guardianship demonstrated that Bierstedt was incompetent at the time the land was sold, thereby creating a presumption of lack of testamentary capacity. As a result, because the testator did not have the testamentary capacity to, in effect, work a change in the will, the sale could not be considered to manifest an intention on the part of the testator to modify the will. Therefore, no ademption occurred.

Similarly, in Estate of Wolfe, 208 N.W.2d 923 (Iowa 1973), this court considered whether the destruction of property which was the subject of a specific bequest, contemporaneous with the death of the testator, worked an ademption. In this case, the testator had specifically bequeathed his automobile, a 1969 Buick Electra, to his brother. The testator was killed in an automobile accident in which his automobile was a total loss. Insurance proceeds that included the value of the auto were paid to the estate. The brother claimed he was entitled to the proceeds. In holding for the brother and against the estate, the court rejected the identity rule and emphasized that the intent of the testator is paramount in determining whether an ademption has occurred. As a result, the court reasoned that where property is missing from the estate because of some act or event involuntary as to the testator, there is no ademption.

In summary, our cases hold that the identity rule will not be rigidly applied in all cases. Under what the court has called the "modified intention theory," the identity rule will not be applied to cases where specifically devised property is removed from the estate through an act that is involuntary as to the testator. This includes cases where the property is sold by a guardian, or conservator, or is destroyed contemporaneously with the death of the testator. Until now, however, we have not had occasion to consider whether ademption occurs when specifically devised property is sold by an attorney-in-fact.

B. . . .

At common law, a power of attorney was revoked by the incapacity of the principal. The durable power of attorney was created to avoid the common law result and provide persons with limited means a cost-effective alternative to guardianship proceedings. All fifty states have now enacted statutes authorizing durable powers of attorney.

While there are many cases in other states involving acts of court-appointed guardians where the testators are incompetent, there are only a few cases dealing with the question of whether acts of an agent pursuant to a durable power of attorney cause ademption of specific bequests. The cases have not reached uniform results.

The first case dealing with the question is Estate of Graham, 533 P.2d 1318 (Kan. 1975). In this case, a specific devise of real estate was sold by an agent pursuant to a power of attorney to support the testator's stay in a rest home. After the death of the testator, the beneficiary of the specific bequest sought the balance of the proceeds remaining in the estate.

The Kansas Supreme Court held that no ademption occurred. The court emphasized that the devise was not conveyed with the full knowledge and consent of the testator during his lifetime. The court noted that it seemed logical that the same legal principles should apply to a conveyance by an attorney-in-fact acting under a power of attorney as are applicable to the acts of a guardian. The court noted that were the rule otherwise, an attorney-in-fact hostile to one of the beneficiaries may adeem a gift through the sale of specifically devised property. The court emphasized, however, that the beneficiary was entitled only to the unexpended balance of the proceeds of specifically devised property.

The Ohio Supreme Court considered this question in Estate of Hegel, 668 N.E.2d 474 (1996). In this case, Hegel sold the principal's house after she had become incompetent pursuant to a durable power of attorney. The principal's will devised the house to Hegel. Upon the principal's death, Hegel claimed entitlement to the cash proceeds of the sale that remained in the principal's estate. The probate court held that the devise had been adeemed by extinction. On appeal, the Court of Appeals of Ohio reversed in a 2-1 decision.

The Ohio Supreme Court reversed the court of appeals in a 4-3 decision and held that the specific devise was adeemed. The majority emphasized that while the Ohio legislature had passed a nonademption statute in regard to the actions of court-appointed guardians, it did not extend the rule to agents acting under durable powers of attorney. The majority further noted that it did not regard those acting under powers of attorney as the same as guardians. The majority indicated that attorneys-in-fact have more freedom and can act without court approval as the principal's alter ego. . . .

ANALYSIS

Although the identity rule has been subject to substantial criticism and has been abandoned or substantially altered in the Uniform Probate Code and the Restatement (Third) of Property, neither party questioned its continued vitality either in the district court or on appeal. See Unif. Probate Code §2-606 (1997) (adopting "'intent' theory" of ademption); Restatement (Third) of Prop.: Wills and Other Donative Transfers §5.2(c) (1999) (specific devise fails if property is not in estate "unless failure of devise would be inconsistent with testator's intent"). Instead, the parties have focused on whether Mary was competent at the time of sale and whether the rule in *Bierstedt* should be extended to cases involving attorneys-in-fact. In this posture, we do not examine the continued vitality of the identity rule, but simply apply the principles established in our case law to the facts of this case. For the reasons expressed below, we hold that the sale of the duplex by an attorney-in-fact under the circumstances presented did not result in ademption of the bequest.

A. . . .

If Mary was incompetent at the time of sale of the duplex, the act would clearly be involuntary as to her. The question then arises whether the rule in *Bierstedt* should be extended to cases involving the sale of specifically devised property by an attorney-in-fact, or whether the extension should be rejected.

We follow the approach in *In re Estate of Graham*. It is true, however, that there are some differences between the appointment of a guardian by a court and the selection of an agent with durable power of attorney by a competent testator prior to the onset of any mental infirmity. For example, in the case of the execution of a durable power of attorney, the principal has the power to choose the agent and to approve the scope of the agent's powers.

The rationale of *Bierstedt*, however, is that ademption does not occur when specifically devised property is sold as a result of acts that are involuntary to the testator. The rationale of our cases is that ademption occurs where a testator had knowledge of a transaction involving a specific devise, realizes the effect of the transaction on his or her estate plan, and has an opportunity to revise the will. Where these elements are not present, no ademption occurs. The focus of analysis is on the testator and whether the testator has made a deliberate decision not to revise the will, and not on the nature of the agency causing the involuntary act.

The legal context[ ] of *In re Estate of Hegel* [is] distinguishable. In [that case], the legislature had stepped in to amend the probate code to specifically exclude acts of guardians from the rule of ademption. The legislative failure to exclude acts of agents pursuant to durable powers of attorney was found to be significant. The Iowa legislature, however, has not taken [similar action]. . . .

B. . . .

In the alternative, assuming that Mary was competent at the time of the duplex's sale, the question arises as to whether an ademption should occur based, not upon the act of the attorney-in-fact in selling the property, but upon the intent of the testator expressed prior to the sale. Specifically, the estate claims that Mary on Memorial Day 1998 knew that her assets would need to be sold for her support and specifically approved of the sale of her residence by her attorney-in-fact. There appears to have been no specific discussion, however, of the sale of the duplex at any time. Further, it is conceded that Mary had no knowledge of the actual sale of the duplex over five years later. Nancy simply sold it without telling her mother in order to avoid aggravating her condition.

We do not question the wisdom of Nancy's decision to sell the property without consulting Mary. Our only concern is the legal consequences that flow from it. This case thus raises the question of what result should occur where the principal is competent, but the attorney-in-fact sells a specific devise without the knowledge of the testator.

If Mary was aware of the transaction, was aware of the impact the transaction had on her estate plan, and did not change her will, ademption would, of course, occur under the identity theory. Here, however, Mary only had a general knowledge that assets may need to be sold for her support at some time in the future. This is simply not the same as contemporaneous knowledge that an asset that is subject to a specific devise has, in fact, been removed from the estate. Most ordinary persons would not run down to the lawyer's office to change their will in light of a remote future contingency that has not been specifically discussed and which may or may not occur in the future. An expression of intent in the indefinite future to sell assets for support is not sufficient to cause ademption under our "modified intention theory" where the testator is not aware that the specific action has taken place.

It is true that Nancy did not sell the duplex until all other sources of revenue had been exhausted for her mother's support. It may well be that, under the circumstances, her mother would have assented to the sale of the duplex in 2003 had she been asked. But under our cases, the relevant issue is not whether Mary would have assented to the sale had she been asked, but rather whether Mary had the opportunity to change her will once she knew that the duplex was no longer part of her estate. Under the record here, she simply did not have that opportunity.

There remains a question of remedy. Gretchen seeks to recover $72,625, or half the proceeds realized upon the sale of the duplex. Some courts have held that where ademption does not occur, the devisee is entitled to the entire value notwithstanding the fact that the proceeds may have been used for the care of the testator. In re Estate of Mason, 397 P.2d 1005, 1007 (Cal. 1965). We have considered the issue, however, and have held that in cases where specific devises are removed from the estate as a result of an involuntary act, the devisee is entitled only to the proceeds which have not been expended on the support of the testator. Stake v. Cole, 133 N.W.2d 714, 717 (Iowa 1965). We see no reason to depart from Iowa precedent. As a result, Coy is entitled to $52,158.69. . . .

CONCLUSION

For the reasons expressed above, we hold that under the facts and circumstances of this case, the sale of the duplex did not cause ademption to the extent that there were specifically identifiable proceeds in the estate at the time of death. The . . . matter is remanded to the district court for proceedings not inconsistent with this opinion.

NOTES AND QUESTIONS

1. *A rule tempered by exceptions — the identity theory.* In jurisdictions following the identity theory, courts and legislatures have developed several escape hatches to avoid ademption in cases where, as in *Anton*, the property is not in the estate because of an accident or the action of someone other than the testator, or where the facts indicate a high likelihood that the testator did not intend for ademption.

Many jurisdictions give the devisee any unpaid amount of a condemnation award for the property or any unpaid fire or casualty insurance proceeds after the property has been destroyed. See UPC §2-608(a) (1969, rev. 1987). Thus, in Estate of Sagel, 901 A.2d 538 (Pa. Super. 2006), where T died in the crash of a small plane that he owned and T's will left the plane and his Rolex watch to his son A, the court held that A was entitled to the insurance proceeds for the destruction of the plane and the watch.

To avoid ademption, some courts will classify the devise as general or demonstrative rather than specific. If *T* devises "100 shares of Tigertail Corporation" to *A*, and *T* owns no shares of Tigertail at death, the court will probably declare this to be a general devise if Tigertail Corporation was a widely held stock traded on a major exchange. *A* is entitled to the value of 100 shares of Tigertail at *T*'s death. On the other hand, if testator had said "*my* 100 shares of Tigertail," the courts usually hold it a specific devise and adeemed to the extent the shares are missing at death. A gift that looks specific might also be declared to be demonstrative and not adeemed. Thus a bequest "of $10,000, more or less, entered on my bank book" has been held demonstrative and thus effective to convey $10,000. Kenaday v. Sinnott, 179 U.S. 606 (1900).

Another route to avoiding ademption under the identity theory is to classify the inter vivos disposition as a mere change in form, not substance. Suppose that after *T* executes her will giving "my 100 shares of Tigertail Corporation" to *A*, Tigertail Corporation merges into Lion Corporation, which retires the Tigertail stock and issues in its place 85 shares of Lion stock for every 100 shares of Tigertail. Most courts hold that a corporate merger or reorganization is only a change in form, not substance, and *A* takes the 85 shares of Lion stock.

Suppose *T* devises "my savings account in the First National Bank" to *A*. After executing her will, *T* closes the savings account at First National and purchases certificates of deposit to obtain a higher rate of interest. Is the change one of form or substance? Compare Parker v. Bozian, 859 So. 2d 427 (Ala. 2003) (change in form only, not adeemed), with Church v. Morgan, 685 N.E.2d 809 (Ohio App. 1996) (adeemed).

2.   *A standard tempered by presumptions and burdens — the intent theory.* The 1990 UPC abandons the identity theory and adopts the intent theory. Thus, in addition to codifying the exceptions to ademption that have proliferated in the identity theory jurisdictions, see UPC §2-606(a)(1)-(4) and (b), it also provides additional exceptions for replacement property, see §2-606(a)(5), and for the pecuniary value of property disposed of during the testator's lifetime if the devisee can show that the testator did not intend ademption. See §2-606(a)(6). The intent theory is also adopted by Restatement (Third) of Property: Wills and Other Donative Transfers §5.2 (1999).

Uniform Probate Code (1990, as amended 1997)

§2-606.   NONADEMPTION OF SPECIFIC DEVISES; UNPAID PROCEEDS OF SALE, CONDEMNATION, OR INSURANCE; SALE BY CONSERVATOR OR AGENT

(a) A specific devisee has a right to the specifically devised property in the testator's estate at death and:

(1) any balance of the purchase price, together with any security agreement, owing from a purchaser to the testator at death by reason of sale of the property;

(2) any amount of a condemnation award for the taking of the property unpaid at death;

(3) any proceeds unpaid at death on fire or casualty insurance or on other recovery for injury to the property;

(4) property owned by the testator at death and acquired as a result of foreclosure, or obtained in lieu of foreclosure, of the security interest for a specifically devised obligation;

(5) real or tangible personal property owned by the testator at death which the testator acquired as a replacement for specifically devised real or tangible personal property; and

(6) if not covered by paragraphs (1) through (5), a pecuniary devise equal to the value as of its date of disposition of other specifically devised property disposed of during the testator's lifetime but only to the extent it is established that ademption would be inconsistent with the testator's manifested plan of distribution or that at the time the will was made, the date of disposition or otherwise, the testator did not intend that the devise adeem.

(b) If specifically devised property is sold or mortgaged by a conservator or by an agent acting within the authority of a durable power of attorney for an incapacitated principal, or if a condemnation award, insurance proceeds, or recovery for injury to the property are paid to a conservator or to an agent acting within the authority of a durable power of attorney for an incapacitated principal, the specific devisee has the right to a general pecuniary devise equal to the net sale price, the amount of the unpaid loan, the condemnation award, the insurance proceeds, or the recovery.

(c) The right of a specific devisee under subsection (b) is reduced by any right the devisee has under subsection (a). . . .

PROBLEMS, QUESTIONS, AND NOTE

1. Under UPC §2-606(a)(5) dealing with replacement property, if *T* executes a will bequeathing "my Ford car" to *A* and later sells the Ford and buys a Rolls-Royce, is *A* entitled to the Rolls? Suppose *T* sold the Ford and bought two cars, a Honda and a Rolls-Royce. What result? Suppose *T* sold the Ford and bought a motorcycle. What result?

If *T* devises Blackacre to *A* and sells it and buys Whiteacre with the proceeds, is *A* entitled to Whiteacre? See Fletcher v. Ellenburg, 609 S.E.2d 337 (Ga. 2005).

2. Aunt Fanny Fox has a collection of Chinese snuff bottles. Snuff bottles were first made in China around 1650 when the First Manchu emperor, Kangzi, began to inhale snuff (powdered tobacco) brought by European traders. Sniffing snuff quickly became popular, and thousands upon thousands of small snuff bottles, each with a tiny spoon, were made to carry around in a pocket. Some snuff bottles were carved from jade, agate, and semi-precious stones; others were made of amber, ivory, and glass, sometimes with a scene painted inside. Ordinary Chinese snuff bottles of the eighteenth and nineteenth centuries can be found today for $800 or so, very good ones for perhaps $3,000; exceptional bottles may fetch $50,000 or more. Since each bottle is unique, each is

Two of Aunt Fanny's Snuff Bottles

individually priced in accordance with its quality of workmanship, rarity, and particular appeal to collectors' tastes.

Aunt Fanny bought her bottles from the 1950s through the 1970s, one at a time, as she ran across one catching her eye. She kept no records as to costs, and the bottles were not insured.

Aunt Fanny's will devises her snuff bottles to Wendy Brown. At Aunt Fanny's death, the snuff bottles are not found in her house. No one knows how many bottles there were. Zoë Preston thinks there were 60 or more; Aunt Fanny displayed only part of her collection at any one time. Wendy recalls seeing "about 20" in Aunt Fanny's display cabinet. Aunt Fanny might have given the bottles away, or sold them, or her nurses may have taken them during her long illness. No one knows for sure.

What are Wendy's rights under the common law identity theory? Under UPC §2-606(a)(6)?

3.   As originally drafted, UPC §2-606(a)(6) was criticized for abandoning the identity theory on the grounds that the intent theory will increase litigation and that it changed the meaning of a bequest of "my diamond ring" to "my diamond ring or its equivalent value," muddying up clear language and inserting a devise the testator did not make. See Mark L. Ascher, The 1990 Uniform Probate Code: Older and Better or More Like the Internal Revenue Code?, 77 Minn. L. Rev. 639 (1993). In 1997, however, §2-606(a)(6) was amended to put the burden on the party opposing ademption, that is, the party seeking the pecuniary value of specifically devised property not in the estate. Does this amendment answer the muddying-the-waters criticism?

For further discussion, see Mary K. Lundwall, The Case Against the Ademption by Extinction Rule: A Proposal for Reform, 29 Gonz. L. Rev. 105 (1994).

2.   Stock Splits and the Problem of Increase

Suppose that T executes a will devising 100 shares of stock of Tigertail Corporation to A. Subsequently, Tigertail Corporation splits its stock three for one. At T's death, T owns 300 shares of Tigertail stock. Does A take 100 shares or 300 shares? The old-fashioned approach was to ask whether the bequest was specific or general. If the court found T intended to bequeath particular shares in T's possession, the bequest was termed specific and A received the specified shares (100) as well as any accretions in a stock split (200). On the other hand, if the court found T did not have in mind particular property of his own but only desired to confer a general benefit, A received only 100 shares of stock.

This mechanical approach misconceives the basic nature of a stock split, which is a change in form, not substance. The shares held after the split represent the same proportional ownership of the corporation as the number of shares held before the split. The market value of 300 shares of Tigertail after the split should be approximately the same as 100 shares before the split. Therefore, most modern courts have discarded the old approach in the case of stock splits and have held that, absent a contrary showing of intent, a devisee of stock is entitled to additional shares received by the testator as a result of a stock split.

Some courts treat stock dividends differently from stock splits. They analogize a stock dividend to a cash dividend and conclude that the devisee cannot logically be awarded the former when he is denied the latter. However, this analogy ignores the fact of corporate finance that after a stock dividend, as after a stock split, the testator's percentage of ownership remains the same.

Under both UPC §2-605 (1990) and Restatement (Third) of Property: Wills and Other Donative Transfers §5.3 (1999), stock dividends are treated the same as stock splits: the beneficiary gets them along with the other shares.

3.   Satisfaction of General Pecuniary Bequests

The doctrine of *satisfaction* (sometimes known as *ademption by satisfaction*) applies when the testator makes a transfer to a devisee after executing the will. If the testator is a parent of the beneficiary (or stands in loco parentis) and sometime after executing the will transfers to the beneficiary property of a similar nature to that devised by the will, there is a rebuttable presumption that the gift is in satisfaction of the devise made by the will. Thus:

> Case 12. T's will devises $50,000 to her son, S, and her residuary estate to her daughter, D. After executing the will, T gives S $30,000. There is a presumption that the gift was in partial satisfaction of the legacy, so that S will take only $20,000 at T's death.

This doctrine, which is akin to the doctrine of advancements under intestacy law (see page 133), usually applies to general pecuniary bequests but not to specific bequests. When specific property (such as a painting or the family Bible) is devised by the terms of the will to a beneficiary, but is given to that beneficiary during the testator's life, usually the gift is treated as adeemed by extinction, not by satisfaction. But see Yivo Institute v. Zaleski, 874 A.2d 411 (Md. 2005) (holding that a specific devise of stock to a charity was adeemed by satisfaction when *T* gave the charity an inter vivos gift of equal value and *T*'s letter agreement with the charity provided for a gift of stock by will or by cash during life).

Because the intent of the testator is frequently difficult to ascertain, some states have enacted statutes requiring that the intention of a testator to adeem by satisfaction must be shown in writing. See Stewart v. Walters, 602 S.E.2d 642 (Ga. 2004). UPC §2-609 (1990) so provides, paralleling its rule on advancements (§2-109, page 135). See also Restatement (Third) of Property: Wills and Other Donative Transfers §5.4 (1999), to similar effect.

4. Exoneration of Liens

When a will makes a specific devise of land, on which there is a mortgage, the question may arise whether the devised land passes free of the mortgage. Suppose that *T*'s will devises Blackacre to her daughter, *A*. At *T*'s death, Blackacre is subject to a mortgage that secures a note on which *T* was personally liable. Does *A* take Blackacre subject to the mortgage, or is she entitled to have the note paid out of residuary assets so that the title will pass to *A* free of the lien? In some states, *A* takes Blackacre free of the mortgage. These jurisdictions apply the common law doctrine of *exoneration of liens*. Under this doctrine, when a will makes a specific disposition of real or personal property that is subject to a mortgage to secure a note on which the testator is personally liable, it is presumed, absent contrary language in the will, that the testator wanted the debt, like other debts, to be paid out of the residuary estate. See Manders v. King, 667 S.E.2d 59 (Ga. 2008). It is unclear, however, whether this presumption accords with the probable intent of the average testator, and the risk is that the residue will be depleted by exonerating the lien.

Dissatisfaction with the exoneration doctrine has led to the enactment, in a majority of states, of statutes reversing the common law rule, as does UPC §2-607 (1990).

5. Abatement

The problem of abatement arises when the estate has insufficient assets to pay debts as well as all the devises; in such a case, some devises must be abated or reduced. By divvying up a limited pie among claimants of different priorities, abatement operates like bankruptcy.

In the absence of any indication in the will how devises should abate or be reduced, devises ordinarily abate in the following order: (1) residuary devises are reduced first, (2) general devises are reduced second, and (3) specific and demonstrative devises are the last to abate and are reduced pro rata. This plan is believed to follow the testator's intent that specific devises be given effect before general devises, and both be given effect before a residuary devise.

But the residuary devisee is often the most important devisee of the testator.

> *Case 13.* T executes a will in which she devises $300,000 to charity *B*, $100,000 to charity *C*, and the residue of her estate to her son, *A*. At the time of the will's execution, *T* has $800,000 in assets. *T* then becomes ill and undergoes an experimental treatment costing $500,000. The treatment fails, and *T* dies with an estate of $300,000. Under traditional abatement rules, *A* takes nothing, *B* takes $225,000, and *C* takes $75,000.

Is it likely that *T* would have wanted the charities, *B* and *C*, to take to the exclusion of her son, *A*? UPC §3-902 (1990) provides that "if the testamentary plan . . . would be defeated by" the usual order of abatement, "the shares of the distributees abate as may be necessary to give effect to the intention of the testator." Under §3-902, what result in Case 13? See In re Estate of Tateo, 768 A.2d 243 (N.J. App. Div. 2001), holding that a specific devise to *T*'s son would not be given priority over general devises to *T*'s daughter and grandchildren.

It is of course preferable to avoid such problems through better drafting. In Case 13, if *T* had devised one-half of the residue of her estate to the charities and the other half to her son *A*, then all three gifts would have adjusted automatically in accord with the size of *T*'s estate. For this reason, it is often wise to make substantial devises in the form of shares of the residue.

6

NONPROBATE TRANSFERS
AND PLANNING FOR INCAPACITY

In this chapter we examine revocable inter vivos trusts, life insurance, pensions, and other legal arrangements that have the effect of passing property at death outside of probate. These modes of nonprobate transfer, taken together, function as a private system of succession that runs in parallel — indeed, competes — with the probate system. In this chapter we also examine the challenge of planning for incapacity, including the use of revocable trusts, powers of attorney, and health care directives for that purpose.

SECTION A.   AN INTRODUCTION TO WILL SUBSTITUTES

The point of departure in examining nonprobate transfers is to ask: What is a will substitute, and why do people find private succession through nonprobate transfer advantageous?

> *John H. Langbein, The Nonprobate Revolution and the*
> *Future of the Law of Succession*
> 97 Harv. L. Rev. 1108 (1984)

Over the course of the twentieth century, persistent tides of change have been lapping at the once-quiet shores of the law of succession. Probate, our court-operated system for transferring wealth at death, is declining in importance. Institutions that administer noncourt modes of transfer are displacing the probate system. Life insurance companies, pension plan operators, commercial banks, savings banks, investment companies, brokerage houses, stock transfer agents, and a variety of other financial intermediaries are functioning as free-market competitors of the probate system and enabling property to pass on death without probate and without will. The law of wills and the rules of descent no longer govern succession to most of the property of most decedents. . . .

In order to validate will-like modes of transfer that lack Wills Act formality and that operate without the mechanisms and protections of probate, we have been pretending that the will substitutes are lifetime transfers. In truth, will substitutes are simply "nonprobate wills" — "wills" that need not comply with the Wills Act. . . .

I.   THE WILL SUBSTITUTES

Four main will substitutes constitute the core of the nonprobate system: life insurance, pension accounts, joint accounts, and revocable trusts. When properly created, each is functionally indistinguishable from a will — each reserves to the owner complete lifetime dominion, including the power to name and to change beneficiaries until death. These devices I shall call "pure" will substitutes, in contradistinction to "imperfect" will substitutes (primarily joint tenancies), which more closely resemble completed lifetime transfers. The four pure will substitutes may also be described as mass will substitutes: they are marketed by financial intermediaries using standard form instruments with fill-in-the-blank beneficiary designations.

The typical American of middle- or upper-middle-class means employs many will substitutes. The precise mix of will and will substitutes varies with individual circumstances — age, family, employment, wealth, and legal sophistication. It would not be unusual for someone in mid-life to have a dozen or more will substitutes in force, whether or not he had a will.

A. LIFE INSURANCE

A propertied person of middle years commonly has several life insurance policies that he has acquired at different times — one or two purchased individually, others obtained as group policies that typically arise out of employment. The beneficiary designation in a life insurance policy serves precisely the function of the designation of a devisee in a will. The label aside, life insurance is functionally indistinguishable from a will, for it satisfies the twin elements of the definition of a will. We say that a will is revocable until the death of the testator and that the interests of the devisees are ambulatory — that is, nonexistent until the testator's death. Unless specially restricted by contract, the life insurance beneficiary designation operates identically.

In the 1960's, Spencer Kimball wrote about "the close similarity" of the execution of a life insurance beneficiary designation "to the making of a will. . . . Just as the will is 'ambulatory,' taking effect only on death, so the beneficiary designation can be changed until death."

B. PENSION ACCOUNTS

Any American who has spent much time in the work force since World War II is likely to have acquired rights in one or more pension accounts, depending upon his employment history and the features of the plans in force where he has worked. The tax laws have also been encouraging him to create supplementary retirement accounts, sometimes arranged through his employer, otherwise in the form of IRA accounts or Keogh plans with any of the many financial intermediaries that offer them. All these pension accounts contain will substitutes — beneficiary designations that pass the owner's interest to the persons of his choice in the event that he dies before exhausting the account in its retirement payout phase.

C. BANK, BROKERAGE, AND MUTUAL FUND ACCOUNTS

In arranging their personal banking, Americans meet another raft of invitations to execute will substitutes. Married persons in particular elect these options widely. The purest of the bank-operated will substitutes are accounts over which the depositor retains explicit lifetime dominion while designating beneficiaries to take on his death. Where local law permits, such arrangements may assume the blatant form of the P.O.D. ("pay on death") account, which was pioneered by the United States Treasury for selling government bonds. . . .

More commonly, the joint bank account — whether savings or checking — is manipulated to do the work of a will. In theory, joint accounts differ from other pure will substitutes: they look more like gifts than like wills. When the owner of property arranges to take title jointly, he supposedly creates a present interest in his donee-cotenant. In the prototypical joint tenancy of realty, the donee receives an interest equal to the donor's, and the donor loses the power to revoke the transfer. Moreover, the commonality-of-use rule requires that the cotenants act together in order to transfer the realty. Joint accounts of personalty, however, "differ from the true joint tenancies as defined in [real] property law, for by the privilege of withdrawal either [cotenant] may consume the account." Accordingly, a depositor may name a cotenant on a bank account but deal with the account as though it were his own. The cotenant may not even know that he has been designated. Depending on his contract with the bank, the depositor may revoke and alter cotenancy designations as freely as he would beneficiary designations under any of the other will substitutes. He may also achieve the same result by closing the account, as he pleases. In this way, joint accounts may be used to approximate the incidents of a will; the cotenancy designation is effectively revocable and ambulatory.

Brokerage houses apply the same mechanism to so-called street accounts. In an account that is nominally joint, the beneficial owner of the securities may deal with them as though he has not made the cotenancy designation, but on the owner's death the cotenant succeeds to the securities or other account proceeds. Investment companies have extended the practice to mutual fund accounts. . . .

D. THE REVOCABLE INTER VIVOS TRUST

Although the revocable trust is the fundamental device that the estate-planning bar employs to fit the carriage trade with highly individuated instruments, the revocable trust also keeps company with the mass will substitutes. Standard-form revocable trusts with fill-in-the-blank beneficiary designations are widely offered in the banking industry and were at one time aggressively promoted in the mutual fund industry. . . .

Either by declaration of trust or by transfer to a third-party trustee, the appropriate trust terms can replicate the incidents of a will. The owner who retains both the equitable life interest and the power to alter and revoke the beneficiary designation has used the trust form to achieve the effect of testation. Only nomenclature distinguishes the remainder interest created by such a trust from the mere expectancy arising under a will. Under either the trust or the will, the interest of the beneficiaries is both revocable and ambulatory.

E. IMPERFECT WILL SUBSTITUTES

The "pure" will substitutes are not the only instruments of the nonprobate revolution; "imperfect" will substitutes — most prominent among them the common-law joint tenancy — also serve to transfer property at death without probate. Joint tenancies in real estate and in securities are quite common; joint tenancies in automobiles and other vehicles are also fairly widespread. Because they ordinarily effect lifetime transfers, joint tenancies are "imperfect" rather than "pure" will substitutes. When the owner of a house, a car, a boat, or a block of IBM common stock arranges to take title jointly, his cotenant acquires an interest that is no longer revocable and ambulatory. Under the governing recording act or stock transfer act, both cotenants must ordinarily join in any subsequent transfer. Yet like the pure will substitutes, joint tenancy arrangements allow the survivor to obtain marketable title without probate: under joint tenancy, a death certificate rather than a probate decree suffices to transfer title. . . .

By providing a nonprobate mode of transfer for realty and securities, the joint tenancy operates in conjunction with the pure will substitutes to make total avoidance of probate feasible for persons of ordinary or even substantial means. . . .

II. THE HIDDEN CAUSES OF THE NONPROBATE REVOLUTION

The typical propertied decedent in modern America leaves a will and many will substitutes. The will substitutes differ from the ordinary "last will and testament" in three main ways. First, most will substitutes — but not all — are asset-specific: each deals with a single type of property, be it life insurance proceeds, a bank balance, mutual fund shares, or whatever. Second, property that passes through a will substitute avoids probate. A financial intermediary ordinarily takes the place of the probate court in effecting the transfer. Third, the formal requirements of the Wills Act — attestation and so forth — do not govern will substitutes and are not complied with. Of these differences, only probate avoidance is a significant advantage that transferors might consciously seek.

————————————

The increasing popularity of will substitutes raises two key legal questions. First, should Wills Act formalities be required of will substitutes? Second, should the rules of construction and other principles applicable to wills be applied to will substitutes? The subsidiary law of wills, which includes rules on creditors' rights, antilapse, simultaneous death, slayers, and revocation-on-divorce, reflects long experience with the problems that arise in interpreting and administering testamentary dispositions. But will substitutes are already governed by their own separate bodies of law, such as contract or trust law, which may not be consistent with the law of wills. As we shall see, the modern view is that will substitutes are valid even if not executed with Wills Act formalities, but increasingly will substitutes have been subjected to the subsidiary law of wills. See Restatement (Third) of Trusts: Wills and Other Donative Transfers §§7.1-7.2 (2003).

There also are two key policy and planning questions raised by the growing use of will substitutes. First, what lessons for probate reform can be drawn from the success of will substitutes? The adoption of unsupervised, informal probate procedures, for example, appears to have been prompted in part by the successful experience with unsupervised nonprobate transfers. We discuss informal probate such as under Article 3 of the Uniform Probate Code at pages 43-44. See also Grayson M.P. McCouch, Probate Law and Nonprobate Transfers, 62 U. Miami L. Rev. 757 (2008). Second, given the broad proliferation of will substitutes, how can the law facilitate a unified estate plan? As we shall see, the combined use of the revocable trust and pour-over will has become the technique of choice in many jurisdictions.

SECTION B.   WILL SUBSTITUTES AND THE WILLS ACT

1.   *Revocable Trusts*

Revocable trusts have come into widespread use as will substitutes, particularly among the moderately and very wealthy. The revocable trust is the most flexible of all will substitutes because the donor can draft both the dispositive and the administrative provisions precisely to the donor's liking. Thus, although we give extended treatment to trusts in general in Chapters 8 through 14, we provide here a thumbnail sketch of key terminology in order to give context to the use of the revocable trust as a will substitute.

A *trust* is, functionally speaking, an arrangement whereby a *trustee* manages property in a *fiduciary* capacity for one or more *beneficiaries*. The trustee holds *legal title* to the property and the beneficiaries hold *equitable title*. The trustee can be one of the beneficiaries of the trust, but the same person cannot be the sole trustee and sole beneficiary, because then the trustee would owe no duties to anyone except himself (see the discussion of merger at page 548).

The person who creates a trust is the *settlor*, *grantor*, or *trustor*. A trust may be created during the settlor's life, in which case it is an *inter vivos* trust. Or it may be created by will, which would make it a *testamentary* trust. An inter vivos trust may be *revocable* or *irrevocable*. By definition, a testamentary trust is always irrevocable and a revocable trust is always inter vivos.

A revocable trust may be created by a *deed of trust*, whereby the settlor *transfers* the property to be held in trust to the trustee. On the settlor's death, the trust property is then distributed or held in further trust, depending on the terms of the trust instrument. While several early cases held a revocable trust created by deed of trust ineffective to transfer property at the settlor's death unless executed with Wills Act formalities, by statute or judicial decision all jurisdictions now allow a revocable trust created by deed of trust to effect a nonprobate transfer on death. See Restatement (Third) of Trusts §25 (2003).

A revocable trust may also be created by a *declaration of trust* where, as the name suggests, the settlor simply *declares* himself to be trustee of certain property for the benefit of himself during his life, with the remainder to pass to others at his death. The settlor retains the power to revoke the trust and the right to the trust income, and as trustee he also controls the management of the trust property. Because there is little discernible change in the settlor's relation to the trust property during lifetime, the question arises, should the declaration of trust be effective to transfer property at the settlor's death without Wills Act formalities?

Farkas v. Williams
Supreme Court of Illinois, 1955
125 N.E.2d 600

HERSHEY, J. . . . The plaintiffs asked the court to declare their legal rights, as co-administrators, in four stock certificates issued by Investors Mutual Inc. in the name of "Albert B. Farkas, as trustee for Richard J. Williams" and which were issued pursuant to written declarations of trust. The decree of the circuit court found that said declarations were testamentary in character, and not having been executed with the formalities of a will, were invalid, and directed that the stock be awarded to the plaintiffs as an asset of the estate of said Albert B. Farkas. Upon appeal to the Appellate Court, the decree was affirmed. See 121 N.E.2d 344 (Ill. App. 1954). We allowed defendants' petition for leave to appeal.

Albert B. Farkas died intestate at the age of sixty-seven years, a resident of Chicago, leaving as his only heirs-at-law brothers, sisters, a nephew and a niece. Although retired at the time of his death, he had for many years practiced veterinary medicine and operated a veterinarian establishment in Chicago. During a considerable portion of that time, he employed the defendant Williams, who was not related to him.

On four occasions (December 8, 1948; February 7, 1949; February 14, 1950; and March 1, 1950) Farkas purchased stock of Investors Mutual, Inc. At the time of each purchase he executed a written application to Investors Mutual, Inc., instructing them to issue the stock in his name "as trustee for Richard J. Williams." Investors Mutual, Inc., by its agent, accepted each of these applications in writing by signature on the face of the application. Coincident with the execution of these applications, Farkas signed separate declarations of trust, all of which were identical except as to dates. The terms of said trust instruments are as follows:

Declaration of Trust — Revocable. I, the undersigned, having purchased or declared my intention to purchase certain shares of capital stock of Investors Mutual, Inc. (the Company), and having directed that the certificate for said stock be issued in my name as trustee for Richard J. Williams as beneficiary, whose address is 1704 W. North Ave. Chicago, Ill., under this Declaration of Trust Do Hereby Declare that the terms and conditions upon which I shall hold said stock in trust and any additional stock resulting from reinvestments of cash dividends upon such original or additional shares are as follows:

(1) During my lifetime all cash dividends are to be paid to me individually for my own personal account and use; provided, however, that any such additional stock purchased under an authorized reinvestment of cash dividends shall become a part of and subject to this trust.

(2) Upon my death the title to any stock subject hereto and the right to any subsequent payments or distributions shall be vested absolutely in the beneficiary.

(3) During my lifetime I reserve the right, as trustee, to vote, sell, redeem, exchange or otherwise deal in or with the stock subject hereto, but upon any sale or redemption of said stock or any part thereof, the trust hereby declared shall terminate as to the stock sold or redeemed, and I shall be entitled to retain the proceeds of sale or redemption for my own personal account and use.

(4) I reserve the right at any time to change the beneficiary or revoke this trust, but it is understood that no change of beneficiary and no revocation of this trust except by death of the beneficiary, shall be effective as to the Company, for any purpose unless and until written notice thereof in such form as the Company shall prescribe is delivered to the Company at Minneapolis, Minnesota. The decease of the beneficiary before my death shall operate as a revocation of this trust.

(5) In the event this trust shall be revoked or otherwise terminated, said stock and all rights and privileges thereunder shall belong to and be exercised by me in my individual capacity. . . .

The applications and declarations of trust were delivered to Investors Mutual, Inc., and held by the company until Farkas' death. The stock certificates were issued in the name of Farkas as "trustee for Richard J. Williams" and were discovered in a safety-deposit box of Farkas after his death, along with other securities, some of which were in the name of Williams alone. . . .

It is conceded that the instruments were not executed in such a way as to satisfy the requirements of the statute on wills; hence, our inquiry is limited to whether said trust instruments created valid inter vivos trusts effective to give the purported beneficiary, Williams, title to the stock in question after the death of the settlor-trustee, Farkas. To make this determination we must consider: (1) whether upon execution of the so-called trust instruments defendant Williams acquired an interest in the subject matter of the trusts, the stock of defendant Investors Mutual, Inc., (2) whether Farkas, as settlor-trustee, retained such control over the subject matter of the trusts as to render said trust instruments attempted testamentary dispositions.

First, upon execution of these trust instruments did defendant Williams presently acquire an interest in the subject matter of the intended trusts?

If no interest passed to Williams before the death of Farkas, the intended trusts are testamentary and hence invalid for failure to comply with the statute on wills. Restatement of the Law of Trusts, §56. But considering the terms of these instruments we believe Farkas did intend to presently give Williams an interest in the property referred to. For it may be said, at the very least, that upon his executing one of these instruments, he showed an intention to presently part with some of the incidents of ownership in the stock. Immediately after the execution of each of these instruments, he could not deal with the stock therein referred to the same as if he owned the property absolutely, but only in accordance with the terms of the instrument. He purported to set himself up as trustee of the stock for the benefit of Williams, and the stock was registered in his name as trustee for Williams. Thus assuming to act as trustee, he is held to have intended to take on those obligations which are expressly set out in the instrument, as well as those fiduciary obligations implied by law. In addition, he manifested an intention to bind himself to having this property pass upon his death to Williams, unless he changed the beneficiary or revoked the trust, and then such change of beneficiary or revocation was not to be effective as to Investors Mutual, Inc., unless and until written notice thereof in such form as the company prescribed was delivered to them at Minneapolis, Minnesota. An absolute owner can dispose of his property, either in his lifetime or by will, in any way he sees fit without notifying or securing approval from anyone and without being held to the duties of a fiduciary in so doing.

It seems to follow that what incidents of ownership Farkas intended to relinquish, in a sense he intended Williams to acquire. . . . It is difficult to name this interest of Williams, nor is there any reason for so doing so long as it passed to him immediately upon the creation of the trust.[1] As stated in 4 Richard Powell, The Law of Real Property, at page 87: "Interests of beneficiaries of private express trusts run the gamut from valuable substantialities to evanescent hopes. Such a beneficiary may have any one of an almost infinite variety of the possible aggregates of rights, privileges, powers and immunities."

An additional problem is presented here, however, for it is to be noted that the trust instruments provide: "The decease of the beneficiary before my death shall operate as a revocation of this trust." The plaintiffs argue that the presence of this provision removes the only possible distinction which might have been drawn between these instruments and a will. Being thus conditioned on his surviving, it is argued that the "interest" of Williams until the death of Farkas was a mere expectancy. Conversely, they assert, the interest of Farkas in the securities until his death was precisely the same as that of a testator who bequeaths securities by his will, since he had all the rights accruing to an absolute owner.

Admittedly, had this provision been absent the interest of Williams would have been greater, since he would then have had an inheritable interest in the lifetime of Farkas. But to say his interest would have been greater is not to say that he here did not have a beneficial interest, properly so-called, during the lifetime of Farkas. The provision purports to set up but another "contingency" which would

---

1. The idea of an interest smaller than any interest you can name, but nonetheless an interest, brings to mind the mathematical concept of the infinitesimal, developed by Isaac Newton and Gottfried Wilhelm von Leibniz. Although scorned by Bishop Berkeley as "ghosts of departed quantities," infinitesimals proved very useful in differential calculus.

Would it be a good idea for the Illinois legislature to settle the matter by passing a statute providing that, if a settlor retained the powers Farkas retained, the beneficiary would be deemed to receive an infinitesimal interest? Should the legislature give the interest a name, such as a *farkas*, since the court finds naming so difficult? — Eds.

serve to terminate the trust. The disposition is not testamentary and the intended trust is valid, even though the interest of the beneficiary is contingent upon the existence of a certain state of facts at the time of the settlor's death. (Restatement of the Law of Trusts, §56, cmt. f.) In an example contained in the previous reference, the authors of the Restatement have referred to the interest of a beneficiary under a trust who must survive the settlor (and where the settlor receives the income for life) as a contingent equitable interest in remainder. . . .

Second, did Farkas retain such control over the subject matter of the trust as to render said trust instruments attempted testamentary dispositions?

In each of these trust instruments, Farkas reserved to himself as settlor the following powers: (1) the right to receive during his lifetime all cash dividends; (2) the right at any time to change the beneficiary or revoke the trust; and (3) upon sale or redemption of any portion of the trust property, the right to retain the proceeds therefrom for his own use.

Additionally, Farkas reserved the right to act as sole trustee, and in such capacity, he was accorded the right to vote, sell, redeem, exchange or otherwise deal in the stock which formed the subject matter of the trust.

We shall consider first those enumerated powers which Farkas reserved to himself as settlor.

It is well established that the retention by the settlor of the power to revoke, even when coupled with the reservation of a life interest in the trust property, does not render the trust inoperative for want of execution as a will. . . .

A more difficult problem is posed, however, by the fact that Farkas is also trustee, and as such, is empowered to vote, sell, redeem, exchange and otherwise deal in and with the subject matter of the trusts. . . .

In the instant case the plaintiffs contend that Farkas, as settlor-trustee, retained complete control and dominion over the securities for his own benefit during his lifetime. It is argued that he had the power to deal with the property as he liked so long as he lived and owed no enforceable duties of any kind to Williams as beneficiary. . . .

That the retention of the power by Farkas as trustee to sell or redeem the stock and keep the proceeds for his own use should not render these trust instruments testamentary in character becomes more evident upon analyzing the real import and significance of the powers to revoke and to amend the trust, the reservation of which the courts uniformly hold does not invalidate an inter vivos trust.

It is obvious that a settlor with the power to revoke and to amend the trust at any time is, for all practical purpose, in a position to exert considerable control over the trustee regarding the administration of the trust. For anything believed to be inimicable to his best interest can be thwarted or prevented by simply revoking the trust or amending it in such a way as to conform to his wishes. Indeed, it seems that many of those powers which from time to time have been viewed as "additional powers" are already, in a sense, virtually contained within the overriding power of revocation or the power to amend the trust. Consider, for example, the following: (1) the power to consume the principal; (2) the power to sell or mortgage the trust property and appropriate the proceeds; (3) the power to appoint or remove trustees; (4) the power to supervise and direct investments;

and (5) the power to otherwise direct and supervise the trustee in the administration of the trust. Actually, any of the above powers could readily be assumed by a settlor with the reserved power of revocation through the simple expedient of revoking the trust, and then, as absolute owner of the subject matter, doing with the property as he chooses. Even though no actual termination of the trust is effectuated, however, it could hardly be questioned but that the mere existence of this power in the settlor is sufficient to enable his influence to be felt in a practical way in the administration of the trust. . . .

In the case at bar, the power in Farkas to vote, sell, redeem, exchange or otherwise deal in the stock was reserved to him as trustee, and it was only upon sale or redemption that he was entitled to keep the proceeds for his own use. Thus, the control reserved is not as great as in those cases where said power is reserved to the owner as settlor. For as trustee he must so conduct himself in accordance with standards applicable to trustees generally. It is not a valid objection to this to say that Williams would never question Farkas' conduct, inasmuch as Farkas could then revoke the trust and destroy what interest Williams has. Such a possibility exists in any case where the settlor has the power of revocation. Still, Williams has rights the same as any beneficiary, although it may not be feasible for him to exercise them. Moreover, it is entirely possible that he might in certain situations have a right to hold Farkas' estate liable for breaches of trust committed by Farkas during his lifetime. In this regard, consider what would happen if, without having revoked the trust, Farkas as trustee had given the stock away without receiving any consideration therefor, had pledged the stock improperly for his own personal debt and allowed it to be lost by foreclosure or had exchanged the stock for another security or other worthless property in such manner as to constitute gross impropriety and gross negligence. In such instances, it would seem in accordance with the terms of these instruments that Williams would have had an enforceable claim against Farkas' estate for whatever damage had been suffered. Contrast this with the rights of a legatee or devisee under a will. The testator could waste the property or do anything with it he wished during his lifetime without incurring any liability to those designated by the will to inherit the property. . . .

Another factor often considered in determining whether an inter vivos trust is an attempted testamentary disposition is the formality of the transaction. Historically, the purpose behind the enactment of the statute on wills was the prevention of fraud. The requirement as to witnesses was deemed necessary because a will is ordinarily an expression of the secret wish of the testator, signed out of the presence of all concerned. The possibility of forgery and fraud are ever present in such situations. Here, Farkas executed four separate applications for stock of Investors Mutual, Inc., in which he directed that the stock be issued in his name as trustee for Williams, and he executed four separate declarations of trust in which he declared he was holding said stock in trust for Williams. The stock certificates in question were issued in his name as trustee for Williams. He thus manifested his intention in a solemn and formal manner.

For the reasons stated, we conclude that these trust declarations executed by Farkas constituted valid inter vivos trusts and were not attempted testamentary dispositions. It must be conceded that they have, in the words of Mr. Justice Holmes in Bromley v. Mitchell, 30 N.E. 83 (Mass. 1892), a "testamentary look." Moreover, it must be admitted that the line should be drawn somewhere, but after a study of this case we do not believe that point has been reached. . . .

Reversed and remanded, with directions.

QUESTIONS

1. To determine the validity of the trust, the court applied two tests: (1) whether Williams acquired a present interest when the trust was created, and (2) whether Farkas retained so much control over the trust property that he still owned it at death, rendering the trust testamentary. What is the difference?

2. Taking notice of the four separate transactions with Investors Mutual, Inc., and the four separate declarations of trust, the court concluded that Farkas "manifested his intention in a solemn and formal manner." Were these alternative formalities essential to the court's holding? Does the involvement of a neutral financial intermediary ensure reliability?

3. What duties did Farkas as trustee owe Williams as beneficiary? What equitable interest was created in Williams? Given that Farkas retained the power to revoke the trust, and to take back the trust property, what sense would it make to hold Farkas liable for breach of trust? See Moon v. Lesikar, 230 S.W.3d 800 (Tex. App. 2007).

Uniform Trust Code (2000, as amended 2004)

§603.   SETTLOR'S POWERS; POWERS OF WITHDRAWAL

(a) While a trust is revocable [and the settlor has capacity to revoke the trust], rights of the beneficiaries are subject to the control of, and the duties of the trustee are owed exclusively to, the settlor.

(b) During the period the power may be exercised, the holder of a power of withdrawal has the rights of a settlor of a revocable trust under this section to the extent of the property subject to the power.

Linthicum v. Rudi
Supreme Court of Nevada, 2006
148 P.3d 746

HARDESTY, J.   In this appeal, we consider whether revocable inter vivos trust beneficiaries have the right to challenge amendments to the trust, when made by the settlor during the settlor's lifetime. Because we conclude that a beneficiary's interest in a revocable inter vivos trust is contingent at most, we hold that, generally, these beneficiaries lack standing to challenge the settlor's lifetime amendments. Instead, to challenge the settlor's capacity to make amendments, revocable inter vivos trust beneficiaries must follow the procedures set forth in Nevada's guardianship statutes. . . .

FACTS

Appellants Ernette and Myrna Linthicum are the brother and sister-in-law, respectively, of Claire Linthicum-Cobb. In 2002, Cobb executed a will and a revocable inter vivos trust. As settlor, Cobb named herself trustee and reserved the power to revoke or amend the trust throughout her lifetime without having to notify any beneficiary. Cobb named Ernette and Myrna the primary beneficiaries of the trust upon Cobb's death. Additionally, Cobb named Ernette and Myrna successor trustees upon Cobb's death or incapacity. Finally, the trust stated that the trust would become irrevocable upon Cobb's death.

In 2004, Cobb executed a new will and a restatement/amendment to the trust. The amended trust replaced Ernette and Myrna as successor trustees with respondent Arnold Rudi, the nephew of Cobb's deceased husband. Also, the amended trust allegedly named Rudi as the sole beneficiary. Under the amended trust, Cobb remained the current trustee and retained the power to revoke the trust. Thus, the amended trust was still a revocable inter vivos trust.

After Cobb named Rudi the sole successor trustee, Rudi and Guardianship Services of Nevada petitioned for co-guardianship of Cobb's person and estate because Cobb was possibly delusional and paranoid. Ernette and Myrna objected to Rudi's appointment as a co-guardian; Rudi's petition for guardianship was later withdrawn. The district court granted Guardianship Services' petition for guardianship because it found that some of Cobb's actions had resulted in self-neglect and potential self-harm.

Subsequently, Ernette and Myrna filed a complaint alleging that the amended trust was a product of incapacity and/or undue influence, and they sought a constructive trust and/or cancellation of the amended trust. As to undue influence, Ernette and Myrna alleged that Rudi had a confidential relationship with Cobb and participated in executing the amended trust.

Rudi filed a motion to dismiss the complaint . . . asserting that Ernette and Myrna had failed to state a claim upon which relief could be granted because they lacked standing to challenge the amended trust. Specifically, Rudi argued that a will contest cannot be maintained until the testator dies, and since Cobb was still alive at the time, Ernette and Myrna lacked a present legal interest in the will and the trust. Rudi also argued that Ernette and Myrna could not assert any damages resulting from the amended trust.

Ernette and Myrna simultaneously filed an opposition to Rudi's motion to dismiss and a motion for the appointment of themselves as guardians ad litem. Ernette and Myrna argued that they had standing because the amended trust was presently operative and effectual. Moreover, they argued that even if they could not challenge Cobb's will until after her death, it was necessary to challenge the amended trust during Cobb's lifetime to ensure that her wishes for the administration of her estate were observed while she was incapacitated. Finally, if the court concluded that they did not have standing, they asked that they be appointed as guardians ad litem.

The district court granted Rudi's motion to dismiss, without prejudice, finding that Ernette and Myrna lacked standing to challenge the amended living trust because Cobb was still alive; the court also denied Ernette and Myrna's motion to be appointed guardians ad litem. In denying a subsequent rehearing motion, the district court explained that Ernette's and Myrna's interest was at best contingent and would only vest if they survived Cobb. . . . Ernette and Myrna appealed.

DISCUSSION

Ernette and Myrna argue that Nevada statutory law allows them to challenge Cobb's revocable inter vivos trust during Cobb's lifetime and that the district court erred by granting Rudi's motion to dismiss. Specifically, Ernette and Myrna argue that Nev. Rev. Stat. ("NRS") 164.015, NRS 153.031(1)(a) and NRS 153.031(1)(d) allow interested persons to challenge the validity of a revocable trust while the settlor is still alive. We disagree. . . .

NRS 164.015(1) permits "an interested person" to petition the court for proceedings "concerning the internal affairs of a nontestamentary trust" and to obtain "any appropriate relief provided with respect to a testamentary trust in NRS 153.031." NRS 153.031(1)(a) and NRS 153.031(1)(d) allow a trustee or beneficiary of a trust to petition the court to determine the existence of the trust and the validity of a trust provision, respectively. However, neither of these statutes directly addresses revocable inter vivos trusts, such as the trust in this case. Moreover, these statutes specifically refer to petitions by interested persons. Because the trust at issue is a revocable inter vivos trust and Cobb retained the ability to revoke the trust during her lifetime, Ernette and Myrna have at most a contingent interest that has not yet vested. Consequently, Ernette and Myrna are not interested persons within the meaning of NRS 164.015 and NRS 153.031.

In so concluding, we embrace the holdings of other jurisdictions that have considered the matter. In a case from Ohio, Lewis v. Star Bank, 630 N.E.2d 418, 419 (Ohio App. 1993), the beneficiaries of a revocable inter vivos trust sued the trustee for an alleged breach of fiduciary duty for failing to give pre-death tax and estate-planning advice to the settlor. The Ohio Court of Appeals determined that while the settlor was alive, pursuant to the terms of the trust itself, she had reserved the right to modify or revoke the trust. The court further concluded that as long as the settlor had that right and other "indicia of retained ownership" during her lifetime, the beneficiaries did not have an absolute entitlement to any portion of the trust while the settlor was alive. Since the beneficiaries' interests were subject to complete divestment while the settlor was alive, the court held that the beneficiaries were not in privity with the settlor or the trustee and could not maintain their lawsuit.

Similarly, in Ullman v. Garcia, 645 So. 2d 168, 169 (Fla. Dist. App. 1994), a Florida appellate court cited a Florida statute that prevented revocable trusts from being contested before the settlor's death. Although the court relied in part on a statute, it also elaborated upon the reasoning behind this rule, much of which underlies our holding today. The Florida court noted that the devisee of a revocable trust does not enjoy any control over ownership of the trust until the settlor's death.[2] Because the settlor has an absolute right to terminate the trust at any time and distribute the trust property as he or she sees fit, named beneficiaries to a revocable trust are only "potential devisees." The court also observed that a revocable trust is "a unique instrument" that has "no legal significance until the [settlor]'s death." . . .

Nevada statutes do not contemplate beneficiaries to a revocable inter vivos trust challenging the trust until the settlor's death. Furthermore, such beneficiaries have only a contingent interest, at most, while the settlor is still alive. That interest does not vest until the settlor's death. Other jurisdictions addressing the issue have held similarly. For these reasons, we conclude that Ernette and Myrna lack standing to challenge Cobb's revocable inter vivos trust while Cobb is still alive. . . .

To the extent that Ernette and Myrna's concerns center on Cobb's capacity, those concerns are more appropriately addressed under Nevada's guardianship statutes, NRS Chapter 159, in [a] separate action brought under those statutes, rather than through their appointment as guardians ad litem in the litigation against Cobb's trust. . . .

CONCLUSION

Because we conclude that a beneficiary's interest in a revocable inter vivos trust is contingent at most, we conclude that Ernette and Myrna lack standing to challenge Cobb's revocable inter vivos trust during Cobb's lifetime. Additionally, we conclude that Ernette and Myrna must follow the procedures created by the Legislature when it modified Nevada's guardianship statutes in 2003, if they wish to pursue a remedy in this matter. Accordingly, we affirm the district court orders.

QUESTIONS, NOTES, AND PROBLEM

1. In *Farkas*, the court held that the trust was effective to pass property to Williams on the settlor's death because during the settlor's life an enforceable interest had passed to Williams. In *Linthicum*, the court held that the interest of a beneficiary in a revocable trust is contingent and unenforceable during the settlor's lifetime. How can these decisions be reconciled? See Hoggan v. Hoggan, 169 P.3d 750 (Utah 2007); Restatement (Third) of Trusts §25, cmt. b (2003).

What recourse do Ernette and Myrna have to challenge the amendment to Cobb's revocable trust? Uniform Trust Code (UTC) §604 (2000) provides that a

2. The *devisee* of a revocable trust? See the discussion of the term devisee at page 41. — Eds.

person may bring suit to challenge a revocable trust, but only after the trust becomes irrevocable by reason of the settlor's death.

2.   Consistent with the weight of modern authority, UTC §603, page 403, provides that while the settlor is alive the trustee of a revocable trust owes duties only to the settlor. See also Restatement (Third) of Trusts §74 (2007), to similar effect. Under modern law, would Farkas as trustee have owed any duties to Williams as beneficiary? Suppose Farkas had named a third party trustee who looted the trust without Farkas's knowledge but while Farkas was alive and competent. If Farkas died without having discovered the looting, would Williams have any recourse against the trustee?

Suppose Farkas was incompetent while the third party trustee looted the trust. Would a guardian or conservator appointed by the court have standing to sue on Farkas's behalf? See id., cmts. a(2) and e. Would the fiduciary of Farkas's estate or Williams or both have standing after Farkas's death? See Siegel v. Novak, 920 So. 2d 89 (Fla. App. 2006); Alan Newman, Revocable Trusts and the Law of Wills: An Imperfect Fit, 43 Real Prop., Tr. & Est. L.J. 523, 531-537 (2008).

3.   Should a trustee of a revocable trust have a duty to inform a beneficiary of an amendment by the settlor that removes the beneficiary if the trustee thinks that the amendment was made under suspicious circumstances? See JP Morgan Chase Bank, N.A. v. Longmeyer, 275 S.W.3d 697 (Ky. 2009).

2.   *Payable on Death Contracts and Other Nonprobate Transfers*

In re Estate of Atkinson
Probate Court of Huron County, Ohio, 1961
175 N.E.2d 548

YOUNG, J.   This matter arises out of exceptions filed by the widow of the decedent to the inventory and appraisement of his estate. The facts are simple and not in dispute.

The decedent, during his lifetime, made deposits in the Willard United Bank, and took three certificates of deposit, as follows:

  1. Certificate of Deposit No. 1403, issued June 25, 1957, in the amount of $5,500.00, registered as follows: "Walter S. Atkinson, P.O.D. Mrs. Patricia Burgeois."
  2. Certificate of Deposit No. 1798, issued October 1, 1957, in the amount of $2,000.00, registered as follows: "Walter S. Atkinson, P.O.D. Mrs. Maxine Burdette."
  3. Certificate of Deposit No. 1881, issued February 3, 1959, in the amount of $1,000.00, registered as follows: "Walter S. Atkinson, P.O.D. Mrs. Patricia Burgeois."

It is conceded by both parties that the letters "P.O.D." are an abbreviation meaning "payable on death", and that it was the intent of the decedent that the certificates of deposit should be payable upon his death to the person whose name follows the letters "P.O.D."

On September 30, 1957, the decedent made a will making various provisions, including legacies to Maxine Burdette and Patricia Burgeois, who are his daughters by a former marriage, and specifically providing that his widow, Emma Atkinson, should not share in his estate.

After the death of the decedent, the widow elected to take [her spousal forced share of the decedent's estate].[3] The certificates of deposit not being listed in the inventory and appraisement [of the decedent's estate], she filed the exceptions which are the subject of this action.

It is the contention of the widow that these certificates of deposit must be considered as part of the decedent's estate for the purpose of computing her statutory twenty percent exemption, and her share of the decedent's estate.

It is the contention of the daughters that these certificates of deposit passed to them by force of the language in which they were registered immediately upon the death of the decedent, and cannot be considered as being any part of his estate.

The serious problem is whether adding the words "payable on death" to a certificate of deposit is not invalid as being contrary to the statute of wills, Section 2107.03, Ohio Revised Code, which provides as follows:

> Except oral wills, every last will and testament shall be in writing, but may be handwritten or typewritten. Such will shall be signed at the end by the party making it or by some other person in such party's presence and at his express direction, and be attested and subscribed in the presence of such party, by two or more competent witnesses, who saw the testator subscribe, or heard him acknowledge his signature.

The daughters contend that there is no difference between the certificates of deposit marked "P.O.D." and bank accounts or securities which are listed in the names of two persons or the survivor, which have been held effective to pass title to the survivor upon the death of a co-owner, even though they were not executed with the necessary formalities to make a testamentary disposition.

There appears to be surprisingly little authority upon this precise point. However, an examination of the cases leads inevitably to the conclusion that the contention of the daughters cannot stand, but that the registration of the certificates of deposit in this case is an ineffectual attempt at a testamentary disposition of the deposits involved.

The precise question has only once been decided in this state, in the case of Waltbillig v. Burke, 17 Ohio. App. 444 (1923). In that case the decedent's account in the Employees Saving Fund of the Pennsylvania Lines was marked

> that in the event of my death, all deposits standing to my credit in said Savings Fund, and all interest due thereon, shall be paid to my wife Bridget Burke.

The court held that this was invalid as a testamentary disposition, and awarded the deposit to the decedent's administrator, and not to his wife. . . .

---

3. We take up the spousal forced share in Chapter 7. — Eds.

It is clear in the present matter that there was no present interest of any kind created in the decedent's daughters by the language used in the certificate of deposit. On the contrary, the words "pay on death" are clearly testamentary. . . .

A hasty search of the authorities outside of Ohio discloses the case of Vercher v. Roy, 171 La. 524, 131 So. 658 (La. 1930), in which the court holds that a certificate of deposit payable to the order of Vercher, or in case of his death to Roy, did not give Roy any right to the proceeds on the death of Vercher, the depositor.

It is therefore the finding of this court that the exceptions to the inventory and appraisement are well taken, and must be allowed. An entry may be drawn accordingly, with exceptions to the executrix.

Estate of Hillowitz
Court of Appeals of New York, 1968
238 N.E.2d 723

FULD, C.J.   This appeal stems from a discovery proceeding brought in the Surrogate's Court by the executors of the estate of Abraham Hillowitz against his widow, the appellant herein. The husband had been a partner in an "investment club" and, after his death, the club, pursuant to a provision of the partnership agreement, paid the widow the sum of $2,800, representing his interest in the partnership. "In the event of the death of any partner," the agreement recited, "his share will be transferred to his wife, with no termination of the partnership." The executors contend in their petition that the above provision was an invalid attempt to make a testamentary disposition of property and that the proceeds should pass under the decedent's will as an asset of his estate. The widow maintains that it was a valid and enforcible contract. Although the Surrogate agreed with her, the Appellate Division held that the agreement was invalid as "an attempted testamentary disposition" (264 N.Y.S.2d 868 (A.D. 1965)).

A partnership agreement which provides that, upon the death of one partner, his interest shall pass to the surviving partner or partners, resting as it does in contract, is unquestionably valid and may not be defeated by labeling it a testamentary disposition. . . . We are unable to perceive a difference in principle between an agreement of this character and one, such as that before us, providing for a deceased partner's widow, rather than a surviving partner, to succeed to the decedent's interest in the partnership. . . .

These partnership undertakings are, in effect, nothing more or less than third-party beneficiary contracts, performable at death. Like many similar instruments, contractual in nature, which provide for the disposition of property after death, they need not conform to the requirements of the statute of wills. . . . Examples of such instruments include (1) a contract to make a will . . . ; (2) an inter vivos trust in which the settlor reserves a life estate . . . ; and (3) an insurance policy . . . .

In short, members of a partnership may provide, without fear of running afoul of our statute of wills, that, upon the death of a partner, his widow shall be entitled to his interest in the firm. This type of third-party beneficiary contract is not invalid as an attempted testamentary disposition. . . .

The order of the Appellate Division should be reversed, with costs in this court and in the Appellate Division, and the order of the Surrogate's Court reinstated.

QUESTIONS

1. In both *Atkinson* and *Hillowitz*, the decedent entered into a contract with a pay-on-death (POD) provision, but only one was held valid. Can these conflicting outcomes be reconciled? Was the POD designation in *Hillowitz* more reliable than in *Atkinson*?

2. In *Hillowitz*, the court analogized a partnership agreement under which a deceased partner's interest passes to the surviving partners to one in which a deceased partner's interest passes to the decedent's surviving spouse. Is the analogy sound? Is it relevant that in the first arrangement the surviving partners take pursuant to a bargained-for exchange, whereas in the second arrangement the spouse takes as the donee of a gratuitous transfer? Are there any better rationales that the court might have relied upon?

John H. Langbein, The Nonprobate Revolution and the Future of the Law of Succession
97 Harv. L. Rev. 1108 (1984)

The essential difference between a gift and a will can be simply stated: a gift is a lifetime transfer, ordinarily effected by present delivery of the property, whereas a will transfers property only on the transferor's death. . . . [T]he pure will substitutes fall . . . clearly on the will side of the gift/will line. Each maintains the transferor's complete lifetime dominion and creates no interest in the transferee until the transferor's death. Nevertheless, the case law that has legitimated the pure will substitutes treats them as lifetime transfers. The main stratagem has been to identify some so-called "present interest" in the transferee, acquired during the lifetime of the transferor, which makes the transferee a donee and distinguishes the will substitute from a will. . . .

The odor of legal fiction hangs heavily over the present-interest test. We see courts straining to reach right results for wrong reasons and insisting that will-like transfers possess gift-like incidents. Courts have used such doctrinal ruses to validate not only the revocable inter vivos trust, but the other will substitutes as well. Why is a transfer by life insurance policy or by pension plan not void for violation of the Wills Act? Because the beneficiary's interest is "vested" during the transferor's lifetime. But how can it be vested when the transferor may freely revoke the beneficiary's interest? Well, the power to revoke simply makes the interest "vested subject to defeasance." What is the difference between the revocable and ambulatory interest created by a will, and a vested but defeasible interest in life insurance or pension proceeds? None at all, except for the form of words. Similarly, the joint bank account created merely as a probate avoidance device has been treated as a true joint tenancy, despite the depositor's power to exercise total lifetime dominion over the account. Of the pure will substitutes, only the transparently labelled P.O.D. account has persistently failed the present-interest test and has had to depend for the most part upon statutory validation.

_____

The modern law no longer denies the will-like nature of the will substitutes; it has come to validate them expressly. In 1969, the Uniform Probate Code authorized POD designations in all contracts, and all but a few states have followed suit. Jeffrey A. Schoenblum, 2008 Multistate Guide to Estate Planning at Table 5.01. In 1989, the Uniform Transfer on Death Security Registration Act was promulgated, permitting securities to be registered in a transfer-on-death (TOD) form. As with the POD designation, TOD registrations are now allowed in nearly all states. Schoenblum, supra. Today most banks, brokerage houses, mutual funds, and other such financial intermediaries allow POD and TOD designations on their customers' accounts. With a POD or TOD designation, the property held in the account passes outside of probate. The current POD provision in the UPC follows. Restatement (Third) of Property: Wills and Other Donative Transfers §7.1 (2003) is to similar effect.

Uniform Probate Code (1990, as amended 1998)

§6-101. Nonprobate Transfers on Death

A provision for a nonprobate transfer on death in an insurance policy, contract of employment, bond, mortgage, promissory note, certificated or uncertificated security, account agreement, custodial agreement, deposit agreement, compensation plan, pension plan, individual retirement plan, employee benefit plan, trust, conveyance, deed of gift, marital property agreement, or other written instrument of a similar nature is nontestamentary. This subsection includes a written provision that:

(1) money or other benefits due to, controlled by, or owned by a decedent before death must be paid after the decedent's death to a person whom the decedent designates either in the instrument or in a separate writing, including a will, executed either before or at the same time as the instrument, or later;

(2) money due or to become due under the instrument ceases to be payable in the event of death of the promisee or the promisor before payment or demand; or

(3) any property controlled by or owned by the decedent before death which is the subject of the instrument passes to a person the decedent designates either in the instrument or in a separate writing, including a will, executed either before or at the same time as the instrument, or later.

QUESTIONS

1. If UPC §6-101 had been in force in Ohio when *Atkinson* was decided, what result? Would it have been necessary in *Farkas* to consider whether Williams had an enforceable interest in the trust if §6-101 had been applicable?

2. Explicit statutory validation of POD and TOD designations has many advantages. But what are the costs? What of the evidentiary, cautionary, protective, and channeling functions served by the Wills Act? Are the formalities of a writing and signature typically associated with POD and TOD designations sufficient to satisfy these functions? Does the presence of a neutral financial institution, as is typical for bank and brokerage POD accounts, ensure reliability? For further discussion of these and related questions, see James Lindgren, Abolishing the Attestation Requirement for Wills, 68 N.C. L. Rev. 541, 556-557 (1990); Kent D. Schenkel, Testamentary Fragmentation and the Diminishing Role of the Will: An Argument for Revival, 41 Creighton L. Rev. 155 (2008).

NOTE: A TRANSFER ON DEATH (TOD) DEED FOR REAL PROPERTY?

Suppose *T*, the owner of Blackacre, records a deed that purports to convey Blackacre "to *T*, transfer on death to *A*." *T* dies intestate, leaving *B* as her sole heir. Who takes Blackacre, *A* or *B*? The issue is whether real property can be passed at death outside of probate by a TOD deed. Professor Gary explains:

> A transfer-on-death deed or TOD deed, also known as a beneficiary deed, allows the owner of real property to execute a deed that names the beneficiary who will succeed to ownership at the owner's death. The execution of a TOD deed creates no current interest in the beneficiary and is not a completed gift for property or tax purposes. The owner can revoke the designation at any time, but if the owner records the deed and does not revoke it, the beneficiary will be able to obtain title to the property at the owner's death without going through probate. The cost of using a TOD deed is modest, both at the time of the deed's creation and recordation and at the time . . . the transfer to the beneficiary occurs. The option of using a TOD deed also may eliminate the unintended consequences that sometimes occur when a property owner uses a joint tenancy with right of survivorship to avoid probate for real property. [Susan N. Gary, Transfer-on-Death Deeds: The Nonprobate Revolution Continues, 41 Real Prop., Prob. & Tr. J. 529, 532 (2006).]

An increasing number of states — twelve as of this writing[4] — have enacted statutes that expressly validate the transfer of real property by TOD deed, and a Uniform Real Property Transfer on Death Act is slated for promulgation in the summer of 2009. Under the existing statutes and the current draft of the Uniform Act, in order to be valid, a TOD deed must be recorded before the transferor's death. Does the recording of a written deed satisfy the evidentiary, cautionary, protective, and channeling functions served by the Wills Act?

4. TOD deeds for real property have been validated in Missouri, Kansas, Ohio, New Mexico, Arizona, Nevada, Colorado, Arkansas, Wisconsin, Montana, Oklahoma, and Minnesota. The Kansas statute is examined in Estate of Roloff, 143 P.3d 406 (Kan. App. 2006).

SECTION C.   WILL SUBSTITUTES AND THE SUBSIDIARY LAW OF WILLS

1. Introduction

Restatement (Third) of Property: Wills and Other Donative Transfers (2003)

§7.2   APPLICATION OF WILL DOCTRINES TO WILL SUBSTITUTES

Although a will substitute need not be executed in compliance with the statutory formalities required for a will, such an arrangement is, to the extent appropriate, subject to substantive restrictions on testation and to rules of construction and other rules applicable to testamentary dispositions.

COMMENT

a. Rationale. [A] will substitute serves the function of a will. It shifts the right to possession or enjoyment to the donee at the donor's death. In this sense, a will substitute is in reality a nonprobate will. A will substitute is therefore, to the extent appropriate, subject to substantive restrictions on testation and to rules of construction and other rules applicable to testamentary dispositions. Substantive restrictions on testation constitute important policies restricting disposition of property after the owner's death that should not be avoidable simply by changing the form of the death-time transfer. By contrast, rules of construction and other interpretative devices aid in determining and giving effect to the donor's intention or probable intention and hence should apply generally to donative documents. . . .

Historically, some of the rules of construction were formulated only for wills because wills then constituted the principal means of transmitting property at death. Some rules of construction were placed in the probate code, which led the legislature to draft them as rules applicable to wills. As will substitutes have proliferated and become alternative means of passing property at death, legislatures and courts have sometimes been slow to expand the scope of these rules to transactions to which they should be fully applicable in policy. This Restatement (along with the Restatement Third, Trusts, the Revised Uniform Probate Code, and the Uniform Trust Code) moves toward the policy of unifying the law of wills and will substitutes.

QUESTION

What criteria should apply in determining whether it is "appropriate" to subject a will substitute "to rules of construction and other rules applicable to testamentary dispositions," that is, to the subsidiary law of wills?

2. *Revocable Trusts*

The revocable trust is the most will-like of all the will substitutes. Thus, it is not surprising that the courts have applied to revocable trusts subsidiary rules from the law of wills such as abatement or ademption when there is not enough trust property to satisfy the provisions calling for distribution on the death of the set-tlor (abatement) or the trust does not include a specific item of property that is to be distributed to a particular beneficiary (ademption). See Handelsman v. Handelsman, 852 N.E.2d 862 (Ill. App. 2006) (abatement); Wasserman v. Cohen, 606 N.E.2d 901 (Mass. 1993) (ademption). Discerning the appropriateness of applying other subsidiary rules, however, has proved more challenging. See Alan Newman, Revocable Trusts and the Law of Wills: An Imperfect Fit, 43 Real Prop., Tr. & Est. L.J. 523 (2008).

IN RE ESTATE AND TRUST OF PILAFAS, 836 P.2d 420 (Ariz. App. 1992): In 1982, Steve J. Pilafas executed a will and revocable inter vivos trust. Twice he updated both, the last revisions coming about a month before his death. Pilafas named himself as trustee, and he funded the trusts with substantial assets, including "a Phoenix residence and his interest in a note and deed of trust on a mobile home park. . . . The trust corpus also included other real property, an agreement of sale, and, eventually, a promissory note payable to the trustee and secured by a deed of trust on real property that decedent acquired on June 2, 1988."

The lawyer who drafted the final will and revised trust documents gave both to Pilafas after their execution. Pilafas died in 1988. "Subsequently, the decedent's son, appellee James S. Pilafas, unsuccessfully searched decedent's house and belongings for the original will and trust documents. No information of record indicates their possible whereabouts." Because the will and trust documents were last known to be in possession of the decedent, the question arose, would a presumption of revocation apply to one or both instruments?

> Appellees claim that decedent revoked his will because that document could not be found in a diligent search of his personal effects and papers after his death. This argument relies on the common law presumption that a testator destroyed his will with the intention of revoking it if the will is last seen in the testator's possession and cannot be found after his death.[5]
>
> In response, appellants contend that the common law presumption never arose in this case because appellees proffered insufficient evidence that the will was last seen in decedent's possession or that it could not be found after decedent's death. We disagree. In support of their motion for summary judgment, appellees submitted affidavits tending to prove that decedent took possession of his original will after he executed it; that he meticulously kept important documents; and that appellee James S. Pilafas diligently searched decedent's home after his death and was unable to find the original will. In response, appellants offered no evidence undermining the factual basis for the common law presumption. In our opinion, the trial court correctly determined that decedent revoked his will and died intestate. . . .
>
> Appellees ask us to extend to revocable inter vivos trusts the common law presumption that a will last seen in the testator's possession that cannot be found after his death has been revoked. Appellees' reliance on this common law presumption is misplaced, however, if decedent's trust agreement was not susceptible to revocation by physical destruction.

---

5. On the presumption of revocation, see Harrison v. Bird, page 287. — Eds.

Unlike the execution of a will, the creation of a trust involves the present transfer of property interests in the trust corpus to the beneficiaries. George G. Bogert and George T. Bogert, Trusts & Trustees §998 (2d ed. rev. 1983). "These interests cannot be taken from [the beneficiaries] except in accordance with a provision of the trust instrument, or by their own acts, or by a decree of a court." Id. Even a revocable trust vests the trust beneficiary with a legal right to enforce the terms of the trust. The terms of the trust also limit the powers of the settlor and trustee over the trust corpus, even when the settlor declares himself trustee for the benefit of himself and others.

The terms of decedent's trust agreement governing revocation provide: "The Settlor may at any time or times during the Settlor's lifetime by instrument in writing delivered to the Trustee amend or revoke this Agreement in whole or in part." Appellants argue that under this provision decedent could exercise his power to revoke the trust only through an "instrument in writing delivered to the Trustee." We agree. . . .

Appellees claim to discern a trend in the law toward wholesale application of the law of wills to revocable trusts. This trend is logical and justified, appellees argue, because revocable trusts often serve as substitutes for wills and the same rules should apply to both. As evidence of this trend, appellees cite decisions that apply statutory rules affecting lapsed bequests and post-will divorce to provisions in revocable inter vivos trusts. See, e.g., Clymer v. Mayo, 473 N.E.2d 1084, 1093-94 (Mass. 1985); Miller v. First Nat'l Bank & Trust Co., 637 P.2d 75, 77-78 (Okla. 1981). These decisions, however, involve trust provisions that as a practical matter operate only after the settlor's death. In contrast, the provisions of decedent's inter vivos trust transferred present remainder interests to the trust beneficiaries, who are entitled to insist on full compliance with the terms of the trust instrument. We see no cogent reason the settled and predictable common law rules governing the revocation of trusts should be generally displaced by the distinct statutory rules for the revocation of wills.[6]

Because appellees presented no evidence showing that decedent complied with the required method of revocation, the inter vivos trust was not revoked and remained valid.

PROBLEMS AND QUESTION

1.   Suppose that Pilafas had executed a subsequent will that expressly revoked the inter vivos trust, and that this will is found among Pilafas's papers at death. Does it revoke the trust? Has it been delivered to the trustee? See In re Estate of Lowry, 418 N.E.2d 10 (Ill. App. 1981). Suppose that a bank were trustee. What result? See Connecticut Gen. Life Ins. Co. v. First Natl. Bank of Minneapolis, 262 N.W.2d 403 (Minn. 1977). Suppose that the will stated the testator's intent "to dispose of all property that I have the right to dispose of by will" but did not expressly revoke the trust. What result? See Gardenhire v. Superior Court, 26 Cal. Rptr. 3d 143 (App. 2005).

2.   Suppose Pilafas tore both his will and trust into many pieces. What result as to the will? What result as to the trust? See Salem United Methodist Church v. Bottorff, 138 S.W.3d 788 (Mo. App. 2004).

---

6. Because we hold that the decedent's trust agreement could not have been revoked by physical destruction, we need not decide whether the common law presumption that a lost will last seen in the testator's possession was revoked by physical destruction may apply under some circumstances to revocable inter vivos trusts. We also need not decide whether Arizona's Statute of Frauds, A.R.S. §44-101, would have required a written instrument to revoke the decedent's trust.

3. Would the result in *Pilafas* or in the foregoing problems change if the trust instrument provided that the trust was revocable but did not specify a particular mode of revocation? See Restatement (Third) of Trusts §63 (2003); UTC §602(c) (2000, rev. 2001).

State Street Bank and Trust Co. v. Reiser
Appeals Court of Massachusetts, 1979
389 N.E.2d 768

KASS, J. State Street Bank and Trust Company (the bank) seeks to reach the assets of an inter vivos trust in order to pay a debt to the bank owed by the estate of the settlor of the trust. We conclude that the bank can do so.

Wilfred A. Dunnebier created an inter vivos trust on September 30, 1971, with power to amend or revoke the trust and the right during his lifetime to direct the disposition of principal and income. He conveyed to the trust the capital stock of five closely held corporations. Immediately following execution of this trust, Dunnebier executed a will under which he left his residuary estate to the trust he had established.

About thirteen months later Dunnebier applied to the bank for a $75,000 working capital loan. A bank officer met with Dunnebier, examined a financial statement furnished by him and visited several single family home subdivisions which Dunnebier, or corporations he controlled, had built or were in the process of building. During their conversations, Dunnebier told the bank officer that he had controlling interests in the corporations which owned the most significant assets appearing on the financial statement. On the basis of what he saw of Dunnebier's work, recommendations from another bank, Dunnebier's borrowing history with the bank, and the general cut of Dunnebier's jib, the bank officer decided to make an unsecured loan to Dunnebier for the $75,000 he had asked for. To evidence this loan, Dunnebier, on November 1, 1972, signed a personal demand note to the order of the bank. The probate judge found that Dunnebier did not intend to defraud the bank or misrepresent his financial position by failing to call attention to the fact that he had placed the stock of his corporations in the trust.

Approximately four months after he borrowed this money Dunnebier died in an accident. His estate has insufficient assets to pay the entire indebtedness due the bank. . . .

During the lifetime of the settlor, . . . the bank would have had access to the assets of the trust. When a person creates for his own benefit a trust for support or a discretionary trust, his creditors can reach the maximum amount which the trustee, under the terms of the trust, could pay to him or apply for his benefit. Restatement (Second) of Trusts §156(2) (1959). This is so even if the trust contains spendthrift provisions. Restatement (Second) of Trusts §156(1) (1959). Under the terms of Dunnebier's trust, all the income and principal were at his disposal while he lived.

We then face the question whether Dunnebier's death broke the vital chain. His powers to amend or revoke the trust, or to direct payments from it, obviously died with him, and the remainder interests of the beneficiaries of the trust became vested. The contingencies which might defeat those remainder interests could no longer occur. . . .

As an estate planning vehicle, the inter vivos trust has become common currency. Frequently, as Dunnebier did in the instant case, the settlor retains all the substantial incidents of ownership because access to the trust property is necessary or desirable as a matter of sound financial planning. Psychologically, the settlor thinks of the trust property as "his," as Dunnebier did when he took the bank's officer to visit the real estate owned by the corporation whose stock he had put in trust. . . . In other circumstances, persons place property in trust in order to obtain expert management of their assets, while retaining the power to invade principal and to amend and revoke the trust. It is excessive obeisance to the form in which property is held to prevent creditors from reaching property placed in trust under such terms.

This view was adopted in United States v. Ritter, 558 F.2d 1165, 1167 (4th Cir. 1977). In a concurring opinion in that case Judge Widener observed that it violates public policy for an individual to have an estate to live on, but not an estate to pay his debts with. The Internal Revenue Code institutionalizes the concept that a settlor of a trust who retains administrative powers, power to revoke or power to control beneficial enjoyment "owns" that trust property and provides that it shall be included in the settlor's personal estate. I.R.C. §§2038 and 2041.

We hold, therefore, that where a person places property in trust and reserves the right to amend and revoke, or to direct disposition of principal and income, the settlor's creditors may, following the death of the settlor, reach in satisfaction of the settlor's debts to them, to the extent not satisfied by the settlor's estate, those assets owned by the trust over which the settlor had such control at the time of his death as would have enabled the settlor to use the trust assets for his own benefit. . . .

So ordered.

NOTES

1. In *Reiser*, had Dunnebier not transferred his stock to the trust, then as property owned by him at death it would have been included in his probate estate and been subject to the claims of his creditors. The same result obtains under the court's holding that the trust property is subject to the claims of Dunnebier's creditors to the extent that those claims could not be satisfied out of his probate estate. This is the prevailing view. See Livesay v. Carolina First Bank, 665 S.E.2d 158 (N.C. App. 2008) (upholding statute giving settlor's creditors rights against revocable trust at settlor's death). Both Restatement (Third) of Trusts §25, cmt. e (2003), and UTC §505(a)(3) (2000), are in accord.

2.   All nonprobate assets are *not* created equal when it comes to satisfying the debts of the decedent. Though creditors generally enjoy the right to reach revocable trusts, the beneficiaries of some other nonprobate transfers are protected from having to pay the decedent's creditors. The creditors of a joint tenant cannot reach the jointly held property after the joint tenant's death because the decedent's interest is treated as having vanished. Life insurance proceeds are usually exempt from the insured's creditors if payable to a spouse or child, and the same is generally true of retirement benefits. U.S. savings bonds with a POD beneficiary may also be exempt. See Elaine H. Gagliardi, Remembering the Creditor at Death: Aligning Probate and Nonprobate Transfers, 41 Real Prop., Prob. & Tr. J. 819 (2007).

UPC §6-102, added in 1998, permits the decedent's creditors to reach nonprobate transfers (except joint tenancies in real estate), such as revocable inter vivos trusts and joint bank accounts, if the probate estate is insufficient to pay the debts.

3.   Of all the subsidiary rules from the law of wills, the applicability of *lapse* rules and *antilapse* statutes to interests in trust has been the most controversial. We take this issue up in connection with our treatment of future interests and trust construction in Chapter 13 at page 859.

3. *Life Insurance*

Life insurance contracts have long been effective to transfer property on death without Wills Act formalities. Indeed, the long and benign experience with life insurance was cited by the drafters of the original, 1969 version of UPC §6-101 as a basis for validating POD contracts more broadly. More difficult has been the question of the extent to which life insurance contracts should be subject to the subsidiary law of wills. Before turning to that question, however, we pause to provide a basic sketch of the operation of life insurance and its utility in modern estate planning. Large amounts of money are at stake. In 2007, roughly 375 million life insurance policies were in force with a total face value of $19.5 trillion.

Life insurance is a euphemism for death insurance. The principal purpose is to shift the financial risk of premature death to an insurance company. By buying into a pool with other people worried about the same risk, those who do not die prematurely in effect pay off those who do.

Life insurance is particularly effective at replacing lost income. For a person with dependents, experts often recommend buying life insurance worth at least six to ten times annual income. So someone who makes $50,000 a year should have $300,000 to $500,000 in life insurance. This rule of thumb is designed not to generate a figure that will replace all lost income, but rather to achieve what for many would be an affordable level of insurance. Life insurance is also commonly purchased as part of a buy/sell agreement involving partnership or other closely held business interests, for example to provide the surviving partners with enough cash to buy out the deceased partner's share.

Whole life insurance, also called *ordinary* or *straight* life insurance, is a combination product involving both life insurance and a savings plan. Such a policy eventually becomes *paid up* or *endowed*, after which no further premiums are owed. See Robert J. Lynn and Grayson M.P. McCouch, Introduction to Estate Planning 124-125 (5th ed. 2004). There are newer variations on whole life policies, called *universal* life or *variable* life, which also combine life insurance with a savings account, but that allow more investment options or greater flexibility.

The simplest and most common type of life insurance is called *term* insurance. A term policy contains no savings feature. It is instead a contract whereby the insurance company is obligated to pay the named beneficiary if the insured dies within the policy's stated term of years — commonly 1, 5, 10, 20, or even 30 years. Because there is no savings feature, there is no cash surrender value for a term policy. Some term policies allow for conversion to permanent insurance at a future time irrespective of subsequent changes in the insured's heath.

Because there is no cash surrender value, and because the insured might not die within the stated term, term policies usually cost less than comparable whole life policies, which enables the insured to buy more coverage. Healthy, young adults can usually obtain 20- or 30-year term policies, covering the period of acute vulnerability before the insured's children are self-sufficient, at a relatively low cost. For example, for a level premium of around $100 a month for 30 years, a 30-year old woman in excellent health can obtain a $2 million 30-year term life insurance policy.

"No, but I can tell you the meaning of whole or term life insurance."

Depending on the policy terms, the owner of the life insurance policy, or the beneficiary after the insured's death, may select different *settlement options* for the receipt of death benefits, including a lump sum, an annuity, interest for years followed by payment of the principal, or periodic payments of interest and principal. For modest estates, these settlement options can provide some of the flexibility that trusts provide for more substantial estates.

We turn now to the applicability of the subsidiary law of wills to life insurance policies, focusing on the problem of revocation on divorce.

COOK v. EQUITABLE LIFE ASSURANCE SOCIETY, 428 N.E.2d 110 (Ind. App. 1981): Douglas Cook purchased a whole life insurance policy, naming his wife at the time, Doris, as the beneficiary. Douglas and Doris divorced. The divorce decree made no mention of the life insurance policy, and Douglas failed to change the beneficiary designation after the divorce. Nine months later, on Christmas Eve, Douglas married Margaret, with whom he later had a son, Daniel. Eleven years later Douglas made a holographic "Last Will & Testimint [sic]" providing as follows:

> Being of sound mind do Hereby leave all my Worldly posessions to my Wife and son, Margaret A. Cook & Daniel Joseph Cook. being my Bank Accounts at Irwin Union Bank & trust to their Welfair my Insurance policys with Common Welth of Ky. and Equitable Life. all my machinecal tools to be left to my son if He is Interested in Working with them If not to be sold and money used for their welfair all my Gun Collection Kept as long as they, my Wife & Son and then sold and money used for their welfair

Douglas died three years later. Because the court assumed that Douglas's designation of Doris as the beneficiary of his life insurance policy was not revoked by their subsequent divorce, the issue was whether Douglas could change the beneficiary designation by will. The policy terms required a written notice to the company to change the beneficiary.

Clearly it is in the interest of insurance companies to require and to follow certain specified procedures in the change of beneficiaries of its policies so that they may pay over benefits to persons properly entitled to them without subjection to claims by others of whose rights they had no notice or knowledge. Certainly it is also in the interest of beneficiaries themselves to be entitled to prompt payment of benefits by insurance companies which do not withhold payment until the will has been probated in the fear of later litigation which might result from having paid the wrong party. . . .

[In this case there has been no] showing that the insured had done all within his powers or all that reasonably could have been expected of him to comply with the policy provisions respecting a change of beneficiary, but that through no fault of his own he was unable to achieve his goal. . . . There is no indication that Douglas took any action in the fourteen years between his divorce from Doris and his death, other than the making of the will, to change the beneficiary of his life insurance policy from Doris to Margaret and Daniel. Surely, if Douglas had wanted to change the beneficiary he had ample time and opportunity to comply with the policy requirements. . . .

We may be sympathetic to the cause of the decedent's widow and son, and it might seem that a departure from the general rule in an attempt to do equity under these facts would be

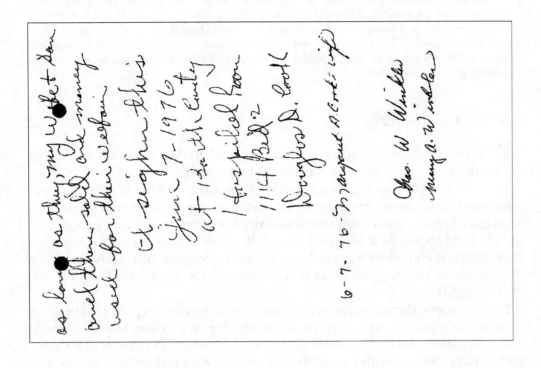

Will of Douglas Cook

noble. Nevertheless, such a course is fraught with the dangers of eroding a solidly paved pathway of the law and leaving in its stead only a gaping hole of uncertainty. Public policy requires that the insurer, insured, and beneficiary alike should be able to rely on the certainty that policy provisions pertaining to the naming and changing of beneficiaries will control except in extreme situations. We, therefore, invoke a maxim equally as venerable as the one upon which appellants rely in the determination of this cause: Equity aids the vigilant, not those who slumber on their rights.

QUESTION AND NOTES

1.   Consider the reproduction of Douglas Cook's holographic will. Is it fair to say, as the court said, that he slumbered on his rights?

2.   *Cook* presents the regrettably common problem of what to do with a will substitute that names an ex-spouse as beneficiary. In many states, the statute that revokes a will provision for a divorced spouse does not apply to the designation of the divorced spouse in a life insurance contract or other nonprobate transfer. *Cook* reflects the majority approach in such states. See Susan N. Gary, Applying Revocation-on-Divorce Statutes to Will Substitutes, 18 Quinnipiac Prob. L.J. 83, 90-100 (2004).

In other states, the revocation-on-divorce statute expressly applies to specified nonprobate transfers such as revocable trusts. See, e.g., Ohio Rev. Code Ann. §5815.31 (2008); Okla. Stat. Ann. tit. 60, §175 (2008). UPC §2-804 (1990, rev. 2002), page 306, provides that divorce revokes dispositions in favor of the divorced spouse in "a governing instrument," which is defined in §1-201 to include revocable inter vivos trusts as well as other will substitutes, such as life insurance, pension plans, and POD and TOD contracts. Had *Cook* involved UPC §2-804, the result would have been different.

Regardless of the state of the statutory law, the lawyer representing a party in a divorce proceeding should address death benefits explicitly in the divorce agreement.

3.   Two problems have arisen in the application of statutes such as UPC §2-804. First, there is a lingering question whether the statute may constitutionally be applied to an insurance beneficiary designation made before the effective date of the statute. Most but not all courts have upheld retroactive application. Compare Buchholz v. Storsve, 740 N.W.2d 107 (S.D. 2007) (upholding retroactive application), with Whirlpool Corp. v. Ritter, 929 F.2d 1318 (8th Cir. 1991) (retroactive application unconstitutional). Second, the application of statutes such as UPC §2-804 to federally regulated pension accounts and employer-provided life insurance has been curtailed by Egelhoff v. Egelhoff, page 426.

NOTE: A SUPERWILL?

Would it be a good idea to permit a *superwill*, that is, to allow the testator's will to trump the beneficiary designations in all nonprobate transfers? A superwill could resolve the problem of updating beneficiary designations across the testator's many and sometimes forgotten nonprobate instruments. But what would be the drawbacks? Would the superwill draw the otherwise expeditious nonprobate modes of transfer into probate, holding up payment until the will is held valid?

There is precedent of sorts for the superwill concept. A power to revoke an inter vivos trust created by the decedent can be exercised by will, if the trust so provides. And a power of appointment given the decedent over a trust created by another person can be exercised by the will of the decedent. If the decedent can change the beneficiary of a trust by will, why not the beneficiary of a contract? See Cynthia J. Artura, Superwill to the Rescue? How Washington's Statute Falls Short of Being a Hero in the Field of Trust and Probate Law, 74 Wash. L. Rev. 799 (1999); Roberta R. Kwall and Anthony J. Aiello, The Superwill Debate: Opening the Pandora's Box?, 62 Temp. L. Rev. 277 (1989). See also Wash. Rev. Code §§11.11.003-11.11.901 (2008) (superwill statute).

Restatement (Third) of Property: Wills and Other Donative Transfers §7.2, cmt. e (2003) endorses a modified superwill concept:

> Insurance contracts, multiple-party accounts, pension accounts, and other will substitutes commonly require the account owner to follow a particular procedure for altering or amending the beneficiary designation, such as completing a form supplied by the financial intermediary or other payor. Such a term governs as a matter of the contract between the account owner and the financial intermediary or payor. It sometimes happens that the account owner misunderstands this requirement and attempts to revoke the beneficiary designation by will. The courts are divided about whether to enforce the account term, thereby defeating the account owner's later contrary expression of donative intent.
>
> In such cases, when the financial intermediary or other payor has paid the beneficiary of record on the account in good faith before learning of the later inconsistent designation in the will, the account term is effective to protect the financial intermediary or payor from liability to the beneficiary designated in the will. In such circumstances, that intended beneficiary is remitted to an action in restitution against the account-designated beneficiary who received the payment.
>
> When the financial intermediary or payor receives notice of the inconsistent beneficiary designation contained in the subsequent will before paying the beneficiary of record on the account, the financial intermediary or payor should pay the proceeds as directed under the will, notwithstanding the failure of the account owner to comply with the account term specifying account-specific procedures for revocation or alteration. If the financial intermediary or payor is uncertain about the priority or effectiveness of the attempted revocation or alteration by will, the financial intermediary or payor may discharge its responsibilities by interpleading and/or paying the proceeds into court.
>
> When a designation by will supersedes a designation contained in the instrument of account, the proceeds remain separate from probate property and pass in accordance with the provisions of the nonprobate account, unless the language of the later will expresses an intent that the account proceeds are to become part of the probate estate.

4. Pension and Retirement Accounts

The federal government has long permitted a death beneficiary to be named on U.S. savings and war bonds. Beginning in the early 1960s, Congress permitted death beneficiaries to be put on various types of retirement plans, including pension and profit-sharing, 401(k), and several types of individual retirement accounts (IRAs). Substantial wealth is held in these plans. Data compiled by the Federal Reserve show that by year-end 2008, private pension plans held $4.6 trillion in assets and public retirement plans held $3.5 trillion. Two-thirds of the public plan assets were in state and local government plans; the rest were in federal plans. IRAs, meanwhile, held $4.7 trillion in assets at year-end 2007, and insurance companies held $2.1 trillion in annuity reserves at year-end 2008.

John H. Langbein, The Twentieth-Century Revolution in Family Wealth Transmission
86 Mich. L. Rev. 722 (1988)

Pension funds are [an] artifact of the new forms of wealth that arose in consequence of the breakup of older, family-centered modes of production. Neither on the prairie nor in the cities of Abraham Lincoln's day had anybody ever heard of a pension fund. Your life expectancy was such that you were unlikely to need much in the way of retirement income. If you did chance to outlive your period of productive labor, you were in general cared for within the family.

Not only is the need for a retirement income stream relatively recent, but so too is the mode of wealth that now supplies it. Pension funds are composed almost entirely of financial assets — the instruments of financial intermediation — that distinctively modern form of property that was still of peripheral importance in the last century. . . .

The way to begin thinking about the pension revolution is to grasp the magnitude of the underlying demographic phenomena that brought it about. Life expectancy a hundred years ago was about forty-five years. Today, it is seventy-five years and climbing. . . .

Not only have the demographics altered so that the elders are routinely surviving for long intervals beyond their years of employment, but in consequence of the transformation in the nature of wealth, their property has taken on a radically altered character. That family farm or family firm that was the source of intrafamilial support in former times has become ever more exceptional. Most parental wealth (apart from the parents' own human capital) now takes the form of financial assets, which embody claims upon those large-scale enterprises that have replaced family enterprise. . . .

In propertied families, today's elderly no longer expect much financial support from their children. The shared patrimony in farm or firm that underlay that reverse transfer system in olden times has now largely vanished. Instead, people of means are expected to foresee the need for retirement income while they are still in the workforce, and to conduct a program of saving for their retirement. Typically, these people have already undertaken one great cycle of saving and dissaving in their lives — that program by which they effected the investment in human capital for their children. Just as that former program of saving was oriented toward a distinctively modern form of wealth, human capital, so this second program centers on the other characteristic form of twentieth-century wealth, financial assets.

A priori, we might expect that individuals would be left to save for retirement without government guidance, much as they are left alone to save and spend for other purposes, but that has not been the case. Instead, the federal government has intervened by creating irresistible tax incentives to encourage people to conduct much or most of their retirement saving in a special mode, the tax-qualified pension plan.

There are three crucial advantages to conducting retirement saving through a tax-qualified pension plan. First, most contributions to the plan are tax-deferred. When my employer contributes to a qualified pension or profit-sharing plan on my behalf, or when I contribute to a defined contribution plan such as a 401(k) or, in the case of academic personnel, a 403(b), I am saving with pretax dollars. If I am in the 25-percent bracket, the Treasury is contributing to my pension savings plan 25 cents in foregone taxation for my 75 cents in foregone consumption. The second great tax advantage is that the earnings on qualified plan investments accrue and compound on a tax-deferred basis. It is not until the employee retires and begins to receive distributions of his pension savings that he pays income tax on the sums distributed. The third major advantage associated with pension taxation is that, because most retirees have lower taxable income in their retirement years than in their peak earning years, they find that distributions from pension accounts are usually taxed at lower marginal rates. As the progressivity of the income tax has abated in recent years, however, this attribute of the system has become less significant.

As a matter of tax policy, it is open to serious question whether Congress should be granting the level of tax subsidy for pension saving that it now does, but that is a topic for another day. The present point is that the tax attractions of conducting retirement saving through the medium of a tax-qualified pension plan are simply overwhelming. These advantages explain why employers incur the regulatory costs incident to sponsoring these plans; and why employees, especially those in higher tax brackets, prefer to take compensation in the form of pension saving rather than cash wages. The private pension system — this [several]-trillion-dollar savings scheme — is tax driven.

NOTE: DEFINED BENEFIT VERSUS DEFINED CONTRIBUTION PENSION PLANS

Pension plans usually take one of two forms. In a *defined benefit* plan, the employer promises to pay an annuity on retirement — for example, a set percentage of the average of the employee's top three years of wages. An annuity is an annual payment that can be made for a term of years or, more typically, every year for the rest of the beneficiary's life or the lives of the beneficiary and beneficiary's spouse. An annuity therefore shifts the financial risk of living too long (we should all have such problems!) to a pension fund or insurance company. By buying into a pool with other people worried about the same risk, those who die younger pay those who die older. An annuity thus reflects the opposite bet from that of life insurance: with an annuity, if you die sooner than expected, you lose; with life insurance, if you die sooner, you win (sort of). In a defined benefit plan, annuitization replaces succession, because at the death of the annuitant there is nothing left to pass on. Though defined benefit plans are becoming less common in private pension plans, they remain common for government employees.

In a *defined contribution* plan, the employer or the employee or both make contributions to a specific pension account for the employee. Upon retirement, the employee may make withdrawals from the account, subject to various distribution rules. Because the employee owns all the funds in the account, defined contribution plans often lead to lump-sum payouts on the death of the worker and her spouse. The defined contribution plan therefore operates in effect as a tax-advantaged savings account that concludes with a nonprobate transfer. In this way, the defined contribution plan has helped drive the nonprobate revolution. For further discussion, see Edward A. Zelinsky, The Origins of the Ownership Society: How the Defined Contribution Paradigm Changed America (2007); Alicia Munnell et al., The Impact of Defined Contribution Plans on Bequests 268, *in* Death and Dollars: The Role of Gifts and Bequests in America (Alicia H. Munnell and Annika Sunden eds., 2003).

Federal Reserve data on private-sector pension plans show $2.7 trillion in defined contribution plans and $1.9 trillion in defined benefit plans. With a private-sector defined benefit plan, the worker runs the risk that the company will go bankrupt, leaving the worker with a reduced pension funded by the federal Pension Benefit Guarantee Corporation. With a defined contribution plan, on the other hand, the worker directly bears market risk and the consequences of poor choices in allocating her pension account among different investment vehicles. See James M. Poterba, Individual Decision Making and Risk in Defined Contribution Plans, 13 Elder L.J. 285 (2005).

Pension plans have long been subject to a complex overlay of federal regulation, most significantly the Employee Retirement Income Security Act of 1974 (ERISA). The question thus arises, does the federal regulation of pension plans preempt the state subsidiary law of wills?

Egelhoff v. Egelhoff
Supreme Court of the United States, 2001
532 U.S. 141

THOMAS, J.   A Washington statute provides that the designation of a spouse as the beneficiary of a nonprobate asset is revoked automatically upon divorce. We are asked to decide whether the Employee Retirement Income Security Act of 1974 (ERISA), 29 U.S.C. §1001 et seq., pre-empts that statute to the extent it applies to ERISA plans. We hold that it does.

I

Petitioner Donna Rae Egelhoff was married to David A. Egelhoff. Mr. Egelhoff was employed by the Boeing Company, which provided him with a life insurance policy and a pension plan. Both plans were governed by ERISA, and Mr. Egelhoff designated his wife as the beneficiary under both. In April 1994, the Egelhoffs divorced. Just over two months later, Mr. Egelhoff died intestate following an automobile accident. At that time, Mrs. Egelhoff remained the listed beneficiary under both the life insurance policy and the pension plan. The life insurance proceeds, totaling $46,000, were paid to her.

Respondents Samantha and David Egelhoff, Mr. Egelhoff's children by a previous marriage, are his statutory heirs under state law. They sued petitioner in Washington state court to recover the life insurance proceeds. Respondents relied on a Washington statute that provides:

> If a marriage is dissolved or invalidated, a provision made prior to that event that relates to the payment or transfer at death of the decedent's interest in a nonprobate asset in favor of or granting an interest or power to the decedent's former spouse is revoked. A provision affected by this section must be interpreted, and the nonprobate asset affected passes, as if the former spouse failed to survive the decedent, having died at the time of entry of the decree of dissolution or declaration of invalidity. Wash. Rev. Code §11.07.010(2)(a) (1994).

That statute applies to "all nonprobate assets, wherever situated, held at the time of entry by a superior court of this state of a decree of dissolution of marriage or a declaration of invalidity." §11.07.010(1). It defines "nonprobate asset" to include "a life insurance policy, employee benefit plan, annuity or similar contract, or individual retirement account." §11.07.010(5)(a).

Respondents argued that they were entitled to the life insurance proceeds because the Washington statute disqualified Mrs. Egelhoff as a beneficiary, and in the absence of a qualified named beneficiary, the proceeds would pass to them as Mr. Egelhoff's heirs. In a separate action, respondents also sued to recover the pension plan benefits. Respondents again argued that the Washington statute disqualified Mrs. Egelhoff as a beneficiary and they were thus entitled to the benefits under the plan. . . .

Courts have disagreed about whether statutes like that of Washington are preempted by ERISA. To resolve the conflict, we granted certiorari.

II

. . . ERISA's pre-emption section, 29 U.S.C. §1144(a), states that ERISA "shall supersede any and all State laws insofar as they may now or hereafter relate to any employee benefit plan" covered by ERISA. We have observed repeatedly that this broadly worded provision is "clearly expansive." New York State Conference of Blue Cross & Blue Shield Plans v. Travelers Ins. Co., 514 U.S. 645, 655 (1995). But at the same time, we have recognized that the term "relate to" cannot be taken "to extend to the furthest stretch of its indeterminacy," or else "for all practical purposes pre-emption would never run its course." Ibid.

We have held that a state law relates to an ERISA plan "if it has a connection with or reference to such a plan." Shaw v. Delta Air Lines, Inc., 463 U.S. 85, 97 (1983). Petitioner focuses on the "connection with" part of this inquiry. Acknowledging that "connection with" is scarcely more restrictive than "relate to," we have cautioned against an "uncritical literalism" that would make preemption turn on "infinite connections." *Travelers*, supra, at 656. Instead, "to determine whether a state law has the forbidden connection, we look both to 'the objectives of the ERISA statute as a guide to the scope of the state law that Congress understood would survive,' as well as to the nature of the effect of the state law on ERISA plans." California Div. of Labor Standards Enforcement v. Dillingham Constr., N.A., Inc., 519 U.S. 316, 325 (1997), quoting *Travelers*, supra, at 656.

Applying this framework, petitioner argues that the Washington statute has an impermissible connection with ERISA plans. We agree. The statute binds ERISA plan administrators to a particular choice of rules for determining beneficiary status. The administrators must pay benefits to the beneficiaries chosen by state law, rather than to those identified in the plan documents. The statute thus implicates an area of core ERISA concern. In particular, it runs counter to ERISA's commands that a plan shall "specify the basis on which payments are made to and from the plan," §1102(b)(4), and that the fiduciary shall administer the plan "in accordance with the documents and instruments governing the plan," §1104(a)(1)(D), making payments to a "beneficiary" who is "designated by a participant, or by the terms of [the] plan." §1002(8). In other words, unlike generally applicable laws regulating "areas where ERISA has nothing to say," *Dillingham*, 519 U.S. at 330, which we have upheld notwithstanding their incidental effect on ERISA plans, this statute governs the payment of benefits, a central matter of plan administration.

The Washington statute also has a prohibited connection with ERISA plans because it interferes with nationally uniform plan administration. One of the principal goals of ERISA is to enable employers "to establish a uniform administrative scheme, which provides a set of standard procedures to guide processing of claims and disbursement of benefits." Fort Halifax Packing Co. v. Coyne, 482 U.S. 1, 9 (1987). Uniformity is impossible, however, if plans are subject to different legal obligations in different States.

The Washington statute at issue here poses precisely that threat. Plan administrators cannot make payments simply by identifying the beneficiary specified by the plan documents. Instead they must familiarize themselves with state statutes so that they can determine whether the named beneficiary's status has been "revoked" by operation of law. And in this context the burden is exacerbated by the choice-of-law problems that may confront an administrator when the employer is located in one State, the plan participant lives in another, and the participant's former spouse lives in a third. In such a situation, administrators might find that plan payments are subject to conflicting legal obligations.

To be sure, the Washington statute protects administrators from liability for making payments to the named beneficiary unless they have "actual knowledge of the dissolution or other invalidation of marriage," Wash. Rev. Code

§11.07.010(3)(a) (1994), and it permits administrators to refuse to make payments until any dispute among putative beneficiaries is resolved, §11.07.010(3)(b). But if administrators do pay benefits, they will face the risk that a court might later find that they had "actual knowledge" of a divorce. If they instead decide to await the results of litigation before paying benefits, they will simply transfer to the beneficiaries the costs of delay and uncertainty. Requiring ERISA administrators to master the relevant laws of 50 States and to contend with litigation would undermine the congressional goal of "minimizing the administrative and financial burdens" on plan administrators — burdens ultimately borne by the beneficiaries. Ingersoll-Rand Co. v. McClendon, 498 U.S. 133, 142 (1990).

We recognize that all state laws create some potential for a lack of uniformity. But differing state regulations affecting an ERISA plan's "system for processing claims and paying benefits" impose "precisely the burden that ERISA pre-emption was intended to avoid." *Fort Halifax*, supra, at 10. And as we have noted, the statute at issue here directly conflicts with ERISA's requirements that plans be administered, and benefits be paid, in accordance with plan documents. We conclude that the Washington statute has a "connection with" ERISA plans and is therefore pre-empted.

III

Respondents suggest several reasons why ordinary ERISA pre-emption analysis should not apply here. . . .

[R]espondents emphasize that the Washington statute involves both family law and probate law, areas of traditional state regulation. There is indeed a presumption against pre-emption in areas of traditional state regulation such as family law. But that presumption can be overcome where, as here, Congress has made clear its desire for pre-emption. Accordingly, we have not hesitated to find state family law pre-empted when it conflicts with ERISA or relates to ERISA plans. See, e.g., Boggs v. Boggs, 520 U.S. 833 (1997) (holding that ERISA pre-empts a state community property law permitting the testamentary transfer of an interest in a spouse's pension plan benefits).

Finally, respondents argue that if ERISA pre-empts this statute, then it also must pre-empt the various state statutes providing that a murdering heir is not entitled to receive property as a result of the killing. In the ERISA context, these "slayer" statutes could revoke the beneficiary status of someone who murdered a plan participant. Those statutes are not before us, so we do not decide the issue. We note, however, that the principle underlying the statutes — which have been adopted by nearly every State — is well established in the law and has a long historical pedigree predating ERISA. See, e.g., Riggs v. Palmer, 22 N.E. 188 (N.Y. 1889). And because the statutes are more or less uniform nationwide, their interference with the aims of ERISA is at least debatable. . . .

The judgment of the Supreme Court of Washington is reversed, and the case is remanded for further proceedings not inconsistent with this opinion.

It is so ordered.

BREYER, J., dissenting.   . . . The Court has previously made clear that the fact that state law "imposes some burden on the administration of ERISA plans" does not necessarily require pre-emption. De Buono v. NYSA-ILA Medical and Clinical Services Fund, 520 U.S. 806, 815 (1997). Precisely, what is it about this statute's requirement that distinguishes it from the "myriad state laws" that impose some kind of burden on ERISA plans? Ibid.

Indeed, if one looks beyond administrative burden, one finds that Washington's statute poses no obstacle, but furthers ERISA's ultimate objective — developing a fair system for protecting employee benefits. The Washington statute transfers an employee's pension assets at death to those individuals whom the worker would likely have wanted to receive them. As many jurisdictions have concluded, divorced workers more often prefer that a child, rather than a divorced spouse, receive those assets. Of course, an employee can secure this result by changing a beneficiary form; but doing so requires awareness, understanding, and time. That is why Washington and many other jurisdictions have created a statutory assumption that divorce works a revocation of a designation in favor of an ex-spouse. That assumption is embodied in the Uniform Probate Code; it is consistent with human experience; and those with expertise in the matter have concluded that it "more often" serves the cause of "justice." John H. Langbein, The Nonprobate Revolution and the Future of the Law of Succession, 97 Harv. L. Rev. 1108, 1135 (1984).

In forbidding Washington to apply that assumption here, the Court permits a divorced wife, who already acquired, during the divorce proceeding, her fair share of the couple's community property, to receive in addition the benefits that the divorce court awarded to her former husband. To be more specific, Donna Egelhoff already received a business, an IRA account, and stock; David received, among other things, 100% of his pension benefits. David did not change the beneficiary designation in the pension plan or life insurance plan during the 6-month period between his divorce and his death. As a result, Donna will now receive a windfall of approximately $80,000 at the expense of David's children. The State of Washington enacted a statute to prevent precisely this kind of unfair result. But the Court, relying on an inconsequential administrative burden, concludes that Congress required it.

Finally, the logic of the Court's decision does not stop at divorce revocation laws. The Washington statute is virtually indistinguishable from other traditional state-law rules, for example, rules using presumptions to transfer assets in the case of simultaneous deaths, and rules that prohibit a husband who kills a wife from receiving benefits as a result of the wrongful death. It is particularly difficult to believe that Congress wanted to pre-empt the latter kind of statute. But how do these statutes differ from the one before us? Slayer statutes — like this statute — "govern the payment of benefits, a central matter of plan administration." And contrary to the Court's suggestion, slayer statutes vary from State to State in their details just like divorce revocation statutes. Indeed, the "slayer" conflict would seem more serious, not less serious, than the conflict before us, for few, if any, slayer statutes permit plans to opt out of the state property law rule. . . .

For these reasons, I disagree with the Court's conclusion. And, consequently, I dissent.

QUESTIONS AND NOTES

1.   In *Egelhoff*, the majority suggested that slayer rules differ from revocation-on-divorce rules in that the former have "a long historical pedigree" and "are more or less uniform nationwide." Is this a meaningful distinction? Is it descriptively accurate? See pages 149-151.

2.   After *Egelhoff*, by what means could revocation-on-divorce, slayer, and other such subsidiary wills rules be extended to pension plans? Congress could amend ERISA to allow the state law subsidiary law of wills to apply, or to add a set of comparable federal subsidiary rules. Plan administrators could add language to their pension plans to address these issues. Or courts could recognize such rules as part of the federal common law applicable in disputes under ERISA, perhaps by endorsing the versions stated in the Restatement (Third) of Property or Uniform Probate Code, as Professor Gallanis has suggested. See Thomas P. Gallanis, Reform of Qualified Retirement Plans: ERISA and the Law of Succession, 65 Ohio St. L.J. 185 (2004).

Since *Egelhoff*, there has been little congressional attention to the question whether to apply the subsidiary law of wills to death benefits governed by ERISA. To fill the void, the lower federal and state courts have begun to recognize federal common law rules of revocation-on-divorce, slayer, and the like. In Metropolitan Life Ins. Co. v. Johnson, 297 F.3d 558 (7th Cir. 2002), *H* tried to replace his ex-spouse as his beneficiary under his pension plan, but on the beneficiary change form *H* checked the box for the wrong plan. Under Illinois law, the beneficiary change would have been effective under the substantial compliance doctrine. The court held that ERISA preempted Illinois law, but the court went on to hold that federal common law under ERISA also recognized substantial compliance, hence the court upheld the beneficiary change.

In Ahmed v. Ahmed, 817 N.E.2d 424 (Ohio App. 2004), the court applied similar reasoning to the question of whether a slayer may take under an ERISA-regulated insurance policy. The court held that, even though ERISA preempts the Ohio slayer statute, as a matter of federal common law a slayer may not take under an ERISA plan. However, the court did not treat the slayer as having predeceased the victim, which is the usual state law approach, including that of the Ohio statute, but instead directed that the insurance proceeds be paid to the victim's probate estate. See also Connecticut General Life Ins. Co. v. Riner, 351 F. Supp. 2d 492 (W.D. Va. 2005) (holding that "even if ERISA preempts [the state] slayer statute, it still would be inappropriate for the court to allow the slayer to benefit from his wrongdoing").

The question thus arises, has preemption of the state subsidiary law of wills under *Egelhoff* in fact resulted in greater uniformity and ease of administration for ERISA plan death benefits?

3.   For further discussion, see Gallanis, supra; Albert Feuer, Who Is Entitled to Survivor Benefits from ERISA Plans? 40 J. Marshall L. Rev. 919 (2007); Susan N. Gary, Applying Revocation-on-Divorce Statutes to Will Substitutes, 18 Quinnipiac Prob. L.J. 83, 124-126 (2004); Sarabeth A. Rayho, Note, Divorcees Turn About in Their Graves as Ex-Spouses Cash In: Codified Constructive Trusts Ensure an Equitable Result Regarding ERISA-Governed Employee Benefit Plans, 106 Mich. L. Rev. 373 (2007).

5.   *Multiple-Party Bank and Brokerage Accounts*

The various types of multiple-party bank and brokerage accounts include joint and survivor, POD, agency or convenience, and savings (Totten trust) accounts. If an account is joint and survivor, owned by "*A* and *B*, as joint tenants with right of survivorship," either *A* or *B* has the power to draw on the account and the survivor solely owns the balance of the account, which does not pass through probate.

Sometimes, however, something other than a true joint tenancy account is intended. *A*, a bank depositor, may open a joint account with *B*, intending only that *B* receive the balance upon *A*'s death — a POD account disguised as a joint account. Or *A* might intend that *B* have power to draw on the account during *A*'s life only for the convenience of *A*, but not for other purposes and not to receive the balance at *A*'s death — an agency or convenience account disguised as a joint account.

Because banks and brokerage houses often give their customers a joint tenancy form without regard to the customer's particular intention, courts are often left with the problem of discerning which type of account was actually intended.

Varela v. Bernachea
Court of Appeal of Florida, 2005
917 So. 2d 295

PER CURIAM.   . . . [Cristina] Varela and [Carlos Alberto] Bernachea are both Argentinean citizens who met in Buenos Aires in late 2000. They developed a romantic relationship and traveled the world together. Bernachea was an attorney in Argentina for over 30 years, but has since retired and invested in American businesses and real estate. In late 2001, at Bernachea's behest, Varela stopped working and moved into his Sunny Isles Beach condominium where the two began living together. While they were a couple, Bernachea paid all of Varela's expenses and showered her with expensive gifts. Varela claimed that she never knew Bernachea was married. Moreover, she claimed Bernachea held her out as his wife. Bernachea disputed Varela's claims and asserted that Varela knew he had a wife, yet contented herself with being his mistress.

Whatever their true arrangement, on January 4, 2002, Bernachea added Varela as a joint tenant with a right of survivorship to his Merrill Lynch CMA account. Mr. Jorge Herrera, Bernachea's long-time banker, testified that he related the details of the transaction in Spanish and that Bernachea, a former practicing attorney, never stated that he did not understand the legal significance of a joint tenancy with a right of survivorship during the transaction. As a joint owner of the account, Varela received a Visa check card for the account, which she freely used. Herrera and his assistant Ms. Zoraida Rosa both testified below that they never received any instruction to restrict Varela's access to the account — be it via check or check card.

Bernachea took the position below that Varela's access to the Merrill Lynch account was restricted. Specifically, Bernachea testified that the parties maintained a separate joint account with Southtrust because Varela had check writing privileges for the Southtrust account, but lacked such privileges for the CMA account. Varela, on the other hand, testified that she and Bernachea maintained the separate Southtrust account because a Southtrust branch was conveniently located near their condominium, and they accessed the Southtrust account more frequently, largely to pay bills. Thus, the uncontested testimony established that Varela had the ability to access the CMA funds. Bernachea's testimony reflects his confusion, regarding whether Varela could only access the CMA account via her Visa check card, or could additionally access the account via conventional paper check. It was undisputed, however, that the CMA and Southtrust accounts were joint accounts and that the account funds were supplied by Bernachea.

On October 18, 2002, Bernachea suffered a heart attack in his Sunny Isles condominium. Varela called 911 and accompanied Bernachea to the hospital. While Bernachea was hospitalized, Varela stayed with him until Bernachea's daughters arrived from Argentina and barred Varela from both Bernachea's hospital room and his Sunny Isles condominium. Varela willingly vacated the apartment. On October 25, 2002, Varela visited the Merrill Lynch branch on Brickell Avenue. Once there, Varela wrote a $280,000.00 check on the CMA account and deposited it in her own name in a newly opened Merrill Lynch personal account.

A Brickell branch account executive, Mr. Daniel Diaz, called the Coral Gables Merrill Lynch branch to ensure that Varela was authorized to write such a check. Diaz spoke with Herrera, who confirmed that Varela was the joint CMA owner and had the ability to write a check up to the account balance. Nevertheless, two weeks after his release from the hospital Bernachea demanded that Merrill Lynch return the $280,000.00. Merrill Lynch complied and transferred the $280,000.00 into the CMA account. Varela contested this transfer, but Merrill Lynch would not return the funds.

Bernachea subsequently sued Varela and Merrill Lynch to settle the ownership status of the CMA account. . . . The [trial] court [found] that Bernachea was the sole CMA account owner because he lacked donative intent when he added Varela as a joint account owner. Varela appeals from the Final Judgment. We reverse. . . .

When a joint bank account is established with the funds of one person, a gift of the funds is presumed. This presumption may be rebutted only by clear and convincing evidence to the contrary. Spark v. Canny, 88 So. 2d 307 (Fla. 1956); De Soto v. Guardianship of De Soto, 664 So. 2d 66, 67 (Fla. 3d DCA 1995). In the instant case, the trial court erroneously found, in the absence of clear and convincing evidence, that Bernachea rebutted Varela's gift presumption.

The trial court premised its finding on Bernachea's claim that he lacked donative intent. The only evidence in support of this claim was Bernachea's own dubious testimony, claiming he misapprehended the significance of a joint tenancy, and only intended for Varela to possess "restricted" account access. However, Herrera, who the court found was a credible witness, testified that he specifically explained the details of a joint tenancy with a right of survivorship in Spanish without any questions from Bernachea, a former attorney. Thus, the court's finding that "[Bernachea] did not understand the significance of the 'joint tenancy with right of survivorship' . . . in the English form" is inconsistent with the facts and testimony that same court found credible. Moreover, Bernachea admitted that, per his wishes, Varela had the ability to make check card purchases and write checks on the CMA account to the account balance.

Clearly, Bernachea did not rebut Varela's gift presumption when he openly admitted that he gave Varela access to their joint account via check card. Contrary to Bernachea's attempt to define a distinction, there is no principled distinction between paper checks and check cards. In fact, the check card's raison d'être is its status as a convenient replacement for paper checks. This modern reality conflicts with the trial court's holding that unfettered account access via check card, represents "restricted status." Moreover, in direct contrast to the court's conclusion, Herrera and Rosa testified that Varela's account access was never restricted. Additionally, both Merrill Lynch branches approved Varela's $280,000.00 check because she was a joint account owner with the ability to write checks up to the account balance.

The Record does not support the trial court's finding, as a matter of law, that Bernachea demonstrated an absence of donative intent. Moreover, Bernachea failed to rebut the presumption that he intended to give Varela an equal interest in their joint bank account. Accordingly, we reverse the Final Judgment and remand with instructions to enter judgment for Varela, awarding her a one-half interest in the October, 25, 2002, CMA account balance.

NOTES, PROBLEMS, AND QUESTION

1. If a convenience or POD account is intended, during the depositor's life the other tenant is not entitled to treat the funds as her own. This was the dispute in *Varela*. Similar issues can arise at the depositor's death. If a convenience account is intended, the survivor is not entitled to the balance on the death of the depositor. See Franklin v. Anna National Bank, 488 N.E.2d 1117 (Ill. App. 1986). The obvious difficulty is in proving that the depositor did not intend a joint and survivor account if the depositor signed a joint and survivor form. Many courts, as in *Varela*, apply a presumption that a present gift is intended when a joint account is established and require clear and convincing evidence to rebut

the presumption. In some states, the presumption of a gift is conclusive, and evidence to the contrary is not admissible. See Robinson v. Delfino, 710 A.2d 154 (R.I. 1998). Substantial authority holds that the law of the account's situs, not the law of the deceased depositor's domicile, controls. See Barboza v. McLeod, 853 N.E.2d 192 (Mass. 2006).

2. The UPC provisions for multiple-party bank accounts are found in §§6-201 through 6-227. The UPC authorizes a joint tenancy account with the right of survivorship, an agency account, and a POD account. Short forms for banks to use in establishing each type of account are provided.

Under the UPC, joint accounts belong to the parties during their joint lifetimes "in proportion to the net contribution of each to the sums on deposit, unless there is clear and convincing evidence of a different intent." UPC §6-211(b). Extrinsic evidence is admissible to show that a joint account was opened solely for the convenience of the depositor. UPC §§6-203, 6-204, 6-212, cmt.

3. Suppose *W* opens an account with *H* as joint tenants with right of survivorship. Can a general creditor of *H* recover against assets deposited in the joint account by *W*? See Enright v. Lehmann, 735 N.W.2d 326 (Minn. 2007).

Suppose that *W* opens the account intending to create a convenience account and not a gift. If *H* withdraws money from this account and deposits it in a POD account for the benefit of his children from a prior marriage, does *W* have recourse *H*'s estate or *H*'s children? See Estate of Cowling v. Estate of Cowling, 847 N.E.2d 405 (Ohio 2006).

4. Under the common law of wills, a devisee is required to survive the testator in order to take; if the devisee predeceases, the gift is said to lapse unless an antilapse statute applies. Should the common law lapse rules and the antilapse statutes be applied to POD bank accounts and contracts?

The UPC imposes a requirement of survivorship on beneficiaries of POD bank accounts (§6-212), as well as on beneficiaries of securities in TOD registration (§6-307), but not on beneficiaries of POD contracts generally (§6-101). However, the UPC includes an antilapse provision for POD designations, which substitutes the descendants of the named beneficiary who does not survive the benefactor. See UPC §2-706 (1990, rev. 2008), which parallels the UPC antilapse provision for wills in §2-603, discussed at pages 366-374.

5. *The savings account (or Totten) trust.* In the landmark case of In re Totten, 71 N.E. 748 (N.Y. 1904), *O* made deposits in a savings account in the name of "*O*, as trustee for *A*." *O* retained the right to revoke the trust by withdrawing the funds at any time during his life. Since *A* is entitled only to the amount on deposit at *O*'s death, in practical effect *A* is merely a POD beneficiary of a "trust" of a savings account. The court upheld this arrangement as not testamentary, declaring that a "tentative" revocable trust had been created at the time of the deposit. At *O*'s death, any funds in the account belong to *A*. Savings account trusts, often known as *Totten trusts*, have been accepted in almost all states. See Restatement (Third) of Trusts §26 (2003) (calling them "tentative trusts"). Under the UPC, the Totten trust is abolished as a formal category and is instead treated as a POD account.

SECTION D.   POUR-OVER WILLS AND REVOCABLE TRUSTS IN MODERN ESTATE PLANNING

1. Introduction

The will has yielded to the revocable trust as the central instrument governing property transfer at death in contemporary practice. The revocable trust has eclipsed the will not only because it avoids probate, but also because it allows the settlor to consolidate under one instrument the dispositive plan for all her property, probate and nonprobate. To do so, the settlor designates the trustee of her revocable trust as the beneficiary of all her will substitutes and names the trustee as the beneficiary under her will (called a *pour-over will*). To change her estate plan later, the settlor need only amend her revocable trust. In this way, the revocable trust has come to function as the will did in the days before the proliferation of will substitutes. See also Kent D. Schenkel, Testamentary Fragmentation and the Diminishing Role of the Will: An Argument for Revival, 41 Creighton L. Rev. 155 (2008) (proposing reform to reunify transfer on death).

In this section we consider the rise of the revocable trust and pour-over will, and we take a closer look at the advantages and disadvantages of revocable trusts (often called *living trusts*). While the revocable trust may have advantages for many clients, for some it will be unsuitable.

2. Norman Dacey and Avoiding Probate

Perhaps no single person has done more to advance the rise of the revocable trust than Norman F. Dacey, author of a runaway bestseller, How to Avoid Probate! The first edition, published in 1965, opened with a slashing attack on lawyers who benefit from the probate system:

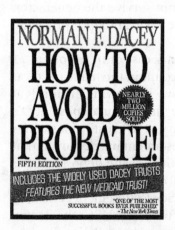

> The probate system, conceived generations ago as a device for protecting heirs, has now become their greatest enemy. Almost universally corrupt, it is essentially a form of private taxation levied by the legal profession upon the rest of the population. All across the land, both large and small estates are being plundered by lawyers specializing in "probate practice." [1st ed. at 15.]

After denouncing the "extortionate" legal fees and other disadvantages of probate, Dacey offered a way to avoid the problem completely: Declare yourself trustee of all your property, with the trust property to pass to named beneficiaries upon your death. In other words, do what Albert Farkas did in

Farkas v. Williams, page 398. Dacey's book contains do-it-yourself trust and will forms designed for various kinds of assets and different family situations.

The legal profession was not amused by Dacey's book. The New York County Lawyers' Association sought an injunction to ban the sale of the book in New York on the grounds that Dacey, a nonlawyer, was giving legal advice. The New York Court of Appeals held that Dacey's readers were not his clients because the book was sold to the public at large and no relationship of personal trust and confidence arose. New York County Lawyers' Assn. v. Dacey, 234 N.E.2d 459 (N.Y. 1967). Dacey then sued the New York County Lawyers' Association for $5 million in damages for interfering with his right to free speech. He lost. Dacey v. New York County Lawyers' Assn., 423 F.2d 188 (2d Cir. 1969). Dacey also sued the Florida Bar Association for publishing a book review that Dacey thought was libelous. Dacey v. Florida Bar, Inc., 427 F.2d 1292 (5th Cir. 1970). He lost again. This litigation, of course, helped to promote the book. Eventually, Dacey sold two and a half million copies before the book finally went out of print after the fifth edition in 1993.

Subsequently, to avoid income tax on the royalties, Dacey moved to Ireland, but lawyers had their revenge when the Commissioner of Internal Revenue (a lawyer!) pursued Dacey and forced him to pay back taxes and penalties. Dacey v. Commissioner, T.C. Memo 1992-187. In 1988, Dacey renounced his U.S. citizenship and became a citizen of Ireland. He died in London in 1994. Now dead for more than 15 years, Dacey remains a polarizing figure and a common target for defenders of the probate system. In William P. DeFeo, Avoiding Probate Court: A Judge's Perspective, 19 Quinnipiac Prob. L.J. 53 (2005), the author, a probate court judge in Connecticut, calls Dacey's book "little more than a clever exploitation of the shapeless fears and suspicions people have for the law and for the people who administer it."

Since Dacey first published his book, there has been a groundswell of public demand for a simpler and less costly probate system. Reform has occurred in many states, often in the form of adoption of the Uniform Probate Code, particularly its informal probate and small estate procedures (see pages 43-44 and 46-47). It is fair to suggest that How to Avoid Probate!, and its astonishing reception by the public, served as a catalyst for probate reform. The reforms to date, however, have not deprived the revocable trust of all of its advantages in bypassing probate. In some states, probate remains relatively costly, time-consuming, and public. See Paula A. Monopoli, American Probate: Protecting the Public, Improving the Process (2003).

NOTE: THE MARKETING OF LIVING TRUSTS AND UNAUTHORIZED PRACTICE OF LAW

The public demand for revocable trusts has sparked an industry of sorts that markets living trusts directly to the public. Lawyers have fought these purveyors of living trusts, alleging unauthorized practice of law, with notable success. See

Angela M. Vallario, Living Trusts in the Unauthorized Practice of Law: A Good Thing Gone Bad, 59 Md. L. Rev. 595 (2000).

In Cleveland Bar Association v. Sharp Estate Services, Inc., 837 N.E.2d 1183 (Ohio 2005), the Ohio Supreme Court issued a permanent injunction against a group of nonlawyers who had been marketing revocable trusts and related estate planning documents, including in-home sales presentations to prospective customers. The court ordered the nonlawyers to turn over a list of their customers to the local bar association and to pay a fine of $1,027,260. The court instructed the bar association to contact the customers to advise them of the unauthorized practice of law and to suggest "that the clients may want to consult with a lawyer of their choice, at their expense, to confirm that the respondents' documents are suitable and appropriate for them." The fine was calculated by multiplying the number of plans sold in the state, 468, with their cost, $2,195. In a companion case, the court suspended from practice for six months a lawyer who had been assisting the nonlawyers. Disciplinary Counsel v. Wheatley, 837 N.E.2d 1188 (Ohio 2005).

Lawyers in Illinois have an additional weapon: the criminal law. In 1993, Illinois enacted a statute providing that the "assembly, drafting, execution, and funding of a living trust" by a nonlawyer or by a corporation not authorized to do trust business is an unlawful business practice. The statute makes a first-time violation a misdemeanor and a further violation a felony. 815 Ill. Comp. Stat. Ann. §505/2BB (2008). In Landheer v. Landheer, 891 N.E.2d 975 (Ill. App. 2008), the court read this statute to render void a trust amendment drafted by a nonlawyer, though it said that a settlor could lawfully prepare her own trust documents, even if she is not a lawyer.

What about a will-drafting computer program, such as Quicken WillMaker Plus, or an online Web site such as LegalZoom.com, which generates will and trust forms according to the user's answers to a set of standard questions? The Texas State Bar won an injunction against the sale of Quicken's will drafting program in Texas, but the legislature quickly changed the law to allow computer drafting programs as long as they "clearly and conspicuously state that the products are not a substitute for the advice of an attorney." Unauthorized Practice of Law Comm. v. Parsons Tech., Inc., 179 F.3d 956 (5th Cir. 1999). In Franklin v. Chavis, 640 S.E.2d 873 (S.C. 2007), the court held that filling in the blanks in a will form generated by computer software for someone else constituted unauthorized practice of law. See also Brent L. Barringer, Note, When Cyberlawyering Fails: What Remedies Are or Should be Available to Those Harmed from Relying on "Self-Help" Legal Software?, 2005 U. Ill. J.L. Tech. & Poly. 171; Margaret Hensler Nicholls, Note, A Quagmire of Internet Ethics Law and the ABA Guidelines for Legal Website Providers, 18 Geo. J. Legal Ethics 1021 (2005).

The rise of a lay industry to meet consumer demand for living trusts to avoid probate contains an obvious lesson: Reform probate and the law of wills so that a will can have the attributes of a revocable trust. If this were done, the living trust business would collapse. But until it is done, suppressing nonlawyers who are giving the public what it wants, while some lawyers are not, is unlikely to succeed.

3. *Consequences During Life of Settlor*

(a) *Property management by fiduciary.* A third party trustee may be selected to manage a funded revocable trust, with duties under modern law that run only to the settlor. This may be desirable, for example, if the settlor wants to be relieved of the burdens of financial management. On the other hand, when property is put in trust, some inconveniences may arise. Third parties such as banks and transfer agents may want to see a copy of the trust instrument to verify that the trustee has the power to engage in the transaction.

(b) *Keeping title clear.* A revocable trust is useful in keeping separate property that a husband or wife or both do not want to be commingled with their other assets. For example, a husband and wife may want to establish separate revocable trusts of property that each brings to the marriage or acquires by inheritance. Doing so avoids uncertainties over ownership and consequent problems upon divorce or death.

Spouses who move from a community property state to a separate property state sometimes create a revocable trust for their community property to preserve their ability to qualify for a stepped-up income tax basis on *all* the property when one spouse dies (see pages 514-515).

(c) *Income and gift taxes.* Under the federal income, gift, and estate tax systems, assets in a revocable trust are treated as still owned by the settlor. When the revocable trust is created, it is not treated as a completed gift to the beneficiaries (see Chapter 15). Despite what you may have read in the advertisements by self-proclaimed estate planners, a well-drafted will (with proper titling of the testator's property) can save just as much in estate taxes as can a well-drafted revocable trust.

(d) *Dealing with incompetency.* Increased longevity has brought with it an increased chance that a person's last days (or perhaps months or years) will be spent in a state of mental or physical disability, requiring some form of fiduciary administration of the person's property. Many persons are reluctant to have a spouse or parent formally adjudicated an incompetent. Moreover, guardianship or conservatorship proceedings are cumbersome and expensive, and invite unwanted publicity. Even the modern UPC §5-406 stipulates an elaborate court procedure protecting the alleged incompetent.

A revocable trust can be used in planning for the contingency of incapacity. The settlor may be a co-trustee, with the trust instrument providing that either co-trustee alone may act with respect to the trust property. Or the trust instrument may provide that the other co-trustee shall act as sole trustee if the settlor becomes incompetent. Or the settlor may be the sole trustee, but in the event of incapacity, a named successor trustee automatically takes over. The trust instrument should normally include a mechanism for determining the settlor's competence, for example by requiring a unanimous vote of the settlor's spouse, children, and doctor. Such provisions reduce the risk of litigation and allow the settlor, in advance, to select the successor fiduciary. When Groucho Marx was in his 80s, he was declared incompetent by a court, against his wishes. He had been living with a woman named Erin Fleming, who said he preferred her as his guardian if he had to have one. After a messy court fight, with the newspapers titillating readers with intimate family details, a relative of Marx was appointed guardian.

A custodianship account for securities or other assets is sometimes used to relieve a person of the burdens of property management, but a custodianship is an agency relationship that normally terminates on the disability or death of the principal. By contrast, a revocable trust continues during the settlor's incapacity and can provide for disposition or continued management of the trust property at the settlor's death. The revocable trust holds a similar advantage over the durable power of attorney, a subject we take up at page 448.

4. *Consequences at Death of Settlor: Avoidance of Probate*

(a) *Costs*. Property transferred during life to a revocable trust avoids probate because legal title to the property passes to the trustee. There is no need at the death of the settlor to change the title to the trust property by probate administration. Although trustee's fees may be payable, if, for example, a professional trustee is named, these fees are typically smaller than the total cost of going through probate.

But lawyers may charge more to draft a revocable trust than a will, particularly when there are related pour-over documents. In addition, transferring title of property to the trustee may entail certain costs such as stock transfer or deed recording fees.

(b) *Delays*. In an estate administration, the property may be in the executor's possession and control for a substantial period of time, perhaps even years. Under a revocable trust, income and principal can be disbursed to the beneficiaries more quickly. Further, because the rules governing property management by trustees are often more liberal than those applicable to executors, it is frequently easier for a trustee to deal with an ongoing business in the form of a partnership or sole proprietorship, and for a trustee to exercise options, borrow money, and participate in reorganizations.

(c) *Creditors*. In probate a short-term statute of limitations is applicable to creditors (see page 44). If creditors do not file claims within a short period after the testator's death, the creditors are forever barred. In many states there is no similar short-term limitations period for revocable trusts; the limitations period is the normal one applicable to the particular claim. Where it is important to cut off the rights of creditors — as might be true with professionals such as doctors or lawyers where the statute of limitations on malpractice runs from discovery — probate may hold an advantage over the revocable trust.

(d) *Publicity*. A will is a public record, open to disappointed heirs, newspaper reporters, and the just plain curious. Any inventory of property and the named beneficiaries are generally there for all the world to see. Because an inter vivos trust is not recorded in a public place, the nature of the settlor's property and the names of the beneficiaries need not be disclosed to the public, and perhaps not even to any public officials (except the tax authorities, whose records are subject to strict taxpayer-confidentiality rules). Hence, revocable trusts can be especially attractive to persons desiring privacy. Such persons include personalities trying to keep out of the tabloids and persons of great wealth who fear kidnapping or other victimization of their beneficiaries or theft of their art collections, jewels, or other property. See Frances H. Foster, Trust Privacy, 93 Cornell L. Rev. 555 (2008).

In Estate of Hearst, 136 Cal. Rptr. 821 (App. 1977), William Randolph Hearst had created a testamentary trust to care for his descendants and relatives. After Patty Hearst was kidnapped by the Symbionese Liberation Army, the trustees asked the court to cut off public access to the probate files in Hearst's estate, fearing that radicals would find hitherto unnoticed members of the family and the location of their homes and properties. The court agreed to restrict public access while the Hearst family was in danger of attack. If W.R. Hearst had created a revocable inter vivos trust of his property, the family records would have been private without the need for a special ruling.

(e) *Ancillary probate*. If the settlor owns real property located outside the domiciliary state, an ancillary probate in the situs state will be necessary to pass title to the property. To avoid ancillary probate, which may be cumbersome and expensive, the out-of-state real property can be transferred to a revocable inter vivos trust during the settlor's life, eliminating the need for ancillary probate at the owner's death.

(f) *Avoiding restrictions protecting family members*. In many states the surviving spouse's elective share has been extended to revocable trusts created by the decedent spouse. See Sullivan v. Burkin, page 488. Nonetheless, a disgruntled spouse might be able to create a funded revocable trust in some other state that does not recognize the spouse's right to reach the trust, thereby defeating the spouse's elective share. In a similar vein, it may be possible to use a funded revocable trust to put assets beyond the reach of a child born out of wedlock, protected by a pretermission statute, whom the client does not wish to mention in his will. Pretermission statutes typically apply only to probate property. See Kidwell v. Rhew, page 536.

(g) *Avoiding restrictions on testamentary trusts*. A testamentary trust is a trust created by a will. It is sometimes called a *court trust* because it comes into being by an order of the probate court that supervises the administration of the estate. In many states this court continues to supervise the administration of the testamentary trust after the estate is closed. An inter vivos trust, by contrast, is created by the settlor during lifetime and comes into being without any court order. It is not subject to court supervision unless the beneficiary, the trustee, or some other interested party brings suit to settle some trust matter.

In most states a trustee of a testamentary trust has a duty to account to the court. Judicial approval of a trustee's accounts is often a time-consuming and expensive procedure. It may require the appointment of guardians ad litem to represent unborn and unascertained beneficiaries. In some states the cumbersome formal accounting may be avoided by making use of a funded revocable trust.

(h) *Choosing the law of another jurisdiction to govern.* As a general rule, the settlor of an inter vivos trust of personal property may choose the state law that is to govern the trust. (If a trust asset is land, the law of the state where the land is located governs.) The settlor typically can choose the law of the domicile of the settlor or of the beneficiaries, or the law of the state where the trust is administered. A testator may not have this freedom of choice. Many states apply the law of the settlor's domicile to a testamentary trust, because it was created by a will probated in that state, regardless of the testator's intent that the law of another state apply. To avoid undesirable trust law in the state of the settlor's domicile, the settlor may want to create an inter vivos trust in another state. For example, the settlor of an inter vivos trust can create a trust in a state that has abolished the Rule Against Perpetuities, a subject we take up at page 905.

UPC §2-703 (1990) changes the old law and provides that the testator may select the state law to govern the meaning and legal effect of his will, including trusts created by the will, unless that law is contrary to the domiciliary state's law protecting the surviving spouse or any other public policy of the domiciliary state. This provision aligns testamentary choice of law rules with those generally used for inter vivos trusts, and, where adopted, it lessens the need to create an inter vivos trust to achieve some benefit available in some other state. It is not wholly clear, however, when applying foreign law to the will of a domiciliary testator would violate public policy of the domiciliary state.

(i) *Lack of certainty in the law.* Where a revocable trust is used as a substitute for a will, the law may be less certain in solving a problem that arises than it would be in the case of a will. The subsidiary law of wills — dealing with divorce, adoption, lapse, ademption, simultaneous death, apportionment of death taxes, and creditors' rights — may or may not apply to revocable trusts, depending on the rule and the jurisdiction. Most of these issues can be solved by appropriate drafting, but only if the drafter anticipates the problem.

(j) *Avoiding will contests.* A revocable trust, like a will, can be contested for lack of mental capacity and undue influence. In practice, however, it is likely to be considerably more difficult to set aside a funded revocable trust than a will on these grounds. In the first place, the heirs of the decedent may not be entitled even to see the trust instrument unless they file a lawsuit.[7] They are thereby forced to incur significant legal fees just to see the settlor's estate plan. Second, if a trust continues as an ongoing operation for several years, generating monthly or yearly statements and perhaps sales of assets and reinvestments, a jury or a court will be reluctant to set the trust aside. Hence, if a will contest is foreseen, creating a revocable trust of the client's property may be advisable, a strategy discussed in Chapter 3 at page 206.

(k) *Estate taxation.* As mentioned above, there are no significant federal estate tax advantages to a revocable trust. The assets of a revocable trust are included in

---

7. On the rights of trust beneficiaries and the settlor's heirs to examine the trust instrument, see Fletcher v. Fletcher, page 739.

the gross estate of the settlor under §2038 of the Internal Revenue Code of 1986. See Chapter 15.

(l) *Controlling surviving spouse's disposition.* When one spouse wants assurance that the surviving spouse's property will be disposed of in accordance with a mutual estate plan, both spouses can create a revocable trust of their property to become irrevocable upon the death of the first spouse. The trust may provide, for example, that all the income shall be payable to the surviving spouse, with the right of the surviving spouse to dip into principal if necessary to support him, and upon the surviving spouse's death the trust principal shall be divided equally between, say, the husband's son and the wife's daughter by prior marriages. This use of the revocable trust may be especially attractive in second marriages and is much preferable to trying to control the surviving spouse's disposition by contract (see pages 325-334).

(m) *Perceived complexity.* Some clients are never completely comfortable with the thought of someone else (a third-party trustee) holding legal title to "their" property, despite retaining the power to unwind the arrangement. Because the ultimate goal of estate planning is peace of mind for an informed client, the client's discomfort with a revocable trust, whether or not rational, can be a deal breaker.

5. Pour-Over Wills

The concept of a *pour-over will* is simple. *O* sets up a revocable inter vivos trust naming *X* as trustee. *O* then executes a will devising the residue of his estate to *X*, as trustee, to hold under the terms of the trust. The *pour-over* by will of probate assets into an inter vivos trust allows *O* to establish an inter vivos trust that can serve as a single receptacle for all the settlor's probate and nonprobate property. The testators in both *Pilafas* and *Reiser*, for example, executed pour-over wills to transfer their residuary estates to the inter vivos trusts they had created.

When the law in this area was first developing, two theories were useful in validating a pour-over of probate assets into an inter vivos trust. The first was *incorporation by reference.* A will can incorporate by reference a document in existence at the time the will is executed. See page 310. However, a will cannot incorporate amendments to the document made after the will is executed. Hence, if the trust instrument is amended after the will is executed, the probate assets will either be disposed of in accordance with the terms of the trust instrument as it stood at the time of execution of the will and not as subsequently amended, *or*, if this would not be in accordance with testator's intent, will pass by intestacy. A further difficulty is that a trust instrument incorporated by reference into the will gives rise to a testamentary trust at the death of the settlor (the trust instrument itself is incorporated into and made part of the will), which undermines the point of pouring over into a nonprobate vessel.

The second theory was the doctrine of *independent significance* (see page 323). Under this doctrine a will may dispose of property by referring to some act that has significance apart from disposing of probate assets — in this context, by reference to an inter vivos trust that disposes of assets transferred to the trust during life. Under this doctrine the trust instrument does not have to be in existence when the will is executed, but the trust must have some assets in it before the time of the testator's death. Under the doctrine of independent significance, the assets poured over into the inter vivos trust, like the assets transferred to the trust during life, are subject to the terms of (and are treated as an addition to) the inter vivos trust. The will can pour over assets to the trust as amended after execution of the will.

Note the difference between independent significance and incorporation by reference: Independent significance requires that the inter vivos trust have some *property transferred to it during life*, which the trust disposes of; incorporation by reference requires that the *trust instrument be in existence at the time the will is executed*. Neither permit a pour-over into an unfunded inter vivos trust, whether drafted before or after the execution of the will.

Because of the limitations and uncertainties of these doctrines and frequent embarrassing errors by lawyers, estate planners sought the enactment of legislation permitting a will to pour over probate assets into an unfunded inter vivos trust.

Uniform Probate Code (1990)

§2-511.   TESTAMENTARY ADDITIONS TO TRUSTS

(a) A will may validly devise property to the trustee of a trust established or to be established (i) during the testator's lifetime by the testator, by the testator and some other person, or by some other person, including a funded or unfunded life insurance trust, although the settlor has reserved any or all rights of ownership of the insurance contracts, or (ii) at the testator's death by the testator's devise to the trustee, if the trust is identified in the testator's will and its terms are set forth in a written instrument, other than a will, executed before, concurrently with, or after the execution of the testator's will or in another individual's will if that other individual has predeceased the testator, regardless of the existence, size, or character of the corpus of the trust. The devise is not invalid because the trust is amendable or revocable, or because the trust was amended after the execution of the will or the testator's death.

(b) Unless the testator's will provides otherwise, property devised to a trust described in subsection (a) is not held under a testamentary trust of the testator, but it becomes a part of the trust to which it is devised, and must be administered and disposed of in accordance with the provisions of the governing instrument setting forth the terms of the trust, including any amendments thereto made before or after the testator's death. . . .

The Uniform Testamentary Additions to Trusts Act (UTATA), in its original 1960 form, validated a pour-over of probate assets into an inter vivos trust only if the trust instrument was executed (signed) before or concurrently with the will. The original Uniform Act did not require that some property be transferred to the inter vivos trust during life. If the trust instrument was executed before or concurrently with the will, the probate assets could be poured over into the inter vivos trust as subsequently amended. The trust funded at death by the pour-over was treated as an inter vivos trust — that is, as having come into existence before the testator's death. This gave pour-over trusts the advantages of inter vivos trusts.

The 1990 UPC deleted the original act's requirement that the trust instrument be executed before or concurrently with the will. UPC §2-511(b), and the conforming 1991 revision to UTATA, permits the trust instrument to be executed or amended after the will. Thus, a testator's will can pour over the testator's probate assets to "a trust with the First National Bank as trustee, which I will execute," if the testator thereafter executes the trust instrument.

QUESTIONS

Given that UTATA now permits a pour-over to a trust that is created *after* the will is executed, why does UPC §2-510, codifying the doctrine of incorporation by reference (page 310), continue to require a writing to be in existence when it is incorporated into a will? Is there any reason why a signed letter or other document should be treated differently from a signed trust instrument?

CLYMER v. MAYO, 473 N.E.2d 1084 (Mass. 1985): Clara Mayo, a professor of psychology at Boston University, executed a will in 1963 designating her husband, James, as the primary beneficiary. In 1964 she named James as the beneficiary of her B.U. group life insurance policy. In 1965 she made him the beneficiary of her B.U. retirement plans, which were administered by TIAA-CREF, the leading company administering university pensions in the United States. On February 2, 1973, Clara executed a new will and a new revocable trust. Under the new will, the bulk of her estate was to pour over into the new revocable trust. James was the life beneficiary under the trust, with remainder interests in Clara's nieces and nephews until the last of them turned 30, and then the trust assets were to be distributed to Boston University and Clark University to support graduate education of women.

On the same day that she executed her new will and trust, Clara named the trustees of her revocable trust as the beneficiary of her B.U. life insurance policy. Later, she designated the trustees as the beneficiary of her TIAA-CREF retirement plans. In so doing, Clara unified the disposition of all of her property through her new revocable trust.

In 1978, Clara and James divorced. Clara thereupon changed the beneficiary designation of her life insurance to Marianne LaFrance, but left the trust as the beneficiary of her pension plans, and left James as the principal beneficiary under the trust. In 1981 Clara died, leaving her parents as her only heirs.

The first issue was the validity of the trust. If the trust was invalid, then the devise in Clara's will to the trust would fail, and Clara's parents would take as her intestate heirs. Under traditional law, a trust must contain property, known as the *res*, to be valid. However, UTATA validates unfunded trusts that are intended to be funded by a pour-over will if the trust agreement is executed before the testator's death. Applying the Massachusetts version of UTATA, the court held that the bequest to the inter vivos trust was valid even though the trust was unfunded. As an alternative holding, the court concluded that the trust did have a res, namely, the right to receive the insurance and pension plan proceeds.

The next issue was whether James's interest in the trust was revoked as a result of the divorce. By statute Massachusetts revokes an ex-spouse's interests under the testator's will. The question here was whether this statute, which by its terms spoke only of wills, should be applied to Clara's inter vivos revocable trust since Clara employed the trust as a will substitute.

> [T]he trust had no practical significance until her death in 1981. The decedent executed both her will and indenture of trust on February 2, 1973. She transferred no property or funds to the trust at that time. The trust was to receive its funding at the decedent's death, in part through her life insurance policy and retirement benefits, and in part through a pour-over from the will's residuary clause. [James], the proposed executor and sole legatee under the will, was also made the primary beneficiary of the trust. . . .
>
> During her lifetime, the decedent retained power to amend or revoke the trust. Since the trust was unfunded, her cotrustee was subject to no duties or obligations until her death. Similarly, it was only as a result of the decedent's death that [James] could claim any right to the trust assets. It is evident from the time and manner in which the trust was created and funded, that the decedent's will and trust were integrally related components of a single testamentary scheme. For all practical purposes the trust, like the will, "spoke" only at the decedent's death. For this reason Mayo's interest in the trust was revoked by operation of G.L. c. 191, §9 [providing that divorce revokes an ex-spouse's interests under a will], at the same time his interest under the decedent's will was revoked.
>
> "Divorce usually represents a stormy parting, where the last thing one of the parties wishes is to have an earlier will carried out giving everything to the former spouse." Raymond Young, Probate Reform, 18 B.B.J. 7, 11 (1974). To carry out the testator's implied intent, the law revokes "any disposition or appointment of property made by the will to the former spouse." It is indisputable that if the decedent's trust was either testamentary or incorporated by reference into her will, Mayo's beneficial interest in the trust would be revoked by operation of the statute. . . .
>
> [We conclude] that the legislative intent under G.L. c. 191, §9, is that a divorced spouse should not take under a [revocable] trust executed in these circumstances. In the absence of an expressed contrary intent, that statute implies an intent on the part of a testator to revoke will provisions favoring a former spouse. It is incongruous then to ignore that same intent with regard to a trust funded in part through her will's pour-over at the decedent's death. As one law review commentator has noted, "[t]ransferors use will substitutes to avoid probate, not to avoid the subsidiary law of wills. The subsidiary rules are the product of centuries of legal experience in attempting to discern transferors' wishes and suppress litigation. These rules should be treated as presumptively correct for will substitutes as well as for wills." John H. Langbein, The Nonprobate Revolution and the Future of the Law of Succession, 97 Harv. L. Rev. 1108, 1136-1137 (1984).

Restricting our holding to the particular facts of this case — specifically the existence of a revocable pour-over trust funded entirely at the time of the decedent's death — we conclude that G.L. c. 191, §9, revokes Mayo's interest under [the trust].[8]

Accordingly, James took nothing and the nieces' and nephews' interests became possessory, with the remainder to be divided between Clark University and Boston University upon the youngest of the nieces and nephews reaching the age of 30.

NOTE

Where a settlor names the trustee of her inter vivos trust as the beneficiary of her life insurance policy but does not add any other funds or assets to the trust, the inter vivos trust is called an *unfunded life insurance trust*. If the settlor adds other assets to the inter vivos trust, it is called a *funded inter vivos trust*. An unfunded life insurance trust as well as a funded trust are valid inter vivos trusts. In the former case, the trust *res* (property) is the trustee's contingent right to receive the proceeds of the policy. This interest is potentially valuable, for if the insured dies without changing the policy beneficiary, the trustee will be entitled to the policy proceeds. This is true even though the right is fragile in the sense that the insured, while still alive, might change the beneficiary designation.

SECTION E.   JOINT TENANCIES IN REALTY

Joint tenancy and *tenancy by the entirety* are common and popular methods of avoiding the cost and delay of probate. Perhaps most family homes in this country are owned by husband and wife either in joint tenancy or tenancy by the entirety. Upon the death of one joint tenant or tenant by the entirety, the survivor owns the property absolutely, freed of the decedent's interest in the property. The common law theory is that the decedent's interest vanishes at death, and therefore no probate is necessary because no interest passes to the survivor at death. Joint tenancies and tenancies by the entireties are ordinarily covered in first-year courses in property. Only three features of joint tenancies need be mentioned here.

---

8. As an alternative ground the appellants argue that the terms of the Mayos' divorce settlement, in which Mayo waived "any right, title or interest" in the assets that later funded the decedent's trust, amount to a disclaimer of his trust interest. We decline to base our holding on such reasoning because a disclaimer of rights "must be clear and unequivocal." Second Bank-State St. Trust Co. v. Yale Univ. Alumni Fund, 156 N.E.2d 57 (Mass. 1959), and we find no such disclaimer in the Mayos' divorce agreement.

First, the creation of a joint tenancy in land gives the joint tenants equal interests upon creation. Unlike joint tenancies in personalty (for example, bank and brokerage accounts), joint tenancies in land require the agreement of all tenants to take most important actions. A person who transfers land into a joint tenancy cannot, during life, revoke the transfer and cancel the interest given the other joint tenant. In that sense, a joint tenancy in land is an imperfect will substitute because it is not revocable. But this may be changing. In Brousseau v. Brousseau, 927 A.2d 773 (Vt. 2007), the court entertained a suit to undo a transfer of land in joint tenancy.

Second, a joint tenant cannot devise her share by will. If a joint tenant wants someone other than the other joint tenant to take her share at death, she must sever the joint tenancy during life, converting it into a tenancy in common. Under the common law vanishing theory of joint tenancy, there is no interest for the decedent's will to operate upon.

Third, a creditor of a joint tenant generally must seize the joint tenant's interest, if at all, during the joint tenant's life. In almost all states, the joint tenant's interest vanishes at death, leaving nothing for the creditor to reach. See Jeffrey A. Schoenblum, 2008 Multistate Guide to Estate Planning at Table 9.04.

SECTION F. PLANNING FOR INCAPACITY

In this section we return to the problem of planning for incapacity. As we have seen, the revocable trust is among the more flexible tools for the orderly management of an incapacitated client's property (see pages 439-440). In the material that follows, we consider the durable power of attorney, another tool for surrogate property management for an incapacitated person, and then we turn to the problem of heath care decisions and the disposition of the body.

1. *The Durable Power of Attorney*

An ordinary power of attorney creates an agency relationship whereby the agent, called an *attorney-in-fact* (though the agent need not be, and often is not, a lawyer), is given a written authorization to act on behalf of the principal. The power of attorney instrument potentially solves one of the common problems encountered by agents conducting business for their principals, namely, supplying sufficient evidence of the agent's authority to induce third parties to transact with the agent. However, a simple power of attorney is limited by the traditional rule of agency law that the agent's authority terminates on the principal's incapacity. For this reason an ordinary power of attorney is of little use in planning for incapacity. Enter the *durable power of attorney*.

Unlike an ordinary power of attorney, a *durable* power continues throughout the incapacity of the principal until the principal dies. A durable power is authorized by UPC §§5-501 to 5-505 (1990) and by statutes in all states. Durable powers are controlled by the common law of agency as modified by the power-of-attorney statutes. The principal, if competent, can terminate the durable power at any time, and the attorney-in-fact owes the principal the *fiduciary duties* of *loyalty*, *care*, and *obedience*. Durable powers must be created by a written instrument, and in some states witnessed or notarized.

The holder of a durable power is somewhat like a trustee, but there are important differences. First, a durable power ceases when the principal dies. Hence the holder of the power can make no transfers after the principal's death. A durable power is not a means of avoiding probate. In contrast, a trust can continue after the settlor's death, transferring property without probate. The trustee can be given authority to take action after the settlor's death to cure defects in the estate plan that surface for the first time when all the relevant facts are known.

Second, if an agent dies, the power terminates unless a successor agent is named by the principal. If a trustee dies, a successor trustee is appointed by a court.

Third, a trustee has title to the trust assets and generally has all the powers of an outright owner. The trustee can sell and reinvest the trust property. The law of trustees' powers and duties is well developed and well known. In contrast, an attorney-in-fact does not own the property, and traditional agency law strictly construes express powers and sparingly implies other powers. See Jones v. Brandt, 645 S.E.2d 312 (Va. 2007).

Fourth, third parties more readily deal with trustees than with agents, including an attorney-in-fact. Banks and other financial institutions, uncertain of an agent's authority and unfamiliar with a durable power, sometimes refuse to deal with an agent holding a durable power of attorney, though they can be compelled by law to do so.

The upshot is that durable powers are useful for persons seeking a way of dealing with incompetency without creating a trust, but trusts are more flexible and satisfactory for most clients. Durable powers of attorney have, nonetheless, become an extremely popular device for dealing with incapacity among persons of modest means. Unfortunately, there is potential for significant abuse of durable powers of attorney. This has led to increased litigation and proposals for reform.

In re Estate of Kurrelmeyer
Supreme Court of Vermont, 2006
895 A.2d 207

BURGESS, J. . . . In 1996, Louis Kurrelmeyer executed two durable general powers of attorney to appoint his wife, Martina Kurrelmeyer, and his daughter, Nancy Kurrelmeyer, as attorneys-in-fact. Louis Kurrelmeyer was competent at the time he executed the powers of attorney. In December of 2000, Martina, pursuant to her powers under the durable power of attorney, executed a document establishing the "Louis H. Kurrelmeyer Living Trust," with herself and Nancy as co-trustees. Days after she created the trust, Martina transferred certain real estate owned by her husband, the "Clearwater" property, to herself and Nancy as co-trustees of the trust. At the time of the creation of the living trust and the transfer of the Clearwater property, Louis Kurrelmeyer was no longer competent. Mr. Kurrelmeyer died testate a year later, and Martina was appointed executrix of his estate.

Louis Kurrelmeyer's last will and testament, executed in 1980, contained a specific provision for the Clearwater property. Under the will, Martina would take a life estate in the property, with responsibility for taxes and upkeep, and upon her death the property would pass to Mr. Kurrelmeyer's surviving children as joint tenants with rights of survivorship. In contrast, the terms of the trust provide Martina additional rights with regard to the property. Under the terms of the trust, Martina may occupy the home as long as she wishes and the trust is permitted to pay the expenses on the property should she fail to do so. The trustees would be required, however, on Martina's unilateral request, to sell the home, with the sale proceeds to be used either to purchase another home for Martina or, alternatively, to be added to the trust principal. Additionally, the trust provides that all income from the trust property would be paid to Martina, as well as so much of the principal as the trustees deem necessary and proper for her support. Upon Martina's death, the trust principal would be distributed to Louis's children, if they survived him, with any deceased child's share to be distributed to that child's descendants or held in trust until such descendants reached the age of twenty-five. The trust requires that there be at least one other trustee serving so long as Martina is serving as a co-trustee, and the co-trustees must act by mutual agreement.

During the probate administration of Louis Kurrelmeyer's estate, his son, Louis Kurrelmeyer Jr., objected to the exclusion of the Clearwater property from the inventory completed by Martina Kurrelmeyer. Claiming that Martina exceeded her authority in creating the trust, Louis Jr. asked the probate court to set aside the trust and include the Clearwater property in the probate estate to be distributed in accordance with Mr. Kurrelmeyer's will.[9] The probate court upheld the trust, and the children appealed to the superior court.

Martina Kurrelmeyer moved for summary judgment, arguing the creation of the trust and transfer of the Clearwater property to the trust were authorized under the broad authority granted to her by the durable power of attorney. The children moved for a judgment in their favor, arguing that the power of attorney did not authorize creation of a revocable trust, that the transfer of the Clearwater

---

9. At the time of his death, Louis Kurrelmeyer had three surviving children — Louis Jr., Nancy, and Ellen. Nancy subsequently passed away, and Ellen became executrix of Nancy's estate. Additionally, the trust designates Ellen as Nancy's successor co-trustee. . . . For the sake of simplicity, and because counsel for Louis Jr., Ellen, and Nancy's Estate have represented the children's interests as aligned in this appeal, as well as in the appeal to the superior court, we refer to appellees collectively as "the children."

property to the trust was a breach of Martina's fiduciary duty because it constituted self-dealing, and that the transfer violated the gift-giving proscription of the power of attorney. . . .

Granting summary judgment for the children, the superior court concluded that the power of attorney did not authorize Martina to create a trust. . . . Martina appealed. . . .

I.

We first address Martina's claim that the trial court erred in concluding as a matter of law that the power of attorney did not authorize her to create a trust on Louis Kurrelmeyer's behalf. We disagree with the superior court's characterization of the power of attorney as ambiguous, and find that the express language of the power of attorney authorized the attorney-in-fact to create a trust. . . .

The trial court invoked a doctrine of strict construction, relied upon in some jurisdictions, to seemingly resolve any arguable ambiguity against the attorney-in-fact claiming delegation. We are not persuaded that strict construction, rather than a construction to effect the principal's intent, is a preferred method of determining the scope of a power of attorney. See Restatement (Second) of Agency §34, cmt. h (1958) (noting that while it is often stated that formal instruments denoting an agent's authority should be strictly construed, "[t]here should be neither a 'strict' nor a 'liberal' interpretation, but a fair construction which carries out the intent as expressed"). . . . Accordingly, we will not apply a rule of narrow construction to particular words and phrases used in the power of attorney, but will examine the express terms and the context of the instrument as a whole to give effect to the principal's intent. . . .

To determine whether the power of attorney authorized Martina to create a trust, we look to Mr. Kurrelmeyer's "written authorization," entitled "Durable General Power of Attorney." As its title suggests, this power of attorney is indeed "general" and quite broad. The power of attorney was to survive, and be unaffected by, the principal's subsequent disability or incompetence. It authorizes Martina, as attorney-in-fact, to act in the principal's name "in any way which I myself could do, if I were personally present, with respect to the following matters to the extent that I am permitted by law to act through an agent." Among the delineated powers, the first subsection authorizes the agent "to add all of my assets deemed appropriate by my said attorney to any trust of which I am the Donor" by transferring in trust a variety of types of property, including stocks, bonds, bank accounts, real estate, and "other assets or property of any kind" owned by the principal. The subsection immediately following provides:

In *addition*, I authorize my said attorney to: (i) execute *and deliver any assignments, stock powers, deeds or trust instruments*; (ii) sign my name to any instrument pertaining to or required in connection with the transfer of my property; (iii) give full receipts and discharges; (iv) re-register the title to stock certificates, bonds, notes, bills and other securities; (v) change the name on bank, brokerage and commodity accounts; (vi) withdraw any or all funds standing in my name in any bank; (vii) endorse and deliver any checks, drafts, certificates of deposit, notes or other instruments . . . ; (viii) change life insurance beneficiaries . . . (ix) elect lump sum or optional settlements of life insurance . . . ; (x) convey any real estate, interest in real estate, any mortgages and notes or any beneficial interest in real estate which I may own or have any interest in; and (xi) record deeds of conveyance in the appropriate land records. (emphasis supplied).

The text continues, authorizing the attorney-in-fact to examine and obtain copies of the principal's will. The attorney is authorized to "make gifts to members of my family (other than himself or herself) whom my said attorney has reason to believe I would have wished to benefit, but my said attorney shall not give any more than $10,000.00 per year to any one donee." Among other powers, the attorney-in-fact is also granted unrestricted access to, and an unrestricted right to remove, the contents from "any and all warehouses, safe deposit boxes, drawers, and vaults" owned in the principal's name alone and in common with others. The attorney-in-fact is authorized to disclaim interests in property on behalf of the principal, to convey title to his motor vehicles, to "convey any and all real estate owned by [the principal] to any person or entity," and, finally, the attorney-in-fact is authorized

[t]o do and perform all and every act and thing whatsoever necessary to be done in the premises, as fully to all intents and purposes as I might or could do if personally present, with full power of substitution and revocation, hereby ratifying and confirming all that my said attorney may do pursuant to this power.

We conclude that the express terms of the power of attorney unambiguously grant the attorney-in-fact the authority to create a trust and to add assets to a trust to accomplish estate planning objectives. The first subsection, empowering the attorney to add any and all assets to a trust of which he is the donor, does refer to a trust already in existence, but does not suggest lack of authority to create a new trust when considered together with the second subsection—granting the power "to execute and deliver . . . trust instruments" expressly in addition to adding assets to existing trusts. The phrase "trust instrument" is commonly understood to refer to the document that brings the trust into existence. Just as a subsequent provision authorizes the attorney-in-fact to "execute . . . deeds" and "easements," which we commonly read to include granting and conveying lands and creating rights of way, so too may the attorney-in-fact create a trust under the provision authorizing the attorney to "execute . . . trust instruments." Where a power is broadly drawn to include the authority to transact all business on behalf of the principal and delineates a variety of general acts, each particular task within the grant of authority need not be spelled out in exacting detail. Given the express language granting the authority to execute trust instruments, particularly in the context of the breadth of the attorney's other express powers, including, ultimately, her authority to fully substitute herself for the principal to do all things "whatsoever necessary . . . to all intents and purposes" as the principal "might or could do if personally present," we find that the agent's authority under this power of attorney includes the authority to create a trust on the principal's behalf.

II.

Alternatively, the children argue that, even if the principal intended to authorize the attorney-in-fact to create a trust, the power to create a trust is personal to the settlor and non-delegable as a matter of law. We agree that certain acts may require personal performance as a matter of public policy, statutory law, or under the terms of an agreement. See Restatement (Second) of Agency §17, cmt. b ("The making of affidavits as to knowledge and the execution of wills are illustrations of acts commonly required by statute to be done personally."). We do not agree, however, that delegation of authority to create a trust through a durable general power of attorney to serve the interests of the principal violates public policy as a matter of law, even when a trust's dispositive terms may serve a function similar to that of a will.

The use of a revocable living trust serves a number of legitimate purposes. Restatement (Third) of Trusts §25, cmt. a (2003). For example, revocable trusts are widely used in estate planning and asset management as a means to avoid the costs and delays associated with probate administration, as a means to provide property management for settlors late in life by establishing trustees and successor trustees to assume continuing responsibility, and as a means to maintain privacy and flexibility in the management of assets beyond the life of the settlor. Revocable trusts allow the settlor to retain the ability to use the assets for support during lifetime, provide for ongoing asset management, and preserve the estate for the settlor's intended beneficiaries.

The fact that the trust here was created by an agent does not affect its legitimacy. See *id.* §11(5) ("Under some circumstances, an agent under a durable power of attorney or the legal representative of a property owner who is under disability may create a trust on behalf of the property owner."); see also *id.*, cmt. f (noting that despite restrictions against making a will for an incompetent person, it is proper for a principal to authorize an agent to create or modify a revocable inter vivos trust "to serve purposes that are financially advantageous to the estate, such as probate avoidance and managerial efficiency"). The children fail to demonstrate any sufficiently countervailing evil to compel this Court to declare such powers of attorney contrary to public policy and void as a matter of law. . . .

For the same reason that trusts can be beneficial to an estate, we are not persuaded on the current record that this trust is necessarily an invalid usurpation of the principal's last will and testament. The trial court was concerned that, by conveying Clearwater to the trust, Martina did "indirectly what she [could] not do directly," that is, alter the will by depriving the children of their expected inheritance of Clearwater's appreciation. When the principal expressly granted his attorney-in-fact the power to convey realty from his estate, he must have anticipated that the terms of his will might be so altered. It is not clear, then, why conveyance of Clearwater to a trust would be a per se impermissible alteration of the will, when the power of attorney expressly authorized Martina to convey any real estate outright to others. Therefore, these additional arguments do not persuade us that the trust must be rendered void as a matter of public policy.

III.

The question of whether Martina's actions breached her fiduciary duties remains. Even though we conclude that Martina had authority from her principal to create a trust on his behalf, her authority to act under that power was not limitless. A fiduciary duty of loyalty is implied in every agency as a matter of law. The attorney-in-fact was prohibited from making gifts to herself by the express language of the power of attorney and was also prohibited from using the agency for her own benefit or the benefit of others except as authorized.

The children complained below that Martina's conveyance of the Clearwater property to the trust provided no benefit to Louis Kurrelmeyer, served no apparent tax or estate planning purpose, and was prohibited by the gifting provision of the power of attorney as well as by Martina's fiduciary duty of loyalty to her principal. Martina argued, in response, that the trust and conveyance were justified by generally recognized and prudent tax and estate planning objectives, that the conveyance of Clearwater to the trust could not, as a matter of law, constitute a gift prohibited by the power of attorney, and that the co-trustee approval requirement was a safeguard against any self-dealing.

Concluding, erroneously, that creating any new trust was void as beyond the authority of the attorney-in-fact, the superior court did not reach the additional question of whether the trust and conveyance were valid, as claimed by Martina, or a breach of fiduciary duty as claimed by the children. The court recognized general proscriptions against self-dealing by attorneys-in-fact and trustees, but did not address the parties' particular factual or legal claims on this topic. . . . [T]he parties do not appear to agree upon facts material either to Martina's contention that the dispositive terms of the trust and the conveyance of the Clearwater property were justified as prudent estate planning or to the children's contentions that the terms of the trust and the transfer of property were unauthorized self-dealing.

Therefore, we remand the case to the superior court for further proceedings to consider whether there was a breach of a fiduciary duty on the part of Martina Kurrelmeyer, as agent, in light of all the relevant circumstances at the time the trust was executed.

Reversed and remanded for further proceedings not inconsistent with this decision.

NOTES, QUESTIONS, AND PROBLEM

1. *Epilogue.* On remand, the trial court upheld the validity of the trust:

> We find that the wife's acts in creating the trusts and conveying the primary residence to them were fully in keeping with the principal's (decedent's) intent to give her full beneficial ownership of the house, including the right to sell it so as to purchase another house and live somewhere else. The wife's conveyance into the trusts carried out her husband's wishes and intentions, which had been discussed and formulated with [an] estate plan[ning] attorney, who credibly testified here. . . . Decedent's overarching goal was to provide for his surviving

wife. Her acts as his attorney-in-fact were in full accord therewith. . . . [Because] she did carry out the intention of her now deceased husband, . . . there was no breach of fiduciary duty — she remained loyal to her principal's intentions. [Estate of Kurrelmeyer, Vermont Superior Court, Chittenden County, No. 1079-03 CnCiv (Dec. 30, 2008).]

The trial court's decision was on appeal to the state supreme court as this book went to press.

2. Is the distinction drawn in *Kurrelmeyer* — between an agent's making a will versus making a revocable trust and transferring property to it — meaningful? Do not both have the effect of modifying the principal's estate plan? Why allow the principal to delegate to an agent the power to do one but not the other? The majority view is that an agent acting under a power of attorney cannot make, amend, or revoke the principal's will, but the agent may create, modify, or revoke a trust if the power to do so is expressly granted in the power of attorney instrument. See Alan Newman, Revocable Trusts and the Law of Wills: An Imperfect Fit, 43 Real Prop., Tr. & Est. L.J. 523, 527-531 (2008). See also UTC §602(e) (2000, rev. 2001).

In some states a guardian or conservator appointed by the court has the power not only to make, amend, or revoke a trust for the ward, but also to make, amend, or revoke the ward's will. If challenged, under the *substituted judgment* standard the guardian or conservator must show that the ward probably would have undertaken the same action. See UPC §5-411 (1990). In Murphy v. Murphy, 78 Cal. Rptr. 3d 784 (App. 2008), the court held that a judicial substituted judgment order during the ward's life precluded a post-death challenge to the estate plan as modified by a conservator if the contestant had notice of the lifetime proceeding. See also Americans for the Arts v. Ruth Lilly Charitable Remainder Annuity Trust #1, discussed at page 718.

3. For comprehensive treatments of the durable power of attorney, see Karen E. Boxx, The Durable Power of Attorney's Place in the Family of Fiduciary Relationships, 36 Ga. L. Rev. 1 (2001); Carolyn L. Dessin, Acting as Agent under a Financial Durable Power of Attorney, 75 Neb. L. Rev. 574 (1996). See also Nina A. Kohn, Elder Empowerment as a Strategy for Curbing the Hidden Abuses of Durable Powers of Attorney, 59 Rutgers L. Rev. 1 (2006). Professor Dessin writes:

> Once a financial durable power of attorney is validly executed, it can be an extremely powerful document, authorizing an agent to perform virtually any act with respect to the principal's property that the principal could perform. This breadth of power coupled with few required execution formalities creates a fear of overreaching by unscrupulous agents. [Dessin, supra, 75 Neb. L. Rev., at 582.]

Professor Dessin's fears about the abuse of durable powers can be confirmed by searching under "durable power of attorney" in Lexis or Westlaw, where a disturbing number of cases involve misappropriation by the agent — usually a friend or relative of the principal. The very lack of oversight and ease of use that make powers of attorney so attractive in planning for incapacity make them easy to abuse. For a cautionary tale, see In re Winthrop, 848 N.E.2d 961 (Ill. 2006), in which the court suspended a lawyer from practice for two years for his role in facilitating an agent's misuse of a power drawn by the lawyer.

4. Whether an agent under a power of attorney may make *gifts* raises particular difficulties. Many courts require the power to make gifts to be explicit, and they subject the agent's exercise of such a power in favor of the agent to close fiduciary scrutiny, requiring the gift clearly to be in the principal's best interests. See Archbold v. Reifenrath, 744 N.W.2d 701 (Neb. 2008); Estate of Ferrara, 852 N.E.2d 138 (N.Y. 2006).

A related issue is whether the agent can change the principal's POD or TOD designations, or whether a sale by the agent of specifically devised property causes ademption. Suppose *B*, an agent under a power of attorney from *T* and the residuary beneficiary under *T*'s will, converts *T*'s POD accounts, which named *A* as the POD beneficiary, to ordinary accounts in *T*'s name. *T* dies. Is *B* entitled to the property? If so, does *A* have recourse against *B* for breach of fiduciary duty? Compare Crosby v. Luehrs, 669 N.W.2d 635 (Neb. 2003), with In re Estate of Anton, page 381.

For a thoughtful treatment of the tax consequences of gifts and other transfers by an agent acting under a power of attorney, see Bridget J. Crawford, Tax Avatars, 2008 Utah L. Rev. 793. See also Peter B. Tiernan, Agent's Powers in a Durable Power of Attorney Can Result in Unexpected Tax, 32 Est. Plan. 34 (Dec. 2005).

5. In 2006, the Uniform Law Commission promulgated a new Uniform Power of Attorney Act, so far enacted in Idaho and New Mexico. It is intended to reconcile the divergent state laws on powers of attorney and to address the recurring problem areas in their use. Under the new act, the clumsy term *attorney-in-fact* is replaced with the more intuitive term *agent* (§102), and, in contrast to current law, all powers of attorney are presumed to be durable unless the instrument states otherwise (§104). The act specifies the agent's fiduciary duties, addressing a split in the existing law, which draws variously on agency and trust law, and it resolves which duties are mandatory and which may be overridden by the terms of the instrument (§114). The act provides that if the power to do so is stated expressly in the instrument, the agent may create, amend, revoke, or terminate an inter vivos trust; may make gifts; and may create or change survivorship rights or beneficiary designations (§201). The act contains a statutory short form (§301), which must be accepted by a third party unless certain exceptions are met, most notably if the third party makes or knows of a report to the local adult protective services office stating a good faith belief that the principal may be subject to physical or financial abuse, neglect, exploitation, or abandonment by the agent (§120).

For further discussion by the act's reporter, see Linda S. Whitton, Navigating the Uniform Power of Attorney Act, 3 NAELA J. 1 (2007); Linda S. Whitton, The New Uniform Power of Attorney Act: Balancing Protection of the Principal, the Agent, and Third Persons, 41 Heckerling Inst. on Est. Plan. ch. 9 (2007). See also Linda S. Whitton, Durable Powers as an Alternative to Guardianship: Lessons We Have Learned, 37 Stetson L. Rev. 7 (2007).

2. *Directives Regarding Health Care and Disposition of the Body*

a. Advance Directives: Living Wills, Health Care Proxies, and Hybrids

The Supreme Court has held that each person has a constitutional right to make health care decisions for herself, including the right to refuse medical treatment. Cruzan v. Director, Mo. Dept. of Health, 497 U.S. 261 (1990). If state law requirements are met, a person may state her wishes about terminating medical treatment or may appoint an agent to make the decision for her. Where a person's wishes are not clearly expressed, the state may assert an interest in favor of preserving life and prevent the withdrawal of treatment. In resolving a conflict over the wishes of an incompetent individual, the law relies on advance directives and default rules in the absence of an advance directive.

Advance directives are of three basic types: (1) *instructional directives*, such as a *living will* or a commonly used form known as a *Medical Directive*, which specify either generally or by way of hypothetical examples how one wants to be treated in end-of-life situations or in the event of incompetence; (2) *proxy directives*, such as a *health care proxy* or *durable power of attorney for health care*, which designate an agent to make health care decisions for the patient (the power of the agent does not expire with the principal's incompetency); and (3) *hybrid* or *combined directives* incorporating both of the first two approaches, directing treatment preferences and designating an agent to make substituted decisions.

By permission of Chip Bok and Creators Syndicate, Inc.

Rebecca Dresser, Precommitment: A Misguided Strategy for
Securing Death with Dignity
81 Tex. L. Rev. 1823 (2003)

Studies of advance directives point to several practical problems. First, advance directives are rarely completed. Second, most of the directives that are completed fail to convey meaningful information. Third, people making directives often have a poor understanding of what they are deciding. In particular, they may not envision how they could experience their decisions in a future incapacitated state. . . .

Advance directives have been endorsed for more than thirty years, and [the federal Patient Self-Determination Act] has required since 1991 that hospitals and other health care organizations notify patients of their right to make a directive. Nevertheless, relatively few people complete directives. Researchers generally report that less than 25% of people have directives, though some studies have found higher completion levels among selected groups with serious illnesses. . . .

Most people completing directives do not attempt to issue detailed instructions for the variety of situations that could befall them. Instead, they supply only a general indication of how they would like to be treated. Such directives furnish little information to clinicians and families seeking to resolve actual treatment issues. . . .

To remedy the problem of imprecision, health professionals have created documents that elicit more specific information about treatment preferences. The most well-known of these is the Medical Directive, which sets forth six hypothetical clinical situations involving different physical and mental impairments and six categories of life-sustaining interventions. Even these documents may supply inadequate guidance, however. For example, the Medical Directive may not indicate how a person's wishes would apply in an actual treatment situation, because not all treatment situations fit neatly into one of thirty-six scenarios. . . .

Most people simply cannot predict all the medical conditions that the future might bring, much less understand what would be the possible harms and benefits of interventions targeting those conditions. . . .

A related problem is that a person's preferences regarding future life-sustaining treatment may change over time. Several studies have measured the stability of advance directive preferences over periods of up to two years. Most find what they label "moderate" stability. . . .

Changed preferences point to a further problem, which is that people do a poor job of predicting their preferences in situations they have never experienced.

NOTES

1.   Every state has statutes providing for advance direction of health care, but these vary in the particulars and often require specific forms. The lawyer advising a client to execute a directive should consult local law. See Jeffrey A. Schoenblum, 2008 Multistate Guide to Estate Planning at Table 7.

The Uniform Health-Care Decisions Act, promulgated in 1993, takes a hybrid approach, including forms that create a durable power of attorney for health care and offer the person a chance to indicate how aggressively he would like to be treated. The agent must make decisions in accordance with the patient's wishes. The health care provider must follow the instructions except where contrary to the provider's conscience or contrary to generally accepted medical practice.

2.   On the difficulties in a child's making end-of-life decisions for a parent, see Ray D. Madoff, Autonomy and End-of-Life Decision-Making, Trial, Dec. 2006, at 36. For a discussion of recourse available when an advance directive is not followed, see Carol J. Wessels, Treated with Respect: Enforcing Patient Autonomy by Defending Advance Directives, 6 Marq. Elder's Advisor 217 (2005). See also Marsha Garrison, The Empire of Illness: Competence and Coercion in Health-Care Decision Making, 49 Wm. & Mary L. Rev. 781 (2007) (arguing for protective doctrines to ensure voluntariness as a precondition to enforcement of health care instructions).

When making health care decisions for an incompetent patient, an agent for health care decisions is held to a *substituted judgment* standard of what the patient has chosen or would have chosen in that situation. Some commentators have suggested that, instead of or in addition to this standard, the agent should act in the *best interests* of the patient. In end-of-life situations, however, it is often unclear what the patient would have wanted or what is in the best interests of the patient. See Conservatorship of Wendland, 28 P.3d 151 (Cal. 2001), in which the conservator could not meet the clear and convincing evidentiary standard of what the conservatee would have wanted or the best interests of the conservatee.

In the absence of an advance directive designating an agent, responsibility for an incompetent patient's decisions regarding health care usually falls to the patient's spouse or next of kin, subject to the state's interest in preserving life. To give a clear order of priority among potential decision makers, many states have enacted a statutory hierarchy. The Uniform Health-Care Decisions Act is representative. It provides that in the absence of an advance directive, decisions are authorized to be made by surrogates in the following order: (1) the spouse, unless legally separated; (2) an adult child; (3) a parent; or (4) an adult brother or sister. If there is more than one person in a class, the majority controls.

For an argument that same-sex partners should be added to the hierarchy of health care surrogates, see Rebecca K. Glazer, Equality at the End: Amending State Surrogacy Statutes to Honor Same-Sex Couples' End-of-Life Decisions, 13 Elder L.J. 255 (2005).

Bush v. Schiavo
Supreme Court of Florida, 2004
885 So. 2d 321

PARIENTE, C.J.   The narrow issue in this case requires this Court to decide the constitutionality of a law passed by the Legislature that directly affected Theresa Schiavo, who has been in a persistent vegetative state since 1990. This

Court . . . concludes that the law violates the fundamental constitutional tenet of separation of powers and is therefore unconstitutional both on its face and as applied to Theresa Schiavo. Accordingly, we affirm the trial court's order declaring the law unconstitutional.

FACTS AND PROCEDURAL HISTORY . . .

As set forth in the Second District's first opinion in this case, which upheld the guardianship court's final order,

> Theresa Marie Schindler was born on December 3, 1963, and lived with or near her parents in Pennsylvania until she married Michael Schiavo on November 10, 1984. Michael and Theresa moved to Florida in 1986. They were happily married and both were employed. They had no children.
>
> On February 25, 1990, their lives changed. Theresa, age 27, suffered a cardiac arrest as a result of a potassium imbalance. Michael called 911, and Theresa was rushed to the hospital. She never regained consciousness.
>
> Since 1990, Theresa has lived in nursing homes with constant care. She is fed and hydrated by tubes. The staff changes her diapers regularly. She has had numerous health problems, but none have been life threatening.[10] In re Guardianship of Schiavo, 780 So. 2d 176, 177 (Fla. Dist. 2001) (*Schiavo I*).

For the first three years after this tragedy, Michael and Theresa's parents, Robert and Mary Schindler, enjoyed an amicable relationship. However, that relationship ended in 1993 and the parties literally stopped speaking to each other. In May of 1998, eight years after Theresa lost consciousness, Michael petitioned the guardianship court to authorize the termination of life-prolonging procedures. By filing this petition, which the Schindlers opposed, Michael placed the difficult decision in the hands of the court.

---

10. A devotee of romantic movies, Theresa (Terri) avoided high school dances — including her prom — because she was self-conscious about her weight. But she slimmed down during her senior year. After graduation she enrolled in a local community college, where she fell in love with the handsome and popular Michael Schiavo. In 1984, Terri and Michael married after a little more than a year of dating.

Terri Schiavo

Sadly, life does not always follow the template of a romantic movie. There are reports that "Mr. Schiavo was a penny pincher who kept track of the mileage on his wife's car and yelled at her for spending money on haircuts . . . . The couple worked opposite hours — she all day, he late into the night." With His Wife in Limbo, Husband Can't Move, N.Y. Times, Nov. 2, 2003, §1, at 18. According to Terri's brother, parents, and others, Terri was even contemplating a divorce in the year before her heart attack:

> The Schindlers say that on Feb. 25, 1990, Mrs. Schiavo told her brother that she and Mr. Schiavo had had a violent argument — a claim Mr. Schiavo denies. Mr. Schiavo has said his wife was asleep when he arrived home from work around 2 A.M. . . . [O]n "Larry King Live," he said that he awoke at 4:30 and heard a thud. It was his wife, whom he found on the floor, he said.
>
> By the time paramedics arrived, Mrs. Schiavo's heart had not pumped for perhaps 10 minutes, doctors found. The prevailing theory is that she had an undiagnosed potassium deficiency, possibly due to extreme weight loss or even, her husband has said, bulimia. She had gone from over 200 pounds in high school to 110. [Id.]

Terri Schiavo did not leave an advance directive. — Eds.

After a trial, at which both Michael and the Schindlers presented evidence, the guardianship court issued an extensive written order authorizing the discontinuance of artificial life support. The trial court found by clear and convincing evidence that Theresa Schiavo was in a persistent vegetative state and that Theresa would elect to cease life-prolonging procedures if she were competent to make her own decision. This order was affirmed on direct appeal, see *Schiavo I*, 780 So. 2d at 177, and we denied review. See In re Guardianship of Schiavo, 789 So. 2d 348 (Fla. 2001). . . .

In affirming the trial court's order, the Second District concluded by stating:

> In the final analysis, the difficult question that faced the trial court was whether Theresa Marie Schindler Schiavo, not after a few weeks in a coma, but after ten years in a persistent vegetative state that has robbed her of most of her cerebrum and all but the most instinctive of neurological functions, with no hope of a medical cure but with sufficient money and strength of body to live indefinitely, would choose to continue the constant nursing care and the supporting tubes in hopes that a miracle would somehow recreate her missing brain tissue, or whether she would wish to permit a natural death process to take its course and for her family members and loved ones to be free to continue their lives. After due consideration, we conclude that the trial judge had clear and convincing evidence to answer this question as he did. . . .

[After two years of further litigation, which resulted in the original decision being upheld, "Theresa's nutrition and hydration tube was removed on October 15, 2003." Six days later the Florida legislature passed Chapter 2003-418, which authorized the governor of Florida to stay the removal of nutrition and hydration on facts that matched the *Schiavo* case. Governor Jeb Bush immediately issued "executive order No. 03-201 to stay the continued withholding of nutrition and hydration from Theresa. The nutrition and hydration tube was reinserted pursuant to the Governor's executive order." After successful lower court challenges to the statute by Michael, the Florida Supreme Court issued this decision.]

ANALYSIS

We begin our discussion by emphasizing that our task in this case is to review the constitutionality of chapter 2003-418, not to reexamine the guardianship court's orders directing the removal of Theresa's nutrition and hydration tube, or to review the Second District's numerous decisions in the guardianship case. . . .

The language of chapter 2003-418 is clear. It states[:] . . .

> (1) The Governor shall have the authority to issue a one-time stay to prevent the withholding of nutrition and hydration from a patient if, as of October 15, 2003:
>   (a) That patient has no written advance directive;
>   (b) The court has found that patient to be in a persistent vegetative state;
>   (c) That patient has had nutrition and hydration withheld; and
>   (d) A member of that patient's family has challenged the withholding of nutrition and hydration.
>
> (2) The Governor's authority to issue the stay expires 15 days after the effective date of this act, and the expiration of the authority does not impact the validity or the effect of any stay issued pursuant to this act. The Governor may lift the stay authorized under this act at any time.

A person may not be held civilly liable and is not subject to regulatory or disciplinary sanctions for taking any action to comply with a stay issued by the Governor pursuant to this act.

(3) Upon issuance of a stay, the chief judge of the circuit court shall appoint a guardian ad litem for the patient to make recommendations to the Governor and the court. . . .

ENCROACHMENT ON THE JUDICIAL BRANCH . . .

Under the express separation of powers provision in our state constitution, "the judiciary is a coequal branch of the Florida government vested with the sole authority to exercise the judicial power," and "the legislature cannot, short of constitutional amendment, reallocate the balance of power expressly delineated in the constitution among the three coequal branches." Children A, B, C, D, E, & F, 589 So. 2d 260, 268-69 (Fla. 1991). . . .

In this case, the undisputed facts show that the guardianship court authorized Michael to proceed with the discontinuance of Theresa's life support after the issue was fully litigated in a proceeding in which the Schindlers were afforded the opportunity to present evidence on all issues. This order as well as the order denying the Schindlers' motion for relief from judgment were affirmed on direct appeal. The Schindlers sought review in this Court, which was denied. Thereafter, the tube was removed. Subsequently, pursuant to the Governor's executive order, the nutrition and hydration tube was reinserted. Thus, the Act, as applied in this case, resulted in an executive order that effectively reversed a properly rendered final judgment and thereby constituted an unconstitutional encroachment on the power that has been reserved for the independent judiciary. . . .

When the prescribed procedures are followed according to our rules of court and the governing statutes, a final judgment is issued, and all post-judgment procedures are followed, it is without question an invasion of the authority of the judicial branch for the Legislature to pass a law that allows the executive branch to interfere with the final judicial determination in a case. That is precisely what occurred here and for that reason the Act is unconstitutional as applied to Theresa Schiavo.

DELEGATION OF LEGISLATIVE AUTHORITY

In addition to concluding that the Act is unconstitutional as applied in this case because it encroaches on the power of the judicial branch, we further conclude that the Act is unconstitutional on its face because it delegates legislative power to the Governor. . . .

In enacting chapter 2003-418, the Legislature failed to provide any standards by which the Governor should determine whether, in any given case, a stay should be issued and how long a stay should remain in effect. Further, the Legislature has failed to provide any criteria for lifting the stay. This absolute, unfettered discretion to decide whether to issue and then when to lift a stay makes the Governor's decision virtually unreviewable. . . .

CONCLUSION . . .

The trial court's decision regarding Theresa Schiavo was made in accordance with the procedures and protections set forth by the judicial branch and in accordance with the statutes passed by the Legislature in effect at that time. That decision is final and the Legislature's attempt to alter that final adjudication is unconstitutional as applied to Theresa Schiavo.... [W]e affirm the circuit court's final summary judgment.

It is so ordered.

NOTES AND QUESTION

1. *Aftermath*. After the U.S. Supreme Court denied Governor Jeb Bush's petition for certiorari and three days after Terri Schiavo's feeding tube was removed, Congress passed an ambiguously worded statute, signed into law on March 21, 2005, just two days after it was formally introduced. The statute was designed to give the federal courts jurisdiction to intervene in the *Schiavo* case. On March 24, 2005, however, the Court denied a motion to stay the Florida Supreme Court's order in *Schiavo*. Terri Schiavo died on March 31, 2005.

On June 13, 2005, the local medical examiner released his autopsy report. He found that the immediate cause of Terri's death was dehydration, that Terri's brain was about half the size of normal, that she was blind before her death, and that her condition before death was consistent with her having been in a persistent vegetative state.

2. Michael's treatment choices took precedence over those of Terri's parents, the Schindlers, because Michael had been named by the court as her guardian. In the absence of this appointment, Michael's directions would still have governed her care because in Florida, as in most states, the patient's spouse has priority over the patient's parents. Fla. Stat. §765.401 (2008).

3. In the years since Terri Schiavo's death, much has been written about the legal maneuvers and the larger issues involved in her case, too much to be summarized here. The curious student who enters "Terri Schiavo" into Lexis or Westlaw will find plenty of matches. Meanwhile, Michael Schiavo and the Schindler family have each published books telling their respective sides of the story. See Michael Schiavo and Michael Hirsh, Terri: The Truth (2006); Mary Schindler, Robert Schindler, Suzanne Schindler Vitadamo, and Bobby Schindler, A Life That Matters: The Legacy of Terri Schiavo (2006).

4. Polls show overwhelmingly that most Americans would not want to be kept alive if there were no hope of recovery. The question thus arises, if a particular patient's wishes are not known, but under the circumstances most patients would choose to forgo continued treatment, should the default rule be no treatment — in Professor Lindgren's formulation, death by default? See James Lindgren, Death by Default, 56 Law & Contemp. Probs. 185 (Summer 1993).

NOTE: EUTHANASIA AND ASSISTED SUICIDE

By referendum in 1994, Oregon became the first (and still only) U.S. state to authorize physician-assisted suicide. Under the Oregon Death with Dignity Act, a physician is relieved of criminal and civil liability for prescribing a lethal dose of medicine to an adult if certain conditions are met. The adult must suffer from an incurable disease that is likely to produce death within six months, must make multiple separate requests (at least one in writing), must notify her next of kin, and must survive two waiting periods (one 15 days, the other 2 days). Or. Rev. Stat. §§127.800 et seq. Through year-end 2008, a total of 341 people have died under the Oregon law since it took effect in late 1997. The overwhelming majority had terminal cancer, and most died at home. The Oregon law, and similar legislation in the Netherlands, is examined in Jackson Pickett, Can Legalization Improve End-of-Life Care? An Empirical Analysis of the Results of the Legalization of Euthanasia and Physician-Assisted Suicide in the Netherlands and Oregon, 16 Elder L.J. 333 (2009).

In Gonzales v. Oregon, 546 U.S. 243 (2006), the U.S. Supreme Court upheld the Oregon law against a U.S. Justice Department interpretation of the federal Controlled Substances Act, which would have extended federal criminal liability to physicians acting under the state law.

b.   Disposition of the Body

(1) *Postmortem remains.* Historically, a person other than a monarch has had little say about what is done to his body after death. The body was not considered to be property, so it was not disposable by will; nor was it owned by the decedent's estate or by his family. Until the twentieth century, burials were regarded as a matter of "sentiment and superstition" and were left to the jurisdiction of the church. With the rise of secularism, courts began to exercise a "benevolent discretion" to carry out the wishes of the deceased person, provided those wishes do not conflict unreasonably with the desires of the living. This power, in some states codified by mortal remains legislation, has been exercised in such a way that a person now has something more than a hope, but far less than an assurance, that his wishes will be carried out at death if the family objects.[11] If a person dies by violence or in

---

11. In Meksrus Estate, 24 Pa. Fiduc. 249 (Orph. Ct. 1974), a testamentary direction to inter diamonds, jewelry, and paintings with the decedent's body was held to be against public policy and void. Such a provision, if enforced, the court thought, "is almost certain to tempt some people and invite others to overt action to procure the" buried treasure.

Professor Foster collects more recent, celebrity examples of disputes over postmortem disposition:

> For nearly three months, the body of the self-styled "Godfather of Soul," James Brown, lay refrigerated in a secret location while his children, disputed wife, and executors fought over his final resting place.
> Evangelist Billy Graham and his wife, Ruth, had an even more unfortunate experience. Unlike . . . James Brown, the Grahams were still alive when their children engaged in "a struggle worthy of the Old Testament" over where to bury the elderly couple.
> Red Sox legend Ted Williams suffered the ultimate indignity. After a family feud over his body, the once "Splendid Splinter" became a frozen, cracked head in an Arizona cryonics laboratory. With a greasy scrap of paper and a blind faith in the "miracles" of modern medicine, John Henry Williams consigned his father to the ranks of the living dead. Today, a great American hero is literally and figuratively suspended between life and death and "may never rest in peace." [Frances H. Foster, Individualized Justice in Disputes over Dead Bodies, 61 Vand. L. Rev. 1351, 1352-1354 (2008).]

suspicious circumstances, however, statutes in all states require an autopsy regardless of the wishes of the deceased person or next of kin.

NOTE

For thoughtful examinations of the tension between honoring the wishes of the deceased and the preferences of the survivors, see Frances H. Foster, Individualized Justice in Disputes over Dead Bodies, 61 Vand. L. Rev. 1351 (2008); Tanya K. Hernandez, The Property of Death, 60 U. Pitt. L. Rev. 971 (1999). For reform proposals, see Ann M. Murphy, Please Don't Bury Me Down in That Cold Cold Ground: The Need For Uniform Laws on the Disposition of Human Remains, 15 Elder L.J. 381 (2007); Tracie M. Kester, Uniform Acts — Can the Dead Hand Control the Dead Body? The Case for a Uniform Bodily Remains Law, 29 W. New Eng. L. Rev. 571 (2007). See also Thomas A. Robinson, Stop! Are You Sure You Want to Throw Grandpa's Body Away?, 63 U. Miami L. Rev. 37 (2008) (considering whether bodies should be preserved, flash frozen, for the future).

---

(2) *Organ donation.* With the advent first of dissection, then of cadaver organ transplantation, the first principle of law, medicine, and ethics — saving human life — became a relevant consideration in the disposition of the dead. To increase the quantity of cadaver organs for transplantation, all states have enacted some form of the Uniform Anatomical Gift Act, first promulgated in 1968, later revised in 1987, and again in 2006. This act permits a person to give her body to any hospital, physician, medical school, or body bank for research or transplantation. It also permits a gift of a body, or parts thereof, to any specified individual for therapy or transplantation needed by the individual. Under the original Uniform Anatomical Gift Act of 1968, the gift can be made by a duly executed will or by a card carried on the person if the card is "signed by the donor in the presence of two witnesses who must sign the document in his presence." Under the 1987 and 2006 revisions, the witnessing requirement was eliminated so that only a signature on a card would be required. In many states, additional legislation has been enacted providing for an organ donation form to be affixed to the back of a driver's license, which is also allowed under the 1987 and 2006 revisions of the Uniform Act. The 2006 revision clarifies and expands the class of persons who can make a gift of a deceased person's body or parts to include agents under a power of attorney for health care.

The various anatomical gift statutes have had little effect on easing the shortage of organs. By year-end 2008, there were roughly 100,000 people on the national waiting list to receive an organ donation. In 2008, nearly 28,000 transplants were made from 14,000 donors. In the arresting formulation of the Prefatory Note to the 2006 revision of the Uniform Act, "Every hour another person in the United States dies because of the lack of an organ to provide a life saving organ transplant."

There are many reasons for the shortage of organs: (a) the difficulty of imagining one's death and others' using one's organs; (b) the fear that physicians might hasten a person's death in order to obtain organs;[12] (c) unwillingness to be cut open after death, sometimes because of religious belief; and (d) simply not thinking about the matter. Organ shortages remain acute in spite of the driver's license donor statutes and improved hospital counseling of bereaved families.

A number of commentators, and some entrepreneurs ready to buy and sell organs, have suggested that a market in human organs be established. A market, after all, is the traditional way of allocating scarce resources. In 1984, however, Congress forbade the sale of human organs. National Organ Transplant Act, 42 U.S.C. §274e (2008). The British Parliament outlawed the sale of human organs in 1989, after a public outcry over the sale of a kidney to a Londoner for £2,000 by a Turkish peasant flown to London for the operation. N.Y. Times, Aug. 1, 1989, §B, at 5. See also Annie Cheney, Body Brokers: Inside America's Underground Trade in Human Remains (2006).

Suppose that the federal government gave a tax deduction to the estate of any cadaver organ donor. Should that be prohibited as a sale? See Joseph B. Clamon, Tax Policy as a Lifeline: Encouraging Blood and Organ Donation Through Tax Credits, 17 Annals Health L. 67 (2008); Lisa Milot, The Case Against Tax Incentives for Organ Transfers, 45 Willamette L. Rev. 67 (2008). Suppose that health insurance companies, as a result of collective bargaining or governmental requirement, offered lower premiums to persons who agreed to donate their organs at death. Would this be a sale? In 2007, South Carolina lawmakers debated legislation that would give prison inmates a credit against their sentences in return for an organ donation. Would this be a sale? Would it be ethical?

For arguments in favor of a futures market in cadaver organs, see, e.g., Richard A. Epstein, The Human and Economic Dimensions of Altruism: The Case of Organ Transplantation, 37 J. Leg. Stud. 459 (2008); Elizabeth E. Appel, Blue Redefining Stewardship Over Body Parts, 21 J.L. & Health 75 (2008); Lloyd Cohen, Increasing the Supply of Transplant Organs: The Virtues of a Futures Market, 58 Geo. Wash. L. Rev. 1 (1989); Henry Hansmann, The Economics and Ethics of Markets for Human Organs, 14 J. Health Pol. Poly. & L. 57 (1989).

A government report in 1986 urged states to adopt statutes requiring hospitals to request from families of prospective donors at the time of death permission to remove organs for transplantation. A federal regulation of the same year made this "routine request" a condition of hospital Medicare eligibility. See U.S. Dept. of Health & Human Services, Report of Task Force on Organ Transplantation (Apr. 1986). Although most states have enacted "routine request" statutes, because of difficulties families have in facing such requests in times of shock and grief, the routine request approach has not been successful enough to relieve the shortage of organs.

---

12. In a case that received national media attention, a California doctor was acquitted in late 2008 of the charge that he hastened the death of a donor to harvest the donor's organs. See Jesse McKinley, Surgeon Cleared of Harming Man to Rush Organ Removal, N.Y. Times, Dec. 19, 2008, at A30.

Others have favored establishing a nationwide system whereby every individual must answer the question: Do you give your organs for transplantation upon your death? The question could be required to be answered upon an application for a driver's license. This system is called "mandated choice."

A significant increase in the quantity of cadaver organs available for transplantation might result if the default rule were switched in favor of presuming that the deceased person has consented to donation. Under such a "presumed consent" or "opt-out" system, usable organs would be routinely removed from cadavers unless, before the time of removal, an objection were entered, either by the deceased person during life or immediately after the decedent's death by the next-of-kin knowing of the decedent's objection.

In support of a presumption of donation, Professors Sunstein and Thaler argue that this would set the default rule closer to people's preferences:

> In many nations — Austria, Belgium, Denmark, Finland, France, Italy, Luxembourg, Norway, Singapore, Slovenia, and Spain — people are presumed to consent to allow their organs to be used, after death, for the benefit of others; but they are permitted to rebut the presumption, usually through an explicit notation to that effect on their drivers' licenses. In the United States, by contrast, those who want their organs to be available for others must affirmatively say so, also through an explicit notation on their drivers' licenses. The result is that in "presumed consent" nations over 90 percent of people consent to make their organs available for donation, whereas in the United States, where people have to take some action to make their organs available, only 28 percent elect to do so. We hypothesize that this dramatic difference is not a product of deep cultural differences, but of the massive effect of the default rule. Hence we would predict that a European-style opt-out rule in the United States would produce donation rates similar to those observed in the European countries that use this rule. Note in this regard that by one report, over 85 percent of Americans support organ donation — a statistic that suggests opt-outs would be relatively rare. [Cass R. Sunstein and Richard H. Thaler, Libertarian Paternalism Is Not an Oxymoron, 70 U. Chi. L. Rev. 1159, 1192 (2003).]

The median opt-out rate in countries with organ donation as the default is a staggeringly low 1 percent. In Belgium, organ donation increased 119 percent in the first three years after the implementation of the law. Should an opt-out rule be adopted in the United States? The 2006 revision to the Uniform Anatomical Gift Act preserved the traditional opt-in approach. See David Orentlicher, Presumed Consent to Organ Donation: Its Rise and Fall in the United States, 61 Rutgers L. Rev. 295 (2009).

NOTE: ELDER LAW

The field of elder law, dealing with legal problems of the elderly, began to develop in the 1990s. Elder law deals with a wide range of issues facing the elderly, including health care, asset preservation, Medicaid eligibility, retirement, competency and guardianship, discrimination, elder abuse, and housing and institutionalization. Practitioners in this area deal with many personal health issues, such as nursing home care and continuing care retirement communities.

On the property side, lawyers can help with pension plans and Social Security, estate planning, durable powers of attorney, conservatorships, and trusts to preserve assets if the elderly person is admitted into a state institution. For a taste of this field, see Lawrence A. Frolik and Alison McChystal Barnes, Elder Law (4th ed. 2007); John J. Regan, Rebecca C. Morgan and David M. English, Tax, Estate and Financial Planning for the Elderly (looseleaf, through 2008); A. Kimberley Dayton, Molly M. Wood, and Julia A. Belian, Elder Law: Readings, Cases, and Materials (3d ed. 2007). See also Lawrence A. Frolik, The Law of Later-Life Health Care and Decision Making (2006).

Representing an elderly client with diminishing capacity can be a special challenge. See A. Frank Johns, Older Clients with Diminishing Capacity and Their Advance Directives, 39 Real Prop., Prob. & Tr. J. 107 (2004). In 2002, the American Bar Association revised Rule 1.14 of the Model Rules of Professional Conduct (Client with Diminished Capacity) to give guidance to lawyers who deal with clients of any age with diminished capacity. For discussion, see ACTEC Commentaries on the Model Rules of Professional Conduct 131-139 (4th ed. 2006).

7

RESTRICTIONS ON THE POWER OF DISPOSITION: PROTECTION OF THE SPOUSE AND CHILDREN

SECTION A. RIGHTS OF THE SURVIVING SPOUSE

1. Introduction to Marital Property Systems

In the United States, two basic marital property systems exist: the system of *separate property*, originating in the common law of England, and the system of *community property*, originating in Continental Europe and brought to this country by French and Spanish settlers. The fundamental difference between these systems is that under the common law, husband and wife own separately all property each acquires (except those items one spouse has agreed to put into joint ownership with the other), whereas under community property, husband and wife own all acquisitions from earnings after marriage in equal, undivided shares. There are, to be sure, many variations among the states adhering to one or another of these systems, and community property ideas have made noticeable inroads into the common law separate property system. Nonetheless, separate property and community property are quite different ways of thinking about marital property ownership. The former stresses the individual's autonomy over her earnings; the latter stresses sharing of earnings between husband and wife as economic partners.

Community property developed throughout the continent of Europe, purportedly spread by Germanic tribes after the fall of Rome. From these western countries it was taken by European settlers to Central and South America, Mexico, and states along the southern and western borders of the United States. It is odd, then, that in England — separated from the continent by only a 21-mile-wide channel of water — there arose the very different separate property system.

Why the English resisted so powerful an idea as the sharing principle of community property has intrigued scholars for generations. The most plausible explanations connect the separate property system with the highly centralized

English feudal system, dominated by a powerful king, which required succession of power (land) from father to son and fealty between a (male) lord and a (male) tenant. Women were supported by their husbands, but they were denied an ownership share of, or power over, their husbands' property. Whatever the reason for its existence, the English separate property system became well entrenched by the fourteenth century and was taken by the English settlers to the eastern seaboard of the United States, from where it spread westward.

Under the separate property system, whatever the worker earns is his or hers. There is no automatic sharing of earnings. If one spouse is the wage earner while the other spouse works in the home, the wage-earning spouse will own all the property acquired during marriage (other than gifts or inheritances from others or gifts by the wage earner to the homemaker). Thus, a crucial issue under a separate property system is what protection against disinheritance should be given the surviving spouse who works in the home or works at a lower-paying job? All but one of the separate property states answer this question by giving the surviving spouse, by statute, an *elective share* (or *forced share*) in the estate of the deceased spouse. The elective share is not, however, limited to property acquired with earnings. It is enforceable against all of the decedent spouse's property, though as we shall see, nonprobate transfers pose challenges in implementing this idea.

A community property system has long existed in eight states (Arizona, California, Idaho, Louisiana, Nevada, New Mexico, Texas, and Washington), and Wisconsin adopted such a system in 1984. These states contain more than one-quarter of the U.S. population. The fundamental principle of community property is that all earnings of the spouses, and property acquired from those earnings, are community property unless both spouses agree to separate ownership. Each spouse is the owner of an undivided one-half interest in the community property. The death of one spouse dissolves the community. The deceased spouse owns and has testamentary power over his or her half of the community; the surviving spouse already owns the other half.

A simple illustration shows the difference between the principles underlying the separate property and the community property systems:

> *Case 1. H* works outside the home, earning $50,000 a year. *W* works in the home, earning no wages. At the end of 20 years, *H* has through savings of his earnings bought a house in his name, a life insurance policy payable to his daughter, and $100,000 of stocks in his name. Under a separate property regime, during life *W* owns none of that property. At *H*'s death, *W* has an elective share (usually one-third) of the house and the stocks but perhaps not the insurance policy because it is not in *H*'s probate estate. In a community property state, *W* owns half of *H*'s earnings during life, and thus at *H*'s death *W* owns one-half of the acquisitions from earnings (the house, the insurance proceeds, and the stocks). If *W* dies first, *W* can dispose of her half of the community property by will. In a separate property state, if *W* dies first, she has no property to convey.

In the late twentieth century, many academics came to favor community property. In 1983, the Uniform Law Commission promulgated the Uniform Marital Property Act. The act adopts community property principles, though it avoids the phrase *community property* and uses *marital property* instead. See Kathy T. Graham,

Community Property States (2008)

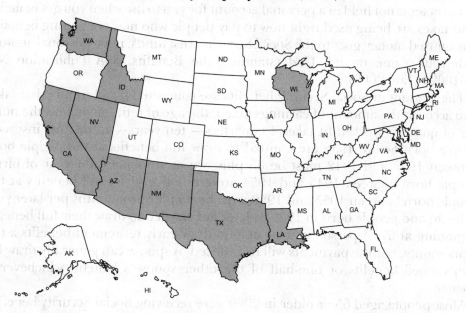

The Uniform Marital Property Act: A Solution for Common Law Property Systems?, 48 S.D. L. Rev. 455 (2003). Wisconsin is the only state to have adopted the act. Wis. Stat. Ann. §§766.001-766.097 (2008).

In 1998, Alaska enacted a statute permitting married couples to elect to hold their property as community property. Alaska Stat. §§34.77.010-34.77.160 (2008). This seems a good idea. It gives married couples a chance to choose the system of marital property ownership that they prefer.

In examining the surviving spouse's rights, we turn first to rights of the surviving spouse to *support*, which (except for dower) are generally the same in both separate property and community property states. We then turn to the central topic: the right of the surviving spouse to a *share* in the decedent spouse's property or in the marital property.

2.   Rights of Surviving Spouse to Support

a.   Social Security

In the 1930s, Congress established the Social Security system, under which retirement benefits are paid to a worker and the worker's surviving spouse. In 2009, workers paid 6.2 percent of their earnings up to $106,800 into the system, matched by another 6.2 percent paid by their employers. In addition, there is a 2.9 percent Medicare tax split between employer and employee. Self-employed workers paid the entire 15.3 percent (6.2 + 6.2 + 2.9 = 15.3) themselves.

Taxes paid into the Social Security system are used to pay current benefits to people who have already retired or are disabled, to survivors of predeceased workers, and to the dependents of Social Security beneficiaries. "The money you pay in taxes is not held in a personal account for you to use when you get benefits. Your taxes are being used right now to pay people who now are getting benefits. Any unused money goes to the Social Security trust funds, not a personal account with your name on it." Understanding the Benefits, SSA Publication No. 05-10024 (Jan. 2009).

The amount of Social Security benefits are computed by a formula that takes into account the amount of earnings taxed, the age of retirement, and the number of quarters worked (it takes 40 quarters—ten years—to be fully insured). People born before 1938 are entitled to draw full benefits at 65; people born between 1938 and 1942 must be 65 plus two months per later year of birth; people born between 1943 and 1954 are entitled to draw full benefits at 66; people born between 1955 and 1959 must be 66 plus two months per later year of birth; and people born in 1960 or later are entitled to draw their full benefits beginning at 67. A person may be able to draw early retirement benefits a few years sooner, but the payments will be reduced. A spouse can generally draw his own earned benefits or one-half of the other spouse's benefit, whichever is greater.

Most people aged 65 or older in 2009 were receiving Social Security benefits, with an average monthly benefit of $1,153 for retired workers and $1,876 for retired couples. If a worker dies, generally the surviving spouse will then receive the worker's full monthly benefits. Workers have no power to transfer their right to benefits to any other person. A divorced former spouse of the worker has a right to benefits if the marriage lasted for 10 years or longer. The average monthly benefit for nondisabled surviving spouses in 2009 was $1,112. Understanding the Benefits, supra.

NOTE

The current Social Security regime raises issues of gender equity. As Professors Frolik and Barnes observe, "[d]ivorce is common, and because two-thirds of all divorces occur within ten years of the wedding, a majority of divorcees are not entitled to retirement or disability based on their former husbands' work records." Lawrence A. Frolik and Alison McChrystal Barnes, Elder Law: Cases and Materials 188 (4th ed. 2007). There is also reason to question whether families in which one spouse worked should receive more benefits than families in which both spouses worked when the total amounts paid into the system by each family are the same.

    Case 2. H1 earns $80,000 a year, while his wife W1 works in the home. H1 retires and starts receiving Social Security benefits, but then dies in a boating accident with his neighbor, H2. Under the current system, W1 receives H1's full monthly retirement benefits, based on H1's $80,000 salary, until she dies.

    Case 3. H2 and W2, the neighbors of the couple in Case 2, each earn $40,000 a year. Both H2 and W2 retire and both receive Social Security benefits. Then H2 dies in the boating accident with *H1*. *W2* is entitled to receive only her own Social Security benefit, based on her $40,000 salary, or her deceased husband's benefits based on his $40,000 salary, whichever is larger — but not both.

W2's benefits in Case 3 will be smaller than *W1*'s in Case 2 even though both marriages paid equal amounts into the system based on equal overall wages.

b.   Employee Pension Plans

Pension plans funded by self-employed individuals, employers, or jointly funded by employer and employee contributions mushroomed in the twentieth century. Data compiled by the Federal Reserve show that by year-end 2008, private pension plans held $4.6 trillion in assets and public pension plans held $3.5 trillion. Two-thirds of the public plan assets were held for the future benefit of state and local government employees; the rest were for federal employees. In Chapter 6, we introduced pension plans and examined their operation as a mode of nonprobate transfer (see pages 423-432). We consider now the rights of a surviving spouse over the decedent spouse's pension accounts.

Most private pension plans are governed by the federal Employee Retirement Income Security Act of 1974 (ERISA), which preempts inconsistent state law. As amended by the Retirement Equity Act in 1984, ERISA requires that the spouse of an employee have survivorship rights if the employee predeceases the spouse. The purpose is to insure a stream of income to surviving spouses. If a plan pays its primary benefits as an annuity rather than a lump sum (see page 425), in most cases it must be paid as a joint and survivor annuity to the employee and his spouse (so the survivor spouse continues to receive payments regardless of which spouse dies first), unless the nonemployee spouse consents to some other form of payment of the retirement benefit, such as in a lump sum. If the employee dies before retirement, the surviving spouse may be entitled to a preretirement survivor annuity. For a summary of spousal rights in pensions, see John H. Langbein, Susan J. Stabile, and Bruce A. Wolk, Pension and Employee Benefit Law 271-282 (4th ed. 2006).

A spouse may waive her rights to benefits under the employee's pension plan, but ERISA discourages waivers with strict rules regarding their validity. For example, waiver requires the written consent of the "spouse," and one who is not yet a spouse cannot so consent. Hence premarital agreements cannot waive ERISA-covered pension rights. In addition, workers under the age of 35 cannot effectuate a waiver of spousal benefits. See Langbein, Stabile, and Wolk, supra, at 275-277.

NOTE AND PROBLEM

1.   In Boggs v. Boggs, 520 U.S. 833 (1997), a first wife had a community property share in her husband's pension, which, under community property law, she

could devise to whomever she pleased. She devised her share to her husband for life and then to her three sons. The husband married again after his first wife's death. Upon his death, the Supreme Court held that his pension benefits must be used to support his second wife, rather than be paid to the sons as named beneficiaries, in order to carry out ERISA's object to protect surviving spouses. ERISA preempted state community property law to the extent state law allowed the first wife to make a testamentary transfer of her interest in her husband's pension and make it unavailable to a second wife. See Cynthia A. Samuel and Katherine S. Spaht, Fixing What's Broke: Amending ERISA to Allow Community Property to Apply Upon the Death of a Participant's Spouse, 35 Fam. L.Q. 425 (2001).

2.   *W* designates *H* as the death beneficiary of her employer's pension plan. Subsequently *W* divorces *H* but does not change her beneficiary designation. Then *W* dies. Is *H* entitled to the death benefits? See Egelhoff v. Egelhoff, page 426. What result if *W* had remarried? If *W* had changed the death beneficiary to her sister, *S*, after the divorce?

c. Homestead

Most states have a homestead law that is designed to secure the family home to the surviving spouse and minor children, free of the claims of the decedent's creditors. See Jeffrey A. Schoenblum, 2008 Multistate Guide to Estate Planning at Table 6.01. Such a homestead is frequently called a *probate homestead*. Although the details of these laws vary considerably, the surviving spouse will often have the right to occupy the family home (or maybe the family farm) for his lifetime. In some states, the homestead must be established by the decedent during life, usually by filing a declaration of homestead in some public office; in other states, the probate court has the power to set aside real property as a homestead. The amount of the homestead exemption is ridiculously small in some states and provides little protection to the surviving spouse. Uniform Probate Code §2-402 (1990, rev. 2008) recommends $22,500, subject to the cost of living adjustment formula in §1-109. But in several states the homestead exemption is substantial and may even exempt the family home from the claims of all creditors and devisees, regardless of its value. The right to occupy the homestead is usually given in addition to any other rights the surviving spouse has in the decedent's estate. See Carolyn S. Bratt, Family Protection Under Kentucky's Inheritance Laws: Is the Family Really Protected?, 76 Ky. L.J. 387 (1988).

d. Personal Property Set-Aside

Related to homestead is the right of the surviving spouse (and sometimes of minor children) to receive tangible personal property of the decedent up to a certain value. UPC §2-403 (1990, rev. 2008) sets the limit at $15,000, subject to the cost of living adjustment formula in §1-109. These items, which are also exempt from creditors' claims, usually include household furniture and clothing, but may also include a car and farm animals. The set-aside is usually subject to several conditions and limitations, but, if these are met, the decedent usually has no power to deprive the surviving spouse of the exempt items.

e. Family Allowance

Every state has a statute authorizing the probate court to award an allowance for maintenance and support of the surviving spouse (and often of dependent children). The allowance may be limited to a fixed period (typically one year), or it may continue thereafter while the will is being contested or for the entire period of administration. As with the homestead and personal property set-aside, any family allowance is in addition to whatever other interests pass to the surviving spouse.

In some states, the maximum allowance that can be awarded is fixed by statute. In other states, a reasonable allowance tied to the spouse's standard of living is permitted. UPC §2-404 (1990) provides for a reasonable allowance, which cannot continue beyond one year if the estate is inadequate to pay creditors. Maintenance of the decedent's spouse and dependent children is not allowed after the estate is closed. UPC §2-405 authorizes the personal representative to determine the family allowance up to a stated limit without court order but subject to judicial review.

Later in this chapter, we examine proposals to import to the United States the broader system of family maintenance that is used in England, Australia, New Zealand, and most Canadian provinces (see pages 521-527). These jurisdictions grant the court discretion to override the terms of the decedent's will and to distribute some or all of the estate to the decedent's family and other dependents if the court determines that they deserve a larger share than is provided for in the will.

f. Dower and Curtesy

At common law, a widow had *dower* in all land of which her deceased husband had been seised during marriage and that was inheritable by the descendants of husband and wife. Dower entitles the widow to a life estate in one-third of her husband's qualifying land. Thus:

> *Case 4. H*, married to *W*, buys Blackacre, taking title in himself in fee simple. *H* subsequently dies. *W* is entitled to a life estate in one-third of Blackacre. If *W* had predeceased *H*, her dower interest would be extinguished.

The right of dower attaches the moment the husband acquires title to land or upon marriage, whichever is later. Dower remains inchoate until the husband's death, when it becomes possessory. Once inchoate dower has attached, the husband cannot sell the land free and clear of the wife's dower interest. In Case 4, if *H*, after buying Blackacre, had conveyed it to *A*, *A* would take title subject to *W*'s dower, and if and when *W* survived *H*, *W* would be entitled to a life estate in one-third of Blackacre (now owned by *A*). No purchaser, bona fide or not, can cut off the wife's dower without her consent.

In feudal times, when land was the chief form of wealth, dower provided generous support to the widow of a propertied man. But today, when most wealth takes the form of intangible personal property (such as stocks and bonds) and human capital (arising from education and training), dower may provide no protection at all. Dower has been abolished in the great majority of states,[1] and it functions today primarily to make the signatures of both spouses a practical requirement to the sale of one spouse's land.

At common law, a husband had a support interest in his wife's lands, called *curtesy*. It was comparable to dower except (1) the husband did not acquire curtesy unless children were born of the marriage, and (2) the husband was given a life estate in the entire parcel, not merely in one-third. Curtesy survives today in a handful of states, but in most of these it is only a label given to the support interest of the husband, which in fact has been made identical with the wife's support interest.

3. Rights of Surviving Spouse to a Share of Decedent's Property

a. The Elective Share and Its Rationale

All but one[2] of the separate property states give the surviving spouse, in addition to any support rights mentioned above, an *elective share* (sometimes called a *forced share*) of the decedent's property. The term *elective share* arose because the

---

1. In only four jurisdictions — Arkansas, Kentucky, Michigan, and Ohio — does dower exist as it was known to the common law. In all of these except Michigan, dower has been extended to the husband as well as the wife. Statutes similar to Michigan's, providing dower for a wife but not for a husband, were found to violate the Equal Protection Clause in Stokes v. Stokes, 613 S.W.2d 372 (Ark. 1981), and Boan v. Watson, 316 S.E.2d 401 (S.C. 1984). However, in In re Estate of Miltenberger, 737 N.W.2d 513 (Mich. App. 2007), a Michigan appellate court upheld the Michigan statute, and over a strong dissent the state supreme court denied review. 753 N.W.2d 219 (Mich. 2008). In Ohio and Michigan, the surviving spouse must elect to take dower, or to take a statutory share of the decedent's estate, or to take a share under the decedent's will. As the statutory elective share is almost always greater than dower, dower is rarely elected.

2. Georgia is the only separate property state without an elective share statute, though it does mandate at least one year of support for the spouse. Professor Chaffin, a leading authority on Georgia wills law, approved of this on the ground that the vast majority of husbands do support their wives after death and the elective share permits the surviving spouse to wreck a sound estate plan. Verner F. Chaffin, A Reappraisal of the Wealth Transmission Process: The Surviving Spouse, Year's Support and Intestate Succession, 10 Ga. L. Rev. 447, 464-470 (1976). See also Jeffrey N. Pennell, Minimizing the Surviving Spouse's Elective Share, 32 Heckerling Inst. on Est. Plan. ch. 9 (1998), reporting infrequent disinheritance of spouses, and in most such cases a sound planning explanation, based on a review of probate court records of Georgia decedents in 1996 and 1997.

Not all of Professor Chaffin's students were convinced. In Note, Preventing Spousal Disinheritance in Georgia, 19 Ga. L. Rev. 427 (1985), the author argued for equitable distribution of a portion of the decedent's property to the surviving spouse. Observing that the Georgia Supreme Court adopted equitable distribution upon divorce on its own after the Georgia legislature failed to act, the note suggests that the court should atone for a supine legislature by extending equitable distribution to termination of marriage by death. But see Terry L. Turnipseed, Why Shouldn't I Be Allowed to Leave My Property to Whomever I Choose at My Death? (Or How I Learned to Stop Worrying and Start Loving the French), 44 Brandeis L.J. 737 (2006) (arguing for abolition of elective share statutes).

"Now read me the part again where I disinherit everybody."
Drawing by Peter Arno.
© The New Yorker Collection 1940 Peter Arno from cartoonbank.com.

statutes typically provide the surviving spouse with an election. The spouse can take under the decedent's will or the spouse can renounce the will and take a fractional share of the decedent's estate.

The primary policy justification for the elective share is that the surviving spouse contributed to the decedent's acquisition of wealth and deserves to have a portion of it. On this view, the elective share implements the partnership theory of marriage. A second but more narrow policy justification is to provide the surviving spouse with adequate support. Although both the *partnership* and *support* theories justify the existence of *an* elective share, they are often in tension when it comes to designing *the* elective. To make this point more concrete, let us consider a few examples.

What percentage and of what property? The partnership theory militates toward awarding the surviving spouse one-half of the decedent's property acquired during the marriage, whereas the support theory often justifies a smaller share but would apply it to all the decedent's property. The support theory might also or alternatively justify the survivor receiving all of the decedent's property up to a set amount. Which of these approaches would provide the surviving spouse with a larger amount depends on the aggregate value of the decedent's property and how much of it was acquired during the marriage. The typical elective share is one-third of all of the decedent spouse's probate property plus certain nonprobate transfers. The marriage may have lasted one hour[3] or 50 years; the surviving spouse may have considerably more property than the decedent spouse; and the decedent spouse's property may have been acquired mainly before or during the marriage. In most separate property states, the elective share fraction, and the property to which it applies, is the same in all of these cases.

Is the election personal to the surviving spouse? Suppose *H* dies leaving a will that excludes *W*. Before *W* exercises her right of election, she dies. Should *W*'s personal representative be allowed to renounce *H*'s will and take a forced share? If the answer is Yes, then *W*'s elective share of *H*'s property will pass to *W*'s heirs or devisees. If the answer is No, then all of *H*'s property will pass to *H*'s devisees. Under the support theory, the answer should be No, because after her death *W* has no need for support. Under the partnership theory, the answer should be Yes, because *W* is entitled to direct the disposition of her share of the property accumulated by the marital partnership. In most states, and under UPC §2-212(a) (1990, rev. 2008), the answer is No.

Can the elective share be satisfied with a life interest in property held in trust? Under the support theory, the answer should be Yes, because the surviving spouse requires support only during life. Under the partnership theory, the answer should be No, because the surviving spouse should have complete dominion over the survivor's share of the partnership property. Today only two states, Connecticut and Rhode Island, limit the surviving spouse to a life estate.

Caution. There is no subject in this book on which there is more statutory variation than the surviving spouse's elective share. For a survey, see Jeffrey A. Schoenblum, 2008 Multistate Guide to Estate Planning at Table 6. Even most of the states adopting the 1969 or 1990 UPC provisions, which had the purpose of bringing uniformity, made important substantive changes in the elective share provisions. There are many reasons for this: different opinions about how much the surviving spouse deserves under various circumstances, including length of marriage, existence of children, and her own wealth; differences about what

---

3. Or less. In Estate of Neiderhiser, 2 Pa. D. & C.3d 302 (1977), the groom dropped dead during the marriage ceremony, after he and the bride had each said "I will" (equal in other marriage ceremonies to "I do"). The court held that marriage is a contract that becomes binding upon the exchange of vows, and the bride was entitled to an elective share in the groom's estate. In 2004, a woman in France was permitted to marry her deceased fiancé. The marriage was retroactive to the night before the groom's death. See Craig S. Smith, A Love That Transcends Death Is Blessed by the State, N.Y. Times, Feb. 19, 2004, at A4. For an argument that heirs and devisees ought to be allowed to challenge deathbed marriages, see Terry L. Turnipseed, How Do I Love Thee, Let Me Count the Days: Deathbed Marriages in America, 96 Ky. L.J. 275 (2007-2008).

property of the decedent should be subject to the elective share; and the inability of legislators to decide definitively what is the purpose of the elective share — partnership or support — and to carry this purpose through to its logical ends. See Laura A. Rosenbury, Two Ways to End a Marriage: Divorce or Death, 2005 Utah L. Rev. 1227, 1245-1261.

Uniform Probate Code (1990, as amended 2008)

ARTICLE II, PART 2
ELECTIVE SHARE OF SURVIVING SPOUSE

GENERAL COMMENT
THE PARTNERSHIP THEORY OF MARRIAGE

The partnership theory of marriage, sometimes also called the marital-sharing theory, is stated in various ways. Sometimes it is thought of "as an expression of the presumed intent of husbands and wives to pool their fortunes on an equal basis, share and share alike." Mary Ann Glendon, The Transformation of Family Law 131 (1989). Under this approach, the economic rights of each spouse are seen as deriving from an unspoken marital bargain under which the partners agree that each is to enjoy a half interest in the fruits of the marriage, i.e., in the property nominally acquired by and titled in the sole name of either partner during the marriage (other than in property acquired by gift or inheritance). A decedent who disinherits his or her surviving spouse is seen as having reneged on the bargain.[4] Sometimes the theory is expressed in restitutionary terms, a return-of-contribution notion. Under this approach, the law grants each spouse an entitlement to compensation for non-monetary contributions to the marital enterprise, as "a recognition of the activity of one spouse in the home and to compensate not only for this activity but for opportunities lost." Id. See also American Law Institute, Principles of Family Dissolution §4.09 Comment c (2002).

No matter how the rationale is expressed, the community-property system, including that version of community law promulgated in the Model Marital Property Act, recognizes the partnership theory, but it is sometimes thought that the common-law system denies it. In the ongoing marriage, it is true that the basic principle in the common-law (title-based) states is that marital status does not affect the ownership of property. The regime is one of separate property. Each

---

4. Judge Posner puts the point thusly, if anachronistically:

Another limitation on the power of a testator is the provision, found in the inheritance laws of all states, forbidding him to disinherit his widow completely. The limitation has an economic justification. The husband's wealth at death is likely, as we know, to be a product, in part, of the wife's work even if she never had any pecuniary income. Without statutory protection against disinheritance of her rightful share of her husband's estate, women could negotiate with their husbands for contractual protection (contracts to make bequests are enforceable). The statutory provision minimizes transaction costs. [Richard A. Posner, Economic Analysis of Law §18.8 (7th ed. 2007).]

— Eds.

spouse owns all that he or she earns. By contrast, in the community-property states, each spouse acquires an ownership interest in half the property the other earns during the marriage. By granting each spouse upon acquisition an immediate half interest in the earnings of the other, the community-property regimes directly recognize that the couple's enterprise is in essence collaborative.

The common-law states, however, also give effect or purport to give effect to the partnership theory when a marriage is dissolved by divorce. If the marriage ends in divorce, a spouse who sacrificed his or her financial-earning opportunities to contribute so-called domestic services to the marital enterprise (such as child rearing and homemaking) stands to be recompensed. All states now follow the equitable-distribution system upon divorce, under which "broad discretion [is given to] trial courts to assign to either spouse property acquired during the marriage, irrespective of title, taking into account the circumstances of the particular case and recognizing the value of the contributions of a nonworking spouse or homemaker to the acquisition of that property. Simply stated, the system of equitable distribution views marriage as essentially a shared enterprise or joint undertaking in the nature of a partnership to which both spouses contribute — directly and indirectly, financially and nonfinancialy — the fruits of which are distributable at divorce." John D. Gregory, The Law of Equitable Distribution ¶1.03, at p. 1-6 (1989).

The other situation in which spousal property rights figure prominently is disinheritance at death. . . . Elective-share law in the common-law states, however, has not caught up to the partnership theory of marriage. Under typical American elective-share law, including the elective share provided by the original [1969] Uniform Probate Code, a surviving spouse may claim a one-third share of the decedent's estate — not the 50 percent share of the couple's combined assets that the partnership theory would imply.

Although we speak of a surviving *spouse's* elective share, in the vast majority of cases it is in actuality a *widow's* share. As a matter of historical fact, men have earned more than women, but women tend to outlive men, so the prototypical situation to which the elective share is applicable is a propertied dead husband and poorer widow. Viewed in this manner, the real test of whether the elective-share system implements the partnership theory comes when the wife predeceases her husband — and it fails this test. If the wife dies before her husband, she cannot dispose of any of the marital partnership property titled in her husband's name. Suppose, for example, that H owns $500,000 in acquisitions from his earnings and W owns $100,000 from her earnings. If W dies first, W can dispose of only her $100,000 (and H may even have an elective share in that). If the couple had community property, W could dispose of her half of the $600,000 total by will.

NOTE: THE ESTATE TAX MARITAL DEDUCTION
AND THE DEPENDENCY OF WOMEN

In the 1940s, with a steep increase in federal income tax rates to finance World War II, the income tax advantages of community property became very clear in a "traditional" married couple consisting of a "breadwinner" and a "homemaker." The earnings of the breadwinner were taxable one-half to the breadwinner and one-half to the homemaker (who owned one-half). Because of the graduated step-up in brackets, the total tax on earnings split between a husband and wife each reporting $50,000 could be considerably less than the one tax on the breadwinner's earnings of $100,000 in a separate property state. Similarly, federal estate taxes in community property states were lower because only the breadwinner's half of the community property was taxable at the breadwinner's death whereas all the breadwinner's earned property was taxable at death in separate property states.

To reap these federal tax advantages, Michigan, Nebraska, Oklahoma, Oregon, and Pennsylvania adopted community property in the 1940s. Several more states had community property bills in the legislative hoppers. But this revolution in marital property was not to be. In 1948, Congress — a virtually all-male club[5] — intervened. Congress amended the Internal Revenue Code to eliminate the tax advantages of community property. The five states that had switched to community property repealed or abrogated their statutes. See Carolyn Jones, Split Income and Separate Spheres: Tax Law and Gender Roles in the 1940s, 6 Law & Hist. Rev. 259 (1988). See also Stephanie Hunter McMahon, To Save State Residents: States' Use of Community Property for Federal Tax Reduction, 1939-1947, 27 Law & Hist. Rev. (forthcoming 2009).

To remove the income tax advantage, Congress permitted married couples to split their earned income equally between them by filing a joint return.[6] Congress solved the estate tax problem by giving the husband an estate tax marital deduction, up to 50 percent of the value of his estate, for property left to his surviving wife in a form comparable to the outright ownership that a wife would have under community property.

The word "comparable" is the rub. To equate the position of the separate property wife exactly with the community property wife, the former must end up with *outright ownership* of one-half her husband's earnings. Yet, for Congress to provide a powerful tax incentive for a husband to devise his widow outright ownership of half of his property was highly objectionable to (mostly male) estate planners and trust officers in separate property states. They thought the

5. In the 80th Congress beginning in January 1948, there were 96 senators (all men) and 435 Representatives (6 women). Congress remains a mostly male club. At the opening of the 111th Congress in January 2009, only 17% of the members of the Senate and the House of Representatives were women (though Nancy Pelosi, a woman, was the Speaker of the House).

6. Community property still has an income tax advantage in that upon the death of the first spouse all of the community property gets a stepped-up basis (eliminating any potential income tax on appreciation in the property), even though only one-half is included in the decedent spouse's estate tax return. With separate property, only the property included in the decedent spouse's estate receives a stepped-up basis.

husband should have the right to put the widow's share in trust for her without suffering a tax disadvantage. The thinking was that a homemaker, without business experience, might be incapable of managing her inherited wealth. Never mind that widows in California, Texas, and other community property states had long been legally entrusted with managing their property after their husbands' deaths, with no noticeable adverse consequences to them.[7] Congress effected a compromise: If a husband gave his wife a *life estate* (support) with the *power to appoint* the property to anyone she wished at her death (equivalent to complete ownership at her death), this arrangement would be deemed comparable to a fee simple and would qualify for the marital deduction.

In 1982, the federal estate tax marital deduction was changed to incorporate a completely new principle: Interspousal transfers will not be taxed at all, provided the donor spouse gives the donee spouse at least a life estate in the property. A gift of a fee simple or its purported equivalent (a life estate coupled with a general power of appointment) is no longer required for the marital deduction. The marital deduction is unlimited in amount.

The earlier version of the marital deduction provided a tax incentive to the donor spouse to give the surviving spouse support and an ownership share of the decedent spouse's property (even though complete control of that share could be postponed until the surviving spouse's death). The current marital deduction requires only that the donor spouse create a trust giving his surviving spouse support for life to avoid transfer taxation (called a QTIP trust). Thus, viewed through the precise eye of the marital deduction provisions only, the homemaker (or the spouse with lower earnings) appears further now than before from being treated as well as her counterpart in community property states. Professor Mary Moers Wenig put it crisply: "With QTIP, the new federal law of dower was born." Mary M. Wenig, "Taxing Marriage," 6 S. Cal. Rev. L. & Women's Stud. 561 (1997).

For further discussion, see the debate between Professors Gerzog, Zelenak, and Dodge: Wendy C. Gerzog, The Marital Deduction QTIP Provisions: Illogical and Degrading to Women, 5 UCLA Women's L.J. 301 (1995); Lawrence Zelenak, Taking Critical Tax Theory Seriously, 76 N.C. L. Rev. 1521 (1998); Wendy C. Gerzog, The Illogical and Sexist QTIP Provisions: I Just Can't Say It Ain't So, 76 N.C. L. Rev. 1597 (1998); Joseph M. Dodge, A Feminist Perspective on the QTIP Trust and the Unlimited Marital Deduction, 76 N.C. L. Rev. 1729 (1998). See also Donna Litman, The Interrelationship Between the Elective Share and the Marital Deduction, 40 Real Prop., Prob. & Trust J. 539 (2005); Mary L. Fellows, Wills and Trusts: "The Kingdom of the Fathers," 10 J.L. & Inequality 137 (1991); Mary M. Wenig, The Marital Property Law of Connecticut: Past, Present and Future, 1990 Wis. L. Rev. 807.

---

7. But see the "widow's election," page 510.

b.   Same-Sex Marriage and Domestic Partners

Marriage brings a variety of legal and economic consequences, mostly beneficial, to a surviving spouse. A married partner may be entitled to Social Security
benefits based on the other partner's earnings, to pension rights from the other
partner's job, and to an elective share of the other partner's estate. Transfers to a
married partner can also qualify for federal estate and gift tax marital deductions. Unmarried surviving partners, even those in a relationship that approximates marriage, have none of these benefits.

In Estate of Cooper, 592 N.Y.S.2d 797 (App. Div. 1993), appeal dismissed by
624 N.E.2d 696 (N.Y. 1993), the decedent devised all his estate to his surviving
same-sex partner except for certain real property, comprising 80 percent of the
value of the estate, which the decedent gave to a former lover. The surviving partner petitioned to elect against the decedent's will, reasoning that he lived in "a
spousal-type situation" with the decedent for more than three and half years.
"Except for the fact that we were of the same sex, our lives were identical to that
of a husband and wife. We kept a common home; we shared expenses; our friends
recognized us as spouses; we had a physical relationship." The petitioner argued
that it was unconstitutional for the state to deny him a spouse's elective share,
even though he did not formally qualify as a spouse, on the theory that the state's
failure to recognize same-sex marriage was unconstitutional. The court denied
the petition. But see Estate of Ranftle, N.Y.L.J., Feb. 4, 2009, at 34 (N.Y. Surrogate's Court decision recognizing out-of-state same-sex marriage).

More recently, public opinion has begun moving toward a consensus in favor
of legal recognition for same-sex couples (see page 78). As this book went to press,
same-sex marriage was recognized in Connecticut, Iowa, New Hampshire,
Maine, Massachusetts, and Vermont. Hence, in these states a surviving spouse of
a same-sex marriage is entitled to an elective share of the decedent spouse's
estate. Civil unions with spousal-like rights for the surviving partner are recognized in California[8] and New Jersey. Similar rights for domestic partners are
recognized in District of Columbia, Hawaii (called reciprocal beneficiaries),
Nevada, Oregon, and Washington. Benefits under federal law, however, continue
to be denied to same-sex married couples.

For further discussion, including treatment of the criteria for qualifying as a
domestic partner and the conflicts of law problems arising from the patchwork of
state laws on same-sex marriage, civil unions, and domestic partnerships, see
pages 77-79.

---

8. For five months in 2008, same-sex marriage was recognized in California. See footnote 6 at page 78.

c. Incompetent Surviving Spouse

Should the representative of an incompetent surviving spouse be permitted to take a forced share on behalf of the surviving spouse? Under the support theory, if the incompetent surviving spouse does not need the property for her support, the representative should be barred from doing so. Under the partnership theory, the representative should be entitled to do so because the forced share represents the surviving spouse's portion of the marital partnership property, which ultimately should pass to the surviving spouse's heirs or devisees.

In re Estate of Cross
Supreme Court of Ohio, 1996
664 N.E.2d 905

On August 23, 1992, Carroll R. Cross died testate leaving his entire estate to his son, Ray G. Cross, who was not a child of the surviving spouse. At the time of his death, Beulah Cross, the surviving spouse, was apparently close to eighty years old, was suffering from Alzheimer's disease, and was living in a nursing home paid by Medicaid. Due to Mrs. Cross's incompetency, she was unable to make an election under R.C. 2106.01 as to whether she should take against her husband's will. Therefore, pursuant to R.C. 2106.08, the probate court appointed a commissioner, who investigated the matter and determined that the court elect for Mrs. Cross to take her intestate share under R.C. 2105.06 and against the will. As a result of this election, Mrs. Cross would receive twenty-five thousand dollars in spousal allowance and one-half of the net estate, which was approximately nine thousand dollars. Following a hearing before a referee, Judge John E. Corrigan of the probate court elected for Mrs. Cross to take against decedent's will.

Decedent's son appealed the probate court's decision. While the appeal was pending, Mrs. Cross died. The court of appeals, with one judge dissenting, reversed, finding that the election to take against the will was against Mrs. Cross's best interest and was not necessary to provide her adequate support, since the cost of her nursing home care was already covered by Medicaid. Rosemary D. Durkin, Administrator of the Estate of Beulah Cross, filed a notice of appeal to this court, as did intervenor, Cuyahoga County Board of Commissioners.

SWEENEY, J.   At issue in this case is whether Judge Corrigan abused his discretion in electing for decedent Carroll Cross's surviving spouse, who depended solely upon Medicaid benefits for her support and care, to take against the will and under R.C. 2105.06. For the following reasons, we uphold the election made by Judge Corrigan for Mrs. Cross, and reverse the decision of the court of appeals.

Where a surviving spouse is under a legal disability, the probate court is given the authority under R.C. 2106.08 to appoint a suitable person to ascertain the surviving spouse's adequate support needs and to compare the value of the surviving spouse's rights under the will with the value of her rights under the statute of descent and distribution. R.C. 2106.08 further provides that the court may elect for the surviving spouse to take against the will and under R.C. 2105.06 "only if it finds, after taking into consideration the other available resources and the age, probable life expectancy, physical and mental condition, and present and reasonably anticipated future needs of the surviving spouse, that the election to take under 2105.06 of the Revised Code is necessary to provide adequate support for the surviving spouse during his life expectancy."

Prior to the amendment of former R.C. 2107.45 (now renumbered R.C. 2106.08), effective December 17, 1986, the probate court made its determination of whether to elect to take under the will or against the will based upon which provision was "better for such spouse." In essence, the court based its decision on which provision was more mathematically advantageous to the surviving spouse. See In re Estate of Cook, 249 N.E.2d 799, 802 (Ohio 1969). However, in passing R.C. 2106.08, the General Assembly moved away from a simple mathematical calculation, taking into consideration such factors as other available resources, age, life expectancy, physical and mental condition, and the surviving spouse's present and future needs. In either case, the probate court must ascertain what the surviving spouse would have done for her financial benefit had she been competent to make the decision herself. See In re Estate of Hinklin, 586 N.E.2d 130, 132 (Ohio App. 1989).

In this case, the court of appeals . . . , in striking down the election made by Judge Corrigan for Mrs. Cross to take against the will, . . . ignored Medicaid eligibility requirements. . . .

[E]ligibility for Medicaid benefits is dependent upon a recipient's income or available resources. Ohio Adm. Code 5101:1-39-05. The term "resources" includes "property owned separately by the person, his share of family property, and property devised to him from a parent or spouse." Ohio Adm. Code 5101:1-39-05(A)(4). This also encompasses "those resources in which an applicant/recipient has a legal interest and the legal ability to use or dispose of. . . ." Ohio Adm. Code 5101:1-39-05(A)(8).

Mrs. Cross clearly had a legal interest in and the ability to use or dispose of her intestate share under her right to take against the will. Thus, she had available to her a potential resource for Medicaid eligibility purposes. This is critical to the facts presented, since the Medicaid rules specifically state that the nonutilization of available income renders a Medicaid applicant or recipient ineligible for benefits. According to Ohio Adm. Code 5101:1-39-08(A)(2), "A basic tenet of public assistance is that all income must be considered in determining the need of an individual for public assistance. Potential income must be explored prior to approving medicaid. An individual who does not avail himself of a potential income is presumed to fail to do so in order to make himself eligible for public assistance. Such nonutilization of income available upon request constitutes ineligibility . . . ."

As applied to this case, in order to maintain Mrs. Cross's Medicaid eligibility and to continue to have her nursing home expenses provided for by public assistance, Judge Corrigan was required to elect for Mrs. Cross to take against the will and to receive her intestate share. Otherwise, if the election was to take under the will, Mrs. Cross would receive no income and would be deemed ineligible for benefits for failing to avail herself of a potential income. Thus, the election to take against the will was necessary for Mrs. Cook's future support and met the requirements of R.C. 2106.08. We find that the probate court, by appointing a commissioner to investigate the matter and by electing for Mrs. Cross to take against the will, was correct in its actions. Through his decision, Judge Corrigan acted in the best interests of this surviving spouse and protected the interests of all litigants coming before him. Consequently, Judge Corrigan did not abuse his discretion in electing for Mrs. Cross to take against the will.

Accordingly, we reverse the judgment of the court of appeals and reinstate the judgment of the probate court.

NOTES AND QUESTIONS

1. The guardian of an *incompetent surviving spouse* can elect against the decedent's will if it is in the "best interests" of the spouse. A minority of states hold that the guardian should elect to take against the will if it is to the surviving spouse's economic benefit, calculated mathematically. A majority of states hold, as did the court in *Cross*, that all the surrounding facts and circumstances should be taken into consideration by the probate court. The majority view allows the guardian to take into account the preservation of the decedent's estate plan and whether the surviving spouse would have wanted to abide by her dead spouse's will.

The 1969 UPC took a different approach. Section 2-203 provided that the probate court, acting for an incompetent, could order election against the spouse's will only "after finding that exercise is necessary to provide adequate support for the protected person during his probable life expectancy." This implements the view that the elective share is for the support of the surviving spouse, not the protection of the surviving spouse's partnership share.

The 1990 UPC continued the view that the elective share is for support when the spouse is incompetent, but it implemented this view in a new way. UPC §2-212 (1990, rev. 2008) provides that if a representative elects the elective share for an incompetent surviving spouse, the portion of the elective share that exceeds what the decedent spouse provided for the survivor must be placed in a *custodial trust* for the benefit of the surviving spouse. The trustee is given the power to expend income and principal for the surviving spouse's support, but upon the spouse's death the trustee must transfer the trust property to the residuary devisees under the will of the predeceased spouse or to the predeceased spouse's heirs. Thus, the decedent spouse can prevent an incompetent surviving spouse's representative from upsetting the decedent's estate plan. The official comment to §2-212 says its purpose is "to assure that that part of the elective share is devoted to the personal economic benefit and needs of the surviving spouse, but not to the economic benefit of the surviving spouse's heirs or devisees."

Why does a surviving spouse who happens to be incompetent at the decedent's death deserve, in recognition of the survivor's contribution to the marriage, only support and not an ownership share that will pass to the survivor's heirs or devisees?

Similar questions arise in the case of a *surviving spouse who dies* before exercising the right of election. In most states, and under UPC §2-212, the right of election may only be exercised by the surviving spouse or a representative of the surviving spouse during the surviving spouse's life. In Wilson v. Wilson, 197 P.3d 1141 (Or. App. 2008), the court held that a claim for an elective share filed by a representative on behalf of an incompetent surviving spouse was extinguished by the death of the surviving spouse. The court reasoned that the representative's authority to claim the surviving spouse's elective share was dependent on the surviving spouse's need for support, which ended with her death.

2. *Creditors and Medicaid eligibility.* The majority rule is that ordinary creditors of the surviving spouse cannot compel the surviving spouse to take a forced share. See Aragon v. Snyder, 715 A.2d 1045 (N.J. Super. 1998). However, the value of the elective share will be counted toward the surviving spouse's "available resources" in determining the surviving spouse's eligibility for Medicaid. See I.G. v. Department of Human Services, 900 A.2d 840 (N.J. App. 2006). As a result, in most cases involving election by a representative for an incompetent spouse, the need to preserve benefits eligibility drives the result.

For further discussion of the elective share and Medicaid eligibility, see Julia Belian, Medicaid, Elective Shares, and the Ghosts of Tenures Past, 38 Creighton L. Rev. 1111 (2005). For more on the use of trusts to preserve eligibility for governmental benefits, see pages 638-641.

3. *Abandonment.* In a minority of states the elective share is denied to individuals who abandoned or refused to support the deceased spouse. See, e.g., N.Y. Est. Trusts & Powers Law §5-1.2 (2008). Proving abandonment, however, can be tricky. Compare Purce v. Patterson, 654 S.E.2d 885 (Va. 2008) (finding that husband abandoned his wife, even though they mutually agreed to separate, because husband showed a lack of support for wife before and after the separation), with In re Riefberg's Estate, 446 N.E.2d 424 (N.Y. 1983) (finding that wife, who excluded husband from marital home and lived separately, did not abandon husband).

If the rationale for the elective share is sharing the economic fruits of marriage, should one spouse lose that share upon leaving the other? Should the elective share apply only to property the abandoned spouse owned on the date of abandonment? In most community property states, if the couple separates, the earnings of both spouses continue to be community property until divorce. In California, however, earnings acquired after separation are not community property.

d. Property Subject to the Elective Share

The original elective share statutes gave the surviving spouse a fractional share, usually one-third, of the decedent's *estate*. In this context, the term estate was understood to mean the *probate estate*. With the increasing importance of nonprobate modes of transfer (see Chapter 6), however, the question arose whether the elective share should be extended to nonprobate transfers. Consider the following case study:

> *Case 5. W*, a successful lawyer, wishes to leave the bulk of her fortune to her daughter, *D*, rather than to her tedious husband, *H*, even though she amassed this fortune during the marriage. Knowing of *H*'s right of election against her probate estate, *W* transfers $2.9 million to *X* in trust to pay income to *W* for life and the remainder to *D* on *W*'s death. *W* retains the right to revoke the trust. *W* then dies without having done so. *W*'s will leaves her entire probate estate, worth $100,000, to *H*. Can *H* elect to take against the $2.9 million that, under the terms of the trust, will pass outside of probate to *D*?

In Case 5, unless *H*'s forced share reaches *W*'s revocable trust, it is possible for *W* to achieve a near disinheritance of *H* while still leaving him *all* of her probate estate. Notice also that if nonprobate transfers are reachable by the elective share, then the surviving spouse is protected from disinheritance by nonprobate transfers even if the decedent dies intestate.

In this section we consider (1) the judicial responses to the question whether nonprobate transfers may be reached by the elective share, then (2) some illustrative legislative responses, and finally (3) the approaches of the 1969 and 1990 Uniform Probate Codes, the latter as revised in 2008.

(1) JUDICIAL RESPONSES

Sullivan v. Burkin

Supreme Judicial Court of Massachusetts, 1984
460 N.E.2d 572

WILKINS, J.[9]   Mary A. Sullivan, the widow of Ernest G. Sullivan, has exercised her right, under G.L. c. 191, §15, to take a share of her husband's estate. By this action, she seeks a determination that assets held in an inter vivos trust created by her husband during the marriage should be considered as part of the estate in determining that share. A judge of the Probate Court for the county of Suffolk rejected the widow's claim and entered judgment dismissing the complaint. The widow appealed, and, on July 12, 1983, a panel of the Appeals Court reported the case to this court.

In September, 1973, Ernest G. Sullivan executed a deed of trust under which he transferred real estate to himself as sole trustee. The net income of the trust was payable to him during his life and the trustee was instructed to pay to him all or such part of the principal of the trust estate as he might request in writing from time to time. He retained the right to revoke the trust at any time. On his death,

---

9. Justice Herbert Wilkins, who was one of the intellectual leaders of the Massachusetts court in recent decades, made a specialty of trust cases. He wrote the opinion in Sullivan v. Burkin, as well as Beals v. State Str. Bank & Tr. Co., page 813; Loring v. Marshall, page 832; and Dewire v. Haveles, page 863. From 1996 through 1999, Justice Wilkins was Chief Justice, a position once held by his father. — Eds.

the successor trustee is directed to pay the principal and any undistributed income equally to the defendants, George F. Cronin, Sr., and Harold J. Cronin, if they should survive him, which they did. There were no witnesses to the execution of the deed of trust, but the husband acknowledged his signatures before a notary public, separately, as donor and as trustee.

The husband died on April 27, 1981, while still trustee of the inter vivos trust. He left a will in which he stated that he "intentionally neglected to make any provision for my wife, Mary A. Sullivan and my grandson, Mark Sullivan." He directed that, after the payment of debts, expenses, and all estate taxes levied by reason of his death, the residue of his estate should be paid over to the trustee of the inter vivos trust. The defendants George F. Cronin, Sr., and Harold J. Cronin were named coexecutors of the will. The defendant Burkin is successor trustee of the inter vivos trust. On October 21, 1981, the wife filed a claim, pursuant to G.L. c. 191, §15, for a portion of the estate.[10]

Although it does not appear in the record, the parties state in their briefs that Ernest G. Sullivan and Mary A. Sullivan had been separated for many years. We do know that in 1962 the wife obtained a court order providing for her temporary support. No final action was taken in that proceeding. The record provides no information about the value of any property owned by the husband at his death or about the value of any assets held in the inter vivos trust. At oral argument, we were advised that the husband owned personal property worth approximately $15,000 at his death and that the only asset in the trust was a house in Boston which was sold after the husband's death for approximately $85,000.

As presented in the complaint, and perhaps as presented to the motion judge, the wife's claim was simply that the inter vivos trust was an invalid testamentary disposition and that the trust assets "constitute assets of the estate" of Ernest G. Sullivan. There is no suggestion that the wife argued initially that, even if the trust were not testamentary, she had a special claim as a widow asserting her rights under G.L. c. 191, §15. If the wife is correct that the trust was an ineffective testamentary disposition, the trust assets would be part of the husband's probate estate. In that event, we would not have to consider any special consequences of the wife's election under G.L. c. 191, §15, or, in the words of the Appeals Court, "the present vitality" of Kerwin v. Donaghy, 59 N.E.2d 299 (Mass. 1945).

We conclude, however, that the trust was not testamentary in character and that the husband effectively created a valid inter vivos trust. . . . A trust with remainder interests given to others on the settlor's death is not invalid as a testamentary disposition simply because the settlor retained a broad power to

10. As relevant to this case, G.L. c. 191, §15, provides:

The surviving husband or wife of a deceased person . . . within six months after the probate of the will of such deceased, may file in the registry of probate a writing signed by him or by her . . . claiming such portion of the estate of the deceased as he or she is given the right to claim under this section, and if the deceased left issue, he or she shall thereupon take one third of the personal and one third of the real property . . . except that . . . if he or she would thus take real and personal property to an amount exceeding twenty-five thousand dollars in value, he or she shall receive, in addition to that amount, only the income during his or her life of the excess of his or her share of such estate above that amount, the personal property to be held in trust and the real property vested in him or her for life, from the death of the deceased. . . .

modify or revoke the trust, the right to receive income, and the right to invade principal during his life. . . . We believe that the law of the Commonwealth is correctly represented by the statement in Restatement (Second) of Trusts §57, Comment h (1959), that a trust is "not testamentary and invalid for failure to comply with the requirements of the Statute of Wills merely because the settlor-trustee reserves a beneficial life interest and power to revoke and modify the trust. The fact that as trustee he controls the administration of the trust does not invalidate it."[11]

We come then to the question whether, even if the trust was not testamentary on general principles, the widow has special interests which should be recognized. Courts in this country have differed considerably in their reasoning and in their conclusions in passing on this question. . . .

The rule of Kerwin v. Donaghy, 59 N.E.2d 299 (Mass. 1945), is that

> [t]he right of a wife to waive her husband's will, and take, with certain limitations, "the same portion of the property of the deceased, real and personal, that . . . she would have taken if the deceased had died intestate" (G.L. [Ter. Ed.] c. 191, §15), does not extend to personal property that has been conveyed by the husband in his lifetime and does not form part of his estate at his death. Fiske v. Fiske, 53 N.E. 916 (Mass. 1899). Shelton v. Sears, 73 N.E. 666 (Mass. 1905). In this Commonwealth a husband has an absolute right to dispose of any or all of his personal property in his lifetime, without the knowledge or consent of his wife, with the result that it will not form part of his estate for her to share under the statute of distributions (G.L. [Ter. Ed.] c. 190, §§1, 2), under his will, or by virtue of a waiver of his will. That is true even though his sole purpose was to disinherit her.

In the *Kerwin* case, we applied the rule to deny a surviving spouse the right to reach assets the deceased spouse had placed in an inter vivos trust of which the settlor's daughter by a previous marriage was trustee and over whose assets he had a general power of appointment. The rule of Kerwin v. Donaghy has been adhered to in this Commonwealth for almost forty years and was adumbrated even earlier.[12] The bar has been entitled reasonably to rely on that rule in advising clients. In the area of property law, the retroactive invalidation of an established principle is to be undertaken with great caution. We conclude that, whether or not Ernest G. Sullivan established the inter vivos trust in order to defeat his wife's right to take her statutory share in the assets placed in the trust and even though he had a general power of appointment over the trust assets, Mary A. Sullivan obtained no right to share in the assets of that trust when she made her election under G.L. c. 191, §15.

We announce for the future that, as to any inter vivos trust created or amended after the date of this opinion, we shall no longer follow the rule announced in

---

11. Thus the Massachusetts court, like other courts, agrees with Farkas v. Williams, page 398, that a revocable inter vivos trust is valid to pass property at death without Wills Act formalities. — Eds.

12. In early opinions, this court considered an intent to deny inheritance rights to be a ground for invalidating an inter vivos transfer, but in the first part of this century it abandoned that position. . . .

Opinions in this Commonwealth, and generally elsewhere, considering the rights of a surviving spouse to a share in assets transferred by the deceased spouse to an inter vivos trust have analyzed the question on grounds of public policy, as if establishing common law principles. These opinions have not relied in any degree on what the Legislature may have intended by granting a surviving spouse certain rights in the "estate" of a deceased spouse.

Kerwin v. Donaghy. There have been significant changes since 1945 in public policy considerations bearing on the right of one spouse to treat his or her property as he or she wishes during marriage. The interests of one spouse in the property of the other have been substantially increased upon the dissolution of a marriage by divorce. We believe that, when a marriage is terminated by the death of one spouse, the rights of the surviving spouse should not be so restricted as they are by the rule in Kerwin v. Donaghy. It is neither equitable nor logical to extend to a divorced spouse greater rights in the assets of an inter vivos trust created and controlled by the other spouse than are extended to a spouse who remains married until the death of his or her spouse.

The rule we now favor would treat as part of "the estate of the deceased" for the purposes of G.L. c. 191, §15, assets of an inter vivos trust created during the marriage by the deceased spouse over which he or she alone had a general power of appointment, exercisable by deed or by will. This objective test would involve no consideration of the motive or intention of the spouse in creating the trust. We would not need to engage in a determination of "whether the [spouse] has in good faith divested himself [or herself] of ownership of his [or her] property or has made an illusory transfer" (Newman v. Dore, 9 N.E.2d 966 (N.Y. 1937)) or with the factual question whether the spouse "intended to surrender complete dominion over the property" (Staples v. King, 433 A.2d 407, 411 (Me. 1981)). Nor would we have to participate in the rather unsatisfactory process of determining whether the inter vivos trust was, on some standard, "colorable," "fraudulent," or "illusory."

What we have announced as a rule for the future hardly resolves all the problems that may arise. There may be a different rule if some or all of the trust assets were conveyed to such a trust by a third person. . . . If the surviving spouse assented to the creation of the inter vivos trust, perhaps the rule we announce would not apply. We have not discussed which assets should be used to satisfy a surviving spouse's claim. We have not discussed the question whether a surviving spouse's interest in the intestate estate of a deceased spouse should reflect the value of assets held in an inter vivos trust created by the intestate spouse over which he or she had a general power of appointment. That situation and the one before us, however, do not seem readily distinguishable. . . . Nor have we dealt with other assets not passing by will, such as a trust created before the marriage or insurance policies over which a deceased spouse had control.

The question of the rights of a surviving spouse in the estate of a deceased spouse, using the word "estate" in its broad sense, is one that can best be handled by legislation. See Uniform Probate Code, §§2-201, 2-202, 8 U.L.A. 74-75 (1983). See also Uniform Marital Property Act, §18 (1983), which adopts the concept of community property as to "marital property." But, until it is, the answers to these problems will "be determined in the usual way through the decisional process." Tucker v. Badoian, 384 N.E.2d 1195, 1201 (Mass. 1978) (Kaplan, J., concurring).

We affirm the judgment of the Probate Court dismissing the plaintiff's complaint.

So ordered.

BONGAARDS v. MILLEN, 793 N.E.2d 335 (Mass. 2003): In 2003, the Supreme Judicial Court of Massachusetts faced one of the key questions left open by its decision in *Sullivan*, namely, what of a trust created by a third party over which the decedent spouse had a general power of appointment?

Jean Bongaards was the life tenant of a trust established by her mother. Under the terms of the trust, Jean had a limited power of appointment over the remainder, and during her life she could have terminated the trust, whereupon the entire corpus would have been paid to her (i.e., Jean held a general lifetime power of appointment). Jean never exercised her right to terminate. Instead, ten days before her death, she appointed the trust remainder to her sister Nina. Having been left out of Jean's will,[13] her husband George claimed an elective share against her estate. Reasoning that the trust corpus, which included the $1.4 million apartment building in which they lived,[14] would have been treated as marital property subject to equitable division on divorce, George argued that it should be included in her estate for determining the amount of his elective share.

Rejecting George's claim, the court held that "the trust property at issue here is . . . not subject to the plaintiff's elective share for the simple reason that the trust was created by a third party, [Jean's mother], and not by Jean. The rule announced in *Sullivan* applies only to assets of a trust 'created during the marriage by the deceased spouse.'" The court continued:

> Indeed, there does not appear to be any ambiguity in the Legislature's use of the term "estate of the deceased" in G.L. c. 191, §15. In context, "estate of the deceased" refers to the decedent's probate estate — the will being waived by the surviving spouse would ordinarily be the operative instrument that would divide the decedent's probate estate, and a spouse dissatisfied with the will's provisions for that division could instead opt for the statutory division of that same "estate." Absent any ambiguity in the term "estate of the deceased" . . . , there would be no basis to interpret that term to mean anything other than the decedent's probate estate.
>
> Regardless whether changing times and the modern array of possible will substitutes may make it advisable to expand the term beyond the mere probate estate, we are not at liberty to update statutes merely because, in our view, they no longer suffice to serve their intended

---

13. Jean Bongaards explicitly disinherited her husband: "My failure to provide in this will for my husband, George Bongaards, is intentional, and not due to accident or mistake, and is not a reflection of any lack of regard or appreciation on my part." SJC Case Challenges Antiquated Inheritance Law, Boston Globe, Feb. 9, 2003, at B1.

14. George did receive a summer house on Cape Cod because he and Jean had owned it in joint tenancy. And a $39,905 bank account was also included in her estate, subject to George's elective share. Bongaards v. Millen, 2003 WL 25316205 (Mass. Prob. & Fam. Sept. 23, 2003) (trial order). But the apartment building in which they had lived for 30 years passed instead to Jean's sister Nina and Nina's children.

The trust at issue was created by Jean's mother, Josephine D'Amore, an Italian immigrant and single mother. Although Josephine spoke English, she could not read it. But she could cook. She owned a successful restaurant in the North End of Boston, which enabled her to buy substantial buildings and put them in separate trusts for each of her six children. After George and Jean moved into the first floor of Jean's building in 1965, George paid rent to Josephine, and after Josephine's death, to Jean. The lawyer for Jean's sister Nina told a reporter that the property was always meant to stay in Josephine's family: "George Bongaards knew that his whole life. He admitted it repeatedly in his depositions, yet when his wife died, he ignored that and decided to try and get a piece of the building." Boston Globe, Feb. 9, 2003, supra.

purpose. This is particularly true when the Legislature itself has recently considered numerous proposals to modernize the elective share statute, with differing approaches regarding how the elective share should be harmonized with contemporary concepts of marriage and property, and has yet to adopt any of them. See Note, Marital Property Reform in Massachusetts: A Choice for the New Millennium, 34 New Eng. L. Rev. 261, 270-271, 337-338 (1999) (outlining various proposals to reform elective share statute submitted to Legislature between 1991 and 1999). That the current version of the statute is woefully inadequate to satisfy modern notions of a decedent spouse's obligation to support the surviving spouse or modern notions of marital property does not authorize us to tinker with the statute's provisions in order to remedy those inadequacies. It is up to the Legislature to choose between the complex — and apparently controversial — options for modernizing this outdated scheme, not up to us to modernize it piecemeal according to our views of what remedies should be made available to a disinherited spouse.

It could be argued that *Sullivan* already represents such a tinkering with the definition of "estate" for purposes of G.L. c. 191, §15, and that ordinary principles of statutory construction should therefore not prevent us from continuing the process begun in *Sullivan*. However, that justification for a significant expansion of the term "estate" in G.L. c. 191, §15, ignores the fact that *Sullivan* merely closed a loophole through which spouses had been able to evade §15. As articulated in *Sullivan*, what was to remain part of the "estate" subject to the elective share was property that previously belonged to the deceased spouse. But for the spouse's artificially distancing the property from that "estate" by the creation of a trust while still, for all practical purposes, retaining absolute control over and use of the property, the property would have been part of the deceased spouse's probate, and hence the elective share, "estate." In other words, *Sullivan* kept in the elective share "estate" property that would ordinarily have been in that "estate," refusing to give effect to a spouse's attempt to remove that property from the elective share "estate" but still retain access to it by means of a "trust."

It is one thing for this court to plug loopholes to prevent a spouse's evasion of the elective share statute. It is quite another to expand the reach of the elective share statute itself and, by so doing, frustrate the intent of a third party who is a stranger to the marriage. The recognition in *Sullivan* that property in a trust created by a third party presents "a different situation" from property in a trust "created during the marriage by the deceased spouse," was not some hypertechnical distinction. A third party has no obligation to support someone else's spouse, and property owned by a third party has never been part of someone else's spouse's elective share "estate." Thus, when a third party places that property in a trust, the property is not being removed — artificially or otherwise — from that elective share "estate." The property was never in that "estate" in the first place. . . . The proposed revision of the definition of "estate" to include trust property that was never, prior to the trust's creation, the property of either spouse is not designed merely to prevent evasion of the elective share statute. Rather, it would represent a judicially created expansion of the reach of the statute. It goes far beyond the modest prophylactic measure announced in *Sullivan* and cannot be justified as a mere "extension" of *Sullivan*.

NOTES AND PROBLEMS

1. In Sullivan v. Burkin, the court rejected several tests applied in various states to determine which nonprobate transfers are subject to the surviving spouse's election. The first, and most famous, is the *illusory transfer* test laid down by Newman v. Dore, 9 N.E.2d 966 (N.Y. 1937) (now superseded by statute in New York, see page 495). In *Newman*, the court upheld a widow's claim that a revocable inter vivos trust established by her husband during their marriage was

"illusory" and invalid.[15] After some years of uncertainty and confusion about the holding in *Newman*, courts following *Newman* held that an "illusory" revocable trust is a valid trust, but it counts as part of the decedent's assets subject to the elective share; the trustee may have to contribute some of the trust assets to make up the elective share. The illusory transfer test is the most widely adopted of the judicial tests for subjecting nonprobate property to the elective share. See Dreher v. Dreher, 634 S.E.2d 646 (S.C. 2006) (applying the illusory transfer test, as codified by state statute).

What kind of ownership rights retained by the decedent make a transfer illusory was left unclear in *Newman* and was little clarified in later cases. The key is said to be the amount of control retained by the decedent spouse. See Sieh v. Sieh, 713 N.W.2d 194 (Iowa 2006). But how much is too much? Are any of the following nonprobate transfers illusory? Would it matter if these property arrangements were made before or after marriage?

(a) *H* owns an insurance policy naming his two daughters as beneficiaries. *H* has the rights to cash in the policy and to change the beneficiaries.

(b) *H* has an account with a stock brokerage house, which holds all his stocks as custodian. *H* has named his daughters as payable-on-death beneficiaries of the account.

(c) *H* has two bank accounts: one naming his daughters as payable-on-death beneficiaries, and a second a joint account with his daughters.

(d) *H* bought Blackacre and took title with his daughters in joint tenancy.

2.   Some states adopted an *intent to defraud* test. In determining whether the decedent intended to defraud his surviving spouse of her elective share, some look for subjective intent. Others look for objective evidence of intent: the control retained by the transferor, the amount of time between the transfer and death, and the degree to which the surviving spouse is left without an interest in the decedent's property or other means of support.

Still other states consider whether the decedent had a *present donative intent* to transfer an interest in the property. This test focuses not on what the transferor retained, but on whether the transferor intended to make a present gift. Factors similar to those weighed in the intent-to-defraud test appear to be used in applying this test.

In Karsenty v. Schoukroun, 959 A.2d 1147 (Md. 2008), the court adopted a multifactor balancing test absorbing elements from the various judicial approaches, effectively assuring that future results will be highly fact-sensitive. The lesson: Lawyers should advise clients to exercise extreme caution in making nonprobate transfers without the other spouse's consent that might have the effect of diminishing the other spouse's elective share.

---

15. The facts of Newman v. Dore are unusual. The husband was 80 and his wife in her 30s when they married. After four years of marriage, the wife sued for separation on the grounds that she could no longer abide her husband's perverted sexual habits. The record did not make clear what the octogenarian's alleged perversions were, though a newspaper story indicates that he received monkey glands by surgical transplant. Indignant over his wife's allegations, the husband instructed his lawyer to disinherit her. The separation action was still pending at his death. See Elias Clark, Louis Lusky, Arthur W. Murphy, Mark L. Ascher, and Grayson M.P. McCouch, Gratuitous Transfers 146-147 (5th ed. 2007).

3.   In most states, a *revocable trust* created by the decedent spouse is included in determining the surviving spouse's elective share, a position endorsed by Restatement (Third) of Property: Wills and Other Donative Transfers §9.1, cmt. j (2003). In a few holdouts, revocable trusts and other such nonprobate transfers are not subject to the elective share. See Jeffrey A. Schoenblum, 2008 Multistate Guide to Estate Planning at Table 6.03.

4.   Suppose *H* and *W*, both 65 years of age, live in State Red. In State Red, a surviving spouse can include a revocable inter vivos trust created by the decedent in the decedent's assets subject to the elective share. In State Blue, a revocable inter vivos trust is not reachable by the surviving spouse. *H* takes a trip to State Blue and sets up a revocable inter vivos trust there, naming a State Blue bank as trustee. The trust instrument provides that the law of State Blue shall govern the trust. *H* transfers almost all his assets to the State Blue trustee. *H* dies domiciled in State Red. Can *W* reach the assets in the inter vivos trust in State Blue? Compare National Shawmut Bank v. Cumming, 91 N.E.2d 337 (Mass. 1950) (applying law of trustee's domicile to defeat elective share claim of spouse domiciled out of state), with In re Clark, 236 N.E.2d 152 (N.Y. 1968) (applying law of state where couple were domiciled, deeming it to have paramount interest).

UPC §2-202(d) (1990, rev. 2008) provides that the law of the decedent's domicile shall govern the right to take an elective share of property located in another state. But not all states agree. In Estate of Pericles, 641 N.E.2d 10 (Ill. App. 1994), the court applied the standard conflict of laws rule that the law of the state where real property is located governs the elective share in such real property. See generally 1 Jeffrey A. Schoenblum, Multistate and Multinational Estate Planning §§10.02-10.05 (25th ann. ed. 2008).

(2) STATUTORY SCHEMES

Dissatisfied with vague tests laid down by courts, many states have enacted statutes providing objective criteria for determining what nonprobate transfers are subject to the elective share. These statutes reject the judicially crafted illusory transfer and other similar tests, favoring instead a list of specified nonprobate transfers that are added to the probate estate to constitute a *net estate* or an *elective estate* or an *augmented estate* against which the surviving spouse's elective share is applied. We treat here the representative New York and the interesting Delaware approaches, both of which may be contrasted with the Uniform Probate Code schemes discussed in the next section.

(a)   New York

In 1965, New York became the first state to enact a net estate type approach, replacing the illusory transfer test developed by the courts with a statutory scheme that subjects some nonprobate transfers to the elective share. The New York statute now gives the surviving spouse $50,000 or one-third of the decedent's net estate, whichever is greater, plus a personal property set-aside (page 474). N.Y. Est. Powers & Trusts Law §5-1.1-A (2008).

In New York, the decedent's net estate that is subject to the elective share includes the probate estate and the following nonprobate transfers:

(1)   gifts causa mortis (gifts of tangible personal property contingent on death);

(2)   gifts made within one year before death, except gifts not exceeding the amount of the gift tax annual exclusion ($13,000 in 2009);

(3)   savings account (Totten) trusts;

(4)   joint bank accounts, to the extent of the decedent's contribution;

(5)   joint tenancies and tenancies by the entireties, to the extent of the decedent's contribution;

(6)   property payable on death to a person other than the decedent;

(7)   lifetime transfers in which the decedent retained possession or life income or a power to revoke or a power to consume, invade, or dispose of the principal;

(8)   pension plans or the like; and

(9)   any property over which the decedent had a general power of appointment enabling him to appoint the property to whomever he pleases.

The amount of the elective share is reduced by deducting the value of any interest, other than a life estate, that passes from the decedent to the surviving spouse by intestacy, by will, or by will substitute.

(b)   Delaware

Delaware takes a different and more elegant approach. It defines the property subject to the elective share as all property includible in the decedent's gross estate under the federal estate tax, whether or not an estate tax return is filed. If a nonprobate transfer is taxable at death (as are revocable trusts, POD contracts, and joint tenancies), the surviving spouse can reach it. Del. Code Ann. tit. 12, §902 (2008). This approach has the advantage of incorporating into elective share law the inclusion principles of federal estate tax law, which evolved out of long experience with decedents trying to avoid estate tax by lifetime transfers. The federal tax authorities pay little attention to the distinction between probate and nonprobate transfers, and focus instead on the question whether an economic benefit is transferred from the decedent to another person.

For discussion and approval of using the federal estate tax laws to govern the elective share, see Susan N. Gary, Marital Partnership Theory and the Elective Share: Federal Estate Tax Law Provides a Solution, 49 U. Miami L. Rev. 567 (1995); Sidney Kwestel and Rena C. Seplowitz, Testamentary Substitutes: Retained Interests, Custodial Accounts and Contractual Transactions—A New Approach, 38 Am. U. L. Rev. 1 (1988). For treatment of what nonprobate transfers are subject to federal estate taxation, see Chapter 15.

(3)   THE UNIFORM PROBATE CODE

(a)   *The 1969 Uniform Probate Code*

Inspired by New York's innovations, the 1969 UPC introduced the concept of the *augmented estate* (the probate estate augmented with certain nonprobate transfers). UPC §2-202 (1969). The surviving spouse is entitled to an elective share of one-third of the augmented estate. The augmented estate includes the probate estate and the following nonprobate and inter vivos transfers made without consideration at any time *during the marriage*:

(1) any transfer under which the decedent retains the right to possession or income from the property;

(2) any transfer which the decedent can revoke or invade or dispose of the principal for his own benefit;

(3) any transfer in joint tenancy with someone other than the spouse;

(4) any transfer made within two years before death exceeding $3,000 per donee per year ($3,000 was, at the time, the maximum amount exempt from the federal gift tax under the annual exclusion; it is now $13,000); and

(5) property given to the surviving spouse during life, including a life estate in a trust, and property received by the spouse at death derived from the decedent, such as life insurance and pensions.

The purpose of augmenting the probate estate with items (1) through (4) was, in the words of the official comment, "to prevent the owner of wealth from making arrangements which transmit his property to others by means other than probate deliberately to defeat the right of the surviving spouse to a share." The augmented estate expressly excluded life insurance payable to a person other than the surviving spouse on the questionable ground that "it is not ordinarily purchased as a way of depleting the probate estate and avoiding the elective share of the spouse."

The 1969 UPC includes in the augmented estate property given to the surviving spouse by the decedent during life (item 5 listed above). The purpose of this innovation is to prevent a spouse who has been well provided for by lifetime or nonprobate transfers from electing against the will and claiming more than a fair share. Thus:

> *Case 6. H*, married to *W*, owns the family home in joint tenancy with *W* (the house is worth $80,000 at *H*'s death). *H* owns insurance on his own life in the amount of $100,000, payable to *W*. During life *H* transfers $200,000 to a trust to pay *H* the income for life, then to pay *W* the income for life, then to pay the principal to *H*'s children. *H* dies, leaving a probate estate of $100,000, which he devises to his children. In a majority of states the elective share system does not take into account the property given *W. W* can elect to take a fractional share of *H*'s probate estate regardless of how much she has received from *H* by nonprobate routes.

To be equitable, the 1969 UPC includes gifts to the spouse in the decedent's augmented estate, crediting them against the elective share to which the surviving spouse is entitled.

The 1969 UPC augmented estate approach was adopted and remains in effect in quite a few states. In addition, the concept of augmenting the probate estate with transfers *during marriage* that the decedent continued to have control over influenced other states in revising their elective share systems even if they did not adopt the UPC.

(b) The 1990 Uniform Probate Code and 2008 Amendments

The 1990 UPC completely redesigned the elective share and the augmented estate so that it achieved results closer to those of a community property system, which the revisers took to be the desideratum. The central idea of the 1990 UPC elective share is to add up all the property of both spouses and split it according to a percentage based on the length of the marriage. The revisers believed that this would result in treating spouses in common law jurisdictions in roughly the same way they are treated in community property jurisdictions (assuming that the spouses have only community property and each spouse owns half of their community property assets).

The 1990 UPC also adds to the augmented estate many transfers made before marriage, as well as transfers during marriage, where the decedent retained substantial control of the property. It also includes property or powers received from others. In this respect, the 1990 UPC resembles the Internal Revenue Code, which subjects to estate taxation property transferred by the decedent during life over which the decedent retained substantial control as well as property subject to a general power of appointment given the decedent by others.

The purpose of the augmented estate under the 1990 UPC is no longer, as under the 1969 UPC, to protect against "fraud on the widow's share," but rather "to bring elective-share law into line with the partnership theory of marriage," tempered by a minimum support obligation in the form of a $50,000 supplemental elective-share amount. The official comment explains:

> The general effect of implementing the partnership theory in elective-share law is to increase the entitlement of a surviving spouse in a long-term marriage in cases in which the marital assets were disproportionately titled in the decedent's name; and to decrease or even eliminate the entitlement of a surviving spouse in a long-term marriage in cases in which the marital assets were more or less equally titled or disproportionately titled in the surviving spouse's name. A further general effect is to decrease or even eliminate the entitlement of a surviving spouse in a short-term, later-in-life marriage (typically a post-widowhood remarriage) in which neither spouse contributed much, if anything, to the acquisition of the other's wealth, except that a special supplemental elective-share amount is provided in cases in which the surviving spouse would otherwise be left without sufficient funds for support. [UPC Art. II, Part 2, gen. cmt. (1990, rev. 2008).]

As revised in 2008, the UPC elective share provides for an equal split of marital property, but the proportion of each spouse's property that is deemed marital, includible in the augmented estate subject to division, is phased in based on the length of the marriage. The supplemental elective-share amount was also increased to $75,000 and made subject to the inflation adjustment rules of UPC §1-109 (2008). Many of the 2008 amendments were presaged in Lawrence W. Waggoner, The Uniform Probate Code's Elective Share: Time for a Reassessment, 37 U. Mich J.L. Ref. 1 (2003). Professor Waggoner, the reporter for the 1990 UPC drafting committee, also served as the reporter for the 2008 amendments.

Uniform Probate Code (1990, as amended 2008)

§2-202. ELECTIVE SHARE

(a) [Elective-Share Amount.] The surviving spouse of a decedent who dies domiciled in this State has a right of election, under the limitations and conditions stated in this Part, to take an elective-share amount equal to 50 percent of the value of the marital-property portion of the augmented estate. . . .

§2-203. COMPOSITION OF THE AUGMENTED ESTATE; MARITAL-PROPERTY PORTION

(a) . . . [T]he value of the augmented estate . . . consists of the sum of the values of all property, whether real or personal, movable or immovable, tangible or intangible, wherever situated, that constitute:

(1) the decedent's net probate estate [defined in §2-204];

(2) the decedent's nonprobate transfers to others [defined in §2-205];

(3) the decedent's nonprobate transfers to the surviving spouse [defined in §2-206]; and

(4) the surviving spouse's property and nonprobate transfers to others [defined in §2-207].

(b) The value of the marital-property portion of the augmented estate consists of the sum of the values of the four components of the augmented estate as determined under subsection (a) multiplied by the following percentage:

If the decedent and the spouse were married to each other:	The percentage is:
Less than 1 year	3%
1 year but less than 2 years	6%
2 years but less than 3 years	12%
3 years but less than 4 years	18%
4 years but less than 5 years	24%
5 years but less than 6 years	30%
6 years but less than 7 years	36%

If the decedent and the spouse were married to each other:	*The percentage is:*
7 years but less than 8 years	42%
8 years but less than 9 years	48%
9 years but less than 10 years	54%
10 years but less than 11 years	60%
11 years but less than 12 years	68%
12 years but less than 13 years	76%
13 years but less than 14 years	84%
14 years but less than 15 years	92%
15 years or more	100%

In funding the elective share amount, the UPC credits the surviving spouse with nonprobate transfers to the surviving spouse and marital assets that are already owned by the surviving spouse. UPC §2-209 (1990, rev. 2008). Thus:

> *Case 7. H* and *W* have been married for 18 years, so under UPC §§2-202 and 2-203, 100 percent of the augmented estate is marital property subject to the surviving spouse's elective share of 50 percent. *H*'s augmented estate consists of:

(a)	$100,000	probate estate, devised to *A*
(b)	$150,000	nonprobate transfers to others than *W*
(c)	$ 25,000	life insurance payable to *W*
(d)	$ 50,000	*H*'s half interest in joint tenancy held with *W*
(e)	$ 75,000	*W*'s property
(f)	$ 50,000	*W*'s half interest in the joint tenancy
	$450,000	

> *W* has an elective share of 50 percent of the whole, or $225,000. Since *W* owns $75,000 in her own name, this amount is credited against her elective share, reducing it to $150,000. Also credited against the elective share are $25,000 in life insurance received by *W*, $50,000 for *H*'s half of the joint tenancy, and $50,000 for *W*'s half of the joint tenancy. Thus, the amount of *W*'s elective share payable out of *H*'s probate estate and nonprobate transfers is $25,000.

Although the drafters wanted the UPC elective share to resemble the results of a community property system, some differences remain. The 1990 UPC augmented estate, even as revised in 2008, includes all property of both spouses, and not only property acquired from earnings. Community property, owned equally by the spouses, includes only earnings and acquisitions from earnings. It does not apply to property brought to the marriage or acquired by gift or inheritance, which is the separate property of the acquiring spouse (so long as it is kept separate). The decedent spouse can dispose of his separate property any way he likes; the surviving spouse has no claim to it.

The drafters justified including all property of the spouses in the augmented estate on the grounds that it avoids problems of classifying property as community (earned) or separate, particularly when the couple has mixed their property. On the other hand, by including all property of the spouses in the elective share, the UPC in its current form makes it impossible for one spouse to keep his property acquired before marriage or by inheritance free from the elective share of the other spouse without the consent of the other spouse.

The 1990 UPC elective share provisions have been adopted in about one-fifth of the states, mainly in the Great Plains. See Jeffrey A. Schoenblum, 2008 Multistate Guide to Estate Planning at Table 6.03.

QUESTIONS AND NOTE

1. Should *life insurance* owned by the decedent be subject to the elective share? The 1969 UPC exempted it. The 1990 UPC includes it, a decision left undisturbed by the 2008 amendments. The life insurance industry has fought this, just as it has fought allowing the policy beneficiary to be changed by will. What is the reason for the opposition?

2. For further analysis and discussion of the UPC augmented estate, see Susan N. Gary, The Oregon Elective Share Statute: Is Reform an Impossible Dream?, 44 Willamette L. Rev. 337 (2007); Stephanie J. Willbanks, Parting Is Such Sweet Sorrow, But Does It Have to Be So Complicated? Transmission of Property at Death in Vermont, 29 Vt. L. Rev. 895 (2005); Angela M. Vallario, Spousal Election: Suggested Equitable Reform for the Division of Property at Death, 52 Catholic U. L. Rev. 519 (2003); Alan Newman, Incorporating the Partnership Theory of Marriage into Elective-Share Law: The Approximation System of the Uniform Probate Code and the Deferred-Community-Property Alternative, 49 Emory L.J. 487 (2000).

e. Must the Surviving Spouse Accept a Life Estate?

Once the amount of the elective share has been determined, the surviving spouse is usually credited (or, in legal language, *charged*) with the value of all other interests given her by the will (or will substitute). If those amounts do not satisfy the elective share, the difference must be made up either by pro rata contributions from all the other beneficiaries (the majority and UPC rule) or from the residuary estate.

Suppose that the decedent has left the surviving spouse a life estate in a certain amount of property. Must the surviving spouse accept the life estate or its value in partial satisfaction of her elective share? Under the original 1969 UPC and the law of most states, if the surviving spouse renounces the life estate and elects to take her share in fee simple, she is *not* charged for the value of the life estate. In 1975, the 1969 UPC was amended to provide that a surviving spouse who rejects the life estate *is* charged an amount equal to one-half the total value of the property subject to the life estate.

Charging the surviving spouse with the value of the life estate was carried over into the 1990 UPC. The practical effect of so charging the surviving spouse is to force the surviving spouse to take the life estate given her by the decedent's will. The object of the UPC revisers was to cause as little distortion in the decedent's estate plan as possible. Under heavy criticism from commentators, in 1993 the UPC was amended to provide that a life estate renounced by the surviving spouse is not charged against her elective share. UPC §2-209 (1990, rev. 1993). See Ira M. Bloom, The Treatment of Trust and Other Partial Interests of the Surviving Spouse Under the Redesigned Elective-Share System: Some Concerns and Suggestions, 55 Alb. L. Rev. 941 (1992).

Two states offer *only* a life estate as the elective share. See Conn. Gen. Stat. §45a-436 (2008) (one-third life estate in probate property); R.I. Gen. Laws §33-25-2 (2008) (life estate in all real estate). Under these schemes, a surviving spouse can take under the will or elect to take a life estate as the forced share.

f. Waiver

The right of election allows the surviving spouse to take his statutory share in spite of the will of the decedent spouse. The question thus arises, can the spouses agree to waive the survivor's elective share? The prototypical waiver occurs in a *premarital agreement* (sometimes also called a *prenuptial* or *antenuptial agreement*), which is as much the province of the trusts and estates lawyer as it is the matrimonial lawyer. Whatever marriages do not end by divorce necessarily end by death.

All separate property states will enforce a waiver of the right of election by premarital agreement, and most will also enforce a waiver agreed to during the marriage (a *postnuptial agreement*). See Jeffrey A. Schoenblum, 2008 Multistate Guide to Estate Planning at Table 6.04. Yet there remains concern that these agreements may not reflect an arm's-length bargain — or even if they do, that they may still be inequitable.

In just over half the states, the enforceability of a premarital agreement is governed by the Uniform Premarital Agreement Act (1983). The UPAA overrides the presumption of fraud that some courts attached to a premarital agreement if, in the court's view, the agreement made inadequate provision for a spouse in light of the other spouse's wealth. See In re Estate of Martin, 938 A.2d 812 (Me. 2008). Under the UPAA, the party opposing enforcement must prove that the agreement either (1) was not voluntary, or (2) was unconscionable when executed and the party opposing enforcement did not have fair and reasonable disclosure of the other party's property and finances. It is also a good practice for each spouse to have independent counsel, and this is required in some states.

UPC §2-213 (1990, rev. 1993) adopts the enforcement standard of the UPAA and extends it to both prenuptial and postnuptial agreements.

Uniform Probate Code (1990, as amended 1993)

§2-213.   WAIVER OF RIGHT TO ELECT AND OF OTHER RIGHTS

(a) The right of election of a surviving spouse and the rights of the surviving spouse to homestead allowance, exempt property, and family allowance, or any of them, may be waived, wholly or partially, before or after marriage, by a written contract, agreement, or waiver signed by the surviving spouse.

(b) A surviving spouse's waiver is not enforceable if the surviving spouse proves that:

(1) he [or she] did not execute the waiver voluntarily; or

(2) the waiver was unconscionable when it was executed and, before execution of the waiver, he [or she]:

(i) was not provided a fair and reasonable disclosure of the property or financial obligations of the decedent;

(ii) did not voluntarily and expressly waive, in writing, any right to disclosure of the property or financial obligations of the decedent beyond the disclosure provided; and

(iii) did not have, or reasonably could not have had, an adequate knowledge of the property or financial obligations of the decedent.

(c) An issue of unconscionability of a waiver is for decision by the court as a matter of law.

(d) Unless it provides to the contrary, a waiver of "all rights," or equivalent language, in the property or estate of a present or prospective spouse or a complete property settlement entered into after or in anticipation of separation or divorce is a waiver of all rights of elective share, homestead allowance, exempt property, and family allowance by each spouse in the property of the other and a renunciation by each of all benefits that would otherwise pass to him [or her] from the other by intestate succession or by virtue of any will executed before the waiver or property settlement.

Reece v. Elliott
Court of Appeals of Tennessee, 2006
208 S.W.3d 419

FRANKS, J.   Plaintiff's Declaratory Judgment suit to declare the antenuptial agreement invalid was dismissed by the Trial Court which held the agreement enforceable. On appeal, we affirm.

Plaintiff, widow of Eugene Reece, filed this declaratory judgment action against Linda Elliott and Diane Dempsey, Individually and as Co-Executrixes of the Estate of Eugene Reece.

Plaintiff stated that she was the surviving widow of Eugene Reece, that they had married on December 4, 1999, and Reece died intestate on July 5, 2003. Contemporaneously with the filing of this action, plaintiff applied for statutory benefits as surviving widow and attached a copy of the antenuptial agreement dated November 29, 1999. She sought a declaration regarding the rights and liabilities of the parties, and also sought rescission of the document based upon her late husband's failure to make a full disclosure regarding his assets and financial condition.

The Agreement attached states that Mr. Reece and petitioner had an interest in real and personal property identified in the attached lists, and that the property listed would be considered the separate property of each. The document further states that each party had children of prior marriages, and that each party desired to provide for his/her children from previous marriages by maintaining separate property and relinquishing marital property rights in the other's property. The document also states that each party recognized his/her right to dissent from the will of the other, and that each party waived that right as to said separate property. The parties affirmed in the document they had each consulted with and had the opportunity to consult with counsel, that they understood the full import of the document, and that a full disclosure of assets had been made.

Exhibit A to the document lists the separate property of Mr. Reece, and includes a residence in Ohio, its contents, and three vacant lots there. It also includes 230 acres in Morgan County, 1687 shares of JH Routh Packing Company stock, a promissory note due from Routh, various automobiles and equipment, a brokerage account at Fidelity, bank accounts at Citizens Bank in Tennessee and Ohio, and school bonds. Exhibit B is a list of separate property of petitioner, and it lists a residence in Knoxville and the contents thereof, a Grand Cherokee Laredo, a brokerage account at First Tennessee, an IRA, U.S. savings bonds, and a savings account and CD at First Tennessee. Values are not listed for every item.

In the defendants' Answer, they relied on the antenuptial agreement, and the defenses of estoppel, laches, release and waiver. During the trial, plaintiff testified that attorney James Brooks prepared the antenuptial agreement and she only met him when she picked it up. She testified that she consulted with an attorney, Debra Graham, who read over the document. She testified that the list of her property was prepared by her and then taken to Mr. Brooks to be typed up and attached to the agreement. She testified that Mr. Reece told her he had worked as a truck driver for Routh Packing Company, and he owned stock in the company. She testified the agreement set forth a number of shares of stock and that when she read the agreement, she saw his list of property, and saw that Routh Packing owed him $357,000.00. She testified that she fully understood those items would not belong to her in the event of his death, and that she would have no interest in his separate property. She went over the appropriate list with her attorney and did not have any questions. She signed the agreement in the attorney's office, and the attorney's staff notarized her signature.

She further testified that she was not aware of any items of property that Reece failed to disclose, and that it did not matter if Reece owned 87 shares of stock or 1,687 shares, they were his. She said she did not know what she would have done if she had known the stock was worth a lot of money. She acknowledged that she did not discuss with her attorney the need to find out what the stock was worth, and that she did not know what the stock was worth in 1999. She elaborated that when she met with her attorney she did not consider having the attorney find out what the husband's value in Routh Packing was, because it was not a consideration, and that she did not disclose the values of her property on her list, but she told him what they were worth. She acknowledged that she did not ask Reece what the stock was worth because it was not important to her at the time because he was going to keep it anyway.

Following trial, the Trial Court stated that it was obvious from looking at Mr. Reece's list of property that he was a wealthy man, without taking into account the value of the stock, and that in the Court's opinion, the lack of value stated on the stock was not fatal to the agreement. The Court reiterated that the parties had entered into the agreement knowingly, they each had their own attorney, and that everything was revealed on the list and the wife could have investigated any items that she wanted to. He noted that nothing was hidden, and the wife herself did not put values on several of her assets, admitting that it was not important, because they both agreed the assets would go to their respective children. The Court found that the law required each party to have a clear idea of the nature and extent of the other's assets, which the Court found to be the case, and entered Judgment, finding the antenuptial agreement was valid and enforceable and dismissed plaintiff's action. . . .

[Plaintiff appealed, asking whether her husband's] failure to disclose the value of the stock would render the antenuptial agreement invalid and unenforceable?

Prenuptial/antenuptial agreements are favored by public policy in Tennessee, and will be upheld so long as the parties enter into the agreements voluntarily and knowledgeably. Tenn. Code Ann. § 36-3-501 deals with antenuptial or prenuptial agreements, and states:

> Notwithstanding any other provision of law to the contrary, . . . any antenuptial or prenuptial agreement entered into by spouses concerning property owned by either spouse before the marriage that is the subject of such agreement shall be binding upon any court having jurisdiction over such spouses and/or such agreement if such agreement is determined, in the discretion of such court, to have been entered into by such spouses freely, knowledgeably and in good faith and without exertion of duress or undue influence upon either spouse. The terms of such agreement shall be enforceable by all remedies available for enforcement of contract terms.

Plaintiff's sole argument is that she did not enter into the agreement with full knowledge of the value of the deceased's assets, because there was no value disclosed regarding the stock in Routh Packing Company.

In the case of Randolph v. Randolph, 937 S.W.2d 815 (Tenn. 1996), the Supreme Court interpreted the term "knowledgeably" as meaning that the proponent of the agreement had to prove that a full and fair disclosure of the nature, extent and value of the party's holdings was provided, or that such disclosure was unnecessary because the spouse had independent knowledge of the same. The Court said:

> The extent of what constitutes "full and fair" disclosure varies from case to case depending upon a number of factors, including the relative sophistication of the parties, the apparent

fairness or unfairness of the substantive terms of the agreement, and any other circumstance unique to the litigants and their specific situation. While disclosure need not reveal precisely every asset owned by an individual spouse, at a minimum, full and fair disclosure requires that each contracting party be given a clear idea of the nature, extent and value of the other party's property and resources. Though not required, a fairly simple and effective method of proving disclosure is to attach a net worth schedule of assets, liabilities and income to the agreement itself. [Id. at 821.]

The Court also noted that while it was not required, representation by independent counsel was also a factor to take into account, and possibly the "best evidence that a party has entered into [an] antenuptial agreement voluntarily and knowledgeably." Id. at 822. . . .

In cases where antenuptial agreements have been enforced, we have made clear that the basic question which must be answered is whether the spouse was misled, where the proponent of the agreement makes a fair disclosure, even if it not 100% exhaustive, and the spouse had the opportunity to ask questions and discover the extent of the other's holdings but failed to do so due to lack of interest, then the agreement has been held valid.

Here plaintiff had full knowledge that her husband was a man of wealth, as shown by the list of assets that was provided. The fact that there was no value listed for one particular asset, even though it was significant, would not invalidate the agreement that she entered freely. She consulted with independent counsel and admitted to clearly understanding what the agreement meant, and that she would have no claim to any of these assets. She had the opportunity to ask questions about the assets, and did not have her counsel investigate, stating that it "did not matter" because she knew the assets would not be hers. She admitted that her husband was never dishonest with her, and was very straightforward and open with her about his financial dealings and never misled her. The disclosure in the agreement demonstrates the husband's wealth, and the wife did not avail herself of the opportunity to ask him the value of the stock, nor make any independent investigation. We agree with the Trial Court that the wife was not misled, and under these circumstances, we agree with the Trial Court that the agreement entered is binding and enforceable on plaintiff. . . .

The Trial Court's Judgment is affirmed.

NOTES, PROBLEMS, AND QUESTIONS

1. *Fair and reasonable disclosure.* A commonly litigated question is whether the party challenging the premarital agreement can be charged with constructive knowledge of the other party's property in satisfaction of the requirement of fair and reasonable disclosure. See In re Estate of Martin, 938 A.2d 812 (Me. 2008) (charging *W* with constructive knowledge based on her access to *H*'s financial records); Pulley v. Short, 261 S.W.3d 701 (Mo. App. 2008) (charging *W* with knowledge of extent and nature of *H*'s property based on tours of *H*'s real estate properties and a schedule, given to *W*, of those properties).

To avoid a subsequent challenge based on inadequate disclosure, it is advisable to prepare a schedule of each party's assets, including a good faith valuation of each asset, and to attach the schedule to the agreement. A cautionary tale that reinforces the prudence of this practice is provided by In re Estate of Davis, 213 S.W.3d 288 (Tenn. App. 2006). In that case, the court held a premarital agreement invalid for insufficient disclosure:

> The question is whether Wife made a full and fair disclosure of the nature, extent, *and* value of her holdings. Assuming that Wife did make a list of her holdings, the Agreement unequivocally states that such a list did "not purport to be all inclusive, the values set forth on which do not purport to be necessarily accurate but rather are estimates." Since Wife's list cannot be located, assuming there was a list, we are unable to determine if that missing list actually was sufficiently detailed such that there was a full and fair disclosure to Husband of Wife's holdings. [Id. at 297.]

2. *Independent counsel.* In 1988, Barry Bonds, the current holder of Major League Baseball's single-season records for home runs, walks, on-base percentage, and slugging percentage, took his fiancée, Susann ("Sun") Margreth, to execute a premarital agreement just before they caught a plane to Las Vegas to be married. The agreement, which waived Sun's rights to Barry's current and future property, was explained to Sun by Barry's lawyers. Sun did not have independent counsel. She later claimed that her English skills were limited (she was born in Sweden). After having two children together, Barry and Sun separated in 1994. Sun contested the premarital agreement. The California Supreme Court held that Sun's lack of independent counsel did not render her waiver involuntary. In re Marriage of Bonds, 5 P.3d 815 (Cal. 2000). The following year

Barry Bonds

the California legislature amended its enactment of the UPAA to require independent counsel (or a written, knowing waiver) and seven days' notice before signing. Cal. Fam. Code §1615 (2008).

An increasing number of jurisdictions now require independent counsel, or the opportunity for independent counsel, as a condition for the enforcement of a premarital agreement. See In re Estate of Kinney, 733 N.W.2d 118 (Minn. 2007) (contrasting former common law rule with new statutory rule that requires "opportunity to consult with legal counsel"). Under the UPAA, the absence of independent counsel is not, by itself, enough to invalidate a premarital agreement, but it is a relevant factor in assessing voluntariness and adequacy of disclosure. UPAA §6, cmt.

3.   *Postnuptial versus prenuptial agreements.* In some states postnuptial waivers of the right of election are subject to closer scrutiny than premarital waivers or are not enforced at all. Is there a sound policy basis for differential treatment of pre- and postnuptial agreements? Do not the parties usually have more information after marriage? See Sean Hannon Williams, Postnuptial Agreements, 2007 Wis. L. Rev. 827.

4.   *Critical literature.* As we have seen, current law favors the enforcement of prenuptial agreements subject to procedural safeguards in the form of disclosure and perhaps independent counsel. For a critique of this "mythification of procedural fairness," see Judith T. Younger, Lovers' Contracts in the Courts: Forsaking the Minimum Decencies, 13 Wm. & Mary J. Women & L. 349 (2007).

For an argument that prenuptial agreements are inequitable by their very nature, albeit focusing chiefly on divorce and not death, see Jeffrey G. Sherman, Prenuptial Agreements: A New Reason to Revive an Old Rule, 53 Clev. St. L. Rev. 359 (2005-2006). For a more sympathetic take, see Arlene G. Dublin, Prenups for Lovers: A Romantic Guide to Prenuptial Agreements (2001).

4.   *Rights of Surviving Spouse in Community Property*[16]

a.   Basic Information

Nine states, containing more than one-fourth of the population of the United States, have a system of community property (see pages 470-471). Community property in the United States is a community of acquests: Husband and wife own the earnings and acquisitions from earnings of both spouses during marriage in undivided, equal shares. Anything bought with such earnings is community property. Property that is not community property is the separate property of one spouse or the other or, in the case of a tenancy in common or joint tenancy, of both. Separate property includes property acquired before marriage and property acquired during marriage by gift or inheritance. In Idaho, Louisiana, and Texas, income from separate property is community property. In the other community property states, income from separate property retains its separate character. Where the characterization of the property is doubtful, there is a strong presumption that the property is community property.

Where property has been commingled, or acquired from both separate and community funds, states often have a rule about how to characterize the property in a particular situation. For example, if a husband uses his earnings after marriage to pay premiums on a life insurance policy acquired before marriage, some states, applying the inception-of-title rule, hold the policy remains the husband's

---

16. The editors gratefully acknowledge the assistance of Professor Joshua C. Tate of SMU Dedman School of Law in updating the treatment of community property in this and the next section.

separate property and the community is entitled only to a return of premiums paid with interest. Other states apply a pro rata share rule to insurance policies, dividing the policy proceeds between separate and community property according to the proportion of payments paid.

To avoid tracing problems, couples can make agreements regarding the character of their property. By agreement they may change separate property into community property, or they may change community property into a joint tenancy, a tenancy in common, or sole ownership of one spouse. Couples sometimes agree that all their property is held as community property to achieve the favorable income tax treatment given community property. Upon the death of one spouse, the entire value of community property receives a stepped-up basis for determining capital gains when the property is eventually sold. Any appreciation in value between acquisition and the date of the spouse's death is never taxed as capital gain. If the property is not community property, only the decedent's interest in the property receives a stepped-up basis.[17]

Either spouse can dispose of his or her half of the community assets at death. The surviving spouse owns the other half, which is not, of course, subject to testamentary disposition by the deceased spouse. The one-half of the community property belonging to the deceased spouse may be devised to whomever the decedent pleases, the same as separate property.

Because community property belongs to both spouses even when title appears on its face to be in the name of one spouse, problems arise over which spouse can manage the property and deal with third persons respecting the property. These problems may concern sale, leasing, or mortgaging the property or subjecting the property to creditors. Each community property state has statutes on this matter. Although these statutes differ in many details, we can indicate broadly the management roles. In Texas, the wife has sole management power over her earnings kept separate and the husband sole power over his. If the earnings are commingled, they are subject to the joint management of the spouses. In California and most other community property states, either the husband or wife, acting alone, has the power to manage community property. Statutes, however, ordinarily require both spouses to join in transfers or mortgages of community real property.

In exercising management power, one spouse may sell community property to a purchaser for a valuable consideration, but a spouse cannot freely give away

---

17. *The Alaska Community Property Trust.* Couples not domiciled in Alaska can transfer their personal property into an Alaska Community Property Trust and provide in the trust agreement that the property is community property. Alaska Stat. §34.77.100 (2008). This trust, appointing as trustee a bank in Alaska (thus ensuring a local fee), will be governed by Alaska law if the settlors so intend. A major advantage of an Alaska Community Property Trust is that it apparently enables residents of noncommunity property states to take advantage of Internal Revenue Code §1014(b)(6), which provides that, upon the death of one spouse the entire community property is given a stepped-up basis (the value of the property on the date of the spouse's death). The surviving spouse will thus have to pay no tax on capital gain incurred before the decedent's death if she sells the property. No ruling by the Internal Revenue Service has yet been made, however, as to whether property in an Alaska Community Property Trust created by nonresidents is community property under I.R.C. §1014(b)(6). See Ira Mark Bloom, How Federal Transfer Taxes Affect the Development of Property Law, 48 Clev. St. L. Rev. 661, 671-672 (2000).

community property. States give various remedies to the nondonor spouse in the case of a gift to a third party. Thus:

> *Case 8.* *H*, married to *W*, purchases a life insurance policy on his life with his earnings. The policy is community property. *H* names *A* as beneficiary. Upon *H*'s death, what are *W*'s rights in the policy proceeds? In California, *W* is entitled, after *H* dies, to set aside the gift to the extent of one-half. (During *H*'s life, *W* is entitled to set aside an entire gift and reclaim the property for the community, but, after *H* dies, a gift by *H* during life of community property is treated as if it were a devise by *H* of his half share.) In Texas, the manager of community property (*H* in this instance) can make reasonable gifts to others, but excessive gifts are deemed in fraud of the other spouse's rights. If the court finds the gift to have been in fraud of *W*'s rights, *W* is entitled to half the policy proceeds. The other community property states divide between the California and Texas views, sometimes with variations.

Almost all community property states follow the theory that husband and wife own equal shares in each item of community property at death. Thus, if *H* and *W* own Blackacre (worth $50,000) and Whiteacre (worth $50,000), each owns a half share in each tract. *W*'s will cannot devise Blackacre to *H* and Whiteacre to *D*, her daughter by a previous marriage, even if *H* would end up receiving property equal to the value of his community share. (Divorce is different. In most community property states, the divorce court may award specific items of community property to one spouse or the other, provided each spouse ends up with an equitable share of the aggregate value of community property.)

In jurisdictions applying a reasonable gifts rule to lifetime transfers and an item theory to death transfers, should nonprobate transfers to a person other than the spouse be treated as inter vivos transfers or death transfers? If they are death transfers, the surviving spouse is entitled to one-half of each. If they are inter vivos transfers, the surviving spouse may set aside only those transfers deemed unreasonable. See Stanley M. Johanson, Revocable Trusts and Community Property: The Substantive Problems, 47 Tex. L. Rev. 537, 576-578 (1969).

b. Putting the Survivor to an Election

An estate planning device, known as the *widow's election*, developed in community property states in the days when the husband was the manager of community property and the wife was seen as a homemaker without business experience, whatever the realities. Even after statutes gave the wife equal management power, many wives went into business, and gender-neutral terms were widely adopted, the name "widow's election" is still used to describe this election plan, which may be applicable to widowers as well as to widows. In explaining the widow's election, we shall assume the husband dies first, which is true more often than not.

A widow's election involves a will executed by the husband devising *all* the community property in trust to pay the income to his wife for life, with remainder to others on the wife's death, and requiring the wife to elect between surrendering her half of the community property and taking under the husband's will. If the widow wants to share in her husband's trust, she must surrender her community property. The object of the widow's election is to create, at the death of the husband, one trust of all the community property — both the husband's half and the wife's half — paying the widow all the income for her life. To do this, the widow must consent to the transfer of her share of the community property by electing to take under the will. If the widow so elects, the situation is treated as though the widow transferred her one-half community interest to the trust in exchange for receiving a life estate in her husband's one-half community interest. If, instead, the widow elects against the will, she takes the one-half interest in community property to which she is entitled by law, but she forfeits the life estate in the husband's half of the community property devised to her by her husband's will.

The widow's election may have estate and gift tax advantages, which flow from the fact that the widow has made an exchange for consideration, receiving a life estate in her husband's half of the community property in exchange for transferring a remainder interest in her half of the community property. However, there is a possible income tax disadvantage such that most estate planners do not recommend a forced widow's election plan. See John R. Price, Contemporary Estate Planning §§9.23-9.39 (2008 ed.).

An alternative to a forced widow's election is a plan by husband and wife to transfer all the community property into a revocable trust, paying income to husband and wife for their joint lives and for the life of the survivor, remainder to their children or to others. The revocable trust becomes irrevocable upon the death of one spouse. This has none of the possible estate and gift tax benefits of a forced widow's election because it is not an exchange of the widow's property for consideration. But it does not have an income tax disadvantage. The joint revocable trust plan may be attractive to couples who want unified trust management of the community property after the death of one of the spouses and assurances that the trust corpus will pass to their descendants upon the death of the surviving spouse. See John H. Martin, The Joint Trust: Estate Planning in a New Environment, 39 Real Prop., Prob. & Tr. J. 275 (2004); Melinda S. Merk, Joint Revocable Trusts for Married Couples Domiciled in Common-Law Property States, 32 Real Prop., Prob. & Tr. J. 345 (1997).

5. *Migrating Couples and Multistate Property Holdings*

The traditional conflict of laws rules used to determine which state law governs marital property are these:

(1) The law of the situs controls problems related to land.
(2) The law of the marital domicile at the time that personal property is acquired controls the characterization of the property (that is, as separate or community).
(3) The law of the marital domicile at the death of one spouse controls the survivor's marital rights.

The application of these rules is briefly examined below. For further discussion, see 1 Jeffrey A. Schoenblum, Multistate and Multinational Estate Planning §10.21 (25th ann. ed. 2008); Karen E. Boxx, Community Property Across State Lines: Square Pegs and Rounds Holes, Prob. & Prop., Jan./Feb. 2005, at 9.

It should be noted that although the state of the situs has the power to control its land, it may choose to apply the law of the marital domicile. UPC §2-202(d) (1990, rev. 2008), for example, provides that the rights of a spouse to an elective share in land located in the state shall be governed by the law of the decedent's domicile at death.

a. Moving from a Separate Property State to a Community Property State

If a couple acquires property in a separate property state and moves to a community property state, serious problems of fairness to the surviving spouse may arise. Under traditional doctrine, the ownership of movable property is determined by the laws of the state where the couple is domiciled when the property is acquired. Thus, if the husband is the wage earner, all of the property is the husband's in a separate property state. The wife is protected by the elective share scheme. When the couple moves to a community property state, the property remains the husband's and is now characterized as the husband's separate property.[18] If the couple remains domiciled in the community property state until the husband dies, the law of the state of domicile at date of death governs the disposition of movable property. If neither spouse works in the community property state, there may be no community property for the surviving spouse. Hence, as a result of the move, the wife loses the protection of the elective share system provided by the state where the movable property was acquired and is not protected by the system of community property (which she would have been if the couple had been domiciled in the community property state when the husband was working).

Several community property states give a remedy to the surviving spouse in this situation. These states have a concept of *quasi-community property*. Quasi-community property is property owned by the husband or the wife acquired while domiciled elsewhere, which would have been characterized as community property if the couple had been domiciled in the community property state when the property was acquired. Real property situated outside the state is not treated as quasi-community property because the spouse retains in it any forced share or dower given by the law of the situs.[19] During the continuance of the marriage,

---

18. If the husband moves unilaterally to a community property state, leaving the wife behind in the separate property state, community property jurisdictions differ in their treatment of the husband's subsequent earnings. See Jasmine B. Bertrand, Comment, What's Mine Is Mine Is Mine: The Inequitable Intersection of Louisiana's Choice-of-Law Provisions and the Movables of Migratory Spouses, 79 Tul. L. Rev. 493, 502-512 (2004).

19. The surviving spouse of a couple domiciled in a separate property state who buy land in a community property state may have the same elective share in the land as she would have in land in the domiciliary state. See Cal. Prob. Code §120 (2008).

quasi-community property is treated for most purposes as the separate property of the acquiring spouse. However, in a state that recognizes quasi-community property for probate purposes, one-half of the quasi-community property belongs to the surviving spouse at death; generally the other half is subject to testamentary disposition by the decedent.[20] A few community property states, including Texas, currently use the concept of quasi-community property only in divorce actions and not in the division of decedents' estates.[21]

Quasi-community property, where recognized, is analogous to an elective share in the deceased spouse's property acquired from earnings while domiciled in another state. See Cal. Prob. Code §§66, 101 (2008); Idaho Code §15-2-201 (2008); La. Civ. Code Ann. art. 3526 (2008); Wash. Rev. Code Ann. §§26.16.220-230 (2008) (quasi-community property extended to "surviving domestic partners").

> *Case 9.* H and W are domiciled in Illinois. H saves $500,000 from his earnings, which he invests in stocks and bonds. In Illinois this is his separate property. H and W then retire to California. The stocks and bonds become quasi-community property in California. Upon H's death, W owns one-half of the stocks and bonds. If W dies first, she cannot dispose of any part of this wealth by will; H owns it all. If, instead, H and W had moved to Texas, on H's death W would have no interest in the assets brought from Illinois.

To prevent a spouse from attempting to defeat the survivor's quasi-community property rights by inter vivos transfers, the surviving spouse may have the right to reach one-half of any nonprobate transfer of quasi-community property where the decedent retained possession or enjoyment, or the right to income, or the power to revoke or consume, or a right of survivorship. See Cal. Prob. Code §102 (2008); Idaho Code §15-2-202 (2008).

b. Moving from a Community Property State to a Separate Property State

Suppose that a husband and wife who have acquired community personal property move to a separate property state. What is the effect of this move on the community property? Generally, a change in domicile from a community property state to a separate property state does not change the preexisting property rights of the husband or wife. Community property continues to be community property when the couple and the property move to a separate property state.

---

20. If the nonacquiring spouse dies first, the quasi-community property belongs absolutely to the acquiring spouse; the nonacquiring spouse has no testamentary power over it.

21. Arizona, New Mexico, and Texas have adopted the quasi-community property concept for purposes of equitable division upon divorce. Quasi-community property is treated the same as community property in that situation. Ariz. Rev. Stat. §25-318 (2008); N.M. Stat. Ann. §40-3-8 (2008); Tex. Fam. Code §7.002 (2008). These states do not apply the quasi-community concept to marriages ending in death. See Mark Patton, Note, Quasi-Community Property in Arizona: Why Just at Divorce and Not Death?, 47 Ariz. L. Rev. 167 (2005).

The Uniform Disposition of Community Property Rights at Death Act (1971), enacted in 14 separate property states, provides that community property brought into the state (and all property — including land in the state — traceable to community property) remains community property for purposes of testamentary disposition, unless the spouses have agreed to convert it into separate property. Under the Uniform Act, community property brought into the state is not subject to the elective share. See Stanley M. Johanson, The Migrating Client: Estate Planning for the Couple from a Community Property State, 9 U. Miami Inst. Est. Plan. ¶¶800 et seq. (1975). On the other hand, in a state that has not adopted the Uniform Act, a court might automatically convert any community property the spouses exchange in that state into a form of common law joint ownership. See Jeremy T. Ware, Section 1014(B)(6) and the Boundaries of Community Property, 5 Nev. L.J. 704, 716-717 (2005).

Any couple moving community property into a separate property state should be careful to preserve its community nature, if doing so is desirable. If the community property is sold and the proceeds used to purchase other assets, title to the new property should be taken in the name of husband and wife as community property. If resistance from transfer agents, bankers, or title companies — who may know little about community property — is met, the husband and wife should take title in the name of both spouses, at the same time executing a written agreement reciting their intention to retain the asset as community property. Or the spouses may preserve the community character of their property by creating a revocable trust of the community property and stating in the trust instrument that all property of the trust is community property. If the inbound separate property state has not enacted the Uniform Act, it may be advisable to select the law of a community property state to govern the trust.

Because lawyers in separate property states sometimes lack understanding of the community property system, they may recommend to couples who are bringing community property into a separate property state that they change the title to joint tenancy or some other separate property form. If this is done with the intent of changing community property into a common law concurrent interest, the income tax advantage of community property is lost and the lawyer could be liable for malpractice. An example:

> *Case 10.* H and W, domiciled in Texas, buy property for $100,000. Since the property is paid for out of H and W's earnings, it is community property. At H's death several years later, the property is worth $300,000. Under the federal estate tax law, one-half the value of the community property ($150,000) is subject to estate tax at H's death (but it qualifies for the marital deduction if devised to W, thus incurring no estate taxation). *Note, however, the income tax consequences.* At the death of one spouse, the *entire* value of community property acquires a stepped-up basis for income tax purposes, that is, its value at H's death ($300,000). Internal Revenue Code of 1986, §§1014(a) and 1014(b)(6). If W sells the property after H's death for $325,000, she will pay income tax only on $25,000 capital gain.
>
> Suppose that before H dies, H and W move to Massachusetts. A Massachusetts lawyer advises them to change the title to the property to H and W as joint tenants. H and W do this.

Then *H* dies, and the property is worth $300,000. The estate tax consequences of joint tenancy are the same as if the property had remained community property, but the income tax consequences are very different. Only one-half the value of joint tenancy property receives a stepped-up basis at *H*'s death. Rev. Rul. 68-80, 1968-1 C.B. 348. *W*'s new basis is $50,000 (her half of the old basis) plus $150,000 (stepped-up basis on *H*'s half) or $200,000. If *W* sells the property for $325,000, she will pay an income tax on $125,000 capital gain. Income tax on $100,000, which could have been avoided, is the result of advice by a lawyer unknowledgeable about community property.

Another form of community property has been adopted in most community property states — community property with a right of survivorship (as in a joint tenancy). Under this form, the decedent spouse cannot dispose of his share of the community property by will; it passes under a right of survivorship to the surviving spouse. This new form of community property is now an option in Arizona, California, Idaho, Nevada, New Mexico, Texas, Washington, and Wisconsin (called survivorship marital property). The purpose is to avoid probate costs on the passage of the decedent's half of community property to the surviving spouse — in effect making community property with right of survivorship nonprobate property. Because community property cannot be held in a common law joint tenancy, spouses in community property states previously had to partition community property into separate property before they could create a right of survivorship.

6. *Spouse Omitted from Premarital Will*

Changes in circumstances between execution of a will and the testator's death may render the will stale in various respects. The rules pertaining to the revocation of provisions for a spouse on divorce, lapse and antilapse, and ademption and abatement, among others, are perhaps best understood as mechanisms by which the law undertakes to mitigate the stale will problem. See Adam H. Hirsch, Text and Time: A Theory of Testamentary Obsolescence, 86 Wash. U. L. Rev. 609 (2009). Another rule in this vein protects a surviving spouse from unintentional disinheritance through a premarital will.

At common law, a premarital will was revoked on marriage or on marriage followed by the birth of issue. This obsolete rule, although still in force in a few states, has been overridden in most states by statutes that give a surviving spouse who is omitted from a premarital will a spousal intestate share but otherwise leave the premarital will intact. The purpose of these statutes is to correct for the decedent spouse's probable mistake in failing to update the premarital will. The statutes thus state default rules that can be overcome by evidence that the decedent spouse did not mistakenly omit the surviving spouse in the premarital will. The question thus arises, what evidence is sufficient to show that omitting the surviving spouse was not a mistake?

In re Estate of Prestie
Supreme Court of Nevada, 2006
138 P.3d 520

HARDESTY, J.   In this appeal, we consider whether an amendment to an inter vivos trust can rebut the presumption that a pour-over will is revoked as to an unintentionally omitted spouse. . . .

FACTS

In 1987, California residents Maria and W.R. Prestie were married in Las Vegas, Nevada. Maria and W.R. were divorced two years later yet maintained an amiable relationship. W.R. was later diagnosed with macular degeneration and moved to Las Vegas, where he purchased a condominium. Maria also moved to Las Vegas, although she initially resided in a separate residence.

In 1994, W.R. simultaneously executed in California a pour-over will and the W.R. Prestie Living Trust (the inter vivos trust). The pour-over will devised W.R.'s entire estate to the trust. W.R.'s son, appellant Scott Prestie, was named both the trustee and a beneficiary of the inter vivos trust. Neither the will nor the inter vivos trust provided for Maria.

As W.R.'s sight worsened, Maria provided care for W.R. by taking him to his doctor appointments, cooking, and cleaning his condominium. In 2000, Maria moved into W.R.'s condominium to better assist him with his needs. In 2001, W.R. amended the inter vivos trust to grant Maria a life estate in his condominium upon his death.[22] A few weeks later, Maria and W.R. were married for a second time. W.R. passed away approximately nine months later.

Maria eventually petitioned the district court for, among other things, a one-half intestate succession share of W.R.'s estate on the ground that W.R.'s will was revoked as to her under Nev. Rev. Stat. ("NRS") 133.110 (revocation of a will by marriage). Specifically, Maria argued that because she married W.R. without entering into a marriage contract and after he had executed his will, the will was revoked as to her because it did not contain a provision providing for her or a provision expressing an intention to not provide for her.

The probate commissioner found that W.R.'s will was executed before he remarried Maria in 2001 and that the amendment granting Maria a life estate in the condominium was to the inter vivos trust, not to W.R.'s will. The probate commissioner also concluded that, under NRS 133.110, W.R. and Maria did not have a marriage contract and W.R.'s will did not provide for Maria or express an intent to not provide for Maria. Therefore, the probate commissioner recommended that W.R.'s will be revoked as to Maria. The district court subsequently entered an order adopting the probate commissioner's report and recommendations, and Scott Prestie appeals.

---

22. The amendment to the inter vivos trust was erroneously labeled a codicil. See Nev. Rev. Stat. ("NRS") 132.070 (stating that a codicil is an addition to a will).

DISCUSSION

On appeal, . . . Scott argues that . . . W.R.'s amendment to the inter vivos trust rebutted the presumption of revocation of W.R.'s will as to Maria. . . .

NRS 133.110 provides for surviving spouses who are unintentionally omitted from their spouse's will:

> If a person marries after making a will and the spouse survives the maker, the will is revoked as to the spouse, unless provision has been made for the spouse by marriage contract, or unless the spouse is provided for in the will, or in such a way mentioned therein as to show an intention not to make such provision; and no other evidence to rebut the presumption of revocation shall be received.

Scott argues that W.R.'s amendment to the inter vivos trust, which gave Maria a life estate in W.R.'s condominium, means that Maria has been provided for under NRS 133.110. Moreover, Scott contends that W.R.'s amendment to the inter vivos trust rebuts the presumption of revocation under NRS 133.110. We disagree with both of these arguments. . . .

NRS 133.110 is unambiguous, and we have previously explained that it "provides for the presumptive revocation of a will if the testator marries after executing his will and his spouse survives him, unless he has provided for the surviving spouse by marriage contract, by provision in the will, or has mentioned her in such a way as to show an intention not to provide for her." Leggett v. Estate of Leggett, 494 P.2d 554, 556-57 (Nev. 1972). "The sole purpose of [NRS 133.110] is to guard against the unintentional disinheritance of the surviving spouse." Id. at 557. Thus, the *only evidence* admissible to rebut the presumption of revocation for the purposes of NRS 133.110 is a marriage contract, a provision providing for the spouse in the will, or a provision in the will expressing an intent to not provide for the spouse.

Accordingly, we reject the notion that an amendment to a trust, which provides for the spouse, is admissible to rebut the presumption of a will's revocation.[23] The plain language of NRS 133.110 dictates otherwise, and "we will not engraft, by judicial legislation, additional requirements upon the clear and unambiguous provisions of NRS 133.110." *Leggett*, 494 P.2d at 557.

W.R. executed his will before remarrying Maria; consequently, Maria could invoke the protections afforded to a spouse under NRS 133.110. Scott concedes that W.R.'s amendment to the inter vivos trust does not constitute a marriage contract and that no other marriage contract providing for Maria exists. Likewise, it is undisputed that W.R.'s will did not contain a provision providing for Maria or a provision expressing an intent to not provide for her. Thus, the district court properly concluded that W.R.'s will is revoked as to Maria, as none of the three limited exceptions contained in NRS 133.110 is present. . . .

---

23. We are cognizant of the fact that modern estate planning regularly utilizes revocable inter vivos trusts with pour-over wills. This approach to estate planning usually results in amendments, if any, being made to the revocable trust and not the pour-over will. Given the clear and unambiguous language of NRS 133.110, we caution that a testator must modify his or her will in order to avoid the consequences resulting from the unintentional omission of a surviving spouse pursuant to NRS 133.110.

CONCLUSION

We conclude that an amendment to an inter vivos trust cannot serve to rebut the presumption that a will is revoked as to an unintentionally omitted spouse. NRS 133.110 unambiguously permits three exceptions to rebut the presumption of revocation, and an amendment to an inter vivos trust is clearly not one of them. . . . Accordingly, we affirm the district court's order.

Uniform Probate Code (1990, as amended 1993)

§2-301. ENTITLEMENT OF SPOUSE; PREMARITAL WILL

(a) If a testator's surviving spouse married the testator after the testator executed his [or her] will, the surviving spouse is entitled to receive, as an intestate share, no less than the value of the share of the estate he [or she] would have received if the testator had died intestate as to that portion of the testator's estate, if any, that is neither devised to a child of the testator who was born before the testator married the surviving spouse and who is not a child of the surviving spouse nor devised to a descendant of such a child or passes under sections 2-603 or 2-604 to such a child or to a descendant of such a child, unless:

(1) it appears from the will or other evidence that the will was made in contemplation of the testator's marriage to the surviving spouse;

(2) the will expresses the intention that it is to be effective notwithstanding any subsequent marriage; or

(3) the testator provided for the spouse by transfer outside the will and the intent that the transfer be in lieu of a testamentary provision is shown by the testator's statements or is reasonably inferred from the amount of the transfer or other evidence.

(b) In satisfying the share provided by this section, devises made by the will to the testator's surviving spouse, if any, are applied first, and other devises, other than a devise to a child of the testator who was born before the testator married the surviving spouse and who is not a child of the surviving spouse or a devise or substitute gift under sections 2-603 or 2-604 to a descendant of such a child, abate as provided in section 3-902.

QUESTIONS, PROBLEM, AND NOTES

1. In *Prestie*, was Maria omitted from her husband's estate plan, or just his will? Put otherwise, was her omission from her husband's will mistaken? In determining whether Maria was "provided for in the will," why not look at the terms of the trust into which the will poured over? Why not look beyond the face of the will to determine whether the omission of a spouse was intentional? See Erickson v. Erickson, page 345; In re Estate of Bay, 105 P.3d 434 (Wash. App. 2005) (applying premarital will statute that provides an intestate share unless

there is clear and convincing evidence that a smaller or no share is more in keeping with the decedent's intent).

What result in *Prestie* if UPC §2-301 had been applicable? Is it likely that the failure to account for nonprobate transfers in the Nevada premarital will statute reflects a considered legislative policy judgment?

Suppose W.R. made a bequest to Maria in his will executed prior to their remarriage. Would Maria still qualify as an omitted spouse? See In re Estate of Moi, 151 P.3d 995 (Wash. App. 2006).

2. Why did Maria seek a spousal intestate share under the premarital will statute instead of an elective share? Nevada, where the case arose, is a community property state.

When a surviving spouse elects against a will, in many states the spouse is entitled to include nonprobate assets as part of the decedent's estate (called the "augmented estate" by the UPC). A spouse omitted from a will made before marriage is not able to reach nonprobate assets; her share is solely of the probate estate. Why is this? Why treat the situations differently?

If the surviving spouse is richer than the decedent spouse, effectively the surviving spouse has no forced share under the 1990 UPC and its 2008 amendments (see pages 498-501). But a richer surviving spouse omitted from a premarital will can take an intestate share. Why are these situations treated differently?

3. If *H* marries *W* some years after making his will leaving everything to his daughter by a previous marriage, under UPC §2-301 *W* is not entitled to an intestate share in *H*'s estate. She must elect to take against the will, where her share may be less than an intestate share. Mongold v. Mayle, 452 S.E.2d 444 (W. Va. 1994) (interpreting UPC). On the other hand, if *H* had left his property by will to his alma mater, *W* would take an intestate share. What is the reason for this?

SECTION B. RIGHTS OF DESCENDANTS OMITTED FROM THE WILL

1. *Protection from Intentional Omission*

a. The Domestic Approach

In all states except Louisiana, a child or other descendant has no statutory protection against intentional disinheritance by a parent. There is no requirement that a testator leave any property to a child, not even the proverbial one dollar.[24]

24. At common law, a child omitted from his parent's will had no remedy. It may have been thought that it was necessary to leave the heir a shilling to disinherit him effectively, but Blackstone says that this was an error. 2 William Blackstone, Commentaries *502. Blackstone says "cutting the heir off with a shilling" is traceable to a Roman law notion that the testator had lost his memory or mind unless he gave some legacy to each child.

*"Everything I have, son, I have because your grandfather left
it to me. I see now that that was a bad thing."*

Indeed, it is extremely common for married testators to leave their entire estate to their surviving spouse, with their children receiving property only if the testator's spouse predeceases the testator.

Even though a parent has the power to disinherit children, unless the parent does so in favor of a surviving spouse, the parent should think twice or, better, three times, before exercising the power. Several doctrines have been flexibly used to protect children, with the consequence that disinheritance is almost always a risky affair. A will disinheriting a child virtually invites a will contest. As we saw in Chapter 3, "testamentary capacity," "undue influence," and "fraud" are subtle and elastic concepts that judges and juries can use to rewrite the testator's distributive plan in order to "do justice." In contests by disinherited children, judges and juries are frequently influenced by their sympathies for the children. This is well known to practicing lawyers, who will often advise the devisees to agree to an out-of-court settlement with a disinherited child.

QUESTIONS AND NOTES

1. Would a forced share for children reduce the number of will contests? Professor Langbein suggests that "the American rule, by allowing liberal disinheritance of children, creates the type of plaintiff who is most prone to bring these actions." John H. Langbein, Book Review: Will Contests, 103 Yale L.J. 2039, 2042 (1994). Even so, he prefers "the American position of liberal testamentary freedom to disinherit children who turn out to be . . . disappointing and unsavory." Id.

Professor Tate makes another argument for the power to disinherit a child. Drawing on the writings by economists on the so-called strategic bequest motive, and echoing Jeremy Bentham (see page 17), Tate argues that the power of disinheritance gives an older parent or grandparent leverage to induce children and grandchildren to provide care for the parent or grandparent in old age. See Joshua Tate, Caregiving and the Case for Testamentary Freedom, 42 U.C. Davis L. Rev. 129 (2008).

2. *Louisiana.* The Louisiana forced share for children, which is derived from French law, is called a *legitime.* It protects against the disinheritance of children under 23, the mentally infirm, and the disabled. La. Const. Art. 12, §5 (2008); La. Civ. Code Ann. §1493 (2008). Prior to a constitutional amendment in 1995, the forced share extended to all children. See Vincent D. Rougeau, No Bonds but Those Freely Chosen: An Obituary for the Principle of Forced Heirship in American Law, 1 Civ. L. Comment. 3, 1 (2008); Max Nathan, Jr., Forced Heirship: The Unheralded "New" Disinherison Rules, 74 Tul. L. Rev. 1027 (2000); Katherine S. Spaht, The Remnant of Forced Heirship: The Interrelationship of Undue Influence, What's Become of Disinherison, and the Unfinished Business of the Stepparent Usufruct, 60 La. L. Rev. 637 (2000).

The Louisiana forced share for children is not absolute. It makes provision for disinheriting a child for "just cause," including:

> (1) The child has raised his hand to strike a parent, or has actually struck a parent; but a mere threat is not sufficient.
> (2) The child has been guilty, towards a parent, of cruel treatment, crime, or grievous injury. . . .
> (6) The child, being a minor, has married without the consent of the parent. . . .
> (8) The child, after attaining the age of majority and knowing how to contact the parent, has failed to communicate with the parent without just cause for a period of two years. . . .
> [La. Civ. Code Ann. §1621(A) (2008).]

The cause for disinheriting the child must have existed at the time of the will's execution.

b. A Look Abroad: Family Maintenance Statutes

Another way of providing support to both children and spouses is a discretionary system in which the court has the power to order distributions from the estate to the decedent's dependents based on their need and prevailing societal views of the morality of the decedent's estate plan. New Zealand pioneered such an approach in 1900. England, Australia, and most Canadian provinces now have similar legislation.

Under the English statute, which is representative, the decedent's property may be used to support those who were dependent upon the decedent during lifetime. Eligible dependents include the decedent's spouse or civil partner, former spouse or civil partner who has not remarried or formed a subsequent civil partnership, children, and any other person who was being maintained by the decedent. See United Kingdom Inheritance (Provisions for Family and Dependants) Act 1975, §1(1) (rev. 2004). Note, then, that the rules examined in this subsection apply not only to children but to spouses and civil partners as well. A spouse or civil partner is entitled to a financial provision "as would be reasonable in all the circumstances of the case" for a husband or wife or civil partner "to receive, whether or not that provision is required for his or her maintenance." Id. §1(2)(a)-(aa). Other eligible dependents such as children are entitled to receive such financial provision "as it would be reasonable in all the circumstances of the case for the applicant to receive for his maintenance." Id. §1(2)(b).

Lambeff v. Farmers Co-operative Executors & Trustees Ltd.

Supreme Court of South Australia, 1991
56 S.A.S.R. 323, 1991 WL 1121294

MATHESON, J. The plaintiff is the only daughter of George Lambeff who died at Ceduna on 23 March 1989, aged 63. She claims provision from his estate pursuant to the provisions of the Inheritance (Family Provision) Act 1972.

The last will and testament of the deceased was made on 14 March 1988 and probate was granted to the defendants on 15 November 1989. They were the executors named in the will. The second and third defendants were the only sons of the deceased. The will directed that upon payment of debts and funeral expenses the whole estate should be held upon trust for the two sons in equal shares absolutely. As at the date of swearing of the first affidavit of the trust manager of the first defendant, namely, 28 February 1990, the estimated value of the assets in the estate was $220,058.87. As at 24 December 1990, he deposed that the value of the net estate was $209,522.76. The major assets were a home unit at 15/17 MacFarlane Street, Glenelg North, valued at approximately $50,000, in which the deceased's former de facto wife, Barbara Lambeff, the mother of his two sons, lived, and a leasehold property at Ceduna, upon which there was an old stable, 18 powered caravan sites and a sand mine, and valued at $144,500. In addition, the deceased was the joint owner of a property at 13 Park Terrace, Ceduna with Barbara Lambeff, the capital value of which, according to the Valuer-General, was $120,000. The deceased lived with Barbara Lambeff from about 1956 to 1980 with several separations. She is not a party to these proceedings.

The deceased married the plaintiff's mother in Czechoslovakia on 28 June 1945 and the plaintiff was born there on 21 June 1946. The deceased, the plaintiff's mother and the plaintiff moved to Perth in the State of Western Australia in July 1950. The deceased and his wife separated in 1956, and in or about that year he commenced an association with Barbara Lambeff and moved to Ceduna where the deceased lived until his death. On 3 October 1957, the second defendant, Nicholas George Lambeff, was born and on 5 April 1961 the third defendant, Christopher Jordan Lambeff, was born. The deceased worked in Perth as a builder and continued so to work at Ceduna after setting up house there.

The plaintiff attended high school until the end of second year and then did a secretarial course at a technical college in Perth. Her mother married Leons Romanovskis in Perth on 29 December 1965. The plaintiff remained with her mother until October 1966, and then moved to Melbourne where she has lived and worked ever since. Her mother and her stepfather moved to Adelaide in about November 1974. At the time of her father's death, the plaintiff was employed by Scottish Amicable Life Assurance Society. Since the merger of that company with Colonial Mutual Life Assurance Society Ltd., the plaintiff has been working as a marketing officer. She proofreads marketing literature, assists with advertising and performs a variety of tasks within the marketing department. Her gross salary is $33,000. She has purchased a flat at 13 Hawkesburn Road, South Yarra. It cost $78,000 and the mortgage was $66,000. It will be repaid when she is 60. It was valued in January 1990 at $120,000. Her only other assets are clothes, furniture and jewellery. She is unmarried and has had no children.

It is convenient here to quote from the plaintiff's affidavit . . . :

> When I overcame my distress at being abandoned by my father in 1960, I wrote to him on three occasions, the first being in 1967, endeavouring to re-establish contact with him. I received no acknowledgment of the letters and interpreted this behaviour to be his total rejection of me. My letters were written at about five-yearly intervals. I believe the lack of response from my father at the time was due to the animosity he harboured towards my mother and/or the influence held over him by his de facto wife, Barbara. . . .

The defendant, Nicholas Lambeff, is 33 years of age. He has a wife and two children. They are expecting their third child. Nicholas Lambeff left school after attempting second year high school twice. He has four restricted building licences. He said that from about the age of 10 he worked for the deceased, helping him establish the caravan park, the largest asset of the estate. He said that any remuneration he received for his services was inadequate when compared with the number of hours he worked. He stated that he continued to help the deceased until his death because he had told him on many occasions that one day the caravan park would belong to him. He and his family have lived in the caravan park for about the last 15 years. He says that he and his wife have managed it since 1980, and for their livelihood they rely on the income earned from it and from some irregular contract work. His wife has no formal qualifications, but has assisted with the running of the caravan park and has worked as an assistant in a local chemist shop on a casual basis. They do not own any real estate. Their assets are worth approximately $27,500.

The defendant, Christopher Lambeff, is 30 years of age. He has a de facto wife and two children. He left school after failing fourth year high school, and has no qualifications. He also worked for his father from an early age in the caravan park. He has had various labouring jobs. His de facto wife has been a governess and a teacher's aide, but has not worked since the birth of their first child. They have no real estate. Their assets are worth approximately $30,350. They have been living at 13 Park Terrace, Ceduna, rent free, in the house now registered in the name of Barbara Lambeff. . . .

Section 7 of the Inheritance (Family Provision) Act states:

> (1) Where —
>   (a) a person has died domiciled in the State or owning real or personal property in the State; and
>   (b) by reason of his testamentary dispositions or the operation of the laws of intestacy or both, a person entitled to claim the benefit of this Act is left without adequate provision for his proper maintenance, education or advancement in life,
> the Court may in its discretion, upon application by or on behalf of a person so entitled, order that such provision as the Court thinks fit be made out of the estate of the deceased person for the maintenance, education or advancement of the person so entitled. . . .
>   (3) The Court may refuse to make an order in favour of any person on the ground that his character or conduct is such as, in the opinion of the Court, to disentitle him to the benefit of this Act, or for any other reason that the Court thinks sufficient. . . .

The plaintiff's case is that she was left without adequate provision for her proper advancement in life.

I was referred to the judgment of King, C.J., in Estate of Puckridge (1978) 20 S.A.S.R. 72. His Honour said (at 77):

> The words "advancement in life" have a wide meaning and application and there is nothing to confine the operation of the provision to an early period of life in the members of the family. In McCosker v. McCosker (1957), 97 C.L.R. 566, the expression was held to be wide enough to embrace the provision of capital for the poultry farming business of a claimant. The word "proper" is of considerable importance and means proper in all the circumstances of the case. The circumstances include the size of the estate, the needs of the applicants, the nearness or remoteness of the applicants' blood and personal relationship to the deceased, any special claims which the applicants may have on the bounty of the deceased, and competing claims of others.

In Bosch v. Perpetual Trustee Co. Ltd., [1938] A.C. 463 at 478-479, their Lordships said:

> . . . that in every case the court must place itself in the position of the testator and consider what he ought to have done in all the circumstances of the case, treating the testator for that purpose as a wise and just, rather than a fond and foolish, husband or father.

As Dixon, C.J., said in Blore v. Lang (1960), 104 C.L.R. 124 at 128: "Some moral claim to which a wise and just testator might be expected to respond must exist, but it may rise out of relationship." . . .

I agree . . . that there are now two totally separate family units. I also agree that upon the evidence the plaintiff has a secure, well-paid job, that she has a substantial equity in her flat and that she has no dependants. She has good prospects of benefiting from the estates of her mother and stepfather, although the poor health of her stepfather raises a question mark over that. The deceased's sons, on the other hand, have little in the way of assets and they have families to support. The estate is by no means large. They are, however, both young and fit.

It may well be that the plaintiff has established that she has a special claim upon the estate within the meaning of some of the earlier cases. I do not need to find one, because I do not think it is necessary to show such a claim on a statute worded as is the South Australian statute. . . .

The plaintiff was abandoned by the deceased at the age of 10, and had no support from him thereafter. She later made efforts to befriend her father. She has done nothing to disentitle herself. It is true that she has acquitted herself reasonably well in life without her father's support, but I think she would have done better with proper support for her advancement in life. I think her claim succeeds, but in all the circumstances the provision should be modest. I order that the defendants pay her a legacy of $20,000 out of the estate.

PROBLEM AND NOTES

1.   Suppose you are a lawyer in South Australia. *T*, a married man with assets worth $2 million, comes to your office and wants to leave half of his estate to charity, a quarter to his second wife *W2*, and the remaining quarter split between his two children from his first marriage. *T* explains that *W2* already has substantial assets and that his children both have good jobs and solid finances. *T* has heard about the family maintenance statute and wants you to provide an estate plan that will be hard for any of his dependents to challenge successfully. What do you advise?

2.   Professor Foster summarizes the debate over extending the family maintenance model of the English Commonwealth to the United States:

> Proponents laud the model's flexibility, which they claim allows estate distribution to be "tailored to individual need" and "evolving lifestyles." They also cite the "strong ethical appeal" of the family maintenance model. They praise this approach for exalting the moral principle that familial responsibility does not terminate at death. They stress that the model addresses ethical issues on an individual level as well. The family maintenance model authorizes courts to evaluate on a case-by-case basis the morality of both the decedent's dispositive scheme and the claims of survivors. Proponents argue that by promoting private support of dependents the model not only provides moral guidance but also performs a vital social welfare function. They conclude that the family maintenance model offers the optimal mechanism to secure meaningful protection of family members with the least intrusion on freedom of testation. Unlike the alternative foreign and U.S. entitlement-based systems, they argue, the family maintenance scheme "does not apply automatically" but rather comes into play only upon petition by qualifying "aggrieved claimants."

For critics of the family maintenance model, judicial discretion is a "terrible price" to pay for improved support of dependents. They view the model as fundamentally unsuited to the U.S. environment. They claim adoption of its discretionary scheme would be ill-advised, even "frightening" given the peculiarities of the U.S. probate system — a system, they argue, that is comprised of multiple, local probate courts, staffed often by lay judges chosen on the basis of politics rather than merit. For opponents, the costs of a discretionary redistribution scheme are also unacceptable. They contend it would "promote litigation," increase "information and administrative costs," and "deplete estates." Critics also argue that the family maintenance model would introduce such complexity and unpredictability into the U.S. probate process that it would undermine estate planning and obstruct simple, orderly transfer of property rights. [Frances Foster, Linking Support and Inheritance: A New Model from China, 1999 Wis. L. Rev. 1199, 1213-1215.]

After reviewing the experience with family maintenance statutes in England and Canada, Professor Knaplund argues against family maintenance in the United States:

> Because a court's role is to determine if the testator's reasons for omitting a spouse or child were valid and rational, a court is required to examine highly personal details of the family's history. . . .
> Such a system in the United States would likely mean frequent litigation and delay in the distribution of estates or pay-off settlements in many cases. New York decided not to enact a family maintenance system more than forty years ago, citing fear of excessive litigation. As Professor Glendon has argued, the American experience "with discretionary distribution on divorce should make us extremely wary of any system that would encourage a variety of friends and relatives to challenge wills and permit a probate judge to rearrange estate plans."[25] In addition, a family maintenance system violates our country's professed belief in freedom of testation, which allows a testator a great deal of latitude in choosing to whom to leave his estate. [Kristine S. Knaplund, Grandparents Raising Grandchildren and the Implications for Inheritance, 48 Ariz. L. Rev. 1, 14, 16 (2006).]

What do you think?

3. Some scholars recommend forced shares for children, such as Louisiana provides in some circumstances, while others suggest discretionary family maintenance systems, such as in the English Commonwealth. Compare Deborah A. Batts, I Didn't Ask to Be Born: The American System of Disinheritance and a Proposal for Change in a System of Protected Inheritance, 41 Hastings L.J. 1197 (1990) (recommending forced share legislation for children), with Ronald Chester, Disinheritance and the American Child: An Alternative From British Columbia, 1998 Utah L. Rev. 1 (recommending a Commonwealth family maintenance system), and Ronald Chester, From Here to Eternity? Property and the Dead Hand 75-92 (2007). See also Shelly Kreiczer-Levy, The Mandatory Nature of Inheritance, 53 Am. J. Juris. 105 (2008); Michelle Harris, Why a Limited Family Maintenance System Could Help American "Grandfamilies," 3 NAELA J. 239 (2007) (favoring family maintenance, responding to Professor Knaplund);

25. Mary Ann Glendon, Fixed Rules and Discretion in Contemporary Family Law and Succession Law, 60 Tul. L. Rev. 1165, 1189 (1986).

Helene S. Shapo, "A Tale of Two Systems": Anglo-American Problems in the Modernization of Inheritance Legislation, 60 Tenn. L. Rev. 707 (1993).

2. *Protection from Unintentional Omission*

We turn now to pretermission statutes, designed to prevent the *unintentional* disinheritance of descendants. It was such a statute that induced Calvin Coolidge, noted for economy of language,[26] to add an opening phrase to his will — the shortest will of any president of the United States. Coolidge's will read in its entirety:

"The White House"
Washington
Will of Calvin Coolidge of Northampton,
Hampshire County, Massachusetts

Not unmindful of my son John, I give all my estate both real and personal to my wife Grace Coolidge, in fee simple — Home at Washington, District of Columbia this twentieth day December, A.D. nineteen hundred and twenty six.

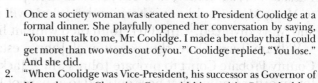

/s/ Calvin Coolidge

26. Many stories are told about Coolidge, who regularly slept 11 hours a day, including a 2- to 4-hour nap almost every afternoon. H.L. Mencken said that Coolidge's "chief feat" was "to sleep more and say less" than any other president. Paul F. Boller, Jr., Presidential Anecdotes 234, 243-244 (rev. ed. 1996). Here are some of our favorite stories about "Silent Cal":

President Calvin Coolidge exercising in the gym of the House of Representatives, 1923.

1. Once a society woman was seated next to President Coolidge at a formal dinner. She playfully opened her conversation by saying, "You must talk to me, Mr. Coolidge. I made a bet today that I could get more than two words out of you." Coolidge replied, "You lose." And she did.

2. "When Coolidge was Vice-President, his successor as Governor of Massachusetts, Channing Cox, paid him a visit. Cox asked how Coolidge had been able to see so many visitors a day when he was Governor, but always leave the office at 5:00 P.M., while Cox himself found he often left as late as 9:00 P.M. 'Why the difference?' he asked. 'You talk back,' said Coolidge."

3. Coolidge once explained to his successor, Herbert Hoover, how to deal with "long-winded visitors": "If you keep dead still they will run down in three or four minutes."

4. In 1933 when Dorothy Parker, *New Yorker* writer and Algonquin Roundtable regular, heard the news that President Coolidge had died suddenly, she quipped, "How can they tell?" [Id. at 235, 239-241.]

In an October 2000 survey of 78 prominent historians, law professors, and political scientists, Calvin Coolidge ranked 25th among American presidents, one place below Bill Clinton. Coolidge was among the more controversial presidents, with a substantial minority of scholars listing him as underrated. See James Lindgren and Steven G. Calabresi, Rating the Presidents of the United States, 1789-2000: A Survey of Scholars in Political Science, History, and Law, 18 Const. Comment. 583 (2001).

Signed by me on the date above in the presence of the testator and of each other as witnesses to said will and the signature thereof.

/s/ *Everett Sanders*

/s/ *Edward T. Clark*

/s/ *Erwin C. Geisser*

Gray v. Gray
Supreme Court of Alabama, 2006
947 So. 2d 1045

SEE, J.   William Terry Gray, the executor of the estate of John Merrill Gray II ("John"), appeals the probate court's judgment finding that John Merrill Gray III ("Jack") is entitled to receive a share of John's estate under Ala. Code §43-8-91 (1975). . . .

BACKGROUND

In 1981, John executed his will. At that time, John was married to Mary Rose Gray and had two children from a prior marriage, Robert B. Gray and Monica L. Muncher. John's will devised all of his estate to his wife Mary and did not include his two children. In 1984, John and Mary gave birth to John Merrill "Jack" Gray III. In 1989, John and Mary divorced. John and Mary's divorce judgment and property settlement included a provision creating a trust for Jack, which states that "[o]ne-half of all assets, inheritance or disbursements of any kind received by the Husband from his mother's estate shall be placed in trust for his son, Jack." Pursuant to Ala. Code §43-8-137, even though John's will devised all of his estate to Mary, Mary would not inherit under John's will upon his death because John and Mary divorced.[27] In 2004, John died without having changed his will.

William Terry Gray, the executor of John's estate, petitioned the Jefferson County Probate Court to probate John's will.[28] Jack petitioned the probate court for an order finding that he is entitled to a share of John's estate under Ala. Code §43-8-91, which provides . . . :

(a) If a testator fails to provide in his will for any of his children born or adopted after the execution of his will, the omitted child receives a share in the estate equal in value to that which he would have received if the testator had died intestate unless:

(1) It appears from the will that the omission was intentional;

(2) When the will was executed the testator had one or more children and devised substantially all his estate to the other parent of the omitted child; or

---

27. Section 43-8-137 revokes "any disposition . . . made by the will to" a divorced former spouse "unless the will expressly provides otherwise. Property prevented from passing to a former spouse because of revocation by divorce . . . passes as if the former spouse failed to survive the decedent." — Eds.

28. William Terry Gray, the executor, was also the testator's brother and the contingent taker under the will. — Eds.

(3) The testator provided for the child by transfer outside the will and the intent that the transfer be in lieu of a testamentary provision be reasonably proven. . . .

The executor moved the probate court to dismiss Jack's petition. The executor argued that Ala. Code §43-8-91(a)(2) applies because John had two children when he executed his will and devised substantially all of his estate to Jack's mother, Mary. Therefore, the executor argued, Jack was not entitled to his intestate share of John's estate. The executor also argued that Ala. Code §43-8-91(a)(3) applies because, he argued, John provided for Jack in a nontestamentary transfer in lieu of a testamentary transfer when he established a trust in Jack's favor upon his divorce from Jack's mother. . . .

The probate court granted Jack's petition, holding that Jack is entitled to a distribution from John's estate equal in value to the share he would have received had John died intestate. The executor appeals. . . .

Analysis . . .

We recognize the instruction of Ala. Code §43-8-2, that the Probate Code be "liberally construed" to promote its underlying purposes, one of which is to "make effective the intent of a decedent in the distribution of his property." However, Ala. Code §43-8-91(a)(2) does not place before the courts the issue of the decedent's intent, in contrast with §43-8-91(a)(1) and (a)(3). Those provisions preclude the omitted child's inheritance under the will when "[i]t appears from the will that the omission was intentional" or "[t]he testator provided for the child by transfer outside the will and the intent that the transfer be in lieu of a testamentary provision be reasonably proven." In §43-8-91(a)(2), the legislature has made assumptions regarding the testator's intent where the two stated factors are present. The courts are not invited to make further inquiry, as we are in §43-8-91(a)(1) and (a)(3). . . .

Section 43-8-91 states that, if a child is born subsequent to the execution of a will and the will fails to provide for the child, the omitted child is entitled to a share of the testator's estate, except in certain circumstances. One of those exceptions is that an omitted child is not entitled to a share of the estate if "[w]hen the will was executed the testator had one or more children and devised substantially all his estate to the other parent of the omitted child."[29]

In 1981, when John executed his will, he had two children by a prior marriage, and his will devised all of his estate to Jack's mother Mary. Therefore, §43-8-91(a)(2) applies, and Jack may not receive a share of John's estate.

---

29. Ala. Code §43-8-91(a)(2) does not distinguish an omitted child whose "other parent" is divorced from the testator after the testator executed his or her will from an omitted child whose "other parent" was divorced from the testator before the testator executed his or her will. The legislature could have limited §43-8-91(a)(2) to only one of those categories by including language to that effect.

Jack argues that the exception in §43-8-91(a)(2) should not apply to him because, he says, §43-8-91(a)(2) "does not appear to contemplate a situation wherein the testator has children, divorces their mother, remarries, executes a will that makes no provision for any children whatsoever, than [sic] has a child with that second wife." Jack's brief, at 8-9. However, §43-8-91(a)(2) states only two conditions for excluding an omitted child from an intestate share of the testator's estate: (1) the testator had one or more children at the time he executed his will, and (2) the testator's will devised substantially all of the testator's estate to the other parent of the omitted child. Because the statute is one of substance and is in derogation of the common law, we must construe it strictly and not extend its reach beyond its terms. Jack's argument, therefore, fails. The fact that John's other children were from a prior marriage is immaterial under §43-8-91. Thus, Jack does not escape the exclusion found in §43-8-91(a)(2). Accordingly, Jack is not entitled to receive a share of John's estate under §43-8-91. . . .

Because, as §43-8-91(a) makes clear, the entire provision is dealing only with omitted children who are "born or adopted after the execution of [the testator's] will," to adopt the construction [advanced in the dissent] that it is intended to apply only to a child "then in being" is to give to the statute a meaning opposite of what it says. We will leave such rewriting to the legislature, whose job it is to amend or repeal statutes. . . .

There is no ambiguity in this statute. . . . [E]ven if there were ambiguity, while the result provided by the legislature may or may not be the one that those of us on this Court would have provided, it certainly does not reach the level of absurdity required before this Court is compelled to conclude that the legislature meant something other than what its words convey.[30]

CONCLUSION . . .

Because we are reversing the probate court's order based on Ala. Code §43-8-91(a)(2) and remanding the case to the probate court for further proceedings, we pretermit consideration of the executor's remaining arguments.

Reversed and Remanded.

LYONS, J., dissenting. . . . The legislature created an exception to the rule permitting an omitted child to inherit when, at the time of the execution of the will, the testator, as a parent of one or more children, devises substantially all his estate to "the other parent of the omitted child." §43-8-91(a)(2). The only rational basis for such an exception is an intent to deny relief to a child then in being who is omitted from the will and whose other parent, under the terms of the will, is entitled to a devise and to whom, ostensibly, the omitted child can look for an inheritance. Also, without such an exception, an omitted child born after the

_____

30. The legislature might well have assumed that in a case like this one it could anticipate that the child would be protected in the divorce proceeding, either directly or by a distribution of a share of the marital assets to the custodial parent. In this case, as we have previously noted, Jack was provided for in the divorce proceeding by the creation of a trust.

execution of the will could inherit in the face of a testator's decision to favor the other parent of his then existing children to the exclusion of such children. In light of this circumstance, there is no reasonable basis on which to suggest that, had the testator executed a new will after Jack's birth, he would have been disposed to treat Jack any differently than the children he had previously excluded. . . .

Any other construction would reach an absurd result, which we are compelled to avoid. I would therefore read the exception set forth in §43-8-91(a)(2) as inapplicable to this proceeding because, at the time of the execution of the will, there was no "*other* parent of an omitted child" or, in other words, the testator had no parenting relationship with the devisee and therefore no basis to assume from the terms of his will an attitude of favoring her to the exclusion of *their* children.

Uniform Probate Code (1990, as amended 1993)

§2-302. OMITTED CHILDREN

(a) Except as provided in subsection (b), if a testator fails to provide in his [or her] will for any of his [or her] children born or adopted after the execution of the will, the omitted after-born or after-adopted child receives a share in the estate as follows:

(1) If the testator had no child living when he [or she] executed the will, an omitted after-born or after-adopted child receives a share in the estate equal in value to that which the child would have received had the testator died intestate, unless the will devised all or substantially all of the estate to the other parent of the omitted child and that other parent survives the testator and is entitled to take under the will.

(2) If the testator had one or more children living when he [or she] executed the will, and the will devised property or an interest in property to one or more of the then-living children, an omitted after-born or after-adopted child is entitled to share in the testator's estate as follows:

(i) The portion of the testator's estate in which the omitted after-born or after-adopted child is entitled to share is limited to devises made to the testator's then-living children under the will.

(ii) The omitted after-born or after-adopted child is entitled to receive the share of the testator's estate, as limited in subparagraph (i), that the child would have received had the testator included all omitted after-born and after-adopted children with the children to whom devises were made under the will and had given an equal share of the estate to each child.

(iii) To the extent feasible, the interest granted an omitted after-born or after-adopted child under this section must be of the same character, whether equitable or legal, present or future, as that devised to the testator's then-living children under the will.

(iv) In satisfying a share provided by this paragraph, devises to the testator's children who were living when the will was executed abate ratably. In abating the devises of the then-living children, the court shall preserve to the maximum extent possible the character of the testamentary plan adopted by the testator.

(b) Neither subsection (a)(1) nor subsection (a)(2) applies if:

(1) it appears from the will that the omission was intentional; or

(2) the testator provided for the omitted after-born or after-adopted child by transfer outside the will and the intent that the transfer be in lieu of a testamentary provision is shown by the testator's statements or is reasonably inferred from the amount of the transfer or other evidence.

(c) If at the time of execution of the will the testator fails to provide in his [or her] will for a living child solely because he [or she] believes the child to be dead, the child is entitled to share in the estate as if the child were an omitted after-born or after-adopted child.

(d) In satisfying a share provided by subsection (a)(1), devises made by the will abate under Section 3-902.

QUESTIONS, NOTES, AND PROBLEMS

1. Why did the majority in *Gray* not consider whether Jack was in fact mistakenly omitted from the will? Was Jack mistakenly omitted from the will? In view of the trust created by the testator for the benefit of Jack, could not the case have been resolved on the basis of Ala. Code §43-8-91(a)(3)?

Pretermitted heir statutes can be classified as "Missouri" type or "Massachusetts" type. Under a Missouri-type statute, the statute usually is drawn to benefit children "not named or provided for" in the will. Hence, it must appear from the will itself that the omission of a child or other heir was intentional. Extrinsic evidence of intent is not admissible. Under a Massachusetts-type statute, the child takes "unless it appears that such omission was intentional and not occasioned by any mistake." Extrinsic evidence is admitted to show the presence or absence of an intent to disinherit. See Annot., 88 A.L.R.2d 616 (1963, rev. 2008).

2. The Alabama omitted child statute at issue in *Gray* was based on the 1969 UPC. What result if UPC §2-302 (1990, rev. 1993) had been applicable?

3. When *T* executes her will, she has two living children, *A* and *B*. Her will devises $7,500 to each child. *T* then has another child, *C*. *T* dies. To what amount is *C* entitled under current UPC §2-302? The official comment says *C* is entitled to $5,000 taken one-half from *A*'s devise (reducing it to $5,000) and one-half from *B*'s. Suppose that *T* had devised $10,000 to *A* and $5,000 to *B*. What would *C* take and where would it come from? How would the analysis change, if at all, under the 1969 UPC?

4. In 1983, René executed a will providing for his three children, each by name. In 1984, René had a fourth child, a daughter Patricia. In the summer of 1986, René executed a codicil making minor changes to his will, but neglecting to add Patricia. In December 1986, René died. The state's pretermitted child statute, based on the 1969 UPC, applies to children born or adopted after the will was executed. Is Patricia entitled to a pretermitted child share? In Azcunce v.

Estate of Azcunce, 586 So. 2d 1216 (Fla. App. 1991), the court held that the execution of the codicil republished the will as of the date of the codicil, hence Patricia was not pretermitted. Is this a sound application of the doctrine of republication by codicil (see page 308)? See Restatement (Third) of Property: Wills and Other Donative Transfers §9.6, cmt. e (2003).

––––––––––––––––

Pretermitted child statutes follow one of two patterns. Some, like UPC §2-302, protect only children born or adopted *after* execution of the will. Other statutes operate in favor of children *alive when the will was executed* as well as afterborn children. Under these latter statutes the failure to name all of the testator's living children invites a challenge under the pretermitted child statute. This problem is acute in the minority of states in which the statute applies not just to *children* but also to *descendants*.

In Estate of Laura, 690 A.2d 1011 (N.H. 1997), Edward executed a will expressly disinheriting his grandsons Richard and Neil. Neil died, leaving two children, Cecelia and Neil, III. Then Edward died. The applicable pretermitted heir statute provided as follows:

> Every child born after the decease of the testator, and every child or issue of a child of the deceased not named or referred to in his will, and who is not a devisee or legatee, shall be entitled to the same portion of the estate, real and personal, as he would be if the deceased were intestate.

The question was whether the great-grandchildren, Cecelia and Neil, III, were barred from taking as pretermitted heirs under the statute by Edward's express disinheritance of their father, Neil. The court held that a testator who names a descendant in an effort to disinherit him has referred to, and thus disinherited, the descendants of the named descendant also.

Contrast *Laura* with Estate of Treloar, 859 A.3d 1162 (N.H. 2004) and Boucher v. Lizotte, 161 A. 213 (N.H. 1932). In *Treloar*, Josiah named "my son-in-law Leon," the husband of the testator's predeceased daughter, Evelyn, as executor of Josiah's will, but Josiah neglected to mention Andrew and Peter, the children of Evelyn and Leon. The court held that the use of the term "son-in-law" in identifying Leon, thus only indirectly referencing Evelyn (and in a fiduciary appointment to boot), was insufficient to preclude application of the pretermitted heir statute to Andrew and Peter. In *Boucher*, by contrast, the testator made a bequest to "Marianna, wife of my son Alphonse." The court held that this reference to Alphonse was sufficient to preclude application of the pretermitted heir statute to Alphonse's children.

While the reference in *Treloar* was less specific than in *Boucher*, is this distinction meaningful for determining whether the grandchildren were mistakenly omitted? Does it matter that in *Laura* there was a clause explicitly disinheriting the ancestor of the claimant?

NOTE

Suppose you are in a state like New Hampshire, which has a broad pretermission statute that covers not just children but also descendants. Must you rewrite your will every time a new grandchild or great-grandchild is born? The answer is No. In most states, pretermission can be avoided by providing for contingent shares to your descendants with representation. Thus, none of your descendants would be pretermitted if you devise the residue of your estate "to my husband, *H*, if he survives me by 90 days, or if not, to such of my descendants as survive me by 90 days, per stirpes."[31] You need not mention your descendants by name; you simply make them contingent takers *if* their parents should predecease you.

NOTE: ANNA NICOLE SMITH AND BLANKET DISINHERITANCE OF CHILDREN

In a jurisdiction where the pretermission statute applies to children born before the execution of the will, what provision would you recommend including in a will so as to cut out an existing child without mentioning the child by name or suggesting his existence? The question may arise, for instance, if the testator has a child unknown to his current spouse. Courts have been sticklers in requiring the testator to indicate clearly an intention to disinherit such a child, either by express words or by necessary implication. In Estate of Robbins, 756 A.2d 602 (N.H. 2000), the will provided: "Except as otherwise expressly provided by this will, I intentionally make no provisions for the benefit of any other heir of mine." The court held that this language did not disinherit a natural and an adopted child.

The question whether a blanket disinheritance clause is sufficient to block the application of a pretermitted heir statute garnered considerable press attention after the death of Vickie Lynn Marshall, better known as Anna Nicole Smith. In 2001, Smith executed a will in which she stated that "I have one child Daniel Wayne Smith" and left her entire estate "in trust for my child." The will also contained a blanket disinheritance clause:

> Except as otherwise provided in this Will, I have intentionally omitted to provide for my spouse and other heirs, including future spouses and children and other descendants now living and those hereafter born or adopted, as well as existing future stepchildren and foster children.

On September 7, 2006, Smith gave birth to a daughter, Dannielynn Hope. Three days later, her son Daniel, then age 20, died. Five months later, on February 8, 2007, Anna died of what the coroner's report termed "combined drug toxicity." The question thus arose, would Dannielynn take from Smith's estate?

---

31. *Caution:* You would still need to attend to the lapse rules and antilapse statutes (page 358) and to define what form of per stirpital or other representation is intended (page 868).

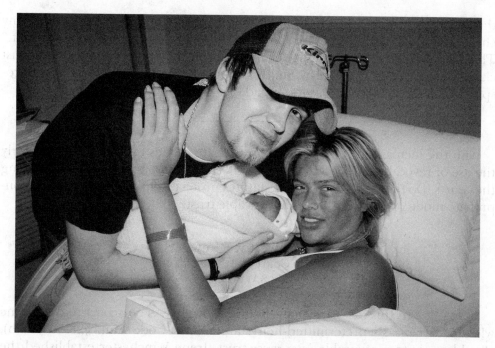

Anna Nicole Smith with her son, Daniel, and newborn daughter, Dannielynn.
Anna Nicole Smith/ANS/Getty Images

Under Cal. Prob. Code §21620 (2008), "if a decedent fails to provide in a testamentary instrument for a child of [the] decedent born or adopted after the execution of all of the decedent's testamentary instruments, the omitted child shall receive a share in the decedent's estate equal in value to that which the child would have received if the decedent had died without having executed any testamentary instrument." However, this provision is qualified by Cal. Prob. Code §21621 (2008), which provides that a "child shall not receive a share of the estate" if the "decedent's failure to provide for the child in the decedent's testamentary instruments was intentional and that intention appears from the testamentary instruments." Dannielynn's claim thus appeared to turn on whether the blanket disinheritance clause indicated that she was intentionally omitted from the will.

Or maybe not. Even if the disinheritance clause precluded application of the pretermitted child statute, Dannielynn's brother, Daniel, the sole named beneficiary, predeceased Smith without descendants. With no descendants of Daniel to be substituted for him by operation of the antilapse statute, and no other residuary taker named in the will, would Dannielynn take the entire estate as Smith's sole heir in intestacy? Or would the express disinheritance clause nonetheless prevent Dannielynn from taking by intestacy as well?

On March 4, 2008, the trial court ruled that Dannielynn was the sole beneficiary of the trust under the will. Although Smith's will left her entire estate "in trust for my child," and it stated that her only child was Daniel, the trust provisions in the will also referred to "my child*ren*" and used other plural language such as "*their* accustomed manner of living" (emphasis added). In resolving this ambiguity in favor of including Dannielynn, the court relied on a declaration of the drafting attorney, who said that although Smith "did not expect to have any children in the future, if she did, she wanted them to share equally in the trust." The purpose of the disinheritance clause, said the attorney, was to guard against claims against Smith's estate by Smith's estranged mother or others. "In retrospect, the language I used was too broad."

With the increasing popularity of nonprobate modes of transfer, particularly the use of revocable inter vivos trusts as will substitutes, a new question is facing the courts. Do the pretermitted heir statutes protect a child omitted from a nonprobate mode of transfer such as a revocable trust?

Kidwell v. Rhew
Supreme Court of Arkansas, 2007
268 S.W.3d 309

GLAZE, J. In this case, appellant Renda Kidwell asks our court to determine whether Arkansas's pretermitted-heir statute, Ark. Code Ann. §28-39-407(b), should apply to a revocable *inter vivos* trust. Irene Winchester established the Irene Winchester Revocable Trust on January 25, 2000. The trust named Winchester as trustee and her daughter, appellee Margie Rhew, as successor trustee upon Winchester's death. Winchester conveyed various parcels of property to the trust during her life, including tracts of real property in Jackson and White counties.

Although Winchester created the trust, she never executed a will, and she died intestate on March 14, 2004. Following her death, Kidwell was appointed as special administrator of Winchester's estate on October 15, 2005. As special administrator, Kidwell identified three separate assets that were potentially includable in Winchester's estate, including the parcels of real estate that had been transferred to the trust during Winchester's lifetime. On September 26, 2006, Kidwell petitioned the Probate Division of the White County Circuit Court for an injunction against Rhew, preventing Rhew from disposing of the property "until rightful ownership shall be determined." In a brief supporting her motion for injunction, Kidwell argued that the pretermitted-heir statute should apply to "dispositions made by testamentary will substitutes, such as an inter vivos trust."

The circuit court entered an order on March 13, 2007, rejecting Kidwell's argument and finding that §28-39-407(b) was "clear on its face and, by explicit terms, applies only to wills and not to trusts created during the life of the settlor." Accordingly, the court denied Kidwell's request to receive an intestate share of Winchester's estate; the court also discharged Kidwell as administrator of the estate and declared that the estate was closed. Kidwell filed a timely notice of appeal, and now raises three points for reversal; however, because each of her three arguments are similar, we treat them together in this opinion.

The fundamental question in this case involves the interpretation of §28-39-407(b). . . . The first rule in considering the meaning and effect of a statute is to construe it just as it reads, giving the words their ordinary and usually accepted meaning in common language. When the language of a statute is plain and unambiguous, there is no need to resort to rules of statutory construction. Moreover, the probate court is a court of special and limited jurisdiction, having only such jurisdiction and powers as are conferred by the constitution or by statute, or are necessarily incident to the exercise of the jurisdiction and powers granted, and the authority and jurisdiction of probate courts are to be strictly construed.

A pretermitted heir is a "child or spouse who has been omitted from a will, as when a testator makes a will naming his or her two children and then, sometime later, has two more children who are not mentioned in the will." Black's Law Dictionary 742 (8th ed. 2004). Arkansas's pretermitted-heir statute provides as follows:

> If, *at the time of the execution of a will,* there is a living child of the testator, or living child or issue of a deceased child of the testator, whom the testator shall omit to mention or provide for, either specifically or as a member of a class, the testator shall be deemed to have died intestate with respect to the child or issue. The child or issue shall be entitled to recover from the devisees in proportion to the amounts of their respective shares, that portion of the estate which he or she or they would have inherited had there been no will. Ark. Code Ann. §28-39-407(b) (emphasis added).

The purpose of the pretermitted-child statute is to avoid the inadvertent or unintentional omission of children or issue of deceased children unless an intent to disinherit is expressed in the will. This court has stated that the object of the statute is "to prevent injustice to a child or descendant from occurring by reason of the forgetfulness of a testator who might, at the time of making his will, overlook the fact that he had such child or descendant." Petty v. Chaney, 661 S.W.2d 373, 374 (Ark. 1983).

On appeal, Kidwell argues that, "if Irene Winchester's testamentary disposition of her estate had been by a Last Will and Testament containing the same terms of the Irene Winchester Revocable Trust, Renda Kidwell would have rights as a pretermitted heir." The immediate and obvious difficulty with that argument is that Winchester *did not* dispose of her property by way of a will. Instead, Winchester disposed of her property through an *inter vivos* trust.

A will and a trust are two different things entirely. A will is a disposition of property to take effect upon the death of the maker of the instrument. See Edmundson v. Estate of Fountain, 189 S.W.3d 427 (Ark. 2004); Faith v. Singleton, 692 S.W.2d 239 (Ark. 1985). A trust, on the other hand, is a fiduciary relationship in which one person is the holder of the title to property subject to an equitable obligation to keep or use the property for the benefit of another. See, e.g., Halliburton Co. v. E.H. Owen Family Trust, 773 S.W.2d 453 (Ark. 1989). As the terms are not interchangeable, it follows that the pretermitted-heir statute, which speaks only in terms of the "execution of a will," does not apply in instances in which there is no will.

Nonetheless, Kidwell argues that this court should look to the Restatement (Second) of Property, Donative Transfers §34.2 (1992), which provides as follows:

(2) If the donative transfer is under a substitute for a will, or under a transfer revocable by the donor at the time of the donor's death, and an issue of the donor who would take a share of the donor's property on the donor's death intestate is omitted as a beneficiary, in the absence of a statute in the controlling state, the policy of the statute in the controlling state applicable to an omitted issue in a will should be applied by analogy to the omitted issue in the substitute for a will, or in the transfer revocable by the donor at the time of the donor's death.

Kidwell urges the court to adopt this language, claiming that when there is no controlling case law, this court will "consistently rely on the Restatements." However, Kidwell fails to note that the Statutory Note and Reporter's Notes on Section 34.2 do not favor her position. The preface to the Statutory Note to Section 34.2 points out that the statutes cited therein "are applicable in terms only to wills. No statutes have been found which apply generally to any omitted intestate beneficiary. In addition, no statutes were found that extend the policy governing the omitted child statutes to will substitutes." Further, the Reporter's Note to Section 34.2 states the following:

> No cases have been found in which the protections by statute or case law afforded to a child omitted from a will have been extended to apply to a child omitted from a will substitute used as a comprehensive dispositive plan. Courts that have addressed the issue have decided against expanding the policy.

We decline to adopt the Restatement's provisions. According to its clear language and express terms, Arkansas's statute applies only to wills. When the language of the statute is clear and unambiguous, there is no need to resort to rules of statutory construction, as Kidwell would have us do. See City of Fort Smith v. Carter, 216 S.W.3d 594 (Ark. 2005). Here, the pretermitted-heir statute speaks only in terms of wills, and not of trusts, and Kidwell cites no convincing authority that would compel this court to reach the conclusion she urges. Accordingly, we affirm the trial court's finding that §28-39-407(b) applies only to wills and not to trusts created during the life of the settlor.

NOTES AND QUESTIONS

1. Most pretermitted heir statutes refer only to wills and not to revocable trusts. To the extent that the question has been litigated, the reported appellate cases are in accord with *Kidwell* that such statutes cannot be applied to a revocable trust used as a will substitute. See In re Estate of Jackson, 194 P.3d 1269 (Okla. 2008); Robbins v. Johnson, 780 A.2d 1282 (N.H. 2001).

The California pretermitted heir statute, Cal. Prob. Code §§21620-21621 (2008), uses the term "testamentary instrument" instead of will. What result in *Kidwell* under the California statute? See Cal. Prob. Code §21601 (2008) (defining "testamentary instruments" to include the decedent's will or revocable trust, and "estate" to include property held in a revocable trust that becomes irrevocable on the death of the decedent).

2.   Should the pretermitted heir statutes be amended to apply to a revocable trust used as a will substitute? Do not the same policies that underpin the statutory protection against mistaken omission from a will apply equally to mistaken omission from a revocable trust? Restatement (Third) of Trusts §25, cmt. e (2003) endorses the application of pretermitted heir statutes to revocable trusts used as will substitutes:

> Sound policy suggests that a property owner's choice of form in using a revocable trust rather than a will as the central instrument of an estate plan should not deprive that property owner and the objects of his or her bounty of appropriate aids and safeguards intended to achieve likely intentions. Thus, although a particular statute of this general type fails to address trusts that are revocable but nontestamentary, the legislation should ordinarily be applied as if trust dispositive provisions that are to be carried out after the settlor's death had been made by will.

What about other nonprobate transfers such as joint bank accounts, payable-on-death contracts, and insurance contracts? Should these too be subjected to the pretermission statutes? Does the asset-specific nature of these transfers counsel a different policy? See Alan Newman, Revocable Trusts and the Law of Wills: An Imperfect Fit, 43 Real Prop., Tr. & Est. L.J. 523, 550 (2008).

TRUSTS: INTRODUCTION AND CREATION

> Of all the exploits of Equity the largest and the most important
> is the invention and development of the Trust. . . .
> It seems to us almost essential to civilization, and yet there is
> nothing quite like it in foreign law.
>
> FREDERIC W. MAITLAND
> *Equity: A Course of Lectures* 23
> (*John Brunyate 2d ed. 1936*)

SECTION A.   INTRODUCTION

1.   Background

A *trust* is, functionally speaking, an arrangement whereby a *trustee* manages property as a *fiduciary* for one or more *beneficiaries*. The trustee holds *legal title* to the trust property and, in the usual trust, can sell the property and replace it with property the trustee thinks is more desirable. The beneficiaries hold *equitable title* and, in the usual trust, are entitled to payments from the trust income and sometimes from the trust corpus as well.

History. The ancestor of the modern trust is the medieval *use* (from a corruption of the Latin word *opus*, meaning benefit). Legal historians have traced the use back to the middle of the thirteenth century when the Franciscan friars came to England. Because the friars were forbidden to own property, benefactors conveyed land to friends of the friars, to hold to the use of the friars. Thus *O*, owner of Blackacre, would *enfeoff A* and his heirs to hold Blackacre *to the use of* the friars. By this transfer, the legal fee simple passed to the *feoffee to uses*, *A*, who held it for the benefit of the *cestui que use*, the mendicant order. The cestui que use took possession of Blackacre, but the legal title was held by *A*.

Although there is some evidence that ecclesiastical courts enforced early uses, initially uses were not enforceable in the civil courts. Since no common law form of action existed whereby the cestui could bring an action against the feoffee, the law courts — paralyzed by the rigidity of their procedures — offered no relief. *A* could expel the friars (or whomever the intended beneficiaries happened to be) and use the property to benefit himself. This state of affairs appeared to be unconscionable to the chancellor, the "keeper of the king's conscience," who began to compel feoffees to uses to perform as they had promised. In effect, the chancellor used his equitable powers to protect the interests of the cestui que use.

Once the chancellor enforced uses, removing the risk of faithless feoffees, the use became increasingly popular. Landowners found that all sorts of benefits could be accomplished by putting legal title in a feoffee to uses. For example, prior to the Statute of Wills in 1540, land could not be devised by will; it necessarily descended to the eldest son. Landowners seeking relief from this forced primogeniture rule turned to the use: *O* would enfeoff Blackacre to *A* and his heirs to the use of *O* during *O*'s lifetime and then to the use of such persons as *O* might appoint by will. The chancery courts enforced such arrangements, making them viable will substitutes that, unlike conventional wills, could be used to avoid the primogeniture rule. Landowners also used uses to avoid feudal death taxes (known as *feudal incidents*), which resulted in a dramatic decline in tax collections. It was this use of the use — avoiding taxes — that brought on the Statute of Uses.

Searching for a way to restore his feudal incidents and replenish his treasury, Henry VIII endeavored to abolish the use. Henry interested himself personally in a lawsuit in the courts, which resulted in a decision putting into doubt the legality of the use generally. Fearing that uses might become unenforceable, with drastic consequences for the cestuis (the beneficiaries), Parliament, on Henry's urging, reluctantly enacted the Statute of Uses in 1535. By this statute, which became effective in 1536, legal title was taken away from the feoffee to uses and given to the cestui que use. In the words of the time, the use was "executed," that is, each equitable interest was converted into a legal interest. The former cestuis — now clothed with legal title — could breathe easy, but they had to pay the king his due upon death.

Then again, maybe not. Although the purpose of the Statute of Uses was to abolish uses, imaginative lawyers found holes in the statute. Courts eventually held that the statute did not operate if the feoffee to uses (the trustee) was given *active duties* to perform (that is, if he had duties beyond simply holding title to the property). This interpretation of the statute permitted chancery to reassert its equitable jurisdiction over uses under the new name of "trust."[1]

---

1. For the history of the development of the trust, see Frederic W. Maitland, Equity: A Course of Lectures (John Brunyate 2d ed. 1936). See also Gregory S. Alexander, The Transformation of Trusts as a Legal Category, 1800-1914, 5 Law & Hist. Rev. 303 (1987); John H. Langbein, The Contractarian Basis of the Law of Trusts, 105 Yale L.J. 625 (1995); Amy Morris Hess, George Gleason Bogert, and George Taylor Bogert, The Law of Trusts and Trustees §§2-6 (3d ed. 2007); 1 Austin Wakeman Scott, William Franklin Fratcher, and Mark L. Ascher, Scott and Ascher on Trusts §§1.1-1.9 (5th ed. 2006).

Trust Purposes. "The purposes for which we can create trusts are as unlimited as our imagination." 1 Austin Wakeman Scott, William Franklin Fratcher, and Mark L. Ascher, Scott and Ascher on Trusts §1.1, at 4 (5th ed. 2006). The diverse purposes for which the trust may be used range from a simple estate plan to provide for a surviving spouse and children in accordance with their respective needs, to commercial enterprises such as mutual funds, pensions, and various structured finance transactions. Lawyers have found many uses for the trust, particularly in situations where there are many beneficiaries or owners and it is desirable to avoid fragmented management of the property. The crucial point is that the trust provides *managerial intermediation*. Because the trustee manages the property on behalf of the beneficiary, the trust "separate[s] the benefits of ownership from the burdens of ownership." Id.

Although *business trusts* have considerable transactional and capital-market importance, our present focus — and the primary focus of the remainder of this book — is on *private trusts* that are created *gratuitously* for the benefit of individual beneficiaries. We do, however, say a few words about the commercial uses of the trust at pages 555-557. Trusts for *charitable purposes* are the subject of Chapter 11.

Private trusts can be used to effect countless forms of gratuitous wealth transfer. Here are five common uses of such trusts in estate planning:

Case 1. Revocable trusts. O declares herself trustee of property for the benefit of O for life, and then on O's death to pay the principal to O's descendants. O retains the power to revoke the trust. This revocable trust avoids the delays, costs, and publicity of probate. The use of the revocable trust as a will substitute is discussed in Chapter 6.

Case 2. Testamentary marital trusts. The federal estate tax law permits a deduction for property given to the surviving spouse (see Chapter 15). The following structure qualifies for the marital deduction: H devises property to X in trust to pay the income to W for her life, and then on her death to pay the principal to H's children. No estate taxes are payable at H's death. Such a trust might be particularly useful if W needs professional money management or is the stepparent of H's children and might not bequeath the property to them if it were left to her outright.

Case 3. Trusts for incompetent persons. O's son A is mentally or physically impaired and is unable to manage his property. O transfers property to X in trust to support A for life, remainder to A's descendants, and if A dies without descendants, to O's daughter B.

Case 4. Trusts for minors. The federal gift tax law allows a tax-free gift of $13,000 per year per donee. An outright gift to a minor creates special problems, however, as the minor is legally unable to manage her property. To permit annual tax-free gifts of $13,000 to his minor daughter A, O creates a trust to use the income and principal for the benefit of A before she reaches 21, and to pay A the principal when she reaches 21. Every year O can make a tax-free gift of $13,000 to the trustee for A.

Case 5. Discretionary trusts. T devises property to X in trust. The trust agreement gives X absolute discretion to pay any amount of income or principal to A, or for A's benefit. Or, X might be given discretion to pay trust income to any one or more of a class of persons, such as A and her descendants, and to distribute the trust property to A's descendants at A's death. Discretionary trusts are useful in lessening the tax burden on family wealth by distributing income to the members of the family in the lowest tax brackets; in preventing creditors of the beneficiary from reaching trust property; and in preserving flexibility to account for changes in future circumstances.

These skeletal examples barely scratch the surface of the myriad donative uses to which trusts are amenable.

Statistics. Trusts arise from private agreement without the need for state involvement. Consequently, hard data on the use of trusts in practice is patchy, but there is some. Federal law requires banks and other trust institutions that are part of the Federal Reserve System to make annual reports of their trust holdings. These reports indicate roughly $760 billion held in roughly 1.25 million private and charitable trust accounts as of year-end 2006. These eye-popping figures necessarily understate the total number of trusts and the aggregate value of trust property because they exclude all trusts for which the trustee is not an institution in the Federal Reserve System.

Another source of data on trust usage is trust income tax returns. Many trustees must file a federal tax return, Form 1041, each year that the trust earns income. Aggregating the figures reported on these returns for trusts that are clearly identifiable as irrevocable and not subject to the control of the donor yields some staggering sums. In filing-year 2007, the Internal Revenue Service received more than 2 million such returns reporting $142.5 billion in gross income, $3.7 billion in fiduciary fees paid, and $1.6 billion in attorney, accountant, and other professional services fees paid. Because these figures exclude many other trusts — including all revocable trusts — they too necessarily understate trust usage in practice.

In summary: Trusts are big business indeed!

Sources of Law. The evolution of modern American trust law has been influenced heavily by a handful of key, nonjudicial authorities, and lately trust law has increasingly become statutory law. Perhaps the most influential of the nonjudicial authorities have been the First and Second Restatements of Trusts, published in 1935 and 1959 respectively. The reporter for both, Professor Austin Wakeman Scott of Harvard, also published a multivolume treatise that tracked the organization of the Restatements and cited them constantly. Together, the Restatements and Scott's closely allied treatise, plus the competing multivolume treatise by Professor George Gleason Bogert of the University of Chicago, came to be cited regularly by courts and commentators. Several states, most notably California, have enacted statutes based on various provisions of the Restatements.

Today the Scott treatise, now renamed Scott and Ascher on Trusts, is maintained by Professor Mark L. Ascher of the University of Texas, and the Bogert treatise is being updated under the supervision of Professor Amy Morris Hess of the University of Tennessee. The Restatement, too, has been updated. The first two volumes of the Restatement (Third) of Trusts were published in 2003. The third volume, which supersedes an interim 1992 volume on trust investment law, was published in 2007. The fourth and final volume of the Restatement (Third) of Trusts is now in progress, with associate reporters Professor Thomas P. Gallanis of the University of Minnesota and Professor Randall W. Roth of the University of Hawaii joining reporter Professor Edward C. Halbach, Jr. of the University of California, Berkeley.

Professor Austin Wakeman Scott   **Professor George Gleason Bogert**

Another engine for trust law reform is the Uniform Law Commission, which has promulgated quite a few uniform acts pertaining to trust law. The Uniform Trustee Powers Act (1964) modernized the law of trustees' powers by providing statutory validation of the expansion of trustees' powers commonly found in well-drafted trust instruments. Article VII of the 1969 Uniform Probate Code provided a modest codification of the law of trust administration. The Uniform Statutory Rule Against Perpetuities (1986), now in force in about half the states, reformed the Rule Against Perpetuities. The Uniform Prudent Investor Act, which has been broadly enacted since its promulgation in 1994, updated the law of trust investment. The Uniform Principal and Income Act, promulgated originally in 1931 but subsequently revised in 1962 and again in 1997, updated the law governing the allocation of investment returns between life and remainder beneficiaries. See John H. Langbein, Why Did Trust Law Become Statute Law in the United States?, 58 Ala. L. Rev. 1069 (2007). See also Mary Louise Fellows and Gregory S. Alexander, Forty Years of Codification of Estates and Trusts Law: Lessons for the Next Generation, 40 Ga. L. Rev. 1049 (2006).

This process of codification culminated with the promulgation in 2000 of the Uniform Trust Code (UTC), for which Professor David M. English of the University of Missouri served as reporter. The first systematic, national codification of American trust law, the UTC has been well received by state legislatures. As of this writing, the UTC has been enacted in 21 jurisdictions: Alabama, Arizona, Arkansas, District of Columbia, Florida, Kansas, Maine, Missouri, Nebraska, New Hampshire, New Mexico, North Carolina, North Dakota, Ohio, Oregon, Pennsylvania, South Carolina, Tennessee, Utah, Virginia, and Wyoming.

Uniform Trust Code Adoptions (2008)

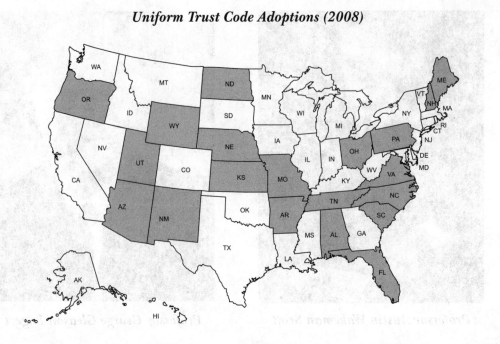

Current information on the UTC, including enactment tracking, is available online at www.utcproject.org.

In general, the drafters of the UTC codified the prevailing common law rules of American trust law. On some issues, however, the drafters took the additional steps of updating or reforming existing law — or even offering their own innovations. For discussions by the reporter and by a member of the drafting committee, see David M. English, The Uniform Trust Code (2000): Significant Provisions and Policy Issues, 67 Mo. L. Rev. 143 (2002), and John H. Langbein, The Uniform Trust Code: Codification of the Law of Trusts in the United States, 15 Tr. L. Intl. 66 (2001). Throughout the remainder of this book, we often reproduce or at least describe the UTC provisions relevant to the particular topic under discussion. In areas in which the UTC diverges from the common law or introduces innovation, you should think carefully about whether the UTC approach is better than traditional law and any alternative you can imagine. Enacting jurisdictions have sometimes made changes to the UTC not only to account for the idiosyncrasies of local practice, but also, and more interestingly, in response to disagreement with policy choices encoded in the UTC.

A note about the structure of the UTC: Most of the UTC's provisions state default rules that may be overridden by the terms of the trust instrument. The only exceptions are the mandatory rules scheduled in UTC §105(b), such as the overriding duty to follow the terms of the trust and to act in good faith. See John H. Langbein, Mandatory Rules in the Law of Trusts, 98 Nw. U. L. Rev. 1105 (2004).

For the most part, the Restatement (Third) of Trusts likewise codifies prevailing common law trust rules, but not always. Especially with respect to the rights of the beneficiary's creditors to trust assets and the rules of trust modification and termination, the latest Restatement takes positions that depart from both traditional law and the more modest innovations of the UTC. For these provisions, you should consider whether the Restatement's approach will lead to better outcomes than traditional law, the UTC, or any alternative reform you can imagine. For a discussion of the Restatement (Third) of Trusts and the modern uniform laws pertaining to trusts, see Edward C. Halbach, Jr., Uniform Acts, Restatements, and Trends in American Trust Law at Century's End, 88 Cal. L. Rev. 1877 (2000).

NOTE: FOREIGN TRUST LAW

In the epigraph that opens this chapter, the great scholar of the common law Frederic W. Maitland asserts that "there is nothing quite like [the trust] in foreign law." This refrain, that the trust is uniquely a creature of Anglo-American common law, is often repeated. However, given the trust's manifest usefulness in both donative transfers and commercial transactions, skepticism seems appropriate. If the trust is so useful, would not other legal systems have developed something similar? The answer is Yes. A trust-like device — the *fideicommissum* — existed in Roman law. The English judges who developed the trust may have been influenced by the German *treuhand*. In Hindu law, one finds a trust-like device called *benami*. In Islamic law one finds the *waqf*. A useful summary, plus references to apposite scholarly discussion, may be found in 1 Austin Wakeman Scott, William Franklin Fratcher, and Mark L. Ascher, Scott and Ascher on Trusts §1.10 (5th ed. 2006).

Today there is trust law in China and Japan, and trusts or trust-like devices are found in a host of other countries, including some that follow the civil law tradition. See Alon Kaplan and Barbara R. Hauser, Trusts in Prime Jurisdictions (2d ed. 2006) (collecting essays on trust laws across the world). In a similar vein, the 1985 Hague Convention on the Law Applicable to Trusts and on Their Recognition was established to provide guidance on the recognition of, and choice of law for, trusts in jurisdictions that lack a native trust law. See Emmanuel Gaillard and Donald T. Trautman, Trusts in Non-Trust Countries: Conflicts of Laws and the Hague Convention on Trusts, 35 Am. J. Comp. L. 307 (1987).

2.   *The Parties to a Trust*

A trust ordinarily involves at least three parties: the settlor, the trustee, and one or more beneficiaries. But three different persons are not necessary for a trust. One person can wear two hats, or sometimes even all three.

a.   **The Settlor**

The person who creates a trust is the *settlor* or *trustor* or *grantor*. The word *settlor* comes from our ancestors, who said the person makes a settlement in trust. The trust may be created during the settlor's life, in which case it is an *inter vivos* trust, or it may be created by will, in which case it is a *testamentary* trust. An inter vivos trust may be created either by a *declaration of trust* in which the settlor declares that he holds certain property in trust, or by a *deed of trust* in which the settlor transfers property to another person as trustee.

Case 1 above is an illustration of a declaration of trust. Under a declaration of trust, the settlor is the trustee. Unlike an outright gift, a declaration of trust of personal property requires neither delivery nor a deed of gift. The donor need only manifest an intention to hold the property in trust. (If the trust is to be funded with real property, however, the Statute of Frauds requires a writing.)

The settlor of the trust may also be a trustee and a beneficiary. Thus:

> *Case 6. O* executes a written declaration of trust declaring herself trustee of Whiteacre, to pay the income derived from Whiteacre to herself for life, and then on her death Whiteacre is to pass to *A*. Even though *O* is the sole settlor, sole trustee, and sole income beneficiary, this is a valid trust because there is an additional beneficiary, *A*.

In order to have a valid trust, the trustee must owe equitable duties to someone other than herself. If *O* were the sole trustee and also the sole beneficiary, the equitable and legal titles would *merge*, leaving *O* with absolute legal title. UTC §402(a)(5) (2000); Restatement (Third) of Trusts §69 (2003). Merger rarely occurs, however, because most trusts have different beneficiaries at some point in the life of the trust. In Case 6, *O* owes equitable duties to *A* even though *A* is not entitled to a distribution from the trust until *O* has died.

If the settlor is not the trustee, a deed of trust or actual delivery of the trust property to the trustee is necessary. In Case 6, if *O* wanted to make her lawyer, *L*, trustee, *O* would have to deed Whiteacre to *L* as trustee.

If a trust is created by will, the settlor cannot, of course, be the trustee. The trustee of a testamentary trust will necessarily be someone other than the settlor.

Our previous focus in Chapter 6 was on the use of revocable inter vivos trusts as will substitutes, primarily declarations of trust in which the settlor serves as the original trustee and retains the power to revoke the trust. Our focus now shifts to irrevocable trusts managed by a trustee other than the settlor.

b. The Trustee

A trust may have one trustee or several trustees. A trustee may be an individual or a corporation. A trustee may be a third party, the settlor, or a beneficiary. Thus:

> *Case 7. H* devises property to *W* in trust to pay the income to *W* for life, and then on *W*'s death the property is to pass to *H*'s children. This is a valid trust. Although *W* is both the trustee and a beneficiary, *W* is not the sole beneficiary. Because *H*'s children have a remainder interest, they can bring an action against *W* to enforce her duties as trustee.

If the settlor intends to create a trust but fails to name a trustee, the court will appoint a trustee. Restatement (Third) of Trusts §§31, 34 (2003). If a will names someone as trustee but the named person refuses the appointment or dies while serving as trustee, and the will does not make provision for a successor trustee, the court will appoint a successor trustee. This rule is sometimes stated: *A trust will not fail for want of a trustee*.[2] Thus:

> *Case 8. T* dies leaving a will that devises his residuary estate in trust, to pay the income to *A* for life, and then on *A*'s death to distribute the trust property to *B*. However, the will does not name anyone as trustee. Because *T*'s will clearly manifests an intention to create a trust, the court will appoint a trustee to carry out *T*'s trust purposes. (If the trust is created by a deed of trust and no trustee is named, the trust may fail for want of a transferee or for want of delivery.)

In order to have a trust, the trustee must have some active duties to perform. If the trustee has no duties at all, the trust is said to be "passive" or "dry," the trust fails, and the beneficiaries acquire legal title to the trust property. Findings of a passive trust are increasingly rare in modern practice. 1 Austin Wakeman Scott, William Franklin Fratcher, and Mark L. Ascher, Scott and Ascher on Trusts §3.4 (5th ed. 2006).

The central feature of the trust is *bifurcation*: The trustee holds legal title to the trust property, but the beneficiaries have the equitable, or beneficial, interests. Two categories of issues arise from this splitting of legal and equitable ownership of property: (1) the resulting effect on the rights of third parties with respect to the trust property, and (2) the rights of the beneficiary with respect to the trust property and against the trustee.

Third-Party Rights: Asset Partitioning. The trust is not a freestanding legal entity with the power to sue, be sued, and transact in its own name. Instead the trustee sues, is sued, and transacts in his capacity as such. Crucially, however, although the trustee has legal title to the trust property, a personal creditor of the trustee has no recourse against the trust property. Restatement (Second) of Trusts §308 (1959). Likewise, a creditor of the trustee *as trustee* — which is to say a person who transacts with the trustee in regard to trust property — has recourse against the trust property, but not against the trustee's personal property. UTC §1010 (2000). Thus:

> *Case 9. T* devises Blackacre in trust to *X* to pay income to *A* for life and the remainder to *B* on *A*'s death. *X* contracts to sell Blackacre to *Y* for $100,000. *Y* may enforce the contract to buy Blackacre by suit against *X* in *X*'s capacity as trustee, and *X* takes the proceeds from the sale of Blackacre as trustee, not personally. If *Z* has a judgment against *X* for an injury caused by *X*'s negligence unrelated to the trust, *Z* has no recourse against Blackacre or the proceeds from the sale of Blackacre.

---

2. This rule does not apply if the court finds (or if the trust instrument specifies) that the trust powers were *personal to the named trustee*. If it is determined that the settlor intended the trust to continue only as long as the person designated as trustee continues to serve, the trust terminates when the named person ceases to serve as trustee. This exception, however, is rarely invoked. In the usual case, the primary purpose of the settlor is to have the trust continue for the indicated purposes and not to have the particular person, and only that person, serve as trustee. See 1 Austin Wakeman Scott, William Franklin Fratcher, and Mark L. Ascher, Scott and Ascher on Trusts §§5.3.1, 5.5.2 (5th ed. 2006); 2 id., at §11.4.1.

Some older authorities, such as Restatement (Second) of Trusts §§244, 261 (1959), provide that the trustee is personally liable for the debts and other obligations arising from the management of the trust property, but offset that liability with a corresponding right of the trustee to indemnification from the trust fund. This older view no longer reflects modern practice and is rejected by UTC §1010. See also 4 Scott and Ascher on Trusts, supra, at §§26.1-26.7. Accordingly, from the perspective of persons outside of the settlor-trustee-beneficiary triangle, the modern law of trusts in effect splits the trustee into "two distinct legal persons: a natural person contracting on behalf of himself, and an artificial person acting on behalf of the beneficiaries." Henry Hansmann and Reinier Kraakman, The Essential Role of Organizational Law, 110 Yale L.J. 387, 416 (2000). See also Henry Hansmann and Ugo Mattei, The Functions of Trust Law: A Comparative Legal and Economic Analysis, 73 N.Y.U. L. Rev. 434 (1998).

The Beneficiary's Rights: The Fiduciary Obligation. By splitting legal and equitable ownership, the trust puts managerial authority in the hands of the trustee, but it is the beneficiaries, not the trustee, who bear the consequences of the trustee's good or bad decisions. See Robert H. Sitkoff, An Agency Costs Theory of Trust Law, 89 Cornell L. Rev. 621 (2004). To safeguard the beneficiary against mismanagement or misappropriation by the trustee, the trustee is held to a *fiduciary* standard of conduct.

The fiduciary obligation in trust law includes duties of loyalty, prudence, and a host of subsidiary rules that reinforce the duties of loyalty and prudence. Unless the trust provides otherwise, under the *duty of loyalty* the trustee must administer the trust solely in the interest of the beneficiaries; self-dealing is sharply limited and often prohibited altogether. Under the *duty of prudence*, the trustee is held to an objective standard of care in managing the trust property. Important *subsidiary rules* include: the *duty of impartiality* between classes of beneficiaries, such as income beneficiaries who want high yields and remainderpersons who want appreciation in values; the *duty not to commingle* the trust property with trustee's own property; and the *duty to inform and account* to the beneficiaries.

A trustee who breaches her fiduciary duties may be denied compensation, subjected to personal liability, and removed as trustee. In Chapter 10, we give extended consideration to important problems in trust administration and to the distinctive nature of the fiduciary office.

Because a trustee has onerous duties and is exposed to significant potential liability, the law does not impose upon a person the office of trustee unless the person accepts.[3] At common law, once a person accepts appointment as trustee,

---

3. In Daniel M. Schuyler, The Fiduciary Must Know The Law, 56 Nw. U. L. Rev. 177, 189 (1961), Professor Schuyler expressed the problem thus:

> The trustee's job, I think does not
> afford him such a happy lot.
> In return for modest fees
> he's subject to a constant squeeze.
> And written in the trustee's bible
> is the rule: "You're always liable."
> In view of this how can it be
> that anyone would be a trustee?

the person can be released from office only with the consent of the beneficiaries or by a court order. However, UTC §705 (2000, rev. 2001) modifies this rule to allow for resignation by a trustee with 30 days notice to all interested parties. Well drafted trusts often contain a provision to similar effect.

NOTE: INDIVIDUAL VERSUS CORPORATE TRUSTEES

What considerations should the settlor have in mind when choosing a trustee? Trustee selection usually follows one of two patterns. In the first, the settlor asks a trusted friend or relative to serve. This person, an *individual trustee*, typically agrees to serve out of a sense of friendship or moral obligation, not to receive trustee's fees. An individual trustee usually costs less than a corporate trustee, and, more importantly, often has a strong sense of the settlor's wishes. But the individual may be inexperienced in portfolio management, eventually become too elderly or incompetent to do a good job, or die before the end of the trust's term, in which case trustee succession becomes an issue. Well drafted trusts provide for trustee succession, but not all trusts are well drafted.

In the second selection pattern, the settlor names a *corporate trustee*, such as a bank or trust company. Almost every large bank has a trust department that is experienced in portfolio management and trust administration. Banks have deep pockets, which means that a recovery of damages is likely in the case of breach. Institutional bureaucracy provides the beneficiary with additional safeguards, as do federal and state banking regulations. See 12 C.F.R. §§9 et seq. (2008). But the cost of expertise, deep pockets, and institutional safeguards is higher fees. In addition, trust companies are sometimes perceived as being unresponsive to the beneficiaries and highly inflexible, a point to which we will return in Chapter 9 in connection with the law of trustee removal.

The modern rule governing trustee compensation, followed by UTC §708 (2000) and Restatement (Third) of Trusts §38 (2003), entitles the trustee to "reasonable compensation." The older rule, still followed in some states, is to award the trustee an annual commission set by a statutory formula (usually a percentage of the trust corpus, or percentage of trust income, or some combination of the two). See Mary F. Radford, George Gleason Bogert, and George Taylor Bogert, The Law of Trusts and Trustees §975 (3d ed. 2006). However, the rules governing trustee compensation are defaults that may be displaced by contrary agreement, and corporate trustees typically insist upon agreement to their published or other negotiated fee schedule before agreeing to serve.[4]

---

4. The current fee schedule for the Delaware-based Wilmington Trust Company, for example, is as follows: Subject to a minimum annual fee of $10,000, 1 percent for the first $2 million, plus 0.75 percent for the next $3 million, plus 0.5 percent for the next $5 million, and 0.35 percent for the next $10 million. Accounts in excess of $20 million are individually negotiated. Under this schedule, the annual fee for a $3 million trust would be $27,500 and for a $10 million trust would be $67,500.

In weighing the pros and cons of individual versus corporate trustees it is useful to consider more specifically what exactly it is that a trustee does. Professor Langbein suggests that trusteeship may be broken down into three roles: investment, administration, and distribution.

> *Investment* includes not only the initial selection of securities or other assets, but also the tasks of monitoring the investments for continuing suitability, investing new funds, and voting the shares. *Administration* includes the range of accounting, reporting, and tax filing. The responsibility for taking custody of securities is another branch of trust administration. Unusual trust assets may require other administrative work — maintaining and leasing real estate, insuring and safekeeping the Picasso and the diamond tiara, and so forth. *Distribution* is sometimes mechanical, but trust investments often bestow upon trustees the discretion to spray, sprinkle, invade, accumulate, terminate, and so forth. Distribution, therefore, requires interpreting and applying the sometimes complex language of the trust instrument; and it commonly involves contact with the current beneficiaries, in order to keep abreast of their needs and circumstances. [John H. Langbein, The Uniform Prudent Investor Act and the Future of Trust Investing, 81 Iowa L. Rev. 641, 665 (1996).]

A trusted friend or relative of the settlor who knows the settlor's values and the beneficiaries' circumstances is likely to excel at the distribution function, but might be ignorant of portfolio management and weak at administration. A corporate trustee may have expertise in portfolio management and administration, but might lack the family-specific knowledge that bears on crafting a sensible distribution policy. Accordingly, it is not uncommon for the settlor to name *co-trustees*, sometimes an individual and an institution, with the idea that the co-trustees will have complementary strengths and weaknesses. The modern law also encourages *delegation* by the trustee to experts on matters outside of the trustee's competence, a subject we take up at page 721.

A more recent method of fragmenting trusteeship is to name a *trust protector* who is given specific powers, such as to order distributions, replace the trustee, or modify the trust in light of changed circumstances. In a *directed trust*, the trustee, perhaps serving at a reduced commission,[5] is responsible for administration but otherwise must follow the directions of a third party, such a named investment advisor or distribution committee. We take up the ramifications of trust protectors and directed trusts at pages 651 and 723 respectively. The increasing importance of delegation and the growing popularity of trust protectors and directed trusts reflect the reality that a single person or entity often lacks expertise in one or more aspects of trusteeship. See Sheldon G. Gilman, How and When to use Trust Advisors Most Effectively, 35 Est. Plan. 30 (2008).

Another development is the rise of the *private trust company*, a company formed specifically to serve as trustee of one or more trusts created by a single family. By creating a private trust company, a wealthy individual or family can consolidate the various functions of trusteeship that might otherwise be parceled out through

---

5. The current fee schedule for the Wilmington Trust Company provides for commissions in directed trusts — trusts for which the Company is not responsible for portfolio management — that are 60 percent of the company's standard fees. See supra note 4.

delegation, protectors, and directed trusts. This might be desirable if the family wants to retain control over a family business or has other nonfinancial objectives. See John P.C. Duncan, The Private Trust Company: It Has Come of Age, Tr. & Est., Aug. 2003, at 49; Rachel Emma Silverman, Matters of Trust: Super-Rich Set Up Companies, Wall St. J., Aug. 4, 2007, at B1. Quite a few states have enacted statutes accommodating private trust companies, and in August 2008 the Internal Revenue Service issued a notice clarifying the associated income and transfer tax consequences. IRS Notice 2008-63, 2008-31 I.R.B. 261.

For further discussion of individual versus corporate trustees, compare I. Mark Cohen, Appreciating Individual Trustees, Tr. & Ests., Dec. 2006, at 32, with Barbara Hauser, Appreciating Corporate Trustees, Tr. & Ests., Aug. 2005, at 52.

c.   The Beneficiaries

Trust beneficiaries hold equitable interests. Generally speaking, this means that the beneficiaries have rights that originated in chancery and have different characteristics from legal interests. The beneficiaries have a claim against the trustee personally for breach of trust. But this personal claim has no higher priority than the claims of the trustee's other creditors. Thus, equity gives the beneficiaries additional remedies relating to the trust property itself. If the trustee wrongfully disposes of the trust property, the beneficiaries can recover the property unless it has come into the hands of a bona fide purchaser for value. If the trustee disposes of trust property and acquires other property with the proceeds of sale, the beneficiaries can enforce the trust on the newly acquired property.

Private trusts almost always create successive beneficial interests. Trust income is often payable to a beneficiary (or class of beneficiaries) for life, perhaps to be followed by life interests in another class of beneficiaries, with the trustee to distribute the trust property to yet another class of beneficiaries upon termination of the trust. The creation of a trust therefore usually involves the creation of one or more equitable future interests as well as a present interest in the income.

> *Case 10. O* transfers securities worth $100,000 to *X* in trust, to pay the income to *A* for life and then to *B* for life. On the death of the survivor of *A* and *B*, the trustee is to distribute the trust principal to *B*'s descendants then living. *X* has legal title to the trust property and has a fiduciary duty to manage and invest it for the benefit of the named beneficiaries. *A* has an equitable life estate. *B* has an equitable remainder for life. *B*'s descendants have an equitable contingent remainder in fee simple. *O* has an equitable reversionary interest. If on the death of the survivor of *A* and *B* there are no descendants of *B* then living, the trust property will revert to *O* (or to *O*'s successors if *O* has died in the meantime).

Today, most life estates and future interests are equitable rather than legal interests; they are created in trusts. Legal life estates and future interests in tangible or intangible personal property are rare and almost always unwise. Legal life estates and future interests in land are sometimes encountered. These too are almost always unwise. A trust with equitable interests is a much more flexible and useful means of giving successive interests in property than are legal interests.

NOTE: A TRUST COMPARED WITH A LEGAL LIFE ESTATE

A person who wants to give another a life estate may give the donee either a legal life estate or create a trust with the donee as life beneficiary. A legal life tenant has possession and control of the property, whereas a trustee, not the life beneficiary, has legal title to the trust property. Let us compare a legal life estate ("to *A* for life, remainder to *A*'s descendants") with an equitable life estate ("to *X* in trust for *A* for life, remainder to *A*'s descendants"). Is a legal life estate more or less desirable than a trust?

Legal life estates. The legal life tenant has no power to sell a fee simple unless such a power is granted in the instrument creating the life estate. Otherwise, to sell a fee simple *all* the remainderpersons and reversioners must agree to the sale or the life tenant must obtain judicial approval. The same analysis pertains to obtaining a mortgage or leasing the property. No banker is so foolish as to lend money with only a life estate as security, and prospective lessees will be wary of signing a lease that is limited to the duration of the life tenancy. Still another problem is waste. The life tenant may want to take oil out of the land, cut timber, or take down a still usable building. But each of these actions may constitute waste, entitling the remainderpersons to an injunction or damages.

If land is involved, someone must pay taxes and maintain the property. The general rule is that the life tenant has a duty to pay taxes and keep the property in repair, but only to the extent the income from the property is adequate to cover those charges. Life estates in personal property also pose problems. Personal property often requires expert management (think of stocks, bonds, and other financial assets). The application of the law of waste to life estates in personal property is uncertain, and thus insufficient to protect the remainderpersons from misappropriation or mismanagement by the life tenant.[6]

If the life tenant gets into debt, the creditor can seize the life estate and sell it. Of course, very little may be realized upon sale. Likely the creditor will buy it on judicial sale for a small amount, and if the life tenant lives a long time the creditor reaps a windfall. If the debtor is a remainderperson, the creditor may be able to seize the remainder and sell it. As with the life estate, the remainder may sell for very little, and the creditor usually will be the purchaser.

Many other problems may arise: trespassers may damage the property; the government may exercise eminent domain; a third party may be injured on the premises. If the respective rights of the life tenant and the remainderpersons are not covered in the governing document, they may end up being decided in expensive court proceedings.

Equitable life estates (i.e., a trust). All of the foregoing difficulties are resolved or mitigated by using a trust. If a house held in trust needs a new roof or if a plot of

---

6. Pennsylvania has abolished life estates in personalty, converting the life tenant into a trustee. Pa. Cons. Stat. Ann. tit. 20, §6113 (2008). Statutes in a handful of other states require the life tenant to account like a trustee, and in some states the courts may require the life tenant to give security. The Pennsylvania approach was endorsed by the late Professor A. James Casner in his classic treatise on property law. See American Law of Property §2.27, at 172 (1952).

land should be sold for development, the trustee usually has broad enough powers to act promptly to benefit the trust and its beneficiaries, allocating the costs and benefits fairly between life and remainder beneficiaries. Even if the settlor creates a wide array of exotic beneficial interests such as a life tenant, multiple remainders, and a variety of executory interests, when those interests are in trust, third parties need deal only with the trustee. See Thomas W. Merrill and Henry E. Smith, The Property/Contract Interface, 101 Colum. L. Rev. 773, 847-849 (2001). The trustee can mortgage, lease, and otherwise transact in relation to the trust property. Trust law supplies a law of fiduciary administration that spells out the trustee's duties in managing trust property and in balancing the interests of life and remainder beneficiaries. And, unlike a legal estate, an equitable estate can be put out of the reach of creditors, protecting an incautious beneficiary from himself.

In summary: When one considers all the problems that may arise in the future, one finds that a trust is almost always preferable to a legal life estate.

QUESTIONS AND NOTE

1.   In view of the disadvantages of a legal life estate, why not convert all legal life estates into trusts by statute? What purposes are served in having two bodies of law, one applicable to legal life estates and one applicable to life estates in trust?

2.   The English Law of Property Act of 1925 abolished the legal life estate. Today only two kinds of legal estates can exist in England: the fee simple absolute in possession and the leasehold. Apart from leaseholds, all life estates and future interests of every kind (remainders, executory interests, reversions, possibilities of reverter, rights of entry) are equitable interests. The holder of the possessory interest holds the property in trust for the other interested parties. See C. Dent Bostick, Loosening the Grip of the Dead Hand: Shall We Abolish Legal Future Interests in Land?, 32 Vand. L. Rev. 1061 (1979); Ronald H. Maudsley, Escaping the Tyranny of Common Law Estates, 42 Mo. L. Rev. 355 (1977).

3.   Commercial Uses of the Trust

Although this book is focused primarily on the use of the trust in gratuitous wealth transfer, it is worth pausing to consider the extraordinary role of the trust in the commercial world. In the late 1800s and early 1900s, before the corporate form had matured, large-scale business enterprises regularly organized in trust form — the common law *business trust*. John D. Rockefeller's infamous Standard Oil Company was organized as a trust, not a corporation. The prevalence of the business trust explains why we have antitrust law, not competition or monopoly law, as it is known abroad.

Unlike the corporation of the late 1800s and early 1900s, the common law business trust was only lightly regulated, so entrepreneurs used the business trust to escape the comparatively much heavier regulation of the corporate form. Using the business trust for this purpose was so pronounced in Massachusetts, where corporate ownership of real estate was prohibited, that the term *Massachusetts trust* became synonymous with business trust.

Over the course of the twentieth century, with the rise of permissive and enabling corporate law, the corporation became the entity of choice for business enterprises. Even so, the trust remains a vital cog in the modern economy. Among other purposes, the trust today is a preferred form of organization for mutual funds and asset securitization, and federal law imposes a mandatory trust form on employee pension funds. See John H. Langbein, The Secret Life of the Trust: The Trust as an Instrument of Commerce, 107 Yale L.J. 165 (1997). Thus:

> *Case 11. Mutual fund. T*, an investment professional, approaches *A, B, C*, and others like them and agrees to pool certain of their assets in a common fund to be managed by *T. A, B, C*, and the other investors each receive tradable shares in the fund in an amount proportional to their investment. By structuring their collective investment in this way, *A, B, C*, and the others are able to take advantage of economies of scale, obtain professional portfolio management, and achieve a more diversified portfolio than each could have individually. In managing the portfolio, *T* is subject to a fiduciary obligation to *A, B, C*, and the other investors in the fund. *Note*: Mutual funds are subject to regulation under the Investment Company Act of 1940 and other federal securities laws.
>
> *Case 12. Asset securitization. O*, a bank, regularly makes loans both to individuals and to businesses. The individual loans are secured by mortgages on the individuals' homes. The business loans are unsecured. *O* sells all its rights to payments under its entire portfolio of individual loans to *T* as trustee of an asset securitization trust. To pay for those rights, *T* sells equitable ownership shares in the trust to investors *A, B*, and *C*. Because the rights to payments under the individual loans are segregated in the trust, *A, B*, and *C* may ignore the risk attending to *O*'s business loans. In this way, *O* is able to realize the full value of its portfolio of individual loans notwithstanding its risk on the business loans. Once the transaction is complete, *T* manages the portfolio of individual loans subject to a fiduciary obligation to *A, B*, and *C*.
>
> *Case 13. Pension fund. E* hires *A* to work for *E* in *E*'s business. Under the terms of the employment contract, *E* agrees to pay a weekly wage to *A* and to contribute an amount representing 10 percent of *A*'s weekly wage to a pension trust for the benefit of *A*, payable to *A* upon her retirement. Until *A*'s retirement, the pension trust is managed by a professional trustee who is subject to a fiduciary obligation to *A*. *Note*: Most employee pension trusts are subject to the federal Employee Retirement Income Security Act of 1974 (ERISA).

Pension funds and mutual funds combined hold nearly $20 trillion, and the asset securitization industry is said to be worth in excess of $1 trillion. From the perspective of aggregate size, therefore, the commercial uses of the trust appear to exceed by a wide margin the use of the trust in gratuitous wealth transfer. Compare the figures on donative trusts at page 544.

Thirty states have codified the business trust, thereby creating the *statutory business trust*. Uniform Statutory Trust Entity Act pref. note (2008 Ann. Meeting Draft). Today, most structured finance transactions and mutual funds that make use of the business trust employ a statutory trust rather than one arising under the common law. The leading business trust statute is the Delaware Statutory Trust Act of 1988, Del. Code Ann. tit. 12, §§3801 et seq. (2008). A uniform act, the Uniform Statutory Trust Entity Act, is now in draft form and is slated for promulgation in late 2009.

For further examination of the trust as a mode of business organization, see Langbein, supra; Steven L. Schwarcz, Commercial Trusts as Business Organizations: Unraveling the Mystery, 58 Bus. Law. 559 (2003); Robert H. Sitkoff, Trust as "Uncorporation": A Research Agenda, 2005 U. Ill. L. Rev. 31.

SECTION B.   CREATION OF A TRUST

1. Intent to Create a Trust

No particular form of words is necessary to create a trust. Not even the word *trust* or *trustee* is required. The sole question is whether the grantor manifested an intention to create a trust relationship. UTC §402(a)(2) (2000); Restatement (Third) of Trusts §13 (2003). A person unfamiliar with trust law may therefore intend to create a trust; the focus is on function rather than form. A transfer of property to an individual to hold "for the use and benefit" of another person manifests an intention to create a trust. See 1 Austin Wakeman Scott, William Franklin Fratcher, and Mark L. Ascher, Scott and Ascher on Trusts §4.2 (5th ed. 2006).

LUX v. LUX, 288 A.2d 701 (R.I. 1972): In 1968, Philomena Lux died testate. Litigation ensued over whether she devised certain property to her grandchildren outright or in trust. The pertinent provisions of her will were as follows:

> 2. All the rest, residue and remainder of my estate, real and personal, of whatsoever kind and nature, and wherever situated, of which I shall die seized and possessed, or over which I may have power of appointment, or to which I may be in any manner entitled at my death, I give, devise and bequeath to my grandchildren, share and share alike.
> 3. Any real estate included in said residue shall be maintained for the benefit of said grandchildren and shall not be sold until the youngest of said grandchildren has reached twenty-one years of age.
> 4. Should it become necessary to sell any of said real estate to pay my debts, costs of administration, or to make distribution of my estate or for any other lawful reason, then, in that event, it is my express desire that said real estate be sold to a member of my family.

Based on this language, the court concluded that "Philomena intended that her real estate be held in trust for the benefit of her grandchildren." The court explained:

> In reaching this conclusion, we must emphasize that there is no fixed formula as to when a testamentary disposition should be classified as an outright gift or a trust. The result reached depends on the circumstances of each particular case.

We are not unmindful of the formal requirements necessary for the creation of a testamentary trust. It is an elementary proposition of law that a trust is created when legal title to property is held by one person for the benefit of another. . . . However, no particular words are required to create a testamentary trust. The absence of such words as "trust" or "trustee" is immaterial where the requisite intent of the testator can be found. . . . A trust never fails for lack of a trustee. . . .

When the residuary clause in the instant case is viewed in its entirety, it is clear that Philomena did not give her grandchildren a fee simple title to the realty. It appears that she, realizing the nature of this bequest and the age of the beneficiaries, intended that someone would hold and manage the property until they were of sufficient age to do so themselves. The property is income-producing and apparently she felt that the ultimate interest of her grandchildren would be protected if the realty was left intact until the designated time for distribution. The use of the terms "shall be maintained" and "shall not be sold" is a strong indication of Philomena's intent that the property was to be retained and managed by some person for some considerable time in the future for the benefit of her son's children. This is a duty usually associated with a trustee. We therefore hold that Philomena's will does create a trust on her real estate.

Having found the trust, the question of who shall serve as trustee is easily answered. The general rule is that, unless a contrary intention appears in the will or such an appointment is deemed improper or undesirable, the executor would be named to the position of trustee.

Jimenez v. Lee
Supreme Court of Oregon, 1976
547 P.2d 126

O'CONNELL, C.J.   This is a suit brought by plaintiff against her father[7] to compel him to account for assets which she alleges were held by defendant as trustee for her. Plaintiff appeals from a decree dismissing her complaint.

Plaintiff's claim against her father is based upon the theory that a trust arose in her favor when two separate gifts were made for her benefit. The first of these gifts was made in 1945, shortly after plaintiff's birth, when her paternal grandmother purchased a $1,000 face value U.S. Savings Bond which was registered in the names of defendant "and/or" plaintiff "and/or" Dorothy Lee, plaintiff's mother. It is uncontradicted that the bond was purchased to provide funds to be used for plaintiff's educational needs. A second gift in the amount of $500 was made in 1956 by Mrs. Adolph Diercks, one of defendant's clients. At the same

---

7. Jason Lee, the defendant in Jimenez v. Lee, was elected to the Oregon Court of Appeals in 1974, unseating an incumbent judge. As a result of the bitter campaign, a newspaper reporter sued the state bar under Oregon's open records law to reveal its disciplinary records on Jason Lee. In 1975, Lee filed for the Oregon Supreme Court seat of Chief Justice O'Connell, who was retiring in 1976. The decision in Jimenez v. Lee, written by Chief Justice O'Connell, was handed down on March 18, 1976. The next day, March 19, Jason Lee withdrew from the Supreme Court race. In June 1976, the Supreme Court decided the reporter's lawsuit and ordered the Jason Lee disciplinary records opened to the public. Lee's files weighed fifteen pounds and revealed many complaints. A public letter of reprimand, for ambulance chasing and for directing his secretary as a notary to execute false acknowledgments, had been issued to Lee in 1965.

Judge Jason Lee did not resign from the Court of Appeals. In 1980, while still sitting on that court, Lee died of a heart attack. Lee's will left all his property to his second wife, Merie. If Merie predeceased him (she didn't), his will devised his property in trust for his grandchildren: "I leave nothing but my love to my children."

The information in this footnote was furnished to the editors by Professor Valerie Vollmar of Willamette University College of Law. — Eds.

time Mrs. Diercks made identical gifts for the benefit of defendant's two other children. The $1,500 was deposited by the donor in a savings account in the names of defendant and his three children.

In 1960 defendant cashed the savings bond and invested the proceeds in common stock of the Commercial Bank of Salem, Oregon. Ownership of the shares was registered as "Jason Lee, Custodian under the Laws of Oregon for Betsy Lee [plaintiff]." At the same time, the joint savings account containing the client's gifts to defendant's children was closed and $1,000 of the proceeds invested in Commercial Bank stock.[8] Defendant also took title to this stock as "custodian" for his children.

The trial court found that defendant did not hold either the savings bond or the savings account in trust for the benefit of plaintiff and that defendant held the shares of the Commercial Bank stock as custodian for plaintiff under the Uniform Gift to Minors Act.[9] Plaintiff contends that the gifts for her educational needs created trusts in each instance and that the trusts survived defendant's investment of the trust assets in the Commercial Bank stock.

It is undisputed that the gifts were made for the educational needs of plaintiff. The respective donors did not expressly direct defendant to hold the subject matter of the gift "in trust" but this is not essential to create a trust relationship. It is enough if the transfer of the property is made with the intent to vest the beneficial ownership in a third person. That was clearly shown in the present case. Even defendant's own testimony establishes such intent. When he was asked whether there was a stated purpose for the gift, he replied: "Mother said that she felt that the children should all be treated equally and that she was going to supply a bond to help with Elizabeth's educational needs and that she was naming me and Dorothy, the ex-wife and mother of Elizabeth, to use the funds as may be most conducive to the educational needs of Elizabeth." Defendant also admitted that the gift from Mrs. Diercks was "for the educational needs of the children." There was nothing about either of the gifts which would suggest that the beneficial ownership of the subject matter of the gift was to vest in defendant to use as he pleased with an obligation only to pay out of his own funds a similar amount for plaintiff's educational needs.

Defendant himself demonstrated that he knew that the savings bond was held by him in trust. In a letter to his mother, the donor, he wrote: "Dave and Bitsie [plaintiff] & Dorothy are aware of the fact that I hold $1,000 each for Dave & Bitsie in trust for them on account of your E-Bond gifts." It is fair to indulge in the presumption that defendant, as a lawyer, used the word "trust" in the ordinary legal sense of that term. . . .

Having decided that a trust was created for the benefit of plaintiff, it follows that defendant's purchase of the Commercial Bank stock as "custodian" for

---

8. The specific disposition of the balance of this account is not revealed in the record. Defendant testified that the portion of the gift not invested in the stock "was used for other unusual needs of the children." Defendant could not recall exactly how the money was used but thought some of it was spent for family vacations to Victoria, British Columbia, and to satisfy his children's expensive taste in clothing.

9. The Uniform Transfers to Minors Act, which is the successor to the Uniform Gifts to Minors Act, is examined at pages 138-139. — Eds.

plaintiff under the Uniform Gift to Minors Act was ineffectual to expand defendant's powers over the trust property from that of trustee to that of custodian.[10]

Defendant's attempt to broaden his powers over the trust estate by investing the trust funds as custodian violated his duty to the beneficiary "to administer the trust solely in the interest of the beneficiary." Restatement (Second) of Trusts §170, p. 364 (1959).

The money from the savings bond and savings account are clearly traceable into the bank stock. Therefore, plaintiff was entitled to impose a constructive trust or an equitable lien upon the stock so acquired. Plaintiff is also entitled to be credited for any dividends or increment in the value of that part of the stock representing plaintiff's proportional interest. Whether or not the assets of plaintiff's trust are traceable into a product, defendant is personally liable for that amount which would have accrued to plaintiff had there been no breach of trust. Defendant is, of course, entitled to deduct the amount which he expended out of the trust estate for plaintiff's educational needs. However, before he is entitled to be credited for such expenditures, he has the duty as trustee to identify them specifically and prove that they were made for trust purposes. A trustee's duty to maintain and render accurate accounts is a strict one. . . .

Defendant did not keep separate records of trust income and trust expenditures. He introduced into evidence a summary of various expenditures which he claimed were made for the benefit of plaintiff. It appears that the summary was prepared for the most part from cancelled checks gathered together for the purpose of defending the present suit. This obviously did not meet the requirement that a trustee "maintain records of his transactions so complete and accurate that he can show by them his faithfulness to his trust." . . .

Defendant contends that even if a trust is found to exist and that the value of the trust assets is the amount claimed by plaintiff there is sufficient evidence to prove that the trust estate was exhausted by expenditures for legitimate trust purposes. Considering the character of the evidence presented by defendant, it is difficult to understand how such a result could be reached. As we noted above, the trust was for the educational needs of plaintiff. Some of the expenditures made by defendant would seem to fall clearly within the purposes of the trust. These would include the cost of ballet lessons, the cost of subscribing to a ballet magazine, and other items of expenditure related to plaintiff's education. But many of the items defendant lists as trust expenditures are either questionable or clearly

---

10. If defendant were "custodian" of the gifts, he would have the power under the Uniform Gift to Minors Act, Ore. Rev. Stat. (O.R.S.) §126.820, to use the property "as he may deem advisable for the support, maintenance, education and general use and benefit of the minor, in such manner, at such time or times, and to such extent as the custodian in his absolute discretion may deem advisable and proper, without court order or without regard to the duty of any person to support the minor, and without regard to any other funds which may be applicable or available for the purpose." As custodian defendant would not be required to account for his stewardship of the funds unless a petition for accounting were filed in circuit court no later than two years after the end of plaintiff's minority. O.R.S. §126.875. As the trustee of an educational trust, however, defendant has the power to use the trust funds for educational purposes only and has the duty to render clear and accurate accounts showing the funds have been used for trust purposes. See O.R.S. §128.010; Restatement (Second) of Trusts §172 (1959).

outside the purpose of an educational trust. For instance, defendant seeks credit against the trust for tickets to ballet performances on three different occasions while plaintiff was in high school. The cost of plaintiff's ticket to a ballet performance might be regarded as a part of plaintiff's educational program in learning the art of ballet, but defendant claims credit for expenditures made to purchase ballet tickets for himself and other members of the family, disbursements clearly beyond the purposes of the trust. . . .

The case must, therefore, be remanded for an accounting to be predicated upon a trustee's duty to account, and the trustee's burden to prove that the expenditures were made for trust purposes. . . . In determining whether defendant has met this strict burden of proof, the trial court must adhere to the rule that all doubts are resolved against a trustee who maintains an inadequate accounting system.

The decree of the trial court is reversed and the cause is remanded for further proceedings consistent with this opinion.

NOTE

The stakes in disputes over a transferor's intent to create a trust usually boil down to the applicability of the fiduciary obligation. In *Jimenez*, because the court determined that the father held the property in trust, he was subject to liability for breach of his fiduciary duties. See also Wilson v. Wilson, 154 P.3d 1136 (Kan. App. 2007) (upholding an award of punitive damages for father's breach of fiduciary duty in holding property for children under the Uniform Transfers to Minors Act). We examine the law of fiduciary administration in Chapter 10.[11]

---

11. Even without having studied Chapter 10, you are now in a position to evaluate the following Ann Landers exchange of May 23, 2002, which bears a striking similarity to Jimenez v. Lee.

Ann Landers

> Dear Ann Landers: I am a 15-year-old girl. When my sister and I were born, my parents set up college accounts with our parents named as trustees. My parents divorced seven years ago, and my mother discovered that Dad had gone into those accounts and withdrawn half the balances. He opened new savings accounts for my sister and me, listing himself as the sole trustee.
>
> My sister recently discovered that her account has no money in it. When I asked Dad to see my balance statement, he was evasive and said I was "too young to understand." He would not let me withdraw any money from the account. I'm pretty sure he has spent all of it. My mother cannot possibly afford to pay for all our college expenses. How can I approach Dad about what's going on without hurting his feelings? Is there any way I can get the money back?
>   — Loving Daughter in North Carolina
>
> Dear Daughter: Don't be so worried about hurting Dad's feelings. He should be honest with you about the money so you can prepare for your future.
>
> If the funds are gone, there is no way you can get them back. Ask your father point-blank if there is money left in the account and how much. Tell him you need to know so you can start saving for college as soon as possible. Meanwhile, be prepared to check out student loans and scholarships at state universities. Lack of money is no reason to miss out on a college education.

If Ann Landers had asked you what advice she should give Loving Daughter, what would you have said?

NOTE: PRECATORY LANGUAGE

In a surprisingly large number of cases, the testator expresses a "wish," "hope," or "recommendation" that property be used by the devisee in some particular manner. The problem is that this language does not clearly indicate whether the testator intended to create a trust, with fiduciary duties imposed on the devisee, or merely an unenforceable moral obligation. If the language indicates the latter, it is called *precatory*. Courts sometimes speak of *precatory trusts*, meaning unenforceable dispositions of this sort.

In Colton v. Colton, 127 U.S. 300 (1888), the testator devised his entire estate to his wife and then continued, "I recommend to her the care and protection of my mother and sister, and request her to make such gift and provision for them as in her judgment will be best." The question thus arose, did the testator's wife take the entire estate outright, or did she take it subject to a trust for the benefit of the testator's mother and sister?

> On the one hand, the words may be merely those of suggestion, counsel, or advice, intended only to influence, and not to take away, the discretion of the legatee growing out of his right to use and dispose of the property given as his own. On the other hand, the language employed may be imperative in fact though not in form, conveying the intention of the testator in terms equivalent to a command, and leaving to the legatee no discretion to defeat his wishes, although there may be a discretion to accomplish them by a choice of methods, or even to define and limit the extent of the interest conferred upon his beneficiary. [Id., at 312-313.]

After parsing the language of the will and the context in which the will was drafted, the Court concluded that the testator intended to create an enforceable trust.

As illustrated by the *Colton* case, to fathom the testator's intent the language of the governing document must be construed in light of all the circumstances. The result: great uncertainty and much litigation. Compare County of Suffolk v. Greater N.Y. Councils, Boy Scouts of Am., 413 N.E.2d 363 (N.Y. 1980) ("my wish," precatory), with Levin v. Fisch, 404 S.W.2d 889 (Tex. 1966) ("my desire," mandatory under the circumstances).

The lesson: Be clear in your drafting. For example, "I wish, but do not legally require, that *C* permit *D* to live on the land."

For further discussion, see Frank L. Schiavo, Does the Use of "Request," "Wish," or "Desire" Create a Precatory Trust or Not?, 40 Real Prop., Prob. & Tr. J. 647 (2006), surveying judicial treatment of precatory words and expressions, and Alyssa A. DiRusso, He Says, She Asks: Gender, Language, and the Law of Precatory Words in Wills, 22 Wis. Women's L.J. 1 (2007), presenting an empirical study of gender differences in the use of precatory words and discussing the relevance of those differences for discerning testator's intent.

NOTE

Another distinction deserves mention: the difference between a trust and an *equitable charge*. If a testator devises property to a person, subject to the payment of a certain sum of money to a third person, the testator creates an equitable charge, not a trust. An equitable charge creates a security interest in the transferred property; there is no fiduciary relationship. The relationship between the holder of the charge and the beneficiary is more in the nature of a debtor and secured creditor. See 1 Austin Wakeman Scott, William Franklin Fratcher, and Mark L. Ascher, Scott and Ascher on Trusts §2.3.6 (5th ed. 2006).

To make an outright gift of personal property, as compared to a gift in trust, generally the donor must deliver the property to the donee and the donee must accept the gift. But delivery can be constructive or symbolic, rather than physical, and courts generally infer acceptance from the absence of refusal or disclaimer. A *constructive delivery* gives the donee the means of obtaining the property, such as a key. A *symbolic delivery* gives the donee something symbolic of the object, for example a written instrument handed over when manual delivery is impractical. See Restatement (Third) of Property: Wills and Other Donative Transfers §§6.1 and 6.2, cmt. g (2003).

The foregoing rules concerning gifts collide with the law of trust formation when a donor intends to make a gift but fails to satisfy all the requirements of an outright gift, particularly delivery. In such a case the question arises, can the failed gift be saved by recharacterizing it as a declaration of trust? A declaration of trust, unlike an outright gift, does not require delivery because the settlor is also the trustee and thus already has possession. In addition, a declaration of trust can be made orally (subject to the statute of frauds). All that is necessary is that the donor manifest an intention to hold the property in trust.

The Hebrew University Association v. Nye
Supreme Court of Connecticut, 1961
169 A.2d 641

KING, J.   The plaintiff obtained a judgment declaring that it is the rightful owner of the library of Abraham S. Yahuda, a distinguished Hebrew scholar who died in 1951. The library included rare books and manuscripts, mostly relating to the Bible, which Professor Yahuda, with the assistance of his wife, Ethel S.

Yahuda, had collected during his lifetime.[12] Some of the library was inventoried in Professor Yahuda's estate and was purchased from the estate by his wife. There is no dispute that all of the library had become the property of Ethel before 1953 and was her property when she died on March 6, 1955, unless by her dealings with the plaintiff between January, 1953, and the time of her death she transferred ownership to the plaintiff. While the defendants in this action are the executors under the will of Ethel, the controversy as to ownership of the library is, in effect, a contest between two Hebrew charitable institutions, the plaintiff and a charitable trust or foundation to which Ethel bequeathed the bulk of her estate.

The pertinent facts recited in the finding may be summarized as follows: Before his death, Professor Yahuda forwarded certain of the books in his library to a warehouse in New Haven with instructions that they be packed for overseas shipment. The books remained in his name, no consignee was ever specified, and no shipment was made. Although it is not entirely clear, these books were apparently the ones which Ethel purchased from her husband's estate. Professor Yahuda and his wife had indicated to their friends their interest in creating a scholarship research center in Israel which would serve as a memorial to them. In January, 1953, Ethel went to Israel and had several talks with officers of the plaintiff, a university in Jerusalem. One of the departments of the plaintiff is an Institute of Oriental Studies, of outstanding reputation. The library would be very useful to the plaintiff, especially in connection with the work of this institute. On January 28, 1953, a large luncheon was given by the plaintiff in Ethel's honor and was attended by many notables, including officials of the plaintiff and the president of Israel. At this luncheon, Ethel described the library and announced its gift to the plaintiff. The next day, the plaintiff submitted to Ethel a proposed

---

12. In P.E. Spargo, Sotheby's, Keynes and Yahuda: The 1936 Sale of Newton's Manuscripts, the author writes:

> Abraham Shalom Ezekiel Yahuda . . . published his first book, *Kadmoniyyot ha-Aravim* ("Arabs' Antiquities") at the age of fifteen . . . . An extraordinarily competent linguist[,] he published extensively on theological matters as well as on Jewish-Arab relations. During his life Yahuda travelled widely and acquired an extensive and valuable collection of books and manuscripts. He died in New Haven, Connecticut, in 1951, but such was the high regard in which he was held that a year after his death his body was moved to Israel where he was given a state burial in Har-Menuhoth, Jerusalem, resting place of Israel's leaders. [Id., at 125, *in* The Investigation of Difficult Things: Essays on Newton and the History of the Exact Sciences 115 (P.M. Harman and Alan E. Shapiro eds., 1992).]

In addition to the rare religious texts remarked upon by the court, Yahuda's collection — appraised at the time of the litigation at $80,000 — included original documents signed by Napoleon and many of the nonscientific papers of Sir Isaac Newton. Yahuda competed with the British economist John Maynard Keynes for the acquisition of these Newton papers, and each wound up with impressive collections. Yahuda's collection, which included extensive writings by Newton on alchemy, theology, and the bible, was characterized by Albert Einstein in a letter to "My Dear Yahuda" as "a most interesting look into the mental laboratory of this unique thinker." Today, the Yahuda collection is held by the Jewish National and University Library in Jerusalem and the Keynes collection is held by King's College at the University of Cambridge. — Eds.

Professor
Abraham S. Yahuda

newspaper release which indicated that she had made a gift of the library to the plaintiff. Ethel signed the release as approved by her. From time to time thereafter she stated orally, and in letters to the plaintiff and friends, that she "had given" the library to the plaintiff. She refused offers of purchase and explained to others that she could not sell the library because it did not belong to her but to the plaintiff. On one occasion, when it was suggested that she give a certain item in the library to a friend, she stated that she could not, since it did not belong to her but to the plaintiff.

Early in 1954, Ethel began the task of arranging and cataloguing the material in the library for crating and shipment to Israel. These activities continued until about the time of her death. She sent some items, which she had finished cataloguing, to a warehouse for crating for overseas shipment. No consignee was named, and they remained in her name until her death. In October, 1954, when she was at the office of the American Friends of the Hebrew University, a fundraising arm of the plaintiff in New York, she stated that she had crated most of the miscellaneous items, was continuously working on cataloguing the balance, and hoped to have the entire library in Israel before the end of the year. Until almost the time of her death, she corresponded with the plaintiff about making delivery to it of the library. In September, 1954, she wrote the president of the plaintiff that she had decided to ship the library and collection, but that it was not to be unpacked unless she was present, so that her husband's ex libris could be affixed to the books, and that she hoped "to adjust" the matter of her Beth Yahuda and her relations to the plaintiff. A "beth" is a building or portion of a building dedicated to a particular purpose.

The complaint alleged that the plaintiff was the rightful owner of the library and was entitled to possession. It contained no clue, however, to the theory on which ownership was claimed. The prayers for relief sought a declaratory judgment determining which one of the parties owned the library and an injunction restraining the defendants from disposing of it. The answer amounted to a general denial. The only real issues raised in the pleadings were the ownership and the right to possession of the library. As to these issues, the plaintiff had the burden of proof. The judgment found the "issues" for the plaintiff, and further recited that "a trust [in relation to the library] was created by a declaration of trust made by Ethel S. Yahuda, indicating her intention to create such a trust, made public by her." We construe this language, in the light of the finding, as a determination that, at the luncheon in Jerusalem, Ethel orally constituted herself a trustee of the library for future delivery to the plaintiff. The difficulty with the trust theory adopted in the judgment is that the finding contains no facts even intimating that Ethel ever regarded herself as trustee of any trust whatsoever, or as having assumed any enforceable duties with respect to the property. The facts in the finding, in so far as they tend to support the judgment for the plaintiff at all, indicate that Ethel intended to make, and perhaps attempted to make, not a mere promise to give, but an executed, present, legal gift inter vivos of the library to the plaintiff without any delivery whatsoever.

Obviously, if an intended or attempted legal gift inter vivos of personal property fails as such because there was neither actual nor constructive delivery, and the intent to give can nevertheless be carried into effect in equity under the fiction that the donor is presumed to have intended to constitute himself a trustee to make the necessary delivery, then as a practical matter the requirement of delivery is abrogated in any and all cases of intended inter-vivos gifts. Of course this is not the law. A gift which is imperfect for lack of a delivery will not be turned into a declaration of trust for no better reason than that it is imperfect for lack of a delivery. Courts do not supply conveyances where there are none. This is true, even though the intended donee is a charity. The rule is approved in 1 Scott, Trusts §31.

It is true that one can orally constitute himself a trustee of personal property for the benefit of another and thereby create a trust enforceable in equity, even though without consideration and without delivery. 1 Scott, op. cit. §28; §32.2, p. 251. But he must in effect constitute himself a trustee. There must be an express trust, even though oral. It is not sufficient that he declare himself a donor. 1 Scott, op. cit. §31, p. 239; 4 id. §462.1. While he need not use the term "trustee," nor even manifest an understanding of its technical meaning or the technical meaning of the term "trust," he must manifest an intention to impose upon himself enforceable duties of a trust nature. Cullen v. Chappell, 116 F.2d 1017 (2d Cir. 1941); Restatement (Second), 1 Trusts §§23, 25; 1 Scott, op. cit., pp. 180, 181. There are no subordinate facts in the finding to indicate that Ethel ever intended to, or did, impose upon herself any enforceable duties of a trust nature with respect to this library. The most that could be said is that the subordinate facts in the finding might perhaps have supported a conclusion that at the luncheon she had the requisite donative intent so that, had she subsequently made a delivery of the property while that intent persisted, there would have been a valid, legal gift inter vivos. . . . The judgment, however, is not based on the theory of a legal gift inter vivos but on that of a declaration of trust. Since the subordinate facts give no support for a judgment on that basis, it cannot stand.

[The court remanded the case for a new trial at which the plaintiff could present its case on other theories than a declaration of trust.]

The Hebrew University Association v. Nye
Superior Court of Connecticut, 1966
223 A.2d 397

PARSKEY, J.   Most of the facts in this case are recited in Hebrew University Assn. v. Nye, 169 A.2d 641 (Conn. 1961). Additionally, it should be noted that at the time of the announcement of the gift of the "Yahuda Library" the decedent gave to the plaintiff a memorandum containing a list of most of the contents of the library and of all of the important books, documents and incunabula. . . .

The plaintiff claims a gift inter vivos based on a constructive or symbolic delivery. . . . For a constructive delivery, the donor must do that which, under the circumstances, will in reason be equivalent to an actual delivery. It must be as nearly perfect and complete as the nature of the property and the circumstances will permit. The gift may be perfected when the donor places in the hands of the donee the means of obtaining possession of the contemplated gift, accompanied with acts and declarations clearly showing an intention to give and to divert himself of all dominion over the property. It is not necessary that the method adopted be the only possible one. It is sufficient if manual delivery is impractical or inconvenient. Constructive delivery has been found to exist in a variety of factual situations: delivery of keys to safe deposit box; pointing out hiding places where money is hidden; informal memorandum.

Examining the present case in the light of the foregoing, the court finds that the delivery of the memorandum coupled with the decedent's acts and declarations, which clearly show an intention to give and to divest herself of any ownership of the library, was sufficient to complete the gift. If the itemized memorandum which the decedent transmitted had been incorporated in a formal document, no one would question the validity of the gift. But formalism is not an end in itself. "Whatever the value of the notion of forms, the only use of the forms is to present their contents." Holmes in Justice Oliver Wendell Holmes — His Book Notices and Uncollected Letters and Papers, p. 167 (Shriver Ed.). This is not to suggest that forms and formalities do not serve a useful and sometimes an essential purpose. But where the purpose of formalities is being served, an excessive regard for formalism should not be allowed to defeat the ends of justice. The circumstances under which this gift was made — a public announcement at a luncheon attended by a head of state, accompanied by a document which identified in itemized form what was being given — are a sufficient substitute for a formal instrument purporting to pass title. . . .

The court recognizes, in arriving at this result, that it is abrogating in some respects the requirement of delivery in a case involving an intended gift inter vivos. Obviously, it would be neither desirable nor wise to abrogate the requirement of delivery in any and all cases of intended inter-vivos gifts, for to do so, even under the guise of enforcing equitable rights, might open the door to fraudulent claims. But neither does it mean that the present delivery requirement must remain inviolate. "Equity is not crippled . . . by an inexorable formula." Marr v. Tumulty, 256 N.Y. 15, 21 (1931). If it be argued that hard cases make bad law, the short response is, not while this court sits. . . .

Rules of law must, in the last analysis, serve the ends of justice or they are worthless. For a court of equity to permit the decedent's wishes to be doubly frustrated for no better reason than that the rules so provide makes no sense whatsoever. "The plastic remedies of the chancery are moulded to the needs of justice."

Accordingly, judgment may enter declaring that the plaintiff is the legal and equitable owner of the "Yahuda Library" and has a right to the immediate possession of its contents.

NOTES AND QUESTION

1.   The Scott treatise, favoring doctrinal purity, disapproves of cases where the intention to make a gift seems plain and the gift fails for lack of delivery, but the court recasts the gift as a declaration of trust in order to save it.

If the donor manifests the intention to make a gift but delivers neither the property, a deed of gift, nor any other instrument evidencing the gift, the gift is generally incomplete. . . . It frequently happens, therefore, that an intended gift fails for lack of delivery. In such a case, the donee may urge the court to recharacterize the imperfect gift as a complete and irrevocable declaration of trust by the donor. Especially when the intent to make a gift is clear, the temptation to uphold the transaction by finding that the donor intended a trust can be strong, since it is so easy to create a trust. It may be that the requirement of delivery is merely a relic from a time in which symbolism was more important than intention. But if we do away with the delivery requirement for a gift, there is no need to call a gift a declaration of trust. On the other hand, if sound policy underlies the delivery requirement, if it draws a helpful line between transactions that are inchoate and those that are final, it ought not be possible to evade the requirement by the simple device of calling a failed gift a declaration of trust, especially given the fact that the donor clearly never intended to create a trust. Thus, although courts have occasionally found that donors intended to create trusts on evidence that showed only an intention to make a gift, they have much more frequently refused to do so. [1 Austin Wakeman Scott, William Franklin Fratcher, and Mark L. Ascher, Scott and Ascher on Trusts §5.1, at 232-233 (5th ed. 2006).]

But see Sarajane Love, Imperfect Gifts as Declarations of Trust: An Unapologetic Anomaly, 67 Ky. L.J. 309 (1979), taking the opposite view.

2.   Restatement (Third) of Trusts §16 (2003) provides: "If a property owner intends to make an outright gift inter vivos but fails to make the transfer that is required in order to do so, the gift intention will not be given effect by treating it as a declaration of trust." But comment d to §16 fuzzes up the picture:

If the manifestations of intention provide reliable, objective evidence of a deceased property owner's intended purpose and there is no indication that this purpose has been abandoned, the conduct and words ordinarily are interpreted as intending a type of transaction that would be effective to accomplish this purpose under the circumstances. That is, the preferred interpretation in marginal cases of this type is not that the property owner was merely expressing an intention to make a gift in the future but rather that the owner intended a declaration of trust. (If tenable under the circumstances, it is also possible that marginal acts that might or might not constitute delivery would be treated as a delivery based on a finding that they were in fact undertaken with the intention of making a present, outright gift.)

With admirable candor and greater clarity, Restatement (Third) of Property: Wills and Other Donative Transfers §6.2, cmt. yy (2003) provides that "a gift of personal property can be perfected on the basis of donative intent alone if the donor's intent to make a gift is established by clear and convincing evidence." Under this approach, noncompliance with the formality of delivery can be excused as harmless error if there is clear and convincing evidence of donative intent. The analogy is to excusing noncompliance with will execution formalities (see pages 253-264).

3.   For a comprehensive and learned comparative study of the treatment of gifts under the common law and the civil law, see Richard Hyland, Gifts: A Study in Comparative Law (2009).

2. *Necessity of Trust Property*

The usual definition of a trust includes three elements: a trustee, a beneficiary, and *trust property*. Under traditional law, a trust cannot exist without trust property, often called the *res*.[13] The res, however, need not be land or a hefty chunk of money. The trust res may be one dollar or one cent or it may be any interest in property that can be transferred. Restatement (Third) of Trusts §40, cmt. b (2003). Contingent remainders, leasehold interests, choses in action, royalties, life insurance policies — anything that is called property — may be put in trust. The critical question is whether a court will call the particular claim property.

Unthank v. Rippstein
Supreme Court of Texas, 1964
386 S.W.2d 134

STEAKLEY, J. Three days before his death C.P. Craft penned a lengthy personal letter to Mrs. Iva Rippstein. The letter was not written in terms of his anticipated early death; in fact, Craft spoke in the letter of his plans to go to the Mayo Clinic at a later date. The portion of the letter at issue reads as follows:

> Used most of yesterday and day before to "round up" my financial affairs, and to be sure I knew just where I stood before I made the statement that I would send you $200.00 cash the first week of each month for the next 5 years, provided I live that long, also to send you $200.00 cash for Sept. 1960 and thereafter send that amount in cash the first week of the following months of 1960, October, November and December. [opposite which in the margin there was written:]
>
> I have stricken out the words "provided I live that long" and hereby and herewith bind my estate to make the $200.00 monthly payments provided for on this Page One of this letter of 9-17-60.

Mrs. Rippstein, Respondent here, first sought, unsuccessfully, to probate the writing as a [holographic] codicil to the will of Craft. The Court of Civil Appeals held that the writing was not a testamentary instrument which was subject to probate. In re Craft Estate, 358 S.W.2d 732 (Tex. App. 1962). We refused the application of Mrs. Rippstein for writ of error with the notation "no reversible error." See Rule 483, Texas Rules of Civil Procedure.

The present suit was filed by Mrs. Rippstein against the executors of the estate of Craft, Petitioners here, for judgment in the amount of the monthly installments which had matured, and for declaratory judgment adjudicating the liability of the executors to pay future installments as they mature. The trial court granted the motion of the executors for summary judgment. The Court of Civil

---

13. As we saw in Chapter 6, the sole exception to the property requirement is under legislation such as the Uniform Testamentary Additions to Trusts Act for an inter vivos trust that is to be funded by a pour-over will. See pages 444-447.

Appeals reversed and rendered judgment for Mrs. Rippstein, holding that the writing in question established a voluntary trust under which Craft bound his property to the extent of the promised payments; and that upon his death his legal heirs held the legal title for the benefit of Mrs. Rippstein to that portion of the estate required to make the promised monthly payments.

In her reply to the application for writ of error Mrs. Rippstein states that the sole question before us is whether the marginal notation constitutes "a declaration of trust whereby [Craft] agrees to thenceforth hold his estate in trust for the explicit purpose of making the payments." She argues that Craft imposed the obligation for the payment of the monies upon all of his property as if he had said "I henceforth hold my estate in trust for [such] purpose." She recognizes that under her position Craft became subject to the Texas Trust Act in the management of his property. Collaterally, however, Mrs. Rippstein takes the position that it being determinable by mathematical computation that less than ten per cent of the property owned by Craft at the time he wrote the letter would be required to discharge the monthly payments, the "remaining ninety per cent remained in Mr. Craft to do with as he would." Her theory is that that portion of Craft's property not exhausted in meeting his declared purpose would revert to him by way of a resulting trust eo instante with the legal and equitable title to such surplus merging in him.

These arguments in behalf of Mrs. Rippstein are indeed ingenious and resourceful, but in our opinion there is not sufficient certainty in the language of the marginal notation upon the basis of which a court of equity can declare a trust to exist which is subject to enforcement in such manner. The uncertainties with respect to the intention of Craft and with respect to the subject of the trust are apparent. The language of the notation cannot be expanded to show an intention on the part of Craft to place his property in trust with the result that his exercise of further dominion thereover would be wrongful except in a fiduciary capacity as trustee, and under which Craft would be subject to suit for conversion at the hands of Mrs. Rippstein if he spent or disposed of his property in a manner which would defeat his statement in the notation that a monthly payment of $200.00 in cash would be sent her the first week of each month. It is manifest that Craft did not expressly declare that all of his property, or any specific portion of the assets which he owned at such time, would constitute the corpus or res of a trust for the benefit of Mrs. Rippstein; and inferences may not be drawn from the language used sufficient for a holding to such effect to rest in implication. The conclusion is compelled that the most that Craft did was to express an intention to make monthly gifts to Mrs. Rippstein accompanied by an ineffectual attempt to bind his estate in futuro; the writing was no more than a promise to make similar gifts in the future and as such is unenforceable. The promise to give cannot be tortured into a trust declaration under which Craft while living, and as trustee, and his estate after his death, were under a legally enforceable obligation to pay Mrs. Rippstein the sum of $200.00 monthly for the five-year period. . . .

The judgment of the Court of Civil Appeals is reversed and that of the trial court is affirmed.

QUESTIONS AND NOTES

1. What policies are served by refusing to give effect to C.P. Craft's written intent? Where there is a written instrument making a gratuitous promise, which shows unambiguously that the donor intended to be legally bound, should the court give it effect as a declaration of trust? What would be the trust res? See Jane B. Baron, The Trust Res and Donative Intent, 61 Tul. L. Rev. 45 (1986), arguing that the trust res requirement, supported by unconvincing rationales, too often defeats donative intent.

The letter in *Unthank* was refused probate as a holographic will on the grounds that it was not a testamentary instrument. Would the result change under Uniform Probate Code §2-502(b)-(c) (1990, rev. 2008), page 227, as interpreted in Estate of Kuralt, page 280, or under UPC §2-503, page 258.

2. *Trusts distinguished from debts.* The requirement of an identifiable trust res distinguishes a trust from a debt. A trustee is a fiduciary who holds *specifically identified* property for the benefit of another. The trust property must be kept separate from the trustee's own funds. A *debt* involves a personal obligation to pay *a sum of money* to another. The crucial factor in distinguishing between a trust relationship and an ordinary debt is whether the recipient of the assets is entitled to use them as his own and commingle them with his own assets. Restatement (Third) of Trusts §5, cmt. k (2003); 1 Austin Wakeman Scott, William Franklin Fratcher, and Mark L. Ascher, Scott and Ascher on Trusts §2.3.8 (5th ed. 2006).

Money deposited in a bank ordinarily creates a debt; the money is not segregated from the bank's general funds. The chose in action against the bank can serve as a res if the depositor declares a trust or transfers it in trust to another.

3. *Resulting trusts.* In *Unthank*, Iva Rippstein argued that C.P. Craft, after transferring all his property into trust, had a resulting trust in the amount of his property not required to meet the payments to her. A resulting trust is an *equitable reversionary interest* that arises by operation of law in two situations, the first of which was at issue in the case: (1) where an express trust fails or makes an incomplete disposition (see Restatement (Third) of Trusts, supra, §8), or (2) where one person pays the purchase price for property and causes title to the property to be taken in the name of another person who is not a natural object of the bounty of the purchaser (see Restatement (Third) of Trusts, supra, §9). Thus:

> *Case 14.* O devises property to X in trust to pay the income to A for life, and on A's death to distribute the property to A's descendants. A dies without descendants. Because the remainder to A's descendants fails, X holds the remainder on resulting trust for O's heirs or devisees.
>
> *Case 15.* B purchases Blackacre with money supplied by A. Unless B can show that A intended to make a gift to B, B holds title to Blackacre on resulting trust for A, often called a *purchase money resulting trust.*

In both settings the transferee is not entitled to the beneficial interest, so the interest "is said 'to result' (that is, it reverts) to the transferor or to the transferor's estate or other successor(s) in interest." Restatement (Third) of Trusts, supra, §7. Once a resulting trust is found, the trustee must convey the property to the beneficial owner upon demand.

BRAINARD v. COMMISSIONER, 91 F.2d 880 (7th Cir. 1937): In December 1927, Brainard orally stated, before his wife and mother, that he declared a trust of his expected profits from stock trading during 1928 for the benefit of his wife, mother, and two minor children, ages one and three. However, Brainard "agreed to assume personally any losses resulting from the venture." In 1928, Brainard traded in stock under his own name and turned a profit. After deducting $10,000 as his trustee's fee, which he paid himself and declared as income on his income tax return, the remaining profits were divided into equal shares and credited on Brainard's books to the benefit of the four beneficiaries. The beneficiaries reported the profits credited to their shares of the trust on their respective 1928 income tax returns.

The question presented was whether Brainard's 1927 declaration created a valid trust over the future 1928 profits. If the trust did not arise until after Brainard credited the 1928 profits on his books to the four beneficiaries or if the trust had no rights to those profits until 1928, then those profits accrued to him personally before the transfer in trust. Under the applicable tax law, those profits would be taxable in 1928 to Brainard. If, however, the trust arose in December 1927 when the oral declaration was made, and the profits arose in the trust, then they would be taxable in 1928 to the beneficiaries.

The court held that the trust did not arise until after the profits were credited on Brainard's books on the grounds that there was no res at the time of the declaration of trust. "It is clear that [Brainard], at the time of his declaration, had no property interest in 'profits in stock trading in 1928, if any,' because there were none in existence at that time. . . . It is obvious that the respective profits came into existence when and if such stocks were sold at a profit in 1928." Where there is no res at the time of a declaration of trust, the settlor must manifest anew his intent to create a trust when the res comes into being. During "such intervening time . . . [Brainard] must be considered as the sole owner of the profits and they were properly taxed to him as a part of his income."

Speelman v. Pascal
Court of Appeals of New York, 1961
178 N.E.2d 723

DESMOND, C.J.   Gabriel Pascal, defendant's intestate who died in 1954, had been for many years a theatrical producer. In 1952 an English corporation named Gabriel Pascal Enterprises, Ltd., of whose 100 shares Gabriel Pascal owned 98, made an agreement with the English Public Trustee who represented the estate of George Bernard Shaw. This agreement granted to Gabriel Pascal Enterprises, Ltd., the exclusive world rights to prepare and produce a musical play to be based on Shaw's play "Pygmalion" and a motion picture version of the musical play. The agreement recited, as was the fact, that the licensee owned a film scenario written by Pascal and based on "Pygmalion." In fact Pascal had, some time previously, produced a nonmusical movie version of "Pygmalion" under rights obtained by Pascal from George Bernard Shaw during the latter's lifetime. The 1952 agreement required the licensee corporation to pay the Shaw estate an initial advance and thereafter to pay the Shaw estate 3% of the gross receipts of the musical play and musical movie with a provision that the license was to terminate if within certain fixed periods the licensee did not arrange with Lerner[14] and Loewe or other similarly well-known composers to write the musical play and arrange to produce it. Before Pascal's death in July, 1954, he had made a number of unsuccessful efforts to get the musical written and produced and it was not until after his death that arrangements were made, through a New York bank as temporary administrator of his estate, for the writing and production [by Lerner and Loewe] of [a musical based on Pygmalion,] the highly successful "My Fair Lady." Meanwhile, on February 22, 1954, at a time when the license from the Shaw estate still had two years to run, Gabriel Pascal, who died four and a half months later, wrote, signed and delivered to plaintiff a document as follows:

Dear Miss Kingman

This is to confirm to you our understanding that I give you from my shares of profits of the Pygmalion Musical stage version five per cent (5%) in England, and two per cent (2%) of my shares of profits in the United States. From the film version, five per cent (5%) from my profit shares all over the world.

As soon as the contracts are signed, I will send a copy of this letter to my lawyer, Edwin Davies, in London, and he will confirm to you this arrangement in a legal form.

This participation in my shares of profits is a present to you in recognition for your loyal work for me as my Executive Secretary.[15]

Very sincerely yours,

Gabriel Pascal

---

14. Alan Jay Lerner, dying in 1986, left what might be called a delicious bequest:

Third: I give and bequeath to Benjamin Welles, if he survives me, and Sydney Gruson, if he survives me, the sum of $1,000.00 each. The purpose of this modest remembrance is to defray the cost of one evening's merriment to be devoted to cheerful recollections of their departed friend.

The abstemious Bernard Shaw, vegetarian and teetotaller, who scathingly denounced the "artificial happiness, artificial courage, and artificial gaiety" provided by alcohol, would not have been amused. — Eds.

15. Pascal's loyal "Executive Secretary" is portrayed somewhat differently by Pascal's widow, Valerie, in her book, The Disciple and His Devil (1970). Marianne Speelman, also known as Zaya Kingman, was half Chinese and half Irish and the exotically beautiful widow of a Dutch banker who had made a fortune in China. She invited Gabriel Pascal to dinner in March of 1953 and that same night began a torrid love affair (id. at 252). As a result of her herb teas and food prepared with "life elixir," Pascal experienced "prodigious sexual powers" and felt as if he were flying. Marianne wrote that anybody who had ever made love to her could never again be satisfied with any other woman (id. at 255). Valerie states that soon after delivering the document in this case (id. at 297), Pascal attempted to break off his volcanic affair and, under the influence of an Indian mystic, renounced his fleshly desires forever (id. at 299). Spent, Pascal died some four months later. — Eds.

Marianne Speelman (Zaya Kingman)

The question in this lawsuit is: Did the delivery of this paper constitute a valid, complete, present gift to plaintiff by way of assignment of a share in future royalties when and if collected from the exhibition of the musical stage version and film version of "Pygmalion"? A consideration was, of course, unnecessary. . . .

The only real question is as to whether the 1954 letter above quoted operated to transfer to plaintiff an enforcible right to the described percentages of the royalties to accrue to Pascal on the production of a stage or film version of a musical play based on "Pygmalion." We see no reason why this letter does not have that effect. It is true that at the time of the delivery of the letter there was no musical stage or film play in existence but Pascal, who owned and was conducting negotiations to realize on the stage and film rights, could grant to another a share of the moneys to accrue from the use of those rights by others. There are many instances of courts enforcing assignments of rights to sums which were expected thereafter to become due to the assignor. A typical case is Field v. Mayor of New York, 6 N.Y. 179 (1852). One Bell, who had done much printing and similar work for the City of New York but had no present contract to do any more such work, gave an assignment in the amount of $1,500 of any moneys that might thereafter become due to Bell for such work. Bell did obtain such contracts or orders from the city and money became due to him therefor. This court held that while there was not at the time of the assignment any presently enforcible or even existing chose in action but merely a possibility that there would be such a chose of action, nevertheless there was a possibility of such which the parties expected to ripen into reality and which did afterwards ripen into reality and that, therefore, the assignment created an equitable title which the courts would enforce. . . . The cases cited by appellant (Young v. Young, 80 N.Y. 422 (1880); Vincent v. Rix, 248 N.Y. 76 (1928)) are not to the contrary. In each of those instances the attempted gifts failed because there had not been such a completed and irrevocable delivery of the subject matter of the gift as to put the gift beyond cancellation by the donor. In every such case the question must be as to whether there was a completed delivery of a kind appropriate to the subject property. . . . In our present case there was nothing left for Pascal to do in order to make an irrevocable transfer to plaintiff of part of Pascal's right to receive royalties from the productions. . . .

Judgment affirmed.

NOTES, PROBLEMS, AND QUESTIONS

1. What doctrinal, factual, or other distinction justifies the different results reached in *Brainard* and *Speelman*? In terms of ritual and evidentiary policies, are the cases consistent?

"An expectation or hope of receiving property in the future, or an interest that has not come into existence or has ceased to exist," does not qualify as a res sufficient to create a *trust*. Restatement (Third) of Trusts §41 (2003). However, a person may *assign* future earnings from an existing contract. The theory is that the future yield of an existing property right can be transferred even though property to be acquired in the future cannot be. In the *Speelman* case, Pascal had exclusive rights (a license) from the Shaw estate to make a musical version of Pygmalion.

2. In which of the following cases has there been an effective transfer? Compare them with what happened in *Brainard* and *Speelman*.

(a) *O* orally declares to *A*: "I give you five percent of the profits of a musical play based upon Shaw's Pygmalion, if I produce it and if there are any profits."

(b) *O* orally declares himself trustee for one year of all stocks he owns, with any profits from stock trading to go to *A*. See Barnette v. McNulty, 516 P.2d 583 (Ariz. App. 1973).

(c) In a notarized writing, *O* declares himself trustee for the benefit of *A* of any profits *O* makes from stock trading during the next calendar year.

(d) *O* orally declares himself trustee for the benefit of *A* of five percent of the profits, if there are any, of a musical play that *O* is writing, based upon Shaw's Pygmalion.

NOTE: TAXATION OF GRANTOR TRUSTS

In Brainard v. Commissioner, page 572, the settlor of the trust sought to obtain an income tax advantage by creating a trust of his future profits from stock trading. If a valid trust were created, these profits would be taxable to the trust beneficiaries, at a lower bracket, and not to the settlor. This kind of transfer, avoiding income tax to the settlor on future income, is not available to a taxpayer today.

In Helvering v. Clifford, 309 U.S. 331 (1940), the Supreme Court held that, where a taxpayer declared a trust of securities for five years with income payable to another for the five-year term but with the settlor retaining complete control over the principal and reversion of the corpus at the end of five years, the taxpayer could be treated as owner, and taxed on the income, by the federal taxing authorities. Subsequently, the Treasury Department issued regulations spelling out in detail the circumstances under which the settlor of a trust would be taxable on the trust income on the ground of retained dominion and control (the "Clifford regulations"). These were in turn supplanted by amendments to the Internal Revenue Code itself. Sections 671-677 of the Code now govern the circumstances when the settlor is taxable on trust income because of retained dominion and control. Where the settlor wants to avoid being taxed on the trust income, care must be taken to avoid these sections.

Sections 671-677 define what are called *grantor trusts* — trusts in which the income is taxable to the settlor (grantor) because the settlor has retained substantial control and is deemed by the Code still to be the owner of the trust assets. We have noted earlier, at page 439, that trust income of a revocable trust is taxable to the settlor. A revocable trust is an example of a grantor trust. I.R.C. §676. Now we attend to grantor trusts where the settlor retains not a right to revoke the trust but some lesser power. See Robert T. Danforth, The Use of Grantor Trusts in Estate Planning, Tax Mgmt. Ests., Gifts & Tr. J. 103 (Mar./Apr. 2006).

Under the grantor trust provisions of the Code, there is a *spousal attribution rule*: A settlor is treated as holding any power or interest that is held by the settlor's spouse if the spouse is living with the settlor at the time the property is transferred into trust.

Where the grantor has a *reversionary interest*, either in the corpus or in the income, and the reversionary interest at the inception of the trust exceeds 5 percent of the value of the corpus or the income, the trust is a grantor trust, and the income from the trust is taxable to the settlor. I.R.C. §673. There is one important exception. The settlor is exempt from this rule if she creates a trust for a minor lineal descendant, who has the entire present interest, and the settlor retains a reversionary interest that will take effect only upon the death of the lineal descendant under the age of 21. I.R.C. §673(b). The drafting moral here is clear. Except in the one case mentioned, when drafting an irrevocable trust for shifting income taxes on assets, do not leave a reversionary interest of any value in the settlor.

Where the *settlor* or a *nonadverse party* is given discretionary power over income or principal exercisable without the consent of an adverse party, the trust is a grantor trust, and the income is taxable to the settlor. I.R.C. §674. Thus:

> *Case 16.* O creates a trust, with herself and the First National Bank as co-trustees, to pay the income to O's two children in such amounts as the trustees shall determine or to accumulate it, and, on the death of O's two children, to distribute the principal to O's grandchildren then living. The trustees earn $70,000 income the first year, which the trustees distribute equally to O's two children. The $70,000 income is taxable to O, the settlor of a grantor trust, *and* O has made a gift to each child of $35,000. Each gift qualifies for a $13,000 annual gift tax exclusion, so O has made a taxable gift to each child of $22,000. (On the gift tax exclusion, see Chapter 15.) The amount received by O's children is not income to them because it is a gift from O.

There are two major exceptions to §674. The first is that a discretionary power to distribute, apportion, or accumulate income or to pay out principal can be given to an *independent* trustee without adverse tax consequences to the settlor. I.R.C. §674(c). If in Case 16 the First National Bank had been named sole trustee, the income would not be taxable to O. It is important to distinguish between an independent trustee and a nonadverse party. An independent trustee is one who is not related or subordinate to the settlor nor subservient to her wishes. A nonadverse party is a person who lacks a substantial beneficial interest that would be adversely affected by the exercise or nonexercise of the power.

The second major exception to §674 permits (a) a power to be given the settlor or any trustee to distribute *principal* pursuant to a "reasonably definite standard which is set forth in the trust instrument," or (b) a power to be given any trustee other than the settlor or the settlor's spouse to distribute *income* pursuant to a "reasonably definite external standard which is set forth in the trust instrument." I.R.C. §674(b)(5)(A) and (d).

Another type of grantor trust is one where certain administrative powers can be exercised for the benefit of the settlor rather than for the beneficiaries of the trust. Generally, the settlor will be subject to tax on the income if there is a power exercisable by the settlor or a nonadverse party (1) to purchase trust property for less than an adequate consideration, (2) to borrow trust property without adequate security, (3) to vote or acquire stock in a corporation in which the settlor has a significant voting interest, or (4) to reacquire the trust principal. Any of these indicia of dominion and control may be sufficient to tax the settlor on the trust income. See I.R.C. §675.

The category of grantor trusts also includes a trust where the settlor, a nonadverse party, or an independent trustee has the power to distribute trust income to the settlor or the settlor's spouse. I.R.C. §677(a). Under §677, income is not taxable to the settlor merely because the trustee *may* distribute it for the support of a beneficiary (other than the settlor's spouse) whom the settlor is legally obligated to support. If the trust property is in fact used to discharge the settlor's legal obligation, however, the settlor is taxable on the income to the extent income is actually so used. I.R.C. §677(b). Thus:

> *Case 17.* O transfers property to the First National Bank in trust to pay the income in its discretion for the support of O's children. Even though the trustee has discretion to use the income for the support of O's minor children (thereby discharging O's legal obligation of support), O is taxable on the income only to the extent it is actually so applied. If the income used for the support of O's children is in excess of the amount O is legally obligated to provide, the excess income is not taxable to O.

In Case 17, a provision could be inserted in the trust instrument prohibiting any distributions by the trustee that would discharge the settlor's legal obligation of support. Such a provision would prevent taxation of the income to the settlor and would not, as a practical matter, interfere with any trust distribution by the trustee.

Any lawyer creating an inter vivos trust should pay close attention to I.R.C. §§671-677 and the relevant regulations if the settlor desires to shift taxation on the income to the trust or its beneficiaries. The lawyer should also keep in mind that although the income tax and the estate and gift taxes are not exactly parallel, if the settlor is treated as owner and taxable on trust income, there is a good chance that the trust assets will be subject to estate taxation at the settlor's death. See the discussion of I.R.C. §§2036 and 2038 in Chapter 15.

3. *Necessity of Trust Beneficiaries*

A trust must have one or more ascertainable beneficiaries. UTC §402(a)(3) (2000); Restatement (Third) of Trusts §44 (2003). The reason: There must be someone to whom the trustee owes fiduciary duties, someone who can call the trustee to account. Underpinning this beneficiary principle is the policy that a private trust must be for the benefit of the beneficiaries. See John H. Langbein, Mandatory Rules in the Law of Trusts, 98 Nw. U. L. Rev. 1105 (2004).

There are several exceptions, however. A charitable trust, unlike a private trust, need not have an ascertainable beneficiary to be valid (we take up charitable trusts in Chapter 11). The beneficiaries of a private trust may be unborn or unascertained when the trust is created. Thus, a trust created by O, who is childless, for the benefit of her future children would be valid. The courts would protect the interests of the unborn children from improper acts of the trustee. On the other hand, if at the time the trust becomes effective the beneficiaries are too indefinite, the attempted trust will fail for want of ascertainable beneficiaries.

Clark v. Campbell
Supreme Court of New Hampshire, 1926
133 A. 166

SNOW, J.   The ninth clause of the will of deceased reads:

My estate will comprise so many and such a variety of articles of personal property such as books, photographic albums, pictures, statuary, bronzes, bric-a-brac, hunting and fishing equipment, antiques, rugs, scrapbooks, canes and masonic jewels, that probably I shall not distribute all, and perhaps no great part thereof, during my life by gift among my friends. Each of my trustees is competent by reason of familiarity with the property, my wishes and friendships, to wisely distribute some portion at least of said property. I therefore give and bequeath to my trustees all my property embraced within the classification aforesaid in trust to make disposal by the way of a memento from myself, of such articles to such of my friends as they, my trustees, shall select. All of said property, not so disposed of by them, my trustees are directed to sell and the proceeds of such sale or sales to become and be disposed of as a part of the residue of my estate.

The question here reserved is whether . . . the bequest for the benefit of the testator's "friends" must fail for the want of certainty of the beneficiaries.

By the common law there cannot be a valid bequest to an indefinite person. There must be a beneficiary or a class of beneficiaries indicated in the will capable of coming into court and claiming the benefit of the bequest. This principle applies to private but not to public trusts and charities. The basis assigned for this distinction is the difference in the enforceability of the two classes of trusts. In the former there being no definite cestui que trust to assert his right, there is no one who can compel performance, with the consequent unjust enrichment of the trustee; while in the case of the latter, performance is considered to be sufficiently secured by the authority of the attorney-general to invoke the power of the courts. . . .

That the foregoing is the established doctrine seems to be conceded, but it is contended in argument that it was not the intention of the testator by the ninth clause to create a trust, at least as respects the selected articles, but to make an absolute gift thereof to the trustees individually. . . . It is a sufficient answer to this contention that the language of the ninth clause does not warrant the assumed construction. . . . When the clause is elided of unnecessary verbiage the testator is made to say: "I give to my trustees my property (of the described class) in trust to make disposal of to such of my friends as they shall select." It is difficult to conceive of language more clearly disclosing an intention to create a trust.

It is further sought to sustain the bequest as a power. The distinction apparently relied upon is that a power, unlike a trust, is not imperative and leaves the act to be done at the will of the donee of the power. But the ninth clause by its terms imposes upon the trustees the imperative duty to dispose of the selected articles among the testator's friends. If, therefore, the authority bestowed by the testator by the use of a loose terminology may be called a power, it is not an optional power but a power coupled with a trust to which the principles incident to a trust so far as here involved clearly apply. . . .

We must, therefore, conclude that this clause presents the case of an attempt to create a private trust. . . .

The question presented, therefore, is whether or not the ninth clause provides for definite and ascertainable beneficiaries so that the bequest therein can be sustained as a private trust. . . .

Like the direct legatees in a will, the beneficiaries under a trust may be designated by class. But in such case the class must be capable of delimitation, as "brothers and sisters," "children," "issue," "nephews and nieces." A bequest giving the executor authority to distribute his property "among his relatives and for benevolent objects in such sums as in their judgment shall be for the best" was sustained upon evidence within the will that by "relatives" the testator intended such of his relatives within the statute of distributions as were needy, and thus brought the bequest within the line of charitable gifts and excluded all others as individuals. Goodale v. Mooney, 60 N.H. 528, 536 (1881). Where a testator bequeathed his stocks to be apportioned to his "relations" according to the discretion of the trustee, to be enjoyed by them after his decease, it was held to be a power to appoint amongst his relations who were next of kin under the statute of distribution. . . .

In the case now under consideration the cestuis que trust are designated as the "friends" of the testator. The word "friends" unlike "relations" has no accepted statutory or other controlling limitations, and in fact has no precise sense at all. Friendship is a word of broad and varied application. It is commonly used to describe the undefinable relationships which exist not only between those connected by ties of kinship or marriage, but as well between strangers in blood, and which vary in degree from the greatest intimacy to an acquaintance more or less casual. . . . There is no express evidence that the word is used in any restricted sense. The only implied limitation of the class is that fixed by the boundaries of the familiarity of the testator's trustees with his friendships. If such familiarity could be held to constitute such a line of demarcation as to define an ascertainable group, it is to be noted that the gift is not to such group as a class, the members of which are to take in some definite proportion (1 Jarman, Wills, 534; 1 Schouler, Wills, s. 1011) or according to their needs, but the disposition is to "such of my friends as they, my trustees, may select." No sufficient criterion is furnished to govern the selection of the individuals from the class. The assertion of the testator's confidence in the competency of his trustees "to wisely distribute some portion" of the enumerated articles "by reason of familiarity with the property, my wishes and friendships," does not furnish such a criterion. . . . Where an executor was given direction to distribute in a manner calculated to carry out "wishes which I have expressed to him or may express to him" and such wishes had been orally communicated to the executor by the testator, the devise could not be given effect as against the next of kin. Olliffe v. Wells, 130 Mass. 221, 224, 225 (1881). Much less can effect be given to the uncommunicated wishes of the testator here.

It was the evident purpose of the testator to invest his trustees with the power after his death to make disposition of the enumerated articles among an undefined class with practically the same freedom and irresponsibility that he himself would have exercised if living; that is, to substitute for the will of the testator the will and discretion of the trustees. Such a purpose is in contravention of the policy of the statute which provides that "no will shall be effectual to pass any real or personal estate . . . unless made by a person . . . in writing, signed by the testator or by some one in his presence and by his direction, and attested and subscribed in his presence by three or more credible witnesses." P.L., c. 297, §2.

Where a gift is impressed with a trust ineffectively declared and incapable of taking effect because of the indefiniteness of the cestui que trust, the donee will hold the property in trust for the next taker under the will, or for the next of kin by way of a resulting trust. . . . The trustees therefore hold title to the property enumerated in the paragraph under consideration, to be disposed of as a part of the residue, and the trustees are so advised. . . .

Case discharged.

NOTE AND QUESTIONS

1.   Professor Scott argued that where there is a transfer in trust for members of an indefinite class of persons such as to the testator's friends, no enforceable trust is created, but the transferee has a discretionary power to convey the property to such members of the class as he may select. 2 Austin Wakeman Scott, William Franklin Fratcher, and Mark L. Ascher, Scott and Ascher on Trusts §12.9 (5th ed. 2006). In other words, the transferee has a *power of appointment*. See also Restatement (Third) of Trusts §46 (2003), adopting this view.

A valid power of appointment may have a definite class of beneficiaries (e.g., "my descendants") or it may not (e.g., "anyone except the donee or her creditors or her estate"). The test of validity is: If the class of beneficiaries is described such that some person might reasonably be said to answer the description, the power is valid. An appointment is invalid, however, if it cannot be determined whether the appointee answers the description.

In trusts today, beneficiaries are often given powers of appointment, that is, a power to distribute the trust property. *T* may devise his residuary estate in trust "for my wife *W* for life, and then to distribute the trust assets to such of my descendants as my wife appoints by will." The power of appointment is discretionary; it is a nonfiduciary power. If *W* fails to exercise the power, the trust property passes to *T*'s heirs upon *W*'s death. Powers of appointment are treated in Chapter 12.

In Clark v. Campbell, the court held that the testator did not create a power of appointment because the power was given to *trustees*, whose powers over the trust property are held in a fiduciary capacity. As such, the testator created not an optional power but a "power coupled with a trust" to which the trust law requirement of definite or ascertainable beneficiaries applied. By contrast, if the power of selection had been given "to my sister Polly and my friend Herbert" and not "to Polly and Herbert, *trustees* (or *executors*)," it would have been a valid nonfiduciary power of appointment.

What is the drafting moral here? See Restatement (Third) of Trusts, supra, cmt. d.

2.   The will of Marilyn Monroe, the actress and celebrity icon whose death in 1962 was ruled a probable suicide, contained the following clause: "I give and bequeath all of my personal effects and clothing to Lee Strasberg,[16] or if he should predecease me, then to my Executor hereinafter named, it being my desire that he distribute these, in his sole discretion, among my friends, colleagues and those to whom I am devoted." Did Monroe intend to create a trust? If so, did Monroe designate an ascertainable beneficiary? See Alyssa A. DiRusso, He Says, She Asks: Gender, Language, and the Law of Precatory Words in Wills, 22 Wisc. Women's L.J. 1, 1-3 (2007). See also Shaw Family Archives v. CMG Worldwide, page 10.

In re Searight's Estate
Ohio Court of Appeals, Ninth District, 1950
95 N.E.2d 779

HUNSICKER, J.   George P. Searight, a resident of Wayne county, Ohio, died testate on November 27, 1948. Item "third" of his will provided:

> I give and bequeath my dog, Trixie, to Florence Hand of Wooster, Ohio, and I direct my executor to deposit in the Peoples Federal Savings and Loan Association, Wooster, Ohio, the sum of $1000.00 to be used by him to pay Florence Hand at the rate of 75 cents per day for the keep and care of my dog as long as it shall live. If my dog shall die before the said $1000.00 and the interest accruing therefrom shall have been used up, I give and bequeath whatever remains of said $1000.00 to be divided equally among those of the following persons who are living at that time, to wit: Bessie Immler, Florence Hand, Reed Searight, Fern Olson and Willis Horn.

At the time of his death, all of the persons, and his dog, Trixie, named in such item third, were living.

Florence Hand accepted the bequest of Trixie, and the executor paid to her from the $1000 fund, 75 cents a day for the keep and care of the dog. The value of Trixie was agreed to be $5.

The Probate Court [held item third valid]. . . . The questions presented by this appeal on questions of law are:

---

16. Before his death in 1982, Lee Strasberg achieved considerable notoriety in his own right as an actor and acting coach in the method acting tradition. In 1952, he was named the artistic director of the prestigious Actor's Studio, a position that he held until his death. In addition to Monroe, Strasberg's students included James Dean, Robert DeNiro, Jane Fonda, Dustin Hoffman, Paul Newman, and Al Pacino. The Actor's Studio is perhaps best known today as the home of James Lipton, the sycophantic host of the Bravo cable network's Inside the Actor's Studio, in which Lipton conducts astonishingly obsequious celebrity interviews that are at times weirdly riveting. In 2007, Lipton published an autobiography, entitled Inside "Inside," in which he admitted to working in France after World War II as a *mec*, which in English would be translated as pimp, except that the *mec* works for the prostitute. Lipton reports (id. at 138) that he "did a thriving business," primarily organizing sex shows for American tourists. "As the clients' personal guide," Lipton writes (id. at 139), "I was obliged to stay with them. . . . It was my first experience as a producer, and I have to say that, in the many times this ritual was performed, I never had a complaint from the audience." — Eds.

1. Is the testamentary bequest for the care of Trixie (a dog) valid in Ohio —
    (a) as a proper subject of a so-called "honorary trust"?
    (b) as not being in violation of the rule against perpetuities? . . .

1(a). . . . We do not have, in the instant case, the question of a trust established for the care of dogs in general or of an indefinite number of dogs, but we are here considering the validity of a testamentary bequest for the benefit of a specific dog. This is not a charitable trust, nor is it a gift of money to the Ohio Humane Society or a county humane society, which societies are vested with broad statutory authority, Section 10062, General Code, for the care of animals.

Text writers on the subject of trusts and many law professors designate a bequest for the care of a specific animal as an "honorary trust"; that is, one binding the conscience of the trustee, since there is no beneficiary capable of enforcing the trust.

The rule in Ohio, that the absence of a beneficiary having a legal standing in court and capable of demanding an accounting of the trustee is fatal and the trust fails, was first announced in Mannix, Assignee v. Purcell, 19 N.E. 572 (Ohio 1888) . . . .

In 1 Scott on the Law of Trusts, Section 124, the author says:

> There are certain classes of cases similar to those discussed in the preceding section in that there is no one who as beneficiary can enforce the purpose of the testator, but different in one respect, namely, that the purpose is definite. Such, for example, are bequests for the erection or maintenance of tombstones or monuments or for the care of graves, and bequests for the support of specific animals. It has been held in a number of cases that such bequests as these do not necessarily fail. It is true that the legatee cannot be compelled to carry out the intended purpose, since there is no one to whom he owes a duty to carry out the purpose.
>
> Even though the legatee cannot be compelled to apply the property to the designated purpose, the courts have very generally held that he can properly do so, and that no resulting trust arises so long as he is ready and willing to carry it out. The legatee will not, however, be permitted to retain the property for his own benefit; and if he refuses or neglects to carry out the purpose, a resulting trust will arise in favor of the testator's residuary legatee or next of kin. . . .

The object and purpose sought to be accomplished by the testator in the instant case is not capricious or illegal. He sought to effect a worthy purpose — the care of his pet dog.

Whether we designate the gift in this case as an "honorary trust" or a gift with a power which is valid when exercised is not important, for we do know that the one to whom the dog was given accepted the gift and indicated her willingness to care for such dog, and the executor proceeded to carry out the wishes of the testator.

> Where the owner of property transfers it upon an intended trust for a specific noncharitable purpose and there is no definite or definitely ascertainable beneficiary designated, no trust is created; but the transferee has power to apply the property to the designated purpose, unless he is authorized by the terms of the intended trust so to apply the property beyond the period of the rule against perpetuities, or the purpose is capricious. I Restatement of the Law of Trusts, Section 124.

To call this bequest for the care of the dog, Trixie, a trust in the accepted sense in which that term is defined is, we know, an unjustified conclusion. The modern authorities, as shown by the cases cited earlier in this discussion, however, uphold the validity of a gift for the purpose designated in the instant case, where the person to whom the power is given is willing to carry out the testator's wishes. Whether called an "honorary trust" or whatever terminology is used, we conclude that the bequest for the care of the dog, Trixie, is not in and of itself unlawful.

1(b). In Ohio, by statute, Section 10512-8, General Code, the rule against perpetuities is specifically defined, and such statute further says: "It is the intention by the adoption of this section to make effective in Ohio what is generally known as the common law rule against perpetuities."

It is to be noted, in every situation where the so-called "honorary trust" is established for specific animals, that, unless the instrument creating such trust limits the duration of the trust — that is, the time during which the power is to be exercised — to human lives, we will have "honorary trusts" established for animals of great longevity, such as crocodiles, elephants and sea turtles. . . .

If we then examine item third of testator's will, we discover that, although the bequest for his dog is for "as long as it shall live," the money given for this purpose is $1000 payable at the rate of 75¢ a day. By simple mathematical computation, this sum of money, expended at the rate determined by the testator, will be fully exhausted in three years and 238 1/3 days. If we assume that this $1000 is deposited in a bank so that interest at the high rate of 6% per annum were earned thereon, the time needed to consume both principal and interest thereon (based on semiannual computation of such interest on the average unused balance during such six month period) would be four years, 57 1/2 days.

It is thus very apparent that the testator provided a time limit for the exercise of the power given his executor, and that such time limit is much less than the maximum period allowed under the rule against perpetuities.

We therefore conclude that the bequest in the instant case for the care of the dog, Trixie, does not, by the terms of the creating instrument, violate the rule against perpetuities. . . .

The judgment of the Probate Court is affirmed.

NOTES AND QUESTION

1. In *Searight's Estate*, the Department of Taxation of Ohio argued that an inheritance tax was levied on the amount used for the care of Trixie. Ohio General Code §5332 levied a tax on all property passing to a "person, institution or corporation." In an omitted portion of the opinion, the court decided that a dog was none of these, and no inheritance tax was levied on the amount used for Trixie's care. A tax was levied, however, on the contingent amount passing to the five persons on the death of Trixie.

In the probate court proceedings, the Department also argued that a dog is personal property and a thing of value and should have been taxed as an inheritance of Florence Hand. The executor of the estate of George P. Searight testified:

> If the Court please: I am an innocent bystander of this situation and am not personally interested one way or the other except to be right. Let me say this to the Court, — I wrote this provision in the Will, and frankly, the question as to whether the dog was taxable or not was never considered. I had no idea we would have such a problem. When the time came to make the Will George was concerned that when something happened to him that the dog was not to go to the dog pound. In fact he had as much affection for his dog as for his relatives. He lived with the dog and lived down there like a recluse.
>
> So far as the tax matter is concerned, let me take Mr. Annat's last contention, so far as taxing the dog as a thing of value. The dog may have a value of two, three or five dollars. It has no value other than that of a mongrel fox-terrier dog. Frankly I would say it could be argued that the fair market value of the dog was zero. If Florence tried to sell the dog I don't think she could give it away. On the contention of whether or not it is a thing of value I am not disposed to argue. Whether it can be sold, I don't know. I do know this, — George had it and I know there was some question about Florence taking it, and only because he made that instruction in the Will she took it.

The parties settled the matter by agreeing that the dog had a value of $5 and Florence Hand owed a tax on that.

The executor's final accounting reported that $255.75 was distributed to Florence Hand for the care of Trixie, who died on October 30, 1949, after being struck by a car. The balance of the $1,000 was divided among the five legatees.

2.   After you study the Rule Against Perpetuities in Chapter 14, consider whether the court's assumption of a 6 percent interest rate is consistent with the orthodox understanding of the Rule (it isn't). Relatedly, in deciding the perpetuities question, why did the court not take into account the fact that Trixie had died before the court's decision was rendered?

NOTE: TRUSTS FOR PETS AND OTHER NONCHARITABLE PURPOSES

The primary exception to the rule that a trust must have an ascertainable beneficiary is for charitable trusts. A trust that is for a *charitable purpose*, such as the relief of poverty, the advancement of education or religion, or the promotion of health, is valid as a *charitable trust*. Because a charitable trust lacks an ascertainable beneficiary who can enforce the trust, the state attorney general has the power to enforce the trust. We take up charitable trusts, including creation and enforcement, in Chapter 11.

In *Searight's Estate*, the question was whether a trust for a *pet animal* was valid. Such a trust is not valid under traditional analysis, because it is neither for the benefit of an ascertainable beneficiary (which includes people but not dogs) nor for a charitable purpose (caring for a single dog is not a charitable purpose). The lack of an ascertainable beneficiary nixes not only trusts for the benefit of a pet animal, but also any *noncharitable purpose trust*. Yet people regularly seek to establish trusts for the preservation of tombs, monuments, or graves, and for the saying of masses, in addition to trusts for pet animals. The question thus arises, why not adapt the law of trusts to allow for noncharitable purpose trusts, or at least to allow such a trust so long as its purpose is not capricious or against public policy?

The question is perhaps most pressing in the case of trusts for pet animals. Pet owners often have intense and loving relationships with their pets. See Gerry W. Beyer, Pet Animals: What Happens When Their Humans Die?, 40 Santa Clara L. Rev. 617 (2000), reporting that 79 percent of pet owners share a bed with their pets and 37 percent carry photos of their pets in their wallets. It should come as no surprise, therefore, that even a quick look at the archives of almost any major media outlet reveals countless anecdotes of pet owners who want to provide for the welfare of their pets after the owner's death.[17]

Leona Helmsley and Trouble

17. Perhaps the most famous recent example is provided by the will of Leona Helmsley, the luxury hotelier and New York real estate magnate who was dubbed the "Queen of Mean" by the tabloids for her harsh treatment of employees and who served an 18-month stint in federal prison for tax evasion. According to the testimony of a housekeeper, Helmsley had said, "We don't pay taxes. Only the little people pay taxes."

In her will Helmsley left $12 million in trust for the benefit of her dog, Trouble, a Maltese poodle that Helmsley called Princess. Helmsley directed that upon Trouble's death, the dog should be interred next to her in the Helmsley Mausoleum, a direction that is unlikely to be followed because New York law prohibits burial of animals in human cemeteries. Helmsley left $3 million in trust for the perpetual care and maintenance of the Mausoleum, directing the trustees to arrange for the Mausoleum "to be acid washed or steam cleaned at least once a year."

Helmsley also made a few modest bequests to humans. She gave $100,000 to her chauffeur; $5 million outright plus a life interest in a $10 million trust to her brother; and $5 million outright plus a life interest in a $5 million trust to two of her four grandchildren (the other two she expressly disinherited). The favored grandchildren's respective rights to distributions from their trusts were conditioned on their each visiting their father's grave at least once a year. Helmsley directed that "a register to be signed by each visitor" be "placed in the Helmsley Mausoleum," and that the trustees "shall rely on" the register exclusively "in determining whether" the grandchildren satisfied the visitation requirement. One wonders whether the grandchildren could satisfy the visitation condition for two years at a time by signing the register just before and just after the clock strikes 12 on New Year's Eve.

The remainder of the Helmsley fortune, estimated to be worth somewhere between $4 billion and $8 billion, was left to a charitable trust that she had created previously. To make her wishes for the charitable trust clear, in 2003 Helmsley signed a "Mission Statement" that said that the trustees should support (1) "the provision of care for dogs," and (2) "the provision of medical and health care services for indigent people, with emphasis on providing care to children." In 2004, Helmsley signed a superseding Mission Statement that dropped the purpose of medical care for the indigent but preserved the purpose of provision of care for dogs. Helmsley, it may truly be said, left her fortune to the dogs — or so she tried. In February 2009, a New York court ruled that under the terms of the trust the Mission Statements did not bind the trustees. Two months later, the trustees announced their first set of distributions, $136 million in all, of which only $1 million went to canine-related causes.

No stranger to controversy during life, Leona Helmsley provoked strong reactions at death, too. The New York Times characterized Helmsley as a "posthumous control freak." In an op-ed discussing the Helmsley will, Professor Madoff lamented that through the tax deduction for bequests to charitable trusts, "American taxpayers subsidize the whims of the rich and fulfill their fantasies of immortality." Ray D. Madoff, Dog Eat Your Taxes?, N.Y. Times, July 9, 2008, at A23. The New York Post covered the story with the headline "Rich Bitch," a term subsequently recycled by Jeffrey Toobin, Rich Bitch: The Legal Battle Over Trust Funds for Pets, New Yorker, Sept. 29, 2008, at 38. Even Donald Trump, Helmsley's rival in the New York real estate scene, weighed in. Through a spokesperson Trump said, "The dog is the only thing that loved her and deserves every single penny of it."

Two solutions to the problem of a trust for a noncharitable purpose have evolved: (a) the common law honorary trust and (b) the statutory purpose trust.

(a) *The honorary trust.* Following the lead of §124 of the First and Second Restatements of Trusts, many courts allow a donor to create what has come to be known as an *honorary trust*. This approach was followed in *Searight's Estate*. In an honorary trust, the transferee is not under a legal obligation to carry out the settlor's stated purpose, hence the qualifier *honorary*, but if the transferee declines, she is said to hold the property upon a resulting trust and the property reverts to the settlor or the settlor's successors. 2 Austin Wakeman Scott, William Franklin Fratcher, and Mark L. Ascher, Scott and Ascher on Trusts §12.11 (5th ed. 2006).

Suppose that an honorary trust was funded with far more money than its purpose could reasonably need. Would such a trust fail as capricious? See Restatement (Third) of Trusts §47, cmt. e (2003).

In drafting an honorary trust, care must be taken not to offend the Rule Against Perpetuities. In a state that has retained the common law Rule, an honorary trust for a noncharitable purpose is void if it can last beyond all relevant lives in being at the creation of the trust plus 21 years — and even if the honorary trust is for a pet animal, the pet is *not* a relevant measuring life. Inasmuch as cockatoos can live to be 80, and tortoises have been known to live for over 150 years, this poses drafting challenges. For a thoughtful examination of trusts for purposes and the Rule Against Perpetuities, see Adam J. Hirsch, Trusts for Purposes: Policy, Ambiguity, and Anomaly in the Uniform Laws, 26 Fla. St. U. L. Rev. 913, 930-950 (1999).

(b) *The statutory purpose trust.* Today most states have enacted statutes that permit a trust for a pet animal or other noncharitable purpose for a given amount of time and for the perpetual care of a grave site. Many of these statutes are based on Uniform Trust Code §§408-409 (2000) or Uniform Probate Code §2-907 (1990, rev. 1993). Under the UTC and UPC provisions, the court is authorized to reduce the amount of the trust property if the court determines that it exceeds the amount required for the intended use. To resolve the problems of enforcement that arise when the trustee does not owe duties to a person who can call the trustee

---

Meanwhile, one of Trouble's former handlers, who claimed to have suffered permanent nerve damage when Trouble bit her hand, threatened to bring suit in view of Trouble's newly inherited wealth. The handler's prior suit against Helmsley had been dismissed on the ground that the handler's injuries fell within the Worker's Compensation Law, which bars tort suits against an employer for injuries suffered at work. More disturbingly, after Helmsley's death Trouble began receiving death threats. It was decided, therefore, to move Trouble out of the New York area. A team of security guards took Trouble — code named Bubble by her protection detail — to Florida by private jet to live with a Helmsley employee at the employee's Sarasota residence.

But what of the two disinherited grandchildren and Trouble's trust? The grandchildren contested Helmsley's will on the grounds of lack of capacity. A quick settlement was reached under which they shared a $6 million payout and the trust for Trouble was reduced to $2 million. Like most states, New York has a statute that validates trusts for pet animals but authorizes the court to reduce the size of the trust if it "substantially exceeds the amount required for the intended use." N.Y. Est. Powers & Trusts Law §7-8.1(d) (2008). The court based the reduction to $2 million on an estimate by Trouble's keeper of yearly expenses (including $100,000 for security and $8,000 for grooming) and on an analysis by Trouble's veterinarian of the dog's likely life expectancy. Said Rachel Hirschfeld, a trusts and estates lawyer who specializes in pet trusts: "One of the great moments in my life was when the judge awarded two million in the Helmsley case. It's not the reduction that's important; it's that the judge said two million was appropriate. It's a landmark case, for a judge to be able to say that we have a case for that amount of money." Toobin, supra, at 41.

to account, both the UTC and the UPC follow the lead of trusts for the benefit of minors and other incompetents and provide for enforcement by a person appointed by the settlor or the court.

Perhaps the oddest pet trust statute is in Washington. Under the Washington statute, a trust for a pet animal is valid, but only if the animal has vertebrae. Wash. Stat. §11.118.010 (2008). Seattle attorney Wendy Goffe tells us that the vertebrae limitation was inserted by a legislator who for obscure reasons was worried about wasting resources on guardians ad litem for ant farms. The bar association's draft of the bill, reports Goffe, did not discriminate against ants, slugs, or any other invertebrates, though now such animals will have to be provided for by an out-of-state trust.

The California pet trust statute is also noteworthy, but for a different reason. Starting in 2009, under Cal. Prob. Code. §15212 a trust for the benefit of a pet animal alive at the settlor's death is valid for the life of the animal. The trust is enforceable not only by a person designated in the trust instrument or by the court, but also by "any person interested in the welfare of the animal or any non-profit charitable organization that has as its principal activity the care of animals." Is this a good idea?

Further reading. For an illuminating examination of the policies underlying the law governing noncharitable purpose trusts, see Adam J. Hirsch, Bequests for Purposes: A Unified Theory, 56 Wash. & Lee L. Rev. 33 (1999). Professor Hirsch points out that the law divides bequests for purposes into three categories — (1) charitable, (2) not charitable but not harmful, and (3) antisocial — and treats each category differently. He argues that, apart from a tiny number of bequests for harmful purposes (such as the payment of criminal fines, as in Thrupp v. Collett, 53 Eng. Rep. 844 (M.R. 1858)), bequests for all sorts of purposes, whether deemed charitable or not, merit enforcement because they provide either social utility or personal utility to the settlor. The challenging issue under Hirsch's approach is to distinguish the merely capricious, which he would allow, from the harmful, which he would not. See also Rachel Hirschfeld, Ensure Your Pet's Future: Estate Planning for Owners and Their Animal Companions, 9 Marq. Elder's Advisor 155 (2007), examining the development of the law on pet trusts and providing planning tips.

4. Necessity of a Written Instrument

Standing alone, the law of trusts does not require a writing to create a valid trust. On the contrary, an inter vivos oral declaration of trust over personal property is enforceable. Restatement (Third) of Trusts §20 (2003). However, the Wills Act requires that a testamentary trust (that is, a trust created by will) be in writing, and the Statute of Frauds requires an inter vivos trust of land to be in writing. Problems sometimes arise, therefore, when someone attempts to create an oral trust for disposition of property at death, or to create an oral inter vivos trust of land.

a. Oral Trusts for Disposition at Death

In re Estate of Fournier
Supreme Judicial Court of Maine, 2006
902 A.2d 852

DANA, J.   Faustina Fogarty appeals from a judgment entered in the Aroostook County Probate Court denying her petition for a declaratory judgment that she was the beneficiary of an oral trust created by her brother, the late George Fournier. . . .

I. BACKGROUND

In 1998 or 1999, Fournier asked a couple who were friends with him if they would "hold some money for him." They said they would, and Fournier delivered two boxes, each containing $200,000 cash, to their home.[18] Fournier asked them to hold the $400,000 in secret until his death and then deliver it to his sister, Faustina Fogarty. Fournier explained that Fogarty "needed it more" than his other sister, Juanita Flanigan.[19] Although he requested secrecy from his friends, Fournier told both Flanigan and her daughter that his friend was holding money for him.

Fournier died in 2005, survived by Fogarty and Flanigan. Under his will, Fogarty was appointed the personal representative of his estate.[20] Upon learning of

---

18. Rick Solman, the winning counsel in *Fournier*, explains:

> George Fournier was a bachelor and a bit of a recluse. As it turns out, he regularly kept hundreds of thousands of dollars hidden in various places throughout his home. No one knows how, when, or where he accumulated his money, but he was a very frugal spender.
>
> He became friends with a Josephat Madore, who was employed in the transportation department at the local school. Later, Josephat and his wife, Yvette, took it upon themselves to check on George from time to time, to take him to medical appointments, etc.
>
> Although they were never social friends, George trusted the Madores and eventually asked them to hold $400,000 in cash until his death. He also appointed Josephat as his attorney-in-fact under a general power of attorney.
>
> It is unclear why George did not prepare a written trust agreement. Perhaps he did not want to spend the money. The evidence suggests that George didn't want the government to tax the money on his death. He told the Madores that he had already paid taxes on the money once.

George Fournier

> George did have a will, which was prepared by an attorney subsequent to the delivery of the cash to the Madores. However, there was no reference in the will to the cash held by the Madores or the trust. [Email from Rick Solman to Robert H. Sitkoff, dated August 14, 2008.]

— Eds.

19. Apparently in recognition of Fogarty's financial need, Fournier gave her a gift of $100,000 in 2002.

20. Fournier's will, dated January 10, 2000, provided for a variety of cash bequests (including a gift of $5 to his sister Rose); gave his Maine residence to his sister Juanita Flanigan and his nephew Curtis King; gave a separate Maine property, "including the boats, buildings, garages and other outbuildings" to Faustina Fogarty; and gave the residue in equal shares to Flanigan, Fogarty, and King. — Eds.

Fournier's death, Fogarty and her son met privately with the couple, and the husband gave Fogarty the money. Fogarty petitioned for a declaratory judgment to establish that during his lifetime Fournier had created an oral trust for her benefit. Following a hearing, the court denied her petition and she brought this appeal.

II. DISCUSSION

A. THE LAW

"A trust may be created by [t]ransfer of property to another person as trustee during the settlor's lifetime." 18-B Maine Revised Statutes (M.R.S.) §401(1) (2005). Section 402(1) provides, in pertinent part:

> A trust is created only if:
>
> A. The settlor has capacity to create a trust;
> B. The settlor indicates an intention to create the trust;
> C. The trust has a definite beneficiary . . . ;
> D. The trustee has duties to perform; and
> E. The same person is not the sole trustee and sole beneficiary.

Although a trust need not be in writing, the creation of an oral trust must be established by clear and convincing evidence. 18-B M.R.S. §407. . . .

B. THE EVIDENCE PRESENTED AT THE HEARING

At the hearing, the husband engaged in the following colloquy with Fogarty's attorney:

Q: [W]hat instructions did Mr. Fournier give you in regard to this money?
A: Hold that money until he's dead. Return the money to [Fogarty], and that's what I did.
Q: Did Mr. Fournier tell you who the money was for?
A: He just said [Fogarty]. Nobody else. . . .
Q: Did Mr. Fournier tell you why he wanted the money to go to his sister [Fogarty]? . . .
A: . . . He said [Fogarty] had a big family, that she's the one that would need more money, you know? And then he mentioned a couple of names, you know? He said [Flanigan] was a wealthy woman, [and h]e didn't want Curtis [King] to get the money.[21] . . .
Q: At any time did Mr. Fournier tell you that he wanted part of this 4 hundred thousand to go to [Flanigan], or anybody else?
A: The only thing he told me was money had to go to [Fogarty]. . . .

---

21. "George reportedly felt that Curtis had wasted the inheritance he had received when his mother (George's sister) had died." Email from Solman to Sitkoff, supra. — Eds.

Q: . . . Was the only time he talked about the four hundred thousand the first time he brought it to you[?]

A: Never talked about the four hundred thousand beside that[.]

The wife testified as follows:

> I asked [Fournier] what are we supposed to do with this money if something happens to you [and h]e says it would go to [Fogarty]. . . . And after a year or two I asked [Fournier] are you ready to take back your money, [and] he says, no, leave it where it is[, i]t's for [Fogarty]. I feel she needs it more. Because I knew he had another sister, and I asked about the other sister. He said the other sister, she's well off. She has plenty of money, and I feel [Fogarty] would need it more.

Flanigan's daughter testified that Fournier told her about the money, saying: "If anything should happen to me, I am giving [the husband] some money to hold for me." Additionally, Flanigan testified that Fournier told her that the husband was holding money for her and Fogarty.

C. THE COURT'S FACTUAL FINDINGS AND LEGAL CONCLUSIONS

The [probate] court found that Fournier instructed the couple that, upon his death, they should "deliver the money to Faustina Fogarty, the personal representative named in his Will." The court reasoned that, in telling Flanigan's daughter about the money,[22] Fournier evinced an intent that the money pass through his estate. The court further reasoned, somewhat inconsistently, that, in giving Fogarty $100,000 in 2002, Fournier decreased her financial need, potentially obviating the need for a trust for her benefit.

Applying 18-B M.R.S. §402(1), the court concluded that, despite Fournier's instructions to the couple, no trust had been created. The court ordered that the $400,000 was part of Fournier's estate.

D. ANALYSIS

While we discern no error in the court's finding that Fournier instructed the couple to deliver the money to Fogarty, we discern clear error in its finding that Fogarty was to take the money as personal representative. Neither Fournier's discussion with Flanigan's daughter, nor his previous gift to Fogarty contradicts the overwhelming evidence (provided primarily by the couple) that Fournier intended Fogarty to take the money in her individual capacity.

Applying 18-B M.R.S. §402(1) to the foregoing findings, we conclude that Fournier created an oral trust in which the couple was to hold the money during his lifetime and turn it over to Fogarty personally after his death.

The entry is: Judgment vacated and remanded to the Probate Court for entry of a judgment in favor of Faustina Fogarty.

---

22. Although Flanigan testified that Fournier told her the husband was holding money "for the two of us," the court does not appear to have credited Flanigan's testimony. Indeed, the court found that Flanigan had "recently suffered a stroke and [was] still in the process of recovery" and that her "memory [was] not good."

NOTES AND QUESTIONS

1. *Epilogue.* Six weeks after the Maine Supreme Judicial Court rendered its decision in *Fournier*, Juanita Flanigan petitioned the probate court for a new trial on the basis of a note found by a real estate agent in an unlocked metal box under a bureau in George Fournier's home. In a variety of ink and pencil notations, the note, evidently written by Fournier, referenced $400,000 that was to be used to "reimburse" Flanigan, Faustina Fogarty, and Curtis King, though King's name was crossed out. The note was not signed by Fournier and was dated about a year after Fournier gave Josephat Madore and his wife the disputed $400,000 in cash, but it was signed by Madore. The probate court granted Flanigan's petition and, after a new trial, ruled that the $400,000 should be divided among Flanigan, Fogarty, and King, concluding that the note showed that the oral trust was for the benefit of all three. On appeal, the Supreme Judicial Court of Maine affirmed, among other things taking notice of the fact that, per footnote 20 above, Fournier left the residue of his estate to Flanigan, Fogarty, and King in equal shares. In re Estate of Fournier, 966 A.2d 885 (Me. 2009).

Subsequently Discovered Note Written by George Fournier

2. An oral trust of personal property is valid in all but a handful of states. UTC §407 (2000), applied in *Fournier*, provides: "Except as required by a statute other than this [Code], a trust need not be evidenced by a trust instrument, but the creation of an oral trust and its terms may be established only by clear and convincing evidence."

As in *Fournier*, an oral trust may be proved by oral testimony and, once proved, the trust is enforceable even if it provides for the disposition of property on the death of the settlor. In such a case, does the requirement of clear and convincing evidence satisfy the evidentiary, cautionary, and ritual functions that underpin the Wills Act formalities normally required for a testamentary disposition? How can the outcome in *Fournier* be squared with cases such as In re Groffman, page 228, and Stevens v. Casdorph, page 229, in which a signed will was denied probate because it did not strictly comply with the applicable Wills Act attestation provisions? Does *Fournier* provide an argument in favor of reforming the strict compliance rule? Does the epilogue in *Fournier* provide a cautionary tale against allowing oral trusts to pass property at death?

Olliffe v. Wells
Supreme Judicial Court of Massachusetts, 1881
130 Mass. 221

[Ellen Donovan died in 1877 leaving a will devising her residuary estate to the Rev. Eleazer M.P. Wells "to distribute the same in such manner as in his discretion shall appear best calculated to carry out wishes which I have expressed to him or may express to him." Wells was named executor. Ellen's heirs brought suit, claiming the residue should be distributed to them. In his answer, Wells stated that Ellen Donovan, before and after the execution of the will, had orally expressed to him her wish that her estate be used for charitable purposes, and especially for the poor, aged, infirm, and needy under the care of Saint Stephen's Mission of Boston.[23] Wells further stated that he desired and intended to distribute the residue for these purposes. The parties agreed that the facts alleged in the answer should be taken as true.]

GRAY, C.J.   Upon the face of this will the residuary bequest to the defendant gives him no beneficial interest. It expressly requires him to distribute all the property bequeathed to him, giving him no discretion upon the question whether he shall or shall not distribute it, or shall or shall not carry out the intentions of the testatrix, but allowing him a discretionary authority as to the manner only in which the property shall be distributed pursuant to her intentions. The will declares a trust too indefinite to be carried out, and the next of kin of the testatrix

---

23. Eleazer Mather Porter Wells, born in 1783, entered Brown University at the age of 22 but was dismissed as a result of a practical joke played on a professor by his roommates. (O tempora! O mores!) Thereafter he was deeply affected by a profound religious experience, including voices in the night saying, "Go and do my work." At age 40, Wells entered the ministry, becoming an Episcopal priest. In 1843, at age 60, Wells opened St. Stephen's Mission. From here he provided food, nursing care, clothing, and shelter for the poor of the West End of Boston. On one occasion he was able to keep the fire at the mission going by burning 100 old volumes of Voltaire's writings, which had been given to the mission. These proved good kindling, and Wells is quoted as having said, "Well, even the worst of men are put to good uses for the benefit of others." The great Boston fire of 1872 destroyed St. Stephen's Mission, and for the remaining years of his life Wells worked to revitalize the mission to no avail.

The Rev. Wells

Wells died in 1878 at age 95. A resolution adopted by the clergy of the Episcopal Diocese of Massachusetts paid tribute to Wells as

> [a] clergyman of stainless reputation and incorruptible integrity; an enthusiast in his sacred calling, especially in his self-selected mission to the destitute and afflicted, the outcast and the erring. . . . The work of Dr. Wells, continued so long a period at St. Stephen's Mission in Boston, and as the trusted almoner of very many of his fellow citizens, and withal his pure and consistent life as a man of God and of unremitting prayer, furnish a splendid commendation of religion.

Information supplied by Mark J. Duffy, Archivist of the Episcopal Diocese of Massachusetts, in a letter to Jesse Dukeminier dated April 13, 1982.

To what extent, if any, does the court's decision in Olliffe v. Wells turn on the facts that St. Stephen's Mission had been destroyed and the "trusted almoner"had died before the case reached the Supreme Judicial Court?

must take by way of resulting trust, unless the facts agreed show such a trust for the benefit of others as the court can execute. Nichols v. Allen, 130 Mass. 211. . . .

It has been held in England and in other States, although the question has never arisen in this Commonwealth, that, if a person procures an absolute devise or bequest to himself by orally promising the testator that he will convey the property to or hold it for the benefit of third persons, and afterwards refused to perform his promise, a trust arises out of the confidence reposed in him by the testator and of his own fraud, which a court of equity, upon clear and satisfactory proof of the facts, will enforce against him at the suit of such third persons. . . .

Upon like grounds, it has been held in England that, if a testator devises or bequeaths property to his executors upon trusts not defined in the will, but which, as he states in the will, he has communicated to them before its execution, such trusts, if for lawful purposes, may be proved by the admission of the executors, or by oral evidence, and enforced against them. . . . And in two or three comparatively recent cases it has been held that such trusts may be enforced against the heirs or next of kin of the testator, as well as against the devisee. . . . But these cases appear to us to have overlooked or disregarded a fundamental distinction.

Where a trust not declared in the will is established by a court of chancery against the devisee, it is by reason of the obligation resting upon the conscience of the devisee, and not as a valid testamentary disposition by the deceased. Cullen v. Attorney General, L.R. 1 H.L. 190. Where the bequest is outright upon its face, the setting up of a trust, while it diminishes the right of the devisee, does not impair any right of the heirs or next of kin, in any aspect of the case; for if the trust were not set up, the whole property would go to the devisee by force of the devise; if the trust setup is a lawful one, it enures to the benefit of the cestuis que trust; and if the trust setup is unlawful, the heirs or next of kin take by way of resulting trust.

Where the bequest is declared upon its face to be upon such trusts as the testator has otherwise signified to the devisee, it is equally clear that the devisee takes no beneficial interest; and, as between him and the beneficiaries intended, there is as much ground for establishing the trust as if the bequest to him were absolute on its face. But as between the devisee and the heirs or next of kin, the case stands differently. They are not excluded by the will itself. The will upon its face showing that the devisee takes the legal title only and not the beneficial interest, and the trust not being sufficiently defined by the will to take effect, the equitable interest goes, by way of resulting trust, to the heirs or next of kin, as property of the deceased, not disposed of by his will. Sears v. Hardy, 120 Mass. 524, 541, 542. They cannot be deprived of that equitable interest, which accrues to them directly from the deceased, by any conduct of the devisee; nor by any intention of the deceased, unless signified in those forms which the law makes essential to every testamentary disposition. A trust not sufficiently declared on the face of the will cannot therefore be set up by extrinsic evidence to defeat the rights of the heirs at law or next of kin. . . .

Decree for the plaintiffs.

NOTE

Olliffe v. Wells is the origin of the distinction between a *secret* and a *semisecret* trust, followed by most states, although it is rejected in several states and in England. The distinction is this: If Ellen Donovan had left a legacy to the Reverend Wells absolute on its face, without anything in the will indicating an intent to create a trust, a promise by the Reverend Wells to Ellen Donovan to use the legacy for St. Stephen's Mission would be enforceable by a constructive trust imposed upon Wells. This is called a secret trust because the will indicates no trust. Courts admit evidence of the promise for the purpose of preventing the Reverend Wells from unjustly enriching himself by pocketing the legacy. Having admitted proof of the promise, they remedy the unjust enrichment by imposing a constructive trust on Wells for the benefit of St. Stephen's Mission.

On the other hand, if the will indicates that the Reverend Wells is to hold the legacy in trust but does not identify the beneficiary (as was true in Olliffe v. Wells), a semisecret trust is created. Because the will shows on its face an intent not to benefit Wells personally, it is not necessary to admit evidence of Wells's promise in order to prevent his unjust enrichment. Such evidence is excluded, and the legacy to Wells fails.

Restatement (Third) of Trusts §18, cmt. c (2003), and Restatement (Third) of Restitution §46, cmt. g (T.D. No. 5, 2007), both take the view that a constructive trust should be imposed in favor of the intended beneficiary in the semisecret, as well as secret, trust situation. Nonetheless, the weight of authority in the United States follows Olliffe v. Wells.

b.   Oral Inter Vivos Trusts of Land

Where *O* conveys land to *X* upon an oral trust to pay the income to *A* for life and upon *A*'s death to convey the land to *B*, the Statute of Frauds in virtually every state prevents the enforcement of the express trust. Is *X* permitted to keep the land? The cases split between permitting *X* to retain the land, on the ground that the Statute of Frauds forbids proof of the oral trust, and imposing a constructive trust on *X* to prevent his unjust enrichment. See 1 Austin Wakeman Scott, William Franklin Fratcher, and Mark L. Ascher, Scott and Ascher on Trusts §6.11 (5th ed. 2006), providing extensive discussion and citation to authority. See also Restatement (Third) of Trusts §24, cmts. h-j (2003). Most decisions have permitted *X* to retain the land. However, a constructive trust for the beneficiaries will be imposed where the transfer was wrongfully obtained by fraud or duress; where the transferee, *X*, was in a confidential relationship with the transferor; or where the transfer was made in anticipation of the transferor's death, and most of the cases involve one of these situations.

More common than an oral trust for a third party is an oral trust for the benefit of the transferor. Indeed, judging by the cases, a surprising number of persons

put title to land in another, relying upon the transferee's oral promise to reconvey. Some of the transferors are attempting to avoid their creditors or spouses or
to achieve some tax benefit. Of course, any lawyer knows these transferors are
asking for trouble, and human nature being what it is, usually they get it.

A comparison of Hieble v. Hieble, 316 A.2d 777 (Conn. 1972), with Pappas v.
Pappas, 320 A.2d 809 (Conn. 1973), is instructive. In *Hieble*, a mother transferred
title to certain real property from herself alone to herself in joint tenancy with her
son and daughter. The mother was fearful of a return of cancer and wanted to
avoid probate. The son and daughter agreed to reconvey the property to the
mother if she remained healthy. Several years later, after the son refused to reconvey his interest, the mother brought suit. The court concluded that a constructive
trust should be imposed on the basis of the oral agreement and the confidential
relationship of the parties.

In *Pappas*, Andrew Pappas, age 67, married a 23-year-old woman while on a
visit to Greece. On their return, marital difficulties arose, and just prior to the
wife's suing for divorce, Andrew conveyed certain real estate to his son. The son
agreed to transfer the property back to Andrew once his marital difficulties were
over. In the divorce action, Andrew testified that he made the conveyance for consideration in satisfaction of certain financial and other obligations. Immediately
after the divorce action was concluded Andrew demanded a reconveyance from
the son, who refused. The court held that a constructive trust could not be
imposed upon the son because Andrew, in misrepresenting the nature of the
transfer in the divorce action, had perpetrated a fraud on the court and therefore
did not have "clean hands."

9

RIGHTS TO DISTRIBUTIONS
FROM THE TRUST FUND

> The law, in its majestic equality, forbids the rich as well as the poor to
> sleep under bridges, to beg in the streets, and to steal bread.
>
> ANATOLE FRANCE
> *Le Lys Rouge, ch. 7 (1894)*

This chapter addresses the rights of a beneficiary, or a creditor of the beneficiary, to a distribution from the trust fund. As we shall see, even if a beneficiary is insolvent and entitled to a distribution, often a creditor of the beneficiary cannot compel the trustee to distribute trust assets to satisfy the beneficiary's debt. This chapter also addresses the rules that govern when a trust may be modified or terminated, which set the boundaries on the court's power to alter the terms of the trust and sometimes affect creditor rights. The easier it is for a beneficiary to obtain a modification or termination of the trust, the more the trust property looks like the beneficiary's own property, and the stronger is the case for enforcing the claims of the beneficiary's creditors against the beneficiary's interest in the trust. Finally, this chapter examines when a court may remove the trustee, which raises many of the same considerations as modification and termination.

SECTION A.   RIGHTS OF THE BENEFICIARY TO DISTRIBUTIONS

Trusts can be divided into mandatory trusts and discretionary trusts. In a *mandatory trust*, the trustee must make specified distributions to an identified beneficiary. Thus:

> *Case 1. O* transfers property to *X* in trust to distribute all the income to *A*. This is a mandatory trust. The trustee has no discretion to choose either the person who will receive the distribution or the amount to be distributed.

In a *discretionary trust*, the trustee has discretion over distributions. Discretionary trusts may be drafted in limitless variety. Thus:

> *Case 2. O* transfers property to *X* in trust to distribute all the income to one or more members of a group consisting of *A*, *A*'s spouse, and *A*'s descendants, in such amounts as the trustee determines. This is a kind of discretionary trust known as a *spray trust*. The trustee must distribute all the income currently, but has discretion to determine which beneficiaries get it and in what amounts. Some discretionary trusts also authorize the trustee to accumulate income and add it to principal. These are known as *sprinkle trusts*. In many discretionary trusts the trustee's discretion is subjected to a standard of review, such as one that authorizes the trustee only to make distributions as is necessary for the beneficiary's support and maintenance. This is a form of discretionary trust known as a *support trust*.

Through a discretionary trust, the settlor can *postpone* and *delegate* to the trustee the decisions of to whom to make distributions, in what amounts, and when. Postponing and delegating such decisions is often sensible because no settlor can foresee all the changes that will occur with the passage of time. On the other hand, with discretion comes the need for a mechanism to police the exercise of that discretion. Enter the *fiduciary obligation*. Although we defer systematic examination of fiduciary administration until Chapter 10, it is worth considering here fiduciary governance of the trustee's exercise of discretionary distribution powers.

Marsman v. Nasca
Massachusetts Appeals Court, 1991
573 N.E.2d 1025

DREBEN, J. This appeal raises the following questions: Does a trustee, holding a discretionary power to pay principal for the "comfortable support and maintenance" of a beneficiary, have a duty to inquire into the financial resources of that beneficiary so as to recognize his needs? If so, what is the remedy for such failure? . . .

1. *Facts.* We take our facts from the findings of the Probate Court judge, supplemented on occasion by uncontroverted evidence. . . .

Sara Wirt Marsman died in September, 1971, survived by her second husband, T. Frederik Marsman (Cappy), and her daughter by her first marriage, Sally Marsman Marlette. Mr. James F. Farr, her lawyer for many years, drew her will and was the trustee thereunder.[1] . . .

---

1. The will provided for two trustees; however, one resigned in April, 1972, and thereafter Farr acted as sole trustee. [James F. Farr, who died in 1993, was a prominent trusts and estates lawyer in Boston and the author of a leading practitioner's handbook, James F. Farr and Jackson W. Wright, Jr., An Estate Planner's Handbook (4th ed. 1979). He was also the author of the sixth edition of Augustus Peabody Loring's Trustee's Handbook, first published in 1898 and the Bible of Boston trustees for several generations, referred to by the court in footnote 4, below. — Eds.]

Sara's will provided in relevant part:

> It is my desire that my husband, T. Fred Marsman, be provided with reasonable maintenance, comfort and support after my death. Accordingly, if my said husband is living at the time of my death, I give to my trustees, who shall set the same aside as a separate trust fund, one-third (1/3) of the rest, residue and remainder of my estate . . . ; they shall pay the net income therefrom to my said husband at least quarterly during his life; and after having considered the various available sources of support for him, my trustees shall, if they deem it necessary or desirable from time to time, in their sole and uncontrolled discretion, pay over to him, or use, apply and/or expend for his direct or indirect benefit such amount or amounts of the principal thereof as they shall deem advisable for his comfortable support and maintenance.

[The remainder interest was given to Sara's daughter Sally, who was Cappy's stepdaughter, and to Sally's family.]

The will also contained the following exculpatory clause: "No trustee hereunder shall ever be liable except for his own willful neglect or default."

During their marriage, Sara and Cappy lived well and entertained frequently. Cappy's main interest in life centered around horses. An expert horseman, he was riding director and instructor at the Dana Hall School in Wellesley until he was retired due to age in 1972.[2] Sally, who was also a skilled rider, viewed Cappy as her mentor, and each had great affection for the other. Sara, wealthy from her prior marriage, managed the couple's financial affairs. She treated Cappy as "Lord of the Manor" and gave him money for his personal expenses, including an extensive wardrobe from one of the finest men's stores in Wellesley.

In 1956, Sara and Cappy purchased, as tenants by the entirety, the property in Wellesley which is the subject of this litigation. Although title to the property passed to Cappy by operation of law on Sara's death, Sara's will also indicated an intent to convey her interest in the property to Cappy. In the will, Cappy was also given a life estate in the household furnishings with remainder to Sally.

After Sara's death in 1971, Farr met with Cappy and Sally and held what he termed his "usual family conference" going over the provisions of the will. At the time of Sara's death, the Wellesley property was appraised at $29,000, and the principal of Cappy's trust was about $65,600.

---

2. Boston Globe, Feb. 26, 1987, at 59:

T. Frederik Marsman, 85, of Wellesley, former director of horse riding at the Dana Hall School, died Tuesday at his home after a long illness.

A native of the Netherlands, Mr. Marsman received his equestrian training under several European masters. He was a captain when he came to this country in 1926 with the Netherlands Army Show Team. Shortly after the trip, Mr. Marsman, who was called Cappy, returned to the United States as the manager of the Grayholm Stables in Rhode Island. During his 12 years there, he became a well-known figure in the ring shows of the East Coast.

One of the pioneers in developing dressage in this country, Mr. Marsman was the trainer and rider of Gygeo and Green Mountain, two champion dressage horses of the 1920s and 1930s. He held championships in dressage, jumping and four-in-hand driving.

For 30 years he was director of riding at Dana Hall School in Wellesley and at Teela-Wooket Camps in Vermont. He also was a judge in many national and Canadian horse shows.

— Eds.

Captain T. Frederik Marsman (Cappy)

Cappy continued to live in the Wellesley house but was forced by Sara's death and his loss of employment in 1972 to reduce his standard of living substantially. He married Margaret in March, 1972, and, shortly before their marriage, asked her to read Sara's will, but they never discussed it. In 1972, Cappy took out a mortgage for $4,000, the proceeds of which were used to pay bills. Farr was aware of the transaction, as he replied to an inquiry of the mortgagee bank concerning the appraised value of the Wellesley property and the income Cappy expected to receive from Sara's trust.

In 1973, Cappy retained Farr in connection with a new will. The latter drew what he described as a simple will which left most of Cappy's property, including the house, to Margaret. The will was executed on November 7, 1973.

In February, 1974, Cappy informed [Farr] that business was at a standstill and that he really needed some funds, if possible. Farr replied in a letter in which he set forth the relevant portion of the will and wrote that he thought the language was "broad enough to permit a distribution of principal." Farr enclosed a check of $300. He asked Cappy to explain in writing the need for some support and why the need had arisen. The judge found that Farr, by his actions, discouraged Cappy from making any requests for principal.

Indeed, Cappy did not reduce his request to writing and never again requested principal. Farr made no investigation whatsoever of Cappy's needs or his "available sources of support" from the date of Sara's death until Cappy's admission to a nursing home in 1983 and, other than the $300 payment, made no additional distributions of principal until Cappy entered the nursing home.

By the fall of 1974, Cappy's difficulty in meeting expenses intensified.[3] Several of his checks were returned for insufficient funds, and in October, 1974, in order that he might remain in the house, Sally and he agreed that she would take over the mortgage payments, the real estate taxes, insurance, and major repairs. In return, she would get the house upon Cappy's death.

Cappy and Sally went to Farr to draw up a deed. Farr was the only lawyer involved, and he billed Sally for the work. He wrote to Sally, stating his understanding of the proposed transaction, and asking, among other things, whether Margaret would have a right to live in the house if Cappy should predecease her. The answer was no. No copy of the letter to Sally was sent to Cappy. A deed was executed by Cappy on November 7, 1974, transferring the property to Sally and her husband Richard T. Marlette (Marlette) as tenants by the entirety, reserving a life estate to Cappy. No writing set forth Sally's obligations to Cappy.

The judge found that there was no indication that Cappy did not understand the transaction, although, in response to a request for certain papers by Farr, Cappy sent a collection of irrelevant documents. The judge also found that Cappy clearly understood that he was preserving no rights for Margaret, and that neither Sally nor Richard nor Farr ever made any representation to Margaret that she would be able to stay in the house after Cappy's death. . . .

Sally and Marlette complied with their obligations under the agreement. Sally died in 1983, and Marlette became the sole owner of the property subject to Cappy's life estate. Although Margaret knew before Cappy's death that she did not have any interest in the Wellesley property, she believed that Sally would have allowed her to live in the house because of their friendship. After Cappy's death in 1987, Marlette inquired as to Margaret's plans, and, subsequently, through Farr, sent Margaret a notice to vacate the premises. Margaret brought this action in the Probate Court.

After a two-day trial, the judge held that [Farr] was in breach of his duty to Cappy when he neglected to inquire as to the latter's finances. She concluded that, had Farr fulfilled his fiduciary duties, Cappy would not have conveyed the residence owned by him to Sally and Marlette. The judge ordered Marlette to convey the house to Margaret and also ordered Farr to reimburse Marlette from the remaining portion of Cappy's trust for the expenses paid by him and Sally for the upkeep of the property. If Cappy's trust proved insufficient to make such payments, Farr was to be personally liable for such expenses. Both Farr and Marlette appealed from the judgment, from the denial of their motions to amend the

---

3. After Sara's death, Cappy's income was limited, particularly considering the station he had enjoyed while married to Sara. In 1973, including the income from Sara's trust of $2,116, his income was $3,441; in 1974 it was $3,549, including trust income of $2,254; in 1975, $6,624, including trust income of $2,490 and social security income of $2,576. Margaret's income was also minimal; $499 in 1974, $4,084 in 1975, including social security income of $1,686. Cappy's income in 1976 was $8,464; in 1977, $8,955; in 1978, $9,681; in 1979, $10,851; in 1980, $11,261; in 1981, $12,651; in 1982, $13,870; in 1983, $12,711; in 1984, $12,500; in 1985, $12,567; in 1986, $12,558. The largest portion from 1975 on came from social security benefits.

findings, and from their motions for a new trial. Margaret appealed from the denial of her motion for attorney's fees. . . . [W]e agree with the judge that Sara's will imposed a duty of inquiry on the trustee, but we disagree with the remedy and, therefore, remand for further proceedings.

2. *Breach of trust by the trustee.* Contrary to Farr's contention that it was not incumbent upon him to become familiar with Cappy's finances, . . . Sara's will clearly placed such a duty upon him. In his brief, Farr claims that the will gave Cappy the right to request principal "in extraordinary circumstances" and that the trustee, "was charged by Sara to be wary should Cappy request money beyond that which he quarterly received." Nothing in the will or the record supports this narrow construction. To the contrary, the direction to the trustees was to pay Cappy such amounts "as they shall deem advisable for his comfortable support and maintenance." This language has been interpreted to set an ascertainable standard, namely to maintain the life beneficiary "in accordance with the standard of living which was normal for him before he became a beneficiary of the trust." Woodberry v. Bunker, 268 N.E.2d 841 (Mass. 1971).

Even where the only direction to the trustee is that he shall "in his discretion" pay such portion of the principal as he shall "deem advisable," the discretion is not absolute. "Prudence and reasonableness, not caprice or careless good nature, much less a desire on the part of the trustee to be relieved from trouble . . . furnish the standard of conduct." Boyden v. Stevens, 188 N.E. 741 (Mass. 1934).

That there is a duty of inquiry into the needs of the beneficiary follows from the requirement that the trustee's power "must be exercised with that soundness of judgment which follows from a due appreciation of trust responsibility." Id. In Old Colony Trust Co. v. Rodd, 254 N.E.2d 886 (Mass. 1970), the trustee sent a questionnaire to each potential beneficiary to determine which of them required assistance but failed to make further inquiry in cases where the answers were incomplete. The court agreed with the trial judge that the method employed by the trustee in determining the amount of assistance required in each case to attain "comfortable support and maintenance" was inadequate. There, as here, the trustee attempted to argue that it was appropriate to save for the beneficiaries' future medical needs. The court held that the "prospect of illness in old age does not warrant a persistent policy of niggardliness toward individuals for whose comfortable support in life the trust has been established. The payments made to the respondent and several other beneficiaries, viewed in light of their assets and needs, when measured against the assets of the trust show that little consideration has been given to the 'comfortable support' of the beneficiaries."

Farr, in our view, did not meet his responsibilities either of inquiry or of distribution under the trust. The conclusion of the trial judge that, had he exercised "sound judgment," he would have made such payments to Cappy "as to allow him to continue to live in the home he had occupied for many years with the settlor" was warranted.

3. *Remedy against Marlette.* [The trial judge ordered Marlette to convey the house to Margaret on the theory that, had Farr not been in breach of trust, Cappy would have died owning the house and thus would have been able to devise it to Margaret. This court vacated that order because Sally and Marlette were bona

fide purchasers without notice. The conveyance to Sally and Marlette was supported by consideration, and Sally and Marlette did not have notice of Farr's breach of trust.]

4. *Remainder of Cappy's trust.* The amounts that should have been expended for Cappy's benefit are, however, in a different category. More than $80,000 remained in the trust for Cappy at the time of his death. As we have indicated, the trial judge properly concluded that payments of principal should have been made to Cappy from that fund in sufficient amount to enable him to keep the Wellesley property. . . . The remedy in such circumstances is to impress a constructive trust on the amounts which should have been distributed to Cappy but were not because of the error of the trustee. Even in cases where beneficiaries have already been paid funds by mistake, the amounts may be collected from them unless the recipients were bona fide purchasers or unless they, without notice of the improper payments, had so changed their position that it would be inequitable to make them repay. Here, the remainder of Cappy's trust has not yet been distributed, and there is no reason to depart from the usual rule of impressing a constructive trust in favor of Cappy's estate on the amounts wrongfully withheld. . . .

That Cappy assented to the accounts is also no bar to recovery by his estate. The judge found that he was in the dark as to his rights to receive principal for the upkeep of the home. An assent may be withdrawn by a judge "if it is deemed improvident or not conducive to justice." Swift v. Hiscock, 183 N.E.2d 875, 877 (Mass. 1962). [In addition, the accounts had not been approved by the court.][4] . . .

The amounts to be paid to Cappy's estate have not been determined. On remand, the Probate Court judge is to hold such hearings as are necessary to determine the amounts which should have been paid to Cappy to enable him to retain possession of the house.

5. *Personal liability of the trustee.* . . . [The] difficult question is the effect of the exculpatory clause. As indicated in part 3 of this opinion, we consider the order to Marlette to reconvey the property an inappropriate remedy. In view of the judge's finding that, but for the trustee's breach, Cappy would have retained ownership of the house, the liability of the trustee could be considerable.

Although exculpatory clauses are not looked upon with favor and are strictly construed, such "provisions inserted in the trust instrument without any overreaching or abuse by the trustee of any fiduciary or confidential relationship to the settlor are generally held effective except as to breaches of trust 'committed in bad faith or intentionally or with reckless indifference to the interest of the beneficiary.'" New England Trust Co. v. Paine, 59 N.E.2d 263 (Mass. 1945). The actions of Farr were not of this ilk and also do not fall within the meaning of the term used in the will, "willful neglect or default."

---

4. . . . In Loring, A Trustee's Handbook §62 (Farr rev. 1962) the author states: "[P]reparing annual accounts, signed by the adult beneficiaries and allowing them to continue without adjudication is an unsafe procedure for the trustee." [On informal accountings, see page 749. — Eds.]

Farr testified that he discussed the exculpatory clause with Sara and that she wanted it included. Nevertheless, the judge, without finding that there was an overreaching or abuse of Farr's fiduciary relation with Sara, held the clause ineffective. Relying on the fact that Farr was Sara's attorney, she stated: "One cannot know at this point in time whether or not Farr specifically called this provision to Sara's attention. Given the total failure of Farr to use his judgment as to [C]appy's needs, it would be unjust and unreasonable to hold him harmless by reason of the exculpatory provisions he himself drafted and inserted in this instrument."

Assuming that the judge disbelieved Farr's testimony that he and Sara discussed the clause, although such disbelief on her part is by no means clear, the conclusion that it "would be unjust and unreasonable to hold [Farr] harmless" is not sufficient to find the overreaching or abuse of a fiduciary relation which is required to hold the provision ineffective. See Restatement (Second) of Trusts §222, Comment d (1959). We note that the judge found that Sara managed all the finances of the couple, and from all that appears, was competent in financial matters.

There was no evidence about the preparation and execution of Sara's will except for the questions concerning the exculpatory clause addressed to Farr by his own counsel. No claim was made that the clause was the result of an abuse of confidence.

The fact that the trustee drew the instrument and suggested the insertion of the exculpatory clause does not necessarily make the provision ineffective. Restatement (Second) of Trusts §222, Comment d. No rule of law requires that an exculpatory clause drawn by a prospective trustee be held ineffective unless the client is advised independently.

The judge used an incorrect legal standard in invalidating the clause. While recognizing the sensitivity of such clauses, we hold that, since there was no evidence that the insertion of the clause was an abuse of Farr's fiduciary relationship with Sara at the time of the drawing of her will, the clause is effective. . . .

The judgment is vacated, and the matter is remanded to the Probate Court for further proceedings to determine the amounts which, if paid, would have enabled Cappy to retain ownership of the residence. Such amounts shall be paid to Cappy's estate from the trust for his benefit prior to distributing the balance thereof to the [remainder beneficiaries].

So ordered.

NOTES AND QUESTIONS

1. *Duty to inquire.* In *Marsman,* because the trust instrument entitled Cappy to so much of the trust principal as the trustee deemed advisable for Cappy's "comfortable support and maintenance," the court held that Farr was under a duty to inquire into Cappy's needs and circumstances. This is a standard interpretation that one imagines was known to Farr. See 3 Austin Wakeman Scott, William Franklin Fratcher, and Mark L. Ascher, Scott and Ascher on Trusts §18.2.2 (5th ed. 2007). Why did Farr's request that Cappy explain his need for funds in writing not satisfy this duty?

2.   *The beneficiary's other resources.* A troublesome source of litigation is whether a trustee, in exercising a discretionary power to use income or principal for the beneficiary's support, may consider the other resources available to the beneficiary. In *Marsman*, this question was answered expressly by the terms of the trust, which directed the trustees to consider "the various available sources of support" for Cappy. Where not dealt with in the trust instrument expressly, the law is in flux.

> When the terms of the trust require the trustee to pay to or apply for the beneficiary so much as is necessary for maintenance or support, but fail to provide whether the trustee is to take into account the beneficiary's other resources, it is unclear what the usual inference ought to be. Many cases, as well as the Restatement (Second) of Trusts, have concluded that the usual inference ought to be that the settlor intended for the beneficiary to receive support, even if the beneficiary has other resources. The Restatement (Third) of Trusts, however, concludes that the usual inference ought to be that the settlor intended for the trustee to take the beneficiary's other resources into account in determining the level of support to which the beneficiary is entitled. [Scott and Ascher on Trusts, supra, §13.2.4.]

3.   *Conservative trustees.* There is a tendency for trustees to be conservative in making discretionary distributions to beneficiaries. Why?

4.   *Professional responsibility.* James F. Farr rendered legal services for Sara, Cappy, Sally, and Marlette, all more or less at the same time. It may be appropriate for one lawyer simultaneously to represent multiple members of the same family, but much depends on the circumstances.

> A lawyer who is asked to represent multiple clients regarding related matters must consider at the outset whether the representation involves or may involve impermissible conflicts, including ones that affect the interests of third parties or the lawyer's own interests. The lawyer must also bear this concern in mind as the representation progresses: What was a tolerable conflict at the outset may develop into one that precludes the lawyer from continuing to represent one or more of the clients. [ACTEC Commentaries on the Model Rules of Professional Conduct 92 (4th ed. 2006) (Rule 1.7).]

Under Model Rule of Prof. Conduct 1.7(b) (2002), multiple clients with adverse interests can consent to concurrent representation by the same lawyer, provided that their consent is "informed" and the lawyer "reasonably believes" that he "will be able to provide competent and diligent representation to each affected client." Did Farr have a tolerable conflict that became intolerable when Cappy and Sally were on opposite sides of the house sale? Is it reasonable for a lawyer to believe that he could properly represent parties on opposite sides of a negotiated transaction?

NOTE: EXTENDED DISCRETION

If a trustee has simple discretion, the courts will not interfere with the judgment of the trustee so long as the trustee acts reasonably and in good faith. However, when the instrument purports to free the trustee from some or all of these limitations by use of adjectives such as *sole, absolute,* or *uncontrolled,* problems in construction may arise. At one extreme are instruments that purport to give unlimited discretionary power to the trustee, as in *Marsman.* But a discretionary power to be exercised in the trustee's sole or absolute or uncontrolled discretion is not in fact absolute or uncontrolled. As Judge Learned Hand remarked:

> [N]o language, however strong, will entirely remove any power held in trust from the reach of a court of equity. After allowance has been made for every possible factor which could rationally enter into the trustee's decision, if it appears that he has utterly disregarded the interests of the beneficiary, the Court will intervene. Indeed were that not true, the power would not be held in trust at all; the language would be no more than a precatory admonition. [Stix v. Commissioner, 152 F.2d 562, 563 (2d Cir. 1945).]

What, then, are the limitations on the trustee's freedom when the trustee has "absolute" or "uncontrolled" discretion? Professor Scott argued for a subjective standard, emphasizing the trustee's "good faith" and proper motives, and dispensing with the requirement of reasonableness. He wrote into the Restatement a standard of whether the trustee has acted "in a state of mind in which it was contemplated by the settlor that he would act. . . . [T]he trustee will not be permitted to act dishonestly, or from some motive other than the accomplishment of the purposes of the trust, or ordinarily to act arbitrarily without an exercise of his judgment." Restatement (Second) of Trusts §187, cmt. j (1959). Some courts, relying on the Restatement's good faith standard, declare that the trustee must not act arbitrarily or capriciously, seemingly bringing in a reasonableness test under the guise of other words. Other courts apply a reasonableness test even when the discretion is "absolute."

Under Uniform Trust Code (UTC) §814 (2000, rev. 2004), "Notwithstanding the breadth of discretion granted to a trustee in the terms of the trust, including such terms as 'absolute,' 'sole,' or 'uncontrolled,' the trustee shall exercise a discretionary power in good faith and in accordance with the terms and purposes of the trust and the interests of the beneficiaries." Restatement (Third) of Trusts §50, cmt. c (2003), provides that "words such as 'absolute' or 'unlimited' or 'sole and uncontrolled' are not interpreted literally. Even under the broadest grant of fiduciary discretion, a trustee must act honestly and in a state of mind contemplated by the settlor. Thus, the court will not permit the trustee to act in bad faith or for some purpose or motive other than to accomplish the purposes of the discretionary power." See also id., at §87, cmt. d.

In the final analysis, it appears that the difference between simple and absolute discretion is one of degree and that the trustee's action must not only be in good faith but also to some extent reasonable, with more elasticity in the concept of reasonableness the greater the discretion given in the instrument. For further discussion, see Robert T. Danforth, Article Five of the UTC and the Future of Creditors' Rights in Trusts, 26 Cardozo L. Rev. 2551, 2580-2586, 2597-2602 (2006); Alan Newman, Spendthrift and Discretionary Trusts: Alive and Well Under the Uniform Trust Code, 40 Real Prop., Prob. & Tr. J. 567, 601-618 (2005).

NOTE: EXCULPATORY CLAUSES

In *Marsman*, the testamentary trust Farr drafted for Sara included an *exculpatory clause* (sometimes called an *exoneration clause*), excusing the trustees (and so Farr himself!) from liability except for "willful neglect or default." The court upheld the clause because there was no evidence that it had resulted from an abuse of confidence reposed by Sara in Farr. The court put the burden of proving abuse on Margaret, and she could not satisfy it.

Do you think it is ethical to include an exculpatory clause in a trust you draft that names you as the trustee? Who should have the burden of proving that the clause did or did not arise from a freely bargained agreement with a fully informed client? See ACTEC Commentaries on the Model Rules of Professional Conduct 95 (4th ed. 2006) (discussing Rule 1.7 and appointment of scrivener as fiduciary); Paula A. Monopoli, Drafting Attorneys as Fiduciaries: Fashioning an Optimal Ethical Rule for Conflicts of Interest, 66 U. Pitt. L. Rev. 411 (2005). To borrow an idea from the literature of contract law, if the settlor's lawyer is also named trustee, does the danger of abusive insertion of an exculpatory clause call for a penalty default rule whereby the lawyer has the burden of proving the absence of abuse? Professors Ayres and Gertner explain the concept:

> Penalty defaults are designed to give at least one party to the contract an incentive to contract around the default rule and therefore to choose affirmatively the contract provision they prefer. In contrast to the received wisdom, penalty defaults are purposefully set at what [one or both] parties would not want — in order to encourage the parties to reveal information to each other. [Ian Ayres and Robert Gertner, Filling Gaps in Incomplete Contracts: An Economic Theory of Default Rules, 99 Yale L.J. 87, 91 (1989).]

This is the strategy taken by Uniform Trust Code §1008(b) (2000):

> An exculpatory term drafted or caused to be drafted by the trustee is invalid as an abuse of a fiduciary or confidential relationship unless the trustee proves that the exculpatory term is fair under the circumstances and that its existence and contents were adequately communicated to the settlor.

Putting the burden on a trustee who was also the settlor's lawyer to show that the settlor had affirmative knowledge of the clause and its meaning helps to ensure that the clause was not unwittingly embraced by the settlor. See In re Dentler Family Trust, 873 A.2d 738, 744 (Pa. Super. 2005).

The position of the UTC is endorsed by Restatement (Third) of Trusts §96, cmt. d (T.D. No. 5, 2009) and is supported by considerable authority. In Rutanen v. Ballard, 678 N.E.2d 133 (Mass. 1997), decided subsequent to *Marsman*, the court refused to enforce an exculpatory provision on the ground that the draftsperson/trustee had not adequately advised the settlor about the clause. See also 4 Austin Wakeman Scott, William Franklin Fratcher, and Mark L. Ascher, Scott and Ascher on Trusts §24.27.4, at 1809 (5th ed. 2007), stating that "the court may properly call upon an attorney who drafts a will or other instrument naming the attorney as trustee, and inserts a provision relieving the attorney of liability for breach of trust, to show that the settlor freely and knowingly consented to inclusion of the provision."

Thus far we have been supposing that the settlor's lawyer drafted the trust instrument and is named as trustee. Suppose instead that the named trustee is a bank and the settlor uses a trust form supplied by the bank that includes an exculpatory provision. The majority view appears to be that the same presumption of abuse applies and the "provision relieving the trustee of liability for breach of trust is ineffective unless the settlor fully understood the nature of the provision and freely agreed to it." Id. However, unlike a case where the settlor names her lawyer as trustee, a settlor who names a third party as trustee is perhaps less vulnerable to abuse if represented by a lawyer who does not have a personal stake in the exculpatory provision. Indeed, the official comment to UTC §1008 takes the position that, "If the settlor was represented by independent counsel, the settlor's attorney is considered the drafter of the instrument even if the attorney used the trustee's form. Because the settlor's attorney is an agent of the settlor, disclosure of an exculpatory term to the settlor's attorney is disclosure to the settlor."

For an exculpatory clause that was not inserted as a result of abuse, the question arises whether the law should impose an outer limit on the scope of permissible exculpation. In McNeil v. McNeil, 798 A.2d 503, 509 (Del. 2002), the trust provided that the trustees' decisions were "not subject to review by any court." Observing that courts "flatly refuse to enforce provisions relieving a trustee of all liability," the court reviewed the trustees' actions nonetheless. The reason: "A trust in which there is no legally binding obligation on a trustee is a trust in name only and more in the nature of an absolute estate or fee simple grant of property."

Generally speaking, the line is drawn just short of bad faith, reckless indifference, and intentional or willful neglect. An exculpatory clause that purports to immunize the trustee for any such conduct will not be enforced. See Scott and Ascher on Trusts, supra, at §24.27.3; UTC §§1008(a)(1), 105(b)(2); Restatement (Third) of Trusts, supra, §96. In New York, by statute, an attempted grant of immunity to a testamentary trustee for failure to exercise *reasonable* care is deemed contrary to public policy and void. N.Y. Est. Powers & Trusts Law §11-1.7(a)(1) (2008).

For further discussion, see John H. Langbein, Mandatory Rules in the Law of Trusts, 98 Nw. U. L. Rev. 1105, 1123-1125 (2004); Melanie B. Leslie, Trusting Trustees: Fiduciary Duties and the Limits of Default Rules, 94 Geo. L.J. 67 (2005); David Horton, Unconscionability in the Law of Trusts, 84 Notre Dame L. Rev. 1675 (2009).

NOTE: MANDATORY ARBITRATION CLAUSES

Suppose the trust instrument provides that all disputes between the trustee and the beneficiary must be resolved by arbitration. Can the beneficiary nonetheless bring an action in court against the trustee for breach of trust? The authorities are scarce and contradictory.

In Schoneberger v. Oelze, 96 P.3d 1078 (Ariz. App. 2004), the court allowed the beneficiary to litigate in court in spite of the trust's mandatory arbitration provision, explaining that the settlor "may not unilaterally strip trust beneficiaries of their right to access the courts absent their agreement." See also In re Calomiris, 894 A.2d 408 (D.C. 2006), to similar effect. A Florida statute enacted in 2007 takes the opposite view, mandating the enforcement of a provision requiring "arbitration of disputes . . . between or among the beneficiaries and a fiduciary under [a] will or trust." Fla. Stat. §731.401 (2008).

Given that an exculpatory clause eliminating fiduciary liability in the absence of bad faith, reckless indifference, and intentional or willful neglect is generally enforceable, why not enforce a mandatory arbitration clause? Many lawyers and legal scholars believe that arbitration is a simpler and quicker means of resolving disputes than litigation. On this view, arbitration is a mode of enforcing the trust, not a mode of defeating enforcement.

Because there is considerable interest in trust arbitration clauses among practitioners, it seems likely that in the coming years there will be new developments. In the meantime, for further discussion see Michael P. Bruyere and Meghan D. Marino, Mandatory Arbitration Provisions: A Powerful Tool to Prevent Contentious and Costly Trust Litigation, But Are They Enforceable?, 42 Real Prop., Prob. & Tr. J. 351 (2007); Bridget A. Longstrom, Bruce M. Stone, and Robert W. Goldman, Resolving Disputes with Ease and Grace, 31 ACTEC J. 235 (2005).

SECTION B.   RIGHTS OF THE BENEFICIARY'S CREDITORS

The rich have — at least in Anglo-American history — continually sought ways to secure their property to their children and grandchildren so that it remains safe from the accidents of fortune and bad management. The fee tail and, later, the strict settlement were the standard devices used in England to keep land in the family. The spendthrift trust, an American invention not recognized in England, and the discretionary trust, which is recognized throughout the common law world, are their ideological descendants. Both provide a means of making property available to the beneficiary but unavailable to the beneficiary's creditors. In this section, we explore the asset protection features of trust law by examining the rights of the beneficiary's creditors to the trust property in (1) *discretionary trusts*, (2) *spendthrift trusts*, and (3) *self-settled asset protection trusts*.

1. *Discretionary Trusts*

Traditional law differentiates between two species of discretionary trusts: the *pure discretionary trust*, in which the trustee has absolute, sole, or uncontrolled discretion over distributions to the beneficiary, and the *support trust*, in which the trustee is obligated to make distributions as necessary for the beneficiary's needs. Still a third permutation, not formally recognized as a separate category by traditional law but nonetheless common in practice, is a trust that combines an explicit statement of unfettered discretion with a distribution standard. Such a trust, an example of which was at issue in *Marsman*, has been aptly dubbed a *discretionary support trust*. See Evelyn Ginsberg Abravanel, Discretionary Support Trusts, 68 Iowa L. Rev. 273 (1983).

Under traditional law, a creditor of a beneficiary of a *pure discretionary trust* has no recourse against the beneficiary's interest in the trust. The creditor cannot, by judicial order, compel the trustee to pay him. The theory is that, because the beneficiary has no right to compel a distribution, neither does the beneficiary's creditor. Restatement (Second) of Trusts §155, cmt. b (1959).

Although a creditor cannot compel the trustee to satisfy a debt of the beneficiary if the trust is discretionary, the creditor may be entitled to a court order directing the trustee to pay the creditor before making any further distributions to the beneficiary. By this procedure, a creditor can deprive the beneficiary of trust distributions even though the creditor will not necessarily be paid. This cutting-off-income procedure was approved in the leading case of Hamilton v. Drogo, 150 N.E. 496 (N.Y. 1926), which involved a discretionary trust established by the will of the dowager Duchess of Manchester to provide her spendthrift son, the ninth duke,[5] freedom from the travails of penury. Andrews, J., explained how the rule worked:

> We may not interfere with the discretion which the testatrix has vested in the trustee any more than her son may do so. Its judgment is final. But at least annually this judgment must be exercised. And if it is exercised in favor of the duke [the beneficiary], then there is due him the whole or such part of the income as the trustee may allot to him. After such allotment, he may compel its payment. At least for some appreciable time, however brief, the award must precede the delivery of the income he is to receive, and during that time the lien of the execution attaches. [Id. at 497.]

Because the trustee is said to exercise discretionary authority a moment in time before actually making a distribution, it is important to know what acts constitute an exercise of discretion. Crediting the beneficiary's account on the trustee's books or making an oral or written declaration to the beneficiary may be a sufficient act to exercise the power, thereby enabling the creditor to seize that portion of the trust property while it is still in the hands of the trustee. Thus, while a creditor cannot compel a trustee to make a discretionary distribution, the creditor can

---

5. William Angus Drogo Montagu, ninth Duke of Manchester, "had been kept so short of cash as a boy, with pocket money of one penny a day, that he grew up with no real sense of its value. On an allowance of £400 a year at Cambridge, he ran up debts totalling £2,000. He spent much time in America, Africa, and India, avoiding creditors, looking for a rich wife, and sponging off his friends." David Cannadine, The Decline and Fall of the British Aristocracy 403 (1990). After the ninth duke's death, the Manchester family fortunes continued in an irreversible decline set in motion by three spendthrift dukes in a row (the seventh, eighth, and ninth). All the family land was sold off to support high living. The tenth duke moved to Kenya seeking a new fortune, but Kenyan independence sank that venture. The eleventh duke became an alligator hunter in Australia, but after a while he moved back to England where he became a business consultant in Bedford.

obtain an order effectively requiring that, *if* any distributions are to be made from the trust, the creditor shall be paid before the beneficiary.

QUESTIONS AND PROBLEM

1.   Is it true that the beneficiary of a pure discretionary trust never has a right to compel a payment? Is not *some* form of judicial review of the trustee's conduct always available to the beneficiary?

2.   Why is the procedure for cutting off income sanctioned in Hamilton v. Drogo helpful to the beneficiary's creditor even though the trustee can simply stop making distributions?

3.   *T* devises a fund in trust to *X* to pay or to apply for the benefit of *A* so much of the income as *X* determines in *X*'s uncontrolled discretion, and then on *A*'s death to pay to remainder to *B*. *C*, a creditor of *A*, obtains a Hamilton v. Drogo style order directing *X* to pay *C* before paying *A*. Can *X* make use of the "apply for the benefit of" language of the trust to circumvent the order by paying directly for goods and services rendered to *A*? See Wilcox v. Gentry, 867 P.2d 281 (Kan. 1994); Restatement (Second) of Trusts, supra, §155, cmt. i.

Under traditional law, the beneficiary of a *support trust* cannot alienate her interest. Nor can creditors of the beneficiary reach the beneficiary's interest, except suppliers of necessaries, who may recover through the beneficiary's right to support. Restatement (Second) of Trusts, supra, §154. There is also considerable authority for the proposition that children and spouses may enforce claims for child support and alimony against a beneficiary's interest in a support trust. Restatement (Second) of Trusts, supra, §157. Accordingly, under traditional law a support trust insulates the trust property from some but not all of the beneficiary's creditors.

In contrast to pure discretionary trusts and support trusts, both of which are recognized as distinct categories by traditional law, the hybrid *discretionary support trust* is not regarded as a distinct category. But such trusts are quite common in practice, which has led to needless litigation over the categorization of the trust as discretionary or support. In general, although a discretionary support trust is arguably a variant on the support trust theme, for the purpose of creditor rights the courts have tended to treat it like a pure discretionary trust, foreclosing claims by the beneficiary's creditors. Abravanel, supra, 68 Iowa L. Rev. at 281.

Both the Restatement (Third) of Trusts and the UTC collapse the distinction between discretionary trusts and support trusts, unifying the rules regarding creditors' rights for all trusts in which the trustee has any discretion over payments irrespective of whether the trustee's discretion is uncontrolled or subject to a standard or both. The reporter's notes to the Restatement explains the rationale:

Not only is the supposed distinction between support and discretionary trusts arbitrary and artificial, but the lines are also difficult — and costly — to attempt to draw. Attempting to do so tends to produce dubious categorizations and almost inevitably different results (based on fortuitous differences in wording or maybe a "fireside" sense of equity) from case to case for beneficiaries who appear, realistically, to be similarly situated as objects of similar settlor intentions. . . .

The fact of the matter is that there is a continuum of discretionary trusts, with the terms of distributive powers ranging from the most objective (or "ascertainable," I.R.C. §2041) of standards (pure "support") to the most open ended (e.g., "happiness") or vague ("benefit") of standards, or even with no standards manifested at all (for which a court will probably apply "a general standard of reasonableness"). And these trusts use an unlimited variety of combinations of such terms or standards, with any standard or combination about as likely as another to be accompanied by language of extended discretion (such as "absolute" or "sole and uncontrolled") or by a requirement that other resources of the beneficiary must, or must not (or that they may but need not) be considered by the trustee in exercising its discretion. All of these possibilities are subject to the same general principle that courts will interfere only to prevent abuse. [Reporter's note to Restatement (Third) of Trusts §60, cmt. a (2003)].

Although the Restatement and the UTC unify the rules of creditor rights in all forms of discretionary trusts, they state different substantive rules. Restatement (Third) of Trusts §60 (2003) takes the position that, "if the terms of a trust provide for a beneficiary to receive distributions in the trustee's discretion, a transferee or creditor of the beneficiary is entitled to receive or attach any distributions the trustee makes or is required to make in the exercise of that discretion." By contrast, UTC §504 (2000, rev. 2004) provides that, subject to an exception for claims by children and spouses for child support and alimony, a creditor of a beneficiary cannot compel a discretionary distribution even if the beneficiary could compel such a distribution.

Uniform Trust Code (2000, as amended 2004)

§504.   DISCRETIONARY TRUSTS; EFFECT OF STANDARD

(a) In this section, "child" includes any person for whom an order or judgment for child support has been entered in this or another State.

(b) Except as otherwise provided in subsection (c), whether or not a trust contains a spendthrift provision, a creditor of a beneficiary may not compel a distribution that is subject to the trustee's discretion, even if:

(1) the discretion is expressed in the form of a standard of distribution; or

(2) the trustee has abused the discretion.

(c) To the extent a trustee has not complied with a standard of distribution or has abused a discretion:

(1) a distribution may be ordered by the court to satisfy a judgment or court order against the beneficiary for support or maintenance of the beneficiary's child, spouse, or former spouse; and

(2) the court shall direct the trustee to pay to the child, spouse, or former spouse such amount as is equitable under the circumstances but not more than the amount the trustee would have been required to distribute to or for the

benefit of the beneficiary had the trustee complied with the standard or not abused the discretion.

(d) This section does not limit the right of a beneficiary to maintain a judicial proceeding against a trustee for an abuse of discretion or failure to comply with a standard for distribution.

(e) If the trustee's or cotrustee's discretion to make distributions for the trustee's or cotrustee's own benefit is limited by an ascertainable standard, a creditor may not reach or compel distribution of the beneficial interest except to the extent the interest would be subject to the creditor's claim were the beneficiary not acting as trustee or cotrustee.

PROBLEM AND QUESTION

T devises property to *X* in trust to pay so much of the income and principal to *A* as *X* determines is necessary for *A*'s comfortable support and maintenance. *A* is insolvent. *X* refuses to make a distribution to *A*. *B*, a general creditor of *A*, sues *X* on the theory that, since *A* is insolvent, it would be an abuse of *X*'s discretion as trustee not to make a distribution to *A*, and thus *B* is entitled to stand in *A*'s shoes and receive that distribution. What result under traditional law? What result under UTC §504? What result under Restatement (Third) of Trusts §60? Before you conclude that *B* wins under the Restatement, consider comment e to §60:

> On the other hand, a trustee's refusal to make distributions might not constitute an abuse as against an assignee or creditor even when, under the standards applicable to the power, a decision to refuse distributions to the beneficiary might have constituted an abuse in the absence of the assignment or attachment. This is because the extent to which the designated beneficiary might actually benefit from a distribution is relevant to the justification and reasonableness of the trustee's decision in relation to the settlor's purposes and the effects on other beneficiaries. Thus, the balancing process typical of discretionary issues becomes, in this context, significantly weighted against creditors, and sometimes against a beneficiary's voluntary assignees.

In practice, will the Restatement lead to different results than the UTC? Will it lead to more litigation?

NOTE: PROTECTIVE TRUSTS

Suppose a settlor wants the beneficiary to have a mandatory right to regular payments out of the trust fund, but also wants the asset-protection features of a discretionary trust. Particularly in a jurisdiction that does not recognize spendthrift trusts, this settlor should consider a mandatory trust subject to a protective provision. In such a *protective trust*, the trustee is directed to pay income to *A*, but if *A*'s creditors attach *A*'s interest, *A*'s mandatory income interest is automatically changed to a discretionary interest. The trustee then has discretion to apply the income for *A*'s benefit, and the creditors of *A* cannot demand any part of it. See Restatement (Third) of Trusts §57 (2003).

In England, which does not enforce spendthrift provisions, protective trusts are so common that, under §33 of the Trustee Act of 1925, 15 & 16 Geo. 5, ch. 19, the court will insert a protective provision into any trust for which the settlor manifested an intent to create a protective trust. In the words of a leading text on English trust law: "Discretionary trusts thus have the advantage of protecting beneficiaries from themselves besides the obvious advantage of flexibility. However, there is the corresponding disadvantage that such trusts create uncertainty for a beneficiary since he has no fixed entitlement . . . . To tackle this disadvantage there arose the protective trust." David J. Hayton and Charles Mitchell, Hayton and Marshall Commentary and Cases on the Law of Trusts and Equitable Remedies 273-277 (12th ed. 2005).

2. Spendthrift Trusts

A beneficiary of a spendthrift trust cannot voluntarily alienate her interest. Nor can her creditors reach her interest in the trust. This is true even if the trust provides for mandatory payments to the beneficiary. A spendthrift trust is created by imposing a disabling restraint upon the beneficiaries and their creditors. Restatement (Third) of Trusts §58 (2003); UTC §502 (2000). Thus:

> *Case 3.* *T* devises property to *X* in trust to pay the income to *A* for life and on *A*'s death to distribute the property to *A*'s descendants. A clause in the trust provides that *A* may not transfer her interest in the trust and that it may not be reached by *A*'s creditors. By this trust, *A* is given a stream of income that *A* cannot alienate and her creditors cannot reach.

In many jurisdictions, a trust is not spendthrift unless the settlor expressly inserts a spendthrift clause. But spendthrift provisions are routinely included in professionally drafted trusts, if only by rote inclusion of formbook boilerplate, and a growing number of jurisdictions no longer require an express spendthrift provision. Jeffrey A. Schoenblum, 2008 Multistate Guide to Estate Planning at Table 9.05, Part 1, Column 2. In New York, all trusts are spendthrift with respect to income unless the settlor expressly makes the beneficiary's interest transferable. N.Y. Est. Powers & Trusts Law §7-1.5 (2008).

The two decisions largely responsible for the spendthrift trust doctrine are Nichols v. Eaton, 91 U.S. 716 (1875), and Broadway Natl. Bank v. Adams, 133 Mass. 170 (1882). In Nichols v. Eaton, Justice Miller inserted an elaborate dictum upholding spendthrift trusts: "Why a parent, or one who loves another, and wishes to use his own property in securing the object of his affection, as far as property can do it, from the ills of life, the vicissitudes of fortune, and even his own improvidence, or incapacity for self-protection, should not be permitted to do so, is not readily perceived." In Broadway Natl. Bank v. Adams, the Massachusetts court upheld the spendthrift trust.

The spendthrift trust arises from the settlor's right to condition the terms of her transfer. In the words of a 1909 decision of the Supreme Court of Pennsylvania:

> [The spendthrift trust] allows the donor to condition his bounty as suits himself so long as he violates no law in so doing. When a trust of this kind has been created, the law holds that the donor has an individual right of property in the execution of the trust; and to deprive him of it would be a fraud on his generosity. For the law to appropriate a gift to a person not intended would be an invasion of the donor's private dominion. It is always to be remembered that consideration for the beneficiary does not even in the remotest way enter into the policy of the law. It has regard solely to the rights of the donor. Spendthrift trusts can have no other justification than is to be found in considerations affecting the donor alone. They allow the donor to so control his bounty, through the creation of the trust, that it may be exempt from liability for the donee's debts, not because the law is concerned to keep the donee from wasting it, but because it is concerned to protect the donor's right of property. [In re Morgan's Estate, 72 A. 498, 499 (Pa. 1909).]

The underlying policy question, on which American law diverges from the English law,[6] is whether to allow the dead hand to restrain alienation of the beneficial interest. Consider the following two cases:

> *Case 4. X*, a successful businessman, enjoys good health and is now entering his eightieth year. His son, *A*, spoiled by the luxury afforded to him during his youth, runs up a host of debts and has no job. Because *X* is still alive and in possession of his fortune, he is able to provide *A* with a comfortable style of living despite *A*'s debts. *A*'s creditors have no recourse against *X*'s assets.
>
> *Case 5. Y*, a successful businessman, died at an early age, survived by his son, *B*. Spoiled by his early life of luxury and damaged by the tragic early loss of his father, *B* has run up a host of debts and has no job. Because *Y* died intestate, *B* inherited a large share of *Y*'s fortune. However, these funds have either been lost through *B*'s mismanagement or have been attached by *B*'s creditors.

As articulated by Justice Miller, the argument for allowing the spendthrift trust is that it puts *Y* in the same position as *X*, allowing both to protect their children from improvidence.

The spendthrift trust has been sharply criticized. John Chipman Gray, the great oracular property teacher at Harvard, was so outraged at the introduction of spendthrift trusts that he was moved to write his Restraints on the Alienation of Property, first published in 1883, in refutation of Nichols v. Eaton. "The general introduction of spendthrift trusts would be to form a privileged class, who could indulge in every speculation, could practice every fraud, and, provided they kept on the safe side of the criminal law, could yet roll in wealth. They would be an aristocracy, though certainly the most contemptible aristocracy with which a country was ever cursed." John C. Gray, Restraints on the Alienation of Property §262 (1883). In spite of Gray's strictures, by the time the second

---

6. Under the leading case of Brandon v. Robinson, 34 Eng. Rep. 379 (Ch. 1811), a disabling restraint is not enforceable in England or the Commonwealth, though as we have seen the beneficiary's interest in an English trust can be protected from creditors by making it discretionary.

edition of his book was published, the battle was lost. "State after State has given in its adhesion to the new doctrine . . . . And yet I cannot recant." Id. at iv-v (2d ed. 1895).

Today the spendthrift trust is recognized throughout the United States. Helene S. Shapo, George Gleason Bogert, and George Taylor Bogert, The Law of Trusts and Trustees §222, at 421 (3d ed. 2007). The modern debate over the spendthrift trust has shifted to the question whether to make exceptions for certain classes of creditors, such as tort victims or spouses and children.

Scheffel v. Krueger
Supreme Court of New Hampshire, 2001
782 A.2d 410

DUGGAN, J.   In 1998, the [plaintiff, Lorie Scheffel, individually and as mother of Cory C.,] filed suit in superior court asserting tort claims against the defendant, Kyle Krueger. In her suit, the plaintiff alleged that the defendant sexually assaulted her minor child, videotaped the act and later broadcasted the videotape over the Internet. The same conduct that the plaintiff alleged in the tort claims also formed the basis for criminal charges against the defendant.[7] The court entered a default judgment against the defendant and ordered him to pay $551,286.25 in damages. To satisfy the judgment against the defendant, the plaintiff sought an attachment of the defendant's beneficial interest in the Kyle Krueger Irrevocable Trust (trust).

The defendant's grandmother established the trust in 1985 for the defendant's benefit. Its terms direct the trustee to pay all of the net income from the trust to the beneficiary, at least quarterly, or more frequently if the beneficiary in writing so requests. The trustee is further authorized to pay any of the principal to the beneficiary if in the trustee's sole discretion the funds are necessary for the maintenance, support and education of the beneficiary. The beneficiary may not invade the principal until he reaches the age of fifty, which will not occur until April 6, 2016.

The beneficiary is prohibited from making any voluntary or involuntary transfers of his interest in the trust. Article VII of the trust instrument specifically provides:

> No principal or income payable or to become payable under any of the trusts created by this instrument shall be subject to anticipation or assignment by any beneficiary thereof, or to the interference or control of any creditors of such beneficiary or to be taken or reached by any legal or equitable process in satisfaction of any debt or liability of such beneficiary prior to its receipt by the beneficiary.

---

7. Having been turned in by his wife, who found the incriminating videotape among Krueger's belongings in their bedroom, Krueger was convicted of "eighty counts of aggravated felonious sexual assault, seven counts of attempted aggravated felonious sexual assault, two counts of felonious sexual assault, and one count of simple assault." State v. Krueger, 776 A.2d 720 (N.H. 2001). — Eds.

Asserting that this so-called spendthrift provision barred the plaintiff's claim against the trust, the trustee defendant moved to [dismiss the plaintiff's claim]. The trial court ruled that under N.H. Rev. Stat. ("RSA") 564:23 (1997), this spendthrift provision is enforceable against the plaintiff's claim and dismissed [the plaintiff's claim]. . . .

We first address the plaintiff's argument that the legislature did not intend RSA 564:23 to shield the trust assets from tort creditors, especially when the beneficiary's conduct constituted a criminal act. . . . "We interpret legislative intent from the statute as written, and therefore, we will not consider what the legislature might have said or add words that the legislature did not include." Rye Beach Country Club v. Town of Rye, 719 A.2d 623 (N.H. 1998).

We begin by examining the language found in the statute. RSA 564:23, I, provides:

> In the event the governing instrument so provides, a beneficiary of a trust shall not be able to transfer his or her right to future payments of income and principal, and a creditor of a beneficiary shall not be able to subject the beneficiary's interest to the payment of its claim.

The statute provides two exceptions to the enforceability of spendthrift provisions. The provisions "shall not apply to a beneficiary's interest in a trust to the extent that the beneficiary is the settlor and the trust is not a special needs trust established for a person with disabilities," RSA 564:23, II, and "shall not be construed to prevent the application of RSA 545-A or a similar law of another state [regarding fraudulent transfers]," RSA 564:23, III. Thus, under the plain language of the statute, a spendthrift provision is enforceable unless the beneficiary is also the settlor or the assets were fraudulently transferred to the trust. The plaintiff does not argue that either exception applies.

Faced with this language, the plaintiff argues that the legislature did not intend for the statute to shield the trust assets from tort creditors. The statute, however, plainly states that "a creditor of a beneficiary shall not be able to subject the beneficiary's interest to the payment of its claim." RSA 564:23, I. Nothing in this language suggests that the legislature intended that a tort creditor should be exempted from a spendthrift provision. Two exemptions are enumerated in sections II and III. Where the legislature has made specific exemptions, we must presume no others were intended. "If this is an omission, the courts cannot supply it. That is for the Legislature to do." Brahmey v. Rollins, 179 A. 186 (N.H. 1935).

The plaintiff argues public policy requires us to create a tort creditor exception to the statute. The cases the plaintiff relies upon, however, both involve judicially created spendthrift law. See Sligh v. First Natl. Bank of Holmes County, 704 So. 2d 1020, 1024 (Miss. 1997); Elec. Workers v. IBEW-NECA Holiday Trust, 583 S.W.2d 154, 162 (Mo. 1979). In this State, the legislature has enacted a statute repudiating the public policy exception sought by the plaintiff. This statutory enactment cannot be overruled, because "[i]t is axiomatic that courts do not question the wisdom or expediency of a statute." Brahmey, 179 A. 186, 192-93. Therefore, "[n]o rule of public policy is available to overcome [this] statutory rule." Id. . . .

Finally, the plaintiff asserts that the trial court erred in denying her request that the trust be terminated because the purpose of the trust can no longer be satisfied. The plaintiff argues that the trust's purpose to provide for the defendant's support, maintenance and education can no longer be fulfilled because the defendant will likely remain incarcerated for a period of years. The trial court, however, found that the trust's purpose "may still be fulfilled while the defendant is incarcerated and after he is released." The record before us supports this finding.

Affirmed.

SHELLEY v. SHELLEY, 354 P.2d 282 (Or. 1960): *T*'s will left his residuary estate in trust for his son, Grant. The income was to be paid to Grant for life. In addition, the trustee was to begin distributing corpus to Grant after he reached age 30 in amounts that the trustee and other named persons deemed Grant capable of investing properly. The trustee was also given discretion to distribute corpus to Grant or his children "in case of any emergency arising whereby unusual and extraordinary expenses are necessary" for their "proper support and care." Grant's interest in the trust was made inalienable by a spendthrift clause:

> Each beneficiary hereunder is hereby restrained from alienating, anticipating, encumbering, or in any manner assigning his or her interest or estate, either in principal or income, and is without power so to do, nor shall such interest or estate be subject to his or her liabilities or obligations nor to judgment or other legal process, bankruptcy proceedings or claims of creditors or others.

Grant married twice and divorced twice, leaving two children by each marriage. Both divorce decrees obligated Grant to make child support payments, and the second decree also called for alimony payments. Grant subsequently disappeared, and the trustee bank filed an interpleader in response to claims made against the trust by Grant's children and former wives for satisfaction of his support and alimony obligations.

> The question on this appeal is whether the spendthrift provision will be given effect to bar the claims of the beneficiary's children for support and the plaintiff's claim for alimony. In Cogswell v. Cogswell, 167 P.2d 324, 335 (Or. 1946), we held that the spendthrift provision of a trust is not effective against the claims of the beneficiary's former wife for alimony and for support of the beneficiary's child. . . .
>
> The defendant bank concedes that the *Cogswell* case is controlling in the case at bar, but asks us to overrule it on the ground that it is inconsistent with our own cases recognizing the testator's privilege to dispose of his property as he pleases and, further, that it is inconsistent with various Oregon statutes expressing the same policy of free alienation. If we should accept the premise urged by the defendant bank, that a testator has an inviolable right to dispose of his property as he pleases subject only to legislative restriction, the conclusion is inevitable that the testator may create in a beneficiary an interest free from all claims, including those for support and alimony.
>
> But the premise is not sound. The privilege of disposing of property is not absolute; it is hedged with various restrictions where there are policy considerations warranting the limitation. . . . Not all of these restrictions are imposed by statute. The rule against perpetuities, the rule against restraints on alienation, the refusal to recognize trusts for capricious

purposes or for illegal purposes, or for any purpose contrary to public policy, are all instances of judge-made rules limiting the privilege of alienation. Many others could be recited. It is within the court's power to impose upon the privilege of disposing of property such restrictions as are consistent with its view of sound public policy, unless, of course, the legislature has expressed a contrary view. Our own statutes do not purport to deal with the specific question before us, that is as to whether there should be limitations on the owner's privilege to create a spendthrift trust.

Having concluded that it had the power to make exceptions to the general rule that a spendthrift clause bars the claims of the beneficiary's creditors, the court turned to the specific claims presented in this case.

> The question is whether a person should be entitled to enjoy the benefits of a trust and at the same time refuse to pay the obligations arising out of his marriage.
>
> We have no hesitation in declaring that public policy requires that the interest of the beneficiary of a trust should be subject to the claims for support of his children. . . . Certainly the defendant will accept the societal postulate that parents have the obligation to support their children. If we give effect to the spendthrift provision to bar the claims for support, we have the spectacle of a man enjoying the benefits of a trust immune from claims which are justly due, while the community pays for the support of his children. We do not believe that it is sound policy to use the welfare funds of this state in support of the beneficiary's children, while he stands behind the shield of immunity created by a spendthrift trust provision. To endorse such a policy and to permit the spectacle which we have described above would be to invite disrespect for the administration of justice. . . .
>
> The justification for permitting a claim for alimony is, perhaps, not as clear. The adjustment of the economic interests of the parties to a divorce may depend upon a variety of factors, including the respective fault of the parties, the ability of the wife to support herself, the duration of the marriage, and other considerations. Whether alimony is to be granted and its amount are questions which are determined in light of these various interests. It is probably fair to say that the duties created by the marriage relation, at least as they are evaluated upon the termination of the marriage, are conceived of as more qualified than those arising out of the paternal relationship. On the theory that divorce terminates the husband's duty to support his former wife and that she stands in no better position than other creditors, some courts have held that the spendthrift provision insulates the beneficiary's interest in the trust from her claim. Recognizing the difference in marital and parental duties suggested above, it has been held that a spendthrift trust is subject to the claims for the support of children but free from the claims of the former wife. . . . A majority of the cases, however, hold that a spendthrift provision will not bar a claim for alimony. . . .
>
> The duty of the husband to support his former wife should override the restriction called for by the spendthrift provision. The same reason advanced above for requiring the support of the beneficiary's children will, in many cases, be applicable to the claim of a divorced wife; if the beneficiary's interest cannot be reached, the state may be called upon to support her.

The court thus held that Grant's interest in the trust *income* was subject to the claims of his children and former wives.

With respect to the trust *principal*, the analysis was different because Grant's interest was discretionary.

> The question of the claimants' rights to reach the corpus of the trust involves other considerations. For the reasons heretofore stated, the beneficiary's interest in the corpus is not made immune from these claims. But, by the terms of the trust, the disbursement of the

corpus is within the discretion of the trustee (or, in some instances subject to the approval of others), and, therefore, Grant Shelley's right to receive any part of the corpus does not arise until the trustee has exercised his discretion and has decided to invade the corpus.

Accordingly, the court held that Grant's former wives could not reach the trust corpus. Grant's children likewise could not enforce their claim against their father's rights to the trust corpus. However, the trust also named Grant's children as beneficiaries in an emergency, so they could receive payment directly from the trust, not as Grant's creditors, but as beneficiaries themselves.

> The trust directed and authorized the trustee, in the exercise of its sole discretion . . . , to make disbursements for the use and benefit not only of Grant Shelley, but also for his children. The disbursements were to be made "in case of any emergency arising whereby unusual and extraordinary expenses are necessary for the proper support and care of my said son, or said children." Here the children are named as beneficiaries of the trust and need not claim derivatively through their father. However, they are entitled to a share of the corpus only if, in the trustee's discretion, it is determined that an emergency exists. The defendant bank contends that the expenses of supporting Grant Shelley's children claimed in this case were for the usual and ordinary costs of support and do not, therefore, constitute "unusual and extraordinary expenses" within the meaning of the trust provision. . . . We disagree with defendant's interpretation. We construe the clause to include the circumstances involved here, i.e., where the children are deserted by their father and are in need of support. We think that the testator intended to provide that in the event that the income from the trust was not sufficient to cover disbursements for the support and care of either the son or his children an "emergency" had arisen and the corpus could then be invaded.

Uniform Trust Code (2000, as amended 2005)

§502. SPENDTHRIFT PROVISION

(a) A spendthrift provision is valid only if it restrains both voluntary and involuntary transfer of a beneficiary's interest.

(b) A term of a trust providing that the interest of a beneficiary is held subject to a "spendthrift trust," or words of similar import, is sufficient to restrain both voluntary and involuntary transfer of the beneficiary's interest.

(c) A beneficiary may not transfer an interest in a trust in violation of a valid spendthrift provision and, except as otherwise provided in this [article], a creditor or assignee of the beneficiary may not reach the interest or a distribution by the trustee before its receipt by the beneficiary.

§503. EXCEPTIONS TO SPENDTHRIFT PROVISION

(a) In this section, "child" includes any person for whom an order or judgment for child support has been entered in this or another State.

(b) A spendthrift provision is unenforceable against:

(1) a beneficiary's child, spouse, or former spouse who has a judgment or court order against the beneficiary for support or maintenance;

(2) a judgment creditor who has provided services for the protection of a beneficiary's interest in the trust; and

(3) a claim of this State or the United States to the extent a statute of this State or federal law so provides.

(c) A claimant against which a spendthrift provision cannot be enforced may obtain from a court an order attaching present or future distributions to or for the benefit of the beneficiary. The court may limit the award to such relief as is appropriate under the circumstances.

NOTES AND QUESTIONS

1.   In Shelley v. Shelley, the court held that the trust established for Grant Shelley was subject to the claims of his children and former wives. In Scheffel v. Krueger, the court held that the trust established for Kyle Krueger was not subject to the claims of the child whom Krueger had sexually assaulted. Can these results be reconciled? Should the law recognize a distinction between ordinary contract creditors (such as lenders) and involuntary creditors (such as tort victims and children)?

> In many of the cases that have held that the terms of the trust can put the interest of a beneficiary beyond the reach of creditors, the courts have laid some stress on the fact that the creditors had only themselves to blame for extending credit to such a person. The courts have said that before extending credit the creditors could have ascertained the extent and character of the debtor's resources. In this respect, however, the situation of a tort creditor is quite different from that of a contract creditor. The pedestrian who is about to be hit by an automobile has no opportunity to investigate the credit of the driver or to avoid being injured, no matter what the driver's resources are. [3 Austin Wakeman Scott, William Franklin Fratcher, and Mark L. Ascher, Scott and Ascher on Trusts §15.5.5 (5th ed. 2007).]

If spendthrift trust law were to recognize a distinction between voluntary and involuntary creditors, on which side of the line would spouses fall?

2.   Although spendthrift trusts are now recognized throughout the United States, the states diverge on whether to allow exceptions for certain classes of creditors and a handful of other related questions. A brief treatment follows.[8]

(a) *Children and spouses.* Judgments for child or spousal support, or both, can be enforced against the debtor's interest in a spendthrift trust in the majority of states and under UTC §503(b)(1) (2000, rev. 2005) and Restatement (Third) of Trusts §59(a) (2003). In a substantial minority of states, however, a spouse or child

---

8. For deeper and more systematic recent discussions, see Timothy J. Vitollo, Uniform Trust Code Section 503: Applying Hamilton Orders to Spendthrift Interests, 43 Real Prop., Tr. & Est. L.J. 169 (2008); Alan Newman, The Rights of Creditors of Beneficiaries Under the Uniform Trust Code: An Examination of the Compromise, 69 Tenn. L. Rev. 771 (2002). For discussions of creditor rights in spendthrift and other trusts with particular focus on recent criticisms of the UTC by a handful of asset protection lawyers, compare Robert T. Danforth, Article Five of the UTC and the Future of Creditors' Rights in Trusts, 26 Cardozo L. Rev. 2551 (2006), and Alan Newman, Spendthrift and Discretionary Trusts: Alive and Well Under the Uniform Trust Code, 40 Real Prop., Prob. & Tr. J. 567 (2005), with Jeffrey A. Schoenblum, In Search of a Unifying Principle for Article V of the Uniform Trust Code: A Response to Professor Danforth, 26 Cardozo L. Rev. 2609 (2006). For modern commentary on spendthrift trusts and creditor rights more generally, see Anne S. Emanuel, Spendthrift Trusts: It's Time to Codify the Compromise, 72 Neb. L. Rev. 179 (1993); Adam Hirsch, Spendthrift Trusts and Public Policy: Economic and Cognitive Perspectives, 73 Wash. U. L.Q. 1 (1995).

or both cannot reach a spendthrift trust to satisfy a judgment for support. For a meticulous survey of the law across the states, see Timothy J. Vitollo, Uniform Trust Code Section 503: Applying Hamilton Orders to Spendthrift Interests, 43 Real Prop., Tr. & Est. L.J. 169, 185-192 (2008). See also Carolyn L. Dessin, Feed a Trust and Starve a Child: The Effectiveness of Trust Protective Techniques Against Claims for Support and Alimony, 10 Ga. St. U. L. Rev. 691 (1994).

Following the traditional view, the court in *Shelley* held that the beneficiary's children and former spouses could not reach Grant Shelley's *discretionary* interest in the trust. UTC §504(c), page 612, would change this result if the trustee has abused her discretion. Is this a sensible reform? Does your answer depend on whether the state recognizes an exception to spendthrift trusts for children, spouses, and former spouses?

(b) *Tort victims.* Whether a spendthrift clause bars recovery by a tort victim against the tortfeasor's interest in a spendthrift trust is not entirely settled, though the trend is against recovery. In Scheffel v. Krueger, the court held the spendthrift clause effective against a tort creditor. So too did the court in Duvall v. McGee, 826 A.2d 416 (Md. 2003). In Jackson v. Fidelity & Deposit Company of Maryland, 608 S.E.2d 901 (Va. 2005), the court refused to create an exception for debts arising from breach of fiduciary duty. In Sligh v. Sligh, 704 So. 2d 1020 (Miss. 1997), discussed in Scheffel v. Krueger, the court held that a tort creditor could enforce a judgment against the tortfeasor's interest in a spendthrift trust or in a discretionary trust, but the very next year the state legislature enacted the Family Trust Preservation Act, which reversed *Sligh* and exempted spendthrift trusts from tort creditors. Miss. Code Ann. §91-9-503 (2008). In Georgia, tort victims are entitled to enforce a judgment against the tortfeasor's interest in a spendthrift trust. Ga. Code Ann. §53-12-28(c) (2008).

UTC §503 does not recognize an exception for tort creditors, and the official comment makes clear that this omission was deliberate. Will widespread adoption of the UTC put an end to the possibility of a common law spendthrift exception for tort creditors? See Mary Louise Fellows and Gregory S. Alexander, Forty Years of Codification of Estates and Trusts Law: Lessons for the Next Generation, 40 Ga. L. Rev. 1049, 1075 (2006), arguing in the affirmative.

The position of Restatement (Third) of Trusts, supra, §59 is fuzzier. The text of §59 does not recognize an exception for tort creditors, but comment a(2) to that section contemplates that "evolving policy" might "justify recognition of other exceptions." The comment then continues: "The nature or a pattern of tortious conduct by a beneficiary . . . may on policy grounds justify a court's refusal to allow spendthrift immunity to protect the trust interest and the lifestyle of that beneficiary, especially one whose willful or fraudulent conduct or persistently reckless behavior causes serious harm to others."

(c) *Furnishing necessary support.* The traditional rule is that a person who has furnished the beneficiary with necessary services or support can reach the beneficiary's interest in a spendthrift trust (the paradigmatic examples are physicians and grocers). See Scott and Ascher on Trusts, supra, §15.5.2. This exception is carried forward in Restatement (Third) of Trusts, supra, §59(b), but it is rejected by UTC §503. The official comment to §503 explains: "Most of these cases involve claims by governmental entities, which the drafters concluded are better handled by the enactment of special legislation as authorized by subsection (b)(3)."

A related exception of venerable origin, recognized by Restatement (Third) of Trusts, supra, §59(b), cmt. d, and UTC §503(b)(2), is for persons who provide services necessary to protect the beneficiary's interest in the trust. The official comment to UTC §503 explains: "This exception allows a beneficiary of modest means to overcome an obstacle preventing the beneficiary's obtaining services essential to the protection or enforcement of the beneficiary's rights under the trust."

(d) *Federal tax lien.* The United States can reach the beneficiary's interest to satisfy a tax claim against the beneficiary. Federal tax law trumps state spendthrift trust rules. Scott and Ascher on Trusts, supra, §15.5.4, at 1000-1002. Whether a state can reach the beneficiary's interest to satisfy a state tax claim depends on the applicable state statute. UTC §503(b)(3) and Restatement (Third) of Trusts §59, cmt. a(1), are in accord with respect to both federal and state tax claims.

(e) *Excess over amount needed for support.* In New York, the beneficiary's creditors can reach that part of spendthrift trust income in excess of the amount needed for the support and education of the beneficiary. N.Y. Est. Powers & Trusts Law §7-3.4 (2008). Several states have copied this statute. In determining what is necessary for the support of the beneficiary and what is excess (and thus reachable by creditors), courts developed a *station-in-life rule*. Creditors can reach only the amount in excess of what is needed to maintain the beneficiary in his station in life. Does this make sense? The station-in-life rule rendered these excess-income statutes relatively useless to the creditors of beneficiaries who are accustomed to luxury.[9]

(f) *Percentage levy, spendthrift caps.* In a few states a creditor is permitted to reach a certain percentage (say, between 10 and 30 percent) of the trust income of the spendthrift trust beneficiary in a garnishment proceeding ordinarily applicable to wage earners. See, e.g., Cal. Prob. Code §15306.5 (2008) (25 percent). A handful of states cap the amount of income or principal that can be shielded by a spendthrift provision. See, e.g., Okla. Stat. Ann. tit. 60, §175.25 (2008) (providing that trust income due to the beneficiary in excess of $25,000 per year is subject to garnishment by creditors).

---

9. John Chipman Gray was even more scornful of the New York scheme than of spendthrift trusts generally:

> It may be said that, if the Courts have been wrong in tolerating spendthrift trusts, a remedy is to be found in the legislatures. If the remedy is like that applied in New York, it is, if not worse, more disgusting than the disease. . . . The Statutes of New York, as interpreted by the Courts, provide that the surplus of income given in trust beyond what is necessary for the education and support of the beneficiary shall be liable for his debts. . . . The Court takes into account that the debtor is "a gentleman of high social standing, whose associations are chiefly with men of leisure, and who is connected with a number of clubs," and that his income is not more than sufficient to maintain his position according to his education, habits, and associations.
>
> To say that whatever money is given to a man cannot be taken by his creditors is bad enough; at any rate, however, it is law for rich and poor alike; but to say that from a sum which creditors can reach one man, who has lived simply and plainly, can deduct but a small sum, while a large sum may be deducted by another man because he is "of high social standing" . . . is to descend to a depth of as shameless snobbishness as any into which the justice of a country was ever plunged. [John C. Gray, Restraints on the Alienation of Property x-xi (2d ed. 1895).]

3. *Pension trusts*. The federal Employee Retirement Income Security Act of 1974 (ERISA), 29 U.S.C. §1056(d)(1) (2008), requires that "Each pension plan [covered by the act] shall provide that benefits provided under the plan may not be assigned or alienated." ERISA also provides that these benefits may be reached for child support, alimony, or marital property rights. Id. at §1056(d)(3). The principle underlying these provisions is that the employee's future retirement security should be protected even at the expense of current non-family creditors. See John H. Langbein, Susan J. Stabile, and Bruce A. Wolk, Pension and Employee Benefit Law 268-271 (4th ed. 2006). See also John Hennigan, Rousey and the New Retirement Funds Exemption, 13 Am. Bankr. Inst. L. Rev. 777 (2005); John K. Eason, Retirement Security Through Asset Protection: The Evolution of Wealth, Privilege, and Policy, 61 Wash. & Lee L. Rev. 159 (2004).

Under traditional law, the settlor's creditors are entitled to recover against so much of the trust property as the trustee could, under any circumstances, pay the settlor (see below). Does the protection from creditors of *earned wealth* located in pension plans and other retirement accounts compensate for limiting the asset protection of spendthrift and discretionary trusts to *inherited* wealth?

NOTE: BANKRUPTCY LAW AND TRUST ASSET PROTECTION

The efficacy of a spendthrift or discretionary trust to provide the beneficiary with a fund that cannot be attached by the beneficiary's creditors depends ultimately on whether federal bankruptcy courts will respect state trust law. Viewed from this perspective, the asset protection features of state trust law function only at the sufferance of Congress, which thus far has chosen to allow them. The Bankruptcy Code excludes from the debtor's bankruptcy estate any beneficial interest in trust that is not alienable "under applicable nonbankruptcy law," which includes state trust law. 11 U.S.C. §541(c)(2) (2008). The question thus arises, should the Bankruptcy Code be amended to allow tort judgments or claims for alimony and child support to be enforced against a bankrupt beneficiary's interest in a spendthrift or discretionary trust? Is this a question on which there should be a national policy set at the federal level?

For further discussion of the federal role in the development of state trust asset protection rules, see John K. Eason, Developing the Asset Protection Dynamic: A Legacy of Federal Concern, 31 Hofstra L. Rev. 23 (2002).

3. Self-Settled Asset Protection Trusts

Under traditional law, the settlor cannot shield assets from creditors by placing them in a trust for the settlor's own benefit. Even if the trust is discretionary, spendthrift, or both, the settlor's creditors can reach the maximum amount that under any circumstances the trustee could pay to the settlor or apply for the settlor's benefit. Thus:

> *Case 6. O*, a surgeon, transfers property to *X* in trust to pay so much of the income and prin-
> cipal to *O* as *X* determines in *X*'s sole and absolute discretion. Five years later, *O* botches a rou-
> tine surgery, causing grievous injury to the patient, *A. A* may enforce an award of damages
> against the entire corpus of the trust, because *X* could, in *X*'s discretion, pay the entire corpus
> to *O*. This is true even if the trust instrument provides that *O*'s interest may not be assigned
> or reached by *O*'s creditors (a spendthrift clause). Nor does it matter that *O*'s right to the trust
> assets is subject to *X*'s discretion.

The traditional rule is carried forward in Restatement (Third) of Trusts
§§58(2), 60, cmt. f (2003) and UTC §505 (2000).

Why is protection from creditors available only to recipients of *inherited* wealth
and not also to persons who *earn* wealth and then create a self-settled trust? The
usual answer is that the protective justification for allowing a donor to insulate a
gift from the claims of the donee's creditors collapses when the donor and the
donee are one and the same. Professor Sterk explains: "[A]lthough courts and
legislatures have had some sympathy for property owners seeking to protect their
imprudent or profligate children, the notion that property owners ought to be
able to protect themselves against their own profligacy, at the expense of their
creditors, has been much harder to swallow." Stewart E. Sterk, Asset Protection
Trusts: Trust Law's Race to the Bottom?, 85 Cornell L. Rev. 1035, 1043-1044
(2000).

Suppose, however, that a state were to authorize a self-settled trust against
which the settlor's creditors had no recourse. Would such an innovation attract
trust business to the state? Believing that the answer is Yes, quite a few offshore
jurisdictions and at least eleven U.S. states have enacted statutes that reverse the
traditional rule, thereby giving rise to the *self-settled asset protection trust* (APT). If
such a statute were applicable in Case 6 above, *A* would have no recourse against
the trust assets even if *O* admitted to botching *A*'s surgery and put up no defense
in the malpractice suit.

In the 1980s, a host of offshore jurisdictions — including Bahamas, Barbados,
Belize, Bermuda, Cayman Islands, Cook Islands, Cyprus, Gibraltar, Grenada,
Liechtenstein, Mauritius, Nevis, Samoa, St. Lucia, and Turks and Caicos —
amended their trust laws to allow the creation of a self-settled trust against which
the settlor's creditors have virtually no recourse. The Cook Islands' International
Trusts Act of 1984 (last amended in 1999) is representative. The Act validates *self-
settled spendthrift trusts*, provided that the settlor-beneficiary is not a resident. As
Professor Sterk has observed, this qualification is "a sure sign that the purpose of
the statute was to attract foreign capital." Sterk, supra, 85 Cornell L. Rev. at 1048.
The Act also provides that no judgment rendered by a foreign court against a
Cook Islands trust, or against the settlor, trustee, or beneficiary of a Cook Islands
trust, will be enforced by a Cook Islands court. Although it has been conjectured
that the value of offshore APTs exceeds $1 trillion, no reliable empirical study of
such trusts exists.

The APT migrated onshore in 1997 in the form of an innovative Alaska statute
drafted by a prominent New York trust lawyer, his brother (the head of the Alaska
Trust Company), and an Alaska lawyer. The three had the idea while fishing

Asset Protection Trust States (2008)

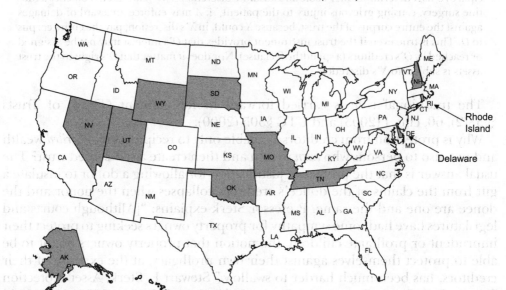

together in Alaska. Under the Alaska statute, the settlor's creditors have no recourse against the settlor's interest in a self-settled spendthrift trust so long as the initial transfer was not fraudulent. Alaska Stat. §34.40.110 (2008). Delaware followed later that year. See Del. Code Ann. tit. 12, §§3570-3576 (2008). The official synopsis of the Delaware Act states that it "is similar to legislation recently enacted in Alaska. It is intended to maintain Delaware's role as the most favored domestic jurisdiction for the establishment of trusts." H.R. 356, 139th Gen. Assemb., 71 Del. Laws 159 (1997). Since then, Missouri, New Hampshire, Nevada, Oklahoma, Rhode Island, South Dakota, Tennessee, Utah, and Wyoming have also passed statutes that validate some form of APT, bringing the count to eleven states.[10] See David G. Shaftel, Comparison of the Twelve Domestic Asset Protection Statutes, 34 ACTEC J. 293 (2009) (surveying the statutes, noting uncertainty about Colorado).

The political dynamic driving the validation of APTs is similar to that which drives the movement to abolish the Rule Against Perpetuities. See pages 905-910. Local bankers and lawyers, who stand to benefit from an influx of trust assets, have lobbied for legislation validating APTs. However, the settlor's motivation for the use of an APT is different from the settlor's motivation for using a perpetual trust. The perpetual trust is used to provide for future generations; the

---

10. Some commentators have read an older statute in Colorado as authorizing APTs against future creditors, see Colo. Rev. Stat. Ann. §38-10-111 (2008), but in dicta the Colorado Supreme Court has rejected that interpretation. In re Cohen, 8 P.3d 429, 432-434 (Colo. 1999).

"The doctor's lawyer will see you now."

APT is used to limit the settlor's personal liability exposure. See Lynn M. LoPucki, The Death of Liability, 106 Yale L.J. 1 (1996).

The extent to which the APT is actually used in practice is unclear. Anecdotes abound of doctors and corporate executives who, in the face of rising insurance premiums, have opted to drop their coverage in favor of moving their assets into an APT. See Rachel Emma Silverman, A Fortress for Your Money: How to Guard Against Lawsuits and Other Claims on Assets, Wall St. J., July 15, 2006, at B1. On this account, the APT might be reckoned as a form of self-help tort reform.

On the other hand, a recent empirical study of trust fund location based on federal banking data from 1985 through 2003 found only "tentative evidence that validating APTs increases a state's trust business." In contrast to the repeal of the Rule Against Perpetuities, which had an observable effect on the location of roughly $100 billion in trust assets, the authors concluded that the "data do not yet allow us to confirm or deny the existence of a significant domestic APT business." Robert H. Sitkoff and Max M. Schanzenbach, Jurisdictional Competition for Trust Funds: An Empirical Analysis of Perpetuities and Taxes, 115 Yale L.J. 356, 411-412, 415 (2005).

As yet, there are no reported appellate cases on the enforceability of a domestic APT in a state that has not adopted an APT statute. There are, however, appellate cases on the enforceability of an offshore APT.

Federal Trade Commission v. Affordable Media, LLC
United States Court of Appeals, Ninth Circuit, 1999
179 F.3d 1228

WIGGINS, J. A husband and wife, Denyse and Michael Anderson, were involved in a telemarketing venture that offered investors the chance to participate in a project that sold such modern marvels as talking pet tags and water-filled barbells by means of late-night television. Although the promoters promised that an investment in the project would return 50 per cent in a mere 60 to 90 days, the venture in fact was a Ponzi scheme,[11] which eventually unraveled and left thousands of investors with tremendous losses. . . .

While the investors' money was lost in the fraudulent scheme, the Andersons' profits from their commissions remained safely tucked away across the sea in a Cook Islands trust. When the [Federal Trade] Commission brought a civil action to recover as much money as possible for the defrauded investors, the Andersons . . . claimed that they were unable to repatriate the assets in the Cook Islands trust because they had willingly relinquished all control over the millions of dollars of commissions in order to place this money overseas in the benevolent hands of unaccountable overseers, just on the off chance that a law suit might result from their business activities. The learned district court was skeptical . . . and [chose] to grant the Commission its requested preliminary relief.

An old adage warns that a fool and his money are easily parted. This case shows that the same is not true of a district court judge and his common sense. After the Andersons refused to comply with the preliminary injunction by refusing to return their illicit proceeds, the district court found the Andersons in civil contempt of court. The Andersons appealed. . . .

I

Sometime after April 1997, Denyse and Michael Anderson became involved with The Sterling Group ("Sterling"). Sterling sold such imaginative products as the "Aquabell," a water-filled dumbbell, the "Talking Pet Tag," and a plastic wrap dispenser known as "KenKut" by means of late-night television commercials broadcast between the hours of 11:00 P.M. and 4:00 A.M. The Andersons formed

---

11. The term *Ponzi scheme* derives from Charles Ponzi's infamous swindle in the early 1920s. Ponzi discovered that, under the Universal Postal Convention then in effect, it was possible to buy a stamp in Europe that was worth a few cents more in the United States than it cost in Europe. Claiming that he would exploit this opportunity for postal arbitrage, Ponzi solicited investors with promises of returns on the order of 50 percent in 45 days. Investors were given tradable notes on which, for a time, Ponzi made good. But he did so by paying off the earlier investors with the proceeds raised from later investors. Ponzi did not actually undertake substantial postal arbitrage, and in view of the transaction costs, no wonder. Having taken in a reported $15 million from investors, it would have required a phalanx of workers to process, and an armada of vessels to transport, the billions of stamps necessary to achieve his promised returns. Ultimately, as in the case of all Ponzi schemes, Ponzi's scheme collapsed. Investors recovered only twelve cents on the dollar, and Ponzi wound up serving a stint in prison — neither his first nor his last. Today the term *Ponzi scheme* is used to describe any scam in which subsequent receipts are used to make good on promises to earlier investors. Doing so gives the scam the appearance of genuine returns and the con artist a measure of credibility. For a vivid portrayal of Ponzi and the original Ponzi scheme, see Francis Russell, Bubble, Bubble — No Toil, No Trouble, 24 Am. Heritage 74 (Feb. 1973). — Eds.

Financial Growth Consultants, LLC ("Financial") to serve as the primary telemarketer of media units, an investment that afforded purchasers the opportunity to receive a portion of the profits generated from the sales of Sterling's outlandish products. Financial's telemarketers thereupon set about locating prospective investors in the media unit scheme.

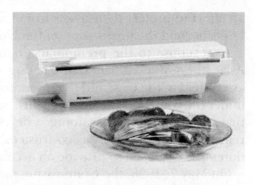

KenKut plastic wrap dispenser and a wrapped plate of strawberries.

The media units sold for $5,000. Each media unit entitled the investor to participate in the sale of Sterling's products from 201 of the late-night commercials. Each product sold for $20.00. The investor would receive $7.50 for each product sold during his 201 commercials, up to a maximum of five products per commercial. According to Financial's telemarketers, the investors would likely receive $37.50 per commercial (from five products sold during each commercial) for a total of $7,537.50 — an astronomical fifty percent return in sixty to ninety days. Financial, for its part, would receive forty-five percent of the investor's $5,000.00 investment, an amount that the Andersons assert is the industry standard.

It appears that Financial's telemarketers were especially skilled at marketing the media units. Financial may have raised at least $13,000,000 from investors in the media-unit scheme, retaining an estimated $6,300,000 in commissions for itself. Perhaps unsurprisingly to those not involved in the media-unit project, it turned out that Sterling could not sell enough Talking Pet Tags and Aquabells to return the promised yields to the media-unit investors. Instead, it appears that Sterling used later investors' investments to pay the promised yields to earlier investors — a classic Ponzi scheme.

On April 23, 1998, the Federal Trade Commission (the "Commission") filed a complaint in the United States District Court for the District of Nevada, charging the Andersons, Financial, and others with violations of the Federal Trade Commission Act (the "Act") and the Telemarketing Sales Rule for their participation in a scheme to telemarket fraudulent investments to consumers. Upon motion by the Commission, the district court issued an ex parte temporary restraining order against the defendants. After hearings on April 30 and May 8, 1998, the district court entered a preliminary injunction against the defendants, which incorporated the provisions of the temporary restraining order. Both the temporary restraining order and the preliminary injunction required the Andersons to repatriate any assets held for their benefit outside of the United States.

In July, 1995, the Andersons had created an irrevocable trust under the law of the Cook Islands. The Andersons were named as co-trustees of the trust, together with AsiaCiti Trust Limited ("AsiaCiti"), a company licensed to conduct trustee services under Cook Islands law. Apparently, the Andersons created the trust in an effort to protect their assets from business risks and liabilities by placing the assets beyond the jurisdiction of the United States courts. . . .

In response to the preliminary injunction, the Andersons faxed a letter to AsiaCiti on May 12, 1998, instructing AsiaCiti to provide an accounting of the assets held in the trust and to repatriate the assets to the United States to be held under the control of the district court. AsiaCiti thereupon notified the Andersons that the temporary restraining order was an event of duress under the trust, removed the Andersons as co-trustees under the trust because of the event of duress, and refused to provide an accounting or repatriation of the assets.[12] . . .

On May 7, 1998, the Commission moved the district court to find the Andersons in civil contempt for their failure to comply with the temporary restraining order's requirements that they submit an accounting of their foreign assets to the Commission and to repatriate all assets located abroad. At a hearing on June 4, 1998, the district court found the Andersons in civil contempt of court for failing to repatriate the trust assets to the United States and failing to provide an accounting of the trust's assets. The district court, however, continued the hearing until June 9, then until June 11, and finally until June 17, in an effort to allow the Andersons to purge themselves of their contempt. In attempting to purge themselves of their contempt, the Andersons attempted to appoint their children as trustees of the trust, but AsiaCiti removed them from acting as trustees because the event of duress was continuing. At the June 17 hearing, the district court indicated that it believed that the Andersons remained in control of the trust and rejected their assertion that compliance with the repatriation provisions of the trust was impossible. At the close of the June 17 hearing, the district judge ordered the Andersons taken into custody because they had not purged themselves of their contempt. The Andersons timely appealed the district court's issuance of the preliminary injunction and finding them in contempt. We affirm the district court.

II

[The court upheld the preliminary injunction.]

III

The next issue on appeal is the district court's finding the Andersons in contempt for refusing to repatriate the assets in their Cook Islands trust. . . . Based

---

12. The Andersons' trust created the circumstances in which a foreign trustee would refuse to repatriate assets to the United States by means of so-called duress provisions. Under the trust agreement, an event of duress includes "[t]he issuance of any order, decree or judgment of any court or tribunal in any part of the world which in the opinion of the protector will or may directly or indirectly, expropriate, sequester, levy, lien or in any way control, restrict or prevent the free disposal by a trustee of any monies, investments or property which may from time to time be included in or form part of this trust and any distributions therefrom." Upon the happening of an event of duress, the trust agreement provides that the Andersons would be terminated as co-trustees, so that control over the trust assets would appear to be exclusively in the hands of a foreign trustee, beyond the jurisdiction of a United States court . . . . [Footnote relocated. — Eds.]

on the record before us, we find that the district court did not abuse its discretion in holding the Andersons in contempt. . . .

The temporary restraining order required the Andersons, in relevant part, to "transfer to the territory of the United States all funds, documents and assets in foreign countries held either: (1) by them; (2) for their benefit; or (3) under their direct or indirect control, jointly or singly." These provisions were continued in the preliminary injunction. It is undisputed that the Andersons are beneficiaries of an irrevocable trust established under the laws of the Cook Islands. The Andersons do not dispute that the trust assets have not been repatriated to the United States. Instead, the Andersons claim that compliance with the temporary restraining order is impossible because the trustee, in accordance with the terms of the trust, will not repatriate the trust assets to the United States.

A party's inability to comply with a judicial order constitutes a defense to a charge of civil contempt. The Andersons claim that the refusal of the foreign trustee to repatriate the trust assets to the United States, which apparently was the goal of the trust, makes their compliance with the preliminary injunction impossible.

Although the Andersons assert that their "inability to comply with a judicial decree is a complete defense to a charge of civil contempt, *regardless of whether the inability to comply is self-induced*" (emphasis added), we are not certain that the Andersons' inability to comply in this case would be a defense to a finding of contempt. It is readily apparent that the Andersons' inability to comply with the district court's repatriation order is the intended result of their own conduct — their inability to comply and the foreign trustee's refusal to comply appears to be the precise goal of the Andersons' trust. The Andersons claim that they created their trust as part of an "asset protection plan." These "[s]o-called asset protection trusts are designed to shield wealth by moving it to a foreign jurisdiction that does not recognize U.S. judgments or other legal processes, such as asset freezes." Debra Baker, Island Castaway, ABA Journal, October 1998, at 55. The "asset protection" aspect of these foreign trusts arises from the ability of people, such as the Andersons, to frustrate and impede the United States courts by moving their assets beyond those courts' jurisdictions:

> Perhaps most importantly, situs courts typically ignore United States courts' demands to repatriate trust assets to the United States. A situs court will not enforce a United States order from a state court compelling the turnover of trust assets to a creditor that was defrauded under United States law, or assets that were placed into a self-settled spendthrift trust.

James T. Lorenzetti, The Offshore Trust: A Contemporary Asset Protection Scheme, 102 Com. L.J. 138, 143-144 (1997).

Because these asset protection trusts move the trust assets beyond the jurisdiction of domestic courts, often times all that remains within the jurisdiction is the physical person of the defendant. Because the physical person of the defendant remains subject to domestic courts' jurisdictions, courts could normally utilize their contempt powers to force a defendant to return the assets to their jurisdictions. Recognizing this risk, asset protection trusts typically are designed so that a defendant can assert that compliance with a court's order to repatriate the trust assets is impossible:

> Another common issue is whether the client may someday be in the awkward position of either having to repatriate assets or else be held in contempt of court. A well-drafted [asset protection trust] would, under such a circumstance, make it impossible for the client to repatriate assets held by the trust. Impossibility of performance is a complete defense to a civil contempt charge.

Barry S. Engel, Using Foreign Situs Trusts for Asset Protection Planning, 20 Est. Plan. 212, 218 (1993).

Given that these offshore trusts operate by means of frustrating domestic courts' jurisdiction, we are unsure that we would find that the Andersons' inability to comply with the district court's order is a defense to a civil contempt charge. We leave for another day the resolution of this more difficult question because we find that the Andersons have not satisfied their burden of proving that compliance with the district court's repatriation order was impossible. It is well established that a party petitioning for an adjudication that another party is in civil contempt does not have the burden of showing that the other party has the capacity to comply with the court's order. Instead, the party asserting the impossibility defense must show "categorically and in detail" why he is unable to comply.

In the asset protection trust context, moreover, the burden on the party asserting an impossibility defense will be particularly high because of the likelihood that any attempted compliance with the court's orders will be merely a charade rather than a good faith effort to comply. Foreign trusts are often designed to assist the settlor in avoiding being held in contempt of a domestic court while only feigning compliance with the court's orders . . . .

With foreign laws designed to frustrate the operation of domestic courts and foreign trustees acting in concert with domestic persons to thwart the United States courts, the domestic courts will have to be especially chary of accepting a defendant's assertions that repatriation or other compliance with a court's order concerning a foreign trust is impossible. Consequently, the burden on the defendant of proving impossibility as a defense to a contempt charge will be especially high. . . .

The Andersons claim that they have "demonstrated to the district court 'categorically and in detail' that they can not comply with the repatriation section of the preliminary injunction." The district court was not convinced and neither are we. While it is possible that a rational person would send millions of dollars overseas and retain absolutely no control over the assets, we share the district court's skepticism. The district court found, notwithstanding the Andersons' protestations, that

> As I look at the totality of the scheme of what I see before me at this time, I have no doubt that the Andersons can if they wish to correct this problem and provide the means of putting these funds in a position that they can be accountable if the final determination of the Court is that the funds should be returned to those who made these payments.

We cannot say that this finding was clearly erroneous. The Andersons had previously been able to obtain in excess of $1 million from the trust in order to pay their taxes. Given their ability to obtain, with ease, such large sums from the trust, we share the district court's skepticism regarding the Andersons' claim that they cannot make the trust assets subject to the court's jurisdiction.

Moreover, beyond this general skepticism concerning the Andersons' lack of control over their trust, the specifics of the Andersons' trust indicate that they retained control over the trust assets. These offshore trusts allow settlors, such as the Andersons, significant control over the trust assets by allowing the settlor to act as a cotrustee or "protector" of the trust.[13] When the settlors retain this type of control, however, they can jeopardize the asset protection scheme because they will be subject to a U.S. court's personal jurisdiction and be forced to exercise their control to repatriate the assets.

The district court's finding that the Andersons were in control of their trust is well supported by the record given that the Andersons were the protectors of their trust. A protector has significant powers to control an offshore trust. A protector can be compelled to exercise control over a trust to repatriate assets if the protector's powers are not drafted solely as the negative powers to veto trustee decisions or if the protector's powers are not subject to the anti-duress provisions of the trust.[14] The Andersons' trust gives them affirmative powers to appoint new trustees and makes the anti-duress provisions subject to the protectors' powers, therefore, they can force the foreign trustee to repatriate the trust assets to the United States.

Perhaps the most telling evidence of the Andersons' control over the trust was their conduct after the district court issued its temporary restraining order ordering the repatriation of the trust funds. . . . After the Andersons claimed that compliance with the repatriation provisions of the temporary restraining order was impossible, the Commission revealed to the court that the Andersons were the protectors of the trust. The Andersons immediately attempted to resign as protectors of the trust. This attempted resignation indicates that the Andersons knew that, as the protectors of the trust, they remained in control of the trust and could force the foreign trustee to repatriate the assets.

---

13. The office of the trust protector is a creature of the trust instrument. Its purpose is to provide flexibility and a check on the trustee. The protector is often given the power to remove and replace the trustee or to make modifications to the trust in light of changed circumstances. For more on trust protectors, see page 651. — Eds.

14. . . . In provisions of the trust agreement that the Andersons conveniently fail to reference, the trust agreement makes clear that the Andersons, as protectors, have the power to determine whether or not an event of duress has occurred: "For the purpose of determining whether an Event of Duress has occurred pursuant to paragraph (c) and paragraph (d) of this clause (1)(a)(vi) of this Deed, *the written certificate of the Protector to that effect shall be conclusive.*" Trust Agreement (emphasis added). Moreover, the very definition of an event of duress that the Andersons assert has occurred makes clear that whether or not an event of duress has occurred depends upon the opinion of the protector: "The issuance of any order, decree or judgement of any court or tribunal in any part of the world *which in the opinion of the Protector* will or may directly or indirectly, expropriate." Trust Agreement (emphasis added). Therefore, notwithstanding the provisions of the trust agreement that the Andersons point to, it is clear that the Andersons could have ordered the trust assets repatriated simply by certifying to the foreign trustee that in their opinion, as protectors, no event of duress had occurred. . . . [Footnote relocated. — Eds.]

Because we see no clear error in the district court's finding that the Andersons remain in control of their trust and could repatriate the trust assets, the district court did not abuse its discretion in holding them in contempt. We, therefore, affirm the district court's finding the Andersons in contempt. Given the nature of the Andersons' so-called "asset protection" trust, which was designed to frustrate the power of United States' courts to enforce judgments, there may be little else that a district court judge can do besides exercise its contempt powers to coerce people like the Andersons into removing the obstacles they placed in the way of a court. Given that the Andersons' trust is operating precisely as they intended, we are not overly sympathetic to their claims and would be hesitant to overly-restrict the district court's discretion, and thus legitimize what the Andersons have done.

Affirmed.

IN RE LAWRENCE, 279 F.3d 1294 (11th Cir. 2002): Two months after he created an offshore asset protection trust in Mauritius funded with $7 million, Stephan Jay Lawrence lost a securities law arbitration proceeding, which resulted in a $20.4 million judgment against him. Lawrence then filed for bankruptcy. The bankruptcy court ordered Lawrence to turn over to the bankruptcy trustee the assets held in the offshore trust. Lawrence did not comply, so on October 5, 1999, the court held Lawrence in contempt and jailed him pending compliance with the turnover order.

On appeal, Lawrence argued that, because he had no control over the offshore trust fund, compliance with the turnover order was impossible and hence he should be released. Lawrence stressed that he had been removed as a beneficiary under a duress provision in the trust that extinguished his interest in the event of bankruptcy. The court rejected this argument. Under the terms of the trust, Lawrence retained the authority to appoint trustees, and these trustees would have the discretion to reinstate Lawrence as a beneficiary. Once restored as a beneficiary, the new trustees could distribute the entire trust fund to Lawrence. The court was therefore unimpressed with the duress provision. "The sole purpose of this provision appears to be an aid to the settlor to evade contempt while merely feigning compliance with the court's order. . . . [W]here the person charged with contempt is responsible for the inability to comply, impossibility is not a defense to the contempt proceedings."

NOTES AND QUESTIONS

1. *Epilogue.* Over the Christmas holiday in 1998, less than a month before the Ninth Circuit heard oral argument in *Affordable Media,* the district court purged the Andersons of their contempt, freeing them after six months in jail. In September 1999, two months after the Ninth Circuit rendered its decision and almost a year after the Andersons were freed, the FTC brought suit in the Cook Islands against AsiaCiti Limited, the trustee of the Andersons' offshore trust. The parties settled the Cook Islands litigation in 2002 for $1.2 million, the

equivalent of six cents on the dollar; the FTC had sought $20 million. The settlement proceeds went to a fund for defrauded customers.

On December 13, 2006, after six years, two months, and 28 days of incarceration, Stephan Jay Lawrence, a graduate of MIT and once a hotshot options trader on Wall Street, was finally released. Observing that "[s]ix years is longer than most terms of imprisonment for serious federal crimes," the judge concluded that "Lawrence has come to value his money (whatever may be left) more than his liberty."

2.   Professor Danforth describes the more common features of an offshore APT:

> First, if the APT is properly established in a foreign country, in most cases a court in the United States will lack personal jurisdiction over the trustee. . . . Second, many offshore jurisdictions recognize the role of a trust "protector," a person granted special non-fiduciary powers to control the administration of the trust, with respect to such matters as removal and replacement of trustees, control over discretionary actions of the trustees, etc. By use of the trust protector mechanism, a settlor is able to vest in some trusted person substantial control over trust administration, while at the same [time] being able to resist the claim that the settlor himself or herself (whose actions will be subject to the authority of a United States court) retains such control. . . . Third, many offshore APTs include a so-called duress clause, under which the trustee is directed to ignore any directions received from a settlor or trust protector who is under duress [, which is defined to include] . . . a United States court's order. Finally, most offshore APTs also include a "flight" clause, under which the trustee is authorized to change the situs of the trust, change the applicable law, and move the trust assets to a new jurisdiction, if a claim against the trust threatens to be successful. [Robert T. Danforth, Rethinking the Law of Creditors' Rights in Trusts, 53 Hastings L.J. 287, 309-310 (2002).]

Does the validation of the contempt power in *Affordable Media* and *Lawrence* signal the end of the offshore APT? Professor Sterk thinks not:

> Civil contempt sanctions . . . do not appear to offer a stable long-term solution . . . . First, when the Andersons created their Cook Islands trust, they retained broad powers over the trust funds as trust protectors. . . . The Ninth Circuit seized upon these powers, which settlors typically do not include in offshore trusts, as evidence that the Andersons had power to arrange repatriation of trust assets. . . .
>
> Second, *Affordable Media* fails to answer one critical question: For how long will a court be willing to incarcerate an offshore trust settlor for civil contempt? . . . Penalties for civil contempt are designed to coerce the contemnor into compliance with the court's order. If incarceration will not induce compliance, the foundation for imprisonment collapses. [Stewart E. Sterk, Asset Protection Trusts: Trust Law's Race to the Bottom?, 85 Cornell L. Rev. 1035, 1102-1104 (2000).]

Among lawyers who specialize in asset protection, *Affordable Media* and *Lawrence* are viewed as cautionary tales on how not to draft an offshore APT. In each the crucial blunder was giving the settlor, over whom a domestic court would have jurisdiction, affirmative powers to override or to replace the offshore trustee.

As a practical matter, even a poorly structured APT, offshore or domestic, may give the settlor additional leverage in negotiating with creditors. Eric Henzy, who represented the plaintiff in In re Brooks, 217 B.R. 98 (Bankr. D. Conn. 1998), explains: "In *Brooks* we got a judgment essentially voiding this offshore trust. We then settled for approximately fifty cents on the dollar, because the enforcement problems were so significant." Roundtable Discussion, 32 Vand. J. Transnatl. L. 779, 786 (1999).

3. Should the law draw a distinction between (a) an APT established before any claims against the settlor are pending, threatened, or expected, that leaves the settlor with enough funds to pay anticipated debts, and (b) an APT established after a claim is pending, threatened, or expected, that is funded with virtually all of the settlor's assets? Under *fraudulent transfer* law, codified in the widely adopted Uniform Fraudulent Transfer Act (1984), it is actual fraud to make a transfer with the intent to hinder, delay, or defraud creditors. It is constructive fraud to make a transfer without receiving equivalent value in exchange if the debtor is insolvent or if the transfer leaves the debtor with "unreasonably small assets" or with insufficient assets to pay anticipated further debts. A creditor is defined to include persons holding even contingent, disputed, and unmatured rights to payment.

4. A majority of states privileges claims by *spouses* and *children* against ordinary spendthrift trusts. Suppose there is a claim by a spouse or child of the settlor against the settlor's interest in an APT. Some but not all of the APT statutes carve out an exception for claims by spouses and children. What result under one of the statutes without such an exception? Speaking of a self-settled asset protection trust located in the Bahamas, the court in Breitenstine v. Breitenstine, 62 P.3d 587, 593 n.1 (Wyo. 2003), stated in dicta that "the use of such trusts to avoid alimony, child support, and a fair division of marital property upon divorce is reprehensible to us." The court did not reach the issue whether to recognize an exception for claims by spouses and children, because it found that the underlying transfer to the trust was a fraudulent transfer under state law.

5. *Bankruptcy.* The effectiveness of a self-settled APT depends on its enforceability in federal bankruptcy court. As we have seen (see page 624), the Bankruptcy Code excludes from the debtor's bankruptcy estate any beneficial interest in trust that is not alienable "under applicable nonbankruptcy law." 11 U.S.C. §541(c)(2) (2008). Taken literally, this provision would appear to include the settlor's beneficial interest in an APT, just as it protects a beneficiary's interest in a third-party settled spendthrift or discretionary trust and many pension plans.

In 2005, during debate over the Bankruptcy Abuse Prevention and Consumer Protection Act passed later that year, the Senate considered but ultimately rejected an amendment to §541(c)(2) that would have included in the bankruptcy estate assets in excess of $125,000 put by the debtor into a self-settled trust for the benefit of the debtor within ten years of the bankruptcy filing. See John K. Eason, Policy, Logic, and Persuasion in the Evolving Realm of Trust Asset Protection, 27 Cardozo L. Rev. 2621, 2667-2677 (2006). Does the failure of the 2005 amendment signal congressional approval of the APT? Probably not. As Professor Eason has shown, "opposition to that amendment likely had as much to do with a desire to get the Act through the Senate without complicating amendments as it did with any particular endorsement of [domestic APTs]." Id. Moreover, Congress did pass an amendment that provides that the trustee in bankruptcy can recover property transferred by the debtor to a self-settled trust for the benefit of the debtor within ten years of the bankruptcy filing if the transfer was made with actual intent to hinder, delay, or defraud a creditor. 11 U.S.C. §548(e)(1) (2008). Although this amendment adds little protection for creditors not already present in ordinary state fraudulent transfer law (which is applicable in bankruptcy), it augments the fraudulent transfer rules within the Bankruptcy Code, 11 U.S.C. §548, by providing a longer recovery window than is typical.

6. *Professional responsibility.* Is it proper for a lawyer to assist in creating an APT, or in pursuing other forms of asset-protection planning? Any lawyer involved in an effort to delay, hinder, or defraud a client's existing or foreseeable creditors is asking for trouble. First, there is Model Rule of Prof. Conduct 1.2(d) (2002): "A lawyer shall not counsel a client to engage, or assist a client, in conduct that the lawyer knows is criminal or fraudulent." Second, some states have recognized new theories of recovery such as conspiracy to convey property fraudulently and intentional interference with the contract rights of a third party, actions that may enable a creditor to assert a claim against the debtor's lawyer. Third, there is potential for a malpractice claim if the strategy proves to be ineffective. Finally, various criminal laws are potentially applicable in the case of overly aggressive asset-protection planning. See generally Henry J. Lischer, Jr., Professional Responsibility Issues Associated with Asset Protection Trusts, 39 Real Prop., Prob. & Tr. J. 561 (2004); Denis A. Kleinfeld and Salvador C. Orofino, Nailing the Lawyer for His Debtor-Client's Sins, 144 Tr. & Est. 36 (Nov. 2005).

On the other hand, is it proper for a lawyer *not* to talk to clients about APTs and other asset-protection devices? In Richard W. Nenno, Planning with Domestic Asset-Protection Trusts, Part I, 40 Real. Prop., Prob. & Tr. J. 263, 284-286 (2005), the author writes: "Attorneys cannot assume that they will escape ethical problems simply by choosing not to participate in asset-protection planning because the Model Rules and Model Code require attorneys to represent their client zealously. . . . [A]ttorneys might face exposure if they do not advise the client to [engage in asset-protection planning] and creditors later reach the client's assets."

7. *Literature.* There is a robust literature that considers bankruptcy law, fraudulent transfer law, choice of law principles, federal constitutional principles, and other doctrinal issues raised by APTs and other asset-protection devices. In addition to the articles cited above, see also Richard C. Ausness, The Offshore Asset Protection Trust: A Prudent Financial Planning Device or the Last Refuge of a Scoundrel?, 45 Duq. L. Rev. 147 (2007); Karen E. Boxx, Gray's Ghost — A Conversation about the Onshore Trust, 85 Iowa L. Rev. 1195 (2000); Randall J. Gingiss, Putting a Stop to "Asset Protection" Trusts, 51 Baylor L. Rev. 987 (1999); Henry J. Lischer, Jr., Domestic Asset Protection Trusts: Pallbearers to Liability, 35 Real Prop., Prob. & Tr. J. 479 (2000); Elena Marty-Nelson, Offshore

Asset Protection Trusts: Having Your Cake and Eating It Too, 47 Rutgers L. Rev. 11 (1994); Richard W. Nenno, Planning With Domestic Asset-Protection Trusts: Part II, 40 Real Prop., Prob. & Tr. J. 477 (2005). See also Adam J. Hirsch, Fear Not the Asset Protection Trust, 27 Cardozo L. Rev. 2685 (2006); John E. Sullivan III, Gutting the Rule Against Self-Settled Trusts: How the New Delaware Trust Law Competes with Offshore Trusts, 23 Del. J. Corp. L. 423 (1998).

NOTE: TRUSTS FOR THE STATE-SUPPORTED

A person qualifies for Medicaid and public support benefits only if the person has relatively few financial resources. The amounts of assets and income that will disqualify an applicant vary from state to state. The question arises whether trusts benefiting a person will be counted as resources available for the support of the person if he applies for public support.

Federal law draws a distinction between *self-settled trusts* (generally included when assessing financial need) and *trusts created by third parties* (generally not included). The typical case of the former arises when a person seeks to guard against the consumption of the person's assets by long-term care expenses that would otherwise be covered by a government benefit program. The typical case of the latter arises when a person seeks to provide resources for the supplemental needs of a child or other loved one who is otherwise eligible for government benefits without undermining the beneficiary's eligibility for those benefits.

Self-settled trusts. For Medicaid purposes, a trust is self-settled, and therefore generally considered in the qualification decision, "if assets of the individual were used to form all or part of the corpus of the trust" and the trust was established by the individual, by the individual's spouse, or by a person or court with legal authority to act on behalf of, or on request of, the individual or the individual's spouse. 42 U.S.C. §1396p(d) (2008). If the trust is revocable by the individual, the principal and all income of the trust are considered resources available to the individual. If the trust is irrevocable, any income or principal that under any circumstances could be paid to or applied for the benefit of the individual are considered resources of the individual. Hence, in the case of a discretionary trust, the Medicaid applicant is deemed to have resources in the maximum amount that could be distributed to him, assuming full exercise of discretion by the trustee in his favor. See Masterson v. Department of Soc. Serv., 969 S.W.2d 746 (Mo. 1998).

There are two important exceptions. First, a discretionary trust created by the will of one spouse for the benefit of the surviving spouse is not deemed a resource available to the surviving spouse. 42 U.S.C. §1396p(d)(2)(A) (2008). This makes it possible for one spouse to create a wholly discretionary trust for the benefit of the surviving spouse, who may qualify for Medicaid if the survivor's other resources are below the eligibility amount. See Pohlmann v. Nebraska Department of Health and Human Services, 710 N.W.2d 639 (Neb. 2006). Second, a trust will not be considered a resource available to the Medicaid applicant if it is established for a disabled individual from the individual's property, by a parent, grandparent, or guardian of the individual or by a court, and the trust provides that the state will receive upon the individual's death all amounts remaining in the trust up to the amount equal to the total medical assistance paid by the state. 42 U.S.C. §1396p(d)(4)(A) (2008). This makes it possible, after an accident in which an individual is disabled, to settle the proceeds of a tort recovery in a trust to provide supplemental care for the individual above what the state provides, if the trust reimburses the state out of the trust assets at the individual's death.

Because self-settled trusts generally prevent qualification for Medicaid, individuals who want to preserve their life savings for their descendants will sometimes impoverish themselves by giving the bulk of their property to their descendants, outright or in trust, usually retaining only enough property to cover the anticipated cost of their own care until they qualify for Medicaid. In such cases there is a period of ineligibility that may last up to 60 months. See Note, Long-Term Care Financing Crisis — Recent Federal and State Efforts to Deter Asset Transfers as a Means to Gain Medicaid Eligibility, 74 N.D. L. Rev. 383 (1998).

Trusts that are not self-settled. With respect to trusts established by a third person for the benefit of the applicant, Medicaid regulations provide that trust income or principal is "considered available both when actually available and when the applicant or recipient has a legal interest in a liquidated sum and has the legal ability to make such sum available for support and maintenance." 45 C.F.R. §233.20(a)(3)(ii)(D) (2008). Thus, if a mandatory or support trust is created, wherein the beneficiary has the legal right to compel the distribution of income, such income is treated as a resource available to the beneficiary. But if a discretionary trust is created, the trust is not considered a resource available to the individual in applying for Medicaid unless it was intended to be used for the applicant's support. See Corcoran v. Department of Soc. Servs., 859 A.2d 533 (Conn. 2004).

If a trust has been set up by a third party for an institutionalized beneficiary, the courts have generally followed the common law rules applicable to creditors of beneficiaries of mandatory, support, and discretionary trusts. If the beneficiary has a right to trust income or principal, the state can reach it. At common law, a spendthrift clause is unenforceable against the state because the state is furnishing necessaries to the institutionalized beneficiary. In a similar vein, although Uniform Trust Code §503 (2000, rev. 2005) does not recognize an exception for those who provide the beneficiary with necessary support, the exception under §503(b)(3) for claims by the state would address cases in which the state provided necessary support. See generally Alan Newman, Spendthrift and Discretionary Trusts: Alive and Well Under the Uniform Trust Code, 40 Real Prop., Prob. & Tr. J. 567, 618-626 (2005), discussing special and supplemental needs trusts under the UTC.

Most of the litigation concerns discretionary trusts. Generally, the state cannot reach discretionary trusts, nor consider them when determining eligibility for public benefits. Many discretionary trusts are hybrids, however, combining the purpose of support with discretion in the trustee (e.g., "to provide for the comfort and support of my daughter in the trustee's sole and absolute discretion"). If a beneficiary of a discretionary trust can, under some conceivable circumstances, obtain a court order requiring payment to the beneficiary, it is possible that the trust assets may be reached by the state. See In re Barkema Trust, 690 N.W.2d 50 (Iowa 2004).

Settlors who want to provide only benefits that the state is unable or unwilling to provide can establish a *supplemental needs trust*. If structured properly, the state cannot reach the trust assets. See Miller v. Department of Mental Health, 442 N.W.2d 617 (Mich. 1989). For an examination of the history behind, and current regulation of, supplemental needs trusts, see John J. Campbell, Preserving Public Benefits in Physical Injury Settlements: Special-Needs Trusts and Beyond, 2 NAELA J. 367 (2006); Joseph A. Rosenberg, Supplemental Needs Trusts for People with Disabilities: The Development of a Private Trust in the Public Interest, 10 B.U. Pub. Int. L.J. 91 (2004).

This is an evolving area of the law involving unsettled questions of public policy at both state and federal levels, increasing pressures on the public purse, and hard-to-predict judicial interpretations of trust language. Practitioners must use great caution in advising clients who want to create a trust that the state cannot reach. See Pack v. Osborn, 881 N.E.2d 237 (Ohio 2008), holding that the law at the time of the Medicaid application, not the law at the time the trust is created, controls for eligibility determination. See also In re Myers, 127 P.3d 325 (Kan. 2006), upholding the public censure for incompetence of a lawyer who drafted trusts that failed to protect the trust assets from being counted as resources available to the clients in determining their Medicaid eligibility.

For further discussion, see Sebastian V. Grassi, Jr., Estate Planning for a Special Needs Child Requires Special Attention, 34 Est. Plan. 28 (Dec. 2007); Clifton B. Kruse, Jr., Third-Party and Self-Created Trusts: Planning for the Elderly and Disabled Client (3d ed. 2002).

PROBLEMS

1. Barbara is a developmentally disabled person. Her mother, Edith, neglected Barbara and failed to provide her with Social Security benefits that Edith had received on behalf of Barbara. Upon suit by Barbara's aunt, her guardian, a consent decree was entered ordering Edith to fund a trust for the benefit of Barbara with $150,000 Edith had inherited from her sisters. Edith complied by creating a discretionary trust for Barbara with a spendthrift provision. The trust agreement named Edith as settlor. It directed the trustee to terminate the trust immediately should any agency providing support for Barbara attempt to reach it. Can the trust assets be reached by the state to provide for Barbara's care? See Hertsberg Trust v. Department of Mental Health, 578 N.W.2d 289 (Mich. 1998).

2. Wendy and Howard Brown's elder daughter, Sarah, has been injured in an automobile accident that left her unable to care for herself or manage her affairs. Sarah has been placed in a nursing home. The cost of the nursing home is $40,000 a year. Sarah received $200,000 in insurance proceeds. Howard, as

Sarah's conservator, has applied for Medicaid. (For more on the Brown family, see pages 49-58.)

Howard and Wendy want your advice on (a) what to do with the $200,000, and (b) what provisions they should make in their wills to provide more comfortable support for Sarah than the minimum provided by Medicaid. Advise them. See Stell v. Boulder County Dept. of Soc. Servs., 92 P.3d 910 (Colo. 2004); Gold v. United Health Servs. Hosp., Inc., 746 N.E.2d 172 (N.Y. 2001); Cricchio v. Pennisi, 683 N.E.2d 301 (N.Y. 1997).

3.   Your client is 70 years old and has just been diagnosed with Alzheimer's disease. Although she is still capable of making decisions for herself, her doctor says that this will change within the next few years, and that eventually she will require a great deal of care for the rest of her life, which could be another 20 years or more. Your client has asked what she can do to preserve her $1 million estate for the benefit of her descendants. What advice would you give?

SECTION C.   MODIFICATION AND TERMINATION OF TRUSTS

1.   *Introduction*

If the settlor and all the beneficiaries consent, an irrevocable trust may be modified or terminated. The trustee cannot object. Such a right exists even if the trust contains a spendthrift clause.

If, however, the settlor is dead or does not consent, the question arises whether the beneficiaries can modify or terminate the trust if they all agree. Let us look first at the law in England. In Saunders v. Vautier, 49 Eng. Rep. 282 (1841), the English court held that a trust can be terminated at any time if all the beneficiaries are adult and sui juris and all consent. In the 1950s, at the behest of trust beneficiaries who urgently sought to modify trusts to escape serious tax disadvantages, Parliament enacted the Variation of Trusts Act of 1958, 6 & 7 Eliz. 2, ch. 53, §1, which greatly expanded the power of courts to modify or terminate trusts. The act provides that a court may consent to modification or termination of a trust on behalf of incompetent, minor, or unborn beneficiaries whenever the court finds it beneficial to those beneficiaries. Nearly all Commonwealth countries have adopted a similar rule. Paul Matthews, The Comparative Importance of the Rule in Saunders v. Vautier, 122 L.Q. Rev. 266, 282 (2006).

What has happened in England and the Commonwealth countries is that, after the settlor's death, the trust is regarded as the beneficiaries' property, not as the settlor's property — and the dead hand continues to rule only by the sufferance of the beneficiaries. As Mummery, L.J., explained, "The principle recognises the rights of beneficiaries . . . to overbear and defeat the intention of a testator or settlor." Goulding v. James, 2 All E.R. 239, 247 (C.A. 1997). Concurring in the same case, Sir Ralph Gibson added, "it is not clear to me why evidence of the intention of the testator can be of any relevance whatever. . . . The fact that a testator would not have approved or would have disapproved very strongly does not alter the fact that the beneficiaries are entitled in law to do it." Id. at 252.

Recall that England does not recognize the spendthrift trust. In rejecting the spendthrift trust, the English courts made the beneficiary's interest alienable regardless of the settlor's intent (though the beneficiary's interest can still be shielded against creditors through a discretionary or protective trust). The same antipathy to the dead hand explains the English law of modification and termination. "The court [in Saunders v. Vautier] explicitly connected the question of a beneficiary's power to compel termination in anticipation of the time prescribed by the trustor with the question of the beneficiary's power to alienate his equitable interest. Since no valid restraint could be imposed upon an equitable fee, a provision postponing possession of the trust estate could not be given effect." Gregory Alexander, The Dead Hand and the Law of Trusts in the Nineteenth Century, 37 Stan. L. Rev. 1189, 1201 (1985).

Modification and termination of trusts in England is strikingly different from the practice in this country. In the United States, the traditional rule is that a trust cannot be terminated or modified prior to the time fixed for termination by petition of all the beneficiaries if termination or modification would be contrary to a *material purpose* of the settlor. The leading case establishing this rule is Claflin v. Claflin, 20 N.E. 454 (Mass. 1889), and the rule, which was preserved in Restatement (Second) of Trusts §337 (1959), is often referred to as the *Claflin doctrine*. In that case, a trust was established for testator's son, with principal to be paid to the son at age 30. After age 21, the son sued to terminate the trust, pointing out that he was the sole beneficiary. Echoing Justice Miller's elaborate dictum upholding spendthrift trusts in Nichols v. Eaton, page 614, the court refused to permit termination, as this would violate the intent of the testator:

> [A] testator has a right to dispose of his own property with such restrictions and limitations, not repugnant to law, as he sees fit, and . . . his intentions ought to be carried out, unless they contravene some positive rule of law, or are against public policy. . . . It cannot be said that these restrictions upon the plaintiff's possession and control of the property are altogether useless, for there is not the same danger that he will spend the property while it is in the hands of the trustees as there would be if it were in his own. [*Claflin*, 20 N.E. at 456.]

The *Claflin* doctrine applies to modification or termination by consent of the beneficiaries. An alternative basis for modification or termination is an unanticipated change in circumstances. Under the *equitable deviation* doctrine, the court will permit the trustee to deviate from the administrative terms of a trust when compliance would defeat or substantially impair the accomplishment of the purposes of the trust on account of changed circumstances not anticipated by the settlor. It is not enough to show that deviation would be more advantageous or better for the beneficiaries than continuing compliance; deviation must be necessary to accomplish the purpose of the trust. Restatement (Second) of Trusts, supra, §167, cmt. b.

Accordingly, American irrevocable trusts have proved quite difficult to amend or terminate without the settlor's consent, something that is, of course, hard to obtain from the settlor of a testamentary trust. The question thus arises, should the *Claflin* and deviation doctrines be relaxed to allow for freer modification and termination?

2.   Deviation and Changed Circumstances

IN RE TRUST OF STUCHELL, 801 P.2d 852 (Or. App. 1990): In his 1947 will, J.W. Stuchell created a testamentary trust for his family. The petitioner, Edna Rogers Harrell, was one of the two surviving life beneficiaries. Upon the death of the last life beneficiary, the principal of the trust was to be distributed to Edna's children or their descendants per stirpes. At the time of the litigation, Edna had four children.

> One of petitioner's four children, John Harrell (Harrell), is a mentally retarded 25 year old who is unable to live independently without assistance. His condition is not expected to improve, and he will probably require care and supervision for the rest of his life. . . .
>
> In December, 1989, petitioner requested the court to approve, on behalf of Harrell, an agreement, which had been approved by the other income beneficiary and remaindermen, to modify the trust. If the trust is not modified, Harrell's remainder will be distributed directly to him if he survives the two life-income beneficiaries. If and when that happens, his ability to qualify for public assistance will be severely limited. The proposed modification provides for the continuation of the trust, if Harrell survives the two life-income beneficiaries, and contains elaborate provisions that are designed to avoid his becoming disqualified, in whole or in part, for any public assistance programs. The stated purpose is to ensure that the trust funds be used only as a secondary source of funds to supplement, rather than to replace, his current income and benefits from public assistance.

Citing the deviation rule of Restatement (Second) Trusts §167 (1959), which provides that the court may "permit the trustee to deviate from a term of the trust if owing to circumstances not known to the settlor and not anticipated by him compliance would defeat or substantially impair the accomplishment of the purposes of the trust," Edna's lawyer argued that the court should permit the proposed modification. Citing comment b to that section, which states that deviation will not be permitted "merely because such deviation would be more advantageous to the beneficiaries," the court denied the petition:

> Even assuming that the Restatement rule were to be adopted as the law in Oregon, it is clear that the limitation imposed by the comment would preclude permitting the proposed amendment, the only purpose of which is to make the trust more advantageous to the beneficiaries. The most obvious advantage would be to the three remaindermen who have consented to the amendment.
>
> There being no statutory or common law authority for a court to approve the proposed agreement modifying the trust, the trial court did not err in dismissing the petition.

QUESTIONS

Do you think that the testator, who did not anticipate John Harrell's special needs, would have objected to the proposed modification once those needs became apparent? Why did the court not regard this as the relevant question?

Courts have been much more liberal in permitting trustees to deviate from *administrative* directions in the trust, because of an unanticipated change of circumstances, than they have been in permitting modification of *distributive* provisions. See Mary F. Radford, George Gleason Bogert, and George Taylor Bogert, The Law of Trusts and Trustees §994 (3d ed. 2006).

In 1911, Joseph Pulitzer's will created a trust for the benefit of his descendants. Pulitzer bequeathed to the trustees shares of stock in a corporation publishing the World newspapers (including one of the major papers of the day, the New York World), and his will provided that the sale of these shares was not authorized under any circumstances. After several years of large and increasing losses from the publication of the World, the trustees in 1931 petitioned the court to approve a sale of the shares. The court held that, even though sale was prohibited by Pulitzer, it had the power to authorize sale in circumstances where the trust estate was in jeopardy, and it approved the sale. In re Pulitzer, 249 N.Y.S. 87, 94 (Sur. Ct. 1931), aff'd mem., 260 N.Y.S. 975 (App. Div. 1932).

If an unanticipated change in circumstances can justify deviating from an administrative provision, why not from a distributive provision? Are not distributive provisions also vulnerable to the effects of an unanticipated change in circumstances? In 1990, California enacted a statute that authorized the court to "modify the administrative *or dispositive* provisions of the trust or terminate the trust if, owing to circumstances not known to the settlor and not anticipated by the settlor, the continuation of the trust under its terms would defeat or substantially impair the accomplishment of the purposes of the trust." Cal. Prob. Code §15409 (2008) (emphasis added). Other states followed, confirming the applicability of equitable deviation to administrative terms and providing statutory warrant for its application to dispositive terms. See Austin Wakeman Scott, William Franklin Fratcher, and Mark L. Ascher, Scott and Ascher on Trusts §§16.4, 33.4 (5th ed. 2006).

Both Restatement (Third) of Trusts §66 (2003) and Uniform Trust Code §412 (2000) adopt the modern view of equitable deviation as applicable to both administrative and dispositive terms. They also reduce the threshold for deviation from a showing of substantial impairment of the purposes of the trust to a showing that the deviation "will further the purposes of the trust."

Restatement (Third) of Trusts (2003)

§66.   POWER OF COURT TO MODIFY: UNANTICIPATED CIRCUMSTANCES

(1) The court may modify an administrative or distributive provision of a trust, or direct or permit the trustee to deviate from an administrative or distributive provision, if because of circumstances not anticipated by the settlor the modification or deviation will further the purposes of the trust.

(2) If a trustee knows or should know of circumstances that justify judicial action under Subsection (1) with respect to an administrative provision, and of the potential of those circumstances to cause substantial harm to the trust or its beneficiaries, the trustee has a duty to petition the court for appropriate modification of or deviation from the terms of the trust.

Uniform Trust Code (2000)

§412.   MODIFICATION OR TERMINATION BECAUSE OF UNANTICIPATED CIRCUMSTANCES
        OR INABILITY TO ADMINISTER TRUST EFFECTIVELY

(a) The court may modify the administrative or dispositive terms of a trust or terminate the trust if, because of circumstances not anticipated by the settlor, modification or termination will further the purposes of the trust. To the extent practicable, the modification must be made in accordance with the settlor's probable intention.

(b) The court may modify the administrative terms of a trust if continuation of the trust on its existing terms would be impracticable or wasteful or impair the trust's administration.

(c) Upon termination of a trust under this section, the trustee shall distribute the trust property in a manner consistent with the purposes of the trust.

In re Riddell
Court of Appeals of Washington, 2007
157 P.3d 888

PENOYAR, J.   The Trustee of a consolidated trust, Ralph A. Riddell, appeals the trial court's denial of his motion to modify the trust and create a special needs trust on behalf of a trust beneficiary, his daughter, Nancy I. Dexter, who suffers from schizophrenia affective disorder and bipolar disorder. . . .

FACTS

George X. Riddell and Irene A. Riddell were husband and wife with one child, Ralph. George's Last Will and Testament left the residue of his estate in trust for the benefit of his wife, his son, his daughter-in-law, and his grandchildren.

George also created an additional trust (the Life Insurance Trust) for their benefit. Irene's Last Will and Testament left the residue of her estate in trust for the benefit of her son; her son's wife, Beverly Riddell; and her grandchildren.

The trusts contained a provision in which, upon the death of Ralph and Beverly, George and Irene's grandchildren would receive the trust's benefits until the age of thirty-five when the trusts would terminate and the trustee would distribute the principal to the grandchildren. Ralph is currently the Trustee. George and Irene are both deceased.

Ralph and Beverly have two children, Donald H. Riddell and Nancy. Both Donald and Nancy are more than thirty-five years old. Donald is a practicing attorney and able to handle his own financial affairs. Nancy suffers from schizophrenia affective disorder and bipolar disorder; by 1991 she received extensive outpatient care; and by 1997 she moved to Western State Hospital. She is not expected to live independently for the remainder of her life.

Both Ralph and Beverly are still living. Upon their death, the trusts will terminate because Nancy and Donald are both over the age of thirty-five; Nancy will receive her portion of her grandparents' trust principal, which is approximately one half of $1,335,000.

The Trustee, Ralph, . . . filed a petition in superior court, asking the trial court to consolidate the trusts and to modify the trust to create a "special needs" trust on Nancy's behalf, instead of distributing the trust principal to her. He explained that, under the current trust, when her parents die, Nancy's portion of the principal will be distributed to her and the trust will terminate. He argued that a special needs trust is necessary because, upon distribution, Nancy's trust funds would either be seized by the State of Washington to pay her extraordinary medical bills or Nancy would manage the funds poorly due to her mental illness and lack of judgment. He argued that the modification would preserve and properly manage Nancy's funds for her benefit.

The trial court granted the motion to consolidate the trusts but denied the motion to modify. It stated that it did not have the power to modify the trust unless unanticipated events existed that were unknown to the trust creator that would result in defeating the trust's purpose. The trial court found that the trust's purpose was "to provide for the education, support, maintenance, and medical care of the beneficiaries" and that a modification would only "permit[ ] the family to immunize itself financially from reimbursing the State for costs of [Nancy's medical] care." Relying on the Restatement (Second) of Trusts, it stated that it would not allow a modification "merely because a change would be more advantageous to the beneficiaries." . . .

Ralph moved for reconsideration, arguing that . . . the Restatement (Third) of Trusts gave the trial court . . . the authority to modify the consolidated trust into a special needs trust. Ralph argued that, because the grandparents directed the trust proceeds to be distributed to their grandchildren when they reach the age of thirty-five, the settlors intended that their grandchildren attain a level of responsibility, stability, and maturity to handle the funds before receiving the distribution. He also argued that due to Nancy's mental illness, allowing a distribution to her would defeat the settlors' intent and the trust's purpose.

The trial court denied the motion for reconsideration. It . . . agreed that the Restatement (Third) of Trusts . . . allowed the court to modify an administrative or distributive protection of a trust if, because of circumstances the settlor did not anticipate, the modification or deviation would further the trust's purpose. It then stated:

> I believe that there is a showing here that there is a circumstance that was, perhaps, not anticipated by the original settler [sic]; however, the purpose of the trust is to provide for the general support and medical needs of the beneficiaries. I think that modifying the trust in a fashion that makes some of those assets less available for that purpose than they would be under the express language of the trust presently is not consistent with the purpose of the trust.

The trial court reasoned that because the trust was written to provide for "medical care" and because creating a special needs trust would make some money unavailable for medical care expenses, the modification was inconsistent with the trust's purpose. Ralph now appeals.

ANALYSIS . . .

Ralph contends that the trial court erred in declining to modify the trust. He explains that a modification would further the trust's purpose because, if George and Irene had anticipated that Nancy would suffer debilitating mental illness requiring extraordinary levels of medical costs and make her incapable of managing her money independently, they would not have structured the trust to leave a substantial outright distribution of the trust principal to her. He contends that the settlors instead would have established a special needs trust to protect the funds because Nancy's medical bills would be extraordinary and covered by state funding. . . .

In Niemann v. Vaughn Community Church, 113 P.3d 463 (Wash. 2005), our Supreme Court held that trial courts may use "equitable deviation" to make changes in the manner in which a trust is carried out. The court outlined the two prong approach of "equitable deviation" used to determine if modification is appropriate. The court "may modify an administrative or distributive provision of a trust, or direct or permit the trustee to deviate from an administrative or distributive provision, if [1] because of circumstances not anticipated by the settlor [2] the modification or deviation will further the purposes of the trust." Niemann, 113 P.3d at 470. In Niemann, the court adopted the Restatement (Third) of Trusts and noted that the Restatement (Third) requires a lower threshold finding than the older Restatement and gives courts broader discretion in permitting deviation of a trust.

The first prong of the equitable deviation test is satisfied if circumstances have changed since the trust's creation or if the settlor was unaware of circumstances when the trust was established. Restatement (Third) of Trusts §66, cmt. a. Upon a finding of unanticipated circumstances, the trial court must determine if a modification would tend to advance the trust purposes; this inquiry is likely to involve a subjective process of attempting to infer the relevant purpose of a trust from the general tenor of its provisions. Id. cmt. b.

The reason to modify is to give effect to the settlor's intent had the circumstances in question been anticipated. Id. cmt. a. Courts will not ordinarily deviate from the provisions outlined by the trust creator but they undoubtedly have the power to do so, if it is reasonably necessary to effectuate the trust's *primary* purpose. Niemann, 113 P.3d at 471. . . .

In this case, the trial court did not issue formal factual findings, but it stated in the oral ruling that there was a showing of a changed circumstance in this case. This meets the first prong. The settlor's intent is also a factual question. The trial court found in its oral ruling that the "stated" purpose of the trust is to provide for the beneficiaries' education, support, maintenance, and medical care. Thus, it found that this trust's primary purpose was to provide for Nancy during her lifetime. Because the trust was to terminate at age thirty-five, it was also the settlors' intent that Nancy have the money to dispose of as she saw fit, which would include any estate planning that she might choose to do.

There is no question that changed circumstances have intervened to frustrate the settlors' intent. Nancy's grandparents intended that she have the funds to use as she saw fit. Not only is Nancy unable to manage the funds or to pass them to her son, but there is a great likelihood that the funds will be lost to the State for her medical care. It is clear that the settlors would have wanted a different result.

In 1993, as part of the Omnibus Budget Reconciliation Act, Congress set forth a requirement for creating special needs trusts (or supplemental trusts), intended to care for the needs of persons with disabilities and preserve government benefits eligibility while allowing families to provide for the supplemental needs of a disabled person that government assistance does not provide. The Act exempted certain assets from those assets and resources counted for the purposes of determining an individual's eligibility for government assistance. Pub. L. 103-66, §13611(b), codified at 42 U.S.C. §1396p(d)(4)(A). A supplemental needs trust is a trust that is established for the disabled person's benefit and that is intended to supplement public benefits without increasing countable assets and resources so as to disqualify the individual from public benefits.

In this case, the trial court was concerned with fashioning a trust for Nancy that would allow the family to shield itself for "reimbursing the State" for the costs of her medical care due to her disability. But in 1993, Congress permitted the creation of special needs trusts in order to allow disabled persons to continue to receive governmental assistance for their medical care. Special needs trusts were created in order to allow disabled persons to continue receiving governmental assistance for their medical care, while allowing extra funds for assistance the government did not provide. Given this legal backdrop, the trial court should not have considered any loss to the State in determining whether an equitable deviation is allowed. The law invites, rather than discourages, the creation of special needs trusts in just this sort of situation. The proper focus is on the settlors' intent, the changed circumstances, and what is equitable for these beneficiaries.

George and Irene both died without creating a special needs trust but did not know of Nancy's mental health issues or how they might best be addressed. They clearly intended to establish a trust to provide for their grandchildren's general support, not solely for extraordinary and unanticipated medical bills.

A special needs trust may be established by a third party or by the disabled person that would be benefited by the trust. Trusts established or funded by the disabled person are subject to 42 U.S.C. §1396p(d)(4)(A), which entitles the State to receive all remaining trust amounts upon trust termination for medical assistance paid on behalf of the disabled beneficiary. However, the State is not entitled to receive payback upon termination of a third party special needs trust for medical assistance provided for the disabled beneficiary. Here, the trust was established and funded by George and Irene Riddell for the beneficiary Nancy Dexter. It is a third party special needs trust. The trust is not subject to State assistance payback and is not required to have a payback provision.

We remand to the trial court to reconsider this matter and to order such equitable deviation as is consistent with the settlors' intent in light of changed circumstances.

QUESTIONS, PROBLEM, AND NOTES

1. Should a trustee who is or should be aware of circumstances justifying modification have a duty to petition the court? Put more directly, if Ralph had not petitioned for modification, would he have been in breach of duty to Nancy? See Restatement (Third) of Trusts §66(2), cmt. e (2003).

2. In 1950, *T* devised a fund worth $120,000 in trust to *X* to pay *A* and *B* each $100 per month for their lives and then to pay the remainder to a charity, *C*. In 2001, observing that the trust corpus had grown to $3.5 million and arguing that this growth was an unanticipated change in circumstances, *A*, *B*, and *C* petitioned jointly for an order terminating the trust and directing the trustee to pay $150,000 each to *A* and *B* and the $3.2 million balance to *C*. What result under traditional law? What result under UTC §412, page 645? See Estate of Somers, 89 P.3d 898 (Kan. 2004).

3. By making modification more freely available, will the extension of equitable deviation to distributive provisions dissuade potential settlors from establishing a trust in the first place? Does your analysis depend on whether the court's power to modify is limited, as under UTC §412(a), to effecting the settlor's probable intent in view of changed circumstances? See also Restatement (Third) of Trusts, supra, §66, cmt. a, which provides: "The objective is to give effect to what the settlor's intent probably would have been had the circumstances in question been anticipated."

Although modification of an administrative or dispositive term under paragraph (a) of UTC §412 must accord with the settlor's probable intent, deviation from an administrative term that has become "wasteful" under paragraph (b) is not so limited. But what counts as waste? Compare the statement of *cy pres* for charitable trusts in UTC §413, discussed at page 763, which adds "wasteful" to the traditional grounds for cy pres of illegality, impracticability, and impossibility.

4. *Combination and division of trusts; uneconomic trusts.* In *Riddell*, the court consolidated several similar trusts. The usual reason for consolidation is efficiency. Combining multiple related trusts can eliminate redundant costs and achieve efficiencies in investment. The mirror-image scenario is presented by the division of a trust into one or more separate trusts. Division may be sensible if the trust's beneficiaries have different tax or investment considerations or the number of beneficiaries makes administration of the trust unwieldy. Well-drafted trusts typically include provisions that authorize the trustee to combine or divide. Nonjudicial combination and division is also expressly authorized by statute in some states, Restatement (Third) of Trusts, supra, §68, and UTC §417.

In a similar vein, statutes in many states, Restatement (Third) of Trusts, supra, §66, cmt. d, and UTC §414 (2000), authorize the termination of a trust if its value has declined such that continued operation of the trust no longer makes economic sense.

5. *Drafting advice.* With the passage of time there often will be changes in the named beneficiaries' needs and abilities, in the tax laws, and in different types of investment opportunities. When you are drafting a trust that is to last well into the future, you should consider giving a beneficiary or an independent third party — sometimes called a *trust protector* (see below) — the power to modify or terminate the trust. See Jeffrey N. Pennell, Wealth Transfer Planning and Drafting ch. 4, at 2-6 (2005).

6. *Decanting.* If the trustee has a discretionary power to distribute the trust corpus for the benefit of the beneficiary, or if a third party has such a power, it may be possible to exercise the power to form a new trust that has updated terms or that is subject to the laws of another state. This practice, known as *decanting* — that is, pouring over all the assets of one trust into another trust — is an increasingly popular method of freshening a trust that has become stale with the passage of time. Recently enacted statutes in Alaska, Delaware, Florida, New York, South Dakota, and Tennessee expressly validate decanting, subject to specified conditions. For further discussion, see Alan S. Halperin and Lindsay N. O'Donnell, Modifying Irrevocable Trusts: State Law and Tax Considerations in Trust Decanting, 42 Heckerling Inst. on Est. Plan. ch. 13 (2008).

7. *Mandatory law?* Extending the facts in *Pulitzer*, page 644, Professor Langbein removes the unanticipated circumstances and posits the following hypothetical:

Suppose . . . that the settlor in *Pulitzer* had foreseen and recited in the trust instrument the danger that the newspaper might become unprofitable, and he directed the trustees to continue operating it anyhow. In the actual case, the court refused to consider the possibility that a settlor of such "sagacity and business ability" could have intended "from mere vanity" to keep the newspaper operating at the expense of the trust. But suppose he had. Suppose the settlor spelled out that he foresaw the possibility that the paper would cease to be economically viable, but he wanted it maintained regardless of the impairment of the interests of the beneficiaries. [John H. Langbein, Mandatory Rules in the Law of Trusts, 98 Nw. U. L. Rev. 1105, 1118-1119 (2004).]

In such a case, should the court nonetheless authorize the sale of the newspaper stock?

The broader question raised by Langbein's hypothetical is whether the settlor should be permitted to make the trust's terms immutable, that is, to opt out of the law of modification and termination. UTC §105(b)(4) provides that the settlor cannot vary the rules of trust modification and termination, including the power of the court under §412(b) to modify an administrative term that is "wasteful." We take up the related question of settlor-mandated investment directions at pages 717-720.

NOTE: REFORMATION AND MODIFICATION TO ACHIEVE TAX OBJECTIVES

Lately the courts have become increasingly receptive to petitions seeking to reform or modify a trust in order to obtain income or estate tax advantages. See Pond v. Pond, page 981. Sometimes the courts have corrected a lawyer's error in drafting the instrument that, if left uncorrected, would result in a tax inefficiency. In other cases the courts have modified the trust because an unanticipated change in circumstance has frustrated the settlor's tax objectives.

The former is an application of *reformation*, an equitable remedy that conforms the instrument to what the settlor actually intended at the time of its execution. The innovation here, discussed previously in Chapter 5 at pages 343-357, is extending the reformation concept to testamentary trusts. Reformation to correct mistakes is authorized by UTC §415 (2000); Restatement (Third) of Property: Wills and Other Donative Transfers §12.1 (2003); and Uniform Probate Code (UPC) §2-805 (2008).

In contrast, modification to achieve the settlor's probable intent in light of changed circumstances is an application of *equitable deviation*, which as we have seen has been extended to distributive provisions. Equitable deviation to achieve the settlor's probable tax objectives is specifically authorized by UTC §416; Restatement (Third) of Property, supra, §12.2; and UPC §2-806.

NOTE: TRUST PROTECTORS

Having gained increased prominence as a check on trustees in offshore trusts, the use of a trust protector is becoming more common in domestic trusts as a response to the reality that the donor of a gift cannot foresee all of the problems or opportunities that her family might face after the gift is made. Like powers of appointment (see Chapter 12), naming a trust protector and arming that person with broad powers builds flexibility into what might otherwise be a rigid trust. Thus:

Case 7. T devises property to *X*, a bank, in trust to pay the income to *A* for life and on *A*'s death to distribute the property to *A*'s descendants. *T* also names her trusted friend *P*, who lacks the skills to serve as the trustee herself, as the trust protector. *T* authorizes *P*, as trust protector: (1) to replace *X* with another corporate fiduciary; (2) to approve modifications to the trust's administrative and dispositive provisions (including increases to *A*'s lifetime share); (3) to terminate the trust; and (4) to select a successor trust protector. In so doing, *T* ensures that the trust's terms and administration can be adapted by someone familiar with *T*'s values in light of the family's evolving circumstances.

In Case 7, if *A*'s needs change or a different arrangement becomes more tax efficient, *P* can modify the trust accordingly. If *X* proves to be lackadaisical in responding to *A*'s needs or if *X* manages the trust portfolio poorly, *P* can fire *X* and replace it with another bank or trust company that promises to be more responsive. The use of trust protectors is ratified by UTC §808 (2000) and statutes in a handful of states including Alaska, Delaware (called "trust advisors"), and South Dakota.

On the other hand, adding a trust protector to the mix raises potential issues. Suppose *P* cuts a deal with *A* whereby *P* instructs *X* to increase *A*'s lifetime payments and in return *A* gives *P* a share of the increased payments. Do the remainder beneficiaries, *A*'s descendants, have a claim against *P* for breach of duty? Does *X*, as trustee, have an obligation enforceable by the remainder beneficiaries to verify the good faith of *P*'s instructions? Suppose that *P* is aware that *X* is self-dealing or otherwise in breach of the terms of the trust. Does *A* have a claim against *P* if *P* fails to exercise *P*'s power to remove *X*? As yet, there are no reported appellate cases on these and related questions, and the statutes are few and contradictory.

UTC §808(d) provides that a person who has the power to direct the trustee "is presumptively a fiduciary who, as such, is required to act in good faith with regard to the purposes of the trust and the interests of the beneficiaries." However, because this provision is not included in the schedule of mandatory rules in UTC §105, it may be overridden by the terms of the trust. Restatement (Third) of Trusts §75, cmts. c and e (2007) take the position that a trust protector is generally a fiduciary. The Alaska trust protector statute provides that a trust protector is presumptively *not* a fiduciary. Alaska Stat. §13.36.370(d) (2008). Under the Delaware statute, a trust protector is presumptively a fiduciary, but the trustee has no duty to monitor the protector or to notify the beneficiary if the trustee disagrees with the protector's judgment. Del. Code tit. 12, §3313(a), (f) (2008).

For discussion of trust protectors and the many unresolved doctrinal and policy questions surrounding their use, see Stewart E. Sterk, Trust Protectors, Agency Costs, and Fiduciary Duty, 27 Cardozo L. Rev. 2761, 2763 (2006); Alexander A. Bove, Jr., The Trust Protector: Trust(y) Watchdog or Expensive Exotic Pet?, 30 Est. Plan. 390 (2003). See also Gregory S. Alexander, Trust Protectors: Who Will Watch the Watchmen?, 27 Cardozo L. Rev. 2807 (2006), and Jeffrey Evans Stake, A Brief Comment on Trust Protectors, 27 Cardozo L. Rev. 2813 (2006) (providing commentary on Sterk's analysis), and the related discussion of *directed trusts* at page 723.

3. *Claflin and Material Purpose*

Under the *Claflin* doctrine, if continuance of the trust without modification or termination is necessary to carry out a *material purpose* of the settlor, the beneficiaries cannot compel modification or termination. The difficulty is in determining what is a material purpose of the settlor. In general, a trust cannot be terminated if it is a spendthrift trust, if the beneficiary is not to receive the principal until attaining a specified age (that is, enjoyment is postponed), if it is a discretionary trust, or if it is a trust for support of the beneficiary. Such provisions are usually deemed to state a material purpose of the settlor. Petitions to terminate a trust that provides for successive beneficial interests have proved more vexing.

In re Estate of Brown
Supreme Court of Vermont, 1987
528 A.2d 752

GIBSON, J. The trustee of a testamentary trust appeals an order of the Washington Superior Court granting the petition of the lifetime and residual beneficiaries of the trust to terminate it and to distribute the proceeds to the life tenants. We reverse.

The primary issue raised on appeal is whether any material purpose of the trust remains to be accomplished, thus barring its termination. The appellant/trustee also raises the closely related issue of whether all beneficiaries are before the court, i.e., whether the class of beneficiaries has closed.

Andrew J. Brown died in 1977, settling his entire estate in a trust, all of which is held by the trustee under terms and conditions that are the subject of this appeal. The relevant portion of the trust instrument provides:

> (3) The . . . trust . . . shall be used to provide an education, particularly a college education, for the children of my nephew, Woolson S. Brown. My Trustee is hereby directed to use the income from said trust and such part of the principal as may be necessary to accomplish this purpose. Said trust to continue for said purpose until the last child has received his or her education and the Trustee, in its discretion, has determined that the purpose hereof has been accomplished.
>
> At such time as this purpose has been accomplished and the Trustee has so determined, *the income from said trust and such part of the principal as may be necessary shall be used by said Trustee for the care, maintenance and welfare of my nephew, Woolson S. Brown and his wife, Rosemary Brown, so that they may live in the style and manner to which they are accustomed, for and during the remainder of their natural lives.* Upon their demise, any remainder of said trust, together with any accumulation thereon, shall be paid to their then living children in equal shares, share and share alike. (Emphasis added.)

The trustee complied with the terms of the trust by using the proceeds to pay for the education of the children of Woolson and Rosemary Brown. After he determined that the education of these children was completed, the trustee began distribution of trust income to the lifetime beneficiaries, Woolson and Rosemary.

On June 17, 1983, the lifetime beneficiaries petitioned the probate court for termination of the trust, arguing that the sole remaining purpose of the trust was to maintain their lifestyle and that distribution of the remaining assets was necessary to accomplish this purpose. The remaindermen, the children of the lifetime beneficiaries, filed consents to the proposed termination. The probate court denied the petition to terminate, and the petitioners appealed to the Washington Superior Court. The superior court reversed, concluding that continuation of the trust was no longer necessary because the only material purpose, the education of the children, had been accomplished. This appeal by the trustee followed. . . .

An active trust may not be terminated, even with the consent of all the beneficiaries, if a material purpose of the settlor remains to be accomplished. Restatement (Second) of Trusts §337 (1959). This Court has invoked a corollary of this rule in a case where partial termination of a trust was at issue. In re Bayley Trust, 250 A.2d 516, 519 (Vt. 1969).

As a threshold matter, we reject the trustee's argument that the trust cannot be terminated because it is both a support trust and a spendthrift trust. It is true that, were either of these forms of trust involved, termination could not be compelled by the beneficiaries because a material purpose of the settlor would remain unsatisfied. See Restatement (Second) of Trusts §337.

The trust at issue does not qualify as a support trust. A support trust is created where the trustee is directed to use trust income or principal for the benefit of an individual, but only to the extent necessary to support the individual. 2 A. Scott, Scott on Trusts §154, at 1176; G. Bogert, Trusts and Trustees §229, at 519 (2d ed. rev. 1979). Here, the terms of the trust provide that, when the educational purpose of the trust has been accomplished and the trustee, in his discretion, has so determined, "the income . . . and such part of the principal as may be necessary shall be used by said Trustee for the care, maintenance and welfare of . . . [Rosemary and Woolson Brown] so that they may live in the style and manner to which they are accustomed. . . ." The trustee has, in fact, made the determination that the educational purpose has been accomplished and has begun to transfer the income of the trust to the lifetime beneficiaries. Because the trustee must, at the very least, pay all of the trust income to beneficiaries Rosemary and Woolson Brown, the trust cannot be characterized as a support trust.

Nor is this a spendthrift trust. "A trust in which by the terms of the trust or by statute a *valid restraint on the voluntary and involuntary transfer of the interest* of the beneficiary is imposed is a spendthrift trust." Restatement (Second) of Trusts §152(2). (Emphasis added.) While no specific language is needed to create a spendthrift trust, id. at Comment c, here the terms of the trust instrument do not manifest Andrew J. Brown's intention to create such a trust. . . .

Although the issue as to whether a material purpose of the trust remains cannot be answered through resort to the foregoing formal categories traditionally imposed upon trust instruments, we hold that termination cannot be compelled here because a material purpose of the settlor remains unaccomplished. In the interpretation of trusts, the intent of the settlor, as revealed by the language of the instrument, is determinative. In re Jones, 415 A.2d 202, 205 (Vt. 1980).

We find that the trust instrument at hand has two purposes. First, the trust provides for the education of the children of Woolson and Rosemary Brown. The Washington Superior Court found that Rosemary Brown was incapable of having more children and that the chance of Woolson Brown fathering more children was remote; on this basis, the court concluded that the educational purpose of the trust had been achieved.

The settlor also intended a second purpose, however: the assurance of a life-long income for the beneficiaries through the management and discretion of the trustee. We recognize that, had the trust merely provided for successive beneficiaries, no inference could be drawn that the settlor intended to deprive the beneficiaries of the right to manage the trust property during the period of the trust. Estate of Weeks, 402 A.2d 657, 658 (Pa. 1979) (quoting Restatement (Second) of Trusts §337 Comment f). Here, however, the language of the instrument does more than create successive gifts. The settlor provided that the trustee must provide for the "care, maintenance and welfare" of the lifetime beneficiaries "so that they may live in the style and manner to which they are accustomed, *for and during the remainder of their natural lives*." (Emphasis added.) The trustee must use all of the income and such part of the principal as is necessary for this purpose. We believe that the settlor's intention to assure a life-long income to Woolson and Rosemary Brown would be defeated if termination of the trust were allowed. . . .

Because of our holding regarding the second and continuing material purpose of the trust, we do not reach the question of whether the trial court erred in holding that the educational purpose of the trust has been accomplished.

Reversed; judgment for petitioners vacated and judgment for appellant entered.

QUESTIONS AND NOTE

1.   Because all trusts interpose a trustee between the beneficiary and the trust fund, would not the early termination of any trust offend the settlor's material purpose under the reasoning in *Brown*? If not, what precisely is the material purpose that would have been offended by early termination?

2.   The Scott treatise summarizes the cases as follows:

In the . . . typical case in which the trust has multiple, successive beneficiaries, it can be . . . difficult to determine whether early termination would defeat a material trust purpose. The cases indicate that if the settlor's only purpose in creating the trust was to preserve the trust principal during the life of an income beneficiary, for eventual enjoyment by a remainder beneficiary, early termination ordinarily does not defeat a material trust purpose. In contrast, the cases also indicate that, if the settlor intended to protect the life beneficiary against his or her own mismanagement, termination before the life beneficiary's death would defeat a material trust purpose. Whether this, or any other material purpose, was among the settlor's purposes in creating the trust is, of course, a question of interpretation of the trust instrument, in light of all the circumstances. [5 Austin Wakeman Scott, William Franklin Fratcher, and Mark L. Ascher, Scott and Ascher on Trusts §34.1, at 2207 (5th ed. 2008).]

Is it clear that the settlor in *Brown* did not want Woolson and Rosemary to have managerial control over the trust property? Because the trust did not contain a spendthrift limitation, Woolson and Rosemary could have sold their interests in the trust to another in return for a lump-sum payment. They also could have assigned their interests to their children. If they had done so, could the children have terminated the trust?

———————————

Just as the law of deviation has been liberalized in recent years, so too has the *Claflin* doctrine. Statutes in several states have relaxed the conditions under which a trust may be modified by request of the beneficiaries. Some of these statutes weaken the material purpose limitation. Others authorize modification or termination by consent of only some of the beneficiaries. Both Restatement (Third) of Trusts §65 (2003) and Uniform Trust Code §411 (2000, rev. 2004) follow the new liberalizing trend, though the rules stated under each differ in several important respects.

Restatement (Third) of Trusts (2003)

§65. TERMINATION OR MODIFICATION BY CONSENT OF BENEFICIARIES

(1) Except as stated in Subsection (2), if all of the beneficiaries of an irrevocable trust consent, they can compel the termination or modification of the trust.

(2) If termination or modification of the trust under Subsection (1) would be inconsistent with a material purpose of the trust, the beneficiaries cannot compel its termination or modification except with the consent of the settlor or, after the settlor's death, with authorization of the court if it determines that the reason(s) for termination or modification outweigh the material purpose.

Uniform Trust Code (2000, as amended 2004)

§411. MODIFICATION OR TERMINATION OF NONCHARITABLE IRREVOCABLE TRUST BY CONSENT

. . . (b) A noncharitable irrevocable trust may be terminated upon consent of all of the beneficiaries if the court concludes that continuance of the trust is not necessary to achieve any material purpose of the trust. A noncharitable irrevocable trust may be modified upon consent of all of the beneficiaries if the court concludes that modification is not inconsistent with a material purpose of the trust.

[(c) A spendthrift provision in the terms of the trust is not presumed to constitute a material purpose of the trust.]

(d) Upon termination of a trust under subsection . . . (b), the trustee shall distribute the trust property as agreed by the beneficiaries.

(e) If not all of the beneficiaries consent to a proposed modification or termi-nation of the trust under subsection . . . (b), the modification or termination may be approved by the court if the court is satisfied that:

(1) if all of the beneficiaries had consented, the trust could have been modi-fied or terminated under this section; and

(2) the interests of a beneficiary who does not consent will be adequately protected.

NOTES AND QUESTIONS

1.   *The continued role of the material purpose standard.* Restatement (Third) of Trusts §65(2) follows the handful of state statutes such as Cal. Prob. Code §15403 (2008) that permit modification or termination on petition of the beneficiaries if the reason for the modification or termination outweighs any conflicting mate-rial purpose of the settlor. See Boys and Girls Club of Petaluma v. Walsh, 87 Cal. Rptr. 3d 413 (App. 2008). In contrast, UTC §411(b) hews closer to the traditional *Claflin* doctrine, preserving the material purpose threshold.

In the introduction to this section, we suggested that the English law of modi-fication and termination of trusts is very different from the law in this country. If the Restatement's balancing test takes hold, will this remain true? Notice that under the balancing test it is still necessary to determine the settlor's purpose and whether that purpose is material. To that end, the Restatement advises:

> Material purposes are not readily to be inferred. A finding of such a purpose generally requires some showing of a particular concern or objective on the part of the settlor, such as concern with regard to a beneficiary's management skills, judgment, or level of maturity. Thus, a court may look for some circumstantial or other evidence indicating that the trust arrangement represented to the settlor more than a method of allocating the benefits of property among multiple intended beneficiaries, or a means of offering to the beneficiaries (but not imposing on them) a particular advantage. Sometimes, of course, the very nature or design of a trust suggests its protective nature or some other material purpose. [Restatement (Third) of Trusts, supra, §65, cmt. d.]

The Restatement goes on to take the position that the "mere fact that the set-tlor has created a trust for successive beneficiaries does not prevent the benefi-ciaries from terminating or modifying the trust to reallocate the beneficial interests among themselves if they wish to do so." Id. Would *Brown* be decided dif-ferently under the new Restatement?

2.   *Spendthrift trusts and material purpose.* Contrary to existing case law, both Restatement (Third) of Trusts §65, cmt. e and UTC §411(c) provide that the exist-ence of a spendthrift clause is *not* presumed to constitute a material purpose of the trust. Rather, in the words of the Restatement, a spendthrift clause "may sup-ply some indication that the settlor had a material purpose — a protective purpose — that would be inconsistent with allowing" modification or termina-tion, but the clause, by itself, is not sufficient to establish a material purpose. The drafters of the UTC and the Restatement justified this reform on the

grounds that the existence of a spendthrift clause often reflects rote duplication of formbook language, not a considered judgment by the settlor. In 2004, however, the Uniform Law Commission put §411(c) in brackets, signaling that uniformity is unnecessary or cannot be achieved, in response to the provision's chilly reception by the state legislatures. Several enacting jurisdictions deleted the provision or reversed the presumption so that a spendthrift clause would be assumed to state a material purpose.

3. *Unanimity of the beneficiaries.* UTC §411(e) provides a mechanism for obtaining modification or termination by consent of only *some* of the beneficiaries, provided that the "interests of a beneficiary who does not consent will be adequately protected." By contrast, Restatement (Third) of Trusts §65, cmt. b takes the position that consent must be obtained from or on behalf of *all* the potential beneficiaries.

4. *Literature.* For further examination of trends in modification and termination of private trusts, see Alan Newman, The Intention of the Settlor Under the Uniform Trust Code: Whose Property Is It, Anyway?, 39 Akron L. Rev. 649, 657-669 (2005); Ronald Chester, Modification and Termination of Trusts in the 21st Century: The Uniform Trust Code Leads a Quiet Revolution, 35 Real Prop., Prob. & Tr. J. 697 (2001); Julia C. Walker, Get Your Dead Hands Off Me: Beneficiaries' Right to Terminate or Modify a Trust Under the Uniform Trust Code, 67 Mo. L. Rev. 443 (2002); David M. English, The Uniform Trust Code (2000): Significant Provisions and Policy Issues, 67 Mo. L. Rev. 143, 169-176 (2002).

NOTE: REVOCABLE VERSUS IRREVOCABLE TRUSTS

Under traditional law a trust created by a written instrument is irrevocable unless there is an express or implied provision that the settlor reserves the power to revoke.[15] In some states, however, including California and Texas, the opposite presumption holds. A trust is revocable unless declared to be irrevocable. UTC §602(a) (2000) adopts the minority rule: "Unless the terms of a trust expressly provide that the trust is irrevocable, the settlor may revoke or amend the trust." According to Professor Langbein, the UTC approach will better satisfy expectations:

> This change will be of no practical importance in the world of professionally drafted trust instruments, because no competent drafter ever leaves that question to default law. Rather, a well-drafted trust spells out that the trust is revocable or irrevocable. Accordingly, the change made by the Code will be of importance primarily for "kitchen table trusts," that is, for instruments drafted by non-lawyers (or dreadful lawyers). In such cases, the Code's intuition is that the settlor's intention is mostly to use the trust as a will substitute, and that, accordingly, the trust was meant to be revocable. [John H. Langbein, The Uniform Trust Code: Codification of the Law of Trusts in the United States, 15 Tr. L. Intl. 66, 70 (2001).]

---

15. For bank account (Totten) trusts, the presumption is reversed: Revocability is presumed. See page 435.

Restatement (Third) of Trusts §63, cmt. c (2003) states a fuzzier rule: An inter vivos trust is presumed to be revocable if the settlor retains an interest in the trust property such as a power of withdrawal, but is otherwise presumed to be irrevocable.

A related question is whether a revocable trust, particularly when used as a will substitute, can be revoked by will. Unless the terms of the trust so provide, the traditional answer is No. UTC §602(c)(2)(A) reverses this rule on the grounds that doing so better comports with expectations. In cases where "the terms of the trust do not provide a method or the method provided in the terms is not expressly made exclusive," revocation is permitted by "a later will or codicil that expressly refers to the trust or specifically devises property that would otherwise have passed according to the terms of the trust." See also Restatement (Third) of Trusts, supra, §63, cmt. h, to similar effect, and Restatement (Third) of Property: Wills and Other Donative Transfers §7.2, cmt. e (2003), which takes the position that "a revocable trust may be revoked or amended by a later will."

4.   Trustee Removal

As a technical matter, trustee removal has traditionally been viewed as a remedy for breach of trust, not a modification of the trust's terms. We nonetheless treat trustee removal here because, as with trust modification and termination, removal often presents a tension between the interests of the settlor and the interests of the beneficiary. The difficult task is to set the threshold for removal high enough that the trustee can carry out the settlor's wishes in spite of a contrary preference of one or more of the beneficiaries, but not so high that shirking or mismanagement by the trustee cannot be adequately deterred or remedied. Robert H. Sitkoff, An Agency Costs Theory of Trust Law, 89 Cornell L. Rev. 621, 663-664 (2004).

The balance struck by traditional law is to permit removal only for cause. The court may remove a trustee who is dishonest or who has engaged in a serious breach of trust, but not one who has committed a minor breach or who has a simple disagreement with the beneficiary. Trustees who were chosen by the settlor, as compared to those named by a court, are even less readily removed — there is something of a thumb on the scale for them. If the settlor was aware of an asserted ground for removal at the time of naming the trustee, that ground will not serve as a basis for the later removal of the trustee unless the trustee is entirely unfit to serve. 2 Austin Wakeman Scott, William Franklin Fratcher, and Mark L. Ascher, Scott and Ascher on Trusts §§11.10, 11.10.1 (5th ed. 2006). Accordingly, even if the beneficiary is dissatisfied with the performance of the trustee or believes that another trustee will better manage the trust, the court will not normally replace the trustee unless the trustee is guilty of a serious breach of trust or is shown to be unfit to serve.

Some have argued that the inability of beneficiaries to change trustees lessens competition among trust companies, contributes to higher trustees' fees, and leads to a cautious, even indifferent, style of trust management. Proponents of freer trustee removal also point to the proliferation of bank mergers and acquisitions, which sometimes causes a new trust officer, one unknown to the settlor and unfamiliar with the beneficiaries, to be assigned to the trust.

Today, well-drafted trusts often include a provision that overrides the default law of trustee removal by providing a mechanism for the beneficiaries to remove the trustee so long as the replacement is a corporate trustee independent of the beneficiaries. A power to remove and replace the trustee can also be retained by the settlor (subject to tax considerations) or given to a third party (sometimes called a *trust protector*, see page 651). The question thus arises, should the default law of trustee removal be reformed to match the terms that are regularly included in professionally drafted trusts?

Uniform Trust Code (2000)

§706.   REMOVAL OF TRUSTEE

(a) The settlor, a cotrustee, or a beneficiary may request the court to remove a trustee, or a trustee may be removed by the court on its own initiative.

(b) The court may remove a trustee if:

(1) the trustee has committed a serious breach of trust;

(2) lack of cooperation among cotrustees substantially impairs the administration of the trust;

(3) because of unfitness, unwillingness, or persistent failure of the trustee to administer the trust effectively, the court determines that removal of the trustee best serves the interests of the beneficiaries; or

(4) there has been a substantial change of circumstances or removal is requested by all of the qualified beneficiaries, the court finds that removal of the trustee best serves the interests of all of the beneficiaries and is not inconsistent with a material purpose of the trust, and a suitable cotrustee or successor trustee is available.

(c) Pending a final decision on a request to remove a trustee, or in lieu of or in addition to removing a trustee, the court may order such appropriate relief under Section 1001(b) as may be necessary to protect the trust property or the interests of the beneficiaries.

Davis v. U.S. Bank National Association
Missouri Court of Appeals, 2007
243 S.W.3d 425

SULLIVAN, J.   U.S. Bank National Association (Appellant) appeals from the trial court's summary judgment in favor of Harold A. Davis (Respondent). We affirm.

FACTUAL AND PROCEDURAL BACKGROUND

On May 3, 1967, Respondent's grandfather, Lorenz K. Ayers (Ayers), now deceased, executed a Living Trust Agreement (the Trust), pursuant to which Ayers appointed himself and Mercantile Trust Company, National Association (Mercantile), as Co-Trustees. On December 26, 1972, Ayers executed a Trust Indenture, pursuant to which Ayers appointed Mercantile as the Trustee[16] and Respondent as the income beneficiary of the Trust, entitled to receive the entire net income of the Trust for life. Upon Respondent's death, the principal of the Trust is to be divided among Respondent's then living children in equal shares and distributed to each child (in trust if under the age of 21 and "outright" if 21). Respondent currently has two children, Dillon A. Davis (Son) and Marguerite S. Davis (Daughter). The Trust provides that if Respondent has no surviving children upon his death, Respondent's share of the Trust "shall pass to his or her heirs at law who are direct descendants of [Ayers]." In the event that there are no heirs at law who are direct descendants of Ayers at the time of Respondent's death, the principal passes free of trust to Lafayette College, Easton, Pennsylvania.

On May 15, 2006, Respondent filed a petition (the Petition) . . . seeking the removal of Appellant as Trustee, the appointment of U.S. Trust Company of Delaware (UST) as successor Trustee, and an order transferring the Trust assets to UST. . . .

After hearing arguments . . . the circuit court [granted Respondent's Motion for Summary Judgment and] . . . ordered the removal of Appellant as Trustee and appointed UST as successor Trustee of the Trust. This appeal follows. . . .

DISCUSSION

In 2004, the General Assembly enacted [the Missouri Uniform Trust Code], effective January 1, 2005. . . . Relevant to our discussion is Section 456.7-706.2(4) [based on UTC §706(b)(4)], which provides for the removal of a trustee without any showing of wrongdoing by the trustee:

> . . . The court may remove a trustee if: . . .
> (4) . . . removal is requested by all of the qualified beneficiaries and in either such case the party seeking removal establishes to the court that:
> (a) removal of the trustee best serves the interests of all of the beneficiaries;
> (b) removal of the trustee is not inconsistent with a material purpose of the trust; and
> (c) a suitable cotrustee or successor trustee is available and willing to serve.

In the instant case, Respondent's petition and motion for summary judgment alleged that all four elements of Section 456.7-706.2(4) were satisfied: the "qualified beneficiaries" of the Trust, as defined by Section 456.1-103(20) are Respondent, Son and Daughter; UST is available and willing to serve as successor

---

16. Appellant is the successor by merger to Mercantile, and has been the sole current Trustee of the 1967 Trust and the 1972 Trust since 2001.

corporate Trustee; removal of Appellant as Trustee was not inconsistent with a material purpose of the Trust; UST will charge lower fees and allow an independent investment adviser which is in the best interests of the beneficiaries; Respondent is a resident of Pennsylvania, and lives within a thirty-minute drive to UST and the investment advisor; Appellant is located in Missouri; [and] the proposed investment advisor has a complete understanding of Respondent and his family's unique personal financial situation and how the Trust co-ordinates with his family's financial objectives . . . .

In its Memorandum in Opposition to Respondent's Motion for Summary Judgment, Appellant maintained that a conflict of interest existed between Respondent and Son and Daughter . . . and therefore, Respondent could not represent the interests of Son and Daughter pursuant to Section 456.3-303; Respondent had failed to name necessary and indispensable parties to the lawsuit; Respondent had failed to show removal of the Trustee would best serve the interests of the beneficiaries; removal of the Trustee would be inconsistent with a material purpose of the Trust; and Respondent's Motion for Summary Judgment was premature as discovery was needed. . . .

POINT I

In its first point [on appeal], Appellant asserts that Respondent's failure to join all of the remainder beneficiaries of the Trust as parties to his lawsuit deprived the court of subject matter jurisdiction. This assertion is incorrect. Section 456.7-706.2(4) only requires that "qualified beneficiaries" be joined in an action to remove a trustee. . . . [Under Section 456.1-103(2), based on UTC §103(13), the term "qualified beneficiary"]

> means a beneficiary who, on the date the beneficiary's qualification is determined:
>   (a) is a permissible distributee;
>   (b) would be a permissible distributee if the interests of the permissible distributees described in paragraph (a) of this subdivision terminated on that date; or
>   (c) would be a permissible distributee if the trust terminated on that date. . . .

Respondent and Son and Daughter are the permissible distributees if Respondent's interest or the Trust terminated at the time of the filing of this suit. As such, Respondent and Son and Daughter are all of the qualified beneficiaries of the Trust. The remote remainder beneficiaries of the Trust are not qualified beneficiaries. All of the qualified beneficiaries were before the Court and therefore, all of the necessary parties were before the court. . . .

POINT II

In its second point, Appellant alleges that Respondent could not virtually represent Son and Daughter under Section 456.3-303(4).[17] We disagree. . . .

---

17. Section 456.3-303(4), which is based on UTC §303(6), provides: "To the extent there is no conflict of interest between the representative and the person represented or among those being represented with

In the instant case, Respondent and Son and Daughter have substantially identical interests which are not in conflict with regard to removing Appellant as Trustee and implementing UST as Trustee. UST is within a thirty-minute drive of Respondent and Son and Daughter's house; changing the domicile of the Trust to Delaware would avoid out of state income tax being paid on Trust income; UST has a complete understanding of Respondent and his family's unique personal financial situation; and UST will charge lower fees than Appellant. . . .

Appellant maintains that there is an inherent conflict of interest between income beneficiaries and residual beneficiaries. However, this assertion has no basis in Missouri law. Further, Section 456.3-303(4) requires any conflict of interest to be "with respect to a particular question or dispute." As such, the determination as to the existence of a conflict of interest is undertaken on a case by case basis. In this case, we have found none, and Appellant has not shown us otherwise.

Accordingly, we find that Respondent demonstrated that there is no conflict of interest between himself and Son and Daughter with regard to changing the Trustee, and thus he could virtually represent them in doing so. Appellant presented no facts putting this issue into dispute. . . .

POINT III

In its third point, Appellant maintains that there remain issues of fact as to whether or not removing the Trustee is in the best interests of all of the beneficiaries. Appellant claims that it presented facts in opposition to Respondent's summary judgment motion which called into question the validity of the reduced trustee fee which Respondent claimed would be achieved by Appellant's removal and replacement with UST.

In conjunction with his motion for summary judgment, Respondent submitted the affidavit of investment advisor Daniel M. McDermott, President of McDermott Advisory Group, LLC (McDermott). McDermott's affidavit includes the numbers he used to calculate all of Appellant's fees and the numbers used to calculate UST's fees and the investment management fees. His affidavit demonstrates how he calculated the annual savings of $10,259.55 by switching from Appellant to UST, resulting from a fee that is 23.94% lower than that being charged by Appellant, and the information on which such calculations were based. The documents reflecting the numbers he used in his calculation are attached to his affidavit. [A bank officer] testified by affidavit that he had reviewed McDermott's calculations and that McDermott's calculations accurately reflect the published fee schedule of UST and that the fees were properly applied in the calculation. Appellant did not dispute the numbers presented by McDermott, but rather merely criticized them as hearsay and speculative. However, Respondent

---

respect to a particular question or dispute . . . a parent may represent and bind the parent's minor or unborn child if a conservator, conservator ad litem, or guardian for the child has not been appointed." — Eds.

presented documentary evidence in the form of published rates of the fees as currently charged. Under the statute, Respondent merely has to show that the change in Trustee somehow inured to his and the other beneficiaries' benefit. . . .

Appellant claims that the change in trustee is inconsistent with the material purpose of the Trust as the Trust clearly did not contemplate the change, but does contemplate keeping the same Trustee in the same state. Not only does this argument speculate as to what the Trust "contemplates" without any evidentiary support, but it is also irrelevant, because the statutory scheme provides for the change of Trustee as long as the terms of the Trust do not prohibit it, and the terms of the Trust in this case do not. See Section 456.7-706.2(4)(b). . . .

Respondent presented factually supported reasons why it would be beneficial to him and Son and Daughter to remove the present Trustee in lieu of UST and Appellant does not put any of those reasons into dispute. Nor does Appellant present us with any additional fact issues. Therefore, there are no remaining disputed factual matters into which Appellant is entitled to conduct more discovery. Additionally, Appellant presents no evidentiary support for its argument that its removal as Trustee is inconsistent with a material purpose of the trust. . . .

CONCLUSION

The trial court's judgment is affirmed.

NOTES, QUESTIONS, AND PROBLEM

1. In *Davis*, the court removed the trustee on the basis of the "removal is requested by all of the qualified beneficiaries" clause of UTC §706(b)(4). Under that provision the question is "whether there is another entity that, for some reason, may perform better or provide different and more desirable benefits as administrator, or is otherwise better suited to serve as fiduciary for a particular trust." In re Fleet Natl. Bank's Appeal from Prob., 837 A.2d 785, 796-797 (Conn. 2004). In authorizing removal without a showing of wrongdoing or even mediocre performance, does the UTC tip the balance too far in favor of the beneficiaries? Is the requirement that removal not be "inconsistent with a material purpose of the settlor" enough to protect the settlor's intent?

UTC §706(b)(4) also authorizes removal on the basis of "a substantial change of circumstances." Might removal have been available in *Davis* on the grounds that the current trustee was the successor entity after a merger with the original trustee named by the settlor?

2. In addition to the removal without fault provisions of paragraph (b)(4), UTC §706 implements two other important reforms. First, paragraph (a) gives the settlor standing to petition for the trustee's removal. Under traditional law the settlor of an irrevocable trust did not have such a right. Second, paragraph (b)(3) authorizes removal for "persistent failure of the trustee to administer the

trust effectively." The official comment states that "a long-term pattern of mediocre performance, such as consistently poor investment results when compared to comparable trusts," might warrant removal under paragraph (b)(3). Professor Langbein contends that this provision responds "to the concern that under traditional law beneficiaries have had little recourse when trustee performance has been indifferent, but not so egregious as to be in breach of trust." John H. Langbein, The Uniform Trust Code: Codification of the Law of Trusts in the United States, 15 Tr. L. Intl. 66, 76 (2001).

Because UTC §706 is not included in the schedule of rules made mandatory by §105(b), it may be overridden by contrary provisions in the trust instrument. For a careful parsing of UTC §706, see Alan Newman, The Intention of the Settlor Under the Uniform Trust Code: Whose Property Is It, Anyway?, 39 Akron L. Rev. 649, 694-698 (2005).

3.   *Duties of a successor trustee. O* conveys a fund to *X* in trust, naming *Y* as the successor trustee. After *X* engages in self-dealing, the court grants the beneficiary's petition to remove *X*, and *Y* succeeds *X* as trustee. The beneficiary then discovers that *X* had also imprudently managed the trust portfolio. Can the beneficiary hold *Y* liable for *X*'s imprudence? The answer is No. A successor trustee is not personally liable to the beneficiary for a breach by a prior trustee unless the successor trustee unreasonably failed to discover and rectify the prior breach. Thus, *Y* might be held liable if she continued *X*'s imprudent investment practices or if, without good cause, she failed to pursue a viable claim against *X* for *X*'s breaches. However, *Y*'s liability in such a case would arise out of *Y*'s independent breach in unreasonably failing to remedy *X*'s prior blunders. See 4 Austin Wakeman Scott, William Franklin Fratcher, and Mark L. Ascher, Scott and Ascher on Trusts §24.28 (5th ed. 2007).

4.   For thoughtful examinations of contemporary issues in trustee removal, see Newman, supra; Gayle B. Wilhelm, Changing Horses: Some Thoughts About Removal of Trustees, 18 Quinnipiac Prob. L.J. 273 (2005); Ronald Chester and Sarah Reid Ziomek, Removal of Corporate Trustees Under the Uniform Trust Code and Other Current Law: Does a Contractual Lense Help Clarify the Rights of Beneficiaries?, 67 Mo. L. Rev. 241 (2002).

NOTE: VIRTUAL REPRESENTATION

Trusts and estates litigation often involves the interests of one or more minor, unborn, or unascertained beneficiaries. The question thus arises, how are the interests of such a beneficiary to be protected? As we have seen (see Note 3 at page 252), in some circumstances the court will appoint a guardian ad litem to protect those interests. An alternative approach is *virtual representation* by a party with similar interests. UTC §304 (2000) provides: "Unless otherwise represented, a minor, incapacitated, or unborn individual, or a person whose identity or location is unknown and not reasonably ascertainable, may be represented by and bound by another having a substantially identical interest with respect to the particular question or dispute, but only to the extent there is no conflict of interest between the representative and the person represented."

The UTC extends the concept of virtual representation, which may be traced back to eighteenth century England, in two important ways. First, the UTC allows for representation not only in judicial proceedings but also in obtaining consent of the beneficiaries without judicial involvement. Hence, the UTC authorizes representation not only in litigation but also in transactions. Second, UTC §303, the Missouri version of which was at issue in *Davis*, allows a parent to represent a minor or unborn child, even if the parent does not have a similar personal interest, so long as there is no conflict of interest between the parent and the child "with respect to [the] particular question or dispute."

For further discussion of the history of virtual representation and its operation under the UTC, see Martin D. Begleiter, Serve the Cheerleader — Serve the World: An Analysis of Representation in Estate and Trust Proceedings and Under the Uniform Trust Code and Other Modern Trust Codes, 43 Real Prop., Tr. & Est. L.J. 311 (2008).

10

TRUST ADMINISTRATION:
THE FIDUCIARY OBLIGATION

> [T]he normal private trust is essentially a gift, projected on the plane
> of time and so subjected to a management regime.
>
> BERNARD RUDDEN
> *in 44 Mod. L. Rev. 610 (1981) (book review)*

SECTION A.   INTRODUCTION

A donor cannot foresee all of the problems or opportunities that her family might
face after a gift is made. And if the donor makes her gift outright, she cannot be
certain that the beneficiary will use the property as the donor intended. The use
of a trust ameliorates these problems by interposing a trustee between the beneficiary and the property. Perhaps the beneficiary is disabled or has special needs,
or is very young, or is very old, or is feckless or profligate, or lacks skills in property management. Or perhaps the settlor wants to ensure professional management of the family fortune given the possibility that a future beneficiary might be
incapable of responsibly managing property. (And note also that we have not yet
mentioned the various tax reasons for using trusts.) The crucial point, to borrow
the words of the Scott treatise, is that the trust makes it "possible to separate the
benefits of ownership from the burdens of ownership." 1 Austin Wakeman Scott,
William Franklin Fratcher, and Mark L. Ascher, Scott and Ascher on Trusts §1, at
4 (5th ed. 2006).

This virtue, however, can also be a vice. If the trust property is invested wisely
and produces handsome returns, the beneficiary, not the trustee, reaps most of
the gains. And if the trust property is invested poorly or is stolen by the trustee or
others, the beneficiary, not the trustee, suffers the immediate consequences of the

depletion in the trust fund. Putting aside reputational concerns and feelings of moral obligation (which is not to say that these considerations are unimportant), the problem is that the trustee lacks a direct financial incentive to act with loyalty and care in administering the trust fund. The primary doctrinal answer to this problem, which is the focus of this chapter, is the *fiduciary obligation*. The fiduciary obligation in trust law comprises duties of *loyalty*, *prudence*, and a host of *subsidiary rules* that reinforce the duties of loyalty and prudence.

John H. Langbein, Rise of the Management Trust
Tr. & Est., Oct. 2004, at 52

From Conveyancing to Financial Management

The trust first developed for an age in which real estate was the principal form of wealth. We can trace the Lord Chancellor enforcing trusts (then called "uses") as far back as the 14th century. Until the later 17th century, the owner of freehold land was not allowed to pass the land by will and, thus, on the owner's death, the land had to descend by intestacy. The trust was a conveyancing device that defeated both the rigidities of intestacy (which still included primogeniture) and the burdensome taxes (called feudal incidents) that pertained when land passed on intestacy. The owner of land (the settlor) transferred the land to trustees to hold for the settlor for life and, on his death, to transfer the land to those survivors and in those shares specified in the terms of the trust. Then, as now, the trust served as a will substitute. In this way, landowners could use the trust "to make decent provision for their wives, daughters, and younger sons and to prevent escheat (when the landholder was not survived by descendants)." . . .

Today's trust has ceased to be a conveyancing device for land and has become, instead, a management device for holding a portfolio of financial assets. The management trust is a response to the radical change away from family real estate as the dominant form of personal wealth. As the jurist Roscoe Pound observed in an arresting epigram, "Wealth in a commercial age is made up largely of promises." Most modern wealth takes the form of financial assets: equities, bonds, mutual fund shares, insurance contracts, pension and annuity interests, and bank accounts. Today's trust typically holds a portfolio of these complex financial assets, which are contract rights against the issuers. Such a portfolio requires skilled and active management. Investment decisions must be made and monitored, the portfolio rebalanced and proxies voted. Unusual assets, such as close corporation or partnership interests, commonly require even more active and specialized administration. By contrast, under the old conveyancing trust that held ancestral land, the beneficiaries commonly lived on the land and managed it. The trustees were, in truth, more stakeholders than managers; they were, in effect, nominees, with no serious powers or duties.

FROM AMATEUR TO PROFESSIONAL TRUSTEESHIP

The transformation in the nature of wealth that led to the management trust brought about a parallel transformation in trusteeship.

Trustees of old were unpaid amateurs, that is, family and community statesmen who lent their names and honor to a conveyancing dodge. Writing in the last years of the 19th century, the great legal scholar Frederic W. Maitland could still observe that "[a]lmost every well-to-do-man was a trustee."

Private trustees still abound, but the prototypical modern trustee is the fee-paid professional whose business is to enter into and carry out trust agreements. These entities thrive on their expertise in investment management, trust accounting, taxation, regulation and fiduciary administration. . . .

OVERCOMING TRUSTEE DISEMPOWERMENT

Another profound transformation that was essential to bring about the modern management trust was a reorientation in the way trust law went about the task of protecting trust beneficiaries. Because the trustee nominally owns the trust property, the trust relationship, by necessity, puts the beneficiaries of a trust at the peril of trustee misbehavior; a trustee could, for example, misappropriate or mismanage the trust's assets.

Protecting the beneficiary against those dangers has always been the central concern of trust law. In the early centuries of the trust, when trustees were mostly stakeholders of ancestral land, it was relatively easy to keep them in check, simply by disabling them from doing much with the trust property. Thus, trust default law deliberately supplied no trustee powers. The trustee had only those powers that the trust instrument expressly granted, which were typically few, as the trustee's job was usually just to hold and convey to the remainderpersons. Stakeholder trustees did not need to transact. . . .

Trustee disempowerment was, therefore, the original system of beneficiary safeguard in the law of trusts, and it worked well enough as long as trustees had nothing much to do beyond standing as nominee owners of family land. But when the portfolio of financial assets displaced family land as the characteristic form of family wealth held in trust, disempowerment became quite counterproductive. The modern trustee conducts a program of investing and managing financial assets that requires extensive discretion to respond to changing market forces.

Two great steps were needed to adapt trust law to the rise of the management trust: Disempowerment had to be abandoned, and a new system of beneficiary safeguard had to be devised.

Broad empowerment legislation, such as the Uniform Trustees' Powers Act (1964), is now widespread. Such statutes authorize trustees to engage in every conceivable transaction that might enhance the value of trust assets (and professionally drafted instruments commonly contain such powers). The Uniform Trust Code (2000) completes this development, reversing the common law rule and providing the trustee [in §815] with "all powers over the trust property which an unmarried competent owner has over individually owned property."

THE RISE OF FIDUCIARY LAW

Equipping trustees with transactional power was only half the job of adapting the law to the needs of the management trust. The other half was the development of a substitute system of beneficiary safeguard. Trustees with transactional power necessarily have the power to abuse as well as to advance the interests of beneficiaries. To prevent abuse, trustees were subject to duties, protective in nature, which were elaborated into a new body of law that we now recognize as trust fiduciary law.

All trust fiduciary law rests on two core principles, the care norm (the duty of prudent administration) and the loyalty norm (the duty to administer the trust for the benefit of the beneficiary). The many subrules — for example, the duties to keep and disclose records; to collect, segregate, earmark and protect trust properly; to enforce and defend claims; to be impartial among multiple beneficiaries — are all applications of prudence and loyalty.

The modern law of trust administration is so centered on fiduciary law that we tend not to remember how recently that body of law has developed. . . . [A] quick look at the classical treatises tells the story. . . . Not until treatises by Thomas Lewin (16 editions from 1837 to 1964) in England, and John N. Pomeroy (five editions, from 1881 to 1941) in the United States do we find coverage of what we now recognize as fiduciary issues, although still in a cramped fashion, somewhat as an afterthought. The success of mid-century treatises by George G. Bogert and Austin W. Scott in running Pomeroy off the American market results from their extensive coverage of the new trust law, that is, of trust fiduciary law.

To be sure, principles of trust fiduciary law can be traced well back to the 18th century. Keech v. Sandford,[1] the foundational case on what we now generalize as the duty of loyalty, was decided in 1726. The outline of early trust investment law also was articulated in the 18th and early 19th centuries. But these doctrinal impulses were not matters of great consequence until the last century or so. Only when financial assets came to displace ancestral land from the typical trust, and when empowerment triumphed over disempowerment, did trustees come routinely to exercise the levels of discretion over trust property that bring the fiduciary standards of care and loyalty into operation. As a practical matter, therefore, trust fiduciary law has been 20th-century and, now, 21st-century law.

NOTE: AGENCY COSTS AND THE FIDUCIARY OBLIGATION

Safeguarding the beneficiary against mismanagement or misappropriation by the trustee presents what the law-and-economics literature calls a *principal-agent*

---

1. 2 Eq. Cas. Abr. 741, Sel. Cas. Ch. 61, 25 Eng. Rep. 223 (1726). . . .

or *agency problem*. Suppose a real estate agent is working on a 5 percent commission. Such an agent will have no specific financial incentive to undertake even $10 of additional effort to increase the sale price by $100 because the payoff to the agent of doing so would be only $5 (5 percent of $100). However, this $10 investment would have been worthwhile from the perspective of the homeowner because the payoff to the homeowner on the $10 investment would be $95 (the $100 increase in price minus the $5 increase in the agent's commission). See Frank H. Easterbrook and Daniel R. Fischel, The Economic Structure of Corporate Law 91 (1991). In this example, the property owner is the *principal*, the real estate agent is the *agent*, and the inefficiencies resulting from their misaligned interests are called *agency costs*.

Agency problems arise whenever one person, the principal, engages another person, the agent, to undertake discretionary but imperfectly observable actions that affect the wealth of the principal. The concern is that in exercising this discretionary authority, the agent will favor his own interests over those of the principal. Agency problems are endemic in market economies because no one has the time and skills to do everything for themselves, so delegation to an agent is a necessary evil. Professor Langbein put the point into the context of trust law as follows: "Inserting a trustee between the beneficiary and the donative interest is manifestly clumsy and costly. The donor who structures a gift in this way expects compensating advantages." John H. Langbein, The Contractarian Basis of the Law of Trusts, 105 Yale L.J. 625, 632 (1995).

The application of *agency theory* to law is perhaps most fully developed in the study of corporations. There the model is of shareholders as principals and managers as agents. On this account, much of the law of corporate governance can be understood as endeavoring to minimize agency costs in the shareholder/manager relationship. Among the arsenal of agency-cost minimizing weapons in corporate law and practice are (1) the shareholders' right to vote on the composition of the board of directors, (2) the corporate fiduciary obligation, and (3) the corporate takeover market.

Agency costs are likewise a problem in trust governance. Both market conditions and the needs of the beneficiary will vary over time. It is therefore impractical for the settlor and the trustee to include in the trust instrument a detailed specification of precisely what the trustee should do in all possible future scenarios. Enter the *fiduciary obligation*:

> The fiduciary principle is an alternative to direct monitoring. It replaces prior supervision with deterrence, much as the criminal law uses penalties for bank robbery rather than pat-down searches of everyone entering banks. Acting as a standard-form penalty clause in every agency contract, the elastic contours of the fiduciary principle reflect the difficulty that contracting parties have in anticipating when and how their interests may diverge. [Frank H. Easterbrook and Daniel R. Fischel, Corporate Control Transactions, 91 Yale L.J. 698, 702 (1982).]

Because of the need for nimble management to address changing market conditions and the evolving needs of the beneficiaries, modern trust law gives the trustee broad and expansive powers. However, the trustee's exercise or nonexercise of those powers is subject to after-the-fact judicial scrutiny for compliance with the trustee's fiduciary duties on pain of damages and disgorgement remedies. See Restatement (Third) of Trusts §§70, 86 (2007). The duty of *prudence* prescribes an objective standard of care and the duty of *loyalty* proscribes misappropriation. These core principles are augmented by a host of fiduciary subrules.

Unlike the corporate fiduciary obligation, the fiduciary obligation in trust law is not backstopped by the beneficiary's ability to replace the trustee easily (on trustee removal, see page 659) or by the unfettered freedom to sell her beneficial interest (on spendthrift and other disabling restraints, see page 609). The threat of fiduciary litigation is therefore the primary legal device for minimizing agency costs in trust governance, and courts tend to apply the fiduciary obligation in trust law with greater vigor than in corporate law. See Robert H. Sitkoff, Trust Law, Corporate Law, and Capital Market Efficiency, 28 J. Corp. L. 565 (2003).

An important challenge in applying agency theory to trust law is ascertaining the identity of the principal. Thus far we have been speaking of the trustee's fiduciary obligation to the beneficiary. This is consistent with traditional doctrine. In an irrevocable trust, only the beneficiary has standing to bring suit against the trustee for breach of duty.[2] See Restatement (Third) of Trusts §94(1) (T.D. No. 5, 2009); 4 Austin Wakeman Scott, William Franklin Fratcher, and Mark L. Ascher, Scott and Ascher on Trusts §24.4.1 (5th ed. 2007).

But a private trust created gratuitously for the benefit of one or more beneficiaries is a vehicle for effecting the settlor's donative intent. The question thus arises, should not the settlor also be viewed as a principal? The traditional answer is Yes. In many respects American trust law regards the settlor as the primary principal. The beneficiary cannot easily remove the trustee, modify or terminate the trust, or sell her beneficial interest. On each of those questions, American trust law respects the settlor's intent to subject the beneficiary's gift to the trust. See Alan Newman, The Intention of the Settlor Under the Uniform Trust Code: Whose Property Is It, Anyway?, 38 Akron L. Rev. 649 (2005).

For more on the application of agency theory to trust law, see Robert H. Sitkoff, An Agency Costs Theory of Trust Law, 89 Cornell L. Rev. 621 (2004); Jonathan R. Macey, Private Trusts for the Provision of Private Goods, 37 Emory L.J. 295 (1988); A.I. Ogus, The Trust as Governance Structure, 36 U. Toronto L.J. 186 (1986).

---

2. There has lately been erosion of this limitation in the context of donor standing to enforce charitable trusts (see Smithers v. St. Luke's-Roosevelt Hospital Center, page 776) and donor standing to seek removal of the trustee (see Uniform Trust Code §706, page 660). Notice also the limitation to irrevocable trusts. Under modern law, the trustee of a revocable trust owes duties only to the settlor. Compare Farkas v. Williams, page 398, with Uniform Trust Code §603, page 403, and Linthicum v. Rudi, page 403.

NOTES AND QUESTION

1. *What of morality?* Economics — the dismal science — is hardly the only mode of analysis for throwing light on the nature and function of the fiduciary obligation. Even a fleeting examination of the cases reveals that they are rife with the language of morality and fairness, not the cold balancing of costs and benefits. Perhaps the most famous example is this passage in Meinhard v. Salmon, 164 N.E. 545 (N.Y. 1928), written by Judge Cardozo:

> Many forms of conduct permissible in a work-a-day world for those acting at arms length, are forbidden to those bound by fiduciary ties. A trustee is held to something stricter than the morals of the market place. Not honesty alone, but the punctilio of an honor the most sensitive, is then the standard of behavior. As to this there has developed a tradition that is unbending and inveterate. Uncompromising rigidity has been the attitude of courts of equity when petitioned to undermine the rule of undivided loyalty by the "disintegrating erosion" of particular exceptions. . . . Only thus has the level of conduct for fiduciaries been kept at a level higher than that trodden by the crowd. It will not consciously be lowered by any judgment of this court. [164 N.E. at 546.]

Is this conception of the fiduciary obligation inconsistent with an agency theory of fiduciary duties?

2. *Amateurs versus professional trustees.* For a discussion of considerations relevant to choosing between an amateur trustee (such as a friend or relative) and a professional trustee (such as a bank or trust company), see page 551. That discussion also includes a summary of the law of trustee compensation and the three main functions of modern trusteeship: *administration, distribution,* and *investment.*

3. *Literature.* There is a surfeit of scholarship that analyzes the fiduciary obligation from a variety of perspectives. For a sampling, see Gregory S. Alexander, A Cognitive Theory of Fiduciary Relationships, 85 Cornell L. Rev. 767 (2000); Rob Atkinson, Obedience as the Foundation of Fiduciary Duty, 34 J. Corp. L. 43 (2008); Henry N. Butler and Larry E. Ribstein, Opting Out of Fiduciary Duties: A Response to the Anti-Contractarians, 65 Wash. L. Rev. 1 (1990); Robert Cooter and Bradley J. Freedman, The Fiduciary Relationship: Its Economic Character and Legal Consequences, 68 N.Y.U. L. Rev. 1045 (1991); Deborah A. DeMott, Beyond Metaphor: An Analysis of Fiduciary Obligation, 1988 Duke L.J. 879; Frank H. Easterbrook and Daniel R. Fischel, Contract and Fiduciary Duty, 36 J.L. & Econ. 425 (1993); Tamar Frankel, Fiduciary Duties as Default Rules, 74 Or. L. Rev. 1209 (1995); Arthur B. Laby, The Fiduciary Obligation as the Adoption of Ends, 56 Buff. L. Rev. 99 (2008); Melanie B. Leslie, Trusting Trustees: Fiduciary Duties and the Limits of Default Rules, 94 Geo. L.J. 67 (2005); L.S. Sealy, Fiduciary Relationships, 1962 Cambridge L.J. 69; J.C. Shepherd, Towards a Unified Concept of Fiduciary Relationships, 97 L.Q. Rev. 51 (1981); D. Gordon Smith, The Critical Resource Theory of Fiduciary Duty, 55 Vand. L. Rev. 1399 (2002); Ernest J. Weinrib, The Fiduciary Obligation, 25 U. Toronto L.J. 1 (1975).

NOTE: POWERS OF THE TRUSTEE

In the twentieth century, legislatures in a large majority of states enacted legislation to broaden trustees' powers. This legislation has usually taken one of two forms:

(1)   An act that permits the settlor to *incorporate by express reference* in the trust instrument all or some enumerated statutory powers. This permits a trust drafter to omit a long and detailed list of trustee powers, incorporating the statutory powers instead.

(2)   A broad trustees' powers act that *grants to trustees basic powers* set forth in the statute, as exemplified by the Uniform Trustees' Powers Act §3(c) (1964). Express incorporation of statutory powers in the trust instrument is unnecessary under this type of statute.

The Uniform Trust Code (UTC) takes the strategy of empowering the trustee to its logical conclusion. In UTC §815 (2000), in addition to the "powers conferred by the terms of the trust," the trustee is authorized to exercise "all powers over the trust property which an unmarried competent owner has over individually owned property" and "any other powers appropriate to achieve the proper investment, management, and distribution of the trust property." In UTC §816, the trustee is given more than two dozen specific transactional powers, including the power to "acquire or sell property," to "deposit trust money in an account in a regulated financial-service institution," to "pay or contest any claim," and to "sign and deliver contracts."

QUESTIONS AND NOTE

1.   Given the sweeping language of UTC §815, why did the drafters also include in §816 a laundry-list of specific powers? Is the enumeration of powers in §816 an unnecessary redundancy?

2.   Regardless of the breadth of the local powers statute, well-drafted trusts almost always include a detailed schedule of powers (for a simple example, see pages 142-143). Why is this practice advisable?

3.   *Duties of third parties dealing with a trustee.* As part of the traditional strategy of protecting the beneficiary by disempowering the trustee, at common law a third party dealing with the trustee was required to inquire whether the trustee in fact had the power to engage in the proposed transaction. If the trustee did not have the power to do so, the third party dealing with the trustee could be held liable by the beneficiary for the trustee's breach. The purpose of this rule was to induce the third party to undertake careful scrutiny of the trust instrument, thereby protecting the beneficiary against overreaching by the trustee. In practice, the effect of the rule was to deter third parties from dealing with a trustee at all.

Most states have abrogated the common law rule by statute, many following Uniform Trustees' Powers Act §7 (1964) or the updated formulation in UTC §1012(a)-(b) (2000):

(a) A person other than a beneficiary who in good faith assists a trustee, or who in good faith and for value deals with a trustee, without knowledge that the trustee is exceeding or improperly exercising the trustee's powers is protected from liability as if the trustee properly exercised the power.

(b) A person other than a beneficiary who in good faith deals with a trustee is not required to inquire into the extent of the trustee's powers or the propriety of their exercise.

Professor English, the reporter for the UTC, explains the rationale for discarding the old rule: "The theory is that trust beneficiaries are helped more by the free flow of commerce than they were by the largely ineffective protective features of former law." David M. English, The Uniform Trust Code (2000): Significant Provisions and Policy Issues, 67 Mo. L. Rev. 143, 208-211 (2002).

For a critical discussion, see Peter T. Wendel, The Evolution of the Law of Trustees' Powers and Third Party Liability for Participating in a Breach of Trust: An Economic Analysis, 35 Seton Hall L. Rev. 971 (2005).

SECTION B. THE DUTY OF LOYALTY

The most fundamental principle of the fiduciary obligation in trust law is the duty of undivided *loyalty* to the beneficiary. The trustee must administer the trust solely in the interest of the beneficiary.

Hartman v. Hartle
New Jersey Court of Chancery, 1923
122 A. 615

FOSTER, V.C. Mrs. Dorothea Geick died testate on April 8, 1921, leaving five children, one of them being the complainant. She named her two sons-in-law executors, and they qualified. Among other matters the will expressly directed her executors to sell her real estate and to divide the proceeds equally among her children.

On February 9, 1922, the executors sold part of the real estate known as the Farm, at public auction, for $3,900 to one of testatrix' sons, Lewis Geick, who actually bought the property for his sister, Josephine Dieker, who is the wife of one of the executors.

On April 11, 1922, Mrs. Dieker sold the property to the defendant Mike Contra (and another, who is not a party to the action) for $5,500, part cash and part on mortgage.

The executors settled their final accounts on April 21, 1922, and at or about that time complainant expressed to the deputy surrogate her dissatisfaction with the price realized from the sale of the farm. About March 21, 1923, she filed her bill in this cause charging the sale of the farm to have been improperly and fraudulently made by the executors to Mrs. Dieker, and further charging that

Mrs. Dieker and the other heirs of the testatrix had agreed at sale, because of slow bidding and inadequate price, to have the farm bid in for the benefit of all the heirs.[3]

At the hearing each and every one of these allegations were shown to be untrue by the great weight of the testimony; and this proof was so conclusive that it left complainant with but one contention to sustain her case, viz. that under the law the sale of the property by the executors and trustee to Mrs. Dieker, the wife of one of them, without previous authority from the court, was illegal and void, and that it should be set aside and the farm resold, or, if that be found impossible because of the sale made by Mrs. Dieker to Contra, an innocent purchaser, then that complainant should have paid to her one-fifth of the $1,600 profits realized by Mrs. Dieker from the sale of the property.

It is the settled law of this state that a trustee cannot purchase from himself at his own sale, and that his wife is subject to the same disability, unless leave so to do has been previously obtained under an order of the court. Scott v. Gamble, 9 N.J. Eq. 218 (1852); Bassett v. Shoemaker, 20 A. 52 (N.J. App. 1890); Bechtold v. Read, 22 A. 1085 (N.J. Ch. 1891). And under the circumstances of the case complainant cannot be charged with laches under the view expressed in Bechtold v. Read, supra.

In view of the fact that the property is now owned by innocent purchasers, a resale cannot be ordered, but, as an alternative, Mrs. Dieker and the executors will be held to account for complainant's one-fifth share of the profits made on the resale of the property under the authority of Marshall v. Carson, 38 N.J. Eq. 250 (1884), and a decree will be advised to that effect.

IN RE GLEESON'S WILL, 124 N.E.2d 624 (Ill. App. 1955): On March 1, 1950, Mary Gleeson leased 160 acres of farm land to Con Colbrook for one year. On March 1, 1951, Gleeson and Colbrook renewed the lease for another year. On February 14, 1952, just two weeks before the second lease was to expire, Gleeson died. In her will, Gleeson devised the land to Colbrook, as trustee, for the benefit of her three children. After Gleeson's death, with the expiration of the second lease imminent, Colbrook remained on the land for another year, until March 1, 1953, though he increased his rent payments from $6 per acre to $10 per acre plus a share of the crops. After the holdover year, he leased the land to another tenant. At issue was whether Colbrook breached his duty of loyalty by holding over from March 1, 1952, until March 1, 1953.

> The Courts of this state have consistently followed a general principle of equity that a trustee cannot deal in his individual capacity with the trust property. . . .
> Petitioner [Colbrook] recognizes the existence of this general rule, but argues that because of the existence of the peculiar circumstances under which the petitioner proceeded, the instant case must be taken to constitute one of the rare exceptions to such rule. The circumstances alluded to as peculiar are pointed out as being the facts that the death of Mrs.

---

3. Personal representatives, executors, and administrators are held to the same fiduciary standards as trustees. See Uniform Probate Code §§3-703 and 3-712 (1990). — Eds.

Gleeson occurred on February 14, 1952, only 15 days prior to the beginning of the 1952 farm year; that satisfactory farm tenants are not always available, especially on short notice; that the petitioner had in the preceding fall of 1951 sown part of the 160 acres in wheat to be harvested in 1952; that the holding over by the trustee and his partner was in the best interests of the trust; that the same was done in an open manner; that the petitioner was honest with the trust; and that it suffered no loss as a result of the transaction.

The court was unimpressed with this argument:

> The good faith and honesty of the petitioner or the fact that the trust sustained no loss on account of his dealings therewith are all matters which can avail petitioner nothing so far as a justification of the course he chose to take in dealing with trust property is concerned.

Colbrook "should have . . . decided whether he chose to continue as a tenant or to act as trustee." The duty of loyalty proscribed his doing both. Accordingly, the court ordered Colbrook to account "for all monies received by him personally as a profit by virtue of his" holdover tenancy on the land "during the 1952 crop year, and to pay the amount of any such profit to the trust."

NOTES AND QUESTIONS

1. *Undivided loyalty and sole benefit.* If the trustee engages in a transaction that involves self-dealing or a conflict between the trustee's fiduciary capacity and personal interests, good faith and fairness to the beneficiaries are not enough to save the trustee from liability. In such a case, *no further inquiry* is made; the trustee's good faith and the reasonableness of the transaction are irrelevant. Restatement (Third) of Trusts §78 (2007); 3 Austin Wakeman Scott, William Franklin Fratcher, and Mark L. Ascher, Scott and Ascher on Trusts §17.2 (5th ed. 2007). The beneficiaries can hold the trustee accountable for any profit made on the transaction, or, if the trustee has bought trust property, can compel the trustee to restore the property to the trust, or, if the trustee has sold his own property to the trust, can compel the trustee to repay the purchase price and take back the property. Scott and Ascher on Trusts, supra, at §17.2.1.1.

The only defenses that the trustee has to a self-dealing or conflicted transaction are that the settlor authorized it in the trust instrument or that the beneficiaries consented after full disclosure. Even then, the trustee must have acted in good faith and the transaction must be fair to the beneficiaries. The purpose is to deter self-dealing and conflicted transactions or to channel the trustee toward seeking advance judicial approval. See Restatement (Third) of Trusts, supra, §§71 and 78, cmts. c(1), c(2), and c(3); UTC §802(b) (2000, rev. 2004); Scott and Ascher on Trusts, supra, §17.2.11.

2. *Justifying the no-further-inquiry rule.* In Robert Cooter and Bradley J. Freedman, The Fiduciary Relationship: Its Economic Character and Legal Consequences, 68 N.Y.U. L. Rev. 1045 (1991), the authors explain that the no-further-inquiry rule uses self-interest to compel the trustee to do what is best for the beneficiary. Because appropriating the trust property is both profitable for

the fiduciary and difficult for the beneficiary to detect, the authors believe that the law appropriately infers disloyalty from the fact of self-dealing.

But is it not possible that some self-dealing or conflicted transactions would have been advantageous for the beneficiaries? If so, then the absolute nature of the no-further-inquiry rule prevents some desirable transactions. One commentator answers that the rule may be justifiable nonetheless if, on balance, "these deals are so frequently undesirable that the costs of extirpating the entire class of transaction (a *rule*) are less than the costs of case-by-case adjudication (the fairness *standard*)." Robert H. Sitkoff, Trust Law, Corporate Law, and Capital Market Efficiency, 28 J. Corp. L. 565, 673-674 (2003).

Restatement (Third) of Trusts, supra, §78, cmt. b, puts the point thus: "Viewed from the beneficiaries' perspective, especially that of remainder beneficiaries, efforts to prevent or detect actual improprieties can be expected to be inefficient if not ineffective. Such efforts are likely to be wastefully expensive and to suffer from time lag and inadequacies of information, from a lack of relevant experience and understanding, and perhaps from want of resources to monitor trustee behavior and ultimately to litigate and expose actual instances of fiduciary misconduct."

3. *Categorical exceptions.* The sole benefit principle, and its enforcement through the no-further-inquiry rule, are not so absolute as they once were. Statutes in most states now allow a corporate trustee to deposit the trust assets with its own banking department and to invest the trust assets in a common trust fund or in a mutual fund that it operates. Another exception, related to the rise of the professional trustee, entitles the trustee to take reasonable compensation even though, strictly speaking, by compensating herself with trust funds the trustee self-deals. These exceptions are codified in UTC §802(f) and (h) and are recognized by Restatement (Third) of Trusts, supra, §78, cmts. c(4), c(6), and c(8).

4. *Retreat from no-further-inquiry?* Taking note of the proliferation of statutory exceptions, and taking his cue from the application of the duty of loyalty in corporate and other fiduciary settings in which the duty is not absolute, Professor Langbein suggests that the no-further-inquiry rule does more harm than good. See John H. Langbein, Questioning the Trust Law Duty of Loyalty: Sole Interest or Best Interest?, 114 Yale L.J. 929 (2005). He argues that advance judicial approval is not practical for certain transactions, hence a conflicted transaction should be sustained if the trustee can prove that the transaction was prudently undertaken in the best interests of the beneficiaries.

Professor Leslie is not convinced. In her view, the no-further-inquiry rule helps offset the structural difficulties confronted by beneficiaries in monitoring the trustee. See Melanie B. Leslie, In Defense of the No Further Inquiry Rule: A Response to Professor John Langbein, 47 Wm. & Mary L. Rev. 541 (2005). Should the law take into account the identity of the trustee, whether the trustee is an amateur individual versus a professional institution? See Melanie B. Leslie, Common Law, Common Sense: Fiduciary Standards and Trustee Identity, 27 Cardozo L. Rev. 2713 (2006); Karen E. Boxx, Distinguishing Trustees and Protecting Beneficiaries: A Response to Professor Leslie, 27 Cardozo L. Rev. 2753 (2006).

The underlying policy question is this: Which governance strategy is better suited to addressing conflicted and self-dealing transactions by a trustee, a best-interests standard with the burden on the trustee (per Langbein), or prohibition subject to a growing list of statutory exceptions (current law)?

5. *Trust pursuit rule.* One of the remedies afforded in equity for a breach of trust is the trust pursuit rule. If the trustee, in wrongfully disposing of trust property, acquires other property, the beneficiary is entitled to enforce a constructive trust on the property so acquired, treating it as part of the trust. The trust pursuit rule is also applied where the property ends up in the hands of a third person, unless the third person is a bona fide purchaser for value and without notice of the breach of trust. If the trustee in breach of trust transfers trust property to a person who takes with notice of the breach of trust, the transferee does not hold the property free of the trust, despite paying full value for the transfer. Likewise, if the trustee in breach of trust transfers trust property and no value is given for the transfer, the transferee does not hold the property free of the trust, despite receiving no notice of the trust. See Scott and Ascher on Trusts, supra, §§24.6, 29.1.1, 29.1.5, and 29.1.6.

In re Rothko
Court of Appeals of New York, 1977
372 N.E.2d 291

COOKE, J. Mark Rothko, an abstract expressionist painter whose works through the years gained for him an international reputation of greatness, died testate on February 25, 1970. The principal asset of his estate consisted of 798 paintings of tremendous value, and the dispute underlying this appeal involves the conduct of his three executors in their disposition of these works of art. In sum, that conduct as portrayed in the record and sketched in the opinions was manifestly wrongful and indeed shocking.

Rothko's will was admitted to probate on April 27, 1970 and letters testamentary were issued to Bernard J. Reis, Theodoros Stamos and Morton Levine.[4]

---

4. The executors were three of Rothko's most intimate companions during his last years. Bernard J. Reis, a certified public accountant who had graduated from law school but had not been licensed to practice law, had acted for years as Rothko's business and professional advisor and confidant. Reis drafted Rothko's will.

Theodoros Stamos was a fellow artist in whose family plot Rothko was buried. Stamos entered into a personal contract with Marlborough Gallery, Inc., on January 1, 1971, whereby Marlborough became Stamos's exclusive art dealer agent for four years at a commission of 50 percent. The Surrogate found "Executor Levine stated, and the court finds, that in a conversation in April, 1970, before the execution of the questioned agreements, executor Stamos related that Marlborough had evidenced interest in his paintings. The conversation led Levine to believe that Stamos was interested in entering into some contractual arrangement with Marlborough which indicated a conflict of interest on the part of Stamos. Levine testified that when he confronted Stamos with the impropriety of such motivation angry exchanges followed." In re Rothko, 379 N.Y.S.2d 923, 940 (Sur. 1975).

Morton Levine, professor of anthropology at Fordham University, was chosen by Rothko to act as guardian of his two children. Kate Rothko came of age soon after her father's death and, at her insistence, Levine was removed as guardian of Christopher Rothko. "It is recognized that Levine was neither an art expert nor an experienced fiduciary but he was an educated man who, despite his educational background and his position as a college professor, failed to exercise ordinary prudence in his performance of fiduciary obligations which he

Hastily and within a period of only about three weeks and by virtue of two contracts each dated May 21, 1970, the executors dealt with all 798 paintings.

By a contract of sale, the estate executors agreed to sell to Marlborough A.G., a
Liechtenstein corporation (hereinafter MAG), 100 Rothko paintings as listed for
$1,800,000, $200,000 to be paid on execution of the agreement and the balance
of $1,600,000 in 12 equal interest-free installments over a 12-year period. Under
the second agreement, the executors consigned to Marlborough Gallery, Inc., a
domestic corporation (hereinafter MNY), "approximately 700 paintings listed on
a Schedule to be prepared," the consignee to be responsible for costs covering
items such as insurance, storage, restoration and promotion. By its provisos,
MNY could sell up to 35 paintings a year from each of two groups, pre-1947 and
post-1947, for 12 years at the best price obtainable but not less than the appraised
estate value, and that it would receive a 50 percent commission on each painting
sold, except for a commission of 40 percent on those sold to or through other
dealers.

Petitioner Kate Rothko, decedent's daughter and a person entitled to share in
his estate by virtue of an election under EPTL §5-3.3,[5] instituted this proceeding
to remove the executors, to enjoin MNY and MAG from disposing of the paintings, to rescind the aforesaid agreements between the executors and said corporations, for a return of the paintings still in possession of those corporations, and
for damages. She was joined by the guardian of her brother Christopher Rothko,
likewise interested in the estate, who answered by adopting the allegations of his
sister's petition and by demanding the same relief. The Attorney General of the
State, as the representative of the ultimate beneficiaries of the Mark Rothko
Foundation, Inc., a charitable corporation and the residuary legatee under decedent's will, joined in requesting relief substantially similar to that prayed for by
petitioner. . . .

Following a nonjury trial covering 89 days and in a thorough opinion, the Surrogate found: that Reis was a director, secretary and treasurer of MNY, the consignee art gallery, in addition to being a coexecutor of the estate; that the testator
had a 1969 inter vivos contract with MNY to sell Rothko's work at a commission
of only 10 percent and whether that agreement survived testator's death was a
problem that a fiduciary in a dual position could not have impartially faced; that
Reis was in a position of serious conflict of interest with respect to the contracts of
May 21, 1970 and that his dual role and planned purpose benefited the Marlborough interests to the detriment of the estate; that it was to the advantage of coexecutor Stamos as a "not-too-successful artist, financially," to curry favor with

---

assumed. Levine's argument at best is a statement that he undertook a responsibility which he was unqualified
to handle." Id. at 942.

On the Rothko litigation, see Lee Seldes, The Legacy of Mark Rothko (1979). — Eds.

5. Mark Rothko devised his residuary estate to the Mark Rothko Foundation, a charitable corporation, with
Reis, Stamos, and Levine named as directors. N.Y. Est., Powers & Trusts Law §5-3.3 (1967) provided that a child
of a testator may set aside a testamentary disposition to charity to the extent it exceeds one-half of the testator's
estate. Kate Rothko set aside the charitable gift in the amount permitted, with the result that one-half of the
residuary gift passed to Rothko's heirs. Hence Kate Rothko, who otherwise was left nothing by Mark Rothko's
will, had standing to attack the action of the executors. N.Y. Est., Powers & Trusts Law §5-3.3 was repealed in
1981 (see Note 6 at page 759). — Eds.

Mark Rothko
Number 22 (1969)
Collection, The Museum of Modern Art, New York

Marlborough and that the contract made by him with MNY within months after signing the estate contracts placed him in a position where his personal interests conflicted with those of the estate, especially leading to lax contract enforcement efforts by Stamos; that Stamos acted negligently and improvidently in view of his own knowledge of the conflict of interest of Reis; that the third coexecutor, Levine, while not acting in self-interest or with bad faith, nonetheless failed to exercise ordinary prudence in the performance of his assumed fiduciary obligations since he was aware of Reis' divided loyalty, believed that Stamos was also seeking personal advantage, possessed personal opinions as to the value of the paintings and yet followed the leadership of his coexecutors without investigation of essential facts or consultation with competent and disinterested appraisers, and that the business transactions of the two Marlborough corporations were admittedly controlled and directed by Francis K. Lloyd. It was concluded that the acts and failures of the three executors were clearly improper to such a substantial extent as to mandate their removal . . . as estate fiduciaries. The Surrogate also found that MNY, MAG and Lloyd were guilty of contempt in shipping, disposing of and selling 57 paintings in violation of the temporary restraining order dated June 26, 1972 and of the injunction dated September 26, 1972; that the contracts for sale and consignment of paintings between the executors and MNY and MAG provided inadequate value to the estate, amounting to a lack of mutuality and fairness resulting from conflicts on the part of Reis and Stamos and improvidence on the part of all executors; that said contracts were voidable and were set aside by reason of violation of the duty of loyalty and improvidence of the executors, knowingly participated in and induced by MNY and MAG; that the fact that these agreements were voidable did not revive the 1969 inter vivos agreements since the parties by their conduct evinced an intent to abandon and abrogate these compacts. The Surrogate held that the present value at the time of trial of the paintings sold is the proper measure of damages as to MNY, MAG, Lloyd, Reis and Stamos. . . . It was held that Levine was liable for $6,464,880 in damages, as he was not in a dual position acting for his own interest and was thus liable only for the actual value of paintings sold MNY and MAG as of the dates of sale, and that Reis, Stamos, MNY and MAG, apart from being jointly and severally liable for the same damages as Levine for negligence, were liable for the greater sum of $9,252,000 "as appreciation damages less amounts previously paid to the estate with regard to sales of paintings." . . . The liabilities were held to be congruent so that payment of the highest sum would satisfy all lesser liabilities including the civil fines and the liabilities for damages were to be reduced by payment of the fine levied or by return of any of the 57 paintings disposed of, the new fiduciary to have the option in the first instance to specify which paintings the fiduciary would accept.

The Appellate Division, in an opinion by Justice Lane, modified to the extent of deleting the option given the new fiduciary to specify which paintings he would accept. Except for this modification, the majority affirmed on the opinion of Surrogate Midonick, with additional comments. Among others, it was stated that the entire court agreed that executors Reis and Stamos had a conflict of interest and divided loyalty in view of their nexus to MNY and that a majority were in agreement with the Surrogate's assessment of liability as to executor Levine and his findings of liability against MNY, MAG and Lloyd. The majority agreed with the Surrogate's analysis awarding "appreciation damages" . . . . Justices Capozzoli and Nunez, in separate dissenting in part opinions, voted to modify and remit to determine the reasonable value of the paintings as of May 1970, when estate contracts with MNY and MAG had their inception in writing.

Since the Surrogate's findings of fact as to the conduct of Reis, Stamos, Levine, MNY, MAG and Lloyd and the value of the paintings at different junctures were affirmed by the Appellate Division, if there was evidence to support these findings they are not subject to question in this Court and the review here is confined to the legal issues raised . . . .

In seeking a reversal, it is urged that an improper legal standard was applied in voiding the estate contracts of May 1970, that the "no further inquiry" rule applies only to self-dealing and that in case of a conflict of interest, absent self-dealing, a challenged transaction must be shown to be unfair. The subject of fairness of the contracts is intertwined with the issue of whether Reis and Stamos were guilty of conflicts of interest. Scott is quoted to the effect that "[a] trustee does not necessarily incur liability merely because he has an individual interest in the transaction . . . . In Bullivant v. First National Bank, 246 Mass. 324, it was held that . . . the fact that the bank was also a creditor of the corporation did not make its assent invalid, *if it acted in good faith and the plan was fair* . . ." (emphasis added here) (II Scott on Trusts, §170.24, p.1384), and our attention has been called to the statement in Phelan v. Middle States Oil Corp. (220 F.2d 593) that Judge Learned Hand found "no decisions that have applied [the no further inquiry rule] inflexibly to every occasion in which the fiduciary has been shown to have had a personal interest that might in fact have conflicted with his loyalty" (p.603).

These contentions should be rejected. First, a review of the opinions of the Surrogate and the Appellate Division manifests that they did not rely solely on a "no further inquiry rule," and secondly, there is more than an adequate basis to conclude that the agreements between the Marlborough corporations and the estate were neither fair nor in the best interests of the estate. . . . The opinions under review demonstrate that neither the Surrogate nor the Appellate Division set aside the contracts by merely applying the no further inquiry rule without regard to fairness. Rather they determined, quite properly indeed, that these agreements were neither fair nor in the best interests of the estate.

To be sure, the assertions that there were no conflicts of interest on the part of Reis or Stamos indulge in sheer fantasy. Besides being a director and officer of MNY, for which there was financial remuneration, however slight, Reis, as noted by the Surrogate, had different inducements to favor the Marlborough interests, including his own aggrandizement of status and financial advantage through sales of almost one million dollars for items from his own and his family's extensive private art collection by the Marlborough interests. Similarly, Stamos benefited as an artist under contract with Marlborough and, interestingly, Marlborough purchased a Stamos painting from a third party for $4,000 during the week in May 1970 when the estate contract negotiations were pending. The conflicts are manifest. Further, as noted in Bogert, Trusts and Trustees (2d ed.), "The duty of loyalty imposed on the fiduciary prevents him from accepting employment from a third party who is entering into a business transaction with the trust" (§543[S], p.573). "While he [a trustee] is administering the trust he must refrain from placing himself in a position where his personal interest or that of a third person does or may conflict with the interest of the beneficiaries" (Bogert, Law of Trusts [Hornbook Series, 5th ed.], p.343). Here, Reis was employed and Stamos benefited in a manner contemplated by Bogert (see also, Meinhard v. Salmon, 249 N.Y. 458, 464, 466-467). In short, one must strain the law rather than follow it to reach the result suggested on behalf of Reis and Stamos.

Levine contends that, having acted prudently and upon the advice of counsel, a complete defense was established.[6] Suffice it to say, an executor who knows that his coexecutor is committing breaches of trust and not only fails to exert efforts directed towards prevention but accedes to them is legally accountable even though he was acting on the advice of counsel (Matter of Westerfield, 32 App. Div. 324, 344; III Scott, Trusts [3d ed.], §201, p.1657). When confronted with the question of whether to enter into the Marlborough contracts, Levine was acting in a business capacity, not a legal one, in which he was required as an executor primarily to employ such diligence and prudence to the care and management of the estate assets and affairs as would prudent persons of discretion and intelligence, accented by "[n]ot honesty alone, but the punctilio of an honor the most sensitive" (Meinhard v. Salmon, 249 N.Y. 458, 464, supra). Alleged good faith on the part of a fiduciary forgetful of his duty is not enough. He could not close his eyes, remain passive or move with unconcern in the face of the obvious loss to be visited upon the estate by participation in those business arrangements and then shelter himself behind the claimed counsel of an attorney . . . .

Further, there is no merit to the argument that MNY and MAG lacked notice of the breach of trust. The record amply supports the determination that they are chargeable with notice of the executors' breach of duty.

The measure of damages was the issue that divided the Appellate Division. The contention of Reis, Stamos, MNY and MAG, that the award of appreciation damages was legally erroneous and impermissible, is based on a principle that an executor authorized to sell is not liable for an increase in value if the breach consists only in selling for a figure less than that for which the executor should have sold. For example, Scott states:

---

6. The three executors sought advice from their legal counsel about entering into the contracts with MAG and MNY. Counsel advised the executors that Reis had a conflict of interest.

By the same letter, this law firm advised the executors that a petition for advance approval of any contracts for liquidation of the estate through Marlborough Galleries would not be entertained by a Surrogate. While it is true, as the law firm advised, that Surrogates do not usually give advance approval concerning matters of business judgment which are within the province of executors, no indication was given that the opposite rule governs when a fiduciary faces a conflict of interest. [In re Rothko, 379 N.Y.S.2d 923, 936 (Sur. 1975).]

Is the law firm liable to executor Levine for negligence? — Eds.

> The beneficiaries are not entitled to the value of the property at the time of the decree if it was not the duty of the trustee to retain the property in the trust and the breach of trust consisted *merely* in selling the property for too low a price (emphasis added) (III Scott, Trusts (3d ed.), §208.3, p.1687).
>
> If the trustee is guilty of a breach of trust in selling trust property for an inadequate price, he is liable for the difference between the amount he should have received and the amount which he did receive. He is not liable, however, for any subsequent rise in value of the property sold (Id., §208.6, pp.1689-1690).

A recitation of similar import appears in comment d under Restatement, Trusts, §205:

> d. Sale for less than value. If the trustee is authorized to sell trust property, but in breach of trust he sells it for less than he should receive, he is liable for the value of the property at the time of the sale less the amount which he received. If the breach of trust consists *only* in selling it for too little, he is not chargeable with the amount of any subsequent increase in value of the property under the rule stated in Clause (c), as he would be if he were not authorized to sell the property (see §208) (emphasis added).

However, employment of "merely" and "only" as limiting words suggests that where the breach consists of some misfeasance, other than solely for selling "for too low a price" or "for too little," appreciation damages may be appropriate. Under Scott (§208.3, pp.1686-1687) and the Restatement (§208), the trustee may be held liable for appreciation damages if it was his or her duty to retain the property, the theory being that the beneficiaries are entitled to be placed in the same position they would have been in had the breach not consisted of a sale of property that should have been retained. The same rule should apply where the breach of trust consists of a serious conflict of interest — which is more than merely selling for too little.

The reason for allowing appreciation damages, where there is a duty to retain, and only date of sale damages, where there is authorization to sell, is policy oriented. If a trustee authorized to sell were subjected to a greater measure of damages he might be reluctant to sell (in which event he might run a risk if depreciation ensued). On the other hand, if there is a duty to retain and the trustee sells there is no policy reason to protect the trustee; he has not simply acted imprudently, he has violated an integral condition of the trust.

"If a trustee in breach of trust transfers trust property to a person who takes with notice of the breach of trust, and the transferee has disposed of the property . . . [i]t seems proper to charge him with the value at the time of the decree, since if it had not been for the breach of trust the property would still have been a part of the trust estate" (IV Scott, Trusts [3d ed.], §291.2). This rule of law which applies to the transferees MNY and MAG also supports the imposition of appreciation damages against Reis and Stamos, since if the Marlborough corporations are liable for such damages either as purchasers or consignees with notice, from one in breach of trust, it is only logical to hold that said executors, as sellers and consignors, are liable also pro tanto. . . .

[S]ince the paintings cannot be returned, the estate is therefore entitled to their value at the time of the decree, i.e., appreciation damages. These are not punitive damages in a true sense, rather they are damages intended to make the estate whole. Of course, as to Reis, Stamos, MNY and MAG, these damages might be considered by some to be exemplary in a sense, in that they serve as a warning to others, but their true character is ascertained when viewed in the light of over-riding policy considerations and in the realization that the sale and consignment were not merely sales below value but inherently wrongful transfers which should allow the owner to be made whole . . . .

The decree of the Surrogate imposed appreciation damages against Reis, Sta-mos, MNY and MAG in the amount of $7,339,464.72 — computed as $9,252,000 (86 works on canvas at $90,000 each and 54 works on paper at $28,000 each) less the aggregate amounts paid the estate under the two rescinded agreements and interest. Appellants chose not to offer evidence of "present value" and the only proof furnished on the subject was that of the expert Heller whose appraisal as of January 1974 (the month previous to that when trial commenced) on a painting-by-painting basis totaled $15,100,000. There was also testimony as to bona fide sales of other Rothkos between 1971 and 1974. Under the circumstances, it was impossible to appraise the value of the unreturned works of art with an absolute certainty and, so long as the figure arrived at had a reasonable basis of computa-tion and was not merely speculative, possible or imaginary, the Surrogate had the right to resort to reasonable conjectures and probable estimates and to make the best approximation possible through the exercise of good judgment and com-mon sense in arriving at that amount . . . . This is particularly so where the con-duct of wrongdoers has rendered it difficult to ascertain the damages suffered with the precision otherwise possible . . . . Significantly, the Surrogate's factual finding as to the present value of these unreturned paintings was affirmed by the Appellate Division and, since that finding had support in the record and was not legally erroneous, it should not now be subjected to our disturbance. . . .

Accordingly, the order of the Appellate Division should be affirmed, with costs to the prevailing parties against appellants, and the question certified answered in the affirmative.

NOTES AND QUESTION

1. *Epilogue.* Bernard Reis, Theodoros Stamos, and Morton Levine were removed as executors of Mark Rothko's will, and Kate Rothko was appointed sole administrator c.t.a.[7] of Rothko's estate. Kate Rothko was not agreeable to the bill for legal services presented by her counsel in the amount of $7.5 million and hired another lawyer to resist its collection out of the estate. In view of the fact that her lawyers had successfully recovered paintings then worth $40 million for the estate, the surrogate allowed the firm a fee of $2.6 million, which was about

---

7. *Administrator c.t.a.* is short for *administrator cum testamento annexo*, which means administrator with the will attached. Although the fiduciary for an estate is typically called an *executor* when there is a will and an *adminis-trator* when the decedent dies intestate, this is not always so. When the testator fails to name an executor or the named executor (and any alternate) is disqualified, the court will appoint an administrator c.t.a.

twice the hourly rate usually charged by the firm. In re Rothko, 414 N.Y.S.2d 444 (Sur. 1979).

Marlborough Gallery paid most of the $9.2 million assessed as damages in the principal case, but Reis, Stamos, and Levine were liable for the estate's legal fees and costs, and Reis filed for bankruptcy in 1978. N.Y. Times, Jan. 26, 1978, at C19. Stamos assigned his house to the Rothko estate, which permitted him to retain a life estate in it.

In 1977, Marlborough Gallery owner Frank Lloyd was indicted on charges of tampering with the evidence in the *Rothko* case by altering a gallery stock book containing the purchase and sale prices of Rothko works. Lloyd, a British subject, was outside the country when the indictment was handed up, and upon his return in 1982 he was tried and convicted on the charges. His sentence required him to set up a scholarship fund and art education programs at his gallery. N.Y. Times, Jan. 7, 1983, at 1.

In 1983, a painting by Rothko sold for $1.8 million at a Sotheby's auction in New York. This price equaled the amount Marlborough A.G. was to pay for 100 paintings under its agreement with Rothko's executors. It was, at the time, the highest price ever paid for a modern work by an American artist. Twenty-four years later, in 2007, one of Rothko's paintings — White Center (Yellow, Pink and Lavender on Rose), owned by David Rockefeller — sold to a mystery buyer at a Sotheby's auction for $72.84 million, again the highest price ever paid for a modern work, shattering the prior record of $27.1 million. See Christopher Benfey, The Branding of Rothko: How His Art Became the Ultimate Luxury Object, Slate, May 22, 2007.

For a retrospective view of the litigation, and the subsequent lives of the parties, see A Betrayal the Art World Can't Forget, N.Y. Times, Nov. 2, 1998, at B1.

2. *Damages and structural conflicts.* The measure of damages applied in the *Rothko* case is sharply criticized in Richard V. Wellman, Punitive Surcharges Against Disloyal Fiduciaries — Is *Rothko* Right?, 77 Mich. L. Rev. 95 (1978). Professor Wellman would limit recovery against the two disloyal fiduciaries and the gallery to restitution (recovering all amounts received by the gallery for sales and resales of the paintings plus interest). Wellman's central point is that appreciation damages (a penalty) may be appropriate where a trustee sells an asset he has no authority to sell but are not appropriate where a trustee has authority to sell (as did Rothko's executors) but is guilty of disloyalty or self-dealing. Wellman continues:

> [T]he wisdom of assessing any penalty can be questioned when a trustee has, or later may be said to have had, personal interests which conflict with his fiduciary duty. In such instances, it will usually be unclear whether the fiduciary has breached his duty of loyalty: liability is decided by hindsight and may arise in countless unforeseen ways. A penalty exceeding the liability of an insurer against controllable losses is simply an unjust remedy for conduct of only uncertain impropriety. Even in *Rothko,* the wrongfulness of the executors' conduct was not self-evident. For example, in 1969 Rothko sold a number of paintings to the gallery at prices comparable to those of the executors' 1970 sale and signed a long-term exclusive consignment contract with the gallery. Further, Rothko knew that Reis and Stamos had personal ties to the gallery. These facts suggest that Rothko wanted his executors to deal with the gallery. [Id. at 113.]

In a similar vein, Professor Langbein suggests that "[c]onflicts of interest are sometimes embedded in the very relationship that induces the settlor to ask the particular individual to serve as trustee." Thus, Langbein asks, "Did the two executors provoke a disloyal conflict, or did they pursue a course of action that Rothko tacitly authorized when he selected fiduciaries who came with an embedded conflict of interest? At this distance from the litigation, these questions that the court did not ventilate are hard to answer." John H. Langbein, The Contractarian Basis of the Law of Trusts, 105 Yale L.J. 625, 665-666 (1995).

Even if one were inclined to accept the argument that Rothko tacitly consented to Reis and Stamos selling the art in a conflicted transaction, would not the terms of the sale still need to be fair to the estate? Consider also that the executors sold all of Rothko's paintings within three weeks of their appointment, without obtaining an independent expert appraisal, and on terms that look favorable to the gallery when viewed with hindsight. Irrespective of the loyalty analysis, did the executors breach the duty of prudence? Although separate principles in theory, it is not uncommon in practice for a breach of the duty of loyalty to be accompanied by a breach of the duty of prudence, and vice versa.

NOTE: CO-TRUSTEES

Under traditional law, if there is more than one trustee of a private trust, the trustees must act as a group and with unanimity, unless the trust instrument provides to the contrary. One of several trustees does not have the power alone to transfer or deal with the property. Since co-trustees must act jointly, a co-trustee is liable for the wrongful acts of a co-trustee to which she has consented or which, by her negligence through inactivity or wrongful delegation, she has enabled the co-trustee to commit. It is improper for one trustee to leave to the others the custody and control of the trust property.

The traditional rule of unanimity is on the way out. In many states, by UTC §703(a) (2000) or other statute, a majority can act if there are three or more trustees. See also Restatement (Third) of Trusts §39 (2003). However, even if unanimity is not required, a co-trustee still has a duty to take reasonable steps to prevent a breach of trust by her co-trustees, if necessary by bringing suit. See UTC §703(g); Restatement (Third) of Trusts, supra, §81.

For a charitable trust, the rule has long been that unanimity of action is not required of the trustees. Action by a majority is valid.

QUESTIONS AND NOTE

1.   What would you, as counsel for Levine, have advised him to do when the conflict of interest of Reis became apparent? Could Levine have escaped liability by resigning? See UTC §705(c) (2000, rev. 2001); Restatement (Third) of Trusts, supra, §36, cmt. d.

2.   Per footnote 6 on page 683, Levine had the advice of a lawyer. Should obtaining and following such advice provide a defense in a later suit for breach of trust? See Restatement (Third) of Trusts, supra, §77, cmt. b(2).

SECTION C.   THE DUTY OF PRUDENCE

> October.
> This is one of the peculiarly dangerous months
> to speculate in stocks in.
> The others are July, January, September, April, November,
> May, March, June, December, August, and February.
> — *Pudd'nhead Wilson's Calendar*
>
> MARK TWAIN
> *The Tragedy of Pudd'nhead Wilson 166 (1900)*

After loyalty, the next great principle of trust fiduciary law is the duty of *prudence*, which imposes on the trustee an objective standard of care. "A trustee shall administer the trust as a prudent person would, by considering the purposes, terms, distributional requirements, and other circumstances of the trust. In satisfying this standard, the trustee shall exercise reasonable care, skill, and caution." UTC §804 (2000).

We have already seen the duty of prudence in action. In Marsman v. Nasca, page 598, the court held the trustee, Farr, liable for failing to investigate the needs of the beneficiary, Cappy, in deciding whether to make a discretionary distribution of principal. Farr failed to "exercise reasonable effort and diligence in planning the administration of the trust, in making and implementing administrative decisions, and in monitoring the trust situation, with due attention to the trust's objectives and the interests of the beneficiaries." Restatement (Third) of Trusts §77, cmt. b (2007). Moreover, a trustee who possesses special skills or expertise, or who procures appointment by claiming to have special skills or expertise, is under a duty to use those special skills or expertise. Id., cmt. e. A prominent member of the Boston bar, Farr was a specialist in trusts and estates matters.

In contemporary trust practice, which is dominated by trusts funded with financial assets, the primary application of the duty of prudence is in the law of trust investment.

1.   *The Prudent Man Rule and the History of Trust-Investment Law*

John H. Langbein and Richard A. Posner,
Market Funds and Trust-Investment Law
1976 Am. B. Found. Res. J. 1

In 1719 the British Parliament authorized trustees to invest in the shares of the South Sea Company. The South Sea "Bubble" burst the next year, share prices fell by 90 percent, and "public confidence in joint stock companies and their securities was destroyed" for the rest of the eighteenth century.[8]

In the period of reaction to the Bubble the standard of prudence in trust investment acquired three notable characteristics. First, the Court of Chancery developed a "court-list" of presumptively proper investment. The courts "repeatedly decided" that "the trustee would be free from liability if he invested . . . in Government three per cent stock [i.e., bonds]." Some chancellors recognized "well-secured" first mortgages on realty as appropriate, although others questioned them well into the nineteenth century. Statutes extended the categories of presumptively proper investments. Lord St. Leonard's Act added East India stock to the court list and confirmed mortgage investments, "provided that such Investment shall in other respects be reasonable and proper." Successive Parliaments added various local and colonial government issues, and in 1889 certain railway debentures and preferred stocks. Most American jurisdictions maintained similar statutory lists into the 1940s. . . .

Second, because investments not on the list were improper unless authorized in the trust instrument, England and many American jurisdictions forbade all trust investment in the securities of private enterprises until late in the nineteenth century, and greatly restricted such investments thereafter. . . .

Third, trust-investment law developed a preoccupation with the preservation of the corpus (principal) of the trust. In the words of a leading case, "the primary object to be attained by a trustee in the matter of investing the funds confided to his control is their safety." . . .

What emerged, in short, was an emphasis on "safe" investments, a category dominated in the mind of the judges and legislators by long-term fixed-return obligations such as mortgages and bonds. This approach to investment by trustees may have made sense in the eighteenth and nineteenth centuries in light of

8. The South Sea Company was granted a monopoly on British trade with the eastern coast of South America, where it was thought that the indigenous population would be willing to trade immense amounts of gold and silver for British manufactured goods. Unfortunately, Spain had control of the area and permitted only one Company ship per year to trade. Worse, this annual voyage occurred only once, in 1717, after which Spain prohibited further trade. Although the company had little or no actual profits, its stock sold briskly, especially after it agreed to take on the entire debt of England. Its stock price quickly rose from £130 before this ridiculous proposal to £310 when the proposal was accepted by Parliament. The company then issued huge amounts of new stock; over £1 million worth sold in just the first few hours after issue.

With outlandish schemes for making great fortunes, other "bubble companies" joined in the action. One company promised an annual 100 percent return on investments in a business that was not even disclosed; the prospectus described the venture simply as, "A company for carrying on an undertaking of great advantage, but nobody to know what it is." After collecting £2,000 on the first day of sales, the anonymous entrepreneur absconded to the Continent, never to be heard from again. Gullible investors bought stock in other imaginative businesses, including ventures for developing "a wheel for perpetual motion," for "extracting silver from lead," and for transmuting "quicksilver [mercury] into a malleable fine metal." Charles MacKay, 1 Extraordinary Popular Delusions and the Madness of Crowds 55-56, 61, 63 (2d ed. 1852).

By the summer of 1720, the South Sea Company's stock was trading at £1,000 per share. Then it became known that the Company's chairman and other insiders had sold their shares. The bubble burst, the stock price dropped 90 percent, and what money was left was eventually distributed to shareholders. Sir Isaac Newton, one of many disappointed investors, lamented, "I can calculate the motions of heavenly bodies, but not the madness of people." For the classic account of the South Sea Bubble and other speculative excesses, see id. at 46-88. — Eds.

two facts which are not true today. First, the capital markets were relatively unde-veloped and the opportunities to make passive, reasonably liquid investments in common stock were therefore limited. Second, there was relatively little inflation in the eighteenth and nineteenth centuries. Although the interest rate on a fixed-income security will include the anticipated rate of inflation, the investor bears the risk—which in an inflationary period is substantial for long-term instruments—that the actual rate of inflation will turn out to be higher than the anticipated rate.

Restatement (Third) of Trusts (2007)

CHAPTER 17. INVESTMENT OF TRUST FUNDS
(THE "PRUDENT INVESTOR RULE")

INTRODUCTORY NOTE

The foundation of trust investment law in the first and second Restatements has been the so-called "prudent man rule" of Harvard College v. Amory, 9 Pick. (26 Mass.) 446, 461 (1830). The opinion admonishes trustees "to observe how men of prudence, discretion and intelligence manage their own affairs, not in regard to speculation, but in regard to the permanent disposition of their funds, considering the probable income, as well as the probable safety of the capital to be invested." Thus, in 1959, the rule of Restatement Second, Trusts §227 directed trustees "to make such investments and only such investments as a prudent man would make of his own property having in view the preservation of the estate and the amount and regularity of the income to be derived." In generally similar lan-guage, influenced by the original Restatement, the prudent-man rule had been adopted at one time by decision or legislation in most American jurisdictions, often displacing the more restrictive, so-called "legal list" statutes.

Unfortunately, much of the apparent and initially intended generality and adaptability of the prudent man-rule was lost as it was further elaborated in the courts and applied case by case. Decisions dealing with essentially factual issues were accompanied by generalizations understandably intended to offer guidance to other courts and trustees in like situations. These cases were subsequently treated as precedents establishing general rules governing trust investments. Specific case results and flexible principles often thereby became crystallized into specific subrules prescribing the types and characteristics of permissible invest-ments for trustees.

Based on some degree of risk that was abstractly perceived as excessive, broad categories of investments and techniques often came to be classified as "specula-tive" and thus as imprudent per se.[9] Accordingly, the exercise of care, skill, and

---

9. The Restatement (Second) of Trusts took the position that investing in stock in any company other than one "with regular earnings and paying regular dividends which may reasonably be expected to continue," buy-ing securities on margin, or buying discounted bonds was presumptively improper, whereas ordinarily "it is

caution would be no defense if the property acquired or retained by a trustee, or the strategy pursued for a trust, was characterized as impermissible.

Knowledge, practices, and experiences in the modern investment world have demonstrated that arbitrary restrictions on trust investments are unwarranted and often counterproductive. For example, understandable concern has existed that widely accepted theories and practices of investment management cannot properly be pursued by trustees under long-standing judicial and treatise statements of the law. Prohibitions that developed under the traditional prudent-man rule have been potential sources of unjustified liability for trustees generally and, more particularly, of inhibitions limiting the exercise of sound judgment by skilled trustees. This is particularly so for trustees whose fiduciary circumstances call for, or at least permit, investment programs that would include some high risk-and-return strategies (such as a venture capital program) or for the use of abstractly high-risk investments or techniques (such as futures or option trading) for the purpose of reducing the risk level of the portfolio as a whole.

These criticisms of the prudent man rule are supported by a large and growing body of literature that is in turn supported by empirical research, well documented and essentially compelling. Much but not all of this criticism is found in writings that have collectively and loosely come to be called modern portfolio theory.

NOTE: PROBLEMS WITH THE PRUDENT MAN RULE

Among the many problems with the constrained *prudent man rule*, in addition to its male chauvinism, was the prevalence of hindsight bias in its application by the courts. If a higher risk investment did not pay off, the trustee faced potential liability for imprudently speculating in stock. Worse still, courts assessed the prudence of each investment in isolation rather than in the context of the portfolio as a whole, exposing the trustee to liability for a decline in the value of one stock even if that stock was part of a properly designed, well diversified portfolio. An investment in a company that makes suntan lotion looks very different if paired with an investment in a company that makes rain umbrellas versus a company that makes beach umbrellas.

An egregious example of hindsight bias is In re Chamberlain's Estate, 156 A. 42, 43 (N.J. Prerog. 1931): "It was common knowledge, not only amongst bankers and trust companies, but the general public as well, that the stock market condition [in August 1929] was an unhealthy one, that values were very much inflated, and that a crash was almost sure to occur." Common knowledge indeed! If most people know that the market will crash tomorrow, then most people will sell their stock today. If it had been common knowledge in August 1929 that a crash was looming, then the crash would have started in August, not October,

---

proper for a trustee to invest in . . . bonds of the United States or of the State or of municipalities, in first mortgages on land, or in corporate bonds." Restatement (Second) of Trusts §227, cmts. f and m (1959). — Eds.

because each person with such knowledge would have started selling in August, before prices collapsed when everyone else started selling. The court's opinion in Chamberlain's Estate defies logic and the teachings of modern financial theory.

During the latter part of the twentieth century, the prudent man rule came under sustained attack from scholars and sophisticated practitioners. Drawing on the theory of efficient capital markets in general, and on modern portfolio theory in particular, this body of work made a compelling case for reform.[10] See Bevis Longstreth, Modern Investment Management and the Prudent Man Rule (1986); John H. Langbein and Richard A. Posner, Market Funds and Trust Investment Law, 1976 Am. B. Found. Res. J. 1; Part II, 1977 Am. B. Found. Res. J. 1.

Nobel laureate Harry M. Markowitz, the father of modern portfolio theory.

By deeming broad swaths of investments to be *safe* or *speculative*, the prudent man rule ignored the reality that risk is correlated with return. In an efficient market, the tradeoff of risk and return is already reflected in a tradable security's price. As compared to less risky investments, higher risk investments must offer a higher return to compensate the buyer for assuming the additional risk. There is no reason to suppose that in all cases the beneficiary will fare better with a trust portfolio that includes only investments with low risk and low returns.

Under the prudent man rule, cautious trustees regularly invested heavily in government and corporate bonds. Although these types of investments have a relatively low risk of *default*, they expose the trust estate to significant *inflation* risk. If the rate of inflation exceeds the interest rate, in real value the trust estate will shrink. A portfolio that includes stocks is more likely to experience a total return

---

10. This is not to say that the ideas advanced by these scholars were initially well received. One particularly amusing episode involved then-Professor Richard Posner:

> One snowy morning last January [1976], a law professor named Richard Posner gave a talk at a conference on pension-fund investing at New York's Plaza Hotel. Posner was far and away the least popular speaker at the conference. As the drift of his message began to get across to the audience, an angry buzz filled the Terrace Room; before he had finished speaking, many in the audience were no longer listening, but denouncing him to others at their tables. Subsequent speakers warmed themselves to the group by starting off with slighting references to Posner's remarks. [A.F. Ehrbar, Index Funds — An Idea Whose Time Is Coming, Fortune, June 1976, at 145.]

that exceeds the rate of inflation — and so does not shrink in real value — than a portfolio comprised exclusively of government and corporate bonds. Consider the following statistics for average annual return from 1926 to 2007 on various investment vehicles:

Large company stocks	12.2%
Long-term corporate bonds	6.2%
Long-term government bonds	5.8%
Treasury bills	3.8%

During the same period, the average annual rate of inflation was 3.1%. 2008 Ibbotson Stocks, Bonds, Bills, and Inflation Classic Yearbook, at Table 2-1. Even after the disastrous year for stock investments in 2008, which is not reflected in the returns through 2007 reported above, the premium earned by stocks over bonds since 1926 remains quite substantial.

NOTE

Despite its many flaws, the prudent man rule endured into the 1990s. In Jeffrey N. Gordon, The Puzzling Persistence of the Constrained Prudent Man Rule, 62 N.Y.U. L. Rev. 52 (1987), the author examines the institutional features of the trust law reform process. Perhaps the most intriguing idea suggested is that the rule survived because it was merely a default. Those who knew of the rule's defects simply opted out of its application to their trusts. The ease with which the rule could be avoided dulled the incentive of those in the know to lobby for law reform. As Langbein and Posner suggest, the unfortunate consequence of this was that, "for most of the [twentieth] century . . . the law has imposed the traditional standards largely on the beneficiaries of those trust settlors who failed to hire competent counsel." Langbein and Posner, supra, 1976 Am. B. Found. Res. J. at 5.

2. *The Prudent Investor Rule and Modern Trust-Investment Law*

In the 1990s, the *prudent man rule* was finally replaced with the modernized — and gender neutral — *prudent investor rule* that reflects the teachings of modern portfolio theory. The old rule quickly received two deathblows. First, in 1992, the American Law Institute published a revision to the trust-investment sections of the Restatement of Trusts. See Restatement (Third) of Trusts: Prudent Investor Rule (1992).[11] Second, in 1994, the Uniform Law Commission promulgated the Uniform Prudent Investor Act (UPIA). The core reforms of the Restatement and

---

11. The 1992 interim volume was superseded and renumbered in 2007 by the third volume of the finalized Restatement (Third) of Trusts.

the UPIA, which implement the teachings of modern portfolio theory, have been adopted in all states, primarily but not exclusively through adoption of the UPIA.

a.　The Prudent Investor Rule

Uniform Prudent Investor Act (1994)

§2.　STANDARD OF CARE; PORTFOLIO STRATEGY; RISK AND RETURN OBJECTIVES

(a) A trustee shall invest and manage trust assets as a prudent investor would, by considering the purposes, terms, distribution requirements, and other circumstances of the trust. In satisfying this standard, the trustee shall exercise reasonable care, skill, and caution.

(b) A trustee's investment and management decisions respecting individual assets must be evaluated not in isolation, but in the context of the trust portfolio as a whole and as a part of an overall investment strategy having risk and return objectives reasonably suited to the trust.

(c) Among circumstances that the trustee shall consider in investing and managing trust assets are such of the following as are relevant to the trust or its beneficiaries:

(1) general economic conditions;

(2) the possible effect of inflation or deflation;

(3) the expected tax consequences of investment decisions or strategies;

(4) the role that each investment or course of action plays within the overall trust portfolio, which may include financial assets, interests in closely held enterprises, tangible and intangible personal property, and real property;

(5) the expected total return from income and the appreciation of capital;

(6) other resources of the beneficiaries;

(7) needs for liquidity, regularity of income, and preservation or appreciation of capital; and

(8) an asset's special relationship or special value, if any, to the purposes of the trust or to one or more of the beneficiaries.

(d) A trustee shall take reasonable steps to verify facts relevant to the investment and management of trust assets.

(e) A trustee may invest in any kind of property or type of investment consistent with the standards of this [Act].

(f) A trustee who has special skills or expertise, or is named trustee in reliance upon the trustee's representation that the trustee has special skills or expertise, has a duty to use those special skills or expertise.

§3.　DIVERSIFICATION

A trustee shall diversify the investments of the trust unless the trustee reasonably determines that, because of special circumstances, the purposes of the trust are better served without diversifying.

NOTES

1. Restatement (Third) of Trusts §90 (2007), superseding Restatement (Third) of Trusts: Prudent Investor Rule §227 (1992), states a standard of care and a duty to diversify similar to UPIA §§2 and 3. The Restatement also provides extensive, discursive commentary on modern portfolio theory, the new rule, and their relationship.

2. *ERISA*. The Employee Retirement Income Security Act of 1974 (ERISA) governs the investment of pension funds by the trustees managing the funds. ERISA applies to all pension funds except state and local pension funds exempt under 29 U.S.C. §1003(b) (2008). The standard governing investments is the prudent investor rule. See 29 U.S.C. §1104(a) (2008), as interpreted in 29 C.F.R. §2550.404a-1(b) (2008). ERISA also provides that the trustee shall discharge his duties "solely in the interest of the participants and beneficiaries." 29 U.S.C. §1104(a)(1) (2008).

Because the trustees of huge pension and employee benefit funds are subject to duties of prudence and loyalty that are analogous to those in ordinary trust law, the law of private trusts is often at issue in ERISA litigation. At the same time, ERISA cases have come to be cited in decisions involving private trusts, and the drafters of the new prudent investor rule explicitly cited the rule's successful prior implementation under ERISA.

For Professor John H. Langbein's sharp criticism of the Supreme Court's botched encounters with the law of private trusts, see The Supreme Court Flunks Trusts, 1990 Sup. Ct. Rev. 20, and What ERISA Means by "Equitable": The Supreme Court's Trail of Error in Russell, Mertens, and Great-West, 103 Colum. L. Rev. 1317 (2003). See also Trust Law as Regulatory Law: The Unum/Provident Scandal and Judicial Review of Benefit Denials Under ERISA, 101 Nw. U. L. Rev. 1315 (2007).

b.   The Rule Explained and Examined

John H. Langbein, The Uniform Prudent Investor Act
and the Future of Trust Investing
81 Iowa L. Rev. 641 (1996)

The Uniform Prudent Investor Act implements a tightly interconnected set of reforms. These adjustments to the legal regime were driven by profound changes that have occurred across the past generation in our understanding of the investment function. This new learning about the investment process is called the theory of efficient markets, or more broadly, Modern Portfolio Theory (MPT). Four Nobel prizes in economics have thus far been awarded for the academic work that identified and verified the theory of efficient markets, and more will come. As I cover the main features of the Uniform Prudent Investor Act, I have the occasion to point out places in which the influence of MPT is much in evidence. I have tried, however, to avoid the forbidding jargon of the efficient

market literature. Lawyers and courts can understand the essential findings of
MPT without mastering betas, capital asset pricing models, correlation coeffi-
cients, and the like. . . .

In giving content to the prudence label, the Act makes three great changes in
the law. All three were presaged in the 1992 Restatement. First, the Act articulates
a greatly augmented duty to diversify trust investments. Next, in place of the old
preoccupation with avoiding speculation, the Act substitutes a requirement of
sensitivity to the risk tolerance of the particular trust, directing the trustee to
invest for "risk and return objectives reasonably suited to the trust." Finally, the
Act reverses the much criticized nondelegation rule of former law and actually
encourages trustees to delegate investment responsibilities to professionals.

A. Diversification

A duty to diversify trust investments has been recognized in American trust law
for about a century. In recent decades the importance of diversification has been
increasingly emphasized among investment professionals, and accordingly, the
trustee's duty to diversify has become more acute — for example, in ERISA, the
1974 federal pension legislation, a fiduciary must diversify the investments of
participants and beneficiaries to minimize risk of loss unless doing so is clearly
imprudent. The 1992 revision of the Restatement of Trusts integrated the duty to
diversify into the very definition of prudent investing. . . .

The Uniform Prudent Investor Act [in section 3] demands that the "trustee
shall diversify the investments of the trust unless the trustee reasonably determines that, because of special circumstances, the purposes of the trust are better
served without diversifying." . . .

The emphasis on diversification also underlies another prominent feature of
the Uniform Act, the portfolio standard of care in section 2(b), which reads: "A
trustee's investment and management decisions respecting individual assets
must be evaluated not in isolation but in the context of the trust portfolio as a
whole . . . ." The official Comment says: "An investment that might be imprudent
standing alone can become prudent if undertaken in sensible relation to other
trust assets, or to other nontrust assets."

This insistence on diversifying investments responds to one of the central findings of Modern Portfolio Theory, that there are huge and essentially costless gains
to diversifying the portfolio thoroughly. To understand why, begin with the obvious truth that some securities are riskier than others. Investors demand to be paid
to bear the greater risk. For example, a start-up computer software company in
Silicon Valley entails a far larger risk of disappointing returns or total failure than
does a seasoned blue chip such as Mobil Oil or General Electric. If you are a
Silicon Valley entrepreneur who wants me to invest in your start-up firm, you must
offer me an expected return (that is, a combination of dividends and capital
appreciation on the securities) that is higher than Mobil or GE will pay me in
order to induce me to invest in your riskier venture. This calculation is called the
risk/return curve: The higher expected return on the investment compensates
me for bearing the greater risk of the investment being disappointing.

Modern Portfolio Theory isolates three distinct components of the risk of own-ing any security: market risk, industry risk, and firm risk. Market risk is common to all securities; it reflects general economic and political conditions, interest rates, and so forth. Industry risk, by contrast, is specific to the firms in a particu-lar industry or an industry grouping. Finally, firm risk refers to factors that touch the fortunes only of the individual firm. Thus, if we take the international oils for an example, we recall that all the producers suffered from the 1973 Arab oil embargo (industry risk), but only Exxon incurred the liabilities arising from the great Alaskan oil spill of March 1989 (firm risk).

The capital market investigators have actually been able to compute the approximate weight of the three elements that comprise the risk of securities ownership. In round numbers, market risk has been reckoned at 30 percent; the risk of industry and other groupings at 50 percent; and firm risk at 20 percent. These numbers underlie the intense preoccupation with diversification as the means of reducing the risk of investing. By definition, market risk cannot be eliminated through diversification, since market risk is common to all securities. But industry risk and firm risk can be reduced greatly through diversification. To continue with the example of the oil industry, contrast an investor who owned only international oil shares in 1973 with an investor whose portfolio was broadly diversified across many industries. The oil embargo damaged the international oils and the automobile and airline industries, but it triggered a boom in domes-tic oils, in coal stocks, in synthetic fuels, in the energy conservation firms, and in the oilfield equipment industry. We see, therefore, that industry risk is often nega-tively correlated. Owning stocks in these other industries would, in part, have off-set the damage to the industries harmed by the embargo.

Likewise, within an industry, diversification reduces risk. Since I cannot predict the Alaskan oil spill, or any other firm-specific hazard, I can lower my exposure to such firm-specific risks by investing not only in Exxon, but also BP, Shell, Mobil, Texaco, and the others. Indeed, it commonly happens that the perfor-mance of firms in the same industry is negatively correlated — the success of one firm comes at the expense of its competitors. Efficient market theory instructs us that it is impossible to outsmart the market by predicting which securities will do better or worse. Owning many securities enhances the chances of offsetting los-ers with winners.

In the literature of Modern Portfolio Theory, a telling expression has been coined to describe what is wrong with underdiversification: *uncompensated risk*. No one pays the investor for owning too few stocks. Recall that when I spoke of the difference between the Silicon Valley start-up and Mobil Oil, I said that the greater risk intrinsic to the start-up was reflected in its expected return. The investor faced with a choice between mature blue chips and an imperiled new venture will prefer the blue chips unless the new venture offers a superior return, a risk premium. Moving out on the risk/return curve in this way, we routinely observe that the investor who bears the greater risk is compensated for it. By con-trast, no one compensates the investor for having a portfolio that neglects to hold securities in enough industries and firms to achieve effective diversification.

Underdiversification entails needless risk, risk that can be avoided by constructing a sufficiently large and representative portfolio.

Diversification tends to push the investor toward very large portfolios. Although much of the benefits of diversification can be achieved with a carefully selected smaller portfolio, optimal diversification probably requires a portfolio containing hundreds of issues. Relatively few investors, or for our purposes, relatively few trust funds have that much money to invest. Accordingly, an investor who seeks to eliminate the uncompensated risk of underdiversification will usually need to invest in some form of pooled investment vehicle, such as mutual funds or bank common trust funds.

B. Sensitivity to the Risk/Return Curve in Place of the Ban on Speculation

The Uniform Prudent Investor Act eliminates the old categoric restrictions on particular types of investments, such as the prohibition on junior mortgages. Section 2(e) of the Act provides: "A trustee may invest in any kind of property or type of investment consistent with the standards of this [Act]." The official Comment explains:

> The universe of investment products changes incessantly. Investments that were at one time thought too risky, such as equities, or more recently, futures, are now used in fiduciary portfolios. By contrast, the investment that was at one time thought ideal for trusts, the long-term bond, has been discovered to import a level of risk and volatility — in this case, inflation risk — that had not been anticipated.

The idea that some securities are intrinsically too risky for trust investors collides with the central findings of Modern Portfolio Theory. MPT teaches that the risk intrinsic to any marketable security is presumptively already discounted into the current price of the security. Hence, on an expected return basis, the risk is compensated risk. Thus, for example, there is no reason to think that the shares of a bankrupt company are mispriced. The securities markets are so efficient at discounting information about future profitability that today's price fully impounds the future prospects for any firm, even a bankrupt firm, on an expected value basis.

Furthermore, the risk of a high-risk investment can be materially reduced through diversification. That is why sophisticated investors who invest in start-up or otherwise fragile firms commonly employ venture capital funds, which spread the risk of failure of any single firm across a portfolio of many firms. The same logic underlies so-called vulture funds that invest in bankrupt or troubled firms. Some of the firms will fail, but many will thrive. A basket of such securities offers the likelihood of a high net return on an expected return basis.

The drafters of the Uniform Prudent Investor Act reasoned that "trust beneficiaries are better protected by . . . emphasis on close attention to risk/return objectives . . . than in attempts to identify categories of investment that are per se prudent or imprudent." The heart of the Act, section 2(b), states that the "trustee's investment and management decisions" are required to "hav[e] risk and return objectives reasonably suited to the trust." The Act recognizes that investment returns correlate strongly with risk. However, as the official Comment explains, "tolerance for risk varies greatly with the financial and other circumstances of the investor, or in the case of a trust, with the purposes of the trust and the relevant circumstances of the beneficiaries." By way of illustration, the Comment observes that if the "main purpose" of the particular trust "is to support an elderly widow of modest means," that trust "will have a lower risk tolerance than a trust to accumulate for a young scion of great wealth."

Thus, the Act aspires to free trustees from the old preoccupation with avoiding speculation. Should we expect to see future trust portfolios stuffed with penny stocks, Polish zloty futures, and Czarist Russian bonds? The answer, of course, is no. For most trusts and trustees, the outer reaches of the risk/return distribution will be every bit as unsuitable as before. What has changed is that the trustee is now able to examine the risk tolerance of each particular trust and to tailor that trust's investment policy accordingly.

C. DELEGATION

The last of the great reforms of the Uniform Prudent Investor Act is to put the final nails in the coffin of the much criticized former rule that forbade trustees to delegate investment and management functions.

NOTE

1. For a comparable discussion of the new Restatement, see Edward C. Halbach, Jr., Trust Investment Law in the Third Restatement, 77 Iowa L. Rev. 1151 (1992). See also Joel C. Dobris, Speculations on the Idea of "Speculation" in Trust Investing: An Essay, 39 Real Prop., Prob. & Tr. J. 439 (2004).

2. For a lucid and accessible introduction to modern finance written for the trusts and estates professional, see Jonathan R. Macey, An Introduction to Modern Financial Theory (2d ed. 1998).

Max M. Schanzenbach and Robert H. Sitkoff,
Did Reform of Prudent Trust Investment Laws
Change Trust Portfolio Allocation?
50 J.L. & Econ. 681 (2007)

"How do you make a small fortune? Give a bank a large one to manage in trust." So goes an old saw about the banking industry that reflects long experience with risk-averse, conservative trust investing by institutional trustees operating under the prudent-man rule of trust investment law. The prudent-man rule favored "safe" investments such as government bonds and disfavored "speculation" in stock, and under the rule the courts assessed the prudence of each investment in isolation rather than in the context of the portfolio as a whole. In the last 20 years, however, all states have replaced the old prudent-man rule with the new prudent-investor rule. Drawing on the teachings of modern portfolio theory, the new prudent-investor rule directs the trustee to invest on the basis of risk and return objectives reasonably suited to the trust and instructs courts to review the prudence of individual investments not in isolation but in the context of the trust portfolio as a whole. The new prudent-investor rule thus abolishes all categorical restrictions on permissible types of investments and clearly rejects the old law's hostility to investment in stock. . . .

This paper investigates the effect of the change from the prudent-man rule to the prudent-investor rule on stock holdings in noncommercial trusts. In the period under study, 35 states adopted the new prudent-investor rule. Using [federal banking] data from 1986-97, we find that after a state's adoption of the prudent-investor rule, trust institutions held about 1.5-4.5 percentage points more stock at the expense of "safe" investments. This shift to stock amounts to a 3-10 percent increase in stock holdings and accounts for roughly 10-30 percent of the overall increase in stock holdings in the period under study. We provide some evidence that the rest of the increase is attributable to stock market appreciation. . . . We [also] show that the increase in stock holdings after adoption of the new law came largely at the expense of favored "safe" investments such as government bonds. . . .

The results of our empirical analysis demonstrate that changes in the default rules of prudent trust investing affected trust portfolio allocation. . . . Further, our results provide the first empirical evidence that . . . trustee behavior is sensitive to changes in trust fiduciary law . . . .

Depending on the approach taken, the point estimates imply that the trust institutions in our sample increased stock holdings by 1.5-4.5 percentage points — an increase of 3-10 percent — after the adoption of the new prudent-investor rule. Our findings, which endure across a variety of identification strategies and numerous robustness checks, explain roughly 10-30 percent of the overall increase in stock holdings in the period under study. The rest of the increase appears to be attributable to stock market appreciation. . . .

This result is more impressive when one considers that (1) for many trusts the new law will not require a [portfolio] reallocation . . . , (2) the new law requires the trustee of a noncomplying trust to reallocate the trust portfolio within a reasonable time given the tax and other transaction costs of reallocation, and (3) the institutional trustees who make up our sample tend to have access to competent legal counsel and standard-form trust agreements with well-drafted opt-out provisions.

Percentage of stock holdings is an interesting outcome variable not only because of the old rule's hostility toward stock but also because it proxies for movement along the risk and return curve. While we cannot be as firm in our conclusions here, the increase in stock holdings after the adoption of the prudent-investor rule suggests movement outward on the risk and return curve. The agency problems in trust law, together with trustee compensation schemes, rigid doctrine, and hindsight bias, combined to make bank trust departments conservative investors under the old law. We cautiously conclude that the new prudent-investor standard is welfare enhancing.

NOTES

1. In their study of the effect of the new prudent investor rule, Professors Schanzenbach and Sitkoff analyzed data collected by federal banking authorities from federally regulated institutional trustees such as banks, savings and loan associations, and certain trust companies. As demonstrated by the following graph, made with that data, there has been a profound shift from government bonds to corporate stock over the past 20 years, with the most pronounced movement coming in the years after the promulgation of the Restatement (1992) and UPIA (1994).

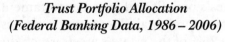

Trust Portfolio Allocation
(Federal Banking Data, 1986 – 2006)

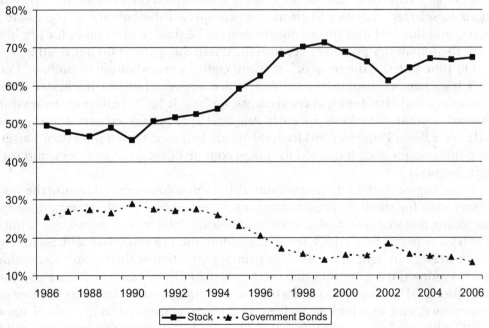

2. In Martin D. Begleiter, Does the Prudent Investor Need the Prudent Investor Act — An Empirical Study of Trust Investment Practices, 51 Me. L. Rev. 28, 70-72 (1999), the author surveyed 239 banking institutions in Iowa about their interpretation of the new Iowa prudent investor rule. Of the 61 institutions replying, a substantial majority indicated that they employed risk and return analysis in making trust investments and that the new prudent investor rule did not flatly prohibit specific investments.

c.   Risk, Return, and Diversification in Practice

In re Estate of Janes
Court of Appeals of New York, 1997
681 N.E.2d 332

LEVINE, J.   Former State Senator and businessman Rodney B. Janes (testator) died on May 26, 1973, survived solely by his wife, Cynthia W. Janes, who was then 72 years of age. Testator's $3,500,000 estate consisted of a $2,500,000 stock portfolio, approximately 71% of which consisted of 13,232 shares of common stock of the Eastman Kodak Company.[12] The Kodak stock had a date-of-death value of $1,786,733, or approximately $135 per share.

Testator's 1963 will and a 1969 codicil bequeathed most of his estate to three trusts. First, the testator created a marital deduction trust consisting of approximately 50% of the estate's assets, the income of which was to be paid to Mrs. Janes for her life. In addition, it contained a generous provision for invasion of the principal for Mrs. Janes's benefit and gave her testamentary power of appointment over the remaining principal. The testator also established a charitable trust of approximately 25% of the estate's assets which directed annual distributions to selected charities. A third trust comprised the balance of the estate's assets and directed that the income therefrom be paid to Mrs. Janes for her life, with the remainder pouring over into the charitable trust upon her death.

On June 6, 1973, the testator's will and codicil were admitted to probate. Letters testamentary issued to petitioner's predecessor, Lincoln Rochester Trust Company, and Mrs. Janes, as coexecutors, on July 3, 1973. Letters of trusteeship issued to petitioner alone. By early August 1973, petitioner's trust and estate officers, Ellison Patterson and Richard Young had ascertained the estate's assets and the amount of cash needed for taxes, commissions, attorneys' fees, and specific bequests.

In an August 9, 1973 memorandum, Patterson recommended raising the necessary cash for the foregoing administrative expenses by selling certain assets, including 800 shares of Kodak stock, and holding "the remaining issues . . . until the [t]rusts [were] funded." The memorandum did not otherwise address investment strategy in light of the evident primary objective of the testator to provide for his widow during her lifetime. In a September 5, 1973 meeting with Patterson and Young, Mrs. Janes, who had a high school education, no business training or experience, and who had never been employed, consented to the sale of some 1,200 additional shares of Kodak stock. Although Mrs. Janes was informed at the meeting that petitioner intended to retain the balance of the Kodak shares, none of the factors that would lead to an informed investment decision was discussed. At that time, the Kodak stock traded for about $139 per share; thus, the

---

12. Rodney B. Janes, born in Rochester on October 21, 1892, served in the New York State Senate from 1939 until 1946, representing the Rochester area. Inquiry by the editors revealed no clear explanation for Janes's high concentration of Kodak stock except for Kodak's being a Rochester company. — Eds.

Rodney B. Janes

estate's 13,232 shares of the stock were worth alm[o]
$1,840,000. The September 5 meeting was the only occasion
where retention of the Kodak stock or any other investment
issues were taken up with Mrs. Janes.

By the end of 1973, the price of Kodak stock had fallen to
about $109 per share. One year later, it had fallen to about $63
per share and, by the end of 1977, to about $51 per share. In
March 1978, the price had dropped even further, to about $40
per share. When petitioner filed its initial accounting in February 1980, the remaining 11,320 shares were worth approximately $530,000, or about $47 per share. Most of the shares were used to fund
the trusts in 1986 and 1987.

In addition to its initial accounting in 1980, petitioner filed a series of supplemental accountings that together covered the period from July 1973 through
June 1994. In August 1981, petitioner sought judicial settlement of its account.
Objections to the accounts were originally filed by Mrs. Janes in 1982, and subsequently by the Attorney-General on behalf of the charitable beneficiaries (collectively, "objectants"). In seeking to surcharge petitioner for losses incurred by
the estate due to petitioner's imprudent retention of a high concentration of
Kodak stock in the estate from July 1973 to February 1980, during which time the
value of the stock had dropped to about one third of its date-of-death value,
objectants asserted that petitioner's conduct violated EPTL 11-2.2(a)(1), the
so-called "prudent person rule" of investment. When Mrs. Janes died in 1986,
the personal representative of her estate was substituted as an objectant.

Following a trial on the objections, the Surrogate found that petitioner, under
the circumstances, had acted imprudently and should have divested the estate of
the high concentration of Kodak stock by August 9, 1973. The court imposed a
$6,080,269 surcharge against petitioner and ordered petitioner to forfeit its com-
missions and attorneys' fees. In calculating the amount of the surcharge, the
court adopted a "lost profits" or "market index" measure of damages espoused
by objectants' expert — what the proceeds of the Kodak stock would have yielded,
up to the time of trial, had they been invested in petitioner's own diversified
equity fund on August 9, 1973.

The Appellate Division modified solely as to damages, holding that "the Surrogate properly found [petitioner] liable for its negligent failure to diversify and
for its inattentiveness, inaction, and lack of disclosure, but that the Surrogate
adopted an improper measure of damages." In a comprehensive opinion by Pre-
siding Justice M. Dolores Denman, the Court held that the Surrogate's finding of
imprudence, as well as its selection of August 9, 1973 as the date by which petitioner should have divested the estate of its concentration of Kodak stock, were
"well supported" by the record. The Court rejected the Surrogate's "lost profits"
or "market index" measure of damages, however, holding that the proper measure of damages was "the value of the capital that was lost" — the difference

ue of the stock at the time it should have been sold and its value
sold. Applying this measure, the Court reduced the surcharge to
granted petitioner and objectants leave to appeal, and now

LIABILITY

Petitioner argues that New York law does not permit a fiduciary to be surcharged for imprudent management of a trust for failure to diversify in the absence of additional elements of hazard, and that it relied upon, and complied with, this rule in administering the estate. Relying on Matter of Balfe, 274 N.Y.S. 284, mod. 280 N.Y.S. 128 (App. Div. 1935), petitioner claims that elements of hazard can be capsulized into deficiencies in the following investment quality factors: "(i) the capital structure of the company; (ii) the competency of its management; (iii) whether the company is a seasoned issuer of stock with a history of profitability; (iv) whether the company has a history of paying dividends; (v) whether the company is an industry leader; (vi) the expected future direction of the company's business; and (vii) the opinion of investment bankers and analysts who follow the company's stock." Evaluated under these criteria, petitioner asserts, the concentration of Kodak stock at issue in this case, that is, of an acknowledged "blue chip" security popular with investment advisors and many mutual funds, cannot be found an imprudent investment on August 9, 1973 as a matter of law. In our view, a fiduciary's duty of investment prudence in holding a concentration of one security may not be so rigidly limited.

New York followed the prudent person rule of investment during the period of petitioner's administration of the instant estate. This rule provides that "[a] fiduciary holding funds for investment may invest the same in such securities as would be acquired by prudent [persons] of discretion and intelligence in such matters who are seeking a reasonable income and the preservation of their capital" (EPTL 11-2.2[a][1]).[13] . . .

No precise formula exists for determining whether the prudent person standard has been violated in a particular situation; rather, the determination depends on an examination of the facts and circumstances of each case. In undertaking this inquiry, the court should engage in "a balanced and perceptive analysis of [the fiduciary's] consideration and action in light of the history of each individual investment, viewed at the time of its action or its omission to act" (Matter of Donner, 626 N.E.2d 922 (N.Y. 1993)). And, while a court should not view each act or omission aided or enlightened by hindsight, a court may, nevertheless, examine the fiduciary's conduct over *the entire course of the investment* in determining whether it has acted prudently. Generally, whether a

---

13. The recently enacted Prudent Investor Act requires a trustee "to diversify assets unless the trustee reasonably determines that it is in the interests of the beneficiaries not to diversify, taking into account the purposes and terms and provisions of the governing instrument" (EPTL 11-2.3[b][3][C]). The act applies to investments "made or held" by a trustee on or after January 1, 1995 and, thus, does not apply to the matter before us (EPTL 11-2.3[a]).

fiduciary has acted prudently is a factual determination to be made by the tr[...]
court.

As the foregoing demonstrates, the very nature of the prudent person standard dictates against any absolute rule that a fiduciary's failure to diversify, in and of itself, constitutes imprudence, as well as against a rule invariably immunizing a fiduciary from its failure to diversify in the absence of some selective list of elements of hazard, such as those identified by petitioner. Indeed, in various cases, courts have determined that a fiduciary's retention of a high concentration of one asset in a trust or estate was imprudent without reference to those elements of hazard (see, Matter of Donner, supra). The inquiry is simply whether, under all the facts and circumstances of the particular case, the fiduciary violated the prudent person standard in maintaining a concentration of a particular stock in the estate's portfolio of investments. . . .

Petitioner's restrictive list of hazards omits such additional factors to be considered under the prudent person rule by a trustee in weighing the propriety of any investment decision, as: "the amount of the trust estate, the situation of the beneficiaries, the trend of prices and of the cost of living, the prospect of inflation and of deflation" (Restatement [Second] of Trusts §227, comment e). Other pertinent factors are the marketability of the investment and possible tax consequences (id., comment o). The trustee must weigh all of these investment factors as they affect the principal objects of the testator's or settlor's bounty, as between income beneficiaries and remainder persons, including decisions regarding "whether to apportion the investments between high-yield or high-growth securities" (Turano and Radigan, New York Estate Administration ch. 14, §P, at 409 [1986]).

Moreover, and especially relevant to the instant case, the various factors affecting the prudence of any particular investment must be considered in the light of the "circumstances of the trust itself rather than [merely] the integrity of the particular investment". . . .

Thus, the elements of hazard petitioner relies upon as demonstrating that, as a matter of law, it had no duty to diversify, suffer from two major deficiencies under the prudent person rule. First, petitioner's risk elements too narrowly and strictly define the scope of a fiduciary's responsibility in making any individual investment decision, and the factors a fiduciary must consider in determining the propriety of a given investment.

A second deficiency in petitioner's elements of hazard list is that all of the factors relied upon by petitioner go to the propriety of an individual investment "exclusively . . . as though it were in its own water-tight compartment," which would encourage a fiduciary to treat each investment as an isolated transaction rather than "in its relation to the whole of the trust estate." Thus, petitioner's criteria for elements of hazard would apply irrespective of the *concentration* of the investment security under consideration in the portfolio. That is, the existence of any of the elements of risk specified by petitioner in a given corporate security would militate against the investment even in a *diversified* portfolio, obviating any need to consider concentration as a reason to divest or refrain from investing. This ignores the market reality that, with respect to some investment vehicles,

self may create or add to risk, and essentially takes lack of diver-
the prudent person equation altogether. ...

ing an investment portfolio in which Kodak represented 71% of
k holdings, and the balance was largely in other growth stocks,
insufficient attention to the needs and interests of the testator's
low, the life beneficiary of three quarters of his estate, for whose
ort and anticipated increased medical expenses the testamentary
ently created. Testimony by petitioner's investment manager, and
by the objectants' experts, disclosed that the annual yield on Kodak stock in 1973
was approximately 1.06%, and that the aggregate annual income from all estate
stockholdings was $43,961, a scant 1.7% of the $2.5 million estate securities portfolio. Thus, retention of a high concentration of Kodak jeopardized the interests
of the primary income beneficiary of the estate and led to the eventual need to
substantially invade the principal of the marital testamentary trust.

Lastly, there was evidence in the record to support the findings below that, in
managing the estate's investments, petitioner failed to exercise due care and the
skill it held itself out as possessing as a corporate fiduciary. Notably, there was
proof that petitioner (1) failed initially to undertake a formal analysis of the estate
and establish an investment plan consistent with the testator's primary objectives; (2) failed to follow petitioner's own internal trustee review protocol during
the administration of the estate, which advised special caution and attention in
cases of portfolio concentration of as little as 20%; and (3) failed to conduct more
than routine reviews of the Kodak holdings in this estate, without considering
alternative investment choices, over a seven-year period of steady decline in the
value of the stock.

Since, thus, there was evidence in the record to support the foregoing affirmed
findings of imprudence on the part of petitioner, the determination of liability
must be affirmed.

II. DATE OF DIVESTITURE

As we have noted, in determining whether a fiduciary has acted prudently, a court
may examine a fiduciary's conduct throughout the entire period during which
the investment at issue was held (see, Matter of Donner, supra). The court may
then determine, within that period, the "reasonable time" within which divesture
of the imprudently held investment should have occurred. What constitutes a reasonable time will vary from case to case and is not fixed or arbitrary. The test
remains "the diligence and prudence of prudent and intelligent [persons] in the
management of their own affairs." Thus, in *Donner*, we upheld both the Surrogate's examination of the fiduciary's conduct throughout the entire period during which the investment at issue was retained in finding liability, and the
Surrogate's selection of the date of the testator's death as the time when the
trustee should have divested the estate of its substantial holdings in high-risk
securities.

Again, there is evidentiary support in the record for the trial court's finding,
affirmed by the Appellate Division, that a prudent fiduciary would have divested

the estate's stock portfolio of its high concentration of Kodak stock by August 9, 1973, thereby exhausting our review powers on this issue. Petitioner's own internal documents and correspondence, as well as the testimony of Patterson, Young, and objectants' experts, establish that by that date, petitioner had all the information a prudent investor would have needed to conclude that the percentage of Kodak stock in the estate's stock portfolio was excessive and should have been reduced significantly, particularly in light of the estate's over-all investment portfolio and the financial requirements of Mrs. Janes and the charitable beneficiaries.

III. DAMAGES

Finally, as to the calculation of the surcharge, we conclude that the Appellate Division correctly rejected the Surrogate's "lost profits" or "market index" measure of damages. Where, as here, a fiduciary's imprudence consists solely of negligent retention of assets it should have sold, the measure of damages is the value of the lost capital. Thus, the Surrogate's reliance on Matter of Rothko in imposing a "lost profit" measure of damages is inapposite, since in that case the fiduciary's misconduct consisted of deliberate self-dealing and faithless transfers of trust property.

In imposing liability upon a fiduciary on the basis of the capital lost, the court should determine the value of the stock on the date it should have been sold, and subtract from that figure the proceeds from the sale of the stock or, if the stock is still retained by the estate, the value of the stock at the time of the accounting. Whether interest is awarded, and at what rate, is a matter within the discretion of the trial court. Dividends and other income attributable to the retained assets should offset any interest awarded.

Here, uncontradicted expert testimony established that application of this measure of damages resulted in a figure of $4,065,029, which includes prejudgment interest at the legal rate, compounded from August 9, 1973 to October 1, 1994. The Appellate Division did not abuse its discretion in adding to that figure prejudgment interest from October 1, 1994 through August 17, 1995, $326,302.66 previously received by petitioner for commissions and attorneys' fees, plus postjudgment interest, costs, and disbursements.

Accordingly, the order of the Appellate Division should be affirmed, without costs.

NOTES AND QUESTIONS

1. *Prudent man or prudent investor?* In footnote 13, page 704, the court stated that it reviewed the trustee's conduct under the old prudent man rule, progressively called the prudent person rule in New York, because the conduct predated the state's new UPIA-based prudent investor rule. The trustee was therefore not subject to the explicit statutory requirement to diversify. Do you accept this at face value? Does not the opinion read as if it were decided under the new law? In the

decades prior to *Janes*, it was often said that New York trustees did not have a duty to diversify. See Note, Trust Fund Investment in New York: The Prudent Man Rule and Diversification of Investments, 47 N.Y.U. L. Rev. 527 (1972). On the other hand, a duty to diversify is detectable in other states as early as Appeal of Dickinson, 25 N.E. 99 (Mass. 1890).

What could the trustee have done to avoid the risk of subsequent judicial review informed by evolving understandings of finance theory and prudent trust investment practices?

2. *What others were doing.* The trustee in *Janes* defended its retention of the Kodak stock on the grounds that Kodak was "an acknowledged 'blue chip' security popular with investment advisors and many mutual funds." According to a story in the New York Times (Aug. 23, 1976, at 45), by the middle of 1976 Kodak remained among the top five holdings of bank trust departments (the other four were IBM, Exxon, General Motors, and AT&T). The question thus arises, why did so many investment professionals remain loyal to Kodak despite its collapsing stock price? The answer might have something to do with the *nifty-fifty* phenomenon of the 1970s. Professor Malkiel explains:

> In the 1970s, . . . investing in blue-chip companies was in. . . . Nothing could be more prudent than to buy their shares and then relax on the golf course while the long-term rewards materialized.
>
> There were only four dozen or so of these premier growth stocks . . . . Their names were familiar — IBM, Xerox, Avon Products, Kodak, McDonald's, Polaroid, and Disney — and they were called the Nifty Fifty. They were "big capitalization" stocks, which meant that an institution could buy a good-sized position without disturbing the market. And because most pros realized that picking the exact correct time to buy is difficult if not impossible, these stocks seemed to make a great deal of sense. So what if you paid a price that was temporarily too high? These stocks were proven growers, and sooner or later the price you paid would be justified. In addition, these were stocks that — like the family heirlooms — you would never sell. Hence they also were called "one decision" stocks. You made a decision to buy them, once, and your portfolio-management problems were over.
>
> These stocks provided security blankets for institutional investors in another way, too. They were so respectable. Your colleagues could never question your prudence in investing in IBM. True, you could lose money if IBM went down, but that was not considered a sign of imprudence . . . .
>
> The end was inevitable. The Nifty Fifty craze ended like all other speculative manias. Sooner or later the same money managers who had worshiped the Nifty Fifty decided that the stocks were overpriced and made a second decision — to sell. In the debacle that followed, the premier growth stocks fell completely from favor. [Burton G. Malkiel, A Random Walk Down Wall Street 66-68 (rev. ed. 2007).]

3. *How much diversification is enough?* In Jonathan R. Macey, An Introduction to Modern Financial Theory 24-26 (2d ed. 1998), the author reviews the literature of financial economics and concludes: "Empirical studies have shown that a small amount of diversification goes a long way. For example, it has been shown that a portfolio of ten stocks provides 88.5 percent of the possible advantages of diversification. A portfolio of 20 stocks provides 94.2 percent of the advantages of diversification. . . . [I]nvestors need a very good excuse for not holding a diversified portfolio, because investors who do not hold such portfolios are

assuming risks that they could easily avoid through diversification." The key point to grasp is that, on average, investors who fail to diversify do not receive higher returns to compensate them for taking on the extra risk of their portfolio suffering from the troubles of just one firm or one industry.

4. *Excuses for not diversifying.* It may be prudent not to diversify or to delay diversification when the tax or other costs of reorganizing the portfolio are likely to outweigh the benefits of diversification. See UPIA §3, cmt. A lack of diversification might be justifiable in the case of a trust that holds a family business, particularly if the business is closely held and not readily marketable. See In re Hyde, 845 N.Y.S.2d 833 (App. Div. 2007). Failure to diversify is likely to be justifiable for a trust that holds the surviving spouse's residence, the family vacation home, the family farm, or other such assets. See In re Trust Created by Inman, 693 N.W.2d 514 (Neb. 2005).

Diversification might not be necessary if the trust is but one component of a larger scheme such that the beneficiary's financial interests are diversified overall. See John H. Langbein, Mandatory Rules in the Law of Trusts, 98 Nw. U. L. Rev. 1105, 1114-1115 (2004).

How is diversification to be obtained in a small trust? The comment to UPIA §3 suggests pooled investments such as mutual funds and common trust funds. It may even be acceptable to invest the entire trust in a single such fund, provided that the trustee exercises due care in choosing and monitoring it.

NOTE: CALCULATING DAMAGES FOR IMPRUDENT INVESTMENT

The core principle in trust remedy law is to put the beneficiary in at least the position that she would have been in had the breach not occurred. This *make-whole* standard is implemented by holding the trustee liable for any losses incurred and gains forgone as a result of the breach. In addition, the trustee is liable for any profit made by the trustee through the breach of trust. See UTC §1002 (2000). The question thus arises, how is the make-whole policy applied in a case of imprudent investment?

In *Janes*, the New York Court of Appeals awarded $4,065,029 in damages as the measure of *capital lost plus interest*. This figure represents the value of the trust's Kodak stock on August 9, 1973, the date by which the trial court found the trustee should have divested, plus compound interest through October 1, 1994, minus the actual value of the trust. The court indicated that the rate of interest, if any, should be set at the discretion of the trial court, though it did not discuss the rate used in this case. Our review of the record on appeal indicates that the interest rate used varied from 6 to 9 percent from year to year.[14] The specific rate used in each year was New York's legal rate of interest in that year. The legal rate of interest is the statutory interest rate that is applied to delayed payment on a

---

14. We thank Professor Kenneth Joyce of the University of Buffalo Law School, State University of New York, for supplying us with the briefs and record on appeal. Professor Joyce was co-counsel on behalf of Mrs. Janes's estate before the New York Court of Appeals.

money judgment. That rate is currently a whopping 9 percent, see N.Y. Civ. Prac. L. & R. §5004 (2008), considerably more than prevailing market interest rates.

There can be wide variance in the interest calculation depending on the rate of interest used and whether interest is compounded. Consider the following table, which shows the value of the trust's Kodak stock on August 9, 1973 ($1,687,647.30), plus interest through October 1, 1994, compounded yearly, at three different plausible rates:

Interest Rate	*Value in 21 Years*
3.1% (the historic average annual rate of inflation)	$ 3,218,579.15
5.8% (the historic average annual return on long-term government bonds)	$ 5,560,617.05
9% (the current New York legal rate)	$10,444,242.68

Is the legal rate of interest a good proxy for the rate of return that the trust portfolio would have experienced? Are there other policies, such as simplicity, in favor of using this rate? What considerations are relevant in choosing the rate of interest?

The alternative to capital lost plus interest is *total return damages*. The total return approach requires the finder of fact, usually with the assistance of expert testimony, to compare the actual performance of the imprudent portfolio against the performance of a hypothetical prudent portfolio, and to award damages in the amount of the difference, perhaps adjusting for taxes and other expenses and distributions.

The trial court in *Janes* awarded total return damages of $6,080,269. In the trial court's view, this figure represented the amount "of the difference between what the estate actually received from the Kodak stock and what the estate would have received if the stock had been sold in August of 1973 and reinvested" in a prudent portfolio. For the model of a prudent portfolio, the trial court looked to the performance of "the bank's own diversified equity fund," of which less than 3 percent was invested in Kodak. Like the choice of interest rate in the capital lost plus interest calculation, the choice of model portfolio is critical for a total return computation. In this case, other models produced measures of damages ranging between $4,065,029 and $7,530,547. In re Judicial Settlement of the Account of Lincoln First Bank, 630 N.Y.S.2d 472 (Sur. 1995).

Although rejected by the Court of Appeals in *Janes*, the total return approach is endorsed by Restatement (Third) of Trusts: Prudent Investor Rule §§205, 208-211 (1992) and implicitly by UTC §1002. The Scott treatise explains:

> It has often been thought that the appropriate remedy . . . was to hold the trustee liable for the initial amount of the loss, plus statutory interest. Indeed, such a remedy may be appropriate when the time between the breach and the remedy is short and the relevant interest rate closely reflects the income yield of comparable trusts. Yet such a remedy nearly always misses the mark, and often badly, when the interval between the breach and the remedy is substantial. If the applicable interest rate is lower than the total return (including both income and capital appreciation) that the trust would have earned in the absence of the

breach, such a remedy plainly undercompensates the loss. By the same token, if the relevant interest rate is higher than what the trust's total return would have been, such a remedy may yield overcompensation. . . .

These days, courts seem increasingly willing to calculate the trust estate's total loss not by reference to an initial loss, increased by statutory interest, but by reference to the more general concept of what it would take to make the trust estate whole. . . .

In most cases, . . . determining what it would take to make the trust estate whole requires inquiry into what the trust *likely would have earned*, in the absence of the breach of trust. In some cases, . . . it may be necessary to inquire into the actual total return during the relevant period of one or more comparable trusts on part or all of their holdings. For example, one or more breaches of trust may have had a substantial adverse impact on the trust's overall productivity as when the trustee has improperly failed to invest or diversify any of the trust estate. . . . It may even be appropriate to refer to the performance of one or more market indices, in determining what it will take to make the trust estate and its beneficiaries whole. [4 Austin Wakeman Scott, William Franklin Fratcher, and Mark L. Ascher, Scott and Ascher on Trusts §24.9 (5th ed. 2007).]

Which approach better fits the new prudent investor rule? Are there other relevant considerations, such as simplicity of application or transparency for appellate scrutiny?

In considering the trustee's failure to diversify in *Janes*, what is the relevance, if any, of the fact that Kodak stock comprised over 70 percent of the testator's pre-death $2.5 million stock portfolio? Did Janes implicitly consent to the trustee's retention of the Kodak stock? Suppose Janes had expressly consented to the trustee's retention of the Kodak stock or, even more difficult, that in his will he instructed the trustee to retain the stock. Would such a clause save the trustee from liability for failing to diversify?

Uniform Prudent Investor Act (1994)

§1.   PRUDENT INVESTOR RULE

(a) Except as otherwise provided in subsection (b), a trustee who invests and manages trust assets owes a duty to the beneficiaries of the trust to comply with the prudent investor rule set forth in this [Act].

(b) The prudent investor rule, a default rule, may be expanded, restricted, eliminated, or otherwise altered by the provisions of a trust. A trustee is not liable to a beneficiary to the extent that the trustee acted in reasonable reliance on the provisions of the trust.

§4.   DUTIES AT INCEPTION OF TRUSTEESHIP

Within a reasonable time after accepting a trusteeship or receiving trust assets, a trustee shall review the trust assets and make and implement decisions concerning the retention and disposition of assets, in order to bring the trust portfolio into compliance with the purposes, terms, distribution requirements, and other circumstances of the trust, and with the requirements of this [Act].

Wood v. U.S. Bank, N.A.
Court of Appeals of Ohio, 2005
828 N.E.2d 1072

PAINTER, J.   This case turns on a question of law that has received little judicial attention in Ohio. Does a trustee have a duty to diversify the assets of a trust when the language of the trust authorizes retention of a specific asset, namely stock in the corporate trustee?

We hold that even if the trust document allows the trustee to "retain" assets that would not normally be suitable, the trustee's duty to diversify remains unless there are special circumstances. Of course, a trustee's duty to diversify may be expanded, restricted, eliminated, or otherwise altered by the terms of the trust. But this statement is true only if the instrument creating the trust clearly indicates an intention to abrogate the common-law, now statutory, duty to diversify. . . .

I. THE TRUST

[The] husband [of plaintiff-appellant, Dana Barth Wood ("Wood")], John Wood II (we will use his first name because there are other Woods in the case), was a prominent Cincinnati attorney with estate-planning experience. John created a trust worth over $8 million. Wood was a beneficiary of the trust. John served as trustee during his lifetime and named Star Bank the successor trustee. Star Bank, formerly First National Bank of Cincinnati, later became Firstar Bank. U.S. Bank is the successor-in-interest to First National, Star, and Firstar. At this writing at least, it is still U.S. Bank. Because it was the language used through most of the trial, we refer to the trustee as "Firstar" and the disputed stock as "Firstar stock." Nearly 80 percent of the trust assets were in Firstar stock. The rest was mostly Cincinnati Financial Corporation stock. . . .

The trust specifically gave Firstar the power "[t]o retain any securities in the same form as when received, including shares of a corporate Trustee . . . , even though all of such securities are not of the class of investments a trustee may be permitted by law to make and to hold cash uninvested as they deem advisable or proper." The unfortunate wording of this sentence makes it unclear whether the "advisable or proper" — a redundant couplet — applied to the cash only, not the other assets. Grammatically, that is the meaning. Luckily, our holding makes it unnecessary to construe this language; but we caution that this type of fuzzy drafting can create problems.

The trust did not last long — John had directed the trustee to distribute almost all the trust assets to the beneficiaries after paying the debts and expenses of the estate. Beginning in early 1998, Firstar had custody of the trust assets.

II. Reverse Diversification

Shortly after John's death, Firstar's trust officers and the beneficiaries (including Wood) met to discuss the estate. . . .

At the meeting, Firstar recommended selling some stock to pay the debts and expenses of the estate and retaining the remainder pending the eventual distribution to the beneficiaries free of trust. The debts and expenses were nearly $4 million; the trust itself contained approximately $8 million, of which roughly $6 million was in Firstar stock. This plan did not call for selling any Firstar stock other than what was necessary to cover the taxes and other debts. Firstar trust officers premised the plan on Firstar stock's strong earnings momentum at the time, so it called for a sale of two-thirds of Cincinnati Financial stock and only about ten percent of the Firstar stock.

Since the original composition of the trust was 82 percent Firstar stock and 18 percent Cincinnati Financial stock, selling more of the Cincinnati Financial stock meant that the final trust was approximately 86 percent Firstar stock and only 14 percent Cincinnati Financial stock. The trust officers and Sean Wood (one of the other beneficiaries) testified that the parties agreed to the distribution plan. Firstar estimated that it would take 18 to 20 months to finalize the estate. At trial, Wood agreed that she had seen the distribution plan and did not object to it at the meeting. But she emphasized that she had asked Firstar to diversify once the stock started increasing in value.

Firstar held the assets during this time and did not diversify. . . . Firstar focused primarily on liquidating non-Firstar stock to raise estate-tax funds. Though approximately half of the Cincinnati Financial stock was sold (for around $1 million), only about ten percent of the Firstar stock was sold. Thus, Firstar stock made up an even higher percentage of the trust assets after the liquidation because there was so much of it to begin with.

Because of a Firstar merger, Firstar's stock increased from about $21 per share in October 1998 to almost $35 per share in early 1999. In April 1999, Wood asked Firstar to sell some of the stock. Harvey Knowles, Wood's advisor, also requested diversification. Neither Wood nor her attorneys and financial advisors made any written request that Firstar diversify the trust assets. Firstar did not sell any stock as a result of these requests.

Firstar's stock price plunged beginning in mid-1999. And by mid-2000, it was worth only $16 per share. It was around this time that Firstar made the final distribution to the beneficiaries. According to expert testimony based on calculations using an average mutual fund as the basis for estimating value, Firstar's failure to diversify cost Wood $771,099.

III. A Lawsuit, A Jury Trial, and An Appeal

Wood sued Firstar, asserting that Firstar had violated Ohio law by failing to diversify the assets of the trust. . . . Wood claimed that, under [the Ohio UPIA], Firstar had a mandatory duty to diversify absent special circumstances. She also argued that Firstar had made no attempt to show special circumstances that would have relaxed its mandatory duty to diversify and that no such circumstances existed. . . .

Wood proposed jury instructions based on the UPIA. The trial court rejected the statute-based instructions, and over Wood's objections, the trial court adopted Firstar's abuse-of-discretion and estoppel instructions.

The jury returned a verdict against Wood. . . .

IV. To Diversify or Not to Diversify?

Because the issue of a trustee's duty to diversify is dispositive, we first address [this issue]. Wood argues that the trial court erred by providing the jury with an abuse-of-discretion standard and by refusing to instruct the jury in accordance with [the Ohio UPIA]. . . .

We must therefore first determine whether Firstar had a duty to diversify. Duties owed by a trustee to the beneficiaries are well established. "A trustee shall diversify the investments of a trust unless the trustee reasonably determines that, because of special circumstances, the purposes of the trust are better served without diversifying." R.C. 1339.54(B). This duty may be expanded, restricted, eliminated, or otherwise altered by the trust instrument. R.C. 1339.52(C). This duty, imposed by the UPIA, is the same one recognized by the common law; the common law is now codified.

V. It Means What It Says — And Nothing More

The language of John's last trust was unambiguous. It granted Firstar the power to retain its own stock in the trust even though Firstar would ordinarily not have been permitted to hold its own stock. Specifically, Firstar had the power "[t]o retain any securities in the same form as when received, including shares of a corporate Trustee . . . , even though all of such securities are not of the class of investments a trustee may be permitted by law to make and to hold cash uninvested as they deem advisable or proper."

Wood now presents "The Rule of Undivided Loyalty" to support her claim that the retention language in the trust did not lessen Firstar's duty to diversify. This rule states that "[t]he foremost duty which a fiduciary owes to its beneficiary is undivided loyalty." Ledbetter v. First State Bank & Trust Co., 85 F.3d 1537, 1540 (11th Cir. 1996). This rule prohibits the trustee's ownership of its own stock. Id. But it does not apply to prohibit ownership when the trustor gives the trustee the "authority to retain stock received from the trustor." Id. at 1544; see also Restatement (Third) of Trusts §227(b) and 229, cmt. d (1992). The only restriction to the exception is that the trustee "must not act in bad faith or abuse its discretion." Id. But because the trustee still has the duty to act prudently, and diversification is normally called for, the retention language in this case did not affect the duty to diversify.

The retention clause merely served to circumvent the rule of undivided loyalty. The trust did not say anything about diversification. And the retention language smacked of the standard boilerplate that was intended merely to circumvent the rule of undivided loyalty — no more, no less. There were significant tax consequences that precluded John from diversifying by selling the Firstar stock during his lifetime, but that hurdle was removed upon his death. Had John wanted to eliminate Firstar's duty to diversify, he could simply have said so. He could have mentioned that duty in the retention clause. Or he could have included another clause specifically lessening the duty to diversify. But he did not. We hold that the language of a trust does not alter a trustee's duty to diversify unless the instrument creating the trust clearly indicates an intention to do so.

Wood also cites [Ohio UPIA §§3 and 4]. As we have already said, these provisions codified the common law, imposing mandatory investment standards upon the trustee, including the duty to diversify. Under [Ohio UPIA §3], there is a single exception for the duty to diversify. This duty arises when the trustee "reasonably" determines that that there are "special circumstances." In this case, the question of special circumstances was never presented to the jury, even though identifying special circumstances was the only way that Firstar could possibly have been relieved of its duty to diversify.

In response, Firstar cites [Ohio UPIA §1, which states that the prudent investor rule] "may be expanded, restricted, eliminated, or otherwise altered, without express reference to these sections by the instrument creating a trust." [It also] states, "A trustee is not liable to a beneficiary of a trust to the extent the trustee acted in reasonable reliance on the provisions of the trust."

The Third Restatement of Trusts states, "In making and implementing investing decisions, the trustee has a duty to diversify the investments unless, under the circumstances, it is not prudent to do so." Restatement (Third) of Trusts: Prudent Investor Rule §227(b) (1992). And with regard to a trustee's duty regarding original investments, the comments to the Restatement indicate that a broad generalization is not enough to relieve a trustee of its duty to diversify:

> A general authorization in an applicable statute or in the terms of the trust to retain investments received as a part of a trust estate does not ordinarily abrogate the trustee's duty with respect to diversification or the trustee's general duty to act with prudence in investment matters. [Restatement (Third) of Trusts: Prudent Investor Rule §229, cmt. d (1992).]

This is precisely what the retention language here was — a general authorization. The Restatement continues,

> The terms of the trust, however, may permit the trustee to retain all the investments made by the settlor, or a larger proportion of them than would otherwise be permitted. Thus, a trust may be created by a will that directs or authorizes the trustee to retain all of the securities bequeathed to the trustee; or the will may provide that any or all such securities or some specific securities may be retained, as the trustee deems proper, without regard to the ordinary requirement of diversification. [Id.]

But the retention language here did not give the necessary authorization or direction.

We hold that to abrogate the duty to diversify, the trust must contain specific language authorizing or directing the trustee to retain in a specific investment a larger percentage of the trust assets than would normally be prudent. The authorization to "retain" here was not sufficient — it only authorized the trustee to retain its own stock — something it could not otherwise do. . . .

The instructions here stated, "The normal rule is that a trustee shall diversify the investments of a trust. If by the terms of the trust the trustee is permitted but not directed to retain investments originally transferred to the trust, the trustee is not liable for retaining them where there is no abuse of discretion in doing so. The trustee is not liable for the exercise of its discretion so long as the trustee acts in good faith and does not abuse its discretion. An abuse of discretion occurs if the trustee acts dishonestly or with an improper motive or fails to use his judgment or acts beyond the bounds of a reasonable judgment."

Under the facts of this case, we reject this instruction — it virtually assured a verdict for Firstar, as there were no allegations of dishonesty or fraud. . . .

VI. Timing and Special Circumstances . . .

A trustee who is authorized to retain assets but sells them is not liable merely because the securities later rise in value, or vice versa. Trustees should not be judged on hindsight. Few would become trustees if they were liable every time they did not sell stock at the most propitious chance. But the problem here is that the trust would have benefited even more if Firstar had simply performed its duty to diversify. Wood's argument is not based on hindsight — it is simply based on Firstar's duty to diversify, absent special circumstances.

The "special circumstances" language generally refers to holdings that are important to a family or a trust. For example, in In re Trust Created by Inman, 693 N.W.2d 514 (Neb. 2005) the Nebraska Supreme Court recently held that there was no duty to diversify when the asset in question was a piece of farmland that had a special meaning to the family. We realize that Firstar stock is not farmland. But perhaps it had a special relationship to the family or to the trust. Or perhaps it did not. Further, this was not the case of a controlling interest in a family business — which might normally be an example of special circumstances. Either way, this question was for the jury. But the trial court's instructions improperly removed that question from the jury's consideration.

Because of the trial court's erroneous instruction here, the jury was not given the proper legal standard. The proper jury instruction would have simply quoted the appropriate statutory language, changing the ambiguous (to laypeople) *shall* to the proper *must*: "A trustee must diversify the investments of a trust unless the trustee reasonably determines that, because of special circumstances, the purposes of the trust are better served without diversifying."

Wood requested the proper instruction under the UPIA. The trial court's instructions did not achieve the same purpose: they did not even mention the "special circumstances" language, the only way that Firstar could have gotten around its duty in this case.

Given the improper law to apply, the jury could have come only to the conclusion that it did — namely, that Firstar had not "abused its discretion" in retaining the Firstar stock. But with the proper instructions, the jury may have gone the other way. Thus, we must order a new trial. We sustain Wood's second assignment of error. . . .

Judgment reversed and cause remanded.

NOTE: PERMISSIVE VERSUS MANDATED RETENTION OF INCEPTION ASSETS AND THE DUTY TO DIVERSIFY

It is important to distinguish between a term in the trust that *authorizes* the trustee to retain inception assets irrespective of diversification and one that *requires* the trustee to do so. Influenced by the central lesson of modern portfolio theory that failing to diversify is almost always folly, the courts tend to hold that a *permissive authorization* to retain an undiversified portfolio does not excuse the trustee from liability for failing to diversify in the absence of good reasons not to diversify.

In First Ala. Bank of Huntsville, N.A. v. Spragins, 475 So. 2d 512 (Ala. 1985), the court held that the trustee acted imprudently by maintaining a "portfolio that contained an inordinate amount of the Bank's holding company stock, in violation of sound management practices," despite authorization in the trust instrument for the trustee to manage the trust portfolio "regardless of any lack of diversification." Said the court: "We do not perceive, from the language of this trust, that the donor intended by his 'lack of diversification' provision to authorize acts of imprudence in the management of the trust to the point of disregarding the interests of the beneficiaries, the sole purpose of the trust arrangement in the first instance." See also Rutanen v. Ballard, 678 N.E.2d 133 (Mass. 1997); Robertson v. Central Jersey Bank & Trust Co., 47 F.3d 1268 (3d Cir. 1995).

A permissive retention clause may, however, justify a slower reallocation of the trust portfolio. In Nelson v. First Natl. Bank and Trust Co. of Williston, 543 F.3d 432 (8th Cir. 2008), at issue was a revocable trust with a 90 percent concentration in a single publicly traded company. The plaintiffs argued that the trustee, a bank, should have divested the trust of this concentration within two weeks of the trust's becoming irrevocable by reason of the settlor's death. The court rejected this argument based on a clause in the trust instrument that provided that "any investment made or retained by the trustee in good faith shall be proper." In the two weeks after the settlor's death, the trustee consulted with a lawyer and an accountant, and scheduled a meeting with the beneficiaries. In view of these actions, the court concluded: "Whether or not a trustee acting without the additional protections of this trust would have been obligated to consider immediate liquidation" of the concentration, "the plaintiffs have not produced evidence that [the trustee's] failure to contemplate that step was the result of dishonesty, improper motive, or other bad faith."

Be careful not to conflate *power* with *duty*. Even if the trustee has the power to retain certain assets, the exercise of that power must accord with the trustee's duties of prudence and loyalty. Restatement (Third) of Trusts §91, cmt. f (2007) explains:

> [T]he fact that an investment is permitted does not relieve the trustee of the fundamental duty to act with prudence. The fiduciary must still exercise care, skill, and caution in making decisions to acquire or retain the investment. . . .
>
> Whether and to what extent a specific investment authorization may affect the normal duty to diversify the trust portfolio can be a difficult question of interpretation. Because permissive provisions do not abrogate the trustee's duty to act prudently and because diversification is fundamental to prudent risk management, trust provisions are strictly construed against dispensing with that requirement altogether. Nevertheless, a relaxation in the degree of diversification may be justified under such an authorization by special opportunities for the trust or by special objectives of the settlor. . . .
>
> For this added risk, despite the presence of a permissive provision of this type, some reasonable justification must be found in the settlor's intentions or purposes or in some special opportunity (based, for example, on special skills) available to the trust.

What about a *mandatory instruction* to retain the trust's inception assets or language that otherwise exempts the trustee from the duty to diversify? Will the courts give effect to such language? The canonical authorities say Yes. See 4 Austin Wakeman Scott, William Franklin Fratcher, and Mark L. Ascher, Scott and Ascher on Trusts §19.3.3 (5th ed. 2007). On closer inspection, however, the matter turns out to be complex.

In *Wood*, the court assumed that the settlor could have opted out of the duty to diversify, but it held that the settlor had not done so. In Americans for the Arts v. Ruth Lilly Charitable Remainder Annuity Trust #1, 855 N.E.2d 592 (Ind. App. 2006), the court held that the trust instrument did exempt the trustee from the duty to diversify, but in that case the instrument was drafted by the settlor's conservator, the beneficiaries had opportunity but declined to object to the terms of the trust, and the trustee did in fact undertake to diversify.[15] In neither

---

15. The facts in *Ruth Lilly* were unusual indeed. The settlor, Ruth Lilly, a great-granddaughter of the founder of Eli Lilly & Company, was under a conservatorship. Her conservator, National City Bank, petitioned the probate court for permission to rework Ruth's estate plan on the grounds that at her death her $1 billion estate would incur needless tax liability and would invite burdensome litigation. (On the power of a guardian or conservator to change the ward's estate plan, see note 2 at page 455.) The new estate plan included certain trusts for which National City would serve as trustee. After a hearing the probate court approved the new plan and the trusts were created and funded with $286 million in Eli Lilly stock. In the ensuing months, National City began divesting the trusts of the Eli Lilly stock, and within a year the trusts were "fully diversified." National City then filed an accounting. Two of the beneficiaries objected, arguing that the bank diversified too slowly. Over the course of the year the stock price declined significantly.

The trusts provided that the trustee could "retain indefinitely" the trust's inception assets and that "any investment made or retained by the trustee in good faith shall be proper despite any resulting risk or lack of diversification." Citing *Wood* for the proposition that a settlor can abrogate the duty to diversify if that intent is stated clearly enough, the court held that the trusts "contain precisely the type of language suggested by the *Wood* court, inasmuch as they include a clause explicitly lessening the duty to diversify." The court also emphasized, however, that the plaintiffs had notice of the terms of the trusts in the earlier probate court hearing. At that hearing, the plaintiffs were represented by big-time lawyers, including Cravath, Swaine & Moore, at a cost of nearly $250,000 paid out of Ruth's estate. Yet the plaintiffs did not raise any objections to the diversification language at the hearing. The plaintiffs, it would seem, were hoisted by their own petards.

case was the court confronted squarely with a concentrated portfolio defended by an unrepentant trustee on the grounds that the settlor expressly required retention of the concentration. See also Jeffrey A. Cooper, Speak Clearly and Listen Well: Negating the Duty to Diversify Trust Investments, 33 Ohio N.U. L. Rev. 903 (2007) (critical survey of recent cases in which the court "found that the settlor did not effectively negate the trustee's default duty to diversify").

Restatement (Third) of Trusts, supra, §91, takes the position that the trustee "has a duty to conform to the terms of the trust directing or restricting investments by the trustee." However, §91 also states that this duty is subject to §66, page 645, which puts on the trustee an affirmative duty to petition the court to modify or deviate from an administrative term if the trustee knows of circumstances justifying modification or deviation and the term as written would "cause substantial harm to the trust or its beneficiaries." Given the clear folly of failing to diversify in most circumstances, does not this provision put on the trustee a duty to challenge almost any instruction not to diversify? See Scott and Ascher on Trusts, supra.

Suppose that the settlor directs the trustee not to sell the trust's inception assets, in this case the stock of a company that the settlor founded. If the trustee can show that the company had become unprofitable, should the court authorize the trustee to sell the stock in that company? See Matter of Pulitzer, 249 N.Y.S. 87 (Sur. 1931), aff'd mem., 260 N.Y.S. 975 (App. Div. 1932), discussed at page 644. Suppose that the settlor directs the trustee to invest only in first mortgages and government bonds and forbids investment in corporate stock. If the trustee can show that in an inflationary economy the value of the trust estate will decline by investing in fixed-value obligations, should the court authorize the trustee to invest in stock? See In re Trusteeship Agreement with Mayo, 105 N.W.2d 900 (Minn. 1960); Toledo Trust Co. v. Toledo Hosp., 187 N.E.2d 36 (Ohio 1962).

The underlying issue is whether the courts should disregard a mandated investment strategy if the strategy is unsound. Professor Langbein argues in the affirmative:

> What is happening in [these cases] is that the settlor is imposing his supposed investment wisdom on the trust in circumstances in which the investment strategy is objectively stupid and imprudent. We now know that the advantages of diversifying a portfolio of securities are so great that it is folly not to do it. . . . [When] the trust assets are cash or cash-equivalent, in the sense that diversification can be achieved at little cost, I believe that the courts will come to view the advantages of diversification as so overwhelming that the settlor's interference with effective diversification will be found to be inconsistent with the requirement that a private trust must be for the benefit of the beneficiary. [John H. Langbein, The Uniform Prudent Investor Act and the Future of Trust Investing, 81 Iowa L. Rev. 641, 664-665 (1996).]

The principle that a private trust must be for the benefit of the beneficiaries — recognized by UTC §§105(3) and 404 (2000) and Restatement (Third) of Trusts, supra, §27(2) — is rooted in the traditional rule against trusts for capricious purposes. In Langbein's view, a trust for the purpose of maintaining certain assets is not for the benefit of the beneficiaries and should be no more enforceable than an instruction to waste or destroy the trust property. See John H. Langbein, Mandatory Rules in the Law of Trusts, 98 Nw. U. L. Rev. 1105, 1111-1117 (2004).

Professor Cooper is not convinced. He argues that application of the benefit-the-beneficiary principle to mandated investment strategies is misguided:

> Many investment restrictions are not the undesirable remnants of irrational dead hands, but are carefully-designed provisions intended to further a living settlor's unique estate planning goals. Applying an objective, dispassionate test of "benefit" would cut too deeply, setting aside these important restrictions as freely as it would set aside those imposed by less thoughtful trust settlors. . . . The interpersonal aspects of wealth transmission would be frustrated, as personal visions of trust settlors become subjugated to the dispassionate dictates of modern investment theory. [Jeffrey A. Cooper, Empty Promises: Settlor's Intent, the Uniform Trust Code, and the Future of Trust Investment Law, 88 B.U. L. Rev. 1165, 1169-1170 (2008).]

Can these conflicting views be reconciled? Is the argument for respecting the "interpersonal aspects" of trusts weaker as applied to an administrative term than to a dispositive term?

Time may be running out for the courts to address these questions. In at least three states, recent legislation explicitly validates the enforceability of a settlor's instruction not to diversify. See Del. Code tit. 12, §3303(a) (2008); N.H. Rev. Stat. §564-B:9-901(b) (2008); S.D. Code, tit. 55, §55-5-8 (2008). See also Mont. Code Ann. §72-34-605(2) (2008) (recognizing exception for certain types of land and family businesses).

PROBLEM AND QUESTION

1. *Revocable trusts.* In 1990, T conveys 1,500 shares of Enron stock in trust to X. The trust instrument provides that the trust may be revoked or amended by written instrument delivered to X. T then instructs X in writing to retain the Enron stock, and X does so. In 2001, Enron files for bankruptcy in the wake of public disclosure of sundry accounting frauds at the company. The stock price drops to zero. In 2002, T sues X for breach of the duty of prudence, arguing that X should have diversified the portfolio or at least warned T of the inherent danger in failing to diversify. What result? See McGinley v. Bank of America, 109 P.3d 1146 (Kan. 2005).

2. *Beneficiary authorization.* Suppose the beneficiary consents, in writing, to an undiversified portfolio and agrees not to seek to surcharge the trustee for losses from a lack of diversification. Should such an agreement be enforced? See In re Saxton, 712 N.Y.S.2d 225 (App. Div. 2000).

NOTE: SOCIAL INVESTING

Can trustees invest the trust assets to accomplish goals unrelated to the trust? For example, can trustees refuse to invest in the stock of a corporation that manufactures cigarettes or publishes textbooks that teach the theory of evolution? Or can a labor union pension fund invest in projects that provide jobs to the union members (pension fund investment being subject to a similar standard of prudence)? Do such investments breach the duty of undivided loyalty to the fund beneficiaries? Are they prudent? The official comment to UPIA §5 takes the position that "[n]o form of so-called 'social investing' is consistent with the duty of loyalty if the investment activity entails sacrificing the interests of trust beneficiaries — for example, by accepting below-market returns — in favor of the interests of the persons supposedly benefitted by pursuing the particular social cause."

For further discussion of social investing in trust law, see Joel C. Dobris, SRI — Shibboleth or Canard (Socially Responsible Investing, That Is), 42 Real Prop., Prob. & Tr. J. 755 (2008); John H. Langbein and Richard A. Posner, Social Investing and the Law of Trusts, 79 Mich. L. Rev. 72 (1980). See also Michael S. Knoll, Ethical Screening in Modern Financial Markets: The Conflicting Claims Underlying Socially Responsible Investment, 57 Bus. Law. 681 (2002).

d. Delegation

Under traditional law, the trustee was not permitted to delegate matters that the trustee could reasonably be required personally to perform. Restatement (Second) of Trusts §171 (1959). Because this rule was understood to bar the trustee from delegating the power to select investments, see id., cmt. h., it gave rise to two types of cases. In the first, a trustee who was ignorant of investment matters would obtain expert advice and then, given the trustee's ignorance, would go though a charade of exercising independent judgment, concluding that — surprise! — the expert's advice was sound and should be followed. This type of case amounted to a de facto delegation, but the trustee's conduct would be upheld. In the second type of case, an ignorant trustee would obtain expert advice but not go through the charade of exercising independent judgment. This trustee would be held in breach of trust. See John H. Langbein, Reversing the Nondelegation Rule of Trust-Investment Law, 59 Mo. L. Rev. 105 (1994).

Prudent people seek help when dealing with matters beyond their ken. No one would fault a trustee who delegates to a plumber responsibility to fix a leaky pipe in one of the trust's properties. Why is portfolio management different? Just as the beneficiary is better off if a trustee who knows nothing about pipes hires a plumber to fix a leak, is not the beneficiary likewise better off if a trustee who knows nothing about portfolio management delegates to an investment specialist?

The drafters of the prudent investor rule took the occasion of the UPIA and the new Restatement to reverse the old nondelegation rule, replacing it with a rule that permits delegation subject to a duty of care, skill, and caution in *selecting*, *instructing*, and *monitoring* the agent. This new rule is now the law in nearly all states, and it is extended to all aspects of trust administration by UTC §807 (2000) and Restatement (Third) of Trusts §80 (2007).

Uniform Prudent Investor Act (1994)

§9.   DELEGATION OF INVESTMENT AND MANAGEMENT FUNCTIONS

(a) A trustee may delegate investment and management functions that a prudent trustee of comparable skills could properly delegate under the circumstances. The trustee shall exercise reasonable care, skill, and caution in:

(1) selecting an agent;

(2) establishing the scope and terms of the delegation, consistent with the purposes and terms of the trust; and

(3) periodically reviewing the agent's actions in order to monitor the agent's performance and compliance with the terms of the delegation.

(b) In performing a delegated function, an agent owes a duty to the trust to exercise reasonable care to comply with the terms of the delegation.

(c) A trustee who complies with the requirements of subsection (a) is not liable to the beneficiaries or to the trust for the decisions or actions of the agent to whom the function was delegated.

(d) By accepting the delegation of a trust function from the trustee of a trust that is subject to the law of this State, an agent submits to the jurisdiction of the courts of this State.

COMMENT

. . . If the trustee delegates effectively, the beneficiaries obtain the advantage of the agent's specialized investment skills or whatever other attributes induced the trustee to delegate. But if the trustee delegates to a knave or an incompetent, the delegation can work harm upon the beneficiaries.

Section 9 . . . is designed to strike the appropriate balance between the advantages and the hazards of delegation. Section 9 authorizes delegation under the limitations of subsections (a) and (b). Section 9(a) imposes duties of care, skill, and caution on the trustee in selecting the agent, in establishing the terms of the delegation, and in reviewing the agent's compliance.

The trustee's duties of care, skill, and caution in framing the terms of the delegation should protect the beneficiary against overbroad delegation. For example, a trustee could not prudently agree to an investment management agreement containing an exculpation clause that leaves the trust without recourse against reckless mismanagement. Leaving one's beneficiaries remediless against willful wrongdoing is inconsistent with the duty to use care and caution in formulating the terms of the delegation. . . .

Although subsection (c) of the Act exonerates the trustee from personal responsibility for the agent's conduct when the delegation satisfies the standards of subsection 9(a), subsection 9(b) makes the agent responsible to the trust. The beneficiaries of the trust can, therefore, rely upon the trustee to enforce the terms of the delegation.

PROBLEM, QUESTIONS, AND NOTE

1.   In 1999, *T* devises a fund in trust to *X* for the benefit of *A*. At *A*'s suggestion, *X* delegates responsibility for managing the trust's investment portfolio to *Y*, a reputable investment advisor. *Y*, also acting at *A*'s suggestion, invests the trust fund exclusively in technology stocks. In 2000, the technology bubble bursts and the value of the trust fund collapses. *A* sues *X* for improper delegation to *Y*. At the trial, *X* testifies that "when I put somebody in charge of something, I don't second guess them. You either get rid of him or leave it go. I left it go." What result? Does *A*'s role in the delegation and portfolio selection undermine *A*'s case? See O'Neill v. O'Neill, 865 N.E.2d 917 (Ohio App. 2006).

2.   Suppose the trustee lacks particular skills such that under the circumstances a prudent person would normally delegate to an expert. Does the trustee's duty of prudence *require* the trustee to delegate in such a case? See Restatement (Third) of Trusts §80, cmt. d(1) (2007).

3.   If the trustee exercises due care in selecting, instructing, and monitoring the agent, but the trust suffers a loss as a result of the agent's negligence, the trustee has a cause of action against the agent under UPIA §9(b). In such circumstances, can the beneficiary bring suit directly against the agent? Cf. City of Atascadero v. Merrill Lynch, Pierce, Fenner & Smith, Inc., 80 Cal. Rptr. 2d 329 (App. 1999).

4.   For further discussion, see Robert H. Hayden, Trustee Delegations and the Prudent Investor Act: Filling the Gaps, 32 Rutgers L. Rec. 64 (2008); John H. Langbein, Reversing the Nondelegation Rule of Trust-Investment Law, 59 Mo. L. Rev. 105, 110 (1994).

NOTE: DELEGATED VERSUS DIRECTED TRUSTS

As we have seen, the role of the trustee has evolved from stakeholder with little responsibility to manager with broad investment, administration, and distribution obligations, often discretionary. For the settlor, this poses a dilemma in trustee selection; increasingly, no single person or entity will have all the skills needed to do the job well. A trusted friend or relative might know the beneficiaries and be familiar with the settlor's values, but be ignorant of sound investment practices and weak at administrative work like record keeping. A corporate trustee might have expertise in investment and administration, but be unfamiliar with the family history and present circumstances. Accordingly, in modern practice it has become common to fracture the office of trustee through the appointment of co-trustees and trust protectors. See pages 551-553, 651. To this list of mechanisms for fracturing trusteeship we can now add *delegated* and *directed trusts*, separate concepts that are sometimes confused.

In a *delegated trust*, the responsibilities of trusteeship are divvied up by the trustee. The modern law of delegation encourages a trustee who lacks expertise in a matter to delegate the matter to an expert. For example, an individual trustee who lacks investment prowess has the power — and probably the duty — to delegate the investment function to an investment professional.

In a *directed trust*, the trust instrument provides that the trustee must follow the direction of a third party. In contrast to delegation, in a directed trust it is the settlor who splits up the trustee's responsibilities. Directed trusts most commonly involve a corporate trustee subject to direction on distribution or investment. Thus:

> *Case 1.* O conveys a fund in trust to X, a trust company, for the benefit of O's surviving spouse and descendants. The trust instrument provides that X is responsible for the trust's administration and investments, but that X may only make distributions to the beneficiaries as instructed by a distribution committee consisting of O's surviving spouse, O's lawyer, and O's business partner.
>
> *Case 2.* O conveys a fund in trust to X, a trust company, for the benefit of O's surviving spouse and descendants. The trust instrument provides that X is responsible for the trust's administration and for making discretionary distributions to the beneficiaries, but that X must invest the trust assets as instructed by Y, an investment advisor who has had a long and successful relationship with O. Because X is not responsible for managing the trust's investment portfolio, X agrees to serve at a reduced commission (see footnote 5 at page 552).

In Case 1, O is able to take advantage of X's relative expertise in administration and investment, while putting responsibility for distribution decisions in the hands of trusted people who are well-acquainted with the family. In Case 2, O is able to continue Y's management of the property, which may be desirable if the trust holds only part of the family fortune and Y also manages the rest.

There is considerable overlap between the directed trust and *trust protector* concepts. These are not terms of art with set doctrinal meanings, but rather have evolved out of usage in practice to describe different types of divided trusteeship. Persons given the power to modify or terminate the trust, to remove and replace the trustee, or to change the situs of the trust are usually called trust protectors. When a person other than the trustee is given the power to direct distributions or make investments, the trust is commonly called a directed trust, the trustee is generally said to be a directed trustee, and the person holding the power may be called a trust director or trust advisor, though sometimes the term advisor is used for a protector as well. The definitional boundaries are porous.

Of greater import than the etymology of the vocabulary are the legal consequences of directed trusts and trust protectors. Suppose in Case 1 that O's surviving spouse promises to give O's lawyer a share of any increased distribution to which O's lawyer agrees. Do O's descendants have a claim against the lawyer for breach of duty? Does X, as trustee, have a duty enforceable by O's descendants to verify the good faith of the distribution committee's instructions? Suppose in Case 2 that Y instructs X to make an obviously imprudent investment. Do the beneficiaries have a claim against Y for breach of duty? Does X, as trustee, have a duty enforceable by the beneficiaries to refuse to follow such a direction?

There are no reported appellate decisions addressing these and related questions. Restatement (Third) of Trusts §75 (2007) takes the position that the trustee has a duty to follow a direction of a person if the trust so provides unless the direction "is contrary to the terms of the trust . . . or the trustee knows or has reason to believe that [the direction] violates a fiduciary duty that the power holder owes to the beneficiaries." The comments go on to explain that a person other than a beneficiary who is given the power to direct the trustee presumptively holds that power in a fiduciary capacity, subject to liability to the beneficiary for breach of duty. Id., cmt. c(1). The UTC is similar but a bit more protective of the trustee. Under UTC §808, the trustee must follow a direction unless it is "manifestly" contrary to the terms of the trust or would constitute a "serious" breach of fiduciary duty. What is the difference between a direction that is contrary to the terms of the trust and one that is manifestly so? What is the difference between an ordinary breach of fiduciary duty and one that is serious? Questions like these keep trust officers awake at night.

A handful of states, most prominently Delaware, have enacted statutes that are much more protective of a directed trustee. Under Del. Code Ann. tit. 12, §3313 (2008), the one who directs (called a "trust adviser") is presumptively a fiduciary but the governing instrument can provide otherwise, and the trustee has no duty to monitor or to notify the beneficiary if the trustee has concerns about the direction. The trustee is protected from liability except in cases of the trustee's own willful misconduct. Laws like this are a major reason why Delaware has become such a big player in the national market for trust business.

The curious student wanting to know more about directed trusts should consult the burgeoning practitioner literature. See Mary Clarke and Diana S.C. Zeydel, Directed Trusts: The Statutory Approaches to Authority and Liability, 35 Est. Plan. 14 (Sept. 2008); Sheldon G. Gilman, Effective Use of Trust Advisors Can Avoid Trustee Problems, 35 Est. Plan. 18 (Mar. 2008); Richard W. Nenno, Directed Trusts: Can Directed Trustees Limit Their Liability?, Prob. & Prop., Nov./Dec. 2007, at 45; Dennis I. Belcher, Not My Fault — The Devil Made Me Do It! Responsibilities and Duties of a Delegating or Directed Trustee, 41 Heckerling Inst. on Est. Plan. ch. 13 (2007); Al W. King and Pierce H. McDowell, Delegated vs. Directed Trusts, Tr. & Ests., July 2006, at 26. See also the discussion of trust protectors at page 651.

SECTION D. IMPARTIALITY AND THE PRINCIPAL AND INCOME PROBLEM

Perhaps the most important subrule in trust fiduciary law is the duty of *impartiality*. This duty is implicated when a trust has two or more beneficiaries. The duty of impartiality is this: In investing, managing, and distributing the trust property, the trustee must strike a balance between the beneficiaries, giving due regard to their respective interests. UTC §803 (2000); Restatement (Third) of Trusts §79 (2007).

The duty of impartiality is unfortunately named. It does not in fact require impartiality in the sense of equality. The trustee must take into account any preferences that the settlor may have expressed in the governing instrument or in some other manner, and must also consider the various and sometimes conflicting interests of the beneficiaries. After giving due regard to these interests, the trustee must act accordingly. In some circumstances, this will require the trustee to favor one beneficiary over another.

Howard v. Howard
Court of Appeals of Oregon, 2007
156 P.3d 89

ORTEGA, J.   This appeal arises from a dispute between the income beneficiary and a remainder beneficiary of trusts established by the late Leo Howard. Marcene Howard, the income beneficiary for life, is Leo's widow; Coy Howard, the remainder beneficiary, is Leo's son. Coy contends that the trial court erred by instructing the trustee not to consider Marcene's other assets in administering and making investment decisions for the trust.

Leo and his first wife had three children, including Coy. After his first wife's death, Leo married Marcene, who had two children from her prior marriage. Leo and Marcene married in 1961. They had no children together.

Leo and Marcene did their estate planning together. In 1992, they went to an attorney, Fredricks, for the preparation of trust agreements to replace their earlier wills. Those trust agreements gave the trustee discretion to invade the principal when necessary to support the surviving spouse. Leo and Marcene transferred 60 percent of their property to Leo's trust and 40 percent to Marcene's, so that 60 percent of the total estate would go to Leo's three children and 40 percent to Marcene's two children, resulting in an equal share for each child.

In 1999, Leo and Marcene amended the 1992 trust agreements in their entirety, and Leo's trust instrument made the following provisions. After Leo's death, in the event that Marcene survived Leo, his pecuniary assets were to be divided into two trusts, the Leo L. Howard Family Trust (the Family Trust) and the Howard Marital Trust (the Marital Trust). The trustee was to distribute a "non-marital share" — the maximum amount that could pass free of the federal estate tax — to the Family Trust and the residue to the Marital Trust. The trust instrument states Leo's intention that the marital share would qualify for the federal estate tax marital deduction and directs that the trust instrument be interpreted consistently with that intent. The trust instrument further provides that Marcene may require the trustee "to make any unproductive property in any marital trust productive or to convert it to productive property within a reasonable time."

The trust instrument provides that, during Marcene's lifetime, the net income of both trusts is to be distributed to her, and no distributions of principal are to be made from either trust. On Marcene's death, the residue of the Marital Trust is to be distributed to the Family Trust, which is to be divided among Leo's surviving children and the surviving issue of his children who predecease Leo and

Marcene. The trust instrument states, "I intentionally make no provision herein for any of my stepchildren."

Some sections of the trust instrument explicitly refer to consideration of the beneficiaries' needs and other resources. Article 3.2 provides, in the event of Leo's incapacity during his lifetime, for distribution of income and principal necessary to meet his or Marcene's needs. Article 8.3(b) requires the trustee to retain the share of any surviving issue of any deceased child of Leo until the issue turns 25; until that time, the trustee is to pay the beneficiary "such amounts of income and principal of the share as [the t]rustee shall determine to be necessary for his or her health, education, support and maintenance." Article 10.5 states, "In making discretionary distributions, [the t]rustee may, but is not required to, consider any other income, support, or property available to the beneficiary."

Another section of the trust instrument addresses the comparative interests of the various beneficiaries. Article 11.19 states, "My support, comfort, companionship, enjoyment and desires shall be preferred over the rights of the remaindermen. After my death, in the event my spouse survives me, my spouse's support, comfort, companionship, enjoyment and desires shall be preferred over the rights of the remaindermen."

The trial court admitted, as evidence regarding the 1999 amendments, notes and testimony by Fredricks, who prepared the trust instrument. In a file note about the 1999 amendments, Fredricks memorialized a discussion that he had had with Leo and Marcene. Fredricks wrote that they

> looked at the fact that the estates ha[d] grown considerably over the last few years and . . . determined . . . that there be no distributions of principal for the benefit of the spouse after one of the spouses is deceased.
>
> Leo and Marcene both felt that the survivor would have substantial assets of his or her own in their own trust over which they could draw upon the principal, and also, would be receiving all of the net income of both the family trust and the marital trust which should be more tha[n] sufficient to take care of the survivor.

Fredricks testified that Article 11.19 of the trust instrument was included because the 1999 amendments eliminated discretionary distributions of principal and both Marcene and Leo "had a central desire to make sure that the other was adequately provided for." Fredricks had explained to Leo and Marcene that Oregon law usually requires a trustee to be impartial between the income beneficiary and the remainder beneficiaries and that Article 11.19 overrides that rule and "slants . . . questionable decisions in favor of the income beneficiary, with the thought being that basically they were interested in first providing for one another and then for the [remainder beneficiaries]."

Fredricks never told Leo and Marcene that the trustee could not consider the surviving spouse's other resources when applying Article 11.19. However, in his view, Article 11.19 did not provide for Marcene's needs only, nor did it require the trustee to consider Marcene's assets in providing for her. Fredricks also explained to Leo and Marcene that, after the death of one spouse, there would be no way to continue balancing the assets in Leo's and Marcene's respective trusts to maintain the earlier 60-40 split.

Leo died in January 2002. As pertinent here, he was survived by Marcene, two of his children, and the three children of his deceased daughter. Marcene and Coy served as cotrustees of Leo's trusts but came to disagree about the interpretation of certain trust provisions. Marcene petitioned for an interpretation of the trusts' terms and for the proper administration of their assets. . . .

After the hearing, the trial court concluded that, . . . when the interests of Marcene and the remainder beneficiaries conflict, her interests take precedence. The court also determined that the growth of the corpus was not the trusts' primary object. The court instructed the trustee that Marcene's "personal income and assets and financial posture . . . [are] not relevant to the administration of the trust and [are] to have no bearing whatsoever on the considerations of the [t]rustee[.]" On appeal, Coy assigns error only to that last instruction.

Although a trustee owes a duty to any remainder beneficiaries as well as to the life income beneficiary, the trustee must carry out those duties in light of any preference expressed in the trust instrument. We construe trust instruments in accordance with the trustor's intent by looking at the entire instrument and, if possible, giving effect to all of the instrument's provisions. Here, we conclude that the trial court was correct in its determination that Leo did not intend to require the trustee to consider Marcene's other financial resources when administering the assets of the trusts.

As Marcene points out, the trust instrument requires the trustee to pay all the net trust income to her, without any reference to her other resources or her needs, although Articles 3.2 (governing distributions if Leo had become incapacitated), 6.2(b) and 8.3(b) (governing distributions to a beneficiary who has not attained the age of 25), and 10.5 (governing discretionary distributions) explicitly refer to consideration of the beneficiaries' needs and other resources. That drafting choice appears deliberate: If Leo had wished the trustee to consider Marcene's other resources, the trust instrument demonstrates that he knew how to give such an instruction.

Nonetheless, Coy contends that, unless Marcene's other resources are considered, the trustee cannot comply with Leo's intent to pass the remainder of his estate to his own children and not to provide for his stepchildren. Coy notes the potential for Marcene "(1) to divert as current income proceeds that otherwise would be available to grow principal for Leo's biological issue and (2) through gifts made directly or indirectly out of this income to her own children, to make her biological issue *de facto* [remainder beneficiaries] of the Leo Howard Trust." Marcene concedes that, under the trial court's unchallenged instructions to the trustee, "it is clear that growth of the principal may not be eliminated entirely." She points out, however, that Article 11.19 of the trust instrument makes her "support, comfort, companionship, enjoyment and desires" a higher priority than the rights of the remainder beneficiaries. Marcene contends that an investment strategy focused on preserving assets for distribution to the remainder beneficiaries would not comply with Article 11.19.

We agree with Marcene. The trust instrument states that Leo intended to make no provision for his stepchildren, not that he intended to require consideration of Marcene's other resources or to limit Marcene's income or ability to make gifts to her children. Accordingly, Leo's decision not to provide for his stepchildren circumscribes neither his direction of trust income to Marcene nor, under Article 11.19, his preference for her interests over those of the remainder beneficiaries. Coy's argument simply is too attenuated in light of Leo's other clear directives regarding income for Marcene. . . .

The trust instrument unambiguously provides that Marcene's other resources are not relevant to the administration of the trust, and the trial court therefore did not err in its instruction to the trustee.

Affirmed.

NOTES AND QUESTIONS

1.   Commonly the settlor wants to favor his surviving spouse, assuring the spouse comfortable support during her life, with whatever is left passing to the settlor's descendants when the surviving spouse dies. In *Howard*, the complication was the blended family. Both the husband and the wife had children from prior marriages. In such a case, what language would you recommend to assure comfortable support for the surviving spouse while preserving relative equality between the separate familial lines of descent? What if the surviving spouse is closer in age to the decedent's children than to the decedent? Who should be the trustee of such a trust? Do these circumstances argue for an institutional trustee?

2.   *The impecunious surviving spouse.* A recurring fact pattern in modification cases involves a surviving spouse who cannot live comfortably on the income from a trust created at the other spouse's death, and asks a court to permit the invasion of principal for support. Unless all the remainder beneficiaries consent, which is complicated if there are minor or unborn beneficiaries, relief is denied unless the trust is construed to contain an express or implied power to invade principal. See 5 Austin Wakeman Scott, William Franklin Fratcher, and Mark L. Ascher, Scott and Ascher on Trusts §33.4, at 2178 (5th ed. 2007). Do you think it likely that, by denying the surviving spouse's petition in such cases, the court is giving effect to the settlor's probable intent? See 31 A.L.R.3d (1970, rev. 2009).

In some states, the problem of the impecunious surviving spouse has been ameliorated by statute. See N.Y. Est. Powers & Trusts Law §7-1.6(b) (2008) (giving court discretion to make allowance from principal to provide sufficient support for income beneficiary, if court is satisfied that such invasion effectuates the intention of the settlor). See also Scott and Ascher on Trusts, supra, §33.4, at 2182 (citing other statutes).

3.   Suppose that there is an ambiguity in the trust instrument that can be resolved in a manner favorable to either the income beneficiary or the remainder beneficiary, but not both. In petitioning for a judicial construction, can the trustee argue in favor of one interpretation or the other? See Northern Trust Co. v. Heuer, 560 N.E.2d 961 (Ill. App. 1990).

Although impartiality problems can arise in a trust with concurrent beneficiaries, the most common impartiality problem is presented by a trust with successive beneficiaries. Suppose *T* devises a fund in trust to *X* "to pay the income to *A* for life and then the principal to *B* on *A*'s death." Although the overall interests of *A* and *B* are closely aligned on matters such as self-dealing or embezzlement by *X*, their interests in the investment of the trust fund may be at odds. The problem is that under traditional fiduciary rules respecting allocation to *income* and *principal*, the particular *form* of the trust's investment return determines its classification. The income beneficiary, *A*, will prefer investments that produce returns that are classified as income while *B*, the principal beneficiary, will prefer investments that produce returns that are classified as principal.

Under traditional principal and income accounting rules, cash dividends on common stock and interest on bonds are classified as income, but appreciation in the stock or bond price goes to principal.[16] Thus, if the trustee opts to invest in a stock that does not pay a dividend (in which case the stock's price will appreciate faster because profits will accumulate within the company), then the principal beneficiary is advantaged at the expense of the income beneficiary. If the trustee opts to invest in a bond that pays interest but does not otherwise appreciate in value, then the income beneficiary is advantaged at the expense of the principal beneficiary. As a matter of economic reality, however, the assignment of some forms of investment return to principal and other forms of return to income is arbitrary. The consequence is that the income and principal beneficiaries are advantaged or disadvantaged by dint of the trustee's allocation of the trust fund between investments that produce income (as defined) versus appreciation of principal (as defined).

The embrace of modern portfolio theory by the prudent investor rule has brought into sharp focus the arbitrariness of allocating certain investment proceeds to income and others to principal based on the form of the proceeds in question. Paying too much attention to the *form* of the investment return will sometimes collide with the larger aim of maximizing the *total return* subject to the risk tolerances of the beneficiaries and the purpose of the trust. Just as a pound of lead weighs as much as a pound of feathers, tax considerations aside, a dollar of profit in one form is equal to a dollar of profit in another — a buck is a buck.

---

16. The 1962 Uniform Principal and Income Act is representative of the traditional approach. To income the 1962 Act allocates: (1) rent; (2) interest on loans and bonds; (3) cash dividends on stock; (4) net profits from a business or farming operation; (5) royalties from natural resources (except 27 1/2 percent allocated to principal); and (6) royalties from patents and copyrights (but not in excess of 5 percent per year of inventory value).

To principal, increasing the corpus of the trust, the 1962 Act allocates: (1) proceeds from sale of property; (2) proceeds of insurance on property; (3) stock splits and stock dividends; (4) corporate distributions from a merger or acquisition; (5) payment of bond principal; (6) royalties from natural resources (27 1/2 percent); and (7) royalties from patents and copyrights in excess of 5 percent of inventory value.

Restatement (Third) of Trusts (T.D. No. 5, 2009)

CHAPTER 23. ACCOUNTING FOR PRINCIPAL AND INCOME

INTRODUCTORY NOTE

Fundamental change in prevailing principal-and-income accounting rules became inevitable with the widespread adoption of the Uniform Prudent Investor Act, which was promulgated in 1994 to provide a ready means of codifying the Restatement Third of Trusts investment principles. The "prudent investor rule" encourages trustees to invest for optimal total return (i.e., to make a reasonable effort to achieve the highest total return that is suitable to the trust's purposes and the circumstances of the trust and its beneficiaries, especially risk tolerance). Yet, under many circumstances, the combination of traditional rules of principal-and-income accounting and the trustee's duty of impartiality . . . constrains the ability of trustees to invest for suitable total return.

Commentators recognized that, collectively, all beneficiaries of a trust would be expected to benefit if the investment and distribution functions were separated, so that the trustee could invest for an optimal total return and then make distribution decisions that would be reasonably appropriate to the terms and purpose of the trust and to the diverse present and future interest of the beneficiaries.

Legislatures responded. Forty-five states and the District of Columbia have now (2009) adopted all or portions of the 1997 Uniform Principal and Income Act, with its adjustment power (id. §104) and stated goal of harmonizing principal-and-income accounting with prudent investing. . . . To serve essentially the same objective, 28 states now (2009) have some form of unitrust-conversion statute, usually as an alternative accompanying the adjustment power.

In re Matter of Heller
Court of Appeals of New York, 2007
849 N.E.2d 262

ROSENBLATT, J.   In September 2001, New York enacted legislation that transformed the definition and treatment of trust accounting income. The Uniform Principal and Income Act (EPTL art. 11-A) and related statutes (L. 2001, ch. 243), including the optional unitrust provision (EPTL 11-2.4), are designed to facilitate investment for total return on a portfolio. The appeal before us centers on the optional unitrust provision, which permits trustees to elect a regime in which income is calculated according to a fixed formula and based on the net fair market value of the trust assets. We hold that a trustee's status as a remainder beneficiary does not in itself invalidate a unitrust election made by that trustee . . . .

I.

In his will, after making certain other gifts of personal property and money, Jacob Heller created a trust to benefit his wife Bertha Heller (should she survive him) and his children.[17] Heller provided that his entire residuary estate be held in trust during Bertha's life. He appointed his brother Frank Heller as trustee and designated his sons Herbert and Alan Heller as trustees on Frank's death. Every year Bertha was to receive the greater of $40,000 or the total income of the trust. Heller named his daughters (Suzanne Heller and Faith Willinger, each with a 30% share) and his sons and prospective trustees (Herbert and Alan Heller, each with a 20% share) as remainder beneficiaries.

Jacob Heller died in 1986, and his wife Bertha survives him. When Heller's brother Frank died in 1997, Herbert and Alan Heller became trustees. From that year until 2001, Bertha Heller received an average annual income from the trust of approximately $190,000. In March 2003, the trustees elected to have the uni-trust provision apply, pursuant to EPTL 11-2.4(e)(1)(B)(I). As required by EPTL 11-2.4(e)(1)(B)(III), they notified trust beneficiaries Bertha Heller, Suzanne Heller and Faith Willinger. The trustees sought to have unitrust treatment applied retroactively to January 1, 2002, the effective date of EPTL 11-2.4. As a result of that election, Bertha Heller's annual income was reduced to approxi-mately $70,000.

Appellant Sandra Davis commenced this proceeding, as attorney-in-fact for her mother Bertha Heller, and on August 1, 2003 moved for summary judgment, seeking, among other things, an order annulling the unitrust election and revok-ing the letters of trusteeship issued to Herbert and Alan Heller. . . . Surrogate's Court . . . denied . . . her motion seeking annulment of the unitrust election itself and other relief.

Davis appealed Surrogate's Court's order, and Herbert and Alan Heller cross-appealed. The Appellate Division affirmed the order to the extent that it denied Davis's summary judgment motion . . . . It also granted leave to appeal and cer-tified the following question to us: "Was the opinion and order of [the Appellate Division] dated August 15, 2005, properly made?" We conclude that it was and now affirm.

II.

The 2001 legislation that forms the subject of this appeal was designed to make it easier for trustees to comply with the demands of the Prudent Investor Act of 1994. In addition to enacting EPTL article 11-A (Uniform Principal and Income Act), the Legislature both added EPTL 11-2.3(b)(5) to the Prudent Investor Act and included the optional unitrust provision, EPTL 11-2.4.

Under the former Principal and Income Act, a trustee was required to balance the interests of the income beneficiary against those of the remainder beneficiary, and was constrained in making investments by the act's narrow definitions of income and principal. A trustee who invested in nonappreciating assets would

---

17. Notice the reference to *his* children. Bertha was a second spouse. In correspondence with the editors, Gary B. Friedman, counsel for the appellant, reported as follows: "The marriage was long — 26 years — and Jacob died 22 years before Bertha. Before the unitrust conversion it was a fairly close family. The trustees and the other 2 remainderpersons were children from the first marriage." — Eds.

ensure reasonable income for any income beneficiary, but would sacrifice growth opportunities for the trust funds, as inflation eroded their value; if the trustee invested for growth, remainder beneficiaries would enjoy an increase in the value of the trust at the expense of income beneficiaries. Moreover, the need to invest so as to produce what the former Principal and Income Act defined as income led to investment returns that failed to represent the benefits envisaged as appropriate by settlors.

The Prudent Investor Act encourages investing for total return on a portfolio. Unless the governing instrument expressly provides otherwise, the act requires that trustees "pursue an *overall* investment strategy to enable the trustee to make appropriate present and future distributions to or for the benefit of the beneficiaries under the governing instrument, in accordance with risk and return objectives reasonably suited to the *entire* portfolio" (EPTL 11-2.3[b][3][A] [emphasis added]).

The 2001 legislation allows trustees to pursue this strategy uninhibited by a constrained concept of trust accounting income. First, the Prudent Investor Act now authorizes trustees

> to adjust between principal and income to the extent the trustee considers advisable to enable the trustee to make appropriate present and future distributions in accordance with clause (b)(3)(A) if the trustee determines, after applying the rules in article 11-A, that such an adjustment would be fair and reasonable to all of the beneficiaries, so that current beneficiaries may be given such use of the trust property as is consistent with preservation of its value (EPTL 11-2.3[b][5][A]).

A trustee investing for a portfolio's total return under the Prudent Investor Act may now adjust principal and income to compensate for the effects of the investment decisions on distribution to income beneficiaries. Alternatively, the optional unitrust provision lets trustees elect unitrust status for a trust (EPTL 11-2.4), by which income is calculated according to a fixed formula.

In a unitrust pursuant to EPTL 11-2.4, an income beneficiary receives an annual income distribution of "four percent of the net fair market values of the assets held in the trust on the first business day of the current valuation year," for the first three years of unitrust treatment. This is true regardless of the actual income earned by the trust. Starting in the fourth year, the value of the trust assets is determined by calculating the average of three figures: the net fair market value on the first business day of the current valuation year and the net fair market values on the first business days of the prior two valuation years. Income generated in excess of this amount is applied to principal.

Under the 2001 legislation, then, a trustee may invest in assets, such as equities, that outperform other types of investment in the long term but produce relatively low dividend yields for an income beneficiary, and still achieve impartial treatment of income and remainder beneficiaries. The trustee may accomplish this either by adjusting as between principal and income or by electing unitrust status with the result that the income increases in proportion to the value of the principal. If a trust's assets are primarily interests in nonappreciating investments producing high yields for income beneficiaries, a unitrust election may initially result in a substantial decrease in the distribution to any income beneficiary, at least until the portfolio is diversified. This case presents such a scenario.

III.

Davis argues that the trustees are barred as a matter of law from electing unitrust status because they are themselves remainder beneficiaries, and that, in any case, they may not elect unitrust status retroactively to January 1, 2002. The Appellate Division held that the legislation does not impede unitrust election by an interested trustee, that such an election is not inconsistent, per se, with common-law limitations on the conduct of fiduciaries and that the statute permits trustees to select retroactive application. We agree.

EPTL 11-2.3(b)(5), the 2001 statute that gives trustees the power to adjust between principal and income, expressly prohibits a trustee from exercising this power if "the trustee is a current beneficiary or a presumptive remainderman of the trust" or if "the adjustment would benefit the trustee directly or indirectly". Tellingly, the Legislature included no such prohibition in the simultaneously enacted optional unitrust provision, EPTL 11-2.4. Moreover, in giving a list of factors to be considered by the courts in determining whether unitrust treatment should apply to a trust, the Legislature mentioned no absolute prohibitions, and created a presumption in favor of unitrust application. We conclude that the Legislature did not mean to prohibit trustees who have a beneficial interest from electing unitrust treatment.

It is certainly true that the common law in New York contains an absolute prohibition against self-dealing, in that "a fiduciary owes a duty of undivided and undiluted loyalty to those whose interests the fiduciary is to protect" (Birnbaum v. Birnbaum, 539 N.E.2d 574 (N.Y. 1989)). "The trustee is under a duty to the beneficiary to administer the trust solely in the interest of the beneficiary" (Restatement (Second) of Trusts §170(1) (1959)). In this case, however, the trustees owe fiduciary obligations not only to the trust's income beneficiary, Bertha Heller, but also to the other remainder beneficiaries, Suzanne Heller and Faith Willinger. That these beneficiaries' interests happen to align with the trustees' does not relieve the trustees of their duties to them. Here, we cannot conclude that the trustees are prohibited from electing unitrust treatment as a matter of common-law principle.

That the trustees are remainder beneficiaries does not, by itself, invalidate a unitrust election. Nevertheless, a unitrust election from which a trustee benefits will be scrutinized by the courts with special care. In determining whether application of the optional unitrust provision is appropriate, it remains for the Surrogate to review the process and assure the fairness of the trustees' election, by applying relevant factors including those enumerated in EPTL 11-2.4(e)(5)(A).[18]

---

18. N.Y. Est. Powers & Trusts Law §11-2.4(e)(5)(A) (2008) provides that, in determining whether unitrust conversion is appropriate, the following factors should be considered:

Application of these factors here presents questions of fact precluding summary judgment. . . .

Accordingly, the order of the Appellate Division should be affirmed, with costs, and the certified question answered in the affirmative.

NOTES AND QUESTIONS

1. *Adjustment power.* A revised Uniform Principal and Income Act was promulgated in 1997. The revisions were designed to address the tension between investing the trust portfolio for the highest total return and the duty to produce an appropriate amount of income for the income beneficiary. As revised, the Act continues the traditional approach whereby the particular form of the return determines the beneficiary's return. But to free the trustee's hand in crafting a portfolio for total return, §104 of the Act gives the trustee the power to reallocate between income and principal if the trustee concludes that total return investing leads, under the traditional principal and income accounting rules, to unfair results. This *statutory adjustment power* is a default rule, operational only if the settlor does not provide otherwise. See also Restatement (Third) of Trusts §113 (T.D. No. 5, 2009) (recognizing a common law power of adjustment).

2. *Unitrust.* A different solution to the problem of fair allocation is the *unitrust.* The unitrust idea, which comes from the charitable remainder unitrust discussed at page 988, is that the settlor will set the percentage of the value of the trust principal that must be paid to the income beneficiary each year. The trust principal is revalued each year. Thus, if the income beneficiary is entitled to 5 percent of the value of the trust principal and the principal is worth $1 million, the income beneficiary receives $50,000. If the value of the trust principal increases in the next year to $1,200,000, the income beneficiary is entitled to $60,000.

The unitrust lets the settlor determine the percentage of the total return that is to be paid to the income beneficiary, leaving it to the trustee to maximize the trust's total return irrespective of the form in which that return takes. The percentage need not be fixed; the settlor might key the percentage to the rate of inflation or prevailing interest rates. Many lawyers advise that the settlor smooth the payouts by requiring that the payout percentage be multiplied by a three-year rolling average value of the trust.

In states that permit the conversion of a traditional principal and income trust into a unitrust, the payout percentage is usually set by statute, typically between 3

(i) the nature, purpose, and expected duration of the trust;
(ii) the intent of the creator of the trust;
(iii) the identity and circumstances of the beneficiaries;
(iv) the needs for liquidity, regularity of payment, and preservation and appreciation of capital;
(v) the assets held in the trust; the extent to which they consist of financial assets, interests in closely held enterprises, tangible and intangible personal property, or real property; the extent to which an asset is used by a beneficiary; and whether an asset was purchased by the trustee or received from the creator of the trust.

— Eds.

to 5 percent, and it is applied to a rolling average value over the prior few years, usually three. See Restatement (Third) of Trusts, supra, §113, cmt. c.

3. *Trustee-beneficiary.* The statutory adjustment power is usually denied to a trustee who is also a beneficiary of the trust. See Uniform Principal and Income Act §104(c)(7). In *Heller*, the court held that such a trustee-beneficiary may, however, convert to a unitrust, subject to judicial review to "assure the fairness of the trustees' election." In reaching this result, the court emphasized the duty owed by the trustees to the other remainder beneficiaries. Was this fact critical? Would the outcome be different if the trustees were the only remainder beneficiaries?

4. *Federal tax law.* A host of federal income, gift, and estate tax laws are keyed to definitions of income and principal under state trust fiduciary law. New treasury regulations, effective January 2, 2004, provide that what is deemed income by the exercise of an adjustment power or application of a unitrust percentage will generally be treated as income for federal tax purposes, provided that the power of equitable adjustment or the unitrust percentage is sanctioned by state statute and the amount deemed income is within 3 to 5 percent of the total value of the trust. See Richard W. Nenno, The Power to Adjust and Total-Return Unitrust Statutes: State Developments and Tax Considerations, 42 Real Prop., Prob. & Tr. J. 657 (2008).

5. *Literature.* For further discussion, see S. Alan Medlin, Limitations on the Trustee's Power to Adjust, 42 Real Prop., Prob. & Tr. J. 717 (2008); Christopher P. Cline, The Uniform Prudent Investor and Principal & Income Acts: Changing the Trust Landscape, 42 Real Prop., Prob. & Tr. J. 611 (2008); Joel C. Dobris, Why Five? The Strange, Magnetic, and Mesmerizing Affect of the Five Percent Unitrust and Spending Rate on Settlors, Their Advisors, and Retirees, 40 Real Prop., Prob. & Tr. J. 39 (2005); Alyssa A. DiRusso and Kathleen M. Sablone, Statutory Techniques for Balancing the Financial Interests of Trust Beneficiaries, 39 U.S.F. L. Rev. 261 (2005).

SECTION E.   SUBRULES RELATING TO THE TRUST PROPERTY

In this section, we continue our examination of the subsidiary rules of trust fiduciary law by looking at several that relate to the trustee's care of the trust property. These subsidiary rules give specific content to the broad, overarching duties of loyalty and prudence as applied to recurring, common sets of facts and circumstances.

1. Duty to Collect and Protect Trust Property

A trustee has the duty to *collect* and *protect* trust property without unnecessary delay. See UTC §809 (2000); Restatement (Third) of Trusts §76(2)(b) (2007). What is unreasonable delay depends on the circumstances.

When a testamentary trust is established, the trustee should collect the assets from the executor as promptly as circumstances permit. In addition, a testamentary trustee owes a duty to the beneficiaries to examine the property tendered by the executor to make sure it is what the trustee ought to receive. This means the trustee must look at the acts of the executor and require the executor to redress any breach of duty that diminished the assets intended for the trust. See UTC §812; Restatement (Third) of Trusts, supra, §76, cmt. d. This is a specific application of the trustee's duty to enforce and defend claims of the trust. See UTC §811.

2.   Duty to Earmark Trust Property

A trustee has a duty to *earmark* trust property. See UTC §810(c) (2000); Restatement (Third) of Trusts §84, cmt. d (2007). To earmark property is to designate it as trust property rather than the trustee's own. The reason: If the property is not earmarked, a trustee might later claim that the investments that proved profitable were the trustee's own investments and the investments that lost value were made for the trust.

Assets not subject to registration, such as bearer bonds, fall within an established exception to the earmarking requirement. In such cases, the trustee must keep records indicating that the property belongs to the trust and the property should be kept separate from the trustee's own property. Restatement (Third) of Trusts, supra, §84, cmt. d(2).

Under the older view, where a trustee commits a breach of trust by failing to earmark a trust investment, the trustee is strictly liable for any loss, even if the loss was not caused by the failure to earmark. The more modern view is that a trustee is liable only if the loss results from the failure to earmark and is not liable if the loss results from general economic conditions. See 3 Austin Wakeman Scott, William Franklin Fratcher, and Mark L. Ascher, Scott and Ascher on Trusts §17.11.3 (5th ed. 2007).

3.   Duty Not to Mingle Trust Funds with the Trustee's Own

A trustee is guilty of a breach of trust if the trustee *commingles* the trust funds with his own, even if trustee does not use the trust funds for his own purposes. See UTC §810(b) (2000); Restatement (Third) of Trusts §84, cmt. b (2007). The reason: Commingled trust funds become more difficult to trace and hence subject to the risk that personal creditors of the trustee can reach them. That the personal creditors of the trustee cannot normally reach the assets of the trust is a key feature of trust law. See pages 549-550.

The prohibition against commingling has been partially abrogated in almost all jurisdictions to permit a corporate fiduciary to hold and invest trust assets in a common trust fund. Building on this trend, UTC §810(d) allows all trustees to make a joint investment from separate trusts, provided that "the trustee maintains records clearly indicating the respective interests." The rationale for both reforms is to allow trustees to take advantage of economies of scale. Neither permit commingling with the trustee's own assets. See Restatement (Third) of Trusts, supra, §84, cmt. c.

As with a breach of the duty to earmark, there is a divergence of views regarding the extent of a trustee's liability for commingling. The older view is that a trustee is strictly liable, even though the loss would have occurred had there been no commingling. More recent authority holds a trustee liable only to the extent the commingling caused the loss. See 3 Austin Wakeman Scott, William Franklin Fratcher, and Mark L. Ascher, Scott and Ascher on Trusts §17.11.1 (5th ed. 2007).

SECTION F.   DUTY TO INFORM AND ACCOUNT

1. *Duty to Inform*

The trustee has a duty to inform the beneficiaries of the existence of the trust and significant developments pertaining to the administration of the trust, and to respond promptly to a request by a beneficiary for information reasonably related to the beneficiary's interests in the trust. 3 Austin Wakeman Scott, William Franklin Fratcher, and Mark L. Ascher, Scott and Ascher on Trusts §17.5 (5th ed. 2007). The existence of this duty gives the beneficiary a stick with which to compel disclosure by the trustee.

Uniform Trust Code (2000, as amended 2004)

§813.   DUTY TO INFORM AND REPORT

(a) A trustee shall keep the qualified beneficiaries of the trust reasonably informed about the administration of the trust and of the material facts necessary for them to protect their interests. Unless unreasonable under the circumstances, a trustee shall promptly respond to a beneficiary's request for information related to the administration of the trust.

(b) A trustee:

(1) upon request of a beneficiary, shall promptly furnish to the beneficiary a copy of the trust instrument;

(2) within 60 days after accepting a trusteeship, shall notify the qualified beneficiaries of the acceptance and of the trustee's name, address, and telephone number;

(3) within 60 days after the date the trustee acquires knowledge of the creation of an irrevocable trust, or the date the trustee acquires knowledge that a formerly revocable trust has become irrevocable, whether by the death of the

settlor or otherwise, shall notify the qualified beneficiaries of the trust's existence, of the identity of the settlor or settlors, of the right to request a copy of
the trust instrument, and of the right to a trustee's report as provided in subsection (c); and

(4) shall notify the qualified beneficiaries in advance of any change in the
method or rate of the trustee's compensation.

(c) A trustee shall send to the distributees or permissible distributees of trust
income or principal, and to other qualified or nonqualified beneficiaries who
request it, at least annually and at the termination of the trust, a report of the trust
property, liabilities, receipts, and disbursements, including the source and
amount of the trustee's compensation, a listing of the trust assets and, if feasible,
their respective market values. Upon a vacancy in a trusteeship, unless a cotrustee
remains in office, a report must be sent to the qualified beneficiaries by the
former trustee. A personal representative, [conservator], or [guardian] may send
the qualified beneficiaries a report on behalf of a deceased or incapacitated
trustee.

(d) A beneficiary may waive the right to a trustee's report or other information
otherwise required to be furnished under this section. A beneficiary, with respect
to future reports and other information, may withdraw a waiver previously
given. . . .

Fletcher v. Fletcher
Supreme Court of Virginia, 1997
480 S.E.2d 488

COMPTON, J.   In this chancery proceeding arising from a dispute over an inter
vivos trust, we consider the extent of a trustee's duty to furnish information about
the trust instrument and about other documents relating to the trust.

The facts are presented on appeal by a Rule 5:11 agreed statement of facts.
During their lifetimes, J. North Fletcher and Elinor Leh Fletcher, his wife, residents of Fauquier County, accumulated substantial assets.

Following Mr. Fletcher's death in 1984, Mrs. Fletcher executed a revocable,
inter vivos "Trust Agreement" in December 1985 in which she placed all her
assets. The ten-page document, containing nine articles, named her as both
"Grantor" and "Trustee." In August 1993, the Grantor modified the Trust Agreement by executing a "Trust Agreement Amendment." The five-page Amendment
replaced Article Six of the Trust Agreement with a new Article Six.

The Trust Agreement as amended (the Trust Agreement) contains, among
other things, specific provisions for the establishment of a number of trusts upon
the Grantor's death, including three separate trusts for the respective benefit of
appellee James N. Fletcher, Jr., an adult child of the Grantor, and his two
children, Andrew N. Fletcher, born in 1972, and Emily E. Fletcher, born in 1976
(sometimes collectively, the beneficiaries). The three separate trusts were to be in
the amount of $50,000 each. The Trust Agreement appointed appellant Henry
L. Fletcher, another adult child of the Grantor, and appellant F & M

Bank-Peoples Trust and Asset Management Group, formerly Peoples National Bank of Warrenton, as successor Trustees to act upon the Grantor's death.

Under the Trust Agreement, the Trustees are authorized, in their discretion, to expend for the benefit of James N. Fletcher, Jr., such amounts of the net income and principal of the $50,000 trust as may be necessary to provide him adequate medical insurance and medical care during his lifetime, or until such time as the trust is depleted. In the event the trust is still in existence at Fletcher's death, then the Trustees are required to transfer and pay over to his surviving children his or her proportionate share of the balance of the remaining principal and income.

Under the Trust Agreement, the Trustees also are authorized, in their discretion, to expend for the benefit of Fletcher's children such amounts of the income and principal of each of the $50,000 trusts as they deem advisable.

The Grantor died in June 1994. Upon her death, the Trust Agreement became irrevocable, and the successor Trustees assumed their duties. They established the three $50,000 trusts, and the beneficiaries have benefited from them.

In June 1995, beneficiary James N. Fletcher, Jr., instituted the present proceeding against the Trustees. In a bill of complaint, the plaintiff alleged that the December 1985 instrument recites that the Grantor "transferred, assigned and set over certain cash and securities which were . . . described in a schedule entitled 'A' attached to the trust agreement." The plaintiff further alleged that, upon his mother's death, he was advised that the assets had been transferred to "a new trust" with the defendants as Trustees.

The plaintiff also asserted that he "requested details from the defendants of both the December 3, 1985 trust and the trust created with the assets of that trust upon his mother's death," and that the Trustees have refused to comply with his request. He further asserted that he has been provided with only pages 1, 8 and 9 of the 1985 instrument and "two pages" from the Amendment. The plaintiff also asserted that "without a listing of the precise terms of both trust agreements or a complete listing of the assets of these trusts," he is "unable to determine whether or not the trust estate is being properly protected."

Plaintiff also alleged that Trustee Henry L. Fletcher "has repeatedly made a point of justifying his failure to disclose the requested information . . . by stating that it was his mother's request that the trust terms and dealings be kept confidential, even from the beneficiaries." Further, the plaintiff asserts that Trustee Fletcher "has failed to produce any written direction from [their mother] with respect to the confidentiality." This situation, along with other facts, according to the allegations, has resulted in "an extremely strained relationship between" the brothers.

Concluding, the plaintiff alleged that because he lacks the "relevant information" sought, "he is unable to determine whether or not either trustee is properly performing their duties as a trustee according to law." Thus, he asked the court to compel the Trustees "to provide full and complete copies of all trust instruments in their possession that relate to the two trusts referred to herein."

In a demurrer, the Trustees asserted that the bill of complaint failed to state a cause of action. In an answer, the Trustees denied that any "new trust" was created upon the Grantor's death, and asserted that the Trust Agreement remained in effect following the death. The Trustees asserted, however, that upon the death, "separate trusts were created under the express terms of the Trust Agreement," and that the plaintiff has been provided with "all provisions of the Trust Agreement relating to him and his children, along with regular accountings relating to his interest under the Trust Agreement." In sum, the Trustees denied the plaintiff is entitled to the information sought.

In October 1995, pursuant to an agreed order, the Trustees filed the Trust Agreement under seal with the court, to be examined only by the court.

Subsequently, the trial court heard argument on the demurrer and, during the hearing, ruled that the plaintiff was entitled to see all provisions of the Trust Agreement. The court noted that the plaintiff's "interests as a child of" the Grantor and as "a beneficiary of her trust outweighed the arguments advanced" by the Trustees.

Accordingly, in a January 1996 final order, the court said it was of opinion that the plaintiff "has an absolute right to complete copies of the Trust Agreement and all amendments referred to in the pleadings and associated documents." Thus, the court ordered the Trustees to provide the plaintiff with "full and complete copies of the Trust instruments that are referred to in the Bill of Complaint filed in this cause." The Trustees appeal.

The Trustees contend the trial court erred in finding that the plaintiff had an absolute right to review complete copies of the Trust Agreement and in ordering them to provide plaintiff with such copies. Emphasizing that the trust instrument established three separate trusts, the Trustees argue the trial court's order "ignores the fiduciary duty of confidentiality between the Trustees and other beneficiaries under the . . . Trust Agreement." Noting the use of revocable trusts in planning disposition of assets upon death, the Trustees say that following a grantor's death, "the trustees handle the trust assets for the various beneficiaries, in accordance with the grantor's instruction, in a manner appropriate for each beneficiary taking into account the unique circumstances applicable to each beneficiary."

Continuing, the Trustees observe that a grantor, as here, often "directs the trustee to segregate trust assets into separate trusts for the benefit of different beneficiaries." See Code §55-19.3 (trustee may divide a trust into two or more separate trusts). According to the Trustees, "Segregation of a trust into separate trusts for different beneficiaries not only segregates the assets, but also segregates the trustee's duties to the different beneficiaries." The Trustees say that a "trustee has a continuing duty to the grantor to fulfill the trustee's obligations under the trust agreement. The trustee also has a fiduciary duty to the beneficiaries of each trust established under the agreement. The trustee's duties to the beneficiaries of each separate trust do not overlap."

The Trustees point out the plaintiff has not alleged any wrongdoing on their part "nor has he alleged that he has any interest under the . . . Trust Agreement other than his interest in a separate trust established for his benefit." The Trustees state they have provided the plaintiff with copies of the portions of the Trust

Agreement that pertain to the establishment and administration of the separate trusts, have submitted a copy of the Trust Agreement to the trial judge so the court may determine whether they have disclosed to the plaintiff all relevant information, and have provided regular accountings to the beneficiaries with respect to their separate trusts. The Trustees argue that the family relationship and the "specter" of disharmony, standing alone do not create a right in the plaintiff to compel disclosure. Finally, the Trustees argue "the trial court's Order compelling disclosure violates the public policy that permits individuals to ensure privacy of their affairs through the use of inter vivos trust agreements in lieu of wills."

We do not agree with the Trustees' contentions. They place too much emphasis upon the duties of trustees while neglecting the rights of beneficiaries.

This is a case of first impression in Virginia. The parties have not referred us to any cases elsewhere that are factually apposite, and we have found none. Nevertheless, text writers and the Restatement articulate settled principles that are applicable.

"The beneficiary is the equitable owner of trust property, in whole or in part. The trustee is a mere representative whose function is to attend to the safety of the trust property and to obtain its avails for the beneficiary in the manner provided by the trust instrument." Bogert, The Law of Trusts and Trustees §961, at 2 (Rev. 2nd ed. 1983). The fact that a grantor has created a trust and thus required the beneficiary to enjoy the property interest indirectly "does not imply that the beneficiary is to be kept in ignorance of the trust, the nature of the trust property and the details of its administration." Bogert, §961, at 2.

Therefore, "the trustee is under a duty to the beneficiary to give him upon his request at reasonable times complete and accurate information as to the nature and amount of the trust property, and to permit him or a person duly authorized by him to inspect the subject matter of the trust and the accounts and vouchers and other documents relating to the trust." Restatement (Second) of Trusts §173 (1959). Accord Bogert, §961, at 3-4; IIA Scott, The Law of Trusts §173, at 462 (4th ed. 1987). Indeed, "where a trust is created for several beneficiaries, each of them is entitled to information as to the trust." Scott, §173, at 464.

And, even though "the terms of the trust may regulate the amount of information which the trustee must give and the frequency with which it must be given, the beneficiary is always entitled to such information as is reasonably necessary to enable him to enforce his rights under the trust or to prevent or redress a breach of trust." Restatement §173, cmt. c. See In re Estate of Rosenblum, 328 A.2d 158, 164-165 (Pa. 1974).

Turning to the present facts, we observe that the appellate record fails to establish that the Grantor directed the Trustees not to disclose the terms of the entire Trust Agreement to the beneficiaries. The trust instrument, which we have examined, does not mention the subject. Although the Trustees assert the Grantor orally gave such instructions, the plaintiff questions this fact. And, there was no evidentiary hearing below to decide the matter. Thus, we express no opinion on what effect any directive of secrecy by the Grantor would have on the outcome of this case.

Recognizing the foregoing general principles of the law of trusts, the Trustees nevertheless seek to remove this case from the force of those rules by dwelling on the fact that three separate trusts were created. In essence, the Trustees treat this single integrated Trust Agreement as if there are three distinct trust documents, each entirely independent of the other, a circumstance that simply does not exist.

There is a single cohesive trust instrument based on a unitary corpus. The Trustees seek to avoid the beneficiary's scrutiny of eight pages of the Trust Agreement. They also seek to prevent review of Schedule "A," which lists the cash and securities the Grantor transferred to the trust corpus. This document was not even included in the sealed papers filed with the trial court.

The information not disclosed may have a material bearing on the administration of the Trust Agreement insofar as the beneficiary is concerned. For example, without access to the Trust Agreement (even though there are numerous separate trusts established), the beneficiary has no basis upon which he can intelligently scrutinize the Trustees' investment decisions made with respect to the assets revealed on Schedule "A." The beneficiary is unable to evaluate whether the Trustees are discharging their duty to use "reasonable care and skill to make the trust property productive." Sturgis v. Stinson, 404 S.E.2d 56, 58 (Va. 1991) (quoting Restatement (Second) of Trusts §181 (1959)). Also, the beneficiary is entitled to review the trust documents in their entirety in order to assure the Trustees are discharging their "duty to deal impartially" with all the beneficiaries within the restrictions and conditions imposed by the Trust Agreement. *Sturgis*, 404 S.E.2d at 58.

In sum, we hold that the trial court correctly required the Trustees to disclose the information sought. Thus, the judgment appealed from will be

Affirmed.

QUESTIONS AND NOTES

1. In *Fletcher*, on the settlor's death the trust property was to be divided into three separate trusts. Why did James need access to the provisions of the governing instrument and records of administration relating to the two trusts in which he had no beneficial interest? Suppose Elinor had created three separate revocable trusts, only one of which named James as a beneficiary. Would James have information rights in the other two? Suppose the settlor expressly directs the trustee to disclose to a beneficiary only the provisions of the trust relating to that beneficiary. Should this direction be upheld? UTC §813(b)(1), page 738, provides that upon request the trustee must "promptly furnish to the beneficiary a copy of the trust instrument," but this provision is omitted from the schedule of mandatory rules in §105, so the settlor is free to provide otherwise. See also Restatement (Third) of Trusts §82, cmt. e (2007), which takes the position that "the settlor can limit the trustee's duty to disclose trust provisions or information on a reasonable basis."

Suppose Elinor had amended the trust from time to time before she died. Would James be entitled to see the earlier versions? See Taylor v. Nationsbank Corp., 481 S.E.2d 358 (N.C. App. 1997).

2. *A secret will?* Once a will is offered for probate, it becomes part of the public record. The testator's heirs are entitled to notice of the will's filing and have standing to contest its validity. Newspaper reporters and the just plain curious, too, may examine the will. A revocable trust, by contrast, is normally not filed in court or otherwise made public before or after the settlor's death. Under modern law, while the trust remains revocable the trustee's duties run to the settlor, not the beneficiaries (see pages 403-407), and after the settlor's death there is generally no obligation on the trustee to advise anyone other than the named beneficiaries of even the existence of the trust.

The real issue in *Fletcher* is this: Should the settlor be able to make, in effect, a secret will by using a revocable trust? Implicitly, *Fletcher* holds that the answer is No. See also Cal. Prob. Code §16061.5 (2008), which provides that when a revocable trust becomes irrevocable because of the death of the settlor, the trustee shall provide a complete copy of the terms of the trust to any beneficiary *or heir* of the settlor who requests it. In a related vein, UTC §604 provides a much shorter statute of limitations (120 days instead of 3 years) on an action to contest the validity of a revocable trust after the settlor's death if the trustee serves a copy of the trust instrument on the prospective contestant.

For more and deeper discussion, see the extensive analysis of trust privacy and the distinction between wills and revocable trusts by Professor Frances H. Foster in Trust Privacy, 93 Cornell L. Rev. 555 (2008), and Privacy and the Elusive Quest for Uniformity in the Law of Trusts, 38 Ariz. St. L.J. 713 (2006).

3. *A secret trust?* Should a settlor be able to make a secret trust — a trust unknown to the beneficiary in which the trustee has no duty to give information to the beneficiary? Without knowledge of the existence of the trust and basic information about its administration, the beneficiary cannot effectively protect her interest in the trust. See Foster, 93 Cornell L. Rev., supra, at 606-607. On the other hand, if knowing about the trust would induce the beneficiary to adopt a slothful or profligate lifestyle, might it be in the beneficiary's best interest to conceal the existence of the trust?

Under traditional law, as recognized by Restatement (Second) of Trusts §173, cmt. c (1959) and carried forward by Restatement (Third) of Trusts, supra, §82, cmt. a(2), the settlor may curtail the trustee's duty to give information, but not eliminate it completely. The beneficiary is always entitled to information reasonably related to the beneficiary's interest in enforcing her rights under the trust. The clear analogy is to the mandatory limits on an exculpation clause (see page 607). What differentiates property held in trust from property held outright is that the former is subject to an irreducible core of fiduciary obligation.

Under UTC §105(b)(8)-(9) as originally drafted, the settlor could prevent a beneficiary from learning of the trust's existence only until the beneficiary reached age 25. This provision came under intense criticism from practicing lawyers, and many states that enacted the UTC have rejected it, providing instead that the beneficiary can be kept in the dark until a later age or indefinitely if there is a trust protector or other surrogate to whom information must be given and who has standing to bring suit against the trustee for breach of trust. See Dana G. Fitzsimons, Jr., Navigating the Trustee's Duty to Disclose, Prob. & Prob., Jan./Feb.

2009, at 40 (charting the position of each state). In recognition of this lack of consensus, in 2004 the Uniform Law Commission put §105(b)(8)-(9) in brackets to signal that uniformity is not expected.

Is the naming of a trust protector with rights to information an adequate alternative safeguard against abuse by the trustee? In addition to the articles by Professor Foster cited in the prior note, see T.P. Gallanis, The Trustee's Duty to Inform, 85 N.C. L. Rev. 1595 (2007); Kevin D. Millard, The Trustee's Duty to Inform and Report Under the Uniform Trust Code, 40 Real Prop., Prob. & Tr. J. 373 (2005).

4. *Major transactions.* Should the trustee have an affirmative duty to give the beneficiary advance notice of a major transaction or other arrangement that after the fact would be difficult to unwind? See Allard v. Pacific Natl. Bank, 663 P.2d 104 (Wash. 1983); Restatement (Third) of Trusts, supra, §82, cmt. d.

5. *Trustee's agents.* Does the beneficiary's right to information allow the trustee to examine the communications between the trustee and the trustee's attorney? The cases are sparse and contradictory. Compare Riggs Natl. Bank v. Zimmer, 355 A.2d 709 (Del. Ch. 1976) (allowing the beneficiary to discover attorney-trustee communications because the beneficiary, not the trustee, is the "real" client), with Wells Fargo Bank v. Superior Ct. (Boltwood), 990 P.2d 591 (Cal. 2000) (rejecting the analysis in *Riggs*). The prevailing view in ERISA litigation appears to be in favor of the beneficiaries. See United States v. Mett, 178 F.3d 1058, 1062-1064 (9th Cir. 1999).

UTC §813 does not take a position on this question. The official comment explains that, because of the lack of consensus, the drafters left the question "open for further consideration by the courts."

2. Duty to Account

The law protects a trustee from liability to the beneficiary for breach of trust if the facts underlying the beneficiary's claim are fairly disclosed in an accounting filed with the court, notice of the accounting is properly served on the beneficiary, and the beneficiary does not timely object to the accounting. This rule provides a carrot to encourage the trustee to make regular and substantial disclosure to the beneficiary. Problems arise, however, when the facts underlying a subsequent claim by the beneficiary may not have been fairly disclosed in the accounting.

National Academy of Sciences v. Cambridge Trust Co.
Supreme Judicial Court of Massachusetts, 1976
346 N.E.2d 879

REARDON, J.   This matter is before us for further appellate review, the Appeals Court having promulgated an opinion.

The facts which give rise to the case are essentially as follows. Leonard T. Troland died a resident of Cambridge in 1932 survived by his widow, Florence R.

Troland. By his will executed in April, 1931, he left all of his real and personal property to be held in trust by the Cambridge Trust Company (bank) with the net income of the trust, after expenses, "to be paid to, or deposited to the account of [his wife], Florence R. Troland" during her lifetime so long as she remained unmarried. He further provided that

> [k]nowing my wife, Florence's, generosity and unselfishness as I do, I wish to record it as my intention that she should not devote any major portion of her income under the provisions of this will, to the support or for the benefit of people other than herself. It is particularly contrary to my will that any part of the principal or income of my estate should revert to members of my wife's family, other than herself, and I instruct the trustees to bear this point definitely in mind in making decisions under any of the options of this will.

The testator went on to provide in part that on his wife's death or second marriage the bank would transfer the trusteeship to The National Research Council of Washington, D.C., which the petition alleged to be an agency of the National Academy of Sciences (academy), to constitute a trust to be known as the Troland Foundation for Research in Psychophysics. . . .

The will was allowed, the trust was established as provided by the testator, and the bank paid the income thereof to the widow until her death in 1967. During the period from 1932 to 1945 the widow provided eighteen different mailing addresses for income checks to be transmitted to her by the bank. On February 13, 1945, she married Edward D. Flynn in West Palm Beach, Florida, and failed to advise the bank of her remarriage. Following her remarriage she lived in Perth Amboy, New Jersey. Commencing on April 14, 1944, she directed the bank to forward all her monthly checks to her in care of Kenneth D. Custance, her brother-in-law through marriage to her sister. Over the years these checks were forwarded to two Boston addresses and were made payable to "Florence R. Troland." Custance in turn forwarded the checks to Florence R. Flynn who indorsed them in blank "Florence R. Troland" and returned them to Custance who also indorsed them prior to depositing them in bank accounts in his name maintained at the State Street Bank and Trust Company in Boston and the National Bank of Wareham, Massachusetts. After Florence R. Flynn's death on December 25, 1967, the bank for the first time learned of her remarriage.[19] Throughout her second

---

19. A letter from Thomas Quarles, Jr., a lawyer in Manchester, New Hampshire, discloses some interesting information about the parties in this case. Quarles, who came upon this case while a law student using a prior edition of this book, writes:

Leonard Troland

> My father, Thomas Quarles, Sr., was the trust officer at the Cambridge Trust Company in charge of the Troland trust at the time of Florence Troland's death in 1967. Leonard Troland, the settlor of the trust, was apparently quite a colorful individual. A professor of psychology at Harvard for many years, he was also one of a group that developed the Technicolor motion picture film process. Proceeds from the sale of this invention formed part of the principal of the Troland trust. Mr. Troland apparently had a flair for the theatrical in his personal life as well. In 1932, he reportedly committed suicide by driving his car off the rim of the Grand Canyon at sunset.

> Florence Troland was aware of the limitation in the trust that cut off her interest if she remarried. So was her brother-in-law, Kenneth Custance. Nevertheless, after her remarriage in 1945, he convinced her to keep quiet and to endorse her trust

marriage Florence R. Flynn lived with her husband who was able to provide support for her and who, although aware that she was receiving payments from the trust, was ignorant of the limitation on her rights to receive such payments. . . . The total of all checks collected by Florence R. Flynn following her marriage in 1945 up to the date of her death is $106,013.41. The twelfth through thirty-third accounts of the bank covering that period between her remarriage and October 8, 1966, were presented to the Probate Court for Middlesex County in separate proceedings and allowed. The academy had formal notice prior to the presentation of the twelfth through fourteenth accounts and the eighteenth through thirty-third accounts, and with respect to the fifteenth through seventeenth accounts assented in writing to their allowance. The academy, unaware of the widow's remarriage, did not challenge any of the accounts and they were duly allowed.

The petition brought in the Probate Court by the academy seeks revocation of the seven decrees allowing the twelfth through thirty-third accounts of the bank, the excision from those accounts of "all entries purporting to evidence distributions to or for the benefit of 'Florence R. Troland' . . . subsequent to February 13, 1945," the restoration by the bank to the trust of the amounts of those distributions with interest at the rate of six percent, a final account reflecting the repayments and adjustments, [and] appointment of the academy as trustee . . . .

Following hearing a judge of the Probate Court revoked the seven decrees allowing the twelfth through thirty-third accounts, ordered restoration to the trust of $114,314.18, representing amounts erroneously distributed to Florence R. Flynn plus Massachusetts income taxes paid on those amounts from trust funds, together with interest thereon in the sum of $104,847.17 through March 31, 1973, and interest thereafter at the rate of six percent per annum to the date of restoration in full. . . .

The issues before us have to do with the power of the Probate Court judge to order the revocation of the decrees allowing the twelfth through thirty-third accounts, and the propriety of charging the bank for the amounts erroneously disbursed. . . .

The bank recited in the heading of each of the challenged accounts that the trust was "for the benefit of Florence R. Troland," and stated in schedule E of each account (in the first four accounts specifically as "Distributions to Beneficiary") that monthly payments of $225 or more were made to "Florence R. Troland." The Appeals Court held that these recitals and statements "constituted a continuing

income check over to him. He told her that the money was needed to support a succession of spiritualist churches that he headed in the Onset, Massachusetts area. When Florence died in 1967, Kenneth apparently felt guilty about the years of fraud. At her funeral, he gave Florence's latest trust check to her surviving husband, who contacted the Cambridge Trust Company asking what he should do with it. It was only at that point that the Bank realized that through Mrs. Troland and Mr. Custance's fraud it had paid the wrong beneficiary for 22 years. Fortunately, my father kept his job. He had only been with the Bank for a few years and had only recently taken over the Troland trust. [Letter from Thomas Quarles, Jr., to Jesse Dukeminier, dated Dec. 1, 1986.]

— Eds.

representation by the bank to the academy and to the court that the widow remained 'Florence R. Troland' despite her (then unknown) remarriage to Flynn, and that she remained the sole income beneficiary of the trust." . . . The court further held that those representations were technically fraudulent in that "[t]hey were made as of the bank's own knowledge when the bank had no such knowledge and had made absolutely no effort to obtain it." . . . With these views we find ourselves substantially in accord.

The doctrine of constructive or technical fraud in this Commonwealth is of venerable origin. As we pointed out in Powell v. Rasmussen, 243 N.E.2d 167 (Mass. 1969), the doctrine here was developed in two opinions by Chief Justice Shaw. In Hazard v. Irwin, 18 Pick. 95, 109 (1836), it was defined in the following terms: "[W]here the subject matter is one of fact, in respect to which a person can have precise and accurate knowledge, and . . . he speaks as of his own knowledge, and has no such knowledge, his affirmation is essentially false." This rule was reiterated by Chief Justice Shaw in Page v. Bent, 2 Met. 371, 374 (1841): "The principle is well settled, that if a person make[s] a representation of a fact, as of his own knowledge, in relation to a subject matter susceptible of knowledge, and such representation is not true; if the party to whom it is made relies and acts upon it, as true, and sustains damage by it, it is fraud and deceit, for which the party making it is responsible." In this case the marital status of Mrs. Troland/Flynn was a fact susceptible of precise knowledge, the bank made representations concerning this fact of its own knowledge when it had no such knowledge, and the academy to whom the representations were made relied on them to its detriment. While this standard of fraud in law has been developed primarily in the context of actions seeking rescission of contracts and of tort actions for deceit, we have indicated in past decisions that an analogous standard might be applicable to misrepresentations in the accounts of fiduciaries. See Greene v. Springfield Safe Deposit & Trust Co., 3 N.E.2d 254 (Mass. 1936); Welch v. Flory, 200 N.E. 900 (Mass. 1936); Brigham v. Morgan, 69 N.E. 418 (Mass. 1904). We hold today that "fraud" as used in G.L. c. 206, §24, contemplates this standard of constructive fraud at least to the extent that the fiduciary has made no reasonable efforts to ascertain the true state of the facts it has misrepresented in the accounts. This rule is not a strict liability standard, nor does it make a trustee an insurer against the active fraud of all parties dealing with the trust. Entries in the accounts honestly made, after reasonable efforts to determine the truth or falsity of the representations therein have failed through no fault of the trustee, will not be deemed fraudulent or provide grounds for reopening otherwise properly allowed accounts. However, in the instant case the probate judge found that the bank, through the twenty-two years covered by the disputed accounts, exerted "no effort at all . . . to ascertain if Florence R. Troland had remarried even to the extent of annually requesting a statement or certificate from her to that effect" and that "in administering the trust acted primarily in a ministerial manner and in disregard of its duties as a trustee to protect the terms of the trust." In these circumstances we have little trouble in concluding that the bank's representations as to the marital status of the testator's widow fully justified the reopening of the accounts.

Cases relied on by the bank in which this court refused to allow previously allowed accounts to be reopened are distinguishable in that either they did not involve representations of fact susceptible of precise knowledge but rather questions of judgment and discretion as to matters fully and frankly disclosed in the accounts . . . or that the alleged wrongful acts or mistakes of the trustee were discernible from an examination of the accounts, the trust documents and the law. . . . We adhere to our decisions that it is the duty of beneficiaries "to study the account presented to the Probate Court by the trustee, and to make their objections at the hearing." Greene v. Springfield Safe Deposit & Trust Co., supra, 3 N.E.2d at 257. However, in this case the fact of the widow's remarriage was not discernible from the most scrupulous examination of the accounts, the trust documents and the relevant law, and the bank cannot avoid responsibility here for its misrepresentations by alleging a breach of duty on the part of the academy.

As to the propriety of surcharging the bank for the amounts erroneously disbursed, when a trustee makes payment to a person other than the beneficiary entitled to receive the money, he is liable to the proper beneficiary to make restitution unless the payment was authorized by a proper court. . . . Since, as we have held the decrees allowing the twelfth through thirty-third accounts were revoked properly, the bank thus became liable to the academy to restore to the trust corpus the payments it made to Mrs. Troland/Flynn when she was not entitled to receive them. In addition to the amounts erroneously disbursed, the bank was also properly charged by the Probate Court judge with simple interest on those payments at the legal rate of six percent per annum. . . .

[T]he decree is affirmed.

NOTES, QUESTION, AND PROBLEM

1. *Informal accountings.* Under traditional law, the beneficiary can compel the trustee to provide an accounting. 3 Austin Wakeman Scott, William Franklin Fratcher, and Mark L. Ascher, Scott and Ascher on Trusts §17.4 (5th ed. 2007). To hold down the costs of administration, trust instruments often provide for informal accountings in lieu of judicial accountings. Should such a provision be enforced?

In Jacob v. Davis, 738 A.2d 904 (Md. App. 1999), a remainder beneficiary petitioned for an accounting, partly to examine whether the trustees had impermissibly favored the income beneficiaries. The trust instrument excused the trustee from judicial accountings and provided that an informal account rendered to the adult *income* beneficiaries, if approved in writing by those beneficiaries, "shall be a complete discharge to my Trustee with respect to all matters set forth in the account as fully and to the same extent as though the account had been judicially settled." The court granted the *remainder* beneficiary's petition in spite of this provision. See also In re Shore, 854 N.Y.S.2d 293 (Sur. 2008) (explaining that "there is a basic reason that such a provision cannot be enforced, namely that accountability is an essential element of all fiduciary relationships").

This reasoning is criticized by David Westfall, Nonjudicial Settlement of Trustees' Accounts, 71 Harv. L. Rev. 40 (1957). Professor Westfall argues that if the income beneficiaries can be given a power of appointment that diminishes or destroys the remainder, there is no reason not to give effect to a clause permitting the income beneficiary to absolve the trustee from further accountability.

Restatement (Third) of Trusts §83, cmt. d (2007) takes the position that a provision "that the trustee need only account or submit reports to a designated person . . . and that the approval of the trustee's account or report by that person shall discharge the trustee from liability" is effective if "(i) the other person in giving approval acts neither in bad faith nor in casual disregard of the interests or rights of the nonassenting beneficiaries and (ii) the accounting appropriately discloses material issues about the trustee's conduct." The designated person's approval of an informal accounting is subject to judicial review for abuse. The trustee also remains under a duty to provide to the beneficiary upon reasonable request information related to the beneficiary's interest in the trust.

2.   UTC §813, page 738, strikes an interesting balance. Section 813(c) generally requires the trustee to provide an annual report, but because this provision is not made mandatory by §105, the settlor may release the trustee from this requirement. Under §813(d), the beneficiaries may likewise waive their right to reports or other information, but this waiver can always be withdrawn later. Further, "a waiver of a trustee's report or other information does not relieve the trustee from accountability and potential liability for matters that the report or other information would have disclosed." UTC §813, cmt.

3.   *O* transfers property to *X* in trust to pay the income to *A* for life, remainder to *A*'s children. *A* is now 42 years old, is not married, and has no descendants. To hold down trust expenses, *A* seeks to have the trustee account nonjudicially to her, agreeing to indemnify the trustee against any objections to its administration that might subsequently be made by a remainderperson. Should the trustee agree to this? See UTC §§111, 1009 (2000, rev. 2004).

11

CHARITABLE TRUSTS

SECTION A. INTRODUCTION

In this chapter, we explore the *charitable trust*, one of the several permissible forms of charitable organization. In general, the same rules that pertain to the formation and governance of a private trust apply likewise to a charitable trust — except that a charitable trust must be for the benefit of a *charitable purpose*, not an ascertainable beneficiary; a charitable trust is exempt from the Rule Against Perpetuities and is therefore more easily modified under the *cy pres* doctrine; and the *state attorney general*, not an ascertainable beneficiary, is the principal party with standing to enforce a charitable trust.

Most charities are structured as nonprofit corporations rather than as trusts. However, much of the law of charitable gifts, nonprofit corporations, and charitable foundations derives from the law of charitable trusts. See Evelyn Brody, Charity Governance: What's Trust Law Got to Do with It?, 80 Chi.-Kent L. Rev. 641 (2005). Accordingly, the principles applicable to charitable trusts explored in this chapter have a broader, more general application across the charity and nonprofit sector — and real money is at stake. In 2006, there were 1.6 million tax-exempt, charitable organizations on file with the IRS, reporting assets of $2.4 trillion and revenue of $1.2 trillion.

SECTION B. NATURE OF CHARITABLE PURPOSES

The fundamental distinction between a private trust and a charitable trust is that where a private trust must be for the benefit of an ascertainable beneficiary, a charitable trust instead must have a valid *charitable purpose*.

Shenandoah Valley National Bank v. Taylor
Supreme Court of Appeals of Virginia, 1951
63 S.E.2d 786

MILLER, J.   Charles B. Henry,[1] a resident of Winchester, Virginia, died testate on the 23rd day of April, 1949. His will dated April 21, 1949, was duly admitted to probate and the Shenandoah Valley National Bank of Winchester, the designated executor and trustee, qualified thereunder.

Subject to two inconsequential provisions not material to this litigation, the testator's entire estate valued at $86,000, was left as follows:

> Second: All the rest, residue and remainder of my estate, real, personal, intangible and mixed, of whatsoever kind and wherever situate, . . . I give, bequeath and devise to the Shenandoah Valley National Bank of Winchester, Virginia, in trust, to be known as the "Charles B. Henry and Fannie Belle Henry Fund," for the following uses and purposes:
>
> (a) My Trustee shall invest and reinvest my trust estate, shall collect the income therefrom and shall pay the net income as follows:
>
> (1) On the last school day of each calendar year before Easter my Trustee shall divide the net income into as many equal parts as there are children in the first, second and third grades of the John Kerr School of the City of Winchester, and shall pay one of such equal parts to each child in such grades, to be used by such child in the furtherance of his or her obtainment of an education.
>
> (2) On the last school day of each calendar year before Christmas my trustee shall divide the net income into as many equal parts as there are children in the first, second and third grades of the John Kerr School of the City of Winchester, and shall pay one of such equal parts to each child in such grades, to be used by such child in the furtherance of his or her obtainment of an education.

By paragraphs (3) and (4) it is provided that the names of the children in the three grades shall be determined each year from the school records, and payment of

---

1. The testator, Charles B. Henry, operated a fruit and vegetable stand until shortly before his death. In earlier years, in addition to the stand, he hawked fruits and vegetables through the town from a horse-drawn wagon.

A number of years before his death he lost his only child, a very pretty little daughter. This, so I am told, profoundly affected him, causing him to become more and more a recluse and this became even more pronounced after the death of his wife, who predeceased him by some years. Along with this increasing withdrawal from general social intercourse, there seems to have developed an increasing tendency to become miserly. This was indicated by such things as avoidance of use of electric lights except when absolutely necessary and making the produce which was no longer salable a substantial part of his diet.

Nonetheless, perhaps because of memory of his own deceased child, he seems to have maintained a strong affection for children generally. As a fruit vendor, he was widely known among the older generation of local citizens.

He saved and hoarded his money and made some investments, and I recollected being told by someone, possibly an official of the Shenandoah Valley Bank that when the Great Depression struck, he was frantic to the point of unnatural frenzy at the depreciation of his investments.

My firm received the case as a result of the complainant being the babysitter for my partner's sister and brother-in-law and was the second or third cousin to Charlie Henry. For some time she had been helping to look after him and bringing him food, undoubtedly with that expectation so often disappointed that he would remember her in his will; in fact, I recollect that she claimed that he had flatly promised to do so or by artful insinuation had convinced her that he would. Her disappointment and resulting ire prompted her to seek counsel. [Letter to the editors, dated July 7, 1975, from the Hon. Robert K. Waltz, winning counsel in the *Taylor* case and later circuit court judge in Virginia.]

— Eds.

the income to them "shall be as nearly equal in amounts as it is practicable" to arrange.

Paragraph (5) provides that if the John Kerr School is ever discontinued for any reason the payments shall be made to the children of the same grades of the school or schools that take its place, and the School Board of Winchester is to determine what school or schools are substituted for it.

Under clause "Third" the trustee is given authority, power, and discretion to retain or from time to time sell and invest and reinvest the estate, or any part thereof, as it shall deem to be the best interest of the trust.

The John Kerr School is a public school used by the local school board for primary grades and had an enrollment of 458 boys and girls so there will be that number of pupils or thereabouts who would share in the distribution of the income.

The testator left no children or near relatives. Those who would be his heirs and distributees in case of intestacy were first cousins and others more remotely related. One of these next of kin filed a suit against the executor and trustee, and others challenging the validity of the provisions of the will which undertook to create a charitable trust. . . .

The sole question presented is: does the will create a valid charitable trust?

Construction of the challenged provisions is required and in this undertaking the testator's intent as disclosed by the words used in the will must be ascertained. If his dominant intent as expressed was charitable, the trust should be accorded efficacy and sustained.

But on the other hand, if the testator's intent as expressed is merely benevolent, though the disposition of his property be meritorious and evince traits of generosity, the trust must nevertheless be declared invalid because it violates the rule against perpetuities. . . .

Authoritative definitions of charitable trusts may be found in 4 Pomeroy's Equity Jurisprudence, 5th Ed., sec. 1020, and Restatement of the Law of Trusts, sec. 368, p.1140. The latter gives a comprehensive classification definition. It is:

> Charitable purposes include:
>
> (a)   the relief of poverty;
> (b)   the advancement of education;
> (c)   the advancement of religion;
> (d)   the promotion of health;
> (e)   governmental or municipal purposes; and
> (f)   other purposes the accomplishment of which is beneficial to the community.

In the recent decision of Allaun v. First National Bank, 56 S.E.2d 83 (Va. 1949), the definition that appears in 3 M.J., Charitable Trust, sec. 2, p.872, was approved and adopted. It reads:

> "A charity," in a legal sense, may be described as a gift to be applied, consistently with existing laws, for the benefit of an indefinite number of persons, either by bringing their hearts under the influence of education or religion, by relieving their bodies from disease, suffering or

constraint, by assisting them to establish themselves for life, or by erecting or maintaining public building or works, or otherwise lessening the burdens of government. It is immaterial whether the purpose is called charitable in the gift itself, if it is so described as to show that it is charitable. Generally speaking, any gift not inconsistent with existing laws which is promotive of science or tends to the education, enlightening, benefit or amelioration of the condition of mankind or the diffusion of useful knowledge, or is for the public convenience is a charity. It is essential that a charity be for the benefit of an indefinite number of persons; for if all the beneficiaries are personally designated, the trust lacks the essential element of indefiniteness, which is one characteristic of a legal charity. (190 Va. p.108.) . . .

In the law of trusts there is a real and fundamental distinction between a charitable trust and one that is devoted to mere benevolence. The former is public in nature and valid; the latter is private and if it offends the rule against perpetuities, it is void. "It is quite clear that trusts which are devoted to mere benevolence or liberality, or generosity, cannot be upheld as charities. Benevolent objects include acts dictated by mere kindness, good will, or a disposition to do good. . . . Charity in a legal sense must be distinguished from acts of liberality or benevolence. To constitute a charity the use must be public in its nature." Zollman on Charities, sec. 398, p.268.

We are, however, reminded that charitable trusts are favored creatures of the law enjoying the especial solicitude of courts of equity and a liberal interpretation is employed to uphold them. Zollman on Charities, sec. 570, p.391; 2 Bogert on Trusts, sec. 369, p.1129. . . .

Appellant contends that the gift . . . not only meets the requirements of a charitable trust as defined in Restatement of the Law of Trusts, supra, but specifically fits two of those classifications, viz.:

> (b) trusts for the advancement of education;
> (f) other purposes the accomplishment of which is beneficial to the community.

We now turn to the language of the will for from its context the testator's intent is to be derived. Sheridan v. Krause, 172 S.E. 508 (Va. 1934). Its interpretation must be free from and uninfluenced by the unyielding rule against perpetuities. Yet, when the testator's intent is ascertained, if it is found to be in contravention of the rule, the will, in that particular, must be declared invalid. . . .

In paragraphs (1) and (2), respectively, of clause "Second" in clear and definite language the discretion, power and authority of the trustee in [the trustee's] disposition and application of the income are specified and limited. Yearly on the last school day before Easter and Christmas each youthful beneficiary of the testator's generosity is to be paid an equal share of the income. In mandatory language the duty and the duty alone to make cash payments to each individual child just before Easter and Christmas is enjoined upon the trustee by the certain and explicit words that it "shall divide the net income . . . and shall pay one of such equal shares to each child in such grades."

Without more, that language, and the occasions specified for payment of the funds to the children being when their minds and interests would be far removed from studies or other school activities definitely indicate that no educational purpose was in the testator's mind. It is manifest that there was no intent or belief that the funds would be put to any use other than such as youthful impulse and desire might dictate. But in each instance immediately following the above-quoted language the sentence concludes with the words or phrase "to be used by such child in the furtherance of his or her obtainment of an education." It is significant that by this latter phrase the trustee is given no power, control or discretion over the funds so received by the child. Full and complete execution of the mandate and trust imposed upon the trustee accomplishes no educational purpose. Nothing toward the advancement of education is attained by the ultimate performance by the trustee of its full duty. It merely places the income irretrievably and forever beyond the range of the trust.

Appellant says that the latter phrase, "to be used by such child in furtherance of his or her obtainment of an education," evinces the testator's dominant purpose and intent. Yet it is not denied that the preceding provision "shall divide the net income into as many equal parts . . . and shall pay one of each equal parts to such child" is at odds with the phrase it relies upon. The appended qualification, it says, however, discloses a controlling intent that the 450 or more shares are to be used in the furtherance of education, and it was not really intended that a share be paid to each child so that he or she could during the Christmas and Easter holidays, or at any other time, use it "without let or hindrance, encumbrance or care." With that construction we cannot agree. In our opinion, the words of the will import an intent to have the trustee pay to each child his allotted share. If that be true, — and it is directed to be done in no uncertain language — we know that the admonition to the children would be wholly impotent and of no avail.

In construing wills, we may not forget or disregard the experiences of life and the realities of the occasion. Nor may we assume or indulge in the belief that the testator by his injunction to the donees intended or thought that he could change childhood nature and set at naught childhood impulses and desires.

Appellant asserts that literal performance of the duty imposed upon it — pay to each child his share — would be impracticable and should not be done. Its position in that respect is stated thus: "We do not understand that under the law of Virginia a court would pay money for education into the hands of children who are incapable of handling it." It then says that the funds could be administered by a guardian or under sec. 8-751, Code, 1950 (where the amounts are under $500), a court could direct payment to be made to the recipient's parents.

With these statements, we agree. But because the funds could be administered under applicable statutes has no bearing upon nor may that device be resorted to as an aid to prove or establish the testator's intent. We are of opinion that the testator's dominant intent appears from and is expressed in his unequivocal direction to the trustee to divide the income into as many equal parts as there are children beneficiaries and pay one share to each. This expressed purpose and intent is inconsistent with the appended direction to each child as to the use of his respective share and the latter phrase is thus ineffectual to create an educational trust. The testator's purpose and intent were, we think, to bestow upon the children gifts that would bring to them happiness on the two holidays, but that falls short of an educational trust.

If it be determined that the will fails to create a charitable trust for *educational purposes* (and our conclusion is that it is inoperative to create such a trust), it is earnestly insisted that the trust provided for is nevertheless charitable and valid. In this respect it is claimed that the two yearly payments to be made to the children just before Christmas and Easter produce "a desirable social effect" and are "promotive of public convenience and needs, and happiness and contentment" and thus the fund set up in the will constitutes a charitable trust. 2 Bogert on Trusts, sec. 361, p.1090, and 3 Scott on Trusts, sec. 368, p.1972. . . .

Numerous cases that deal with and construe specific provisions of wills or other instruments are cited by appellant to uphold the contention that the provisions of this will, without reference to and deleting the phrase "to be used by such child in the furtherance of his or her obtainment of an education" meet the requirements of a charitable trust.

Upon examination of these decisions, it will be found that where a gift results in mere financial enrichment, a trust was sustained only when the court found and concluded from the entire context of the will that the ultimate intended recipients were poor or in necessitous circumstances.

A trust from which the income is to be paid at stated intervals to each member of a designated segment of the public, without regard to whether or not the recipients are poor or in need, is not for the relief of poverty, nor is it a social benefit to the community. It is a mere benevolence — a private trust — and may not be upheld as a charitable trust. Restatement of the Law of Trusts, sec. 374, p.1156: " . . . if a large sum of money is given in trust to apply the income each year in paying a certain sum to every inhabitant of a city, whether rich or poor, the trust is not charitable, since although each inhabitant may receive a benefit, the social interest of the community as such is not thereby promoted."

In 2 Bogert on Trusts, sec. 380, we find:

> As previously stated, gifts which are mere exhibitions of liberality and generosity, without regard to their effect upon the donees, are not charitable. There must be an amelioration of the condition of the donees as a result of the gift, and this improvement must be of a mental, physical, or spiritual nature and not merely financial. Thus, trusts to provide gifts to children, regardless of their need, or to make Christmas gifts to members of a certain class, without consideration of need or effect, are not charitable. . . . (p. 1218.)
>
> Gifts which are made out of mere sentiment, and will have no practical result except the satisfying of a whim of the donor, are obviously lacking in the widespread social effect necessary to a charity. (p. 1219.)

Nor do we find any language in this will that permits the trustee to limit the recipients of the donations to the school children in the designated grades who are in necessitous circumstances, and thus bring the trust under the influence of the case styled Appeal of Eliot, 51 A. 558 (Conn. 1902).

The conclusion there reached was that where a trust is set up and a class is designated as beneficiary which generally contains needy persons, the testator will be presumed to have intended as recipients those members of the class who are in necessitous circumstances.

Payment to the children of their cash bequests on the two occasions specified would bring to them pleasure and happiness and no doubt cause them to remember or think of their benefactor with gratitude and thanksgiving. That was, we think, Charles B. Henry's intent. Laudable, generous and praiseworthy though it may be, it is not for the relief of the poor or needy, nor does it otherwise so benefit or advance the social interest of the community as to justify its continuance in perpetuity as a charitable trust. . . .

No error is found in the decrees appealed from and they are affirmed.

NOTES AND QUESTIONS

1. *Charitable purpose.* To be classified as *charitable*, a trust must be for the relief of poverty or for the advancement of education, religion, health, or governmental or other purpose that is sufficiently beneficial to the community to justify the preferential treatment afforded to a charitable trust. See Restatement (Third) of Trusts §28 (2003); Uniform Trust Code §405 (2000). See also 6 Austin Wakeman Scott, William Franklin Fratcher, and Mark L. Ascher, Scott and Ascher on Trusts §38.7 (5th ed. 2009), collecting authority on other purposes beneficial to the community. The list of charitable purposes is of venerable origin, deriving from the Statute of Charitable Uses, 43 Eliz. I, c. 4 (1601).

It is sometimes said — erroneously — that a trust is charitable if it has many beneficiaries. On the contrary, a trust is not charitable merely because it benefits a class of persons. Thus, a trust to benefit sick or needy employees is charitable (because it furthers health and relieves poverty), but a trust for the general benefit of employees is not charitable. Likewise, a trust to pay the salary of a law professor is charitable (because it furthers an educational purpose), but a trust for the general benefit of lawyers is not charitable. See Scott and Ascher on Trusts, supra, §38.9.1.

A trust may be a valid charitable trust although the persons who directly benefit are limited in number. Thus, a trust awarding scholarships or prizes for educational achievement is charitable, even if only one or two students will benefit. But a trust to educate a particular person or named persons is not charitable. Nor is a trust to educate the descendants of the settlor charitable. Restatement (Third) of Trusts §28, cmt. a(1) (2003); In re Estate of Keenan, 519 N.W.2d 373 (Iowa 1994). On the other hand, a trust to provide scholarships has been held charitable even if the settlor's family is given preference. United Bank, Inc. v. Blosser, 624 S.E.2d 815 (W. Va. 2005). And a trust to send a specific person through medical school upon her promise to practice in the testator's hometown has been held charitable. Estate of Carlson, 358 P.2d 669 (Kan. 1961).

A trust may be a valid charitable trust although the settlor delegates the selection of charitable purpose to the trustee. Thus, *O* may convey a fund, in trust, to *X* for such charitable purpose or purposes as *X* shall select. Restatement (Third) of Trusts, supra, §28, cmt. a.

For a comprehensive analysis of charitable gifts and of the difficulties courts have had in defining charitable, see Mary Kay Lundwall, Inconsistency and Uncertainty in the Charitable Purposes Doctrine, 41 Wayne L. Rev. 1341 (1995).

2.   *The Rule Against Perpetuities.* Mr. Henry's "candy trust" was invalid ab initio because it violated the Rule Against Perpetuities (see Chapter 14). Had the trust qualified as charitable, it would have been valid and could have lasted forever. See also Marsh v. The Frost Natl. Bank, 129 S.W.3d 174 (Tex. App. 2004), holding that a bequest "to provide a million dollar trust fund for every American 18 years or older" by accumulating income for 346 years on the proceeds from the sale of certain property was not charitable and hence violated the Rule Against Perpetuities.

During the latter part of the twentieth century, and continuing into the present, a majority of states modified the common law Rule Against Perpetuities by adopting a form of wait-and-see, whereby courts wait to see if, in light of actual instead of possible events, the interest will in fact vest or fail within the perpetuities period, or by abrogating the rule altogether with respect to trusts for which the trustee has the power of alienation. How would these reforms alter the result, if at all, in *Taylor*? For careful, indeed fastidious, analysis, see Adam J. Hirsch, Trusts for Purposes: Policy, Ambiguity, and Anomaly in the Uniform Laws, 26 Fla. St. U. L. Rev. 913, 930-950 (1999).

3.   *Trusts for noncharitable purposes.* Under traditional law, a trust not for a charitable purpose must have one or more ascertainable (and human) beneficiaries to be valid. This rule has been relaxed to permit a trust for a *noncharitable purpose* provided that the purpose is not capricious. Many courts recognize *honorary trusts*, where the trustee has the power, but not a duty, to apply the trust property to the settlor's stated purpose. If the trustee does not do so, then the property reverts on resulting trust to the settlor or the settlor's heirs or devisees.

Today, most states have enacted statutes that expressly permit a trust for the benefit of a pet animal or for another noncharitable purpose such as the preservation of graves or the saying of masses. Many of these *statutory purpose trust* provisions are based on UTC §§408-409 (2000) or Uniform Probate Code §2-907 (1990, rev. 1993). For further discussion, see pages 585-588.

4.   *Trusts to benefit a political party.* It is against public policy to endow perpetually a political party, so a trust to promote the success of a particular political party is not charitable. However, a trust for the improvement of the structure and methods of government, in a manner advocated by a particular political party, is charitable. Hence, a trust to advance "the principles of socialism and those causes related to socialism," including supporting candidates for public office espousing socialistic views, has been held charitable. In re Estate of Breeden, 256 Cal. Rptr. 813 (App. 1989).

A trust with the purpose of bringing about a change in the law may be charitable, provided the purpose is not to bring about those changes by illegal means, such as revolution or illegal lobbying. Restatement (Third) of Trusts §28, cmt. l (2003). In Register of Wills for Baltimore City v. Cook, 216 A.2d 542 (Md. 1966), the court upheld a trust to support the passage of the Equal Rights Amendment, rejecting Jackson v. Phillips, 96 Mass. 539 (1867), which held a trust in support of women's suffrage not charitable.

5. *Drafting advice.* The lawyer drawing a will making a gift to charity should make sure of the exact legal name of the charity, and if the client wants an estate tax charitable deduction, whether the charity is tax-exempt under the Internal Revenue Code. A purpose deemed charitable by a state court may not always qualify for a federal estate tax charitable deduction. See Principles of the Law of Nonprofit Organizations §210, reporter's notes (C.D. No. 5, 2007), describing and contrasting requirements of state law and federal tax law.

Trusts for *benevolent* or *philanthropic* purposes should be avoided. Some older cases held that these words are broader than *charitable*, and, if so, the trust may fail as a charitable trust because the income can be used for noncharitable purposes. Modern cases tend to construe these words to be synonymous with charitable, and in a state that has adopted UTC §409, it is possible that the benevolent or philanthropic purpose might qualify as a valid trust for a noncharitable purpose, but out of caution these terms should be avoided nonetheless.

6. *Mortmain statutes.* Most states once had statutes permitting spouses and children to set aside death-bed wills making gifts to charity (traceable to the medieval fear of overreaching by priests taking the last confession and will). Some of these statutes restricted the share of an estate that could be left to charity even when the will was executed years before death. These statutes have all been either repealed or declared unconstitutional as a denial of equal protection of the law or on substantive due process grounds. See Restatement (Third) of Property: Wills and Other Donative Transfers §9.7 (2003). Today, claims of overreaching by a charity, religious or otherwise, are litigated as ordinary undue influence matters. See Jeffrey G. Sherman, Can Religious Influence Ever Be "Undue" Influence?, 73 Brooklyn L. Rev. 579 (2008), arguing that "all relationships between a testator and her religious or spiritual advisor" be deemed "per se 'confidential relationships' for purposes of litigating any will contest."

NOTE: SHAW'S ALPHABET TRUSTS

George Bernard Shaw, winner of the 1925 Nobel Prize for Literature, was long interested in reforming the English alphabet so that letters, singly and in combination, would have only one pronunciation. He pointed out that fish could be spelled "ghoti" if the "gh" were pronounced like the "gh" in "enough," "o" like the "o" in "women," and "ti" like "ti" in "notion." (He did not note that Shaw could be spelled "pshaw.") Shaw devised the residue of his estate to his executor, in trust for 21 years, to develop a new alphabet of 40 letters and to propagandize for its adoption. Upon the termination of the alphabet trusts "or if and so far as such trusts shall fail through judicial decision," the principal was to be distributed one-third to the British Museum "in acknowledgment of the incalculable value to me of my daily resort to the reading room of that institution at the beginning of my career," one-third to the National Gallery of Ireland, and one-third to the

Royal Academy of Dramatic Art. The court held the alphabet trust was not for the advancement of education nor beneficial to the community, and therefore it was not a charitable trust. The court further held that the devise could not be treated as a private trust because it was not in favor of an ascertainable beneficiary. The court referred to Restatement of Trusts §124 (1935), which approves treating such a gift as a power, and stated that it was

> not at liberty to validate this trust by treating it as a power. . . . The result is that the alphabet trusts are, in my judgment, invalid, and must fail. It seems that their begetter suspected as much, hence his jibe about failure by judicial decision. I answer that it is not the fault of the law, but of the testator, who failed almost for the first time in his life to grasp the problem or to make up his mind what he wanted. [In re Shaw, 1 All E.R. 745, 759 (Ch. 1957).]

The case was appealed, but while the appeal was pending a compromise was effected by which a sum was set aside to employ a phonetic expert to develop a phonetic alphabet, transliterate Shaw's play Androcles and the Lion into the new alphabet, and publish the transliterated play.

SECTION C.   MODIFICATION OF CHARITABLE TRUSTS: CY PRES

Under the *cy pres* doctrine, if the settlor's exact charitable purpose becomes illegal, impossible, or impracticable, the court may direct the application of the trust property to another charitable purpose that approximates the settlor's intention. Cy pres is shorthand for the Norman French phrase *cy pres comme possible*, meaning "as nearly as possible." The doctrine addresses the risk that, because a charitable trust may have a perpetual existence, changed circumstances will render the trust's original purpose obsolete. See Restatement (Third) of Trusts §67, cmt. a (2003).

In England there was a royal prerogative power of cy pres as well as a judicial doctrine of cy pres. Under the prerogative power, charitable gifts were expected to comply with public policy as established by the king. Any deviations were corrected by the crown, regardless of the testator's intent. In Da Costa v. De Pas, 27 Eng. Rep. 150 (Ch. 1754), a Jewish testator left money in trust to form an assembly for the purpose of teaching Jewish law and religion. The trust encouraged a religion other than the state religion and was referred to the king by the chancellor for instructions. Applying prerogative cy pres, the king allotted the money to instruct foundlings in the Christian religion.

Largely as a reaction to the abuse of prerogative cy pres by the crown, disregarding entirely the probable wishes of the settlor, courts in this country were reluctant to adopt judicial cy pres. It, too, could be abused. As the nineteenth century receded into history, however, various changes in circumstances made it difficult or impractical to administer charitable trusts as specifically intended by the donors. A nineteenth-century trust to care for old horses retired from pulling fire wagons and streetcars could not be administered for those purposes in the twentieth century. Hence, American courts finally came to accept a judicial doctrine of cy pres.

In re Neher
Court of Appeals of New York, 1939
18 N.E.2d 625

LOUGHRAN, J.   The will of Ella Neher was admitted to probate by the Surrogate's Court of Dutchess County December 22, 1930. Paragraph 7 thereof made these provisions:

> I give, devise and bequeath my home in Red Hook Village, on the east side of South Broadway, consisting of house, barn and lot of ground . . . to the incorporated Village of Red Hook, as a memorial to the memory of my beloved husband, Herbert Neher, with the direction to said Village that said property be used as a hospital to be known as "Herbert Neher Memorial Hospital." The trustees of the Village of Red Hook, consisting of the President and the Trustees, shall constitute the managing board with full power to manage and operate said hospital as they deem wise for the benefit of the people of Red Hook, and each succeeding Board of Trustees shall constitute the Board of Trustees for said hospital, so that any person duly elected and qualified or duly appointed and qualified as a President or Trustee of the said Village of Red Hook shall be a trustee of said hospital during such person's lawful term of office, and shall be succeeded as a trustee on the hospital board by his successor on the Village Board.

All her other estate Mrs. Neher gave to relatives and friends.

On September 1, 1931, the trustees of Red Hook (hereinafter called the village) resolved to "accept the real property devised and bequeathed by the Will of Ella Neher, deceased, according to the terms of the Will of said Ella Neher."

In March, 1937, the village presented to the Surrogate's Court its petition asserting that it was without the resources necessary to establish and maintain a hospital on the property devised to it by the testatrix and that a modern hospital theretofore recently established in the neighboring village of Rhinebeck adequately served the needs of both communities. The prayer of this petition was for a decree "construing and reforming paragraph Seven of the last Will and Testament of said decedent directing and permitting your petitioner to receive said property and to erect and maintain thereon a building for the administration purposes of said Village to be known and designated as the Herbert Neher Memorial Hall, with a suitable tablet placed thereon expressing such memorial."

This petition the Surrogate denied on the single ground "that to read into the will a general intention to devote the property to charitable purposes instead of an intention to limit the use of the property to the operation of a hospital, would do violence to the expressed testamentary design of Mrs. Neher." The Appellate Division has affirmed the Surrogate. The village brings the case here by our leave. This gift was not a gift to a particular institution. There was to be no singular object of the bounty. This gift was one to a whole community — "to the incorporated Village of Red Hook." The idea initially expressed by the testatrix was that her home should be dedicated to the village in the name of her husband. The only question is whether this first stated design of beneficence at large is necessarily to be denied prime import, because of the words that immediately follow — "with the direction to said Village that said property be used as a hospital to be known as 'Herbert Neher Memorial Hospital.'" This last phrase, it is to be noticed, gave no hint in respect of a predilection for any certain type of the manifold varieties of medical or surgical care. Nor did the will make any suggestion as to management or control, save that the village trustees (as such) were designated as a governing board. So great an absence of particularity is a strong circumstance against the view that the instruction of the testatrix was of the substance of the gift.

When paragraph 7 of the will is taken as a whole, the true construction, we think, is that the paramount intention was "to give the property in the first instance for a general charitable purpose rather than a particular charitable purpose, and to graft on to the general gift a direction as to the desires or intentions of the testator as to the manner in which the general gift is to be carried into effect." Parker, J., in Matter of Wilson, [1913] 1 Ch. 314, 321. Such a grafted direction may be ignored when compliance is altogether impracticable and the gift may be executed cy pres through a scheme to be framed by the court for carrying out the general charitable purpose.

The order of the Appellate Division and the decree of the Surrogate's Court should be reversed and the matter remitted to the Surrogate's Court for further proceedings in accordance with this opinion, without costs.

QUESTION, PROBLEMS, AND NOTES

1. "[U]nder the cy pres doctrine, a court is required to award the funds to a charity that most resembles the one that was to be the recipient of the trust. In addition to examining the named entity's purpose, a court must also consider the locality of the intended charity and the nature of the population that would be served by the gift." Estate of Elkins, 888 A.2d 814 (Pa. Super. 2005).

Was permission to use the property in *Neher* "to erect and maintain . . . a building for the administration purposes of [the] Village" an approximation of the settlor's intention as nearly as possible? Compare UTC §413(a)(3) (2000), which provides that when applying cy pres the court may "modify or terminate the trust by directing that the trust property be applied or distributed, in whole or in part, *in a manner consistent with the settlor's charitable purposes*" (emphasis added).

2. *T* devises a fund in trust to the city of *X* to maintain a flower garden in a designated location in a city park. Thirty years later, *X* removes the garden to make room for a vacation resort and petitions the court to apply cy pres to allow *X* to recreate the flower garden elsewhere in the park. What result? What is the relevance, if any, of the fact that *X* caused the impossibility that is the basis for its

cy pres petition? See Kolb v. City of Storm Lake, 736 N.W.2d 546 (Iowa 2007) (allowing cy pres).

T devises property to *X* as trustee to pay the income to his niece *A* and, on *A*'s death, to pay the principal to the dental school that *T* had graduated from 50 years earlier. *T* dies. Two years later, while *A* is still alive, the dental school is closed and its resources are absorbed by the medical school and hospital of the same university. Eight years later, *A* dies, survived by a daughter, *B*. *B* argues that, because the dental school no longer exits, the gift fails and the trust property should revert to her on resulting trust as *T*'s successor. In response, the university asks the court to apply cy pres on the ground that, though it no longer offers the basic degree in dental medicine, it continues to offer dental treatment for patients and post-graduate education in dentistry through its medical school and hospital. What result? See Obermeyer v. Bank of Am., 140 S.W.3d 18 (Mo. 2004) (allowing cy pres).

3. *The expansion of cy pres.* In recent years the Uniform Law Commission and the American Law Institute have advanced several reforms to the cy pres doctrine that would increase the frequency with which courts could apply the doctrine.

(a) *"Wasteful" as a basis for cy pres.* Section 413(a) of the Uniform Trust Code allows for cy pres if a particular charitable purpose becomes "unlawful, impracticable, impossible to achieve, or *wasteful*" (emphasis added). See also Restatement (Third) of Trusts §67 (2003), and Principles of the Law of Nonprofit Organizations §§240, 440 (C.D. No. 5, 2007), which likewise include "wasteful" as a basis for cy pres. We take up the addition of "wasteful" as a basis for cy pres in connection with the Buck Trust at page 765.

(b) *Presumption of general charitable intent.* Another reform advanced by the UTC and Restatement (Third) of Trusts is a presumption of general charitable intent. Under traditional law, before a court can invoke cy pres to modify the specifics of the donor's charitable gift, the party seeking cy pres must show that the donor had a general charitable intent. See Ronald Chester, George Gleason Bogert, and George Taylor Bogert, The Law of Trusts and Trustees §436 (3d ed. 2005). Whether the donor had a general charitable intent was the main issue in *Neher*. UTC §413 and Restatement (Third) of Trusts, supra, §67 shift the burden to the party opposing cy pres to show that the donor did not have a general charitable intent.

By creating a presumption in favor of general charitable intent, the UTC and Restatement also resolve a question that had existed in charitable trusts with a gift over — for example, "to *X* University so long as Trusts and Estates is taught in the law school, and if not, then to *Y* Hospital for the care of cancer patients." Some courts have taken the view that, in such a case, the settlor had a specific charitable intent and an alternative specific charitable intent, and thus the gift over precludes the application of cy pres to the primary gift. The alternative view is that the presence of a gift over is only one factor to be weighed in ascertaining the settlor's intent. See Ronald Chester, Cy Pres or Gift Over? The Search for Coherence in Judicial Reform of Failed Charitable Trusts, 23 Suffolk U. L. Rev. 41 (1989). Principles of the Law of Nonprofit Organizations, supra, §440(d), appears to split the difference. It says that "if the gift instrument provides for a gift over to an alternative charitable beneficiary, . . . the court may not apply cy pres in favor of the initial donee unless the alternative beneficiary is also subject to, and unable to perform, a restriction. The alternative beneficiary is entitled to notice and may participate in the determination of whether to modify the restriction."

4.   Because cy pres ultimately seeks to vindicate the settlor's general intent, it has been justified as intent-implementing. Judge Posner explains:

> A policy of rigid adherence to the letter of the donative instrument is likely to frustrate both the donor's purposes and the efficient use of resources. . . . [Suppose that a donor] had given the city a tuberculosis sanitarium . . . . As the incidence of tuberculosis declined and advances in medical science rendered the sanitarium method of treating tuberculosis obsolete, it would have become clear that the facilities would be more valuable in another use. . . . [E]nforcement would in all likelihood be contrary to the purposes of the donor, who intended by his gift to contribute to the cure of disease, not to perpetuate useless facilities.
>
> The foregoing discussion may seem tantamount to denying the competence of a donor to balance the value of a perpetual gift against the cost in efficiency that such gifts frequently impose. But since no one can foresee the future, a rational donor knows that his intentions might eventually be thwarted by unpredictable circumstances and may therefore be presumed to accept implicitly a rule permitting modification of the terms of the bequest in the event that an unforeseen change frustrates his original intention. . . .
>
> When the continued enforcement of conditions in a gift to charity is no longer economically feasible, because of illegality . . . or opportunity costs . . . , the court, rather than declaring the gift void . . . , will authorize the administrators of the donee institution to apply the assets to a related (cy pres) purpose within the general scope of the donor's intent. [Richard A. Posner, Economic Analysis of Law §§18.3-18.4, at 545-546 (7th ed. 2007).]

5.   Many commentators favor expanding the use of judicial cy pres to change charitable trust provisions to maximize community benefits as required by changing community needs. See Rob Atkinson, The Low Road to Cy Pres Reform: Principled Practice to Remove Dead Hand Control of Charitable Assets, 58 Case W. Res. L. Rev. 97 (2007); Rob Atkinson, Reforming Cy Pres Reform, 44 Hastings L.J. 1111 (1993); Alex M. Johnson, Jr., Limiting Dead Hand Control of Charitable Trusts: Expanding the Use of the Cy Pres Doctrine, 21 U. Haw. L. Rev. 353 (1999); Alex M. Johnson, Jr. and Ross D. Taylor, Revolutionizing Judicial Interpretation of Charitable Trusts: Applying Relational Contracts and Dynamic Interpretation to Cy Pres and America's Cup Litigation, 74 Iowa L. Rev. 545 (1989); Ronald Chester, Cy Pres: A Promise Unfulfilled, 54 Ind. L.J. 407 (1979). See also Iris J. Goodwin, Ask Not What Your Charity Can Do for You: Robertson v. Princeton Provides Liberal-Democratic Insights into the Dilemma of Cy Pres Reform, 51 Ariz. L. Rev. 75 (2009).

Other commentators are less sanguine about the ability of courts to give effect to the settlor's general intention. See Jonathan R. Macey, Private Trusts for the Provision of Private Goods, 37 Emory L.J. 295 (1988). See also Eric G. Pearson, Comment, Reforming the Reform of the Cy Pres Doctrine: A Proposal to Protect Testator Intent, 90 Marq. L. Rev. 127 (2006).

In Peter Luxton, Cy-Pres and the Ghost of Things That Might Have Been, 1983 Convey. 107, the author suggests that courts give greater importance to the testator's intention in the early years of the trust but, at the end of the perpetuities period, treat the property as dedicated to charity. Luxton's argument raises the following question: Should cy pres be applied more liberally after the period governed by the Rule Against Perpetuities has expired? See Johnson, supra, 21 U. Haw. L. Rev., at 355-356, for an argument in the affirmative.

SAN FRANCISCO CHRONICLE: THE BUCK TRUST

Beryl Buck, a childless widow, died in 1975. She was a resident of Marin County, California, the most affluent of the counties in the San Francisco Bay Area. Known as the "hot-tub capital of the world," Marin is in fact one of the nation's wealthiest counties.

Mrs. Buck's will left the residue of her estate to the San Francisco Foundation, a community trust administering charitable funds in Marin and four other counties in the San Francisco Bay Area (Alameda, Contra Costa, San Francisco, and San Mateo).[2] The will directed that these funds, to be known and administered as the Leonard and Beryl Buck Foundation,

> shall always be held and used for exclusively non-profit charitable, religious, or educational purposes in providing care for the needy in Marin County, California, and for other non-profit charitable, religious, or educational purposes in that county.

At the time of Mrs. Buck's death, the largest asset in her estate consisted of a block of stock in Beldridge Oil Company, a privately held company with rich oil reserves in Southern California, founded by her father-in-law. In 1975, this stock was worth about $9 million, but soon thereafter, in 1979, Shell Oil won a bidding war and bought the stock in the Buck Trust for $260 million. The corpus increased to well over $300 million by 1984, all of which was directed by Mrs. Buck's will to be spent on 7 percent of the Bay Area's residents in rich Marin County — a sudden embarrassment of riches that seemed to threaten the integrity of the San Francisco Foundation in administering charitable dollars equitably in the Bay Area. In 1984, the Foundation brought suit seeking judicial authorization to spend some portion of Buck Trust income in the other four counties of the Bay Area.

---

2. A bequest to a community trust qualifies as charitable. The Scott treatise explains:

> These trusts are ordinarily created by the execution of an elaborate trust instrument under which named trustees undertake to hold property in trust for charitable purposes. The terms of the trust usually provide that its purposes are to be determined from time to time by a selected group of citizens who are to act as a distribution committee. Indeed, one of the purposes of these trusts it to provide flexibility in selecting charitable purposes. Instead of determining at the outset a single charitable purpose, the committee is to determine from time to time what the community's greatest needs are, and to provide for them. A community trust ordinarily begins with small contributions; thereafter, members of the community are invited to make further contributions by will or otherwise. [5 Austin Wakeman Scott, William Franklin Fratcher, and Mark L. Ascher, Scott and Ascher on Trusts §37.2.4, at 2388 (5th ed. 2008).]

The Foundation's petition for cy pres rested upon the following theory: The enormous increase in the value of principal was a posthumous "surprise," a change in circumstances raising substantial doubt whether Mrs. Buck, if she had anticipated such an event, would have limited her beneficence to Marin County. This "surprise" warranted inquiry into what Mrs. Buck would have done had she anticipated the bonanza. The Foundation argued that she would not have limited her beneficence to Marin County because (a) she selected as trustee a foundation administering funds for the benefit of five counties; (b) other philanthropists, as shown by the 50 largest American charitable foundations (with the sole exception of the Buck Trust), reach out beyond their parochial origins as their resources grow and they seek to serve a more populous and diverse slice of humanity, following a principle of proportionality; and (c) in the face of such an increase in wealth, the donor would be less interested in a small geographical area and more interested in the efficiency of the charitable dollar. This, the Foundation argued, was the philanthropic standard followed by almost all the great philanthropists of wealth equal to Mrs. Buck's posthumous fortune.

The Foundation's action proved to be throwing fat into a fire. Marin County officials were outraged. One called the Foundation "grave-robbing bastards" and characterized the cy pres petition as a "criminal attack upon the sanctity of wills." Marin officials were joined by the Marin Council of Agencies (a consortium of Marin County nonprofit agencies) in opposing the petition. Forty-six individuals and charitable organizations in the other four counties (called "Objector-Beneficiaries") were allowed to intervene to object to the Marin-only limitation. The attorney general of California, as supervisor of charitable trusts, also intervened, arguing against cy pres and asking whether the Foundation was in violation of its fiduciary duties for bringing such a suit and ought to be removed as trustee.

The case caused an uproar in San Francisco, with the local newspaper columnists pulling out all the stops. At first, the commentators were incensed at all that money being spent in rich Marin, but then — on second thought — public opinion began to coalesce behind the idea that Mrs. Buck had the right to do with her property as she wished, and the San Francisco Foundation became an object of calumny.

Near the close of the respondent's case, after nearly six months of trial, the Foundation resigned as trustee, and the court dismissed the Foundation's cy pres petition. In the course of its opinion refusing to apply cy pres, not officially reported but reprinted in 21 U.S.F.L. Rev. 691 (1987), the trial court said:

> The Restatement (Second) of Trusts, section 399 at 297, describes the cy pres doctrine as follows: "If property is given in trust to be applied to a particular charitable purpose and *it is or becomes impossible or impracticable or illegal to carry out the particular purpose,* and if the settlor manifested a more general intention to devote the property to charitable purposes, the trust will not fail but the court will direct the application of the property to some charitable purpose which falls within the general charitable intention of the settlor. (Emphasis added). . . ."
>
> Ineffective philanthropy, inefficiency and relative inefficiency, that is, inefficiency of trust expenditures in one location given greater relative needs or benefits elsewhere, do not

constitute impracticability. . . . Such situation is not the equivalent of impossibility; nor is there any threat that the operation of the trust will fail to fulfill the general charitable intention of the settlor.

To the extent that concepts of effective philanthropy or efficiency relate to achieving the greatest benefit for the cost incurred they should not form the basis for modifying a donor's wishes. No law requires a testator to make a gift which the trustees deem efficient or to constitute effective philanthropy. Moreover, calculating "benefit" involves inherently subjective determinations; thus, what is "effective" or "efficient" will vary, depending on the interests and concerns of the person or persons making the determination. Cy pres does not authorize a court to vary the terms of the bequest merely because the variation will accommodate the desire of the trustee.

To the extent that the term efficiency embraces the concept of relative need, it is not an appropriate basis for modifying the terms of a testamentary trust. If it were otherwise, all charitable gifts, and the fundamental basis of philanthropy would be threatened, as there may always be more compelling "needs" to fill than the gift chosen by the testator. Gifts to Harvard or Stanford University, for example, could fail simply because institutions elsewhere are more needy. Similarly, needs in the Bay Area cannot be equated with the grueling poverty of India or the soul-wrenching famine in Ethiopia. Moreover, a standard of relative need would interpose governmental regulation on philanthropy because courts would be required to consider questions of comparative equity, social utility, or benefit, perhaps even wisdom, and ultimately substitute their judgments or those of the trustees for those of the donors.

The cy pres doctrine should not be so distorted by the adoption of subjective, relative, and nebulous standards such as "inefficiency" or "ineffective philanthropy" to the extent that it becomes a facile vehicle for charitable trustees to vary the terms of a trust simply because they believe that they can spend the trust income better or more wisely elsewhere, or as in this case, prefer to do so. There is no basis in law for the application of standards such as "efficiency" or "effectiveness" to modify a trust, nor is there any authority that would elevate these standards to the level of impracticability.

No appeal was taken from the trial court decision in *Buck*. The trial court ordered the creation of the Marin Community Foundation, which would replace the San Francisco Foundation in administering the Buck Trust.

The new foundation is governed by seven trustees, two appointed by the Marin County Board of Supervisors, one by the Marin Council of (Nonprofit) Agencies, one by the president of the University of California, one by the Interfaith Council of Marin, one by relatives of Mrs. Buck's husband, and one by the Marin Community Foundation board. The trial judge chose three Marin-based research institutes to divide a substantial portion of the income from the trust: The Buck Center on Aging, The Institute on Alcohol and Other Drug Problems, and The Marin Educational Institute.

Professor Simon is highly critical of the supervisory role assumed by the trial court over the Buck Trust at the end of the trial:

> The extraordinary command role the court reserved for itself over the decision-making process . . . violates the basic concept of private philanthropy and disregards the role assigned to charitable trustees in the nonprofit sector. . . .
>
> [I]t is not obvious that these programs would have been preferred by the donor over distributions to neighboring Bay Area counties served by the [San Francisco] Foundation. . . . [T]he fact that she picked a community foundation focused on the Bay Area as the instrument of her charity cannot be ignored when shaping a cy pres solution. [John G. Simon, American Philanthropy and the Buck Trust, 21 U.S.F.L. Rev. 641, 666-668 (1987).]

The Foundation Directory (2008) reports that the Marin Community Foundation, created out of the Buck Trust, had $1.1 billion in assets as of June 30, 2006 and made $51.6 million in grants in fiscal-year 2006. The San Francisco Foundation, without the Buck Trust, had assets of $1 billion as of June 30, 2007 and made $88.7 million in grants in fiscal-year 2007.

QUESTION, NOTE, AND PROBLEM

1. Suppose the San Francisco Foundation's petition for cy pres was filed today in a state that has adopted UTC §413(a) (2000) and was based on a theory of waste. What result?

Professor English, the reporter for the UTC, has written that cases of waste would "normally involve situations where the funds allocated to the particular charitable scheme far exceed what is needed." David M. English, The Uniform Trust Code (2000): Significant Provisions and Policy Issues, 67 Mo. L. Rev. 144, 179 & n.164 (2002). See also Restatement (Third) of Trusts §67, cmt. c(1) (2003), which provides that if the trust property so "exceeds what is needed for the particular charitable purpose . . . that the continued expenditure of all of the funds for that purpose . . . would be wasteful," then a court "might broaden the purposes of the trust." For example, the court might "direct application of the surplus funds to a like purpose in a different community."

2. *T* devises a fund in trust to the city of *X* for the beautification of three cemeteries and the upkeep of certain identified cemetery plots. Thirty-five years later, *X* petitions the court for cy pres to allow *X* to redirect $50,000 of the trust's $75,000 corpus to capital improvements for the three cemeteries. *X* argues that $25,000 is more than sufficient for the beautification of the cemeteries and the upkeep of the identified plots, hence retention of the additional $50,000 in the trust would be wasteful. What result? See In re Trust of Lowry, 885 N.E.2d 296 (Ohio App. 2008) (denying cy pres).

NOTE: CY PRES VERSUS ADMINISTRATIVE DEVIATION

Cy pres should be contrasted with *administrative deviation*. A court will permit deviation in the administrative terms of a trust — private or charitable — when compliance would defeat or substantially impair the accomplishment of the purposes of the trust on account of changed circumstances not anticipated by the donor. See 5 Austin Wakeman Scott, William Franklin Fratcher, and Mark L. Ascher, Scott and Ascher on Trusts §37.3.3 (5th ed. 2008), discussing the applicability of deviation to charitable trusts. It is sometimes said in shorthand that cy pres allows for modification of the donor's stated purpose (the donor's "ends"), whereas deviation focuses on the donor's prescribed rules of administration (the donor's "means"). See Principles of the Law of Nonprofit Organizations §440, cmt. A (C.D. No. 5, 2007). It is not always clear, however, what is an administrative term and what is a central purpose—and courts have been known to interpret "administrative" broadly on appealing facts.

The Uniform Trust Code further blurs the line between cy pres and deviation. Under UTC §412 (2000), page 645, the "court may modify the administrative *or dispositive* terms of a trust" (emphasis added). In City of Augusta v. Attorney General, 943 A.2d 582 (Me. 2008), the court authorized deviation from the terms of a charitable trust created in 1815 for the benefit of a high school. The court allowed the trustee to sell the land on which the high school had been located but could no longer be maintained on account of dangerous conditions that could not be repaired, and to apply the proceeds to a new high school located elsewhere. The court rejected the argument that deviation was limited to administrative terms, holding that UTC §412 expressly authorizes deviation from dispositive provisions if, owing to changed circumstances, such deviation would further the purposes of the trust. See also South Carolina Department of Mental Health v. McMaster, 642 S.E.2d 552 (S.C. 2007), authorizing deviation so that the state department of mental health could sell an asylum held in charitable trust on the condition that the proceeds be applied for the benefit of mentally ill patients in other facilities.

Anticipating cases such as these, Professor Chester observed that in view of the extension of deviation to dispositive terms, a separate provision for cy pres might prove to be an unnecessary redundancy. "Events that make continuation of the trust as is 'impracticable,' 'impossible,' 'illegal' or 'wasteful' seem to be just the types of 'unanticipated circumstances' necessary to trigger [deviation]." Ronald Chester, Modification and Termination of Trusts in the 21st Century: The Uniform Trust Code Leads a Quite Revolution, 35 Real Prop., Prop. & Tr. J. 697, 708-709 (2001).

PHILADELPHIA STORY: THE BARNES FOUNDATION

The Barnes Foundation, in the Philadelphia suburb of Merion, was created by Dr. Albert Barnes. Dr. Barnes was a chemist who invented Argyrol, which became a leading treatment for colds, also prescribed as eyedrops for newborn babies to prevent blindness. Argyrol earned Dr. Barnes a great fortune, which he spent buying art in the early years of the twentieth century. He descended on Paris, checkbook in hand, and, haunting the garrets and artists' studios in Montparnasse, bought dozens of paintings directly from artists. He amassed a collection of over 180 Renoirs, 100 Cézannes, 60 Matisses, 40 Picassos, and works by dozens of other artists. Today this collection, which has been characterized as perhaps "the greatest private art collection in American history," is valued in the billions of dollars. Jeffrey Toobin, Battle for the Barnes, The New Yorker, Jan. 21, 2002, at 34. Dr. Barnes hung his 2,000 pieces of art five or six atop each other in a gallery he built in Merion. "At first glance, the display . . . looks almost haphazard. Paintings are lined up next to and above one another, sometimes inches apart, and they are labeled with only a single word on their frames." Id.

Barnes Foundation Gallery. **Top: Seurat,** *Models.* **Bottom: Cézanne,**
***Card Players and Girl.* Upper left: Cézanne,** *The Drinker.* **Lower left:**
Cézanne, *Still Life with Bottle.* **Upper right: Corot,** *Woman in Gray.*
Lower right: Cézanne, *Leda and the Swan.*

Son of a butcher in South Philadelphia, Dr. Barnes was high-hatted by Philadelphia Main Line society and by art critics and scholars who panned his art. As a result, he would not permit them in to see the paintings after his collection became celebrated. He barred entry to all except "plain people, that is, men and women who gain their livelihood by daily toil in shops, factories, schools, and stores." Dr. Barnes admitted some scholars and literati on a selective basis. A few others were able to sneak in disguised as chauffeurs, miners, or workmen.

Dr. Barnes had unconventional theories about art education, developed with John Dewey. To further these theories, the Barnes Foundation was set up as an educational institution, not as an art gallery. The curriculum consisted solely of instruction in Barnes's aesthetic theories. Classes in Barnesian aesthetics were open to students for two hours in the afternoon.

When Dr. Barnes died in 1951, the Barnes Foundation bylaws were set in stone. No painting was ever to be moved from where he hung it. No painting was to be sold or loaned. No painting could be added to the collection, and paintings from other galleries could not be exhibited there. The gallery was to be open to the general public only on Saturdays from September through June. Entrance fees were prohibited (remember: Dr. Barnes wanted only "plain people" to see his pictures). Also prohibited were "any society functions commonly designated receptions, teas, dinners, or banquets," public or private. The trustees were permitted to invest only in government bonds. Barnes mandated that the rules were "unamendable and shall never be amended in any manner whatsoever."

In 1961, the Pennsylvania attorney general brought a lawsuit, forcing the Barnes Gallery to open its doors to the general public two and one-half days a week in order to keep its charitable tax-exempt status. This suit was instigated by pressure from the Philadelphia Inquirer, which was then owned by Walter Annenberg, a noted art collector himself.

In 1988, upon the death of the last trustee appointed by Dr. Barnes, control of the Barnes Foundation passed to Lincoln University, a small, historically black college in Chester County, Pennsylvania. (Justice Thurgood Marshall was a graduate.) During his life, Barnes had always admired and enjoyed African American culture and art, and he gave Lincoln the power to nominate the trustees who would run his foundation after the death of his associates. The new trustees found the 1925 gallery in a sad state of disrepair. With an endowment of only $10 million, the income could pay for only half the guards needed. Thus, half the gallery was open for two hours, the public was then shooed out, and after the guards moved to the other half, the public was readmitted to the other half for two hours.

The new trustees looked around for ways of restoring the facility and generating income. In the 1990s, they brought a series of lawsuits asking the court to authorize deviation from Barnes's rigid rules. These petitions were opposed by a small group of former Barnes Foundation students, who adamantly opposed even the slightest deviation from what they regarded as Dr. Barnes's vision. The court authorized the trustees to open the gallery to the public three-and-a-half days a week during the whole year and to charge a $5 admission fee. The trustees were given greater discretion in investing the Barnes Foundation funds to produce a higher yield, and the trustees were permitted to hold fundraising events in the gallery, even though Dr. Barnes had forbidden this. The trustees also asked for the power to sell some pictures, but this brought a great outcry. The trustees then proposed, and the court approved, a world tour of 50 priceless masterworks from the collection to be shown in Washington, Paris, Toronto, Tokyo, Ft. Worth, and Philadelphia. The tour netted the Foundation about $17 million, of which $12 million were used to modernize the gallery. For those who could not see the paintings on the world tour, the trustees produced a CD-ROM, with photographs in color.

The world tour drew record crowds, more in Paris than had ever before lined up to see an art show. But the world tour brought protests from some Philadelphians, who were outraged that Dr. Barnes's intent had been violated in so many ways. The protestors — particularly the neighbors in Merion — were angry that the Barnes Foundation had been transformed from an educational institution serving a few into a museum drawing thousands of people in cars. Dr. Barnes, they said, must be spinning in his grave. But, maybe not. At the end of the tour, the paintings were rehung in the Barnes Gallery exactly as the eccentric Dr. Barnes had hung them — with some of the greatest works placed near the ceiling, difficult to see but hung according to his aesthetic theories.

The latest round in the "Battle for the Barnes" began in 2002. Explaining that the Foundation's financial condition had become so dire as to threaten its survival, the trustees again asked the court to authorize deviation from Barnes's rules, this time to permit moving the collection from the recently modernized Merion building to a new facility to be built in Philadelphia, close to the Philadelphia Museum of Art. The relocation plan was hatched as part of a deal between the trustees and the Pew Charitable Trusts and the Lenfest Foundation, both mainstays of Philadelphia philanthropy. The plan called for Pew and Lenfest to help the trustees raise $150 million for the construction of the new facility and to replenish the Barnes Foundation's depleted endowment. In the meantime, Pew and Lenfest provided the Foundation with $3.1 million in bridge financing and paid the costs associated with the litigation.

In January 2004, the court ruled that "the present location of the gallery is not sacrosanct, and relocation may be permitted *if necessary*." But the evidence before it did not make out a case of necessity. The court had harsh words for the trustees over what it regarded as an unwillingness to consider selling some of the paintings that were not part of the public display. "[T]he possibility of selling some of these holdings has been dismissed by The Foundation as too little, too shortsighted, or unethical. The move to Philadelphia has been floated as the only lifeboat in the entire sea. Since the outside charities are footing The Foundation's legal bills in these hearings, we accept their single-option theory as the product of zealous advocacy." The court also had unkind words for the attorney general's office, which did little more than support the Foundation, "cheering on its witnesses. . . . The course chosen by the Office of the Attorney General prevented the court from seeing a balanced, objective presentation of the situation, and constituted an abdication of that office's responsibility."

Over the course of six days of hearings in late September 2004, which produced more than 1,200 pages of testimony, the trustees tried again — this time with more success. On December 13, 2004, the court ruled that the trustees had met their burden of proof and granted their petition. Although the plan calls for moving the art collection to Philadelphia, the Foundation will retain the Merion facility, which had undergone a $12 million renovation during the world tour. Said the court: "The irony of converting a state-of-the-art gallery into perhaps the most expensive administration building in the history of nonprofits is not lost to us. Looking to the future, it is of the utmost importance that the Board of Trustees steer The Foundation so that another such irony does not surface ten or fifteen years hence."

In 2007, after the Barnes Foundation signed a lease for the land in downtown Philadelphia on which the new gallery would be built, a group calling itself the "Friends of the Barnes Foundation," joined by Montgomery County (where Merion is located), filed a petition to reopen the 2004 judgment authorizing the gallery's move. Two reasons were given for reopening the decision. First, sometime after the 2004 decision, it was discovered that the 2002 state budget included a roughly $100 million appropriation for the construction of a new facility in Philadelphia to house the Barnes collection. The fact of this appropriation had not been presented to the court in the 2004 hearing. Second, in June of 2007, just before the petition to reopen the judgment was filed, Montgomery County offered to buy the Foundation's land in lower Merion for $50 million, to lease the property back to the Foundation, and to rezone the property to allow for more visitors and thus increased admissions revenues to the Foundation. The Foundation rejected the proposal on the grounds that the move to Philadelphia was at that point irreversible.

After a hearing in March of 2008 in which the Attorney General sided with the Foundation, the court denied the petitions in May of that year. Calling the Friends' petition "a 231 paragraph diatribe, rampant with scattershot accusations, arguments, and conjecture," the court held that both the Friends and the County lacked standing. However, the court also denied the Foundation's and Attorney General's request that they be reimbursed for their costs by the petitioners. In the court's view, the "filings were made in good faith, and the events that precipitated the filings (the state budget appropriations' coming to light and the County's offer to explore the purchase/lease-back arrangement) were of sufficient import that the attempt to reopen the issues was not arbitrary."

Neither the County nor the Friends appealed. Meanwhile the Foundation, supported in part by a pledge of $30 million from the state, held a symbolic groundbreaking at the site of the new facility on October 15, 2008. See Inga Saffron, Barnes Stages Symbolic Groundbreaking on Parkway, Phila. Inq., Oct. 16, 2008, at B1. And so the Barnes saga continues.

QUESTION AND NOTES

1. Would you, as a judge, have approved the trustees' deviations from Dr. Barnes's by-laws? See Bruce H. Mann, In the End, a Move Was Only Way Out, Phila. Inq., Dec. 15, 2004, at A23.

2. For a recent, book-length telling of the Barnes Foundation saga, see John Anderson, Art Held Hostage: The Story of the Barnes Collection (2003). See also Jonathan Scott Goldman, Just What the Doctor Ordered? The Doctrine of Deviation, The Case of Doctor Barnes's Trust and the Future Location of the Barnes Foundation, 39 Real Prop., Prob. & Tr. J. 711 (2005); Heinrich Schweizer, Settlor's Intent vs. Trustee's Will: The Barnes Foundation Case, 29 Colum. J.L. & Arts 63 (2005); Ilana H. Eisenstein, Comment, Keeping Charity in Charitable Trust Law: The Barnes Foundation and the Case for Consideration of Public Interest in Administration of Charitable Trusts, 151 U. Pa. L. Rev. 1747 (2003). For a portrait of the irascible Dr. Barnes, see Howard Greenfield, The Devil and Dr. Barnes (1987).

NOTE: DISCRIMINATORY TRUSTS

Charitable trusts have been created to furnish benefits to members of a particular race, gender, or religion. Usually, benefits under these trusts are restricted to "whites" or to "men." Such trusts have been the subject of considerable litigation since the 1960s. See 6 Austin Wakeman Scott, William Franklin Fratcher, and Mark L. Ascher, Scott and Ascher on Trusts §39.5.5 (5th ed. 2009). For example, after Amherst College refused a bequest to be used for scholarships for Protestant boys on account of the religious restriction, the court removed the clause. Howard Sav. Inst. v. Peep, 170 A.2d 39 (N.J. 1961). The court reasoned that the testator's primary charitable purpose was to benefit the college.

If the trustee of a racially restrictive trust is a governmental body (such as a public school granting scholarships to whites), courts have held that the administration of the trust in a racially discriminatory manner is discriminatory state action forbidden by the Equal Protection Clause of the Constitution, making the racial restriction unenforceable. The question then becomes: Would the settlor prefer the trust to continue without the racial restriction or to terminate? Applying cy pres or the deviation doctrine, most courts have held that the settlor would prefer the charitable trust to continue without the racial restriction. See Trammell v. Elliott, 199 S.E.2d 193 (Ga. 1973) (bequest to a public institution for the benefit of "poor white boys and girls" given effect minus the racial limitation).

A contrary example is provided by the infamous cases of Evans v. Newton, 382 U.S. 296 (1966), and Evans v. Abney, 396 U.S. 435 (1970). In the 1966 decision, the Supreme Court held that Senator Augustus O. Bacon's bequest of land to the City of Macon in trust for a park for "white people" was unconstitutional, regardless of whether it was administered by a governmental body or private trustees, because the park was a public institution. In the 1970 decision, however, the Court upheld the determination of the Georgia courts that the trust could not be modified, and the property passed on resulting trust to Bacon's heirs, on the grounds that Bacon would have preferred the trust to fail rather than operate free of the racial limitation.

Where the trustee is a private individual and not a public body, enforcing the racial restriction is usually not unconstitutional as discriminatory state action. See In re Wilson, 452 N.E.2d 1228 (N.Y. 1983). For an interesting argument that racial and gender restrictions are unconstitutional even if the trustee is a private individual, see James W. Colliton, Race and Sex Discrimination in Charitable Trusts, 12 Cornell J.L. & Pub. Poly. 275 (2003).

Even if there is no federal constitutional difficulty, a racially restrictive trust may nonetheless run afoul of some federal or state law forbidding racial discrimination. If so, the question arises whether the court should apply cy pres and strike the racial restriction. Most courts have done so. In Home for Incurables of Baltimore City v. University of Md. Med. Sys. Corp., 797 A.2d 746 (Md. 2002), the court removed a racial restriction, illegal under state law, in a charitable bequest to the Home for Incurables of Baltimore City for the benefit of "white patients who need physical rehabilitation." The will also contained an alternative bequest to the University of Maryland in the event that the Home found the racial limitation "not acceptable." The alternative bequest was not subject to a racial limitation. The court held that the Home should take the bequest free from the racial limitation on the grounds that, by ordering the proceeds be paid to the University, the court would be giving effect to the illegal racial discrimination.

Restricting the benefits of a private charitable trust to one gender does not violate the U.S. constitution, but it too may violate other federal or state laws prohibiting gender discrimination. In such cases, courts have removed the gender restriction under the power of cy pres. See In re Certain Scholarship Funds, 676 A.2d 1325 (N.H. 1990) (invoking cy pres to remove gender and religious limitations to bring the trust in line with the state constitution).

A new question is facing the courts: Is a charitable trust run by a public body that gives scholarships exclusively to black persons constitutional? In Podberesky v. Kirwan, 38 F.3d 147 (4th Cir. 1994), the Fourth Circuit held that state university scholarships for blacks were invalid under the Equal Protection Clause unless they were justifiable to remedy present effects of past discrimination. In Grutter v. Bollinger, 539 U.S. 306 (2003), however, the Supreme Court upheld the University of Michigan Law School's race-conscious admissions policy on the ground that the school had a compelling state interest in obtaining a diverse student body. To the extent that achieving a racially diverse class requires not just admitting a diverse group of applicants, but also providing enough funding to nonwhite admittees to induce them to matriculate, does *Grutter* implicitly overrule *Podberesky*? This seems an issue that will likely be litigated. See Chris Chambers Goodman, Beneath the Veil: Corollaries on Diversity and Critical Mass Scholarships from Rawls' Original Position of Justice, 13 Wash. & Lee J. Civil Rts. & Soc. Just. 285 (2007); Paul Horwitz, Grutter's First Amendment, 46 B.C. L. Rev. 461, 537-539 (2005); Helen Norton, Stepping Through Grutter's Open Doors: What the University of Michigan Affirmative Action Cases

Mean for Race-Conscious Government Decisionmaking, 78 Temp. L. Rev. 543, 548-560 (2005).

SECTION D. SUPERVISION OF CHARITABLE TRUSTS

The fiduciary duties that apply to a trustee of a private trust also apply to a trustee of a charitable trust. However, because a charitable trust must be for a charitable purpose rather than an ascertainable beneficiary, the difficult question arises, who will enforce those fiduciary duties? Without an ascertainable beneficiary with a financial interest in the trust, who ensures that the trustee acts in accord with the settlor's charitable purpose and refrains from abuse or breach of fiduciary obligation?

CARL J. HERZOG FOUNDATION, INC. v. UNIVERSITY OF BRIDGEPORT, 699 A.2d 995 (Conn. 1997): In 1986, the Carl J. Herzog Foundation made a gift to the University of Bridgeport to provide scholarships to nursing students. In 1991, the University closed its nursing school and added the funds to its general endowment. The Herzog Foundation brought suit for an injunction to reestablish the scholarships or to give the money to the Bridgeport Area Foundation, which was prepared to administer nursing scholarships.

The court held that the donor of a charitable gift has no standing to enforce the terms of the gift unless the donor had expressly reserved the right to do so. The exclusive enforcement power is in the state attorney general, who alone has standing to enforce the terms of the gift. The court quoted Restatement (Second) of Trusts §391 (1959):

> A suit can be maintained for the enforcement of a charitable trust by the Attorney General or other public officer, or by a co-trustee, or by a person who has a special interest in the enforcement of the charitable trust, but not by persons who have no special interest or by the settlor or his heirs, personal representatives or next of kin.

Accordingly, because the Herzog Foundation had not expressly retained a reversionary interest, the court held that the Foundation did not have standing as donor to challenge the University of Bridgeport's use of the donated funds.

Smithers v. St. Luke's-Roosevelt Hospital Center
Supreme Court, Appellate Division, New York, 2001
723 N.Y.S.2d 426

ELLERIN, J. The issue before us is whether the estate of the donor of a charitable gift has standing to sue the donee to enforce the terms of the gift. We conclude that in the circumstances here present plaintiff estate does have the necessary standing. . . .

R. Brinkley Smithers

Plaintiff Adele Smithers is the widow of R. Brinkley Smithers, a recovered alcoholic who devoted the last 40 years of his life to the treatment and understanding of the disease of alcoholism.[3] In 1971 Smithers announced his intention to make a gift to defendant St. Luke's-Roosevelt Hospital Center (the "Hospital") of $10 million over time for the establishment of an alcoholism treatment center (the "Gift"). In his June 16, 1971 letter to the Hospital creating the Gift, Smithers stated, "Money from the $10 million grant will be supplied as needed. It is understood, however, that the detailed project plans and staff appointments must have my approval."

According to the complaint, the Hospital agreed to use the Gift to expand its treatment of alcoholism to include, following five days of detoxification in the hospital, "rehabilitation in a free-standing, controlled, uplifting and non-hospital environment," that is, a "therapeutic community" removed from the hospital setting. With $1 million from the first installment of the Gift, the Hospital purchased a building at 56 East 93rd Street in Manhattan to house the rehabilitation program, and in 1973 the Smithers Alcoholism Treatment and Training Center opened there.[4]

Smithers thereafter remained involved in the management and affairs of the Smithers Center. At times, according to the complaint, the Hospital sought to avoid its obligations under the terms of the Gift, and its relationship with Smithers was an uneasy one. On July 31, 1978, Smithers wrote that the Hospital had "not lived up to my letter of intent," and that "[u]nder the circumstances no funds

3. From the age of 46 until his death at 86, Brink Smithers and the Christopher D. Smithers Foundation — which Brink Smithers and his mother, Mabel Brinkley Smithers, created and named after his father (an investment banker who helped finance the creation of IBM) — gave over $40 million for the research and treatment of alcoholism. He also helped fund the National Council on Alcoholism and Drug Dependence and served variously as its president, chairman, and treasurer. In 1970, Smithers played an important role in the enactment of the federal legislation that created the National Institute on Alcohol Abuse and Alcoholism. — Eds.

4. The 56 East 93rd Street building is a 55-room Upper East Side mansion that had previously served as the Algerian Embassy and had once been owned by Broadway impresario Billy Rose. Patients were assigned to rooms with vaulted ceilings and mahogany doors. Because of its celebrity patients, including novelists John Cheever and Truman Capote and former New York Mets (and then New York Yankees) Dwight Gooden and Darryl Strawberry, the Center developed a reputation as the "alcoholism clinic to the stars." The Center treated approximately 4,000 patients annually, and its program served as the model for other treatment centers such as the Betty Ford Center in California. — Eds.

The Smithers Alcoholism Center, Rehabilitation Unit, 56 East 93rd Street

or stock will be forthcoming from me." Only slightly more than half of the Gift had been made at that time.

In 1981 the president of the Hospital, Gary Gambuti, commenced discussions with Smithers in an effort to induce him to complete the Gift. . . .

Over the next two years, Gambuti repeatedly assured Smithers that the Hospital would strictly adhere to the terms of the Gift and carry out Smithers's intent in making it. Only when Smithers was completely satisfied of the Hospital's intentions did he agree to complete the Gift, which he accomplished in an October 24, 1983 letter, stating:

> This final contribution is subject to the following restrictions . . . [I]t is my intention that my final contribution be set aside as an endowment fund, (the "Smithers Endowment Fund"). The income is to be used exclusively for the support of the Smithers Center, to the extent necessary for current operations, and any unused income remaining at the end of each calendar year is to be accumulated and added to principal. Principal of the Smithers Endowment Fund is not to be expended for any purpose except for remodeling or rebuilding the administration section and out-patient floor at the Building on 58th Street, and for construction, repairs or improvements with respect to any other building space at any time used directly in connection with the Smithers Center. Such capital expenditures should be considered as secondary to the endowment function and should in no event exceed in the aggregate one half of the initial value of the Smithers Endowment Fund.

Beneath Smithers's signature is the following paragraph signed and dated by Gambuti:

> The contribution of the number of shares of IBM Stock referred to above by R. Brinkley Smithers is gratefully accepted, *subject to the restrictions set forth in this letter,* in full satisfaction of any outstanding pledge or other obligation. (Emphasis added.)

The existing rehabilitation services, which Smithers included in his definition of the Smithers Center and which the Hospital's acceptance of the Gift encompassed, were housed in the free-standing Smithers building and, according to the complaint, were intended always to be housed in *a* free-standing facility. . . .

In late 1992, the Hospital asked Mrs. Smithers to organize a "Silver Anniversary Gala," in honor of her husband and herself, to raise funds for restoration of the building and for a scholarship program for Smithers Center patients in need of financial assistance. From 1992 to March 1995, she and, until his death in January 1994, [Mr.] Smithers successfully solicited millions of dollars' worth of donated goods and services for a total restoration of the building and organized the fundraiser, scheduled for April 1995. Then, in March 1995, just over a year after Smithers's death, the Hospital announced that it planned to move the Smithers Center into a hospital ward and sell the East 93rd Street building. The Hospital directed Mrs. Smithers, a month and a half before the fundraiser was scheduled to be held, to cancel the event. The Hospital's announced intentions aroused Mrs. Smithers's suspicions. . . . Mrs. Smithers notified the Hospital of her objections to the proposed relocation of the program and demanded an accounting of the Smithers Center's finances. . . .

[I]n May 1995 the Hospital disclosed that it had been misappropriating monies from the Endowment Fund since before Smithers's death, transferring such monies to its general fund where they were used for purposes unrelated to the Smithers Center. Mrs. Smithers notified the Attorney General, who investigated the Hospital's plan to sell the building and discovered that the Hospital had transferred restricted assets from the Smithers Endowment Fund to its general fund in what it called "loans." The Attorney General demanded the return of these assets and in August 1995 the Hospital returned nearly $5 million to the Smithers Endowment Fund, although it did not restore the income lost on those funds during the intervening years.

In the next three years, Mrs. Smithers tried to negotiate a resolution with the Hospital. The Attorney General participated in the negotiations, seeking . . . "to effectuate a settlement that would resolve the plaintiff's concerns and benefit the Smithers Alcoholism Program." . . . [These] negotiations proved unsuccessful . . . .

In July 1998, the Attorney General entered into an [agreement] with the Hospital. Under the terms of this [agreement] the Hospital agreed to make no more transfers or loans from Gift funds for any purpose other than the benefit of the Smithers Center and to return to the Gift fund $1 million from the proceeds of any sale of the building.[5] The Attorney General did not require the Hospital to return the entire proceeds of such a sale, because he found that, contrary to Mrs. Smithers's contention, the terms of the Gift did not preclude the Hospital from selling the building.

Two months later, Mrs. Smithers commenced this suit to enforce the conditions of the Gift and to obtain an accounting by the Hospital of its handling of the Endowment Fund and property dedicated to the Smithers Center. The Hospital and the Attorney General were named, *inter alia*, as defendants. Mrs. Smithers had obtained Special Letters of Administration from the Nassau County Surrogate's Court appointing her the Special Administratrix of Smithers's estate for the purpose of pursuing claims by the estate against the Hospital in connection with its administration of the Smithers Center. . . .

The Hospital . . . moved to dismiss the complaint for lack of standing. The Attorney General also moved to dismiss for lack of standing and for failure to state a cause of action. [The Supreme Court, which in New York is a trial court, dismissed Mrs. Smithers's complaint.]

On appeal, the Attorney General's office, having reevaluated the matter "under the direction of the newly elected Attorney General,"[6] reversed its position and urged this Court to remand for a hearing on the merits to determine whether or not the building was subject to gift restrictions. If it were, then all proceeds of the sale would be subject to the same restrictions and could not be used for the Hospital's general purposes. . . . [T]he Attorney General urged that the issue of Mrs. Smithers's standing to bring the suit need not, and should not, be reached in this action, since he certainly had standing and had joined with her in seeking reversal and remand. . . .

While this appeal was pending, the Attorney General and the Hospital reached another agreement. This agreement raised some issues for the first time, but it brought the position of the Attorney General and the Hospital on other issues into accord with Mrs. Smithers's position. For example, the Hospital agreed to allocate the entire net proceeds of the sale of the building to the restricted purposes of the Gift and to restore the income lost as a result of the transfer of Gift funds to its general fund. Reversing his position again, the Attorney General returned to his predecessor's contention that Mrs. Smithers has no standing to bring this suit, and asked this Court to modify the decision dismissing the complaint for lack of standing so as to hold only that plaintiff does not have standing

---

5. In fact the hospital sold the 56 East 93rd Street mansion in 1999 to the all-girls, Manhattan-based Spence School for $15 million, an eye-popping $14 million more than the $1 million sum that the agreement with the attorney general required the hospital to return to the Gift fund. Cerisse Anderson, Donor's Widow Wins Right to Sue Over Gift, N.Y.L.J. 1 (Apr. 6, 2001). — Eds.

6. The new attorney general was Eliot Spitzer. The son of a wealthy New York real estate magnate, Spitzer graduated Harvard Law School and then worked as an assistant district attorney in Manhattan and for a big New York law firm before entering politics. As attorney general, Spitzer gained notoriety for his aggressive pursuit of alleged wrongdoing in the securities industry. Soon thereafter, Spitzer was elected governor of New York by a record margin, but resigned after admitting to be the person identified as "Client 9" in a 47-page FBI affidavit filed in connection with the prosecution of the so-called Emperor's Club prostitution ring. See Alan Feuer and Ian Urbina, Client 9 in Room 871: Notes on a Rendezvous, N.Y. Times, Mar. 11, 2008, at B1. — Eds.

as special administratrix of the donor's estate and affirm, as modified, on that narrow ground. . . .

The sole issue before us is whether Mrs. Smithers, on behalf of Smithers's estate, has standing to bring this action. The Attorney General maintains that, with a few exceptions inapplicable here, standing to enforce the terms of a charitable gift is limited to the Attorney General. Most recently, the Attorney General has urged that, pursuant to the above-mentioned proposed settlement stipulation between himself and the Hospital, he has achieved all the relief that is appropriate in this case. . . .

The question of whether the donor who is living and can maintain his or her own action need rely on the protection of the Attorney General to enforce the terms of his gift . . . was addressed in Associate Alumni of the General Theological Seminary of the Protestant Episcopal Church in the United States of America v. The General Theological Seminary of the Protestant Episcopal Church in the United States, 57 N.E. 626 (N.Y. 1900). . . .

> The general rule is "If the trustees of a charity abuse the trust, misemploy the charity fund, or commit a breach of the trust, the property does not revert to the heir or legal representative of the donor unless there is an express condition of the gift that it shall revert to the donor or his heirs, in case the trust is abused, but the redress is by bill or information by the attorney-general *or other person having the right to sue*." . . .

[The *Associate Alumni* case] explicitly forecloses the conclusion that the Attorney General's standing in these actions is exclusive. . . .

Supreme Court incorrectly characterized Mrs. Smithers as one who "positions herself as the champion and representative of the possible beneficiaries of the Gift," with no tangible stake because she has no position or property to lose if the Hospital alters its administration of the Gift. Mrs. Smithers did not bring this action on her own behalf or on behalf of beneficiaries of the Smithers Center. She brought it as the court-appointed special administratrix of the estate of her late husband to enforce his rights under his agreement with the Hospital through specific performance of that agreement. Therefore, the general rule barring beneficiaries from suing charitable corporations has no application to Mrs. Smithers. Moreover, the desire to prevent vexatious litigation by "irresponsible parties who do not have a tangible stake in the matter and have not conducted appropriate investigations" has no application to Mrs. Smithers either. Without possibility of pecuniary gain for himself or herself, only a plaintiff with a genuine interest in enforcing the terms of a gift will trouble to investigate and bring this type of action. Indeed, it was Mrs. Smithers's accountants who discovered and informed the Attorney General of the Hospital's misdirection of Gift funds, and it was only after Mrs. Smithers brought her suit that the Attorney General acted to prevent the Hospital from diverting the entire proceeds of the sale of the building away from the Gift fund and into its general fund. The Attorney General, following his initial investigation of the Hospital's administration of the Gift, acquiesced in the Hospital's sale of the building, its diversion of the appreciation realized on the sale, and its relocation of the rehabilitation unit, even as he ostensibly was demanding that the Hospital continue to act "in accordance with the donor's gift." Absent Mrs. Smithers's vigilance, the Attorney General would have resolved the matter between himself and the Hospital in that manner and without seeking permission of any court.

The donor of a charitable gift is in a better position than the Attorney General to be vigilant and, if he or she is so inclined, to enforce his or her own intent. Smithers was the founding donor of the Smithers Center, which he established to carry out his vision of "first class alcoholism treatment and training." In his agreement with the Hospital he reserved to himself the right to veto the Hospital's project plans and staff appointments for the Smithers Center. He and Mrs. Smithers remained actively involved in the affairs of the Smithers Center until his death, and she thereafter. During his lifetime, when Smithers found that, as he wrote on July 31, 1978, "[c]ertain things that were definitely understood were not carried out" by the Hospital, he decided not to donate the balance of the Gift. It was only when the Hospital expressly agreed to the various restrictions imposed by Smithers that he completed the Gift. The Hospital's subsequent unauthorized deviation from the terms of the completed Gift commenced during Smithers's lifetime and was discovered shortly after he died. To hold that, in her capacity as her late husband's representative, Mrs. Smithers has no standing to institute an action to enforce the terms of the Gift is to contravene the well settled principle that a donor's expressed intent is entitled to protection and the longstanding recognition under New York law of standing for a donor such as Smithers. We have seen no New York case in which a donor attempting to enforce the terms of his charitable gift was denied standing to do so. Neither the donor nor his estate was before the court in any of the cases urged on us in opposition to donor standing. The courts in these cases were not addressing the situation in which the donor was still living or his estate still existed. Cf. Herzog Foundation v. University of Bridgeport, 699 A.2d 995 (Conn. 1997).

Moreover, the circumstances of this case demonstrate the need for co-existent standing for the Attorney General and the donor. The Attorney General's office was notified of the Hospital's misappropriation of funds by Mrs. Smithers, whose accountants performed the preliminary review of the Hospital's financial records, and it learned of the Hospital's closing of the detox unit — a breach, according to the Attorney General, of a specific representation — from Mrs. Smithers's papers in this action. Indeed, there is no substitute for a donor, who has a "special, personal interest in the enforcement of the gift restriction" (Note, Protecting the Charitable Investor: A Rationale for Donor Enforcement of Restricted Gifts, 8 B.U. Pub. Int. L.J. 361 (1999)). Mrs. Smithers herself, who the Supreme Court found had no position to lose if the Hospital altered its administration of the Gift, has her own special, personal interest in the enforcement of the Gift restrictions imposed by her husband, as is manifest from her own fund-raising work on behalf of the Smithers Center and the fact that the gala that she organized and that the Hospital ultimately cancelled was to be in her honor as well as her husband's. In any event, the Attorney General's interest in enforcing gift terms is not necessarily congruent with that of the donor. The donor seeks to

have his or her intent faithfully executed, which by definition will benefit the beneficiaries, and perhaps also to erect a tangible memorial to himself or herself. In
the June 16, 1971 letter to the Hospital in which Smithers created the Gift, he
wrote that it "is to be used to set up the Smithers Alcoholism Treatment and Training Center." . . . We conclude that the distinct but related interests of the donor
and the Attorney General are best served by continuing to accord standing to
donors to enforce the terms of their own gifts concurrent with the Attorney
General's standing to enforce such gifts on behalf of the beneficiaries thereof.

Mrs. Smithers, appointed the Special Administratrix of Smithers's estate for
the purpose of pursuing claims by the estate against the Hospital in connection
with its administration of the Smithers Center, therefore has standing to sue the
Hospital for enforcement of the Gift terms. . . .

Order, Supreme Court, New York County, modified, on the law, to grant plaintiff's motion for a preliminary injunction to the extent of staying disbursement of
the proceeds of the sale of the East 93rd Street building, to deny defendants'
motion to dismiss the complaint and to reinstate the complaint, and otherwise
affirmed, without costs.

FRIEDMAN, J., dissenting.   . . . [The issue on appeal] is whether Adele Smithers, as the representative of her husband's estate, has standing to bring this action
seeking to enforce the terms of a charitable gift given by her husband, the funding of which was completed approximately 12 years before this action was commenced. Because I believe that plaintiff does not have standing, I respectfully
dissent.

In considering the subject of standing, I begin with the observation that, when
a charitable gift is made, without any provision for a reversion of the gift to the
donor or his heirs, the interest of the donor and his heirs is permanently
excluded. Accordingly, in the absence of a right of reverter, the right to seek
enforcement of the terms of a charitable gift is restricted to the Attorney
General . . . .

The New York general rule on standing is not only consistent with the
common-law approach (see Herzog Foundation v. University of Bridgeport,
supra), but also with the approach taken by the Restatement (Second) of Trusts
(see §§391[e] & [f]). . . .

In holding that standing is generally restricted to the Attorney General, our
courts have pointed out that a limited standing rule is necessary to protect charitable institutions from "vexatious litigation" by parties who do not have a tangible
stake in the outcome of the litigation. While the majority believes that this concern does not apply to Mrs. Smithers because her motives are altruistic (and I
agree that they are), the limited standing rule enunciated by our Court of Appeals
is a prophylactic one that does not permit a case-by-case inquiry into the subjective motivations of the party commencing the action. . . .

[I]t is uncontroverted that the estate was not the donor of the gift. Thus, even if
pure donor standing were recognized (as the majority concludes), this could not
be a basis for granting standing to Mr. Smithers's estate. Next, to the extent that

Mr. Smithers may have had standing based upon his right to exercise discretionary control over the gift, i.e., via the right to appoint key staffing positions, that
right was personal to him, abated upon his death, and did not devolve to his
estate. Hence, as plaintiff concedes that the estate has no right to exercise control
over the gift, this may not be a basis of standing. Finally, since it is uncontroverted
that the estate does not have a right of reverter in the gift or, in fact, any right
to control the gift by way of appointment to staff positions or otherwise, it follows that there is no retained interest that could support a claim of standing. In
view of this, I fail to perceive the legal basis for the majority's grant of standing to
plaintiff. . . .

Accordingly, I vote to affirm the order dismissing the complaint.

NOTES, QUESTIONS, AND PROBLEM

1. *Epilogue.* The nursing school at issue in *Herzog* was closed because the
University of Bridgeport ran into severe financial trouble. In 1992, an affiliate of
the Rev. Sun Myung Moon's Unification Church bailed out the University and
took control of it. At about the same time, the law school of the University of
Bridgeport pulled up stakes and resettled at Quinnipiac College in Hamden,
Connecticut.

The alcoholism center at issue in *Smithers* was renamed the Addiction Institute
of New York as part of a settlement between the hospital, Mrs. Smithers, and the
Smithers Foundation. Mrs. Smithers retained the exclusive right to use the Smithers name in connection with the treatment of alcoholism and substance abuse; the
hospital promised to use any remaining proceeds from the $15 million sale of the
56 East 93rd Street building for the treatment of alcoholism; and the hospital
agreed to return approximately $6 million for redirection by Mrs. Smithers and
the Foundation to a new donee that would use the funds for a new, free-standing
substance abuse facility. In 2008, the Smithers Alcoholism Treatment and Training Center was opened at the St. John's Riverside Hospital facility in Yonkers,
New York.

In 2003, the probate court with jurisdiction over Mr. Smithers's estate ruled
that Mrs. Smithers was entitled to be reimbursed for her legal fees in the litigation against St. Luke's-Roosevelt Hospital Center. Although the "decedent's probate estate had no direct economic stake in the hospital proceedings," the court
was satisfied that Mrs. Smithers "undertook this litigation with the best of
motives, desiring nothing more than to vindicate her late husband's life's work
that was allegedly being ignored by St. Luke's-Roosevelt Hospital." Estate of
Smithers, 760 N.Y.S.2d 304, 307 (Sur. 2003).

Since Mr. Smithers's death, Mrs. Smithers, as the president of the Smithers
Foundation, has continued her husband's efforts to fight alcoholism. For a pro-
file of the indefatigable Mrs. Smithers, see Michael Unge, Making Her Pitch:
Darryl Strawberry's Ongoing Battle with Substance Abuse Is Just One of the
Causes Adele Smithers Has Made Her Own, Newsday, Aug. 15, 1999, at G16.

2. *State attorneys general and charitable trusts.* The court in *Herzog* followed the traditional rule that a settlor does not have standing to enforce the terms of the trust — private or charitable — unless the settlor retains an interest in the trust property. For a private trust, therefore, in the absence of a reversionary interest in the settlor, only the beneficiary has standing to bring suit against the trustee.

Because a charitable trust must be for the benefit of a charitable purpose rather than an ascertainable beneficiary, such a trust lacks a beneficiary with standing in court and a financial incentive to police the trustee. The question thus arises, if not the settlor, who enforces the terms of a charitable trust? Professor Brody strikes at the heart of the problem: "In the case of an entity having no owners and established for the benefit of indefinite beneficiaries, who is the principal on whom the law can rely to monitor the agents and enforce the charitable purposes?" Evelyn Brody, The Limits of Charity Fiduciary Law, 57 Md. L. Rev. 1400, 1429 (1998).

The law has traditionally answered this question by giving the state attorney general, as *parens patriae*, standing to bring suit against the trustee of a charitable trust. See Ronald Chester, George Gleason Bogert, and George Taylor Bogert, The Law of Trusts and Trustees §411 (3d ed. 2005). But is supervision by the state attorneys general sufficient to ensure that the trustee of a charitable trust acts in accord with the settlor's charitable purpose and refrains from abuse or breach of fiduciary duty? Professor Gary suggests that the answer is No.

> While the powers of the attorney general are substantial, the extent of the supervision the attorney general provides is limited. . . . In some states, several assistant attorneys general form a charitable division of the attorney general's office. . . . In other states, however, one assistant attorney general supervises the nonprofit sector as only one part of his or her assignment. Hawaii has reported 0.5 attorneys working with charities, and many states do not list any attorneys specifically assigned to charitable matters. . . .
>
> [I]nquiries or complaints from dissenting board members, employees, beneficiaries or other members of the public, including the press, are much more likely to trigger investigations than reviews of annual reports conducted in the attorney general's office. In determining which cases to pursue, the attorneys consider the amount involved, the size of the organization, the impact on the public, and the egregiousness of the conduct. The worst abuses receive attention, but many problems probably go undetected or unaddressed. The attorneys general perform an important supervisory role in the charitable sector, but other forms of supervision are both necessary and desirable. [Susan N. Gary, Regulating the Management of Charities: Trust Law, Corporate Law, and Tax Law, 21 U. Haw. L. Rev. 593, 622-624 (1999).]

See also Garry W. Jenkins, Incorporation Choice, Uniformity, and the Reform of Nonprofit State Law, 41 Ga. L. Rev. 1113, 1128-1130 (2007), reporting the results of a fresh survey of state attorneys general revealing meager resources allocated to charity oversight.

Other scholars have emphasized that the state attorney general, who is typically elected, tends to have little interest in supervising charities because such efforts rarely advance the attorney general's political career. On this view, unless an alleged breach of trust garners enough media attention to achieve political salience, actual scrutiny of a charitable trust by the attorney general is unlikely. In the usual case there is simply not enough of a political payoff to the attorney general to warrant the diversion of resources from other initiatives. Once again, Professor Brody provides the apt summation: "Political cynics believe that 'A.G.' stands not for 'attorney general' but for 'aspiring governor.'" Evelyn Brody, Whose Public? Parochialism and Paternalism in State Charity Law Enforcement, 79 Ind. L.J. 937, 946 (2004).

3.   *The emergence of settlor standing.* Why not grant settlors standing concurrent with the attorney general to bring suit to enforce a charitable trust? Twenty years before *Smithers*, Professor Hansmann argued in favor of donor standing to enforce charitable gifts:

> [I]t makes sense to deny standing to [donors] only if the consequence would be large numbers of spite suits, strike suits, or suits filed through sheer idiocy — which are presumably what the courts and commentators have in mind when they raise the specter of "harassing" litigation — or of suits that, though based on a real grievance, are feebly litigated and thus do more harm than good. Yet it appears extraordinarily unlikely that suits of this nature would ever become a sufficiently significant problem to outweigh the benefits of enlisting [donors] into the enforcement effort. [Henry B. Hansmann, Reforming Nonprofit Corporation Law, 129 U. Pa. L. Rev. 497, 609 (1981).]

Although a departure from traditional law, the decision in *Smithers* appears to reflect a trend toward the recognition of settlor standing. See 5 Austin Wakeman Scott, William Franklin Fratcher, and Mark L. Ascher, Scott and Ascher on Trusts §37.3.10, at 2450-2454 (5th ed. 2008), citing the "impressive and growing authority" for the proposition "that the settlor can enforce a charitable trust." See also Ronald Chester, George Gleason Bogert, and George Taylor Bogert, The Law of Trusts and Trustees §415, at 68-69 (3d ed. 2005) (observing that "the traditional rule of no settlor enforcement is under attack").

In addition to New York, the list of states that now recognize settlor standing to enforce a charitable trust includes California, see L.B. Research & Educ. Found. v. UCLA Found., 29 Cal. Rptr. 3d 710, 716-717 (App. 2005), as well as the more than 20 that have adopted a variant of Uniform Trust Code §405(c) (2000) or similar legislation. UTC §405(c) provides that "[t]he settlor of a charitable trust . . . may maintain a proceeding to enforce the trust." Settlor standing to enforce a charitable trust is also endorsed by Restatement (Third) of Trusts §94 (T.D. No. 5, 2009). Perhaps the most forceful embrace of settlor standing is in Delaware, which by statute in 2005 not only authorized the settlor to enforce a trust, but also to "designate a person or persons, whether or not born at the time of such designation," to do so as well. Del. Code Ann., tit. 12, §3303(b) (2008).

There has been less movement toward donor standing for restricted gifts not made in trust. See Dodge v. Trustees of Randolph-Macon Woman's College, 661 S.E.2d 805 (Va. 2008) (refusing to apply the UTC provisions on charitable trusts to a charity organized as a corporation rather than a trust).

4.   *T* gives a fund in trust to *X* University to support a public policy school that emphasizes training for government service. After *T*'s death, the school uses the fund to support other departments in addition to the public policy school. In a state that has adopted UTC §405(c), does the executor of *T*'s estate have standing to sue *X* for breach? If so, does the right pass to *T*'s residuary takers? Suppose, for example, that *T* left his entire estate in equal shares to his children *A* and *B*. What result if *A* wants to bring suit against *X* but *B* does not? Does it matter whether *A* seeks return of the fund versus an injunction compelling *X* to comply with the terms of the gift? Will the right pass from *A* and *B* to their respective successors? Alternatively, suppose the donor was not a natural person but rather an institution, as in *Herzog*. Does such a donor retain standing rights in perpetuity?

In Evelyn Brody, From the Dead Hand to the Living Dead: The Conundrum of Charitable-Donor Standing, 41 Ga. L. Rev. 1183 (2007), Professor Brody surveys the open doctrinal issues surrounding donor standing and discusses their probable treatment in the forthcoming Principles of the Law of Nonprofit Organizations, a project of the American Law Institute for which Brody is the reporter. See also Ben Gose, Terms of Endowment, Chron. Phil., Nov. 15, 2007, at 10 (describing a lawsuit against Princeton brought by the heirs of a donor who made a $35 million contribution in 1961, valued in 2008 at nearly $900 million, for breach of restrictions on the use and management of the funds).

5.   For further discussion of donor standing and cognate issues, see Rob Atkinson, Unsettled Standing: Who (Else) Should Enforce the Duties of Charitable Fiduciaries?, 23 J. Corp. L. 655 (1998); Ronald Chester, Grantor Standing to Enforce Charitable Transfers Under Section 405(c) of the Uniform Trust Code and Related Law: How Important Is It and How Extensive Should It Be?, 37 Real Prop., Prob. & Tr. J. 611 (2003); Iris J. Goodwin, Standing to Enforce Charitable Gifts: Civil Society vs. Donor Empowerment, 58 Vand. L. Rev. 1093 (2005); Edward C. Halbach, Jr., Standing to Enforce Trusts, 62 U. Miami L. Rev. 713 (2008); Craig Kaufman, Sympathy for the Devil's Advocate: Assisting the Attorney General When Charitable Matters Reach the Courtroom, 40 Real Prop., Prob. & Tr. J. 705 (2005); Reid Kress Weisbord, Reservations About Donor Standing: Should the Law Allow Charitable Donors to Reserve the Right to Enforce a Gift Restriction?, 42 Real Prop., Prob. & Tr. J. 245 (2007).

The emphasis thus far has been on the role of the donor in charitable supervision as a remedy for chronic lackadaisical enforcement by the state attorneys general. The mirror-image worry, discussed in the literature most prominently by Professor Evelyn Brody, is that when the attorney general does intervene in the operation of a charity, he will be tempted to curry favor with local voters by imposing parochial local preferences even at the expense of the trust's charitable purpose. See Evelyn Brody, Whose Public? Parochialism and Paternalism in State Charity Law Enforcement, 79 Ind. L.J. 937 (2004).

THE SWEETEST PLACE ON EARTH: HERSHEY'S KISS-OFF[7]

The largest confectionary in North America, the Hershey Company makes such familiar goodies as Kit Kats, Reese's Pieces, Milk Duds, and of course, Hershey's Chocolate Bars, Kisses, and Syrup. The Company is based in Hershey, Pennsylvania, a town that fancies itself "The Sweetest Place On Earth," where Cocoa Avenue intersects with Chocolate Avenue and the streetlights are shaped like Hershey's Kisses. Also based in the town of Hershey is the Milton Hershey School, a boarding school that enrolls, feeds, and clothes 1,700 needy children whose families have an average income of just under $14,000. The School's operations are funded by the Milton Hershey School Trust, a Pennsylvania charitable trust that as of 2007 was worth roughly $8.2 billion, more than all but the six largest domestic university endowments.

The Company, the School, and the Trust were all founded about a century ago by Milton S. Hershey. For Hershey, an uncommonly gifted confectioner, the lure of chocolate — the rich, sensual, and satisfying food derived from the cocoa bean — was irresistible. Chocolate had long been a pleasure of the upper class, but because it was so difficult to mass produce and ship in an edible and economically viable form, few others had ready access to it. Milk chocolate, a solid form of chocolate with a pleasing taste that could be mass produced and widely distributed at bearable cost, was the holy grail of chocolate making. The trick was to induce the water-based milk to combine with the fatty, oil-based cocoa.

Hershey's solution was to boil the milk to the brink of souring, which explains the hallmark bitter, harsh taste of Hershey's milk chocolate. Although panned by chocolate connoisseurs — who preferred the more subtle flavors of European chocolates such as Cadbury, Lindt, and Nestlé — for many Americans, Hershey's grittier chocolate was their first encounter with the substance, and it was memorable. Hershey's chocolate became America's chocolate. And the town of Hershey became a model company town.

Hershey then turned his attention to the School, which he founded with his wife Catherine in 1909. Because Milton and Catherine never had children of their own, the students enrolled in the School became their surrogate children. As Milton later explained: "Well, I have no heirs; so I decided to make the orphan boys of the United States my heirs." Joël Glenn Brenner, The Emperors of Chocolate: Inside the Secret World of Hershey and Mars 117 (1999).

In 1918, three years after Catherine died, Milton Hershey transferred substantially all of his assets — including his stock in the Company, then worth $60 million — to the Trust. Today, the Trust provides the School with an endowment that is remarkable not only for its size but even more so for its breathtaking lack of diversification. Of the Trust's $8.2 billion corpus, $3.4 billion (41 percent) is invested in the stock of the Hershey Company, representing roughly one-third of

---

7. Adapted from Jonathan Klick and Robert H. Sitkoff, Agency Costs, Charitable Trusts, and Corporate Control: Evidence from Hershey's Kiss-Off, 108 Colum. L. Rev. 749 (2008).

Milton S. Hershey and the Orphan Boys

the Company's outstanding shares and, thanks to a dual-class stock structure, three-quarters of the shareholder votes.

Increasingly aware of the perils of an undiversified portfolio, and after getting a nudge from the Pennsylvania Attorney General's office, the trustees decided to sell the Trust's interest in the Company. In July 2002, when the Wall Street Journal broke the news of the trustees' plan, investors bid up the Company's stock price by 25 percent from $62.50 to $78.30.

The thought of cashing out at a premium price pleased the trustees, but Hershey residents and workers took a different view. They organized a "Derail the Sale" campaign, which included yard signs with slogans such as "The Hershey Trust — An Oxymoron" and "Don't Shut Down Chocolate Town." They asked D. Michael Fisher, the Pennsylvania Attorney General and the Republican candidate for governor in the looming November gubernatorial election, to remove the trustees and to block the sale.

Invoking his powers as attorney general, Fisher petitioned the local court with jurisdiction over the Trust to enjoin the sale. At the hearing, the main witness was former Hershey CEO Richard Zimmerman, who predicted that an acquiring company would seek to cut costs by shutting down less efficient manufacturing plants. "And I suspect," testified Zimmerman, "that one would start with the [main Hershey] plant that's nearly a hundred years old." In Zimmerman's view, although these actions might improve the profitability of the combined company, "there are very many more things in life more important than money."

Calling Zimmerman's testimony "persuasive" and noting the "symbiotic relationship among the School, the community, and the Company," the judge enjoined the sale. On appeal, the trustees' lawyers argued that nothing in the Deed of Trust indicated that Milton and Catherine Hershey wanted the Trust to maintain its ownership of the Company, or to undertake responsibility for the economic health of the local community, or to provide continuing employment for the Company's workers. On the contrary, the only interest named in the Deed of Trust was that of the School. The Deed of Trust also gave the trustees "full power and authority to invest" the trust assets.

In reply, the Attorney General conceded that the Trust was "imprudently" undiversified "and that it would be 'desirable' for the Trust to diversify its holdings." But he also argued that "there was no testimony that it needs to do so immediately, within the next few days or weeks." By contrast, "the current employees of Hershey Foods would be worse off under an acquisition than they are now," and the sale of the Company "would seriously impair, if not destroy, the symbiotic relationship which has existed for many decades among the company, the School and its Trust, and the other institutions which together carry on Milton Hershey's unique vision."

While waiting for the appellate court to render a decision, the trustees gathered in a hotel in Valley Forge, Pennsylvania, to discuss their options. They had set a deadline of a few days earlier for bids for the Company. The top bid was from the Wm. Wrigley Jr. Company: $12.5 billion in cash and stock, or about $89 per share. According to subsequent media reports, the trustees' Valley Forge session was "emotional," "rancorous," and "sometimes teary," with the trustees feeling "embittered" by what they perceived to be "pressure" from the Attorney General's office to diversify followed by the Attorney General's heated opposition. The trustees felt "overwhelmed by the outcry of protest from the community." The chairman of the board of trustees, who had received death threats, had been living with an armed guard assigned to his home. The trustees deliberated for ten hours. William Wrigley delivered a "moving" speech in which he promised a commitment to the Hershey community and to keep the Hershey factories open. Just before midnight, however, the trustees announced that they had voted 10 to 7 to reject Wrigley's bid and all the other bids too.

Investors took a dim view of the sale's cancellation. The Company's stock tumbled to $65 per share the next day, down 12 percent from the prior day's closing price of $73.81. Hershey residents and workers, however, received the news with a mix of relief and joy. "All I can say is hooray," one resident told the Associated Press. "I still want this company to be around for my grandchildren, so they can work here when they're old enough," said another. Kathy Taylor, a former town supervisor who helped spearhead the "Derail the Sale" movement, offered a more blunt assessment to the New York Times: "Our cash cow is safe; we're feeling really great." In something of an anticlimax, later that day the appellate court upheld the trial judge's injunction by a 4-to-1 vote.

Aftermath. After the trustees abandoned the sale, the trial judge dissolved the injunction but ordered the trustees to give the Attorney General's office "prompt written notice" of any future intention to sell the Trust's controlling interest in the Company. The judge also criticized the trust board as being too large and too "distant and disconnected from the charitable interests they serve." Soon thereafter, Fisher announced that the seven trustees who had voted in favor of continuing the sale, as well as three others who had opposed the sale, would be stepping down in favor of four new board members, all hailing from central Pennsylvania.

Fisher, meanwhile, lost the gubernatorial election by a margin of almost 10 percent, and this in spite of running television ads in which he claimed to have saved over 6,000 Hershey jobs. The following year President George W. Bush nominated Fisher to be a circuit judge for the United States Court of Appeals for the Third Circuit. The Senate confirmed Fisher's appointment on December 9, 2003.

On November 6, 2002, the Governor signed an amendment to the Pennsylvania prudent investor statute. The amendment requires the trustees of a charitable trust "in making investment and management decisions" to consider "the special relationship of [a trust asset] and its economic impact as a principal business enterprise on the community." It also bars the trustee of a charitable trust "holding a controlling interest in a publicly traded business corporation received as an asset from the settlor" from selling that controlling interest without first notifying the Attorney General and the Pennsylvania employees of the business. If the Attorney General challenges the sale, the amendment puts the burden on the trustee to "prove by clear and convincing evidence" that the sale "is necessary to maintain the economic viability of the corporation and [to] prevent a significant diminution of trust assets or to avoid an impairment of the charitable purpose of the trust." The amendment, which was transparently directed at the Hershey Trust, was well received in Pennsylvania. The State Senate majority leader captured the local view: "We have to be active and protect our economic assets."

Since the 2002 amendment to the state's prudent investor rule, the Company's stock price has experienced a steady decline. In early 2007, after continued erosion of market share to competitors such as Mars, the Company announced that it would lay off 1,500 workers (12 percent of its workforce) and open a new factory in Mexico — a cruel irony given Wrigley's pledge to preserve the local Hershey factories. Later that year, the trustees forced a shakeup in the Company's top leadership and expressed dissatisfaction with the Company's "unsatisfactory performance." Yet the trustees also pledged to maintain the Trust's controlling interest in the Company, citing among other things their obligations under the state's prudent investor rule. And so the Company, the Trust, and the School trudge ahead, inextricably entwined, with the Trust unable to diversify and the Company — unlike Mars, which announced that it would be merging with the Hershey Company's former suitor Wrigley — unable to realize the synergies of a merger.

QUESTION AND NOTES

1.   Is the Hershey Trust a good candidate for cy pres under UTC §413(a) on the grounds of waste? In spite of the Trust's mushrooming corpus, the School

"served no more children at the start of 2005 than it did in 1963." Michael D'Antonio, Hershey: Milton S. Hershey's Extraordinary Life of Wealth, Empire, and Utopian Dreams 266 (2006).

2.   Professor Brody is sharply critical of the role played by all three branches of the Pennsylvania government in the Hershey Trust's aborted 2002 diversification plan:

> The Hershey case shows each of the three branches of Pennsylvania government acting illegitimately. The attorney general practically treated the Hershey assets as his election campaign funds. The Orphans' Court's long experience with the Hershey Trust only served to continue a history of usurping the board's discretion — and this time it was even less justifiable, relating as it did to making prudent investments rather than to programs. Moreover, the particular local nature of the supervising court can compound the risk of parochialism, as one journalist observed: "That the directors should live anyplace beside Hershey seemed an affront to Morgan, a 71-year-old judge on retired status who has spent 30 years on Common Pleas Court of Dauphin County, of which the Orphans' Court is a division, and who attended college and law school at Dickinson, just a few miles from Hershey in Carlisle." Finally, the legislature singled out the Trust and effectively appropriated to the local community locked-in control of a publicly traded corporation — without, of course, rising to the level of a "taking" requiring payment of compensation. [Evelyn Brody, Whose Public? Parochialism and Paternalism in State Charity Law Enforcement, 79 Ind. L.J. 937, 998-999 (2004).]

Although agreeing with Brody about the demerits of the "inflexible legislative" response to the aborted sale, Professor Sidel is more sympathetic to the actions of the attorney general and consideration of local preferences:

> [T]he system did work. It provided a framework for a dynamic reconsideration of what the *parens patriae* interest really is, informed not entirely by isolated regulators conferring with legal texts but necessarily, forcefully informed by public attitudes, the views of those directly affected, and broader representational forces. While that process occurred during, and appears to have been influenced by, a political and electoral process, that political process served as a transmission belt for public attitudes to be conveyed, for more information to be ascertained, and ultimately for a result to be achieved that directly addressed the questions of fiduciary duty and trustee responsibility with which the Hershey Trust Board wrestled. Here the changing nature of public interest under *parens patriae*, and the influence of political dialogue, was not an unfortunate concomitant or product of the process — it was integral to it, and, I would argue resulted in a better and more informed solution. [Mark Sidel, The Struggle for Hershey: Community Accountability and the Law in Modern American Philanthropy, 65 U. Pitt. L. Rev. 1, 59-60 (2003).]

3.   In a recent article, Professors Klick and Sitkoff undertook an econometric analysis of the Hershey Company's stock price movements during the 2002 sale window. They estimate that the attorney general's intervention to block the sale wiped out $2.7 billion in shareholder wealth, of which the Trust's share was $850 million. The $850 million figure equates roughly to $67,000 per Hershey resident. Concluding that canceling the sale was not in the best interests of the Trust, the Company, or the Company's other shareholders, they also question whether blocking the sale was in the best interests of the community:

[S]uppose that there was no doubt that the Hersheys would have wanted to favor the community in the event of surplus funds, and suppose further that the law allowed the trustees to take into account the interests of the community in such a scenario. Even then, it is hardly obvious that maintaining control of the Company would be an efficient way to benefit the community or subsidize life in Hershey. For example, the Trust could have sold its interest in the Company, thereby realizing the $850 million gain and diversifying its portfolio, and then it could have paid out every dollar of that $850 million gain to the local community, either in cash or through a program of community enrichment. In this scenario, the community would have received an actual $850 million transfer from the Trust, the Company would thereafter be subject to the pressures of the takeover market, and the Trust would have at least achieved salutary portfolio diversification. . . . Instead, the Trust was forced to maintain its interest in the Company (and so an undiversified portfolio), the community did not receive a cash transfer, and the Company remained [under the control of] the trustees. The bill for this inefficiency came due in early 2007 when . . . the Company announced that it [was transferring jobs to a new plant in Mexico]. [Jonathan Klick and Robert H. Sitkoff, Agency Costs, Charitable Trusts, and Corporate Control: Evidence from Hershey's Kiss-Off, 108 Colum. L. Rev. 749, 824-825 (2008).]

NOTE: STANDING FOR PERSONS WITH SPECIAL INTERESTS

A person with a special interest as a beneficiary may be able to enforce a charitable trust. The person must show that he is entitled to receive a benefit under the trust that is not available to the public at large or to an average beneficiary. 5 Austin Wakeman Scott, William Franklin Fratcher, and Mark L. Ascher, Scott and Ascher on Trusts §37.3.10, at 2440-2450 (5th ed. 2008).

For example, an elderly, indigent widow living in a charitable home for the aged has been held to have standing to sue the board of trustees who, because of the costs of operating an obsolete facility, proposed to relocate the residents elsewhere. Hooker v. The Edes Home, 579 A.2d 608 (D.C. 1990). A parishioner can sue to enforce a trust for the benefit of his church. Gray v. St. Matthews Cathedral, 544 S.W.2d 488 (Tex. App. 1976). A minister can sue to enforce a trust to pay the salary of the clergy of his church. First Congregational Socy. v. Trustees, 40 Mass. (23 Pick.) 148 (1839).

On the other hand, a person who is merely eligible within the trustee's discretion for a benefit from a charitable trust does not have special interest standing. Gene Kauffman Scholarship Foundation, Inc. v. Payne, 183 S.W.3d 620 (Mo. App. 2006); Schalkenbach Found. v. Lincoln Found., 91 P.3d 1019 (Ariz. App. 2004). Nor does the alumni association of a private school have standing to enforce a charitable trust for the benefit of the school. In re Milton Hershey School, 911 A.2d 1258 (Pa. 2006). Nor does a charity with a similar purpose have standing to enforce a charitable trust on the theory that the charity will have an increased burden if the trust is mismanaged. In re Public Benev. Trust of Crume, 829 N.E.2d 1039 (Ind. App. 2005). Nor, in the usual case, does a student have standing to sue college trustees. Russell v. Yale University, 737 A.2d 941 (Conn. App. 1999).

Special interest standing extends only so far as the person's special interest. Thus, a senior citizen center has special interest standing to enforce a pledge to contribute funds from a charitable trust, but not to enforce the terms of the trust generally. In re Clement Trust, 679 N.W.2d 31 (Iowa 2004).

NOTES

1. *Relator standing.* Another, if rarely used, mechanism for charity enforcement is suit by the attorney general "on the relation" of a private party who does not have individual standing. Such a suit is brought by the party and at the party's expense, but in the name of the attorney general and subject to the control of the attorney general. See Restatement (Third) of Trusts §94, cmt. e (T.D. No. 5, 2009); Ronald Chester, Improving Enforcement Mechanisms in the Charitable Sector: Can Increased Disclosure of Information Be Utilized Effectively, 40 New Eng. L. Rev. 447, 472-473 (2006).

2. *The English Charity Commission.* In contrast with the American approach, which gives the state attorneys general principal responsibility for overseeing charities, in the United Kingdom there is a Charity Commission. Initially established by the Charitable Trusts Act of 1853, the Commission currently has nine members and is authorized to intervene in the administration of charities to police misconduct or mismanagement. In addition, the Commission serves as the registrar of charities and offers advice to the trustees of charitable entities. For further discussion, see 5 Austin Wakeman Scott, William Franklin Fratcher, and Mark L. Ascher, Scott and Ascher on Trusts §37.3.10, at 2436-2437 (5th ed. 2008); Debra Morris, New Charity Regulation Proposals for England and Wales: Overdue or Overdone?, 80 Chi.-Kent L. Rev. 779 (2005).

Drawing on the English model, several American commentators have urged the creation of a specialized agency charged with supervising charities in the United States. See, e.g., Joel L. Fleishman, The Foundation: A Great American Secret: How Private Wealth Is Changing the World 256-259 (2007); James J. Fishman, Wrong Way Corrigan and Recent Developments in the Nonprofit Landscape: A Need for New Legal Approaches, 76 Fordham L. Rev. 587, 591-598 (2007).

3. *Charitable trust monitors.* Professor Geoffrey Manne has put forward an intriguing variant on the enforcement of charitable trusts — namely, "the creation of private, for-profit monitoring companies" that would contract with charitable organizations "to monitor both the financial and charitable aspects of the nonprofit's operation. The monitoring companies would be granted, by contract, the right to sue in order to rectify perceived violations of a nonprofit's fiduciary duties or the terms of its charter." In Manne's view, reputation effects and the desire to attract business, which is to say a profit motive, would give the monitoring companies appropriate incentives to police charitable organizations. Geoffrey A. Manne, Agency Costs and the Oversight of Charitable Organizations, 1999 Wis. L. Rev. 227. Interestingly, in recent years a growing number of for-profit, donor-advising firms have been formed. These firms provide donors with advice in making charitable donations and undertake follow-up monitoring of

the recipient's use of the funds. See Rachel Emma Silverman and Sally Beatty, Doing Due Diligence on Your Donations — As Charitable Giving Grows, So Do Services for Donors Who Want Evidence That Their Money is Having an Impact, Wall St. J., Dec. 20, 2007, at D1.

Although there are subtle differences between the rules to qualify as charitable under state trust law versus under federal tax law, in the usual case a trust that is charitable under state law will also qualify as charitable under federal tax law. Consequently, through the tax code — and its enforcer, the Internal Revenue Service — the federal government has come to play an increasingly important role in the supervision of charitable trusts and other charitable entities.

HAWAII JOURNAL: THE BISHOP ESTATE

The Bishop Estate was established in 1884 as a charitable trust under the will of Princess Bernice Pauahi Bishop, the last descendant of King Kamehameha I, Hawaii's first and most powerful king. The trust assets include a $10 billion endowment and 350,000 acres of non-income-producing land described by the trustees as "63 miles of ocean frontage, 100 miles of streams, historic fishponds, forests and lava fields . . . that are deeply tied to the Hawaiian culture." The New York Times has called Bishop Estate, "a feudal empire so vast that it could never be assembled in the modern world." N.Y. Times, Oct. 14, 1997, at A1.

The princess's will directed that there be five trustees, appointed by the justices of the Supreme Court of Hawaii, which, in those days when Hawaii was a monarchy, also served as the probate court. The trustees were to erect two schools, one for boys and one for girls, and to expend the annual income of the trust on the maintenance of the schools. Two schools were built shortly after the princess's death, but many decades later they were combined in a single school for boys and girls known as the

Princess Bernice Pauahi Bishop

©H.L. Chase, Bishop Museum

Kamehameha Schools.[8] A Bishop Estate trusteeship has long been a coveted position in Hawaii. During the 1990s, the trustees paid themselves annual fees of nearly $1 million each and engaged in trust business with friends, relatives, and political associates. Jurisdiction for probate matters had long since passed from the supreme court to the probate court, but the justices continued to select the Bishop Estate trustees, insisting that they were acting "unofficially."

As the twentieth century was nearing its end, the Bishop Estate trustees, supreme court justices, key legislators, and the governor had what might charitably be described as a cozy relationship (others called it corrupt). To be appointed as a justice on the supreme court, a candidate had to be put on an approved list by the judicial selection commission, a majority of whose members were picked by the president of the senate, speaker of the house, chief justice of the supreme court, and the governor. Trustees who served in the 1990s included a president of the senate, speaker of the house, chief justice of the supreme court, and the governor's closest associate.

The trustees' gilt-edged world began to unravel when one of the trustees intervened high-handedly in the day-to-day running of the Schools. She soon was calling the teachers incompetent and countermanding decisions of the Schools' president and principals. She ordered that no Hawaiian word be taught — or even uttered on campus — unless the word existed in 1884, the year the princess died, and she commanded that nothing in writing leave the campus until it had been personally approved by her, creating a long backlog of important communications. When students protested, she summoned the student body president to her downtown office for a two-hour, closed-door interrogation, asking him how he would feel if she wrote a letter to Princeton (where he had been offered a scholarship) denouncing him as a rabble-rouser. Eventually, the Kamehameha ohana (community) revolted. Teachers and students were threatened with sanctions if they participated, but alumni marched, 1,000 strong, through downtown Honolulu, stopping at the supreme court building to ask that the justices do something about the situation.

Then came the spark that ignited the firestorm that was soon to engulf the trustees. On August 9, 1997, the Honolulu Star Bulletin published "Broken Trust," a 6,500-word essay written by four prominent kupuna (elders) of the native Hawaiian community (a senior federal district judge; a retired state judge; a former principal of the Kamehameha Schools; and the head trustee of the Queen Liliuokalani Trust) and Professor Randall W. Roth of the University of Hawaii Law School. The essay began, "The time has come to say, 'no more.'"

8. Although the will does not limit admission to native Hawaiians, with minor exceptions that has always been the policy. In 2003, a non-native Hawaiian brought suit in federal court, arguing that his civil rights were violated when the school rejected his application on the basis of race. The district court ruled in favor of the Kamehameha Schools. On appeal, the Ninth Circuit reversed, ruling in favor of the anonymous plaintiff by a vote of 2 to 1, but on rehearing en banc the court reversed and ruled in favor of the Schools by a vote of 8 to 7. Doe v. Kamehameha Schools/Bernice Pauahi Bishop Estate, 470 F.3d 827 (9th Cir. 2006). In 2007, while a petition for certiorari was pending before the U.S. Supreme Court, the trustees settled the lawsuit for $7 million. On August 6, 2008, an almost identical suit was filed in federal court against the Kamehameha Schools by four new plaintiffs. Earlier the same day the Schools filed suit in state court against the plaintiff in the first suit, alleging a breach of the settlement's confidentiality provisions.

Reviewing the basics of trust law and judicial selection, the authors described how Bishop Estate trusteeships had become "political plums" that sullied the process for selecting justices, accused the Bishop Estate trustees of specific breaches of trust, and called for an investigation of trustee selection and performance. The article triggered a public outcry for reform, which prompted the state attorney general, Margery Bronster, to launch an investigation into the trustees' actions.

A few months after the "Broken Trust" article appeared, a court-appointed master found numerous irregularities in the administration of the Bishop Estate. For example, investment decisions had been "ad hoc," based more on relationships than due diligence and conventional financial analysis. There was no overall plan or apparent effort to diversify investments. The trustees had taken out full-page ads claiming a 17 percent return on investment for the three years under review, but the master determined that the actual return had been 1 percent. The master discovered that the trustees had earlier moved $350 million of income into corpus without noting it in their records or disclosing it in financial statements or annual reports to the court. He was also troubled that trustees created conflicts of interest by investing trust money in private deals in which they had a personal stake.

In addition to employing flawed investment practices and short-changing Kamehameha Schools, the trustees and their associates also received private benefits. Most of the trustees accepted free golf memberships from country clubs leasing Bishop Estate land. One pocketed substantial director fees and stock options from a company in which the Estate held a large block of stock. Another used Estate personnel to perform personal services and accepted trips to the Super Bowl and the Olympics in private jets from persons doing business with the Estate. One trustee "recused" himself as trustee in order to negotiate a deal on behalf of an organization that was buying land from the Estate. And a highly placed employee of the Estate (a powerful state senator) charged $28,000 to the Estate's credit card in casinos and sex clubs in Las Vegas and Honolulu. (When this was discovered by the attorney general's investigation, the trustees gave the employee a retroactive bonus in the amount he needed to repay the Estate and to cover his taxes on the total bonus.) Two trustees were indicted on charges that they received kickbacks in a real estate deal involving the trust and a trustee's brother-in-law.

There were death threats and a sex scandal that was as bizarre as it was tragic. A security guard caught one of the trustees having sex with an Estate attorney in the toilet cubicle in a hotel men's room. The attorney, a married woman, killed herself the next day. One week later, the trustee reportedly took an overdose of sleeping pills, but he survived.

Meanwhile, the trustees hired dozens of big-name lawyers, paying them millions in fees from Estate funds. According to a court-appointed master who later reviewed the legal invoices, "One can easily conclude, as this Master has, that a strategy was adopted to obstruct the legal process, to delay wherever possible, to object wherever possible, to utilize so many lawyers and so many arguments that the opposition would be overwhelmed and would choose to give up. . . . [M]illions of dollars of trust funds were wasted." Through their friends in the legislature, some of whom were on the Estate payroll, the trustees retaliated against Attorney General Bronster. In April 1999, the state senate refused to confirm her to a second term in office.

Enter the Internal Revenue Service. In 1995, the Internal Revenue Service began a full audit of the Estate. On December 31, 1998, the IRS issued its findings that the Estate was not being operated primarily for charitable purposes; that it had become directly involved in local and national political campaigns; that trustee fees were grossly in excess of the value of the trustees' services; and that there had been numerous instances of private benefit from trust assets. Concluding that the abuse had been serious and widespread, the IRS revoked the Estate's charitable tax exemption retroactively and refused to communicate further with the trustees. However, the IRS took the unprecedented step of advising the probate court that it would reconsider its position if certain conditions were satisfied, including the immediate resignation or removal of the trustees. Because the immediate cost of a retroactive revocation would have been nearly $1 billion, the probate court had no real choice but to accept the IRS's offer. Within a matter of days the court replaced all five trustees. See Todd S. Purdum, For $6 Billion Hawaii Legacy, a New Day, N.Y. Times, May 15, 1999, at A1.

Two separate court-appointed masters recommended that the court impose millions of dollars in surcharges, and the attorney general prepared to sue the former trustees on behalf of the charity for nearly $200 million in damages. There was also widespread speculation that the justices might also be sued for breach of fiduciary duty in their selection of the Bishop Estate trustees. Although jurists normally enjoy judicial immunity, this immunity applies only to judicial acts like deciding cases, not ministerial and nonjudicial acts — and the justices had long insisted that they had been acting "unofficially" in choosing the trustees.

Aftermath. The probate court established a new selection process for trustees: a panel of seven committee members, chosen by the probate court, would screen applicants and provide a short list of candidates to the court, which would then make the selection. In addition, the court ordered the trustees to turn over day-to-day control of the Estate's operations to qualified professionals; capped the trustees' fees at $97,500 ($120,000 for the chair); prohibited politicians from serving as a trustee or even serving on the screening committee; and ordered the new trustees to adopt a strict conflicts of interest policy, hire an internal auditor, follow generally accepted accounting principles, develop a strategic plan, adopt new investment policies and practices, and spend an average of 4 percent of the Estate's endowment value each year on the charitable mission.

The new attorney general, the current and former trustees, and the many lawyers who had represented the former trustees entered into a "global settlement" that brought an abrupt end to the controversy. The settlement was financed not by the individuals involved, but by a payout on a $25 million insurance policy that the former trustees had acquired years earlier using Estate funds. Under the settlement, the former trustees did not return any of their (excessive) compensation, make good on any of the surcharges that the masters had recommended, or pay any of the damages sought by the attorney general. Similarly, the lawyers for the former trustees were allowed to keep all of their fees, including fees charged for research into ways to avoid state and federal oversight by moving the trust's situs to an Indian reservation in South Dakota. Numerous records were sealed. Proponents of the settlement and the sealing of records said that it would promote "closure" and "healing." Critics said it would sweep under the rug evidence of further corruption.

The new trustees have increased dramatically the amount of money spent each year, not just on Kamehameha Schools, which now have three campuses and together represent the largest independent school in the country, but also on outreach efforts. These efforts include critically important support for public charter schools in areas heavily populated by native Hawaiians. Early indications are that these charter schools and other outreach activities are having a profoundly positive impact on a large number of Hawaiian children.

In 2006, two of the original "Broken Trust" essay authors published an engrossing, page-turner of a book that provides a gripping behind-the-scenes account of the whole Bishop Estate controversy. See Samuel P. King and Randall W. Roth, Broken Trust: Greed, Mismanagement and Political Manipulation at America's Largest Charitable Trust (2006). For a more staid, scholarly review of selected Bishop Estate issues, see Symposium, The Bishop Estate Controversy, 21 U. Haw. L. Rev. 353-714 (1999). For a comprehensive summary of legal issues and other background materials, see www.BrokenTrustBook.com.

NOTES AND QUESTIONS

1.   Much of the federal regulation of charitable entities traces to the Tax Reform Act of 1969. See Marion R. Fremont-Smith, Governing Nonprofit Organizations: Federal and State Law and Regulation 238-300 (2004), surveying the substantive provisions of the tax code pertaining to charities. Perhaps the most important is I.R.C. §4942, which imposes substantial tax penalties on private charitable foundations (but not on publicly supported charities) that do not expend annually an amount equal to 5 percent of the value of the endowment. Currently, many administrative expenses, including board member salaries, count toward the 5 percent distribution requirement. Proposals to amend the tax code to exclude administrative expenses have been unsuccessful in part because of opposition from nonprofit organizations.

Another provision of the tax code, known as the excess business holdings rule, bars a foundation from holding in excess of 20 percent of a business. I.R.C. §4943. Also enacted in 1969, this provision put many foundations under salutary pressure to diversify. An exception is the Hershey Trust, which qualifies as a "supporting organization" exempt from both the excess business holdings rule and the 5 percent minimum payout rule. See Evelyn Brody, Whose Public?

Parochialism and Paternalism in State Charity Law Enforcement, 79 Ind. L.J. 937, 987-988 (2004).

For a discussion of recent proposals to expand federal charitable oversight, see Marion R. Fremont-Smith, The Search for Greater Accountability of Nonprofit Organizations: Recent Legal Developments and Proposals for Change, 76 Fordham L. Rev. 609, 631-643 (2007). For a spirited argument in favor of more stringent regulation of the private charitable foundation, the "mechanism by which American taxpayers subsidize the whims of the rich and fulfill their fantasies of immortality," see Ray D. Madoff, Dog Eat Your Taxes?, N.Y. Times, July 9, 2008, at A23 (referencing Leona Helmsley's beneficence toward her dog, Trouble, and dogs more generally, discussed at pages 586-587). For discussion of "why, in the real world, it is rare for lawyers representing charitable organizations to report abuses to outside authorities," see Samuel P. King and Randall W. Roth, Erosion of Trust, 93 ABA J. 48 (2007).

2. The federal tax law compels charities to make yearly disclosure of their assets, investments, and disbursements. In 2008, the required filing by tax-exempt organizations — IRS Form 990 — was redesigned to require even more disclosure in a more reader-friendly format.

> The form, which nonprofits must continue to make available to donors and others on request, will now include a top summary page listing comparative financial information — revenues and expenses — over a two-year period. The next page requires charities to detail their organization's accomplishments during the past year, moving that information closer to the front of the form than before. Other sections ask charities to provide more-detailed information about fund raising, governance and compensation for top executives and trustees. [Mike Spector, New IRS Rules Help Donors Vet Charities: Revised Tax Form Will Make Nonprofits Reveal More About How They Spend, Wall St. J., May 29, 2008, at D1.]

3. Another idea sometimes discussed is to require charities to spend down all of their funds, thereby forcing them to appeal continually for new donations. Judge Posner explains:

> Even when no unforeseen contingencies materialize, perpetual charitable gifts raise an economic issue that echoes the concern with the separation of ownership and control in the modern business corporation. A charitable foundation that enjoys a substantial income, in perpetuity, from its original endowment does not compete in any product market or in the capital markets and has no stockholders or other owners. Its board of trustees is self-perpetuating and is accountable to no one for the performance of the enterprise. (Although state attorneys general have legal authority over the administration of charitable trusts, it is largely formal.) And as neither the trustees nor the staff have the kind of property right in the foundation's assets or income that would give them a strong incentive to maximize value, the carrot is missing along with the stick.
>
> The incentives to efficient management of foundation assets could be strengthened by a rule requiring charitable foundations to distribute every gift received, principal and interest, including the original endowment, within a short, specified period of years. The foundation would not be required to wind up its operations within the period; it could continue indefinitely. But it would have to receive new gifts from time to time in order to avoid exhausting all of its funds. Since donors are unlikely to give money to an enterprise known to be slack, the necessity of returning periodically to the market for charitable donations would give trustees and managers of charitable foundations an incentive they now lack to conduct

a tight operation. Foundations — mostly religious and educational — that market their services or depend on continuing charitable support, and are therefore already subject to some competitive constraints, could be exempted from the exhaustion rule.

The objections to the suggested rule are that it is unnecessary — donors are already free to limit the duration of their charitable bequests — and that it might therefore . . . reduce the incentives to make charitable gifts. A counterargument is that many perpetual foundations were established at a time when the foundation was a novel institution. A person creating one at that time may not have been able to foresee the problem of inefficient and unresponsive management that might plague a perpetual foundation as a result of the peculiar set of constraints (or rather lack of constraints) under which they operate. [Richard A. Posner, Economic Analysis of Law §18.5, at 547 (7th ed. 2007).]

Perhaps the most prominent example of a charity that has voluntarily undertaken to spend down its endowment is the Gates Foundation, a charitable trust created by Microsoft founder Bill Gates and his wife Melinda. In December 2006, six months after the investment guru Warren Buffett pledged $31 billion to the Foundation — a gift that would roughly double the Foundation's endowment — the Foundation announced that it would terminate 50 years after the death of the survivor of its three principal patrons. See Sally Beatty, Gates Foundation Sets Time Frame to Spend Assets, Wall St. J., Dec. 1, 2006, at A10.

4.   The rise of great charitable trusts in the United States came after industrial growth in the late nineteenth century produced enormous fortunes. Capital in charitable trusts continued to mushroom during the twentieth century, partly, or perhaps principally, because the federal government permits gifts to charity during life to be deducted from the donor's taxable income and gifts to charity at death to be deducted from the donor's taxable estate. Today, charities own property worth billions of dollars. The Foundation Directory (2008) reports that the 10,000 largest U.S. grant-making foundations (measured by total giving) have total assets in excess of $530 billion. Of these, 8,745 have assets of at least $1 million, and 7,199 have assets totaling $5 million or more. Twenty-nine have assets exceeding $2 billion each. The following table shows the top ten.

Foundation	Endowment in Billions of Dollars
Bill & Melinda Gates Foundation	33.1
The Ford Foundation	13.7
J. Paul Getty Trust	10.1
The Robert Wood Johnson Foundation	10.1
The William and Flora Hewlett Foundation	8.5
W.K. Kellogg Foundation	8.4
Lilly Endowment Inc.	7.6
The David and Lucile Packard Foundation	6.4
John D. and Catherine T. MacArthur Foundation	6.2
The Andrew W. Mellon Foundation	6.1

Source: The Foundation Directory (David G. Jacobs, ed., 20th ed. 2008).

These figures do not include assets of universities, museums, libraries, churches, and other charitable institutions that are not grant-making foundations. The following table shows the ten largest university endowments as of 2008, five of which are in excess of $15 billion.

University	Endowment in Billions of Dollars
Harvard	36.6
Yale	22.9
Stanford	17.2
Princeton	16.3
University of Texas	16.1
Massachusetts Institute of Technology	10.1
University of Michigan	7.6
Northwestern University	7.2
Columbia University	7.1
Texas A&M	6.7

Source: National Association of College and University Business Officers, 2008 Endowment Study.

For further discussion of the "hundreds of billions of dollars in endowments and other charity reserves," see Evelyn Brody, Charitable Endowments and the Democratization of Dynasty, 39 Ariz. L. Rev. 873 (1997). See also Susan N. Gary, Charities, Endowments, and Donor Intent: The Uniform Prudent Management of Institutional Funds Act, 41 Ga. L. Rev. 1277 (2007), discussing the Uniform Acts pertaining to the investment and management of charitable endowments.

12

POWERS OF APPOINTMENT: BUILDING FLEXIBILITY INTO TRUSTS

> The power of appointment is the most efficient dispositive device that
> the ingenuity of Anglo-American lawyers has ever worked out.
>
> W. BARTON LEACH
> *in Powers of Appointment,*
> *24 A.B.A. J. 807 (1938)*

SECTION A. INTRODUCTION

The settlor of a trust cannot foresee all of the problems or opportunities that might arise in the future. Consequently, well-drafted trusts often contain *powers of appointment*, typically in the trust beneficiaries. A power of appointment gives the person who holds the power the ability to distribute the trust property. Thus, through a power of appointment, the settlor is able to *postpone* and *delegate* decisions about who should receive trust property. Powers of appointment allow the settlor to leave it to others in the future to deal flexibly with changing circumstances — with births, deaths, and marriages; with the ability of children to manage property; with changes in the economy and investment returns; and with changes in the law.

1. *Terminology and Types of Powers of Appointment*

To understand the law of powers of appointment, you must first learn the terminology and relationships. The person who creates the power of appointment is the *donor* of the power; the person who holds the power is the *donee*. The persons in whose favor the power may be exercised are the *objects* of the power (the objects are sometimes also called the *permissible appointees*). When a power is exercised in favor of someone, that person becomes an *appointee*. The persons who will eventually receive the property if the donee fails to exercise the power of appointment are called *takers in default of appointment* or, simply, *takers in default*. The property subject to the power is the *appointive property*. See Restatement (Third) of Property: Wills and Other Donative Transfers §17.2 (T.D. No. 5, 2006).

All powers can be divided into general powers and special powers. A *general power* is, in the language of the Internal Revenue Code, "a power which is exercisable in favor of the [donee], his estate, his creditors, or the creditors of his estate."[1] Under the federal estate and gift tax laws, any power that is not a general power is classified as a special power. Thus, a *special power* is a power not exercisable in favor of the donee, his estate, his creditors, or the creditors of his estate. Prevailing professional usage of these terms is in accord with their meanings under the tax code, though the terms *limited power* and *nongeneral power* have become increasingly common synonyms for *special power*.

Although it is sometimes said that the objects of a general power of appointment are necessarily broader than the objects of a special power, this is not true. Consider:

> *Case 1. T* devises property to *X* in trust to distribute the income and principal to such of the creditors of *A* as *A* shall appoint by deed. Because *A* can appoint to her creditors, *A* is the donee of a general power of appointment.
>
> *Case 2. T* devises property to *X* in trust to pay the income and principal to any person whom *A* appoints by deed or by will except that *A* may not appoint to herself, her estate, her creditors, or the creditors of her estate. Because *A* cannot appoint to herself, her creditors, her estate, or the creditors of her estate, *A* is the donee of a special power of appointment.

Case 1 involves a general power even though *A* can only appoint to her creditors. Case 2 involves a special power even though the objects of the power number in the billions.[2]

A general power of appointment may permit the donee to do most of the things that an owner of the fee simple could do. This is clearest in the case of a general power *presently exercisable*. Thus:

> *Case 3. T* devises property to *X* in trust to pay the income to *A* for life, or until such time as *A* appoints, and to distribute the principal to such person or persons as *A* shall appoint either by deed during *A*'s lifetime or by will. If *A* does not exercise the power of appointment, at *A*'s death *X* is to distribute the principal to *B. T* is the donor. *A* is the donee of a general power of appointment exercisable by deed or will. *B* is the taker in default of appointment.

---

1. Internal Revenue Code of 1986 §2041(b) (estate tax). The comparable definition under the federal gift tax is in §2514(c). The Code goes on to exclude from the definition of a general power a power to consume principal "limited by an ascertainable standard relating to the health, education, support, or maintenance" of the donee, a power held with an adverse party, and certain powers created prior to 1942. Id. §§2041(b)(1)(A)-(C) and 2514(c)(1)-(3).

2. The confusion reflects old law. Restatement (First) of Property §320 (1940) took the position that the objects of a special power could not constitute an "unreasonably large" number. That position is contrary to the definition of special power in the tax code, which has prevailed. See Restatement (Third) of Property: Wills and Other Donative Transfers §17.3, cmt. b (T.D. No. 5, 2006).

In Case 3, *A* is very close to being absolute owner of the property: the only thing that stands between *A* and absolute ownership is a piece of paper *A* can sign at any time. To acquire title, *A* has merely to write, "I hereby appoint to myself." Even though *A* can acquire absolute ownership at any time, however, *A* does not have ownership until the power is exercised in *A*'s favor. If *A* does not exercise the power, the property will pass to the taker in default, *B*, and not to *A*'s heirs. If the creating instrument does not name a taker in default, under traditional law the property reverts to the donor or the donor's estate if the power is not exercised.

The most common example of a special power is one that limits the objects to members of the donor's or donee's family. Thus:

> *Case 4. T* devises property to *X* in trust to pay the income to *A* for life, and on *A*'s death to distribute the principal to such one or more of *A*'s descendants as *A* shall appoint by will. If *A* does not exercise the power of appointment, at *A*'s death *X* is to distribute the principal to *A*'s then living descendants, such descendants to take per stirpes.

There is a profound difference between the general power presently exercisable in Case 3 and the special power in Case 4. In Case 4, *A* occupies a position similar to that of *T*'s agent. *A* can exercise the power to benefit *A*'s descendants, but *A* cannot appoint the property in such a way as to benefit *A* or *A*'s estate.[3]

Powers of appointment may be exercisable either by deed or by will as in Cases 2 and 3, by deed alone as in Case 1, or by will alone as in Case 4. When exercisable by will, the power is called a *testamentary* power; when exercisable during life, the power is called a *lifetime* (or *inter vivos*) power.

To be accurate, we should point out that a power of appointment may be created not only in a beneficiary, but also in any other person.[4] Under traditional law, therefore, a trustee who has discretion to pay income or principal to a beneficiary, or discretion to spray income among a group of beneficiaries, has a special power of appointment. However, Restatement (Third) of Property, supra, §17.1, cmt. g, and Restatement (Third) of Trusts §50, cmt. a (2003), reclassify such a power as "a fiduciary distributive power." Discretionary fiduciary powers in trustees are treated in Chapter 9.

In this chapter, we are primarily concerned with nonfiduciary powers of appointment held by beneficiaries of trusts.

---

3. The existence of the power can, however, benefit *A* by assuring filial devotion:

> It doubtless occurred to the testator that by restraining a disposition of his property except by will, which is in its nature revocable, [his widow] would, to the end of her life, retain the influence over, and secure the respect of, the several objects of his bounty, which he intended her to have — a result less likely to be accomplished if power were given her to dispose of the property by deed or other irrevocable act to take effect in her lifetime. [Hood v. Haden, 82 Va. 588, 591 (1886).]

4. The testator may not, however, create a power of appointment in the judge overseeing the probate of the testator's will. See In re Last Will and Testament of McSwain, 946 So. 2d 417 (Miss. App. 2006) (rejecting such a power on the grounds that a judge cannot be empowered to act arbitrarily).

2. The Relation-Back Doctrine: Does the Appointive Property Belong to the Donor or the Donee?

At common law, a power of appointment was viewed as merely empowering the donee to do an act *for* the donor. The appointee was deemed to receive the appointive property directly from the donor, not the donee. This is known as the *relation-back doctrine*. Though the doctrine still applies to special powers of appointment, it no longer is consistently applied to general powers of appointment.

The limits of the relation-back doctrine are perhaps most clearly brought into view by asking whether a creditor of the donee has any recourse against the appointive property. In the case of a special power of appointment, the rule is that a creditor of the donee cannot reach the appointive property. Restatement (Third) of Property: Wills and Other Donative Transfers §22.1 (T.D. No. 5, 2006). This rule is easily explained: Since the donee can reap no personal pecuniary benefit, neither can the donee's creditors.[5]

But what about a creditor of a donee of a presently exercisable general power? The difficulty, to borrow the words of the Restatement, is that even though the holder of such a power "is not the technical owner of the appointive property, the donee is in substance the owner." Id. at §17.4, cmt. f.

Irwin Union Bank & Trust Co. v. Long
Indiana Court of Appeals, 1974
312 N.E.2d 908

LOWDERMILK, J. On February 3, 1957, Victoria Long, appellee herein, obtained a judgment in the amount of $15,000 against Philip W. Long, which judgment emanated from a divorce decree. This action is the result of the filing by appellee of a petition in proceedings supplemental to execution on the prior judgment. Appellee sought satisfaction of that judgment by pursuing funds allegedly owed to Philip W. Long as a result of a trust set up by Laura Long, his mother.

Appellee alleged that the Irwin Union Bank and Trust Company (Union Bank) was indebted to Philip W. Long as the result of its position as trustee of the trust created by Laura Long. On April 24, 1969, the trial court ordered that any income, property, or profits, which were owed to Philip Long and not exempt from execution should be applied to the divorce judgment. Thereafter, on February 13, 1973, the trial court ordered that four percent (4%) of the trust corpus of the trust created by Laura Long which benefited Philip Long was not exempt from execution and could be levied upon by appellee and ordered a writ of execution. . . .

---

5. Judges have sometimes been known, however, to bend the rule when the creditor's circumstances are compelling. In In re Marriage of Chapman, 697 N.E.2d 365 (Ill. App. 1998), the life beneficiary of a trust had a special lifetime power to appoint trust principal to his descendants. The court held that the children of the donee who had a support order were able to reach the trust principal.

The pertinent portion of the trust created by Laura Long is as follows, to-wit:

ITEM V C

Withdrawal of Principal

When Philip W. Long, Jr. has attained the age of twenty-one (21) years and is not a full-time student at an educational institution as a candidate for a Bachelor of Arts or Bachelor of Sciences degree, Philip W. Long shall have the right to withdraw from principal once in any calendar year upon thirty (30) days written notice to the Trustee up to four percent (4%) of the market value of the entire trust principal on the date of such notice, which right shall not be cumulative.

The primary issue raised on this appeal is whether the trial court erred in allowing execution on the 4% of the trust corpus.

Appellant contends that Philip Long's right to withdraw 4% of the trust corpus is, in fact, a general power of appointment. Union Bank further contends that since Philip Long has never exercised his right of withdrawal, pursuant to the provisions of the trust instrument, no creditors of Philip Long can reach the trust corpus. Appellant points out that if the power of appointment is unexercised, the creditors cannot force the exercise of said power and cannot reach the trust corpus in this case. . . .

Appellee argues that Philip has absolute control and use of the 4% of the corpus and that the bank does not have control over that portion of the corpus if Philip decides to exercise his right of withdrawal. Appellee argues that the intention of Laura Long was to give Philip not only an income interest in the trust but a fixed amount of corpus which he could use as he saw fit. Thus, Philip Long would have a right to the present enjoyment of 4% of the trust corpus. A summation of appellee's argument, as stated in her brief, is as follows: "So it is with Philip — he can get it if he desires it, so why cannot Victoria get it even if Philip does not desire it?" . . .

The leading case on this issue is Gilman v. Bell, 99 Ill. 144, 150, 151 (1881), wherein the Illinois Supreme Court discussed powers of appointment and vesting as follows:

No title or interest in the thing vests in the donee of the power until he exercises the power. It is virtually an offer to him of the estate or fund, that he may receive or reject at will, and like any other offer to donate property to a person, no title can vest until he accepts the offer, nor can a court of equity compel him to accept the property or fund against his will, even for the benefit of creditors. If it should, it would be to convert the property of the person offering to make the donation to the payment of the debts of another person. Until accepted, the person to whom the offer is made has not, nor can he have, the slightest interest or title to the property. So the donee of the power only receives the naked power to make the property or fund his own. And when he exercises the power, he thereby consents to receive it, and the title thereby vests in him, although it may pass out of him *eo instanti*, to the appointee.

Contrary to the contention of appellee, it is our opinion that Philip Long has no control over the trust corpus until he exercises his power of appointment and gives notice to the trustee that he wishes to receive his 4% of the trust corpus.

Until such an exercise is made, the trustee has the absolute control and benefit of the trust corpus within the terms of the trust instrument. . . .

The trust as a whole is set up to give the grandchildren of Laura Long the substantial portion of the assets involved. We note with interest that the percentage of corpus which Philip Long may receive is carefully limited to a percentage less than that which would be includable in the gross estate of Philip Long should he die within a year in which he had allowed his power of appointment to lapse.[6] . . .

The trust created in the will of Laura Long, in our opinion, has the legal effect of creating a [general] power of appointment in Philip Long under Item V C of the trust.

Philip Long has never exercised his power of appointment under the trust. Such a situation is discussed in II Scott on Trusts, §147.3 as follows:

> Where the power is a special power, a power to appoint only among a group of persons, the power is not beneficial to the donee and cannot, of course, be reached by his creditors. Where the power is a general power, that is, a power to appoint to anyone including the donee himself or his estate, the power is beneficial to the donee. If the donee exercises the power by appointing to a volunteer, the property appointed can be reached by his creditors if his other assets are insufficient for the payment of his debts. But where the donee of a general power created by some person other than himself fails to exercise the power, his creditors cannot acquire the power or compel its exercise, nor can they reach the property covered by the power, unless it is otherwise provided by statute.

Indiana has no statute which would authorize a creditor to reach property covered by a power of appointment which is unexercised.

In Gilman v. Bell, supra, the court analyzed the situation where a general power of appointment was unexercised and discussed the position of creditors of the donee of the power as follows:

> But it is insisted, that, conceding it to be a mere naked power of appointment in favor of himself, in favor of creditors he should be compelled by a court of equity to so appoint, or be treated as the owner, and the property subjected to the payment of his debts. The doctrine has been long established in the English courts, that the courts of equity will not aid creditors in case there is a non-execution of the power.

Appellee concedes that if we find that Philip Long had merely an unexercised power of appointment then creditors are in no position to either force the exercise of the power or to reach the trust corpus. Thus, it is clear that the trial court erred . . . .

Reversed and remanded.

---

6. Philip Long had a general power of appointment over 4 percent of the trust corpus. At his death, that amount would be included in his gross estate because he could have appointed it to himself in the year of his death. I.R.C. §2041(a)(2). However, none of the trust corpus attributable to lapses of this power in prior years would be included in his gross estate because those lapses did not exceed the greater of $5,000 or 5 percent of the trust corpus (the so-called "five-or-five" rule). I.R.C. §2041(b)(2), discussed in Chapter 15. — Eds.

NOTES AND QUESTION

1. *Creditors of a donee of a general power.* The decision in *Long* is in accord with the traditional view that the donee of a general power has no property interest in the appointive property. As Lord Justice Fry said: "The power of a person to appoint an estate to himself is, in my judgment, no more his 'property' than the power to write a book or to sing a song." In re Armstrong, 17 Q.B.D. 521, 531 (1886). See also Restatement (Second) of Property: Donative Transfers §13.2 (1986).

But if the donee of a presently exercisable general power can reach the appointive property simply by appointing it to himself, one might reasonably ask, should not the donee's creditors be able to reach it? A growing number of legislatures apparently think so. By statute, many states "now treat property that is subject to a general power of appointment as belonging to the donee, even if the power has never been exercised," including "for purposes of allowing the donee's creditors to reach the trust property." 3 Austin Wakeman Scott, William Franklin Fratcher, and Mark L. Ascher, Scott and Ascher on Trusts §14.11.3, at 889-890 (5th ed. 2007).

The common law has moved in the same direction. Under the modern view, which is adopted by Restatement (Third) of Property: Wills and Other Donative Transfers §22.3 (T.D. No. 5, 2006), Uniform Trust Code (UTC) §505(b)(1) (2000), and Restatement (Third) of Trusts §56, cmt. b (2003), a creditor of the donee of a *presently exercisable* general power of appointment is permitted to reach the appointive property, albeit sometimes with the qualification that the creditor must first exhaust the donee's own property. Some states that follow the modern view, and the Restatements (Third) of Property and Trusts (but not the UTC, which is deliberately silent), also allow the donee's creditors to reach the appointive property of a *testamentary* general power of appointment, but only at the donee's death.

For further discussion, see Ira Mark Bloom, Powers of Appointment under the Restatement (Third) of Property, 33 Ohio N.U. L. Rev. 755, 779-790 (2007).

2. *Federal tax and bankruptcy law.* The states that follow the modern view have brought their law of creditor rights to appointive property into alignment with the federal tax and bankruptcy laws. Property subject to a general power of appointment is treated as belonging to the donee for federal estate and gift tax purposes. Likewise, under federal bankruptcy law, a general power presently exercisable passes to the donee's trustee in bankruptcy. 11 U.S.C. §541(b)(1) (2008).

3. *Self-settled general power.* If the donee of a general power is also the donor of the power, the donor-donee's creditors may reach the appointive assets. See Restatement (Third) of Property, supra, §22.2; Scott and Ascher on Trusts, supra, §15.4.1. This principle fits neatly with the traditional rules respecting creditor rights in self-settled trusts (see page 624).

4. *Surviving spouse of the donee.* The traditional view is that the donee's surviving spouse has an elective share against only the donee's *probate* estate, and because appointive property is not part of the donee's probate estate, the donee's

surviving spouse cannot reach it. Further, even though most states have extended the elective share to reach quite a few nonprobate transfers, in many states appointive property is still not available to the surviving spouse. See Bongaards v. Millen, page 492. However, Uniform Probate Code §2-205(1)(A) (1990, rev. 2008) changes this rule with respect to any property over which the decedent had a lifetime general power of appointment. New York Est. Powers & Trusts Law §5-1.1-A(b)(1)(H) (2008), and statutes in a handful of other states, are to the same effect, as is Restatement (Third) of Property, supra, §23.1. See generally Margaret M. Mahoney, Elective Share Statutes: The Right to Elect Against Property Subject to a General Power of Appointment in the Decedent, 55 Notre Dame L. Rev. 99 (1979).

3.   Tax Considerations for Powers of Appointment

The holder of a *general power of appointment* is treated as the owner of the appointive property for tax purposes. The income from the appointive property is taxable to the donee (Internal Revenue Code of 1986 (I.R.C.) §678), and if the donee exercises the power during life, the resulting transfer of the appointive property is subject to gift taxation as if the donee had personally made a gift of that property (I.R.C. §2514). If the donee dies without exercising the power while alive, the appointive property is subject to estate taxation whether or not the donee exercises the power by will. I.R.C. §2041. On the other hand, property subject to a *special power of appointment* is *not* treated as owned by the donee for tax purposes. Whether the donor will prefer the tax consequences of a general or special power depends on the circumstances.

Estate tax advantages of special powers. By carefully tailoring a special power of appointment, the donor can give the donee the functional equivalent of ownership of the appointive property without causing the donee to be treated as owner for federal tax purposes.

Suppose that *T* wants to devise property to her daughter, *A*, but *T* does not want *A* to be treated as owner of the property for estate tax purposes when *A* dies. Although *T* cannot escape taxation at *T*'s own death, taxation can be avoided on *A*'s eventual death. To that end, *T* might structure the devise as follows:

(1)   *T*'s will transfers the legal title to the property to *A* as trustee. *As trustee, A* can manage the property, deciding when to sell and in what to reinvest. If the trustee's powers are broadly drafted, *A* can manage the property almost as if she owned it herself.

(2)   *T*'s will gives to *A*, not as trustee but *as a beneficiary*:
    (a) the right to receive all the income;
    (b) a special power of appointment exercisable by deed or will to appoint the trust property to anyone *A* desires except herself, her creditors, her estate, or the creditors of her estate;

      (c) a power to consume the trust property as needed to maintain the standard of living to which *A* is accustomed;[7] and

      (d) a power to withdraw each year $5,000 or 5 percent of the corpus, whichever is greater, whether or not *A* needs it.[8]

(3)   If *T* wants to provide for the possibility of distributions that would *increase* *A*'s accustomed standard of living, *T* could also give someone else — a trusted friend, perhaps — an unlimited power to appoint trust property to *A* at any time and for any reason.

None of the above powers given to *A*, individually or collectively, causes *A* to be treated as the owner of the trust property for purposes of the federal estate tax. Yet these powers give *A* almost as much control over the trust fund as she would have had if she had received the property outright.

Generation-skipping transfer tax advantages of special powers. In 1986, Congress enacted a generation-skipping transfer (GST) tax to deal with estate tax avoidance like that described above. I.R.C. §§2601-2663, discussed in Chapter 15. Under current law, a GST tax is imposed on the death of a life tenant of a younger generation than the settlor's (on *A*'s death in the above example). However, careful use of the GST tax exemption ($3.5 million in 2009) makes it possible to use planning arrangements such as those described above without incurring a GST tax. The exemption makes possible the use of a *dynasty trust*, which is exempt from estate and GST taxes for the duration of the trust (beginning with *A*'s generation and continuing until the trust terminates). In the above example, in 2009 *T* could create a trust of $3.5 million for her daughter *A* and *A*'s descendants, giving special powers to each generation with the trust to endure for as long as is legally possible in the jurisdiction. In a state that has abolished the Rule Against Perpetuities, such a trust can endure forever, a subject we take up in Chapter 14. If *T* is married, she and her husband (using his $3.5 million exemption) can transfer a total of $7 million in such a transfer-tax-exempt dynasty trust.

7. In general, property subject to a general power of appointment is included in the donee's federal gross estate at death and thus is subject to estate taxation. And if a power to consume permits the donee to appoint the property to herself during life, then it is a general power of appointment. However, I.R.C. §2041(b)(1)(A) creates an important exception to this rule: "A power to consume, invade, or appropriate property for the benefit of the decedent which is limited by an ascertainable standard relating to the health, education, support, or maintenance of the decedent shall not be deemed a general power of appointment." Accordingly, the tax question respecting each power to consume is this: Is the power at hand limited by an ascertainable standard relating to the health, education, support, or maintenance of the decedent? If it is not so limited, the property subject to the power is included in the donee's gross estate. The lawyer drafting a power to consume should carefully track the words of §2041(b)(1)(A) or the regulations. Consider that a power to consume for the donee's "comfort, welfare, or happiness" is not limited by the requisite standard, but a power to consume "to maintain the standard of living to which the donee is accustomed" is limited by the requisite standard. See Estate of Vissering v. Commissioner, page 969, citing numerous cases involving this question.

8. Under a "five-or-five" power, the type of power involved in Irwin Union Bank & Trust Co. v. Long, page 806, $5,000 or 5 percent of the corpus (whichever is greater) will be included in the estate of the donee to the extent the power is not exercised in the year of the donee's death. I.R.C. §2041(b)(2), discussed in Chapter 15. This is a small price to pay for the flexibility gained by granting the power.

Tax reasons to use a general power of appointment. There are times when the settlor will prefer the tax treatment of a general, rather than special, power of appointment. For example:

> *Case 5.* H devises property to X in trust to pay the income to W and, on W's death, to distribute the principal to such person or persons as W by her will appoints, including to W's estate or the creditors of W's estate. H's devise qualifies for the *marital deduction*; no federal estate taxes are payable on the property at H's death. However, since W has a general power, the property is subject to estate taxation on W's death. In effect, the marital deduction permits taxation to be postponed until the death of the surviving spouse.

Settlors sometimes also use general powers of appointment to qualify for the $13,000 annual exclusion from gift taxation. I.R.C. §2503(b). Such planning is discussed in Chapter 15.

SECTION B.   CREATION OF A POWER OF APPOINTMENT

To create a power of appointment, the donor must manifest an intent to do so, either expressly or by implication. It is not necessary that the words "power of appointment" or "appoint" be used. A power of appointment confers *discretion* on the donee, who may choose to exercise the power or not, and is to be distinguished from a direct nondiscretionary disposition by the donor. Thus:

> *Case 6.* Aunt Fanny executes a will in 2009 giving her tangible personal property "to my niece Wendy Brown, to dispose of in accordance with a letter addressed to Wendy dated January 4, 2008, which is in my safe-deposit box, and which I incorporate by reference herein." Aunt Fanny has incorporated the letter by reference and the tangible personal property must be distributed in accordance therewith. Wendy is a trustee who has a fiduciary duty to follow Aunt Fanny's instruction; Wendy does not have a power of appointment.

Words that merely express a wish or desire are *precatory*. They do not create a power of appointment in the absence of other circumstances indicating a contrary intent. If in Case 6 Aunt Fanny had left her tangible personal property to Wendy "with the request but not the legal obligation that she give some of the property to my other relatives," Wendy would take the property free of trust. The precatory words would create neither a trust nor a power of appointment.

For further discussion and helpful illustrations, see Restatement (Third) of Property: Wills and Other Donative Transfers §18.1 (T.D. No. 5, 2006).

SECTION C.   EXERCISE OF A POWER OF APPOINTMENT

1. *Introduction*

Restatement (Third) of Property: Wills and Other Donative Transfers
(T.D. No. 5, 2006)

§19.1 GENERAL REQUISITES FOR EXERCISE OF A POWER OF APPOINTMENT

A power of appointment is exercised to the extent that:

(1) the donee manifests an intent to exercise the power in an otherwise effective document;

(2) the donee's expression of an intent to appoint satisfies the formal requirements of exercise imposed by the donor and by applicable law; and

(3) the donee's appointment constitutes a permissible exercise of the power.

§19.2 DETERMINING THE DONEE'S INTENT TO EXERCISE

Whether or not the donee has manifested an intent to exercise a power of appointment is a question of construction.

COMMENT:

b. Capable drafting. Capable drafting will leave no doubt regarding the donee's intent to appoint or not to appoint. Ideally, the donee or the donee's drafting agent will have the instrument creating the power at hand, and will formulate the language intended to express the donee's intent in light of the creating instrument.

A recurring theme in this book is that wasteful litigation often finds its genesis in poor drafting. Sadly, the question of whether the donee of a power of appointment intended to exercise the power is no exception. In reviewing the materials that follow, consider how the lawyer could have avoided the need for subsequent litigation by drafting a clearer governing instrument.

2. *Exercise by Residuary Clause in Donee's Will*

Beals v. State Street Bank & Trust Co.
Supreme Judicial Court of Massachusetts, 1975
326 N.E.2d 896

WILKINS, J.   The trustees under the will of Arthur Hunnewell filed this petition for instructions, seeking a determination of the proper distribution to be made of a portion of the trust created under the residuary clause of his will. A judge of the Probate Court reserved decision and reported the case to the Appeals Court on the pleadings and a stipulation of facts. We transferred the case here.

Arthur Hunnewell died, a resident of Wellesley,[9] in 1904, leaving his wife and four daughters. His will placed the residue of his property in a trust, the income of which was to be paid to his wife during her life. At the death of his wife the trust was to be divided in portions, one for each then surviving daughter and one for the then surviving issue of any deceased daughter. Mrs. Hunnewell died in 1930. One of the four daughters predeceased her mother, leaving no issue. The trust was divided, therefore, in three portions at the death of Mrs. Hunnewell. The will directed that the income of each portion held for a surviving daughter should be paid to her during her life and on her death the principal of such portion should "be paid and disposed of as she may direct and appoint by her last Will and Testament duly probated." In default of appointment, the will directed that a daughter's share should be distributed to "the persons who would be entitled to such estate under the laws then governing the distribution of intestate estates."

This petition concerns the distribution of the trust portion held for the testator's daughter Isabella H. Hunnewell, later Isabella H. Dexter (Isabella). Following the death of her mother, Isabella requested the trustees to exercise their discretionary power to make principal payments by transferring substantially all of her trust share "to the Dexter family office in Boston, there to be managed in the first instance by her husband, Mr. Gordon Dexter." This request was granted, and cash and securities were transferred to her account at the Dexter office. The Hunnewell trustees, however, retained in Isabella's share a relatively small cash balance, an undivided one-third interest in a mortgage and undivided one-third interest in various parcels of real estate in the Commonwealth, which Isabella did not want in kind and which the trustees could not sell at a reasonable price at the time. Thereafter, the trustees received payments on the mortgage and proceeds from occasional sales of portions of the real estate. From her one-third share of these receipts, the trustees made further distributions to her of $1,900 in 1937, $22,000 in 1952, and $5,000 in 1953.

In February, 1944, Isabella, who was then a resident of New York, executed and caused to be filed in the Registry of Probate for Norfolk County an instrument which partially released her general power of appointment under the will of her father. Isabella released her power of appointment "to the extent that such power empowers me to appoint to any one other than one or more of the . . . descendants [surviving me] of Arthur Hunnewell."[10]

---

9. The town of Wellesley, and the college, are named after Isabella Welles Hunnewell, Arthur's mother. — Eds.

10. Isabella did this to avoid federal estate taxes. In 1942 the Internal Revenue Code was changed to provide that property subject to a general power created before 1942 was includible in the donee's federal taxable estate if the power was exercised. However, Congress permitted powers created before 1942 to be released partially (converting them into special powers) without adverse tax consequences, if the conversion took place before 1951. Thus, by this partial release Isabella kept limited control over the property and avoided estate taxes. — Eds.

On December 14, 1968, Isabella, who survived her husband, died without issue, still a resident of New York, leaving a will dated May 21, 1965.[11] Her share in the trust under her father's will then consisted of an interest in a contract to sell real estate, cash, notes and a certificate of deposit, and was valued at approximately $88,000. Isabella did not expressly exercise her power of appointment under her father's will. The residuary clause of her will provided in effect for the distribution of all "the rest, residue and remainder of my property" to the issue per stirpes of her sister Margaret Blake, who had predeceased Isabella.[12] The Blake issue would take one-half of Isabella's trust share, as takers in default of appointment, in all events. If, however, Isabella's will should be treated as effectively exercising her power of appointment under her father's will, the Blake issue would take the entire trust share, and the executors of the will of Isabella's sister Jane (who survived Isabella and has since died) would not receive that one-half of the trust share which would go to Jane in default of appointment.

In support of their argument that Isabella's will did not exercise the power of appointment under her father's will, the executors of Jane's estate contend that (1) Massachusetts substantive law governs all questions relating to the power of appointment, including the interpretation of Isabella's will; (2) the power should be treated as a special power of appointment because of its partial release by Isabella; and (3) because Isabella's will neither expresses nor implies any intention to exercise the power, the applicable rule of construction in this Commonwealth is that a general residuary clause does not exercise a special power of appointment. The Blake issue, in support of their argument that the power was exercised, contend that (1) Isabella's will manifests an intention to exercise the power and

---

11. N.Y. Times, Sept. 28, 1894, at 5:

HARRIMAN — HUNNEWELL

BOSTON, Mass., Sept. 27. — The beautiful country seat of Mr. and Mrs. Arthur Hunnewell, at Wellesley, was a scene of joy and festivity yesterday, when their daughter, Miss Isabella, was married to Herbert M. Harriman of New-York. The ceremony was performed by the Rev. Leighton Parks, pastor of the Emanuel Church. There were no bridesmaids. The groom's brother, Joseph, was best man.

The ushers were Lawrence Kip of New-York, Belmont Tiffany of New-York, Edgar Scott of Philadelphia, Columbus Baldwin of New-York, Gordon Dexter, and W. S. Patten. Of the bridegroom's kinsfolk there were present: His mother, Mr. and Mrs. Border Harriman, and Mr. and Mrs. Oliver Harriman.

The wedding breakfast was spread beneath the grand old trees which dot the lawn before the mansion. At the expiration of a short wedding trip Mr. and Mrs. Harriman will reside in New-York.

Isabella Hunnewell and Herbert Harriman were divorced twelve years later. Isabella married twice more. Her second marriage, to J. Searlo Barclay, ended in divorce. Her third marriage was to Gordon Dexter, "a Boston businessman, clubman and yachtsman" who evidently had been an usher at her first wedding. Isabella survived Gordon, living to the age of 97. N.Y. Times, Dec. 16, 1968, at 47. — Eds.

12. The significant portion of the residuary clause reads as follows:

All the rest, residue and remainder of my property of whatever kind and wherever situated (including any property not effectively disposed of by the preceding provisions of this my will and all property over which I have or may have the power of appointment under or by virtue of the last will and testament dated November 27, 1933 and codicils thereto dated January 7, 1935 and January 8, 1935 of my husband, the late Gordon Dexter) . . . I give, devise, bequeath and appoint in equal shares to such of my said nephew GEORGE BATY BLAKE and my said nieces MARGARET CABOT and JULIA O. BEALS as shall survive me and the issue who shall survive me of any of my said nephew or nieces who may predecease me, such issue to take per stirpes.

that no rule of construction need be applied; (2) the law of New York should govern the question whether Isabella's will exercised the power and, if it does, by statute New York has adopted a rule that a special power of appointment is exercised by a testamentary disposition of all of the donee's property; and (3) if Massachusetts law does apply, and the will is silent on the subject of the exercise of the power, the principles underlying our rule of construction that a residuary clause exercises a general power of appointment are applicable in these circumstances.

1. We turn first to a consideration of the question whether Isabella's will should be construed according to the law of this Commonwealth or the law of New York.[13] There are strong, logical reasons for turning to the law of the donee's domicil at the time of death to determine whether a donee's will has exercised a testamentary power of appointment over movables. Most courts in this country which have considered the question, however, interpret the donee's will under the law governing the administration of the trust, which is usually the law of the donor's domicil. . . . This has long been the rule in Massachusetts.[14]

If the question were before us now for the first time, we might well adopt a choice of law rule which would turn to the substantive law of the donee's domicil, for the purpose of determining whether the donee's will exercised a power of appointment. However, in a field where much depends on certainty and consistency as to the applicable rules of law, we think that we should adhere to our well established rule. Thus, in interpreting the will of a donee to determine whether a power of appointment was exercised, we apply the substantive law of the jurisdiction whose law governs the administration of the trust.

2. Considering the arguments of the parties, we conclude that there is no indication in Isabella's will of an intention to exercise or not to exercise the power of appointment given to her under her father's will. A detailed analysis of the various competing contentions would not add to our jurisprudence.[15] In the absence of an intention disclosed by her will construed in light of circumstances known to her when she executed it, we must adopt some Massachusetts rule of construction to resolve the issue before us. The question is what rule of construction. We are

---

13. The applicable rules of construction where a donee's intention is not clear from his will differ between the two States. In the absence of a requirement by the donor that the donee refer to the power in order to exercise it, New York provides by statute that a residuary clause in a will exercises not only a general power of appointment but also a special power of appointment, unless the will expressly or by necessary implication shows the contrary. 17B McKinney's Consol. Laws of N.Y. Anno., E.P.T.L., c. 17-b, §10-6.1 (1967). See Matter of Hopkins, 259 N.Y.S.2d 565 (Surr. Ct. 1964). "Necessary implication" exists only where the will permits no other construction. Matter of Deane, 151 N.E.2d 184 (N.Y. 1958). In Massachusetts, unless the donor has provided that the donee of the power can exercise it only by explicit reference to the power, a general residuary clause in a will exercises a general power of appointment unless there is a clear indication of a contrary intent. . . . However, in Fiduciary Trust Co. v. First Natl. Bank, 181 N.E.2d 6 (Mass. 1962), we held that a general residuary clause did not exercise a special testamentary power of appointment in the circumstances of that case.

14. Of course, the law of the donee's domicil would be applied if the donor expressed such an intention. . . .

15. Isabella's residuary clause disposed of her "property." Because the trustees had agreed to distribute her trust portion to her and had largely done so and because, in a sense, she had exercised dominion over the trust assets by executing the partial release, a reasonable argument might be made that she regarded the assets in her portion of the trust as her "property." However, a conclusion that she intended by implication to include assets over which she had a special power of appointment within the word "property" is not justifiable because her residuary clause refers expressly to other property over which she had a special power of appointment under the will of her husband.

unaware of any decided case which, in this context, has dealt with a testamentary general power, reduced to a special power by action of the donee.

3. We conclude that the residuary clause of Isabella's will should be presumed to have exercised the power of appointment. We reach this result by a consideration of the reasons underlying the canons of construction applicable to general and special testamentary powers of appointment. Considered in this way, we believe that a presumption of exercise is more appropriate in the circumstances of this case than a presumption of nonexercise.

When this court first decided not to extend to a special power of appointment the rule of construction that a general residuary clause executes a general testamentary power (unless a contrary intent is shown by the will), we noted significant distinctions between a general power and a special power. Fiduciary Trust Co. v. First Natl. Bank, 181 N.E.2d 6 (Mass. 1962). A general power was said to be a close approximation to a property interest, a "virtually unlimited power of disposition," while a special power of appointment lacked this quality. We observed that a layman having a general testamentary power over property might not be expected to distinguish between the appointive property and that which he owns outright, and thus "he can reasonably be presumed to regard this appointive property as his own." On the other hand, the donee of a special power would not reasonably regard such appointive property as his own: "[h]e would more likely consider himself to be, as the donor of the power intended, merely the person chosen by the donor to decide who of the possible appointees should share in the property (if the power is exclusive), and the respective shares of the appointees."

Considering the power of appointment given to Isabella and her treatment of that power during her life, the rationale for the canon of construction applicable to general powers of appointment should be applied in this case. This power was a general testamentary power at its inception. During her life, as a result of her request, Isabella had the use and enjoyment of the major portion of the property initially placed in her trust share. Prior use and enjoyment of the appointive property is a factor properly considered as weighing in favor of the exercise of a power of appointment by a will. Fiduciary Trust Co. v. First Natl. Bank, supra. Isabella voluntarily limited the power by selecting the possible appointees. In thus relinquishing the right to add the trust assets to her estate, she was treating the property as her own. Moreover, the gift under her residuary clause was consistent with the terms of the reduced power which she retained. In these circumstances, the partial release of a general power does not obviate the application of that rule of construction which presumes that a general residuary clause exercises a general power of appointment.

4. A decree shall be entered determining that Isabella H. Dexter did exercise the power of appointment, partially released by an instrument dated February 25, 1944, given to her by art. Fourth of the will of Arthur Hunnewell and directing that the trustees under the will of Arthur Hunnewell pay over the portion of the trust held under art. Fourth of his will for the benefit of Isabella H. Dexter, as follows: one-third each to George Baty Blake and Julia O. Beals; and one-sixth

each to Margaret B. Elwell and to the estate of George B. Cabot. The parties shall be allowed their costs and counsel fees in the discretion of the probate court.

So ordered.

NOTES AND PROBLEM

1. *Choice of law.* When the appointive asset is land, the choice of law for interpreting a power of appointment is straightforward: The law of the jurisdiction where the land is located governs. But when the appointive property is not land and the donor and donee live in different jurisdictions, the choice of law is more complex. In *Beals,* despite the "strong, logical reasons" for applying the law of the donee's domicile in determining whether the donee properly exercised a testamentary power of appointment, the court instead followed the traditional view and looked to the law of the donor's domicile.

There is respectable authority, however, that takes the opposite view. In White v. United States, 680 F.2d 1156 (7th Cir. 1982), the court held that the law of the donee's domicile governs issues concerning the donee's intention to exercise a power of appointment by will. The court said: "We recognize the special need for certainty and consistency in laws affecting trusts [citing *Beals*], but fail to see how that end is promoted by perpetuation of a legal fiction that confuses lawyers and laymen alike." See also Toledo Trust Co. v. Santa Barbara Foundation, 512 N.E.2d 664 (Ohio 1987); Estate of McMullin, 417 A.2d 152 (Pa. 1980).

Restatement (Third) of Property: Wills and Other Donative Transfers §19.1, cmt. e (T.D. No. 5, 2006), sides with the minority: "In the absence of a provision in the instrument creating the power, the law of the donee's domicile governs whether the donee has effectively exercised a power of appointment." See also Restatement (Second) of Conflict of Laws §275 (1971), to similar effect.

The lawyer drafting the document should consider whether it is wise to avoid possible conflict of laws problems by specifying that the law of a particular state is to control in resolving any legal controversy. If an inter vivos trust includes a power of appointment, the donor might logically choose to select the law of the domicile of the donor or the donee or of the state where the trust is administered. If the power is created by a testamentary trust, the states are split. Some states permit the donor's intention to control. Other states apply the law of the donor's domicile.

For a meticulous examination of choice of law issues regarding powers of appointment, see 1 Jeffrey A. Schoenblum, Multistate and Multinational Estate Planning §17.08 (25th ann. ed. 2008).

2. *Residuary clauses and testamentary powers of appointment.* Should a residuary clause presumptively exercise a general or special power of appointment? The large majority of jurisdictions takes the position that a residuary clause does *not* presumptively exercise a power of appointment held by the testator. States adhering to the majority rule differ on whether contrary intent may be shown

only by reference to the face of the will or whether extrinsic evidence may also be examined.

Restatement (Third) of Property, supra, §19.4, presumes that a residuary clause does not exercise a power "*unless* the power in question is a general power and the donor did not provide for takers in default or the gift-in-default clause is ineffective" (emphasis added). The drafters reasoned that the donor normally expects the gift-in-default clause to control in the absence of "clear evidence of [the donee's] intent to appoint." But if the donor did not provide for takers in default or the gift-in-default clause is ineffective, then it "seems more in accord with the donor's probable intent for the donee's residuary clause to be treated as exercising the power." Id., cmt. a. The same reasoning underpins the similar rule stated in UPC §2-608 (1990), which is excerpted below.

In a minority of jurisdictions, a residuary clause exercises a general power of appointment unless a contrary intent affirmatively appears. In a few jurisdictions — New York is the leading example — a residuary clause exercises a special power of appointment if the residuary devisees are objects of the power. See Will of Block, 598 N.Y.S.2d 668 (Surr. 1993).

At the time of the *Beals* case, Massachusetts adhered to the minority rule, but, in 1978, its legislature adopted the majority rule. See Mass. Gen. Laws Ann. ch. 191, §1A(4) (2008).

For further discussion, see Susan F. French, Exercise of Powers of Appointment: Should Intent to Exercise Be Inferred from a General Disposition of Property?, 1979 Duke L.J. 749; Sheldon F. Kurtz, Powers of Appointment Under the 1990 Uniform Probate Code: What Was Done — What Remains to Be Done, 55 Alb. L. Rev. 1151, 1162-1172 (1992).

3. *H* devises property to *X* in trust to pay *W* all the income for life and then, on *W*'s death, to pay the remainder to such person or persons as *W* names by will or, in default of appointment, to Grandson and Granddaughter. *W* executes a will appointing the trust property to Daughter. *W* dies, but her will is not offered for probate within the state's limitations period for the probate of a will. *X* petitions the court for instructions on whether to pay the remainder to Daughter or to Grandson and Granddaughter. What result? See Lumbard v. Farmers State Bank, 812 N.E.2d 196 (Ind. App. 2004). Suppose that, instead of a will, *W* attempted to appoint the corpus to Daughter in a revocable trust that became irrevocable on *W*'s death. What result? See Restatement (Third) of Property, supra, §19.9, cmt. b.

Uniform Probate Code (1990)

§2-608. EXERCISE OF POWER OF APPOINTMENT

In the absence of a requirement that a power of appointment be exercised by a reference, or by an express or specific reference, to the power, a general residuary clause in a will, or a will making general disposition of all of the testator's property, expresses an intention to exercise a power of appointment held by the testator only if (i) the power is a general power and the creating instrument does not contain a gift if the power is not exercised or (ii) the testator's will manifests an intention to include the property subject to the power.

§2-704.   POWER OF APPOINTMENT; MEANING OF SPECIFIC REFERENCE REQUIREMENT

If a governing instrument creating a power of appointment expressly requires that the power be exercised by a reference, an express reference, or a specific reference, to the power or its source, it is presumed that the donor's intention, in requiring that the donee exercise the power by making reference to the particular power or to the creating instrument, was to prevent an inadvertent exercise of the power.

NOTES, QUESTION, AND PROBLEM

1.   *Specific reference requirement.* To prevent an unintentional exercise of a power of appointment, the donor will sometimes provide that the power can be exercised only by an instrument, executed after the date of the creating instrument, that refers specifically to the power. Courts have supported this practice by strictly requiring a "specific reference" to the creating document. Thus, where a wife was given a power of appointment by her husband's will executed in 1982, and her 1967 will specifically exercised a power given to her in a similar will executed by her husband in 1966, since revoked, the court held that the wife had not exercised the power created by her husband's 1982 will. Estate of Hamilton, 593 N.Y.S.2d 372 (App. Div. 1993). See also Smith v. Brannan, 954 P.2d 1259 (Or. App. 1998) (reaching the same result on similar facts).

Would the wills in *Hamilton* and *Smith* today be good candidates for reformation under Erickson v. Erickson, page 345; Restatement (Third) of Property: Wills and Other Donative Transfers §12.1 (2003), discussed at page 351; and Uniform Probate Code §2-805 (2008), page 351?

Another argument for saving the donee's exercise could be based on Restatement (Third) of Property: Wills and Other Donative Transfers §19.10 (T.D. No. 5, 2006), which recognizes substantial compliance with the donor's requirements of exercise, "including a requirement that the instrument of exercise make reference or specific reference to the power." The courts in both *Hamilton* and *Smith*, however, expressly rejected the argument that the equitable principle of approximation, on which the Restatement's substantial compliance rule is based, could save the ineffective exercise.

2.   *Blanket-exercise clause.* Suppose that the donee's residuary clause gives all her property "and all property over which I have a power of appointment" to *A*. Does this exercise the power under a specific reference requirement? In Estate of Shenkman, 737 N.Y.S.2d 39 (App. Div. 2002), the court held that a

blanket-exercise clause was ineffective to exercise a power that required a specific reference. See also Schwartz v. Baybank Merrimack Valley, N.A., Trustee, 456 N.E.2d 1141 (Mass. App. 1983) (collecting authority).

In the usual case, the same result would obtain under UPC §2-704. The official comment explains: "Under this section, mere use by the donee of a blanket-exercise clause would be ineffective to exercise the power because such a clause would not make a sufficient reference to the particular power." However, if it could be shown by extrinsic evidence that the donee intended to exercise the power by the blanket-exercise clause, the power would be exercised. See also Restatement (Third) of Property, supra, §19.10, cmt. d.

NOTE: LAPSE—APPOINTEE DIES BEFORE DONEE DIES

In the *Beals* case, the court held that the donee, Isabella, exercised her power in favor of the descendants of her sister, Margaret Blake, who had predeceased Isabella. Suppose that Isabella's will had been executed during Margaret's lifetime, and Isabella had exercised the power by appointing to Margaret. If Margaret had predeceased Isabella, would Margaret's descendants take the appointive property under the antilapse statute? In a handful of states, such as California and those that have adopted UPC §2-603 (1990, rev. 2008), the antilapse statute expressly applies to the exercise of a power of appointment. Under such a statute, Margaret's descendants would take in her place.

But what would be the result in a state in which the antilapse statute does not expressly apply to a power of appointment? Under the leading case of Thompson v. Pew, 102 N.E. 122 (Mass. 1913), the antilapse statute would apply. See also Restatement (Third) of Property: Wills and Other Donative Transfers §19.12 (T.D. No. 5, 2006). For a deep and meticulous analysis, see Susan F. French, Application of Antilapse Statutes to Appointments Made by Will, 53 Wash. L. Rev. 405, 417-428 (1978).

Suppose that Isabella had a special power to appoint among her nephews and nieces and that she exercised the power by appointing to the descendants of a niece who had predeceased her. What result? Since Isabella could have appointed to the niece, with the descendants of the niece taking the appointive property under the antilapse statute, why not permit Isabella to appoint directly to the descendants? Restatement (Third) of Property, supra, §19.12 provides that takers substituted by an antilapse statute are regarded as objects of the power. See also French, supra, at 428-431.

Suppose that Isabella had a general testamentary power created by her husband's will and had appointed to her husband's nephew, who predeceased Isabella, leaving descendants. Would the descendants of the deceased nephew take under the antilapse statute? Under Restatement (Third) of Property, supra, §19.12, the antilapse statute applies "as if the appointed property were owned by either the donor or the donee." See also French, supra, at 417-421.

3. Limitations on the Exercise of a Power of Appointment

Appointment in further trust and creation of new powers of appointment. In almost all jurisdictions, a donee of a *general* power of appointment can appoint outright or in further trust and can create new powers of appointment. Because the donee of a general power could first appoint to herself or to her estate and then, by a second instrument or a second clause in her will appoint in further trust, it would make little sense to forbid the donee to appoint in further trust when she uses only a single instrument or a single clause in her will. See 1 Austin Wakeman Scott, William Franklin Fratcher, and Mark L. Ascher, Scott and Ascher on Trusts §3.1.2, at 142-143 (5th ed. 2006); Restatement (Third) of Property: Wills and Other Donative Transfers §19.13 (T.D. No. 5, 2006).

Traditionally, the donee of a *special* power has not been allowed to appoint in further trust, unless the governing instrument expressly permits appointment in trust for the benefit of the objects of the power. The modern and better view is that the donee of a special power can indeed appoint in further trust. See In re Chervitz Trust, 198 S.W. 3d 658 (Mo. App. 2006); Estate of Reisman, 702 N.W. 2d 658 (Mich. App. 2005). This approach is endorsed by Scott and Ascher on Trusts, supra, at 144-145, and Restatement (Third) of Property, supra, §19.14.

A similar analysis pertains to the question whether the donee of a special power can create a new power of appointment. Suppose T gives a power to A to appoint among A's descendants. Can A exercise the power by creating in his daughter B a life estate plus a special power to appoint among B's descendants (who are, of course, objects of the original power)? Because A could appoint outright to B, it seems sensible to permit A to appoint to B something less than absolute ownership. Yet some cases hold that the creation of a new power is an impermissible delegation of the special power. See 5 American Law of Property §23.49 (1952).

Restatement (Third) of Property, supra, §19.14, cmt. e takes the position that the donee of a special power can create a general power in an object of the special power or create a special power in any person to appoint to an object of the original special power. The latter situation includes an appointment in further trust, giving the trustee discretionary power to appoint to the objects.

Exclusive versus nonexclusive powers. A special power may be exclusive or nonexclusive. If it is *exclusive*, the donee can appoint all the property to one or more members of the class of permissible appointees, excluding other objects. If the power is *nonexclusive*, the donee must appoint some amount to each object.

Whether a power is exclusive or nonexclusive depends upon the intention of the donor as revealed by the governing instrument. Language such as "to any one or more" or "to such of" is usually held to create an exclusive power; language such as "to all and every one" or "to each and every one" is usually held to create a nonexclusive power. Thus:

> *Case 7.* T bequeaths a fund to X in trust for A for life, remainder as A shall appoint by will "to each and every one" of A's children. A has three children, B, C, and D. The power is nonexclusive, so A must give some amount each to B, C, and D if A exercises the power.

Case 8. *T* bequeaths a fund to *X* in trust for *A* for life, remainder as *A* shall appoint by will "to any one or more" of *A*'s children. *A* has three children, *B*, *C*, and *D*. The power is exclusive, so *A* can appoint all the property to *C*.

In Hargrove v. Rich, 604 S.E.2d 475 (Ga. 2004), the court held that the use of the conjunction "and" in a power to appoint to the donee's "brothers or sisters or her nieces and nephews, or descendants of deceased nieces and nephews," created a nonexclusive power that prohibited appointment "in favor of one niece to the exclusion of other nieces and nephews."

If the donor's intent cannot be determined, the outcome will turn upon the presumption adhered to in the jurisdiction. Restatement (Third) of Property, supra, §17.5, takes the sensible position that a power of appointment is presumptively exclusive.

You must readily see the great difficulty with a nonexclusive power: How much must the donee give each object of the power? Could the donee in *Hargrove* appoint $1 to each of her other nieces and nephews and the rest to her favored niece? In a few states, the amount cannot be too small because of the "illusory appointment" rule requiring that each permissible appointee receive a "reasonable benefit." Restatement (Third) of Property, supra, §17.5, cmt. j. There is only one reported American decision, however, in which an appellate court actually struck down an appointment as illusory — and that decision is nearly a century old. See Barrett's Executor v. Barrett, 179 S.W. 396 (Ky. 1915) (holding three appointments of $1,000 each illusory when the fourth appointee received the remaining $147,000).

4. Fraud on a Special Power

An appointment in favor of a person who is not an object of the power is invalid. An appointment to an object for the purpose of circumventing the limitation on the power is a "fraud on the power" and is void to the extent it is motivated by such purpose. See Restatement (Third) of Property: Wills and Other Donative Transfers §19.16 (T.D. No. 5, 2006).

PROBLEM

Elsa Milliken held a special testamentary power to appoint among her "kindred," and in default of appointment the property was to pass to Elsa's descendants or, if none, to the donor's heirs. Elsa, who had no descendants, wanted to appoint $100,000 to her husband, but he was not an object of the power. So she approached her cousin, Paul Curtis, and told him that she would leave him $150,000 for himself and an additional $100,000, which she wanted him to give to her husband. Paul said he would be happy to sign a paper to that effect. Elsa's attorney prepared a letter, directed to her and signed by Paul, that read: "I am informed that by your last will and testament you have given me and bequeathed to me the sum of Two Hundred and Fifty Thousand Dollars ($250,000). In the event that you should predecease me and I should receive the bequest before mentioned, I hereby promise and agree, in consideration of the said bequest, that I will pay to your husband, Foster Milliken, Jr., the sum of One Hundred Thousand Dollars ($100,000) out of the said bequest which you have given to me by your said will." Elsa died leaving a will appointing $250,000 to Paul. Is Paul entitled to $250,000, $150,000, or zero? See In re Carroll's Will, 8 N.E.2d 864 (N.Y. 1937). See also Restatement (Third) of Property, supra, at §19.16, cmt. e.

5. *Ineffective Exercise of a Power of Appointment*

When the donee intends to exercise a power of appointment, but the exercise is ineffective for some reason, it may be possible to carry out the donee's intent through the doctrines of allocation or capture.

a. **Allocation**

The doctrine of *allocation* (also known as *marshalling*) applies when *appointive property* and *property owned by the donee* are disposed of under a common dispositive instrument (usually the donee's will). The doctrine's purpose is to give effect to the donee's intent when the appointive property cannot go where the donee intended. Typical cases applying allocation involve an ineffective appointment to a nonobject of a power or an appointment that violates the Rule Against Perpetuities. It is important to realize that, where assets are allocated by a court, the donee could have provided for the allocation in specific language. In applying the doctrine, the court is merely doing what the court thinks the donee would have done but for the ineptness of the donee's lawyer.

The doctrine of allocation is: If the donee *blends* both the appointive property and the donee's own property in a common disposition, the blended property is allocated to the various interests in such a way as to increase the effectiveness of the disposition. The blending may consist of a residuary clause disposing of both appointive property and owned property. Thus:

Case 9. A holds a special testamentary power created by her father to appoint trust property among *A*'s descendants. The trust property is worth $100,000. *A* also owns outright $350,000. *A*'s will provides:

I give all my property, including any property over which I have a power of appointment under the will of my father, as follows: (1) I give $100,000 to my daughter-in-law, *B*, widow of my deceased son, *S*, and (2) I give all the rest to my daughter, *D*.

Since *B* is not an object of the special power, none of the trust property can be allocated to her. But under the doctrine of allocation, *B* would take $100,000 of *A*'s property, and *D* would take the trust property plus the other $250,000 of *A*'s property.

If, in Case 9, *A* had owned assets of only $50,000, *B* would receive only $50,000 because the trust property cannot be allocated to *B*. To satisfy completely the ineffective appointment, allocation requires that the donee have property of her own sufficient to substitute for the appointive property.

Now suppose that there had been no blending clause, and *A* had tried to appoint the trust property to *B*, and her own property to *D*. Under traditional law, since *A* did not blend the property, the appointment would fail, and none of *A*'s own property could be allocated to *B*. However, under Restatement (Third) of Property: Wills and other Donative Transfers §19.19, cmt. a (T.D. No. 5, 2006), the doctrine of allocation may apply even if "the donee has not blended owned and appointing assets in a common disposition." In eliminating the blending requirement, the drafters reasoned that the "use of a blending clause is more the product of the forms used by the donee's lawyer than of any deliberate decision by the donee." Id.

The Restatement (Third) of Property also relaxes the requirement of a common dispositive instrument by treating as a single instrument the donee's will, any codicils thereto, and any revocable trust that becomes irrevocable on account of the donee's death. Treating the donee's will, codicils, and revocable trusts as a single instrument sensibly reflects the reality that modern estate plans often combine a pour-over will with one or more revocable trusts.

b.   Capture

If the donee of a power makes an ineffective appointment, and the donee's intent cannot be given effect through *allocation*, to whom should the appointive property pass? The general rule is that it passes to the takers in default of appointment, or, if there are none, then to the donor's estate. But there is one important exception: the doctrine of *capture*. Capture applies only to general powers and only when the attempted exercise of the general power is ineffective or incomplete.

Capture occurs when the donee of a general power "manifests an intent to assume control of the appointive property for all purposes and not merely for the limited purpose of giving effect to the expressed appointment." Restatement (Second) of Property: Donative Transfers §23.2 (1986). The doctrine of capture rests upon the idea that, since the donee of a general power could appoint to her estate, the appointive property should pass to her estate if she would prefer that in case of an ineffective appointment. Ineffective appointments raising the issue of whether capture applies usually involve the lapse of an appointment to a dead appointee, or a violation of the Rule Against Perpetuities, or a failure of the donee to comply with some prescribed formality in exercising the power.

The intent of the donee to assume control of the appointive property for all purposes is most commonly manifested by provisions in the donee's will that *blend* the owned property of the donee with the appointive property. As with the doctrine of allocation, the requisite blending can occur in a residuary clause disposing of both the appointive property and the donee's own assets or in an introductory clause stating that the donee intends the appointive property to be treated as her own property. Thus:

> *Case 10. A* is the donee of a general power under the will of *X. A*'s will provides:
>
> > I give all my property and any property over which I have a power of appointment under the will of *X* as follows: (1) $10,000 to my friend *B* [who predeceases *A*, with no antilapse statute applicable]; (2) $15,000 in trust for my dog Trixie [which violates the Rule Against Perpetuities and fails also for lack of an ascertainable beneficiary (a dog is not a valid beneficiary)]; and (3) all the rest to *C*.
>
> *A* has captured the appointive property by blending it with her own. *C* takes everything, including the appointive property.

On the theory that a valid gift-in-default clause is more likely to represent the donor's intent than capture, Restatement (Third) of Property: Wills and Other Donative Transfers §19.21 (T.D. No. 5, 2006) alters the doctrine of capture as follows. If the donee of a general power does not effectively exercise the power, the appointive property passes to the takers in default of appointment under the donor's governing instrument. If there is no such provision, or if the provision is ineffective, the appointive property passes to the donee or the donee's estate.

SECTION D.   RELEASE OF A POWER OF APPOINTMENT

The donor of a testamentary power usually intends to protect the donee from an indiscreet or unwise exercise of the power during life; that the power is testamentary ensures that the donee is free to exercise discretion up until the moment of death. Hence, the donee of a testamentary power of appointment — or any other power not presently exercisable — cannot enter into an enforceable *contract* to make an appointment in the future.[16] The promisee may, however, obtain restitution of the value that the promisee gave the donee in consideration for the donee's (unenforceable) promise. In such a case, restitution is based on the donee's unjust enrichment. If the law afforded specific performance or damages

---

16. On the other hand, if the donee promises to exercise a testamentary power in a certain way, and the donee's will exercises the power as promised, the exercise is not rendered invalid merely because the donee could not have been compelled to exercise the power in that way. Benjamin v. Morgan Guar. Tr. Co., 609 N.Y.S.2d 276 (App. Div. 1994).

for breaches of such contracts, the donee of a testamentary power could in effect exercise the power during life by contracting to exercise it. See Restatement (Third) of Property: Wills and Other Donative Transfers §21.2, cmt. a (T.D. No. 5, 2006).

Although a contract to exercise a testamentary power is not enforceable, a similar result can sometimes be obtained by *releasing* the power of appointment. Thus:

> *Case 11. T* devises property in trust for *A* for life, then as *A* by will appoints, and in default of appointment, to *A*'s children equally. By releasing her power of appointment, *A* could effectively grant to her children an indefeasibly vested remainder. Although *A* could not make an enforceable *contract* to appoint to her children, she achieved her objective by a *release*.

Powers of appointment have generally been made releasable in all jurisdictions either by judicial decision or by statute with respect to the whole or any part of the appointive property, and in such manner that reduces or limits the permissible appointees. See Restatement (Third) of Property, supra, at §§20.1 and 20.2.

Seidel v. Werner

New York Supreme Court, Special Term, New York County, 1975
364 N.Y.S.2d 963,
aff'd on opinion below, 376 N.Y.S.2d 139

SILVERMAN, J.   Plaintiffs, trustees of a trust established in 1919 by Abraham L. Werner, sue for a declaratory judgment to determine who is entitled to one-half of the principal of the trust fund — the share in which Steven L. Werner, decedent (hereinafter "Steven"), was the life beneficiary and over which he had a testamentary power of appointment. The dispute concerns the manner in which Steven exercised his power of appointment and is between Steven's second wife, Harriet G. Werner (hereinafter "Harriet"), along with their children, Anna G. and Frank S. Werner (hereinafter "Anna" and "Frank") and Steven's third wife, Edith Fisch Werner (hereinafter "Edith").

Anna and Frank claim Steven's entire share of the trust remainder on the basis of a Mexican consent judgment of divorce,[17] obtained by Steven against Harriet

---

17. Before the liberalization of American divorce law and the spread of the no-fault divorce in the 1970s, couples wanting to end their marriage often found it necessary to travel to another state or even to another country. Nevada emerged as the domestic leader in this jurisdictional competition for divorces, so much so that "'Going to Reno' became almost a synonym for getting a divorce." Lawrence M. Friedman, A Dead Language: Divorce Law and Practice Before No-Fault, 86 Va. L. Rev. 1497, 1504-1505 (2000). Mexico was among the more popular international destinations. The number of Mexican divorces granted to couples in which at least one of the spouses was born in the United States increased from 230 in 1926 to over 4,300 in 1955, representing roughly one-third of all divorces in Mexico that year. Paul H. Jacobson, American Marriage and Divorce 108-109 (1959). For those not inclined, or wealthy enough, to travel and establish a temporary residency elsewhere, New York's especially severe statute, under which evidence of adultery was necessary for a divorce decree, prompted what has come to be called "soft-core adultery." Professor Friedman explains:

> This involved a little drama performed in a hotel. The cast of characters included the husband, a woman (generally a blonde who was hired for the occasion), and a photographer, of course. An article in

on December 9, 1963, which incorporated by reference and approved a separation agreement, entered into between Steven and Harriet on December 1, 1963. That agreement included the following provision:

> 10. The Husband shall make, and hereby promises not to revoke, a will in which he shall exercise his testamentary power of appointment over his share in a trust known as "Abraham L. Werner Trust No. 1" by establishing with respect to said share a trust for the benefit of the aforesaid Children, for the same purposes and under the same terms and conditions, as the trust provided for in Paragraph "9" of this Agreement, insofar as said terms and conditions are applicable thereto.

Paragraph 9 in relevant part provides for the wife to receive the income of the trust, upon the death of the husband, for the support and maintenance of the children, until they reach twenty-one years of age, at which time they are to receive the principal in equal shares.

On March 20, 1964, less than four months after entry of the divorce judgment, Steven executed a will in which, instead of exercising his testamentary power of appointment in favor of Anna and Frank, he left everything to his third wife, Edith:

> First, I give, devise and bequeath all of my property . . . including . . . all property over which I have a power of testamentary disposition, to my wife, Edith Fisch Werner.

Steven died in April 1971 and his Will was admitted to probate by the Surrogate's Court of New York County on July 11, 1973.

(1) Paragraph 10 of the Separation Agreement is a contract to exercise a testamentary power of appointment not presently exercisable (EPTL 10-3.3) and as such is invalid under EPTL 10-5.3, which provides as follows:

> (a) The donee of a power of appointment which is not presently exercisable or of a postponed power which has not become exercisable, cannot contract to make an appointment. Such a contract, if made, cannot be the basis of an action for specific performance or damages, but the promisee can obtain restitution of the value given by him for the promise unless the donee has exercised the power pursuant to the contract.

---

the New York Sunday Mirror magazine section, published in 1934, had the intriguing title: "I was the Unknown Blonde in 100 New York Divorces." The "unknown blonde" usually charged $50 for her work. She was in fact a woman named Dorothy Jarvis, who (according to the Mirror) had "retired as a professional co-respondent in view of her forthcoming marriage to a man she met while performing her role."

Whatever sins the blonde may have committed in her young life, sex with the men who paid her was not among them. She simply played a part in a sordid little drama. She went to a hotel room with the man. There would be a certain amount of undressing. At some point, they would hear a knock on the door — a maid with towels, or the bellboy bringing a telegram. This too was a charade of course. When the door opened, the photographer would burst into the room and take pictures. A study of about 500 cases in the 1930s revealed the following fascinating facts: In 23 cases the man was totally nude; in 2 he was wrapped in a towel; in 8, he wore a nightgown; in 119, he was in his "B.V.D. or underwear"; bathrobe or dressing gown accounted for another 101; pajamas, 227 cases; in 4 he was wearing a "kimono." The woman was nude no less than 55 times (twice she only wore a brassiere); she was in a "negligee" 67 times; underwear 26 times; "chemise," 24 times; nightgown, 126; pajamas, 73; bathrobe or dressing gown, 32; "kimono," 68. [Friedman, supra, at 1511-1513.]

— Eds.

This is a testamentary power of appointment. The original trust instrument provided in relevant part that: "Upon the death of such child [Steven] the principal of such share shall be disposed of as such child shall by its last will direct, and in default of such testamentary disposition then the same shall go to the issue of such child then surviving per stirpes. . . ." It is not disputed that New York law is determinative of the validity of Paragraph 10 of the Separation Agreement; the Separation Agreement itself provides that New York law shall govern.

The reasoning underlying the refusal to enforce a contract to exercise a testamentary power was stated by Justice Cardozo in the case of Farmers' Loan & Trust Co. v. Mortimer, 114 N.E. 389, 390 (N.Y. 1916):

> The exercise of the power was to represent the final judgment, the last will, of the donee. Up to the last moment of his life he was to have the power to deal with the share as he thought best. . . . To permit him to bargain that right away would be to defeat the purpose of the donor. Her command was that her property should go to her son's issue unless at the end of his life it remained his will that it go elsewhere. It has not remained his will that it go elsewhere; and his earlier contract cannot nullify the expression of his final purpose.

See also In re Estate of Brown, 306 N.E.2d 781 (N.Y. 1973).

(2) The question then is whether entry of the Mexican divorce decree, incorporating the Separation Agreement, alters this result; I do not think it does. . . .

[The court held that the Mexican divorce decree was not controlling, because, first, it did not direct Steven to exercise his power of appointment but merely approved the separation agreement as fair and reasonable, and, second, the Mexican court did not pass on or consider rules of New York property law.]

(3) As indicated, the statute makes a promise to exercise a testamentary power in a particular way unenforceable. However, EPTL 10-5.3(b) permits a donee of a power to release the power, and that release, if in conformity with EPTL 10-9.2, prevents the donee from then exercising the power thereafter.

Under the terms of the trust instrument, if Steven fails to exercise his power of appointment, Anna and Frank (along with the children of Steven's first marriage) take the remainder, i.e., the property which is the subject of Steven's power of appointment. Therefore, Harriet, Anna and Frank argue that at a minimum Steven's agreement should be construed as a release of his power of appointment, and that Anna and Frank should be permitted to take as on default of appointment.

There is respectable authority — by no means unanimous authority, and none binding on this Court — to the effect that a promise to appoint a given sum to persons who would take in default of appointment should, *to that extent*, be deemed a release of the power of appointment. See Restatement of Property §336 (1940); Simes & Smith, The Law of Future Interests §1016 (1956).

This argument has the appeal that it seems to be consistent with the exception that the release statute (EPTL 10-5.3(b)) carves out of EPTL 10-5.3(a); and is also consistent with the intentions and reasonable expectation of the parties at the time they entered into the agreement to appoint, here in the separation agreement; and that therefore perhaps in these circumstances the difference between what the parties agreed to and a release of the power of appointment is merely one of form. Whatever may be the possible validity or applicability of this argument to other circumstances and situations, I think it is inapplicable to this situation because:

(a) It is clear that the parties did not intend a release of the power of appointment. Cf. Matter of Haskell, 300 N.Y.S.2d 711 (Sup. Ct. 1969). Indeed, the agreement — unlike a release of a power of appointment — expressly contemplates that something will be done by the donee of the power in the future, and that that something will be an exercise of the power of appointment. Thus, the agreement, in the very language said to be a release of the power of appointment, says (Par. 10): "the Husband *shall* make . . . a will in which he *shall exercise* his testamentary power of appointment. . . ." (emphasis added).

(b) Nor is the substantial effect of the promised exercise of the power the same as would follow from release of, or failure to exercise, the power.

(i) Under the separation agreement, the power is to be exercised so that the entire appointive property shall be for the benefit of Anna and Frank; under the trust instrument, on default of exercise of the power, the property goes to all of Steven's children (Anna, Frank and two children of Steven's first marriage). Thus the agreement provides for appointment of a greater principal to Anna and Frank than they would get in default of appointment.[18]

(ii) Under the trust instrument, on default of exercise of the power, the property goes to the four children absolutely and in fee. The separation agreement provides that Steven shall create a *trust*, with *income* payable to *Harriet as trustee*, for the support of Anna and Frank until they both reach the age of 21, at which time the principal shall be paid to them or the survivor; and if both fail to attain the age of 21, then the principal shall revert to Steven's estate. Thus, Anna and Frank's interest in the principal would be a defeasible interest if they did not live to be 21; and indeed at Steven's death they were both still under 21 so that their interest was defeasible.

(iii) Finally, under the separation agreement, as just noted, if Anna and Frank failed to qualify to take the principal, either because they both died before Steven or before reaching the age of twenty-one, then the principal would go to Steven's estate. Under the trust instrument, on the other hand, on default of appointment and an inability of Anna and Frank to take, Steven's share of the principal would not go to Steven's estate, but to his other children, if living, and if not, to the settlor's next of kin.

In these circumstances, I think it is too strained and tortuous to construe the separation agreement provision as the equivalent of a release of the power of appointment. If this is a release then the exception of EPTL 10-5.3(b) has swallowed and destroyed the principal rule of EPTL 10-5.3(a). . . .

18. In 1977, two years after this case, the legislature amended N.Y. Est. Powers & Trusts Law §10-5.3(b) to provide that a release is valid "except that where the donor designated persons or a class to take in default of the donee's exercise of the power, a release with respect to the appointive property must serve to benefit all those so designated as provided by the donor." — Eds.

Accordingly, I hold that the separation agreement is not the equivalent of a total or partial release of the power of appointment.

(4) Anna and Frank also seek restitution out of the trust fund of the value given by them in exchange for Steven's unfulfilled promise. EPTL 10-5.3(a) provides that although the contract to make an appointment cannot be the basis for an action for specific performance or damages, "the promisee can obtain restitution of the value given by him for the promise unless the donee has exercised the power pursuant to contract."

Anna and Frank's remedy is limited, however, to the claim for restitution that they have (and apparently have asserted) against Steven's estate. They may not seek restitution out of the trust fund, even if their allegation that the estate lacks sufficient assets to meet this claim were factually supported, because the trust fund was not the property of Steven, except to the extent of his life estate, so as to be subject to the equitable remedy of restitution, but was the property of the donor of the power of appointment until it vested in someone else. Farmers' Loan & Trust Co. v. Mortimer, 114 N.E. 389, 390 (N.Y. 1916).

(5) Finally, Edith moves for summary judgment that she is entitled to receive Steven's share of the trust fund on the ground that Steven exercised his testamentary power in her favor in his will of March 20, 1964, in the provision quoted at the beginning of this decision.

Since there are no factual questions raised as to Steven's exercise of his testamentary power of appointment in Edith's favor in that will provision, and since each of the other defendants' conflicting claims to the share of trust principal has been dismissed, Edith's motion for summary judgment is granted.[19]

(6) Accordingly, on the motions for summary judgment I direct judgment declaring that defendant Edith Fisch Werner is entitled to the one-half share of Steven L. Werner in the principal of the Abraham L. Werner trust; to the extent that the counterclaims and cross-claims asserted by Harriet, Anna and Frank seek relief other than a declaratory judgment, they are dismissed.

QUESTION

Steven Ludwig Werner was a lawyer and, at the time of his death, a professor of labor relations at Cornell. If Steven had known, when he agreed to the divorce settlement, that the contract to appoint the trust fund was unenforceable, was his

19. Edith Fisch, Steven's third wife and the prevailing party in Seidel v. Werner, was a major figure in the New York trusts and estates community. The first woman to be awarded a J.S.D. by Columbia Law School, Fisch was also the first woman to be a law professor in New York state, serving as an assistant professor of law at New York Law School from 1963 to 1965. In addition to teaching and practicing law, Fisch also published books on cy pres and evidence, and later a book on charities that was dedicated to the memory of "Steven L. Werner, lawyer, teacher and scholar." One wonders, might Edith have given Steven the idea that his contract to appoint could be ignored?

The editors gratefully acknowledge Professor Ronald Chester of the New England School of Law, who brought Fisch's background to our attention. — Eds.

conduct unethical, fraudulent, or clever? If you think it would have been illegal or unethical, what would the remedy be?

SECTION E.   FAILURE TO EXERCISE A POWER OF APPOINTMENT

1.   *Failure to Exercise a General Power*

Under traditional law, if the donee of a *general* power of appointment fails to exercise it, the appointive property passes to the takers in default of appointment. If there is no such provision in the document creating the power, the property reverts to the donor or the donor's estate. See Restatement (Second) of Property: Donative Transfers §24.1 (1986).

A somewhat more complicated rule is stated in Restatement (Third) of Property: Wills and Other Donative Transfers §19.22 (T.D. No. 5, 2006): If there is no gift-in-default clause or if the clause is ineffective, the property reverts to the donor or the donor's estate *only* if the donee "expressly refrained from exercising the power." Under this approach, every general power of appointment in effect comes with an implied gift in default of appointment to the donee or the donee's estate.

2.   *Failure to Exercise a Special Power*

If the donee of a *special* power of appointment fails to exercise it, and there is no gift in default of appointment, the appointive property may — if the objects are a defined and limited class — pass to the objects of the power. Otherwise, the property reverts to the donor or the donor's estate.

Loring v. Marshall
Supreme Judicial Court of Massachusetts, 1985
484 N.E.2d 1315

WILKINS, J.   This complaint, here on a reservation and report by a single justice of this court, seeks instructions as to the disposition of the remainder of a trust created under the will of Marian Hovey. In Massachusetts Inst. of Technology v. Loring, 99 N.E.2d 854 (Mass. 1951), this court held that the President and Fellows of Harvard College, the Boston Museum of Fine Arts, and Massachusetts Institute of Technology (the charities) would not be entitled to the remainder of the trust on its termination. The court, however, did not decide, as we now must, what ultimate disposition should be made of the trust principal.

Marian Hovey died in 1898, survived by a brother, Henry S. Hovey, a sister, Fanny H. Morse, and two nephews, John Torrey Morse, Third, and Cabot Jackson Morse. By her will, Marian Hovey left the residue of her estate in trust, the income payable in equal shares to her brother and sister during their lives. Upon her brother's death in 1900, his share of the income passed to her sister, and, upon her sister's death in 1922, the income was paid in equal shares to her two nephews. John Torrey Morse, Third, died in 1928, unmarried and without issue. His share of the income then passed to his brother, Cabot Jackson Morse, who remained the sole income beneficiary until his death in 1946.

At that point, the death of the last surviving income beneficiary, Marian Hovey's will provided for the treatment of the trust assets in the following language:

> At the death of the last survivor of my said brother and sister and my two said nephews, or at my death, if none of them be then living, the trustees shall divide the trust fund in their hands into two equal parts, and shall transfer and pay over one of such parts to the use of the wife and issue of each of my said nephews as he may by will have appointed; provided, that if his wife was living at my death he shall appoint to her no larger interest in the property possessed by me than a right to the income during her life, and if she was living at the death of my father, he shall appoint to her no larger interest in the property over which I have a power of disposition under the will of my father than a right to the income during her life; and the same limitations shall apply to the appointment of income as aforesaid. If either of my said nephews shall leave no such appointees then living, the whole of the trust fund shall be paid to the appointees of his said brother as aforesaid. If neither of my said nephews leave such appointees then living the whole trust fund shall be paid over and transferred in equal shares to the Boston Museum of Fine Arts, the Massachusetts Institute of Technology, and the President and Fellows of Harvard College for the benefit of the Medical School; provided, that if the said Medical School shall not then admit women to instruction on an equal footing with men, the said President and Fellows shall not receive any part of the trust property, but it shall be divided equally between the Boston Museum of Fine Arts and the Massachusetts Institute of Technology.[20]

The will thus gave Cabot Jackson Morse, the surviving nephew, a special power to appoint the trust principal to his "wife and issue" with the limitation that only income could be appointed to a widow who was living at Marian Hovey's death.[21] Cabot Jackson Morse was survived by his wife, Anna Braden Morse, who was living at Marian Hovey's death, and by his only child, Cabot Jackson Morse, Jr., a child of an earlier marriage, who died in 1948, two years after his father. Cabot Jackson Morse left a will which contained the following provisions:

> *Second:* I give to my son, Cabot Jackson Morse, Jr., the sum of one dollar ($1.00), as he is otherwise amply provided for.

20. The parties have stipulated that at the relevant time the Harvard Medical School admitted women to instruction on an equal footing with men. [Women were permitted to attend Harvard Medical School beginning on September 26, 1944. N.Y. Times, Sept. 26, 1944, at 20. This amounts to something of a posthumous triumph for Marian Hovey, who in 1878 had offered Harvard a $10,000 endowment on the condition that it admit women to the medical school. Harvard demurred. — Eds.]

21. We are concerned here only with "property possessed" by the testatrix at her death and not property over which she had "a power of disposition under the will of [her] father." That property was given outright to his widow under the residuary clause of the will of Cabot Jackson Morse.

Third: The power of appointment which I have under the wills of my aunt, Marian Hovey, and my uncle, Henry S. Hovey, both late of Gloucester, Massachusetts, I exercise as follows: I appoint to my wife, Anna Braden Morse, the right to the income during her lifetime of all of the property to which my power of appointment applies under the will of Marian Hovey, and I appoint to my wife the right during her widowhood to the income to which I would be entitled under the will of Henry S. Hovey if I were living.

Fourth: All the rest, residue and remainder of my estate, wherever situated, real or personal, in trust or otherwise, I leave outright and in fee simple to my wife, Anna Braden Morse.

In Welch v. Morse, 81 N.E.2d 361 (Mass. 1948), we held that the appointment of a life interest to Anna Braden Morse was valid, notwithstanding Cabot Jackson Morse's failure fully to exercise the power by appointing the trust principal. Consequently, the trust income following Cabot Jackson Morse's death was paid to Anna Braden Morse until her death in 1983, when the principal became distributable. The trustees thereupon brought this complaint for instructions.

The complaint alleges that the trustees

are uncertain as to who is entitled to the remainder of the Marian Hovey Trust now that the trust is distributable and specifically whether the trust principal should be paid in any one of the following manners: (a) to the estate of Cabot Jackson Morse, Jr. as the only permissible appointee of the remainder of the trust living at the death of Cabot Jackson Morse; (b) in equal shares to the estates of Cabot Jackson Morse, Jr. and Anna Braden Morse as the only permissible appointees living at the death of Cabot Jackson Morse; (c) to the estate of Anna Braden Morse as the only actual appointee living at the death of Cabot Jackson Morse; (d) to the intestate takers of Marian Hovey's estate on the basis that Marian Hovey failed to make a complete disposition of her property by her will; (e) to Massachusetts Institute of Technology, Museum of Fine Arts and the President and Fellows of Harvard College in equal shares as remaindermen of the trust; or (f) some other disposition.

Before us each named potential taker claims to be entitled to trust principal.

In our 1951 opinion, Massachusetts Inst. of Technology v. Loring, 99 N.E.2d 854, we explained why in the circumstances the charities had no interest in the trust:

The rights of the petitioning charities as remaindermen depend upon the proposition that Cabot J. Morse, Senior, did not leave an "appointee" although he appointed his wife Anna Braden Morse to receive the income during her life. The time when, if at all, the "whole trust fund" was to be paid over and transferred to the petitioning charities is the time of the death of Cabot J. Morse, Senior. At that time the whole trust fund could not be paid over and transferred to the petitioning charities, because Anna Braden Morse still retained the income for her life. We think that the phrase no "such appointees then living" is not the equivalent of an express gift in default of appointment, a phrase used by the testatrix in the preceding paragraph.

In Frye v. Loring, 113 N.E.2d 595 (Mass. 1953), the court reiterated that the charities had no interest in the trust fund.

It is apparent that Marian Hovey knew how to refer to a disposition in default of appointment from her use of the terms elsewhere in her will. She did not use those words in describing the potential gift to the charities. A fair reading of the will's crucial language may rightly be that the charities were not to take the principal unless no class member who could receive principal was then living (i.e., if no possible appointee of principal was living at the death of the surviving donee). Regardless of how the words "no such appointees then living" are construed, the express circumstances under which the charities were to take did not occur. The question is what disposition should be made of the principal in the absence of any explicit direction in the will.

Although in its 1951 opinion this court disavowed making a determination of the "ultimate destination of the trust fund," the opinion cited the Restatement of Property §367(2) (1940), and 1 A. Scott, Trusts §27.1 (1st ed. 1939) to the effect that, when a special power of appointment is not exercised and absent specific language indicating an express gift in default of appointment, the property not appointed goes in equal shares to the members of the class to whom the property could have been appointed. . . . [S]ee 5 American Law of Property §23.63, at 645 (A.J. Casner ed. 1952 & Supp. 1962) ("The fact that the donee has failed to apportion the property within the class should not defeat the donor's intent to benefit the class").

Applying this rule of law, we find no specific language in the will which indicates a gift in default of appointment in the event Cabot Jackson Morse should fail to appoint the principal. The charities argue that the will's reference to them suggests that in default of appointment Marian Hovey intended them to take. On the other hand, in Welch v. Morse, 81 N.E.2d 361, we commented that Marian Hovey's "will discloses an intent to keep her property in the family." The interests Marian Hovey gave to her sister and brother were life interests, as were the interests given to her nephews. The share of any nephew who died unmarried and without issue, as did one, was added to the share of the other nephew. Each nephew was limited to exercising his power of appointment only in favor of his issue and his widow.[22] We think the apparent intent to keep the assets within the family is sufficiently strong to overcome any claim that Marian Hovey's will "expressly" or "in specific language" provides for a gift to the charities in default of appointment.[23] . . .

[The charities argued that the principle of res judicata was not applicable because the attorney general, the supervisor of public charities, was not a party to Massachusetts Inst. of Technology v. Loring, 99 N.E.2d 854 (Mass. 1951). The court rejected this argument and held that "the public interest in protecting the charities' rights was fully accommodated by the Justices of this court in its prior decision."]

---

22. The gift to any widow was to be a life interest if she were living at Marian Hovey's death.

23. The nominal distribution made to his son in the donee's will provides no proper guide to the resolution of the issues in this case. We are concerned here with the intention of Marian Hovey, the donor of the special power of appointment. The intentions of the donee of the power of appointment are irrelevant in constructing the donor's intent. Similarly, those who rely on language in Frye v. Loring, 113 N.E.2d 595 (Mass. 1953), as instructive in resolving questions in this case miss the point that Cabot Jackson Morse's intention with regard to his exercise of the power of appointment is irrelevant in determining his aunt's intention concerning the consequences of his partial failure to exercise that power.

What we have said disposes of the claim that the trust principal should pass to Marian Hovey's heirs as intestate property, a result generally disfavored in the interpretation of testamentary dispositions. . . . The claim of the executors of the estate of Anna Braden Morse that her estate should take as the class, or at least as a member of the class, must fail because Marian Hovey's will specifically limits such a widow's potential stake to a life interest.

A judgment shall be entered instructing the trustees under the will of Marian Hovey to distribute the trust principal to the executors of the estate of Cabot Jackson Morse, Jr. The allowance of counsel fees, costs, and expenses from the principal of the trust is to be in the discretion of the single justice.

So ordered.

NOTE

The theory of the court in Loring v. Marshall was that there was an *implied gift in default of appointment* to the potential appointees. This theory is adopted by Restatement (Third) of Property: Wills and Other Donative Transfers §19.23 (T.D. No. 5, 2006).

Another approach is to say that Cabot Jackson Morse had an *imperative* special power of appointment. A special power is imperative when the creating instrument manifests an intent that the permissible appointees be benefited even if the donee fails to exercise the power. If a special power is imperative, the donee must exercise it or the court will divide the assets equally among the potential appointees. The term *imperative power* is used in Cal. Prob. Code §613 (2008) and N.Y. Est. Powers & Trusts Law §10-3.4 (2008), but is rejected by Restatement (Third) of Property, supra, §17.1, cmt. k.

13

CONSTRUCTION OF TRUSTS:
FUTURE INTERESTS

SECTION A.   INTRODUCTION

Today, future interests arise primarily in trusts. Lawyers who deal with trusts must therefore be familiar with future interests, including common constructional and other problems with their use.

The basic conceptual idea underlying the law of future interests is that a future interest is treated as a "thing."[1] In your introductory course in property, you were introduced to the reification of abstractions, particularly the fee simple. You probably now speak of a fee simple as a *bundle* of rights. Indeed, once you have been introduced to property law, it is hard not to think of a fee simple in any way but as a thing. The owner may transfer *it*, creditors may seize *it*, *it* passes on death, and so forth. Future interests are reified in the same manner.

This chapter examines the law of future interests. We consider how to tailor future interests to achieve settlor's intent, and how to avoid intent-defeating technical rules and common problems of ambiguous language.

---

1. Compare the White King speaking to Alice about the two Messengers:

   "And I haven't sent the two Messengers, either. They're both gone to the town. Just look along the road and tell me if you see either of them."
   "I see nobody on the road," said Alice.
   "I only wish *I* had such eyes," the King remarked in a fretful tone. "To be able to see Nobody! And at that distance too! Why, it's as much as *I* can do to see real people, by this light!"

   Lewis Carroll, Through the Looking-Glass, ch. 7.

SECTION B. CLASSIFICATION OF FUTURE INTERESTS

1. *Types of Future Interests*

The future interests recognized by our legal system are:

1. Interests in the *transferor* known as:
    a. Reversion
    b. Possibility of reverter
    c. Right of entry (also known as power of termination)
2. Interests in a *transferee* known as:
    a. Vested remainder
    b. Contingent remainder
    c. Executory interest

These interests are called *future* interests because a person who holds one of them is not entitled to possession or enjoyment of the property currently, but may or will become entitled to possession in the future. Nevertheless, a person who has a future interest has present rights and liabilities. Take this case: *O* conveys Blackacre "to *A* for life, then to *B*." *B* has a remainder, which *B* can sell or give away. *B*'s creditors can reach it. *B* can enjoin *A* from committing waste or doing other acts that impair the value of *B*'s right to future possession. If *B* dies before *A*, the value of *B*'s remainder passes to *B*'s heirs or devisees and is subject to federal estate taxation. But because *B* does not have the right to present possession of Blackacre, we call *B*'s interest a "future interest."

Any estate that may be created in possession, such as a fee simple or a life estate, may also be created as a future interest. Hence, *O* may convey "to *A* for life, then to *B* for life, then to *C*." *B* has a remainder for life, and *C* has a remainder in fee simple. By saying that *C* has a remainder in fee simple, we mean that when *C*'s remainder becomes possessory it will be a fee simple.

NOTE: FUTURE INTERESTS REFORM

The mandatory categorization of all future interests into one of the specified categories, and many of the corresponding technical rules of future interests law, are vestiges inherited from England, relics of medieval feudalism that have little relevance in contemporary society. Today, nothing of consequence turns on the categorization of a future interest as an executory interest versus a contingent remainder, or as a possibility of reverter versus a right of entry. Yet these ancient classifications, and their artificial and needless complexity, endure on bar exams and sometimes in real life too.

Over the years there have been multiple calls for reform and confident predictions that reform was just around the corner. Not long after the publication of the

Restatement (First) of Property in 1936, which preserved the ancient rules, Professor Lewis M. Simes, a widely respected authority on the law of future interests at the University of Michigan, predicted that the states were "on the eve of a movement looking toward the improvement and simplification of the law of Future Interests by legislation." Simes reasoned that the new Restatement expressed the "obscure and complicated rules" in such "clear and accurate fashion" that legislation "correcting the difficulties which have been discovered" would surely follow. Lewis M. Simes, Fifty Years of Future Interests, 50 Harv. L. Rev. 749, 783 (1937). Alas, the reform did not come.

In recent years, a new generation of scholars has taken aim at the law of future interests, once again proposing systematic statutory reform. See D. Benjamin Barros, Toward a Model Law of Estates and Future Interests, 66 Wash. & Lee L. Rev. 3 (2009); T.P. Gallanis, The Future of Future Interests, 60 Wash. & Lee L. Rev. 513 (2003). See also Lawrence W. Waggoner, Reformulating the Structure of Estates: A Proposal for Legislative Action, 85 Harv. L. Rev. 729 (1972). Is there hope for future interests law reform any time soon?

The best answer is Perhaps. What is different now is that the reporters for the Restatement (Third) of Property: Wills and Other Donative Transfers, Professors Lawrence W. Waggoner and John H. Langbein, have decided to take on future interests reform. The most recent preliminary draft of the pertinent provisions of the new Restatement (P.D. No. 13, 2008) abolishes the various subcategories (§25.2), simplifies the inquiry whether a future interests is vested or contingent (§25.3), and states more straightforward rules for construction (§§26.1-26.10).

Keep in mind that a Restatement affords persuasive authority only, and its authoritativeness is perhaps most precarious when it advances reform. The future interests provisions of the Restatement (Third) of Property, moreover, are still a work in progress. Nonetheless, in the field of trusts and estates, the Restatements have had considerable influence (see page 544). In the ensuing treatment of future interests law, we will reference the relevant draft sections of the new Restatement where appropriate. Once finalized, the new Restatement might well provide a roadmap for a new uniform act or for direct reform by judges and state legislatures. For future interests buffs, these are interesting times indeed!

2. Future Interests in the Transferor

a. Reversion

Three types of future interests may be retained by the transferor: reversion, possibility of reverter, and right of entry for condition broken. By far the most important of these is the *reversion*. "A reversion is the interest remaining in the grantor, or in the successor in interest of a testator, who transfers a vested estate of a lesser quantum than that of the vested estate which he has." 1 American Law of Property §4.16 (1952). A reversion is never created alone; it is a retained interest that arises by operation of law when the transferor has conveyed a lesser estate than the transferor had. If a reversion is retained in an inter vivos conveyance, it is retained by the grantor. If a reversion is retained by a will, it is retained in the testator's successors, who are substituted by law for the dead transferor.

A reversion cannot be created in a transferee. A future interest created in a transferee must be a remainder or an executory interest.

PROBLEM

T's will devises Blackacre to *A* for life, and the residue of *T*'s property to *B*. What interest does *B* have in Blackacre?

All reversions are *vested* interests. This does not mean, however, that all reversions will become possessory. A reversion following a contingent remainder, for instance, might not become possessory. Thus:

> *Case 1. O* conveys property in trust "to *A* for life, then to *A*'s children who survive *A*." *A*'s children have a contingent remainder. *O* has a *vested reversion*, which will be divested if *A* leaves surviving children.[2]

The reversion in Case 1 may not become possessory, but it is vested in interest. Future interests are deemed vested or not by the arbitrary rules of the common law, not by the certainty or uncertainty of future possession.

b. Possibility of Reverter and Right of Entry

A *possibility of reverter* is the future interest that remains in the grantor who conveys a fee simple determinable. For example, *O* conveys land "to the School Board so long as the land is used for a school." The School Board has a fee simple determinable; *O* has a possibility of reverter, which will become possessory automatically upon the expiration of the determinable fee.

A *right of entry* for condition broken is the future interest that is retained by the grantor who conveys a fee simple subject to a condition subsequent. For example, *O* conveys land "to School Board, but if it ceases to be used for school purposes, *O* has a right to reenter." The School Board has a fee simple subject to condition subsequent; *O* has a right of entry, which *O* has the option to exercise or not.

----

2. *Warning*: Do not call *O*'s interest a contingent reversion or a possibility of reversion. There are no such interests known to law. If you use the latter term, you may end up confusing a reversion with a *possibility of reverter*, an entirely different interest.

3. Future Interests in Transferees

The common law recognizes three types of future interests in transferees: vested remainders, contingent remainders, and executory interests.

a. Remainders

A *remainder* is a future interest in a transferee that will become possessory, if at all, upon the expiration of all prior interests simultaneously created. A remainderperson waits patiently until the preceding estates expire, and then, if the remainder is not contingent, the remainderperson is entitled to possession. To be a remainder, it must only be possible, not necessarily certain, that the future interest will become possessory upon the termination of the preceding estates. Thus:

> *Case 2.* O conveys a fund in trust "for A for life, then to B." B has a remainder that will become possessory upon the expiration of A's life estate. Because it is certain to become possessory, we call it an *indefeasibly vested remainder*. If B dies during A's life, B's remainder, like B's other property, passes under B's will or by intestacy.
>
> *Case 3.* O conveys a fund in trust "for A for life, then to B if B survives A." B has a remainder, for it is possible (but not certain) that B will take the property on A's death. If B is then alive, B will take, and if B is then dead, the property will revert to O. B has a *contingent remainder*.

Remainders are either vested or contingent. A remainder is *vested* if (1) it is given to a presently ascertained person and (2) it is not subject to a condition precedent (other than the termination of the preceding estates). A remainder is *contingent* if (1) it is not given to a presently ascertained person or (2) it is subject to a condition precedent. In Case 3, B's remainder is contingent because it is subject to the condition precedent of surviving A.

Suppose a remainder is given to a class of persons, some but not all of whom are ascertained, and the remainder is not subject to a condition precedent. This remainder is vested in the present members of the class *subject to partial divestment* by additional persons coming into the class. Thus:

> *Case 4.* O conveys a fund in trust "for A for life, then to A's children." If A has no children at the time of the conveyance, the remainder is contingent because the takers are unascertained. On the other hand, if A has a child (let's call her B), B has a *vested remainder subject to partial divestment* (sometimes called a *vested remainder subject to open*). If A has any more children, B's share will be diminished. B's share will depend on how many children, if any, are subsequently born to A. If A has another child (let's call her C), B is partially divested, that is, divested of C's share. The class gift will remain subject to partial divestment (or open) until A's death.

A class gift is not vested subject to partial divestment if it is subject to a condition precedent. In Case 4, if the conveyance had been "to A for life, then to A's children who survive A," the remainder would be contingent even though A had one or more children alive.

Where a remainder is given to a class of persons described as "the heirs of *A* [a living person]," the takers are not ascertained until *A*'s death.

PROBLEMS AND NOTE

1.   *O* conveys a fund in trust "for *A* for life, and on *A*'s death to *A*'s children in equal shares." At the time of the conveyance, *A* has two children, *B* and *C*. Two years later, *D* is born to *A*. After another year has passed, *B* dies intestate and then *A* dies. To whom should the trust assets be distributed? See In re DiBiasio, 705 A.2d 972 (R.I. 1997); Coleman v. Coleman, 500 S.E.2d 507 (Va. 1998).

2.   In 2006, *O* conveys property in trust "for *A* for life, and on *A*'s death to the heirs of *B*." At the time of the conveyance, *A* and *B* are both alive and *B* has two children, *C* and *D*. If *B* were to die intestate immediately after the conveyance, *C* and *D* would be *B*'s heirs. In 2007, *D* dies, leaving a minor son, *E*, and a will devising all his property to his wife, *W*. In 2009, *B* dies, leaving a will that devises *B*'s entire estate to the American Red Cross. *A* dies in 2011, survived by *C*, *E*, and *W*. To whom should the trust assets be distributed? What result if *B* had died before *D*?

3.   Restatement (Third) of Property: Wills and Other Donative Transfers §§25.3-25.4 (P.D. No. 13, 2008) takes the position that the future interest of a member of a class that is open to new entrants is classified as subject to open and is treated as contingent or vested depending on whether the interest is certain to take effect in possession or enjoyment.

Now we must speak of the difference between a *vested remainder subject to divestment* and a *contingent remainder*, a fundamental distinction in the law of future interests. A vested remainder subject to divestment is a remainder given to an ascertained person, with a proviso that the remainder will be divested if a *condition subsequent* happens. It is not subject to a condition precedent. Whether a remainder is contingent or vested subject to divestment depends solely on the language of the instrument. And, with few exceptions, it depends on *the sequence of words in the instrument*. Interests are classified in sequence as they are written in the instrument. If a condition is incorporated into the gift of the remainder — if it comes, so to speak, between the commas setting apart the remainder — the condition is a condition precedent. But if the remainder is given, and then words of divestment are added, the condition is subsequent. This distinction is best seen by examples.

Case 5. *O* conveys a fund in trust "for *A* for life, then to *B* if *B* survives *A*, and if *B* does not survive *A*, to *C*." *B* has a contingent remainder because the words "if *B* survives *A*" are incorporated into *B*'s gift; they come between the commas. (Of course, if the commas were not there, you would have to decide where the court would mentally insert the commas. The essential idea is that the words "if *B* survives *A*" are part of the gift to *B*.) *C* has an alternative contingent remainder because *C*'s interest is contingent on *B* not surviving *A*.

Case 6. *O* conveys a fund in trust "for *A* for life, then to *B*, but if *B* does not survive *A*, to *C*." *B* has a vested remainder subject to divestment by *C*'s executory interest. Between the commas setting off *B*'s gift there are no words of condition. There is a condition subsequent to *B*'s gift introducing the divesting gift over to *C*.

As Cases 5 and 6 illustrate, you must look very carefully at the exact language used and classify the interests in sequence. *O*'s intent may be identical in both cases, but it has been expressed in different ways, resulting in the creation of different interests.

We now return briefly to the subject of reversions, so that you may see how reversions interact with vested remainders and contingent remainders. To determine when a transferor has a reversion, you can save yourself much trouble by applying this simple Rule of Reversions:

> *O*, owner of a fee simple, will not have a reversion in fee simple if *O* transfers a possessory fee simple or a vested remainder in fee simple. In all other cases where *O* transfers a present possessory interest, *O* will have a reversion in fee simple.

Hence, whenever *O* transfers a life estate, not followed by a vested remainder in fee, *O* has a reversion. If *O* transfers a life estate followed by 100 contingent remainders in fee, but no vested remainder in fee, *O* retains a reversion.

A reversion is a shorthand way of saying that when a vested estate of the same duration is not transferred, "there is either a certainty or a possibility that the right to possession will return to the grantor." When the owner of a fee simple carves out a lesser estate and does not add a vested remainder in fee simple, there is a possibility that the property will be his again.

PROBLEMS AND NOTE

1. *O* conveys property in trust "for *A* for life, then to *B*, but if *B* dies before *A* without descendants surviving *B*, then to *C* at *A*'s death." Does *O* have a reversion? Suppose that *B* dies leaving a surviving child, *D*, and *B*'s will devises all her property to her husband, *H*. Then *D* dies. Then *A* dies. To whom should the trust property be distributed? Cf. Jones v. Hill, 594 S.E.2d 913 (Va. 2004).

2. *O* conveys Blackacre in trust "for *A* for life, then to *B* or her heirs." Subsequently *B* dies, devising her property to *C*. *B*'s heir is *D*. On *A*'s death, who owns Blackacre? See Rowett v. McFarland, 394 N.W.2d 298 (S.D. 1986).

3. Restatement (Third) of Property: Wills and Other Donative Transfers §25.3 (P.D. No. 13, 2008) abolishes the distinction between contingent and vested subject to divestment. It provides that an interest is simply contingent or vested depending on whether the interest is certain to take effect in possession or enjoyment.

b.   Executory Interests

An executory interest differs from a remainder in that it is a *divesting* interest. A remainder never divests a preceding estate prior to its expiration; that is the job of an *executory interest*. An executory interest that may divest another *transferee* if a specified event happens is called a *shifting* executory interest because, if the event happens, the executory interest will shift the property from one transferee to another transferee. In Case 6 above, *C* has a shifting executory interest. An executory interest that may divest the *transferor* in the future if a specified event happens is called a *springing* executory interest because, if the event happens, the property will spring out from the transferor to the transferee. An old example of a springing executory interest at early common law was a marriage arrangement whereby the father of the bride would convey land "to my daughter *A* when she marries *B*." Springing executory interests are rare today.

Executory interests are future interests that would have been enforced by the court of chancery, but not by the law courts, before the Statute of Uses in 1536. The Statute of Uses converted these interests, previously valid only in equity, into legal interests. For an extended treatment of the history of executory interests, see Jesse Dukeminier et al., Property 233-239 (6th ed. 2006).

Executory interests are almost always created in one of the following two basic forms:

> *Case 7. Executory interest divesting a possessory fee simple upon an uncertain event. O* conveys Blackacre "to *A*, but if *A* dies without descendants surviving her, to *B*." *A* has a fee simple subject to divestment by *B*'s shifting executory interest. *B*'s executory interest is subject to a condition precedent (*A*'s death without surviving descendants) and is not certain to become possessory.
>
> *Case 8. Executory interest divesting a vested remainder. O* conveys a fund in trust "for *A* for life, and on *A*'s death to *B*, but if *B* is not then living, to *C*." *B* has a vested remainder in fee simple subject to divestment by *C*'s shifting executory interest. *C*'s executory interest is subject to a condition precedent (*B* dying before *A* dies) and is not certain to become possessory.

The executory interests in Cases 7 and 8 are analogous to contingent remainders, but they are called executory interests because they are divesting interests.

PROBLEMS, NOTE, AND QUESTION

1.   (a) *O* conveys a fund in trust "for *A* for life, then to *A*'s children, but if at *A*'s death *A* is not survived by any children, then to *B*." At the time the trust is created, *A* has no children. What interests are created?

(b) Consider the same facts as in Problem 1(a). A few years later, two children, *C* and *D*, are born to *A*. *C* dies, devising his property to his wife, *W*. *A* dies. To whom should the trust assets be distributed?

2.   *O* conveys a fund in trust "for *A* for life, then to such of *A*'s children as survive *A*, but if none of *A*'s children survive *A*, then to *B*." At the time the trust is

created, *A* has two children, *C* and *D*. Then *C* dies, devising his property to his wife, *W*. *A* dies. To whom should the trust assets be distributed?

3.   *T* devises Blackacre to *A* for life, then to *A*'s children who survive her. The residuary clause of *T*'s will devises to *B* "all the rest and residue of my property, including any of the foregoing gifts in this will that for any reason fail to take effect." What is the state of the title to Blackacre? See Wythe Holt, The Testator Who Gave Away Less Than All He or She Had: Perversions in the Law of Future Interests, 32 Ala. L. Rev. 69 (1980).

4.   *Remainders in default of appointment.* The exercise of a power of appointment is viewed as operating as a condition subsequent on the remainder in default of appointment. If the donee exercises the power, the remainderperson is deprived of his interest. Thus, suppose that *T* devises property in trust "for *A* for life, then to such persons as *A* by will appoints, and if *A* fails to make an appointment, to *A*'s children." Although this language would seem to create a condition precedent, the power is instead treated as a condition subsequent. Thus, this devise is read as if it were "for *A* for life, then to *A*'s children, but if *A* otherwise appoints by will, to such appointees." Assume *A* has one child, *B*. *B* has a vested remainder subject to partial divestment by the birth of other children and also subject to complete divestment by *A*'s exercise of the power of appointment. If *A* has no children, the remainder is contingent because the takers are not ascertained.

5.   *Contingent remainders versus executory interests.* Given that today nothing of consequence turns on the difference between a contingent remainder and an executory interest, should the distinction be abolished? See Restatement (Third) of Property: Wills and Other Donative Transfers §25.2, cmt. c (P.D. No. 13, 2008), answering in the affirmative. See also Jesse Dukeminier, Contingent Remainders and Executory Interests: A Requiem for the Distinction, 43 Minn. L. Rev. 13 (1958).

SECTION C.   CONSTRUCTION OF TRUST INSTRUMENTS

This section has two purposes. The first is to teach the techniques and rules that courts have developed in construing trust instruments. The second is to explore the ambiguities lying hidden in common provisions in wills and trusts. The latter is more important because only by learning to spot ambiguities, and by foreseeing what may happen to the people involved, can you develop the ability to draft an airtight instrument.

1.   *Preference for Vested Interests*

The common law had a strong preference for construing ambiguous instruments as creating a vested rather than a contingent remainder. As Sir Edward

Coke said, "the law always delights in vesting of estates, and contingencies are odious in the law, and are the causes of troubles, and vesting and settling of estates, the cause of repose and certainty." Roberts v. Roberts, 80 Eng. Rep. 1002, 1009 (K.B. 1613). This preference arose in feudal England at a time when contingent interests were barely recognized as interests, and it continued to modern times because of the purportedly desirable consequences of a vested construction. These consequences were:

1. A vested remainder was not subject to the doctrine of *destructibility of contingent remainders* that defeated the grantor's intent. This doctrine provided that a *legal* contingent remainder in *land* was destroyed if it did not vest at or before the termination of the preceding freehold estate. The doctrine is a feudal relic that in all but a tiny handful of states is no longer good law. It is repudiated by Restatement (Third) of Property: Wills and Other Donative Transfers §25.5 (P.D. No. 8, 2008).
2. A vested remainder *accelerated* into possession upon termination of the life estate, solving vexing problems of possession and undisposed income (see below).
3. A vested remainder was *transferable inter vivos*, making land more alienable (see page 851).
4. A vested remainder was not subject to the *Rule Against Perpetuities*, a rule that defeats the grantor's intent (see Chapter 14).

In addition to the different consequences at common law attendant on a classification of an interest as vested or contingent, a new problem has arisen in modern times. In many states, *upon divorce*, a court makes an equitable distribution of a couple's "property," including inherited property. In this context the question arises, is a vested remainder or a contingent remainder in a trust held by one spouse treated as property of that spouse subject to equitable division? The courts appear to agree that an indefeasibly vested remainder is the spouse's property and can be valued in accordance with life expectancy tables (see page 852). On the other hand, a vested remainder subject to divestment if the spouse does not survive the life tenant, or a remainder contingent on surviving the life tenant, is not that spouse's property for purposes of equitable distribution. But if the divesting event or contingency is something other than surviving the life tenant, the courts have struggled with the vested-contingent dichotomy with varying results. See Marc A. Chorney, Interests in Trusts as Property in Dissolution of Marriage: Identification and Valuation, 40 Real Prop., Prob. & Tr. J. 1 (2005); Alan Newman, Spendthrift and Discretionary Trusts: Alive and Well Under the Uniform Trust Code, 40 Real Prop., Prob. & Tr. J. 567, 627-631 (2005).

If your client wants to create a trust with a remainder in a child, you should draft a remainder contingent on surviving to the time of possession if your client wishes to insulate the remainder from the claims of the child's spouse upon divorce.

a.   Acceleration into Possession

Under the common law, a vested remainder accelerates into possession whenever and however the preceding estate ends. A contingent remainder, on the other hand, does not accelerate because the remainderpersons are not entitled to possession until they are all ascertained and any condition precedent has occurred. Thus:

> *Case 9. T* devises property in trust for *W* for life, remainder to *T*'s children (who survive *W*). *W* disclaims the life estate. If the language in parentheses is not included in the instrument, the children of *T* have a vested remainder that accelerates into possession. If the language in parentheses is included, the children of *T* have a contingent remainder that will not accelerate into possession. What is done with the income during *W*'s life?

In at least some cases the rule that a contingent remainder does not accelerate when the life tenant disclaims will not carry out the settlor's intent. In Case 9, for example, the settlor likely postponed the gift to his children merely to give his spouse income during her life. If so, it seems likely that the settlor would not want the trust to continue if the spouse rejects the income. Some courts have decided disclaimer cases based on what the settlor would have intended if the disclaimer had been anticipated, disregarding the technical classification of the remainder as vested or contingent. See Ohio Natl. Bank of Columbus v. Adair, 374 N.E.2d 415 (Ohio 1978). This approach, however, requires almost every case of disclaimer to be litigated. Enter the disclaimer statutes, such as the Uniform Disclaimer of Property Interests Act (UDPIA) (1999, rev. 2006).[3] Under these statutes, the disclaimant is treated as having predeceased the testator (see page 153), and remainders take effect or fail on this assumption.

In re Estate of Gilbert
New York Surrogate's Court, New York County, 1992
592 N.Y.S.2d 224

ROTH, S.   The executor of the estate of Peter Gilbert asks the court to declare null and void a renunciation by Mr. Gilbert's son, Lester, of his interest in two wholly discretionary trusts under decedent's will.

Mr. Gilbert died on March 26, 1989, leaving an estate of over $40,000,000.[4] He was survived by his wife and four children. Under his will, testator, after making certain pre-residuary legacies, created an elective share trust for the life income benefit of his wife. The amount of decedent's generation-skipping transfer (GST)

---

3. In 2002, the UDPIA was incorporated into the Uniform Probate Code as Article 2, Part 11 (§§2-1101–2-1107), replacing former §2-801.

4. Peter Gilbert, born in Austria, fled the Nazis with his family at age seven. Gilbert became a pioneer of cable television and the owner of the Colorado Rockies of the National Hockey League, now the New Jersey Devils. — Eds.

tax exemption was divided into four discretionary trusts, one for the primary benefit of each of his children. The residue of Mr. Gilbert's estate was similarly divided. Upon the death of the widow, the remainder of her trust is to be added in equal shares to the residuary trusts for decedent's children. The trusts are wholly discretionary. Decedent's son, Lester, is therefore a discretionary income beneficiary of two testamentary trusts, one of which will be augmented at the widow's death. Decedent's issue, including Lester's sisters, nieces and nephews as well as Lester's issue (should he have any), are also discretionary beneficiaries of both of Lester's trusts.

Lester, who has no issue, timely served on the executor a notice of renunciation of his "dispositive share in the estate of Peter Gilbert."

The executor, supported by the guardian ad litem for decedent's minor grandchildren, takes the position that Lester's renunciation should be declared invalid. First, he states that permitting the renunciation would violate the testator's intention to provide for Lester. Second, the executor argues that Lester possesses no current property interest and therefore has nothing to renounce. The executor maintains that Lester's renunciation is premature and may be made only if, and at such time as, the trustees exercise their discretion to distribute income or principal to him.

The executor explains decedent's intention as follows:

> Lester, who is approximately 32 years of age, . . . has left the religion of his birth and has for some time lived in Virginia with a small group of people who share a similar religious doctrine. Some months ago he phoned your petitioner and announced that he planned to renounce whatever bequest was left for him. When asked what he planned to do if he were ever taken seriously ill and needed expensive medical care, he responded "Jesus will provide for me."
>
>   The fact that Lester had chosen to alienate himself from his family did not stop the decedent from loving his son or worrying about his future needs. . . . [T]he decedent wanted to know that funds would be available if the Trustees, acting in the manner that they thought the decedent would have acted had he then been living, should ever decide, for example, to pay a medical bill for Lester.

In effect, the executor argues that if the beneficiary of a wholly discretionary trust is permitted to renounce his or her interest, then no trust can ever be created to protect someone who is now disdainful of financial assistance but may in the future be in dire need, or simply have a change of heart.

However, under these circumstances, decedent's intention is not controlling. With respect to every renunciation, the intent to make a transfer is thwarted by the beneficiary who refuses to accept it. But clearly, "the law does not compel a man to accept an estate, either beneficial or in trust, against his will" (Burritt v. Silliman, 13 N.Y. 93, 96 (1855)).

The executor suggests in his memorandum that he might be forced "to inquire into the mental capacity of Lester, since there is no rational reason which explains Lester's conduct." However, the desire to renounce wealth is not necessarily irrational. Presumably, the executor would not argue that a nun who takes a vow of poverty is mentally incompetent. Here, the acceptance of a monetary benefit apparently conflicts with Lester's religious beliefs. It would not be appropriate for the court to determine the validity of those beliefs, even if requested to do so. Furthermore, even if Lester's renunciation were purely whimsical, this would not in itself be sufficient reason either to reject the renunciation or to find him incompetent. In any event, the question of Lester's mental capacity has not been raised. There is no allegation in the petition or in any affidavit that Lester is a person under disability. The court must therefore proceed on the assumption that Lester is competent to make an effective renunciation.

The executor's second argument is that Lester has no current property interest which he can renounce. Rather, the executor maintains that Lester must wait until the trustees exercise their discretion to distribute income or principal to him, at which time, the executor asserts, Lester can renounce the property subject to such exercise of discretion. [The executor analogized these facts to a case in which the beneficiary's creditors try to reach the beneficiary's interest in a discretionary trust. In those cases, courts usually hold that the creditor cannot reach the trust property until a distribution is made. See page 610. The court rejected this argument, reasoning that the better analogy is to a case in which a beneficiary seeks to compel a distribution by the trustee even though the trustee is vested with "absolute," "sole," or some other form of extended discretion. In those cases, courts order a distribution to the beneficiary if the trustee's failure to make one was an abuse of the trustee's discretion. See page 605. Thus, because "Lester may have the right to compel the trustees to distribute trust property to him under certain circumstances," he "has a current interest which could be deemed 'property' for the purpose of an effective renunciation."]

Lester's renunciation also applies to his remainder interest in the elective share trust, which is contingent upon his surviving the widow. As discussed above, any interest, whether or not contingent, is within the scope of the statute. Even if the executor's interpretation is correct and a renunciation must relate to an interest in property, a contingent remainder has historically been recognized as a property interest.

Finally, the guardian ad litem argues that if Lester's renunciation is allowed, the remainder interests in his trusts should not be accelerated. The remainder of Lester's trusts would be payable to his issue. As mentioned earlier, Lester has no issue. If the interests are accelerated, Lester's unborn issue would be cut off and decedent's living grandchildren would lose certain present interests in these trusts. It is noted that acceleration of the trust remainders would have no direct tax consequences and any indirect effects would be relatively minor.

The question is whether under EPTL 2-1.11(d) this court has any discretion to suspend acceleration. Such statute, in relevant part, provides that:

> Unless the creator of the disposition has otherwise provided, the filing of a renunciation, as provided in this section, has the same effect with respect to the renounced interest as though the renouncing person had predeceased the creator or the decedent . . . and shall have the effect of accelerating the possession and enjoyment of subsequent interests.

Thus, it appears that under the language of the statute, the remainder interests in Lester's trusts will be accelerated unless the decedent has "otherwise provided." There is no explicit "otherwise provision" in testator's will, but the guardian ad litem argues that the court should infer an "otherwise provision" from the general language of the will and the circumstances surrounding its execution. . . .

When EPTL 2-1.11 was enacted in 1977, the language regarding acceleration was added to resolve the dispute reflected in a number of conflicting decisions. Those cases looked to testator's intent as the appropriate guideline and determined acceleration on a case-by-case basis, with unpredictable results. It is clear the addition of this language was intended to provide uniformity (see, e.g., Memorandum in Support of Amended Bill, New York State Assembly, L. 1977, ch. 861, Governor's Bill Jacket). To engage in the type of analysis suggested by the guardian ad litem would mean a return to the approach rejected by the Legislature.

Based upon the foregoing, it is concluded that Lester's renunciation is valid as to any and all interests in his father's estate. Lester is thus to be treated as if he predeceased his father without issue.

NOTES, QUESTION, AND PROBLEM

1. Under most disclaimer statutes, the donee of a contingent or defeasibly vested interest may wait up to nine months after the interest becomes indefeasibly vested to disclaim. Under the Uniform Disclaimer of Property Interests Act (UDPIA) (1999, rev. 2006), there is no time limit (see page 153).[5] Hence the contingent remainderperson may decide after the life tenant's death whether to accept the property:

> Case 10. T devises property in trust "for my daughter A for life, then to my granddaughter B if B survives A, and if B does not survive A, to B's descendants." At A's death, B, now age 21, can decide whether to disclaim and let the property pass to B's descendants.[6]

---

5. *Caution:* Under federal tax law, a disclaimer is treated as a gift by the disclaimant to the persons who take as a result of the disclaimer, *unless the disclaimer occurs within nine months after the interest is created* or nine months after the donee reaches 21, whichever is later. I.R.C. §2518(b)(2). Thus, if in Case 10 B does not disclaim within nine months after T dies, for federal tax purposes B is the owner of the remainder, and if B disclaims the remainder at A's death, B makes a taxable gift to B's descendants of the value of the trust assets at A's death.

6. *Disclaimers and the generation-skipping transfer tax.* The federal government imposes a generation-skipping transfer (GST) tax upon any transfer to a grandchild or other person two or more generations removed from the transferor. I.R.C. §§2601-2663 (see Chapter 15). In Case 10, an estate tax may be payable at T's death and a GST tax may be payable at A's death, when possession of the property is transferred to T's granddaughter. Suppose that A disclaims her life estate at T's death. The effect of the disclaimer is that a GST tax would be payable at T's death, when B (the settlor's grandchild) takes possession, rather than at A's death. The GST tax is in addition to the estate tax levied on T's estate. This last point is sometimes difficult for students to understand because it looks, at first glance, like double taxation. But remember the tax policy: a transfer tax is to be imposed on each living generation. Therefore, where a transfer is made to a grandchild, an estate tax is imposed on T's transfer of his estate, and, because the first generation below T has been skipped over and an estate tax at the death of that generation avoided, a GST tax is imposed on the transfer to the second generation below T. Were this not so, a person could avoid estate taxes in a child's estate by transferring

> *Case 11. T* devises property in trust "for my daughter *A* for life, then to *A*'s descendants."
> At *T*'s death, *A* can decide whether to disclaim and let the property pass to *A*'s descendants.

In Case 10, *B*'s disclaimer cuts out *B*'s afterborn descendants, and in Case 11, *A*'s disclaimer cuts out *A*'s afterborn descendants. Is this consistent with *T*'s probable intent? In Case 10, if *B* had not disclaimed, then she would have received the property outright. Subsequently she could have conveyed any, all, or none of the property to some, all, or none of her descendants. Viewed in this manner, it seems likely that *B*'s decision to disclaim at *T*'s death would not frustrate *T*'s intent.

By contrast, in Case 11 if *A* had not disclaimed her share, *A*'s descendants born after *T*'s death would have been entitled to a share of the property. Hence *A*'s disclaimer and its resulting acceleration of the remainder in *A*'s issue might frustrate *T*'s intent. This was the executor's argument in *Gilbert*. The court's answer was that the statute was enacted for the purpose of avoiding litigation over the testator's probable intent. Could this result have been avoided with better drafting?

2.   *T*'s will devises property in separate trusts, one "for my son *A* for life, then to the descendants of *A* and *B*," and the other "for my son *B* for life, then to the descendants of *A* and *B*." If, when *T* dies, *A* has descendants but *B* does not, by disclaiming does *A* cut off *B*'s afterborn descendants from the first trust, thereby ensuring that it will pass entirely to *A*'s descendants? See Pate v. Ford, 376 S.E.2d 775 (S.C. 1989).

3.   *Literature.* For further study of the intersection between disclaimer and acceleration, the impact of the UDPIA, and analysis of the potential for manipulation of the identity of the remainder beneficiaries through strategic disclaimers, see T.P. Gallanis, The Future of Future Interests, 60 Wash. & Lee L. Rev. 513, 523-529 (2003); Adam J. Hirsch, Revisions in Need of Revising: The Uniform Disclaimer of Property Interests Act, 29 Fla. St. U. L. Rev. 109, 170-175 (2001); William P. LaPiana, Some Property Law Issues in the Law of Disclaimers, 38 Real Prop., Prob. & Tr. J. 207, 220-225 (2003). See also Patricia G. Roberts, The Acceleration of Remainders: Manipulating the Identity of the Remaindermen, 42 S.C. L. Rev. 295 (1991).

b. Transferability

At common law, vested remainders, including defeasibly vested ones, were transferable inter vivos, but contingent remainders and executory interests were not. The theory of the early law was that contingent remainders and executory interests were mere chances of ownership. Today, only a few states retain some version of the common law rule of inalienability for contingent interests. The rest

---

property directly to a grandchild. The tax effect of *A*'s disclaimer in Case 10 would be that a GST tax becomes payable earlier — at *T*'s death rather than at *A*'s death. You can see why, with the enactment of the GST tax in 1986, disclaimers became decidedly less popular. For further discussion, see Joan B. Ellsworth, On Disclaimers: Let's Renounce I.R.C. Section 2518, 38 Vill. L. Rev. 693 (1993) (arguing that I.R.C. §2518 (tax treatment of disclaimers) should be repealed now that the GST tax has greatly reduced the tax incentives for using disclaimers).

have repudiated the rule by statute or by judicial decision. A spendthrift clause in the trust instrument, however, can render inalienable any possessory or future interest during the life of the owner of the interest.

Reversions, remainders, and executory interests are descendible and devisable at the death of the owner of the interest if not contingent on surviving to the time of possession. Such a future interest passes to the heirs or devisees of its owner, and this is true even if the trust has a spendthrift clause. In re Townley Bypass Unified Credit Trust, 252 S.W.3d 715 (Tex. App. 2008). Thus:

> *Case 12.* O conveys property in trust "for A for life, then to B," and includes a spendthrift clause that restricts B's right to alienate her interest in the trust. B dies during A's lifetime. B's remainder passes to B's devisees if B leaves a will or to B's heirs if B dies intestate.

A future interest contingent on surviving to the time of possession is not transferable at death. Thus, if in Case 12 O had conveyed a remainder "to B if B survives A," B could not transmit the remainder to another person if B died during A's lifetime.

The federal government subjects to estate taxation the transfer of any property interest. I.R.C. §2033. A future interest, like a possessory estate, is an interest in property and hence is subject to federal estate taxation if *transmissible* at death. *Transmissible* is a term of art meaning transferable by will or intestacy, irrespective of whether the interest is vested or contingent. Thus, in Case 12, if B dies during A's lifetime, the value of B's remainder is subject to estate taxation because it is transmissible.

PROBLEM AND NOTES

1. T's will devises property in trust "for A for life, then to B, and if B does not survive A, to C." If B dies during A's lifetime, is the value of B's remainder includible in B's taxable gross estate under the federal estate tax? If C dies before A and B, is the value of C's future interest includible in C's taxable gross estate?[7]

2. *Valuation of a future interest.* If a future interest is subject to estate taxation, the value of the future interest depends on the life tenant's life expectancy and the market rate of interest. The federal government publishes life expectancy tables and valuation tables for future interests. See I.R.C. §7520. For an explanation of how future interests are valued, see Jesse Dukeminier et al., Property 196-197 (6th ed. 2006).

3. You can give a remainderperson the power to transfer his remainder at death without estate tax exposure by making the remainder contingent on surviving to the time of possession and giving the remainderperson a special power

---

7. *Caution*: As pointed out in the prior footnote, a generation skipping transfer tax may be levied upon a transfer from a trust settlor to the settlor's grandchild. If B is T's child and C is B's child, a GST tax may be incurred at A's death if B predeceases A. At that point there will be a transfer from the settlor to the settlor's grandchild. Therefore, avoiding an estate tax at B's death at the cost of paying a GST tax at A's later death is not necessarily a good idea.

of appointment. Because such a remainder is not transmissible at death, it is not subject to estate taxation. And as we have seen, property subject to a special power is not subject to estate taxation either (see page 810). Here is an example:

> *Case 13.* *T* devises his residuary estate in trust "for *A* for life, then to *B* if *B* survives *A*, and if *B* does not survive *A*, then to such of *B*'s spouse or one or more of *B*'s descendants as *B* appoints by will." *B* has a contingent remainder that is not transmissible and a special power of appointment. If *B* dies during *A*'s life, *B*'s remainder disappears and is not taxable in *B*'s estate. In this event, the property passes on *A*'s death to persons whom *B* appoints or, if *B* fails to appoint, to *T*'s heirs.

c. Requiring Survival to Time of Possession

Under traditional law, there is no requirement that a remainder beneficiary live to the time of possession. The common law rule of construction, which reflects the traditional law's preference for vesting, provides that survival is not an implied condition of the gift. Thus, if the remainder beneficiary dies before the life tenant, the remainder passes to the remainder beneficiary's estate. This is rule of construction, however, that yields to an expression of contrary intent. And in a few specialized situations, hereafter noted, courts have implied a requirement of survival.

The traditional rule of construction that survival is not an implied condition of the gift is reversed by Uniform Probate Code §2-707 (1990, rev. 2008), and it is preserved but criticized by Restatement (Third) of Property: Wills and Other Donative Transfers §26.3 (P.D. No. 13, 2008). Under UPC §2-707, if a remainder beneficiary does not survive to the distribution date, unless the governing instrument provides otherwise a substitute gift is created in the remainder beneficiary's surviving descendants (that is, the antilapse idea from the law of wills is extended to future interests in trust). If there are no surviving descendants of the deceased remainder beneficiary, the property reverts to the settlor's heirs or devisees. Legislation based on UPC §2-707, or otherwise extending the antilapse concept to future interests in trust, has been adopted in one-third of the states. In two states the antilapse statute was extended to trusts by judicial decision, though one was later reversed by statute. Dollar Sav. & Trust Co. v. Turner, 529 N.E.2d 1261 (Ohio 1988), reversed by Ohio Rev. Code Ann. §§2107.01 et seq. (2008); In re Estate of Button, 490 P.2d 731 (Wash. 1971). See Alan Newman, Revocable Trusts and the Law of Wills: An Imperfect Fit, 43 Real Prop., Tr. & Est. J. 523, 542-545 (2008).

In this section we examine both the traditional no-survivorship rule of construction and the new survivorship-plus-antilapse rule of UPC §2-707. We begin with the traditional rule of construction, under which if a vested remainder subject to divestment is created, the courts (as in the next case) read the divesting language strictly and do not expand it to cause divestment in events other than those stated.

FIRST NATIONAL BANK OF BAR HARBOR v. ANTHONY, 557 A.2d 957 (Me. 1989): In 1975 Franklin Anthony created a revocable inter vivos trust, with income payable to the settlor for life, then to his wife Ethel for life, and upon the death of the settlor and his wife Ethel, the trust corpus was to be divided in equal shares among the settlor's children John, Peter, and Dencie. The settlor's wife Ethel died in 1982. In 1983 John died, leaving three children, Deborah, Christopher, and Paul. In 1984 the settlor, Franklin, died. His will devised two-thirds of his estate to his son Peter and one-third to his daughter Dencie. The children of John were excluded from the settlor's will.

John's children claimed John's one-third interest in the corpus of the trust. Peter and Dencie opposed. The lower court held that the gift to John in the trust "lapsed because his interest did not vest until the death of the survivor of the settlor and his wife," and the antilapse statute did not apply to revocable trusts, only to wills, so John's children could not take. The Supreme Judicial Court reversed, holding that "the remainder interest of John M. Anthony was a present, vested interest at the time of the creation of the inter vivos trust." The court explained:

> We note the following: (1) the settlor explicitly retained the right to change his beneficiaries if he wanted to alter the trust's disposition; (2) the settlor imposed no restrictions on what his children could do with their respective shares; (3) aside from his power to revoke or amend the trust, the settlor specifically limited his own benefit to income during his lifetime and payment of certain expenses associated with his death; (4) the settlor made survival an explicit condition of any benefit to his wife, but did not include such language in the case of his children. The unexercised right to make a change in beneficiaries, the absence of any control over how the children might dispose of their shares, and the overall assignment of economic benefits lead us to conclude that this plan of disposition effectively eliminated any further interest of the settlor in the trust principal unless he affirmatively chose to intervene. His failure to change the plan coupled with the omission of a survival requirement in the case of the children's shares, suggests a disposition to a predeceased child's estate rather than a reversion to the settlor's estate. As a result of this construction of the instrument, it may be said that [John's, Peter's, and Dencie's] interests were vested, subject to defeasance or divestment if the settlor chose to amend or revoke the trust or change his beneficiaries. . . .
>
> The trust instrument before us contains no requirement that the remainder beneficiaries survive the life tenants and we see no reason to imply a requirement of survival. Only the settlor's subsequent revocation or substitution would divest the remainder interest.

Accordingly, because John had a vested remainder subject to divestment by the settlor exercising his power of revocation, but the settlor did not exercise that power, John's interest in the trust passed to his children when he died.

NOTES, QUESTIONS, AND PROBLEM

1. *Remainders and lapse rules.* The traditional and still majority rule, followed in *Anthony*, is that a vested remainder in trust passes to the estate of the remainder beneficiary at her death unless the instrument provides expressly that the remainder is divested by her death. In re Estate of Silsby, 914 A.2d 703 (Me. 2006). Under this approach, because there is no lapse, there is no need to bring in the antilapse concept from the law of wills. Baldwin v. Branch, 888 So. 2d 482 (Ala. 2004).

If the court in *Anthony* had implied a condition of survivorship and then applied the antilapse statute, the result would have been the same. Under either the traditional rule or an antilapse theory, John's remainder would pass to his children — his heirs. But in some cases, the two theories would produce different results.

(a) Suppose John dies intestate, survived by a wife and children. Under the transmissible remainder theory, in many states both wife and children share in John's remainder interest as John's heirs, while in others and under Uniform Probate Code §2-102 (1990, rev. 2008), John's wife takes to the exclusion of the children, provided that all the children were hers and John's. Under an antilapse theory, by contrast, only John's children take. Which outcome would John prefer? Which outcome would the settlor, John's father, prefer?

(b) Suppose John leaves a will devising all his property to his wife. Under the transmissible remainder theory, his wife takes the remainder. Under an antilapse theory, only John's children take the remainder. Which outcome would John prefer? Which outcome would the settlor prefer?

(c) Suppose John is not survived by descendants and that by will he devises his property to his wife (or a friend). Under the transmissible remainder theory, John's wife (or other devisee) takes the remainder. Under the antilapse theory of UPC §2-707, the settlor's heirs or devisees take the remainder. Which outcome would John prefer? Which outcome would the settlor prefer?

2. *Avoiding drafting pitfalls.* A good lawyer does not rely on presumptions or default rules, but rather provides expressly what is to happen if an intended beneficiary does not survive to the time of distribution. For a cautionary tale, see Wagner v. DeSalvio, 860 N.Y.S.2d 146 (App. Div. 2008) (trust remainder given to *A*, *B*, and *C*, the settlor's children, "as contingent beneficiaries"; *C* predeceases leaving descendants; court awarded *C*'s share to *A* and *B* on the basis of a New York statute that reallocates ineffective remainders to the surviving remainder beneficiaries).

3. *Taxation of remainders.* A transmissible remainder, like any transferable interest, is subject to federal estate taxation upon the death of the remainderperson (see page 852). Thus, John Anthony's remainder in the revocable trust created by his father would be subject to estate taxation at his death. However, no taxes would be payable because John's remainder could be destroyed unconditionally by his father, meaning that the remainder has a value of zero.

Before 1986, there was a tax advantage in creating remainders contingent on survival to the time of possession. This tax advantage was weakened by the enactment of the generation-skipping transfer tax in 1986 (see Chapter 15). A GST tax, levied at the highest estate tax rate, is payable on the life tenant's death if the trust principal is then payable to the settlor's grandchildren or any other person two or more generations below the settlor. If, in *Anthony*, John Anthony had held a remainder contingent on his survival to the time of possession, no estate tax would be payable on his death, but on the settlor-life tenant's death a GST tax would be levied on the value of the property received by John's children (the settlor's grandchildren).

As noted at the outset of this section, the common law rule of construction that survival is not an implied condition of the gift yields to an expression of contrary intent, and in a few specialized situations, courts imply a requirement of survival.

(a) *Single- versus multigenerational classes.* Although courts do not imply survival requirements in gifts to single-generational classes, such as to "children" or "brothers and sisters," they do imply survival requirements in gifts to multigenerational classes, such as "issue" or "descendants," and apply the concept of representation from inheritance law. Thus, suppose that *T*'s will devises property "to *A* for life, then to *A*'s descendants." *A* has a son, *B*, and a daughter, *C*. *B* predeceases *A*, devising all his property to his wife. *B* is also survived by a daughter, *D*. On *A*'s death, *D* takes *B*'s share by representation; it does not pass to *B*'s wife. Similarly, where there is a gift to the "heirs" of *A*, a survival requirement to the death of *A* is implied. See Restatement (Third) of Property: Wills and Other Donative Transfers §§14.3-14.4, 15.3-15.4, 16.1 (T.D. No. 4, 2004).

(b) *Condition of survival ambiguous regarding time.* When the testator inserts the word "surviving" in a trust instrument, the word is ambiguous unless an additional word or words tell us *at what time* the donee must be surviving. The requirement of survival may relate to surviving the testator, the life tenant, or a preceding remainder beneficiary. Suppose *T* devises property in trust "for *A* for life, then to *B*, but if *B* dies before *A*, to *B*'s surviving children." *B* has two children, *C* and *D*. Then *B* dies. Then *D* dies intestate, survived by a child, *E*. *A* dies. Does *E* share? It depends on whether "surviving" means "surviving *A*," in which case *E* would not share because *D* did not survive *A*, or "surviving *B*," in which case *E* would share because *D* survived *B*. The prevailing view appears to be that "surviving" means surviving to the time of possession, thus excluding *E*. See Restatement (Third) of Property: Wills and Other Donative Transfers §26.4 (P.D. No. 13, 2008); 5 American Law of Property §21.15 (1952).

Suppose *T* conveys property in trust for *T* for life, and then "upon the death of *T*, the trustee shall pay over whatever remains of the trust estate to *T*'s son *A* if he shall then be living. If *T*'s son *A* shall then be deceased, the remains of the trust estate shall be paid to *T*'s then living descendants." *T* dies. Before the trustee distributes the trust property to *A*, *A* dies. *C* and *D*, the surviving children of *A*'s brother *B*, who predeceased both *A* and *T*, argue that "then living" refers to the time of distribution, not *T*'s death, and that they therefore are entitled to the trust property as *T*'s then living descendants. *E*, the beneficiary of *A*'s will, who is unrelated to *T*, argues that "then living" refers to the time of *T*'s death, and hence that he is entitled to the trust property. What result? See Chavin v. PNC Bank, 816 A.2d 781 (Del. 2003). Compare Wilson v. Rhodes, 258 S.W.3d 873 (Mo. App. 2008); Bryan v. Dethlefs, 959 So. 2d 314 (Fla. App. 2007).

(c) *Gift over on death without descendants.* Suppose *T* bequeaths a fund in trust "for *A* for life, then to *B*, but if *B* dies without descendants surviving her, to *C*." Does *T* intend *C* to take only if *B* dies *before A* without descendants? Or does *T* intend *C* to take if *B* dies *at any time* without descendants? The prevailing view favors the first construction, which permits the trust to terminate on *A*'s death. Accordingly, if *B* survives *A*, the trust property is distributed to *B* and *C* can never take. See

Restatement (Third) of Property: Wills and Other Donative Transfers §26.6 (P.D. No. 13, 2008); 5 American Law of Property §21.53 (1952).

Observe also that under the orthodox construction there is no requirement that *C* live to the time of possession. If *B* dies before *A*, and then *C* dies during *A*'s life, *C*'s interest passes to *C*'s heirs or devisees. In a few states a different rule is followed. If a future interest is contingent on an event other than survival to the time of possession (such as "if *B* dies without descendants"), the future interest is also contingent on surviving to the time of possession. See Rushing v. Mann, 910 S.W.2d 672 (Ark. 1995); Lawson v. Lawson, 148 S.E.2d 546 (N.C. 1966). This minority rule, which may be limited to class gifts, is criticized in Patricia G. Roberts, Class Gifts in North Carolina — When Do We "Call the Roll"?, 21 Wake Forest L. Rev. 1 (1985).

Clobberie's Case
Court of Chancery, England, 1677
86 Eng. Rep. 476

In one Clobberie's case it was held, that where one bequeathed a sum of money to a woman, at her age of twenty-one years, or day of marriage, to be paid unto her with interest, and she died before either, that the money should go to her executor; and was so decreed by my Lord Chancellor Finch.[8]

But he said, if money were bequeathed to one at his age of twenty-one years, if he dies before that age, the money is lost.

On the other side, if money be given to one, to be paid at the age of twenty-one years; there, if the party dies before, it shall go to the executors.

NOTES AND PROBLEMS

1.   *The three rules in Clobberie's Case.* The decision in Clobberie's Case is cited routinely for three rules of construction, one for each paragraph of the case report. The first and third rules are widely followed today. They apply to immediate gifts as well as to remainders, and to a gift to a class as well as to a gift to an individual.

Under the first rule in Clobberie's Case, a gift of the *entire income* to a person (or to a class), with principal to be paid at a designated age, indicates that survival to the time of possession is not required. The reason for this rule is that all interests in the property — both income and principal — are given to the same person or persons, with only possession of the principal postponed. When the beneficiary dies before reaching the stated age, there is no point in delaying payment of the principal to the beneficiary's estate. See 5 American Law of Property §21.20 (1952).

---

8. Lord Chancellor Finch was later titled Lord Nottingham and became famous for launching the Rule Against Perpetuities in the Duke of Norfolk's Case. See page 887. — Eds.

Under the third rule in Clobberie's Case, a gift "payable" or "to be paid" at a designated age indicates that survival to the time of possession is not required. If the beneficiary dies before reaching that age, the principal will be paid at the beneficiary's death to the beneficiary's estate, unless someone would be harmed by such payment. If the income is payable to another, for example, the principal cannot be paid to the principal beneficiary's estate until the income beneficiary dies. See id. §21.18. Cf. Blue Ridge Bank and Trust Co. v. McFall, 207 S.W.3d 149 (Mo. App. 2006).

The American cases are split over whether to follow the second rule, which states that a gift "at" a designated age implies a requirement of survivorship to that age. See 5 American Law of Property, supra, at §21.17. The distinction between a legacy "at 21" (survivorship to 21 required) and a legacy "to be paid at 21" (survivorship to 21 is not required) has been criticized by most commentators as a distinction without a difference.

Restatement (Third) of Property: Wills and Other Donative Transfers §26.9 (P.D. No. 13, 2008) takes the position that, unless the governing instrument provides otherwise, any "future interest that is distributable upon reaching a specified age is conditioned on the beneficiary's survival to that age." The Restatement thus rejects the first and third rules in Clobberie's case, and follows the second.

2.   Suppose *T* bequeaths $10,000 "to *A* when *A* attains 21." *A* is age 15 at *T*'s death. Who is entitled to income from the $10,000 before *A* reaches 21? If *A* dies at age 16, does the legacy fail or is *A*'s administrator entitled to demand payment of $10,000 at *A*'s death or when *A* would have reached 21 had *A* lived? See Edward C. Halbach, Jr., Future Interests: Express and Implied Conditions of Survival, 49 Cal. L. Rev. 297, 299-302 (1961); Lumbert v. Estate of Carter, 867 So. 2d 1175 (Fla. App. 2004).

Suppose *T* bequeaths a fund in trust "for *A* for life, then after *A*'s death to *A*'s children, each share payable as each child respectively reaches the age of 30, if he or she has not reached age 30 before *A* dies." A child of *A* dies at age 10 during *A*'s life. What result?

Suppose *T* bequeaths a fund in trust for the benefit of her child Benjamin "until my child attains age 25, at which time the income and principal shall be distributed and paid over to him and the trust shall terminate." *T*'s will did not name a trust beneficiary if Benjamin died under age 25. Benjamin died at 20. Benjamin's heir is his father, who was previously divorced from Ben's mother. What result? See Summers v. Summers, 699 N.E.2d 958 (Ohio App. 1997).

3.   In Goldenberg v. Golden, 769 So. 2d 1144 (Fla. App. 2000), the testator bequeathed a fund in trust for the benefit of his daughter, who was to receive three-fourths of the income, and his two grandchildren, who were to share one-fourth of the income divided equally. Upon his daughter's death, the principal was to be divided equally between his two grandchildren, one-half when each turned 25 and the remainder when each turned 30. At age 44, while the testator's daughter was still alive, one of the grandchildren died intestate, leaving his wife as his only heir. The testator's other grandchild and the deceased grandchild's

wife both argued that each was the successor to the deceased grandchild's interest in the trust. Quoting a decision of the state supreme court that embraced the
first rule in Clobberie's Case, the court held that the deceased grandchild's interest was vested and hence passed to his wife. The court did not discuss the fact that
the deceased grandchild had been entitled to only one-eighth of the trust
income, not the entire income from the share of the principal that he would have
received upon his mother's death.

NOTE: ANTILAPSE RULES FOR FUTURE INTERESTS IN TRUST

The purpose of UPC §2-707 (1990, rev. 2008) is to extend the antilapse concept from the law of wills to future interests in trust. In effect, §2-707 applies the
antilapse statute as if the transferor were a testator who died on the distribution
date. Although a straightforward concept, the implementation in §2-707 is dev-
ilishly complex. The statute provides for two or more alternative future interests,
for which substitute gifts are created, and also provides for tie-breakers where two
groups of substitute takers appear to have equal claims. Even the drafters call the
statute "elaborate and intricate" and acknowledge that understanding it will
require "a few hours" of study. Edward C. Halbach, Jr. and Lawrence W. Waggoner, The UPC's New Survivorship and Antilapse Provisions, 55 Alb. L. Rev.
1091, 1148 (1992).

Nevertheless, the primary changes to the law made by the statute can be summarized neatly. Under UPC §2-707, unless the instrument provides otherwise,
the following rules apply:

1. *Implied condition of survival.* All future interests in trust are contingent on
   the beneficiary's surviving to the date of distribution.
2. *Substitute gift in descendants.* If a remainder beneficiary does not survive to
   the distribution date, a substitute gift is created in the remainder beneficiary's descendants who survive to the date of distribution.
3. *Failed remainders revert to settlor's devisees or heirs.* If a remainder beneficiary
   dies before distribution and leaves no descendants, the remainder fails,
   and, if there is no alternative remainder that takes effect, the trust property
   passes to the settlor's residuary devisees or to the settlor's heirs.

A version of UPC §2-707 or other legislation that applies the antilapse concept
from the law of wills to future interests in trust has been adopted in about one-
third of the states.[9] Moreover, although Restatement (Third) of Property: Wills
and Other Donative Transfers §26.3 (P.D. No. 13, 2008) preserves the traditional

---

9. Alaska, Arizona, Colorado, Florida, Hawaii, Illinois, Iowa, Massachusetts, Michigan, Montana, New
Mexico, North Dakota, Pennsylvania, South Dakota, Tennessee, and Utah. In addition, the antilapse statute was
extended to trusts in Dollar Sav. & Trust Co. v. Turner, 529 N.E.2d 1261 (Ohio 1988), and In re Estate of Button,
490 P.2d 731 (Wash. 1971), though the Ohio case was later overturned by statute. See Ohio Rev. Code Ann.
§§2107.01 et seq. (2008).

rule, it does so only because the drafters were wary that in the absence of authorizing legislation, if a condition of survival was imposed, the courts could not effect a substitute gift in the descendants of a remainder beneficiary who did not survive to possession. All of which is to say that there seems to be a movement, albeit slowly developing and largely dependent on statutory warrant, toward reversing the common law rule of construction and implying a condition of survival with a substitute gift in descendants.

This movement has been controversial. Several scholars have risen in fierce opposition to UPC §2-707. Others, including the statute's drafters, have risen in strong defense of its provisions.[10] To focus the issues and bring the pros and cons of §2-707 into sharper relief, consider the following cases:

> *Case 14.* *T* devises property in trust "for *W* for life, then to my descendants." *T* has three children, *A*, *B*, and *C*. Under both traditional law and UPC §2-707, because *T* has made a gift to a multigenerational class, *A*'s remainder is contingent on *A*'s surviving *W* (see page 856). If *A* dies during *W*'s life, *A*'s remainder is redirected to *A*'s descendants or, if *A* is not survived by descendants, *A*'s share is reallocated to *B* and *C*.
>
> *Case 15.* *T* devises property in trust "for *W* for life, then to my children." *T* has three children, *A*, *B*, and *C*. Under traditional law, because *T* has made a gift to a single-generational class, *A*'s remainder is not contingent on *A*'s surviving *W* (see page 856). If *A* dies during *W*'s life, *A*'s remainder passes to *A*'s heirs or devisees. Under UPC §2-707, *A*'s remainder is contingent on *A*'s surviving *W*. If *A* dies during *W*'s life, *A*'s remainder is redirected to *A*'s descendants or, if *A* is not survived by descendants, *A*'s share is reallocated to *B* and *C*.
>
> *Case 16.* *T* devises property in trust "for *W* for life, then to my daughter *A*." Under traditional law, *A*'s remainder is not contingent on *A*'s surviving *W*. If *A* dies during *W*'s life, *A*'s remainder passes to *A*'s heirs or devisees. Under UPC §2-707, *A*'s remainder is contingent on *A*'s surviving *W*. If *A* dies during *W*'s life, *A*'s remainder is redirected to *A*'s descendants or, if *A* is not survived by descendants, the gift fails and the property reverts to *T*'s heirs or devisees.

In assaying the merits of UPC §2-707, the point of departure is to observe that, of the foregoing case studies, Case 14 comes closest to what is typical in instruments drafted by skilled estate planners. In a typical, well-drafted estate plan, the first spouse to die will leave his property in trust to his surviving spouse for life, with the remainder to such of the settlor's descendants (and perhaps the descendants' spouses) as the settlor's surviving spouse names by will. Giving the surviving spouse a special power of appointment over the remainder is most

---

10. In opposition, see Jesse Dukeminier, The Uniform Probate Code Upends the Law of Remainders, 94 Mich. L. Rev. 148 (1995); Laura E. Cunningham, The Hazards of Tinkering with the Common Law of Future Interests: The California Experience, 48 Hastings L.J. 667 (1997); David M. Becker, Uniform Probate Code §2-707 and the Experienced Estate Planner: Unexpected Disasters and How to Avoid Them, 47 UCLA L. Rev. 339 (1999); David M. Becker, Eroding the Common Law Paradigm for Creation of Property Interests and the Hidden Costs of Law Reform, 83 Wash. U. L.Q. 773 (2005). See also Susan F. French, Imposing a General Survival Requirement on Beneficiaries of Future Interests: Solving the Problems Caused by the Death of a Beneficiary Before the Time Set for Distribution, 27 Ariz. L. Rev. 801 (1985).

In defense, see Edward C. Halbach, Jr. and Lawrence W. Waggoner, The UPC's New Survivorship and Antilapse Provisions, 55 Alb. L. Rev. 1091 (1992); Lawrence W. Waggoner, The Uniform Probate Code Extends Antilapse-Type Protection to Poorly Drafted Trusts, 94 Mich. L. Rev. 2309 (1996). See also Lawrence W. Waggoner, Class Gifts Under the Restatement (Third) of Property, 22 Ohio N.U. L. Rev. 993 (2007); Edward C. Halbach, Jr., Uniform Acts, Restatements and Trends in American Trust Law and Century's End, 88 Cal. L. Rev. 1877 (2000); Mary Louise Fellows and Gregory S. Alexander, Forty Years of Codification of Estates and Trusts Law: Lessons for the Next Generation, 40 Ga. L. Rev. 1049 (2006).

common when all the children of the settlor are also children of the surviving spouse, as is typical in a first marriage. Alternatively, if the life tenant is in an adversarial relationship with the settlor's children, as might be the case if the settlor has children from a prior marriage or if the life tenant is not a surviving spouse, the instrument will commonly provide for a remainder in the settlor's descendants on the death of the life tenant without a power of appointment in the life tenant. In either scenario, under both traditional law and §2-707, there is an implied condition of survival and the share of a predeceasing child of the settlor passes to the predeceasing child's descendants.

A good lawyer does not rely on presumptions or default rules. Instead she makes the client's intent clear by providing expressly what happens if the intended beneficiary does not survive to the time of distribution. The choice between the traditional rule and UPC §2-707 affects outcomes only in cases in which the remainder is given to a single-generation class, such as to "children" as in Case 15, or to a specifically identified person, as in Case 16, but a child or the person does not survive to the distribution date and the trust instrument does not expressly address this possibility. Under traditional law, in such cases the remainder beneficiary has a transmissible remainder that passes to the beneficiary's heirs or devisees. Under §2-707, the remainder passes to the remainder beneficiary's descendants, if any, or otherwise to the settlor's heirs or devisees. Since it is in these scenarios that the shoe pinches, so to speak, let us consider them more closely.

When a remainder is given to children, as in Case 15, one has a nagging suspicion that the drafter carelessly chose the term *children* when the term *descendants* (or *issue*) — incorporating the principle of representation so prominent in the law of inheritance — would have better fit the settlor's intent. Put otherwise, one suspects that the settlor would want a substitute gift in the descendants of a child who does not survive to the distribution date rather than for the remainder to pass through the deceased child's estate to the deceased child's heirs or devisees. UPC §2-707 implements this intuition; its drafters reasoned that the settlor would want to protect a line of descent that has one or more living members on the distribution date. See Restatement (Third) of Property, supra, §23.3, cmt. e. Where you land on the spectrum from sympathy to hostility for §2-707 usually depends on whether you share this intuition.

In the case of a remainder given to a named person, as in Case 16, the analysis is more difficult. When a specific person is named, it is less clear that the settlor would prefer a substitute gift in the person's descendants over the remainder passing to the person's heirs or devisees if the person does not survive to the distribution date. Critics of UPC §2-707 argue that the traditional rule will yield better outcomes because a transmissible remainder functions like a testamentary power of appointment, enabling the beneficiary to choose a successor taker. This successor taker could be the remainder beneficiary's descendants, as is imposed by operation of law under §2-707, but it could also be the beneficiary's spouse, a charity, or anyone else, outright or in further trust, as changed circumstances warrant.

Proponents of §2-707 counter that the relevant perspective is that of the settlor and that, as evidenced by the frequency in well-drafted instruments of alternative gifts to the descendants of a predeceasing remainder beneficiary, most settlors would prefer to keep the share of a predeceasing remainder beneficiary in the same line of descent if there is a living descendant on the distribution date. Powers of appointment in a remainder beneficiary, while not unheard of, are rarer and may still be provided for expressly if that is what the settlor wants. A substitute gift in the remainder beneficiary's descendants has the further benefit of avoiding the possibility of subjecting the remainder to estate taxation when it passes through the deceased beneficiary's estate, though a generation-skipping transfer tax may be due on the death of the life tenant if the substituted takers are the settlor's grandchildren or any other persons two or more generations below the settlor.

A secondary point of contention concerns the question whether *words of survivorship* are sufficient, in the absence of additional evidence, to override a substitution of descendants for a predeceasing remainder beneficiary. UPC §2-707 provides that words of survivorship attached to a future interest are *not* sufficient. Thus, under §2-707, if *T* devises a fund in trust "for *A* for life, then to *B if B survives A*," the words "if *B* survives *A*" do not indicate that the transferor does not want *B*'s descendants substituted for *B* if *B* predeceases *A*. If *B* predeceases *A*, leaving descendants, the descendants take in spite of this language. This rule of construction, which appears also in UPC §2-603 (the antilapse statute applicable to wills treated at pages 366-374), has been sharply criticized by commentators and has received a chilly reception in the legislatures. As with §2-603, some states that have enacted §2-707, such as Massachusetts in 2009, have dropped this provision, and others, such as Arizona and Florida, have modified it to state that words of survivorship *are* a sufficient indication of an intent contrary to a substitute gift in descendants. One wonders whether §2-707 would have taken less fire if the drafters had stopped at implying a condition of survival and imposing a substitute gift in a predeceasing remainder beneficiary's descendants without also adding the complexity of disregarding words of survivorship.

It bears repeating that a good lawyer does not rely on presumptions or default rules, and that these default rules of construction would not come into play for instruments she drafts. Instead, she makes the client's intent clear by providing expressly what happens if the intended beneficiary does not survive to the time of distribution.

2.   *Gifts to Classes*

As you may recall from Chapter 5 (see page 375), a *class gift* arises when the donor is "group minded." The donor is thought to be group minded if she uses a class label in describing the beneficiaries, such as "to *A*'s children" or "to my nephews and nieces." But a class label is not necessary to create a class gift. A gift to beneficiaries who form a natural class but are described by their individual names may be deemed a gift to a class if the court decides, after admitting extrinsic evidence, that the testator would want the survivors to divide the property rather than for a predeceasing beneficiary's share to lapse. See Restatement (Third) of Property: Wills and Other Donative Transfers §§13.1-13.2 (T.D. No. 4, 2004), page 375.

Gifts to classes raise a host of interpretive and constructional problems. We examine here some of the recurring problems under this heading.

a.   Gifts of Income

Dewire v. Haveles
Supreme Judicial Court of Massachusetts, 1989
404 Mass. 274, 534 N.E.2d 782

WILKINS, J.   This petition for a declaration of rights seeks answers to questions arising from an artlessly drafted will that, among its many inadequacies, includes a blatant violation of the rule against perpetuities. . . .

Thomas A. Dewire died in January, 1941, survived by his widow, his son Thomas, Jr., and three grandchildren (Thomas, III, Paula, and Deborah, all children of Thomas, Jr.). His will placed substantially all his estate in a residuary trust. The income of the trust was payable to his widow for life and, on her death, the income was payable to his son Thomas, Jr., the widow of Thomas, Jr., and Thomas Jr.'s children.[11] After the testator's death, Thomas, Jr., had three more children by a second wife. Thomas, Jr., died on May 28, 1978, a widower, survived by all six of his children. Thomas, III, who had served as trustee since 1978, died on March 19, 1987, leaving a widow and one child, Jennifer. Among the questions presented, and the most important one for present purposes, is to whom the one-sixth share of the trust income, once payable to Thomas, III, is now payable.

In his will, the testator stated: "It is my will, except as hereinabove provided, that my grandchildren, under guidance and discretion of my Trustee, shall share equally in the net income of my said estate." At another point, he referred to the trust income being "divided equally amongst my grandchildren." The rule against perpetuities violation occurred because the will provided for the trust's termination "twenty-one years after the death of the last surviving child of my

---

11. The language of the will directing this distribution appears in article third of the will and reads as follows:

Third: To my wife, Mabel G. Dewire, I give, devise and bequeath all the rest, residue and remainder of all the estate of which I shall die seized, for and during the term of her natural life, and upon her decease to my son, Thomas A. Dewire, Jr., and his heirs and assigns, but in trust nevertheless upon the following trusts and for the following purposes:

A. To hold, direct, manage and conserve the trust estate, so given, for the benefit of himself, his wife and children in the manner following, that is to say:

To expend out of the net income so much as may be necessary for the proper care, maintenance of himself and wife conformable to their station in life, and for the care, maintenance and education of his children born to him in his lifetime, in such manner as in his judgment and discretion shall seem proper, and his judgment and discretion shall be final.

said son, Thomas A. Dewire, Jr., when the property of the trust shall be equally divided amongst the lineal descendants of my grandchildren."[12]

There is no explicit provision in the will concerning the distribution of income on the death of a grandchild while the gift of income to grandchildren continues, nor is there any statement as to what the trustee should do with trust income between the death of the last grandchild and the date assigned for termination of the trust twenty-one years later.

Our task is to discern the testator's intention concerning the distribution of a grandchild's share of the trust income on his death. As a practical matter, in cases of this sort, where there is no express intention, we must resort to reasonable inferences in the particular circumstances which on occasion shade into rules of construction that are applied when no intention at all can be inferred on the issue. In this case, the reasonable inference as to the testator's intention is that Jennifer should take her father's share in the income.

Certain points are not in serious controversy and are relatively easy to resolve. The gift of net income to the testator's grandchildren, divided equally or to be shared equally, is a class gift. . . . The class includes all six grandchildren, three of whom were born before and three of whom were born after the testator's death. . . . Because there is a gift over at the end of the class gift, the testator intended the class gift to his grandchildren only to be a gift of a life interest in the income of the trust. . . . The general rule is that, in the absence of a contrary intent expressed in the will or a controlling statute stating otherwise, members of a class are joint tenants with rights of survivorship. Old Colony Trust Co. v. Treadwell, 43 N.E.2d 777, 779 (Mass. 1942). Meserve v. Haak, 77 N.E. 377, 379 (Mass. 1906). See G.L. c. 191, §22 (1986 ed.) (antilapse statute).

This last stated principle becomes important in deciding whether Jennifer, the child of the deceased grandson, takes her deceased father's share in the trust income or whether the remaining class members, the other five grandchildren, take that income share equally by right of survivorship. Jennifer argues, under the general rule, that the will manifests an intent contrary to a class gift with rights of survivorship. We agree with this conclusion. Thus we need not decide, as Jennifer further argues, whether the rule of construction presuming a right of survivorship in class members should be rejected in the circumstances and replaced by a rule based on principles similar to those expressed in the antilapse statute.[13]

---

12. As we shall explain, the possibility that Thomas, Jr., would have a child born after the testator's death was sufficient to cause the violation of the rule against perpetuities. The fact that Thomas, Jr., had children born after the testator's death makes possible a violation of the rule in actual fact.

13. The Massachusetts antilapse statute applies only to testamentary gifts to a child or other relation of a testator who predeceased the testator leaving issue surviving the testator and to class gifts to children or other relations where one or more class member predeceased the testator (even if the class member had died before the will was executed). G.L. c. 191, §22. The rule of construction of §22 is that the issue of a deceased relation take his share by right of representation "unless a different disposition is made or required by the will."

In this case, no class member predeceased the testator, and, therefore, §22 does not explicitly aid Jennifer. The policy underlying §22 might fairly be seen as supporting, as a rule of construction (absent a contrary intent), the substitution of a class member's surviving issue for a deceased class member if the class is made up of children or other relations of the testator. See Bigelow v. Clap, 43 N.E. 1037, 1038 (Mass. 1896). It has been suggested that "[t]he policy of [antilapse] statutes [dealing with the death of a class member after the testator's death] commends itself to decisional law." Restatement (Second) of Property, Donative Transfers §27.3 Com-

Before we explain why the will expresses an intention that, during the term of the class gift, Jennifer, while living, should take her father's share in the income, we discuss the rule against perpetuities problem.[14] The prospect that interests under this will may vest beyond the permissible limit of the rule against perpetuities is not only theoretically possible, it is actuarially likely. The interests of the grandchildren in the trust income vested at their father's death (if not sooner) and, because he was a life in being at the testator's death, those interests vested within the period of the rule. The gift over at the end of the class gift of income to the grandchildren, however, might not vest seasonably because another grandchild could have been born after the testator's death and could be the surviving grandchild. In this case, in fact, the three youngest grandchildren were born after the death of the testator but they are measuring lives for the term of the class gift. The parties agree that the purported gift of the remainder to the lineal descendants of the testator's grandchildren "twenty-one years after the death of the last surviving" grandchild violates the rule against perpetuities in its traditional form and would be void. See Second Bank-State St. Trust Co. v. Second Bank-State St. Trust Co., 140 N.E.2d 201, 205-206 (Mass. 1957). There is no need at this time to decide the question of the proper distribution of trust income or assets at the death of the last grandchild. The question will be acute at the death of the last grandchild, when the class gift of income from the trust will terminate.

The rule against perpetuities problem need not be resolved at this time. It has some bearing, however, on what should be done during the term of the class gift with the one-sixth share of the trust income that is in dispute. We reject the argument that, because of the violation of the rule against perpetuities, the income interests should be treated as being more than life interests. There is no authority for such a proposition. Although the gift over violates the rule against perpetuities in its traditional form and in time may prove to violate it in actual fact, the language providing for such a distribution may properly be considered in determining a testator's intention with respect to other aspects of his will. . . .

We are now in a position to discuss the question whether the class gift of income to grandchildren calls for the payment of income equally to those grandchildren living from time to time (as joint tenants with rights of survivorship) or whether the issue of any deceased grandchild succeeds by right of representation to his income interest. The latter result better conforms with the testator's intentions.

The testator provided that the trust should terminate twenty-one years after the death of his last grandchild. It is unlikely that the testator intended that trust income should be accumulated for twenty-one years, and we would tend to avoid

---

ment i (Tent. Draft No. 9, 1986). If the antilapse statute protects the interests of the issue of a relation who predeceases a testator, there is a good reason why we should adopt, as a rule of construction, the same principle as to a relation of a testator who survives the testator but dies before an interest comes into possession. In the case of a class gift of income from a trust, the interest could be viewed as coming into possession of each income distribution date.

14. In its classic formulation, the rule against perpetuities declares that: "No interest is good unless it must vest, if at all, not later than twenty-one years after some life in being at the creation of the interest." J.C. Gray, The Rule Against Perpetuities §201, at 191 (4th ed. 1942). See Eastman Marble Co. v. Vermont Marble Co., 128 N.E. 177, 182 (Mass. 1920).

such a construction. See Meserve v. Haak, 77 N.E. 377, 378-379 (Mass. 1906). Certainly, we should not presume that he intended an intestacy as to that twenty-one year period. See Anderson v. Harris, 67 N.E.2d 670, 672-673 (Mass. 1946). He must have expected that someone would receive distributions of income during those years. The only logical recipients of that income would be the issue (by right of representation) of deceased grandchildren, the same group of people who would take the trust assets on termination of the trust (assuming no violation of the rule against perpetuities).[15] If these people were intended to receive income during the last twenty-one years of the trust as well as the trust assets on its termination, it is logical that they should also receive income during the term of the class gift if their ancestor (one of the grandchildren) should die. Such a pattern treats each grandchild and his issue equally throughout the intended term of the trust. Where, among other things, every other provision in the will concerning the distribution of trust income and principal (after the death of the testator and his wife) points to equal treatment of the testator's issue per stirpes, there is a sufficient contrary intent shown to overcome the rule of construction that the class gift of income to grandchildren is given to them as joint tenants with the right of survivorship.

Judgment shall be entered declaring that (1) Jennifer Ann Dewire in her lifetime is entitled to one-sixth of the net income of the trust during the period of the class gift of income, that is, until the death of the last grandchild (and a proportionate share of the income of any grandchild who dies leaving no issue), [and] (2) no declaration shall be made at this time concerning the disposition of trust income or principal on the death of the last grandchild of Thomas A. Dewire . . . .

So ordered.

PROBLEM AND NOTE

1. *T* bequeaths a fund in trust to pay the income "to each of my children Gertrude, Charlotte, and John in equal amounts during their lives, and upon the death of the last survivor, to distribute the principal to their descendants per stirpes then living." Gertrude dies. What distribution of income is made? If Charlotte and John receive Gertrude's share, Gertrude's spouse and children are cut off from any benefits they have been receiving from Gertrude's share and the surviving children get richer. See Svenson v. First Natl. Bank of Boston, 363 N.E.2d 1129 (Mass. App. 1977) (devise of income substantially identical except made to testator's servants rather than her children; court held gift of income was a class gift, to be divided by surviving servants); Westervelt v. First Interstate Bank, 551 N.E.2d 1180 (Ind. App. 1990) (holding income goes to surviving child on theory that each child has an implied cross remainder in the other child's share).

---

15. "[T]he property of the trust shall be equally divided amongst the lineal descendants of my grandchildren." "Equally," referring to a multigenerational class, normally means per stirpes. New England Trust Co. v. McAleer, 181 N.E.2d 569, 572 (Mass. 1962).

Under the traditional rule, which was followed in *Svenson* and *Westervelt*, Thomas III's share in *Dewire* would have been paid to the surviving grandchildren, not to his descendants. Of course, the rules of construction that lead to this result can be overcome by contrary intent, and *Dewire* is a rare — but sensible — example of a court finding a contrary intent. Restatement (Third) of Trusts §49, cmt. c(3) (2003), not only approves of this result, but it also modifies the applicable rules of construction so that it would be more common. Under the Restatement, in cases "in which the remainder is to pass to the descendants of the income beneficiaries upon the survivor's death," and one of the income beneficiaries dies, "the normal inference is that the settlor intended the income share to be paid to the issue (if any) of the deceased income beneficiary." See also Restatement (Third) of Property: Wills and Other Donative Transfers §14.1, cmt. g(4) (T.D. No. 4, 2004), to similar effect.

2. *Drafting advice.* When you give income to a class of persons, do not dispose of the principal upon the death of the survivor, which leaves open the question litigated in *Dewire*. Instead, say "upon the death of each life tenant," and go on to provide what is to be done with the individual life tenant's share. See John L. Garvey, Drafting Wills and Trusts: Anticipating the Birth and Death of Possible Beneficiaries, 71 Or. L. Rev. 47 (1992).

b. Gifts to Children, Issue, or Descendants

The law presumes that the word *children* means only the immediate offspring of the parent and does not include grandchildren or more remote descendants.

> *Case 17. T* bequeaths a fund in trust "for my daughter, *A*, for life, then to *A*'s surviving children." At *T*'s death, *A* has two children, *B* and *C*. Subsequently *C* dies, leaving a child, *D*. Then *A* dies survived by *B* and *D*. If *children* means what it says, *B* takes all the trust fund and *D* does not share. So held in In re Gustafson, 547 N.E.2d 1152 (N.Y. 1989), denying *A*'s grandchild a share, over a strong dissent.

In a case such as this, one has a nagging suspicion that the term *children* was used carelessly and that the terms *issue* or *descendants*, incorporating the principle of representation familiar from inheritance law, would have better fit *T*'s intent. This suspicion has given rise to numerous cases, often involving homemade wills, litigating the question whether the testator (drafter?) meant by children persons other than immediate offspring. Some courts, on the basis of other language in the governing instrument or extrinsic circumstances, have held that the donor meant descendants. See also Restatement (Third) of Property: Wills and Other Donative Transfers §14.1, cmt. g (T.D. No. 4, 2004), which provides that a gift to children usually excludes grandchildren and more remote descendants, but may mean issue or descendants if coupled with language of representation or other reasons for so interpreting it.

Where *T* makes a multigenerational gift in trust, such as "to the descendants of *A*," *A*'s descendants presumptively take *by right of representation* and not *per capita*.

Under a per capita distribution, favored by the early law but no longer, all of *A*'s descendants alive on the distribution date take an equal share. Under a representational distribution, only the living descendants of nearest degree in each line of descent take. Thus, if *A* has three children, *B*, *C*, and *D*, and *B* predeceases *A* leaving two children, *E* and *F*, who survive *A*, the property is divided into three shares with *E* and *F* splitting *B*'s third.

The courts vary on what language is sufficient to overcome the presumption that a gift to issue or descendants is to be distributed by right of representation and not per capita. Suppose *T* devises property in trust with the remainder to the descendants of *A*, "share and share alike." Is the remainder distributed per capita, with all living descendants of *A* taking an equal share, including those with a living ancestor in the line of descent, or is it distributed by representation, with only the living descendants of *A* of nearest degree in each line of descent entitled to take? Compare Estate of Goodwin, 739 N.Y.S.2d 239 (Sur. 2002) (per capita), with First Illini Bank v. Pritchard, 595 N.E.2d 728 (Ill. App. 1992) (by representation).

When a distribution is by representation, a further question arises: which version of representation applies: (1) English per stirpes, (2) modern per stirpes, or (3) per capita at each generation (see pages 88-89)? Restatement (First) of Property §303 (1940) took the position, still followed by some courts, that the form of representation encoded in the local intestacy statute should be followed even if the governing instrument used the term *per stirpes*. More recently, there has been movement toward following the form of representation used in the local intestacy statute unless the instrument uses the term *per stirpes*, in which case English per stirpes is followed. The rationale for this approach is to give effect to the probable intention of the drafter, who is thought to have had the traditional English per stirpes system in mind rather than the state's intestacy statute. See UPC §§2-708 and 2-709 (1990, rev. 1993); Restatement (Third) of Property: Wills and Other Donative Transfers §14.4, cmt. c (T.D. No. 4, 2004).

Another question that has sometimes vexed the courts is whether a person *adopted* by *A* is included in a gift by *T* to the children, issue, descendants, or heirs of *A*. Today almost all states presumptively include adopted individuals (and children born out of wedlock) in such gifts, but problems still arise with adult adoptions and with wills and trusts drafted before the presumption of equal treatment for adopted children took hold. For discussion, see pages 102-109, including Minary v. Citizens Fidelity Bank & Trust Co., 419 S.W.2d 340 (Ky. 1967). The new forms of parentage stemming from advances in *assisted reproductive technology*, including the increasing prevalence of *posthumously conceived children*, have likewise raised interpretive difficulties. For discussion, see pages 126-130, including In re Martin B., 841 N.Y.S.2d 207 (Sur. 2008). Under the UPC, terms of relationship in class gifts are construed in accord with the meaning of those terms under the rules of intestate succession. UPC §2-705 (1990, rev. 2008). The UPC provisions pertaining to adoption and assisted reproductive technology, extensively revised in 2008, are treated in Chapter 2, at the referenced pages just given.

Drafting advice. In view of the unsettled state of the law, the clear drafting lesson is that you should define *issue*, *descendants*, *per stirpes*, and other such terms, among other things making clear the representational scheme that is desired. For a cautionary tale, see In re Estate of Damon, 128 P.3d 815 (Haw. 2006), where the court, following UPC §2-709, held that the term *per stirpes* referenced English rather than modern per stirpes, changing the amounts payable to two of the competing claimants by about $120 million.

c. Gifts to Heirs

Estate of Woodworth

California Court of Appeal, Fifth District, 1993
22 Cal. Rptr. 2d 676

DiBiaso, J.   The Regents of the University of California (Regents) appeal from an order of the probate court which rejected their claim to the remainder of a testamentary trust. We will reverse. We will apply the common law preference for early vesting and hold that, absent evidence of the testator's intent to the contrary, the identity of "heirs" entitled to trust assets must be determined at the date of death of the named ancestor who predeceased the life tenant, not at the date of death of the life tenant.

STATEMENT OF CASE AND FACTS

Harold Evans Woodworth died testate in 1971. His will was thereafter admitted to probate; in 1974 a decree of distribution was entered. According to this decree,[16] a portion of the estate was distributed outright to the testator's surviving spouse, Mamie Barlow Woodworth. The balance of the estate was distributed to Mamie Barlow Woodworth and the Bank of America, to be held, administered and distributed in accord with the terms of a testamentary trust established by the will of Harold Evans Woodworth. The life tenant of the trust was Mamie Barlow Woodworth. Among the trust provisions was the following:

> This trust shall terminate upon the death of MAMIE BARLOW WOODWORTH. Upon the termination of this trust, my trustee shall pay, deliver and convey all of the trust estate then remaining, including all accrued and/or undistributed income thereunto appertaining, to MRS. RAY B. PLASS, also known as Elizabeth Woodworth Plass [Elizabeth Plass], whose present address is 90 Woodland Way, Piedmont, California, if she then survives, and if not then to her heirs at law.

Elizabeth Plass was the testator's sister; he also had two brothers who predeceased him. One died without issue. The other was survived by two children,

---

16. The decedent's will was not introduced in the probate court proceedings. A decree of distribution is a conclusive determination of the terms of a testamentary trust and the rights of all parties claiming any interest under it. (Estate of Easter, 148 P.2d 601 (Cal. 1944)).

Elizabeth Woodworth Holden, a natural daughter, and James V. Woodworth, an adopted son.

Elizabeth Plass died in 1980; she was survived by her husband, Raymond Plass. Raymond Plass died testate in 1988. In relevant part, he left the residue of his estate to the Regents for use on the University's Berkeley campus.

Mamie Woodworth, the life tenant, died in 1991. Thereafter, Wells Fargo Bank, as successor trustee of the Woodworth trust, petitioned the probate court pursuant to Probate Code section 17200 to determine those persons entitled to distribution of the trust estate. The petition alleged that "The petitioner [was] uncertain as to whether Elizabeth Plass' 'heirs at law' under [the decree] should be determined as of February 14, 1980, the date of her death, or August 13, 1991, the date of Mamie [Barlow] Woodworth's death."

It is undisputed that (1) as of February 14, 1980, Elizabeth Plass' heirs at law were her husband, Raymond Plass, her niece, Elizabeth Woodworth Holden, and her nephew, James V. Woodworth; and (2) as of August 13, 1991, Elizabeth Plass' heirs at law were Elizabeth Woodworth Holden and James V. Woodworth (the Woodworth heirs). . . .

[T]he probate court concluded that the identity of the heirs entitled to the trust assets must be determined as of the date of death of the life tenant. The probate court therefore ordered the trustee to deliver the remaining trust assets in equal shares to the Woodworth heirs.

DISCUSSION . . .

2. ISSUES

The Regents contend the probate court erroneously failed to apply the general rule of construction which requires that the identity of "heirs" entitled to take a remainder interest be determined as of the date of death of the denominated ancestor, in the absence of any contrary intent expressed by the testator. (See Estate of Stanford, 315 P.2d 681 (Cal. 1957); Estate of Liddle, 328 P.2d 35 (Cal. App. 1958); and Estate of Newman, 229 P. 898 (Cal. App. 1924).) Had the probate court construed the decree in accord with this principle, the Regents would have been entitled to share in the trust assets as a residuary legatee of Raymond Plass, an heir at law of Elizabeth Plass at the time of her death in 1980.

The Woodworth heirs respond by asserting the probate court's decision is consistent with an exception to the general rule which requires that the determination be made at the date of death of the life tenant. (See Wells Fargo Bank v. Title Ins. & Trust Co., 99 Cal. Rptr. 464 (App. 1971); and Estate of McKenzie, 54 Cal. Rptr. 888 (App. 1966).) Under this principle, the Regents have no interest in the trust assets, because Raymond Plass predeceased Mamie Barlow Woodworth.[17]

---

17. It is undisputed that had the testator in this case died on or after January 1, 1985, the Regents would have no claim to the trust assets. Under Probate Code sections 6150 and 6151 which have been in effect since 1985, a devise of a future interest to a class, such as heirs, includes only those who fit the class description at the time the legacy is to take effect in enjoyment.

3. THE EARLY VESTING RULE

Estate of Liddle, supra, 328 P.2d 35, reflects the common law preference for vested rather than contingent remainders. Thus, unless a particular instrument disclosed a different intent on the part of the testator, a remainder to a class of persons, such as children, became vested in the class when one or more of its members came into existence and could be ascertained, even though the class was subject to open for future additional members. (Estate of Stanford, supra, 315 P.2d 681.) Furthermore, the fact that takers of a postponed gift were described by a class designation did not, under the common law rule, give rise to any implied condition of survival.

The circumstances involved in *Liddle* are substantially indistinguishable from those of the present case. In *Liddle*, the remainder of a testamentary trust was to be distributed to the testatrix's attorney or, in the event of his death, the attorney's heirs-at-law. Although the attorney survived the testatrix, he predeceased the life tenant. [His wife was his heir.] The wife's heirs and the administrator of her estate clashed with certain remote cousins of the attorney over the ownership of the trust assets.

The appellate court ruled in favor of the wife's estate. Relying upon statutes, treatises, and case law expressing common law notions, including Estate of Stanford, supra, 315 P.2d 681, the court construed the phrase "heirs at law" according to its technical meaning, that is, the person or persons who are entitled to succeed to the property of an intestate decedent. The *Liddle* court then held the members of this class must be determined as of the death of the named ancestor. The rule was summarized as follows:

> Normally, when a gift has been made to the "heirs" or "next of kin" of a named individual, the donor has said in effect that he wants the property distributed as the law would distribute it if the named person died intestate. Accordingly, the normal time for applying the statute of descent or distribution is at the death of the named individual. This is, however, merely a rule of construction, and if the testator or grantor manifests an intention that the statute be applied either at an earlier or a later time, such intention will be given effect. (*Liddle*, supra.)

The designated ancestor in *Liddle* was the attorney. Because his wife was his intestate heir at the time he died, the court found she was the proper recipient of the trust estate.

4. THE CONTINGENT SUBSTITUTIONAL GIFT EXCEPTION

On the other hand, *Wells Fargo Bank*, supra, 99 Cal. Rptr. 464, reflects the application of an exception to the early vesting principle. In *Wells Fargo Bank*, a woman had conveyed, by a grant deed, a life estate in certain real property to her daughter, with remainders to the grantor's two other children. If the life tenant died without issue and the two other children died without issue before the grantor's death, the instrument provided that the remainder interest in the property would belong to the grantor's "heirs." The trial court determined the heirs should be ascertained as of the date of the grantor's death.

The court of appeal reversed . . . [relying on] Simes & Smith, The Law of Future Interests (2nd ed.) §735, p. 210. . . . [U]nder consideration at the cited portion of this treatise is the situation where "a testator devises a life estate or defeasible fee to *a person who is one of his heirs*, followed by a remainder or executory interest to the testator's heirs." (Simes & Smith, supra, §735, p. 206; emphasis added.) As Simes and Smith point out, in such circumstances, some courts have rejected the general rule that the members of the class are to be determined at the death of the ancestor (i.e., the testator), and instead have applied an exception which identifies the heirs who will take the remainder as those in being upon the death of the holder of the life estate or defeasible fee. The rationale for these decisions is an assumption the testator did not intend to give both a present and a future interest to the same person. (See Simes & Smith, supra, §735, at pp. 206-210.) *Wells Fargo Bank* involved a bequest of the same type as that which is the subject of section 735 of the Simes and Smith treatise. In *Wells Fargo Bank*, the estate of the life tenant would have been entitled to receive a portion of the remainder if the identity of the grantor's heirs was determined at the time of the grantor's death rather than at the date of the life tenant's death. The *Wells Fargo Bank* court essentially adopted the analysis in section 735 of Simes and Smith that: "[I]f the general rule is applied, an incongruous result would be reached by taking the property away from [the holder of the possessory interest] because he died without issue and giving it back to him because of the same reason." (*Wells Fargo Bank*, supra.) . . .

By contrast, in the instant case we do not have a contingent, substituted gift to a class of recipients which includes the deceased interim beneficiary. As in *Liddle*, the class of contingent, substituted heirs does not encompass any prior contingent interim beneficiary. . . .

Thus, we believe the exception to the general rule of early vesting, as implemented in *Wells Fargo Bank*, should not be applied to the remainder interest contained in the decree of distribution here.

5. OTHER CONSIDERATIONS

For the reasons which follow, we find no other justification for departing from *Liddle*. First, there is nothing in the language of the other provisions of the decree of distribution before us which reveals the testator's intent or desire. Since the record does not include Harold Evans Woodworth's will, we cannot resort to it to attempt to divine his wishes.

Second, the fact that the University, an entity, is not a relative of Elizabeth Plass or one of her heirs at law is not material. Unlike the *Wells Fargo Bank* court, we are unwilling to say that application of the general rule "would result in thwarting the expressed intention of the Grantor by distributing the corpus of the trust to persons or entities other than [Elizabeth Plass'] heirs." (*Wells Fargo Bank*, supra) Had the instrument in *Wells Fargo Bank* satisfactorily disclosed the grantor's intentions regarding the distribution of the remainder interest in the property, there would have been no need for the court to have even considered the competing rules of construction in order to decide the case.

It would be pure speculation for us to conclude that Harold Evans Woodworth would not have wanted Raymond Plass to inherit a portion of the trust assets. It appears from the record that Raymond Plass and Elizabeth Plass were married at the time the testator executed his will. It has long been the law in California that a husband is an heir of his deceased wife. Nothing in the decree forecloses the possibility the testator took into account the fact that Elizabeth Plass might predecease, and Raymond Plass might outlive, Mamie Barlow Woodworth, resulting in Raymond Plass' succession to a portion of the trust remainder.

Third, the rule of construction which favors descent according to blood in cases of ambiguity in testamentary dispositions should likewise not determine the result in this case. The general rule favoring early vesting was well-established long before the testator died. We do not think it should be abandoned in order to carry out some purportedly perceived, but entirely speculative, notion about the intent of the testator based upon events which occurred well after the testator's death. (See Estate of McKenzie, supra, 54 Cal. Rptr. 888.) As we noted earlier, it is perfectly conceivable that Harold Evans Woodworth took into account in making his will the possibility that his property would pass to Raymond Plass and thereafter be transferred to strangers to the Woodworth line. . . .

In the absence of any firm indication of testamentary intent, the rules of construction must be implemented in order to insure uniformity and predictability in the law, rather than disregarded in order to carry out a court's ad hoc sense of what is, with perfect hindsight, acceptable in a particular set of circumstances. . . .

Last, none of the other exceptions identified in *Wells Fargo Bank* to the early vesting rule apply under the circumstances of this case. This is not a situation where the "life tenant is the sole heir, but the will devises the remainder to the testator's 'heirs.'" (*Wells Fargo Bank*, supra; Estate of Wilson, 193 P. 581 (Cal. 1920).)

In addition, the language of the decree does not contain any "expression of futurity in the description of the ancestor's heirs" (*Wells Fargo Bank*, supra), such as "my then living heirs-at-law" (Estate of Layton, 19 P.2d 793 (Cal. 1933)). When, as here, "the gift is in terms 'then to the heirs' of a designated person, the word 'then' merely indicates the time of enjoyment and has no significance in relation to the rule [of early vesting]." (Estate of Miner, 29 Cal. Rptr. 601, 606-607 (App. 1963).) . . .

Finally, and contrary to the contention of the Woodworth heirs, we do not find the words "pay to" contained in the instant decree to be equivalent to the word "vest" or otherwise constitute an "expression of futurity" for purposes of determining the identity of the relevant heirs. Rather, the instruction pertains to the time when the recipients of the assets are entitled to have them.

DISPOSITION

Accordingly, we must reverse the probate court's ruling that the Regents have no claim to the assets of the testamentary trust.

The judgment (order) appealed from is reversed.

NOTE

Because a transmissible remainder is subject to the federal estate tax, estate planners in several states have successfully urged legislatures to enact a statute providing that where a remainder is given to a person's *heirs*, the heirs will not be ascertained until the remainder becomes possessory. See also Restatement (Third) of Property: Wills and Other Donative Transfers §16.1 (T.D. No. 4, 2004), to similar effect. Under these statutes, no remainder beneficiary has a transmissible interest because if he dies before the remainder becomes possessory, he will not be alive when heirs are ascertained and, therefore, cannot be an heir. Cal. Prob. Code §6151, referred to in footnote 17 in the *Woodworth* case and now renumbered §21114 (2008), is such a statute. So is UPC §2-711.

Uniform Probate Code (1990, amended in 1993)

§2-711. FUTURE INTERESTS IN "HEIRS" AND LIKE

If an applicable statute or a governing instrument calls for a present or future distribution to or creates a present or future interest in a designated individual's "heirs," "heirs at law," "next of kin," "relatives," or "family," or language of similar import, the property passes to those persons, including the state, and in such shares as would succeed to the designated individual's intestate estate under the intestate succession law of the designated individual's domicile if the designated individual died when the disposition is to take effect in possession or enjoyment. If the designated individual's surviving spouse is living but is remarried at the time the disposition is to take effect in possession or enjoyment, the surviving spouse is not an heir of the designated individual.

NOTE: THE DOCTRINE OF WORTHIER TITLE

Under the doctrine of worthier title, when a settlor transfers property in trust with a life estate in the settlor or in another, and purports to create a remainder in the *settlor's heirs*, it was conclusively presumed that the settlor intended to retain a reversion in himself and not create a remainder in his heirs. The rationale for this *rule of law*, which as such did not yield to a showing of contrary intent, is obscure, but probably it was to ensure that property passed to descendants by descent rather than by purchase (that is, other than by inheritance). Property acquired by inheritance was deemed "worthier" and, perhaps more importantly, feudal lords exacted dues on inheritance but not other forms of transfer.

In England, Parliament abolished this remnant of feudal times in 1833. Inheritance Act, 3 & 4 Wm. IV, c. 106, §3 (1833). In the United States, however, the doctrine was roused from its slumber by Judge Cardozo in Doctor v. Hughes, 122 N.E. 221 (N.Y. 1919), and recast as a *rule of construction* in order to do equity on some particular facts. In so doing, Cardozo revitalized the doctrine as a rule of presumed intent, which can be rebutted by evidence that the settlor did intend to create a remainder in his heirs. Thus:

> *Case 18.* O transfers property to X in trust "to pay the income to O for life, then to distribute the principal to A if A is living, and if A is not living, to distribute the principal to O's heirs." The presumption is that O has a reversion and O's heirs do not have a remainder. O may convey the reversion by will to whomever O chooses.

The states that followed Cardozo's lead and adopted the doctrine as a rule of construction found that it produced a passel of lawsuits involving speculative evidence about whether the settlor intended to create a remainder rather than retain a reversion. As a result, a majority of states have jettisoned the doctrine by statute or by judicial decision, both as a rule of law and as a rule of construction. The doctrine is also rejected by Restatement (Third) of Property: Wills and Other Donative Transfers §16.3 (T.D. No. 4, 2004), Restatement (Third) of Trusts §49, cmt. a(1) (2003), and UPC §2-710 (1990).

Although rejection of the doctrine of worthier title seems sound, it does leave us with the problem of securing the consent of the unascertained heirs of a living settlor to modification or termination of a trust. In Case 18, for example, if O and A want to terminate the trust, they must secure the consent of O's unknown heirs. Statutes in some states abolishing worthier title have dealt with this problem by providing that a trust may be revoked by the settlor and other ascertained beneficiaries when the only other interested persons are the settlor's heirs. See, e.g., N.Y. Est. Powers & Trusts Law §7-1.9(b) (2008).

NOTE: THE RULE IN SHELLEY'S CASE

At common law, if land was conveyed to a grantee for life, then to the *grantee's heirs*, the attempted creation of a contingent remainder in the heirs was not recognized. Instead, the grantee took the remainder. The life estate then merged into the remainder, giving the grantee a possessory fee simple absolute.

Here is a simplified statement of the rule: If

(1)   one instrument (deed, will, or trust)
(2)   creates a life estate in land in A, and
(3)   purports to create a remainder in A's heirs (or the heirs of A's body), and
(4)   the estates are both legal or both equitable,

the remainder becomes a remainder in fee simple (or fee tail) in A. If there is no intervening estate, the life estate merges into the remainder, giving A a fee simple (or fee tail). The rule in Shelley's Case is not a rule of construction. It is a rule of law, hence it applies regardless of the intent of the transferor. Here is an example:

> *Case 19. O* conveys land in trust "for *A* for life, and then to *A*'s heirs." Under the rule in Shelley's Case, *A* (and not *A*'s heirs) has the remainder, which then merges with *A*'s life estate, giving *A* all the equitable interest in the trust. *A* may by will dispose of the land as *A* chooses.

The rule in Shelley's Case has been abolished in nearly all the states as well as in England.[18] See Restatement (Third) of Property: Wills and Other Donative Transfers §16.2 (T.D. No. 4, 2004); Restatement (Third) of Trusts §49, cmt. a(1) (2003). In some states, however, abolition is by recent statute and does not apply retroactively. In these states, cases involving the rule may still crop up from time to time.

For an engaging discussion of the "mystery" in Shelley's Case — "not what it is or why it came to be, but why it stayed so long" — see John V. Orth, The Mystery of the Rule in Shelley's Case, 7 Green Bag 2d 45 (2003).

d. The Class-Closing Rule

(1) Introduction

A central characteristic of a gift to a class of persons, such as "to the children of *B*," is that if *B* is alive and capable of having more children, the persons to whom the class description applies can increase in number. The question thus arises, for how long can the class increase in membership? In a gift "to *B* for life, then to *B*'s children," all of *B*'s children will be alive (or in gestation) when the class is physiologically closed at *B*'s death.[19] But suppose the disposition is "to *A* for life, then to *B*'s children." If *A* dies during *B*'s lifetime, what should be done with the property, given that *B* may have more children?

There are several alternative solutions possible when the class is not closed physiologically, but one or more members of the class stand ready to take their shares. Distribution could be postponed until all possible class members are on

---

18. Brian Simpson, the distinguished English legal historian, had this to say about the place of the rule in Shelley's Case in contemporary England and America:

> [W]hen I studied property law in Oxford in 1952 we still had to know what it was, since otherwise, it was argued with perverse but yet compelling logic, we could not understand what precisely had been abolished. And the rule could and indeed still can apply to legal instruments executed before 1 January 1926.
>
> Elsewhere in the common law world the rule in *Shelley's Case* still enjoys a curious twilight existence. In legal education it flourishes in the American law schools; its archaic nature and sheer incomprehensibility positively attracts some students of property law, who are fascinated by the absurd, whilst utterly repelling others. Those who teach property law can always establish their dominance by teaching the rule, since a high proportion of their class can be relied upon to misunderstand it, and their confusion can always be enhanced by teaching the doctrine of worthier title, another Gothic relic, at the same time. Outside the classroom its status resembles that of the Big Foot, the Yeti, or the Tasmanian Tiger; sightings are still possible. . . . Although American courts cheerfully invent new constitutional and common law doctrines, and abrogate old ones, as the whim takes them, they shrink with a sort of superstitious awe from disrespectful treatment of the sacred rule in *Shelley's Case.* [A.W. Brian Simpson, Leading Cases in the Common Law 41 (1995).]

19. For treatment of posthumous conception and the class-closing rules, on which there is now decisional law and apposite UPC provisions, see pages 126-130.

the scene. Or a partial distribution could be made to *B*'s present children and a "reasonable" portion withheld (until *B*'s death) for possible future distribution to later-born children. Or full distribution could be made to the children now at hand, subject to a requirement that they rebate a portion of each share as *B* has more children. Or the class could be closed at *A*'s death, with full distribution to the present children and the exclusion of all children later born to *B*. See David M. Becker, A Critical Look at Class Gifts and the Rule of Convenience, 42 Real Prop., Prob. & Tr. J. 491 (2007).

The practical problems that would be raised by postponing distribution, or by making a partial or defeasible distribution to existing class members, have led the courts to adopt the last alternative. This is called the *class-closing rule* or the *rule of convenience*. It is a rule of construction, giving way to sufficient evidence of the testator's contrary intent, but it is adhered to more closely than any other rule of construction — so closely, in fact, that it has sometimes been referred to erroneously as a rule of law. See Re Wernher's Settlement Trusts, [1961] 1 All E.R. 184.

Under the class-closing rule, *a class will close whenever any member of the class is entitled to possession and enjoyment of his or her share*. The key point in time is when one member is *entitled* to demand payment. The fact that actual payment may be delayed because of administrative problems does not keep the class open; it closes when the right to payment arises. For discussion and illustrations of the class-closing rule, see Restatement (Third) of Property: Wills and Other Donative Transfers §15.1 (T.D. No. 4, 2004).

When a class is open, persons not yet born can come into the class. When a class is closed, no more members can be added to the class. Note well that this is all we mean when we say that a class is closed: *No person born hereafter can share in the property*.[20] The fact that a class is closed does not mean that all members of the class will share in the property. No additional members can come in, but present class members can drop out by failing to meet some condition precedent that must be met before distribution but after the class is closed.

(2)   Immediate gifts

The class-closing rule can best be understood by examining a series of illustrative cases. In all these cases involving gifts to the children of *B*, it is assumed that *B* is alive at the testator's death. Otherwise the class would be physiologically closed.

Where there is an immediate gift to a class, the class closes as soon as any member can demand possession, either at the testator's death or later. Thus:

---

20. More accurately, we would say that no person *conceived* after this date can share; for here, as elsewhere in property law, a child is treated as in being from the time of conception if later born alive. We speak of birth, but we mean conception. For an adopted child, the time of adoption, not birth, is controlling. Thus an adopted child must be adopted into the class before the class closes. A child in being when the class closes, but subsequently adopted, does not share.

Case 20. T devises $10,000 "to the children of B." B is alive and has two children, C and D. When T dies, the class closes. C and D can demand immediate possession of their shares. From T's estate C is paid $5,000 and D is paid $5,000. If another child is born to B a year later, that child does not share in the bequest.

There is an exception to this rule if no members of the class have been born before the testator's death. Since the testator must have known there were no class members alive at his death, it is assumed that the testator intended all class members, whenever born, to share. In such a case, the class does not close until the death of the designated ancestor of the class. In Case 20, if B had no children born before the testator's death, the class would not close until B's death. See Restatement (Third) of Property: Wills and Other Donative Transfers §15.1, cmt. k (T.D. No. 4, 2004).

Case 21. T bequeaths $10,000 "to the children of B who reach 21." B has children alive, but no child is 21 at T's death. The class will close when a child of B reaches 21.

Case 22. T bequeaths $10,000 "to the children of B, to be paid to them in equal shares as they respectively reach 21." B has children alive, but all are under 21. The gift is vested with payment postponed. The class will close when the eldest child of B reaches 21 or, if the eldest child dies under that age, when the eldest child would have reached 21 had he lived. See Restatement (Third) of Property, supra, §15.1, cmt. m.

PROBLEMS

1. T bequeaths $15,000 "to the children of B who reach 21." At T's death, B has two children, C (age 7) and D (age 4). Three years later, E is born to B. Thereafter, C reaches 21. What distribution is made to C? One year thereafter, F is born to B. D dies at age 20. Is any distribution made? E then reaches 21. Is any distribution made? F then reaches 21. Is any distribution made?

2. A devise of property "to B and her children" is ambiguous. Does B take a life estate and the children a remainder? Or do B and her children take equal shares as tenants in common? Under the rule in Wild's Case, decided in 1599, if B has children at the time of the devise, B and her children take as tenants in common. Some states continue to follow this rule. Others follow a life estate and remainder construction. See David M. Becker, Debunking the Sanctity of Precedent, 76 Wash. U. L.Q. 853, 861-886 (1998). The rule in Wild's Case is repudiated by Restatement (Third) of Property, supra, §14.2, cmt. f. In a jurisdiction that follows the rule in Wild's Case, what effect does the rule of convenience have on B's children conceived after the testator's death?

(3)   Postponed gifts

If the gift is postponed in possession until a life tenant dies, the class will not close under the class-closing rule until the time for taking possession. Thus, a gift to a class of remainder beneficiaries will not close until the life tenant is dead, and it will not then close under the rule of convenience unless one remainderperson is entitled to possession.

> *Case 23.* *T* bequeaths $10,000 "to *A* for life, then to the children of my daughter *B*." The class will not close in any event, under the rule of convenience, until the death of *A*. Suppose that *B* survives *A*. The class will close at *A*'s death if (a) a child of *B* is then alive, (b) a child of *B* predeceased *T* and the gift did not lapse but went to such child's descendants under an anti-lapse statute, or (c) a child of *B* was alive at *T*'s death or was born after *T*'s death and this child predeceased *A*. In each of those cases, a child or the child's representative can demand payment at *A*'s death.

Suppose that in Case 23, at the death of *A*, *B* has not yet had any children. Will the class be left open until the death of *B*, as in the case of an immediate gift to a class where no one has yet been born at the time of taking possession? Restatement (Third) of Property, supra, §15.1, cmt. k, says Yes, but there are few cases on the matter. The Restatement goes on to state, however, that "if the circumstances indicate that it is improbable that there will be any after-conceived or after-adopted class members because of the age or physical condition of the prospective parent," it would be preferable for the gift to fail.

The class-closing rule described above applies only to gifts of principal, not to gifts of income. In a trust to pay income to the children of *B*, the class closes for the payment of income periodically as the income is accrued.

PROBLEMS

1. *T* bequeaths a fund in trust "to pay the income to *A* for life, then to distribute the principal to the children of *B* who reach 21, and in the meantime the children of *B* who are eligible to receive, but have not yet received, a share of the principal are to receive the income." At *A*'s death, *B* is alive and has one child, *C* (age 5). After *A* dies, the following events occur: *D* is born to *B*; *C* reaches 21; one year later, *E* is born to *B*; *D* and, later, *E* reach 21.

(a) After *A*'s death, who is entitled to the income?
(b) When is the first distribution of principal made, to whom, and how much?
(c) How is the principal ultimately divided?

2. *T* bequeaths a fund in trust "to divide the fund among the children of *B*, payable to each at age 21, and in the meantime they are to receive the income." At *T*'s death, *B* is alive and has one child, *C* (age 5). One year later, *C* dies. Is *C*'s administrator entitled to demand immediate distribution of *C*'s share? Would your answer be different if *B* predeceased *T*?

Lux v. Lux
Supreme Court of Rhode Island, 1972
288 A.2d 701

KELLEHER, J.   The artless efforts of a draftsman have precipitated this suit which seeks the construction of and instructions relating to the will of Philomena Lux who died a resident of Cumberland on August 15, 1968. We hasten to add that the will was drawn by someone other than counsel of record. . . .

Philomena Lux executed her will on May 9, 1966. She left her residuary estate to her husband, Anthony John Lux, and nominated him as the executor. Anthony predeceased his wife. His death triggered the following pertinent provisions of Philomena's will:

> Fourth: In the event that my said husband, Anthony John Lux, shall predecease me, then I make the following disposition of my estate: . . .
>
> 2. All the rest, residue and remainder of my estate, real and personal, of whatsoever kind and nature, and wherever situated, of which I shall die seized and possessed, or over which I may have power of appointment, or to which I may be in any manner entitled at my death, I give, devise and bequeath to my grandchildren, share and share alike.
>
> 3. Any real estate included in said residue shall be maintained for the benefit of said grandchildren and shall not be sold until the youngest of said grandchildren has reached twenty-one years of age.
>
> 4. Should it become necessary to sell any of said real estate to pay my debts, costs of administration, or to make distribution of my estate or for any other lawful reason, then, in that event, it is my express desire that said real estate be sold to a member of my family.

Philomena was survived by one son, Anthony John Lux, Jr., and five grandchildren whose ages range from two to eight. All the grandchildren were children of Anthony. The youngest grandchild was born after the execution of the will but before Philomena's death. The son is named in the will as the alternate executor. He informed the trial court that he and his wife plan to have more children. At the time of the hearing, Anthony was 30. The Superior Court appointed a guardian ad litem to represent the interests of the grandchildren. It also designated an attorney to represent the rights of the individuals who may have an interest under the will but who are at this time unknown, unascertained or not in being. . . .

At the time of her death, the testatrix owned real estate valued at approximately $35,000 and tangible and intangible personal property, including bank accounts, that totaled some $7,400. The real estate, which consists of two large tenement houses, is located in Cumberland.

[The court first addressed the issue of whether Philomena made an absolute gift to the grandchildren or if instead the devise was in trust for their benefit. For the reasons detailed at page 857, the court concluded] that Philomena intended that her real estate be held in trust for the benefit of her grandchildren. [Since no trustee was named in the will, the court appointed the executor to the position of trustee. The court then turned to the constructional issue.] . . .

The ascertainment of time within which a person who answers a class description such as "children" or "grandchildren" must be born in order to be entitled to share in a testator's bounty is not an easy matter. In seeking a solution, the court must seek to effectuate the testator's intent. . . .

The rationale for permitting a class to increase in size until the time for distribution stems from a judicial recognition that generally, when a testator describes the beneficiaries of his bounty by some group designation, he has in mind all those persons whenever born who come within the definition of the term used to describe the group. Normally, if he had in mind the individual members of the designated group, he would have described them by name. This recognition is tempered by the presumption that testators usually would not intend to keep the class open at the expense of an indefinite delay in the distribution of the estate. Since there is no good reason to exclude any person who is born before the period of distribution, all such persons are, in the absence of a contrary testamentary intent, deemed to be members of the class. Casner, Class Gifts to Others than to "Heirs" or "Next of Kin": Increase in the Class Membership, 51 Harv. L. Rev. 254 (1938); 5 American Law of Property §§22.40, 22.41 (1952).

Despite our invocation of the rule requiring the class to remain open until the corpus is distributed, we still must determine what Philomena intended when she said that the corpus has to be preserved until the "youngest grandchild" becomes twenty-one.

There are four possible distribution dates depending on the meaning of "youngest." Distribution might be made when the youngest member of the class in being when the will was executed attains twenty-one; or when the youngest in being when the will takes effect becomes twenty-one; or when the youngest of all living class members in being at any one time attains twenty-one even though it is physically possible for others to be born; or when the youngest whenever it is born attains twenty-one. This last alternative poses a question. Should we delay distribution here and keep the class open until the possibility that Philomena's son can become a father becomes extinct? We think not.

We are conscious of the presumption in the law that a man or a woman is capable of having children so long as life lasts. A construction suit, however, has for its ultimate goal the ascertainment of the average testator's probable intent if he was aware of the problems that lead to this type of litigation. Manufacturers National Bank v. McCoy, 212 A.2d 53 (R.I. 1965). It is our belief that the average testator, when faced with the problem presented by the record before us, would endorse the view expressed in 3 Restatement, Property §295, Comment k at 1594 (1940), where in urging the adoption of the rule that calls for the closing of the class when the youngest living member reaches the age when distribution could be made, states:

> When all existent members of the class have attained the stated age, considerations of convenience . . . require that distribution shall then be made and that the property shall not be further kept from full utilization to await the uncertain and often highly improbable conception of further members of the group. The infrequency with which a parent has further children after all of his living children have attained maturity, makes this application of the rule of convenience justifiable and causes it to frustrate the unexpressed desires of a conveyor in few, if any, cases.

We hold, therefore, that distribution of the trust corpus shall be made at any time when the youngest of the then living grandchildren has attained the age of twenty-one. When this milestone is reached, there is no longer any necessity to maintain the trust to await the possible conception of additional members of the class.

Although Philomena declared that the real estate was not to be sold until the youngest grandchildren became twenty-one, her later statements about the necessity of its sale amounted to her awareness that future circumstances might require the liquidation of her real estate sometime prior to the time her youngest grandchild becomes twenty-one. The Superior Court was informed and documentary evidence was introduced which showed such a precipitous drop in the rental income as would warrant a trustee to seek a better investment.

Section 18-4-2(b) provides that, in the absence of any provision to the contrary, every trust shall be deemed to have conferred upon the trustee a discretionary power to sell the trust estate, be it real or personal property. Section 18-4-10 specifically authorizes a trustee, whenever he believes it desirable to sell trust property, to seek the Superior Court's approval for such a transaction.

When the real estate is sold, the proceeds from such sale shall, because of the doctrine of the substitute res, replace the realty as the trust corpus. Industrial National Bank v. Colt, 233 A.2d 112 (R.I. 1957); Dresser v. Booker, 69 A.2d 45 (R.I. 1949).

The impending sale brings into focus the testatrix's "express *desire* that said real estate be sold to a member of my family" (emphasis added). The words "express desire" are purely precatory. We have said that precatory language will be construed as words of command only if it is clear that the testator intended to impose on the individual concerned a legal obligation to make the desired disposition. Young v. Exum, 179 A.2d 107 (R.I. 1962). We think it clear that since Philomena's primary goal was to benefit her grandchildren, we see nothing in the record that would justify a conclusion that she intended that the potential purchasers of her real estate be limited to the members of her family.

Finally, we come to the allocation of income. The will is silent as to this item. Over a half-century ago, we said that if the will shows no intention on the part of the testator that income be accumulated, income is payable to the beneficiary as it accrues. Butler v. Butler, 101 A. 115 (R.I. 1917). This rule has been reaffirmed on many occasions. Should Philomena's son's hope for additional progeny become a reality, the quantum of each share of income received by a grandchild would be reduced as each new member of the class joins his brothers and sisters.

The parties may present to this court for approval a form of judgment in accordance with this opinion, which will be entered in the Superior Court.

(4)   Gifts of specific sums

If a specific sum is given to each member of the class, which is sometimes called a "per capita" gift, the class closes at the death of the testator regardless of whether any members of the class are then alive. Thus:

> *Case 24. T* bequeaths £500 apiece to each child of *A. A* has no children living at *T*'s death. The class closes at *T*'s death, and no child of *A* ever takes anything. Rogers v. Mutch, 10 Ch. Div. 25 ([Eng.] 1878).

> Life looked rosy to *A* as he sat
> By the crepe-draped casket of *T.*
> Five hundred pounds for each child he begat
> Would soon make him wealthy mused he.
> So he married at once, and began procreating
> At five hundred per, he supposed;
> But you know and I know (what hardly needs stating)
> That the class had already closed.
> Mistakes of this sort are bound to arise
> When a client takes actions like these
> Without seeing his lawyer as soon as *T* dies,
> And paying the usual fees.
>
> FRANK L. DEWEY[21]

What is the reason for closing the class at the death of the testator when the gift is of a fixed sum to each member of a class?

---

21. Reproduced from W. Barton Leach, Langdell Lyrics of 1938 (1938).

14

THE RULE AGAINST PERPETUITIES
AND TRUST DURATION

SECTION A.   INTRODUCTION

The classic statement of the Rule Against Perpetuities, formulated with Delphic simplicity by John Chipman Gray, reads:

> No interest [in real or personal property] is good unless it must vest, if at all, not later than twenty-one years after some life in being at the creation of the interest. [John C. Gray, The Rule Against Perpetuities §201, at 191 (4th ed. 1942).]

By virtue of his erudition, his rigorous logic, his magisterial style, and his position as a celebrated teacher of property law at Harvard, Gray became established in the late nineteenth century as not just a leading authority on the Rule but as *the* authority.[1] Because of the deference paid to Gray's work by the courts, the Rule has sometimes been treated as if it were laid down at one time by this one man. In fact, the Rule had a long and involved evolution over many centuries.

From the sixteenth until the nineteenth century, judges struggled against perpetuities without defining exactly what a perpetuity was. The resulting unrefined and ambiguous doctrines were clarified into the Rule Against Perpetuities as we know it starting with the Duke of Norfolk's Case, 22 Eng. Rep. 931 (Ch. 1682).[2] The Earl of Arundel had eight sons. Thomas, the eldest son and heir apparent, was weak in mind and body, and not expected to have children. Hence, the earl assumed that after his own death and the death of Thomas, the earldom and the

---

1. On the role of Gray, see Stephen A. Siegel, John Chipman Gray, Legal Formalism, and the Transformation of Perpetuities Law, 36 U. Miami L. Rev. 439 (1982).
2. For more on the Duke of Norfolk's Case, see Herbert Barry, The Duke of Norfolk's Case, 23 Va. L. Rev. 538 (1937).

estates accompanying it would likely descend to his second son, Henry, and Henry's descendants. If Henry did inherit the earldom at Thomas's death, the earl wanted the barony of Grostock, which he planned to give initially to Henry, to shift to his fourth son, Charles. The earl went to an experienced estate planner (known as a *conveyancer* in those days when land was the chief form of wealth), Sir Orlando Bridgeman. This outstanding member of the bar, who later became Lord Keeper, drew up a set of highly complicated documents that cannot easily be summarized. It is enough to say that the limitation that brought on the Duke of Norfolk's Case boiled down to this: The barony of Grostock was given to Henry, but a shifting executory limitation was created, providing that if the eldest son, Thomas, should die without descendants in the lifetime of Henry, so that Henry inherited the earldom, then the barony would go to Charles.

In 1652, the Earl of Arundel died, and the earldom descended to the mentally defective first son, Thomas. Henry, the second son, then moved into action. He assumed full control of the properties accompanying the title, and he sent Thomas to Padua, in Italy, where he was incarcerated until his death. Henry also engineered the restoration of the title "Duke of Norfolk" to the family. In 1572, Queen Elizabeth I had beheaded the fourth duke for intrigues involving Mary, Queen of Scots, and by attainder all his lands and titles were forfeited.[3] In 1660, Parliament, with the consent of Charles II, restored the dukedom of Norfolk, and the incompetent Thomas became the duke. When Thomas died without descendants in 1677, Henry became the sixth Duke of Norfolk.

After succeeding to the dukedom and its properties, greedy Henry did not want to give up the barony of Grostock. Charles, the fourth son, brought a bill in chancery to enforce his interest. Henry resisted, claiming the gift to Charles was in the nature of a perpetuity and hence void. Sympathetic to the rational estate planning of a landowner with an incompetent eldest son, Lord Chancellor

---

3. The turbulence of the times is reflected in the history of the title of Duke of Norfolk, who is the premier duke, ranking just below the blood royal. The title goes back to the first Earl of Norfolk, one of the Breton followers of William the Conqueror. After several attainders and lapses of the earldom, the dukedom was created anew by Richard II in 1397 and given to his chief supporter, Thomas Mowbray, perhaps best remembered for his quarrel with Henry Bolingbroke, Duke of Hereford (afterward Henry IV), which forms Act I of Shakespeare's Richard II and which resulted in Mowbray's banishment. After four Mowbray dukes, the title lapsed.

In 1483, after the murder of the princes in the Tower, Richard III conferred the dukedom on Sir John Howard, an heir of the Mowbray estates and the first of the Howard dukes. Two years later, "Jack of Norfolk" died fighting for Richard at Bosworth; the title and the estates were forfeited to the victorious Henry Tudor, who ascended the throne as Henry VII. The first duke's son regained royal favor by commanding, in his 70th year, the army that defeated the Scots at Flodden, and in 1514 Henry VIII restored the title. Two nieces of the third duke, Anne Boleyn and Catherine Howard, were wives of Henry VIII, both beheaded for infidelity. Subsequently, the Howard family fell from grace; the third duke's son was executed on a charge of treason, and the duke himself was arrested, stripped of his title, and ordered to be beheaded. During the night before the morning set for execution, Henry VIII died and the duke was spared. Seven years later, Queen Mary released him from prison and restored the dukedom to him. The third duke was succeeded by his grandson, who in turn was executed by Elizabeth I for plotting with Mary Stuart. The fourth duke's son, Philip Howard, inherited the title Earl of Arundel from his mother. Philip's grandson, Henry Howard, the third Howard to hold the title Earl of Arundel, made the disposition at issue in the Duke of Norfolk's Case.

Since the fourteenth century, the Duke of Norfolk has been the hereditary earl marshal of England. The highest ranking Catholic lord of the realm, the duke attends the sovereign upon the opening of Parliament, walking at his or her right hand, and arranges state ceremonies such as coronations, royal marriages, and funerals.

**The Sixth Duke of Norfolk
by Gerard Soest, ca. 1677**

*Reproduced by permission of the
Tate Gallery, London.*

His greed brought on the case
that originated the Rule
Against Perpetuities.

**The First Earl of Nottingham, Lord
Chancellor after Godfrey Kneller, 1680**

*Reproduced by permission of the
National Portrait Gallery, London.*

His decision gave the rich the
power to secure family wealth
for another generation.

Nottingham[4] was of the opinion that Charles's interest would "wear itself out" in a single lifetime (Thomas's) and should not be regarded as a perpetuity. The sole matter of concern, ruled Nottingham, is the time at which a future interest will vest, and if a future interest must vest, if at all, during or at the end of a life in being, it is good. Upon appeal to the House of Lords, after two days of argument in a crowded house with King James II present, the Lords voted overwhelmingly to affirm Nottingham's decision.

In the Duke of Norfolk's Case, Lord Nottingham indicated that a rule against perpetuities should be concerned solely with the time of vesting in the future, but he did not attempt a definitive statement of how long dead-hand rule would be allowed. When asked, "Where will you stop?" he replied, "I will tell you where I will stop: I will stop wherever any visible Inconvenience doth appear." From this beginning—judicial acceptance of tying up land for a single life in being—the judges gradually extended the permissible period of dead-hand rule until, 150 years later, they finally fixed it at lives in being plus 21 years. After further refinement, the period allowed by the Rule was settled in Cadell v. Palmer, 6 Eng. Rep.

---

4. Lord Nottingham, born Heneage Finch, was one of the greatest of English Chancellors and called the "Father of Equity" by Justice Story. He was equally devoted to the law and to his family. When he lost his wife, mother of his 14 children, he comforted himself by taking the Great Seal to bed with him. 4 John Lord Campbell, Lives of the Lord Chancellors 273 (1857).

956 (H.L. 1832, 1833), at any reasonable number of lives in being plus 21 years thereafter plus any actual periods of gestation.

The classic introduction to the Rule for students is Professor W. Barton Leach's famous article, Perpetuities in a Nutshell, 51 Harv. L. Rev. 638 (1938), updated by Leach in Perpetuities: The Nutshell Revisited, 78 Harv. L. Rev. 973 (1965). This lucid article, written in a lively, piquant style by the modern master of the Rule, has introduced generations of students into the magic garden of perpetuities. For a more recent synopsis of the Rule, see Jesse Dukeminier, A Modern Guide to Perpetuities, 74 Cal. L. Rev. 1867 (1986). For an extensive analysis of the methodology for solving perpetuities problems, see David M. Becker, Perpetuities and Estate Planning (1993).

SECTION B.   THE ORTHODOX RULE AGAINST PERPETUITIES

1.   *Summary of the Rule*

a.   **The Rule and Its Policies**

The Rule Against Perpetuities is a restriction on the remote vesting of interests, in trust or otherwise, but it does not apply to charitable trusts, which are privileged with an exemption from the Rule. The fundamental policy assumption of the Rule is that vested interests are not objectionable, but contingent interests are. The Rule Against Perpetuities limits the time during which property can be made subject to a contingent interest to "lives in being plus 21 years."

The Rule is said to have two purposes: (1) to keep property marketable, and (2) to limit dead hand control. Preventing indefinite fracturing of property ownership implements the first purpose. The idea is that ownership of land will be periodically reconstituted into fee simple because all contingent future interests in the property must vest or fail within the perpetuities period.

The dead hand rationale for the Rule is best understood in light of the disagreeable consequences that can arise from unanticipated circumstances. The Rule implements this anti–dead hand policy by curbing future interests that, after some period of time and change in circumstances, tie up the property in potentially disadvantageous arrangements. As Professor Simpson explains, "given that one can, to a limited extent only, foresee the future and the problems it will generate, landowners should not be allowed to tie up lands for periods outside the range of reasonable foresight." A.W.B. Simpson, Legal Theory and Legal History 159-160 (1987).

Measured against its purposes, the Rule is both underinclusive and overinclusive. The Rule is underinclusive because it applies only to contingent interests, but vested interests that will not become possessory for many years can also be compromised by the passage of time. Arguably the rule should limit all future interests, and not merely contingent ones, but history has settled the question differently. The Rule is overinclusive because it applies to contingent interests *in trust* as well as contingent *legal* future interests. If the trustee is given the power to sell the trust property and reinvest the proceeds, as is typical, there is no concern with marketability. Nonetheless, the prevailing academic view is that the Rule does, by and large, effectively prevent tying up property for an inordinate length of time.

Although the Rule began as a device to curb tying up land, it was eventually extended to personal property. Today, because almost all life estates and future interests are *equitable* (i.e., created in trust) rather than *legal* interests, the Rule's primary application is to interests in trusts funded with stocks, bonds, and other financial assets.

All legal and equitable contingent future interests created in *transferees* are subject to the Rule. Thus, all contingent remainders and executory interests come within the ambit of the Rule. Future interests retained by the *transferor*—reversions, possibilities of reverter, and rights of entry—are not subject to the Rule. Should interests retained by the transferor be subject to a durational limit, after which the possessory fee would become absolute? By statute, quite a few states have answered Yes. See Helene S. Shapo, George Gleason Bogert, and George Taylor Bogert, The Law of Trusts and Trustees §214, at 225 (3d ed. 2007).

b.   The Perpetuities Period: Why Lives in Being?

At the time of the formulation of the Rule Against Perpetuities, heads of families—the fathers—were much concerned about securing the family land from incompetent sons. In the Duke of Norfolk's Case, Lord Chancellor Nottingham recognized this concern as legitimate, and he and his successor judges developed the period during which the father's judgment could prevail. The father could realistically and perhaps wisely assess the capabilities of living members of his family, and so, with respect to them, the father's informed judgment, solemnly inscribed in an instrument, was given effect. But the head of the family could know nothing of unborn persons. So the father was permitted control only as long as the life of anyone possibly known to him plus the next generation's minority (i.e., lives in being plus 21 years).[5] See 6 American Law of Property §24.16 (1952).

---

5. Lord Hobhouse put it this way in his lectures on the dead hand:

A clear, obvious, natural line is drawn for us between those persons and events which the Settlor knows and sees, and those which he cannot know or see. Within the former province we may trust his natural affections and his capacity of judgment to make better dispositions than any external Law is likely to make for him. Within the latter, natural affection does not extend, and the wisest judgment is constantly baffled by the course of events. I submit, then, that the proper limit of Perpetuity is that of lives in being at the time when the settlement takes effect. [Arthur Hobhouse, The Dead Hand 188 (1880).]

The period of the Rule includes any actual periods of gestation involved. The Rule thus follows the general principle of property law that a person is in being from the time of conception, if later born alive. We address the treatment of posthumously conceived children under the Rule at page 894.

c.   The Rule Is One of Logical Proof

The essential thing to grasp about the Rule Against Perpetuities is that it is a rule of logical proof. A contingent future interest is void from the outset, if it is not certain that the interest will either *vest or fail* — that one or the other *must* happen — within 21 years after the death of "some life in being at the creation of the interest." The phrase "some life in being" has always puzzled students. Who is the "life in being"? The answer is the life in being can be *any* person if you can prove that the interest will vest or fail within that life or within 21 years after its expiration. This person, if found, is often called the *measuring life*, though the term *validating life* is probably more accurate. The life in being does not set a *measure* for how long the interest may last, rather it *validates* (or its absence invalidates) the interest.

Case 1 shows how to make the necessary proof that an interest will vest or fail within the relevant validating lives.

> *Case 1. O* transfers a fund in trust "to pay the income to *A* for life, then to *A*'s children for their lives, then to pay the principal to *B*." *A* has no children. *A*'s life estate is vested in possession *upon creation*. The remainder to *A*'s children for their lives will vest in possession or, if there are no children, fail *upon A's death*. *B*'s remainder is vested in interest *upon creation*. Thus, all interests created by the transfer are valid.

In Case 1, all interests in the trust either are presently vested or will vest, if at all, within the period allotted by the Rule, so the trust is valid in its entirety. If an interest in trust violates the Rule, the trust is void only to that extent.[6]

As Case 1 shows, the crucial inquiry under the Rule is: When will the interest vest or fail? An interest that is vested upon creation is not subject to the Rule. A contingent interest satisfies the Rule if it will necessarily vest, if at all, either *in possession* or *in interest* within the relevant lives in being plus 21 years. Here are other illustrations of contingent interests that can be proven valid because they will vest or fail within the perpetuities period:

> *Case 2. T* bequeaths $10,000 "to *A*, when she marries" and $5,000 "to *A*'s first child." *A* is unmarried and without children. The bequest to *A* will vest during *A*'s *life*, if at all; it is valid. The bequest to *A*'s first child also will vest during *A*'s *life*, if at all; it is valid.

---

6. This statement must be qualified to allow for the case in which the invalid interest is essential to the coherence of the transferor's dispositive scheme. Under the doctrine of *infectious invalidity*, the court may invalidate the entire transfer if doing so will better approximate the transferor's intentions than invalidating only the offending interest. See Jeffrey A. Schoenblum, 2008 Multistate Guide to Estate Planning at Table 10, question 25, surveying the position of the states on infectious invalidity.

Case 3. O, a teacher, declares a trust of her first edition of Charles Dickens's Bleak House "for the first student in my current Trusts and Estates class to be sworn in as a judge." The gift will vest or fail within the *lives of the students* in the class. The condition precedent will necessarily be met, if it is ever met, before the last surviving student dies.

Case 4. O transfers a fund in trust "to pay the income to A for life, then to pay the principal to A's children who reach 21." The remainder is valid because it will vest, at the latest, *21 years after A's death*, for all A's children must reach 21 within 21 years after A dies (plus a period of gestation).

PROBLEMS

1.   *T* bequeaths a fund in trust "for A for life, then to the first child of A to be admitted to the bar." Is the latter gift valid? If so, who is the validating life?

2.   Compare the following bequests:

(a) To A for life, then to B if B goes to the planet Saturn.

(b) To A for life, then to B if any person goes to the planet Saturn.

(c) To A for life, then to B for life if any person goes to the planet Saturn.

Is B's remainder good in each bequest? Who is the validating life?

d.   When the Lives in Being Are Ascertained

Although Gray said the life in being must be a person alive "at the creation of the interest," it is more accurate to say that the validating life or lives must be in being *when the perpetuities period starts to run*. Generally, the perpetuities period begins when the instrument takes effect. If an interest is created by *will*, the validating life or lives must be in being at the testator's death. If the interest is created by *deed* or *irrevocable trust*, the validating life or lives must be persons in being when the deed or trust takes effect.

Different rules for determining validating lives govern revocable trusts and interests created by the exercise of a power of appointment. If the interest is created by an *inter vivos trust revocable by the settlor alone*, the validating life or lives must be persons in being when the power to revoke terminates. If the power to revoke terminates at the settlor's death, as is usually the case, the validating lives must be persons alive at the settlor's death. The perpetuities period begins when the power to revoke terminates because, so long as one person has the power to revoke the trust and receive absolute title to the trust assets, the property is not tied up.

We take up interests created by the exercise of a power of appointment in Section D.

e.   The Rule and Trust Duration

In Case 1 above, B's remainder is valid because it vests *in interest* upon creation. It does not matter that it may vest *in possession* at the death of A's children, which could be well beyond the relevant lives in being plus 21 years (if *A* has children born after the transfer). The trust is not void even though it might last longer than lives in being at the date of the transfer plus 21 years.

The Rule Against Perpetuities does not directly limit trust duration. It is concerned only with the time when interests vest. The Rule therefore limits the duration of a trust *indirectly*. By requiring that all interests in the trust must vest or fail within the perpetuities period, the identity of all persons with a claim to the property will be ascertained within the period. These ascertained beneficiaries can terminate the trust when the perpetuities period expires. See Restatement (Third) of Trusts §29, cmt. h(1) (2003); Restatement (Second) of Property: Donative Transfers §2.1 (1981). If they do not terminate the trust, the trust principal will be distributed to the principal beneficiaries when the preceding life estates expire.

2.   The Fantastical Characters

Under the what-might-happen possibilities test of the common law Rule, *any* possibility that an interest might vest too remotely invalidates the interest. No matter how ridiculous or improbable the invalidating scenario, an interest that *might* not vest or fail within the perpetuities period is void ab initio. The common law Rule is applied without mercy. The case reports are therefore replete with fantastical characters and imaginary beings.

a.   The Fertile Octogenarian

The *fertile octogenarian*, perhaps the most famous of the fantastical beings that inhabit perpetuities land, usually appears in a two-generation trust such as the following:

> Case 5. *T* bequeaths a fund in trust for her sister "*A* (age 80) for life, then for *A*'s children for their lives, then to distribute the trust assets to *A*'s descendants then living." The law *conclusively presumes* that *A* is capable of having more children. Because of this presumption, the remainder to *A*'s children for their lives may include an afterborn child of *A*, and the remainder to *A*'s descendants might vest on the death of this afterborn child, which is too remote. The remainder to *A*'s descendants is void.

QUESTIONS AND PROBLEMS

1.   Could the remainder to *A*'s descendants in Case 5 be saved by construing "*A*'s children" to refer to *A*'s children living at *T*'s death? Should a court do this?

2.   *T* bequeaths a fund in trust "for *A* for life, then to such of *A*'s nephews and nieces as live to attain the age of 21." At the time of *T*'s death, *A* is living and has a sister, *B*, and four nephews and nieces (the children of *B*), all of whom are under age 21. Is the interest given to *A*'s nephews and nieces valid under the Rule Against Perpetuities? (A clue: The answer is, "It depends.")

3. Keeping in mind the conclusive presumption of fertility, which of the following bequests would be valid? *T* devises Blackacre to Mary Hall, but if the Brooklyn Bridge ever falls —

(a) to the children of Elizabeth Jee now living.

(b) to the children of Elizabeth Jee then living.

(c) to the children of Elizabeth Jee now living who are then living.

NOTE: THE PRESUMPTION OF FERTILITY

If you think the conclusive presumption of fertility is absurd, at what age would you presume women could not bear children?[7] Men? Now that adoption has become widely accepted, is it not theoretically possible that *any* living person could have a child regardless of age and fertility? On the other hand, should not perpetuities law be based on probabilities rather than theoretical possibilities?

By statute, Illinois and New York limit the presumption of fertility in perpetuities law to likely childbearing years (say, between 13 and 65) and permit the introduction of evidence of infertility. These statutes also provide that the possibility that a person may adopt a child is to be disregarded. 765 Ill. Comp. Stat. §305/4(c) (2008); N.Y. Est. Powers & Trusts Law §9-1.3(e) (2008). The position of each of the states on the fertile octogenarian is collected in Jeffrey A. Schoenblum, 2008 Multistate Guide to Estate Planning at Table 10, question 19.

The conclusive presumption of fertility was laid down in the old case of Jee v. Audley, 29 Eng. Rep. 1186 (Ch. 1787). In this case, the Master of the Rolls, Lord Kenyon, said: "I am desired to do in this case something which I do not feel myself at liberty to do, namely, to suppose it impossible for persons in so advanced an age as John and Elizabeth Jee [both septuagenarians] to have children; but if this can be done in one case it may in another, and it is a very dangerous experiment, and introductive of the greatest inconvenience to give a latitude to such sort of conjecture." See A.W. Brian Simpson, Leading Cases in the Common Law 91

---

7. Consider this report of fertile sexagenarians in Europe:

A 67-year-old Spanish woman has become the world's oldest mother after giving birth to twins.

The woman, whose identity has not been revealed by Sant Pau Hospital in Barcelona, gave birth yesterday by caesarian section, having previously undergone in vitro fertilisation in the United States, according to Spanish news agency EFE.

Although she is from the southern region of Andalucia, the mother chose the Barcelona hospital because it specialises in high-risk births.

The woman, who is understood to be a first-time mother, and twins are all doing well, though the babies are both in incubators, a hospital spokeswoman said.

The previous holder of the oldest mother record was Adriana Iliescu, a 66-year-old Romanian who gave birth to baby Eliza Maria in January 2005.

Britain's oldest mother, Dr Patricia Rashbrook, 63, gave birth to a baby, named JJ, after a caesarean section last July.

The mother-of-three and her academic husband John Farrant, from Lewes, East Sussex, went to Russia to use a donor egg implanted with his sperm. [Joanna Vallely, 67-Year Old Sets Record as Oldest Mother with Birth of Twins, The Scotsman, Dec. 31, 2006, at 7.]

The fertile sexagenarians have ceded their record to a fertile septuagenarian. In late 2008, a 70-year-old Indian woman gave birth to a baby girl — and she hopes to have another. See World's Oldest Mum, Rajo Devi, 70, Wants to Have a Second Child, Hindustan Times, Dec. 31, 2008.

(1995), examining the historical context for Jee v. Audley and the understanding of fertility at the time.

Modern medical science makes the fertility question even more difficult on account of the new reproductive technologies. As in Woodward v. Commissioner of Social Security, page 118, the *fertile decedent* is now a reality. The question thus arises, how should the possibility of posthumous parentage be assimilated, if at all, into perpetuities law? Perhaps because myriad contingent future interests in children or descendants would be rendered void by considering the unlimited possibility of posthumous parentage (do you see why?), like the proverbial ostrich with its head in the sand, the courts thus far have ignored the issue. By statute many states disregard the possibility of a child born after a person's death, following §1(d) of the Uniform Statutory Rule Against Perpetuities, page 902. See Schoenblum, supra, at Table 10, question 11.

For further discussion and a proposal for reform pertaining to the application of the Rule to posthumously conceived children, see Sharona Hoffman and Andrew P. Morriss, Birth After Death: Perpetuities and the New Reproductive Technologies, 38 Ga. L. Rev. 575 (2004). See also Kristine S. Knaplund, Postmortem Conception and a Father's Last Will, 46 Ariz. L. Rev. 91, 113-114 (2004); Joshua Greenfield, Note, Dad Was Born a Thousand Years Ago? An Examination of Post-Mortem Conception and Inheritance, With a Focus on the Rule Against Perpetuities, 8 Minn. J.L. Sci. & Tech. 277, 292-301 (2007) (reviewing reform proposals).

NOTE: THE PRECOCIOUS TODDLER

What is the youngest age of procreation presumed by the law?[8] This has never been established. Only one known case has dealt with the issue. In In re Gaite's Will Trusts, 1 All E.R. 459 (Ch. 1949), the court had before it a bequest that would be void only if it were assumed that a person under the age of five could have a child. The court validated the gift, not on the ground of physical impossibility of a person becoming a parent at an age under five, but on the grounds that a child born to so young a person would necessarily be born out of wedlock and hence excluded as a child. Under modern law, however, it is usually presumed in

---

8. The youngest mother on record is Lina Medina of Lima, Peru. On May 14, 1939, at the age of 5, she was delivered of a 6 1/2-pound boy by caesarean section. An investigation revealed that she had been raped by a mentally retarded teenage stepbrother. In a story in the New York Times, April 3, 1963, at 70, one of Lina's obstetricians, Dr. Rolando Colareta, recalled that he and his colleagues were astounded to discover that "although Lina had every aspect of a five-year-old infant, her sexual development corresponded to that of a young lady over 15 years old. . . . Surprising though it seems, we confirmed that Lina had menstrual periods since she was one-month old." Dr. Colareta went on to point out that cases of 12- and 13-year-old mothers were common in the Andes, where Lina came from. "As a matter of fact," he said, "I delivered a child to a 9-year-old girl here last week and it didn't even make the newspapers." The New York Times reported that Lina, then 28 and still unmarried, was working as a secretary. Her son Gerardo, then 23, was living with Lina's parents and studying accounting. Photographs of the pregnant Lina are abundant on the web and can easily be found using Google's images search feature.

construing wills and trusts that references to children and other relatives of a person include children born out of wedlock. Hence the constructional escape from the Rule used by the court in In re Gaite's Will Trusts is probably no longer available. See Jeffrey A. Schoenblum, 2008 Multistate Guide to Estate Planning at Table 10, question 20.

b. The Unborn Widow

The next of the fantastical characters in perpetuities land is the *unborn widow*. Thus:

> *Case 6.* T bequeaths a fund in trust to *H* for life, then to *H*'s widow for life, then the remainder to *H*'s surviving descendants. Even if *H* is married to *W1* at *T*'s death, the marriage might end and then *H* could marry *W2*, who might not have been born before *T*'s death. In such a case, the remainder to *H*'s descendants will not vest until the death of *W2*, which could happen more than 21 years after the death of all lives in being at the time of *T*'s death.

QUESTION, NOTE, AND PROBLEM

1. In Case 6, would it not be sensible to construe the word *widow* to refer to a person in being when the testator died?

An Illinois statute eliminates the unborn widow scenario by providing that "where the instrument creates an interest in the 'widow,' 'widower,' or 'spouse' of another person, [it is presumed] that the maker of the instrument intended to refer to a person who was living at the date that the period of the rule against perpetuities commences to run." 765 Ill. Comp. Stat. §365/4(c)(1)(C) (2008). See also N.Y. Est. Powers & Trusts Law §9-1.3(c) (2008) (similar); Jeffrey A. Schoenblum, 2008 Multistate Guide to Estate Planning at Table 10, question 21 (surveying the authorities on the unborn widow).

2. *T* bequeaths a fund in trust to pay the income "to my son for life, then to my son's widow, if any, for life; then to pay the principal to my son's children, but if no child of my son is alive at the death of the survivor of my son and his widow, then to pay the principal to the American Red Cross." Is any gift invalid? See John H. Morris and W. Barton Leach, The Rule Against Perpetuities 44 (2d ed. 1962).

NOTE: ALTERNATIVE CONTINGENCIES

Under the *alternative contingencies* doctrine, if the testator makes gifts on alternative contingencies, one of which offends the Rule Against Perpetuities and the other of which does not, the gifts are judged separately. The invalid gift fails; the valid gift takes effect if the event happens upon which it is limited.

To illustrate, suppose that *T* bequeaths a fund in trust "to my son *A* for life, then to *A*'s widow for life, then upon the widow's death *or* upon *A*'s death if *A* leaves no widow, to *A*'s descendants." *T* has split the contingencies, making a gift on the widow's death and a separate gift on the death of *A* leaving no widow. The gift on the death of the widow is void. The gift to *A*'s descendants on *A*'s death is valid if *A* actually leaves no widow. However, to trigger the alternative contingencies doctrine, the testator must expressly separate the contingencies. Thus, without the words "or upon *A*'s death if *A* leaves no widow," the gift to *A*'s descendants would be wholly void even though this second contingency is implicit.

c. The Slothful Executor

Another unusual possibility, occasionally overlooked by the drafter, is that a will may not be probated, or an estate distributed, for many years after the testator's death. Distribution of an estate ordinarily is completed soon after the testator's death, but in a few cases the estate has been tied up for many years in litigation or the will has been found many years after the testator dies.

The possibility of remote distribution gives rise to what are known as the *slothful executor* cases. Thus:

> *Case 7. T* devises property "to *T*'s descendants living upon distribution of *T*'s estate." *T*'s purpose is to avoid extra administrative costs and possible taxation in the estates of any of *T*'s descendants who die before *T*'s estate is distributed. However, because *T*'s estate may not be distributed for many years, perhaps after all *T*'s surviving descendants are dead, the gift to *T*'s descendants living at distribution may be held void.[9]

The administrative contingency involved in Case 7 is a true condition precedent: *T*'s will requires *T*'s descendants to survive distribution in order to take. Some administrative contingency cases, however, involve language that ought not to be construed to create a condition precedent to vesting. Examples include "to *A* upon distribution of my estate," "to my descendants when my debts are paid," and "to *A* upon probate of this will." Language of this sort, not requiring survival, should be construed as merely postponing possession and not imposing a condition precedent. See Deiss v. Deiss, 536 N.E.2d 120 (Ill. App. 1989).

The position of each of the states on the slothful executor is surveyed in Jeffrey A. Schoenblum, 2008 Multistate Guide to Estate Planning at Table 10, question 22.

d. The Magic Gravel Pit and Other Marvels

Here are some other extraordinary occurrences in the strange land of perpetuities:

---

9. There are at least two arguments that can be made to save the gift in Case 7. First, it can be argued that distribution of the estate will not be delayed beyond a reasonable time, which necessarily is less than 21 years. See Belfield v. Booth, 27 A. 585 (Conn. 1893). Second, it can be argued that, because the testator did not intend the executor to have the power to select recipients by delaying distribution, the class of descendants will close at the time distribution reasonably should be made. See Estate of Taylor, 428 P.2d 301 (Cal. 1967).

Case 8. The Magic Gravel Pit. T devises his gravel pits to his trustees to work them until the pits are exhausted and then to sell them and divide the proceeds among *T*'s descendants then living. Since the gravel pits might produce gravel for hundreds of years, the gift to *T*'s descendants is void. So held in In re Wood, [1894] 3 Ch. 381, even though the pits were in fact exhausted in six years.

Case 9. The War That Never Ends. During World War II, *T*, whose husband was a German immigrant, devised $20,000 to such of her husband's family in Germany who survive the war. The devise was held void in Brownell v. Edmunds, 209 F.2d 349 (4th Cir. 1953), on the grounds that World War II might not have ended within lives in being plus 21 years.

Case 10. The Birthday Present that Blows Up. T devises a fund in trust for *A* for life, then to such of *A*'s children as reach their respective twenty-first birthdays. Under the common law, a person reaches 21 at the first moment of the day before his twenty-first birthday; the theory is that a person is in existence on the day of his birth, and that on the day before his first birthday he has completed one year. His birthday is the first day of the second year. See Annot. 5 A.L.R.2d 1143 (1949, rev. 2008). In effect, then, this remainder is to such of *A*'s children as shall be living one day after they reach the age of 21. It is thus arguable that this gift exceeds by one day the Rule Against Perpetuities. See W. Barton Leach, The Careful Draftsman: Watch Out!, 47 A.B.A.J. 259 (1961).

The foregoing scenarios do not exhaust the extravagant possibilities that can be dreamed up to invalidate gifts. But together with the previous cases, they should suffice to show how, under the what-might-happen possibilities test of the common law Rule, even the most remote possibilities can invalidate an interest.

SECTION C. PERPETUITIES REFORM

The absurd assumptions that underpin the infamous perpetuities fantasy cases, combined with the Rule's exasperating complexities (several pertaining to class gifts and powers of appointment, deferred until Section D below), have brought the Rule — but not its underlying policy against remote vesting — into disrepute. In the last half of the twentieth century and continuing into the present, extensive debate erupted over whether the Rule should be reformed substantially, or even abolished completely. The reforms can be sorted into four basic kinds: (1) self-help through a saving clause; (2) adoption of the reformation (or cy pres) doctrine; (3) adoption of the wait-and-see doctrine; and (4) abolition of the Rule.

1. Self-Help: Saving Clauses

Because of the ease with which even experienced attorneys can overlook some remote possibility of untimely vesting, experienced estate planners today generally incorporate in trusts they draft a perpetuities *saving clause*[10] to take

---

10. Not savings clause, which is grammatically incorrect. As an adjective, saving — without the s — has the sense of "rescuing." See William Safire, On Language, N.Y. Times Mag., Apr. 2, 1995, at 22, explaining that savings is the sum of separate acts of saving, as in a savings account.

care of any possible violation. Such a clause is not actually intended to govern the duration of the trust, except in the event some overlooked violation of the Rule unexpectedly extends the trust too long. The clause's sole purpose is to ensure that the Rule is not violated.

Here is an example of a saving clause:

> Notwithstanding any other provisions in this instrument, any trust created hereunder shall terminate, if it has not previously terminated, 21 years after the death of the survivor of the beneficiaries of the trust living at the date this instrument becomes effective. In case of such termination, the then remaining principal and undistributed income of the trust shall be distributed to the then income beneficiaries in the same proportions as they were, at the time of termination, entitled to receive the income. The term "beneficiaries" includes persons originally named as beneficiaries in this instrument as well as persons, living at the date this instrument becomes effective, subsequently named as beneficiaries by a donee of a power of appointment over the trust assets exercising such power.

Under this saving clause, the trust terminates 21 years after the death of all beneficiaries, originally or subsequently named as such, who were in being when the trust became effective. The principal is then distributed as provided in the saving clause. Because the trust must end at the end of the perpetuities period (if not sooner), no interest in the trust can violate the Rule Against Perpetuities. The last sentence of the saving clause makes clear that the donee of a power of appointment can change the measuring lives for the trust, provided the donee does not select someone not alive when the trust was created.

NOTES

1. *Twelve healthy babies, Queen Victoria, and Joseph P. Kennedy.* The saving clause presented above uses the trust's beneficiaries as validating lives. But validating lives need not have any connection with the beneficiaries involved. In this imaginative and famous passage, Professor Leach explained that one could therefore have a saving clause keyed to lives of *twelve healthy babies*:

> The settled inclusion of twenty-one years in gross and the admission of extraneous lives bring it about that a testator or settlor, when motivated by vanity, is able to tie up his property, regardless of lives and deaths in his own family, for an unconscionable period — viz., twenty-one years after the deaths of a dozen or so healthy babies chosen from families noted for longevity, a term which, in the ordinary course of events, will add up to about a century. [6 American Law of Property §24.16, at 52 (1952).]

An interesting variant on Leach's twelve-healthy-babies clause is to choose not the children of a family noted for longevity, but rather a family known for fecundity, preferably with a high public profile so that tracking the validating lives is simplified. Thus, the English solicitors developed a *royal lives* saving clause whereby the trust is to continue until 21 years after the death of all the descendants of Queen Victoria (or of George V or of some other British monarch) living at the creation of the trust. The American counterpart, occasionally still found in wills and trusts today, is a saving clause that substitutes Joseph P. Kennedy, the patriarch of the prominent Kennedy family, for Queen Victoria.

2.   For a thorough discussion of saving clauses, see David M. Becker, Perpetuities and Estate Planning 133-184 (1993).

NOTE: ATTORNEY LIABILITY FOR VIOLATING THE RULE

In most states, attorneys are liable to the intended beneficiaries of negligently drafted instruments. See page 62. On the authority of Lucas v. Hamm, 364 P.2d 685 (Cal. 1961), it is sometimes said that it is not malpractice to draft an instrument that violates the Rule Against Perpetuities. In *Lucas*, the court held that an attorney who violated the Rule was not negligent on the specific facts of the case (involving an administrative contingency). Given the ease with which compliance can be assured through use of a saving clause, however, *Lucas* is a shaky precedent at best. Indeed, citing the emergence of the saving clause, a California lower court has warned that *Lucas* is of doubtful validity today. Wright v. Williams, 121 Cal. Rptr. 194, 199 n.2 (App. 1975).

In sum: It is almost certainly malpractice to violate the Rule Against Perpetuities by failing to include a perpetuities saving clause.

2.   *The Reformation (or Cy Pres) Doctrine*

Under the *reformation* (or *cy pres*) doctrine, the court may modify a trust that violates the Rule Against Perpetuities so as to carry out the testator's intent within the perpetuities period. See Jeffrey A. Schoenblum, 2008 Multistate Guide to Estate Planning at Table 10, questions 5-6, surveying the position of the states on reformation. In exercising the power of reformation, a court might insert a saving clause adapted to the particular possibility that causes the gift to be invalid and, in this manner, interfere with the testator's expressed wishes as little as possible. For illustrations of how such a cy pres saving clause would work, see Jesse Dukeminier, A Modern Guide to Perpetuities, 74 Cal. L. Rev. 1867, 1898-1901 (1986).

NOTE

Illinois and New York have adopted by statute specific correctives — in effect, rule-based specific reformation terms — for the most frequent violations of the Rule. Age contingencies in excess of 21 that cause a gift to fail are reduced to 21 for all persons subject to such contingency, and administrative contingencies are presumed to be intended to occur within 21 years. Recall also that in these states the unborn widow is dealt with by a presumption that a gift to a spouse is a gift to a person in being, and the fertile octogenarian is dealt with by a presumption that a woman is incapable of bearing children after a specified age and by the admission of extrinsic evidence of infertility (see pages 863 and 895).

3.   The Wait-and-See Doctrine

In 1947, the Pennsylvania legislature abandoned the what-might-happen possibilities test of the common law Rule. Pa. Stat. Ann. tit. 20, §6104(b) (2008) provides:

> Upon the expiration of the period allowed by the common law rule against perpetuities as measured by actual rather than possible events any interest not then vested and any interest in members of a class the membership of which is then subject to increase shall be void.

Dubbing the Pennsylvania approach "wait-and-see," in 1952 Professor W. Barton Leach strongly endorsed it in a seminal article, Perpetuities in Perspective: Ending the Rule's Reign of Terror, 65 Harv. L. Rev. 721 (1952). The essence of the wait-and-see doctrine is that *we wait and see what actually happens*; we do not invalidate an interest because of what might happen. In effect, the wait-and-see reform replaces the what-*might*-happen test with a what-*does*-happen approach.

Writing from his perch at Harvard with eloquence and wit, and sensing a general unhappiness with the Rule's remote possibilities test, Leach fired up a movement to adopt the wait-and-see doctrine. After Leach first promoted the wait-and-see doctrine, a flood of articles appeared, some in favor of wait-and-see, some against. The primary arguments against wait-and-see were three: (1) inconveniences would arise from not knowing whether an interest was valid or void; (2) wait-and-see was a long step toward extending the control of the dead hand; and (3) in the view of some critics, the common law did not provide any measuring lives for a wait-and-see period. Professor Leach replied to his critics in an entertaining article, Perpetuities Legislation, Hail Pennsylvania!, 108 U. Pa. L. Rev. 1124 (1960).

When Professor James Casner, Leach's colleague at Harvard, was appointed reporter for the Restatement (Second) of Property, he proposed adding wait-and-see to the new Restatement. This prompted Professor Richard R. Powell, who had been the reporter for the prior

Professor W. Barton Leach

Restatement and who, by this point, was 88 years old, to come out of retirement to speak against Casner's proposal. Two annual meetings of the American Law Institute were given to the battle. Ultimately, Casner prevailed, and wait-and-see was written into the new Restatement. Casner's main argument for wait-and-see was that the traditional what-might-happen test penalizes persons who do not avoid the Rule by a saving clause inserted by a lawyer awake to the issue.

The adoption of wait-and-see by the Restatement (Second) of Property provided a renewed stimulus for the wait-and-see movement. Wait-and-see has now been adopted in a majority of states, either by statute or judicial decision.

a. Wait-and-See for the Common Law Perpetuities Period

Professor Leach believed that the common law provided an inherent wait-and-see period: the lives relevant to vesting of the interest plus 21 years. Under this view, the lives that can affect vesting fix the common law perpetuities period applicable to the particular interest. See Jesse Dukeminier, Perpetuities: The Measuring Lives, 85 Colum. L. Rev. 1648 (1985).

Here are some examples of how wait-and-see works for the common law perpetuities period:

> *Case 11. The Fertile Octogenarian. T* bequeaths a fund in trust "for *A* for life, then for *A*'s children for their lives, then to *A*'s descendants then living." At common law, the remainder in fee simple is void because *A* is conclusively presumed to be capable of having another child. Under wait-and-see, *the lives relevant to vesting are A and all of A's descendants living at T's death. A* and *A*'s children are relevant on two scores: They are preceding life tenants, and they can, by procreating, affect the identity of the remainder beneficiaries. *A*'s grandchildren and great-grandchildren in being at *T*'s death are relevant because they are beneficiaries and also, by procreating or dying, they can affect the identity of the class of descendants who take the remainder.
>
> *Case 12. Age Contingency. T* bequeaths a fund in trust "for *A* for life, then to *A*'s children who reach 25." This is void at common law because *A* can leave, at his death, an afterborn child under the age of 4. The class members will not necessarily take fixed shares within 21 years after *A*'s death. *The wait-and-see lives are A and all of A's children living at T's death. A* qualifies as a measuring life on two counts: *A* is the preceding life tenant, and *A*, by begetting a child who shares in the remainder, can affect the identity of the beneficiaries. The children of *A* in being at *T*'s death who are under 25 can, by dying under 25, affect the identity of the class members. Those children over 25 at *T*'s death are identified beneficiaries in whom the gift vests.

The measuring lives for all of the standard cases arising under the Rule are set forth in Dukeminier, supra.

b. The Uniform Statutory Rule Against Perpetuities

The drafters of the Uniform Statutory Rule Against Perpetuities (USRAP) adopted wait-and-see, but they rejected using causally related measuring lives.

Instead they chose a fixed wait-and-see period of 90 years. Professor Waggoner, the principal drafter of the uniform rule, says that the drafters endeavored to approximate "the average period of time that would traditionally be allowed by the wait-and-see doctrine." Lawrence W. Waggoner, The Uniform Statutory Rule Against Perpetuities: The Rationale of the 90-Year Waiting Period, 73 Cornell L. Rev. 157, 162 (1988).

Although critics of USRAP, such as Professor Dukeminier, sharply contested Waggoner's methodology,[11] it is true that USRAP's 90-year period is a fair, if somewhat shorter, approximation of the period produced by using Leach's twelve-healthy-babies clause (page 898), which a skilled lawyer could use as a saving clause.

Under USRAP,[12] all interests are valid for 90 years after creation. At the end of 90 years, any interest that has not vested is reformed by the court so as to best carry out the intention of the long-dead settlor. USRAP has been supported by state bar associations, perhaps because a 90-year wait-and-see period effectively eliminates perpetuities malpractice exposure for a lawyer's entire career. A variant of USRAP is in force in roughly half the states. See Jeffrey A. Schoenblum, 2008 Multistate Guide to Estate Planning at Table 10, question 1.

For further analyses and assessments of USRAP by persons other than Dukeminier and Waggoner, see Ira M. Bloom, Perpetuities Refinement: There Is an Alternative, 62 Wash. L. Rev. 23 (1987); Mary L. Fellows, Testing Perpetuity Reforms: A Study of Perpetuity Cases 1984-89, 25 Real Prop., Prob. & Tr. J. 597 (1990); Amy M. Hess, Freeing Property Owners from the RAP Trap: Tennessee Adopts the Uniform Statutory Rule Against Perpetuities, 62 Tenn. L. Rev. 267 (1995); Ronald C. Link and Kimberly A. Licata, Perpetuities Reform in North Carolina: The Uniform Statutory Rule Against Perpetuities, Nondonative Transfers, and Honorary Trusts, 74 N.C. L. Rev. 1783 (1996).

Uniform Statutory Rule Against Perpetuities
(1986, as amended 1990)

§1. STATUTORY RULE AGAINST PERPETUITIES

(a) [*Validity of Nonvested Property Interest.*] A nonvested property interest is invalid unless:

(1) when the interest is created, it is certain to vest or terminate no later than 21 years after the death of an individual then alive; or

---

11. With ink as their weapon of choice, an epic battle broke out in the law journals between Dukeminier and Waggoner. In addition to Waggoner's Cornell Law Review article cited above, see also Jesse Dukeminier, The Uniform Statutory Rule Against Perpetuities: Ninety Years in Limbo, 34 UCLA L. Rev. 1023 (1987); Lawrence W. Waggoner, Perpetuity Reform, 81 Mich. L. Rev. 1718 (1983); and pages 1648 through 1747, inclusive, of Volume 85 of the Columbia Law Review (1985), spanning five (yes, five!) articles. There is no precise count of the trees sacrificed to the cause.

12. Professor Link finds one aspect of USRAP "puzzling — its pronunciation. Both 'use-rap' and 'us-rap' seem acceptable to its drafter and advocates." Ronald C. Link and Kimberly A. Licata, Perpetuities Reform in North Carolina: The Uniform Statutory Rule Against Perpetuities, Nondonative Transfers, and Honorary Trusts, 74 N.C. L. Rev. 1783, 1789 n.28 (1996).

(2) the interest either vests or terminates within 90 years after its creation. . . .

(d) [*Possibility of Post-death Child Disregarded.*] In determining whether a nonvested property interest . . . is valid . . . , the possibility that a child will be born to an individual after the individual's death is disregarded.

(e) [*Effect of Certain "Later-of" Type Language.*] If, in measuring a period from the creation of a trust or other property arrangement, language in a governing instrument (i) seeks to disallow the vesting or termination of any interest or trust beyond, (ii) seeks to postpone the vesting or termination of any interest or trust until, or (iii) seeks to operate in effect in any similar fashion upon, the later of (a) the expiration of a period of time not exceeding 21 years after the death of the survivor of specified lives in being at the creation of the trust or other property arrangement or (b) the expiration of a period of time that exceeds or might exceed 21 years after the death of the survivor of lives in being at the creation of the trust or other property arrangement, that language is inoperative to the extent it produces a period of time that exceeds 21 years after the death of the survivor of the specified lives. . . .

§3.   REFORMATION

Upon the petition of an interested person, a court shall reform a disposition in the manner that most closely approximates the transferor's manifested plan of distribution and is within the 90 years allowed by Section 1(a)(2), 1(b)(2), or 1(c)(2) if:

(1) a nonvested property interest or a power of appointment becomes invalid under Section 1 (statutory rule against perpetuities);

(2) a class gift is not but might become invalid under Section 1 (statutory rule against perpetuities) and the time has arrived when the share of any class member is to take effect in possession or enjoyment; or

(3) a nonvested property interest that is not validated by Section 1(a)(1) can vest but not within 90 years after its creation. . . .

NOTE: USRAP AND THE GENERATION-SKIPPING TRANSFER (GST) TAX

The Generation Skipping Transfer (GST) tax is payable on a transfer to a person two or more generations removed from the transferor, such as a grandchild. Trusts created before 1986 are excluded from the GST tax by a grandfathering provision. Under Treasury regulations at the time USRAP was drafted, pre-1986 trusts are not subject to the GST tax unless a special power of appointment over the pre-1986 trust is exercised in a manner that postpones vesting of an interest beyond lives in being at the creation of the trust plus 21 years. The purpose of the regulation is to prevent tax exemption from enduring longer than the perpetuities period beginning at the creation of the trust.

After USRAP was promulgated, it was discovered that USRAP contained an unexpected tax trap. In a USRAP jurisdiction, a grandfathered trust loses its GST tax exemption if the donee of a special power of appointment exercises the power so as to violate the common law Rule Against Perpetuities, thus bringing into play the 90-year wait-and-see period, which may extend the trust beyond lives in being at the creation of the trust plus 21 years.

When the USRAP tax trap was brought to the attention of the USRAP drafting committee in 1990, the committee negotiated a solution with the Treasury Department. Treasury accepted the 90-year perpetuities period as the functional equivalent of the common law perpetuities period. Treasury was unwilling, however, to extend a tax exemption to a trust that could continue for either the common law perpetuities period or for 90 years, whichever period turned out to be longer. Doing so could have given an even more substantial extension of the tax exemption as well as give an unfair advantage to longer-of-two-perpetuities-periods trusts available in USRAP states but not in states adhering to the common law. To satisfy Treasury's demand that a clause terminating a trust on the later of the two perpetuities periods be prohibited, USRAP was amended in 1990 by adding §1(e).

USRAP §1(e) provides that when a gift is made on two alternative contingencies, one of which (A) will necessarily vest, if at all, within the common law perpetuities period, and the second of which (B) might vest beyond that period, the language of (B) is rendered inoperative to the extent it produces a period in excess of 21 years after the specified lives in being. When a clause terminates a trust at the conclusion of either the common law perpetuities period or a 90-year period, whichever is later, §1(e) gives effect only to the common law perpetuities period termination date.

After USRAP was amended to add §1(e), Treasury issued a regulation stating that if a special power of appointment in a grandfathered trust were "directly or indirectly" exercised in a manner that attempts to obtain the longer of the two perpetuities periods available under USRAP, the GST tax exemption would be lost. Treas. Reg. §26.2601-1(b)(1)(v)(B)(2) & (D), examples 6 & 7 (1997).

Although the Treasury regulation forbids the exercise of the power in an attempt to obtain the longer of the two USRAP perpetuities periods, it permits the donee to appoint in further trust for 90 years or less. Hence, a grandfathered trust initially governed by the common law perpetuities period may be turned into a 90-year trust by the exercise of a special power of appointment, provided, of course, that the special power may be so exercised under the instrument.

USRAP §1(e) has not been enacted in some states that adopted USRAP before it was amended in 1990. In these states, when a special power in a grandfathered trust is exercised so as to terminate the trust at the end of the common law perpetuities period or 90 years, whichever is later, creating alternative contingencies, the first of which is valid at common law and the second valid under USRAP, the trust may lose its GST tax exemption. See Jesse Dukeminier, The Uniform Statutory Rule Against Perpetuities and the GST Tax: New Perils for

Practitioners and New Opportunities, 30 Real Prop., Prob. & Tr. J. 185, 198-199 (1995).

Lawyers in USRAP states who are dealing with grandfathered trusts should take special care not to violate the common law Rule Against Perpetuities if they decide not to extend the trust for 90 years. If the common law Rule is violated, bringing into play the 90-year wait-and-see period as an alternative trust termination date, this may result in the longer of the two perpetuities periods applying and the loss of GST tax exemption. Id. at 199-202.

As you can see, the interaction of USRAP and the GST tax is a complicated matter, which you will have to unravel if you are advising the donee of a special power in a grandfathered trust. USRAP may save the lawyer from malpractice liability for violating the Rule when the GST tax is not involved, but it does not protect the lawyer from possible liability for negligently losing the GST tax exemption.

4. Abolition of the Rule Against Perpetuities

The Rule Against Perpetuities no longer commands universal respect or fear. Its storied absurdities seem remnants of a bygone age. There is no longer a consensus on how long the dead hand should be permitted to govern. Sparked by a 1986 change in the federal tax code, and coming on the heels of USRAP's departure from the traditional lives in being plus 21 years formulation, a movement to allow perpetual trusts by abolishing the Rule took hold in the 1990s. Today, nearly half the states, including several in which USRAP remains otherwise in force, have effectively abolished the Rule as applied to future interests in trust.

Robert H. Sitkoff and Max M. Schanzenbach, Jurisdictional Competition
for Trust Funds: An Empirical Analysis of Perpetuities and Taxes
115 Yale L.J. 356 (2005)

This Article presents the results of the first empirical study of the jurisdictional competition for trust funds. Based on . . . data assembled from annual reports to federal banking authorities by institutional trustees, we find that the interstate competition for trust funds is both real and intense. Our analysis indicates that, on average, through 2003 a state's abolition of the Rule Against Perpetuities increased its reported trust assets by about $6 billion and its average trust account size by roughly $200,000. To put these figures in perspective, in 2003 the average state had roughly $19 billion in reported trust assets and an average account size of about $1 million. In the timeframe of our data, seventeen states abolished the Rule, implying that through 2003 roughly $100 billion in trust assets have moved as a result of the Rule's abolition. This figure represents about 10% of the total trust assets reported to federal banking authorities in 2003. . . .

I. JURISDICTIONAL COMPETITION FOR TRUST FUNDS . . .

A. THE RULE AGAINST PERPETUITIES . . .

Beginning in the 1950s, dissatisfaction with the Rule's exasperating complexities and absurd assumptions led to reform to stay what Barton Leach famously called "the slaughter of the innocents" in the Rule's "reign of terror." Some states enacted statutory fixes for specific fantasy scenarios, in particular the unborn widow and the fertile octogenarian. Other states authorized the courts to reform instruments that otherwise would have been void *ab initio*. Still other states adopted the so-called wait-and-see principle whereby courts wait to see if, in light of actual instead of possible events, the interest will in fact vest or fail within a specified period. The culmination of the perpetuities reform movement was the 1986 Uniform Statutory Rule Against Perpetuities (USRAP). USRAP, some form of which is now in force in about half the states, provides a wait-and-see period of ninety years and authorizes reformation of instruments that would otherwise violate the Rule. . . .

Even in its reformed versions and buffered by saving clauses, [however,] the Rule requires that contingent interests vest or fail within a specified period. For this reason, prior to its widespread abolition, the Rule continued to represent a practical constraint on trust duration. [Then the Tax Reform Act of 1986 changed everything.]

B. FEDERAL WEALTH TRANSFER TAXES . . .

Prior to 1986, . . . the estate tax could be avoided by using successive life interests. Because a life tenancy terminates at death and the estate tax applies only to the decedent's transferable interests, there is no tax on the death of a life tenant. Thus:

> *Case 2. The Successive Life Estates Loophole. O* creates a trust for the benefit of her daughter *A* for life, and then to *A*'s daughter *B* for life (*O*'s grandchild), with the remainder to *B*'s children (*O*'s great-grandchildren). Although *O* may have to pay a gift or estate tax upon the trust's creation, no estate tax will be levied at the death of *A* or *B*. Not until the death of *B*'s children — *O*'s great-grandchildren — will another estate tax be due.

Congress sought to close the successive-life-estates loophole with the generation-skipping transfer (GST) tax under the Tax Reform Act of 1986. In rough terms, a transfer to a grandchild, great-grandchild, or any other person who is two or more generations below the transferor is a generation-skipping transfer; the GST tax is assessed on such transfers. Hence, in *Case 2*, a GST tax would be payable at the death of *A* and at the death of *B*. The GST tax rate equals the highest rate of the estate tax, currently 47%.[13]

Under the 1986 Act, however, each transferor has a lifetime exemption from the estate and GST taxes, originally $1 million and now $1.5 million, which is

---

13. The maximum rates are as follows: 49% in 2003; 48% in 2004; 47% in 2005; 46% in 2006; and 45% in 2007-2009. I.R.C. §§2641, 2001(c)(2)(B) (2005).

scheduled to grow incrementally to $3.5 million by 2009.[14] Accordingly, a transferor can fund a trust with the amount of the exemption, free from transfer taxes, which will endure as long as state perpetuities law permits. The federal tax code puts no limit on the duration of the transfer tax exemption. Instead, Congress left it to state perpetuities law to limit the duration of a transfer-tax-exempt trust. Thus:

> *Case 3. The Transfer-Tax-Exempt Trust. O* funds a trust with $1.5 million to pay income to *O*'s daughter *A* for life. *A* is given a special power to appoint the trust corpus outright or in further trust to *O*'s descendants or the spouses of such descendants.[15] At *A*'s death, *A* exercises her power over the trust corpus by appointing it in her will to her children *B* and *C* in equal shares and in further trust, giving each a similar special power over the share of each, and so on. Although *O* may have had to pay some gift or estate tax upon creating the trust, no estate, gift, or GST tax will be due on the exercise of *A*'s, *B*'s, or *C*'s special power or the exercise of any other subsequent special power for as long as state perpetuities law permits.

Accordingly, in 1986 state perpetuities law became a highly salient factor in estate planning. The longer the trust in *Case 3* could be extended, the more generations could benefit from the trust fund free from transfer taxes. . . .

C. THE RACE TO ABOLISH THE RAP

For reasons unrelated to the GST tax, Idaho, South Dakota, and Wisconsin had already abolished the Rule Against Perpetuities before 1986. But . . . these states experienced little to no resulting advantage in the jurisdictional competition for trust funds prior to 1986. Then came the Tax Reform Act of 1986. As the practicing bar digested the Act and grasped the nature of the GST tax, it became apparent that making use of the transferor's exemption in a perpetual trust had significant long-term tax advantages. If the trust in *Case 3*, above, were created in Idaho, South Dakota, or Wisconsin, it could continue, free from federal wealth transfer taxation, generation after generation, forever.

As a general matter, prior to 1986 there was little significant variation in trust law across the states. After the GST tax, however, state perpetuities law became a highly salient margin of differentiation. Given prevailing choice-of-law principles and the shift in the nature of wealth from land to financial assets (making trust assets portable), it was only a matter of time until jurisdictional competition sparked a race to abolish the Rule Against Perpetuities.

To ensure that the law of state *B* will govern the validity and administration of a trust created by a settlor who resides in state *A*, lawyers usually advise the settlor not only to provide in the trust instrument that the law of state *B* is to govern, but also to name a trustee located in state *B* and to give that trustee custody of the trust fund. As a result, an out-of-state settlor who wants to invoke the law of state

---

14. The exemption schedule is as follows: through 2003, $1 million; in 2004 and 2005, $1.5 million; in 2006 through 2008, $2 million; and in 2009, $3.5 million. I.R.C. §§2631(c), 2010(c) (2005).

15. Property subject to a special power, as compared with a general power, is not treated as belonging to the holder of the power for tax purposes. [See page 810. — Eds.] . . .

The Rule Against Perpetuities: If You Repeal It, The Money Will Come

B typically will appoint as trustee a bank or trust company located in state *B*.
Therein lies the payoff to state *B* and the political economy of the RAP's demise.
Ever since the perpetuities loophole in the GST tax was understood, abolition of
the RAP has been "pushed by banking associations . . . [that] wish to remain competitive with banks where perpetual trusts are permitted." Joel Dobris put it more
bluntly: "When the bankers want something, they get it."[16] . . .

For a variety of historical reasons, Delaware . . . has long been a trust-friendly
jurisdiction and by 1986 had a disproportionate share of the nation's trust funds.
Indeed, prior to the GST tax, on several occasions Delaware tweaked its perpetuities law to create tax and other advantages to settling a trust in Delaware. So it
was hardly a surprise when in 1995 Delaware became the first state after the
enactment of the GST tax to abolish the Rule as applied to interests in trust. The
bill's official synopsis makes its purpose plain:

> Several states, including Idaho, Wisconsin and South Dakota, have abolished altogether
> their rules against perpetuities, which has given those jurisdictions a competitive advantage
> over Delaware in attracting assets held in trusts created for estate planning purposes. . . .
> The multi-million dollar capital commitments to these irrevocable trusts, and the ensuing
> compound growth over decades, will result in the formation of a substantial capital base in

16. Joel C. Dobris, Changes in the Role and the Form of the Trust at the New Millennium, or, We Don't Have
to Think of England Anymore, 62 Alb. L. Rev. 543, 572 (1998).

Perpetual Trust States (2008)

the innovative jurisdictions that have abolished the rule against perpetuities. Several financial institutions have now organized or acquired trust companies, particularly in South Dakota, at least in part to take advantage of their favorable trust law.

Delaware's repeal of the rule against perpetuities for personal property held in trust will demonstrate Delaware's continued vigilance in maintaining its role as a leading jurisdiction for the formation of capital and the conduct of trust business.[17]

The Delaware statute triggered a race to abolish the Rule.

NOTES AND QUESTION

1. *The perpetual trust states.* As of this writing, perpetual or effectively perpetual trusts appear to be authorized in Alaska (1,000 years), Arizona (500 years), Colorado (1,000 years), Delaware, District of Columbia, Florida (360 years), Idaho, Illinois, Maine, Maryland, Michigan (360 years), Missouri, Nebraska, Nevada (365 years), New Hampshire, New Jersey, North Carolina, Ohio, Pennsylvania, Rhode Island, South Dakota, Tennessee (360 years), Utah (1,000), Virginia, Wisconsin, and Wyoming (1,000 years). We say *appear* because the language of several of the statutes is opaque.

To say that the foregoing states permit perpetual or effectively perpetual trusts is not to say that they have necessarily abolished the Rule. Although

17. H.R. 245, 138th Gen. Assemb. (Del. 1995) (bill synopsis).

some states have indeed abolished the Rule altogether, others have abolished the Rule only as applied to interests in trusts in which the trustee has the power to sell the trust assets and then reinvest the proceeds (that is, for trusts that do not suspend the power of alienation, see Section E below), and still other states have abolished the Rule only as applied to interests in personal property. Perhaps the oddest transmogrification is in the states that have reduced the Rule, which heretofore had been a mandatory rule designed to curtail the dead hand,[18] to a default that applies unless the settlor provides otherwise. For a survey of the mechanisms by which the states have come to validate perpetual trusts, see Lynn Foster, Fifty-One Flowers: Current Perpetuities Law in the States, 22 Prob. & Prop. 30 (July/Aug. 2008).

2.   *Perpetuities and the (state) constitution.* The race to validate perpetual trusts has brought into focus yet another interesting variant across the states. The Rule is enshrined in the constitutions of about one-fifth of the states. See Foster, supra. Hence, it would appear that before those states can jump on the perpetual trust bandwagon, their constitutions will have to be amended. Or maybe not. The constitutions of Arizona, Nevada, North Carolina, Tennessee, and Wyoming all ban "perpetuities," yet each by statute has validated perpetual (or, in effect, perpetual) trusts. Will the courts of those states uphold the perpetual trust statutes against constitutional challenge?

3.   *The role of the GST tax.* To assess the role of the GST tax in sparking the movement to validate perpetual trusts, in a follow-up study Professors Schanzenbach and Sitkoff examined federal banking data on trust accounts prior to the adoption of the GST tax. They concluded that "prior to the GST tax, states that abolished the Rule did not garner more trust business than those that retained the Rule. Taken together, our findings in this and our prior study show that use of the perpetual trust traces to the 1986 GST tax and grew at an increasingly rapid pace thereafter." Max M. Schanzenbach and Robert H. Sitkoff, Perpetuities or Taxes? Explaining the Rise of the Perpetual Trust, 27 Cardozo L. Rev. 2465, 2496 (2006). See also Mary Louise Fellows, Why the Generation-Skipping Transfer Tax Sparked Perpetual Trusts, 27 Cardozo L. Rev. 2511 (2006) (discussing "the dry tinder on which [the GST tax] spark fell").

The swift spread of legislation enabling perpetual trusts, and the extensive use of such trusts in practice, raises the question whether allowing perpetual trusts reflects sound public policy.

---

18. Gray expressed this view in stronger language:

> The Rule Against Perpetuities is not a rule of construction, but a peremptory command of law. It is not, like a rule of construction, a test, more or less artificial, to determine intention. Its object is to defeat intention. Therefore every provision in a will or settlement is to be construed as if the Rule did not exist, and then to the provision so construed the Rule is to be remorselessly applied. [John C. Gray, The Rule Against Perpetuities §629 (4th ed. 1942).]

Jesse Dukeminier and James E. Krier, The Rise of the Perpetual Trust
50 UCLA L. Rev. 1303 (2003)

We are now in a position to consider the policies underlying the Rule Against Perpetuities — in the context of perpetual trusts. There are essentially three concerns, each of which can be stated in terms of a problem arising from a persistent dead hand. The first, the problem of inalienability, is of little importance in our context because it can be avoided by any well-drafted trust. The second, which we shall call the problem of first-generation monopoly, is contentious; we shall satisfy ourselves simply with describing the competing outlooks. The third, the problem of duration, is a catch-all for a host of difficulties that can arise as an uncertain future unwinds . . . .

A. THE PROBLEM OF INALIENABILITY

Transferability (or "alienability") of property promotes efficiency; it allows the movement of resources from lower to higher valued uses through voluntary transactions between buyers and sellers that leave both sides of the bargain better off. So it is unsurprising that free alienability is one of the enduring principles of English, and subsequently American, property law. . . .

[T]rustees almost always have a power to sell the trust property and invest in other assets. In almost all states permitting perpetual trusts, trustees must be given this power by the instrument if it is not granted by statute. A well-drafted trust will grant the power in any event. Hence, perpetual trusts do not give rise to a problem of inalienability; the trust assets are freely marketable.

B. THE PROBLEM OF FIRST-GENERATION MONOPOLY . . .

[In 1955 Professor Lewis Simes described] what we call the problem of first-generation monopoly, meaning by "first generation" the generation of the settlor who sets up a perpetual trust. Simes wrote:

> [I]t is good public policy to allow each person to dispose of his property as he pleases. The policy extends not only to the present generation but to future generations. If we are to permit the present generation to tie up all existing capital for an indefinitely long period of time, then future generations will have nothing to dispose of by will except what they have saved from their own income; and the property which each generation enjoys will already have been disposed of by ancestors long dead. The rule against perpetuities would appear to strike a balance between the unlimited disposition of property by the members of the present generation and its unlimited disposition by members of future generations.[19]

This is an old and appealing sentiment. . . . [Simes] thought that the force of the argument against first-generation monopoly "can scarcely be denied." And yet it can. Professor Thomas Gallanis notes . . . that sentiments about the dead

---

19. Lewis M. Simes, Is the Rule Against Perpetuities Doomed? The "Wait and See" Doctrine, 52 Mich. L. Rev. 179, 191-192 (1953).

hand rest on dubious assumptions about what people actually want.[20] . . . Consider, for example, the likely preferences of the mentally incompetent; of minor children; of bad money managers who lack the discipline to lash themselves to the mast; of people (maybe those same people!) hounded by creditors and vulnerable to bankruptcy; of people, supported by the state, who are beneficiaries of discretionary trusts, which the state cannot touch; of people contemplating divorce and interested in having their property out of reach of the other half; of people who reap nice tax advantages from trusts, including spouses who benefit from the marital deduction, and beneficiaries of tax-exempt dynasty trusts, among others. . . .

Beyond that, one should consider goals other than satisfaction of preferences. A goal of equality, for example, might support placing restraints on the ability of one generation to limit the opportunities of the next; a goal of donative freedom, on the other hand, would cut in the opposite direction. . . .

[E]quality of opportunity is not provided by income alone. As Professors Blum and Kalven pointed out years ago, the gravest source of inequality of opportunity is inequality of human capital, the knowledge and education embodied in individuals.[21] Human capital is created by family cultural influence on children, as well as by education. The knowledge and education of parents and more remote ancestors are passed along from generation to generation. Judge Posner puts the point in another way: "The inheritance of a large amount of money may seem to confer an unfair advantage, but why more unfair than inheriting brains and energy?" . . .

[T]here is an argument that trusts concentrate economic power in the rich or, more accurately, in the trustees for the rich. In the case of trusts, the trustees, not the beneficiaries, have the power of investment. They decide where the trust capital is to be invested . . . . [But] the wealth invested by trustees is only a small fraction of the total amount of risk capital made available by other investors. . . .

Consider finally the argument that the certainty of receiving trust income makes beneficiaries lazy and unproductive. . . . When the Republic was established, England had a "leisure class," composed of nobles and country gentlemen who lived off their land rents and inheritances and refrained from something as low as work. . . . But this country has never had a leisure class like England's. We have no sense of inherited hierarchy. Our work ethic, deeply imbedded from the times of the Puritans, has spared us a class of great drones. . . .

[Our] work ethic is paired with another ethic: The rich should share their wealth with the less fortunate. From the time when great fortunes were accumulated at the end of the nineteenth century to the present, the American rich, to justify their moral instinct, have given great sums to philanthropic enterprises. . . . This tradition of giving, reflecting conceptions about how society should be organized and what benefits the public, continues to this day. . . . [C]haritable support has given us in the United States universities and hospitals and cultural institutions that are the envy of the world. The diversity of privately

20. Thomas P. Gallanis, The Rule Against Perpetuities and the Law Commission's Flawed Philosophy, 59 Cambridge L.J. 284, 287-290 (2000).

21. An excerpt from the Blum and Kalven article appears at page 24. — Eds.

supported philanthropic enterprises is enormous, far greater than in Western European countries where the charitable agenda is largely set and supported by the government. . . .

Perhaps the objection is to the creation of family dynasties, which receive trust income generation after generation.[22] The answer is this: The Rule Against Perpetuities has not prevented the creation of family dynasties. Witness the Rockefellers (now in their fifth generation), the Du Ponts of high dynastic numbering (whose fortune dates from the War of 1812), and the Mellons (with a fortune predating the Civil War). These are extreme cases, but the fact is that smaller fortunes have supported many other families over several generations. Dozens of the lesser rich families have entrenched themselves from generation to generation in communities across the United States. The same is true in England . . . . If family dynasties are to be prevented, only the federal government, through income and death taxes, can do it. As Susan French has noted, the power of the dead hand is always at the sufferance of the living, who are perfectly free to change the laws that created the power in the first place.[23]

C. THE PROBLEM OF DURATION

The longer trusts endure, the more troublesome they become, thanks largely to uncertainty. . . .

1. Change in Circumstances

No one can foresee the future. After some years pass, events never anticipated by trust settlors and their lawyers are likely to occur — for example, changes in the number, needs, and abilities of beneficiaries; changes in tax law and trust doctrine; changes in investment opportunities, in the rate of inflation and the value of the dollar; changes in trustees and the quality of their performance. The welfare of beneficiaries might be reduced in consequence, or economic waste might result. The Rule Against Perpetuities mitigates the difficulty by finally terminating trusts and forcing distribution of assets. Absent the Rule, termination or modification after a change in circumstances must be dealt with in other ways. . . .

2. Trustees

Any number of problems can arise with trustees, and the longer a trust lasts, the greater the burden of these. . . . When settlors choose a trustee, they cannot know the course of future events. This might well lead them to choose a corporate trustee instead of a trusted friend, if for no other reason than that friends eventually die. But then, so too do corporate trustees, in a sense. Their employees pass

22. Recall the quotation attributed to Tocqueville in the excerpt from Oliver, Shapiro & Press, page 18: "What is the most important for democracy is not that great fortunes should not exist, but that great fortunes should not remain in the same hands. In that way there are rich men, but they do not form a class." — Eds.

23. See Susan F. French, Perpetuities: Three Essays in Honor of My Father, 65 Wash. L. Rev. 323, 350-352 (1990).

on, or away; the corporate trustee itself may merge with another company . . . . Beneficiaries, especially beneficiaries of long-term and perpetual trusts, may end up with a trustee of a sort the settlor would never have wished to choose — such as a bank the beneficiaries find to be distant, cold, and unresponsive to their needs. . . .

3. Multiplication of Beneficiaries

When a trust is limited to one hundred years or so, the number of beneficiaries will usually stay a manageable size, even though administrative costs may rise as the class of beneficiaries increases. In a perpetual trust, the number of beneficiaries can multiply relentlessly from generation to generation. If a trust is set up for two children of the settlor and their descendants, and each child has two children — which is pretty close to the statistical average — and each grandchild has two children, and so on down the generations, and each generation is measured by twenty-five years, there will be sixteen beneficiaries of the trust after one hundred years and 256 after two hundred years. Eventually the trust might become unmanageable. But the problem can be avoided if separate trusts can be created for the various beneficiaries . . . .The Uniform Trust Code grants just such a power to trustees, letting them divide a trust into two or more separate trusts without court approval, so long as notice is given to the beneficiaries.

Multiplication of beneficiaries is not such a bad thing, provided it does not result in burdensome and costly trust administration. It tends to dilute the concentration of wealth — unless family wealth increases as fast as the family itself. . . .

IV. THE FUTURE OF PERPETUAL TRUSTS . . .

The short of it is that Congress has come to be in charge of trust duration. The future of perpetual trusts is in its hands, to be dealt with through the tax system. The role of the states is to develop affordable means for modifying and terminating trusts when that is in the best interests of the beneficiaries. We have reached a great turning point in the law of trusts.

NOTES AND QUESTIONS

1. *Modification, termination, and perpetual trusts.* What legislators giveth to the dead hand in the form of perpetual trusts, judges can taketh away in the form of a liberalized common law of trust modification and termination. It seems likely that, in the not-so-distant future, the courts will be confronted by clauses in perpetual trusts that no longer make sense in light of changed circumstances. Will abrogation of the Rule Against Perpetuities boomerang into a more liberal law of modification and termination?

Model forms for perpetual transfer-tax-exempt trusts typically include provisions that give each generation a special power to appoint the remainder to the next generation outright or in further trust as in Professor Sitkoff and

Schanzenbach's Case 3 at page 907. See also Richard W. Nenno, Delaware Dynasty Trusts, Total-Return Unitrusts, and Asset-Protection Trusts 248-249 (2008 ed.), supplying a model trust form that includes such a clause. Well-drafted perpetual trusts also tend to include provisions that simplify the removal of an unresponsive or ineffective trustee. See Robert A. Vigoda, Powers to Replace Trustees: A Key Element of (and Risk to) Dynasty Trusts, 35 Est. Plan. 20 (2008). Should the law be reformed in line with the substance of such clauses, thereby giving all trusts the benefit of the provisions recommended by the elite bar? If so, should the more liberal rules be made mandatory?

The Uniform Trust Code and Restatement (Third) of Trusts state somewhat more flexible rules of modification, termination, and trustee removal than traditional law, see pages 641-658, but they do not go as far as the clauses found in model perpetual trust forms. The introductory note to the relevant sections of the Restatement says, "It is worth noting, however, that this section [on modification and termination of trusts] applies in the common-law context and that different issues — and different planning and drafting considerations — may arise with respect to trusts of indefinite duration in jurisdictions that have adopted legislation to abolish the rule against perpetuities."

Based on a review of the online promotion of perpetual trusts, Professor Tate concludes that, in addition to tax savings, "settlors also wish to protect their wealth from being wasted and to encourage their descendants to be productive members of society." Because liberalization of trust modification and termination law "will have the effect of frustrating" these goals, Tate argues against mandatory liberalizations of modification and termination law. "Mandatory rules providing for easy modification and termination allow the beneficiaries, at each generation, to substitute their own values for those of the settlor. It is not self-evident that the law should favor the values of fourth- or fifth-generation beneficiaries over those of the settlor, whose labor may have made the trust possible." Joshua C. Tate, Perpetual Trusts and the Settlor's Intent, 53 U. Kan. L. Rev. 595, 620-623 (2005).

Professor French disagrees. "By the time that three or four or five generations have passed, . . . it seems self-evident to me that the settlor's views are likely to be so outdated that they will deserve little deference. The fact that the settlor amassed (or inherited) the funds does not give the settlor special ability to predict future conditions and should not justify maintaining the funds for purposes that no longer meet the needs of the beneficiaries." Susan F. French, Perpetual Trusts, Conservation Servitudes, and the Problem of the Future, 27 Cardozo L. Rev. 2523, 2531 n.24 (2007).

Does allowing modification or termination in view of changed circumstances frustrate the settlor's intent if such modification or termination is keyed to a determination of what the settlor would have wanted if she had anticipated the change in circumstances? Should a donor be allowed to create a perpetual trust that cannot be modified even in the face of changed circumstances?

For a lively and entertaining discussion of potential lines of attack for breaking perpetual trusts — "tattoo removal," to borrow the author's amusing analogy — see Joel C. Dobris, Undoing Repeal of the Rule Against Perpetuities, 27 Cardozo L. Rev. 2537 (2006).

2. *Multiplication of beneficiaries.* In January 2000, the Uniform Law Commission issued a press release regarding perpetual, transfer-tax-exempt trusts:

> This movement is ill-advised, says Lawrence W. Waggoner, Director of Research of the Joint Editorial Board for the Uniform Probate Code, because Congress is not likely to allow this loophole to continue indefinitely. In addition, he says, the creation of such trusts is problematic. Over time, the administration of such trusts is likely to become unwieldy and very costly.
>
> Government statistics indicate that the average married couple has 2.1 children. Under this assumption, the average settlor will have more than 100 descendants (who are beneficiaries of the trust) 150 years after the trust is created, around 2,500 beneficiaries 250 years after the trust is created, and 45,000 beneficiaries 350 years after the trust is created. Five hundred years after the trust is created, the number of living beneficiaries could rise to an astounding 3.4 million. [Uniform Law Commission, Uniform Statutory Rule Against Perpetuities Is Law in 26 States: Move of a Few States to Abolish the Rule in Order to Facilitate Perpetual (Dynasty) Trusts Is Ill-Advised.]

Professors Dukeminier and Krier suggest that the problem of multiplying beneficiaries can be avoided with a clause in the trust instrument or a statute that authorizes the trustee to divide the trust into two or more separate trusts. Many states have such a statute, some based on UTC §417 (2000). Restatement (Third) of Trusts §68 (2003) takes the position that a trustee may divide a trust even without specific authorization by statute or in the trust instrument.

On the other hand, if exponential growth in the number of beneficiaries were actually to occur with any frequency, then the power to *terminate* small trusts might prove more important than the power to *divide* the trust into two or more separate trusts. It seems unlikely that the growth in the trust corpus could match an exponential growth in the number of beneficiaries, especially if the current beneficiaries are entitled to the trust income. To this end, UTC §414 (2000) provides that "the trustee of a trust consisting of trust property having a total value less than [$50,000] may terminate the trust if the trustee concludes that the value of the trust property is insufficient to justify the cost of administration." The official comment explains that the $50,000 figure is in brackets "to signal to enacting jurisdictions that they may wish to designate a higher or lower figure."

3. *Literature.* The erosion of the Rule Against Perpetuities has been the subject of robust commentary. In addition to the articles cited above, see Ira Mark Bloom, The GST Tax Tail Is Killing the Rule Against Perpetuities, 87 Tax Notes 569 (2000); Joel C. Dobris, The Death of the Rule Against Perpetuities, or the RAP Has No Friends—An Essay, 35 Real Prop., Prob. & Tr. J. 601 (2000); Note, Dynasty Trusts and the Rule Against Perpetuities, 116 Harv. L. Rev. 2588 (2003); Eric Rakowski, The Future Reach of the Disembodied Will, 4 Pol., Phil. & Econ. 91 (2005); Frederick R. Schneider, A Rule Against Perpetuities for the Twenty-First Century, 41 Real Prop., Prob. & Tr. J. 743 (2007); Stewart E. Sterk, Jurisdictional Competition to Abolish the Rule Against Perpetuities: R.I.P. for the R.A.P., 24 Cardozo L. Rev. 2097 (2003); Angela M. Vallario, Death by a Thousand Cuts: The Rule Against Perpetuities, 25 J. Legis. 141 (1999). See also Ronald Chester, From Here to Eternity? Property and the Dead Hand 23-27 (2007).

On the intersection of federal transfer tax policy and state perpetuities policy more generally, see Ira Mark Bloom, How Federal Transfer Taxes Affect the Development of Property Law, 48 Clev. St. L. Rev. 661 (2000); Robert T. Danforth, The Role of Federalism in Administering a National System of Taxation, 57 Tax Law. 625 (2004).

NOTE: ENGLISH PERPETUITIES LAW

In 1964 England adopted a variant on the wait-and-see approach whereby an interest is good until "it becomes absolutely certain that it must vest in interest, if at all, outside the perpetuity period of 21 years from the death of statutory lives in being or of a period not exceeding 80 years." D.J. Hayton, The Law of Trusts 106 (4th ed. 2003).

In 1998 the English Law Commission issued a report on whether the Rule should be reformed further or abolished. English Law Commission, The Rules Against Perpetuities and Excessive Accumulations, Report No. 251 (1998). Although a "distinguished minority" of experts consulted urged abolition, the Law Commission concluded that some rule was needed to restrict "how far settlors could tie up property for the future." It recommended abolishing the common law Rule Against Perpetuities and replacing it with a rule that any contingent interest that did not actually vest within 125 years would be void. The Law Commission fixed on 125 years because this is probably the longest period that can be obtained under present law by using a royal lives clause. Thus far, Parliament has not acted on the Law Commission's report.

For a somewhat similar proposal in this country to abolish the application of the Rule Against Perpetuities to trusts and to terminate trusts after 120 years, see Paul G. Haskell, A Proposal for a Simple and Socially Effective Rule Against Perpetuities, 66 N.C. L. Rev. 545 (1988). For a searing critique of the Law Commission's focus on intergenerational fairness instead of the Rule's economic consequences, see T.P. Gallanis, The Rule Against Perpetuities and the Law Commission's Flawed Philosophy, 59 Cambridge L.J. 284 (2000).

SECTION D.   TECHNICAL APPLICATION OF THE RULE TO CLASS GIFTS AND POWERS OF APPOINTMENT

1. *Application of the Rule to Class Gifts*

a.   The Basic Rule: All-or-Nothing

Under the Rule Against Perpetuities, a class gift must be valid for all members of the class, or it is valid for none. If the interest of any member possibly can vest too remotely, the entire class gift is bad. This *all-or-nothing* rule was established in Leake v. Robinson, 35 Eng. Rep. 979 (Ch. 1817). The current position of the states on the all-or-nothing rule is surveyed in Jeffrey A. Schoenblum, 2008 Multistate Guide to Estate Planning at Table 10, question 23.

The all-or-nothing rule requires that (1) the class must close and (2) all conditions precedent for every member of the class must be satisfied, if at all, within the perpetuities period. Case 13 illustrates a common class gift that is void under these principles.

> *Case 13.* *T* bequeaths property in trust "for *A* for life, then for *A*'s children for life, and then to distribute the property to *A*'s grandchildren." The remainder to *A*'s grandchildren is void because not every member of the class will be ascertained until the death of *A*'s children, some of whom might not be in being at *T*'s death. If at *T*'s death *A* has a living grandchild, *G*, then *G*'s gift is vested in interest subject to open for afterborn grandchildren, but it is not vested for purposes of the Rule, and it is therefore void. *A remainder that is vested subject to open is not vested for purposes of applying the Rule Against Perpetuities.* The class must be closed before a remainder in a class is vested under the Rule.

Some gifts to a class may be saved, however, through the operation of the *rule of convenience*. Under the rule of convenience, the class will close when any member of the class is entitled to immediate possession and enjoyment, even if the class would not otherwise close physiologically. See page 876. Thus:

> *Case 14.* *O* transfers property in an irrevocable trust "for my daughter *A* for life, then to distribute the principal to my grandchildren." At the time of the transfer *O* has one living grandchild, *G*. Under the rule of convenience, *G* or her administrator is entitled to demand possession of her share at *A*'s death, closing the class and forcing distribution among the grandchildren then living and the estates of grandchildren then dead. The gift is thus valid. If *O* had no grandchild alive at the date of the transfer, the gift to grandchildren would be void.

QUESTION

If the instrument in Case 14 were a will or a revocable trust rather than an irrevocable trust, the gift to the transferor's grandchildren would be valid regardless of whether a grandchild were alive when the instrument became effective. Why? See page 891.

It does not necessarily follow from the closing of the class within the perpetuities period that the gift is valid. Even if every member of the class is ascertained, every member must also satisfy any conditions precedent. For a gift of a fee simple to vest, for example, the ultimate number of takers in the class must be fixed so that the class neither increases nor decreases. Thus:

> *Case 15.* *T* bequeaths property in trust "for *A* for life, then to distribute the property to such of *A*'s children as attain the age of 25." The class will close physiologically at *A*'s death (a life

in being), but the exact share each child of *A* will take cannot be determined until all of *A*'s children have passed 25 or have died under that age. Here is what might happen: Suppose, at *T*'s death, *A* has one child, *C*, age 10. After *T*'s death *A* might have another child, *D*. Before *D* reaches age 4, *A* and *C* might die. Since *D* might meet the condition precedent more than 21 years after the expiration of any relevant life in being at *T*'s death, the remainder fails under the Rule Against Perpetuities.

QUESTION AND PROBLEMS

1. Suppose that in Case 15 a child of *A* is age 25 at *T*'s death. Is the gift good?

2. *T* devises Blackacre "to such of the grandchildren of *A* as shall attain the age of 25." Unless otherwise stated, assume that no grandchild of *A* has reached age 25. Is the gift valid if at *T*'s death:
    (a) *A* is dead?
    (b) *A* and all of *A*'s children are dead?
    (c) *A* is alive and one grandchild of *A* is 25?
    (d) *A* is dead and one grandchild of *A* is 25?
    (e) *A* is dead and the eldest grandchild of *A* is 4?

3. *T* bequeaths a fund in trust "to pay the income to *A* for life, and then in further trust for the grandchildren of *B*, their shares to be payable at their respective ages of 25." Is the gift valid if *T* is survived by *A* and *B* and:
    (a) the eldest grandchild of *B* is 25 at *T*'s death?
    (b) the eldest grandchild of *B* is 10 at *T*'s death?
    (c) the eldest grandchild of *B* is 2 at *T*'s death?
    Suppose that *B* survives *T*, but *A* predeceases *T*, and the eldest grandchild of *B* is 2 at *T*'s death. Is the gift valid?
    Suppose that *A* survives *T*, but *B* predeceases *T*, and the eldest grandchild of *B* is 2 at *T*'s death. Is the gift valid?

b. Exceptions to the All-or-Nothing Rule

There are two important exceptions to the all-or-nothing rule for class gifts: (1) gifts to subclasses and (2) gifts of specific sums to each member of a class. See Jeffrey A. Schoenblum, 2008 Multistate Guide to Estate Planning at Table 10, question 24, surveying the position of the states on the exceptions to the all-or-nothing rule.

(1) Gifts to subclasses

AMERICAN SECURITY & TRUST CO. v. CRAMER, 175 F. Supp. 367 (D.D.C. 1959): Abraham Hazen bequeathed property in trust for his wife for life, then to his "adopted daughter" Hannah for life, then to Hannah's children for their lives. "Upon the death of each [child] the share of the one so dying shall go absolutely to the persons who shall then be her or his heirs at law" under the District of Columbia law of intestate succession.

Abraham died in 1901. At Abraham's death, Hannah had two children, Mary and Hugh. After Abraham's death, Hannah had two more children, Depue and Horace. Hannah died in 1915; Abraham's widow died in 1916. Depue died in 1954. This action was commenced to determine the validity of the remainder following his life estate. While the case was pending, Horace died. A supplemental bill was filed to determine also the validity of the interest following his life estate.

Because the will makes a gift to each child's heirs upon the death of *each* child, and not a gift to the next generation upon the death of *all* of Hannah's children, the court applied the "gifts to subclasses" exception to the class gift rule. The gifts over following the life estates in Depue and Horace were void since neither was alive at Abraham's death. However, the gifts over following the life estates in Mary and Hugh were valid. These "remainders are not affected by the two invalid remainders, since the four remainders are to subclasses and stand (or fall) separately." Under Cattlin v. Brown, 68 Eng. Rep. 1318 (Ch. 1853), "if the ultimate takers are not described as a single class but rather as a group of subclasses, and if the share to which each separate subclass is entitled will finally be determined within the period of the rule, the gifts to the different subclasses are separable for the purpose of the rule." The remainders following the life estates in Depue and Horace being void, this left a reversion in Abraham's estate, which passed to his heirs.

NOTE

In Estate of Coates, 652 A.2d 331 (Pa. Super. 1994), the court held that where there is a trust for *A* for life, then to *A*'s children for their lives, then "to *A*'s grandchildren per stirpes," the subclass doctrine applies even though possession by the grandchildren was postponed until the death of all *A*'s children. The shares of the grandchildren are fixed at the death of each child.

(2)   *Specific sum to each class member*

The other important exception to the all-or-nothing class gift rule applies where there is a gift of a specific sum to each member of the class. In Storrs v. Benbow, 43 Eng. Rep. 153 (Ch. 1853), the testator bequeathed £500 apiece to each grandchild of his brothers, to be paid at age 21. The testator had two brothers living at his death. The court held that, as a matter of construction, applying the ordinary class closing rule applicable to specific sum gifts (see page 883), the gift benefited only grandchildren living at the testator's death. However, in a dictum that has been treated as law ever since, the court also said that if the testator meant to include grandchildren born after his death, the bequest would be valid for all children born to the brothers' children living at the testator's death and invalid for all children of the brothers' afterborn children.

The amount intended to be received by each member of the class is ascertainable without reference to the number of persons in the class, hence each gift is tested separately under the Rule.

2.   *Application of the Rule to Powers of Appointment*

In applying the Rule Against Perpetuities to powers of appointment, it is necessary to separate powers into (a) general powers presently exercisable and (b) general testamentary powers and all special powers.

a.   General Powers of Appointment Presently Exercisable

(1)   *Validity of power*

Because the donee of a presently exercisable general power of appointment can reach the appointive property simply by appointing it to himself, the property is not tied up. Accordingly, the Rule Against Perpetuities requires only that a general inter vivos power become exercisable, or fail, within the perpetuities period. See Restatement (Second) of Property: Donative Transfers §1.2, cmt. h (1983). For example, *T* devises property "to *A* for life, then to *A*'s children for their lives, with a general power in each child, exercisable by deed, to appoint a proportionate share of the corpus." Each child's power is valid because the power in each child will become exercisable at *A*'s death (or, if a child is then a minor, within 21 years thereafter).

(2)   *Validity of exercise*

Similarly, the validity of an interest created by an exercise of the power is determined as if the donee owned the property in fee. The perpetuities period begins to run when the power is exercised.

An unconditional power to revoke a trust is treated as a general power presently exercisable if the holder can exercise the power to revoke for his own benefit. The perpetuities period does not begin to run until the termination of the power. See Restatement (Second) of Property, supra, §1.2.

PROBLEM

O creates a revocable trust "to pay the income to *O* for life, then to pay the income to *O*'s children for their lives, then to distribute the principal to *O*'s grandchildren." Does the gift to grandchildren violate the Rule Against Perpetuities? Would it if the trust were irrevocable?

b.   General Testamentary Powers and Special Powers

Unlike the holder of a presently exercisable general power of appointment, the holder of a testamentary power or a special power does not have an absolute present right to alienate the property. Hence, for perpetuities purposes the donee is not treated as owner. Instead, the donor is treated as still controlling the property through the donee's exercise of the power. In applying the Rule to powers of appointment other than a presently exercisable general power, two questions arise: (1) Is the power itself valid? (2) Are the interests created by the exercise of the power valid?

(1)   Validity of power

For a testamentary power of appointment or a special power of appointment to satisfy the Rule, it must not be possible for the power to be exercised beyond the perpetuities period. Hence, neither a testamentary power nor a special power can be given to an afterborn person unless the exercise of the power is limited to the perpetuities period.

> *Case 16.* T bequeaths a fund in trust "to pay the income to A for life, then to A's children for their lives, and, as each child of A dies, to pay his or her proportionate part of the principal as such child shall appoint by will." At the time of T's death, A has one child, B. Another child, C, is born a year later. The gift to subclasses doctrine applies to the testamentary powers given to A's children because each child has a power exercisable only over the child's portion of the principal at death. The testamentary power given to B is valid because B was in being at T's death. The testamentary power given to C, born after T's death, is void.

A discretionary power of distribution in a trustee is the equivalent of a special power of appointment.

> *Case 17.* T bequeaths a fund in trust "to pay the income to A for life, then in the trustee's discretion to pay the income to A's children during their lives or to accumulate the income and add it to principal." A has no children at T's death. The discretionary power in the trustee to pay or accumulate income is either partially or totally void.

Gray took the position that a discretionary trust did not create one power that was either entirely valid or entirely void, but a succession of annual powers that were exercisable with respect to each year's income. Thus, a discretionary power in a trustee exercisable during lives not in being, as during the lives of A's children in Case 17, could be exercised for 21 years after A's death but no longer. See John C. Gray, The Rule Against Perpetuities §§410.1-410.5 (4th ed. 1942). However, in the few cases in which this issue has been directly before the court, the discretionary power has been held void in its entirety if it is capable of being exercised in favor of persons not in being. See Arrowsmith v. Mercantile-Safe Deposit & Trust Co., 545 A.2d 674 (Md. 1988); Bundy v. United States Trust Co., 153 N.E. 337 (Mass. 1926).

(2)   *Validity of exercise*

(a) Perpetuities period runs from creation of power. Because the donee of a general testamentary power or a special power is regarded as an agent of the donor, any appointment is read back into the instrument creating the power. Accordingly, the perpetuities period applicable to the appointed interests runs from the creation of the power.

Although in most states general testamentary powers are treated like special powers under the Rule, in a few states general testamentary powers are treated like general inter vivos powers. The perpetuities period on the appointed interests runs from the exercise of a general testamentary power. See Jeffrey A. Schoenblum, 2008 Multistate Guide to Estate Planning at Table 10, question 13.

(b) The second-look doctrine. Any interest created by the exercise of a general testamentary power or a special power is void under the common law Rule unless it must vest, if at all, within 21 years after the death of some life in being at the date the power was created. The exercise of the power is read back into the original instrument. However, under the *second-look doctrine*, facts existing on the date of exercise are taken into account. That is, under the second-look doctrine we wait and see how the donee actually appoints the property, and then we determine on the basis of the facts as they exist at the date of the appointment whether the appointive interests will vest or fail within the perpetuities period (computed from the date of creation of the power). Thus:

> *Case 18. T* devises property "to *A* for life, remainder to such persons as *A* appoints by will, outright or in further trust." *A* appoints in further trust "to my children for life, remainder to my grandchildren in fee." We now read *A*'s appointment into the will that created the power. The disposition is treated as though *T*'s will read "to *A* for life, then to *A*'s children for life, then to *A*'s grandchildren in fee." However, under the second-look doctrine we are also allowed to take into account facts existing at the time of *A*'s appointment. If, at *A*'s death, all of *A*'s surviving children were born in *T*'s lifetime, the remainder to the grandchildren is valid because it will vest, if at all, at the death of persons in being at *T*'s death. Otherwise the remainder is void.

NOTE: THE "DELAWARE TAX TRAP"

In Delaware, a statute provides that all interests created by the exercise of *all* powers, *special as well as general*, must vest within 21 years of the death of some life in being at the time the power is *exercised*, not some life in being at the date of creation of the power. Del. Code Ann. tit. 25, §501 (2008). Under the Delaware statute, a new perpetuities period begins each time a special power is exercised. *T* can set up a trust giving her child, *A*, the income for life and a special testamentary power to appoint outright or in further trust among *A*'s descendants. *A* can exercise the power by appointing in further trust for her child, *B*, for life, giving *B* a special testamentary power in favor of *B*'s descendants. *B* can exercise the power by appointing in further trust for her child — and so on down the generations.

Under the federal estate tax, neither a life estate nor property subject to a special power of appointment is taxable at the death of the life tenant or donee of the power. Although the property escapes estate taxation at that time, it will become subject to estate taxation within a generation or two thereafter because the common law Rule Against Perpetuities ultimately calls a halt to successive life estates. In Delaware, however, life estates can be created in indefinite succession through the exercise of successive special powers of appointment.

Out of concern for estate tax avoidance through the use of Delaware trusts, Congress enacted §2041(a)(3) of the Internal Revenue Code. As amended, this statute taxes the appointive assets in the donee's estate if the donee exercises a special power "by creating another power of appointment which under the applicable local law can be validly exercised so as to postpone the vesting of any estate or interest in such property, . . . for a period ascertainable without regard to the date of the creation of the first power."

This provision plugs the tax loophole that would otherwise exist for Delaware trusts — but the general language of the statute creates a tax trap for residents of all states. In any jurisdiction, *if a donee by will exercises a special power in such a manner as to create a general inter vivos power, the property subject to the special power will be includible in the donee's gross estate taxable under the estate tax.* Reread the quoted statutory provision, and you will see that this is so.

Although it was once sound advice never to exercise a special power by creating a general inter vivos power, which would throw the trust assets into the donee's taxable gross estate, such advice is no longer necessarily sound. In 1986, Congress enacted the generation-skipping transfer (GST) tax, which taxes a transfer to a person two generations below the transferor. In the trust above, where the transferor's child, *A*, is given a life estate and a special power of appointment, a GST tax will be levied at *A*'s death if the trust assets pass to the next generation, *unless the trust assets are subject to an estate tax levied on A's estate.* By exercising her special power so as to create a general inter vivos power in her child, *B*, *A* can subject the trust assets to the estate tax and, thus, avoid a GST tax. Whether to pay the estate tax or the GST tax depends on the availability of estate and GST exemptions as well as the current tax rates. The Delaware Tax Trap has therefore turned out to be useful in sophisticated estate planning. See James P. Spica, A Practical Look at Springing the Delaware Tax Trap to Avert Generation Skipping Transfer Tax, 41 Real Prop., Prob. & Tr. J. 165 (2006); Jonathan G. Blattmachr and Jeffrey N. Pennell, Adventures in Generation-Skipping, or How We Learned to Love the "Delaware Tax Trap," 24 Real Prop., Prob. & Tr. J. 75 (1989). See also James P. Spica, A Trap for the Wary: Delaware's Anti-Delaware-Tax-Trap Statute is Too Clever by Half (of Infinity), 43 Real Prop., Tr. & Est. J. 673 (2009).

SECTION E.   OTHER DURATIONAL LIMITS

1.   *The Rule Against Suspension of the Power of Alienation*

Although since the time of Gray it has been settled that the rule against remote vesting is *the* common law Rule Against Perpetuities, it was not clear before Gray whether there was also a common law *rule against suspension of the power of alienation*. The power of alienation is the power to convey title. A suspension of the power of alienation over specified property occurs when no living person, or living persons joined together, can convey an absolute fee.

The rule prohibiting suspension of the power of alienation is distinguishable from the rule against remote vesting. The rule against remote vesting (the common law Rule Against Perpetuities) is directed against contingent interests that may remain contingent beyond lives in being plus 21 years. The rule against suspension of the power of alienation is directed against interests that make the property inalienable. If there is any possibility that the power of alienation will be suspended longer than lives in being plus 21 years, the interests causing such invalid suspension are void ab initio.

Gray insisted that there was no common law rule against suspension of the power of alienation apart from the rule against remote vesting (that is, the Rule Against Perpetuities), and his view ultimately prevailed in the cases. However, in 1830, before the question was settled in the cases, New York enacted legislation forbidding suspension of the power of alienation for more than a specified period. Several other states copied or were influenced by New York's position. See Helene S. Shapo, George Gleason Bogert, and George Taylor Bogert, The Law of Trusts and Trustees §219 (3d ed. 2007).

Today there are two views of when the power of alienation is suspended by the creation of a trust. Under one view, the Wisconsin view, the power of alienation is not suspended if the trustee has the power to sell the trust assets, making them alienable, or if a living person has an unlimited power to terminate the trust. Wis. Stat. §700.16 (2008). This view is taken in many of the states that have authorized perpetual trusts as the *quid pro quo* for the trust's exemption from the Rule Against Perpetuities.

The other view, held in New York, is different. In New York, if a transfer is made in trust, the power of alienation is suspended if *either* the legal fee simple to the specific property held in trust cannot be transferred *or* the owners of all the equitable interests cannot convey an equitable fee simple. In other words, under the New York view the creation of a trust suspends the power of alienation *unless* the trustee is given the power to sell the specific assets *and* the beneficiaries of the trust can convey their interests.[24] However, since all vested and contingent future

---

24. Hence, the New York policy in favor of alienability is directed *both* at the specific assets in the trust *and* at the beneficial interests in the trust. N.Y. Est., Powers & Trusts Law §9-1.1(a) (2008) provides:

interests are assignable or releasable if (1) the holders thereof are ascertainable and (2) there is no express restraint upon alienation, the only interests that suspend the power of alienation in a New York trust in which the trustee has the power to sell the trust property are (a) those subject to an express restraint upon alienation such as a spendthrift clause or (b) those given to unborn or unascertained persons.

The impact of category (a), interests subject to an express restraint upon alienation such as a spendthrift clause, is magnified by New York's statutory presumption that an income beneficiary's interest in trust is inalienable (that is, subject to a spendthrift constraint) unless the settlor expressly provides otherwise. N.Y. Est., Powers & Trusts Law §7-1.5 (2008). If the income beneficiaries' interests are inalienable, the trust suspends the power of alienation during the income beneficiaries' lives. *Hence, the duration of a spendthrift trust in New York is limited to the perpetuities period*. Such a trust is partially or wholly invalid if it can exceed the perpetuities period in duration. Therein lies the most important difference today between the common law Rule Against Perpetuities (which does not directly restrict the duration of trusts) and the New York rule against suspension of the power of alienation.

> *Case 19. T*, domiciled in New York, dies in 2009. She bequeaths a fund in a spendthrift trust "to pay the income to *A* for life, then to pay the income to *A*'s children for their lives, and then to pay the principal to New York University." The gift does not violate the Rule Against Perpetuities. However, the income interests in *A* and *A*'s children are inalienable. Since the power of alienation might be suspended during the lifetime of afterborn persons (*A*'s children born after *T*'s death), the life income interests in *A*'s children are void. The remainder in New York University will be accelerated (unless the court determines that the stricken interests are so crucial to *T*'s dispositive scheme that invalidating the entire bequest would better approximate *T*'s intent[25]).

If, in Case 19, *T* had by her will expressly provided that *A*'s children could alienate their interests, the trust would be wholly valid. The power of alienation would be suspended only during *A*'s lifetime, a life in being. At *A*'s death, all of *A*'s children are in being, and, together with New York University, they can convey a fee simple absolute.

---

(1) The absolute power of alienation is suspended when there are no persons in being by whom an absolute fee or estate in possession can be conveyed or transferred.

(2) Every present or future estate shall be void in its creation which shall suspend the absolute power of alienation by any limitation or condition for a longer period than lives in being at the creation of the estate and a term of not more than twenty-one years. . . .

The rule against remoteness of vesting is also part of New York law. N.Y. Est., Powers & Trusts Law §9-1.1(b) (2008). New York thus has *both* the common law Rule Against Perpetuities *and* the rule against suspension of the power of alienation.

25. This would be an application of the doctrine of *infectious invalidity*, described in footnote 6 at page 890.

NOTE

The current position of each state on the rule against suspension of the power of alienation is collected in Jeffrey A. Schoenblum, 2008 Multistate Guide to Estate Planning at Table 10, question 26.

2. *The Rule Against Accumulations of Income*[26]

Originating in Thellusson v. Woodford, 32 Eng. Rep. 1030 (Ch. 1805), there appears to exist a common law doctrine — *the rule against accumulations of income* — that limits the period during which the settlor may direct the trustee to accumulate and retain income in trust.

At issue in *Thellusson* was the will of Peter Thellusson, a wealthy financier who died in 1797. Thellusson's will provided that the bulk of his considerable estate, plus all the income it would earn during the lives of his nine surviving male descendants, should be accumulated for the ultimate benefit of his oldest surviving male descendant at the end of that period. Thellusson thus deviated substantially from the normal practice in which the father left his estate either to the oldest son or to all the sons equally. "This placed the family in an unprecedented and disturbing situation. Like some perverted tontine, it left some of them, who were themselves unable to enjoy any of the money, postponing by their continuing existence its distribution to those golden lads for whom it seemed destined." Patrick Polden, Peter Thellusson's Will of 1797 and Its Consequences on Chancery Law 4 (2002).

Thellusson's family challenged the will. Speaking through Lord Eldon, the House of Lords concluded that there was no violation of the Rule Against Perpetuities. The interest in Thellusson's oldest male descendant would vest at the end of the specified measuring lives. It mattered not that none of the measuring lives was a beneficiary.

Lord Eldon then turned to the question of whether the bequest violated a separate rule against excessive accumulations of income:

> [A]nother question arises out of this Will; which is a pure question of equity: whether a testator can direct the rents and profits to be accumulated for that period, during which he may direct, that the title shall not vest, and the property shall remain unalienable; and, that he can do so, is most clear law. [*Thellusson*, supra, 32 Eng. Rep. at 1043.]

Thus the House of Lords held that, under the common law, a direction to accumulate income during the period of the Rule Against Perpetuities is valid.

Although sanctioned by the House of Lords in 1805, Thellusson's accumulation plan was quite unpopular, provoking a public outcry against the possibility of accumulated fortunes. One well-known estimate projected that Thellusson's

---

26. Adapted from Robert H. Sitkoff, The Lurking Rule Against Accumulations of Income, 100 Nw. U. L. Rev. 501 (2006).

accumulation would grow from £600,000 to somewhere between £19 and £38.4 million. The family's counsel "came up with the phrase 'posthumous avarice,' which has attached itself to Thellusson's will ever since." Polden, supra, at 144.

Thellusson's accumulation plan was so unpopular that soon after the Lord Chancellor upheld it, before the House of Lords rendered its decision on appeal, Parliament enacted 39 & 40 Geo. 3, c. 98 (1800), known as the Thellusson Act. The Act limits accumulations of income to (1) the life of the settlor; (2) 21 years from the death of the settlor; (3) the minority of any person living (or in gestation) at the time of the settlor's death; or (4) the minority of any person who, upon majority, would be entitled to the income being accumulated. With minor updating, this statutory rule against accumulations remains good law in England today. See Sarah Wilson, Todd & Wilson's Textbook on Trusts 147-148 (7th ed. 2005).

Just as the fear of exponentially growing trust funds inflamed passions about the dead hand in England, Peter Thellusson's "posthumous avarice" was likewise met with hostility in this country. One Pennsylvania judge expressed fear that such a trust might "draw into its vortex all the property in the state." Hillyard v. Miller, 10 Pa. 326, 336 (1849). Several states adopted statutes similar to the Thellusson Act or, in the case of New York and a few other states, an even more restrictive one. See Helene S. Shapo, George Gleason Bogert, and George Taylor Bogert, The Law of Trusts and Trustees §216 (3d ed. 2007).

History, however, has proved the worry over Thellusson's accumulation scheme to have been misplaced. When his grandson Charles died in 1856, Thellusson's trust came to an end, but the predicted vast fortune had not materialized. As Polden aptly observed, "nearly sixty years of accumulation had not produced one million pounds let alone thirty. From being a public menace, Peter Thellusson had become a laughing stock." Polden, supra, at 7.

Not surprisingly, other accumulation plans have also failed. Perhaps the most famous, the design of which (but not the result) was probably known to Thellusson when he executed his will, is Benjamin Franklin's. When Franklin died in 1790, he left two charitable trusts of £1,000 each (about $4,000) that were directed to accumulate income with no payouts for 100 years, then to spend most of the principal for the benefit of public purposes in Boston and Philadelphia, and then to accumulate again for another 100 years. The Boston trust drew less than $5 million into its vortex by 1990 and the Philadelphia trust sucked in less than half that amount.

In the twentieth century, accumulations legislation such as the Thellusson Act fell out of favor. Today, in states with a statutory rule against accumulation of income in private trusts, the accumulation period is typically the same as the period of the Rule Against Perpetuities. See, e.g., Cal. Civ. Code §724 (2008); N.Y. Est. Powers & Trusts Law §9-2.1(b) (2008). Under such a statute Thellusson's will would be upheld.

In part because the English courts did not develop their accumulations rule before American independence, ambiguity remained in states without an accumulations statute about whether there was an American common law rule against accumulations, and if so, for what duration accumulations would be permitted.

This ambiguity was resolved in 1941 by Gertman v. Burdick, 123 F.2d 924 (D.C. Cir. 1941).

At issue in *Gertman* was a bequest in trust to accumulate income during the lives of two named people and then for 21 years after the death of the survivor of them. In a learned opinion by Judge Fred Vinson, who would later become Chief Justice of the United States, the court upheld the bequest: "[A] rule permitting accumulations for as long as the period of the Rule Against Perpetuities . . . has been the common law of this country." Id. at 931. The rule against accumulations was thus recognized as a doctrine independent from the Rule Against Perpetuities, though the accumulations rule's durational limit was that of the applicable perpetuities period.

Because the durational limit under the two rules is the same, compliance with the Rule Against Perpetuities typically ensures compliance with the rule against accumulations — but not always. Here is an example of a transfer that is valid under the Rule Against Perpetuities but offends the rule against accumulations:

> *Case 20.* T bequeaths a fund in trust to X "to pay so much of the income to A during A's life as X may determine, then to pay so much of the income to A's children for their lives as X may determine, then to pay the remainder to B." At T's death, A has no children. A's life estate is vested in possession upon T's death; the life estate in A's children will vest in possession or, if there are no children, fail, upon A's death; and B's remainder is vested in interest upon T's death.

All interests in Case 20 will vest or fail within the perpetuities period (21 years after the death of the survivor of A and B). However, X has discretion to accumulate income in the trust after the perpetuities period expires. This could happen, for example, if after T's death A has a child, C, who survives A and B by more than 21 years. In some states, the accumulation is void as to the excess; in others, the accumulation is void in its entirety. Restatement (Second) of Property §2.2 reporter's note (1983).

With the rise of the perpetual trust, a new question has arisen: Does a perpetual trust that provides for the accumulation of income violate the rule against accumulations? Some states have dealt with the interaction of the rule against accumulations and perpetual trusts by legislation. Delaware abrogated the rule against accumulations. 25 Del. Code §506 (2008). Illinois provides that the accumulations rule does not apply to trusts in which the settlor opts out of the Rule Against Perpetuities. 765 Ill. Comp. Stat. Ann. 315/1 (2008). South Dakota repealed its statutory rule against accumulations. 1998 S.D. Sess. Laws 417.

In states that have not taken legislative action, the law is less clear. Because the common law rule against accumulations absorbs the period of the applicable Rule Against Perpetuities, it is arguable that statutory perpetuities reform likewise reforms the accumulations rule. In 1999, however, the Supreme Judicial Court of Maine held to the contrary in White v. Fleet Bank, 739 A.2d 373 (Me. 1999). At issue in *White* was a holographic will that contained a bequest in trust from which three-fourths of the income would be paid to the testator's lineal descendants and the other one-fourth would be "reinvested annually for the increase of funds in the Trust." The trust was to continue, "following the lines of direct descent, as long as the Trust may be made to endure."

Regarding the Rule Against Perpetuities, the court held that the quoted language was a saving clause such that, under the then-applicable Maine wait-and-see statute, the bequest was valid. It was possible that all future income interests would vest within the perpetuities period. Regarding the rule against accumulations of income, the trustee argued that Maine's wait-and-see perpetuities reform also applied to the accumulations rule. On this approach, which is endorsed by Restatement (Second) of Property, supra, §2.2, the reinvestment clause would be valid for the duration of the perpetuities period, and invalid thereafter. Applied to the facts in *White*, because the reinvestment clause did not reference any life in being, this interpretation would permit 21 years of accumulation.

The court rejected the trustee's argument, holding that the Maine wait-and-see legislation applied only to the Rule Against Perpetuities. The court thus held the reinvestment clause void from the outset because it was not limited to the applicable perpetuities period of 21 years. Since there was no provision for distribution of the trust corpus or accumulated income, the court ordered the property subject to the reinvestment clause to be disbursed to the testator's heirs on resulting trust.

It remains to be seen whether the reasoning in *White* will be followed in a state that has validated perpetual trusts. *White*, after all, involved the application of wait-and-see, not the abolition of the rule. Wait-and-see legislation does not actually lengthen the perpetuities period, it modifies the application of that period. In a state that has abolished the Rule Against Perpetuities, permitting perpetual trusts, the effective period of the Rule is infinite — the perpetuities period itself is modified. Since the common law rule against accumulations of income absorbs the applicable perpetuities period, in such a state the permissible accumulation period is arguably infinite.

NOTE

For a discussion of the policies that underpin the rule against accumulations, chiefly the prevention of distortive accumulations of wealth, see Robert H. Sitkoff, The Lurking Rule Against Accumulations of Income, 100 Nw. U. L. Rev. 501, 513-516 (2008). See also Karen J. Sneddon, Comment, The Sleeper Has Awakened: The Rule Against Accumulations and Perpetual Trusts, 76 Tul. L. Rev. 189 (2001). For a book-length treatment of Peter Thellusson's will and its many ramifications for the development of the law, see Patrick Polden, Peter Thellusson's Will of 1797 and Its Consequences on Chancery Law 4 (2002).

15

WEALTH TRANSFER TAXATION[1]

SECTION A. INTRODUCTION

Death duties have an ancient history and were known to the Greeks, Romans, and Egyptians. Yet for many years the United States levied *death taxes* only temporarily during times of urgent need for revenue. When relations with France deteriorated in 1797, Congress imposed *stamp taxes* on legacies; the taxes disappeared five years later when the revenue crisis had passed. During the Civil War, Congress levied an *inheritance tax*, which was promptly repealed after the war. During the 1890s, seeking revenue to finance military encounters with Spain, Congress again imposed an inheritance tax, and then repealed it when the fighting ended.

During World War I, Congress enacted an *estate tax*, but chose not to repeal it when the fighting stopped, partly because of public hostility toward the enormous family fortunes that had been amassed during the "robber baron" era a generation earlier. In 1932, Congress added a *gift tax* to prevent avoidance of the estate tax through inter vivos transfers to children and others.

Critics of these *wealth transfer taxes* called them socialistic, but that charge fell on deaf ears during the Great Depression. President Franklin D. Roosevelt captured the mood of the country when he declared:

> The desire to provide security for one's self and one's family is natural and wholesome, but it is adequately served by a reasonable inheritance. Great accumulations of wealth cannot be justified on the basis of personal and family security. In the last analysis such accumulations amount to the perpetuation of great and undesirable concentration of control in a relatively

---

1. This chapter was revised for the eighth edition principally by Stephanie J. Willbanks, Professor of Law at Vermont Law School. For a more comprehensive treatment, see Stephanie J. Willbanks, Federal Taxation of Wealth Transfers: Cases and Problems (2d ed. 2008).

few individuals over the employment and welfare of many, many others. . . . [I]nherited economic power is as inconsistent with the ideals of this generation as inherited political power was inconsistent with the ideals of the generation which established our government. [H.R. Rep. No. 1681, 74th Cong., 1st Sess. 2 (1935), 1939-1 C.B. (part 2) 643.]

During the 1930s and 1940s, Congress kept raising the rates on large estates (those in excess of a threshold amount) until the maximum estate tax rate reached 77 percent. There was a separate threshold amount for gift taxation, with rates that were exactly three-quarters of the estate tax rates. In 1976, the gift and estate taxes were unified, so that one rate schedule applied to cumulative gratuitous transfers in excess of a unified threshold amount, whether the transfer was inter vivos or testamentary.

During the 1980s, Congress increased the threshold from $60,000 to $600,000, thereby eliminating estate tax worries for the vast majority of citizens. Congress also lowered the top tax bracket to 55 percent; made the marital deduction unlimited, so that a married couple could transfer any amount of wealth between them tax free; and added a *generation-skipping transfer (GST) tax* that limited so-called dynasty planning (strategies designed to keep wealth within the family for many generations without incurring a wealth transfer tax at each generation).

In 1999 and again in 2000, Congress passed bills that would have permanently repealed the estate and GST taxes, but President William J. Clinton vetoed both bills. In 2001, Congress passed and President George W. Bush signed the Economic Growth and Tax Relief Reconciliation Act (EGTRRA), which repealed the estate and GST taxes entirely, but only for one year, 2010.

"It's a little less amusing when you hear your kids calling it 'the death tax.'"

Under EGTRRA, between 2001 and 2010 the estate and GST tax exemptions (i.e., threshold amounts) increased incrementally from $1 million to $3.5 million,[2] and the maximum tax rate decreased gradually from 55 to 45 percent, with no tax in 2010.[3] Under a sunset provision, however, the exemptions and rates would revert to their 2001 levels on January 1, 2011. A ridiculous consequence was that, absent further Congressional intervention, there would be a strong financial incentive for the family of the wealthy but infirm to maintain their wealthy kin until 2010, in the hope that they would die before 2011.[4] Gift certificates for sky-diving and tickets for trips to dangerous parts of the world might become popular gifts from children to parents in 2010.

With the election of President Barack Obama in 2008, many commentators predicted that the estate and GST taxes would be reinstated for 2010, and that Congress would settle on an exemption amount around $3.5 to $5 million and a maximum rate of around 45 percent. During the presidential campaign, Obama expressed opposition to repealing the estate tax entirely, calling it "the Paris Hilton Tax Break. It's about giving billions of dollars to billionaire heirs and heiresses at a time when American taxpayers just can't afford it." John K. Wilson, The Improbable Quest 156 (2007). Whether the estate tax stays or goes, it is unlikely that it will ever provide more than a relatively small portion of government revenues. In 2007, federal estate and gift taxes together produced roughly $26 billion in revenue, about 1 percent of the total federal revenue that year.

For an engaging discussion of the 2001 legislation and related tax issues, see Michael J. Graetz and Ian Shapiro, Death by a Thousand Cuts: The Fight over Taxing Inherited Wealth (2005).

NOTE: ESTATE AND INHERITANCE TAXES COMPARED

The federal government and some states impose *estate taxes* that are based on the total value of the decedent's probate and nonprobate property (and possibly other property, as discussed below), reduced by deductions for the decedent's debts, transfers to the decedent's spouse or to charity, and various costs of administering the estate. The executor or administrator normally pays the estate tax before making final distributions, so heirs, devisees, and other recipients of estate property do not pay estate taxes, at least not directly.

---

2. The exemption schedule under EGTRRA is as follows: through 2003, $1 million; in 2004 and 2005, $1.5 million; in 2006 through 2008, $2 million; and in 2009, $3.5 million. I.R.C. §§2631(c), 2010(c) (2008).

3. The maximum rates under EGTRRA are as follows: 49% in 2003; 48% in 2004; 47% in 2005; 46% in 2006; and 45% in 2007-2009. I.R.C. §§2641, 2001(c)(2)(B) (2008).

4. The idea that a phase out of the estate tax might affect the timing of death is not as ridiculous as it might first appear. A 2006 study of death rates in Australia just before and after the effective date of Australia's estate tax repeal found that more than "half of those who would have paid the estate tax in its last week of operation managed to avoid doing so" by not dying until the following week. The authors hastened to add, however, that their data was based on formal death records, so "it is possible that the effect we observe reflects misreporting of the death date, rather than changes in the actual timing of deaths." Joshua S. Gans and Andrew Leigh, Toying with Death and Taxes: Some Lessons from Down Under, 3 The Economists' Voice, Issue 6, Article 9, available at http://www.bepress.com/ev/vol3/iss6/art9.

About half of the states levy some sort of death tax in the form of an estate tax, an inheritance tax, or both. See Jeffrey A. Schoenblum, 2008 Multistate Guide to Estate Planning at Tables 15.01 and 15.02. In contrast to an estate tax, which is levied on the decedent's estate, an *inheritance tax* is levied on the transferee. Although the details of state inheritance taxes vary, the amount each beneficiary pays usually depends not only on the value of the property received but also on the beneficiary's relationship to the decedent. Bequests to the decedent's children are usually taxed at lower rates than bequests to nephews and nieces.

Whether an estate tax is preferable to an inheritance tax is debatable. An estate tax is thought to be easier to administer. But an inheritance tax might be fairer because it is based on the amount each beneficiary receives and it favors close relatives. For further discussion, see Anne L. Alstott, Equal Opportunity and Inheritance Taxation, 121 Harv. L. Rev. 469 (2007); Lily Batchelder, What Should Society Expect from Heirs? A Proposal for a Comprehensive Inheritance Tax, 62 Tax L. Rev. — (forthcoming 2009).

NOTE: LIABILITY FOR WEALTH TRANSFER TAXES

The donor has the primary liability for paying the gift tax. If the donor does not pay, the donee is liable for any unpaid amount. The executor or administrator of a decedent's estate has personal liability for payment of the estate tax but is entitled to reimbursement out of the decedent's estate. If there is no administration of the decedent's estate, persons in possession of the decedent's property are liable for the tax. The person who is liable for generation skipping transfer (GST) taxes depends on the form of the transfer. We take up GST taxation at page 989.

Most professionally drafted wills direct the executor to pay the estate taxes out of the residuary estate instead of charging the individual beneficiaries. An executor or administrator who pays the tax is entitled to reimbursement from life insurance beneficiaries for the portion of the tax resulting from the inclusion of the death benefit in the decedent's estate. I.R.C. §2206. Similarly, the executor is entitled to proportionate reimbursement from recipients of property over which the decedent had a general power of appointment. I.R.C. §2207. Other than these two exceptions, the Code does not generally provide for apportionment of estate taxes to the recipients but leaves the matter to state law. A large majority of states follows the rule that, unless the testator provides otherwise, federal estate taxes must be borne by each beneficiary pro rata. A minority of states follow the opposite default rule: The estate tax is paid out of the residuary estate unless the testator provides otherwise. The Uniform Estate Tax Apportionment Act (2003), which has been absorbed into the Uniform Probate Code as Part 9A of Article III, adopts the majority rule. See Douglas A. Kahn, The 2003 Revised Uniform Estate Tax Apportionment Act, 38 Real Prop., Prob. & Tr. J. 613 (2004). See also Ira Mark Bloom, Unifying the Rules for Wills and Revocable Trusts in the Federal Estate Tax Apportionment Arena: Suggestions for Reform, 62 U. Miami L. Rev. 767 (2008).

Wealth transfer taxation is notoriously complex. This chapter merely summarizes the basic rules and some simple estate planning techniques. For more comprehensive coverage, see, e.g., Ray D. Madoff, Cornelia R. Tenney, Martin A. Hall, and Lisa N. Mingolla, Practical Guide to Estate Planning (2009 ed.); Stephanie J. Willbanks, Federal Estate and Gift Taxation: An Analysis and Critique (3d ed. 2004).

For academic proposals to restructure wealth transfer taxes, in addition to the articles by Professors Alstott and Batchelder cited above, see Karen C. Burke and Grayson M.P. McCouch, A Consumption Tax on Gifts and Bequests, 17 Va. Tax Rev. 657 (1998); Joseph M. Dodge, Comparing a Reformed Estate Tax with an Accessions Tax and an Income-Inclusion System, and Abandoning the Generation-Skipping Tax, 56 SMU L. Rev. 551 (2003); Michael J. Graetz, To Praise the Estate Tax, Not to Bury It, 93 Yale L.J. 259 (1983); Edward J. McCaffery, The Uneasy Case for Wealth Transfer Taxation, 104 Yale L.J. 283 (1994); Colloquium on Wealth Transfer Taxation, 51 Tax L. Rev. 357 (1996) (articles discussing McCaffery's proposal to abolish the federal estate and gift tax by Anne L. Alstott, Joseph M. Dodge, Douglas Holtz-Eakin, and Eric Rakowski, with commentaries by others); James R. Repetti, Democracy, Taxes and Wealth, 76 N.Y.U. L. Rev. 825 (2001). See also the collection of papers in Rethinking Estate and Gift Taxation (William G. Gale, James R. Hines, Jr., and Joel Slemrod eds., 2001); Paul L. Caron and James R. Repetti, The Estate Tax Non-Gap: Why Repeal a "Voluntary" Tax?, 20 Stan. L. & Poly. Rev. 153 (2009); Mildred Wigfall Robinson, Transfer Tax Reform After EGTRRA-2001: Reconstruction or Further Deconstruction?, 28 Va. Tax Rev. 391 (2008).

SECTION B.   THE FEDERAL GIFT TAX

1.   Taxable Gifts

Section 2501(a) of the Internal Revenue Code of 1986 imposes a tax on the transfer of property by *gift*, but it does not define the term gift. In general, the courts have held that a gratuitous transfer is subject to gift taxation if the donor has relinquished all "dominion and control" over the property irrespective of the donor's donative intent. Thus, for example, there is no tax upon the funding of a revocable trust, because the settlor of such a trust retains the power to revoke or amend the trust. The transfer is not complete, and the donor does not give up all dominion and control, until after the trust becomes irrevocable. If you have not really given property away, you still own it. Likewise, there is no tax on a gratuitous transfer to an irrevocable trust if the settlor retains the power to shift beneficial interests from one beneficiary to another. As illustrated by the following case, a gratuitous transfer may also be incomplete for gift tax purposes if it is possible that the underlying property will be used to benefit the donor.

Holtz's Estate v. Commissioner
United States Tax Court, 1962
38 T.C. 37

DRENNAN, J. . . . The principal issue for decision is whether taxable gifts resulted from transfers to a trust established by [Leon Holtz, the decedent] by deed of trust dated June 12, 1953, wherein Leon was the settlor and [a Bank] was the sole trustee. The trust instrument provided that the trustee should distribute the net income therefrom and the principal thereof as follows. During the life-time of settlor the income should be paid to him, and as much of the principal as the trustee "may from time to time think desirable for the welfare, comfort and support of Settlor, or for his hospitalization or other emergency needs," should be paid to him or for his benefit. Upon the death of the settlor, if his wife survived him, the income of the trust was to be paid to her during her lifetime, and a simi-lar provision was made for invasion of principal for her benefit during her life-time. The trust was to terminate at the death of the survivor of settlor and his wife and the "then-remaining principal" was payable to the estate of the survivor.

On June 12, 1953, Leon transferred property having a value of $384,117 to the trust, and on January 18, 1955, he transferred an additional $50,000 in cash to the trust. Respondent determined that, as a result of these transfers, Leon made taxable gifts in 1953 in the amount of $263,277.63, and in 1955 in the amount of $35,570, computing the value of the taxable gifts by reducing the value of the property transferred in each instance by the actuarial value of Leon's life estate and reversionary interest in each transfer. Petitioner claims the transfers were not completed gifts and that no part of the value thereof was subject to gift tax. . . .

The Internal Revenue Codes of 1939 and 1954 provide no guideposts for determining when a gift becomes complete for gift tax purposes beyond the direction that "the tax shall apply whether the transfer is in trust or otherwise, whether the gift is direct or indirect, and whether the property is real or personal, tangible or intangible." [I.R.C. §2511(a).] It is well settled in cases involving this issue, however, that the question whether a transfer in trust is a completed gift, and thus subject to gift tax, turns on whether the settlor has abandoned sufficient dominion and control over the property transferred to put it beyond recall. Bur-net v. Guggenheim, 288 U.S. 280 (1933); Estate of Sanford v. Commissioner, 308 U.S. 39 (1939); Smith v. Shaughnessy, 318 U.S. 176 (1943).

Here we do not have a situation where the settlor either reserved the power in himself alone to modify, alter, or revoke the trust and thus revest the trust prop-erty in himself, as in Burnet v. Guggenheim, supra, or reserved the power to alter the disposition of the property or income therefrom in some way not beneficial to himself, as in Estate of Sanford v. Commissioner, supra, or reserved the power in conjunction with someone else to modify, alter, or revoke the trust, as in Camp v. Commissioner, 195 F.2d 999 (C.A. 1, 1952). Leon reserved no rights in himself to change the disposition of the income or principal of the trust as fixed in the trust agreement. However, the trust agreement itself gave the trustee power to pay directly to Leon or for his benefit as much of the principal of the trust as the trustee thought desirable for Leon's welfare, comfort, and support, or for his hospitalization or other emergency needs. The question is whether this discretionary power placed in the trustee by the settlor under the terms of the trust agreement made the gifts of the remainder interests incomplete for gift tax purposes.

A number of cases decided by this and other courts have held that the placing of discretionary power in the trustee to invade corpus makes the gift of corpus incomplete under certain circumstances. The rule of thumb generally accepted seems to be that if the trustee is free to exercise his unfettered discretion and there is nothing to impel or compel him to invade corpus, the settlor retains a mere expectancy which does not make the gift of corpus incomplete. But if the exercise of the trustee's discretion is governed by some external standard which a court may apply in compelling compliance with the conditions of the trust agreement, and the trustee's power to invade is unlimited, then the gift of corpus is incomplete, Commissioner v. Irving Trust Co., 147 F.2d 946 (C.A. 2, 1945), and this is true even though such words as "absolute" and "uncontrolled" are used in connection with the trustee's discretion, provided the external standards are clearly for the guidance of the trustee in exercising his discretion.

The theory behind this rule seems to be that by placing such standards for guidance of the trustee's discretion in the trust agreement itself, the settlor has not actually lost all dominion and control of the trust corpus or put it completely beyond recall because to ignore the implications and purpose for writing the standards into the invasion clause would be an abuse of discretion on the part of the trustee which the trustee would neither desire to do nor be likely to risk doing under State laws . . . .

The rule of thumb appears to be a reasonable application of the general rule established in the *Guggenheim, Sanford*, and *Shaughnessy* cases because where there is a reasonable possibility that the entire corpus might be repaid to the settlor there can be no assurance that anyone else will receive anything in the form of a gift, and if the corpus should happen to be kept intact until the settlor's death, even though the transfer in trust was not subjected to a gift tax, the corpus of the trust will in all likelihood be subjected to the estate tax in the settlor's estate.

Applying the above principles to the facts under consideration here, we conclude that no part of or interest in the property transferred to the trust constituted a completed gift for gift tax purposes when transferred to the trust.

The form of the trust agreement indicates that the principal beneficiary of the income, and the principal if it became desirable for his welfare, comfort, support, or emergency needs, was the settlor. The first instructions to the trustee, as shown by the part of the deed of trust quoted in our Findings of Fact, were to distribute net income and principal to the settlor during his lifetime. Only upon the death of the settlor, and if she survived him, was any provision made for payment of either income or principal to the settlor's wife. And only upon the death of the survivor of settlor and his wife was any provision made for distribution of the "then-remaining principal." The trustee had the unfettered power to use all of the corpus for the benefit of settlor, if it thought that it was desirable for the welfare, comfort, or needs of the settlor. The words used were broad enough to cover about anything Leon might want or need. It is reasonable to assume that the trustee would invade corpus and that it would be required to do so by a court if the welfare, comfort, or needs of the settlor made it seem desirable. Otherwise, there would not have been much reason for including the paragraph giving the trustee power to invade principal. It was entirely possible that the entire corpus might be distributed during the settlor's lifetime and no one other than the settlor would receive any portion thereof. As long as that possibility was present, by reason of the language employed by the settlor, the settlor had not abandoned sufficient dominion and control over the property transferred to make the gift consummate.

In addition to the trust agreement itself, the evidence indicates that the settlor, who was 80 years of age when the trust was established, expressed concern over whether he would have available sufficient funds to meet his needs. He asked the trust officer whether he would have enough money to buy an automobile and the trust officer reassured him by telling him that the trust agreement provided for the payment of all income to him and that he could also have money out of the principal, and that the trustee would be liberal in giving him money out of the principal. While the term "liberal" is not defined, the above conversation indicates the understanding of the parties was that the trustee recognized that principal should be distributed at any time the settlor's needs reasonably justified it. . . .

Decision will be entered for the petitioner.

PROBLEMS AND NOTES

1. *Incomplete gifts.* O establishes an irrevocable trust funded with $500,000 worth of securities. Trust income is to be paid to O for life, "and on O's death the trustee shall distribute the trust property to such of O's descendants as O appoints by will; and in default of appointment, the trustee shall distribute the property to O's descendants then living, per stirpes."

Has O made a taxable gift of the remainder? See Treas. Reg. §25.2511-2(b) (the answer is No, because O retained a power of appointment, so the gift is not yet complete). Suppose that O releases the power of appointment. Does the release result in a taxable gift of the remainder? (The answer is Yes. The value of the remainder interest at the time of the release is subject to gift taxation.) A gift that remains incomplete during the donor's lifetime but is complete on the donor's death is subject to estate taxation at the donor's death.

2. *Consent of adverse party.* O transfers property in trust to pay the income to A for life, and on A's death to distribute the principal to B. O retains the power to revoke or amend the trust instrument in whole or in part, but only with the consent of A. Has O made a taxable gift? The answer is Yes, because the gift is complete. The donee's consent is required for any change. See Camp v. Commissioner, 195 F.2d 999 (1st Cir. 1952). Now suppose instead that O can only revoke or amend with the consent of S, O's spouse, who has no interest in the

trust. Has *O* made a taxable gift? The answer is No, because *S* does not have an interest that is substantially adverse to any revocation or amendment by *O*. Treas. Reg. §25.2511-2(e).

3. *Disclaimers.* Suppose that a donee, heir, or devisee *disclaims* a gratuitous transfer of property (see page 152). Has the disclaimant made a taxable gift to whoever gets the disclaimed property? I.R.C. §2518 provides that a disclaimer is not a gift for purposes of the gift tax if each of the following conditions is met: (a) the disclaimer is in writing, and made either within nine months after the interest is created or within nine months after the disclaimant reaches 21, whichever is later; (b) the disclaimant has not accepted an interest in the disclaimed property or any of its benefits; and (c) as a result of the disclaimer, the property passes without any direction on the part of the disclaimant and passes either to the decedent's spouse or to someone other than the disclaimant.

4. *Literature.* For a discussion of the gift tax with suggestions for reform, see Mitchell M. Gans and Jay A. Soled, Reforming the Gift Tax and Making it Enforceable, 87 B.U. L. Rev. 759 (2007).

NOTE: JOINT TENANCY

When two people who are not husband and wife own property as joint tenants with right of survivorship, the joint tenancy is generally treated like a tenancy in common for gift tax purposes. The theory is that the donee co-tenant receives the same lifetime rights under a joint tenancy as a tenancy in common (indeed, the donee co-tenant can petition to convert the joint tenancy into a tenancy in common at any time). Thus:

> *Case 1.* *O* pays $40,000 for securities, taking title in the name of *O* and *A*. It does not matter whether the title designates *O* and *A* as joint tenants or as tenants in common. In either scenario, *O* has made a gift of one-half the value of the property, or $20,000, to *A*.

A joint and survivor bank account is treated differently. Because a joint tenant can withdraw all funds on deposit, whereas a tenant in common is entitled only to her fractional share, no gift occurs until funds are actually withdrawn by the non-depositing joint tenant. Thus:

> *Case 2.* *O* deposits $40,000 in a joint and survivor bank account. Since *O* can withdraw the entire $40,000, the gift is incomplete. If *A* withdraws funds from the account, a gift from *O* to *A* in the amount withdrawn is complete and therefore subject to gift taxation. By contrast, if *O* and *A* each had deposited $20,000 in the joint account, no gift would be made by either until either *O* or *A* withdrew more than the $20,000 each deposited. Treas. Reg. §25.2511-1(h)(4).

The rules applicable to a joint bank account also apply to a U.S. government bond registered in the name of "*O* or *A*." Under this "or" form of ownership, either *O* or *A* can present the bond for payment. There is no completed gift unless *A* cashes in the bond.

NOTE: INCOME TAX BASIS

An income tax is usually levied on gain realized on the sale of property. The amount of gain is the difference between the taxpayer's *basis* and the selling price. Generally speaking, if the taxpayer purchased the property, his basis is the purchase price. If *O* buys land for $50,000, and sells it for $75,000, the gain of $25,000 is subject to income taxation.

If a donee receives property by *gift* and then sells it, in computing her gain the donee generally takes the donor's basis. For the purpose of computing loss, however, the donee's basis is the value of the property on the date of the gift. I.R.C. §1015. If property is acquired from a *decedent*, the basis of the property for computing both gain and loss is the value of the asset on the decedent's death. Id. §1014. This *stepped-up basis* at death means that any capital gain on property held until death escapes income taxation.[5]

2. *The Annual Exclusion*

I.R.C. §2503(b) generally allows a donor to exclude from gift taxation the first $13,000[6] of value given to each donee during the current year. The purpose of this *annual exclusion* "is to obviate the necessity of . . . reporting numerous small gifts, and . . . to fix the amount sufficiently large to cover in most cases wedding and Christmas gifts and occasionally gifts of relatively small amounts." H.R. Rep. No. 708, 72d Cong., 1st Sess. 29 (1932), 1939-1 C.B. (part 2) 457, 478. Thus:

> *Case 3. A* gives $15,000 each to *B* and *C*, and $5,000 to *D. A* must report a $2,000 taxable gift to each of *B* and *C*. The gift to *D* need not be reported because it does not exceed the annual exclusion.

In addition to the $13,000 annual exclusion, §2503(e) allows an unlimited exclusion for *tuition payments* and *medical expenses* paid on behalf of any person. Hence, through tuition or medical payments, a donor can make substantial gifts to a donee free of gift taxation. The only limit is that the donor must make the payment directly to the service provider. Reimbursement of the donee for payments made by the donee does not qualify.

Present versus future interests. The annual exclusion is available only for gifts of present interests. Future interests do not qualify. Distinguishing between the two is critical, but not always easy.

---

5. Congress repealed §1014 effective in 2010 as part of the price paid for the repeal of the estate and GST taxes in EGTRRA. It also added a new §1022 that imposes a carryover basis for transfers at death. Congress tried repealing §1014 once before, in the Tax Reform Act of 1976. Banks and other financial institutions serving as fiduciaries complained so vehemently that the repeal was reversed before it became effective. It remains to be seen whether the 2001 repeal will suffer the same fate.

6. The annual exclusion was $5,000 from 1932 to 1939, $4,000 from 1939 to 1942, and $3,000 from 1943 to 1981. The Economic Recovery Tax Act of 1981 raised the annual exclusion to $10,000 beginning in 1982 and indexed it for inflation, but only in increments of $1,000. As a result, the amount of the annual exclusion did not rise to $11,000 until 2002. It became $12,000 in 2006 and $13,000 in 2009.

Case 4. O gives property worth $500,000 to *A* for life, remainder to *B*. Based on *A*'s life expectancy, the value of *A*'s life estate at the time of the gift is $325,000 and *B*'s remainder is worth $175,000. *O* is entitled to a $13,000 exclusion for the gift to *A* (a present interest), but not for the gift of the remainder to *B* (a future interest).

Case 5. O creates a trust to pay the income annually among *O*'s three children in such shares as the trustee in her uncontrolled discretion deems advisable. Even though all the income must be distributed each year, none of the beneficiaries has a present interest (as defined for gift-tax purposes), hence *O* is entitled to no annual exclusions.

The disqualification of future interests from the annual exclusion creates special problems when property is given to a minor. A child can be given a doll or a bicycle. But for more substantial gifts, particularly of income-producing financial assets, a sensible donor will not give possession to the child. Instead the property will be given to a guardian or custodian, which qualifies for the annual exclusion, or, usually even better, to a trustee. (See the discussion of guardianship, custodianship, and trusts for minors at pages 136-140.) To allow donors to make annual exclusion gifts to minors in trust, Congress provided in I.R.C. §2503(c) that property transferred in trust for a minor will be treated as though it were a present interest if certain conditions are satisfied.

I.R.C. §2503(c). TRANSFER FOR THE BENEFIT OF MINOR

No part of a gift to an individual who has not attained the age of 21 years on the date of such transfer shall be considered a gift of a future interest in property for purposes of subsection (b) if the property and the income therefrom —

(1) may be expended by, or for the benefit of, the donee before his attaining the age of 21 years, and

(2) will to the extent not so expended —

(A) pass to the donee on his attaining the age of 21 years, and

(B) in the event the donee dies before attaining the age of 21 years, be payable to the estate of the donee or as he may appoint under a general power of appointment as defined in section 2514(c).

To qualify as a §2503(c) trust, the donor must give the trustee the power to expend *all* the income and principal on the donee before the donee reaches 21, and further provide that unexpended income and principal must pass to the donee at 21 or, if the donee dies before reaching 21, to the donee's estate (or as the donee appoints under a general power of appointment). If the trustee has the power to expend only the income on the donee, the value of the income interest, but not the full value of the property, will qualify as a present interest. Herr v. Commissioner, 35 T.C. 732 (1961). In either case, no person other than the minor can have a beneficial interest in the property.

For further discussion of gifts that qualify for the annual exclusion, see Jeffrey G. Sherman, 'Tis a Gift to Be Simple: The Need for a New Definition of "Future Interest" for Gift Tax Purposes, 55 U. Cin. L. Rev. 585 (1987); John G. Steinkamp, Common Sense and the Gift Tax Annual Exclusion, 72 Neb. L. Rev.

106 (1993); Walter D. Schwidetzky, Estate Planning: Hyperlexis and the Annual Exclusion Rule, 32 Suffolk U. L. Rev. 211 (1998).

Crummey powers. A donor may convert what would otherwise be a future interest into a present interest (and thereby qualify for the annual exclusion) by giving a beneficiary of a discretionary trust a power to withdraw property from the trust. The strategy works because a power of withdrawal, even one limited to use within a few days, is a general power of appointment, and the donee of a general power is treated for all tax purposes as the owner of the appointive property. I.R.C. §2041 (see page 967). Thus:

> *Case 6.* Each year *O* transfers $13,000 to *X* in trust to pay so much of the income and principal to *B* as *X* determines in *X*'s uncontrolled discretion until *B*'s 35th birthday. When *B* turns 35, *X* is to pay the remainder to *B* or, if *B* dies prior to the age of 35, then to *C*. Because these gifts are not present interests and do not satisfy the conditions of §2503(c), the annual exclusion is not available. However, if *O* also gives *B* the power to withdraw $13,000 from the trust within 15 days of each gift, then *B* has a present interest and the gift qualifies for the annual exclusion even if *B* does not exercise the power.
>
> *Case 7.* *O* transfers $39,000 to *X* in trust to pay so much of the income and principal to *A*, *B*, or *C* as *X* determines in *X*'s uncontrolled discretion. So long as *O* also provides that each beneficiary has a power to withdraw up to $13,000 each, the transfer qualifies for the annual exclusion, even if the power to withdraw is limited to a short period of time.

The use of temporary withdrawal powers to qualify a gift in trust for the annual exclusion was upheld in Crummey v. Commissioner, 397 F.2d 82 (9th Cir. 1968), and such a power has come to be known as a *Crummey power*. An important question remains: What kind of beneficial interest in the trust must a beneficiary-donee receive along with a Crummey power in order for the transfer to qualify for the annual exclusion?

Estate of Cristofani v. Commissioner
United States Tax Court, 1991
97 T.C. 74

RUWE, J.   Respondent determined a deficiency in petitioner's Federal estate tax in the amount of $49,486. The sole issue for decision is whether transfers of property to a trust, where the beneficiaries possessed the right to withdraw an amount not in excess of the section 2503(b) exclusion within 15 days of such transfers, constitute gifts of a present interest in property within the meaning of section 2503(b).

FINDINGS OF FACT

Petitioner is the Estate of Maria Cristofani, deceased, Frank Cristofani, executor. Maria Cristofani (decedent) died testate on December 16, 1985. . . .

Decedent has two children, Frank Cristofani and Lillian Dawson. Decedent's children were both born on July 9, 1948. They were in good health during the years 1984 and 1985.

Decedent has five grandchildren. Two of decedent's five grandchildren are Frank Cristofani's children. They are Anthony Cristofani, born July 16, 1975,[7] and Loris Cristofani, born November 30, 1978. Decedent's three remaining grandchildren are Lillian Dawson's children. They are Justin Dawson, born December 1, 1972, Daniel Dawson, born August 9, 1974, and Luke Dawson, born November 14, 1981. During 1984 and 1985, the parents of decedent's grandchildren were the legal guardians of the person of their respective minor children. There were no independently appointed guardians of decedent's grandchildren's property. . . .

On June 12, 1984, decedent executed an irrevocable trust entitled the Maria Cristofani Children's Trust I (Children's Trust). Frank Cristofani and Lillian Dawson were named the trustees of the Children's Trust.

In general, Frank Cristofani and Lillian Dawson possessed the following rights and interests in the Children's Trust corpus and income. Under Article Twelfth, following a contribution to the Children's Trust, Frank Cristofani and Lillian Dawson could each withdraw an amount not to exceed the amount specified for the gift tax exclusion under section 2503(b). Such withdrawal period would begin on the date of the contribution and end on the 15th day following such contribution. Under Article Third, Frank Cristofani and Lillian Dawson were to receive equally the entire net income of the trust quarter-annually, or at more frequent intervals. After decedent's death, under Article Third, the Trust Estate was to be divided into as many equal shares as there were children of decedent then living or children of decedent then deceased but leaving issue. Both Frank Cristofani and Lillian Dawson survived decedent, and thus the Children's Trust was divided into two equal trusts [and distributed to Frank and Lillian shortly thereafter]. . . .

Under Article Twelfth, during a 15-day period following a contribution to the Children's Trust, each of the grandchildren possessed the same right of withdrawal as described above regarding the withdrawal rights of Frank Cristofani and Lillian Dawson. Under Article Twelfth, the trustee of the Children's Trust was required to notify the beneficiaries of the trust each time a contribution was received. Under Article Third, had either Frank Cristofani or Lillian Dawson predeceased decedent or failed to survive decedent by 120 days, his or her equal portion of decedent's Children's Trust would have passed in trust to his or her children (decedent's grandchildren).

Under Article Third, the trustees, in their discretion, could apply as much of the principal of the Children's Trust as necessary for the proper support, health,

---

7. In 1999, Anthony Cristofani, 23, and Emma Freeman, 18, students at the University of California in Santa Cruz, were arrested and charged with armed robbery of local shops.

"Cristofani is described by friends as a flamboyant fellow, a philosophical merry prankster. He favored bright clothes, often donning orange shoes and silk shirts, and was known to jump atop a table in the cafeteria and dance, or bellow in Italian. . . . Several students said . . . [Cristofani and Freeman] were not reluctant to test dorm rules, showering together and pushing the limits of social conduct." L.A. Times, Feb.12, 1999, at A1.

Like grandmother, like grandson — pushing the limits of the rules? — Eds.

maintenance and education of decedent's children. In exercising their discretion, the trustees were to take into account several factors, including "The Settlor's desire to consider the Settlor's children as primary beneficiaries and the other beneficiaries of secondary importance."

Decedent . . . transferred, on December 17, 1984, an undivided 33-percent interest in . . . property to the Children's Trust by a quitclaim deed. Similarly, in 1985, decedent transferred a second undivided 33-percent interest . . . to the Children's Trust . . . . Decedent intended to transfer her remaining undivided interest in the . . . property to the Children's Trust in 1986. However, decedent died prior to making the transfer. . . .

The value of the 33-percent undivided interest in the . . . property that decedent transferred in 1984 was $70,000. The value of the 33-percent undivided interest in the . . . property that decedent transferred in 1985 also was $70,000.

Decedent did not report the two $70,000 transfers on Federal gift tax returns. Rather, decedent claimed seven annual exclusions of $10,000 each under section 2503(b) for each year . . . . These annual exclusions were claimed with respect to decedent's two children and decedent's five grandchildren.

There was no agreement or understanding between decedent, the trustees, and the beneficiaries that decedent's grandchildren would not exercise their withdrawal rights following a contribution to the Children's Trust. None of decedent's five grandchildren exercised their rights to withdraw under Article Twelfth of the Children's Trust during either 1984 or 1985. None of decedent's five grandchildren received a distribution from the Children's Trust during either 1984 or 1985.

Respondent allowed petitioner to claim the annual exclusions with respect to decedent's two children. However, respondent disallowed the $10,000 annual exclusions claimed with respect to each of decedent's grandchildren claimed for the years 1984 and 1985. Respondent determined that the annual exclusions that decedent claimed with respect to her five grandchildren for the 1984 and 1985 transfers . . . were not transfers of present interests in property. Accordingly, respondent increased petitioner's adjusted taxable gifts in the amount of $100,000.

OPINION . . .

The section 2503(b) exclusion applies to gifts of present interests in property and does not apply to gifts of future interests . . . . The regulations define a future interest to include "reversions, remainders, and other interests or estates, whether vested or contingent, and whether or not supported by a particular interest or estate, which are limited to commence in use, possession or enjoyment at some future date or time." Sec. 25.2503-3(a), Gift Tax Regs. The regulations further provide that "An unrestricted right to the immediate use, possession, or enjoyment of property or the income from property (such as a life estate or term certain) is a present interest in property. An exclusion is allowable with respect to a gift of such an interest (but not in excess of the value of the interest)." Sec. 25.2503-3(b), Gift Tax Regs.

In the instant case, petitioner argues that the right of decedent's grandchildren to withdraw an amount equal to the annual exclusion within 15 days after decedent's contribution of property to the Children's Trust constitutes a gift of a present interest in property, thus qualifying for a $10,000 annual exclusion for each grandchild for the years 1984 and 1985. Petitioner relies upon Crummey v. Commissioner, 397 F.2d 82 (9th Cir. 1968), revg. on this issue T.C. Memo. 1966-144.

In Crummey v. Commissioner, T.C. Memo. 1966-144, affd. in part and revd. in part 397 F.2d 82 (9th Cir. 1968), the settlors created an irrevocable living trust for the benefit of their four children, some of whom were minors. The trustee was required to hold the property in equal shares for the beneficiaries. Under the terms of the trust, the trustee, in his discretion, could distribute trust income to each beneficiary until that beneficiary obtained the age of 21. . . . In addition, each child was given an absolute power to withdraw up to $4,000 in cash of any additions to corpus in the calendar year of the addition, by making a written demand upon the trustee prior to the end of the calendar year.

Relying on these powers, the settlors claimed the section 2503(b) exclusion on transfers of property to the trust for each trust beneficiary.[8] Respondent permitted the settlors to claim the exclusions with respect to the gifts in trust to the beneficiaries who were adults during the years of the additions. However, respondent disallowed exclusions with respect to the gifts in trust to the beneficiaries who were minors during such years. Respondent disallowed the exclusions for the minor beneficiaries on the ground that the minors' powers were not gifts of present interests in property.

In deciding whether the minor beneficiaries received a present interest, the Ninth Circuit specifically rejected any test based upon the likelihood that the minor beneficiaries would actually receive present enjoyment of the property. Instead, the court focused on the legal right of the minor beneficiaries to demand payment from the trustee. The Ninth Circuit, relying on Perkins v. Commissioner, 27 T.C. 601 (1956), and Gilmore v. Commissioner, 213 F.2d 520 (6th Cir. 1954), stated:

> All exclusions should be allowed under the *Perkins* test . . . . Under *Perkins*, all that is necessary is to find that the demand could not be resisted. We interpret that to mean legally resisted and, going on that basis, we do not think the trustee would have any choice but to have a guardian appointed to take the property demanded. [Crummey v. Commissioner, 397 F.2d at 88.]

The court found that the minor beneficiaries had a legal right to make a demand upon the trustee, and allowed the settlors to claim annual exclusions, under section 2503(b), with respect to the minor trust beneficiaries. . . .

Subsequent to the opinion in *Crummey*, respondent's revenue rulings have recognized that when a trust instrument gives a beneficiary the legal power to demand immediate possession of corpus, that power qualifies as a present

---

8. During the years in *Crummey*, 1962 and 1963, the §2503(b) annual exclusion was $3,000.

interest in property. See Rev. Rul. 85-24, 1985-1 C.B. 329, 330 ("When a trust instrument gives a beneficiary the power to demand immediate possession of corpus, the beneficiary has received a present interest. Crummey v. Commissioner, 397 F.2d 82 (9th Cir. 1968)"); Rev. Rul. 81-7, 1981-1 C.B. 474 ("The courts have recognized that if a trust instrument gives a beneficiary the power to demand immediate possession and enjoyment of corpus or income, the beneficiary has a present interest. Crummey v. Commissioner, 397 F.2d 82 (9th Cir. . . . [1968])."). While we recognize that revenue rulings do not constitute authority for deciding a case in this Court, . . . we mention them to show respondent's recognition that a trust beneficiary's legal right to demand immediate possession and enjoyment of trust corpus or income constitutes a present interest in property for purposes of the annual exclusion under section 2503(b). See Tele-Communications, Inc. v. Commissioner, 95 T.C. 495, 510 (1990). . . .

In the instant case, respondent has not argued that decedent's grandchildren did not possess a legal right to withdraw corpus from the Children's Trust within 15 days following any contribution, or that such demand could have been legally resisted by the trustees. In fact, the parties have stipulated that "following a contribution to the Children's Trust, each of the grandchildren possessed the *same right of withdrawal* as . . . the withdrawal rights of Frank Cristofani and Lillian Dawson." (Emphasis added.) . . .

On brief, respondent attempts to distinguish *Crummey* from the instant case. Respondent argues that in *Crummey* the trust beneficiaries not only possessed an immediate right of withdrawal, but also possessed "substantial, future economic benefits" in the trust corpus and income. . . .

In the instant case, the primary beneficiaries of the Children's Trust were decedent's children. Decedent's grandchildren held contingent remainder interests in the Children's Trust. Decedent's grandchildren's interests vested only in the event that their respective parent (decedent's child) predeceased decedent or failed to survive decedent by more than 120 days. We do not believe, however, that *Crummey* requires that the beneficiaries of a trust must have a vested present interest or vested remainder interest in the trust corpus or income, in order to qualify for the section 2503(b) exclusion. . . .

Although decedent's grandchildren never exercised their respective withdrawal rights, this does not vitiate the fact that they had the legal right to do so, within 15 days following a contribution to the Children's Trust. Events might have occurred to prompt decedent's children and grandchildren (through their guardians) to exercise their withdrawal rights. . . . [W]e fail to see how respondent can argue that decedent did not intend to benefit her grandchildren.

Finally, the fact that the trust provisions were intended to obtain the benefit of the annual gift tax exclusion does not change the result. As we stated in Perkins v. Commissioner, supra,

> regardless of the petitioners' motives, or why they did what they in fact did, the legal rights in question were created by the trust instruments and could at any time thereafter be exercised. Petitioners having done what they purported to do, their tax-saving motive is irrelevant. [Perkins v. Commissioner, 27 T.C. at 606.]

Based upon the foregoing, we find that the grandchildren's right to withdraw an amount not to exceed the section 2503(b) exclusion, represents a present interest for purposes of section 2503(b). Accordingly, petitioner is entitled to claim annual exclusions with respect to decedent's grandchildren as a result of decedent's transfers of property to the Children's Trust in 1984 and 1985.

Decision will be entered for the petitioner.

NOTES

1.   The Internal Revenue Service has not fully accepted the *Cristofani* decision. It has announced that it will challenge attempts to obtain annual exclusions where the substance of the transfer indicates that the donor's purpose was to obtain the annual exclusion and not to benefit the recipient. If the persons with withdrawal rights have only discretionary income interests, remote contingent rights to the remainder, or no beneficial rights whatsoever in the trust property, the Service may challenge the annual exclusions. The IRS has taken the position that the nonexercise of withdrawal rights in such cases may indicate a prearranged understanding with the donor not to exercise the rights. Tech. Adv. Mem. 96-28-004 (July 12, 1996).

For futher discussion, see Marc A. Chorney, Transfer Tax Issues Raised by Crummey Powers, 33 Real Prop., Prob. & Tr. J. 755 (1999); Bradley E.S. Fogel, Back to the Future Interest: The Origin and Questionable Legal Basis of the Use of Crummey Withdrawal Powers to Obtain the Federal Gift Tax Annual Exclusion, 6 Fla. Tax Rev. 189 (2003); Jeffrey S. Kinsler, Has the Internal Revenue Service's Challenge of Semi-Naked Lapsing Powers Become Frivolous?, 15 Widener L.J. 299 (2006).

2.   The children and grandchildren in *Cristofani* may have made taxable gifts when their Crummey powers lapsed. Section 2514(e) provides that a lapse of a general power is considered a gift by the donee of the power, but only to the extent that the amount that could have been appointed (i.e., withdrawn from the trust) exceeds the greater of $5,000 or 5 percent of the aggregate value of the assets out of which the exercise of the lapsed power could have been satisfied. So, for example, the holder of a typical $13,000 Crummey power will be deemed to have made a taxable gift of $3,000 if the trust estate at the time of the lapse is worth $200,000 (5 percent of $200,000 is $10,000, which is greater than $5,000 but $3,000 less than the lapsed amount). Any such gift by the Crummey power holder will not normally qualify for an annual exclusion. Because of this lapsed-power issue, donors often limit the Crummey withdrawal power to the smaller of the following amounts: (a) the power holder's pro rata share of the value of the gift, (b) the annual exclusion amount, and (c) the greater of $5,000 or 5 percent of the aggregate value of the assets out of which the exercise of the lapsed power could have been satisfied. See generally Ray D. Madoff, Cornelia R. Tenney, Martin A. Hall, and Lisa N. Mingolla, Practical Guide to Estate Planning §8.06 (2009 ed.).

3.   *Marital Deductions and Gift Splitting*

Thanks to the *unlimited marital deduction*, enacted in 1981, a husband and wife are able to make gifts of any size to each other without gift or estate taxation. The underlying theory is that the husband and wife should be able to treat their property as belonging to an integrated economic unit, freely transferable between the unit's members. A transfer tax is imposed only when property passes outside the marital unit. For a critique of this policy, see Bridget J. Crawford, One Flesh, Two Taxpayers: A New Approach to Marriage and Wealth Transfer Taxation, 6 Fla. Tax Rev. 757 (2004).

To qualify for the marital deduction, the gift must be outright or in a qualifying *marital trust*. We take up such trusts in connection with the estate tax (see page 972), but consider here the two most important examples:

> *Case 8. Life estate plus power of appointment trust. W* transfers $5 million in trust to pay the income to *H* for life, and on *H*'s death, to distribute the principal as *H* appoints by will. This transfer qualifies for the marital deduction because *H* has both a life estate and a power to appoint to his estate. See I.R.C. §2523(e).
>
> *Case 9. QTIP (qualified terminable interest property) trust. W* transfers $5 million in trust to pay the income to *H* for life, and on *H*'s death, to distribute the principal to *W*'s descendants. *W* may elect under §2523(f) to take a marital deduction ("QTIP election") for the $5 million transfer, excluding it from transfer tax on creation of the trust, but the value of the trust property will be included in *H*'s gross estate at *H*'s death.

Gift splitting. When property is transferred by gift from one spouse to a third person, the transfer is subject to gift taxation. However, if the non-donor spouse consents, §2513 permits the two spouses to report the gift as made one-half by each of them. Thus, if the wife transfers $52,000 to her two daughters, this may be treated—with the husband's consent—as transfers by the wife of $13,000 to each daughter, and transfers by the husband of $13,000 more to each daughter, thereby qualifying for $52,000 of annual exclusion. In this way, a married person can double the size of her annual gift exclusion, albeit only with the consent of the other spouse and at the cost of the other spouse's exclusion. Gift splitting can be quite valuable to married persons of disparate wealth, allowing the wealthier spouse to make use of the poorer spouse's exemption.

SECTION C.   THE FEDERAL ESTATE TAX

1.   *A Thumbnail Sketch*

Although the details are complex, it will suffice for present purposes to say that the federal estate tax is generally imposed on the net value of property owned by the decedent plus the value of property over which the decedent had substantial control.

The first step in complying with the federal estate tax law is to compute the value of the decedent's *gross estate*, as that term is defined in §§2033-2044 of the Code. In addition to the decedent's probate estate (§2033), the gross estate also includes, among other things, lifetime gratuitous transfers over which the decedent retained a possessory interest or control of beneficial enjoyment (§2036), or the power to alter, amend, terminate, or revoke the transfer (§2038), and also any property over which the decedent had a general power of appointment (§2041).

The Code permits certain *deductions* from the gross estate, such as the decedent's debts and other claims against the estate, as well as transfers to the decedent's spouse (the *marital deduction*) and transfers to charity (the *charitable deduction*).

The gross estate minus deductions equals the *taxable estate*. To compute the estate tax, *adjusted taxable gifts* (taxable gifts made after 1976) are first added to the taxable estate. The total of these two amounts is the *tentative estate tax base*, against which a graduated tax rate schedule is applied to produce a *tentative estate tax*. Then gift taxes that were previously paid on post-1976 taxable gifts are subtracted. Finally, various other credits are subtracted. These may include a credit for taxes on prior transfers that were taxed in the estate of another decedent within the preceding ten years, or a credit for foreign death taxes. The most important credit, however, is the *unified credit*. The Code uses the term "applicable exclusion amount" in defining the unified credit, and most lawyers refer to the applicable exclusion amount as the *exemption amount*.

Congress has long exempted a certain amount of property from transfer taxation. In 1954, the exemption was fixed at $60,000. By 1981, that figure had been increased to $600,000. In 1998, Congress enacted an amendment that would have increased the exemption amount in a series of steps until it reached $1 million in 2006. In 2001, however, Congress provided for a more rapid escalation of the exemption and de-coupled the gift tax and estate tax exemption amounts. Under the 2001 law, the gift tax exemption remained at $1 million, but the estate tax exemption was increased as follows: through 2003, $1 million; in 2004 and 2005, $1.5 million; in 2006 through 2008, $2 million; and in 2009, $3.5 million. Any use of the lifetime gift tax exemption also counts against the estate tax exemption.

NOTE: TAX ADVANTAGES OF LIFETIME GIFTS

The annual exclusion from the gift tax is a use-it-or-lose-it benefit that encourages lifetime giving. That is, excluded gifts are not subject to either gift or estate taxes, and they do not reduce the donor's unified credit.

Wealth-transfer taxes also can be saved by using the $1 million gift tax exemption during life rather than saving it for later use to reduce estate taxes. Gifts are valued for tax purposes as of the date of the gift, whereas property included in the gross estate is valued at the time of the decedent's death. By making an inter vivos gift of property, the donor can remove from the gross estate any subsequent appreciation in the property's value (plus any income the property generates) between the date of gift and the date of the donor's death. Such appreciation (and income) is likewise not subject to gift taxation, because it arises subsequent to the gift.

Another advantage of lifetime gifts is that the calculation of gift taxes does not take into account the tax itself (*tax-exclusive*), whereas estate taxes are a function of the taxable estate, an amount that includes any estate taxes that will be payable to the government (*tax-inclusive*). To illustrate, suppose O aims to transfer $1 million to her daughter, A, and, for mathematical simplicity, suppose further that this transfer is subject to a 50 percent rate. For A to receive by gift $1 million, O must part with a total of $1.5 million ($1 million to A and $500,000 to Uncle Sam). Hence, the tax rate on the total amount paid by O is really 33 1/3 percent. In contrast, for O to transfer $1 million to A at death, O must part with $2 million (again supposing a 50 percent rate) to get $1 million into the hands of A.

For discussion of other reasons why lifetime gifts can save the overall taxes, see John R. Price and Samuel A. Donaldson, Price on Contemporary Estate Planning ch. 7 (2008 ed.).

2. The Gross Estate

a. The Probate Estate

Section 2033 provides: "The value of the gross estate shall include the value of property to the extent of the interest therein of the decedent at the time of his death." This includes any property right recognized by state law that is included in the decedent's probate estate, whether tangible or intangible.

b. Spouse's Elective Share

Under §2034, "the value of the gross estate shall include the value of all property to the extent of any interest therein of the surviving spouse, existing at the time of the decedent's death as dower or curtesy, or by virtue of a statute creating an estate in lieu of dower or curtesy." Put otherwise, the value of the gross estate is not diminished by the value of the surviving spouse's statutory rights.

Section 2034 does not apply to community property, because each spouse is the owner of an undivided one-half interest in community assets and has the power of testamentary disposition over only that one-half share.

c. Joint Tenancy

The decedent's interest in a joint tenancy is not taxed under §2033 as part of the probate estate (because the decedent's interest terminates at death), but it may be taxed under §2040. Section 2040 distinguishes between (1) a joint tenancy between persons other than spouses, and (2) a joint tenancy or tenancy by the entirety between husband and wife.

Non-spouses. Where the joint tenants are not married to each other, §2040(a) includes in the gross estate the entire value of property held in joint tenancy, except any part that is attributable to consideration furnished by the surviving joint tenant. This rule also applies to joint bank accounts and government bonds with survivorship provisions. Thus:

> *Case 10.* O pays $40,000 for securities, taking title in the name of O and A as joint tenants. O has made a taxable lifetime gift to A of one-half the value of the property, or $20,000. When O dies several years later, the securities are worth $60,000. Under §2040, the full value of the securities, or $60,000, is includible in O's gross estate. (There is no double taxation, because §2001(b)(2) provides that the tentative estate tax is reduced by the amount of any gift taxes paid on gifts made after 1976.)

If, in Case 10, O had contributed three-fourths of the purchase price of the securities ($30,000) and A one-fourth ($10,000), three-fourths of the $60,000 date-of-death value of the securities, or $45,000, would be included in O's gross estate. But because the burden of showing the amount contributed by the survivor is on the decedent's personal representative, the value of the entire property will be included in the gross estate if the survivor cannot establish the amount of the survivor's contribution. Accordingly, it can be important to keep records showing the source of funds used to acquire or to improve joint tenancy property.

Spouses. The who-furnished-the-consideration test applicable to joint tenancies between non-spouses does not apply to joint tenancies between spouses. When property is held by the decedent and the decedent's spouse as joint tenants with right of survivorship or as tenants by the entirety, one-half of its date-of-death value is includible in the decedent's gross estate regardless of which spouse furnished the consideration for the property's acquisition or improvement. The one-half interest that is included in the decedent's gross estate qualifies for the unlimited marital deduction because it "passes" to the surviving spouse. Therefore, no estate taxes result from the inclusion of the decedent spouse's one-half interest.[9]

d.   Annuities and Employee Death Benefits

Survivor benefits paid under annuity contracts and retirement plans are includible in the decedent's gross estate under §2039 to the extent that the decedent had a right to current or future distributions while still living. However, survivorship benefits that are payable *by statute* to the decedent's spouse or children are not included because the decedent did not have the power to select the beneficiary. Social Security benefits are therefore excludable.

---

9. The surviving spouse, however, receives a stepped-up basis under §1014 (see page 940) for only one-half of the property included in the decedent's gross estate. A married couple can sometimes save income taxes without increasing estate taxes by transferring joint tenancy property to the spouse who is expected to die first. There is no transfer tax because of the unlimited marital deduction, but the survivor will take a stepped-up basis for the entire property, rather than for only half.

e. Life Insurance

Section 2042 requires the inclusion of insurance proceeds on the life of the decedent if (1) the decedent possessed at death any incident of ownership in the policy, or (2) the policy proceeds were payable to the insured's probate estate. Incidents of ownership include the right to change the beneficiary; to surrender, cancel, or assign the policy; or to borrow against the cash surrender value in the policy. With proper planning, therefore, it is often possible to avoid estate taxation on life insurance proceeds.

> *Case 11.* T purchases two life insurance policies on his own life, designating his spouse as the beneficiary of one, and his estate as the beneficiary of the other. Under the terms of both policies, T had the right to change the beneficiary designations at any time. All death benefits payable under both policies are includible in T's gross estate, because T held at least one incident of ownership in each policy at the time of his death. (The amount payable to T's wife, however, qualifies for the marital deduction.)
>
> *Case 12.* T's child, A, purchases a life insurance policy on T's life and designates himself as the beneficiary at T's death. Because T holds no incidents of ownership and the proceeds are not payable to T's probate estate, none of the proceeds are includible in T's gross estate. This is true even if A pays the premiums on the policy with funds given to A by T, for example in the form of annual exclusion gifts.[10]

Lawyers routinely advise clients to shield life insurance proceeds from estate taxes by having the beneficiary buy and own the policy. However, this may not be possible with insurance offered to a worker as an employee benefit, because the worker may not be able to avoid being the owner of the policy.

For further discussion, see Robert B. Smith, Reconsidering the Taxation of Life Insurance Proceeds Through the Lens of Current Estate Planning, 15 Va. Tax Rev. 283 (1995).

PROBLEMS AND NOTE

1.   *H* is the insured under a $500,000 ordinary life insurance policy. The policy was issued in *W*'s name as owner, and *H* has never held any of the incidents of ownership. The policy names *W* as the primary beneficiary and the couple's daughter, *D*, as the contingent beneficiary. *H* dies, and the policy proceeds are paid to *W. H* leaves a will that devises his entire estate to *W* and *D* in equal shares. The will names *W* as executor. Are the policy proceeds includible in *H*'s gross estate?

2.   Consider the same facts as in Problem 1 except that *W* predeceases *H*, leaving a will that devises "all my property" to *H*. On the date of *W*'s death, the cash surrender value of the policy is $100,000. *H* dies a year later, and the $500,000 in policy proceeds are paid to the couple's daughter, *D*, as contingent beneficiary. What are the estate tax consequences in *W*'s estate? In *H*'s estate?

---

10. If in Case 12 *T* had bought the policy and then given it to *A* within three years of *T*'s death, the proceeds would be includible in *T*'s gross estate under §2035(a). See page 966.

3. If a donee of a special power of appointment can appoint trust property that includes a life insurance policy on the donee's life, the donee has an incident of ownership, so the value of the insurance will be included in the donee's gross estate. In drafting special powers, you should take care to exclude such life insurance from the appointive property.

f. Retained Rights or Powers

People sometimes make gifts with strings attached. In such cases, §2036 may require that the donor's gross estate include the property's value on the date of death. Section 2036 provides:

> The value of the gross estate shall include the value of all property to the extent of any interest therein of which the decedent has at any time made a transfer (except in case of a bona fide sale for an adequate and full consideration in money or money's worth), by trust or otherwise, under which he has retained for his life or for any period which does not in fact end before his death —
>
>   (1) The possession or enjoyment of, or the right to the income from, the property, or
>   (2) The right, either alone or in conjunction with any person, to designate the persons who shall possess or enjoy the property or the income therefrom.

Section 2036(a)(1) applies, for example, when the decedent retains a life estate in the transferred property. Although such an interest terminates at death (and therefore is not includible under §2033), the transfer is subjected to estate taxation under §2036 because the decedent retained the right for life to possess and enjoy the property or to receive its income.

Section 2036(a)(2) reaches transfers in which the decedent retains the right to control the beneficial enjoyment of the property. To take an obvious case, when the transferor designates himself as a co-trustee and the trustees have a discretionary power to accumulate trust income or distribute it to the beneficiary, or a power to distribute the income among several beneficiaries in such shares as the trustees determine, the property's date-of-death value must be included in the gross estate. To a considerable extent, as we shall see, §2036(a)(2) overlaps with §2038, which applies to lifetime transfers where the transferor possesses the power to alter, amend, or revoke.

PROBLEMS

1. *O* transfers property to *X* in trust to pay the income to *O* for life and on *O*'s death to distribute the trust assets to *A*. What are the gift and estate tax consequences of this transfer?

2. *O* transfers property to *X* in trust. The trustee has unfettered discretion to pay the income to *O* or to accumulate it and to invade the corpus for *O*'s benefit. On *O*'s death, the trustee is to distribute the trust assets to *A*. What are the gift and estate tax consequences?

Estate of Maxwell v. Commissioner
United States Court of Appeals, Second Circuit, 1993
3 F.3d 591

LASKER, J.   This appeal presents challenges to the tax court's interpretation of section 2036(a) of the Internal Revenue Code, relating to "Transfers with retained life estate." The petitioner, the Estate of Lydia G. Maxwell, contends that the tax court erred in holding that the transaction at issue (a) was a transfer with retained life estate within the meaning of . . . §2036 and (b) was not a bona fide sale for adequate and full consideration under that statute.

The decision of the tax court is affirmed.

I

On March 14, 1984, Lydia G. Maxwell (the "decedent") conveyed her personal residence, which she had lived in since 1957, to her son Winslow Maxwell, her only heir, and his wife Margaret Jane Maxwell (the "Maxwells"). Following the transfer, the decedent continued to reside in the house until her death on July 30, 1986. At the time of the transfer, she was eighty-two years old and was suffering from cancer.

The transaction was structured as follows:

1)   The residence was sold by the decedent to the Maxwells for $270,000;[11]
2)   Simultaneously with the sale, the decedent forgave $20,000 of the purchase price (which was equal in amount to the annual gift tax exclusion to which she was entitled);
3)   The Maxwells executed a $250,000 mortgage note in favor of decedent;
4)   The Maxwells leased the premises to her for five years at the monthly rental of $1,800; and
5)   The Maxwells were obligated to pay and did pay certain expenses associated with the property following the transfer, including property taxes, insurance costs, and unspecified "other expenses."

While the decedent paid the Maxwells rent totalling $16,200 in 1984, $22,183 in 1985 and $12,600 in 1986, the Maxwells paid the decedent interest on the mortgage totalling $16,875 in 1984, $21,150 in 1985, and $11,475 in 1986. As can be observed, the rent paid by the decedent to the Maxwells came remarkably close to matching the mortgage interest which they paid to her. In 1984, she paid the Maxwells only $675 less than they paid her; in 1985, she paid them only $1,033 more than they paid her, and in 1986 she paid the Maxwells only $1,125 more than they paid her.

---

11. The parties have stipulated that the fair market value of the property on the date of the purported sale was $280,000.

Not only did the rent functionally cancel out the interest payments made by the Maxwells, but the Maxwells were at no time called upon to pay any of the principal on the $250,000 mortgage debt; it was forgiven in its entirety. As petitioner's counsel admitted at oral argument, although the Maxwells had executed the mortgage note, "there was an intention by and large that it not be paid." Pursuant to this intention, in each of the following years preceding her death, the decedent forgave $20,000 of the mortgage principal, and, by a provision of her will executed on March 16, 1984 (that is, just two days after the transfer), she forgave the remaining indebtedness.

The decedent reported the sale of her residence on her 1984 federal income tax return but did not pay any tax on the sale because she elected to use the once-in-a-lifetime exclusion on the sale or exchange of a principal residence provided for by 26 U.S.C. §121.

She continued to occupy the house by herself until her death. At no time during her occupancy did the Maxwells attempt to sell the house to anyone else, but, on September 22, 1986, shortly after the decedent's death, they did sell the house for $550,000.

Under I.R.C. §2036(a), where property is disposed of by a decedent during her lifetime but the decedent retains "possession or enjoyment" of it until her death, that property is taxable as part of the decedent's gross estate, unless the transfer was a bona fide sale for an "adequate and full" consideration. 26 U.S.C. §2036.

On the decedent's estate tax return, the Estate reported only the $210,000 remaining on the mortgage debt (following the decedent's forgiveness of $20,000 in the two preceding years). The Commissioner found that the 1984 transaction constituted a transfer with retained life estate — rejecting the petitioners' arguments that the decedent did not retain "possession or enjoyment" of the property, and that the transaction was exempt from section 2036(a) because it was a bona fide sale for full and adequate consideration — , and assessed a deficiency against the Estate to adjust for the difference between the fair market value of the property at the time of decedent's death ($550,000) and the reported $210,000.

The Estate appealed to the tax court, which, after a trial on stipulated facts, affirmed the Commissioner's ruling, holding:

> On this record, bearing in mind petitioner's burden of proof, we hold that, notwithstanding its form, the substance of the transaction calls for the conclusion that decedent made a transfer to her son and daughter-in-law with the understanding, at least implied, that she would continue to reside in her home until her death, that the transfer was not a bona fide sale for an adequate and full consideration in money or money's worth, and that the lease represented nothing more than an attempt to add color to the characterization of the transaction as a bona fide sale.

There are two questions before us: Did the decedent retain possession or enjoyment of the property following the transfer? And if she did, was the transfer a bona fide sale for an adequate and full consideration in money or money's worth?

II

Section 2036(a) provides in pertinent part:

The value of the gross estate shall include the value of all property to the extent of any interest therein of which the decedent has at any time made a transfer (except in case of a bona
fide sale for an adequate and full consideration in money or money's worth), by trust or otherwise, under which he has retained for his life or for any period not ascertainable without
reference to his death or for any period which does not in fact end before his death — (1) the
possession or enjoyment of, or the right to the income from, the property.

In the case of real property, the terms "possession" and "enjoyment" have been
interpreted to mean "the lifetime use of the property." United States v. Byrum,
408 U.S. 125, 147 (1972).

In numerous cases, the tax court has held, where an aged family member transferred her home to a relative and continued to reside there until her death, that
the decedent-transferor had retained "possession or enjoyment" of the property
within the meaning of §2036. As stated in Rapelje v. Commissioner, 73 T.C. 82
(1979): "Possession or enjoyment of gifted property is retained [by the transferor]
when there is an express or implied understanding to that effect among the parties at the time of transfer." . . . In such cases, the burden is on the decedent's
estate to disprove the existence of any adverse implied agreement or understanding and that burden is particularly onerous when intrafamily arrangements are
involved. . . .

As indicated above, the tax court found as a fact that the decedent had transferred her home to the Maxwells "with the understanding, at least implied, that
she would continue to reside in her home until her death." This finding was based
upon the decedent's advanced age, her medical condition, and the overall result
of the sale and lease. The lease was, in the tax court's words, "merely window
dressing" — it had no substance. . . .

We agree with the tax court's finding that the decedent transferred her home
to the Maxwells "with the understanding, at least implied, that she would continue to reside in her home until her death," and certainly do not find it to be
clearly erroneous. The decedent did, in fact, live at her residence until she died,
and she had sole possession of the residence during the period between the day
she sold her home to the Maxwells and the day she died. There is no evidence that
the Maxwells ever intended to occupy the house themselves, or to sell or lease it
to anyone else during the decedent's lifetime. Moreover, the Maxwells' failure to
demand payment by the estate, as they were entitled to do under the lease, of the
rent due for the months following decedent's death and preceding their sale of
the property, also supports the tax court's finding.

The petitioner argues . . . that the decedent's tenancy alone does not justify
inclusion of the residence in her estate, so it argues that the decedent's payment
of rent sanctifies the transaction and renders it legitimate. Both arguments
ignore the realities of the rent being offset by mortgage interest, the forgiveness

of the entire mortgage debt either by gift or testamentary disposition, and the fact that the decedent was eighty-two at the time of the transfer and actually continued to live in the residence until her death which, at the time of the transfer, she had reason to believe would occur soon in view of her poor health.

The Estate relies primarily on Barlow v. Commissioner, 55 T.C. 666 (1971). In that case, the father transferred a farm to his children and simultaneously leased the right to continue to farm the property. The tax court held that the father did not retain "possession or enjoyment," stating that "one of the most valuable incidents of income-producing real estate is the rent which it yields. He who receives the rent in fact enjoys the property." Barlow, 55 T.C. at 671 (quoting McNichol's v. Commissioner, 265 F.2d 667, 671 (3d Cir. 1959)). However, Barlow is clearly distinguishable on its facts: In that case, there was evidence that the rent paid was fair and customary and, equally importantly, the rent paid was not offset by the decedent's receipt of interest from the family lessor. . . .

Barlow itself recognized that where a transferor "by agreement" "reserves the right of occupancy as an incident to the transfer," §2036(a) applies. Barlow, 55 T.C. at 670. . . .

For the reasons stated above, we conclude that the decedent did retain possession or enjoyment of the property for life and turn to the question of whether the transfer constituted "a bona fide sale for adequate and full consideration in money or money's worth."

III

Section 2036(a) provides that even if possession or enjoyment of transferred property is retained by the decedent until her death, if the transfer was a bona fide sale for adequate and full consideration in money or money's worth, the property is not includible in the estate. Petitioner contends that the Maxwells paid an "adequate and full consideration" for the decedent's residence, $270,000 total, consisting of the $250,000 mortgage note given by the Maxwells to the decedent, and the $20,000 the decedent forgave simultaneously with the conveyance.[12]

The tax court held that neither the Maxwells' mortgage note nor the decedent's $20,000 forgiveness constituted consideration within the meaning of the statute. . . .

As to the $250,000 mortgage note, the tax court held that:

> Regardless of whether the $250,000 mortgage note might otherwise qualify as "adequate and full consideration in money or money's worth" for a $270,000 or $280,000 house, the mortgage note here had no value at all if there was no intention that it would ever be paid.

---

12. As noted above, the parties have stipulated that the fair market value of the property on the date of the purported sale was $280,000. The Estate contends that $270,000 was full and adequate consideration for the sale, with a broker, for a house appraised at $280,000. We assume this fact to be true for purposes of determining whether the transaction was one for "an adequate and full consideration in money or money's worth."

> The conduct of decedent and the Maxwells strongly suggest that neither party intended the Maxwells to pay any part of the principal of either the original note or any successor note.

There is no question that the mortgage note here is a fully secured, legally enforceable obligation on its face. The question is whether it is actually what it purports to be — a bona fide instrument of indebtedness — or whether it is a facade. The petitioner argues not only that an allegedly unenforceable intention to forgive indebtedness does not deprive the indebtedness of its status as "consideration in money or money's worth" but also that "[t]his is true even if there was an implied agreement exactly as found by the Tax Court."

We agree with the tax court that where, as here, there is an implied agreement between the parties that the grantee would never be called upon to make any payment to the grantor, as, in fact, actually occurred, the note given by the grantee had "no value at all." We emphatically disagree with the petitioner's view of the law as it applies to the facts of this case. As the Supreme Court has remarked, the family relationship often makes it possible for one to shift tax incidence by surface changes of ownership without disturbing in the least his dominion and control over the subject of the gift or the purposes for which the income from the property is used. Commissioner v. Culbertson, 337 U.S. 733, 746 (1949). There can be no doubt that intent is a relevant inquiry in determining whether a transaction is "bona fide." As another panel of this Court held recently, construing a parallel provision of the Internal Revenue Code, in a case involving an intrafamily transfer:

> when the bona fides of promissory notes is at issue, the taxpayer must demonstrate affirmatively that "there existed at the time of the transaction a real expectation of repayment and an intent to enforce the collection of the indebtedness." Estate of Van Anda v. Commissioner, 12 T.C. 1158, 1162 (1949), aff'd per curiam, 192 F.2d 391 (2d Cir. 1951).

In language strikingly apposite to the situation here, the court stated:

> it is appropriate to look beyond the form of the transactions and to determine, as the tax court did here, that the gifts and loans back to decedent were "component parts of single transactions." Id. . . .

[T]he tax court found that, at the time the note was executed, there was "an understanding" between the Maxwells and the decedent that the note would be forgiven. In our judgment, the conduct of decedent and the Maxwells with respect to the principal balance of the note, when viewed in connection with the initial "forgiveness" of $20,000 of the purported purchase price, strongly suggests the existence of an understanding between decedent and the Maxwells that decedent would forgive $20,000 each year thereafter until her death, when the balance would be forgiven by decedent's will.

To conclude, we hold that the conveyance was not a bona fide sale for an adequate and full consideration in money or money's worth. The decision of the tax court is affirmed.

NOTES

1.   In Wheeler v. United States, 116 F.3d 749 (5th Cir. 1997), the taxpayer, age 60, sold a remainder interest in his ranch to his two sons for the value of a remainder interest set forth in the actuarial tables of the Treasury regulations. The taxpayer reserved a life estate in the ranch and died at age 67. The court held the transfer was for full consideration, and thus the ranch was not part of the transferor's federal gross estate under §2036. Compare Gradow v. United States, 897 F.2d 516 (Fed. Cir. 1990), holding that full and adequate consideration within the meaning of §2036(a) refers to the entire property, not just the portion that is sold. See Ronald H. Jensen, Estate and Gift Tax Effects of Selling a Remainder: Have D'Ambrosio, Wheeler and Magnin Changed the Rules?, 4 Fla. Tax Rev. 537 (1999).

2.   Joseph Grace executes a trust instrument providing for the payment of income to his wife, Janet, for her life, and payment to her of any part of the principal that a majority of the trustees think advisable. Mrs. Grace is given a special testamentary power of appointment over the trust estate. Joseph, his nephew, and a third party are named as trustees. Shortly thereafter, Janet Grace, at Joseph's request, executes a virtually identical trust instrument naming Joseph as life beneficiary. Then Joseph dies. Is the corpus of either trust includible in Joseph's gross estate? In United States v. Estate of Grace, 395 U.S. 316 (1969), the Court held that, under the *reciprocal trust doctrine*, the value of the Janet Grace trust must be included in Joseph's estate. Said the court: "[A]pplication of the reciprocal trust doctrine requires only that the trusts be interrelated, and that the arrangement, to the extent of mutual value, leaves the settlors in approximately the same economic position as they would have been in had they created trusts naming themselves as life beneficiaries."

The reciprocal trust doctrine is rather vague, and the Internal Revenue Service has a mixed record in the litigated cases. See Elena Marty-Nelson, Taxing Reciprocal Trusts: Charting a Doctrine's Fall from Grace, 75 N.C. L. Rev. 1781 (1997).

3.   A settlor who seeks to avoid §2036(a)(2) by naming someone else as trustee or co-trustee should be careful about retaining the power to remove and replace trustees. The settlor can, however, safely retain such a power if the replacement cannot be related or subordinate to the settlor. Rev. Rul. 95-58, 1995-2 C.B. 191.

Old Colony Trust Co. v. United States
United States Court of Appeals, First Circuit, 1970
423 F.2d 601

ALDRICH, J.   The sole question in this case is whether the estate of a settlor of an inter vivos trust, who was a trustee until the date of his death, is to be charged with the value of the principal he contributed by virtue of reserved powers in the trust. The executor paid the tax and sued for its recovery in the district court. All facts were stipulated. The court ruled for the government, 300 F. Supp. 1032, and the executor appeals.

The initial life beneficiary of the trust was the settlor's adult son. Eighty percent of the income was normally to be payable to him, and the balance added to principal. Subsequent beneficiaries were the son's widow and his issue. The powers upon which the government relies to cause the corpus to be includable in the settlor-trustee's estate are contained in two articles. . . .

Article 4 permitted the trustees to increase the percentage of income payable to the son beyond the eighty percent, "in their absolute discretion . . . when in their opinion such increase is needed in case of sickness, or desirable in view of changed circumstances." In addition, under Article 4 the trustees were given the discretion to cease paying income to the son, and add it all to principal, "during such period as the Trustees may decide that the stoppage of such payments is for his best interests."

Article 7 gave broad administrative or management powers to the trustees, with discretion to acquire investments not normally held by trustees, and the right to determine what was to be charged or credited to income or principal, including stock dividends or deductions for amortization. It further provided that all divisions and decisions made by the trustees in good faith should be conclusive on all parties, and in summary, stated that the trustees were empowered, "generally to do all things in relation to the Trust Fund which the Donor could do if living and this Trust had not been executed."

The government claims that each of these two articles meant that the settlor-trustee had "the right . . . to designate the persons who shall possess or enjoy the [trust] property or the income therefrom" within the meaning of section 2036(a)(2) of the Internal Revenue Code of 1954, 26 U.S.C. §2036(a)(2), and that the settlor-trustee at the date of his death possessed a power "to alter, amend, revoke, or terminate" within the meaning of section 2038(a)(1) (26 U.S.C. §2038(a)(1)).

If State Street Trust Co. v. United States, 1 Cir., 1959, 263 F.2d 635, was correctly decided in this aspect, the government must prevail because of the Article 7 powers. There this court, Chief Judge Magruder dissenting, held against the taxpayer because broad powers similar to those in Article 7 meant that the trustees "could very substantially shift the economic benefits of the trusts between the life tenants and the remaindermen," so that the settlor "as long as he lived, in substance and effect and in a very real sense . . . 'retained for his life . . . the right . . . to designate the persons who shall possess or enjoy the property or the income therefrom. . . .'" 263 F.2d at 639-640, quoting 26 U.S.C. §2036(a)(2). We accept the taxpayer's invitation to reconsider this ruling.

It is common ground that a settlor will not find the corpus of the trust included in his estate merely because he named himself a trustee. He must have reserved a power to himself[13] that is inconsistent with the full termination of ownership. The government's brief defines this as "sufficient dominion and control until his death." Trustee powers given for the administration or management of the trust

---

13. The number of other trustees who must join in the exercise of that power, unless the others have antagonistic interest of a substantial nature, is, of course, immaterial. Treas. Reg. §20.2036-1(a)(ii), (b)(3)(i) (1958); §20.2038-1(a) (1958).

must be equitably exercised, however, for the benefit of the trust as a whole. The court in *State Street* conceded that the powers at issue were all such powers, but reached the conclusion that, cumulatively, they gave the settlor dominion sufficiently unfettered to be in the nature of ownership. With all respect to the majority of the then court, we find it difficult to see how a power can be subject to control by the probate court, and exercisable only in what the trustee fairly concludes is in the interests of the trust and its beneficiaries as a whole, and at the same time be an ownership power.

The government's position, to be sound, must be that the trustee's powers are beyond the court's control. Under Massachusetts law, however, no amount of administrative discretion prevents judicial supervision of the trustee. Thus in Appeal of Davis, 1903, 67 N.E. 604 (Mass.), a trustee was given "full power to make purchases, investments and exchanges . . . in such manner as to them shall seem expedient; it being my intention to give my trustees . . . the same dominion and control over said trust property as I now have." In spite of this language, and in spite of their good faith, the court charged the trustees for failing sufficiently to diversify their investment portfolio. The Massachusetts court has never varied from this broad rule of accountability, and has twice criticized *State Street* for its seeming departure. Boston Safe Deposit & Trust Co. v. Stone, 1965, 348 Mass. 345, 351, n.8, 203 N.E.2d 547; Old Colony Trust Co. v. Silliman, 1967, 352 Mass. 6, 8-9, 223 N.E.2d 504. We make it a further observation, which the court in *State Street* failed to note, that the provision in that trust (as in the case at bar) that the trustees could "do all things in relation to the Trust Fund which I, the Donor, could do if . . . the Trust had not been executed," is almost precisely the provision which did not protect the trustees from accountability in Appeal of Davis, supra.

We do not believe that trustee powers are to be more broadly construed for tax purposes than the probate court would construe them for administrative purposes. More basically, we agree with Judge Magruder's observation that nothing is "gained by lumping them together." State Street Trust Co. v. United States, supra, 263 F.2d at 642. We hold that no aggregation of purely administrative powers can meet the government's amorphous test of "sufficient dominion and control" so as to be equated with ownership.

This does not resolve taxpayer's difficulties under Article 4. Quite different considerations apply to distribution powers. Under them the trustee can, expressly, prefer one beneficiary over another. Furthermore, his freedom of choice may vary greatly, depending upon the terms of the individual trust. If there is an ascertainable standard, the trustee can be compelled to follow it. If there is not, even though he is a fiduciary, it is not unreasonable to say that his retention of an unmeasurable freedom of choice is equivalent to retaining some of the incidents of ownership. Hence, under the cases, if there is an ascertainable standard the settlor-trustee's estate is not taxed, . . . but if there is not, it is taxed. . . .

The trust provision which is uniformly held to provide an ascertainable standard is one which, though variously expressed, authorizes such distributions as may be needed to continue the beneficiary's accustomed way of life. . . . On the other hand, if the trustee may go further, and has power to provide for the beneficiary's "happiness," Merchants Nat'l Bank v. Com'r of Internal Revenue, 1943, 320 U.S. 256, or "pleasure," Industrial Trust Co. v. Com'r of Internal Revenue, 1 Cir., 1945, 151 F.2d 592, or "use and benefit," Newton Trust Co. v. Com'r of Internal Revenue, 1 Cir., 1947, 160 F.2d 175, or "reasonable requirement[s]," State Street Bank & Trust Co. v. United States, 1 Cir., 1963, 313 F.2d 29, the standard is so loose that the trustee is in effect uncontrolled.

In the case at bar the trustees could increase the life tenant's income "in case of sickness, or [if] desirable in view of changed circumstances." Alternatively, they could reduce it "for his best interests." "Sickness" presents no problem. Conceivably, providing for "changed circumstances" is roughly equivalent to maintaining the son's present standard of living. . . . The unavoidable stumbling block is the trustees' right to accumulate income and add it to capital (which the son would never receive) when it is to the "best interests" of the son to do so. Additional payments to a beneficiary whenever in his "best interests" might seem to be too broad a standard in any event. In addition to the previous cases see Estate of Yawkey, 1949, 12 T.C. 1164, where the court said, at p.1170, "We can not regard the language involved ['best interest'] as limiting the usual scope of a trustee's discretion. It must always be anticipated that trustees will act for the best interests of a trust beneficiary, and an exhortation to act 'in the interests and for the welfare' of the beneficiary does not establish an external standard." Power, however, to decrease or cut off a beneficiary's income when in his "best interests," is even more troublesome. When the beneficiary is the son, and the trustee the father, a particular purpose comes to mind, parental control through holding the purse strings. The father decides what conduct is to the "best interests" of the son, and if the son does not agree, he loses his allowance. Such power has the plain indicia of ownership control. The alternative, that the son, because of other means, might not need this income, and would prefer to have it accumulate for his widow and children after his death, is no better. If the trustee has power to confer "happiness" on the son by generosity to someone else, this seems clearly an unascertainable standard.

The case of Hays' Estate v. Com'r of Internal Revenue, 5 Cir., 1950, 181 F.2d 169, is contrary to our decision. The opinion is unsupported by either reasoning or authority, and we will not follow it. With the present settlor-trustee free to determine the standard himself, a finding of ownership control was warranted. To put it another way, the cost of holding onto the strings may prove to be a rope burn. State Street Bank & Trust Co. v. United States, supra.

Affirmed.

NOTE: FAMILY LIMITED PARTNERSHIPS

In a typical *family limited partnership* (FLP), an individual transfers most of her property, and her children add modest amounts, to the partnership in exchange for limited partnership interests. The general partner is often a corporation owned by the individual and her children. When the individual's limited partnership interests pass to her children either by inter vivos gift or by will or will substitute, the value of those interests are discounted to reflect a lack of marketability and control, and the gift or estate tax due is reduced accordingly.

Some people consider it illogical that separate interests in a family-owned entity would qualify for a lack-of-control discount, but *fair market value* is defined for tax purposes as "the price at which the property would change hands between a willing buyer and a willing seller, neither being under any compulsion to buy or to sell and both having reasonable knowledge of relevant facts." Treas. Reg. §20.2031-1(b). The IRS once contended that the separate interests of a family-controlled entity should be aggregated for purposes of determining the fair market value of the interests held by the various family members, but eventually it abandoned that position. Rev. Rul. 93-12, 1993-1 C.B. 202.

Although a limited partnership is most commonly used in this estate planning technique, other entities can work just as well. Consider a simple example involving a family corporation:

> *Case 13.* Parent transfers $6 million of publicly traded securities to a new corporation in exchange for all its stock, and then gives one-third of that stock to Son and one-third to Daughter. Parent's will devises the final one-third interest to Son and Daughter in equal shares. Because each one-third block of stock is considered separately for valuation purposes, Parent properly reports two gifts of one-third interests, each of which qualifies for non-marketability and lack-of-control discounts. A reputable appraiser opines that, based on the Code's definition of fair market value, each one-third interest is worth 25 percent less than each shareholder's proportionate share of the underlying property, which means that each gift has a value for tax purposes of only $1.5 million (one-third of $6 million, minus 25 percent). When Parent dies a few months later, the same expert applies the same 25 percent discount in valuing the one-third interest that Parent had kept for himself. Assuming for the sake of mathematical simplicity that the value of the underlying publicly traded securities did not change during this period of time, Parent managed to transfer $6 million of underlying value to Son and Daughter, but a total of only $4.5 million appeared on Parent's gift and estate tax returns. The other 25 percent, $1.5 million, escaped transfer taxation.

The IRS closely scrutinizes FLPs and similar planning arrangements, but for many years it usually lost most of the disputed cases. More recently, the IRS has successfully argued that §2036 requires inclusion in the donor's gross estate of more than just the discounted value of the decedent's remaining partnership interests. Although much depends on the specific facts, some courts have included in the decedent's gross estate the full value of the property that the decedent had transferred to the FLP. Courts reaching this result do so by finding that there was an implied agreement among the family members to allow the decedent to benefit from or exercise control over the property that she contributed to the FLP, or by finding that the FLP lacked a substantial non-tax or business purpose.

In Turner v. Commissioner, 382 F.3d 367 (3d Cir. 2004), the decedent transferred 95 percent of his assets to two FLPs when he was 95 years old. After the transfers, the decedent did not have sufficient assets to support himself. Neither FLP engaged in any real business or commercial activity, and profits earned by the FLPs passed directly to the original owner of the underlying property. The court found that there was an implicit agreement that the decedent could obtain whatever resources he needed for support from the FLPs. The court concluded that the FLPs had been nothing more than "vehicle[s] for changing the form in which the decedent held his property — a recycling of value." Accordingly, the full value of the transferred assets, not the discounted value of the limited partnership interests, were included in the decedent's gross estate.

The outcome was different in Kimbell v. United States, 371 F.3d 257 (5th Cir. 2004). In that case, the court found that there had been substantial non-tax motives for the formation of the FLP, including the decedent's desire to protect her assets from creditors and to retain the assets in a single, well-managed entity rather than dispersing them through distributions to subsequent generations. Similarly, in Estate of Mirowski v. Commissioner, T.C. Memo 2008-74, the court found a substantial business purpose because of the decedent's interest in managing her assets with those of her daughters, positioning the family for investment opportunities not otherwise available, and providing for each of her three daughters on an equal basis. It also helped that the decedent had not relied on the assets of the entity to maintain her lifestyle.

For recent commentary on FLPs and similar devices, see Dwight Drake, Transitioning the Family Business, 83 Wash. L. Rev. 123 (2008); Ronald Aucutt, Yesterday's FLP: To Be Celebrated, Repaired, or Abandoned?, 41 Heckerling Inst. on Est. Plan. ch. 13 (2007); Richard L. Dees, Time Traveling to Strangle Strangi (And Kill the Monster Again), Part 1, 116 Tax Notes 563 (2007), Part 2, 116 Tax Notes 657 (2007), and Part 3, 117 Tax Notes 161 (2007); Wendy C. Gerzog, Bigelow: The Ninth Circuit on FLPs, 117 Tax Notes 1167 (2007); Walter D. Schwidetzky, Family Limited Partnerships: The Beat Goes On, 60 Tax Law. 277 (2007).

g. Revocable Transfers

Section 2038 brings into the gross estate the date-of-death value of interests (usually in inter vivos trusts or other nonprobate transfers) that the decedent had the power to alter, amend, or revoke. Section 2038(a) provides that the value of the gross estate shall include the value of all property:

> To the extent of any interest therein of which the decedent has at any time made a transfer (except in case of a bona fide sale for an adequate and full consideration in money or money's worth), by trust or otherwise, where the enjoyment thereof was subject at the date of his death to any change through the exercise of a power (in whatever capacity exercisable) by the decedent alone or by the decedent in conjunction with any other person (without regard to when or from what source the decedent acquired such power), to alter, amend, revoke or terminate, or when any such power is relinquished during the three-year period ending on the date of the decedent's death.

In addition to bringing revocable transfers into the gross estate, §2038 also reaches transfers over which the decedent held any one of the enumerated powers, even when the power cannot be exercised to benefit the decedent. Thus, if *O* creates an irrevocable trust in which *O*, as co-trustee, has a discretionary power to accumulate or distribute trust income, or a discretionary power to distribute corpus to the income beneficiary, the property is included in *O*'s gross estate under §2038 because *O*'s discretionary power is a power to alter or amend. (*O*'s reserved power would also cause inclusion under §2036(a)(2).)

To a considerable extent, §2038 applies to the same transfers as §2036(a)(2). There are, however, situations covered exclusively by §2038. While §2036(a)(2) covers only a retained right to designate the persons who shall enjoy the property, §2038 applies if the transferor has the power to effect any change, including the time of enjoyment. Hence, §2038 alone applies where the settlor has a power to accelerate enjoyment by a beneficiary. Section 2036(a)(2) applies to powers that are retained by the decedent for her life, while §2038 applies to powers that the decedent has at the moment of death. Section 2038 thus applies to the decedent's ability to change trust beneficiaries in her will even if she could not do so during life.

If the power to alter, amend, revoke, or terminate is given to a third person, the transfer is not taxed under §2038 even if the power is held by a nonadverse party. It is for this reason that a trustee (or trust protector) who is not the settlor can be given broad discretionary powers, including the power to distribute all or a portion of the trust property, without adverse tax consequences to the settlor. However, if a trustee has such a power, and if the transferor has the right to remove the trustee and appoint himself as trustee, the transferor is treated as having the power and §2038 is applicable. Treas. Reg. §20.2038-1(a)(3).

PROBLEMS

1.   *O* transfers property to the First National Bank in trust to pay the income to *O*'s daughter, *A*, for life, and on *A*'s death to pay the principal to *O*'s granddaughter, *B*. *O* retains the power to invade principal for the benefit of *B*. On *O*'s death, is the entire value of the trust corpus includible in *O*'s gross estate under §2038?

2.   What result if *O* in Problem 1 has no power to invade principal but retains the power to direct that all or a portion of trust income be accumulated and added to principal each year?

h.   Reversionary Interests

Individuals making nonprobate transfers sometimes retain reversions in the property in case the nonprobate transfer terminates or fails. In some cases, this will cause the property to be included in the gross estate. Under §2037, the value of property transferred during life is includible in the transferor's gross estate if:

(1) possession or enjoyment of the property can . . . be obtained only by surviving the decedent, and

(2) the decedent has retained a reversionary interest in the property . . . , and the value of such reversionary interest immediately before the death of the decedent exceeds five percent of the value of the property.

Both conditions must be present for §2037 to apply. Thus:

> *Case 14.* H conveys $500,000 to X in trust, to pay income to W for life, then to distribute the trust principal to H if H is then living or, if H is not then living, to his daughter, A, or her descendants. Condition (1) is met. A cannot obtain possession or enjoyment without surviving H. Therefore, if the value of H's reversionary interest exceeded 5 percent of the value of the property (Condition (2)), the value of the trust assets, less the value of W's life estate, will be includible in H's gross estate if H predeceases W. (The value of H's reversionary interest would be measured by the actuarial probability of H outliving W.)

If no beneficiary's enjoyment of the property depends on surviving the decedent, §2037 is inapplicable. Thus, in Case 14 if there were no gift over to A, §2037 would not apply. Only the value of H's reversionary interest would be included under §2033.

Section 2037 can be avoided by eliminating any possibility that the trust property will revert to the settlor or the settlor's estate. This can be accomplished by making sure that some other person will take the property regardless of what contingencies occur.

i.   Transfers Within Three Years of Death

To prevent deathbed transfers designed to avoid estate taxation, §2035 includes in the decedent's gross estate any of the following transfers made within three years of death:

(1)   Any gift tax paid by the decedent or his estate on gifts made within three years of death, or

(2)   any transfer or release of an interest in property if, had such interest been retained, the property would have been included in the decedent's gross estate under any of the following sections of the Internal Revenue Code: §2036 (transfers with retained life estate); §2037 (transfers taking effect at death); §2038 (revocable transfers); or §2042 (life insurance). The gross estate includes the value of any property which would have been included had such transfer or release not been made.

Unless an inter vivos transfer is referred to above, it is not includible in the decedent's gross estate even if made within three years of death. Thus, if O gives Blackacre to A two months before O's death, O has made a taxable gift at the time of transfer, and Blackacre is not included in O's gross estate at death. (The amount of gift tax paid is, however, included in O's gross estate.)

Without §2035, the owner of a life insurance policy on the owner's life would have a strong tax incentive to give the policy away shortly prior to death, perhaps on her deathbed. A holder of a retained life estate would also have a strong tax incentive to release the life estate when death appeared imminent. Thus:

> *Case 15.* In 1999, *O* creates an irrevocable trust of securities worth $300,000, retaining a life estate, with the remainder to *O*'s son, *A*. (This results in a taxable gift to *A* of the value of the remainder, which is computed based on *O*'s life expectancy and the initial value of $300,000.) In 2009, the trust assets are worth $500,000, and *O*, moments before dying, releases her life estate. The release is a taxable gift to *A* of the value of *O*'s life estate in assets worth $500,000. Without §2035, *O*'s release would eliminate transfer tax on the value of a remainder in $200,000 worth of assets. With §2035, the entire $500,000 worth of assets is included in *O*'s gross estate (though the gift tax paid in 1999 is credited against the estate taxes payable at *O*'s death.)

NOTES AND PROBLEMS

1. In some circumstances a deathbed gift may save transfer taxes notwithstanding §2035. The clearest example is a gift that qualifies for the annual gift tax exclusion. Another possibility is to make use of the valuation principles illustrated in Case 13 at page 963. A gift of a minority interest in a closely held family business from a dying parent to her child may qualify for discounts because of its lack of control and marketability. But caution is advised. A gift that reduces *transfer* taxes might be counterproductive for *income* tax purposes. Instead of a *stepped-up basis* at the owner's death, see page 940, the donee might end up with a *carryover basis*, which could be disadvantageous, depending on the circumstances. To advise clients on gratuitous transfers of wealth, lawyers should understand at least the fundamentals of both transfer and income taxation.

2. Suppose that *A* purchases a life insurance policy and names his daughter, *B*, as the beneficiary. If *A* thereafter assigns the policy to *B*, the insurance proceeds will be included in *A*'s gross estate at death if *A* dies within three years of the transfer. On the other hand, if *B* is named as the owner of the policy as well as beneficiary from the beginning, the proceeds of the policy are not includible in *A*'s gross estate at his death, even if he dies within three years. The strategy of having *B* buy the policy in the first instance can work even if *A* pays the premiums, provided the amount of the premiums is less than the annual $13,000 exclusion (premiums paid in excess of the annual exclusion would be a taxable gift).

j. Powers of Appointment

As we saw in Chapter 12, the donor of a *power of appointment* gives the donee a power to appoint certain property (the appointive property) to one or more potential appointees (the objects of the power). Powers of appointment, used primarily in trusts, provide flexibility by allowing the donor to postpone and delegate dispositive decisions to someone who can take changed circumstances into account when deciding who should get the appointive property and when they should get it.

Under §2041, the gross estate includes the value of property over which the decedent at the time of his death held a *general*, but not a *special*, power of appointment. A power is general if it can be exercised in favor of the donee (i.e., the holder of the power), his creditors, his estate, *or* the creditors of his estate.

> *Case 16.* H's will creates a testamentary trust providing for the payment of trust income to H's wife, W, for life and on her death "to pay the trust principal to such person or persons as W appoints by will." On W's death, the value of the trust corpus is includible in her gross estate whether or not W exercises the power of appointment. Although W was restricted to the income from the trust and she could not exercise the power of appointment to benefit herself or her creditors during her lifetime, at death she could exercise the power in favor of her estate or the creditors of her estate.

A power of appointment that is not a general power is called a *special power*, a *limited power*, or a *nongeneral power* (the terms are synonymous, see page 804). Property subject to a special power of appointment held by the decedent is not included in the decedent's gross taxable estate under §2041.[14]

> *Case 17.* H's will creates a testamentary trust providing for the payment of trust income to H's wife, W, for life and on her death "to pay the trust principal to such one or more of W's descendants or spouses of W's descendants as W shall appoint by will." Because W's power of appointment was not a general power, the appointive property is not taxed under §2041, whether or not W exercises the power. Furthermore, the trust property is not included in W's gross estate under either §2033 (because her life estate ended at her death) or §2036 (because the life estate was not "retained," it was given to W by H).

As Case 17 demonstrates, it is possible to give a beneficiary both a life income interest in property and a limited power to control the disposition of the property at death without subjecting the property to estate taxation in the beneficiary's estate. Moreover, it is possible to give someone the power to appoint property to himself during his lifetime without it necessarily being a general power of appointment, if the exercise of the power is limited by an ascertainable standard or is a five-and-five power.

Ascertainable standards. Under §2041(b)(1)(A), "[a] power to consume, invade, or appropriate property for the benefit of the decedent which is limited by an ascertainable standard relating to the health, education, support, or maintenance of the decedent shall not be deemed a general power of appointment." Accordingly, a power in the donee to appoint property for his own benefit will not result in inclusion in the donee's gross estate so long as the power is limited by the quoted ascertainable standards.

Five-and-five power. If the donor does not want to limit the donee's ability to withdraw to an ascertainable standard, the donor could give the donee a general power to withdraw a limited amount from the trust each year. When the donee

---

14. Treas. Reg. §20.2041-1(c)(1) (1958). There is one important, and sometimes useful, exception to this general rule. See the discussion of the Delaware Tax Trap at page 923.

dies, nothing will be in his gross estate if he has in fact exercised the power. If he has not exercised the power, only the amount that can be withdrawn is in his gross estate. §2041(a)(2). Most donors limit the amount to the greater of $5,000 or 5 percent of corpus because §2514(e) provides that the lapse of a power limited to this amount is not a release and thus is not a transfer resulting in gift tax liability. If the donee can withdraw more than $5,000 or 5 percent of corpus, the failure to withdraw could also create estate tax liability if the release results in a transfer that, had the property actually been owned by the donee, would have been included in the donee's gross estate under §§2035, 2036, 2037, or 2038.

NOTE

Special powers of appointment and limited invasion powers (measured by an ascertainable standard or a standard of "the greater of $5,000 or 5 percent") can be employed to create a flexible estate plan that allows for unforeseen circumstances. Contrast such a flexible plan with an old-fashioned settlement of property "to my wife for life, and on her death the remainder to my descendants per stirpes." At the time the transfer is made, the income from the property may appear to ensure that the wife's support and other needs will be met. But if the wife (or one of the couple's children) should encounter unusual medical or other expenses, or if inflation erodes the real value of the income interest, the income from the property may be insufficient to meet the wife's needs. If, on the other hand, the wife is given an "ascertainable standard" or a "5 or 5" invasion power, the corpus of the trust can be used to satisfy the wife's support and other needs whenever trust income proves insufficient. See generally John G. Steinkamp, Estate and Gift Taxation of Powers of Appointment Limited by Ascertainable Standards, 79 Marq. L. Rev. 195 (1995). Careful drafting is essential, not only to avoid estate taxation, but also to give effect to the settlor's intent. See Trent S. Kiziah, Four Chosen Words, 145 Tr. & Est. 26 (Aug. 2006).

Estate of Vissering v. Commissioner
United States Court of Appeals, Tenth Circuit, 1993
990 F.2d 578

LOGAN, C.J.   The estate of decedent Norman H. Vissering appeals from a judgment of the Tax Court determining that he held at his death a general power of appointment as defined by I.R.C. §2041, and requiring that the assets of a trust of which he was cotrustee be included in his gross estate for federal estate tax purposes. The appeal turns on whether decedent held powers permitting him to invade the principal of the trust for his own benefit unrestrained by an ascertainable standard relating to health, education, support, or maintenance. . . .

The trust at issue was created by decedent's mother, and became irrevocable on her death in 1965. Decedent and a bank served as cotrustees. Under the dispositive provisions decedent received all the income from the trust after his mother's death. On decedent's death . . . , remaining trust assets were to be divided into equal parts and passed to decedent's two children or were held for their benefit. . . .

Under I.R.C. §2041 a decedent has a general power of appointment includable in his estate if he possesses at the time of his death a power over assets that permits him to benefit himself, his estate, his creditors, or creditors of his estate. A power vested in a trustee, even with a cotrustee who has no interest adverse to the exercise of the power, to invade principal of the trust for his own benefit is sufficient to find the decedent trustee to have a general power of appointment, unless the power to invade is limited by an ascertainable standard relating to health, education, support, or maintenance. Treas. Reg. §20.2041-1(c), -3(c)(2). See, e.g., Estate of Sowell v. Commissioner, 708 F.2d 1564, 1568 (10th Cir. 1983) (invasion of trust corpus in case of emergency or illness is an ascertainable standard under §2041(b)(1)(A)); see also Merchants Nat'l Bank v. Commissioner, 320 U.S. 256, 261 (1943) (invasion of trust corpus for "the comfort, support, maintenance and/or happiness of my wife" is not a fixed standard for purposes of charitable deductions); Ithaca Trust Co. v. United States, 279 U.S. 151, 154 (1929) (invasion of trust corpus for any amount "that may be necessary to suitably maintain [decedent's wife] in as much comfort as she now enjoys" is a fixed standard for purposes of charitable deduction).

The relevant provisions of the instant trust agreement are as follows:

> During the term of [this trust], the Trustees shall further be authorized to pay over or to use or expend for the direct or indirect benefit of any of the aforesaid beneficiaries, whatever amount or amounts of the principal of this Trust as may, in the discretion of the Trustees, be required for the continued comfort, support, maintenance, or education of said beneficiary.

The Internal Revenue Service (IRS) and the Tax Court focused on portions of the invasion provision providing that the trust principal could be expended for the "comfort" of decedent, declaring that this statement rendered the power of invasion incapable of limitation by the courts.

We look to state law (here Florida's) to determine the legal interests and rights created by a trust instrument, but federal law determines the tax consequences of those interests and rights. . . .

Despite the decision in Barritt v. Tomlinson, 129 F. Supp. 642 (S.D. Fla. 1955), which involved a power of invasion broader than the one before us, we believe the Florida Supreme Court would hold that a trust document permitting invasion of principal for "comfort," without further qualifying language, creates a general power of appointment. Treas. Reg. §20.2041-1(c). See First Virginia Bank v. United States, 490 F.2d 532, 533 (4th Cir. 1974) (under Virginia law, right of invasion for beneficiary's "comfort and care as she may see fit" not limited by an ascertainable standard); Lehman v. United States, 448 F.2d 1318, 1320 (5th Cir. 1971) (under Texas law, power to invade corpus for "support, maintenance, comfort, and welfare" not limited by ascertainable standard); Miller v. United States, 387 F.2d 866, 869 (3d Cir. 1968) (under Pennsylvania law, power to make disbursements from principal in amounts "necessary or expedient for [beneficiary's] proper maintenance, support, medical care, hospitalization, or other expenses incidental to her comfort and well-being" not limited by ascertainable standard); Estate of Schlotterer v. United States, 421 F. Supp. 85, 91 (W.D. Pa. 1976) (power of consumption "to the extent deemed by [beneficiary] to be desirable not only for her support and maintenance but also for her comfort and pleasure" not limited by ascertainable standard); Doyle v. United States, 358 F. Supp. 300, 309-310 (E.D. Pa. 1973) (under Pennsylvania law, trustees' "uncontrolled discretion" to pay beneficiary "such part or parts of the principal of said trust fund as may be necessary for her comfort, maintenance and support" not limited by ascertainable standard); Stafford v. United States, 236 F. Supp. 132, 134 (E.D. Wisc. 1964) (under Wisconsin law, trust permitting husband "for his use, benefit and enjoyment during his lifetime," unlimited power of disposition thereof "without permission of any court, and with the right to use and enjoy the principal, as well as the income, if he shall have need thereof for his care, comfort or enjoyment" not limited by ascertainable standard).

However, there is modifying language in the trust before us that we believe would lead the Florida courts to hold that "comfort," in context, does not permit an unlimited power of invasion. The instant language states that invasion of principal is permitted to the extent "required for the continued comfort" of the decedent, and is part of a clause referencing the support, maintenance and education of the beneficiary. Invasion of the corpus is not permitted to the extent "determined" or "desired" for the beneficiary's comfort but only to the extent that it is "required." Furthermore, the invasion must be for the beneficiary's "continued" comfort, implying, we believe, more than the minimum necessary for survival, but nevertheless reasonably necessary to maintain the beneficiary in his accustomed manner of living. These words in context state a standard essentially no different from the examples in the Treasury Regulation, in which phrases such as "support in reasonable comfort," "maintenance in health and reasonable comfort," and "support in his accustomed manner of living" are deemed to be limited by an ascertainable standard. Treas. Reg. §20.2041-1(c)(2). See, e.g., United States v. Powell, 307 F.2d 821, 828 (10th Cir. 1962) (under Kansas law, invasion of the corpus if "it is necessary or advisable . . . for the maintenance, welfare, comfort or happiness" of beneficiaries, and only if the need justifies the reduction in principal, is subject to ascertainable standard); Hunter v. United States, 597 F. Supp. 1293, 1295 (W.D. Pa. 1984) (power to invade for "comfortable support and maintenance" of beneficiaries is subject to ascertainable standard).

We believe that had decedent, during his life, sought to use the assets of the trust to increase significantly his standard of living beyond that which he had previously enjoyed, his cotrustee would have been obligated to refuse to consent, and the remainder beneficiaries of the trust could have successfully petitioned the court to disallow such expenditures as inconsistent with the intent of the trust instrument. The Tax Court erred in ruling that this power was a general power of appointment includable in decedent's estate.

Reversed and remanded.

QUESTIONS AND NOTE

Norman Vissering consults you regarding his mother's probated will (which was prepared by his prior lawyer). You spot the drafting error (i.e., the use of the word *comfort*). To avoid litigation and the possible inclusion of his mother's trust in Norman's gross estate, would you recommend that he disclaim the power to use principal for "comfort"?

Treas. Reg. §25.2518-3(a)(2) takes the position that

> all interests in the corpus of a trust are treated as a single interest [and] in order to have a qualified disclaimer of an interest in corpus the disclaimant must disclaim all such interests, either totally or as to an undivided portion. Thus, if a disclaimant has a testamentary power of appointment over the trust corpus coupled with either an inter vivos power to invade corpus or an interest as discretionary appointee, a disclaimer by that person can constitute a qualified disclaimer only if both such interests are disclaimed.

Perhaps Norman should decline to serve as a co-trustee. In that case, he would not have a general power of appointment. Does Norman have a good claim for malpractice against his mother's lawyer? See Kinney v. Shinholser, 663 So. 2d 643 (Fla. App. 1995).

3. Deductions

a. The Marital Deduction

Before 1982, the primary purpose of the marital deduction was to equalize the tax treatment of couples residing in separate property and community property states. See pages 481-482. Since 1981, the marital deduction has been based on the theory that gratuitous transfers between spouses should not be subject to wealth-transfer taxation because the spouses are one economic unit. Thus, unlimited amounts of property (other than certain "terminable interests") now can be transferred between spouses without the imposition of either a gift tax or an estate tax.

For an interest in property to qualify for the marital deduction, five requirements must be met:

(1) The decedent must have been survived by his or her spouse.
(2) The surviving spouse must be a citizen of the United States or the property must pass to a *qualified domestic trust* (see page 985).
(3) The value of the interest deducted must be includible in the decedent's gross estate.
(4) The interest must pass from the decedent to the surviving spouse.
(5) The interest must not be a "nondeductible terminable interest" within the meaning of §2056(b).

The first, second, and third requirements are straightforward. The term "passing" in the fourth requirement is defined rather broadly in §2056(c) to include interests passing by will, by inheritance, by trust, by right of survivorship, by dower or elective share, by the exercise or nonexercise of a power of appointment held by the decedent, by designation as a life insurance beneficiary, or by other transfer.

The fifth requirement is the most important and the most productive of litigation. To qualify for the marital deduction, the interest passing to the surviving spouse must be such that it is subject to taxation in the spouse's estate (to the extent not consumed or disposed of by the spouse during life). The marital deduction thus permits the deferral of estate taxation only until the surviving spouse's death. The clearest example of an interest that qualifies for the deduction is an outright gift of property to the spouse (in fee simple and free of trust).

That an interest will eventually be taxed in the surviving spouse's estate does not ensure qualification for the deduction. The interest cannot violate the *nondeductible terminable interest rule*:

> Where, on the lapse of time, on the occurrence of an event or contingency, or on the failure of an event or contingency to occur, an interest passing to the surviving spouse will terminate or fail, no deduction shall be allowed under this section with respect to such interest —
>
>   (A) if an interest in such property passes or has passed (for less than an adequate and full consideration in money or money's worth) from the decedent to any person other than such surviving spouse (or the estate of such spouse); and
>
>   (B) if by reason of such passing such person (or his heirs or assigns) may possess or enjoy any part of such property after such termination or failure of such interest so passing to the surviving spouse. [I.R.C. §2056(b)(1).]

The simplest example of a terminable interest is a legal or equitable life estate given to a surviving spouse, with the remainder to pass to other persons on the spouse's death. Here's why: On the occurrence of an event or contingency — the spouse's death — the interest in question will terminate or fail. Upon such termination, an interest in the property — the remainder interest — will pass from the decedent to persons other than the surviving spouse or her estate. By reason of such passing, the remaindermen may possess or enjoy the property on the termination of the spouse's life estate.

There are, however, five exceptions to the nondeductible terminable interest rule:

(a) Estate trust exception. The estate trust exception to the nondeductible terminable interest rule is included within the statement of the rule. An interest is a nondeductible terminable interest only if, on termination of the spouse's interest, the property passes *to someone other than the surviving spouse or the spouse's estate*. Consequently, a disposition of property "to my husband for life, and on his death to his estate," whether in the form of a legal life estate or in a trust settlement, qualifies for the marital deduction.

The estate trust is seldom used as a means of qualifying for the deduction because of its relative inflexibility. An estate trust also causes the assets to be subject to creditors' claims and administration expenses in the spouse's estate. However, there is one situation in which an estate trust might be desirable, stemming from the requirement that, under a marital deduction power of appointment trust or a qualified terminable interest property trust (a QTIP trust), both discussed below, all trust income must be paid to the surviving spouse for life. If the testator's estate includes *unproductive property*, a marital deduction power of appointment trust or QTIP trust must include a provision authorizing the surviving spouse to compel the trustee to (a) convert the unproductive assets to income-producing property or (b) pay the spouse a reasonable amount out of other trust assets to compensate for lost income. See Treas. Reg. §20.2056(b)-5(f)(5). This could raise a potentially serious problem if, for example, the testator owns closely held stock that does not pay dividends or owns unimproved real estate that is being held for future development. An estate trust might be useful in this situation.

(b) *Limited survivorship exception.* In drafting wills and will substitutes, it is a common practice to include a provision requiring that a beneficiary survive the decedent by a stated period (for example, 30 or 60 days). Section 2056(b)(3) provides that a devise with a limited survival requirement is deductible if (i) the condition of survival is for a period not exceeding six months and (ii) the contingency (the spouse's death within the period) does not in fact occur. In short, a requirement of survival for up to six months can be attached to the interest passing to the spouse without disqualifying it for the marital deduction. (If the spouse does not survive for the stated period, however, no marital deduction will be available, because no interest will actually pass from the decedent to the surviving spouse.)

Suppose *H* devises property to *W* "if she survives the distribution of my estate." Does this qualify for the marital deduction? See Estate of Heim v. Commissioner, 914 F.2d 1322 (9th Cir. 1990) (holding No, because the distribution date could be more than six months after the decedent's death).

(c) *Life estate plus power of appointment exception.* The transfer of a legal or equitable life estate to the decedent's spouse will qualify for the marital deduction if the spouse also receives a power to appoint the trust corpus to herself or to her estate. This exception, provided for in §2056(b)(5), has four technical requirements:

(1)   The surviving spouse must be entitled to all income for life, payable annually or at more frequent intervals. (The trust property must be income producing, or the spouse must have the power to compel the trustee to make the property income producing.)

(2)   The power of appointment must be exercisable in favor of the spouse or her estate — that is, it must be a general power of appointment. (A power in the surviving spouse to appoint only to her creditors or the creditors of her estate, while also a general power of appointment, would not qualify under §2056(b)(5).)

(3)   The power must be exercisable by the spouse "alone and in all events." (A testamentary power of appointment satisfies the "all events" requirement even though it cannot be exercised by the spouse during the spouse's lifetime.)

(4)   The spouse's interest must not be subject to a power in another person to divert the property to someone other than the spouse. Thus, for example, the trustee cannot be given a discretionary power to distribute trust corpus to the couple's children. The spouse can be given the power to appoint to the children as long as she also has the power to appoint to herself.

This important exception to the nondeductible terminable interest rule led to widespread use of the *life estate plus power of appointment trust*, commonly referred to in the literature and in practice as the *marital deduction power of appointment trust*.

(d) *Life insurance with power of appointment exception.* Rules similar to §2056(b)(5) apply to proceeds of life insurance, endowment, or annuity contracts. See §2056(b)(6).

(e) *Qualified terminable interest property (QTIP) exception.* Until 1982, every transfer qualifying for the marital deduction had the effect of giving the surviving spouse the unrestricted power of disposition over the property, either during life or at death. In 1981, Congress noted that this would make it impossible for the decedent spouse to ensure that the property would eventually pass to his or her children, as opposed to the surviving spouse's children. Congress further noted that a spouse could be forced

> to choose between surrendering control of his entire estate to avoid imposition of estate tax at his death or reducing his tax benefits at his death to insure inheritance by the children. The committee believes that the tax laws should be neutral and that tax consequences should not control an individual's disposition of property. Accordingly, the committee believes that a deduction should be permitted for certain terminable interests. [H.R. Rep. No. 4242, 96th Cong., 2d Sess. 161 (1981).]

Congress therefore enacted §2056(b)(7), which allows a marital deduction for a *qualified terminable interest*:

(1)   The spouse must be entitled to all income for life, payable annually or at more frequent intervals, and the trust property must be income producing or the spouse must have the power to compel the trustee to make the property income producing, *and*

(2)   no person (including the spouse) can have the power to appoint the property during the spouse's lifetime to any person other than the spouse.

Because the purpose of the marital deduction is to permit the deferral of estate taxes until the death of the surviving spouse, the allowance of a marital deduction for qualified terminable interest property (QTIP) is conditioned on an *election* to have the property taxed in the surviving spouse's estate under §2044. If it is a lifetime gift, the donor makes the QTIP election; if it is a transfer at death, the decedent's executor makes the election. The tax is borne by the beneficiaries who receive the qualified terminable interest property on the surviving spouse's death. Thus, if a trust is involved, the tax attributable to the interest is paid out of the principal of the QTIP trust.

NOTE

In comparing the QTIP trust with a marital deduction power of appointment trust, observe that both require that all income be payable to the surviving spouse at least annually *for life*. A provision that terminates the spouse's income interest on remarriage disqualifies both a marital deduction power of appointment trust and a QTIP trust from the marital deduction. However, there are two important differences. In a power of appointment trust, the spouse must have the power to appoint the property to herself or her estate. In a QTIP trust, the remainder interest on the spouse's death can go to any beneficiary designated by the settlor or to persons chosen by the spouse exercising a special power of appointment (provided that the persons are permissible objects of the power). Further, in a QTIP trust no one, *including the spouse*, can have the power to appoint the property to anyone other than the spouse during that spouse's lifetime. Invasions of trust principal by the spouse or by a trustee for the spouse are permitted.

A QTIP trust is particularly useful if the spouses have different natural objects of their bounty (e.g., if one of the spouses has children from a prior marriage) or if a spouse is concerned about the prospect that the surviving spouse may remarry and then favor the new spouse.

Estate of Rapp v. Commissioner
United States Court of Appeals, Ninth Circuit, 1998
140 F.3d 1211

FLETCHER, J.[15]   The executor of Mr. Bert Rapp's estate appeals the tax court's determination that a trust established by Mr. Rapp does not qualify as "qualified terminable interest property" (QTIP), as defined by 26 U.S.C. §2056(b)(7). As such, the value of the trust may not be deducted when determining federal estate taxes owed.

We have jurisdiction, 26 U.S.C. §7482, and we affirm.

I

The testator, Mr. Bert Rapp, died in February 1988. He was survived by his wife, Laura Rapp, and two children, Richard and David Rapp. Mr. Rapp willed his one-half of the community property to a trust.[16]

---

15. Judge Betty Binns Fletcher, who sits on the U.S. Court of Appeals for the Ninth Circuit, is a member of a prominent West Coast family with deep connections to the law. Her father and grandfather were lawyers in Washington State. Her husband, Robert Fletcher, is a professor of law emeritus at the University of Washington. Her son, William Fletcher, formerly a professor at the University of California, Berkeley, now sits as a judge on the Ninth Circuit Court of Appeals. Her daughter, Susan Fletcher French, is a professor of law at UCLA Law School and serves as reporter for the Restatement (Third) of Servitudes. Judge Fletcher's brother, nephew, granddaughter and several of her in-laws are also in the law business. — Eds.

16. By law of California, Mrs. Rapp received as her one-half of the community property, property valued at five million dollars.

Judge Betty Fletcher

Richard is the executor of the estate under Mr. Rapp's will and trustee of the trust. All relevant parties are citizens of California. The issue in this case is whether the trust created by Mr. Rapp's will constitutes a QTIP trust, qualifying it for the marital tax deduction. A QTIP is an exception to an exception. Generally, the value of property passed directly from a testator to a surviving spouse is deducted before computing federal estate taxes.[17] 26 U.S.C. §2056(a). However, if the interest passing to the spouse consists only of a life estate or other terminable interest, the value of that interest is not deducted when determining the tax owed. 26 U.S.C. §2056(b). If the terminable interest qualifies as a QTIP, however, the surviving spouse can elect the marital deduction as if the interest passed directly and without restraint to him or her.

The will left by Mr. Rapp did not create a QTIP trust; however, the will as reformed by the California probate court did create a QTIP trust. The primary issue in this case is the effect to be given to the California probate court's reformation.

A

In 1978, Laurence Clark, Mr. Rapp's attorney, prepared wills for both of the Rapps. Mr. Clark was not an estate attorney, but served as a consultant to Mr. Rapp in his business dealings. The 1978 wills were essentially identical to each other, and provided that household furnishings and other personal effects were to be given to the surviving spouse, and that all other property of the testator was to be held in trust during the life of the surviving spouse. The children were to be given the power as co-trustees to distribute such amounts from the principal and income of the trust as they determined necessary for the surviving spouse's health, education and support.[18] Any decision to do so would be in their "absolute discretion." Upon the death of the surviving spouse, the trust was to cease and the remaining assets were to be distributed to the two children or their living issue.

---

17. The tax deduction is in reality a tax deferral since the property is taxed when (or if) it becomes part of the surviving spouse's estate upon that spouse's death.

18. In this action, Richard is the sole trustee; David relinquished his position as co-trustee.

In 1986, Mr. Clark prepared new wills. These wills revoked the 1978 wills but were substantially similar. Again, Mr. and Mrs. Rapp's wills were nearly identical to each other. The trust was to operate as previously described. Article Fifth (b) of Mr. Rapp's will stated:

> If at any time, in the absolute discretion of the Trustee or co-Trustees, my wife, LAURA B. RAPP, should for any reason be in need of funds for her proper health, education and support, the Trustee may in his absolute discretion pay to or apply for the benefit of my wife, such amounts from the principal and income of the trust estate, up to the whole thereof, as the Trustee from time to time may deem necessary or advisable for her use and benefit.

B

The 1986 will of Mr. Rapp was admitted to probate on May 5, 1988. Mrs. Rapp asked the probate court to modify her husband's will so that the trust created by the will would qualify for the marital deduction as a QTIP trust. Her petition to the probate court alleged:

> it was decedent's intention that the Trust created . . . for the benefit of Petitioner [i.e., Mrs. Rapp] during her lifetime was intended to qualify for the QTIP election and that decedent believed that the Trustees would pay all of the income from the Trust, at least annually, to or for the benefit of Petitioner during her lifetime.

She claimed that the trust was a "marital deduction gift" as defined by section 21520(b) of the California Probate Code.[19] Her petition relied upon the probate court's power to modify or terminate a trust upon consent of all parties, Cal. Prob. Code §15403, or its power to modify or terminate a trust due to changed circumstances, Cal. Prob. Code §15409(a).[20]

---

19. California defines a "marital deduction gift" as a transfer of property that is intended to qualify for the marital deduction. Cal. Prob. Code §21520(a). A "marital deduction" is defined as that which meets the federal definition of a transfer under section 2056 of the Internal Revenue Code. Id. at §21520(a).

[Cal. Prob. Code §21522 provides:

If an instrument contains a marital deduction gift:

(a) The provisions of the instrument, including any power, duty, or discretionary authority given to a fiduciary, shall be construed to comply with the marital deduction provisions of the Internal Revenue Code.

(b) The fiduciary shall not take any action or have any power that impairs the deduction as applied to the marital deduction gift.

(c) The marital deduction gift may be satisfied only with property that qualifies for the marital deduction.

— Eds.]

20. Cal. Probate Code §15403 provides:

[Unless continuance of the trust is necessary to carry out a material purpose of the trust] if all beneficiaries of an irrevocable trust consent, they may compel modification or termination of the trust upon petition to the court.

Cal. Probate Code §15409 provides that a court may modify or terminate a trust if:

owing to circumstances not known to the settlor and not anticipated by the settlor, the continuation of the trust under its terms would defeat or substantially impair the accomplishment of the purposes of the trust.

Oral argument was held before the probate court. A guardian ad litem was appointed to represent Richard Rapp's two minor children. No witnesses were called and no documents were introduced into evidence. Richard Rapp did not contest his mother's petition. He did not ask Mr. Clark, creator of the wills, to testify, and Mr. Clark did not appear.[21] The IRS did not receive notice of the hearing and did not appear. The guardian ad litem did not challenge Mrs. Rapp's petition.

The probate court granted Mrs. Rapp's petition. The court modified Article Fifth (b) to read:

> During the lifetime of my wife, LAURA B. RAPP, the Trustee or co-Trustee shall pay the net income from the corpus of the trust annually or at more frequent intervals to or for the benefit of LAURA B. RAPP, during her lifetime. . . . Any income accrued or held undistributed at the time of my wife's death shall be distributed to her estate.

and added the following provision:

> I authorize my executor to elect to treat the trust created under this Article FIFTH, or any portion thereof, as "qualified terminable interest property" in order to obtain the marital deduction for such property for federal estate tax purposes. Whether or not my executors make such an election, I hereby exonerate my executors from any liability resulting from making or failing to make such an election.

This order was entered October 31, 1988, and became final and unappealable as of April 30, 1989.

C

Shortly after the probate court's order was entered, the executor filed with the Internal Revenue Service (IRS) an application for extension of time to file a federal estate tax return. The return normally is due 9 months after a testator's death. The executor noted in his application that he intended to make an election under §2056 for QTIP exemption, but that he could not determine yet which portion of the estate was to be claimed as a QTIP deduction. He also sent a payment of $156,204 as an estimate of the taxes owed on the estate, but offered no explanation as to how he arrived at that figure.

In May 1989, after the probate court's reformation became final, the executor filed the final federal estate tax return. The executor elected to claim a marital QTIP deduction, but only with respect to as much of the estate as would reduce the total estate tax owed to $156,424, the amount that had been previously paid. Thus, the marital deduction claimed on the return totalled $3,683,899.38.

The IRS sent a notice of deficiency to the executor stating that he had failed to substantiate fully the marital deduction claimed. The IRS allowed the deduction

---

21. Mr. Clark initially was retained as counsel for the estate but was subsequently replaced. Although Mr. Clark did not testify at the reformation hearing, he did testify before the tax court at the behest of the government. He indicated that Mr. Rapp specifically intended to create a trust for his children's benefit, and did not wish to leave outright his money to Mrs. Rapp.

only to the extent of the property that passed directly to Mrs. Rapp under Mr. Rapp's will, consisting of the household furnishings and other personal property valued at $435,262.50. The executor appealed the decision and his claim was heard before the tax court.

After hearing argument, the tax court held that the probate court's reformation order was not binding absent an affirmation by the California Supreme Court. In the absence of an affirmation by the California Supreme Court, the tax court considered itself authorized to determine whether the probate court's order was in conformity with California law. After reviewing California law, the tax court concluded that the probate court had erred in reforming Mr. Rapp's will because the will was not ambiguous and there was little or no evidence that Mr. Rapp intended to create a QTIP trust. As such, the tax court held that, for federal estate tax purposes, the trust created by Mr. Rapp was not a QTIP trust, and that the claimed deficiency was correct. . . .

III

The IRS argues, and the tax court agreed, that the probate court's reformation of Mr. Rapp's will is without binding effect for the purpose of determining federal estate taxes owed, unless California's highest court has affirmed the result. Both rely on Commissioner of Internal Revenue v. Estate of Bosch, 387 U.S. 456 (1967). We agree that *Bosch* is controlling.

A

In *Bosch*, the respondent, Mrs. Bosch, filed a federal estate tax return in which she claimed a marital deduction. Id. at 458. The IRS denied the deduction. Mr. Bosch's will had created a trust from which Mrs. Bosch was to receive all income and in which Mrs. Bosch had a general power of appointment. If she declined that appointment, however, half of the corpus of the trust was to go to Mr. Bosch's heirs.

The entire trust would qualify as tax exempt only if Mrs. Bosch retained the general power of appointment. Before Mr. Bosch died, Mrs. Bosch executed a release of her general power of appointment. Thus, whether or not the entire value of the trust was to be taxed depended upon the validity of the release. Before the tax court, Mrs. Bosch claimed that the release was invalid. While those proceedings were pending, Mrs. Bosch sought and received a determination from a New York state court that the release was a nullity under state law. The result was that a larger estate was to go to Mrs. Bosch as the surviving spouse, a diminished inheritance was to go to other beneficiaries, and a larger marital deduction could be claimed.

The issue before the Supreme Court was what effect was to be given to the state court's determination regarding the validity of the release. The Court first noted that neither res judicata nor collateral estoppel applied. Id. at 463. The Court then reviewed the legislative history of the marital deduction statute, and concluded that Congress did not intend state court actions to have a determinative effect on federal tax questions. It noted:

[Congress] said that "proper regard," not finality "should be given to interpretations of the will" by state courts and then only when entered by a court "in a bona fide adversary proceeding." We cannot say that the authors of this directive intended that the decrees of state trial courts were to be conclusive and binding on the computation of the federal estate tax as levied by the Congress. If the Congress had intended state trial court determinations to have that effect on the federal actions, it certainly would have said so — which it did not do.

Id. at 464 (citations omitted). Relying on Erie R.R. Co. v. Tompkins, 304 U.S. 64 (1938), the Court stated:

> when the application of a federal statute is involved, the decision of a state trial court as to an underlying issue of state law should a fortiori not be controlling. . . . If there be no decision by [the State's highest court] then federal authorities must apply what they find to be the state law after giving the "proper regard" to relevant rulings of other courts of the State. In this respect, it may be said to be, in effect, sitting as a state court.

387 U.S. at 465.

This rule remains valid today. . . .

In this case, Mrs. Rapp sought modification in the probate proceeding for the sole purpose of reforming her husband's will so that the trust would qualify as a QTIP trust. As in *Bosch*, the state court proceedings were "brought for the purpose of directly affecting federal estate tax liability," and, as in *Bosch*, the issue before the state court was "determinative of federal estate tax consequences." *Bosch*, 387 U.S. at 462-463. . . .

The tax court properly held that it is not bound by the California probate court's reformation of Mr. Rapp's will as the decision was not affirmed by the California Supreme Court and is contrary to state law. For federal estate tax purposes, therefore, Mrs. Rapp at no time had a QTIP trust, and the deficiency is correct. . . .

We affirm.

Pond v. Pond

Supreme Judicial Court of Massachusetts, 1997
678 N.E.2d 1321

LYNCH, J.   The plaintiff, trustee of the Sidney M. Pond Trust 1991, a revocable trust (trust), filed a complaint in the Probate and Family Court seeking reformation of the trust. The plaintiff alleges that, due to scrivener's errors in the form of omissions and ambiguities, the declaration of trust fails to give effect to the settlor's intent. At the request of the parties a Probate Court judge reserved and reported the case to the Appeals Court pursuant to G.L. c. 215, §13, and Mass. R. Civ. P. 64, 365 Mass. 831 (1974). We granted the plaintiff's application for direct appellate review. See Commissioner of Internal Revenue v. Estate of Bosch, 387 U.S. 456, 465 (1967) (Internal Revenue Service need not accept decisions other than those of State's highest court).

1. BACKGROUND.

We summarize the undisputed facts as presented by the plaintiff.[22] The settlor, Sidney M. Pond, executed his last will and testament on January 17, 1991. On the same day, the settlor executed a declaration of revocable trust, naming himself and his wife as trustees. Then, they transferred virtually all their assets, except the marital home, into the trust. The settlor died on February 26, 1996.[23]

The trust instrument provided that, during the settlor's lifetime, all of the annual income and such principal as the trustees deemed necessary was to be paid to the settlor and his wife. However, the trust made no provision for income or principal to be paid to his wife if she were to survive the settlor. The trust also provided that, on the death of the settlor and his wife, the trust shall terminate and its assets should be distributed in equal shares to their children. If one of the children predeceased the parents, the trust provided that the deceased child's share shall pass "equally and in equal shares to his/her issue by right of representation," when the issue reach the age of thirty.

In his will, the settlor bequeathed all his tangible personal property to his wife and the residue of his estate, both real and personal, to the trust. The tax clause in the will authorized his wife, as executrix, "in her sole, exclusive and unrestricted discretion, to determine whether to elect (under Sec. 2056[b][7] of the Internal Revenue Code of 1954, as amended, or any corresponding provision of state law) to qualify all or a specific portion of the SIDNEY M. POND REVOCABLE TRUST dated January 17, 1991 for the federal estate tax marital deduction and any marital deduction available under the law of the state in which I am domiciled at the time of my death." To qualify under §2056, however, the trust must provide the surviving spouse a "qualifying income interest for life." See §2056(b)(7)(B) of the Internal Revenue Code (I.R.C.). Without the marital deduction, the settlor's estate would have to pay $70,000 in otherwise avoidable taxes.

The plaintiff contends that scrivener's errors are apparent when the purposes of the trust are considered. The plaintiff avers that the settlor created the trust to satisfy the requirements for the marital deduction under §2056(b)(7) of the I.R.C. and the corresponding deduction under G.L. c. 65C, §3A. The plaintiff also contends that, pursuant to this estate plan, the settlor intended for the trust's assets to be used to support his surviving spouse. Due to the omission of an income provision for the surviving spouse, both objectives were thwarted because his wife was left with virtually no assets and the trust does not qualify for the marital deduction.

The plaintiff requests that the court reform the trust instrument to give effect to the settlor's intent. First, the plaintiff asks this court to insert a provision which would grant the surviving spouse the right to the trust's annual income, and discretionary principal payments, during her lifetime. Second, the plaintiff also asks

---

22. Notice of the proposed reformation was served on the Internal Revenue Service and the Attorney General. Neither the Commonwealth nor the IRS filed an appearance.

23. At the time of the settlor's death, the trust was valued at approximately $650,000.

this court to incorporate provisions which would correct the ambiguity in the termination provisions. The beneficiaries of the trust, who were named as defendants, assented to the proposed reformation.[24]

2. DISCUSSION.

The modification of a trust agreement to conform with a settlor's intent with respect to the marital deduction is a matter of State law which this court may properly decide. . . . When a trust instrument fails to embody the settlor's intent because of scrivener's error, it may be reformed on clear and decisive proof of mistake. . . . To ascertain the settlor's intent, we look to the trust instrument as a whole and the circumstances known to the settlor on execution. . . .

The settlor's intent in creating the trust was clearly to qualify for the marital deduction under §2056(b)(7) of the I.R.C. The tax clause in the settlor's will, which was executed on the same day, demonstrates that the settlor thought that the trust qualified for the marital trust deduction.[25] To qualify, the trust must provide the surviving spouse a "qualifying income interest for life." §2056(b)(7)(B). This means the trust must pay income annually or more frequently to the surviving spouse. §2056(b)(7)(B)(ii). Because we read the trust as clearly manifesting an intent that it qualify for a marital deduction, it can only be a scrivener's error that caused a clause to be omitted that would have provided for income to be paid to his wife for life on the death of the settlor.

We are also convinced that the settlor did not intend to deny his wife discretionary use of the principal during her lifetime. The trust was an essential component in the settlor's estate plan. The settlor transferred virtually all his marital assets into this trust. The trust's income and principal were available to the settlor and his wife during his lifetime. The trust, however, omitted any provision for the surviving spouse after the settlor's death. Because we know that the settlor intended to provide income for his wife if he died first and since the trust made principal available for as long as the settlor lived, we conclude that his intent to continue the same arrangement if he should die first is manifest. Babson v. Babson, 371 N.E.2d 430 (Mass. 1980) (considering will as a whole, testator intended to take maximum advantage of estate tax deductions even though word "maximum" not used). This conclusion is buttressed by the settlor's will bequeathing all his tangible property to his wife and naming her executrix of his estate. There is no indication that the settlor intended to deprive his surviving spouse of the trust's assets during her lifetime.

We conclude that there is clear and decisive proof of mistake due to scrivener's error. The settlor's intent was to minimize estate tax payable by establishing a qualifying terminal interest trust. To qualify under §2056, the trust must distribute income to the surviving spouse. While the discretionary principal payments

---

24. The guardians for the minor grandchildren also have assented to the proposed reformation.

25. Under §2056(b)(7) of the I.R.C., qualifying terminal interest property is eligible for a marital deduction in the estate of the settlor if the settlor's executrix so elects. If that election is made and the marital deduction is thus taken in the settlor's estate, the trust property must then be included in the estate of the surviving spouse for Federal estate tax purposes.

are not required under §2056, the estate plan demonstrates an intent to treat both spouses equally. Thus, we agree that the trust should be reformed to give effect to the settlor's intent. . . .

The case is remanded to the Probate and Family Court for entry of a judgment of reformation consistent with this opinion.

So ordered.

NOTE AND PROBLEMS

1. *Reformation to save taxes.* In Pond v. Pond, the court reformed a trust so as to obtain tax advantages potentially lost because of the faulty work of the lawyer. *Reformation* is an equitable remedy that conforms the instrument to what the donor actually intended at the time of execution. The reformation concept is of venerable origin. The innovation here—endorsed by Uniform Probate Code (UPC) §2-805 (2008); Restatement (Third) of Property: Wills and Other Donative Transfers §12.1 (2003); and Uniform Trust Code §415 (2000)—is to apply it to wills and testamentary trusts. See Chapter 5 at pages 345-357 and Chapter 9 at page 651.

Massachusetts has led the way in reforming trusts to obtain tax advantages lost through faulty drafting, though courts in other states have become increasingly amenable to the idea. See 5 Austin Wakeman Scott, William Franklin Fratcher, and Mark L. Ascher, Scott and Ascher on Trusts §33.5 (5th ed. 2008). Note, however, that under Commissioner v. Estate of Bosch, 387 U.S. 456 (1967), the Internal Revenue Service is bound only by a construction or reformation approved by the state's highest court. Massachusetts has a special procedure permitting the parties to go directly from the probate court to the Supreme Judicial Court. Most states do not have such a summary appellate procedure.

Reformation to save taxes is to be contrasted with *modification* of a trust for which an unanticipated change in circumstances has frustrated the settlor's tax objectives. Such a modification may be available under the *equitable deviation* doctrine (see page 651). Equitable deviation to achieve the settlor's probable tax objectives is specifically authorized by UPC §2-806 (2008); Restatement (Third) of Property, supra, §12.2; and UTC §416.

2. *H* by will creates a trust providing *W* with "so much of the net income as she may require to maintain her usual and customary standard of living." Does this qualify for the QTIP deduction? See Estate of Nicholson v. Commissioner, 94 T.C. 666 (1990) (holding No because the surviving spouse was not entitled to *all* trust income).

Suppose the trust gave the trustee the power to accumulate income in excess of the amount necessary for *W*'s "needs, best interests, and welfare." QTIP deduction? See Estate of Ellingson v. Commissioner, 964 F.2d 959 (9th Cir. 1992) (holding Yes because the wife's "best interests" required that she get all trust income regardless of need). Would it matter if the testator's will had provided that his intention was to qualify the trust for the marital deduction? See Wiseley v. United

States, 893 F.2d 660 (4th Cir. 1990) (stating that such a provision is influential in establishing intent).

3.   *W* has creates a revocable trust for herself to avoid probate. The trust contains a provision that in the event of *W*'s incapacity the trustee may make annual gifts of up to $13,000 to members of *W*'s family. *H* dies, devising property to *W*'s revocable trust. Does *H*'s estate qualify for the marital deduction? (Because the trustee has the power to appoint trust property to persons other than *W*, the answer is No.)

Qualified domestic trusts (QDOTs). In providing for a marital deduction that allows a married couple to avoid estate taxation at the death of the first spouse, Congress intended that the deduction would defer rather than eliminate the taxation of first spouse's property. The underlying theory was that property qualifying for the marital deduction at the death of the first spouse would eventually be included in the surviving spouse's gross estate (if not consumed or subjected to gift taxation first). When the surviving spouse is not a citizen of the United States, however, there is a very real possibility that the surviving spouse will not be subject to U.S. estate taxation at death. Accordingly, under §2056(d)(2), property passing to a noncitizen spouse does not qualify for the marital deduction unless the property passes to a qualified domestic trust (QDOT).

The rules for a QDOT are as follows: at least one trustee must be a citizen of the United States or a domestic corporation; the U.S. trustee must have the right to withhold the deferred estate tax on the QDOT assets; and the trust must otherwise qualify for the marital deduction (i.e., it must also be a marital deduction general power of appointment trust or a QTIP trust). If the decedent did not create a QDOT as part of his or her estate plan, the surviving noncitizen spouse or the decedent's personal representative has the option of creating a QDOT after the decedent's death. A court may also reform a trust to comply with the QDOT requirements. To ensure the collection of the deferred estate tax, the Treasury has issued regulations requiring a bond of an individual trustee and requiring securities to be kept in the United States. Treas. Reg. §26.2056A-2(d)(1)(B).

NOTE: TAX PLANNING FOR SPOUSES AND THE CREDIT SHELTER TRUST

In a brief treatment of estate taxation such as this, we cannot cover the many complicated tax avoidance devices that practitioners sometimes recommend to their clients. There is one basic tax-saving strategy, however, with which all lawyers should be familiar. It involves taking full advantage of any exemption (unified credit) that is available at the death of the first spouse to die. Failure to advise your clients of this strategy may well be malpractice. As of 2009, the unified credit was the equivalent of a $3.5 million exemption.

> *Case 18.* W and H each owns property worth $3.5 million. Neither has made any taxable gifts, and both want their combined wealth to benefit the survivor and then, at the survivor's death, to benefit their children in shares to be determined by the surviving spouse. Each makes a will that devises everything to the surviving spouse, or to their descendants per stirpes if there is no surviving spouse. Under these estate plans, when W dies in early 2009 all her property passes to H. Because of the unlimited marital deduction, no taxes are incurred at that time. At H's death later that year, only $3.5 million of H's $7 million estate is sheltered from taxation. H's estate owes more than $1.5 million in estate taxes on the remaining $3.5 million.

In Case 18, W wasted her $3.5 million exemption by leaving her entire estate outright to H, resulting in $1.5 million being paid in taxes rather than to the children.

Avoiding those taxes would have been easy. Indeed, H and W could have arranged for their entire $7 million in wealth to be available to support the survivor and then pass to their children without any transfer taxation. All they needed were wills providing that the first spouse to die would leave his or her $3.5 million estate in trust for the survivor's benefit during life, but with some relatively minor restrictions that would cause the surviving spouse to be treated as not owning the trust corpus when he or she later died. When each spouse dies, his or her $3.5 million in wealth is not taxed because of the $3.5 million exemption. And even though the surviving spouse benefits during life from the trust created by the predeceasing spouse, the trust corpus is not in the survivor's estate because the survivor is not considered its owner.

Because this trust for the survivor bypasses the survivor's estate, it is sometimes called a *bypass* trust. And because this trust makes full use of the first spouse's unified credit to shelter that spouse's property from estate taxation at the second spouse's death, it is also sometimes called a *credit shelter* trust. Note that at the second spouse's death the *entire* credit shelter trust, including any appreciation in trust property that occurred after the first spouse died, passes to the remainder beneficiaries completely free of estate taxation.

What terms might a credit shelter trust include? The surviving spouse could be given most of the benefits that an owner would have, without being treated as owning the trust property at death. The first spouse could, if she wanted, make the surviving spouse the trustee and give him all the income, a power to invade the principal for his own benefit (subject to an ascertainable standard), and a special power to appoint the remainder to such of their descendants as he named in his will.

By using W's $3.5 million exemption when she died and H's $3.5 million exemption when he died, and by sheltering W's estate from being included in H's estate, H and W's entire $7 million dollar joint wealth could have been made available to the surviving spouse and then to their children or other beneficiaries without paying any estate taxes.

Case 19. Same facts as in Case 18, except that *W* devises her entire estate to a credit shelter trust for *H* for life, remainder as *H* appoints by will among *W*'s descendants. This bequest would qualify for the marital deduction as a QTIP trust if *W*'s personal representative were to so elect, but *W*'s will instructs her personal representative not to make a QTIP election. Under these facts, W's entire $3.5 million estate is taxable at her death, but because of her $3.5 million exemption, no estate taxes are incurred. The trust property, including subsequent appreciation, is not taxable at *H*'s death because *H* had only a life estate coupled with a special power of appointment, and no QTIP election was made.

Case 19 illustrates the use of a credit shelter trust where the couple wants the surviving spouse to have fairly extensive rights in and powers over the other spouse's property during the time between their respective deaths. The credit shelter trust could instead give discretion to an independent trustee to distribute the income among family members, possibly reducing income taxes during the surviving spouse's remaining life. Or the first spouse to die could use his or her $3.5 million exemption by bequeathing that amount outright to children or persons other than the surviving spouse.

The key point from an estate planning perspective is to avoid wasting the first spouse's exemption when the size of the spouses' combined wealth approaches the amount of a single exemption. Not surprisingly, lawyers who represent wealthy couples have devised a variety of complex strategies to ensure that any credit shelter trust will be funded with the maximum amount of the exemption (which changes from time to time).

Lately there has been talk of making the exemption amount (that is, the unified credit) portable between the spouses, a reform that would greatly simplify the process of estate planning for spouses by letting the surviving spouse use any exemption that was not used by the first spouse. See Mitchell M. Gans, Jonathan G. Blattmachr, and Austin Bramwell, Estate Tax Exemption Portability: What Should the IRS Do? And What Should Planners Do in the Interim?, 42 Real Prop., Prob. & Tr. J. 413 (2007); Wendy C. Gerzog, Portability of Exemptions, 119 Tax Notes 509 (2008).

b.   The Charitable Deduction

Decedents sometimes want to leave property to charity. Section 2055 allows an unlimited deduction if the gift is properly structured and the organization that received the property qualifies under the Code. See Miranda Perry Fleischer, Charitable Contributions in an Ideal Estate Tax, 60 Tax L. Rev. 263 (2007), discussing the rationale for the charitable deduction and its structure. Specifically, the organization must be

organized and operated exclusively for religious, charitable, scientific, literary, or educational purposes, including the encouragement of art, or to foster national or international amateur sports competition (but only if no part of its activities involve the provision of athletic facilities or equipment), and the prevention of cruelty to children or animals, no part of the net earnings of which inures to the benefit of any private stockholder or individual, which is not disqualified for tax exemption under §501(c)(3) by reason of attempting to influence legislation, and which does not participate in, or intervene in (including the publishing or distributing of statements), any political campaign on behalf of any candidate for public office. [I.R.C. §2055(a)(2).]

If a client wants to make a gift of a remainder interest to charity, special arrangements are required. Except for a remainder in a personal residence or in a farm, a charitable deduction is allowed in calculating federal income, gift, and estate taxes only if the remainder is in an *annuity trust* or a *unitrust,* or part of a *pooled income fund.* I.R.C. §§664(d), 2055(e)(2), and 2522(c)(2).

A charitable remainder *annuity trust* is one under which a fixed sum, which can be no less than 5 percent of the original value of the trust property, is paid at least annually to the non-charitable beneficiary. The income beneficiary of an annuity trust thus receives the same amount each year. A *unitrust* is one under which a fixed percentage, which cannot be less than 5 percent of the trust property, valued annually, is paid to the non-charitable beneficiary. The income beneficiary of a unitrust will thus receive an annual amount that fluctuates as the value of the trust property changes. A *pooled income fund* is set up by a charitable organization and must meet certain specific requirements of the Code. If the trustee or private beneficiary of an annuity trust, a unitrust, or a pooled income fund has a discretionary power to invade principal, the trust does not qualify for a charitable deduction. The objectives of these rules are to reduce the uncertainty involved in valuing the future interest given to charity and to increase the likelihood that an interest will in fact pass to charity on the non-charitable beneficiary's death. However, the rules governing the drafting of these trusts are technical and not intuitive. For example, if estate taxes may be paid from a charitable remainder trust, no charitable deduction is allowable; and if taxes are apportioned by state law or by a clause in the decedent's will, a deduction may be denied. A bequest in trust "to pay all the income to *A* for life, remainder to the *Y* charity" would not generally qualify for the charitable deduction, because such a trust is neither an annuity trust nor a unitrust.

PROBLEM

T's will bequeaths his property to Princeton University and Johns Hopkins University. A codicil grants *T*'s executor the discretion "to compensate persons who have contributed to my well-being or who have otherwise been helpful to me during my lifetime," providing that no single bequest should exceed 1 percent of the estate. The executors determined that only two individuals met the definition of eligible persons and so 98 percent of the estate passed to the universities. Is the estate entitled to a charitable deduction? See Estate of Marine v. Commissioner, 990 F.2d 136 (4th Cir. 1993) (held No, because the charities did not have an indefeasible right at *T*'s death).

SECTION D.   THE GENERATION-SKIPPING TRANSFER TAX

1.   The Nature of the Tax

Until 1986, it was possible for a wealthy person to make transfers in the form of a *dynasty trust*, either during lifetime or by will, that would insulate the transferred property from estate or gift taxation over several generations. *O* might transfer property worth $10 million, in trust, income payable to *O*'s children for their lives, then to the children's children for their lives, then to the grandchildren's children for their lives, and so on down the generations until the applicable Rule Against Perpetuities called a halt. Each beneficiary could be given, in addition to a share of the income, a power to consume principal measured by an ascertainable standard, and a special testamentary power of appointment over his or her share of the trust property, all without estate or gift tax cost. As each beneficiary died, nothing would be taxed in the beneficiary's estate because the beneficiary held only a life estate and special power of appointment. To achieve even greater flexibility the governing instrument could give an independent trustee an unlimited power to distribute trust principal to the beneficiaries, again incurring no additional gift or estate taxes once the trust was funded. Through the careful use of a saving clause, the trust might continue for many generations over a hundred years or more.

In the Tax Reform Act of 1986, Congress severely limited this tax-avoidance technique by subjecting such arrangements to a *generation-skipping transfer* (GST) tax, but only prospectively. The GST tax does not apply to a trust that was irrevocable before 1986.

The rationale for the GST tax is that wealth should be subject to some kind of transfer tax at least once each generation. To implement this idea, the Code imposes a tax on generation-skipping transfers. A *generation-skipping transfer* is a transfer to a skip person, a new term invented by Congress in imposing this tax. A *skip person* is a grandchild or any other person assigned to a generation that is two or more generations below the transferor's generation. I.R.C. §2613(a). The transferor's spouse and children (or other persons in the transferor's generation or the generation just below the transferor's) are *nonskip persons*. Hence, a transfer directly from a grandparent to a grandchild, either outright or as a future interest, is in general subject to the GST tax.

The GST tax is levied on generation-skipping transfers in the form of (1) a taxable termination, (2) a taxable distribution, or (3) a direct skip. A *taxable termination* is the

> termination (by death, lapse of time, release of a power, or otherwise) of any interest in property held in a trust unless —
>
> (A) immediately after such termination, a non-skip person has an interest in such property, or
>
> (B) at no time after such termination may a distribution (including distributions on termination) be made from such trust to a skip person. [I.R.C. §2612(a)(1).]

Here is an example:

> *Case 20. T* bequeaths $8 million in trust for her son *A* for life, remainder to *A*'s children. At *A*'s death, a "taxable termination" takes place. *A*'s life interest terminates and only skip persons (*A*'s children) have an interest in the property. If the income were payable to *T*'s daughter *B* after *A*'s death, there would be no taxable termination upon *A*'s death. However, there would be a taxable termination upon *B*'s subsequent death, when only skip persons would have an interest in the trust.

The purpose of the exceptions in the definition of a taxable termination ((A) and (B) above) is to limit to *one* the number of taxable terminations, per dollar of property, that can occur in each generation below the transferor's. Where, for example, *T* bequeaths the income from a trust to her children, with principal to be distributed to her grandchildren upon the death of her last surviving child, a taxable termination occurs only at the death of the last surviving child. On the other hand, if at the death of one child that child's share is distributed to that child's children, then a taxable termination of a fractional share of the trust principal has occurred (I.R.C. §2612(a)(2)).

A *taxable distribution* occurs whenever any distribution is made from a trust to a skip person (other than a taxable termination or a direct skip). Thus, if in Case 20, *A* had a special power to distribute income or corpus to *A*'s children, a taxable distribution would take place when and if such distribution were actually made.

A *direct skip* is a transfer of property directly to a skip person. Case 21 illustrates a direct skip:

> *Case 21. T* is survived by her son *A* and *A*'s daughter *B*. *T* devises $5 million to her granddaughter *B*. This is a direct skip, because it skips the generation of the son. A GST tax (in addition to the estate tax payable on *T*'s death) is due on *T*'s death. This double taxation follows from the principle that a transfer tax must be paid once per generation (and this direct skip avoids gift and estate taxation at *A*'s generation). Similarly, if *T* had given *B* $5 million during life, she would have incurred both a gift tax and a GST tax at that time.

There are two important exceptions to the principle that a transfer tax (be it an estate tax, gift tax, or GST tax) must be paid once per generation. First, the GST applies only once in the case of *double* (or even *triple*) *skips*. Thus, a transfer of property directly to a great-grandchild incurs only one GST tax despite skipping two generations, and a transfer directly to a great-great grandchild would incur only one GST despite skipping three generations. Second, there is a *deceased parent exception*, which applies to transfers to descendants of the predeceased children of the transferor. If a child of the transferor is dead at the time of the initial transfer, the children of that child (the transferor's grandchildren) are treated as the children of the transferor for GST tax purposes. §2651(e). If the transferor has no lineal descendants, this exception applies to transfers to lineal descendants of the parent of the transferor (first line collaterals).

When GST tax must be paid. A direct skip occurs (and is taxable) on the day the transfer is effective. By contrast, a taxable termination or taxable distribution occurs in the future, sometime after the original transfer in trust. Although in some cases it will be certain when the trust is established that the trust will produce a GST tax in the future, in other cases it will not be certain. Case 22 is an example.

> *Case 22.* T devises property in trust to pay the income to T's child *A* until *A* attains the age of 30, at which time the trustee is to distribute the trust principal to *A*. If *A* dies before reaching age 30, the trustee is to distribute the principal to *A*'s children in equal shares. Whether this trust will produce a generation-skipping transfer will turn on the events that actually occur. If *A* lives to age 30 and receives the trust principal, there is no generation-skipping transfer. If *A* dies before age 30, and the trust principal is distributed to *A*'s children, a taxable termination will occur at that time.

If a trust turns out to produce a generation-skipping transfer, the tax is payable when that transfer occurs.

GST tax rate. All generation-skipping transfers are taxed at a flat rate equal to the highest rate under the federal estate tax. The highest estate tax rate in 2009 is 45 percent.

GST tax base. The amount taxed and the person liable for the tax depend on the type of transfer. Where there is a *direct skip*, the transferor must pay the tax on the amount received by the transferee. The taxation of a direct skip resembles the gift tax in that the base excludes the amount of tax levied (that is, it is *tax-exclusive*, see page 950).

In the case of a *taxable termination* or *taxable distribution*, however, the tax is imposed on a *tax-inclusive* basis (that is, the taxable amount includes the tax, see page 950). In this respect, taxable terminations and distributions resemble the estate tax. Upon a taxable termination, the tax base is the entire property with respect to which the termination occurred. The tax is to be paid out of the trust. Upon a taxable distribution, the tax base is the amount received by the beneficiary, who is liable for the tax.

2.   *Exemption and Exclusions*

Exemption. Section 2631 provides a lifetime exemption of $3.5 million[26] (as of 2009) for each transferor. For inter vivos transfers by a married person, the transferor and her spouse may elect to treat the transfer as made one-half by each spouse (as under §2513 of the gift tax, see page 948). Hence a husband and wife can give away $7 million in generation-skipping transfers in 2009 without incurring any tax.

> *Case 23.* During life, *W* transfers $7 million to a trustee to pay the income to *W*'s children for their lives, then to distribute the principal to *W*'s grandchildren. *H* consents to treating this transfer as having been made half by him, thus using his $3.5 million GST exemption.

---

26. Originally, the exemption amount was $1 million, to be increased by annual cost-of-living adjustments. In 2001, however, Congress amended §2631 to provide that the GST tax exemption amount would be equal to the estate tax exemption amount.

By applying the spouses' total GST tax exemption of $7 million to this transfer, the trust property, including subsequent appreciation, will not be subject to GST taxation now or in the future. Because the maximum exemption available for gift-tax purposes in 2009 is only $1 million, however, this gift incurs gift taxes of $2.25 million (45 percent of $5 million). The gift tax is payable by *W* at the time of the transfer. At the death of *W*'s children, no GST tax is due.[27]

If, in Case 23, *W* had not made an inter vivos transfer but had bequeathed $7 million in trust, only $3.5 million would be exempt from GST tax (because the split-gift provision applies only to inter vivos gifts). In case of a testamentary transfer, to take advantage of the spouse's GST tax exemption, it is necessary to make the spouse a "transferor" for estate tax purposes. If, in Case 23, the trust had been a testamentary trust and *H* had been bequeathed a life estate in half of $7 million transferred by *W* into trust, *H*'s GST tax exemption of $3.5 million could be used.

If the transferor creates more than one generation-skipping trust, or makes generation-skipping transfers in excess of $3.5 million, the transferor or his personal representative can allocate the exemption. If not so allocated, §2632 provides default rules. Generally, the exemption is first allocated to direct skips and then to taxable terminations and taxable distributions. The exemption is allocated to the "property transferred" and not, in the case of taxable terminations and taxable distributions, to specific generation-skipping transfers that occur in the future. This means that with respect to trusts that might produce taxable terminations or taxable distributions, the entire exemption or a fraction thereof must be allocated to the trust at the time of the transfer into trust. It is important to allocate the exemption so as not to waste it on a trust that is uncertain to produce a generation-skipping transfer, when it could be allocated more effectively elsewhere.

Under §2653(b)(1), the exempt fraction of the trust property — determined when the trust is created — remains the same for the duration of the trust. If the trust produces successive skips, the transferor's exemption can eliminate or reduce the GST tax generation after generation. If, for example, a trust provides for payment of income to *T*'s children for their lives, then to *T*'s grandchildren for their lives, and then to distribute the principal to *T*'s great-grandchildren, the transferor's $3.5 million exemption will shelter the trust, wholly or partially, from GST tax for its entire duration, even if the principal of the trust increases in value far beyond the initial $3.5 million.

Exclusions. Section 2642(c)(1) excludes from GST taxation any transfer not subject to the gift tax because of the annual exclusion (see page 940). Hence transfers of $13,000 or less annually to grandchildren usually will not produce a GST tax.[28] Section 2611(b)(1) further excludes any transfers excluded under §2503(e)

---

27. The gift tax exemption remains at $1 million while the estate and GST tax exemptions increase to $3.5 million in 2009.

28. Gifts in trust that qualify for the gift tax annual exclusion do not automatically avoid the GST tax. To avoid this tax, the trust must be for the benefit of only one individual and must be in that individual's gross estate if that individual dies before the trust terminates. I.R.C. §2642(c)(2).

of the gift tax, relating to the direct payment of tuition and medical expenses (see page 940). Hence, a grandparent can pay tuition for a grandchild without making a generation-skipping transfer, or a trust can make tuition or medical payments for a skip person without subjecting such distributions to the GST tax.

NOTE

To reduce taxes, it may be desirable for a non-skip person to be able to decide whether to pay an estate tax or to pay a GST tax on the non-skip person's death. This flexibility may allow the non-skip person to optimize his and his spouse's exemptions, unified credits, and graduated rates. For example, if *O* transfers property in trust for her son *A* for life, then to *A*'s children, and *O* gives *A* a special power to appoint the property to *A*'s wife or to one or more of *A*'s descendants, *A* can control which tax will be applicable at *A*'s death. If *A* wants the property in his gross estate, thereby avoiding a GST tax, *A* can by will exercise the special power by creating a general inter vivos power in his wife. For discussion, see the sources cited at the end of the Note on the "Delaware Tax Trap," page 923.

3. Some Common GST Tax Planning Strategies

To reduce or avoid the generation-skipping transfer tax, certain strategies are fairly obvious and routine in practice:

(a) Use the annual gift tax exclusion of $13,000 per transferee ($26,000 per transferee for a married couple). See page 940.

(b) Use the tax exclusions for tuition and medical expense payments for grandchildren made directly to the educational institution or medical supplier. See page 940.

(c) Use the predeceased parent exception, if applicable to the particular family. See page 990.

(d) Use the GST exemption to establish a dynasty trust for as long as the law allows, thus avoiding an additional transfer tax for as long as the trust continues to exist. This strategy is discussed more extensively in connection with the repeal of the Rule Against Perpetuities, see pages 905-910.

(e) Arrange the property of a married couple so as not to waste the GST exemption of either spouse.

SECTION E. STATE WEALTH TRANSFER TAXES

Should decedents get a reduction in their federal estate taxes to reflect estate or inheritance taxes paid to a state, much as state income taxes are deductible on federal income tax returns? Before 2001, the federal estate tax included a credit for state death taxes. I.R.C. §2011. Congress enacted this credit in the 1920s, when an effort was made to repeal the federal estate tax on the ground that this source of revenue should be reserved to the states. The states responded by enacting death taxes, to take full advantage of the credit, since the credit permitted diversion of federal revenues to the state without increasing the overall taxes that state residents had to pay on death. Up to a limit set by §2011, every dollar paid in state death taxes reduced the federal estate tax bill by a dollar. Indeed, most states had only a *pick-up* (or *sponge*) tax that equaled (to the penny) the amount of the §2011 credit, though some states had an inheritance tax on beneficiaries or an estate tax with a freestanding rate schedule.

The Economic Growth and Tax Relief Reconciliation Act of 2001 threw the state tax systems into turmoil by replacing the §2011 credit with a deduction for state death taxes. I.R.C. §2058. At the same time, the states have been confronted with political pressures to repeal their death taxes, tempered, however, by local budget crunches. States have reacted in several ways. Some have retained their estate or inheritance taxes and a few states have enacted new ones. Other states have decoupled from the current Code and enacted new taxes, but with rates that are almost identical to their old taxes under the now obsolete §2011. About half of the states no longer have any death tax, some because the state has done nothing in response to the 2001 revisions, perhaps expecting Congress to revisit the changes it made — or even to bring back the §2011 credit. See Jeffrey Cooper, Interstate Competition and Sate Death Taxes: A Modern Crisis in Historical Perspective, 33 Pepp. L. Rev. 835 (2006); Jeffrey A. Cooper, John R. Ivimey, and Donna D. Vincenti, State Estate Taxes after EGTRRA: A Long Day's Journey into Night, 17 Quinnipiac Prob. L.J. 317 (2004). The various state transfer tax rules are summarized in Jeffrey A. Schoenblum, 2008 Multistate Guide to Estate Planning at Table 15.

No one can predict the future of the federal wealth transfer tax system. Its fate is bound up in politics, the economy, and budget battles. The fate of state wealth transfer taxes is equally uncertain. Only time will tell whether they are rescued by the federal system, assume a life of their own, or simply die out.

TABLE OF CASES

Principal cases are indicated by italics.

AUTHOR INDEX

INDEX